THE BLUE GUIDES

BLUE GUIDE

NEW YORK

Carol von Pressentin Wright

Atlas of Manhattan, maps and plans

A & C Black Limited
London

W. W. Norton & Company Inc.
New York

Second Edition 1991

Published by A & C Black (Publishers) Limited
35 Bedford Row, London WC1R 4JH
ISBN 0-7136-3169-4 Great Britain
A CIP catalogue record for this book is available from the British Library
Copyright © A & C Black (Publishers) Limited 1991
Copyright © A & C Black (Publishers) Limited 1983 (First Edition)

Published in the United States of America by
W. W. Norton & Company, Inc.
500 Fifth Ave, New York, NY 10110
All rights reserved
Printed in the United States of America

The text of this book is composed in Egyptian.
Composition by The Maple-Vail Book Manufacturing Group.
Manufacturing by Courier Companies Inc.

Library of Congress Cataloging-in-Publication Data
Von Pressentin Wright, Carol.
    New York : atlas of Manhattan, maps, and plans / Carol von
Pressentin Wright.—2nd ed.
        p. cm.—(Blue guide)
    Includes index.
    1. New York (N.Y.)—Description—1981– —Guide-books.   2. New
York
    (N.Y.)—Maps.   I. Title.   II. Series.
    F128.18.V67   1991
    917.47'10443—dc20   90–21262

ISBN 0-393-30486-8

        5 6 7 8 9 0

Carol von Pressentin Wright was born on Staten Island. She holds a Ph.D. in Comparative Literature, which may explain why her first experience with travel writing consisted of editing a scholarly commentary on Dante's *Divine Comedy*. She is currently writing *Museums and Galleries of New York*, also for the Blue Guide series, and has contributed travel writing to the *New York Times*.

Acknowledgments

I would like to thank first of all Susan Benn, who made this project possible in the first place and Jean M. Taylor, without whose generosity I could neither have accomplished the first edition nor sustained the effort necessary for the second.

The black and white route maps are based on maps provided by the City of New York Department of City Planning. The subway map is reprinted with the permission of the New York City Transit Authority.

Various people have made contributions, corrections, and suggestions. Among them are Ruth Abrams, Louella Adams, Beverly Bartow, Elizabeth Bond, Stephen Campbell, Michele Cohen, Aviva Crown, Mary Cunnane, Tom Dance, Nancy Donner, Rosemary C. Erpf, Jo Haggerty, Pat Hildebrand, Joseph Hurley, Alicja Krenta, Virginia Kurshan, Herbert Kurz, Anne Kutscher, Jeanne Lee, Bevin Maguire, Nilda Peraza, Selma Rattner, Gerun Riley, Linda Robinson, Beth Rosenberg, Muriel Samama, Annamarie Sandecki, Ann Scher, Nina Schroeder, James D. Selby, Vivienne Shaffer, Suzanne Stratton, Elyse Topelian, Michael Walker, and Donald Woods. Thanks also to Ken Fritz for timely extraliterary advice.

I am grateful to Miriam Schnier and Polly Mancini for copy editing a long, involved manuscript, meticulously excising errors and other embarrassments. Thanks to Sydney Wolfe Cohen who, with his index, has brought alphabetic order to a multitude of entries. Iva Ashner, one of a select company to have read the book cover to cover, has shepherded it past unforeseen snares on the road to publication. Mildred Marmur, my agent and friend, has confronted the real world for me with great energy, style, and imagination.

Most of all I would like to thank Fred and Catherine Wright, who both have seen more of New York and less of me than they would have in the normal course of events.

A NOTE ON BLUE GUIDES

The Blue Guides series began in 1918, when Muirhead Guide-Books Limited published *Blue Guide London and Its Environs*. Finlay and James Muirhead already had extensive experience of guide-book publishing: before the First World War they had been the editors of the English editions of the German Baedekers, and by 1915 they had acquired the copyright of most of the famous "Red" handbooks from John Murray.

An agreement made with the French publishing house Hachette et Cie in 1917 led to the translation of Muirhead's London Guide, which became the first *Guide Bleu*—Hachette had previously published the blue-covered *Guides Joanne*. Subsequently, Hachette's *Guide Bleu Paris et Ses Environs* was adapted and published in London by Muirhead. The collaboration between the two publishing houses continued until 1933.

In 1931 Ernest Benn took over the Blue Guides, appointing Russell Muirhead, Finlay Muirhead's son, editor in 1934. The Muirheads' connection with Blue Guides ended in 1963 when Stuart Rossiter, who had been working on the Guides since 1954, became house editor, revising and compiling several of the books hmiself.

The Blue Guides are now published by A & C Black, who acquired Ernest Benn in 1984, so continuing the tradition of guide-book publishing which began in 1826 with *Black's Economical Tourist of Scotland*. The Blue Guide series continues to grow: there are now more than 40 titles in print with revised editions appearing regularly and many new Blue Guides in preparation.

Blue Guides is a registered trade mark.

CONTENTS

I BOROUGH OF MANHATTAN / NEW YORK COUNTY

III BOROUGH OF BROOKLYN / KINGS COUNTY

IV BOROUGH OF QUEENS / QUEENS COUNTY

V BOROUGH OF STATEN ISLAND / RICHMOND COUNTY

MAPS

GROUND PLANS

INTRODUCTION

When I first wrote this book and then again when I revised it for this edition, I spent about a year traveling around New York: walking, riding buses and subways, driving, looking at as much of it as I could. I started more or less at the center and gradually worked outward, from midtown to upper and lower Manhattan, to the Bronx, Brooklyn, Queens, and Staten Island. Both times the same thing happened to my perceptions. When I was in midtown its density, energy, and visible commitment to wealth and success made it seem the navel of the universe, the jewel in the crown. The most desirable of all environments seemed to be one of concrete and asphalt, glass and steel. The most desirable of lives seemed to be one of ardent overreaching, for style, for intellectual intensity, for achievement and its rewards.

Eventually I got to the outer reaches of the boroughs, which exist at the boundaries of the gravitational pull of Manhattan. Midtown Manhattan seemed less than ideal. Here on the fringes of the city were places with visible manifestations of nature (other than the weather) and evidence of what the country as a whole probably perceives as "normal" life. From Inwood or the Flatlands or southern Staten Island (admittedly not tourist magnets), 42nd Street looked far away. What seemed like glamour in midtown looked more like glitter from afar and it seemed that the real life of New York took place beyond the unmarked boundaries of midtown. It was all the ordinary people who went about their ordinary lives on whom the frantic midtown energy of New York truly depended. Whether they liked it or not, however, they were in its thrall. If Manhattan were not what it is, the South Bronx, for instance, would be a far different place. So would Brooklyn Heights, to choose a happier example.

This book, therefore, attempts to present New York in all its multiplicity, to the visitor and perhaps even the resident who would like to know more about this wonderful city. The guide covers in detail those places where most tourists focus their energies—the theater district, Wall Street and the World Trade Center, the United Nations, Rockefeller Center, the Statue of Liberty, and the major museums. But it also includes less frequently visited places and places not on the normal tourist beat—residential areas, neighborhoods with interesting pasts but which are not in the forefront of the action today, areas far from the symbolic epicenter of the city, 42nd and Broadway. Walking tours cover Manhattan's most interesting neighborhoods and the major sights in the outer boroughs. Points of interest inconvenient to reach on foot have been organized in gazetteer form: for these you will need either a car or a lot of time and a good map.

Restaurants, hotels, and a few notes on creature comforts and conveniences have been covered briefly for the sake of completeness, but there are more detailed sources on all of these. See the section on tourist information.

The abbreviation **DL** indicates Designated Landmarks, that is, buildings or other sites chosen for their historic, architectural, or cultural value and protected by law from destruction or undue alteration. The symbol ⊙ used on the maps indicates subway stops.

All **telephone numbers** are in area code 212 (Manhattan and the Bronx) unless otherwise indicated.

Glossary of Architectural Terms

ANTHEMION: Stylized honey-suckle form, used in classical and Greek Revival architecture.

ARCHITRAVE: The lowest part of an entablature; in classical architecture it rested directly on a column and usually supported a frieze and cornice.

BARREL-VAULT: A vault in the form of a very deep arch.

CHAMFER: Cut the edge off a corner or rectangular shape, usually at 45 degrees.

CLERESTORY: Part of an interior raised above adjacent rooftops, usually windowed to allow light into the central part of the building. Typically used in Gothic churches, where the nave is built higher than the aisles, allowing windowed clerestory walls above the aisles.

COFFER: Recessed ceiling ornamentation, usually square or polygonal.

COLONNETTE: Small column, used for decorative purposes.

CONSOLE: Ornamental bracket, sometimes of stone, to support cornices, balconies, or other elements.

CORBEL: Block or bracket projecting from a wall to support timbers, girders, or masonry.

CORNICE: A prominent, continuous, horizontal projection surmounting a wall.

CRENELATIONS: Battlements, the toothed ramparts of a medieval fortification designed to protect a shooter or archer.

CRESTING: Decorative coping or ornamental ridge to give a building an interesting skyline.

ENTABLATURE: The upper section of a classical order, resting on the capitals and including the architrave, frieze, and cornice.

GAMBREL ROOF: A gabled roof with two pitches, the upper half gentler, the lower half steeper.

IMPOST: A bracketed piece of masonry projecting from a wall to support an arch or part of a roofing structure.

LINTEL: A beam supporting weight over a window or door opening.

LUNETTE: Area of wall enframed by a vault or arch, often penetrated by a window.

MACHICOLATION: A projecting gallery on top of a castle wall, supported by corbeled arches with an opening through which boiling liquids or missiles can be dropped on attackers.

MANSARD ROOF: Steep attic urban roof which allowed an added story on a building.

MODILLION: A carved scroll of a bracket, placed horizontally.

MULLION: The major support between adjacent panels of glass or doors, or window sash; the vertical strip dividing panes of glass in a window.

NARTHEX: Originally the open porch of a church; now any kind of vestibule to the nave.

OCULUS: Eye or eyelike. A round window.

ORIEL: A high, projecting bay window, supported by corbels or brackets.

PEDIMENT: The triangular gabled end of a temple roof front, in classical architecture supported by the colonnade and often decorated with sculpture.

PENDENTIVE: Triangular piece of a sphere that fills the space between a round dome and the supporting structure.

PERISTYLE: The series of columns surrounding a building or courtyard.

PIER: A vertical supporting structure, the portion of a wall between windows.

PILASTER: Attached, rectangular column used decoratively.

QUOIN: Corner stone of a building.

REREDOS: A background for an altar, often carved.

SPANDREL: The flat space between two arches and the surrounding rectangular framework. Also, the material between the head of one floor's windows and the sill of the next.

TIE-ROD: A tensile member to hold together parts of a building that tend to separate.

TYMPANUM: The sculptured pediment, or triangular end crest, of a Greek or Roman temple. Later the arched space over Romanesque or Gothic doors, often filled with sculpture.

ZIGGURAT: Terraced pyramids used as holy places by the ancient Assyrians and Babylonians. Hence a stepped pyramid.

Further Reading

NONFICTION:

Barlow, Elizabeth. *The Forests and Wetlands of New York City.* Boston: Little, Brown, 1971.

————. *Frederick Law Olmsted's New York.* New York: Praeger, 1972.

These books, by the curator of Central Park, focus on the natural environment of the city and the changes wrought upon it by Olmsted.

Berger, Meyer. *Meyer Berger's New York.* New York: Random House, 1960.

Berger's classic columns reprinted from the *New York Times* of the 1950s.

Blom, Benjamin. *New York: Photographs 1850–1950.* New York: Dutton, 1982.
A fine collection of historic photographs, some familiar, others newly rediscovered.

Caro, Robert A. *The Power Broker: Robert Moses and the Fall of New York.* New York: Knopf, 1974.
Though Caro's indictment of Robert Moses is today undergoing revision, this extensively researched book offers a detailed view of Moses's impact on the physical environment of the city.

Edmiston, Susan and Linda D. Cirino. *Literary New York.* Boston: Houghton Mifflin, 1976.
A borough-by-borough literary history of the city beginning with Giovanni da Verrazano, who commented in 1594 on "its favorable conditions and beauty."

Federal Writers' Project. *New York City Guide.* New York: Random House, 1939. Reprint. New York: Pantheon, 1982.
Published the year of New York's great World's Fair, this classic account of the city was written during the Depression by a group of federally supported writers, including John Cheever.

Fischler, Stan. *Uptown, Downtown.* New York: Hawthorn Books, 1976.
A history of the subways, by a man who has ridden all of its 710 miles.

Gayle, Margot and Michele Cohen. *The Art Commission and the Municipal Art Society Guide to Manhattan's Outdoor Sculpture.* New York: Prentice Hall, 1988.
The definitive work on this subject, for the casual onlooker and the scholar as well.

Kouwenhoven, John A. *The Columbia Historical Portrait of New York.* Garden City, N.Y.: Doubleday, 1953. Reprint. New York: Harper & Row, 1972.

Lockwood, Charles. *Bricks and Brownstone: The New York Row House.* New York: McGraw-Hill, 1972.

Stokes, Isaac Newton Phelps. *The Iconography of Manhattan Island, 1498–1909.* 6 vols. New York: Robert H. Dodd, 1915–1928. Reprint. New York: Arno Press, 1967.
Stokes, architect and member of a prominent New York family, labored on this masterpiece for most of his adult life. The six large, heavy volumes contain reproductions of historic maps and documents as well as a chronology of events, great and small, culled from public and private sources.

Tauranac, John. *Essential New York.* New York: Holt, Rinehart and Winston, 1979.
Carefully researched, opinionated (in the best sense) architectural history and description.

Willensky, Elliott and Norval White. *The AIA Guide to New York City.* 3rd edition. New York: Harcourt Brace Jovanovich, 1988.
This book, which has doubled in size since the first edition

appeared in 1967, is the single best source of information on the city and its architecture, the book on which other observers of the city depend.

FICTON:

Baldwin, James. *Go Tell It on the Mountain.* New York: Knopf, 1953.

Capote, Truman. *Breakfast at Tiffany's.* New York: Random House, 1958.

Doctorow, E. L. *Ragtime.* New York: Random House, 1975.

————. *World's Fair.* New York: Random House, 1986.

Finney, Jack. *Time and Again.* New York: Simon & Schuster, 1970.

This novel is a favorite of New York buffs, the story of a man who shuttles back and forth in time between 1880 and the present; a detailed picture of the city in the 19C.

James, Henry. *Washington Square.* 1881.

One of James's moral tales, set in Greenwich Village, where his aunt lived.

Wharton, Edith. *The Age of Innocence.* 1920.

Wharton won the Pulitzer Prize for this understated indictment of the manners and morals of the privileged classes from which she sprang.

Wolfe, Tom. *The Bonfire of the Vanities.* New York: Farrar Straus & Giroux, 1987.

Wolfe's roman à clef about the nastiness of contemporary New York society.

Arrival in New York

Arrival by Air.

Most international and many domestic flights arrive at **John F. Kennedy International Airport,** known as JFK, facing Jamaica Bay in the S.E. section of the borough of Queens, about 15 miles from midtown Manhattan (an hour's drive if traffic is light to moderate; traffic on the Van Wyck Expressway near the airport, however, is often very heavy). The airport is a complex of terminals serving about 80 airlines, some of which have their own passport control and customs offices, though many international flights are channeled through the International Arrivals Building.

LaGuardia Airport, also in Queens but on the East River about 8 miles (half an hour, under optimal conditions) from midtown, serves shorter domestic flights. Most flights arrive at and depart from the two-level Main Terminal; Delta Airlines has its own terminal; Eastern Air Lines shuttle flights to Washington and Boston are serviced at the Eastern terminal; the Marine Terminal handles the Pan Am shuttle to Washington and Boston as well as commuter and private flights.

Newark International Airport, near Newark Bay in New Jersey, is about 16 miles (45 minutes under normal driving conditions) from midtown. Some international flights originate and terminate there, and its location makes it useful to passengers whose destination is on Manhattan's West Side. The airport has three terminals including the new international arrivals facility and the North Terminal, used by several scheduled airlines.

Transportation to and from Airports

Taxis operate between midtown and all airports. Fares for destinations within the city from JFK and LaGuardia airports are metered (approximately $30 to JFK, $20 to LaGuardia). Fares from Manhattan to Newark Airport in yellow medallion cabs are metered plus a $10 surcharge. Fares from Newark to Manhattan are either metered or charged at a flat rate depending on the taxi (about $50); make sure you agree on a rate before departing. Bridge and tunnel tolls are extra. The metered fare covers all passengers up to four and all luggage except for trunks (50¢ surcharge). Passengers to destinations other than midtown Manhattan should agree upon the fare with the driver before departing. A 50¢ surcharge is in effect in New York yellow medallion taxis between 8 P.M. and 6 A.M. During peak hours uniformed dispatchers are on duty at the three airports to direct travelers to cabs. There is a peak hour share-the-ride discount taxi program at LaGuardia.

Most of the time, however, passengers must hail their own cabs; New Yorkers are assertive in this respect. Only yellow cabs are licensed by the city and they operate at the airports from designated taxi stands. Do not take taxis whose drivers solicit business from the sidewalk; foreigners and people unfamiliar with New York have been grossly overcharged and sometimes intimidated by taxi hustlers. Taxi drivers are required legally to stay inside their cabs except to help with luggage, etc. They will expect a 15–20% tip.

Ground Transportation, Kennedy Airport

Express bus service. Carey Transportation, Inc., operates between airport terminals and five midtown stops: Park Ave between 41st / 42nd Sts, opposite Grand Central Terminal; the Port Authority Bus Terminal Air Trans Center on 42nd St, between Eighth / Ninth Aves; the New York Hilton Hotel, W. 53rd St off Sixth Ave; the Sheraton City Squire Hotel; and the Marriott Marquis Hotel on Broadway, between 45th / 46th Sts. Buses run at least as frequently as every half hour from early morning until late evening; but call Carey for exact schedule: (718) 632-0500.

The **JFK Express** or **"Train to the Plane"** is a special bus-subway combination operating between JFK and Manhattan via downtown Brooklyn. To use this service from the airport to midtown, follow the signs (a blue circle with a white airplane) to the nearest bus stop, from which point an air-conditioned bus takes you to the subway portion of the ride. The subway makes eight stops: Jay St-Borough Hall in Brooklyn, Broadway-Nassau in the Wall St area of Manhattan, Chambers St near the World

Trade Center, W. 4th St in Greenwich Village, and on Sixth Ave (Ave of the Americas) at 34th St, 42nd St, 50th St-Rockefeller Center, and 57th St. The $6.50 fare covers both parts of the ride; coming from the airport, pay the bus conductor; going to the airport, pay $1 (a token) to enter the subway and the remainder to the bus conductor. The service operates daily between 5 A.M. and midnight at approximately 20-minute intervals. No porter service is available. Count on at least 90 minutes, but allow plenty of leeway. **Note:** At the present time (1990) the Department of Transportation is deciding whether to continue this service in the future. Call to check: (718) 330-1234.

Shared minibus service to major hotels in midtown is provided by Giraldo Limousine (tel: 757-6840) and Abbey's Transportation (718\917-6654). The service operates from about 7 A.M. until about 11 P.M. Fares run about $11 per person.

Helicopter

Service provided by New York Helicopter links Manhattan's E. 34th St Heliport (34th St at the East River) with the TWA Terminal. Departures are frequent during the day. The flight (ten minutes) costs (1988) $58. Lower fares available if linked with connecting flights; call the airline carrier. For reservations, tel: (800) 645-3494. Damin Aviation provides helicopter service between midtown and JFK on a charter basis; call 687-6650. Island Helicopter Corporation also provides charter helicopter service; call 683-4575.

Ground Transportation, LaGuardia Airport

Express bus service to Manhattan is provided by Carey Transportation, Inc., which operates between the airport and five stops in Manhattan (the same stops that service Kennedy, see above). Service from Park Ave is nonstop to the airport. Buses run at least as frequently as every half hour from early morning until late evening except to the shuttle terminals, where service is about every hour. For schedule, tel: (718) 632-0500.

Shared minibus service to major midtown hotels is provided by Giraldo Limousine (757-6840) and Abbey's Transportation (718\565-3213). The service operates from about 7 A.M. until about 11 P.M. Fares are currently $8 per person.

Bus / subway combinations. The Triboro Coach Corporation operates the Q33 bus between LaGuardia (Main Terminal) and the 74th St subway station in Jackson Heights (connections to E, F, G, and IRT Flushing #7 train to Manhattan); frequent daytime service, hourly night service. Similar service from the Marine Terminal. Exact change ($1 in coins or token) required for bus. For additional information, tel: (718) 335-1000. Not a recommended route for anyone inexperienced with the subway system.

Helicopter

Damin Aviation provides executive helicopter service daily between Manhattan and LaGuardia on a charter basis; tel: 687-6650. Island Helicopter Corporation also provides charter helicopter service: call 683-4575.

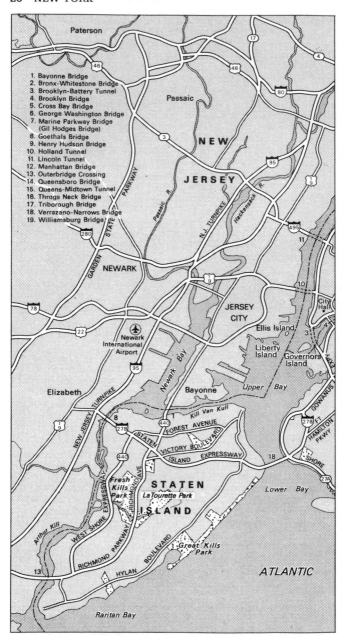

Paterson

1. Bayonne Bridge
2. Bronx-Whitestone Bridge
3. Brooklyn-Battery Tunnel
4. Brooklyn Bridge
5. Cross Bay Bridge
6. George Washington Bridge
7. Marine Parkway Bridge (Gil Hodges Bridge)
8. Goethals Bridge
9. Henry Hudson Bridge
10. Holland Tunnel
11. Lincoln Tunnel
12. Manhattan Bridge
13. Outerbridge Crossing
14. Queensboro Bridge
15. Queens-Midtown Tunnel
16. Throgs Neck Bridge
17. Triborough Bridge
18. Verrazano-Narrows Bridge
19. Williamsburg Bridge

Passaic

NEW

JERSEY

NEWARK

JERSEY CITY

Ellis Island

Liberty Island

Governors Island

City Hall

Newark International Airport

Elizabeth

Newark Bay

Bayonne

Upper Bay

Kill Van Kull

FOREST AVENUE

VICTORY BOULEVARD

STATEN ISLAND EXPRESSWAY

STATEN

ISLAND

Fresh Kills Park

La Tourette Park

Great Kills Park

Lower Bay

ATLANTIC

Arthur Kill

Raritan Bay

GARDEN STATE PARKWAY

NEW JERSEY TURNPIKE

N.J. TURNPIKE

Hackensack R.

Passaic R.

GOWANUS

HAMILTON PKWY

SHORE

WEST SHORE EXPRESSWAY

RICHMOND AVE.

RICHMOND PARKWAY

HYLAN BOULEVARD

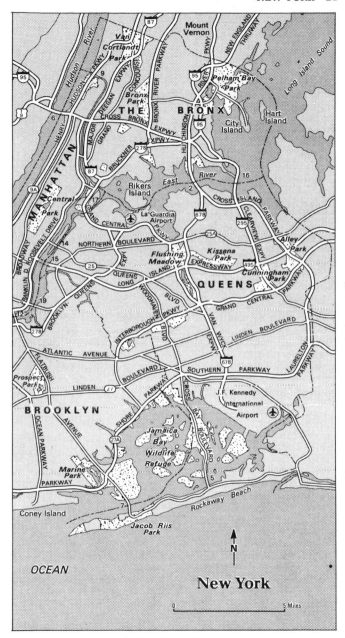

New York

Ground Transportation, Newark Airport

Express bus service. New Jersey Transit provides express motor-coach service between all terminals of the airport and the Port Authority Bus Terminal (Air Trans Center, ground floor, North Wing) at Eighth Ave and 41st St in Manhattan. Buses operate around the clock at about 15 minute intervals. The fare is $5. For information, telephone from New York (201) 460-8444 or from New Jersey (800) 772-2222.

Shared minibus service operates from the airport to midtown hotels in Manhattan from 8 A.M. to midnight at about half-hour intervals Sun through Fri, until 6 P.M. on Sat. Minibuses also available less frequently from hotels to airport. The fare is $11 from the airport, and between $10 and $14 from hotels. For information, call (718) 786-0073 from New York or (201) 961-2535 from New Jersey.

Bus / train combinations to and from New York City are available between Penn Station in Newark and Penn Station (33rd St and Seventh Ave) in Manhattan. For information phone from New York (201) 762-5100 or from New Jersey (800) 772-2222. Airlink buses connect Newark's Penn Station and the airport; telephone from New Jersey (201) 963-2557 or from New York 466-7649.

Helicopter

Service to and from the E. 34th St Heliport (at the East River) in Manhattan is provided by New York Helicopter. Departures from Terminal A (United Airlines Gate #2), frequently throughout the day. Lower fares available when linked to scheduled airline flights; check with airline carrier. For information and reservations call (800) 645-3494. For information on charter service, call Damin Aviation, from New York 687-6650 or from New Jersey (201) 863-7200.

Car rentals. Avis, Hertz, and other major car rental companies maintain offices at the airports. For information call these companies or consult your airline or travel agent.

Parking. All airports maintain large parking lots or structures for long- and short-term parking.

Public transportation to suburban areas. The following carriers provide transportation from JFK and LaGuardia to outlying areas on a regular basis and maintain facilities within the airports:

Long Island (Nassau and Suffolk Counties): Long Island-Airports Limousine 656-7000 or (516) 433-2277. *Westchester County* (N. Y.): Airport Transportation Services 655-4400 or (914) 968-7000. *Orange and Sullivan Counties* (upstate N. Y.): Shortline Flight Catcher Coach (201) 529-3666. *Bergen County* (suburban New Jersey): Fugazy Continental of New Jersey 247-8383 from JFK or 247-5800 from LaGuardia, or Shortline Flight Catcher Coach (201) 529-3666. *Fairfield and New Haven Counties* (Connecticut): Connecticut Limousine 656-8128.

Arrival by Train.

The main railroad stations are *Pennsylvania Station* between Seventh and Eighth Aves, 31st–33rd Sts, and *Grand Central Terminal* at Park Ave and 42nd St. Connections between the terminals must be made on foot (about one mile), by public transportation, or by taxi. The easiest public transportation between Grand Central and Penn Station is the M4 bus (downtown on Fifth Ave two blocks W. of Grand Central) which goes directly to Penn Station. To get from Penn Station to Grand Central, take the M4 bus across 32nd St and up Madison Ave to 42nd St. It is also possible to take the shuttle subway to Times Square and the IRT Broadway-7th Ave (train 1, 2, or 3) to Penn Station, though this route is not recommended to novices with luggage since the Times Square subway station is vast and bleak. Taxis cruise outside both train stations.

Arrival by Bus.

The main terminal is the *Port Authority Bus Terminal* at Eighth Ave and 41st St. There are local bus and subway connections within the station; taxis cruise along Eighth Ave. The immediate neighborhood is no place to linger, especially after dark, and the terminal itself has a resident population of homeless people.

Arrival by Car.

Unless you plan excursions to outlying areas, having a car is no advantage in New York. Traffic can be maddeningly slow. To the uninitiated the city's alternate side of the street parking regulations (parking allowed on one side one day, on the other side the next day) may seem byzantine in their complexity. Finding street parking can be difficult and parking garages are expensive, with midtown rates beginning at $10 for the first hour. Parking tickets are even more expensive. Cars towed from a zone marked "Tow Away Zone" are taken to a West Side pier and impounded; it is costly in time, emotional energy, and money (cash only, currently $100) to retrieve such a vehicle. If you are staying at a hotel, check with the doorman about nearby facilities.

Other hazards to the uninitiated include New York drivers and deteriorating roads. The former are aggressive and impatient but generally predictable. The latter are pocked with bone- and metal-jolting potholes, many impressive in their dimensions. In 1984 the Big Apple Pothole and Sidewalk Protection Corporation, a private firm organized in the wake of a law that made the city liable only for damages caused by registered potholes, catalogued and designated some 750,000 of them.

Getting Around in the City

Walking is the best way to see any city and is generally safe in New York if you use common sense. During the day you can walk almost anywhere, especially with a companion, and at night you can certainly stroll around busy streets. Avoid high crime areas—

Times Square after the theater crowd leaves, Eighth Ave around 42nd St, Harlem, the Lower East Side, the South Bronx—and deserted streets. Do not wander in the parks after dark unless attending a concert or other activity and even then stay with the crowds; do not walk alone in the isolated, remote parts of parks at any time (be cautious of Central Park above 100th St). Do not display money or jewelry; keep bus or subway fares handy so you do not have to dig publicly in wallet or handbag to find change. Traditional advice also includes being alert to your surroundings and looking confident, though no statistics exist as to the effectiveness of this posture.

A more recent pedestrian menace is a corps of bicycle-riding messengers whose profits are directly proportional to the number of jobs completed, and who are therefore deeply committed to speed. Since these cyclists often ride against the flow of traffic and not infrequently run traffic lights, pedestrians should look both ways, carefully, before stepping into the street.

Another problem for walkers, though not usually a danger, is the dramatic increase in the city's population of ''street people'' and beggars. Pedestrians are frequently assailed with requests, some intimidating, for money. In general, it is probably wisest to make an individual policy decision ahead of time and to resist intimidation. The problem is of major proportions and will not go away easily.

A 1978 ordinance, popularly known as the ''pooper scooper'' law, requires dog walkers to clean up after their pets, making foot travel in the city much more pleasant. According to a *New York Times* editorial, an estimated 22,800 tons of dog waste was excreted in the streets in 1983, of which ⅗ was scooped, leaving only 9,000 tons for pedestrians to avoid.

Manhattan's grid system makes it easy to find your way around north of about 14th St. Avenues run north and south and are either named (Park, Lexington) or numbered. Sixth Ave, officially The Avenue of the Americas, is still Sixth Ave to most New Yorkers and a movement to have its name officially changed back to Sixth Ave seems to be making headway. Broadway runs diagonally from the N.W. to the S.E. Traffic on most avenues flows in one direction, with alternate avenues running N. and S., though there are exceptions to this rule. Streets run east and west and are numbered E. or W. of Fifth Ave with the smallest numbers closest to Fifth Ave; thus 12 E. 72nd St lies E. of Fifth Ave but fairly close to it. Traffic generally runs east on even-numbered streets and west on odd-numbered ones, though again there are exceptions. Major crosstown streets with two-way traffic are 14th St, 23rd St, 34th St, 42nd St, 57th St, and 72nd St. Transverses cross Central Park at 65 / 66th St, 79th / 80th St, and 96th / 97th St. Below 14th St the grid system does not exist and streets are laid out unsystematically, reflecting their historical development. Uptown means north; downtown means south; crosstown means either east or west. Midtown is the part of Manhattan from about 34th to 59th Sts.

To find the nearest cross street on any avenue in Manhattan, take the address number, cancel the last digit, divide by two and add or subtract the key number below. Example: Where is 500 Fifth Ave? Cancel the last 0, and divide 50 by 2. To 25 add the key number 18 to get 43. No. 500 Fifth Ave is near 43rd St.

First Ave	Add 3.
Second Ave	Add 3.
Third Ave	Add 10.
Fourth Ave	Add 8.
Fifth Ave	
up to 200	Add 13.
200 to 400	Add 16.
400 to 600	Add 18.
600 to 775	Add 20.
775 to 1286	Eliminate the last digit; do not divide by 2; instead, subtract 18.
1286 to 1500	Add 45.
above 2000	Add 24.
Sixth Ave	Subtract 12.
Seventh Ave	Add 12.
above 110th St	Add 20.
Eighth Ave	Add 10.
Ninth Ave	Add 13.
Tenth Ave	Add 14.
Amsterdam Ave	Add 60.
Broadway	Subtract 30.
Columbus Ave	Add 60.
Lexington Ave	Add 22.
Madison Ave	Add 26.
Park Ave	Add 35.
West End Ave	Add 60.
Central Park West	Divide number by 10 and add 60.
Riverside Drive	Divide number by 10 and add 72.

Taxis. The city fleet has about 11,800 cabs, a statistic difficult to believe during a rainy rush hour; yellow cabs are licensed and regulated by the New York City Taxi and Limousine Commission and may be identified by their color and the medallion in the rear window. Rates, which cover up to four passengers, are posted on the door and are currently (1990) $1.50 for the first ⅕ mile and 25¢ for each additional ⅕ mile; thus a mile ride costs $2.50 before the 15–20% tip. A 50¢ surcharge at night from 8 P.M. to 6 A.M. is in effect on all cabs. Fares to destinations outside the city should be agreed upon before starting. There are a few taxi stands within the city, but most cabs cruise looking for passengers. The lighted sign on top of the car indicates whether the cab is available. To inquire about lost objects, tel: 869-4513; to register complaints, tel: 869-4237 (you must have either the taxi identification number from the lighted roof panel or the driver's identification number, posted inside the cab).

"Gypsy" cabs operate in the outer boroughs and in Manhattan outside the central and downtown districts; they are painted colors other than yellow, often have "livery" license plates, are not authorized to pick up passengers who hail them on the street (although they do), and are not recommended to visitors. In 1984 these cabs, an estimated 35,000 of them, came under city regulation.

Buses are relatively cheap, moderately reliable, and usually pleasant except during rush hours when they are crowded and can be slow, though restricted bus lanes on major avenues help somewhat. The city service operates some four thousand diesel-fueled buses traveling over 200 routes, a network of about 1000 miles. Passengers must have exact change (no bills) or a subway token (available at toll booths in the subway stations) to board. Since many stores will refuse to give change without a purchase, it is wise to stock up on tokens or hoard change. A single ride costs $1.15 and a transfer (free, ask the driver when you board) enables you to change to a second bus whose route crosses yours. Buses stop on demand about every two blocks going up- and downtown and every block crosstown. To signal your desire to get off, press the tape on the bus wall or, on older buses, pull the bell cord. Most buses run on a 24-hour schedule with reduced service at night. Official bus / subway route maps should be available at the Information Booth on the main concourse in Grand Central Station or at the New York Convention & Visitors Bureau located at 2 Columbus Circle (8th Ave / 59th St).

Subways are the fastest but not the most pleasant way to get around. Once the pride of the city, the subway system deteriorated seriously before the current improvement in the reliability of the trains and cleanliness of the stations. Nowadays 94% of the cars are air-conditioned and all are free of graffiti. On the other hand, the subways, like other public facilities within the city, have become makeshift shelters for the homeless, who loiter on the platforms and panhandle in the cars.

The trains run 24 hours a day across a 244-mile route (469 stations) in four boroughs (excluding Staten Island). The fare is $1.15 paid by token (available in booths inside the stations; you can purchase packets of ten tokens, which is advisable since they can be used on buses as well). Maps are posted inside the stations and also in the cars. Free bus / subway system maps are available at the Information Booth in Grand Central Station, the Convention and Visitors Bureau at 2 Columbus Circle, from the New York City Transit Authority, and sometimes in token booths. Routes to outlying areas can be complicated and confusing, but it is easy to travel up- and downtown along major avenues. Rush hours are crowded and unpleasant, best avoided by the claustrophobic. If possible ride the bus instead of the subway late at night, except in company; if you must take the subway during off hours, ride in the car with the conductor or, if there is one, a transit policeman.

SUBWAY SAFETY: The New York subway system has a reputation for crime and filth which though possibly exaggerated is not entirely undeserved. Though some 15,000 felonies are committed in the subway annually, 3.5 million riders use the system daily and survive. Use common sense; be alert to your surroundings; stay with other people; don't go down empty stairwells or ride in empty cars; don't lean over the edge of the platform; if in doubt stay near the conductor, who has a telephone, as does the attendant at the token booth. Beggars, pickpockets, and purse snatchers work the subways as well as the street.

Tourist information. The best source of information is the New York Convention & Visitors Bureau at 2 Columbus Circle (tel: 397-8222), open Mon–Fri 9–6; Sat and Sun 10–6. The bureau offers subway and bus maps, listings of hotels and restaurants, seasonal calendars of events, brochures about points of interest.

For schedules of weekend special events, guided tours, street fairs, etc., check the Friday edition of the *New York Times*. *New York* magazine and *The New Yorker* (issued weekly) have listings of films, concerts, plays, operas, ballets, sporting events, museum and gallery shows, jazz and popular music performances. The Sunday edition of the *New York Times* contains weekly listings of a similar nature.

Hotels

Hotels in New York are expensive by the standards of other American cities and they are often full, particularly during the business week; reserve in advance. The New York Convention & Visitors Bureau (2 Columbus Circle, New York, N.Y. 10019, tel: 397-8222) publishes a list of hotels in the city with current prices as well as a Directory of Vacation Packages, indicating special weekend or seasonal rates; available on request. Better rates may be had at many hotels for the weekends. The following list has been extracted from the Visitors Bureau publication and is offered with the reminder that inflation will undoubtedly have affected the rates.

Luxury Hotels: Double room with bath, $190 and up.

	Address and zip code	Telephone
Doral Tuscany	120 E. 39th St, 10016	686-1600
Drake Swissotel	440 Park Ave at 56th St, 10022	421-0900
Essex House	160 Central Park South, 10019	247-0300
Grand Bay Hotel at Equitable Center	152 W. 51st St, 10019	765-1900
Grand Hyatt New York	Park Ave at Grand Central, 10017	883-1234
Helmsley Palace	455 Madison Ave at 50th St, 10022	888-7000
Helmsley Park Lane	36 Central Park South 10019	371-4000
Inter-Continental New York	111 E. 48th St, 10017	755-5900
Marriott Marquis	1535 Broadway in Times Square, 10019	398-1900
Mayfair Regent	610 Park Ave at 65th St, 10021	288-0800
Morgans	237 Madison Ave, 10016	686-0300
New York Helmsley	212 E. 42nd St, 10017	490-8900
Omni Berkshire Place	21 E. 52nd St, 10022	753-5800
Parker Meridien	118 W. 57th St, 10019	245-5000
The Peninsula Hotel	700 Fifth Ave, 10019	247-2200
The Pierre	Fifth Ave at 61st St, 10021	838-8000
Plaza	Fifth Ave at 59th St, 10019	759-3000

Regency	540 Park Ave at 61st St, 10021	759-4100
Ritz-Carlton	112 Central Park South, 10019	757-1900
Royalton	44 W. 44th St, 10036	869-4400
St. Regis-Sheraton	2 E. 55th St at Fifth Ave, 10022	753-4500
Sheraton Park Avenue	45 Park Ave at 37th St, 10016	685-7676
Surrey	20 E. 76th St near Fifth Ave, 10021	288-3700
United Nations Plaza	1 U.N. Plaza, 44th St and First Ave, 10017	355-3400
Vista International	3 World Trade Center, 10048	938-9100
Waldorf-Astoria	Park Ave at 50th St, 10022	355-3000
Westbury	69th St at Madison Ave, 10021	535-2000

Expensive Hotels: Double room with bath, $140–190.

Barbizon (Golden Tulip)	140 E. 63rd St at Lexington Ave, 10021	838-5700
Beekman Tower	1st Ave at 49th St, 10017	355-7300
Doral Court Hotel	130 E. 39th St, 10016	685-1100
Doral Park Avenue	70 Park Ave at 38th St, 10016	687-7050
Dorset	30 W. 54th St, 10019	247-7300
Dumont Plaza	150 E. 34th St bet. 3rd / Lexington Aves, 10016	481-7600
Eastgate Tower	222 E. 39th St, bet. 2nd / 3rd Aves, 10016	687-8000
Elysee	60 E. 54th St, 10022	753-1066
Halloran House	525 Lexington Ave bet. 48th / 49th Sts, 10017	755-4000
Howard	127 E. 55th St, 10022	826-1100
Lexington	511 Lexington Ave at 48th St, 10017	755-6963
Lyden Gardens	215 E. 64th St bet. 2nd / 3rd Aves, 10021	355-1230
Lyden House	320 E. 53rd St, bet. 1st / 2nd Aves, 10022	888-6070
Madison Avenue Hotel	25 E. 77th St, 10021	744-4300
Mayflower	15 Central Park West at 61st St, 10023	265-0060
New York Hilton	1335 Ave of the Americas at 53rd St, 10019	586-7000
Novotel / New York	226 W. 52nd at Broadway, 10019	315-0100
Omni Park Central	870 Seventh Ave at 56th St, 10019	247-8000
St. Moritz	50 Central Park South, 10019	755-5800
Shelburne Murray Hill	303 Lexington Ave at 37th St, 10016	689-5200
Sheraton Centre	7th Ave at 53rd St, 10019	581-1000
Sheraton City Squire	51st St & 7th Ave, 10019	581-3300
Warwick	65 W. 54th St, 10019	247-2700

Moderate Hotels: Double room with bath, $100–140.

Algonquin	59 W. 44th St, 10036	840-6800
Bedford	118 E. 40th St, 10016	697-4800
Best Western Skyline Motor Hotel	725 10th Ave at 49th St, 10019	586-3400
Beverly	125 E. 50th St, 10022	753-2700
Comfort Inn Murray Hill	42 W. 35th St, 10001	947-0200
Days Inn–New York	440 W. 57th St, 10019	581-8100

Doral Inn	49th–50th St on Lexington Ave, 10022	755-1200
Empire	63rd St & Broadway, 10023	265-7400
Gramercy Park	2 Lexington Ave at 21st St, 10010	475-4320
Helmsley Windsor	100 W. 58th St, 10019	265-2100
Howard Johnson	8th Ave & 51st St, 10019	581-4100
Kitano	66 Park Ave at 38th St, 10016	685-0022
Loews Summit	569 Lexington Ave at 51st St, 10022	752-7000
Madison Towers	22 E. 38th St, 10016	685-3700
Milford Plaza	270 W. 45th St, 10036	869-3600
New York Penta	401 Seventh Ave at 33rd St, 10001	736-5000
Plaza Fifty	155 E. 50th St bet. Lexington / 3rd Aves, 10022	751-5710
Ramada Inn of New York City	8th Ave & 48th St, 10019	581-7000
Roger Smith Winthrop	501 Lexington Ave at 47th St, 10017	755-1400
The Roosevelt	45th St & Madison Ave, 10017	661-9600
Salisbury	123 W. 57th St, 10019	246-1300
San Carlos	150 E. 50th St, 10022	755-1800
Shoreham	33 W. 55th St, 10019	247-6700
Southgate Tower	371 Seventh Ave at 31st St, 10001	563-1800
Travel Inn Motor Hotel	515 W. 42nd St, 10036	695-7171
Wellington	55th St & 7th Ave, 10019	247-3900
Wyndham	42 W. 58th St, 10019	753-3500

Inexpensive Hotels: Double Room with bath for $100 or less. Budget hotels in New York can be depressing; you may get better value slightly away from midtown.

Aberdeen	17 W. 32nd St, 10001	736-1600
Arlington	18 W. 25th St, 10010	645-3990
Century-Paramount	235 W. 46th St at Broadway, 10036	764-5520
Clinton	19 W. 31st St, 10001	279-4017
Collingwood	45 W. 35th St, 10001	947-2500
Consulate	224 W. 49th St, 10019	246-5252
Esplanade	305 West End Ave, 10023	874-5000
Excelsior	45 W. 81st St, 10024	362-9200
Gorham	136 W. 55th St, 10019	245-1800
Grand Union	34 E. 32nd St, 10016	683-5890
Henry Hudson	353 W. 57th St, 10019	265-6100
Iroquois	49 W. 44th St, 10036	840-3080
Mansfield 5th Ave	12 W. 44th St, 10036	944-6050
Milburn	242 W. 76th St	362-1006
Palace International	429 Park Ave South, 10016	532-4860
Pickwick Arms	230 E. 51st St, 10022	355-0300
President	234 W. 48th St, 10036	246-8800
Remington	129 W. 46th St, 10036	221-2600
Stanford	43 W. 32nd St, 10001	563-1480
Times Square Motor Hotel	255 W. 43rd St, 10036	354-7900
Wales	1295 Madison Ave at 92nd St, 10028	876-6000
Washington Square	Washington Square Park, N., 10011	777-9515
Wentworth	59 W. 46th St, 10036	719-2300
Westpark	308 W. 58th St, 10019	246-6440

Special Hotels: In addition to the regular commercial hotels there are special hotels available only to certain visitors.

The *YMCA-Sloane House,* 356 W. 34th St, New York 10001, tel: 760-5850, located near Ninth Ave, accepts both men and women and is popular with students and Europeans. Rooms (some double rooms for couples) are simple but some have private bath. Inquire about weekly student rates. The *YMCA-Vanderbilt Branch,* 224 E. 47th St, New York 10017, tel: 755-2410, located between Second and Third Aves, is also co-ed, has shared bath facilities, a swimming pool, gymnasium, cafeteria, and laundromat. One night's deposit required to reserve; write or call residence director. The *West Side Y,* 5 W. 63rd St, New York 10023, tel: 787-4400, near Lincoln Center, is the most attractive of the YMCAs. It accepts both men and women for a maximum stay of 25 days (reserve daily). A few rooms have private bath. The extensive facilities—cafeteria, two swimming pools, sauna, squash and racquet courts—and good location make this YMCA very popular; write to the residence director well in advance and include one night's deposit to reserve.

Students aged 21 or older arriving in the summer may rent rooms at *International House of New York,* 500 Riverside Drive, New York 10027 (tel: 678-5000), near Columbia University. During the year International House is a student residence, mostly for foreign students though some Americans from Columbia and Barnard live there; it has a low-cost cafeteria, study rooms, and other facilities associated with dormitory life. Bathrooms are communal.

The New York International Youth Hostel at 891 Amsterdam Ave (W. 103rd St) will provide dormitory-style lodgings for travelers of all ages and nationalities. Visitors must carry their own gear and contribute to the upkeep of the hostel by doing small domestic chores, but accommodations are very inexpensive. The hostel also has meeting rooms, a cafeteria, kitchens, and a public restaurant. It occupies a restored red brick Victorian Gothic building (1891), originally the Home for Respectable Indigent Females, designed by Richard Morris Hunt, whose other surviving New York credits include the base of the Statue of Liberty. Tel: 932-2300.

Restaurants

Because of the sheer impossibility of one person's visiting all the restaurants worthy of consideration, this list has been compiled from personal recommendations, newspaper and magazine reviews, and restaurant surveys. It attempts to include the city's most famous, established restaurants, a wide variety of ethnic restaurants, and a number of restaurants located conveniently for the walking tours in the *Guide.* The brief descriptions are intended not as reviews (there is no restaurant on the list that some critic has not praised) but as descriptions, since a list consisting only of names seems of little value.

Those restaurants categorized as expensive will charge $50 or more for a three-course meal excluding alcoholic beverages; moderately expensive restaurants fall into the $35–50 range; moderate restaurants should run from $20–35; and inexpensive restaurants, less than $20. The tax on restaurant meals is currently 8¼%. In some restaurants lunch is a bit less expensive than dinner. Most but not all establishments accept the major credit cards.

Note: Call ahead for credit card policy and information on days and hours of operation (a significant number of restaurants are closed for lunch on weekends, all day Sun, and for vacations during the summer). You may also wish to inquire whether the facilities are accessible to wheelchairs, whether children are welcome, and (especially in small, new, or Chinese restaurants) whether there is a liquor license, since you may bring your own beer or wine if there is not. Make reservations on weekends for all restaurants and at all times for the more expensive ones (though it may be easier for a camel to pass through the eye of a needle than for a newcomer to get a weekend reservation at a currently "hot" restaurant).

Also included are a few restaurants in the outer boroughs, which are all moderately priced unless otherwise indicated.

Many Manhattan restaurants are concentrated in midtown or on the East Side above 59th St. Ethnic restaurants, with the exception of the more expensive Italian and Chinese restaurants, used to be clustered in the old neighborhoods—Little Italy, Chinatown, Yorkville (German and Slavic), and the Lower East Side (Jewish), but this is no longer entirely true. The Upper East Side boasts an abundance of Italian restaurants, but not because there is a significant Italian population. There are Thai restaurants on Eighth Ave in the 40s and Indian restaurants on E. 6th St. Some of the old verities still hold, however. Brooklyn's Atlantic Ave near Court St has Lebanese and other Arab restaurants while Astoria in Queens has Greek ones. Japanese restaurants are concentrated in midtown, near the business district.

Lower Manhattan and TriBeCa

Lower Manhattan was long a gustatorial wasteland, though the situation is improving as the area becomes residential. Good new restaurants now abound in TriBeCa and the South Street Seaport has generated its own eating places. The lunch crowd in the financial district can be overwhelming so eat early or late there if possible.

Arqua. 281 Church St at White St (334-1888). Stylish Italian restaurant, named after an Italian hill town. Northern Italian food; sometimes noisy; adequate service. Moderately expensive.

Bouley. 165 Duane St bet. Greenwich / Hudson Sts (608-3852). Recently arrived French restaurant in TriBeCa, with beautiful surroundings, beautiful appointments, beautiful food. Expensive.

Bridge Cafe. 279 Water St at Dover St (227-3344). Small pub-tavern with pressed-tin ceiling, American and continental food emphasizing seafood specials, vegetable dishes. Often crowded, no reservations. Moderate.

Chanterelle. 2 Harrison St at Hudson St (966-6960). Formerly located in SoHo. Nouvelle cuisine, graceful decor in old building. Expensive.

Ecco. 124 Chambers St bet. West Broadway and Church St (227-7074). TriBeCa Italian; convivial, young crowd of professionals and arty types in former bar. Open late. Moderately expensive.

Fraunces Tavern. 54 Pearl St at Broad St (269-0144). Reconstructed 18C house; famous for history, not food. Stick to simple fare. Closed Sat, Sun. Moderate.

Le Zinc. 139 Duane St bet. West Broadway and Church St (732-1226). An early TriBeCa cafe, named and styled after a Paris bistro. Still attracts a crowd of mostly young clientele. Open late. Moderately expensive.

Montrachet. 239 West Broadway bet. White / Walker Sts (219-2777). French restaurant in recycled TriBeCa industrial building. Softly lit, elegant dining room; dinner only. Expensive.

Odeon. 145 West Broadway at Thomas St (233-0507). An early TriBeCa outpost and celebrity hotspot; now favored by a more conservative set. Nouvelle cuisine in former Art Deco cafeteria. Closely spaced tables; high decibel level. Open late. Expensive.

Tenbrooks. 62 Reade St bet. Church St / Broadway (349-5900). In the far south of TriBeCa; popular bar for neighborhood office workers with more formal dining room. Well-prepared, hearty food including continental dishes, grilled fish and meat, pasta, main-course salads. Moderate.

Thai House Cafe. 151 Hudson St bet. Hubert / Laight Sts (334-1085). Downtown Thai, cheerful and informal. Moderate.

In the South Street Seaport area:

Roebling. Fulton Market mezzanine at South Street Seaport (608-3980). Informal, turn-of-the-century ambience, with crowded singles bar. Ground floor Grille. Seafood, continental, regional American dishes. Moderate.

Sloppy Louie's. 92 South St (509-9694). Formerly grimy, eccentric, and much loved; its present rehabilitation with the opening of the new South St Seaport has not improved it. Fish dishes, chowders, and a bouillabaisse that made the old Sloppy Louie's famous. Moderate.

Sweets. 2 Fulton St near South St (344-9189). In Schermerhorn Row. One of N.Y.'s oldest seafood restaurants. Renovated in 1983 with loss of charm. Fresh, traditional American seafood dishes. Lunch and early dinner (until 8:30). Closed Sat and Sun. Moderate.

In the World Trade Center:

American Harvest. In the Vista International Hotel, Three World Trade Center (432-9334). Comfortable, traditional American decor. American regional dishes offered seasonally. Friendly service. Open for lunch on weekdays, for dinner every day except Sun. Expensive.

The Big Kitchen. One World Trade Center, concourse level (938-1153). Fast-food complex with deli, health food, ice cream, sandwiches; attractive but no frills; crowded at lunch. Good place for children. No dinner weekends. Inexpensive.

The Cellar in the Sky. One World Trade Center, 107th floor (938-1111). Small, romantically dark restaurant in the interior of the tower, offers sophisticated, prix fixe, five-course menu (changes every few weeks) with an aperitif and four wines. Dinner only. Expensive.

Greenhouse Restaurant and Wine Bar. In Vista International Hotel, Three World Trade Center (938-9100). For informal breakfast and lunch or light meals. Sandwiches, salads, simple entrees. Glass, greenery, and skylight roof for view of World Trade Center towers. Lunch daily. Dinner Mon—Sat, Sun brunch. Moderate.

Hors D'Oeuvrerie. One World Trade Center, 107th floor (938-1111). Cocktail lounge with light dishes, fancy appetizers, small portions. Spectacular views. Evening jazz with cover charge. No blue jeans, jacket required. Moderately expensive.

Market Bar and Dining Rooms. One World Trade Center, concourse level (938-1155). Market setting; American food. Expensive.

Windows on the World. One World Trade Center, 107th floor (938-1111). Stunning view, international food, run as a club for weekday lunch (surcharge for nonmembers); very good, but sometimes uneven, food. Best bargain is Sunday buffet (see *Brunch*). Jacket and tie required; no blue jeans. Moderately expensive.

In the World Financial Center:

Au Bon Pain. One World Financial Center (766–9844). Good soups, sandwiches, and breads, pastries, and cookies baked on premises. Self-service. Inexpensive

Au Mandarin. Three World Financial Center (385–0313). Creative Chinese cooking with amiable service. Atrium seating. Moderate.

Donald Sacks. Three World Financial Center (619–4600). Good soups, salads, and pastas as well as more substantial fare. Atrium seating. Moderate.

Edward Moran Bar & Grill. Four World Financial Center (945–2255). Attractive pub with good burgers, raw bar, salads, daily specials. Great views of marina. Seasonal outdoor seating. Inexpensive.

Hudson River Club. Four World Financial Center (786–1500). Elegant, comfortable room overlooking Hudson with excellent American food some of which focuses on ingredients from the Hudson River Valley. Moderately expensive.

Pipeline. Two World Financial Center (945-2755). American food. Great views of the marina but noisy and crowded. Seasonal outdoor seating. Inexpensive.

Winter Garden Cafe. Winter Garden (945–7200). Dining under the palm trees featuring dishes from sun-drenched regions throughout the world, from Mexican pizza to Mediterranean salad. Inexpensive.

Chinatown

Compared to their uptown analogues, most Chinatown restaurants lack refinements of decor, with bare Formica tabletops, fluorescent lights, and paper napkins constituting the main decorative elements. In some restaurants you may be asked to share your table. Toilet facilities are often rudimentary. Many restaurants do not take reservations and some do not take credit cards, so it is wise to phone ahead. Their reputations can be as volatile as dry tinder, with "hot" restaurants attracting long lines of customers for a while only to relapse into relative obscurity. However, the food is often excellent and inexpensive. You can bring your own beer and wine to those restaurants lacking liquor licenses.

Bo Ky. 80 Bayard St near Mott St (406-2292). Vietnamese, with Chinese cooking as well. Small, informal, inexpensive.

Canton. 45 Division St near Market St (226-0921). Large restaurant, seafood specialties, minimal decor; beer sold, but bring your own wine, liquor. Moderate.

Grand Fortune. 194 Canal St near Mott St (267-2221). Attractively prepared dim sum downstairs; counter upstairs for regular Chinese dining. Inexpensive.

Hee Seung Fung also known as H.S.F. 46 Bowery near Canal St (374-1319). Chinatown's largest and formerly most popular dim sum restaurant, now has branches in midtown and on Long Island. Also serves Cantonese food; Chinese decor, bustling. Moderate.

Hong Fat. 63 Mott St (962-9588). Popular noodle house. Open until 5 A.M. Inexpensive.

Hwa Yuan Szechuan Inn. 40 E. Broadway near Market St (966-5534). Szechuan cuisine, hot and spicy. Popular, inexpensive.

King Fung. 20 Elizabeth St near Canal St (964-5256). Large, noisy, colorful Chinese restaurant serving mainly Chinese customers. Cantonese cooking including exotic and unfamiliar dishes. Bring your own alcoholic beverages. Dim sum breakfast and lunch. Inexpensive.

Ko Shing. 7 Division St near Catherine St (966-1713). Rice shop, local clientele. Large portions. Simple cooking. Popular and busy. Inexpensive.

Lan Hong Kok Seafood House. 31 Division St near Catherine St (431-9063). Modest surroundings, fine Cantonese seafood, also meat, vegetable dishes, and dim sum until 4 P.M. Some more exotic dishes only on the Chinese menu. Inexpensive.

The Nice Restaurant. 35 East Broadway at Chatham Sq (406-9510). Large upstairs dining room (extra seating downstairs), brightly lit, popular with local Chinese families. Hong Kong / Cantonese cuisine; expansive menu. No liquor license; waiters do not all speak English. Moderate.

Peking Duck House. 22 Mott St near Pell St (962-8208). Fine Peking duck with the traditional accoutrements; some dim sum; otherwise, hearty, homestyle cooking. Also has uptown branch at 199 Amsterdam Ave, near Lincoln Center. Moderate.

Phoenix Garden. 46 Bowery near Elizabeth St, in the arcade (962-8934). Modest surroundings; sophisticated Cantonese food. Inexpensive.

Saigon Restaurant. 60 Mulberry St near Bayard St (227-8825). Vietnamese food in simple, family-run restaurant. Noteworthy appetizers and cold salads, as well as other specialties of Vietnamese cuisine, which has been described as midway between Chinese and Thai cooking. Inexpensive.

Say Eng Look. 5 East Broadway near Chatham Square (732-0796). Shanghai cuisine; very popular but no reservations. The name means Four Five Six, a winning dice combination in Chinese gambling games. *Four Five Six* (964-5853) at 2 Bowery (corner of Doyers St) is a branch of the same restaurant with a similar menu. Inexpensive.

Silver Palace. 50 Bowery near Canal St (964-1204). Large selection of dim sum served off rolling carts. Often crowded on Sundays. Open all day, 8 A.M.–11 P.M. Inexpensive.

Siu Lam Kung Restaurant. 18 Elizabeth St, S. of Canal St (732-0974). Informal, crowded restaurant with excellent, unusual Cantonese dishes (and a few Szechuan choices). Less hectic for weekday lunch or early (or late) dinner. Inexpensive.

20 Mott Street Restaurant. 20 Mott St (964-0380). Attractive, busy three-level restaurant; large menu features Cantonese specialities including fine roast duck. Beer and plum wine are the only alcoholic beverages. Inexpensive.

Wo Hop. 15–17 Mott St near Chatham Square (962-8617). Cantonese noodle shop serves noodles with pork, chicken, vegetable toppings. Open late. Inexpensive.

Yun Luck Rice Shoppe. 17 Doyers St near Pell St (571-1375). Superior Cantonese food; fluorescent and Formica decor; highly rated by food critics. Inexpensive.

Little Italy

Most of the Italians are gone from Little Italy but the restaurants remain, augmented by a number of new ones that arrived with the neighborhood's *rinascimento*. Many of the older restaurants are family affairs, with plentiful food (the red sauce and garlic kind) served in a convivial atmosphere. The newer ones are likely to be more sophisticated, and also more expensive.

Angelo's. 146 Mulberry St bet. Grand / Hester Sts (966-1277). Pasta, zuppa di pesce, Neapolitan specialities. Moderate.

Benito's (I and II). 174 Mulberry St (226-9171) and 163 Mulberry St (226-9012); bet. Broome / Grand Sts. Another old timer. Sicilian and southern Italian food. Moderate.

Florio's. 192 Grand St bet. Mott / Mulberry Sts (226-7610). Fine pizza in small, sit-down restaurant. Inexpensive.

Il Cortile. 125 Mulberry St bet. Hester / Canal Sts (226-6060). Northern and southern Italian dishes, handsome restaurant with tile floors, pressed tin ceiling. Expensive.

Luna's. 112 Mulberry St (226-8657). Lively and popular spot for Neapolitan cuisine. Moderate.

Puglia. 189 Hester St near Mulberry St (226-8912). Informal, popular with the tourists; hearty Sicilian fare in large portions; long communal tables, lots of noise. Closed Mon. Inexpensive.

Taormina. 147 Mulberry St bet. Grand / Hester Sts (219-1007). Casual, cheerful Italian restaurant with large menu, good pasta dishes, reasonably priced wine list. Moderate.

Cafes and Pastry Shops

Cafe Biondo. 141 Mulberry St bet. Grand / Hester Sts (226-9285).

Caffè Roma. 385 Broome St bet. Mulberry / Mott Sts (226-8413).

Casa Victoria. 126 Mulberry St bet. Hester / Canal Sts (966-2862).

Ferrara's. 195 Grand St bet. Mott / Mulberry Sts (226-6150).

Lower East Side / East Village

Restaurants on the Lower East Side, no gastronomic Eden, reflect their surroundings—far from affluent, ethnically oriented. Those in the Cooper Square neighborhood and in the gentrified parts of the East Village also reflect their surroundings, catering to a younger, more affluent, trendier clientele.

Acme Bar & Grill. 9 Great Jones St bet. Lafayette St / Broadway (420-1934). Home-style southern cooking in funky truck-stop setting. Relaxed, informal, draws young crowd. Inexpensive.

De Robertis. 176 First Ave bet. 10th / 11th Sts (674-7137). Italian bakery and coffeehouse. Tiled floors, old showcases, old-time neighborhood clientele and new arrivals. All pastries baked on the premises. Inexpensive.

Gaylord. 87 First Ave bet. 5th / 6th Sts (529-7990). Indian in East Village, more decorated than the usual in this area; crowded weekends; live Indian music. Curries, vindaloos, tandoori dishes. Inexpensive.

Great Jones Cafe. 54 Great Jones St bet. Lafayette St / Bowery (674-9304). Small, informal cafe with downtown crowd and down-home cooking. Menu written on wall with markers includes hamburgers, enchiladas, occasional Cajun items. No reservations, usually a wait. Inexpensive.

Indian restaurants on Sixth St, E. of Second Ave. In this block are more than a half dozen small, informal Indian restaurants, most run by members of the same family. Among them: *Romna,* 322 E. 6th St (475-9394); *Mitali,* 334 E. 6th St (533-2508); *Anar Bagh Seafood Restaurant,* 338 E. 6th St (529-1937), said to be the best of the group.

Kiev. 117 Second Ave near 7th St (674-4040). Busy, inexpensive restaurant open all day and all night. Eastern European food, blintzes, pirogen, omelettes.

Khyber Pass. 34 St. Marks Place bet. 2nd / 3rd Aves (473-0989). Afghan food, generally rated highly. Exotic Third World decor. Very good value. Pleasant service. Inexpensive.

McSorley's Old Ale House. 15 E. 7th St near 3rd Ave (473-9148). Old-fashioned bar with sawdust on floors, memorabilia on walls; sandwiches, daily specials, ale. Open all night. Inexpensive.

103 Second. 103 Second Ave at 6th St (533-0769). A coffeeshop / restaurant hangout for the recently arrived neighborhood gentry; open all night serving salads, sandwiches, pasta dishes, nouveau American food. Moderate.

Phebe's Place. 361 Bowery near 4th St (473-9008). Actors' hangout; hamburgers, chicken, American food. Inexpensive.

Ratner's. 138 Delancey St bet. Norfolk / Suffolk Sts (677-5588). Famous old-time Jewish dairy restaurant with large menu, fallen from former glories, but one of the few survivors of its kind. Inexpensive.

Sammy's Roumanian Restaurant. 157 Chrystie St near Delancey St (673-0330). Good Jewish restaurant with Roumanian meat dishes, boiled beef, sausages (karnatzlach); avuncular waiters. Moderate.

Second Avenue Delicatessen. 156 Second Ave at 10th St (677-0606). Kosher deli (fans in the ongoing deli competition call it the city's best), with chopped liver, stuffed veal breast, other meat dishes and sandwiches. Moderate.

Sukhothai. 149 Second Ave bet. 9th / 10th Sts (460-5557). Spicy Thai food in upstairs restaurant with English pub decor. Good choice in upwardly mobile neighborhood. English spoken, but not fluently. Dinner only. Inexpensive.

Teresa's. 103 First Ave bet. 6th / 7th Sts (228-0604). Good simple food in the Polish tradition, pirogen and potatoes. Open late. No credit cards. Inexpensive.

Yonah Schimmel Knishes Bakery. 137 E. Houston St near Forsyth St (477-2858). The city's most famous knishery, founded in 1910, retains its original atmosphere. Knishes to take out; also dairy meals in the modest restaurant. Inexpensive.

SoHo

The SoHo renaissance brought an abundance of eating places from the humble to the exalted.

Amazonas. 492 Broome St bet. West Broadway / Wooster St (966-3371). Brazilian with lush decor, tropical fruit drinks, Latin music. Open late. Moderate.

Arturo's Pizzeria. 106 Houston St near Thompson St (475-9828); a good pizzeria. Inexpensive.

Cinco de Mayo. 349 West Broadway bet. Broome / Grand Sts (226-5255). Attractive, popular Tex-Mex in SoHo, with uptown branch. Sometimes crowded. Moderately expensive.

Elephant and Castle. 183 Prince St bet. Thompson / Sullivan Sts (260-3600). Casual but sophisticated branch of Greenwich Village restaurant; omelettes and other egg dishes, quiche, hamburgers. Moderate.

Greene Street. 103 Greene St bet. Prince / Spring Sts (925-2415). Large SoHo loft building, exposed brick walls, plants; very good continental food; top quality jazz and pops in the evenings. Slow service sometimes. Dinner only. Expensive.

Omen. 113 Thompson St bet. Prince / Spring Sts (925-8923). SoHo branch of family-run Kyoto restaurant; wood and brick decor suggestive of a Japanese country inn. Specialty is Omen soup, a spicy broth for plunging vegetables and noodles. Also sashimi and unusual Japanese dishes. No lunch weekdays. Moderate.

Tennessee Mountain. 143 Spring St near Wooster St (431-3993). Homey, attractive setting for down-home cooking. Spareribs, barbecued chicken, fried onion rings, chili. Moderate.

Greenwich Village

Au Troquet. 328 W. 12th St near Hudson St (924-3413). Modest, homey Gallic restaurant in the West Village. Small menu changes periodically, offering well-conceived, well-prepared French cuisine. Service slow sometimes. Dinner only. Moderate.

Black Sheep. 344 W. 11th St, corner of Washington St (242-1010). Bohemian, romantic, archetypal Village restaurant; French country cooking. Two seatings at dinner. Expensive.

Chez Brigitte. 77 Greenwich Ave near 7th Ave (929-6736). Very small, well-established French bistro. Simple, home-cooked food. Excellent value. Inexpensive.

Coach House. 110 Waverly Place bet. Washington Sq. West / 6th Ave (777-0303). Elegant, fine American and European food. Handsome inn-like setting. Dinner only. Expensive.

Cuisine de Saigon. 154 W. 13th Street bet. 6th / 7th Aves (255-6003). Modest Vietnamese restaurant in Greenwich Village townhouse. Dinner only. Moderate.

Da Silvano. 260 Sixth Ave near Bleecker St (982-0090). Italian storefront restaurant, interesting daily specialities, fine pasta; al fresco dining in season. Moderate.

El Coyote. 774 Broadway bet. 9th / 10th Sts (677-4291). Rustic cantina; Tex-Mex food, including generous combination platters. Inexpensive.

El Rincón de España. 226 Thompson St bet. 3rd / Bleecker Sts (475-9891). Spanish restaurant featuring paella, seafood dishes. Dinner only. Inexpensive.

Elephant and Castle. 68 Greenwich Ave bet. 11th / 12th Sts (243-1400). Small and popular; omelettes, quiche, hamburgers. Moderate.

Florent. 69 Gansevoort St, two blocks S. of 14th St bet. Greenwich / Washington Sts (989-5779). In the old meat market, now a bistro. Informal French food, but good value for the money. Popular and busy. Moderate.

Gotham Bar and Grill. 12 E. 12th St near 5th Ave (620-4020). High-ceilinged, multilevel dining room with rose marble bar. Very superior continental food beautifully presented. Expensive.

Harlequin. 569 Hudson St at W. 11th St (255-4950). Authentic Spanish cuisine, fine paella, in stylish, low-key restaurant. Menu also includes French dishes. Moderate.

Il Cantinori. 32 E. 10th St bet. University Place / Broadway (673-6044). Rustic decor, Tuscan and Northern Italian cooking. Expensive.

Il Mulino. 86 W. 3rd St bet. Thompson / Sullivan Sts (673-3783). One of the city's most highly praised Italian restaurants, hence very crowded at peak hours. Expensive.

Jane Street Seafood Cafe. 31 Eighth Ave at Jane St (243-9237). New England charm; clam chowder, broiled seafood. Dinner only. Moderate.

John Clancy's Restaurant. 181 W. 10th St at 7th Ave South (242-7350). Pleasant, low-key restaurant with intimate upstairs dining room. Seafood grilled over mesquite or well-prepared in other less fashionable ways. Extravagant desserts. Dinner only. Expensive.

John's Pizzeria. 278 Bleecker St near 7th Ave (243-1680). Small and mildly rundown. Only whole pizzas; often crowded but very good and justly famous among pizza aficionados who rate it best in city. Inexpensive.

La Boheme. 24 Minetta Lane off MacDougal St bet. Bleecker / W. 3rd Sts (473-6447). French bistro cooking, pasta dishes, French-style pizza in small Village restaurant. Sometimes crowded. Moderate.

La Métairie. 189 W. 10th St at Bleecker St (989-0343). Small neighborhood bistro; informal, good traditional food, superior couscous. Grilled fish, home-made bread. Moderately expensive.

La Tulipe. 104 W. 13th St bet. 6th / 7th Aves (691-8860). Stylish, small French restaurant, nouvelle cuisine; in renovated brownstone. Dinner only. Expensive.

Ray's Original Pizza. Sixth Ave at W. 11th St (243-2253). A stand-up pizzeria with a few tables; whole pies or by the slice. So popular that clones have popped up all over town. Inexpensive.

Rosolio. 11 Barrow St bet. W. 4th St / 7th Ave South (645-9224). Attractive storefront northern Italian restaurant; stylish, casual atmosphere, good service. Very highly rated food. Dinner only. Moderately expensive.

Vandam. 150 Varick St at Vandam St (929-7466). American and French food in 1940s Art Moderne setting; arty clientele later in evening. Dinner and late night supper; no lunch. Moderate.

Vanessa. 289 Bleecker St at 7th Ave South (243-4225). Noisy and often crowded; romantic Art Deco dining room. New American cooking, with stylish but successful food. Dinner only. Expensive.

Zinno. 126 W. 13th St bet. 6th / 7th Aves (924-5182). Large, bustling Italian restaurant featuring simple, Neapolitan food; jazz, piano music. Moderate.

Gramercy Park / Murray Hill: East Side, 14th—42nd Streets

An American Place. 2 Park Ave near 32nd St (684-2122). Offers the full gamut of American cooking from folk favorites (apple pandowdy) to neo-American cuisine (barbecued squab with wild rice). American wines. Prix fixe. Expensive.

Cafe du Parc. 106 E. 19th St near Park Ave South (777-7840). Neo-French cooking in attractive brick-walled restaurant. Grilled things, good fish dishes, luscious desserts. Moderately expensive.

Caliban. 360 Third Ave bet. 26th / 27th Sts (689-5155). Unpretentious restaurant with grilled dishes; attractive, simply prepared food with French accent. Moderate.

East Bay. 491 First Ave at 29th St (683-7770). Sandwiches, blintzes, daily specials. Inexpensive.

El Parador. 325 E. 34th St (679-6812). Small, long-standing, popular Mexican-Spanish restaurant. Moderate.

El Rio Grande. 160 E. 38th St near Lexington Ave (867-0922). Tex-Mex fare in two large, high-ceilinged dining rooms with Southwestern decor. Nachos, guacamole, grilled chicken, shrimp, and steak. Moderate.

Friend of a Farmer. 77 Irving Place bet. Park / 3rd Aves (477-2188). Homey sandwich shop with rural motif, serves wholesome, simple food: apple pie, buckwheat pancakes. Inexpensive.

Hakubai. 66 Park Ave at 38th St in Hotel Kitano (686-3770). Quiet, authentic Japanese restaurant. Moderate.

Health Pub. 371 Second Ave, corner of 21st St (529-9200). Attractive vegetarian restaurant. Borrows dishes from Oriental and European cuisines. No alcohol. Inexpensive.

Hee Seung Fung or *H.S.F.* 578 Second Ave bet. 31st / 32nd Sts (689-6969). Chinese dim sum lunch, also Cantonese food from the menu; newer branch of the Chinatown restaurant of the same name. Moderate.

Park Bistro. 414 Park Ave South bet. 28th / 29th Sts (689-1360). Authentic French bistro food in simple Parisian setting. Moderately expensive.

Pete's Tavern. 129 E. 18th St at Irving Place (473-7676). Great neighborhood bar, Italian and American food. Moderate.

Sal Anthony's. 55 Irving Place near 17th St (982-9030). Large, handsome, flourishing Italian restaurant; all the old standard Italian dishes, competently prepared and served up in generous portions. Moderate.

Salta in Bocca. 179 Madison Ave near 34th St (684-1757). Pleasant Italian restaurant; sometimes hectic at lunch, serene in the evenings; rose-colored walls, white linen, mirrors, flowers. Traditional Italian fare, well-prepared, courteously served. Expensive.

Tatany. 388 Third Ave near 28th St (686-1871). Busy, informal Japanese restaurant with two dining rooms, active sushi bar. Fine seafood, tempura, sushi, shashimi, Japanese pasta dishes. Moderate.

Union Square Cafe. 21 E. 16th St (243-4020). Attractive restaurant in refurbished Union Square area draws business, publishing crowd. Informal, friendly service; well-spaced tables. Stylish French and Italian food, attractively cooked. Moderately expensive.

Z. 117 E. 15th St bet. Park Ave South / Irving Place (254-0960). Greek food; taverna decor. Inexpensive.

Chelsea / Penn Station: West Side, 14th–40th Streets

The Ballroom. 253 W. 28th St near 8th Ave (244-3005). Informal, Spanish decor, tapas (Spanish hors d'oeuvres), bar, classical guitarist. Cooking and service uneven. Cabaret adjoining. Lunch Tues–Fri, closed Sun, Mon. Expensive.

Bistro Bordeaux. 407 Eighth Ave at 31st St (594-6305). Informal, well-prepared French food in bright setting. A good newcomer to the Madison Square Garden area. Moderate.

The Blue Hen. 88 Seventh Ave bet. 15th / 16th Sts (645-3015). American country cooking in a comfortable American farmhouse-style setting. Good-sized portions make this a good value. Moderate.

Chelsea Commons. 463 W. 24th St (929-9424). Bar with hamburgers and simple dishes. Moderate.

Chelsea Trattoria Italiana. 108 Eighth Ave bet. 15th / 16th Sts (924-7786). Modern setting, Italian food, trendy crowd, adequate service. Popular. Moderate.

Empire Diner. 210 Tenth Ave at 22nd St (243-2736). Art Deco interior; simple food. Open 24 hours. Moderate.

Foro Italico. 455 W. 34th St near 9th Ave (564-6619). Good pasta dishes; simpler meat and fish dishes are better. Moderate.

Frank's. 431 W. 14th St bet. 9th / 10th Aves (243-1349). Italian steakhouse, pressed tin on the ceiling, sawdust on the floor; large portions, friendly service. Expensive.

Keen's. 72 W. 36th St bet. 5th / 6th Aves (947-3636). Classic chophouse whose ambience harks back to its days as a gentlemen's club. Mutton chops, grilled dishes, game; pub menu in the barroom until 9:30 P.M. weekdays. Moderately expensive.

Le Madri. 168 W. 18th St at 7th Ave (727-8022). Authentic Italian cooking in a handsome, elegant room with a festive atmosphere. Expensive.

Lola. 30 W. 22nd St near 5th Ave (675-6700) Mostly Caribbean cuisine but with other dishes. Pretty setting though noisy. Expensive.

Manganaro's Hero-Boy. 492 Ninth Ave bet. 37th / 38th Sts (947-7325). In the Ninth Ave market district; no atmosphere whatsoever but famous for over-stuffed hero sandwiches. Closes at 7 P.M. Inexpensive.

Ozeki. 158 W. 23rd St bet. 6th / 7th Aves (620-9152). Sushi and yakitori bars offering raw fish and charcoal grilled meat and seafood specialties, plus tempura, grilled vegetables. Two small, informal dining rooms. Some English spoken by waiters. Closed Sat; dinner only, Sun. Moderate.

Periyali. 35 W. 20th bet. 5th / 6th Aves (463-7890). Superior Greek food in attractive Mediterranean setting. Popular. Some credit cards. Moderate.

Quatorze. 240 W. 14th St near 8th Ave (206-7006). Bistro atmosphere. Simple, well-cooked foods, mostly French. Some credit cards. Moderate.

In the immediate vicinity of Madison Square Garden:

Charley O's at the Garden. 9 Penn Plaza bet. 7th / 8th Aves (947-0222). Chain restaurant with pub atmosphere; full bar. Moderate.

Toots Shor. 233 W. 33rd St bet. 7th / 8th Aves (279-8150). Classic bar for the sporting set; steak and chops. Closed weekends except during major Garden sporting events. Expensive.

Consider also during shopping hours the restaurants in Macy's: The Cellar Grill, Cafe L'Étoile on the third floor, The Fountain on the fifth floor, and The Patio on the eighth floor with sandwiches, soups, etc.

Broadway, Theater District: West Side, 42nd–57th Streets

Audrone's. 342 W. 46th St bet. 8th / 9th Aves (246-1960). On Restaurant Row, French-Continental; crowded before the theater. Moderate.

Bangkok Cuisine. 885 Eighth Ave at 53rd St (581-6370). Atmospheric Thai restaurant. Inexpensive.

Broadway Diner. 1726 Broadway at 55th St (765-0909). Replica of 1940s eatery with Formica counter, tile walls, and chrome accessories. Diner fare—hamburgers, hash, sandwiches. Open 7 A.M. to 12:45 A.M. Inexpensive.

Cabana Carioca. 123 W. 45th St bet. 6th / 7th Aves (581-8088). Colorful upstairs Brazilian restaurant; feijoada, black bean dishes; long reputed the best Brazilian in town. Moderate.

Cafe Un Deux Trois. 123 W. 44th St bet. 6th Ave / Broadway (354-4148). Convivial, noisy restaurant. French-American menu; colorful crowd. Service sometimes inattentive. Moderate.

Caffe Cielo. 881 Eighth Ave bet. 52nd / 53rd Sts (246-9555). Fine Italian cooking. Attentive service. A real find in this area. Busy at lunch and dinner. Moderately expensive.

Chez Josephine. 414 W. 42nd St bet. 9th / 10th Aves (594-1925). Theater Row bistro-cabaret whose decor celebrates Josephine Baker, the sultry 1920s Parisian nightclub singer; clientele includes area musicians who perform on occasion; good bistro food. Moderate.

Curtain Up! 402 W. 43rd St at 9th Ave (564-7272). Soup, burgers, omelettes in outdoor cafe or indoor dining room. Inexpensive / moderate.

Darbar. 44 W. 56th St bet. 5th / 6th Aves (432-7227). Colorful decor includes imposing brass wall hangings; menu features northern Indian Mogul cuisine: lamb dishes, tandoori roasted chicken, fiery curries. Pre- and post-theater dinner. Moderate.

Fuji. 238 W. 56th St bet. Broadway / 8th Ave (245-8594). Restful dining room; well-prepared Japanese food. Moderate.

Jezebel. 630 Ninth Ave at 45th St (582-1045). Storefront, soul food restaurant (corn bread, sweet potato pie, ribs, shrimp, fried chicken); modest surroundings. Moderate.

Joe Allen's. 326 W. 46th St bet. 8th / 9th Aves (581-6464). Casual restaurant; theater clientele; hamburgers, and simple food. Popular at show time. Moderate.

Kiiroi-Hana. 23 W. 56th St bet. 5th / 6th Aves (582-7499). Small Japanese restaurant, fine sushi. Good service, pleasant surroundings. Moderate.

Landmark Tavern. 626 Eleventh Ave at 46th St (757-8595). Irish pub; hearty, traditional food, soda bread. Open until midnight. Moderate.

La Réserve. 4 W. 49th St off Fifth Ave (247-2993). Civilized French restaurant with upgraded cooking. Two dining rooms, softly lit and hung with large paintings of birds and animals. Classically based French cooking with tasteful innovations. Attentive, professional service. Prix fixe. Pre-theater dinner. Expensive.

Lattanzi. 361 W. 46th Street bet. 8th / 9th Aves (315-0980). Straightforward, hearty Roman food in modest, brick-walled restaurant. Moderate.

Le Bernardin. 155 W. 51st St at 7th Ave in Equitable Building (489-1515). Luxurious dining room draws corporate executives at lunch time; menu focuses exclusively on seafood. Fine service, superb food, extensive wine list. Very popular; difficult to get reservations. Expensive.

Le Madeleine. 403 W. 43rd St near 9th Ave (246-2993). Brick-walled bistro with zinc bar; flowers bloom in backyard garden (seasonal). Bistro food; many salads, pastas. Moderate.

Manhattan Island. 482 W. 43rd St at 10th Ave (967-0533). In Manhattan Plaza atop the health club; tropical decor with real foliage; mostly American regional food with pastas, salads, grilled things. Outdoor dining in summer. Some credit cards. Moderate.

Marie-Michelle. 57 W. 56th St near 6th Ave (315-2444). Sophisticated small restaurant with attractive appointments, courteous service, sociable atmosphere. Handsomely presented food, some of it rather elaborate. Good desserts. Moderately expensive.

Maurice. 118 W. 57th St. bet. 6th / 7th Aves in Hotel Parker Meridien (245-7788). Luxurious mirrored, muraled dining room; low noise level; fine distinctive French food. Rated one of the city's best. Expensive.

Orso. 322 W. 46th St bet. 8th / 9th Aves (489-7212). Casual, new-style Sardi's with theatrical and journalistic clientele but better food. Individual pizzas, pasta, grilled dishes, Italian desserts. After-theater supper. Moderate.

Palio. 151 W. 51st St at 7th Ave in Equitable Building (245-4850). Stunning, colorful decor evoking traditional Sienese horse race; opulent appointments. Extensive regional Italian menu. Expensive.

Patsy's Restaurant. 236 W. 56th St bet. Broadway / 8th Ave (247-3491). Neapolitan cuisine in friendly, simple surroundings; old-timer with loyal clientele. Moderately expensive.

Petrossian. 182 W. 58th St at 7th Ave in the Alwyn Court (245-2214). Parisian caviar firm presents exquisite foods—caviar, foie gras—in elegant civilized surroundings. Pre-theater and lunch prix fixe reasonably priced, otherwise expensive.

Pierre au Tunnel. 250 W. 47th St near Broadway (582-2166). Another veteran Theater District restaurant; good French bistro food, good service. Simple and straightforward. Moderate.

Raga. 57 W. 48th St near 6th Ave (757-3450). Beautiful setting, Indian food. Veteran restaurant. Moderately expensive.

Rainbow Room. RCA Building, 30 Rockefeller Plaza, 65th floor (632-5000). *The* celebrity opening of 1987. Gorgeously restored Art Deco trappings, dancing, cabaret; highly touted sophisticated food. Currently crushingly popular. Expensive.

René Pujol. 321 W. 51st St near 8th Ave (246-3023). One of the better low-key French restaurants in the Theater District; cuisine bourgeoise with a few updates; best dishes are humbler ones, seafood; service slow at lunch. Moderate.

Russian Tea Room. 150 W. 57th St near 7th Ave (265-0947). Favored by musicians, theatrical clientele, tourists; lively atmosphere, a landmark; Russian food. Expensive.

Sardi's. 234 W. 44th St bet. 7th / 8th Aves (221-8440). Formerly famous for its theatrical clientele rather than food. Sold (1986) to investment group outside the family, but still a tourist spot. Expensive.

Sea Grill. 19 W. 49th St, in Rockefeller Center near skating rink (246-9201). Faces the rink in winter, outdoor plaza in summer. Except for the Rainbow Room, the most ambitious restaurant at the Center. All kinds of seafood, well prepared and served with style; also some meat dishes. Expensive.

Sea Palace. 608 Ninth Ave bet. 43rd / 44th Sts (307-6340). Two pleasant dining rooms enhanced by greenery. Seafood Thailand style, also curries. Moderate.

Siam Inn. 916 Eighth Ave near 55th St (974-9583). Attractive restaurant, good hot Thai food. Inexpensive.

Sushi Zen. 57 W. 46th St bet. 5th / 6th Aves (302-0707). Small but comfortable restaurant, elegant sushi, shashimi, tempura, and cooked fish and chicken dishes. Moderate.

Tout Va Bien. 311 W. 51st St bet. 8th / 9th Aves (974-9051). Small bistro; French food. Moderate.

"21". 21 W. 52nd St off 5th Ave (582-7200). Haunt of businessmen (lunch), celebrities, and celebrity watchers. Steak, continental cuisine. Expensive.

Restaurants especially suitable for children:

Beefsteak Charlie's. Locations at 1500 Broadway at 44th St (398-1910), 709 Eighth Ave at 45th St (581-0500), and 51st St and Broadway (757-3110). Burgers, chicken, shrimp, salads. Inexpensive.

Carnegie Delicatessen. 854 Seventh Ave at 56th St (757-2245). Famous deli, corned beef, pastrami. Crowded around mealtimes. Avuncular waiters. Also suitable for adults. Open 24 hours. Inexpensive.

Hamburger Harry's. 145 W. 45th St bet. Broadway / 6th Ave (840-0566). As the name suggests, a burger place; different toppings. Inexpensive.

Stage Delicatessen. 834 Seventh Ave near 53rd St (245-7850). Corned beef, pastrami, other deli food; traditional deli waiters. Huge sandwiches. Inexpensive.

Midtown East: 42nd–59th Streets

Akbar. 475 Park Ave bet. 57th / 58th St (838-1717). Romantically decorated northern Indian restaurant; tandoori dishes. Moderate.

Ambassador Grill. 1 United Nations Plaza, First Ave at 44th St (702-5014). Menu emphasizes Gascon dishes. Restaurant favored by diplomats and United Nations personnel; modern downstairs dining room; piano music evenings. Breakfast, lunch, weekend brunch, dinner. Prix fixe. Moderate.

Auberge Suisse. 153 E. 53rd St near Lexington Ave in Citicorp Building (421-1420). Small restaurant; modern decor; Swiss food. Expensive.

Aurora. 60 E. 49th St bet. Park / Madison Aves (692-9292). Posh, comfortable dining room enlivened by Milton Glaser decor; well-spaced tables; low noise level. Outstanding French cooking, fine desserts. Expensive.

Box Tree. 250 E. 49th St bet. 2nd / 3rd Aves (758-8320). Intimate, pretty restaurant; French food; small menu; reservations essential; specify front room. No credit cards. No lunch weekends. Expensive.

Brasserie. 100 E. 53rd St bet. Park / Lexington Aves (751-4840). Open all day and all night, including breakfast, lunch, and after theater. Respectable food and service. Moderate.

Brive. 405 E. 58th St near 1st Ave (838-9393). Elegantly ensconced in an East Side townhouse; nouvelle cuisine based on high-quality ingredients; courteous service. Dinner only. Expensive.

Bukhara. 148 E. 48th St bet. 3rd / Lexington Aves in Helmsley Middletowne Hotel (838-1811). ``Frontier''-style Indian entrées grilled over charcoal or roasted in a tandoor (clay oven). Comfortable dining room with rough sandstone-colored walls, copper and brass accessories. Moderate.

Chalet Suisse. 6 E. 48th St near 5th Ave (355-0855). Established restaurant, country inn decor; Swiss food; fondue. Closed Sat and Sun. Expensive.

Chez Louis. 1016 Second Ave near 53rd St (752-1400). Transported Paris bistro, dimly lit, informal; serves homey bistro food: grilled and baked fish, foie gras, roast chicken, rich desserts. Expensive.

Chikubu Restaurant. 12 E. 44th St (818-0715). Small, neat Japanese restaurant enjoyed by Japanese businessmen; some of the best things reputedly only on Japanese-language menu. Fine broiled dishes, casseroles, shashimi, soups. Moderate.

Christ Cella. 160 E. 46th St near 3rd Ave (697-2479). Formerly recognized as one of New York's two finest restaurants for steak and beef; immense portions; continental cuisine. Expensive.

Dawat. 210 E. 58th St bet. 2nd / 3rd Aves (355-7555). Popular and comfortable Indian restaurant. Kitchen receives mixed reviews. Moderate.

Felidia. 243 E. 58th St bet. 2nd / 3rd Aves (758-1479). Brick-walled, two-level restaurant with expansive northern Italian menu. Superior food, but sometimes crowded and cramped in evenings and occasionally inconsistent; very popular. Expensive.

Four Seasons. 99 E. 52nd St near Park Ave (754-9494). Elegant modern French and regional American food. Handsome decor changes seasonally as does the menu. Upper echelon executives dominate Grill Room at lunch; Pool Room offers more gracious, romantic atmosphere. Prix fixe pre- and post-theater supper. Expensive.

Hatsuhana. 17 E. 48th St near 5th Ave (355-3345). Also at 237 Park Ave, entrance on 46th St bet. Park / Lexington Aves (661-3400). Small, authentic Japanese restaurant; seafood, superb sushi. No reservations; crowded at peak times. Moderately expensive.

Il Nido. 251 E. 53rd St bet. 2nd / 3rd Aves (753-8450). Long an outstanding northern Italian restaurant. Pleasant, not overly formal surroundings. Its blemishes stem from popularity: high noise level, crowding, occasionally self-important waiters. Expensive.

La Côte Basque. 5 E. 55th St near 5th Ave (688-6525). Bastion of Gallic splendor and haute cuisine; opulent dining room, luxuriant floral displays. Fine, classic dishes handsomely presented in ample portions. Prix fixe. Expensive.

Lafayette. 65 E. 56th St (at Park Ave) in Drake Hotel (832-1565). Opened in 1986 and quickly became one of the city's most popular. Elegant modern dining room, soft colors, well-spaced tables, low noise level. Classic French cuisine with Mediterranean overtones. Gracious service. Prix fixe. Expensive.

La Grenouille. 3 E. 52nd St near 5th Ave (752-1495). Another of the city's classic French restaurants. Mirrored dining room, celebrated flower arrangements, haute cuisine. Courteous professional service, highly praised food. Like others of its ilk, has an air of exclusivity. Expensive.

Le Chantilly. 106 E. 57th St near Park Ave (751-2931). Highly rated for its French haute cuisine, formal, sedate. Expensive.

Le Cygne. 55 E. 54th St near Madison Ave (759-5941). One of the most highly rated. Gracious two-level townhouse, rather formal and conservative. Fine French haute cuisine; classic dishes well prepared and elegantly presented; excellent service. Expensive.

Les Tournebroches. 153 E. 53rd St bet 3rd / Lexington Aves (935-6029). In the Citicorp Building; simple French food. Crowded at lunch. Bargain prix fixe dinner, otherwise moderately expensive.

Lutèce. 249 E. 50th St bet. 2nd / 3rd Aves (752-2225). Superb French cuisine in lovely former town house; unpretentious but elegant; generally considered New York's finest French restaurant. Difficult to reserve at peak hours. Expensive.

Ménage à Trois. 134 E. 48th St near Lexington Ave (593-8242). "Grazing" restaurant offers mid-sized portions of pastas, cold dishes, salads, hot dishes, so diners can assemble meals at will. Dining room decorated in muted colors; service slow. Moderate.

Mitsukoshi. 461 Park Ave at 57th St (935-6444). Brightly lit dining room;

elegant kimono-clad waitresses; small sushi bar, private tatami rooms. Excellent sashimi, grilled fish and meat dishes, sushi, tempura. Prix fixe dinners. Expensive.

Nanni. 146 E. 46th St near Lexington Ave (599-9684). Fine northern Italian cuisine; excellent pasta dishes, in lively, noisy restaurant. Expensive.

Oyster Bar & Restaurant. Grand Central Station, lower level, 42nd St near Vanderbilt Ave (490-6650). Tiled and vaulted rooms deep in the station; counter for quick service; long recognized for superior seafood. Perfectly fresh fish, many varieties of oysters in season. Crowded at noon. Closed weekends. Moderate.

Palm. 837 Second Ave at 45th St (687-2953). Grand old steakhouse with sawdust on the floors, cartoons of celebrities on the walls, clamorous atmosphere; blockbuster portions, efficient if brusque service. Crowded. Expensive.

Palm Too across the street from *Palm,* at 840 Second Ave (697-5198). All the above remarks apply.

Pasta & Dreams. 1068 First Ave at 58th St (752-1436). Small, cheerful Italian restaurant with a variety of colorful pasta dishes, salads, and light entrées. Inexpensive.

Prunelle. 18 E. 54th St near 5th Ave (759-6410). Traditional French with nouvelle cuisine influences; game classically prepared. Upscale clientele; elegant understated decor with etched glass partitions, flowers, burled maple fixtures. Expensive.

The Quilted Giraffe. 550 Madison Ave bet. 55th / 56th Sts in AT&T Building (593-1221). Refined, sophisticated, highly applauded nouvelle cuisine in beautifully appointed dining rooms. Reservations necessary well in advance. Expensive.

Seryna. 11 E. 53rd St bet. 5th / Madison Aves (980-9393). Beautiful Japanese restaurant with superior food, some cooked on heated stones. Very popular; pleasant service. Expensive.

Shinbashi. 280 Park Ave at 48th St (661-3915). Japanese restaurant with rock garden; well-prepared familiar specialties. Moderately expensive.

Shun Lee Palace. 155 E. 55th St bet. Lexington / 3rd Aves (371-8844). Outstanding Chinese restaurant with Szechuan dishes, Peking duck, pleasant decor, good service. Moderately expensive.

Sparks. 210 E. 46th St, near 3rd Ave (687-4855). Big, busy steakhouse with a stellar wine list. Outstanding steak, lamb chops, veal chops. Joins Umberto's as site of a famous gangland killing (the sidewalk murder of Paul Castellano in 1985). Expensive.

*Take-Zushi.*71 Vanderbilt Ave bet. 45th / 46th Sts (867-5120). Sushi and sashimi. Central location, two levels, more pleasant downstairs. Crowded; popular for food not decor. Moderately expensive.

Tino's. 801 Second Ave at 43rd St (687-5320). Fine steaks, chops, roasts in modern gray, red, and black restaurant. Cruvinet provides interesting selection of wine by the glass. Expensive.

Toscana. 200 E. 54th St at 3rd Ave (371-8144). Redecorated dramatically, with new menu. Northern Italian food. Good service. Expensive.

Trumpet's. 109 E. 42nd St near Park Ave (850-5999). In Grand Hyatt Hotel, but better than customary hotel fare. Quiet, comfortable atmosphere. Ambitious menu, nouvelle cuisine. Professional service. Expensive.

Wylie's Ribs I. 891 First Ave at 50th St (751-0700). Simple restaurant serving very good barbecued ribs, chicken. Large portions. Open late. Moderate.

Upper East Side, Yorkville: 59th Street and North

Alo Alo. 1030 Third Ave at 61st St (838-4343). Chic Italian restaurant underwritten by Dino de Laurentiis. Colorful, glassed-in room, smartly attired clientele; high noise level. Good Italian food, excellent pastas. Open late. Moderate

Anatolia. 1422 Third Ave bet. 80th / 81st Sts (517-6262). Uptown Turkish, with seafood, lamb dishes, eggplant, kasseri, baklava. Short, fairly priced wine list. Attractive, modern Mediterranean decor. Good service. Moderate.

Arcadia. 21 E. 62nd St bet. 5th / Madison Aves (223-2900). Small bar, attractive dining room with muraled walls. New American cuisine featuring native ingredients, French technique, imaginative combinations. Expensive.

Arizona 206. 206 E. 60th St near 3rd Ave (838-0440). Long, narrow restaurant with rough plaster walls, natural wood fixtures, casual service. Sometimes noisy. Well-prepared southwestern food including grilled dishes and game. Often crowded. Moderate.

Auntie Yuan. 1191A First Ave bet. 64th / 65th Sts (744-4040). Good Chinese food in high-style black dining room; efficient service. Uptown prices; uptown crowd. Expensive.

Azzurro. 1625 Second Ave at 84th St (517-7068). Small, family-run Sicilian restaurant; home-style food prepared with skill, especially good pasta; friendly service. Dinner only. Moderate.

Cafe Pierre. In the Pierre Hotel, Fifth Ave at 61st St (940-8185). Very elegant French restaurant. Breakfast and high tea as well as lunch and dinner. Expensive.

Cafe Trevi. 1570 First Ave bet. 81st / 82nd Sts (249-0040). Pasta and pizza, a few meat and fish dishes served up in informal attractive restaurant. Reservations only for groups larger than six, so there are long lines. Moderate.

Contrapunto. 200 E. 60th St at 3rd Ave (751-8616). Casual, stylish, all-white restaurant featuring many different pastas, a few appetizers. Sometimes hectic. Moderate.

Csarda. 1477 Second Ave at 77th St (472-2892). Home-style Hungarian restaurant with hearty cooking, friendly service. Dinner only. Moderate.

Devon House Ltd. 1316 Madison Ave at 93rd St (860-8294). Two small, low-key, formal, quiet dining rooms. Conservative French and Italian cooking; also more exotic Jamaican-style fare, reflecting the chef's origins. Dinner only. Expensive.

Elaine's. 1703 Second Ave at 88th St (534-8103). Famous for the clientele—writers, journalists, assorted celebrities. Not for the food (mostly Italian) or the service. Expensive.

Fu's. 1395 Second Ave bet. 72nd / 73rd Sts (517-9670). Comfortable, upscale Chinese restaurant with dishes from Szechuan, Shanghai, Hunan, Canton, Peking. Peking duck available daily. Moderate.

Gibbon. 24 E. 80th St near Madison Ave (861-4001). Spacious, pleasant, Japanese food with French influence. Expensive.

Greener Pastures. 117 E. 60th St near Park Ave (832-3212). Health food, imaginative salads, vegetarian dishes. Inexpensive.

Huberts. 575 Park Ave at 63rd St (826-5911). Elegant American, Amerasian cuisine in a restaurant whose success has moved it from Brooklyn, to Gramercy Park, to Park Ave. Sophisticated setting with touches of Japanese decor. Expensive.

Il Monello. 1460 Second Ave near 76th St (535-9310). Established Upper East Side northern Italian; pasta, seafood; pleasant, quiet atmosphere. Expensive.

Kalinka. 1067 Madison Ave bet. 80th / 81st Sts (472-9656). Small neighborhood Russian restaurant with informal dining room and takeout service. Borscht, stuffed cabbage, attractive salads. Wine and beer. Moderate.

La Métairie. 1442 Third Ave at 82nd St (988-1800). Uptown branch of Village bistro. Moderately expensive.

Le Cirque. 58 E. 65th St at Park Ave (794-9292). The ultimate New York celebrity restaurant; superb food; elegant setting; closely spaced tables, which may or may not be a disadvantage. Has maintained its status undiminished since 1974. Expensive.

Le Régence. 37 E. 64th St in Plaza Athénée Hotel (606-4647 / 4648). Formal but not stiff French ambience. Seafood, classic cuisine, graciously updated, professionally served. Expensive.

Melon, J.G. 1291 Third Ave corner of 74th St (744-0585). Neighborhood hamburger place and pub. Not fancy. Open late. Inexpensive.

Mezzaluna. 1295 Third Ave bet. 74th / 75th Sts. (535-9600). Trendy Italian, very popular with the pizza and pasta set. Crowded. Moderate.

Mme. Romaine de Lyon. 29 E. 61st St bet. Madison / Park Aves (758-2422). A standby for egg dishes. More than 500 varieties of omelettes. Moderate.

Paola's. 347 E. 85th St near 1st Ave (794-1890). Another Upper East Side northern Italian, loved by its clientele. Good service, pleasant surroundings. Moderately expensive.

Parioli Romanissimo. 24 E. 81st St bet. 5th / Madison Aves (288-2391). Long a top-flight northern Italian restaurant with highly reputed food; moved from former location and refurbished. Dinner only. Expensive.

Pig Heaven. 1540 Second Ave bet. 80th / 81st Sts (744-4333). Good Chinese food in restaurant with porcine decor. American desserts. Good for children with cosmopolitan tastes. Moderate (i.e., uptown Chinese restaurant prices).

Pinocchio. 170 E. 81st St near 3rd Ave (650-1513). Small, family-run restaurant; home-style Italian cooking. Dinner only. Moderate.

Primavera. 1578 First Ave at 82nd St (861-8608). Mahogany walls, low lights, potted palms, elegant conservative clientele who rate it very highly. A long-time favorite for classic Italian food. Dinner only. Expensive.

Red Tulip. 439 E. 75th St near York Ave (734-4893). Picturesque Hungarian restaurant with lively clientele and robust country cooking. Dinner only, closed Mon. Moderate.

Remi. 323 E. 79th St near 2nd Ave (744-4272). Venetian (the name means "oars"). Handsome decor and pleasant, friendly service. Menu includes risotto, gnocchi, fish, and veal dishes. No lunch. Moderately expensive.

Sam's Cafe. 1406 Third Ave at 80th St (988-5300). American bistro with simple, good-quality food; casual atmosphere. Peopled by celebrity watchers; high noise level. Dinner only. Moderate.

Sel & Poivre. 853 Lexington Ave bet. 64th / 65th Sts (517-5780). Pleasant, low-key bistro with small menu. Friendly service. Dinner only. Moderate.

Sign of the Dove. 1110 Third Ave at 65th St (861-8080). Handsome East Side town house restaurant. Vastly improved food and service. French menu. Elegant and romantic setting. Expensive.

Trastevere. 309 E. 83rd St near 2nd Ave (734-6343). A second location at 155 E. 84th St bet. Lexington / 3rd Aves (744-0210). Minute, family-owned Italian restaurant with small, closely spaced tables. Traditional Italian, Roman specialties prepared with care. Dinner only. Expensive.

Vasata. 339 E. 75th St bet. 2nd / 1st Aves (650-1686). Pleasant Czech restaurant known for roast duck and paprikasch specialties. Closed Mon, dinner only Tues—Sat. Moderate.

Vico. 1603 Second Ave bet. 83rd / 84th Sts (772-7441). Popular, sometimes crowded Upper East Side Italian storefront. Moderately expensive.

Violetta. 1590 First Ave bet. 82nd / 83rd Sts (517-7090). A superior small-scale restaurant among numerous Italian contenders that dot the Upper East Side; friendly service, close quarters. Northern Italian cuisine with Yugoslavian overtones. No lunch. Moderately expensive.

Wilkinson's Seafood Cafe. 1573 York Ave bet. 83rd / 84th Sts (535-5454). Casual dining room with brick walls, woodwork, etched glass, overhead fans.

Young clientele. Imaginatively prepared, high-quality seafood, a few nonmarine entrées. Dinner only. Expensive.

Zarela. 953 Second Ave near 51st St (644-6740). Home-style cooking by one of the city's premier Mexican chefs. Fine appetizers, imaginative entrées ranging in hotness from the mild to the murderous. Good desserts. Moderate.

Lincoln Center: West Side, 59th—72nd Streets

Unfortunately the Lincoln Center area, one of the most popular with visitors, does not offer an array of wonderful dining choices. Understandably, the restaurants closest to the Center are very crowded around concert time, so plan to arrive rather early. See also the listings for Lincoln Center itself.

Andiamo. 1991 Broadway bet. 67th / 68th Sts (362-3315). A welcome addition to Lincoln Center scene; Northern Italian, fresh attractive food in attractive skylit dining rooms. Expensive.

Beijing Duck House. 199 Amsterdam Ave near 69th St (799-5457). One of three branches (the other two are in Chinatown and on the East Side). Peking (or Beijing) duck always available without ordering ahead. Moderate.

Cafe des Artistes. 1 W. 67th St off Central Park West (877-3500). Howard Chandler Christy murals; romantic 1930s decor; French and continental food. Expensive.

Cafe Luxembourg. 200 W. 70th St bet. Amsterdam / West End Aves (873-7411). Art Deco cafe attracts arty late-night crowd and more conservative folk for dinner. Neo-American, Italian, and bistro food: roast chicken, pasta, duck, seafood. Pleasant casual service. Pre-theater prix fixe dinner. No lunch weekdays. Brunch Sat, Sun. Moderately expensive.

Connoisseur. 103 W. 73rd St near Columbus Ave (724-9760). Small basement Chinese restaurant with track lighting, brick walls, gray decor. Better than average food, especially the main courses. Takeout available. Open late. Inexpensive.

Dan Tempura House. 2018 Broadway at 69th St (877-4969). Short on atmosphere, but good tempura, seafood. Inexpensive.

La Boite en Bois. 75 W. 68th St near Columbus Ave (874-2705). Small, popular restaurant with countrified French setting; sometimes very crowded, especially around theater time. Well-prepared bistro dishes, seafood. Reserve well in advance. Dinner only. Moderately expensive.

Lenge Japanese Restaurant. 202 Columbus Ave at 69th St (799-9188). Japanese cuisine; American ambience; quick service. Moderate.

Los Panchos. 71 W. 71st St near Columbus Ave (874-8006). Outdoor tables in season; modest Mexican food in pleasant surroundings; life-sized stuffed burro at the bar. Moderate.

Manhattan Ocean Club. 57 W. 58th St near 6th Ave (371-7777). Serious seafood restaurant in sophisticated modern setting. Daily specials according to market; well-priced intelligent wine list. Open late. Good service. Moderately expensive.

O'Neal's Baloon. 48 W. 63rd St across from Lincoln Center (581-3770). Handy for hamburgers, snacks, and drinks before or after an event at Lincoln Center. Good for children, but crowded around theater time.

Pappardella. 316 Columbus Ave near 75th St (595-7996). Average Upper West Side Italian with outdoor tables in season. Moderately expensive.

Perretti. 270 Columbus Ave bet. 72nd / 73rd Sts (362-3939). Busy neighborhood Italian restaurant and pizzeria. Inexpensive.

Poccino. 1889 Broadway at 63rd St (262-2234). Informal Italian restaurant very close to Lincoln Center. Glass-fronted dining room, modernistic decor. Friendly if slow service. Good pasta. Open late. Moderate.

Shun Lee West. 43 W. 65th St bet. Broadway / Central Park West (595-8895). Large dining room with striking setting; very good Chinese food with dishes from all major Chinese cuisines. Moderately expensive.

Tavern on the Green. In Central Park, near Central Park West and 67th St (873-3200). Spectacular, glittering restaurant with chandeliers and floral displays inside and Central Park outside the windows. Large, eclectic menu; food good but generally rated less successful than the decor. Sometimes large crowds, slow service. Moderately priced pre-theater dinner; otherwise, expensive.

Victor's. 240 Columbus Ave at 71st St (595-8599). Informal, busy Cuban restaurant; sidewalk cafe. Moderate.

Ying. 117 W. 70th St bet. Columbus Ave / Broadway (724-2031). Pleasant Chinese restaurant with backyard garden; Szechuan and other specialties. Moderate.

Upper West Side: 72nd Street and North

The Alameda. 2160 Broadway at 76th St (873-1500). Attractive Mexican restaurant, young clientele, friendly service (many of the waiters seem to be aspiring performers); decor includes copy of Diego Rivera mural. Good salsa, casual Mexican food, margaritas. Moderate.

Alcala. 349 Amsterdam Ave bet. 76th / 77th Sts (769-9600). Spanish tapas bar and restaurant; wood floors and brick walls, which reflect sound. Marble-topped bar, hot and cold appetizers (octopus, mussels, anchovies, vegetables); main courses of Spanish persuasion. Spanish wine list. Closed Mon; dinner only. Moderate.

Amsterdam's Bar & Rotisserie. 428 Amsterdam Ave at 80th St (874-1377). Casual, cafe atmosphere; meat and fish dishes cooked on gas rotisserie in open kitchen. Moderate.

Au Grenier Cafe. 2867 Broadway bet. 111th / 112th Sts (666-3052). Upstairs eatery near Columbia University. Salads, pâtés, steaks and chops, wine by the glass. Popular with students and locals. No dinner weekends. Inexpensive.

Baci. 412 Amsterdam Ave bet. 79th / 80th Sts (496-1550). West Side cousin of Azzurro; small southern Italian family-style restaurant; rather noisy but good food at good prices. Moderate.

Balcony. 2772 Broadway near 107th St (864-8505). Hamburgers, sandwiches, etc.; glassed-in sidewalk cafe. Moderate.

Cavaliere. 108 W. 73rd St off Columbus Ave (799-8282). Geographically within range of Lincoln Center. Italian food, on the light side. Several dining rooms. Prix fixe pre-theater menu offered from 5–6:30. Moderately expensive.

Dock's Oyster Bar and Seafood Grill. Broadway bet. 89th / 90th Sts (724-5588). Informal, tile-walled fish house; oysters and clams, raw or cooked; lobster, homemade coleslaw. Brunch Sun; dinner daily. Moderate.

Empire Szechuan Gourmet. 2574 Broadway at 97th St (663-6004). Spicy and not-so-spicy Szechuan and Hunan fare in modest surroundings. Inexpensive.

Fine & Schapiro. 138 W. 72nd St bet. Broadway / Columbus Ave (877-2874). Delicatessen, sandwiches; within walking distance of Lincoln Center. Inexpensive.

Green Tree Hungarian Restaurant. 1034 Amsterdam Ave at 111th St (864-9106). Hungarian, family-style restaurant near Columbia. Moderate.

Melon, J.G. 340 Amsterdam Ave at 76th St (877-2220). West Side branch of trendy hamburger, sandwich restaurant-pub. Moderate.

Museum Cafe. 366 Columbus Ave at 77th St (799-0150). Straightforward burgers, steaks, sandwiches, fish; pleasant atmosphere; near Museum of Natural History. Moderate.

Sylvia's. 328 Lenox Ave near 126th St (534-9414). Informal friendly restaurant in Harlem noted for soul food. Drive if possible. Inexpensive.

Terrace. 400 W. 119th St near Morningside Drive (666-9490). At the top of Columbia's Butler Hall; fine view; French food; romantic atmosphere. Closed Sun and Mon. Expensive.

Brunch

A New York institution served Sunday and in some restaurants also on Saturday, brunch consists of light lunch or fancy breakfast dishes and drinks. Prices may be somewhat cheaper than at standard weekday meals. Make reservations several days in advance. Most major hotels serve brunch. Call for hours and prices. This list only skims the surface and is subject to change.

Adrienne. 700 Fifth Ave (247-2200) in Theater District.

Ambassador Grill. 1 United Nations Plaza, in Midtown East (355-3400).

Cafe des Artistes. 1 W. 67th St near Lincoln Center (877-3500).

Cafe Luxembourg. 200 W. 70th St near Lincoln Center (873-7411).

Chelsea Central. 227 Tenth Ave in Chelsea (620-0230).

Curtain Up!. 402 W. 43rd St, Theater District (564-7272).

David K's. 1115 Third Ave, Upper East Side (935-1161).

De'Vine. 396 Seventh Ave in Brooklyn (718 \ 499-9861).

Elephant and Castle. 183 Prince St near Sullivan St in SoHo (260-3600); 58 Greenwich Ave bet. 11th / 12th Sts in Greenwich Village (243-1400).

El Rio Grande. 160 E. 38th St, Murray Hill (867-0922).

Fu's. 1395 Second Ave, Upper East Side (517-9670).

Greene Street. 101-103 Greene St bet. Prince / Spring Sts in SoHo (925-2415).

Harlequin. 569 Hudson St in Greenwich Village (255-4950).

Hors d'Oeuvrerie. One World Trade Center, 107th floor, Lower Manhattan (938-1111).

Le Madeleine. 403 W. 43rd St, Theater District, (246-2993).

Mezzogiorno. 195 Spring St in SoHo (331-2112).

Odeon. 145 West Broadway at Thomas St, TriBeCa (233-0507).

Omen. 113 Thompson St, SoHo (925-8923).

Raintree's. 142 Prospect Park West in Park Slope, Brooklyn (718 \ 768-3723).

Remi. 323 E. 79th St, Upper East Side (744-4272).

River Cafe. 1 Water Street, Fulton Ferry, Brooklyn (718 \ 522-5200).

Sarabeth's Kitchen. 1295 Madison Ave, Upper East Side (410-7335).

The Sea Grill. 19 W. 49th St, Rockefeller Center (246-9201).

The Sign of the Dove. 1110 Third Ave, Upper East Side (861-8080).

Tavern on the Green. Central Park near Central Park West and 67th St (873 3200).

Water's Edge. 44th Drive at East River, Queens (718 \ 482-0033).

Windows on the World. One World Trade Center, Lower Manhattan (938-1111).

Open Late

These restaurants serve a complete meal until at least midnight. Hamburger places and pubs serve later.

Acme Bar & Grill. Lower East Side / East Village.

Alo Alo. Upper East Side.

Amsterdam's Bar & Rotisserie. Upper West Side.

Arizona 206 and Cafe. Upper East Side.

Ballroom. Chelsea / Pennsylvania Station.

Bridge Cafe. Lower Manhattan.

Cafe des Artistes. Lincoln Center.

Cafe Luxembourg. Lincoln Center.

Cafe Pierre. Upper East Side.

Cafe Trevi. Upper East Side.

Cafe Un Deux Trois. Theater District.

Carnegie Deli. Theater District.

Century Cafe. Theater District.

Chelsea Central. Chelsea / Penn Station

Chelsea Trattoria Italiana. Chelsea / Penn Station.

Chez Josephine. Theater District.

Chez Louis. Midtown East.

China Grill. Theater District.

Connoisseur. Lincoln Center.

Corner Bistro. Greenwich Village.

Curtain Up!. Theater District.

David K's. Upper East Side.

Dawat. Midtown East.

Devon House Ltd.. Yorkville.

Dock's Oyster Bar and Seafood. Upper West Side.

Felidia. Midtown East.

Four Seasons. Midtown East.

Frank's Restaurant. Chelsea / Penn Station.

Fu's. Upper East Side.

Great Jones Cafe. East Village.

Greene Street Restaurant. SoHo.

Il Cortile. Little Italy.

Jezebel. Theater District.

Jolson's. Theater District.

Khyber Pass. East Village.

Ko Shing. Chinatown.

La Métairie. Greenwich Village, Upper East Side.

Lan Hong Kok Seafood House. Chinatown.

Landmark Tavern. Theater District.

Le Madeleine. Theater District.

Le Zinc. SoHo.

Maxim's. Upper East Side.

McSorley's Old Ale House. Lower East Side / East Village.

Mezzaluna. Upper East Side.

Mezzogiorno. SoHo.

Museum Cafe. Upper West Side.

Odeon. TriBeCa.

Orso. Theater District.

Parioli Romanissimo. Upper East Side.

Pete's Tavern. Gramercy Park / Murray Hill.

Petrossian. Theater District.

Pig Heaven. Upper East Side.

Poccino. Lincoln Center.

Primavera. Upper East Side.

Quatorze. Chelsea / Penn Station.

Remi. Upper East Side.

René Pujol. Theater District.

Sevilla Restaurant and Bar. Greenwich Village.

Shun Lee. Lincoln Center.

Siu Lam Kung. Chinatown.

Tavern on the Green. Lincoln Center.

Teresa's. Lower East Side / East Village.

Tommy Tang's. SoHo / TriBeCa.

Vanessa. Greenwich Village.

Vico. Upper East Side.

The Water Club. Gramercy Park / Murray Hill.

Restaurants with Views

Most restaurants with views are noted exclusively for that; some are expensive, so it may pay to go for drinks and snacks instead of a full meal.

Anna's Harbor Restaurant. 565 City Island Ave, City Island, Bronx (885-1373). Large restaurant with Italian seafood and a view of docks and water (reserve table with view). Moderate.

Beekman Towers Hotel. First Ave at 49th St (355-7300). Glass-enclosed terrace on roof; music, drinks, and snacks. No meals. Moderate.

Harbor View. 1 Cadman Plaza West at Water St, Brooklyn (718 \ 237-2224). Large restaurant with view of the skyline of Manhattan and the East River. Southern Italian food. Piano music on weekends. Moderate.

Rainbow Room. RCA Building, 30 Rockefeller Plaza (757-9090). Classic Art Deco room with wonderful view, good food. Very popular since its reopening in 1987. It is also possible to enjoy the view from the cocktail lounge.

River Cafe. 1 Water St, Brooklyn (718 \ 522-5200). Glorious view of the harbor, Statue of Liberty, and East River bridges; ambience stellar, food very good also. Expensive.

The Terrace. Butler Hall, 400 W. 118th St at Morningside Drive, near Columbia University (666-9490). Fine view of Hudson River and city; good food with French accent; sometimes live chamber music. Expensive.

Top of the Six's. 666 Fifth Ave between 52nd / 53rd Sts (757-6662). Good view, and a good spot for cocktails; hors d'oeuvres served with cocktails Mon–Fri 5–7. Expensive.

The View. 1700 Broadway in Marriott Marquis Hotel bet. 45th / 46th Sts (704-8900). The only revolving restaurant in town; rotates a full circle every 45 minutes; views stretch as far as the New Jersey shoreline. Open for lunch and dinner, pre-theater dinner, also cocktail lounges. French, Italian, American cuisine. Expensive.

The Water's Edge. East River Yacht Club, 44th Drive at the East River (718 \ 482-0033). Good multi-level restaurant with spectacular views of midtown Manhattan and the river; continental cuisine, grilled dishes, seafood. Water taxi service from Manhattan. Expensive.

Windows on the World. One World Trade Center, 107th Floor (938-1111). Stunning room, stunning view; food of higher quality than in most upper floor restaurants. Go early or late. Or enjoy the view from the cocktail lounge (drinks and snacks). Expensive.

Restaurants in the Outer Boroughs

Most restaurants in the outer boroughs are neither as sophisticated nor as expensive as those in Manhattan. Many of those listed below are in ethnic neighborhoods and have informal, even homey atmospheres, straightforward food, friendly service. Some do not take credit cards; some do not have liquor licenses, and you may bring your own beer or wine. Call ahead to make sure.

Restaurants in the Bronx

In City Island: City Island used to be a community whose industry centered around the water. Not surprisingly it has a number of seaside restaurants, many of which cater to the large crowds of tourists and visitors from inland New York who come on the weekends in the warm seasons. *Anna's Harbor Restaurant,* 565 City Island Ave (885-1373); a large restaurant; moderately expensive. *Thwaites Inn,* 536 City Island Ave (885-1023); large, busy, sometimes touristic. *Sammy's Fish Box Restaurant,* 41 City Island Ave (885-0920). *The Lobster Box,* 34 City Island Ave (885-1952). At the far end is *Tony's Pier* at 1 City Island Ave (885-1424).

In Belmont (near the zoo): *Dominick's,* 2335 Arthur Ave (733-2807), a bar with a few tables in front, no menu; small, homey, and famous enough to have lines in front. *Ann & Tony's,* 2407 Arthur Ave (364-8250). *Full Moon Pizzeria,* 602 E. 187th St (584-3451).

In Baychester (near Co-op City): *Il Boschetto,* 1660 E. Gun Hill Rd at Tiemann Ave (379-9335). **In Throg's Neck:** *Amerigo's,* 3587 E. Tremont Ave near Lafayette Ave (824-7766).

Restaurants in Brooklyn

On Atlantic Ave (Arab and Near Eastern restaurants): *Tripoli,* 156 Atlantic Ave near Clinton St (718 \ 596-5800), veteran restaurant, down-to-earth ethnic food. *Moroccan Star,* 205 Atlantic Ave (718 \ 643-0800). Numerous other inexpensive restaurants; bring your own wine or beer.

In Fulton Ferry: *River Cafe,* 1 Water St (718 \ 522-5200); one of the borough's most expensive and elegant. Prices and food compete with those in Manhattan.

Parker's Lighthouse, 1 Main St near Water St (718 \ 237-1555); informal place for seafood, salads, sandwiches; good for kids.

In Coney Island: *Gargiulo's,* 2911 W. 15th St bet. Surf / Mermaid Aves (718 \ 266-4891); once-famous, still popular Italian seafood restaurant. *Totonno's,* 1524 Neptune Ave (718 \ 372-8606); pizzeria open weekends only; inexpensive. **In Brooklyn Heights:** *Tanpopo,* 36 Joralemon St near Columbia Place (718 \ 596-2968); reputedly Brooklyn's best Japanese; moderately expensive. **In Downtown Brooklyn:** (Note: This area is busy during the day deserted at night.) *Gage & Tollner,* 374 Fulton St at Jay St (718 \ 875-5181); seafood in handsome 19C restaurant with landmark interior, moderately expensive. *Junior's,* 386 Flatbush Ave Extension at DeKalb (718 \ 852-5257); deli with famous cheese cake; open late; near Brooklyn Academy of Music but a borderline neighborhood late at night.

In Williamsburg: *Peter Luger Steak House,* 178 Broadway (718 \ 387-7400); famous old steakhouse began as Charles Luger's Cafe, Billiards and Bowling Alley; retains old tavern atmosphere with wood beams, scrubbed tables; moderately expensive. **In Greenpoint:** *Bamonte's,* 32 Withers St (718 \ 384-8831); straightforward Italo-American; popular hangout for local politicians; closed Tues. **In Clinton Hill:** *Joe's Place,* 264 Waverly Ave (718 \ 622-9244). **Near Prospect Park:** *Raintree,* 142 Prospect Park West at 9th St (718 \ 768-3723); small, informal bistro; dinner only. *New Prospect Cafe,* 393 Flatbush Ave (718 \ 638-2148). *Aunt Sonya's,* 1123 8th Ave (718 \ 965-9526).

In Bay Ridge: *Nightfalls,* 7612 3rd Ave bet. 76th / 77th Sts (718 \ 748-8700); elegant sophisticated setting; good neo-American cuisine.

In Bensonhurst: *Tommaso,* 1464 86th St bet. 14th / 15th Aves (718 \ 236-9883); southern Italian cooking with opera also on the weekends; moderately expensive. *Joe's of Avenue U,* 287 Avenue U (718 \ 449-9285); informal southern Italian.

Restaurants in Queens

In Long Island City: *The Bank,* 35-01 Broadway (718 \ 278-4720); southern Italian neighborhood restaurant; fish; moderate. *Los Illusiones,* 36-32 Steinway St, corner of Northern Blvd (718 \ 729-3301); very good Mexican restaurant, patronized by Mexicans and lovers of Mexican food; features music; close to Kaufman-Astoria Studios; moderate. *The Water's Edge,* East River Yacht Club, 44th Drive at the East River (718 \ 482-0033); multi-level restaurant with spectacular views of midtown Manhattan and the river; continental cuisine, grilled dishes, seafood; expensive.

In Astoria (Greek restaurants): *Roumeli Taverna,* 33-04 Broadway, bet. 33rd / 34th Sts (718 \ 278-7533). *Taygetos,* 30-11 30th Ave (718 \ 726-5195). All are moderately priced. Pastry and coffee shops: *Omonoia,* 33-30 Broadway (718 \ 274-6650). *HBH European Cafe,* 29-28 30th Ave (718 \ 274-1609). *Lefkos Pyrgos,* 22-85 31st St (718 \ 932-4423).

Astoria also has Italian and to a lesser extent Czech and Ukrainian populations. *Piccola Venezia,* 42-01 28th Ave near 42nd St (718 \ 721-8470), is a pleasant northern Italian restaurant.

In Flushing: *Villa Bianca,* 167-17 Northern Blvd (718 \ 353-7065); popular Italian; small dining rooms, relaxed ambience; inexpensive. *Stony Wok,* 137-40 Northern Blvd (718 \ 445-8535).

In Corona: *Parkside Restaurant,* 107-01 Corona Ave at 108th St / 51st Ave (718 \ 271-9274); elegant yet relaxed restaurant in old-time Italian neighborhood; next to a small park where elderly Italian men play *bocce;* fine food at moderate prices.

In Forest Hills: *London Lennie's,* 63-88 Woodhaven Blvd (718 \ 894-8084); busy, homey fish house; no reservations so expect to wait during peak hours; no lunch Sat, closed Mon, Tues; no credit cards; moderate. *La Stella,* 102-11 Queens Blvd (718 \ 459-9511), closed Mon.

In Elmhurst: *Jai Ya Thai,* 81-11 Broadway bet. Queens Blvd / 74th St (718 \ 651-1330); casual Thai restaurant; seafood especially good; inexpensive.

Restaurants in Staten Island

Staten Island is no gastronomic paradise except for fanciers of fast food, which may be found in abundance in the malls and shopping centers that dot the island as well as along the major streets. There are also small, family-style Italian restaurants, since Americans of Italian descent make up most of the population. Since many of the museums and other points of interest are community oriented and do not include restaurants, the following list is offered.

Near the zoo: *Forest Inn Restaurant,* 843 Forest Ave not far from Broadway (718 \ 727-6060); snacks, plain food. **Near Snug Harbor:** *R.H. Tugs,* 1115 Richmond Terrace (718 \ 447-6369).

In New Dorp: *Mauro's,* 121 Roma Ave off New Dorp Lane near the beach (718 \ 351-8441); moderately priced Italian restaurant; closed Mon. *Hedges Cafe,* 2561 Hyland Blvd near New Dorp Lane (718 \ 667-3838); cafe serving burgers, fries; active bar; open late; inexpensive. **Near South Beach:** *Basilio Inn,* 2 Galesville Court between the Verrazano Bridge and South Beach (718 \ 447-9292); attractive Italian restaurant in former carriage house. Closed Jan–April. **In Great Kills:** *Buona Pasta,* 3935 Amboy Rd at Giffords Lane (718 \ 967-9385); as the name suggests, good pasta, homestyle; modest surroundings; closed Mon. *Carmen's,* 750 Barclay Ave off Hylan Blvd near Arden Ave overlooking Raritan Bay (718 \ 356-2725); fine view, Mexican food.

Sightseeing Services

The Quarterly Calendar of Events published by the New York Convention & Visitors Bureau contains an inclusive list of commercial sightseeing services. Copies are available at 2 Columbus Circle (59th St at 8th Ave), open weekdays 9–6 and weekends 10–6.

General Tours, available by various means of transportation, are useful for first-time visitors or sightseers with limited time. Among the better known are:

Boat: *Circle Line Sightseeing,* three-hour cruises around Manhattan Island with commentary. Boats leave from Pier 83 at the foot of W. 42nd St at frequent intervals from mid-March to Nov. Tel: 563-3200 for rates and sailing schedule.

The Seaport Line, 19 Fulton St, Suite 307 (406-3434), offers 1½-hour tours of the harbor with close views of the Statue of Liberty on the *Andrew Fletcher,* a sidewheel paddleboat, or the steamship *De Witt Clinton.* The boats, which run daily through Nov 30 (weekends in Dec), depart from the South Street Seaport Museum.

World Yacht Enterprises, Pier 62, foot of W. 23rd St at the Hudson River, offers luxury restaurant-yacht tours for lunch, dinner, and brunch. Reservations necessary. Tel: 929-8540.

Helicopter: *The Island Helicopter Corp.,* located at the foot of 34th St at the East River, offers rides daily from 9 A.M.–5 P.M. and 7 P.M.–9 P.M. Choose from a variety of rides, day or night. Tel: 683-4575.

Manhattan Helicopter Tours leave from the heliport at the foot of W. 30th St on the Hudson River in Manhattan. Daily flights except for Christmas and New Year's Day; reservations required only for groups of ten or more. Call 247-8687 for information, prices, description of available tours.

Bus: *American Sightseeing International / Short Line Tours* leave from the Short Line Terminal at 166 W. 46th St. Tours, aboard glass-topped sightseeing coaches, last from two to eight hours. Tel: 354-4740 for schedule and prices.

The Gray Line offers a choice of bus tours, lasting from two hours to all day and touching major areas of interest. Also coach trips to Atlantic City casinos. Terminal at 8th Ave and 54th St (397-2600).

Crossroads Sightseeing at 701 7th Ave (47th St) has scheduled tours several times daily, except Christmas. There are 2½-hour tours as well as longer routes which include visits to the Empire State Building and the Statue of Liberty. Also Harlem tours and harbor cruises. For ticket prices and information call 581-2828.

Specialized commercial tours include guided visits by bus, van, or car, as well as walking tours, which demand more energy but offer a closer look at one's surroundings. Some of these tours are organized for groups only, but individuals may join if all places are not taken; some will take individuals. Call for information, a description of the tour, and prices.

Backstage on Broadway, 228 W. 47th St (575-8065), offers tours of the nonpublic spaces of Broadway theaters, led by professionals who have worked on Broadway and share their experiences and information. Reservations required.

Those interested in the theater might also enjoy the *Radio City Music Hall tour* at Rockefeller Center (6th Ave at 50th St; call 757-3100 for information), the *Metropolitan Opera tours* (see p. 498) and the *tours of Lincoln Center* (see p. 498).

Brooklyn-Bronx Sightseeing Tours (718 \ 782-7285) offers individual and group tours by car or bus to ethnic neighborhoods in these boroughs, with glimpses of people whose cultural identity shapes their daily lives; the tours visit such Bronx neighborhoods as the Grand Concourse, Kingsbridge, Riverdale, Little Italy, and the South Bronx. In Brooklyn visitors may see, for example, Greenpoint, Hassidic Williamsburg, Flatbush, and Crown Heights. Tours are guided by a lifelong New Yorker with personal experience of these neighborhoods. Call for information and prices.

Doorway to Design sponsors group visits to interior design showrooms normally open only to the trade. Tours might include visits to workrooms of artists and designers, seminars, visits to private homes; call 221-1111.

During the summer months *Guide Service of New York* offers both walking and coach tours to interesting spots all around the city, some off the beaten path: a visit to City Island, an Irish Pub Crawl, with a pub meal and drinks, a Melting Pot tour (Little Italy, Little Ukraine, Brooklyn's Hasidic communities). Tel: 408-3323.

Harlem Spirituals, Inc. offers several different coach tours of Harlem, which have a more personal quality than many commercial tours. Among the choices are a Sunday morning tour through residential areas, the Morris-Jumel mansion, and a Baptist church service with gospel choir (reserve by Saturday); an evening jazz and soul food tour which includes dinner and drinks (reserve 24 hours ahead); and weekday morning tours of residential areas, cultural highlights, and commercial areas of Harlem. For information, tel: 302-2594. Tours leave from midtown Manhattan.

Lou Singer offers customized small tours to anywhere in New York that are more personal than standard bus tours, less expensive than hiring a limousine. Minimum group size is six people, but call to see if you can join an existing group. Tours might include food tours of Lower East Side, Chinatown, or Little Italy; visits to the East Village, Brooklyn churches, old homes, etc. Tel: 718 \ 875-9084 between 7 and 11 P.M.

Those who would rather ride than walk but would prefer something more athletic than a bus ride may join a tour organized by *The Hungry Pedalers,* a group that combines interests in eating and biking. Tours travel at a leisurely pace through ethnic neighborhoods in Manhattan and outlying boroughs and stop for the consumption of local fare. Call 595-5542 or 222-2243.

Adventure on a Shoestring 300 W. 53rd St (265-2663) is a 25-year-old organization whose members visit unusual places within the city: a Fifth Ave mansion, backstage at the Metropolitan Opera, the flower district, a radio broadcast. There is an annual membership fee and a small fee per event; walking tours of interesting neighborhoods are open to nonmembers.

Tours given by museums, cultural organizations, etc.: Many of these are walking tours. Most are quite inexpensive and are led by professionals in the field (architects, historians) rather than by professional tour guides.

The *Lower East Side Historic Conservancy*, 97 Orchard St bet. Delancey and Broome Sts (431-0233), offers a 90-minute walking tour of the Lower East Side designed to illuminate the lives of ordinary people—Jews, Italians—in this neighborhood at the turn of the century. The tour visits schools, synagogues, settlement houses, and other points of interest. The Conservancy also leads occasional tours of the Eldridge St Synagogue.

The *Municipal Arts Society* offers inexpensive three-hour walking tours emphasizing history and architecture (Sundays during warm weather) to such areas as the mansions of Fifth Ave; New York's first suburb, Greenwich Village; and Lower Manhattan. Other walks traverse interesting ethnic neighborhoods (Greenpoint, for example), areas where city planning has had a significant impact (Sunnyside Gardens), or culturally and architecturally interesting areas (the Gothic Revival buildings of the General Theological Seminary). For information and schedule, call 935-3960.

The *Museum of the City of New York* sponsors unusual tours, generally emphasizing history (for example, "Harlem Hejira," a walk in Harlem visiting restaurants, cultural institutions, and churches). Call 534-1672 for information.

The *New-York Historical Society* has recently inaugurated a series of Sunday afternoon walking tours which include Chelsea, Brooklyn Heights, the Upper East and West Sides, Lower Manhattan, and Murray Hill. For tour information call 873-0125.

The *92nd Street Y* organizes artists' hospitality tours; visits to architectural points of interest or ethnic neighborhoods ("River to River on 125th Street," "Snug Harbor Cultural Center"); and visits to exhibitions, some of particular interest to Jewish visitors. Advance registration required. Call 996-1105 for information.

Weekends during warm weather the *Urban Park Rangers* frequently offer free tours through city parks. The Manhattan walks focus on Central Park either for its natural history or as a model of urban planning and park design; also, trips to other parks. For information: 397-3091. For information about the weekend lineup in outer-borough parks call: Brooklyn, (718) 287-3400; the Bronx, 548-7070 or 589-0096; Queens, (718) 699-4294; and Staten Island, (718) 816-5456.

The *Chinatown History Project,* 70 Mulberry St (619-4785), has a slide show and tour of Chinatown that traces its history from colonial times to the present. Groups preferred but individuals may join previously organized groups; telephone for information.

Historical societies in the outer boroughs offer neighborhood, park, and cemetery tours. Call the *Brooklyn Historical Society*, 128 Pierrepont St, Brooklyn (718\624-0890), for information about Brooklyn neighborhood walking tours. The *Queens Historical Society,* 143-35 37th Ave, Flushing (718\939-0647), has planned a self-guided walking tour of the Flushing Freedom Mile, with visits to three historic houses. Send a stamped, self-addressed envelope for brochure or call the society; group tours also can be arranged. The *Bronx County Historical Society,* 3309 Bainbridge Ave, Bronx (881-8900), has a series of walks in neighborhoods as diverse as Riverdale and the South Bronx.

The *Prospect Park Environmental Center,* whose headquarters are at the Picnic House in Prospect Park, Brooklyn (718\788-8549), has a full schedule of walks in Brooklyn neigborhoods, parks, and cemeteries. And the *Staten Island Historical Society,* 441 Clarke Ave, Staten Island (718\351-9414), has walking tours and occasional bus tours.

Theaters

Theater in New York can be divided into three categories: Broadway, Off Broadway, and Off Off Broadway. Proximity to or distance from Broadway in these terms, however, is not merely geographical but also economic and artistic. The Broadway theater represents the Establishment, the center of commercial theater in America. Its houses are located mainly north of Times Square between about 43rd and 53rd Sts; most are large, seating more than a thousand spectators. They have given rise to a special genre, the Broadway Production, usually large in scale, expensive in details of production, star-studded in personnel, and popular in appeal.

While the Off Broadway movement may have originated in the years around World War I when such groups as the Provincetown Players and the Washington Square Players burst upon the scene in Greenwich Village, it truly began to flourish in the early 1950s, notably with Jose Quintero's production in 1952 of Tennessee Williams' *Summer and Smoke,* which had failed four years earlier on Broadway but which became the first major theatrical success south of 42nd St in thirty years. According to Actors' Equity, Off Broadway is defined by an exclusion clause that relegates its theaters (necessarily holding fewer than 300 spectators) to areas outside the Times Square theater district, but which permits smaller work crews and lower wages, allowing for less expensive productions and hence experimentation. Artistically, Off Broadway suggests a place where new actors and directors can work, where new work can be discovered, where Broadway failures can be resuscitated, and where theater companies may develop continuity and consistent artistic policies.

However, as Off Broadway became more successful and less innocent commercially, the Off Off Broadway movement began to flourish, filling the spot that Off Broadway occupied in its early days. Historians trace its beginnings to Alfred Jarry's *King Ubu,* which opened in the Take 3 coffeehouse in Greenwich Village in 1960, or to Ellen Stewart's Cafe La Mama, which opened in a cellar on E. 12th St the same year. Off Off Broadway productions frequently occupy nontheatrical buildings—lofts, churches, coffeehouses—all over the city. Plays tend to be headily experimental or to deal with themes too explosive for Broadway. Companies may be amateur or amateurish, but one of the principles of the movement is to preserve the intimacy between a playwright and his work, where the author may participate in all parts of a production, free from the demands of commercial success. Off Off Broadway productions appeal to a young, artistically daring audience that includes students, artists, and theatrical people interested in getting in at the ground floor.

Tickets: Tickets to Broadway and many Off Broadway productions may be purchased at the box office or from ticket brokers who add a surcharge to the ticket price. Telephone ticket services are *Chargit* (944-9300) for holders of major credit cards, or *Telecharge* (239-2600); both charge additional fees. Half-price tickets available the day of performance may be purchased at **tkts** (Times Square Ticket Center) at W. 47th St and Broadway, or downtown at 2 World Trade Center; tel: 354-5800 (see p. 136 for hours). Prices of Broadway shows range from about $20 to

$60. Off Broadway tickets are cheaper with top prices at about $30; Off Off Broadway events are still less expensive. Standing room is frequently offered for shows that are sold out, sometimes in advance. Check with Chargit or Telecharge. Ticketron, Inc at 777 Third Ave (46th St) will give you the location of your nearest Ticketron outlet (call 399-4444). The service does not tell you the location of the seats you buy; cash only at Ticketron outlets.

The Sunday Arts and Entertainment Guide of the *New York Times*, *The New Yorker* magazine, and *New York* magazine offer extensive listings of current shows and theatrical events.

Broadway Theaters

Ambassador	215 W. 49th St (Broadway / 8th Ave)	239-6200
Barrymore	243 W. 47th St (Broadway / 8th Ave)	239-6200
Belasco	111 W. 44th St (6th / 7th Aves)	239-6200
Biltmore	261 W. 47th St (Broadway / 8th Ave)	582-5340
Booth	222 W. 45th St (Broadway / 8th Ave)	239-6200
Broadhurst	235 W. 44th St (Broadway / 8th Ave)	239-6200
Broadway	1681 Broadway (52nd / 53rd Sts)	239-6200
Brooks Atkinson	256 W. 47th St (Broadway / 8th Ave)	719-4099
Circle in the Square	1633 Broadway (50th / 51st Sts)	239-6200
Cort	138 W. 48th St (6th / 7th Aves)	239-6200
Edison	240 W. 47th St (Broadway / 8th Ave)	302-2302
Eugene O'Neill	230 W. 49th St (Broadway / 8th Ave)	246-0220
Forty-Sixth St	226 W. 46th St (Broadway / 8th Ave)	221-1211
Gershwin	222 W. 51st St (Broadway / 8th Ave)	586-6510
Golden	252 W. 45th St (Broadway / 8th Ave)	239-6200
Helen Hayes	240 W. 44th St (Broadway / 8th Ave)	944-9450
Imperial	249 W. 45th St (Broadway / 8th Ave)	239-6200
Longacre	220 W. 48th St (Broadway / 8th Ave)	239-6200
Lunt-Fontanne	205 W. 46th St (Broadway / 8th Ave)	575-9200
Lyceum	149 W. 45th St (6th / 7th Aves)	239-6200
Majestic	245 W. 44th St (Broadway / 8th Ave)	239-6200
Mark Hellinger	237 W. 51st St (Broadway / 8th Ave)	757-7064
Marquis	1535 Broadway (45th / 46th Sts)	398-8383
Martin Beck	302 W. 45th St (8th / 9th Aves)	246-6363
Minskoff	Broadway at 45th St	944-9300
Music Box	239 W. 45th St (Broadway / 8th Ave)	239-6200

Nederlander	208 W. 41st St	944-9300
	(7th / 8th Aves)	
Neil Simon	250 W. 52nd St	757-8646
	(Broadway / 8th Ave)	
New Apollo	234 W. 43rd St	921-5885
	(7th / 8th Aves)	
Palace	Broadway at 47th St	757-2626
Plymouth	236 W. 45th St	239-6200
	(Broadway / 8th Ave)	
Royale	242 W. 45th St	239-6200
	(Broadway / 8th Ave)	
St. James	246 W. 44th St	398-0280
	(Broadway / 8th Ave)	
Shubert	225 W. 44th St	239-6200
	(Broadway / 8th Ave)	
Virginia, formerly	245 W. 52nd St	977-9370
ANTA	(Broadway / 8th Ave)	
Winter Garden	1634 Broadway	239-6200
	(50th / 51st St)	

Major Off Broadway Theaters

Actors Playhouse	100 Seventh Ave South	691-6226
AMAS Repertory Theater	1 E. 104th St	369-8000
American Place	111 W. 46th St	247-0393
Astor Place	434 Lafayette St	254-4370
Audrey Wood	359 W. 48th St	307-5452
Charles Ludlum	1 Sheridan Square	691-2271
Chelsea Playhouse	519 W. 23rd St	243-0992
Cherry Lane	38 Commerce St	989-2020
Circle in the Square	159 Bleecker St	254-6330
(*Downtown)*		
Circle Repertory Co.	99 Seventh Ave South	924-7100
Douglas Fairbanks	432 W. 42nd St	239-4321
Harold Clurman	412 W. 42nd St	594-2370
Heckscher	1230 Fifth Ave	534-2804
Judith Anderson	422 W. 42nd St	279-4200
Lucille Lortel	121 Christopher St	924-8782
Manhattan Theater Club	321 E. 73rd St	472-0600
Orpheum	126 Second Ave	239-6200
Provincetown Playhouse	133 MacDougal St	777-2571
Public	425 Lafayette St	598-7150
Roundabout / Stage One	333 W. 23rd St	242-7800
Samuel Beckett	410 W. 42nd St	594-2826
Sullivan Street Playhouse	181 Sullivan St	674-3838
Theater of Saint	Lexington Ave	751-4140
Peter's Church	at 54th St	
Top of the Gate	160 Bleecker St	475-5120

Off Off Broadway Theaters

There are over 200 Off Off Broadway theaters scattered through-out the city. Most are small, seating fewer than 100 spectators, and many offer productions only on certain days of the week. Schedules are subject to change, so it is wise to telephone ahead.

Amusements

Concerts, Dance, and Opera

Half-price tickets for operas, concerts, and dance performances are sold when available in the Bryant Park ticket booth, six days a week, Tues–Sun, 12–7 (from 11 A.M. on Wed and Sat for matinees). The booth is located just inside the park close to 42nd St and toward Sixth Ave (382-2323).

Bargemusic at the Fulton Ferry Landing in Brooklyn (718\624-4061) is popular for chamber music and small ensembles.

The Brooklyn Academy of Music (BAM), 30 Lafayette St, Brooklyn (718\636-4100), has a full schedule of music, dance, and drama events through the winter season. Its Next Wave Festival is a premier showcase for contemporary music, dance, and theater. The *Brooklyn Center for the Performing Arts at Brooklyn College* (BCBC), Nostrand and Flatbush Aves, Brooklyn (718\434-1900), also offers a concert season. At the *Brooklyn Museum,* Eastern Parkway and Washington Ave, Brooklyn (718\638-5000), Sunday afternoon concerts are held in the sculpture garden during warm weather.

Carnegie Hall, 154 W. 57th St at 7th Ave (247-7800), is the city's best-loved concert hall, relished both for its acoustics (generally acknowledged to have diminished in quality since its 1987 refurbishing) and its tradition. Major orchestras perform here as well as world-class instrumental soloists and recitalists, both classical and popular. Less prominent artists appear at *Weill Recital Hall at Carnegie Hall* (formerly Carnegie Recital Hall; same telephone number).

City Center, 131 W. 55th St (246-8989), the home of the New York City Ballet before it moved to Lincoln Center, is still known as a center of dance. The Alvin Ailey American Dance Theater, the Joffrey Ballet, the Paul Taylor Dance Company, and the Dance Theater of Harlem appear regularly, while the summe season is usually devoted to foreign companies.

The *Joyce Theater,* 175 Eighth Ave at 19th St (242-0800), an old movie theater gutted and remodeled in 1982, is a welcome newcomer in the Chelsea area and a major center for dance.

The largest facility in the city for music and dance is LINCOLN CENTER FOR THE PERFORMING ARTS, Broadway at 64th St (877-1800). Tickets for Lincoln Center events are available by mail (order at least a month ahead), at the box offices (telephone numbers below), and at most Ticketron outlets.

Alice Tully Hall (362-1911) is the home of the Chamber Music Society of Lincoln Center, and also hosts recitals, films, and small productions requiring a moderately intimate theater. *Avery Fisher Hall* (874-6770) is the home of the New York Philharmonic and the Mostly Mozart Festival; it also hosts visiting orchestras and famous soloists including big name pop and jazz musicians. The *Metropolitan Opera* (362-6000) is the home of the nation's premier opera company and the American Ballet Theater. It also presents visiting ballet companies. The opera season runs from late Sept through mid-April, and the ballet season, divided into two sections, runs from Oct through Nov and again from mid-April through June. The *New York State Theater* (870-5570) is the home of the New York City Opera Company, a "starless" company whose casts feature younger American singers, and of the New York City Ballet, which rose to fame under its late artistic director, George Balanchine. The opera season runs from about late Feb to early May and from early Sept to mid-Nov. The ballet season runs from mid-Nov to the end of Feb, with numerous performances of the *Nutcracker* (get tickets well in advance) in Dec. The spring seasons runs from late April through mid-June.

The *Juilliard Theater* (874-7515), where Juilliard students, orchestras, and dance and theater groups perform, hosts a wide range of concerts, many free. Student recitals are held in Paul Hall (874-0465). Juilliard runs an annual contemporary music festival. Call the school for a schedule.

Also in Lincoln Center is the *Library and Museum of the Performing Arts,* 111 Amsterdam Ave at 65th St (870-1630), a branch of the New York Public Library. During the winter season (Sept–June) there are frequent performances of solo and chamber music, dance, film, and drama. Tickets are free and can be picked up an hour before the performances which begin at 4 P.M. on weekdays and at 2:30 on Sat.

The musical events held in the *Merkin Concert Hall, Abraham Goodman House,* 129 W. 67th St (362-8719), are frequently adventurous, including the work of lesser known composers, concerts on original instruments, ethnic and chamber music, and unusual ensembles (the Soviet Emigré Orchestra, an ensemble from Bukhara in Central Asia, the Chinese Music Ensemble). The Music Today series has featured premiers of contemporary works, some commissioned for the series.

The regular season at Kaufmann Concert Hall in the 92nd St YM-YWHA on Lexington Ave (996-1100) includes a young artists' series, an outstanding chamber music series, occasional operas, many instrumental soloists, lectures, and poetry readings.

Symphony Space, 2537 Broadway at 95th St (864-5400), first a skating rink and then a movie theater, is now a much-needed Upper West Side concert hall. Programs include the inventive and experimental as well as more conventional fare.

Town Hall at 123 W. 43rd St (840-2824), another venerable city institution, offers a wide range of concerts, lectures, and other cultural events.

In addition to the Met and the New York City Opera, many smaller companies offer opera productions throughout the city; some have their own telephone listings; others can be reached only through the theaters in which they are currently performing. The *Amato Opera Theater, Inc.,* 319 Bowery at 2nd St (228-8200), and the *Bel Canto Opera Company,* 30 E. 31st St in the Madison Avenue Baptist Church (535-5231), offer productions from the standard repertoire. *The Light Opera of Manhattan,* 316 E. 91st St (831-2000), known to its devotees as LOOM, serves up the confections of Victor Herbert, Strauss,

Lehar, Gilbert and Sullivan, and other lighthearted composers. Check *New York* magazine, *The New Yorker,* or the Sunday *New York Times* for listings.

Some museums offer concert series with well-known soloists or chamber groups. Notable among them is the *Metropolitan Museum of Art,* Fifth Ave at 82nd St (570-3949). The *Museum of the City of New York,* Fifth Ave at 103rd St (534-1672), offers free Sun afternoon concerts from Oct—May. *The Frick Collection,* 1 E. 70th St (288-0700), has chamber music concerts during the winter.

Church music. The city's churches host a wide range of musical events, with special performances around major religious holidays. Some offer concert schedules on a more regular basis. *Trinity Church* (602-0800) at Broadway and Wall St presents free concerts at 12:45 on Tues, and St. Paul's Chapel (Broadway at Fulton St) has them at 12:10 on Mon and Thurs. *St. Bartholomew's Episcopal Church,* Park Ave at 50th St (744-2500), sometimes offers Sun afternoon choral concerts. *St. Peter's Lutheran Church* in the Citicorp Building, Lexington Ave at 54th St (935-2200), has an extensive jazz program which includes a regular Jazz Vespers at 5 P.M. on Sun and other events. The *Fifth Avenue Presbyterian Church* at 55th St (247-0490) sponsors frequent Sun concerts. Uptown at the *Riverside Church,* Riverside Drive at 122nd St (749-7000), there are carillon concerts Sat noons. The *Cathedral of St. John the Divine,* Amsterdam Ave and 112th St (662-2133), offers an ambitious and wide-ranging program of traditional and experimental performances.

Movie theaters are located all over the city, about 400 of them according to a recent estimate. Seats cannot be reserved and there are often long lines in front of popular, first-run movies. Patrons buy their tickets and then get into the line; be prepared to arrive at least half an hour to 45 minutes before a popular first-run show (call the box office or check the newspaper for times) if you wish to get a good seat. The most expensive movie theaters are the East Side first-run houses, where tickets cost $7 and up (one price for the entire house). Slightly cheaper are the neighborhood theaters which show films that have already had some exposure; increasingly theaters have been divided to show more than one film at a time, an architectural feature usually apparent in the theater's name: anything with numbers after it (Plaza 1, 2, and 3) or anything called Twin, Quad, or Plex. The better theaters in the Times Square area show popular adventure films or comedies while the rest gravitate to sex and violence. In addition to the museums which have film programs, several commercial theaters have established themselves as revival houses, though in the last few years many have either closed or been bought out by chains of first-run theaters. When the Regency (Broadway at 67th St) was bought out by Cineplex Odeon in 1987, a group of regulars demonstrated in front of the theater, complaining that they were being "plexed to death," that the large theater companies were bringing the suburbs into the city. Notable survivors among the dwindling number of revival houses are *Cinema Village,* 22 E. 12th St (924-3363), the *8th St Play-*

house, 52 W. 8th St (674-6515), and the *Theater 80 St. Marks,* 80 St. Marks Place (254-7400).

Among the museums with outstanding film programs are the Museum of Modern Art at 11 W. 53rd St (call 708-9490 for film information), whose offerings are wide-ranging and often organized thematically (Perspectives on French Cinema, or a Louis Malle retrospective, for example). Others are the Whitney Museum, Madison Ave at 75th St (570-0537), the Brooklyn Museum, 200 Eastern Parkway (718 \ 638-5000), the Jewish Museum, Fifth Ave at 92nd St (860-1888), the Museum of Broadcasting, Fifth Ave at 53rd St (752-7684), and The International Center of Photography, Fifth Ave at 94th St (860-1777). The *American Museum of the Moving Image, Zukor Theater,* 34-31 35th St, Astoria, Queens (718 \ 784-4742) has a fine collection of historic films and regular screenings. Call for information about jitney transportation from the Upper East Side.

In addition to the museums, film buffs with historical or esoteric interests might also investigate the film societies, collectives, and other institutions with specialized programs. The *Collective for Living Cinema,* 52 White St (925-2111), dedicated to encouraging independent filmmakers, screens historic and contemporary, often experimental films. *The Film Forum 2* at 57 Watts St (431-1590) has arranged such series as "Before the Code," movies made before the 1934 strictures brought middle-class morality to Hollywood. *Millennium Film Workshop* at 66 E. 4th St (673-0090) screens the work of contemporary filmmakers and offers lectures and other programs. *The Kitchen* at 512 W. 19th St (255-5793) began as a pioneer in video art, and though its programs have expanded, the free Video Viewing Room (changing programs, open Tues–Sat 1–6) is still a good place to see this art form. *The Public Theater* at 425 Lafayette St (598-7171) offers well-chosen classic and contemporary films.

The *New York League for the Hard of Hearing,* 71 W. 23rd St (741-7650) shows captioned films for the hearing-impaired; free to members of the league.

The major colleges and universities within the city have film societies, and many of the international cultural organizations (the Asia Society, the French Institute, Goethe House, the Japan Society, etc.) offer appropriate fare. The weekly film listings in *New York* magazine are especially helpful.

The most important film event in the city is the *New York Film Festival* at Lincoln Center (usually late Sept to mid-Oct), where foreign and American films deserving of special attention get their first American showing; there are also other film festivals at Lincoln Center's Alice Tully Hall. *The New Yorker* and the Sunday edition of the *New York Times* have short reviews of current films.

Art exhibitions. Most art museums are open Tues–Sat 10–5, and Sun 12–5, and many are open one evening per week. The Museum of Modern Art is the only major art museum open on Mon. Galleries, like museums, are usually open Tues–Sat from around 10 or 11 in the morning until 5 or 6 in the afternoon. Many close for part of the summer.

Spectator sports. New York has professional baseball, football, basketball, and hockey teams and enjoys the presence of important tennis tournaments and track and field meets.

BASEBALL. The season runs from early April to Oct with New York's two teams, the Yankees and the Mets, each playing about 75 home games (many at night). The Yankees occupy Yankee Stadium in the Bronx (293-6000), where tickets are on sale daily 9–5; or telephone Ticket World (888-9000).

To reach Yankee Stadium by SUBWAY, take the IRT Lexington Ave (train 4) uptown to 161st St-River Ave or the IND 6th Ave (D train) to the same stop.

CAR: Major Deegan Expressway to Grand Concourse; Grand Concourse N. to 161st St; turn left to Stadium. Car parking available; traffic is usually heavy just before game time.

The stadium is in a borderline neighborhood; the fans sometimes get extremely vocal and have been known to drink large amounts of beer.

The Mets play at Shea Stadium, in the Flushing Meadows-Corona Park area of Queens (718\507-8499). Tickets are available by telephone at Teletron (947-5850) or in person at any Ticketron outlet (call 399-4444 for the nearest branch).

SUBWAY: IRT Flushing line (train 7) to the Willets Point-Shea Stadium stop.

CAR: Grand Central Parkway or Northern Blvd to Flushing Meadows Park; follow signs to Shea Stadium.

BASKETBALL. The New York Knicks play (Oct–April) at Madison Square Garden; for ticket information call the Garden (563-8300).

SUBWAY: IRT Broadway-7th Ave (train 1, 2, or 3) or IND 8th Ave (train A, C, or E) to Penn Station.

BUS: M4 downtown via 5th Ave or any downtown bus with a transfer to the 34th St crosstown bus.

PARKING: Numerous nearby, expensive parking lots.

Rabid fans may also want to see the New Jersey Nets, formerly of New York, who now play in Piscataway, New Jersey; for information call (201) 935-8888.

College basketball has in recent years become popular, with St. John's University (Jamaica, Queens) and other local collegiate teams playing some home games in the Garden. Major tournaments are also played there annually, notably The Big East Tournament and the National Invitation Basketball Tournament (NIT), both held in the spring. For ticket information call the Madison Square Garden box office (563-8300).

BOXING. Once the shrine of boxing, Madison Square Garden still hosts professional boxing and wrestling matches as well as the amateur Golden Gloves tournament (Jan or Feb); tel: 563-8300 for information.

FOOTBALL. The two New York teams, the Jets and the Giants, now both play in the New Jersey Meadowlands. The season runs Sept—Jan. For Jets ticket information, call 421-6600; for Giants ticket information, call (201) 935-8222.

The Meadowlands Sports Complex is located on Route 3 in East Rutherford, New Jersey. To get there by car take the Lincoln Tunnel from Manhattan and follow Route 3 west to exit 16W. Buses run to the stadium from the Port Authority Bus Terminal on game days. Pregame traffic is inevitably heavy so allow extra time.

HORSE RACING. Aqueduct Racetrack in Ozone Park, Queens (season Oct—Dec, Jan—May), and Belmont Racetrack in Elmont on Long Island just beyond the Queens border (season June—July, late Aug—mid-Oct) offer thoroughbred racing. The Belmont Stakes in June is the final leg of the Triple Crown for three-year-olds after the Kentucky Derby and the Preakness Stakes. For ticket information and post time for both tracks call the New York Racing Association, tel: (718) 641-4700.

TRANSPORTATION TO AQUEDUCT. SUBWAY: IND Special Racetrack Express from 42nd St-8th Ave IND station. Service begins approximately two hours before first race.

CAR. Take Belt Parkway toward Kennedy Airport and follow signs for Aqueduct.

EXPRESS BUS SERVICE from 41st St and 7th Ave. For information tel: (718) 641-4700, ext. 306.

TRANSPORTATION TO BELMONT. SUBWAY: IND 6th Ave (E or F train) to Parsons Blvd. Or BMT Jamaica Ave train (J train) to 160th St-Jamaica Ave. Special bus service from both stations to the track. Express bus service from 41st St and 7th Ave. For information tel: (718) 641-4700, ext. 306.

ICE HOCKEY. The New York Rangers play at Madison Square Garden (season Oct—April). For ticket information, telephone the Garden (563-8300). For directions to the Garden, see the entry under Basketball, New York Knicks. The New York Islanders, a suburban team, plays in the Nassau Coliseum in Uniondale, Long Island. For information call (516) 794-4100.

TENNIS. The major event, the U.S. Open Tennis Championships, are played (late Aug—early Sept) at the National Tennis Center in Flushing Meadows, Queens. For ticket information, tel: (718) 271-5100. Tickets for the semifinals and the finals are usually sold out well in advance but it is possible to get tickets for the earlier rounds when more matches are played on a single day. The West Side Tennis Club in Forest Hills, Queens, former host of the U.S. Open, now holds the Tournament of Champions in the spring before the Wimbledon championships (718 \ 268-2300). The Grand Prix Masters Tournament, a major men's indoor event, is held in Madison Square Garden (563-8300) in Jan and in recent years the final of the women's winter tour has taken place in the Garden (same telephone number) in late autumn.

TRACK AND FIELD. Madison Square Garden annually hosts the Wanamaker Millrose Games (late Jan or early Feb). Call 563-8300 for schedule.

Participant sports. Most public parks have playing fields. In Central Park the athletic fields are S. of 66th St on the West Side and N. of the Reservoir in the center of the park.

BICYCLING. During weekends, on holidays, and during most nonrush hours weekdays, vehicular traffic is banned from Central Park except the crosstown transverses.

Commercial rental shops near the park are Gene's Bicycles, 242 E. 79th St bet. 2nd and 3rd Aves (249-9218), Angelo's Bicycle Service, 140 W. 83rd St bet. Columbus and Amsterdam Aves (362-1122), and Bicycle Renaissance, 505 Columbus Ave at 84th St (724-2350).

Near Prospect Park in Brooklyn is Dixon's Bicycle Shop, 792 Union St near 7th Ave (718 \ 636-0067).

GOLF. The city has a surprising number of public golf courses with modest green fees. Telephone ahead to find out approximately how long a wait to expect.

BROOKLYN: Dyker Beach, 86th St and 6th Ave (718 \ 836-9722); Marine Park, 2880 Flatbush Ave (718 \ 338-7113). BRONX: Mosholu, Jerome Ave at Holly Lane (655-9164); Pelham-Split Rock, City Island and Pelham Bay Parkway West (885-1258); Van Cortlandt, Broadway near 242nd St (543-4595). QUEENS: Clearview in Bayside, 202-12 Willets Point Blvd near Clearview Expressway (718 \ 229-2570); Douglaston in Douglaston, Commonwealth Blvd and Marathon Parkway (718 \ 224-6566); Forest Park in Ridgewood, Forest Park West Drive and 80th St (718 \ 296-2442); Kissena in Flushing, Booth Memorial Ave and 164th St (718 \ 939-4594). STATEN ISLAND: LaTourette, 100 London Rd, Forest Hill and Richmond Hill Aves (718 \ 351-1889); Silver Lake, Victory Blvd near Forest Ave (718 \ 447-5686); South Shore, Huguenot Ave and Raily St (718 \ 984-0101).

ICE SKATING. The most memorable place to skate, especially during the Christmas season, is at Rockefeller Center, open from about Nov to March (757-5731). Telephone ahead for schedule as there are several skating sessions daily and the admission price applies only to one session. Admission charge, skate rental; often very crowded.

Other rinks (generally open Nov–March) include the *Wollman Rink* in Central Park (517-4800); admission fee, skate rental. Also in Central Park, Lenox Ave and 110th St, is the *Lasker Memorial Rink;* a shuttle bus to and from the rink operates weekends, stopping on 5th Ave and on Central Park West. For schedule, rates, and bus information tel: 397-3142

Also in Manhattan is the *Rivergate* at 34th St and 1st Ave with daily outdoor skating; admission charge, skate rental (689-0035). Other possibilities are *The Ice Studio,* 1034 Lexington Ave bet. 73rd / 74th St (535-0304) and *Sky Rink Ice Skating,* on the 16th floor at 450 W. 33rd St bet. 9th / 10th Aves (695-6555). Both have instruction and skate rental; call for schedules.

In Brooklyn's Prospect Park the Kate Wollman Memorial Rink is open in season; admission charge, skate rental; bus service around Prospect Park; call (718) 965-6561 for information. In

Queens, the New York City Building at the World's Fair site in Flushing Meadows-Corona Park offers afternoon and evening skating in season (718\271-1996); admission charge, skate rental. On Staten Island there is outdoor skating at the Staten Island War Memorial Rink, Clove Lakes Park, Victory Blvd near Clove Rd; hours vary; tel: (718) 720-1010.

Ponds and lakes: The pond in Central Park near the 73rd St entrance from 5th Ave has winter skating, weather permitting. The water level is lowered to provide safety and to promote early freezing. There are also skating ponds in the other boroughs: Crotona Park Lake and Van Cortlandt Park Lake (Bronx), Prospect Park near Ocean Ave and Lincoln Rd (Brooklyn), Alley Pond Park in Queens Village, Bowne Park in Flushing, Brookville Park in Rosedale, and Tilly Memorial Park in Jamaica (Queens). On Staten Island are Allison Pond in New Brighton, Clove Lakes Park in West Brighton, and Wolfe's Pond Park in Prince's Bay.

RIDING. If you wish to ride in Central Park, call the Claremont Riding Academy, 175 W. 89th St bet. Columbus and Amsterdam Aves (724-5100). In Brooklyn near Prospect Park, the Equestrian Club of Brooklyn, 51 Caton Place off Coney Island Ave near Park Circle (718\438-8849), rents horses for park use. In the Bronx, call the Van Cortlandt Stables, Broadway and W. 254th St (548-9516).

ROLLER SKATING. Skaters in Central Park gather W. of the Mall opposite about 70th St. Indoor rinks in Manhattan include the Roxy Roller Rink, 515 W. 18th St bet. 10th and 11th Aves (675-8300); the Metropolis Roller Skate Club, 241 W. 55th St bet. 7th and 8th Aves (586-4649), and Village Skating at 15 Waverly Place bet. Mercer and Greene Sts in the Village (677-9690).

RUNNING. The New York Road Runners Club, 9 E. 89th St (860-4455) sponsors the New York Marathon in Oct (places filled far ahead) as well as less ambitious races in Central Park on weekends during seasonable weather.

The route of the New York Marathon begins in Ft. Wadsworth, Staten Island, crosses the Verrazano-Narrows Bridge, angles across the Bay Ridge, Sunset Park, Gowanus, and Park Slope sections of Brooklyn before continuing N. through downtown Brooklyn and Williamsburg to Greenpoint. The course passes through the Long Island City area of Queens, over the Queensboro Bridge, N. along First Ave in Manhattan through East Harlem and makes a brief foray through the South Bronx. After crossing the 138th St Bridge over the Harlem River, the course turns S. again for the homestretch, down Fifth Ave through Harlem and Central Park to the Plaza Hotel, across Central Park South and up to the Tavern-on-the-Green on the W. side of the park.

SWIMMING. The Parks Department operates a number of city pools, indoor and outdoor, and while inexpensive they are often very crowded; many are located in poorer neighborhoods and serve as the only means of cooling off for people who lack air conditioning. Two of the more convenient are the John Jay Pool on York Ave and 77th St near the East River (397-3159) and the East 23rd St Pool at 1st Ave and the Franklin Delano Roosevelt Drive (397-3184).

Two YMCAs with fine recreational facilities are the Westside Y at 5 W. 63rd St (787-4400) with pools, a running track, exercise rooms, handball, squash, and racquetball courts, and a sauna; and the Vanderbilt YMCA, 224 E. 47th St bet. 2nd and 3rd Aves (755-2410), also with a pool, gym, and sauna.

TENNIS. The Parks Department maintains public courts for city residents, open mid-April—Oct; seasonal pass available at the Arsenal (in Central Park, 5th Ave at 64th St). Visitors may obtain daily passes at the Central Park Courts which entitle the holder to one hour of tennis on any city-owned court (list available from the Parks Department in the Arsenal). The 26 Har-Tru courts in Central Park are popular and often involve a wait; others on the list may be less well-maintained. Call 360-8133.

Privately owned commercial courts, more expensive in the winter and during prime time, in Manhattan include: Crosstown Tennis, 14 W. 31st St (947-5780); East Side Tennis Ltd, 177 E. 84th St (472-9114); Gramercy Tennis and Racquetball Club, 708 Sixth Ave near 23rd St (691-0110); Randalls Island Indoor Tennis, Parks Department Field House, Randalls Island (534-4845); Tennis Club Grand Central in Grand Central Terminal (867-3841); Wall Street Racquet Club, Wall St at the East River (952-0760). Telephone first to check prices, which are likely to be very high, and to make reservations.

Courts in the outer boroughs are considerably less expensive. The most famous facility is the U.S.T.A. National Tennis Center, Flushing Meadows (718 \ 271-5100), where the national championships are played.

Beaches. New York is not known for its surf but there are 14.9 miles of public beaches within an hour or so of midtown and six city public beaches. Brooklyn: Coney Island Beach and Boardwalk, Manhattan, and Brighton Beaches. Bronx: Orchard Beach and Boardwalk. Queens: Rockaway Beach and Boardwalk. Staten Island: South Beach and Midland Beaches and Franklin D. Roosevelt Boardwalk, Wolfe's Pond Park Beach. Of those within the city limits one of the quieter is *Manhattan Beach* in Brooklyn, just E of Coney Island. Between Manhattan Beach and Coney Island is Brighton Beach, a neighborhood that has become an enclave for recent Soviet emigrés.

PUBLIC TRANSPORTATION: Take the 6th Ave IND (D train) to the Sheepshead Bay stop and transfer to the B1 bus E. to Manhattan Beach. Or walk from the subway stop.

Coney Island, a 3½-mile stretch of Brooklyn on the sea has fallen from its glory days in the early 20th century, but draws huge crowds on hot summer days. Attractions in addition to sand, sun, and salt water, are the Astroland amusement park and the nearby New York Aquarium. See the main entry for Coney Island for additional information and directions.

Orchard Beach in the Bronx fronts on Long Island Sound, not the Atlantic Ocean, and has calm, unruffled waters. Once called the "Riviera of the Bronx," Orchard Beach has recently been restored and cleaned and is divided into about a dozen sections, which tend to be segregated sociologically, one area attracting elderly Jews, others drawing teenage girls, or Puerto Rican families. There are bathhouses, snackbars, and parking for about 6,700 cars.

Take the IRT Lexington Ave local (train #6) to the end of the line; city buses run between the subway station and the beach.

Wolfe's Pond Park, Hylan Blvd and Cornelia Ave in Staten Island (718 \ 390-8000), has a picnic area, snack bars, bathhouses.

Take the Staten Island Ferry to St. George, then S103 bus to Wolfe's Pond Park (a long bus ride).

In Queens across Jamaica Bay is *Jacob Riis Park,* part of the Gateway National Recreation Area operated by the National Park Service. The beach is long and white, and sometimes crowded; boardwalk and playgrounds.

PUBLIC TRANSPORTATION: Take the IND Far Rockaway line (A train) to Broad Channel; change to the Rockaway Park A train and get off at Beach 116th St, the last stop. From here either hike E. to the park (about a 15-minute walk) or take the Q22 bus.

CAR: Take the Belt Parkway east to the Flatbush Ave South exit and continue across the Marine Parkway (Gil Hodges) Bridge to the park. Large parking lot (fee).

Further out on Long Island is JONES BEACH STATE PARK, Wantagh, probably the best public beach in the U.S.; tel: (516) 785-1660, with a 5½-mile beach, boardwalk, pools, refreshment stands, toilet facilities, rental boats, athletic fields, miniature golf, playgrounds.

PUBLIC TRANSPORTATION: The Long Island Railroad offers round-trip train-bus service during the summer from Penn Station (718 \ 454-5477 for further information and schedule).

CAR: Take the Long Island Expressway or the Southern State Parkway to the Meadowbrook State Parkway and follow the signs to the parking lots. Go early in the day to avoid traffic jams and waits at the parking lots which are closed when filled.

Gardens. Contrary to the popular opinion that New York is completely surfaced with unrelieved expanses of asphalt, numerous lovely gardens flourish within the city limits. Most impressive are the *Brooklyn Botanic Garden* (718 \ 622-4433) and the *New York Botanical Garden* (220-8700) in the Bronx, both worth the attention of anyone interested in flora. The former includes 50 acres of beautifully designed, specialized gardens, the most famous of which are the Japanese gardens; new conservatories have just opened. The New York Botanical Garden is renowned for its historic glass conservatories, its rock gardens, and the horticultural richness of its grounds.

In Central Park are the *Conservatory Gardens* off Fifth Ave at 105th St. The southern section is planted in the English style with 3500 perennials that bloom from March through Nov, while the north garden is more formal; inside the entrance gate is a formal lawn with an arbor supporting wisteria. Further south in the park, near the Belvedere Castle, is the small *Shakespeare Garden*, where trees and plants mentioned in the bard's work flourish in relative obscurity.

Two Manhattan museums offer historical gardens in period settings. Within the *Cloisters* (923-3700), the medieval branch of the Metropolitan Museum of Art, arcaded walks border central courtyards landscaped in the manner of the Middle Ages; the landscaped grounds outside the museum walls are at their best in spring and autumn. The *Morris-Jumel Mansion* (923-8008) at Edgecombe Ave and 160th St has a small colonial herb and flower garden, which features only plants grown before 1774. On a smaller scale yet is the herb garden at the *Abigail Adams Smith House* (838-6878) at 421 E. 61st St.

Manhattan mansions with greenery include the *Frick Collection* (288-0700) on Fifth Ave at 70th St, whose three gardens include an inside courtyard with a fountain and tropical foliage. The garden at the *Cooper-Hewitt Museum* (860-6868) remains as it did when Andrew Carnegie built the mansion. Also a period piece of a sort is the Sculpture Garden in the *Museum of Modern Art* (708-9400), designed by Philip Johnson to display sculpture in outdoor light.

Further afield is the *Queens Botanical Garden* (718 \ 886-3800) at 43-50 Main St in Flushing, with 38 acres divided into specialized displays, including herb and bee gardens. The grounds at the *Wave Hill Center for Environmental Studies* at 675 W. 252nd St (549-2055) in the Riverdale section of the Bronx overlook the Hudson River and offer some 28 acres of gardens and horticultural exhibits. The *Bartow-Pell Mansion* (885-1461) in Pelham Bay Park (Bronx) is maintained by the International Garden Club and has a well-kept garden with a fine view of the Long Island Sound. Still burgeoning is the *Staten Island Botanical Garden* on the grounds of Sailors' Snug Harbor, with beautiful lawns and mature shade trees.

Most famous of all perhaps are the *Channel Gardens* at Rockefeller Center, a strip of seasonal plantings imbedded in the walkway between Fifth Ave and the skating rink.

Specialized Museums: The following list groups museums by content. Check the *New York Times, New York* magazine, or *The New Yorker* for notices of changing exhibitions of particular interest.

American Painting	City Hall, the Governors' Room; Metropolitan Museum of Art; Museum of the City of New York; New-York Historical Society; Whitney Museum of American Art; Brooklyn Museum.
Architecture	Museum of Modern Art; Urban Center; Brooklyn Museum (architectural ornaments); Museum of Modern Art.
Bibles	Bible House; Interchurch Center.
Black Art and Culture	Schomburg Center for Research in Black Culture; Studio Museum in Harlem; Bronx Museum of the Arts, Metropolitan Museum (Rockefeller Collection of Primitive Art); Center for African Art.
Books and Manuscripts	Grolier Club; New York Public Library; Pierpont Morgan Library.
Ceramics	American Craft Museum; Asia Society Galleries; Cooper-Hewitt Museum; Frick Collection; Metropolitan Museum of Art; Brooklyn Museum.

Coins, Medals	American Numismatic Society
Costume	Fashion Institute of Technology; Metropolitan Museum of Art; Brooklyn Museum.
Crafts	American Craft Museum; American Museum of Natural History; Cooper-Hewitt Museum; Museum of American Folk Art; Museum of the American Indian.
Decorative Arts	American Craft Museum; Cooper-Hewitt Museum; Metropolitan Museum of Art; Museum of the City of New York; Museum of Modern Art; New-York Historical Society; Brooklyn Museum.
Ethnic Exhibits	American Museum of Immigration; American Museum of Natural History; Asia Society Gallery; Americas Society; China House Gallery; French Institute / Alliance Française; MOCHA; INTAR Latin American Gallery; Japan House; Jewish Museum; Korean Cultural Service; El Museo del Barrio; Museum of the American Indian; Ukrainian Institute of America; Ukrainian Museum; Brooklyn Museum.
European Art 15—19C	Frick Collection; Metropolitan Museum of Art; Brooklyn Museum.
Fire-fighting	New-York Historical Society; New York City Fire Museum.
Furniture	Abigail Adams Smith House; City Hall, The Governor's Room; Fraunces Tavern Museum; Frick Collection; Metropolitan Museum of Art; Morris-Jumel Mansion; Museum of the City of New York; New-York Historical Society; Old Merchant's House; Theodore Roosevelt Birthplace; Bartow-Pell Mansion (Bronx); Brooklyn Museum; Bowne House (Queens).
Graphic Arts	American Institute of Graphic Arts; Metropolitan Museum of Art; Museum of Modern Art.
Jewish Art and History	Educational Alliance; Jewish Museum; Lower East Side Conservancy (The Tenement), Yeshiva University Museum; YIVO Institute for Jewish Research.
Maritime History	Museum of the City of New York; Intrepid Air-Sea-Space Museum, South Street Seaport Museum; City Island Historical Nautical Museum (Bronx); Harbor Defense Museum (Brooklyn).
Medieval Art	The Cloisters; Metropolitan Museum of Art; Pierpont Morgan Library.
Modern Art	Guggenheim Museum; Metropolitan Museum of Art; Museum of Modern Art; New Museum of Contemporary Art; Whitney Museum of American Art.

Musical Instruments	Metropolitan Museum of Art, Museum of the American Piano.
New York History	Abigail Adams Smith Museum; Castle Clinton National Monument; Dyckman House; Federal Hall National Memorial; Fraunces Tavern Museum; Morris-Jumel Mansion; Museum of the City of New York; New-York Historical Society; Old Merchant's House; Theodore Roosevelt Birthplace; South Street Seaport; Museum of Bronx History / Valentine Varian House (Bronx); Van Cortlandt Mansion and Museum (Bronx); Lefferts Homestead (Brooklyn); Brooklyn Historical Society (Brooklyn); New York Public Transit Exhibit (Brooklyn); Bowne House (Queens); Flushing Quaker Meeting House (Queens); Kingsland House (Queens); Queens Museum; Conference House (Staten Island); Richmondtown Restoration (Staten Island).
Oriental Art	Asia Society Galleries; China House Gallery; Japan House Gallery; Metropolitan Museum of Art; Brooklyn Museum; Jacques Marchais Center of Tibetan Art (Staten Island).
Period Rooms	Abigail Adams Smith House; Fraunces Tavern Museum; Frick Collection; Metropolitan Museum of Art; Morris-Jumel Mansion; Museum of the City of New York; New-York Historical Society; Old Merchant's House; Theodore Roosevelt Birthplace; Van Cortlandt Mansion (Bronx); Lefferts Homestead (Brooklyn); Brooklyn Museum; Bowne House (Queens).
Photography	French Cultural Service; International Center of Photography; International Center of Photography / Midtown; Museum of Modern Art.
Science and Technology	American Museum of Natural History; Hayden Planetarium; Con Edison Energy Museum; Children's Museum of Manhattan; Brooklyn Children's Museum; Museum of Holography; Infoquest Center; New York Hall of Science (Queens).
Television	The Kitchen (video art); Museum of Broadcasting.
Theater	Library and Museum of the Performing Arts; Museum of the City of New York (changing exhibitions).
Toys	Aunt Len's Doll and Toy Museum; Museum of the City of New York; Forbes Magazine Galleries.

Calendar of Events

The following calendar gives a general picture of events that recur from year to year, though the dates when holidays are celebrated, exhibitions open, and other activities occur do vary. The Friday *New York Times* carries schedules of weekend events; the New York Convention & Visitors Bureau at Columbus Circle has quarterly calendars with detailed listings and information about parades and other public events.

JANUARY
Conventions and shows usually held in January include the *National Boat Show* and the *Greater New York Auto Show,* both at the Javits Convention Center.

Chinese New Year, celebrated in Chinatown at the end of Jan or early Feb. Parade with dragon dancers, demonstrations of martial arts, fireworks on New Year's Eve, banquets in Chinese restaurants.

Martin Luther King, Jr. Birthday (Mon close to Jan 19).

Ice Capades at Madison Square Garden (late Jan or early Feb).

Collegiate basketball season at Madison Square Garden.

Thoroughbred racing at Aqueduct Racetrack, through mid-May.

FEBRUARY
Black History Month, programs in all boroughs throughout Feb.

International Antique Show at Madison Square Garden.

Annual Exhibition, National Academy of Design.

Westminster Kennel Club Dog Show, Madison Square Garden. A highly social event with well-bred dogs, handlers, and audience.

Washington's and Lincoln's Birthday sales at stores in all boroughs, mid-Feb.

Washington's Birthday Parade on 5th Ave, near Feb 22.

Track and field events at Madison Square Garden; Millrose Games (or in late Jan). National A.A.U. (Amateur Athletic Union) Indoor Track and Field Championships.

MARCH
Big East Basketball Tournament, Madison Square Garden.

St. Patrick's Day Parade, March 17, 5th Ave, from 44th–86th Sts. Bands, marchers from Ireland and elsewhere. Reviewing stand at 65th St.

Ringling Bros. and Barnum & Bailey Circus, Madison Square Garden. The day before the first performance a *Parade of Circus Animals* (10 A.M.) marches from the railroad siding, 12th Ave and 34th St to the Garden. Late March or early April.

Golden Gloves Finals, Madison Square Garden.

National Invitation Basketball Tournament, Madison Square Garden.

Greek National Day Parade, March 25 or a Sat near that date, 5th Ave from 59–79 Sts. School bands, floats, Greek music.

Circle Line boat trips begin season (or early April, until Nov) circumnavigating Manhattan.

APRIL

Easter floral displays at Channel Gardens in Rockefeller Center, at Brooklyn Botanic Garden, and at New York Botanical Garden in the Bronx.

Easter Parade on 5th Ave at noon Easter Sun; informal parade near St. Patrick's Cathedral.

Easter Show at Radio City, seasonal spectacular. Rockettes, dancing Easter bunnies, music on the giant Wurlitzer. Get tickets early.

Baseball season opens for Yankees and Mets.

New York City Ballet spring season opens, New York State Theater in Lincoln Center, through June. American Ballet Theater at Metropolitan Opera House in Lincoln Center through mid-June.

Children's zoo opens at Bronx Zoo.

Stuyvesant Park Festival, 2nd Ave, 15th—17th Sts.

Annual Spring Flower Show, Macy's, 34th St at Herald Square.

Salute to Israel Parade, 5th Ave, Sun mid—late April.

MAY

Martin Luther King, Jr. Parade, 5th Ave.

Bronx Week, dance, concerts, theatrical and athletic events, throughout borough.

Bronx Day Parade, Grand Concourse.

SoHo Festival, Prince St, West Broadway, 6th Ave.

Brooklyn Heights Promenade Art Show, on the Esplanade from Remsen—Clark Sts, one weekend early or mid-May.

Ninth Avenue International Festival, 9th Ave from 37th—57th Sts, 11 A.M.—7 P.M. A large street festival celebrating ethnic groups living on or near 9th Ave. Food—Italian, Greek, Philippine, Chinese, etc.—and entertainment. Two-day festival usually in mid-May.

Norwegian Constitution Day Parade on weekend nearest May 17 in Bay Ridge (Brooklyn) from 67th—90th Sts. Tel: (718) 238-1100.

Ukrainian Festival, E. 7th St between 2nd and 3rd Aves; weekend in mid—late May.

Armed Forces Day, formerly a parade, 5th Ave, 96th—62nd Sts, usually the third Sun in May. Recently, events and exhibits on pier at Intrepid Sea-Air-Space Museum, foot of W. 46th St at Hudson River.

Beaches open officially on Memorial Day, last weekend in May.

Memorial Day Parades in all boroughs.

Washington Square Outdoor Art Show, Greenwich Village, weekends, noon—sundown, late May to early June. Washington Square Park at 4th St and 5th Ave.

Hudson River Day Line begins excursions to Bear Mountain State Park and U.S. Military Academy at West Point. Late May to mid-Sept.

JUNE

Bronx Week Parade along the Grand Concourse in the Bronx.

Celebrate Brooklyn festival, with free music, theater, dance events in Prospect Park, mid-June—Sept.

Metropolitan Opera performances in parks, all five boroughs.

Free outdoor lunch-hour concerts, Rockefeller Center (June—Aug).

Museum Mile Celebration, 5th Ave, 82nd—105th Sts. Museums stay open late, special exhibitions and events, early June.

Feast of St. Anthony of Padua, Sullivan St south of Houston St in Little Italy, early to mid-June. Italian street fair, 6 P.M. to midnight. Procession with image of the saint carried through the streets.

Midwood Mardi Gras, Avenue M, Coney Island—Ocean Aves in Brooklyn.

Belmont Stakes at Belmont Racetrack, Elmont, Long Island.

Puerto Rican Day Parade, 5th Ave, 44th—86th Sts, usually first Sun in June, 11 A.M. Floats, bands, ethnic food at 59th St and 5th Ave.

Fifty-second Street Fair, across town from Lexington—7th Aves.

Flag Day Parade, Fulton and Water Sts to Fraunces Tavern, June 14.

Free outdoor entertainment at World Trade Center, Wed, mid-June—early Sept.

Jewish Festival on Lower East Side, East Broadway bet. Rutgers / Grand Sts, usually the second Sun.

JVC Jazz Festival, late June to early July; famous jazz festival formerly held at Newport, Rhode Island; performances in various halls.

St. Paulinus Festival, N. 8th St and Havemeyer St in Williamsburg, Brooklyn. Italian street festival, late June—mid-July. Procession to Our Lady of Mt. Carmel Church with men carrying a large monument.

Guggenheim Concerts, outdoor band concerts in Damrosch Park, Lincoln Center, evenings 8—10, late June through Aug several nights a week.

JULY

Shakespeare in the Park, Delacorte Theater, Central Park at 81st St. Tickets distributed 6:15 P.M. day of performance; one per person, line forms in early afternoon.

Summerpier jazz concerts at South Street Seaport, free, July—Aug.

Harbor Festival celebrations, end of June through July 4. Events at Battery Park, in the rivers around Lower Manhattan. Parade of ships in the Hudson River, band concerts, hot air balloons, etc. Festival climaxes on July 4 with a half-hour spectacle of fireworks provided by Macy's from barges in the East River. View them from the Franklin Delano Roosevelt Drive, 14th—49th Sts (closed to traffic) or from Brooklyn or Queens, 9:20 P.M. For information call 560-4495.

New York City Opera season, New York State Theater, Lincoln Center, July—Nov.

Mostly Mozart Festival at Lincoln Center, Avery Fisher Hall.

American Crafts Festival at Lincoln Center.

Feast of Our Lady of Mt. Carmel, 116th St and 1st Ave, in former Little Italy; evening celebrations, mid-July.

Festa Italiana in Greenwich Village on Carmine St near Bleecker St, evenings for about a week in late July.

New York Philharmonic concerts in major parks, free, late July—early Aug.

AUGUST

Harlem Week, early- to mid-Aug. Parades, art exhibitions, jazz, dance contests, sports clinics taught by prominent athletes, tours of Harlem landmarks. Tel: 427-3315.

Belmont Racetrack autumn season, end of Aug to mid-Oct.

Governor's Cup Yacht Race, Pier A in Battery Park to Verrazano Bridge and back; late Aug or early Sept.

India Day Parade, Madison Ave.

U.S. Open Tennis Championships at National Tennis Center in Queens. Afternoon and evening matches, late Aug—early Sept.

Tap-O-Mania, mid- or late Aug; 34th St between 7th Ave and Broadway. Another of Macy's contributions to city life, this time a Parade of Tap Dancers, including all who wish to participate. To register as a dancer or find out the rain date, tel: 560-4495.

Greenwich Village Jazz Festival, concerts, films, lectures, about ten days in late Aug.

Festival of the Americas on 6th Ave, 35th—50th Sts.

Lincoln Center Out-of-Doors through Aug, with dance and theater for adults and children in Damrosch Park. Tel: 877-2011.

SEPTEMBER

Washington Square Outdoor Art Show, usually the first two or three weekends in Sept, noon—sundown.

Richmond County Fair, early Sept, grounds of Richmondtown Restoration, Staten Island, 10—5; only true county fair in the city.

Labor Day Parade, 5th Ave / 44th St—3rd Ave / 72nd St, first Mon, morning.

West Indian-American Day Carnevale in Brooklyn. Labor Day weekend with parade on Mon, all day, along Eastern Parkway from Utica Ave to the Brooklyn Museum. Floats, extravagant costumes, West Indian music, dancing in the streets, food.

African-American Day, Adam Clayton Powell Blvd, 111th—142nd St, early afternoon parade.

Baseball season ends (unless World Series is played in New York). *Football season* begins for N.Y. Jets and N.Y. Giants, both at Giants Stadium, Meadowlands, East Rutherford, N.J.

One World Festival Street Fair, St. Vartan's Armenian Cathedral, 2nd Ave at 35th St.

Feast of San Gennaro in Little Italy on Mulberry St between E. Houston St and Worth St, morning—night, about ten days in mid-Sept. Street fair, food and games, procession with saint's image carried through the streets.

Columbus Avenue Festival, all day, Columbus Ave, 66th / 86th Sts.

Lincoln Center New York Film Festival, late Sept to early Oct.

New York Is Book Country, 5th Ave, 48th–57th Sts, and Madison Ave 52nd–53rd Sts, a Sat in mid-Sept, 11–5. Stalls, carts, booths, with publishers, authors, books. Also clowns and balloons.

Steuben Day Parade, third weekend, Sat or Sun, 5th Ave, 61st–86th Sts, noon. Bands, floats, costumed folk dancers march to honor Baron von Steuben who assisted Washington during the Revolutionary War.

Metropolitan Opera and *New York Philharmonic* seasons open at Lincoln Center. Concert season opens at other major halls. Late Sept.

Atlantic Antic, Atlantic Ave from the East River to Flatbush Ave in Brooklyn, Sun in late Sept, 11 A.M.–6 P.M. Arab bazaar with food, music, belly dancing, sometimes camel rides.

Schooner Regatta, South Street Seaport, usually last Sat or first Sat in Oct, late morning.

New York Film Festival, Lincoln Center (late Sept–early Oct).

OCTOBER

Ice skating begins at Rockefeller Center, exact time of opening depends on temperature.

New York Rangers ice hockey season begins, Madison Square Garden, early Oct.

New York Knicks basketball season begins, Madison Square Garden, late Oct or early Nov.

Pulaski Day Parade, 5th Ave, 26th–52nd Sts, Oct 5th or nearest Sun, noon.

Hispanic-American Day Parade, 5th Ave, 44th–79th Sts, usually Sun mid-month, noon.

Columbus Day Parade, 5th Ave, 44th–86th Sts, 11:30 A.M., with Italian-American groups, bands.

Columbus Day sales in major stores.

Fifth Avenue Mile, race from 82nd St to 62nd St, Saturday mid-month, early afternoon.

Second Avenue Autumn Jubilee, 13th–14th Sts.

New York Marathon, 26.2-mile race through the five boroughs, Sun late in Oct or early in Nov. Begins at Verrazano Bridge 10:30 A.M., and finishes at Tavern-on-the-Green in Central Park.

Aqueduct Racetrack winter season, Oct to mid-May, Aqueduct Racetrack, Ozone Park, Queens.

Halloween Parade, Greenwich Village, E. on Houston St from West St to 6th Ave, N. on 6th Ave to 14th St, then to Union Square (Oct 31, early evening).

Fall Antique Show at the Pier, Passenger Ship Terminal, Pier 92; late Oct.

NOVEMBER

Veterans Day Parade, 5th Ave, 39th–24th Sts, Nov 11 (morning).

Women's Professional Tennis Tournament, Madison Square Garden. Mid-month.

Thanksgiving Parade, Thanksgiving Day (last Thurs in month),

Central Park West from 77th–59th St, down Broadway to Macy's at 34th St. Floats, bands, giant helium-filled balloons representing cartoon characters, etc. When the parade reaches Macy's Santa Claus arrives, opening the Christmas season.

Radio City Music Hall Christmas spectacular begins, mid-Nov–early Jan.

Big Apple Circus, tent pitched in Damrosch Park, Lincoln Center.

Hayden Planetarium Christmas show begins, late Nov or early Dec.

Origami tree, American Museum of Natural History, late Nov–Jan.

New York City Ballet, fall season, New York State Theater, Lincoln Center.

DECEMBER

Holiday celebrations include *Christmas tree lightings* at Rockefeller Center, City Hall, other borough halls. *Chanukah candle lighting* at City Hall. *Carol singing* along 5th and Park Aves, also in lobby of Empire State Building. *Brass choirs* at Rockefeller Center.

Christmas windows along 5th Ave. Especially: Lord & Taylor (39th St), Saks Fifth Ave (50th St), F. A. O. Schwarz (58th St). The tree and illuminated angels in the Channel Gardens at Rockefeller Center attract large crowds, especially at night. Office buildings on Park Ave below 50th St often have lavish displays.

Richmondtown Christmas festival at Richmondtown Restoration, Staten Island, early Dec.

Large Christmas tree with 18C Neapolitan carved angels and creche figures in Medieval Sculpture Hall, Metropolitan Museum of Art.

Special holiday displays usually at the Cloisters, Jewish Museum, Museum of the City of New York.

Empire State Building illuminated in red and green holiday lights. (Dec–early Jan).

Chanukah Menorah, Grand Army Plaza, 5th Ave at 59th St.

Master's Men's Tennis Championships, Madison Square Garden.

Christmas Carousel, Lever House, Park Ave at 54th St (Dec–early Jan).

New Year's Eve in Times Square, recommended only for those undaunted by celebratory crowds. At midnight a Big Apple, (formerly a ball was used), descends from the former Times Tower. In Central Park there are *midnight fireworks* and a *midnight run* sponsored by the New York Roadrunners Club.

Children's Activities

Museums. For complete information, hours, etc., check the main entry of each museum, listed in the index.

American Museum of Natural History, Central Park West at 79th St. Animal dioramas, minerals, anthropology exhibits, films most Sat at 2 P.M., Discovery Room. Tel: 873-1300.

Aunt Len's Doll and Toy Museum, 6 Hamilton Terrace (141st St and St. Nicholas Ave). By appointment. The private collection of Lenon Holder Hoyte, whose thousands of dolls and doll accessories have almost taken over her townhouse. Tel: 926-4172.

Brooklyn Children's Museum, 145 Brooklyn Ave in the Crown Heights section of Brooklyn. Fine children's museum with participatory exhibits on technology, natural history, human culture. Tel: (718) 735-4432.

Brooklyn Museum, 200 Eastern Parkway, Brooklyn. Egyptian art, period rooms, costume exhibits. Special activities for children.

Children's Museum of Manhattan, 212 W. 83rd St. Museum with participatory exhibits on art, nature, technology; special events. Excellent for young children. Reservations needed for special events. Tel: 721-1234.

The Cloisters, Fort Tryon Park (Fort Washington Ave near 190th St). Medieval branch of Metropolitan Museum, in romantic neomonastic setting (which some children perceive as a castle) with great views. Tel: 923-3700.

Con Edison Energy Museum, 145 E. 14th St near 3rd Ave. Nice if you're in the area; a walk-through mockup of underground New York, with steam pipes, electrical cables, etc. Tel: 460-6244.

Forbes Magazine Galleries, 62 Fifth Ave at 12th St. Legions of toy soldiers, flotillas of boats, historic documents and memorabilia, a roomful of jewel-encrusted Fabergé baubles, and some of the world's worst trophies. Tel: 620-2389.

Hayden Planetarium, Central Park West at 81st St. Sky shows weekday and weekend afternoons; model of solar system, slide presentation, blacklit gallery. Tel: 496-0900 for show times.

Infoquest Center, AT&T Building, 550 Madison Ave at 56th St. A hands-on science and technology exhibit not unexpectedly emphasizing telecommunications. The best part is the last room structured like a game arcade where children can "create" their own rock videos, use voice communication to guide an electronic mouse through a maze, instruct a robot. Tel: 615-5555.

The *Intrepid Sea-Air-Space Museum,* a decommissioned aircraft carrier refitted as a museum, berthed at Pier 86 on the Hudson River at 46th St. Exhibits highlight human achievement in space, at sea, in the air. Real and model planes, videos and films on flight. Tel: 245-2533.

Lower East Side Walking Tours and Living History Museum, 97 Orchard St bet. Broome / Delancey Sts. Retelling of immigrant experience of many nationalities. Sunday "Peddler's Pack" Walking tour; "Family Matters," historical program Sun afternoons. Tel: 431 0233.

Metropolitan Museum of Art, Uris Center, 5th Ave at 81st St on the ground floor of the Metropolitan. Gallery talks, workshops, special exhibitions geared to introducing young people to art. Also, period rooms, Egyptian art, Chinese garden court, armor. For schedule of children's events: 879-5500.

Museum of Broadcasting, 1 E. 53rd St near 5th Ave (scheduled to move to 23 W. 52nd St in 1990). Audio- and videotapes (radio and TV shows), films, lectures. Tel: 752-4690.

Museum of the American Indian, Broadway at 155th St. Largest collection of Indian artifacts in the world. Tel: 283-2420.

Museum of the City of New York, 5th Ave near 103rd St. Dioramas of early New York, multimedia exhibitions, dolls, toys, dollhouses. Tel: 534-1672.

New York City Fire Museum, 278 Spring St (Hudson and Varick Sts), New York 10013. Tel: 691-1303. Historic collection of firefighting equipment, memorabilia, apparatus.

New-York Historical Society, 170 Central Park West at 77th St. Early American toys, carriages, sleighs, fire trucks, period rooms. Tel: 873-3400.

New York Hall of Science, 111th St and 48th Ave in Flushing Meadows-Corona Park, Queens. Wonderful science museum with hands-on (also feet-on) exhibits, designed to appeal to all children, not only budding Einsteins. Permanent exhibit on light with prisms, mirrors, optical illusions. Tel: (718) 699-0675.

South Street Seaport Museum, 207 Front St, around Fulton St and the East River. Ships, a 19C print shop, a multiscreen seafaring movie, other exhibits focusing on the sea and the port of New York in the 19C. Children's Center at 165 John St. Tel: 669-9400.

Staten Island Children's Museum, Snug Harbor Cultural Center, 1000 Richmond Terrace (Building M), Staten Island. Tel: (718) 273-2060. Another wonderful children's museum, with changing participatory exhibits on art, architecture, science, the humanities; also tours, workshops, Sun performances in winter.

Staten Island Historical Society, Richmondtown Restoration Historical Museum, 441 Clarke Ave, Staten Island. Museum of Childhood has displays of antique toys and dolls, children's furnishings. The restoration offers 96 acres of restored buildings from 17–19C, demonstrations of crafts, trades, domestic life. Tel: (718) 351-1617.

Aquarium and Zoos

New York Aquarium, Boardwalk and W. 8th St, Coney Island, Brooklyn. Whales, seals, penguins, shark tank, electric eel shows; dolphin and sea lion shows daily, May–Sept. Tel: (718) 266-8500.

Barrett Park Zoo (Staten Island Zoo), 613 Broadway near Clove Rd, Staten Island. Zoo set in an 8-acre park, famous for its reptiles, colony of vampire bats, also Children's Zoo with farm animals. Tel: (718) 442-3100.

Bronx Zoo, officially the New York Zoological Park, Southern Blvd and 185th St, Bronx. Large (252-acre), well-maintained zoo with more than 3000 animals, many in open enclosures; fine Children's Zoo (open spring–fall), monorail ride, cable car ride, World of Birds. Tel: 367-1010.

Central Park Zoo, 5th Ave at 64th St. Small (5-acre) urban zoo handsomely remodeled with penguins, polar bears, sea lions, monkeys, red pandas. Also a Children's Zoo. Tel: 360-8287.

Prospect Park Zoo, Flatbush Ave and Empire Blvd, Brooklyn. Small zoo with camels, zebras, bears, lions; Children's Zoo. **Note:** Zoo scheduled for remodeling; tel: 965-6560.

Queens Zoo, 111th St and 56th Ave, Flushing Meadows-Corona Park, Queens. Small-scale modern zoo, pleasant if you are in the neighborhood, for example at the New York Hall of Science. Park telephone number is (718) 699-4254. **Note:** The zoo is currently closed for remodeling.

Tall Buildings with Observation Decks. For further information, hours, prices, etc., check main entry in index.

World Trade Center, Two World Trade Center (Church St, N. of Liberty St). Enclosed deck on 107th floor; also world's highest open-air viewing platform, open weather permitting. Tel: 466-7377.

Empire State Building, 5th Ave at 34th St, Observatories on 86th and 102nd floors. Tel: 736-3100. On the concourse level, one floor down from the main lobby is the *Guinness World Records Exhibit Hall,* with video presentations, models, replicas, photographs of amusing and freakish world records. Tel: 947-2339.

Children who relish high places might also enjoy walking across the Brooklyn Bridge or riding the cable car to Roosevelt Island. See index for access.

Boat Rides

Statue of Liberty Ferry, Battery Park to Liberty Island. Since the centennial celebrations, the Statue is very crowded; go early; if possible take the first boat. For information tel: 732-1236; ticket office, tel: 269-5755.

Staten Island Ferry, from South Ferry. Good views of the Statue of Liberty, Lower Manhattan skyline, Governors Island, and the harbor traffic. Ride is about half an hour each way.

Circle Line, Pier 83, foot of W. 43rd St at Hudson River. Three-hour tour (perhaps too long for smaller children) around Manhattan, April–Nov. Tel: 563-3200.

Seaport Line, from South Street Seaport, Pier 16. Ninety-minute excursions sail by Statue of Liberty; also turn-of-the-century style vessels. Call for schedule, prices. Tel: 669-9400.

Films, Puppet Shows, Story Hours: Children's Entertainment. A number of theater companies specialize in entertainment for and by children. Check the weekly listings in *New York* magazine or the Friday edition of the *New York Times.*

The *Magic Towne House,* 1026 Third Ave near 60th St, has magic shows with comedy geared for children on Sat afternoons. Call for reservations: 752-1165.

Big Apple Circus, one-ring circus held in tent at Lincoln Center during the Christmas season, elsewhere in the summer. Tel: 860-7320.

New York Public Library, branch libraries, including the *Donnell Library Center,* 20 W. 53rd St (621-0636), and the *Library for the Performing Arts at Lincoln Center,* 111 Amsterdam Ave at 65th St (870-1633), have story hours, puppet shows, filmstrips, often on Sat. Call ahead for schedule.

Eeyore's Books for Children, at 2212 Broadway bet. 78th / 79th Sts (362-0634) and 25 E. 83rd St bet. 5th / Madison Aves (988-3404) has free weekend story hours. Call for schedule.

The Cottage Marionette Theatre, Swedish Cottage, Central Park near Central Park West and 81st St, has puppet shows Sat at noon; reservations essential; tel: 988-9093.

South Street Venture, at the Trans-Lux Seaport Theater, 210 Front St (608-7888), is a multiscreen film on the history of the South Street Seaport neighborhood.

Tours, Other Activities

In *Central Park* there are exhibits on weather, geology, and other educational topics at the Central Park Learning Center, Belvedere Castle, 79th St south of the Great Lawn, tel: 772-0210. The Urban Park Rangers in Central Park and other major parks offer tours and naturalist programs; for Central Park, call 397-3091. For other park events that might appeal to children, see the main entry for Central Park in the index.

The South Street Seaport, on the East River at the foot of Fulton St (669-9400), is an attractive reconstruction of the city's 19C port district. Tours of historic buildings and ships; shopping, numerous restaurants, hourly showings of multimedia film on the sea and seaport.

Restaurants for Children. New York has branches of the major fast food chains: McDonald's, Burger King, Steak and Brew, Burger Heaven, Bun & Burger, and Kentucky Fried Chicken. There is a branch of Nathan's Famous (hot dogs and other fast food) at Broadway and 43rd St and an Automat in New York, at 42nd St and Second Ave, not outstanding for the food but for the way it is dispensed. Taco Rico, a Mexican fast food chain, has branches around the city as does the Magic Pan, whose shops feature omelettes and crepes. Children also enjoy the fancier quick service restaurants at the Fulton Market in the South Street Seaport and the establishments in the Big Kitchen at the World Trade Center. Serendipity at 225 E. 60th St (838-3531) has hamburgers, etc., and a wide selection of ice cream desserts and sweets. Rumpelmayer's at 50 Central Park South (755-5800) also has sandwiches, simple main courses, and fancy ice cream desserts, but is expensive. Children with more cosmopolitan tastes might enjoy dining in Chinatown, or at the Tandoor, 40 E. 49th St (752-3334), where some of the dishes are mildly spiced and the surroundings are attractive. Delicatessens and pizzerias abound. America, 9 E. 18th St (505-2110), appeals to the younger set in part for its murals, in part for offering practically everything American including peanut butter sandwiches. The Hard Rock Cafe, 221 W. 57th St (489-6565), is a must see with teenagers, but lines are long.

Useful Information

Emergency telephone numbers

Fire, police, ambulance, first aid	911
Dentist	679-3966
Drug abuse hotline	(800) 522-5353
Poison Control Center	764-7667
Crime Victims' Hotline	577-7777
Physicians' nonemergency referral service	
New York County Med. Society	582-1462
Doctor's Home Referral Service	745-5900
24-hour pharmacy, Kaufman's, Lexington Ave	
at 50th St	755-2266.

Useful telephone numbers

Time	976-1616
Weather	976-1212
Parks and special events	360-1333
Travel information (buses and subways)	330-1234

Telephones. Note: All telephone numbers in this book, unless otherwise indicated, are in area code 212.

The cost of a local call on a public pay telephone is 25¢, payable in nickels, dimes, and quarters. Deposit coins, listen for the dial tone, and dial the seven-digit number. The area code for Manhattan and the Bronx is 212; for Brooklyn, Queens, and Staten Island it is 718. You must dial the digit "1" plus the area code only if you are dialing outside your area (e.g., from Manhattan to Brooklyn). If you expect to be talking long and don't have much change, tell the person you are calling the number of your pay phone so that he or she may return the call when your time has elapsed.

To make a direct long distance call within the U.S., dial the digit "1" + the three-digit area code + the local number. To dial an operator-assisted long distance call (credit card calls, collect calls), dial 0 + the area code + the local number: the operator will come on the line.

To reach the operator, dial 0. For information in Manhattan or the Bronx, dial 411 from Manhattan telephones. For information in Queens, Brooklyn, or Staten Island from Manhattan, dial 1-718-555-1212. For information throughout the U.S. dial 1 + area code + 555-1212.

The code 800 designates a toll free number. To reach such numbers dial the digit 1 + 800 + the seven-digit number.

Note: The city emergency number is 911.

Daylight Saving Time. During the summer months from early April to late Oct, clocks are advanced by one hour. Eastern Standard Time is five hours earlier than Greenwich Mean Time.

Business Hours in offices are usually 9–5, Mon–Fri. Most department stores and specialty shops open at 10, though pharmacies, food stores, etc., open earlier. Many larger stores are open until 9 on Thurs evenings. Banks are open regularly 9–3, sometimes later one day a week, and sometimes on Sat morning from 9–12.

Holidays. Legal holidays are New Year's Day (Jan 1), Martin Luther King Day (Mon near Jan 19), Lincoln's Birthday (Feb 12), Washington's Birthday (Feb 22, but celebrated on or near this date to make a long weekend), Easter Sunday, Memorial Day (May 30, celebrated on or near this date), Independence Day (July 4), Labor Day (first Mon in Sept), Columbus Day (Oct 12, celebrated on or near this date), Veterans Day (Nov 11), Thanksgiving (fourth Thurs in Nov), Christmas (Dec 25). Schools and many businesses are closed on the major Jewish holidays: Passover (March or April), Rosh Hashanah (Sept or Oct) and Yom Kippur (Sept or Oct). Many stores are open on Sun.

Post Offices. The two main post offices in New York are the General Post Office on Eighth Ave at 33rd St (open weekdays 8–6, Sat 8–2, and Sun 9–5) and the Grand Central Post Office, Lexington Ave at 45th St (open weekdays 8–6, Sat 8–2, and Sun 11–3). Branch post offices are located throughout the city; look in the blue section in the Yellow Pages of the telephone book under United States Government, Postal Service; they are generally open 9–5 on weekdays, and Sat mornings 9–12. Mailboxes are on street corners; many hotels will perform postal services.

Climate. New York has a temperate climate but can be very cold in winter when the icy wind whips down the canyonlike streets and very hot in summer when heat radiates off pavements and buildings. With the exception of the subway platforms, however, most public facilities are air-conditioned. The most pleasant seasons are late spring and autumn. The U.S. National Weather Service offers the following statistics (Celsius in parentheses):

84   USEFUL INFORMATION

	Ave. Max. Temp.	Ave. Min. Temp.	Ave. Precip.
January	39° (4)	26° (-3)	2.71 in
February	40° (4)	27° (-3)	2.92
March	48° (9)	34° (1)	3.73
April	61° (16)	44° (7)	3.30
May	71° (22)	53° (12)	3.47
June	81° (27)	63° (18)	2.96
July	85° (29)	68° (20)	3.68
August	83° (28)	66° (19)	4.01
September	77° (25)	60° (16)	3.27
October	67° (19)	51° (11)	2.85
November	54° (12)	41° (5)	3.76
December	41° (5)	30° (-1)	3.53

Clothing. Most better restaurants expect men to wear jackets and ties. Raincoats are useful in spring and autumn. Layered clothing is most appropriate in summer when air conditioning can be chilly or in winter when some restaurants and public places are overheated. Very short skirts or shorts on women may elicit unpleasant remarks. Wear comfortable shoes for walking since there is little respite from the hard pavements.

Tipping. The New York Convention & Visitors Bureau offers the following guidelines. In restaurants the usual tip is 15–20% (many people give double the 8¼% tax added at the end of the bill). In luxury restaurants, it is customary to tip the waiter 15% and to give the captain 5%. Coat-check attendants will expect $1 per coat. Room service waiters and taxi drivers should also receive at least 15% (no less than 25¢ for cab drivers); bellhops will expect about 50¢–$1 per suitcase at hotels depending on the suitcase and the hotel. Porters in airports expect 50¢–$1 per bag. Others to tip include doormen who help with packages or summon a taxi (about $1), hotel chambermaids ($1 or $2 per day), and delivery people ($1 or more, depending on the size of the object delivered). Do not reward rude service.

Alcoholic beverages. Liquor stores are open daily except Sun, holidays, and election days when the polls are open. Beer is sold in grocery stores and delicatessens except on Sun mornings. The legal drinking age is 21. Bars may remain open until 4 A.M.

Toilets are not easy to find in New York. Public facilities, for example on the subways, are often dirty or dangerous. Restaurants are usually unwilling to let noncustomers use their restrooms. Try department stores, museums (especially free ones), hotel lobbies (ask at the desk if necessary), churches and parish houses, libraries, major tourist attractions (Rockefeller Center in the RCA Building, United Nations, etc.), buildings with public atriums (Trump Tower, Citicorp Building).

Consulates and Foreign Government Information Services
Australia, 636 Fifth Ave (245-4000).
Belgium, 50 Rockefeller Plaza (586-5110).
Canada, 1251 Sixth Ave (Ave of the Americas; 586-2400).
France, 934 Fifth Ave (606-3600).
Irish Republic, 580 Fifth Ave (382-2525).

Italy, 690 Park Ave (737-9100).
Netherlands, 1 Rockefeller Plaza (246-1429).
New Zealand, 630 Fifth Ave (698-4650).
South Africa, 425 Park Ave (838-1700).
Switzerland, 444 Madison Ave (758-2560).
United Kingdom, 845 Third Ave (752-8400).
West Germany, 460 Park Ave (308-8700).

Shopping is surely a major tourist attraction and, for some New Yorkers, a hobby, even a way of life. Department stores are known for their wide range of goods and services and offer convenience and ambience but not bargain prices. The most famous and expensive are *Bloomingdale's,* 59th St at Lexington Ave, *Saks Fifth Ave* at 50th St, *Bonwit Teller,* 57th St bet. 5th / Madison Aves, *Henri Bendel,* 57th St bet. 5th / 6th Aves; *Lord & Taylor,* 5th Ave at 39th St; *Bergdorf Goodman,* 57th St and 5th Ave, *Macy's,* Herald Square, 34th St at the intersection of Broadway and 6th Ave, and *Alexander's,* Lexington Ave bet. 58th / 59th Sts, Bloomingdale's less expensive downtown neighbor.

Most shopping areas are in midtown though some outlying neighborhoods are known for special commodities. *Fifth Ave* from about 42nd to 59th Sts is struggling to maintain its elegant ambience; in the lower reaches of this area bookshops, jewelry stores, shoe stores, and other luxury establishments stand side by side with fast food restaurants and tourist traps selling electronic goods, Oriental rugs, cameras, and "artworks," but toward the N. the avenue becomes more sophisticated. South of 42nd St the venerable department store Lord & Taylor anchors the S. end of the shopping district. At 57th St is Trump Tower with its galleries of luxury boutiques and at 59th St, Bergdorf Goodman.

Madison Ave from the high 40s through the 70s and into the 80s (high fashion clothes, books, shoes, accessories, fancy foods) may have replaced Fifth Ave as the city's most elegant and expensive street with *Brooks Brothers* (44th St), a bastion of conservative haberdashery, the southernmost outpost of the strip.

Lexington and Third Aves also have shops and boutiques though they are not generally as elegant as those lining Fifth and Madison Aves. Dealers in musical instruments can be found on 45th St between Sixth and Seventh Aves and also on 48th St in the same crosstown block. There are antique (and junk) shops in the 30s on Second and Third Aves as well as on Columbus Ave in the low 80s. Camera stores, notably *Willoughby's* at 110 W. 32nd St, are clustered in the low 30s W. of Seventh Ave and shops with notions (haberdashery), trimmings, millinery supplies, and similar paraphernalia can be found in the Garment District (mid- to high 30s around Seventh Ave).

While 47th St just off Fifth Ave is "Diamond Street," the premier jewelers are on Fifth Ave itself: *Tiffany's* at 57th St, *Harry Winston* at 56th St; *Van Cleef & Arpels* in Bergdorf Goodman (57th St), and *Cartier's* at 52nd St.

For bargains, and a different kind of atmosphere, try the *Lower East Side,* where women's clothing, shoes, handbags, fabrics, and similar articles cost considerably less than they do uptown; some of the stores offer expensive, high fashion clothing at discount prices; bargaining can lower the price even more. Since most merchants are Jewish, most shops close on Sat but remain open on Sun, the busiest day. Orchard St, with its outdoor displays of goods, is the center of the district. Greenwich Village and SoHo both have boutiques with chic and occasionally outrageous clothing, and SoHo offers a concentration of art galleries as well.

Chronology

1524 Giovanni da Verrazano, working for Francis I of France, explores New York Bay and the North American coastline.

1525 Esteban Gómez explores what was probably the Hudson River for Charles V of Spain.

1609 Henry Hudson, seeking a water route to the Orient for the Dutch East India Company, explores the harbor and sails upriver to the site of Albany.

1613 Adriaen Block and crew overwinter in lower Manhattan, building a new ship after their first, the *Tyger,* burns.

1614 Block explores Long Island Sound, discovers Block Island, and makes the first map of Manhattan.

1624 Thirty Dutch and Walloon families sent by the Dutch West India Company settle in New Netherland, a territory reaching from the Delaware to the Connecticut River.

1625 First permanent settlement is made in lower Manhattan and named New Amsterdam.

1626 Governor General Peter Minuit purchases Manhattan Island from the Indians for 60 guilders (estimated at $24).

1628 First church (Dutch Reformed) founded with arrival of its first minister.

1633 First church built at site of 39 Pearl St.

1636 Settlers Jacques Bentyn and Adrianse Bennett buy land from the Indians in Brooklyn near Gowanus Creek. Jacobus Van Corlaer buys Corlaer's Hook.

1638 First ferry line established from Fulton Ferry in Brooklyn to about Dover St in Manhattan. Earliest Manhattan land grant given to Andries Hudd in what is now Harlem.

1639 Jonas Bronck, a Dane, buys part of the Bronx from the Indians. David de Vries and others settle Staten Island, but are driven out by Indians.

1642 Religious tolerance of New Amsterdam attracts dissidents from New England including John Throgmorton (Throg's Neck) and Anne Hutchinson (Hutchinson River).

1643 Indian uprisings in New Amsterdam, New Jersey, and Staten Island; they continue intermittently until 1655.

1645 First permanent settlement in Queens at Vlisingen (Flushing).

1647 Peter Stuyvesant becomes governor.

1653 New Amsterdam receives charter establishing the municipal government. Peter Stuyvesant builds a fortified wall, river to river, at the present latitude of Wall St, to keep out the British, trading rivals of the Dutch.

1654 First permanent Jewish settlement. Asser Levy and 22 others arrive, fleeing persecution in Brazil.

1655 Flatbush Dutch Reformed Church founded, Long Island's first.

1661 First permanent settlement on Staten Island at Oude Dorp. Bowne House built in Flushing.

1664 The British capture New Amsterdam without a fight and rename it after James, Duke of York, brother of King Charles II.

1665 Thomas Willett becomes first mayor of New York.

1667 Treaty of Breda, closing a second Anglo-Dutch war, confirms Britain's possession of New Netherland.

1673 The Dutch capture New York, again without a fight, and rename it New Orange.

1674 Treaty of Westminster makes New York British once again.

1676 Canal on Broad St filled.

1682 Jews establish cemetery (still extant) at Chatham Square.

1686 The Dongan Charter—first British charter—gives city a form of municipal government that remains in force until modern times.

1689 King James II facing rebellion abdicates and flees to France. Jacob Leisler leads uprising against the British in New York.

1693 Frederick Philipse builds Kingsbridge across Harlem River joining Manhattan Island to the mainland.

1713 First Staten Island ferry.

1725 First newspaper, the *New-York Gazette* founded by William Bradford.

1729 First synagogue of Congregation Shearith Israel built on Beaver St.

1732 First theater opens near present Maiden Lane.

1733 John Peter Zenger publishes the *New-York Weekly Journal,* an antigovernment paper.

1734 Zenger jailed for slander; issues of his paper are publicly burned.

1735 Zenger acquittal establishes precedent for freedom of the press.

1754 King's College, now Columbia University, founded near Trinity Church as city's first college.

1762 Samuel Fraunces buys DeLancey house, opens tavern.

1763 French and Indian War closes with Treaty of Paris, confirming English control of North America.

1765 Stamp Act. Congress meets with delegates from nine colonies in New York and denounces British policies of taxation.

1766 Stamp Act repealed in England. St. Paul's Chapel, oldest remaining church in New York, dedicated. Roger Morris House built, now Morris-Jumel mansion in Harlem.

1767   Townshend Acts, named after British Chancellor of Exchequer, increase taxes and restrict colonial self-government. Although repealed three years later they fuel anti-British sentiment.

1776   Declaration of Independence marks beginning of Revolutionary War. British occupy Brooklyn after Battle of Long Island and take control of all Manhattan by November 17.

1783   Treaty of Paris concludes Revolutionary War as Britain recognizes independence of the 13 colonies. British army leaves New York.

1784   New York City becomes the capital of the state and nation.

1787   Erasmus Hall Academy opens in Flatbush, Brooklyn.

1789   U.S. Constitution ratified. George Washington takes oath as nation's first President in Federal Hall on Wall St.

1790   Federal capital moves to Philadelphia. First census puts city population at 33,000.

1791   Yellow fever epidemic stimulates development of Greenwich Village.

1792   Buttonwood Agreement leads to formation of New York Stock Exchange.

1794   City buys Bellevue, an East River estate, and opens contagious disease hospital.

1796   Robert Fitch tests experimental steamboat on Collect Pond.

1797   Albany becomes state capital. Washington Square purchased as a potter's field.

1798   Yellow fever epidemic claims 2086 lives.

1799   Aaron Burr founds Manhattan Company to provide drinking water, but clause in charter allows him also to found bank.

1800   Alexander Hamilton builds the Grange.

1801   Brooklyn Navy Yard founded.

1803   Cornerstone laid for present City Hall. Yellow fever epidemic.

1806   First New York free school opens.

1807   Robert Fulton demonstrates steamboat *Clermont* on the Hudson River.

1810   Fulton opens steam ferry service to New Jersey.

1811   John Randel, Jr., heads group of commissioners who plan New York's rectilinear street grid, known as the Commissioner's Plan or Randel Survey.

1812   City Hall opens. U.S. declares war on Britain; port suffers in trade war and is fortified against possible British attack.

1814   Treaty of Ghent ends War of 1812.

1816   Village of Brooklyn incorporated on site of present downtown Brooklyn.

1820   New York becomes nation's largest city, with population of 123,706.

1823   City buys site of Bryant Park for another potter's field.

1825   Erie Canal opens, greatly enhancing the importance of New York as a port and making it the gateway to the midwest.

1827   State legislature ends all slavery in New York State.

1828   Washington Square Park laid out in old potter's field.

1829 Large reservoir built on 14th St at the Bowery, one of the numerous stop-gap measures aimed at solving the city's water problems.

1831 New York University founded as University of the City of New York. Gramercy Park laid out.

1832 New York and Harlem Railroad, a horsecar line, opens along the Bowery and Fourth Ave from Prince St to 14th St as city's first railroad.

1834 Village of Brooklyn incorporated as City of Brooklyn.

1835 "Great Fire" destroys 674 buildings near Hanover and Pearl Sts.

1837 Business panic in which city losses total some $60 million. New York and Harlem Railroad reaches Harlem. First steam locomotives added in 1839.

1840 City's population, 312,710.

1841 St. John's College, now Fordham University, founded in the Bronx.

1842 Croton Aqueduct brings water to city; stored in reservoir on site of Bryant Park. John Jacob Astor founds Astor Library. Charles Dickens visits the city.

1843 Potter's field established on Randalls Island.

1846 Potato famine in Ireland swells immigration. Tensions between Catholics and Protestants arise over such issues as aid to parochial schools.

1847 Madison Square Park laid out, replacing old potter's field.

1848 Political uprisings increase immigration from Germany.

1849 Free Academy (chartered 1847), the precursor of City College, opens on Lexington Ave at 23rd St. Astor Place Riot demonstrates incompetence of police force.

1850 P. T. Barnum organizes concert with Jenny Lind at Castle Garden. Giuseppe Garibaldi arrives in Staten Island during period of exile.

1851 *New York Daily Times*, now *New York Times*, begins publication. Hudson River Railroad links New York City and Albany.

1852 William Marcy "Boss" Tweed begins political career as alderman of Seventh Ward.

1853 State legislature authorizes Central Park. World's Fair held at Crystal Palace in Bryant Park.

1855 Castle Garden becomes immigrant station. Construction of large numbers of inhumane tenements leads to tenement reform movement; first model tenement built on Elizabeth and Mott Sts.

1856 City buys land for Central Park.

1857 Another financial panic.

1858 Calvert Vaux and Frederick Law Olmsted chosen to design Central Park; work is begun. Fire destroys Crystal Palace. Macy's founded.

1859 Cooper Union opens. State legislature authorizes Prospect Park. Otis passenger elevator installed in Fifth Avenue Hotel.

1860 City's population reaches 813,669, including large numbers of immigrants.

1861   Civil War begins.

1862   The *Monitor,* an ironclad ship designed by John Ericsson, launched in the Greenpoint section of Brooklyn.

1863   Draft Riots against conscription into the Union Army (those who could pay a $300 fee were exempted) paralyze the city for three days.

1865   Civil War ends. Municipal fire fighting system replaces volunteer companies.

1867   Prospect Park opens in Brooklyn. First tenement house law attempts to set standards for ventilation, sanitation, and room size.

1868   Andrew H. Green proposes consolidation of boroughs. First elevated railroad opens on Greenwich St from the Battery to Cortlandt St, a cable system with both moving and stationary engines.

1869   Rutherford Stuyvesant builds city's first known apartment house on E. 18th St. Potter's field moved to Harts Island, where it remains today. Jay Gould and Jim Fisk corner the gold market.

1870   Work begins on Brooklyn Bridge. First building with passenger elevators (Equitable Life Assurance Building at 120 Broadway; burned 1912). Joseph Warren Beach opens pneumatic subway under Broadway from Warren to Murray Sts. Ninth Ave El reaches 30th St.

1871   Grand Central Depot opens. Boss Tweed arrested, closing a period during which city government reached a low point of inefficiency and corruption.

1873   Financial panic.

1874   P. T. Barnum opens Hippodrome at Madison Square. Part of the Bronx annexed to New York City.

1877   Alfred Tredway White opens model tenement houses in Brooklyn. Museum of Natural History opens at its present site.

1878   Sixth Ave El opens from Rector St to Central Park.

1879   "Dumbbell" tenement plan by James F. Ware wins competition for model tenement sponsored by magazine. Plan condemned by tenement reformers but widely adopted.

1880   Sixth Ave El reaches 155th St. Metropolitan Museum of Art opens. Broadway illuminated by Brush electric arc lamps.

1882   Thomas Edison opens generating plant at 257 Pearl St, making electricity commercially available.

1883   Brooklyn Bridge opens. Metropolitan Opera opens on Broadway between 39th and 40th Sts (demolished 1967). New York Giants baseball team founded.

1885   Elevated railway opens in Brooklyn.

1886   Statue of Liberty inaugurated on Bedloe's (now Liberty) Island. Elevated railway joins Manhattan and Bronx.

1888   Great Blizzard. First building with steel skeleton erected, Tower Building at 50 Broadway.

1890   Madison Square Garden, designed by Stanford White, opens at the N.E. corner of Madison Square.

1891 Carnegie Hall opens. New York Botanical Garden opens in the Bronx.

1892 Immigration station opens on Ellis Island.

1895 Harlem Ship Canal opens along Harlem River with channel dug south of Spuyten Duyvil Creek. Rest of Bronx annexed to New York City.

1898 Greater New York created by joining the five boroughs under a single municipal government. Population of 3.4 million makes it the world's second largest city behind London (4 million).

1899 Bronx Zoo opens. Brooklyn Children's Museum established. Croton Reservoir in Bryant Park razed.

1900 Subway construction begins. Blacks begin moving to Harlem. Census shows tenements house 70% of city's population.

1901 Tenement House Law institutes "New Law" tenements, superseding dumb bell plan. Macy's opens on Broadway.

1903 Williamsburg Bridge opens, making northern Brooklyn accessible to the poor of the Lower East Side.

1904 IRT subway opens from City Hall to W. 145th St.

1905 Municipal Staten Island ferry opens, with 5¢ fare.

1906 Harry K. Thaw, deranged Pittsburgh millionaire, shoots and kills architect Stanford White on the roof of Madison Square Garden.

1908 East River subway tunnel between Bowling Green and Joralemon St links Manhattan and Brooklyn. First Hudson Tube, the McAdoo Tunnel, links Manhattan and Hoboken, New Jersey. IRT Broadway line reaches Kingsbridge section of the Bronx.

1909 Queensboro and Manhattan Bridges open.

1910 Pennsylvania Station opens.

1911 Triangle Shirtwaist Co. fire kills 145. Brooklyn Botanic Garden opens.

1913 The present Grand Central Terminal opens. The Armory Show at the 69th Regiment Armory introduces New York to "modern art."

1916 Nation's first zoning resolution, divides city into residential and commercial areas and restricts height and bulk of buildings.

1923 "Setback" law restricts configuration of tall buildings. New York Yankees move into Yankee Stadium; Babe Ruth hits home run.

1925 Columbia University and Presbyterian Hospital join to form Medical Center at 168th St and Broadway. Stanford White's Madison Square Garden at Madison Square demolished.

1927 Holland Tunnel (for vehicular traffic) opens between New York and New Jersey.

1928 Cornell University and New York Hospital join forces as New York Medical Center, York Ave and E. 70th St. Goethals Bridge and Outerbridge Crossing open linking Staten Island and New Jersey.

1929 Stock market crashes; Great Depression begins.

1931 Empire State Building and George Washington Bridge open. Floyd Bennett Field opens as city's first municipal airport. Bayonne Bridge opens linking Staten Island and New Jersey.

1932 Mayor James J. ("Beau James") Walker resigns after Seabury Investigations reveal rampant corruption.

1933 Fiorello La Guardia elected mayor. IND subway opens to Queens.

1934 New York City Housing Authority formed to clear slums and build low-rent housing.

1935 Work begins on East River Drive.

1936 Triborough Bridge opens. First Houses (Avenue A at E. 3rd St) open.

1938 La Guardia's City Charter of 1936 goes into effect centralizing municipal power and giving full legislative authority to City Council.

1939 North Beach Airport opens; soon renamed for La Guardia. New York World's Fair of 1939–40 opens in Flushing Meadows Park, Queens.

1940 Queens-Midtown Tunnel opens, linking mid-Manhattan and Queens. Brooklyn Battery Tunnel begun.

1941 U.S. enters World War II. New York becomes important as major Atlantic port. Brooklyn Navy Yard operates at full capacity.

1945 World War II ends. Army bomber crashes into Empire State Building. United Nations charter passed.

1946 U.N. selects New York as permanent headquarters. Army plane crashes into Bank of Manhattan Co. building's 58th floor.

1947 Rockefellers donate $5.8 million site of U.N. headquarters. Stuyvesant Town, middle-income housing for returning war veterans and their families, is built by Metropolitan Life Insurance Co. along East River Drive, 14th–20th Sts.

1948 Subway and bus fares rise to 10¢. New York International Airport (opened 1942) greatly expanded; now called Idlewild.

1950 Brooklyn Battery Tunnel opens after construction delay caused by war. City population at all-time high: 7,891,957. Mayor William O'Dwyer, on the verge of exposure for corruption and links with organized crime, is appointed ambassador to Mexico by fellow Democrat, President Harry Truman.

1952 Lever House opens, first of glass-box skyscrapers. Transit Authority established.

1954 Robert F. Wagner elected mayor. Decline of older American cities begins in mid- to late 1950s. Puerto Rican immigration increases as does influx of poor blacks.

1957 Fair Housing Law outlaws racial discrimination. Manhattan-town scandal reveals housing project sponsors have failed to develop site while pocketing tenants' rents.

1958 Brooklyn Dodgers move to Los Angeles. Baseball Giants move to San Francisco.

1959 Ground broken for Lincoln Center.

1960 World Trade Center proposed at estimated cost of $250 million. Completion of Chase Manhattan Bank marks beginning of construction boom in lower Manhattan. Ebbets Field razed for housing project.

1961 New zoning law offers incentives for public amenities, plazas, arcades.

1962 Philharmonic Hall, now Avery Fisher Hall, opens as first building of Lincoln Center for the Performing Arts.

1963 Pennsylvania Station demolished despite protests.

1964 Race riots in Harlem and Bedford-Stuyvesant. World's Fair of 1964–65 opens in Flushing Meadows, Queens. Fair plagued by financial difficulties and controversy but attracts 51 million visitors. Verrazano-Narrows Bridge opens, ending relative isolation of Staten Island.

1965 Landmarks Preservation Commission established to save city's architectural heritage. New laws allow increased Asian, Greek, Haitian, Dominican, etc. immigration. First power blackout.

1966 Ground broken for World Trade Center.

1968 City teachers strike in battle over school decentralization, an issue with racial overtones.

1971 Football Giants move to New Jersey. Construction begins on 63rd St subway tunnel.

1973 Construction of Twin Towers at World Trade Center completed. Welfare Island renamed Roosevelt Island, as redevelopment begins. Section of West Side Highway collapses under weight of dump truck.

1974 Project to replace West Side Highway and to redevelop west side corridor officially named Westway. Opponents file first lawsuit to stop project. City's financial position worsens, as loss of middle class and departure of businesses erode tax base while costs of social services increase.

1975 Cash flow problems and inability to sell more municipal bonds bring city to verge of insolvency. Federal government staves off default on city notes by offering loans. South Bronx becomes symbol of urban despair as 13,000 fires break out in 12-square-mile area.

1977 Power blackout, 25 hours, results in widespread looting, vandalism.

1978 Radio City Music Hall saved from demolition. Supreme Court decision preserves Grand Central Terminal in its present form. *Herald Tribune* ceases publication. Federal government gives city $1.65 billion in long-term loan guarantees.

1980 Census assesses population at 7,086,096, with sharp decline in city's white population, moderate increase in black population, and substantial increase in Hispanic population. Blacks and Hispanics account for 48% of city's population.

1981 City reenters long-term municipal bond market. Construction begins at Battery Park City.

1982 Morosco and Helen Hayes Theaters demolished despite protest as hotel project begins in Times Square. IBM Building opens on Madison Ave.

1983 City celebrates Brooklyn Bridge Centennial. Statue of Liberty restoration begun. Trump Tower opens. *A Chorus Line* sets Broadway record at 3,389th performance. Midtown suffers blackout after fire erupts in electrical substation; 12 blocks of Garment District darkened during crucial marketing week. City enacts "antisliver" law which limits height of buildings that are less than 45 ft wide.

1984 AT&T headquarters opens on Madison Ave. Army Corps of Engineers holds hearings on potential effect of Westway on Hudson River striped bass, whose well-being has provided Westway opponents with means of blocking development.

1985 Columbia University sells land under Rockefeller Center to Rockefeller Group for $400 million. After 12 years of struggle, Westway project ($2.3-billion, 4.2-mile highway) abandoned, because of lack of federal financial support, potential harm to striped bass, hostility of environmentalists and public.

1986 Two British parachutists jump from 86th floor observation deck of Empire State Building, landing two blocks away. Carnegie Hall reopens after complete refurbishing. Statue of Liberty celebrates 100th anniversary amid fireworks, speeches, and parade of tall ships. Corruption probe uncovers kickback schemes involving parking ticket collection contracts; scandal spreads to other city agencies.

1987 Stock market crashes as Dow Jones average plunges 508 points in one day. World Financial Center opens in Battery Park City.

1988 City signs first comprehensive antismoking bill, limiting smoking in public places. Williamsburg Bridge closes for repairs after bridge approaches, long neglected, are deemed unsafe to carry traffic.

1989 David Dinkins is elected first black mayor of the city. B. Altman & Company department store closes after 124 years in business.

1990 Ellis Island reopens to public as museum of immigration.

I BOROUGH OF MANHATTAN / NEW YORK COUNTY

To many people New York is synonymous with Manhattan, a slender island 12.5 miles long, 2.5 miles wide, with a total area of 22.6 square miles, which means that Peter Minuit, who reputedly paid the Indians $24 for it, got it for a little more than a dollar a square mile. It is the third largest borough in population (1,427,533, a drop of 7.3% in the last decade) behind Brooklyn and the Bronx, and the smallest in size. City Hall, the center of the borough politically if not geographically, lies at a latitude of 40° 42′ 26″ and a longitude of 74° 0′ 23″. Its highest altitude is about 268 ft and its lowest, sea level.

Topographically there remain only a few vestiges of Manhattan's appearance before the Dutch came. Southern Manhattan is flat, a coastal plain lying over a fairly shallow stratum of Manhattan schist, the bedrock on which its skyscrapers stand. Again in midtown bedrock lies close to the surface, supporting a second great concentration of towering buildings. A large pond near City Hall and swamps in the West Village and near Turtle Bay have been filled; streams and rivers have been drained, filled, or channeled underground as sewers so that Manhattan from the Battery to Central Park is uniform and undistinguished, with the exception of a few unimpressive rises like Murray Hill.

In its more northerly reaches however the island's natural topography is more evident: in Central Park's outcroppings of Manhattan schist laced with granite intrusions and striated by glacial scratches, in Fort Tryon Park and Inwood Hill Park, two schist ridges bisected by the fault valley that underlies Dyckman Street, in the ridges of Morningside Heights once used by rock climbers to hone their skills, in the valley of W. 125th St slashing diagonally across the regular north-south street grid, and in the glacial potholes of Inwood Hill Park.

Manhattan is encircled by rivers, the Hudson (once called the North River) on the W.; the East River, actually a tidal inlet from Long Island Sound on the E.; and the Harlem River on the N.E., part of which, the Harlem Ship Canal on the N., is an artificial channel dug at the end of the 19C to facilitate navigation.

The island was settled from S. to N., with its oldest neighborhoods in what is today called Lower Manhattan. The first settlement was near Battery Park, an area perhaps attractive to the Dutch, who found its marshy flatness similar to the Dutch lowlands. The Financial District, a residential area for the Dutch, had already begun to assume some public functions after the British took over in 1664. North of it are the Civic Center, Chinatown, and Little Italy, the two latter areas the home of a large immigrant population toward the end of the 19C. South of Houston St is SoHo, once the industrial outpost of Little Italy but more recently a center of the city's artistic life, whose industrial buildings have been converted to studios and apartments and have in the past decade attracted boutiques, restaurants, and establishments similar to those in Greenwich Village directly to

its north. Two nearby neighborhoods today undergoing the gentrification that changed SoHo a decade ago are TriBeCa, an
acronym for the Triangle Below Canal (St), an area S. and W. of
SoHo, and NoHo, a triangular area N. of Houston St between
Mercer St and the Bowery, the part near Broadway sometimes
known, acronymically, as LoBro. The upper reaches of the Lower
East Side, once the home of eastern European immigrants, became
the East Village during the late 1960s, home of many young
people who represented what was then called the counterculture.
The ungentrified parts of the Lower East Side are also known
either as the "Loisaida" (a phonetic spelling) or Alphabet City,
Avenues A–D.

Also S. of midtown are Chelsea, Gramercy Park, Herald Square,
and Murray Hill, all at one time elegant residential districts.
Times Square, as every tourist knows, is in midtown at the S.
edge of the theater district. It has long been notorious for its
neon, pornography, and general honky tonk, but today is poised
on the verge of possibly cataclysmic redevelopment. To its W.
lies an area once known as Hell's Kitchen, the home of successive
immigrant groups. The northern stretches of Hell's Kitchen, lying
roughly between Ninth Ave and the river, from Times Square
north to about 54th St, is nowadays known as Clinton, an area
that will surely undergo significant social change as Times Square
is redeveloped.

In midtown, Fifth Ave divides east from west. In the very
center is Rockefeller Center, hugging Fifth Ave. On the East Side
of midtown lies an important business district with major banks,
corporate headquarters, the advertising industry on Madison
Ave, the long stretch of fine Park Ave apartment houses, and the
posh shops of Fifth and Madison Aves. On the far east, facing
the East River, is the United Nations, focus of the diplomatic
community.

Central Park divides the East Side from the West Side above
59th St. The former includes the elite neighborhoods of Sutton
Place and Beekman Place, the more arriviste apartments, bars,
and restaurants of Second and First Aves, and Yorkville, once an
uptown immigrant neighborhood for Germans, Czechs, and Hungarians, now growing daily more fashionable and expensive.
Above 96th St lies East Harlem, formerly an Italian enclave, now
known as El Barrio or Spanish Harlem.

On the West Side the presence of Lincoln Center for the
Performing Arts has catalyzed the upward mobility of Amsterdam and Columbus Aves, only a few years ago characterized by
humble, service-oriented shops, now chock-full of boutiques and
upscale enterprises, some of which are finding the going difficult
economically. Central Park West and Riverside Drive are the
finest residential areas on the West Side, with their views of
greenery and the Hudson River respectively. North of 96th St are
several large urban renewal projects. Above the park and 110th
St is Morningside Heights, long a middle-class community characterized by its great intellectual and religious institutions.

To the E. and far below Morningside Heights lies the Harlem
plain, embracing the nation's most famous black community.

Hamilton Heights to its N. is the home of C.C.N.Y., the City College of New York, part of the city university system. Upper Manhattan consists of the neighborhoods of Washington Heights and Inwood, both residential. The Cloisters in Fort Tryon Park is the major cultural institution in upper Manhattan. Across the Harlem River is Marble Hill, physically attached to the Bronx, politically a part of Manhattan, to which it was joined before the digging of the Harlem Ship Canal.

1 Statue of Liberty and Ellis Island

The Statue of Liberty National Monument. Liberty Island, New York 10013. Tel: 732-1286.

Boats for the Statue of Liberty leave from Battery Park; the ticket kiosk is located in Castle Clinton, the low red sandstone structure on the W. side of the park. Boats leave at least once hourly, on the hour, all year from 9–4, with additional sailings on the half hour and sometimes beginning at 8:30, during peak season; for schedule information call the Circle Line 269-5755.

In addition to the fee for the ferry, there is a small admission charge to the statue. The round trip by boat takes about 45 minutes. Crowds are often very heavy and the time required to ascend the statue lengthens proportionately. To make the ascent with the shortest waiting time, take the first boat (telephone the Circle Line for exact time of first sailing), stay downstairs on the boat near the gangway, and hurry immediately from the dock to the statue.

Museum in statue interior, with displays on the history and construction of the statue and on immigration. Restrooms in statue base and in restaurant building. Cafeteria, gift shop. Complete access for handicapped visitors to museums, restrooms and restaurant; no wheelchair access above museum level. No facilities for checking parcels, etc., so visitors must carry at all times any paraphernalia they bring to the island or else leave it unguarded.

The crown is a 22-story climb from ground level. An elevator reaches the top of the pedestal but from this level ascent to the crown is by spiral stairway only, the equivalent of 12 stories. Although the statue interior is air-cooled (not air-conditioned) temperatures rise in summer. Visitors with physical disabilities, vertigo, or claustrophobia are urged not to make the climb. There are excellent views (better, actually than from the crown) from the promenade level, above the original Fort Wood, and at the top of the pedestal.

The ****Statue of Liberty** (dedicated 1886, sculptor Frédéric Auguste Bartholdi; DL), surely the most famous piece of sculpture in America, rises in towering majesty on Liberty Island in direct view of ships entering the Upper Bay. A gift of the people of France, the figure stands on a granite pedestal, donated by the American public. Her head is surrounded by a radiant crown, while her feet step forth from broken shackles; in her uplifted right hand is a torch, her left holds a tablet representing the Declaration of Independence.

History. The inspiration for the Statue of Liberty, originally called "Liberty Enlightening the World," comes primarily from two men: Édouard René

Lefebvre de Laboulaye (1811–83), a noted jurist, professor, and authority on U.S. Constitutional history, and Frédéric Auguste Bartholdi (1834–1904), a sculptor of monumental ambitions. Laboulaye, wanting to identify the destiny of France with that of the U.S., the preeminent modern republic, proposed a joint Franco-American monument in 1865 and introduced Bartholdi to the project. The statue's iron skeleton was devised by Alexandre Gustave Eiffel (1832–1923), whose reputation at the time rested with his iron trusswork railway bridges.

The French people raised about $400,000 for the statue, which was constructed in Paris by the firm of Gaget, Gauthier, et Cie and assembled outside Bartholdi's workshops. In 1884 the construction scaffolding was removed and on July 4 the figure was formally presented to the United States; then the statue was dismantled and shipped to New York in 214 crates. On October 28, 1886, President Grover Cleveland dedicated it during spectacular ceremonies climaxed by fireworks and the unveiling of the face. The statue soon became a tourist attraction, a promise of hope offered to immigrants by the New World, and eventually a powerful symbol for the U. S. itself.

As such it has been the target of extremist groups: in 1965 four terrorists attempted to blow off the head and arm holding the torch; in 1971 a group of Vietnam veterans occupied it for a few days as a war protest; in 1980 two men protesting "injustice" climbed the exterior and spent a night enveloped in the folds of the robe.

The centennial year (1986) saw the triumphant unveiling of a restored statue, which had been shrouded for two years in scaffolding. The only visible exterior change is the replacement of the former torch (1916) of glass in a copper grid by a new one gilded with gold leaf as Bartholdi had envisioned. The interior, however, is considerably changed. The corroded iron straps which held the copper skin to the interior framework have been replaced by stainless steel ones, and the connection between the central pylon and the uplifted right arm, swaying since 1916, has been strengthened. The wire mesh that long enclosed the spiral staircase has been cleared away and now the interior of the statue itself, the great volumes of the body and the billowing folds and creases of the robe, soar above the visitor in their full glory. The architectural firm of Swanke Hayden Connell working with Ammann & Whitney, engineers, undertook the restoration.

The unveiling of the statue was climaxed by a July 4 celebration truly American in its exuberant excess. Naval warships fired 21-gun salvos and military planes performed aerobatics over the harbor; a fleet of 150 tall ships— some of them recreations of 18C and 19C traders, fishing schooners, and square-riggers—sailed from the Narrows up the Hudson River to Spuyten Duyvil; a 40,000-shell fireworks display illuminated the harbor at night. Some 25,000 vessels clogged the harbor, including the *Queen Elizabeth 2*, carrying a huge American flag and 800 automobile dealers. Helicopters, jet fighters, and six stately blimps buzzed, soared, and hovered overhead. An estimated 1.5–2 million people jammed the streets and parks, or climbed to the roofs of tall buildings, and crowded into any apartment or office space with a view of the statue. It may have been the city's largest party ever.

The ferry docks at the W. side of **Liberty Island** (renamed in l956), formerly known as Bedloe's Island after Isaac Bedloe who acquired it in 1667 from the English colonial governor.

Before the Revolution it was used as a quarantine station, particularly for smallpox, and from 1746–57 it was owned by Archibald Kennedy, a wealthy merchant, who summered there. The U.S. government acquired it in 1800 to build Fort Wood (1808–11), designed by Col. Jonathan Williams, who also planned Castle Williams on Governors Island and Fort Gibson on Ellis Island. Named after a now obscure hero of the War of 1812, Fort Wood later served as a Civil War recruitment camp and an ordnance depot; in 1877 the government donated it to the Liberty project.

From the boat dock the statue's scale is impressive: height of statue alone, 151 ft; pedestal, 89 ft; height of torch above sea

Enlarging Liberty's hand (1876–81). Bartholdi's clay model of the statue was enlarged in three stages to full scale. The sculptor, bareheaded in the foreground, modified the form each time as increased size created unexpected visual effects. (New York Public Library)

level, 305 ft; weight, 225 tons; waist measurement, 35 ft, width of mouth, 3 ft; length of index finger, 8 ft.

The size of the statue imposed technical difficulties, which Eiffel solved with great ingenuity. He devised an interior framework consisting of a heavy central iron pylon supporting a lightweight system of trusswork that reaches out toward the interior surface of the statue. The hammered copper "skin" of the figure, only $3/32$ of an inch thick, is bound together in sections by steel straps and joined to the trusswork in such a way that it "floats" at the ends of hundreds of flexible attachments and can accommodate both thermal changes and wind.

A broad mall leads from the water to the pedestal designed by Richard Morris Hunt and constructed of concrete and rusticated blocks of Stony Creek granite. The 40 shields ringing the pedestal above the portals were meant to carry the coats-of-arms of the then 40 states.

The cornerstone was laid in 1884, but construction was halted for lack of funds. In 1885 newspaper publisher Joseph Pulitzer launched a funding campaign which in a few months raised over $100,000, mostly in modest donations, while quadrupling the circulation of his financially troubled newspaper.

INTERIOR. In the base of the statue, one floor above ground level, is a museum devoted to the history and construction of the statue and to American immigration. Exhibits of photographs, models, and documents detail the evolution of the concept of Liberty and of Bartholdi's design for the statue, as well as the political maneuvering involved in its execution. Full-scale copper repoussé models of the foot and face graphically illustrate the figure's scale. The next section of the exhibit focuses on the impact of the statue on new arrivals, and the exploitation of the statue as a commercial image or a vehicle for propaganda.

The rest of the museum, formerly known as the Museum of American Immigration, is organized chronologically from the colonial period onward. Exhibits use photographs, costumes, tools, and personal possessions brought from homelands across the sea to suggest the diversity of immigrant backgrounds, the quality of immigrant life, and the contributions of immigrants to American culture. A computerized display allows visitors to look up their own surnames and to locate other families in the country with the same name.

Accessible from the museum level is a promenade on the ramparts of Fort Wood, with superb views of the harbor, Staten Island, New Jersey, and Manhattan.

*Ellis Island National Monument, originally a low-lying sandbar of about 3 acres now enlarged by landfill to 27.5 acres, lies about a mile S.W. of Battery Park in the Upper Bay, not far from the Statue of Liberty.

Note: After extensive renovation the former U.S. Immigration Station at Ellis Island reopened in 1990 as a museum of immigration. The central exhibit is the spectacular Great Hall. Circle Line ferries leave Battery Park hourly at 15 minutes past the hour from 9 to 4 (tel: 269-5755).

It is the site of the former *United States Immigration Station* through which an estimated 12 million immigrants passed on their way to a new life. The turreted, vaguely Byzantine, brick and limestone buildings (1898; Boring & Tilton) were abandoned in 1954 and began to deteriorate rapidly, the natural ravages of weather and damp sea air compounded by vandals who ripped out plumbing and electrical fixtures.

History. The Indians called Ellis Island *Kioshk* (Gull Island); the Dutch bought it in 1630, named it Little Oyster Island, and then ceded it to a patroon—a sort of feudal landowner—who also held title to what is now Hoboken, Staten Island, and Jersey City, but never left Amsterdam to enjoy his territories. During much of the 18C the British called it Bucking Island (etymology unknown), though for a period after 1765 it was known as Anderson's or Gibbet Island, in honor of a pirate named Anderson who was hanged there. At the time of the Revolution it was owned by Samuel Ellis (died 1794), who owned a farm in New Jersey, sold general merchandise in Manhattan, and leased out part of the island to a fisherman's tavern. After his death, the federal government acquired it (1808) from his heirs for a then exorbitant $10,000 to build a fort. Like the three other fortifications built at about this time (see p. 109), it was intended to protect the city from a British naval

The Statue of Liberty under construction in Paris (1881–84). The statue was completely assembled outside sculptor Bartholdi's studio and presented ceremoniously to the U.S. ambassador before being dismantled and shipped. (New York Public Library)

invasion in the War of 1812, but saw no action. Named Fort Gibson in 1814 after an officer killed in the battle of Fort Erie, it is the only one of the four harbor fortifications of which no trace remains. From 1835–90 it served as an ammunition dump, threatening nearby New Jersey residents with the possibility of accidental explosions.

In 1890 when the federal government took over the immigration service, Ellis Island was designated as the site of the main receiving station almost by default: the army did not want immigrants on Governors Island; New Yorkers did not want them on Manhattan, where they were more vulnerable to local swindlers anyhow; and the public considered the use of Bedloe's Island, already the site of the Statue of Liberty, an outrage. An immigrant station, therefore, was built on Ellis Island and opened in 1892. Primarily constructed of Georgia pine, it burned to the ground five years later, fortunately without loss of life, but with the destruction of the immigration records from 1855–90, which had been stored in the powder magazines of the former fort. In 1898 the firm of Boring & Tilton began to construct the present station, while the immigration service returned to the Barge Office in Battery Park, where it had been temporarily housed in 1890–91. The new fireproof buildings opened on December 17, 1900, and that day received 2251 immigrants.

Inside the station federal inspectors processed the immigrants, detaining those who would be physically or mentally incapacitated from earning a living, weeding out paupers, criminals, prostitutes, the insane, and those suffering from contagious diseases or professing such beliefs as anarchy or polygamy. Persons not admitted were either detained (20%) until their cases could be resolved or held for deportation (2%), and so were housed and fed in the dormitories, hospitals, and dining halls.

Until 1902 when President Theodore Roosevelt appointed as Commissioner of Immigration a former Wall Street lawyer, William Williams, immigrants were often abused or robbed, and the concessionaires who operated the food and currency exchange services enriched themselves at the expense of both the immigrants and the government. After Williams' reforms, problems arose primarily from overcrowding. In 1907, the peak year of immigration, 1,004,756 people entered the U.S. through Ellis Island, approximately twice the number the station was designed to handle.

The heavy influx continued until 1915, when World War I closed transAtlantic shipping. During the war Ellis Island served as a detention center for enemy aliens and for immigrants waiting to be deported. In the period of isolationism and racism that followed the war, immigration never reached its earlier level; a series of laws passed in the 1920s imposed an overall annual ceiling (first 358,000, later only 164,000) as well as quotas for particular nationalities, discriminating against Latins, Slavs, and Jews. Under the National Origins Act (1924) immigrants were processed in their own countries and thereafter Ellis Island became gradually underused and increasingly expensive to maintain. Sporadically the government found uses for it—detaining war criminals and enemy aliens during World War II, screening the political beliefs of immigrants, visitors, and foreign seamen seeking shore leave during the McCarthy era in the early 1950s.

In 1954 the last detainee, a Norwegian sailor who had jumped ship, was released; the station closed and the island was vacated. The buildings were put up for sale to the highest bidder with the stipulation that the government approve of the use to which the island be put. The highest bid in 1956 was $201,000 by would-be developers of a luxury convention facility called "Pleasure Island." Later proposals included a Bible college, a gambling casino, and a mental institution. Gradually, however, the government became mindful of the island's historical importance, and in 1965, a few months before a new immigration law was passed abolishing the national origins quotas of the 1920s, it became part of the Statue of Liberty National Monument. In 1970 militant American Indians tried to occupy it to dramatize the destruction of the native population by European immigrants. Later a group of blacks began renovating some of the smaller buildings, avowing their aim to create a rehabilitation center for drug addicts and convicts. In 1976 the island opened to visitors.

In 1982 a commission undertook the present restorations, which currently include only the Main Building and adjacent grounds. An Immigrant Wall of Honor has been erected near the water, paid for by donations from the descendants of those who entered here.

Ellis Island consists physically of two rectangular land masses, largely created by landfill, which are separated by a ferry slip (c. 1890). Directly behind the slip is the *Immigrant Building* (1934), built to accommodate aliens who were temporarily detained, thus segregating them from the criminal and undesirable deportees who constituted much of the island's population in the 1930s; since the volume of immigration fell off at this time, the building was never used for its original purpose. To the left of the slip is the hospital island, whose nearest buildings once served as the pavilions of the *General Hospital* (opened 1902). On the far side of the island are the buildings of the *Contagious Disease Hospital* (completed 1909). The central area, now densely overgrown, was once a recreation area for patients.

To the right of the ferry slip is the original island, now enlarged by landfill, upon which stand the main **Immigrant Receiving Station,** the Baggage and Dormitory Building, the restaurant and laundry building, and the power plant.

The largest and most impressive of the group, the Immigrant Receiving Station (385 ft long, 165 ft wide, corner towers 100 ft tall) is constructed of brick laid in Flemish bond and trimmed with limestone. The two-story arched windows (duplicated on the other side of the structure) once served as doorways, from which a sheltering roof ran to the slip. The Great Hall on the second story (200 × 100 × 56 ft) was designed to handle 5000 immigrants per day. The Guastavino tile ceiling was installed after 1916, when explosions of ammunition stockpiled on nearby New Jersey wharves damaged the earlier roof. The red tile floor was laid at the same time, replacing asphalt. Until 1911 the interior of the hall was divided by iron pipes into a series of pens resembling a cattle run.

2 Lower Manhattan and Battery Park

SUBWAY: IRT Broadway-7th Ave local (train 1 or 9) to South Ferry. IRT Lexington Ave local (train 4 or 5) to Bowling Green. BMT Broadway local (R train) to Whitehall St.

BUS: M1 or M6 via Broadway, M15 via 2nd Ave to South Ferry.

New York City owes its historic supremacy among American cities to its closeness to the sea, and nowhere are these ties more obvious than at the S. tip of Manhattan where the East and Hudson Rivers converge and empty into New York Bay.

The **former U.S. Custom House** (1907; Cass Gilbert; DL) just S. of Bowling Green at the foot of Broadway, occupies the probable site of New York's first permanent European settlement.

In 1624 the Dutch ship *Nieu Nederlandt* deposited eight men on what is now Governors Island and continued upstream to settle others at the present site of Albany. These men, sponsored by the Dutch West India Company, were joined the following year by six families, who brought with them the necessities for subsistence farming. The settlers moved to the S. shore of Manhattan, where

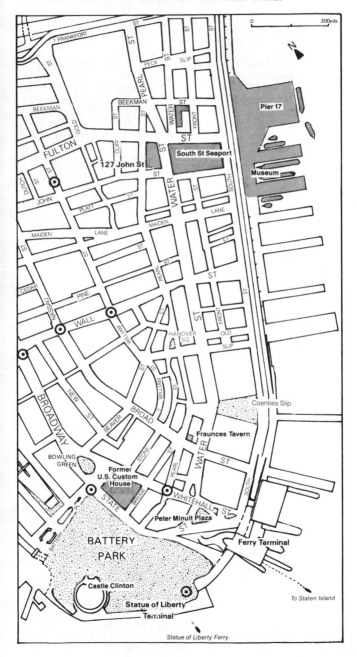

they built rude shelters and a fort to protect themselves from the Indians, who though initially friendly inevitably became hostile later on.

The original fort (1626), Fort Amsterdam, consisted of a crude blockhouse protected by a cedar palisade. As the town grew and alternately fell under the jurisdiction of the Dutch, the British, the Dutch again, and the British once more, the fort was strengthened and appropriately renamed. The last such structure, called Fort George after the reigning British monarch, remained until after the Revolution, when it was torn down (1789) to make way for Government House, a building intended as the residence for the nation's President.

Since New York's hopes to become the nation's permanent capital city did not materialize, Government House became the mansion for the state governor until the state capital was moved to Albany in 1796. The mansion became in turn the Elysian Boarding House, a hotel whose name suggested a level of perfection rarely attained in boarding houses, and then briefly a custom house. Severely damaged by a fire in 1815, it was demolished and replaced by a row of six elegant brick houses, which served first as residences and then, as commerce invaded this residential area, as offices for the principal shipping companies, conferring on the street its nickname, Steamship Row.

Meanwhile the customs service had moved to Wall St, first to the old Federal Hall, later to the building now occupied by Citibank, but as the 19C progressed, these facilities became inadequate. In 1892 the U.S. Treasury bought this plot of land and announced an architectural competition for a new Custom House. Cass Gilbert, although less famous than some of the other contestants, won the competition with a design that symbolized the commercial greatness of the nation and of the city.

EXTERIOR. Adorned with emblems of commerce and the sea, the Custom House facade is a triumph of Beaux-Arts exuberance. In the window arches are heads of the eight "races" of mankind. Above the cornice statues representing twelve great commercial nations of history stare down on the vicissitudes of Broadway, while the head of Mercury, Roman god of commerce, crowns the capital of each of the 44 Corinthian columns encircling the building. Over the main entrance a heroic cartouche by Karl Bitter (1867–1915) bears the arms of the United States.

Gilbert commissioned sculptor Daniel Chester French (1850–1931), best known for his statue of Abraham Lincoln in the Lincoln Memorial (Washington, D.C.), to design the heroic statues of *The Four Continents*. The four limestone sculptures, resting on pedestals at ground level, honor commercial ties that reached the four corners of the globe; from left to right they represent Asia, America, Europe, and Africa.

Asia, shown as the mother of religions, sits withdrawn in contemplation, a small Buddha on her lap, a serpent-wreathed lotus in her right hand, a cross behind her. *America* looks confidently outward, surrounded by symbols of the New World and its vitality. In contrast *Europe,* robed in a Grecian gown, sits enthroned among the achievements of the past: the open book, the globe, the ship's prow, the section of the Parthenon frieze decorating the pedestal. Leaning against her shoulder from the back is a mysterious draped figure, perhaps representing History. *Africa,* a continent as yet unrealized, slumbers heavily between a sphinx and a lion; behind her stands a darkly shrouded figure of uncertain significance.

INTERIOR. After the U.S. Customs Service moved to the World Trade Center in 1973, the building stood empty for long periods. It has been proposed as the home of the Museum of the American Indian, currently in Washington Heights.

*The interior of the former United States Custom House at Bat-
tery Park, designed by architect Cass Gilbert. Completed in
1907, the opulent building expressed the nation's pride in its
greatness as a maritime power. (Cervin Robinson)*

The main entrance leads into a hallway, at either end of which
is a spiral staircase mounting the entire height of the building.
To the right of the main entrance off the hallway, the room
paneled in oak with an elaborately worked ceiling formerly
hosted ceremonial visits of government officials. In the center of
the main floor is the great **Rotunda** (135 ft × 85 ft × 48 ft high),
its oval skylight painted over to comply with blackout regulations
during World War II. Constructed of 140 tons of tile and plaster
(no steel), it was engineered by Rafael Guastavino, whose tile-
work also appears in the Cathedral of St. John the Divine and
Grand Central Station. Just below the dome are *frescoes (1937)
by Reginald Marsh. The eight smaller vertical panels, painted to

resemble niches, display the figures of early explorers of America; the eight larger trapezoidal panels depict the progress of an ocean liner as it enters New York harbor, docks, and unloads its cargo and passengers (including the movie star Greta Garbo, who is shown being interviewed by the press).

The small fenced plot just N. of the main facade of the Custom House is **Bowling Green Park,** the city's first park. During the Dutch colonial period, this area was an open place at the S. end of "De Heere Wegh" ("the Main Street," now Broadway) and was used as a cattle market; hence the name of Marketfield Street, a block east. Later the area became a parade ground and still later a bowling green, leased in 1733 to some citizens for the annual fee of one peppercorn per year. The *Bowling Green Fence* (DL) was built in 1771 to keep the park from collecting "all the filth and dirt in the neighborhood" and to protect an equestrian statue of George III (erected 1766).

The statue of the king, clad in a Roman toga and crowned with a laurel wreath, met an inglorious end on July 9, 1776, when a crowd of patriots, stirred to action by the public reading of the Declaration of Independence, tore it down and dismembered it. The pieces of the gilded lead statue were melted down and cast into bullets which, according to legend, killed 400 British soldiers during the Revolution. The fence has survived better than the statue, although the mob made off with the ornaments which originally capped the fence posts.

No longer harboring the offices of the great transatlantic steamship lines, **Lower Broadway** still maintains fragile ties to its maritime past. No. 1 Broadway (1884; Edward H. Kendall) on the W. side of Bowling Green at Battery Place, occupies the site of the *Archibald Kennedy House* (1771–1882), which was used by George Washington and Gen. Howe during their respective periods of residence in New York during the Revolutionary War. Its tenure as the United States Lines Building is marked by decorative tridents, shells, fish, and other marine motifs on the facade and doorways labeled for first- and cabin-class passengers. The building next door (No. 11 Broadway), built in 1898 (W. & G. Audsley) has amused architectural critics for its eclecticism, the neo-Egyptian pylons on the ground level, the materials and forms of the early Chicago School on the upper stories. The U.S. Post Office at 25 Broadway is the former **Cunard Building** (1921; Benjamin Wistar Morris). Behind the Renaissance facade with its arched entranceways and second-story colonnade lies one of the city's great interiors, reputedly inspired by Raphael's Villa Madama in Rome. The vaulted vestibule inside the doors has ornate ceilings by Ezra Winter and a tall wrought-iron gate by Samuel Yellin. The room beyond, now housing the drab apparatus of the postal service, once proclaimed the romance of steamship travel in a manner suitable to the company that launched the *Queen Mary* and the *Queen Elizabeth*. A dome, 65 ft high, rises loftily above the octagonal room (185 × 74 ft) formerly called the Freight Distribution Hall. The ceiling designs, again by Ezra Winter, were executed by Italian craftsmen brought in for the work; the pendentives supporting the dome are covered with frescoes depicting the ships of Columbus (S.E.), Sir Francis Drake (N.E.), John Cabot (N.W.), and Leif Eriksson (S.W.). The maps of world steamship routes on the N. and S. walls were designed by Barry Faulkner.

Across the street at 26 Broadway is the former *Standard Oil Building* (1922; Carrère & Hastings), built as the home of the Standard Oil Trust Organization, and after the dissolution of the trust (1911), the headquarters of Standard Oil of New York. The facade of this elegant office building curves to follow the contour of Broadway, but the tower, best seen from Battery Park, is aligned with the N.-S. grid of the streets and buildings further uptown, an architectural concession to the uptown skyline. The tower terminates in a structure resembling an oil lamp, which conceals a chimney. Oil lamps also flank the principal entrance, and when Standard Oil had its offices here a bust of John D. Rockefeller stood on the pedestal in the lobby; although the statue is gone, his name and the names of other illustrious company executives adorn the marble walls.

Return S. along Broadway to *Battery Park, whose name recalls a row of cannons which defended the original fort and stood near the present sidewalk W. of the Custom House. Situated on filled land, the park is a pleasant place to escape the shadows and canyons of the financial district and serves as a refuge for office workers at lunch and the occasional sailor temporarily or permanently idle in the port. It offers spectacular views of the harbor and a group of monuments recalling New York's maritime and commercial history. In winter, however, the winds sweeping across it diminish its pleasures, while giving some inkling of the hardships the early settlers must have endured.

Near the intersection of State St, Bowling Green, and Battery Place just outside the fence is the BATTERY PARK CONTROL HOUSE (1904–05; Heins & La Farge; DL), the original entrance and exit for the Bowling Green station of the Lexington Avenue IRT. It is the only kiosk remaining from the city's first subway and a fine example of the influence of the École des Beaux-Arts. Designed by an architectural firm better known for its work on the Cathedral of St. John the Divine, its monumental quality, achieved despite its small scale, suggests the city's pride in its new subway system.

The flagpole near the park entrance is the *Netherlands Memorial Monument,* given to the city in 1926 by the people of that country as a token of affection for the founders of New York. The flagpole base bears a map (now barely visible) of Manhattan in Dutch times and a representation of the legendary Indian receiving $24 for the island (see p. 112). Between the flagpole and Castle Clinton stretches the Eisenhower Mall (1970).

About halfway down the mall, a path leads off behind the hedges to the right toward a bronze *statue of John Ericsson* (1902; Jonathan Scott Hartley), known to students of American naval history as the designer of the ironclad *Monitor,* whose clash with the Confederate frigate *Merrimac* off Hampton Roads, Virginia, in 1862 marked the beginning of the end for wooden warships. Hartley replaced an earlier version (1893) with this statue, which he felt to be superior.

Continue down the main path to Castle Clinton, in front of which stands a bronze statue, *The Immigrants* (1973, dedicated 1983; Luis Sanguino), paying homage to the 8 million immigrants who passed through its gates during its 35 years as the Immigrant Depot Station. It depicts a group of new arrivals in highly dramatic attitudes of hope and despair awaiting entrance to their new land.

*Castle Clinton National Monument (1807; John McComb, Jr.; DL), is the most important structure in the park, its squat red sandstone walls, eight feet thick, raised before the War of 1812 to protect the harbor from a naval invasion.

Castle Clinton National Monument. Battery Park, New York 10004 (c/o 26 Wall St, New York 10005). Tel: 344-7220. Open seven days a week 9–5; closed Christmas Day. Free. Restrooms; gift shop; full handicapped access.

SUBWAY: IRT Broadway-7th Ave local (train 1 or 9) to South Ferry. IRT Lexington Ave local (train 4 or 5) to Bowling Green. BMT Broadway local (R train) to Whitehall St. BUS: M1 or M6 via Broadway, M15 via 2nd Ave to South Ferry.

History. The original fort, first named the West Battery, was situated on an island about 200 ft from the mainland and connected to it by a wooden causeway with a drawbridge. It came into existence during the period of tensions preceding the War of 1812 when British attacks on American ships heightened national awareness of the vulnerability of the coastline. Virtually defenseless at the time, New York began the construction of four forts: Fort Wood on Bedloe's (now Liberty) Island, Fort Gibson on Ellis Island, Castle Williams on Governors Island, and the West Battery here. Built from plans by John McComb, Jr., one of New York's earliest native architects, this fort along with Castle Williams reflected the early 19C conception of coastal defenses, paired fortifications facing one another across a strategic waterway. The walls facing the harbor were pierced by a row of 28 black 32- pounders which could sweep the harbor shore to shore; those facing the land housed powder magazines and officers' quarters. Completed in 1811, the West Battery was untested during the war and fired its guns only for target practice and on commemorative occasions.

After the war it was renamed Castle Clinton after De Witt Clinton, who served during a long and distinguished career both as mayor of the city and governor of the state. In 1824, however, it was renamed again, this time Castle Garden; planted about with flowers and shrubbery, it opened as a place of entertainment, the top of its eight-foot-thick sandstone walls serving as a promenade while the officers' quarters became a bar and refreshment room. Castle Garden audiences watched band concerts, balloon ascensions, fireworks, and scientific demonstrations (Samuel F. B. Morse's "wireless telegraph" was the most famous) and enjoyed gaping at famous people who were publicly received here—for example, the Marquis de Lafayette and Andrew Jackson. In 1845 a roof was added and Castle Garden became a theater for more serious cultural fare, enjoying its greatest night on Sept 11, 1850, when P. T. Barnum staged the American debut of Jenny Lind, the "Swedish Nightingale," before a sellout crowd of more than 6000 people.

After more than a quarter of a century as a theater, Castle Garden closed its doors to the American public and reopened them (1855) to the immigrants streaming in from abroad. By this time the land between the island and Manhattan had been filled, and the immigrant depot had to be fenced off from the rest of the area to exclude swindlers who lurked nearby to prey on the linguistic and economic bewilderment of the new arrivals. The station, which provided medical care, fair currency exchange, and reliable information about jobs, housing, and travel to the interior, welcomed more than 8 million people from 1855–89 when the Immigration Service became a function of the federal government.

Castle Garden was remodeled once more in 1896, this time by the firm of McKim, Mead & White, to open as the New York Aquarium, its tanks at first containing specimens from local waters. In the 1940s, despite the immense popularity of the aquarium, Robert Moses, then Commissioner of Parks, determined to raze the building perhaps as an act of revenge for the defeat of his proposed Brooklyn-Battery Bridge Crossing. A group of concerned citizens fought to save the old fort; it was given breathing space by World War II since all available heavy wrecking equipment was tied up in the war effort. In 1946 Congress declared Castle Clinton a National Monument, and it is now administered by the National Park Service of the U.S. Department of the Interior.

Enter through the main gate. The passageway opens into a circular parade field surrounded by the massive walls of the fort which, on the inside, are faced with brick.

In the center are an information kiosk with a small gift shop and the ticket kiosk for the Circle Line ferry to the Statue of Liberty and Ellis Island (open 9–4 in winter, extended hours in summer; tel: 269-5755). On the left of the entrance passageway a small museum with dioramas and photographic exhibits documents the history of the building.

Return to the park. Follow the path (counterclockwise direction) that encircles Castle Clinton. About a third of the way around, between the fortress and the Fireboat Station, is a *plaque commemorating Emma Lazarus*, who wrote (1883) the famous sonnet, *The New Colossus.*

Although she came from a comfortable, sheltered background and had little actual knowledge of conditions in eastern Europe, Emma Lazarus was stirred by the plight of the Jews persecuted by Czar Alexander II. She saw in Bartholdi's statue a symbol for the freedom that would draw millions of immigrants to this country and thus contributed the poem to a contest as part of the fund-raising efforts for the pedestal.

Along the shoreline runs the *Admiral George Dewey Promenade,* with a spectacular *panorama of New York Harbor. From left to right: Brooklyn Heights, Governors Island (now a U.S. Coast Guard reservation), Staten Island in the distance, Liberty Island with the Statue of Liberty, Ellis Island, and the New Jersey coastline behind it. At the N. end of the promenade on **Pier A** (1884–86; DL) is the **Fireboat Station**. The pier, resting on a complex underwater foundation of concrete blocks, arches, granite sections, and iron girders, is one of the oldest piers remaining in the Hudson River. The tower, originally used as a lookout, now holds a clock donated (1919) by Daniel Reid, one of the founders of U.S. Steel; the clock honors the servicemen who died in World War I. Until 1959 the pier served as headquarters for the Harbor Police, whose duties included escorting incoming dignitaries ashore from their ocean liners. Currently headquarters of the Marine Division of the Fire Department, which has some 150 firefighters and seven vessels, and of Marine Company 1, the pier is slated for redevelopment as a visitors' center.

The promenade leads S. along the shoreline. Beyond Castle Clinton and a few yards inland from the promenade walkway is the *monument to Giovanni da Verrazano* (1909; Ettore Ximenes), a Florentine explorer employed by the king of France, who in 1524 became the first known European to sail into New York harbor. Claiming the land for France, he wrote an enthusiastic description of his surroundings and of the Indians who welcomed him; four years later he set out on a fatal voyage either to South America or to the Caribbean, during which he is said to have been killed and eaten by cannibals. The bronze statue whose pedestal has been altered was donàted by a group of Italian-American citizens who timed their presentation for the Hudson-Fulton Festival to point out that Verrazano got here 85 years before Henry Hudson. The female figure in front of the granite base represents Discovery, a sword in her right hand, formerly a torch in her left, the book of History at her feet.

At about the same time that Verrazano arrived, Esteban Gómez, a Portuguese explorer sailing for Spain, also reached the harbor, but Spain like France seems to have been indifferent to the new territory. In 1609, however, when Henry Hudson looking for a northwest passage to the Orient on behalf of the Dutch East India Company explored the river as far as the site of Albany, the Dutch realized the potential of the new land for the fur trade. In 1613 Adraien Block, a Dutch trader, became the first European to spend any time on Manhattan, when his ship, the *Tyger*, burned and he and his crew were forced to overwinter while constructing a new ship for their return. During excavations for the subway in 1916, the timbers of the *Tyger* were discovered near Dey and Greenwich Sts, an area which had been on the W. shoreline of Manhattan in 1613. They are on view at the Museum of the History of the City of New York. Block is also credited with exploring the Connecticut coast, discovering Long Island and Block Island, and naming Hell Gate, a treacherous stretch of water in the East River.

A few steps further along is the NORWEGIAN MARITIME MEMORIAL (c. 1982), a tribute to the people of the U. S. by the veterans of the Norwegian navy and merchant marine who fought in World War II. During the war years 1100 Norwegian ships hauled supplies between American ports and the war theaters, and many of the sailors looked upon New York, their principal port of call, as their home port. The memorial is constructed from two boulders from the coast of Norway weathered smooth by thousands of years' exposure to sea and wind.

A little further inland is the *Wireless Operators' Memorial*, dedicated to those radio operators who perished at sea, the most famous of whom was Jack Phillips, radioman of the *Titanic*, which struck an iceberg and sank on the night of April 14—15, 1912.

Continue S. to the *East Coast War Memorial* (1961; Albino Manca) with its great bronze eagle facing out to sea; the sculptor claims that he modeled the eagle on pigeons he saw in Washington Square, though the resemblance seems slight. The eight marble pylons bear the names of 4596 Americans who perished in Atlantic coastal waters during World War II. Between the war memorial and the ferry terminal at the S. tip of the park is the *U.S. Coast Guard Memorial*, an 8-ft bronze statue of two guardsmen supporting an injured comrade. The statue (1947; Norman M. Thomas), financed by individual $1 contributions from Coast Guard personnel, was erected after a controversy as to its artistic merit. (The concrete structure nearby is a ventilator for the Brooklyn-Battery Tunnel.)

On the S.W. side of the refreshment stand is a *bust of John*

Wolfe Ambrose (c. 1899, erected 1936; Andrew O'Connor, Jr.), engineer of the Ambrose ship channel, which opened in 1899, the year of its designer's death. The new channel, both deeper and shorter than its predecessor, reduced accidents and opened the harbor to larger ships, including the great luxury liners of the coming decades.

Follow the path leading out of the park toward the E., past the Marine Flagpole. Visible in the central grassy lawn of the park is *Cigarette* (1961; Tony Smith), a black-painted steel sculpture installed in the park in 1980. Continue toward the street.

Just inside the park fence is the *Oyster Pasty Cannon,* discovered during excavations and believed to have been part of the original battery that protected the fort in pre-Revolutionary times.

Continue along the path past the cannon and take the first exit from the park. Cross State St. Herman Melville (1819–91), author of *Moby Dick,* was born at No. 6 Pearl St, near the intersection of State St. The wedge-shaped tower, inserted between two dark, boxy buildings at *17 State St* (1988; Emery Roth & Sons), with its curved wall of mirrored glass facing the street, has been likened to a modern beacon or lighthouse; it replaces the Seamen's Church Institute building, which, when the port of New York was busier, ministered to merchant sailors.

Walk S. on State St. At 7 State St is the Rectory of the Shrine of the Blessed Elizabeth Bayley Seton (originally the **James Watson House**), the only survivor of the time when State St was an upper-crust residential street. Designed in two sections (E. wing 1793, W. wing 1806; DL), it has been attributed to John McComb, Jr. The details of the facade (the interior has been altered) reflect its Georgian and Federal heritage: the marble plaques in the brickwork, the oval windows on the W. wall, the splayed lintels above the rectangular windows. Its most distinctive feature, however, is the curved wooden portico which follows the street line, its tapered Ionic columns said to be made from ships' masts. During the Civil War the Union Army commandeered the house, which overlooked its encampment in the park. After the war an Irish immigrant, Charlotte Grace O'Brien, bought the house and established it as the Mission of Our Lady of the Rosary, a haven for immigrant Irish girls. The Mission now operates the building as a shrine to the Blessed Elizabeth Seton (1774–1821), the first American-born saint, canonized in 1975.

South of State St is **Peter Minuit Plaza,** a small triangular park which contains a *monument to New York's first Jewish immigrants,* a group of Sephardic refugees fleeing persecution in Brazil. Their ship, bound for Holland, was seized by pirates; a few days later the pirates were overtaken by a French frigate whose captain charged the refugees for a voyage to Amsterdam but brought them to New Amsterdam instead. The Jews arrived in September 1654, and despite Peter Stuyvesant's opposition they were allowed to remain and engage in commerce.

Peter Minuit Plaza is named after the Dutch governor, who in 1626 made the most famous real estate deal in the city's history, purchasing the entire island of Manhattan from the Indians for

60 guilders, a sum worth $24 according to traditional rates of exchange.

At or near the present intersection of State and Whitehall Sts stood Peter Stuyvesant's town house, built in about 1657 and renamed Whitehall by the first English governor of New York, Sir Edmund Andros. Before landfill pushed the shoreline outward, the area was a small peninsula projecting into the harbor.

Visible to the S. along the water are two ferry stations. The newer pier (scheduled for demolition) belongs to the **Staten Island Ferry,** the only direct commuting link between the boroughs of Richmond and Manhattan and one of New York's great sightseeing bargains.

To the left of the modern terminal is the **Battery Maritime Building** (1909; DL), at 11 South St, a fine old relic of the days when numerous ferries plied the East River. Constructed of sheet steel and painted green to imitate *verdigris* (compare the Statue of Liberty, whose copper sheeting has weathered to its gray-green color), it is elaborately decorated in the Beaux-Arts style of the period, with rivets, latticework, rosettes, and marine designs. The terminal is most dramatic seen from the water, its open-mouthed arches gaping against the severe geometry of the skyscrapers behind it. Public ferries docked here until 1938, and more recently it has been used by the Coast Guard and the Department of Ports and Terminals.

In 1986 the city accepted a plan to construct a 60-story office building above the Staten Island Ferry terminal, to renovate the two ferry terminals and the South Ferry subway station, and to create a waterfront esplanade.

The *Governors Island ferry* leaves from this terminal; public access to the island, which houses a Coast Guard Station, is limited.

Walk N. along Water St for a view of some of the skyscrapers that radically altered the historic downtown skyline. Two of the most visible are *1 New York Plaza* (1969; William Lescaze & Assocs.) facing Water St between Whitehall and Broad Sts, an office building with a branch of the Chase Manhattan Bank, and *4 New York Plaza* (1968; Carson, Lundin & Shaw) across Broad St to the E., which contains offices and data-processing equipment for the Manufacturers Hanover Trust.

These buildings are the products of a construction boom that began in lower Manhattan in the late 1950s and continued through the 1960s, culminating in the building of the World Trade Center, which opened for tenants in the early 1970s.

During this period the brick and granite warehouses and the small homes that once graced Front and Water Sts were destroyed and the contours of the streets altered in the interests of efficiency and profit; Front St south of Wall St has been absorbed into "superblocks" created by developers seeking ever larger buildings.

In an effort to compensate for the forbidding scale of the new buildings, the city passed the Zoning Resolution of 1961 offering a financial incentive to builders who provided street-level public facilities. For every square foot of "plaza" space, the builder was allowed an additional 10 square feet of floor space. Unfortunately the law lacked significant design requirements, and many of the plazas built during the period suggest that building owners wished to discourage public use. After this became apparent, the city passed an amendment to the Zoning Resolution requiring certain amenities like trees, seating, and shopping facilities.

Continue along Water St (the eastward extension of State St) to Broad St. During the Dutch colonial period **Broad Street** ("de Heere Gracht") was a canal for drainage and shipping, which reached to the present site of Exchange Place. The British filled it about 100 years before the Revolution, by which time it was polluted with sewage, but the extra width of Broad St remains as a reminder of the former canal.

Walk one block inland along Broad St to the corner of Pearl St. **Pearl St,** once on the shore of the East River, was named for the opalescent shells that dotted its beaches. At Bridge St, which joins Pearl St at this intersection, stood the first bridge across the Broad St canal.

On the S.E. corner of Broad and Pearl Sts is the Fraunces Tavern, the most famous of a group of notable old buildings, the **Fraunces Tavern Block,** one of the few full blocks of 18C and 19C buildings to have escaped the successive downtown building booms.

The **Fraunces Tavern** at 54 Pearl St is a reconstruction (1907; William Mersereau; DL) of a mansion built (c. 1719) for Stephen (or Etienne) De Lancey. Since no graphic records have survived, Mersereau's reconstruction was based largely on an analysis of the structure of this building and studies of similar buildings. An advertisement of 1781 describes the house as having "9 spacious rooms plus 5 bedchambers, 13 fireplaces . . . and an exceeding good kitchen, and a spring of remarkable fine water therein."

The De Lanceys, one of New York's wealthy and powerful early families, remained loyal to the king during the Revolution and suffered the confiscation of their property for this lack of political foresight. Even before the war, however, the house had become a warehouse and then a tavern owned by Samuel Fraunces, a West Indian, possibly of French ancestry, who bought the De Lancey house and opened it in 1762 as the Queen's Head Tavern. Fraunces was well-known as a cook, especially for his desserts, which may have influenced George Washington in his selection of the Fraunces Tavern as the scene of the farewell he gave (1783) for his officers when he temporarily retired to private life. Fraunces's abilities later earned him the position of chief steward to Washington, during most of his presidency.

In 1785 Fraunces leased the building to the Department of Foreign Affairs, the Treasury, and the War Department for office space; later he sold it to a Brooklyn butcher. During the 19C the building deteriorated along with the rest of the neighborhood, becoming at its nadir a hotel for transients; after being badly burned several times (1832, 1837, 1852), it remained derelict until its purchase (1904) by the Sons of the Revolution of the State of New York, who restored it to its present condition.

The ground floor contains a restaurant; the two stories above house the **Fraunces Tavern Museum.**

Fraunces Tavern. 54 Pearl Street (Broad St), New York 10004. Tel: 425-1778. Open Mon–Fri, 10–4, specified Sundays 12–4; closed weekends, national holidays except Washington's Birthday; entrance fee after noon.

Changing exhibitions, lectures, audiovisual presentation, children's programs, tours by arrangement. Restrooms. Formal restaurant, separate from museum, on ground floor; informal restaurants close by in neighborhood. Telephone. Gift shop. No wheelchair access. Museum up a flight of steep stairs.

SUBWAY: IRT Lexington Ave express (train 4 or 5) to Bowling Green. IRT 7th Ave local (train 1) to South Ferry. BMT Broadway local (R train) to Whitehall St. IND 8th Ave local (E train) to World Trade Center. BUS: M1 downtown via 5th Ave / Broadway to South Ferry. M6 downtown via 7th Ave / Broadway to South Ferry. M15 downtown via 2nd Ave / Allen St to South Ferry.

On the second floor of the museum are two period rooms: the Long Room, where the farewell actually took place, now refurbished as a late 18C tavern room, and the Clinton Room, furnished as a dining room of the Federal period. Three galleries on the third floor offer changing exhibits on early American history and culture.

Occupying the block between Pearl and S. William Sts and Coenties Alley is 85 BROAD STREET (1983; Skidmore, Owings & Merrill), housing the offices of Goldman Sachs. The huge building uses the air rights from the small-scale Fraunces Tavern Block buildings across the street. Near the Pearl St corner are two exhibits of 17C artifacts (displayed below sidewalk level), unearthed during an archaeological dig required by the Landmarks Preservation Commission when 85 Broad St was constructed.

The area was known to be the historic site of the original Dutch colonial *Stadt Huys* or City Hall, probably located at about 71 Pearl St. The building began as a tavern in about 1641, a five-story gabled structure right at the water's edge, but was converted to the Town Hall when New Amsterdam was granted its municipal charter in 1653. It served not only as a meeting place, but as a jail, a debtors' prison, courthouse, and public warehouse. The British demolished the building in 1699, but part of the foundation was incorporated in a succeeding building. Archaeological excavations uncovered tiles, clay pipes, and parts of a wall and staircase.

Continue along Pearl St; turn right at **Coenties Alley**. The name Coenties (Dutch *Coentje*) is either a nickname for Conraet or a combined form of Conraet and Antje; in any case Conraet and Antje Ten Eyck lived nearby and Conraet ran a tannery on Broad St.

Follow Coenties Alley eastward toward the river. The brick plaza across Water St, formerly Jeannette Park, has been renamed **Vietnam Veterans Plaza**. Dominating it is a greenish glass-brick wall 70 ft long and 14 ft high (1985; William Britt Fellows and Peter Wormser) etched with words written home by American soldiers in Vietnam, parts of speeches, and news dispatches. Once the park was a favorite haunt of idle seamen, a tree-shaded trapezoidal plot of land created when Coenties Slip was filled in the late 19C. Named after the ship *Jeannette*, which took part in the tragic polar expedition of 1879–81, the park originally followed the shape of Coenties Slip.

Return to Coenties Alley and Pearl St. Follow Coenties Alley inland until it ends at **Stone Street**, so named because it was the first paved street in the city (1658). According to tradition, the wife of brewer Stephanus Van Cortlandt (the street was first called Brouwers St) disliked the dust raised by passing vehicles and urged her husband to have the street paved. The present stones, visible here and there under the pavement, were laid in the 19C and are called Belgian blocks after their supposed place of origin.

Follow Stone St to **Mill Lane,** the first intersection on the left, named after a large windmill built by the Dutch in 1626 which stood on the approximate site of Mill Lane and Mill St (now called S. William St).

Used primarily for grinding grain, the mill also had a meeting room on the second story which was rented (1680s) to the city's first Jewish congregation, Shearith Israel. Two millstones from the mill can be seen in the Spanish & Portuguese Synagogue on Central Park West and W. 70th St. In 1729 the congregation, many of whose members were descendants of those refugees from Brazil who had arrived in 1654 (see p. 112), purchased land S. of the mill for 100 pounds sterling plus a loaf of sugar and a pound of tea. Here, at the site of 26 S. William St, they built their first permanent synagogue.

Continue along Stone Street to **Hanover Square.** Named after the English royal family of the Georges, Hanover Square was once a public common in a fine residential district. The most notorious resident was William Kidd, a sea captain hanged in England in 1701 for piracy, who had been a respected citizen in New York, and a contributor to Trinity Church. At the end of the 17C the area was the city's first Printing House Square, home of New York's first newspaper (1725), the *New-York Gazette,* published weekly by William Bradford, whose mortal remains rest in Trinity Churchyard.

Hanover Square was the center of the *Great Fire of 1835,* the most devastating of several serious fires that plagued the city in the early 19C.

On the night of December 17, a gas explosion rocked the area; fed by stockpiles of dry goods and chemicals and whipped by winter winds, the blaze quickly raged out of control. Subzero temperatures froze the fire hoses and by noon the next day the fire had destroyed everything in Hanover Square. When the blaze finally burned itself out, it had destroyed over 20 acres and more than 650 buildings, including all the Dutch colonial structures remaining in downtown New York.

In the square sits a *statue of Abraham De Peyster* (1896; George Edwin Bissell) which formerly graced Bowling Green Park, across Broadway from the house where he was born (1657) into a wealthy mercantile family. Commissioned by his great-great-great-grandson, the bronze statue honors a tireless public servant whose offices included alderman, mayor, chief justice of the colony, colonel of the militia, and acting governor.

India House, at 1 Hanover Square on the S.W. side of the square, is a beautiful old brownstone built from 1851–54 (Richard Carman?; DL) for the Hanover Bank. One of the finest buildings in the Italianate style surviving in the city, India House is important both as a reminder of the elegance to which 19C commercial life could aspire (subsequent tenants were the New

York Cotton Exchange and the shipping firm W. R. Grace and Company) and as a prototype for the New York brownstone row house. India House now belongs to a private men's club.

Walk along Hanover Square (actually a short street) toward the East River. On the S.E. corner of Water St and Old Slip is a large office building known by its address, *55 Water Street*, (1972; Emery Roth & Sons), occupying a four-block "superblock," a zoning concession its builders won by constructing the park on the S. side of the building.

The **East River slips** (Old Slip, Burling Slip, Coenties Slip, and others) were originally docking areas for ships. As the coastline was pushed further out by landfill, breakwaters were built in the river and the slips were dredged to provide adequate draft. Eventually they were filled to create new land, but their rectangular outlines remain in the shape of these streets.

In the middle of Old Slip sits the *former First Precinct Police Station* (1909–11; Hunt & Hunt; DL) designed like a fortified Italian Renaissance palazzo, now containing offices.

Return to Water St. Across Front St is *77 Water Street* (1970; Emery Roth & Sons), an office tower with a whimsical plaza. At its four corners stand four pieces of sculpture (all date from 1969). In the S.W. is a kind of sculptural joke called *Rejected Skin* (William Tarr), inspired by some pieces of aluminum rejected as sheeting for the building and compacted in a scrap yard. George Adamy's work *Month of June* stands in the S.E. In the N.E. is *City Fountains* by Victor Scallo. *Helix* by Rudolph de Harak in the N.W. is made of 120 one-inch-thick stainless steel squares, arranged to create the illusion of a continuous spiral. The building was developed by Melvyn and Robert Kaufman, who became known for their adventurous approach to design; on an Astroturf runway on the roof (visible from other skyscrapers) is *Sopwith 19* (1970; William Tarr), a sculpture of a Sopwith Camel, the World War I fighter plane.

Walk N. on Water St to the intersection of Pine St. On the plaza at 88 Pine St in front of the handsome, aluminum- and glass-clad *Orient Overseas Building,* also known as *Wall Street Plaza* (1973; I. M. Pei & Assocs.), stands a two-part stainless steel sculpture *Moon Gate* (1973; YuYu Yang), a vertical slab with a circular opening facing a polished disc (diameter 12 ft, weight 4000 lb). A nearby tablet recalls the history of the *Queen Elizabeth I,* the Cunard liner which burned in Hong Kong harbor in 1972; Morley Cho, owner of the building, was the last owner of the fabled liner.

Continue N. to **Maiden Lane,** so named by the Dutch, after a footpath used by neighborhood girls on their way to the brook where they washed the laundry. Visible to the E. at 180 Maiden Lane is the *Continental Center* (1983; Swanke Hayden Connell), a 41-story tower sheathed in greenish glass.

Continue N. on Water St. In Jan 1982, during construction of the *National Westminster Bank USA* (1983; Fox & Fowle) at 175 Water St near John St, an archaeological team uncovered thousands of small items—mostly dishes and bottles—in the hull of an 85 × 26-ft 18C merchant ship with a rounded bow, its arrival fixed at sometime after 1746, the date on a ceramic top found below its decks. Since building construction was already delayed a month by the archaeological work, only one side of the ship was removed from the site.

Filling the block between John and Fulton Sts, **127 John Street** (1969; Emery Roth & Sons), another building developed by the Kaufman Organization, beguiles pedestrians with amusing sidewalk artifacts: an immense digital clock, a sculptural phone booth (1972; Albert Wilson) with cutout figures, and a neon tunnel (1972; Rudolph de Harak).

Across the street on the S.E. corner of Water and Fulton Sts (199 Water St) *1 Seaport Plaza* (1984; Swanke Hayden Connell), a 35-story office building towers over the restored South Street Seaport. On the S. and W. where it faces the high rises of the financial district the building has continuous ribbon windows, like those of many modern commercial office buildings. On the N. and E. where the building faces the historic seaport and other 19C buildings the windows are individual openings in a solid wall, echoing the windows of the old seaport buildings framed by stone lintels and sills. In the lobby are three paintings from the "Protractor" series painted in the late 1960s by Frank Stella.

Continue to **Fulton St** and turn right (E.). In the triangle formed by the intersection of Water and Fulton Sts is the **Titanic Memorial,** erected (1913, at the former Seamen's Church Institute building on South St near Jeannette Park) to commemorate those who went down with the *Titanic*.

Follow Fulton St toward the East River. The ***South Street Seaport Museum,** a "museum without walls," is a collection of historic buildings—counting houses, saloons, hotels, warehouses—restored ships, exhibition galleries, and shops clustered around Fulton St on the East River, once the center of the city's maritime industries. The area was restored by the Rouse Company in connection with a commercial development that includes shops, restaurants, offices, and other businesses.

The South Street Seaport Museum. Visitors' Center, 207 Water St, New York 10004. Tel: 669-9424. Open March–Nov weekdays 10–5; weekends 11–5. Dec–March weekdays 11–4; weekends until 5. Closed New Year's Day, Thanksgiving, Christmas. Admission charge. Admission tickets sold until one hour before closing at Visitors' Center, Pier 16 Pilothouse, or A. A. Low Building (171 John St).

Tours, films, children's programs, craft workshops, special events. Harbor excursions in season (964-9082). Sailing cruises aboard the sloop *Pioneer* (669-9416).

Restrooms and telephones in Fulton Market Building, in the Pavilion Building on Pier 17, and on the apron of Pier 15. Restaurants in Fulton Market Building and on Pier 17. Extensive shopping in Pier 17 Pavilion and in Fulton Market Building. Bookstore at 209 Water St. Wheelchair access limited.

SUBWAY: IRT 7th Ave express (train 2 or 3) to Fulton St. IRT Lexington Ave express (train 4 or 5) to Fulton St. BMT Nassau St local (J, M, or Z train) to Fulton St. IND 8th Ave express or local (A or C train) to Broadway-Nassau. The Broadway-Nassau subway station is labyrinthine and confusing. It is easier to walk above ground to Broadway to board the IRT Lexington Ave line.

History. From the first days of settlement until the years after the Civil War, the city's maritime activity focused on the East River, actually an arm of the sea lying on the lee side of Manhattan and less affected than the Hudson by ice floes, flooding, and the prevailing westerlies. During the early 19C Fulton St became a major thoroughfare leading to the Fulton Ferry, which crossed to Brooklyn starting in 1816. The Fulton Market opened in 1822, first as a produce market for Brooklyn and Long Island farmers, eventually as a fish market. When the Erie Canal opened in 1825, flooding New York with mid-western industrial and farm products, 500 new shipping firms came into existence. The China trade, spearheaded by the firm of A. A. Low on Burling Slip (now John St), and the California trade both burgeoned. After the Civil War, however, the area slipped into decline as steamships superseded the clippers and trade moved to the deep-water docks on the Hudson.

In the mid-1960s, after a century of neglect, preservationists began working to save the old port, chartering the museum (1967) and acquiring historic buildings and ships. In 1979 the city approved a plan to merge museum interests with major commercial development and in 1983 a large part of the present restoration opened, including a rehabilitated Schermerhorn Row and a new Fulton Market. In 1985 the large red steel and glass pavilion housing stores and restaurants was constructed on Pier 17.

Begin at **Schermerhorn Row** (1812, 1880, 1983; DL), the architectural centerpiece of the seaport. Peter Schermerhorn, a ship chandler and scion of an old New York family, got the land in 1793 as water lots (between the extremes of high and low tide), filled it, and built 12 red brick commercial buildings with warehouse space downstairs and accounting offices above. The Fulton Ferry began steaming across the river to Brooklyn in 1814 and during the 19C the building on the corner of South St became the Fulton Ferry Hotel; the mansard roof was added in 1868 for extra space. Upstairs at 4 Fulton St is *Sweets,* a venerable seafood restaurant (founded by Abraham M. Sweet in 1847) whose former seedy charm has succumbed to the recent restoration. In the future the upper stories of Schermerhorn Row will see installation of the museum's Port of New York exhibit, a major permanent exhibition which will explore the history of the port and its implications for the city's growth.

Walk around the corner to South St. At 92 South St is *Sloppy Louie's,* another old-timer (1930) and long a favorite with seamen and other locals who prized its bouillabaisse. It too has been cleaned up for the tourist trade.

Continue around the corner to John St. At 167–171 John St stands the former **A. A. Low Building** (1850; DL) built by Abiel Abbot Low, pioneer of the China trade. Low founded his firm in 1840 after three years in Canton learning the trade; ten years later he built this elegant brownstone-faced countinghouse, demolishing the older brick buildings on the site. The cast-iron storefront was made by one of the city's most famous firms, Badger's Architectural Iron Works. The Lows ran a great fleet of China clippers including the *Houqua,* and the *N. B. Palmer,* named respectively for Low's legendary Hong patron during his Canton years, and one of the firm's captains. Today the building contains not teas, silks, and porcelains, but the *Norway Galleries* with long-term changing exhibitions. Next door is the *Children's Center* at 165 John St in a building (1811; DL) leased by flour merchants and grocers during the 19C.

Across the street at *170–176 John St* stands the former BAKER,

South Street in 1898, when sailing vessels still docked in the East River. In the background stands the Brooklyn Bridge, rising above the Fulton Ferry Terminal. (Courtesy of The New-York Historical Society, New York City)

CARVER & MORRELL BUILDING (1840; DL), a Greek Revival commercial building long occupied by a ship chandlery and noteworthy for its granite facing from top to bottom.

Continue along John St, once known as Burling Slip. In 1835 the slip was filled in, but its shape remains, giving the street its unusual width. At Front St turn right and walk toward Fulton St. Directly ahead is the BOGARDUS BUILDING (1983; Beyer Blinder Belle) at 19 Fulton St.

The facade was to have incorporated ironwork from the city's first cast-iron building built by James Bogardus but the pieces were stolen from storage in two separate heists; consequently the modern structure attempts to suggest the appearance of the Bogardus facade using similar materials and proportions. Within are shops and exhibition spaces.

Walk up Fulton St and turn right on Water St. *Nos. 207–211 Water St* (1835–36), with their granite steps, lintels, piers, and cornices, are typical Greek Revival storefronts. Flemish bond brickwork (bricks laid alternately endwise and lengthwise in each course) was declining in fashion when these buildings were constructed but may have been retained because one of the original owners was a mason. *No. 207 Water St* is the **Visitors' Center,** whose changing exhibits of photographs document the seaport and the maritime heritage of the city. In the Book and Chart Shop, 209 Water St, there is a good collection of books on local history, ships, the lore of the sea, and historic preservation. *No. 211 Water St* has been restored to recreate the 19C printing shop of Bowne & Co., Stationers, whose working presses are used for demonstrations, printing classes, and workshops. Next door, *213 Water St* (1868, Stephen D. Hatch; restored 1983) is the SEAPORT GALLERY (gallery talks, changing exhibitions) and the museum library (open to researchers by appointment). The building, in the Italianate style, was constructed as a warehouse for a tin company and has a ground floor facade of cast iron with upper stories faced in limestone.

Continue around the block to the corner of Beekman and Front Sts to the Trans-Lux Seaport Theater (box office at 210 Front St; tel: 608-6696 for show times and prices) whose movies, fast-paced and technically extravagant, touch on the history of South St, seafarers, and the maritime experience. The 104 projectors, 31 auxiliary screens, and 33-speaker audio system do full justice to howling winds, towering surf, and snapping masts. The building was once a fish-processing plant.

To explore the unrestored section of the seaport, walk uptown along Front St. Here the grimy brick and crumbling brownstone, the streets pocked with potholes and littered with trash suggest the obstacles faced by the seaport enthusiasts who worked toward its renaissance. The unrestored area also provides a corrective to the perhaps overly bright, relentlessly commercial atmosphere of the restoration.

No. 142 Beekman Street (1885; George B. Post) was built for a Schermerhorn family descendant in the fish business and is now a seafood restaurant; architecturally appropriate details are the starfish on the tie-rod ends, the cockleshells on the cornice, and the fish wriggling on the terra-cotta keystones.

Continue walking uptown on Front St. Just across the intersection with Peck Slip, on the wall of the power station, is a trompe l'oeil mural (1979; Richard Haas) depicting Federal and Greek Revival buildings with a fanciful arcade through which the Brooklyn Bridge is visible.

Next to the mural is the former *Jasper Ward store* at 45 Peck Slip (1807, restored 1983), built for a politician and real estate speculator. For the first ten years of its life the house faced the water on two sides since Peck Slip was not filled until 1817. On the other corner of Peck Slip (116–119 South St) is the former Meyer's Hotel (1873; John B. Snook), whose name enshrines one Henry L. Meyer, a liquor dealer who ran the place toward the end of the 19C. According to legend Diamond Jim Brady and Annie Oakley hoisted a glass or two on the premises.

Benjamin Peck had a house and wharf here before the Revolution, and in 1763 erected a brick building to house the Peck Slip Market.

Walk inland on Peck Slip to Water St. Turn right. The JOSEPH ROSE HOUSE (1770s), at 273 Water St, the oldest building in the neighborhood and the third oldest in Manhattan (after St. Paul's Chapel and the Morris-Jumel Mansion), is today on the point of collapse. Joseph Rose built it when Water St stood at the water's edge and until 1800, when Front St was extended, he could moor his brig at a wharf virtually at his back door. In the 19C as the neighborhood above Peck Slip became notorious for its dives and brothels, one Kit Burns turned the house into "Sportsmen's Hall," which featured dog and rat fights among other sporting events. Later Burns underwent an unexpected religious conversion and offered the house to a missionary who opened the Water Street Home for Women, a rehabilitation center for repentant prostitutes.

The small wooden building adjacent to the north *(279 Water St)* now houses the Bridge Cafe. It was built (c. 1801) as a grocery store and residence, and in 1888 became a three-family house. The siding and decorative detail date from that period. Overhead is a good view of the Brooklyn Bridge. Return to the movie theater.

In the building at *206 Front St* (1790s, 1880), the Howell family sold groceries and later guns and gunpowder. Next door at 207 Front St the museum administrative offices occupy the oldest building on the block, where in 1797 Benjamin Stratton, Jr., worked as a grocer and cooper.

Across the street is the new (1983; Benjamin Thompson & Assocs.) **Fulton Market Building** devoted primarily to food. Part of the commercial Fulton Fish Market occupies the ground floor facing South St; its activity peaks in predawn hours, when the fish arrives by truck, not boat. An outdoor cafe, produce stalls, upscale fast-food stands, and more formal seafood restaurants stand ready to assuage hunger pains.

Cross South Street to the pier area. On the left at Pier 17 is the "Tin Building" (1907), sheathed in corrugated metal, the fourth home of the FULTON FISH MARKET. The market dates back to 1822 when vendors were allowed to set up their stalls in a wooden building on the site of the present new Fulton Market. Many of the tenants were butchers but there were also produce dealers, fishmongers, sausage makers, and cheese sellers. By 1834, however, the butchers were complaining that the runoff from the upstairs fish-gutting operations was seeping down to their stands, and so the fish dealers were exiled to their own wooden shed on the water, behind which floated fish cars with live fish. This arrangement persisted until the turn of the century when the polluted water of the river poisoned the fish.

The large **Pier Pavilion, Pier 17** (1984; Benjamin Thompson & Assocs.) has shops, more restaurants, more fast food counters, and a large seating area facing the river with wonderful views of the Brooklyn waterfront and the Brooklyn Bridge.

The **Pilothouse** (museum admission and information center) on Pier 16 was salvaged from the steam tugboat *New York Central No. 31,* built for the railroad in 1923 to ferry passenger and freight cars across the rivers. Moored on the N. side of Pier 16 are the tugboat *W. O. Decker* (not open to the public) which once towed barges on Newtown Creek, and the old *Ambrose Light-ship.* Built in 1908, the lightship marked the entrance to New York harbor through the deep-water Ambrose Channel (see p. 112), until it was replaced in 1932 by a tower and beacon. At the end of the pier are two excursion ships of the Seaport Line, the *De Witt Clinton* and the *Andrew Fletcher,* modern boats modeled after their popular 19C predecessors.

On the S. side of the pier is the 1885 schooner, *Pioneer,* which carried iron and steel on the Delaware River. Later, her masts removed, she operated as a power-driven oil tanker until beached as unserviceable; restored and rerigged as a sloop she now makes harbor cruises in summer.

In the slip between Piers 15 and 16 is the **Peking,** a four-masted bark (1911) from Hamburg, Germany, one of the last sailing ships built for commercial purposes. Carrying more than an acre of sail, this swift ship transported general cargo from Europe to South America and brought back nitrates for fertilizer, until the development of synthetic fertilizers made the South American trade economically unfeasible. The **Wavertree** (1885), moored on the N. side of Pier 15, is a square-rigged, iron-hulled ship built in England to carry jute from India to Europe; she was dismasted rounding Cape Horn in 1910 and towed to a remote backwater where a slick of lanoline from a nearby slaughterhouse preserved her hull.

Pier 15, a working pier, is currently closed to the public. Moored here are the *Lettie G. Howard* (1893), a Gloucester fishing schooner, typical of many that formerly brought their catches to the Fulton Fish Market and the *Maj. Gen. William H. Hart,* a steam ferryboat (launched 1925) that carried thousands of passengers daily across the rivers surrounding New York and ended her career on the Governors Island run.

The nearest subways are the IRT Broadway-7th Ave (train 2 or 3), IRT Lexington Ave (train 4 or 5), IND Eighth Ave (A train), and BMT Nassau St line (J, M, or Z train), all of which may be reached through the passages of the Broadway-Nassau St station at Fulton and Nassau Sts. The nearest bus, the M15 at Fulton and Water Sts, runs uptown via 1st Ave.

3 The Financial District and World Trade Center

SUBWAY: IRT 7th Ave express (train 2) to Wall St. IRT Lexington Ave express (train 4 or 5) to Wall St and Broadway. BMT Broadway local (R train) to Rector St.

BUS: M1 (make sure you get one labeled South Ferry). M6 via Broadway / 7th Ave to Rector St.

WHEN TO VISIT: Weekdays during business hours are most interesting. Try to eat lunch early or late, since restaurants in the area are hectic from about noon to 2 o'clock.

*Wall Street, symbol of money and power, is a small street only about a third of a mile long, running between Broadway and the East River.

Once a wall, erected in 1653 during Peter Stuyvesant's tenure, stretched river to river to protect the Dutch town from incursions by its British neighbors to the north. Fortunately for the townspeople the wall was never needed for

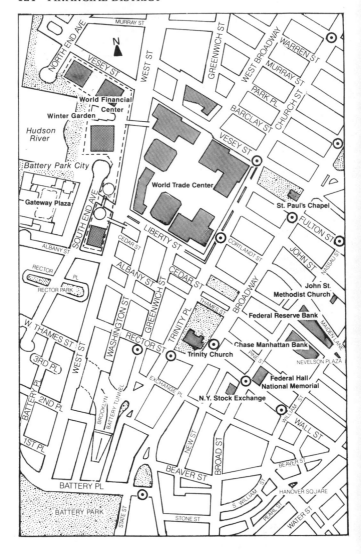

defense, since it suffered the indignities frequently attendant upon municipal projects. The original plan called for a palisade to be made of whole tree trunks sharpened and driven into the ground, but perhaps because of bureaucratic bungling or perhaps because of simple laziness on the part of the builders, the wall was eventually constructed of planks instead. These proved overpoweringly attractive to homeowners as sources of firewood or lumber for household repairs, and so in 1699 the British had the wall torn down as useless.

The imposing buildings give the street a monumental quality, and indeed they are monuments to the titans of finance and industry who built the institutions they represent.

At the head of Wall St on Broadway stands *Trinity Church (1846; Richard Upjohn; DL), once the loftiest building in the neighborhood, now overshadowed by gigantic office buildings.

Trinity Church. Broadway at Wall St, New York 10006. Open weekdays and Sun from about 7:30 A.M.–8:00 P.M.; earlier closing Sat. Gift shop open Mon–Fri 11:30–5:30; Sun 12:30–4; closed Sat. No telephones. Occasional lectures, tours of churchyard; tel: 602-0848. Church accessible to handicapped visitors: a few, small steps up from street level. Restrooms located at the W. end of the church, beyond the chapel, accessible from N. aisle.

Despite modesty in size and conception by today's standards, Trinity Church is probably New York's most famous house of worship because of its dramatic setting. It is also one of the wealthiest as befits a parish situated in a district so unabashedly devoted to Mammon.

The wealth of the parish stems from the original land grant made in 1705 by Queen Anne, which included the land W. of Broadway between Fulton and Christopher Sts, an impressive chunk of lower Manhattan. Although the parish no longer owns the entire parcel, it still has extensive real estate holdings in lower Manhattan. Less lucrative but more picturesque were the rights extended to the church to take over all unclaimed shipwrecks and beached whales.

The present church is the third on the site. The first, finished in 1697, was an attractive stone building facing the river, paid for by all citizens of the colony who were taxed for the construction costs regardless of religious preference. The most famous contributor to the building fund was William Kidd, who was one of New York's most respected citizens before his career as a privateer landed him ignominiously on the gallows in England in 1701. The church burned in the Great Fire of 1776 during the British occupation and remained in ruins until long after the Revolution. A second church (completed 1790) had to be demolished in 1839 after a heavy snowfall compromised the roof.

The building now occupying the site belongs to the Gothic Revival tradition, although its "Gothic" quality pertains to the decoration rather than to the structure. In a medieval church, the buttresses along the nave would support the high walls against the outward thrust of the stone roof vaults, a structural safeguard unnecessary here since the vaults are made of plaster and hung from wooden roof trusses, more or less like any plaster ceiling. Nevertheless, the Gothic elements (the flying buttresses, the stained glass windows, the Gothic tracery, and the medieval inspiration of the sculpture) impressed and pleased 19C New Yorkers. The use of brownstone on the facade, however, drew criticism, since until the construction of Trinity Church brownstone was generally used as a cheap substitute for marble, granite, or limestone. But since Trinity parish could well have afforded marble, the choice was probably made for aesthetic reasons. The Romantic Movement, making itself felt in architecture as well as the other arts, favored the use of dark building materials, which were considered "picturesque" and "natural"— that is, close to the colors of the landscape.

The doors of the church, modeled after the famous Ghiberti doors on the baptistery of the cathedral in Florence, were designed by Richard Morris Hunt and donated by William Waldorf Astor. Karl Bitter, who won the competition for the construction, executed the main doors whose panels illustrate the biblical text, "Thou didst open the Kingdom of Heaven to all believers."

The N. doors, by J. Massey Rhind, depict scenes from the lives of men delivered from trouble and brought to places of rest. The S. doors, by Charles H. Niehaus, present scenes from the history of Manhattan and of Trinity Church.

The stained glass in the chancel window designed by architect Richard Upjohn is among the earliest American examples of that craft, though the glass itself probably comes from Germany. In the baptistery (N. aisle near the entrance) is a 15C Italian altarpiece. The reredos behind the main altar was given by John Jacob and William Astor in memory of their father. Made of Caen stone and marble, it was designed by Frederick C. Withers. The All Saints Chapel on the N. aisle was built in 1913 by architect Thomas Nash. The addition on the S. side contains a small museum with historic documents, communion silver, and changing displays on the history of the parish.

Trinity Church Museum. Broadway and Wall St, New York 10006. Tel: 602-0848. Open Mon–Fri 9–11:45, 1–3:45; Sat 10–3:45; Sun 1–3:45. Closed major holidays. Free.
SUBWAY: IRT 7th Ave express (train 2 or 3) to Wall St. IRT Broadway-7th Ave local (train 1 or 9) to Rector St. IRT Lexington Ave express (train 4 or 5) to Wall St. BMT Broadway local (R train) to Rector St. BUS: M1 downtown via 5th Ave / Broadway to Wall St. M6 downtown via 7th Ave / Broadway to Wall St.

The building is 79 ft wide and 166 ft long; the tower including the spire stands 280 ft above the ground. The first "ring of bells" was received from London in 1797 and is the oldest in New York. Originally the bells were to be swung, but since no tradition of bell ringers exists in the U. S., the bells are now stationary, their clappers connected to a ringing case in a room below the belfry, so that tunes can be played on them.

The church sits in a beautiful *churchyard (DL), its 2½ acres among the few unpaved spots in the Financial District. Some of the gravestones are quite old and striking, their incised frizzle-haired angels and grinning death's heads reminding onlookers of mortality and what lies beyond. The oldest stone belongs to Richard Churcher (N. of church), who died at the age of five in 1681. Others are more elaborate, marking the burial places of renowned figures: Robert Fulton, whose *Clermont* proved that steamboat travel was economically viable; Alexander Hamilton; William Bradford, the publisher of the *New-York Gazette*; and Captain James Lawrence, whose nautical tombstone brings to mind his famous remark about not giving up the ship. Near the Broadway sidewalk on the N. side of the church is the burial place of Charlotte Temple, a young lady of genteel background who was seduced and abandoned by a British officer and immortalized in a long but popular novel by Sarah Haswell Rowson. *Charlotte, A Tale of Truth* was published in 1791 in London, reprinted in Philadelphia in 1794, and quickly went through 160 editions.

The impressive graveyard cross in the center of the N. portion of the cemetery is a monument to the memory of Caroline Webster Astor, queen of New York society at the turn of the century (see pp. 319, 363). At the northeast corner of the plot is a large and very Gothic tribute to the Martyrs of the American Revolution, who died while imprisoned by the British in a sugar-house (see p. 155).

From the W. side of the graveyard, the **American Stock Exchange** at 86 Trinity Place is visible. This handsome Art Deco building (1930; Starrett & Van Vleck) holds the city's second major stock exchange, formerly known as the New York Curb Exchange, because before 1929 its brokers stood on the curb at the N. end of Broad St and signaled with hand and arm movements to their colleagues in the windows of the New York Stock Exchange.

Return to Broadway and walk N. as far as Thames St. The *Trinity Building* and *U.S. Realty Building* at 111 and 115 Broadway (1905 and 1906; Francis H. Kimball; DL) are two fine early-20C Gothic skyscrapers, designed to complement Trinity Church. The Gothic decoration continues inside the lobbies, which have polychromed ceilings, sculptured corbels, and elaborate tracery around the elevators.

Across the street at 120 Broadway, the **Equitable Building** (1915; Ernest R. Graham) has become famous as a landmark in bad design. In order to maximize available rental space and hence profits, the Equitable Building was built 40 stories straight up without setback, filling almost the entire site and darkening the side streets and the windows of adjacent buildings (this problem has been alleviated somewhat by the setback of the new Marine Midland Bank to the north; Pine St, however, is still dark and gloomy). The negative impact of the building spurred the city the following year to pass the *Zoning Resolution of 1916*.

This law, which determined the ''wedding cake'' silhouette of so many early skyscrapers, required buildings above a certain height to set back from the building line. The amount of setback required was determined by running an imaginary plane, the ''sky exposure plane,'' up from the center of the street at a predetermined angle and requiring the profile of the building to remain within this boundary. If carried to its logical conclusion, the regulation would require that very tall buildings, like the Empire State Building, would end either in pyramids or in tiny cubes, but a further provision of the law stated that after setbacks had reduced the building size to 25% of the site, the tower could rise straight up. In 1961 the earlier zoning law was amended in significant ways. First the size of tower allowed to rise straight up without stepping back was enlarged from 25% to 40% of the site. Second, the law established absolute limits on building size. Third, the law offered builders a bonus for including public amenities in their designs.

Walk back toward Wall St. At 100 Broadway is the *Bank of Tokyo*, originally the American Surety Company (1895; Bruce Price), with a row of allegorical stone women above the ground floor by J. Massey Rhind, who did the N. doors of Trinity Church. Although the present owners have gracefully remodeled the building, the lobby still contains its original elaborate ceiling and columns.

At 1 Wall St is the IRVING TRUST COMPANY (1932; Voorhees, Gmelin & Walker, with an addition in 1965), a fine 1930s skyscraper whose exterior detail emphasizes its verticality and whose setbacks illustrate the provisions of the Zoning Resolution of 1916. The curtain wall is designed to suggest fabric folds and is incised with a fabric pattern. The large windows which appear at the top of the faceted tower open into a lounge (not open to the public) with a high faceted ceiling. The Wall St lobby contains Art Deco mosaic decoration by Hildreth Meière in tones of gold, flaming red, and orange.

Continue down Wall St and turn right into Broad St. The ***New York Stock Exchange** (1903; George B. Post; DL) is one reason why New York is the pre-eminent city of the capitalist world.

The New York Stock Exchange. 20 Broad St (visitors' entrance), New York 10005. Tel: 656-5168. Open weekdays from 9:30–4; free; tours every half hour; last tour at 3:30. Accessible to handicapped visitors. Restrooms. Exhibits on the third floor include presentations on the history and evolution of the Exchange, the workings of the stock market, and the impact of technology on trading. Visitors' Gallery overlooking the trading floor; guides explain the hectic activity visible below. For security reasons, visitors are required to have their parcels and baggage X-rayed.

SUBWAY: IRT 7th Ave express (train 2 or 3) to Wall St. IRT Broadway-7th Ave local (train 1 or 9) to Rector St. IRT Lexington Ave express (train 4 or 5) to Wall St. BMT Broadway local (R train) to Rector St. BUS: M1 downtown via 5th Ave / Broadway to Wall St. M6 downtown via 7th Ave / Broadway to Wall St.

Like Federal Hall and the Citibank Building, the Stock Exchange is a "temple," dating from the period when classical architecture was de rigueur for all important public buildings. The sculpture on the pediment is by J. Q. A. Ward and Paul W. Bartlett, and depicts *Integrity Protecting the Works of Man*. The group was designed by Ward, who was elderly at the time, and modeled primarily by Bartlett.

Shortly after the end of the American Revolution, the Congress sitting in Federal Hall issued about $80 million in bonds to pay for the war debt. A central marketplace became necessary for these securities, and after a few years of informal trading outdoors and in coffeehouses, a group of 24 brokers got together and drew up the "Buttonwood Agreement" (May 17, 1792), which marks the formal beginnings of the New York Stock Exchange. The name of the document commemorated a buttonwood or sycamore tree on the N. side of Wall St between William and Pearl Sts near which the brokers used to meet (a tree stands in front of the present Stock Exchange in memory of the origins of the organization).

Walk back toward Wall St. The **Morgan Guaranty Trust Company** (1913; Trowbridge & Livingston; DL) on the right at 23 Wall St was the bank of J. Pierpont Morgan, who more than any other man epitomized Wall St, power, and the stupendous acquisition of wealth. The Wall St facade (about halfway down the building) still bears traces of a tragic unsolved explosion that killed 33 passersby and injured 400 others in 1920. At first, the explosion was believed to be part of a diabolical anarchist plot; another rather fantastic theory attributed it to the ignorance of a junk dealer parked outside the bank who somehow mistook the sticks of dynamite in his wagon for sash weights and inadvertently set them off.

Across the street at 26 Wall St is ***Federal Hall National Memorial*** (1842; Town & Davis with John Frazee; DL), one of the finest Greek Revival buildings in the city and one of New York's most important historic sites, although the great events that took place here predate the present building.

Federal Hall National Memorial. 26 Wall St (Nassau St), New York 10005. Open Mon–Fri 9–5; closed weekends, most federal holidays. Free. Weekly noontime concerts, colonial folk music daily. Gift shop with books, posters, maps, postcards, historical toys. City subway and bus maps available. Restrooms and public telephones on ground floor. No restaurant. Handicapped access from 15 Pine St; restrooms accessible to wheelchairs.

SUBWAY: IRT 7th Ave express (train 2 or 3) to Wall St. IRT Broadway-7th Ave local (train 1 or 9) to Rector St. IRT Lexington Ave express (train 4 or 5) to Wall St. BMT Broadway local (R train) to Rector St. BUS: M1 downtown via 5th Ave / Broadway to Wall St. M6 downtown via 7th Ave / Broadway to Wall St.

A wide flight of steps leads to eight 32-ft fluted Doric columns of Westchester marble that support an architrave and unadorned pediment. On the steps is a statue of George Washington (1883) by John Quincy Adams Ward. There is a second colonnade at the rear entrance to the building on Pine St.

History. In the early 18C the British City Hall (begun 1699; demolished 1812), the successor to the Dutch *Stadt Huys* stood on this site. In that building John Peter Zenger, the argumentative publisher of the *Weekly Journal,* was tried (1735) for libeling the Royal Governor; Zenger's acquittal established a precedent for freedom of the press that would later be reaffirmed in the Bill of Rights.

After the Revolution the Congress met here, first under the Articles of Confederation, but later under the present U.S. Constitution. George Washington was inaugurated here in 1789, more or less on the spot where Ward's statue stands today. The President took the oath of office on the second floor balcony, wearing what was for the period a simple suit.

Well-to-do citizens had contributed $32,000 to renovate the building for the occasion, and Pierre L'Enfant, later one of the principal planners of Washington, D.C., directed the remodeling. The hall was renamed Federal Hall in honor of New York's prestigious position as the nation's capital, although this preeminence did not last long since the federal government was moved to Philadelphia in 1790.

Later the building functioned as the U.S. Custom House and as one of the six government subtreasuries. In 1939 Congress designated the building as a National Historic site, and in 1955 it came under the jurisdiction of the National Park Service.

Inside is a handsome rotunda with one of the vaults from the subtreasury open for display. Beyond the rotunda is a museum of historical exhibits, including an exhibit on New York in 1789 when it was the nation's capital, a display on Washington's inauguration (dioramas, prints, and memorabilia including the rather plain brown suit which he is said to have worn), and an exhibit on the history of the site (models of the building in its various incarnations and a piece of the balcony on which Washington stood during the inaugural ceremonies).

Upstairs in the galleries surrounding the dome are changing exhibits on subjects related to American history as well as a permanent exhibit on the Bill of Rights. On the ground floor are the old coin vaults (1878) dating from the building's period as a U.S. subtreasury, which at the end of the 19C contained as much as 1700 tons of gold and silver coins.

Next door at 30 Wall Street is the *Seamen's Bank for Savings* (1919; York & Sawyer), which incorporates the facade, the foundations, and the bullion vaults of its predecessor, a U. S. Assay Office. Before that a Greek Revival building (1826; Martin E. Thompson) occupied the site, functioning as a bank and later as a U. S. Assay Office. When it was torn down in 1915, its marble facade was dismantled and eventually incorporated in the American Wing of the Metropolitan Museum of Art (see p. 441). The original charter of the Seamen's Bank restricted its clients to sailors, encouraging them to invest their pay instead of squandering it on the transient pleasures of the port of New York.

At 40 Wall St is **Manufacturers Hanover Trust**, a building originally occupied by the Bank of Manhattan (1929; H. Craig Severance & Yasuo Matsui). Planned as the world's tallest building during a period when architects were exercising secrecy and cunning to build higher than their competitors, this building never broke the record; the builders of the Chrysler Building surreptitiously added a stainless steel spire to their structure, previously 2 ft shorter than 40 Wall St, to become victors in the contest—at least until the completion of the Empire State Building. The pyramidal tower and spire atop this bank make it a familiar part of the downtown skyline. (For the history of the Bank of Manhattan, see p. 132).

At 48 Wall St is the *Bank of New York* (1927; Benjamin Wistar Morris), distinguished in the downtown skyline by its Georgian-style cupola. Founded by Alexander Hamilton in 1784, it is the oldest commercial bank in the country; plaques on the W. corner describe its beginnings and the original Wall St wall.

Across the street at 55 Wall St is **Citibank** (formerly the First National City Bank), one of Wall St's most venerable buildings, remarkable for having been constructed in two separate stages. The first section (1842; Isaiah Rogers; DL), a three-story Ionic temple with an imposing domed central hall, belongs to the same period and the same architectural tradition as Federal Hall. The 16 granite columns, quarried in Quincy, Massachusetts, hauled up Wall St by 40 teams of oxen, make an impressive facade for the building, which first served as the new Merchants Exchange, replacing the one destroyed in the Great Fire of 1835. Later used as the custom house, the building was remodeled by the firm of McKim, Mead & White in 1907 when the Custom House at Bowling Green opened. The architects doubled the volume of the building by adding the upper stories, which are surrounded by a tier of Corinthian columns.

Walk back to William St and go a block N. to Pine St. Turn right and continue down the block to *70 Pine Street* (1932; Clinton & Russell), another building recognizable by its top, a Gothic crown with a slender spire. The building used to be known as 60 Wall Tower, laying claim to the more prestigious Wall St address because it was attached to a building on Wall St by an aerial bridge at the sixteenth floor.

Near the E. entrance on Pine St is a large model of the building itself. During the 1920s and 30s, designers made considerable use of sculptural models, and it is possible that the architect, having gone to so much trouble to construct the model, had it installed here (there is another on the Cedar St side). Formerly the Cities Service Building, 70 Pine St has a fine Art Deco lobby, with brown and beige tones of marble, polished aluminum decoration, and Egyptoid elevator doors. The triangular lights in expanding circles above the doors are the logo of the former owner.

Continue down the block and turn right at Pearl St; return to Wall St.

One block E. along Wall St, at the N.W. corner of Wall and Water Sts, is the *site of the Tontine Coffee House,* where members of the infant New York Stock Exchange transacted business before the organization had an official residence. But since nothing marks the site, only those fascinated by the origins of the New York Stock Exchange will find it worth walking the extra block.

Continue along Pearl St to **Beaver St,** named for that furry rodent whose pelts played such a large part in the early economy of the city that it appears on New York's coat of arms along with the sails of a windmill and several barrels of flour.

Follow Beaver St past Hanover Square to *Delmonico's Restaurant* (1891; James Brown Lord) at 56 Beaver St. Sitting imposingly on its triangular plot, the building whose upper stories have been converted to apartments remains an elegant reminder of its distinguished past when it was one of the most highly acceptable places to dine and to be seen. The original Delmonico's opened here in 1827 and was among the first restaurants to offer the public the delights of continental cuisine.

Although New Yorkers were at first cautious about foreign food, the Delmonico brothers eventually succeeded in laying these scruples to rest and in 1846 opened a second establishment, a hotel and restaurant at 25 Broadway. That building, roughly on the site of the present Bowling Green Post Office, was elaborately furnished (rooms cost $10 to $60 per month) and gave its owners "a new and indisputable claim to immortality," according to a contemporary newspaper review.

Across the street at 1 William St is the former headquarters of the Lehman Bros. investment banking firm, originally the Seligman Building (1907; Francis H. Kimball and Julian C. Levi), now the headquarters of the Banca Commerciale Italiana.

Follow South William St (the street name changes at Beaver St), downtown between Delmonico's and the bank. The little alley halfway down the block is **Mill Lane,** whose name commemorates the presence of a flour mill erected by the Dutch West India Company. Upstairs a large loft used as a public meeting place served also as the first house of worship in the community. **William St,** incidentally, takes its name from one of the early settlers, William Beekman, whose family also conferred its name upon Beekman St, near City Hall, and Beekman Place further uptown. This narrow crooked stretch of South William St between Mill Lane and Broad St still (but only barely) preserves some of the flavor of an older New York which may well disappear as renovations and new construction continue.

Walk back on South William and William Sts past the intersection of Wall St, to Pine St. The **Chase Manhattan Bank** (1960; Skidmore, Owings & Merrill), which occupies the enlarged block bounded by Pine, William, Liberty, and Nassau Sts, is now a rather ordinary-looking skyscraper, but in 1960 was considered a remarkable building. First, its presence here was testimony to the bank's decision in the late 1950s to remain downtown when the financial community appeared to be on the brink of flight uptown, a decision that stimulated the rapid growth of the area in the late 1960s. Second, with its severe, unembellished forms and surfaces of glass and steel, the building became the first example in lower Manhattan of the International Style. The outdoor plaza was also the first in the area, a gratuitous act at the time, since the building predates the Zoning Resolution of 1961.

The Chase Manhattan Bank is the successor to the Chase Bank (named after Salmon P. Chase, Secretary of the Treasury under Abraham Lincoln and originator of the national banking system) and the Manhattan Company, formed by Aaron Burr and others. In 1799 Burr and a group of investors organized the Manhattan Water Company, with the apparent intent to provide the city with an adequate, safe water supply. Included in the group's charter was an unobtrusive clause that gave the investors the right to form a bank and engage in various financial activities. Although the Manhattan Water Company did lay several miles of wooden pipe to carry water, its primary interest quickly became banking—and maybe always had been. Alexander Hamilton claimed that Burr used his banking privileges to enhance his political career, and this vociferous and sustained criticism of the bank was yet another source of hostility between the two men.

The plaza, a large expanse of pavement inaccessible from Liberty St, is adorned by Isamu Noguchi's sunken *Japanese garden* whose black basalt rocks were brought from Japan by the sculptor. Originally the fountain was to contain fish, but they had to be rescued from the effects of air pollution and from people's irrepressible desire to throw coins into fountains.

In 1972 the owners installed the sculpture, *Group of Four Trees* by Jean Dubuffet, a 43-ft, 25-ton fabrication supported by a steel skeleton and constructed of fiberglass, aluminum, and plastic resin, materials the artist hoped would withstand the city's toxic environment; the polyurethane paint used on the surface is essentially the same kind used to paint lines on streets.

The work has been called handsome, humane, amusing, and ominous; and critics at the time of its installation were quick to point out the ironic juxtaposition of an institution that epitomizes the moneyed "establishment" and a work by an artist who called himself antibourgeois and anticultural, and claimed to be influenced by children, criminals, and psychotics.

The bank building itself is 813 ft tall, has six underground levels and 60 stories above ground. Excavation began in 1957 but took 20 months since bedrock lay some 25 ft below layers of sand and muck which had to be hardened with chemicals before the site could be blasted. The vault, which weighs 985 tons, reaches down 90 ft below street level and occupies 35,000 square ft of floor space. It is anchored in bedrock to keep it from being washed away in the unlikely event of a tidal wave.

Walk back to William St and continue uptown. The triangular park at the intersection of Maiden Lane and Liberty St is *Louise Nevelson Plaza* and contains a four-piece black sculptural group by Nevelson entitled *Shadows and Flags* donated anonymously in 1978.

Turn left into *Maiden Lane,* once a streamside path where the daughters of the Dutch burghers did the family wash.

The **Federal Reserve Bank** (1924; York & Sawyer; DL) fills the entire block bounded by Maiden Lane, Liberty, William, and Nassau Sts with its massive institutional stolidity. Philip Sawyer, the architect, had studied in Italy, and his design reflects his admiration for the fortified palaces of the great Renaissance families whose wealth and power made them institutions in their own right. The Strozzi Palace in Florence is the principal model for the bank, and the superbly crafted wrought-iron lanterns flanking the doorway on Maiden Lane are almost exact replicas of their Florentine predecessors. Executed by Samuel Yellin (who was responsible for the wrought-iron work in the Cunard Building on lower Broadway), they are considered outstanding examples of the work of a master craftsman.

Beneath the imposing bank are five levels containing offices and bullion vaults, where gold from foreign countries is stored. International transactions are consummated by simply moving the gold from one vault to another without its ever seeing the light of day.

Free tours of the building are available by request at least a week in advance; call the Public Information Office at 720-6130. The tour is popular, so call well ahead.

Walk N. a block on William St to John St. Midblock between William and Nassau Sts stands the **John Street Methodist Church** which in the midst of continual worldly change has steadfastly occupied this property from 1768. It is the oldest Methodist society in the country. The present building (1841; DL; open during the day) is the third on the site and an early example of the Italianate style. The wide board flooring, entrance stairway, pews, and light brackets along the balcony were preserved from an earlier building of 1817, demolished when John St was widened.

The first congregation, composed primarily of Irish Methodist immigrants who had come to this country in the early 1760s, was led by Philip Embury and Barbara Heck. Mrs. Heck, Embury's cousin, came home one day to find her husband, brother, and friends gambling at cards in her kitchen; shocked at such laxity, she broke up the game (an early illustration shows her tossing the cards into the fire), and entreated her cousin, a former preacher, to reassume his duties. Embury began preaching at his home in 1766, but when his living room became too crowded, the group rented the upper story of a Rigging Loft to hold their services. In 1768 the Society purchased this property on John St, and Embury drew up plans for the original chapel, a stone building faced with plaster, which he literally helped build.

One of the early sextons of the church was Peter Williams, a black man whose parents were slaves of a family living on Beekman St. Peter Williams converted to Christianity and became sexton of the church. When his owner returned to England after the Revolution, the church trustees, thinking it embarrassing for a well-known Christian to be sold publicly at auction, bought Williams privately for 40 pounds. He repaid his purchase price over a period of years and was formally emancipated in 1785; he then went into the tobacco business, prospered, and eventually founded the Mother Zion Church, the first black Methodist church in New York.

In the basement of the church are articles dating back to this period; among them the first altar rail, a clock sent by John Wesley, Embury's Bible and lectern.

Walk down John St toward Broadway. Between Maiden Lane and John St along Nassau St is a 26-story office building, **Two Federal Reserve Plaza** (1984; Philip Johnson & John Burgee), whose masonry turrets recall the nearby Federal Reserve Bank. Among its tenants is the **Whitney Museum of American Art, Downtown at Federal Reserve Plaza.**

The Whitney Museum of American Art, Downtown at Federal Reserve Plaza. 2 Federal Reserve Plaza, 33 Maiden Lane (Nassau St), New York 10038. Tel: 943-5655. Open Mon–Fri 11–6. Free. Closed weekends, holidays. Changing exhibitions, lectures, gallery talks (Mon, Wed, Fri at 12:30). No restaurant, no gift shop. Restrooms (ask attendant for key). Accessible to wheelchairs via freight elevator by prior arrangement.
  SUBWAY: IRT 7th Ave express (train 2 or 3) to Fulton St. IRT Lexington Ave express (train 4 or 5) to Fulton St. IND 8th Ave express or local (A or C train) to Broadway-Nassau. BMT Nassau St local (J or M train) to Fulton St. BMT Broadway local (R train) to Fulton St. BUS: M1 marked South Ferry via Fifth Ave / Park Ave South. M6 via 7th Ave / Broadway.

In the arcade leading to the museum entrance is a long-term sculpture installation. Alexander Calder, *The Cock's Comb* (1960); Tony Smith, *One Two Three* (1980), and George Rickey, *Two Lines–Eighteen Feet* (1965). The museum offers five changing exhibitions yearly drawn from the permanent collection of the Whitney Museum and from other sources. The inaugural exhibition, ''Made in the Sixties,'' focused on new developments in that watershed period, and included John Chamberlain's sculpture of crushed and battered automobile bodies, Andy Warhol's serigraphs of Campbell's Soup cans, the hard-edged color painting of Ellsworth Kelly, Frank Stella's shaped canvases, Claes Oldenburg's humorously enlarged soft sculpture, and the Minimalist sculpture of Richard Serra and Donald Judd.

Walk around the corner to the S. on Nassau St and continue back to Liberty St. Turn right. At *55 Liberty Street* (1909; Henry Ives Cobb; DL) is an early skyscraper with Gothic details, one of numerous downtown commercial buildings now converted to housing. The 1970 census counted the full-time population of Lower Manhattan at 500; in 1980 more than 10,000 people lived there.
  At 65 Liberty St, between Liberty Place and Broadway is the former CHAMBER OF COMMERCE OF THE STATE OF NEW YORK (1901; James B. Baker; DL), a fine remnant of the Beaux-Arts tradition, unusual because of the asymmetrical placement of the entrance. Originally three large sculptural groups graced the facade between the columns, but the damage inflicted by air pollution and pigeons forced the removal of the statues.
  At the N.W. corner of Liberty St and Broadway is *One Liberty*

Plaza, the U.S. Steel Building, (1972; Skidmore, Owings & Merrill), notable primarily because it replaced the much-admired Singer Tower (1908; Ernest Flagg), which was the tallest building in the world for 18 months and is still the tallest building ever to be demolished.

On the S.E. corner of the same intersection (Liberty St and Broadway) at 140 Broadway is the *Marine Midland Bank Building* (1967; Skidmore, Owings & Merrill), a smooth, dark building that soars straight up without setbacks (it occupies 40% of its site; the rest is plaza). On the Broadway side stands Isamu Noguchi's red steel and aluminum *Cube* (1973), a 28-ft outdoor sculpture that required a building permit because it is an enclosed mass.

Continue W. on Liberty St toward the Hudson River. On a bench in the small park bounded by Liberty and Cedar Sts, Broadway and Trinity Place sits a bronze businessman, reviewing his correspondence before moving on to his next appointment; entitled *Double Check* (1982; J. Seward Johnson, Jr.), the statue is a popular photo subject for tourists.

Continue down Liberty St to Church St. At 26 Cortlandt St (N.W. corner of Cortlandt and Church Sts) is the *East River Savings Bank* (1934; Walker & Gillette), a fine Art Deco building with a panoramic mural of the East River and its environs as they appeared in 1935 (artist Dale Stetson).

Bounded by Church, Vesey, Liberty, and West Sts and dominating the neighborhood with its huge twin towers and five-acre plaza is the ****World Trade Center** (1976; Minoru Yamasaki and Assocs.; Emery Roth & Sons).

> SUBWAY: IRT Broadway-7th Ave local (train 1 or 9) to Cortlandt St. IND 8th Ave express or local (A or E train) to Chambers St-World Trade Center. BMT Broadway local or express (R or N train) to Cortlandt St-World Trade Center.
>
> BUS: M1, downtown via Fifth Ave / Park Ave South / Broadway to Cortlandt St (make sure you get a bus labeled South Ferry). M6 downtown via 7th Ave / Broadway to Cortlandt St. M10 downtown via 7th Ave. M22 crosstown via Madison / Chambers Sts.

There are restaurants in all price ranges at the Trade Center. Most expensive are Windows on the World and Cellar in the Sky, both at One World Trade Center on the 107th floor (see restaurant listings for additional information). On the 44th floor of the same building is Skydive (938-1958), a modest eatery open weekdays for breakfast and lunch, evenings for drinks. On the concourse level below the plaza are attractive fast food counters in The Big Kitchen (938-1153) whose offerings range from health food to gooey sweets; all are crowded at lunchtime. Also on the concourse level are the Market Bar & Dining Rooms (938-1155), Eat & Drink (432-0395), and The Corner (524-9160), for informal meals. There is a snack bar on the Observation Platform at Two World Trade Center. In the Vista International Hotel are American Harvest and the Greenhouse Restaurant and Wine Bar (see restaurant listings).

The Trade Center has a subterranean parking garage for some 2000 cars (enter from West St; often full) which offers free Saturday parking for shoppers between 10 A.M. and 6 P.M. with purchase. There are currency exchanges on the concourse level, all closed on weekends. In the lobby of One World Trade Center near the entrance to the Vista International Hotel is an airlines ticket center, open weekdays.

On the plaza level of Two World Trade Center is the downtown branch of

tkts, where half-price tickets to Broadway shows are sold on the day of performance (open Mon–Fri 11–5:30; Sat 11–3:30 for evening performances; matinee and Sun tickets available the day before the performance; cash or travelers checks only; tel: 354-5800).

Public toilets are limited. There are restrooms on the Observation Deck and on the 44th floor of One World Trade Center, accessible only after a ticket has been purchased. The public toilets in the PATH station are usable.

The World Trade Center, which brings together businesses and government agencies involved in international trade, was seriously proposed in 1960 and opened for business ten years later.

Return to the plaza, used for lunch-hour picnics, concerts, and special events. Developed by the Port Authority of New York and New Jersey, the Trade Center houses more than 1200 businesses and trade organizations including importers, freight handlers, the U.S. Custom House, steamship lines, and international banks. The resident business population is about 50,000 with another 80,000 people visiting every business day. Virtually a city within a city, the complex has its own medical facility and police station, shops, banks, restaurants, and even a pistol range for Port Authority policemen. Like Battery Park, much of the Trade Center stands on man-made land, once the bed of the Hudson River.

During excavations in this vicinity in 1916, construction workers came across some of the charred timbers of the *Tyger,* the trading ship captained by Adriaen Block (see p. 111) that burned in the harbor in 1613. Block and his followers spent the winter in New Amsterdam and built themselves another vessel, the *Onrust* (usually translated as "Restless"), which carried them back to Holland. A half-century later, in 1967, during excavations for the World Trade Center, workmen unearthed a bronze breech-loading swivel deck gun bearing the mark of the Dutch East India Company (the Dutch West India Company had not been founded in 1613), also probably from the *Tyger,* for the loss of whose cannon Adriaen Block was sued by the Dutch Admiralty. The exhumed relics are now on view at the Museum of the City of New York while the rest of the *Tyger* still lies buried some 20 ft below the World Trade Center.

The excavated dirt and rubble was dumped into the Hudson behind a retaining wall forming 23.5 acres of filled land between Rector and Cortlandt Sts, now part of Battery Park City.

Grouped around a central 5-acre plaza opening on Church St are five major buildings. Along Church St on either side of the plaza are the two Plaza Buildings, **Four and Five World Trade Center,** which serve as product display areas; four commodity exchanges—the New York Cotton Exchange, the New York Mercantile Exchange, the New York Coffee, Sugar and Cocoa Exchange, and the Commodity Exchange, Inc.—are housed in Four World Trade Center, S. side of plaza. A visitors gallery overlooks the trading floor; open Mon–Fri 9:30–3; free; take the elevator to the ninth floor.

At the Church St entrance to the plaza stands the largest free-standing stone carving of modern times, a highly polished, untitled, asymmetrical work (1967–72) of black granite by sculptor Masayuki Nagare.

In the center, surrounded by a fountain, stands the bronze, broken-surfaced *Globe* (1975) by Fritz Koenig. Between the twin towers is a polished stainless steel sculpture by James Rosati entitled *Ideogram* (1973).

Also facing the plaza, between the N. tower and Vesey St, is the **United States Custom House** (Six World Trade Center), which handles the customs and collections activities for the New York-New Jersey port, replacing the old Custom House at Bowling Green.

The most famous buildings at the center are the *Twin Towers, One and Two World Trade Center, each 1350 ft tall, having 104 elevators, 21,800 windows, and an acre of rentable space per floor. In the mezzanine of One World Trade Center facing the plaza hangs a textured wall sculpture (1977–87) entitled *Sky-Gate New York* by Louise Nevelson. A monumental tapestry (35 ft × 20 ft) by Joan Miró hangs in the mezzanine of Two World Trade Center, also facing the plaza.

Like the Brooklyn Bridge and the Empire State Building, the Twin Towers have drawn their share of publicity seekers. The pioneer in this respect (August 1974) was Philippe Petit, a French aerialist, who shot a rope across the gap between the two towers with a crossbow and then walked across the rope. His signature is preserved on the outdoor deck of the Observation Platform. In July 1975 an unemployed construction worker from Queens parachuted from the top of the Trade Center to call attention to the plight of the world's poor. And in May 1977 George Willig, a mountaineer and toy factory employee, scaled the outside of the South Tower using equipment he had designed to fit the tracks of the window-washing apparatus. When Willig arrived at the top some 3½ hours after he began the ascent, the city charged him with "intentionally, willfully, and wrongfully scaling and climbing the South Tower of the World Trade Center" and threatened him with a $250,000 civil suit. On the urging of the mayor, the suit was dropped, and the city amicably settled for a fine of $1.10, a cent per floor, and a promise to refrain from a repeat performance.

*Observation Deck: The observation deck on the 107th floor of Two World Trade Center (the southernmost of the two) offers stunning views of the city, the harbor, New Jersey, and Long Island.

Open daily 9:30–9:30; admission charge; snack bar and restroom facilities. An escalator to the outdoor observation platform is open when wind and weather permit; otherwise visitors may view the surroundings from an enclosed gallery.

Since the windows of the towers cannot be opened, and since buildings so large obviously pose certain dangers to their inhabitants, the interior environment is controlled by a central computer with 6500 sensors that feed it information about the temperature, humidity, and water and power needs.

The maximum permissible sway was determined by carrying out a series of experiments in a Eugene, Oregon, optometrist's office, where subjects who thought they were getting free eye examinations were treated to various amounts of sway to determine what they could tolerate. A maximum of 11 inches of slow or damped sway was deemed acceptable. There is enough aluminum sheeting on the outside of the towers for 9000 houses. Every day building occupants generate 50 tons of garbage (the maximum takeoff weight of a Boeing 737). At full occupancy 2.25 million gallons of water are required per day, and 2.25 million gallons of raw sewage are produced. The buildings require enough electricity to power a city of about 40,000 inhabitants. The Trade Center brings an estimated 43,000 commuters per day to neighborhood transit facilities.

The **Vista International Hotel** (1981; Skidmore, Owings & Merrill) at Three World Trade Center (between Two World Trade Center and the river) is a 22-story luxury facility, the first major hotel built in lower Manhattan since 1836.

Seven World Trade Center (1987; Emery Roth & Sons), bounded by Vesey, Barclay, and Greenwich Sts and West Broadway is the World Trade Center's latest addition. On the Vesey St overpass is Alexander Calder's 25-ton *World Trade Center Stabile* (1971), enlarged from a work entitled *Three Wings*. Calder proposed a 150-ft enlargement; architect Yamasaki suggested a 14-ft sculpture; the current 25-ft figure represents a compromise that favors Yamasaki.

Adjacent to the World Trade Center but not part of it is the **New York Telephone Company Building,** 140 West St between Barclay and Vesey Sts, also known as the **Barclay-Vesey Building** (1926; McKenzie, Voorhees & Gmelin), an office tower and switching center. The first major building by architect Ralph Walker, the Barclay-Vesey Building has long been admired for its arcaded sidewalk along Vesey St (originally a shopping arcade, whose presence represents a compromise between the city, which wanted to widen Vesey St, and the telephone company, which wanted to maximize floor space), and for the lavish Art Deco ornament on the exterior—plant forms, aborigines, baby flutists, elephants with ears spiraling into nautilus shells, and bells (appropriate for the telephone company). Security in the building is tight, but from the entrance you may admire the lobby ceiling paintings (Mack, Jenney & Tyler) illustrating the history of human communications—from the glazed brick reliefs of Babylon to the age of radio. Bronze chandeliers whose shape suggests the general massing of the building draw attention to the location of the elevators, which have handwrought doors.

Return to the Trade Center plaza. Beneath the buildings of the center is a **concourse** level with shops, banks, and restaurants. The Port Authority Trans Hudson (PATH) rail line linking lower Manhattan with New Jersey has its terminal here, and the BMT, IRT, and IND subways all have stops on the concourse level, which is crowded during commuting hours.

Leave the World Trade Center by one of the southern exits which faces Liberty St. The block bounded by Washington and West Sts, Liberty and Cedar Sts is occupied today almost entirely by a parking lot, between whose parked cars rises the solitary **St. Nicholas Greek Orthodox Church** (1820?), a survivor from the 19C when a Middle Eastern colony of Turks, Armenians, Greeks, and especially Syrians lived along Washington St from the Battery to Rector St. As late as the 1930s the congregation observed the ceremony of the Rescue of the Cross each January 6, throwing into the harbor at the Battery a small wooden cross which was rescued by a stalwart swimmer. Construction for the Brooklyn-Battery Tunnel displaced these ethnic colonies; the Greeks crossed the East River to Astoria and the Arabs settled around Atlantic Ave and elsewhere in Brooklyn.

Follow Liberty St across West St to **Battery Park City,* Manhattan's newest neighborhood, rising on 92 acres of man-made land in the Hudson River. The hub of Battery Park City is the WORLD FINANCIAL CENTER, four large office towers occupied by major members of the financial community, with a fifth tentatively planned for the area N. of Vesey St. Apartments, town houses, a marina, parks, shops, and restaurants enrich the area for the projected 25,000 people who will live in its three residential neighborhoods. At the N. end of the site the prestigious Stuyvesant High School will eventually make its new home; at the S. end will be the Museum of Jewish Heritage, a memorial to the Holocaust victims.

History. In the mid-1960s, as commerce fled uptown and the unused Hudson River piers rotted in the water, Gov. Nelson Rockefeller conceived of Battery Park City as a way to revitalize the downtown area and the decaying waterfront, simultaneously providing housing and saving millions of dollars by finding a place to dump the rock and earth excavated from the World Trade Center site. In 1968 the state, which by its riparian rights owned any landfill in the river, created the Battery Park City Authority as a public benefit corporation to develop the area W. of the World Trade Center. An early plan for a futuristic city isolated from the existing downtown area collapsed during the city's fiscal crisis in the mid-1970s.

In 1979 architects Alexander Cooper and Stanton Eckstut created the master plan that determined the present outlines of the area and is responsible in large part for Battery Park City's aesthetic success. This plan required the extension of the existing Manhattan street grid into the landfill area, linking it to the larger city, as well as a north-south Esplanade joining the commercial central area with the residential neighborhoods at both ends. Furthermore the plan laid down design guidelines that assured high architectural quality and emphasized the kind of human scale and variety found in New York's successful older (and tonier) neighborhoods, for example, Gramercy Park or Beekman Place.

North of Liberty St rise the four commercial towers of the **World Financial Center,** each clad in granite and reflective glass, but of different heights and with different roof forms. *One World Financial Center* (1985; Cesar Pelli, design architect; Adamson Assocs., architects), the corporate home of Dow Jones & Co. and Oppenheimer & Co. Forty stories high, it is topped with a sloping rectangular roof.

Walk through the South Gatehouse and its mirror the North Gatehouse (sometimes used for art exhibitions and other public events) to *Two World Financial Center* (1987; Cesar Pelli, design architect; Haines Lundberg Waehler, architects), one of two towers occupied by Merrill Lynch & Co. Recognizable by its domed roof, it is, with 51 stories, the tallest building in the project.

The **Winter Garden** (1988; Cesar Pelli, design architect; Adamson Assocs., architects), the centerpiece of the financial sector, is a glassed-in, barrel-vaulted plaza as large as Grand Central Terminal. Its 45-ft palm trees were imported from California's Mojave desert.

The atrium of the Winter Garden at the World Financial Center, with its 45-foot palm trees and view of the Hudson River, is the most dramatic interior of Battery Park City, Manhattan's newest neighborhood. (Peter Aaron / ESTO; © 1988)

After four years spent beneath a canopy acclimatizing to the limited light they would receive in New York, the trees were hauled in on flat bed trucks and planted while the building was still under construction.

Within the Winter Garden are shops, a cafe, and a performance space for the center's ARTS & EVENTS PROGRAM (call 945-2600 for information; events also held in other locations within the World Financial Center).

Continue on to the pyramidally roofed *Three World Financial Center* (1985; Cesar Pelli, design architect; Adamson Assocs., architects), headquarters of the American Express Company.

Between Three and Four World Financial Center is the glass-roofed, canopied COURTYARD, inspired by European open-air piazzas, with restaurants and cafes. *Four World Financial Center* (1986; Cesar Pelli, design architect; Haines Lundberg Waehler, architects), also occupied by Merrill Lynch & Co., is the last and smallest of the original towers, ending in a truncated stepped pyramid.

Turn around and walk south. The PLAZA, W. of the buildings, borders NORTH COVE, whose marina is devoted to oceangoing yachts, grandiose craft measuring 75–150 ft.

Continue S., walking to the Hudson River beyond Liberty St. Between the Esplanade and South End Ave rises GATEWAY PLAZA (1982; Brown & Gershon), three 34-story towers and three low-rise buildings which were designed before the Cooper Eckstut master plan and were the only buildings constructed according to plans developed during the Rockefeller era.

Continue south. The *Esplanade (1983– ; Cooper & Eckstut) is one of the glories of Battery Park City. A wide, thoughtfully designed walkway, it once more gives pedestrians, after long exile, access to the river. At the intersection of Albany St is Ned Smyth's *The Upper Room* (1987), an elevated bluestone plaza surrounded by terra-cotta columns, which suggests a ruined temple or courtyard. Inside the columns is a long table inlaid with six chess boards. It is part of Battery Park City's public art project, in which artists have created work intrinsic to several sites in the neighborhood.

Continue S. to RECTOR PARK, a residential square surrounded by apartment buildings, designed to recall the quiet elegance of Gramercy Park. At the mouth of the park, facing the Esplanade, is *Rector Gate* (1989; R. M. Fischer), a 43-ft skeletal gateway of stainless steel and decorative metal. A block S., at W. Thames St, is Richard Artschwager's *Sitting / Stance* (1988) with outsized, outdoor furniture in granite, aluminum, and wood.

South Cove (1988; Mary Miss, artist; Stanton Eckstut, architect; Susan Child, landscape architect), landscaped with rock outcroppings and wild plantings, reaches out over the river on pilings.

The S. end of the site is reserved for the Battery Place residential neighborhood, the future *Museum of Jewish Heritage,* and the South Gardens (projected 1992), a design that includes water gardens, hedge gardens, a rose garden, an herb garden, and flower fields.

4 Park Row, City Hall, and the Civic Center

SUBWAY: IRT Broadway-7th Ave (train 1 or 9) to Cortlandt St. IRT 7th Ave (train 2 or 3) to Fulton St. IRT Lexington Ave (train 4 or 5) to Fulton St. IND 8th Ave (A train) to Broadway-Nassau. BMT Broadway local (R train) to Cortlandt St. BMT Nassau St local (J, M, or Z train) to Fulton St.

BUS: M1 via 5th Ave / Broadway, M6 via Broadway, M15 via Park Row, or M102 via 3rd / Lexington Aves.

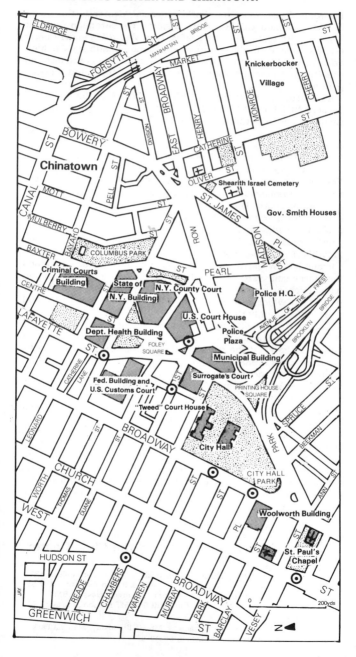

Facing Broadway between Fulton, Church, and Vesey Sts is **St. Paul's Chapel and Churchyard** (1766; Thomas McBean; tower and steeple added 1794, James C. Lawrence; DL), built as a subsidiary chapel of Trinity Church to accommodate worshippers in outlying areas of the city. As the oldest church in the city, a beautiful example of Georgian architecture, and the site of the service following George Washington's inauguration as President, it has rich historical associations.

Short tour at 10 A.M.; free concerts Mon and Thurs at 12:10; for concert information call 602-0760; restroom near original entrance at rear of church.

EXTERIOR. Commonly attributed to Thomas McBean, of whom little is known, St. Paul's shows the influence of St. Martin's-in-the Fields, London, though executed in homely native building materials including masonry of rough, reddish-gray Manhattan schist quarried on the site of the graveyard, and trim of smooth brownstone. When built the church faced W. to the river, but as Broadway became an important thoroughfare, a portico and entrance were added on the E., although the location of the altar made a central entrance unfeasible. On the E. porch with its fluted Ionic columns is *the tomb and monument of Brigadier General Richard Montgomery,* mortally wounded in the Battle of Quebec, Dec 25, 1775, "after a series of successes amidst the most discouraging difficulties," as his epitaph points out. The monument by sculptor Jean Jacques Caffieri pays tribute to his martial skill and the cause of freedom: on the right of the obelisk are a Phrygian cap (given to freed Roman slaves), broken swords, and a club of Hercules with a ribbon inscribed, "Libertas Restituta" ("Liberty Restored").

INTERIOR. The light interior, painted in pale colors, is graced by slender Corinthian columns supporting a barrel-vaulted ceiling. The chancel wall has a beautiful Palladian window glazed with clear glass. The 14 Waterford crystal chandeliers, the organ case, and the elaborately carved pulpit and communion rail all date from before the Revolution. Over the pulpit are three feathers, the emblem of the Prince of Wales. Pierre L'Enfant, best known as city planner of Washington, D.C., may have designed the gilded wooden sunburst behind the altar. At the rear of the church is a *memorial to John Wells* (died 1823), a prominent lawyer, the earliest known marble portrait bust by an American sculptor (1824; John Frazee).

Spared by the Fire of 1776, as old Trinity Church was not, St. Paul's Chapel became the most important Anglican church in the city and was used by George Washington following his inauguration at Federal Hall. The pew where he worshipped, originally canopied, is in the N. aisle; in the S. aisle is the Governor's Pew, reserved first for royal governors, now for the state governor. It is a tribute to the beauty of the church that during the British occupation, while other churches became stables, prisons, and hospitals, St. Paul's Chapel served British officers as their own house of worship.

At the rear of the church is a *burial ground* with gravestones

of moderately prominent early New Yorkers (the most famous
were buried in Trinity churchyard). Among them are: George
Frederick Cooke (died 1812), a famous English actor whose
monument was financed by Edmund Kean, an even more famous
English actor; Etienne Marie Bechet Sieur de Rochefontaine (died
1814), who fought in the American Revolution and emigrated to
New York after the execution of Louis XVI; and Thomas Addis
Emmet (died 1827), Irish patriot and lawyer exiled from British
territory after serving a prison term for treason.

Return to Broadway. Just S. of the church (S.W. corner of Broadway and Fulton St) is the former *American Telephone and
Telegraph Building* (1915–22; William Welles Bosworth), at 195
Broadway, a building with more columns than any other building
anywhere (eight tiers of Ionic, one tier of Doric). In the lobby
(open during business hours) are a plaque memorializing the
inventor of the telephone, Alexander Graham Bell, and a bronze
and marble sculptural work by Chester Beach entitled *Service to
the Nation*. Its central figure, wearing headphones, his hair
frizzled by lightning bolts, is posed before a map of the U.S., its
major cities linked by long distance telephone wires.

Walk N. past *Fulton St,* named after Robert Fulton, entrepreneur of the steamboat, and *Vesey St,* named after William Vesey,
first rector of Trinity Church. *Barclay St,* the next street uptown,
takes its name from the second rector, Henry Barclay, shown on
one of the panels of the S. doors in Trinity Church preaching to
the Indians.

Turn left into Vesey St. At 14 Vesey St between Broadway and
Church St, is the *New York County Lawyers' Association* (1930;
Cass Gilbert; DL), a white marble and limestone neo-Georgian
building. At 20 Vesey St just beyond is the former *Garrison
Building* (1906; Robert D. Kohn; DL), home of the *New York
Evening Post* between 1907 and 1930, with colophons of famous
early printers on the spandrels between windows, and statues
high up on the facade representing the *Four Periods of Publicity*.
They are by Gutzon Borglum, best known for his gigantic portrait
heads of U.S. Presidents at Mt. Rushmore in North Dakota, and
by Estelle R. Kohn, wife of the architect. The top of the building
has been praised as a rare New York example of the Art Nouveau
style in architecture.

Continue to Church St. Turn right and walk a block N. to
Barclay St. **St. Peter's Roman Catholic Church,** at 22 Barclay St
on the S.E. corner of Church St (1838; John Haggerty and
Thomas Thomas; DL) is one of several Greek Revival churches
remaining in lower Manhattan and is historically interesting as
Manhattan's oldest Roman Catholic church, standing on the site
of its predecessor, the first Catholic church in the city. Since the
regulations outlawing Roman Catholicism in Britain applied to
the U.S. during the colonial period it was not until 1785 that the
congregation was able to purchase this land from Trinity Parish
and lay the cornerstone for the original building.

Architecturally the church is interesting because it uses granite
on the facade rather than the softer, more easily carved brown-

stone. The Ionic portico with six massive columns has a low wood-framed pediment containing a central niche with a statue of St. Peter holding the keys to the eternal kingdom.

Return to Broadway. The *Transportation Building* (1927; York & Sawyer), 225 Broadway between Vesey and Barclay Sts, occupies the site of the **Astor House Hotel** (demolished 1915). Built (1834; Isaiah Rogers) by John Jacob Astor, in his declining years, it was the city's first famous hostelry, a monument of Greek Revival architecture and a palace of luxury, including among its conveniences bathing facilities and gaslight on every floor, an indulgence unknown at the time even in the finest mansions. By 1870, however, fashion had deserted lower Broadway and the Astor House began receiving mercantile visitors and a few older people who remembered its finer days.

Continue uptown. The *****Woolworth Building** at 233 Broadway between Barclay St and Park Place was the tallest building in the world when completed (1913; Cass Gilbert; DL); it was eclipsed in 1929 by the tower at 40 Wall St and in 1930 by the Chrysler Building.

The Woolworth Building was officially opened at 7:30 in the evening of April 24, 1913, by President Woodrow Wilson in Washington, who at a signal from a telegrapher pressed a button that illuminated 80,000 light bulbs in the tower in New York. A band on the 27th floor broke into the national anthem and the 800 notables gathered for a banquet broke into sustained applause. The Rev. S. Parkes Cadman, known for the fullness of his prose and the intensity of his sentiments, noted that the building inspired "feelings too deep even for tears" and dubbed it "The Cathedral of Commerce," a nickname that stuck, though modern admirers are generally more subdued in their accolades.

F. W. Woolworth, its builder, enjoyed a classic 19C American rags-to-riches career, starting out as a farm boy and beginning his life's work clerking in a general store.

During this apprenticeship Woolworth became convinced that customers would patronize a store where they could see and even finger the merchandise and where they did not have to haggle over prices with intimidating clerks. After a few false starts he proved himself right in a grand way, opening his first successful five-and-ten-cent store in 1879 and enlarging it eventually into a chain of stores which then permitted him to buy in quantity and offer the consumer better prices. By 1913 he was able to pay $13,500,000 in cash for his building.

The care and attention that Woolworth devoted to the smallest detail of his building (he personally picked out the bathroom fixtures and the mail chutes), the extravagant expenditures for beautiful materials and fine craftsmanship, and the grandiose conception of the whole make the building a monument to its owner's career and a visual delight in a less opulent age.

EXTERIOR. Predating the 1916 zoning restrictions, the building covers its entire site. It rises about 300 ft straight up from the street, its verticality emphasized by the light-colored piers which ascend in an unbroken line straight to the top of the main section. The tower then soars another 400 ft, ending in a delicate crown surrounded by four small towers (total height, 792 ft). At street level around the elaborate doorway arch are carved figures of young men and women at work, performing the labor necessary, according to some observers, to earn the money they need to shop at Woolworth's. Above the second floor are masks representing four centers of civilization—Europe, Africa, Asia, and America—a motif Cass Gilbert used earlier on the Custom House at Bowling Green. On the 26th, 49th, and 51st floors gargoyles represent frogs, bats, pelicans, and other creatures. Flying buttresses and pinnacles surround the gilded crown that tops off the building.

INTERIOR. More than the facade, the interior betrays Woolworth's uninhibited love of spectacle. The walls are covered with golden-toned marble quarried on the Isle of Skyros; the vaulted mosaic ceilings in blue, green, and gold have bird and flower patterns which are intended to recall the mosaics of Ravenna. In the side hallways at the mezzanine level, visible from the main lobby, are murals by C. Paul Jennewein representing *Commerce* and *Labor* (S. and N. respectively). At the end of the entrance corridor is a grand marble staircase with an elaborately carved marble balustrade further ornamented with gilded metalwork.

The only relief in all this magnificence (neither Gilbert nor Woolworth was known for a sense of humor) is offered by a set of sculpted figures beneath the arches leading to the lateral hallways near Broadway. These statues depict Woolworth and some of his builders in appropriate postures. Woolworth clutches a big nickel; Cass Gilbert peers through a pince-nez at a large model of the building; Lewis E. Pierson, president of the Irving Bank, first tenant of the building, gazes at a stock ticker tape; Edward Hogan, the renting agent, negotiates a rental; Gunvald Aus, the structural engineer, measures a girder.

Cross City Hall Park to the intersection of Broadway and Park Row. Between 1842 and 1865 P. T. Barnum's American Museum occupied the S.E. corner of Broadway and Ann St, delighting and deceiving the public with such exhibits as a "Feejee Mermaid," a bearded lady (possibly not a lady at all), and Gen. Tom Thumb, a midget from Bridgeport, Connecticut. The museum burned in 1865 and Barnum went on to organize the "Greatest Show on Earth," a circus that opened in Brooklyn in 1871. James Gordon Bennett's marble New York Herald Building (1866), home of a famous newspaper with a distinguished history, succeeded the museum. The Herald Building was torn down to make way for the predecessor of the present Western Electric Building.

Park Row. In its earliest days Park Row was a center of theatrical activity in the city. The Park Theatre, New York's most famous early playhouse, which faced a small street parallel to Park Row still known as *Theater Alley*, saw the comings and goings of such notable performers as Edmund Kean, Edwin Booth, and Fanny and Charles Kemble. First opened in 1798, burned and refurbished several times, the Park Theatre remained open until 1848 when a final fire and the changing character of the neighborhood closed it forever. Thereafter Park Row became the center of the city's newspaper industry, close to City Hall (political news) and close to the slums of the Lower East Side (sensational human interest stories). In its prime "Newspaper Row," as the street was known, ran from Ann St to Chatham Square and was divided by the approaches to the Brooklyn Bridge into a N. section for the foreign language press and a S. section which belonged to the great New York dailies.

In one grand row facing City Hall Park stood buildings housing four of the city's greatest papers: Joseph Pulitzer's *New York World,* Charles Anderson Dana's *New York Sun,* the *New York Tribune,* founded by Horace Greeley, and the *New York Times,* revitalized by Adolph Ochs. William Randolph Hearst's *New York American* and *New York Evening Journal* spewed forth their successful blend of saccharine and vitriol from offices on William St, and until 1906 the *Evening Post,* once headed by William Cullen Bryant, stood on the S.E. corner of Broadway and Fulton St. When Joseph Pulitzer died in 1911, there were 14 daily newspapers in the city, 12 of which were published on Park Row.

The *Potter Building* (1883; Nathan G. Starkweather) at 38 Park Row on the N.E. corner of Beekman St, converted to apartments in 1979, was designed to be totally fireproof since its predecessor had burned in 1882. Named after its developer, real estate investor Orlando B. Potter, it is constructed of brick, iron, and stone and originally had cast-iron work on the first two stories.

At 41 Park Row between Beekman and Spruce Sts is a building now belonging to Pace University, the former **New York Times Building** (original building, 1857; considerably enlarged and altered, 1889, George B. Post; altered again, 1905, Robert Maynicke). The first home (1858–1904) of the *Times* was both imposing (its height of more than 80 ft gave it a grand panoramic view) and elegant, with plate glass windows on the ground level, elaborately frescoed walls, and marble floors. Its luxury started a trend in newspaper buildings which until then had humbly reflected the status of the industry. It was also fireproof, surviving the blaze that destroyed its neighbor in 1882.

Continue N. on Park Row. The area N. of Nassau and Spruce Sts and Park Row once was known as *Printing House Square,* although the ramps to the Brooklyn Bridge now occupy much of the former open space. A *statue of Benjamin Franklin* (c. 1872; Ernst Plassmann), publisher of the *Pennsylvania Gazette,* was erected when the printing industry dominated the neighborhood.

The New Building (1970; Eggers & Higgins; enlarged 1984) of *Pace University* stands to the E., bounded by Nassau, Frankfort, Gold, and Spruce Sts. Founded in 1906 as an accounting school, Pace University offers courses in the arts and sciences, education, and nursing, as well as business. On the facade facing Park Row is a sculptural relief of welded copper by Henri Azaz entitled *Brotherhood of Man.*

Cross the street to **City Hall Park,** the closest thing New York has to a commons or town green. In Dutch times it was a cow pasture; later it stood at the intersection of the two main arteries of British New York, Broadway which led N. along the W. side of town to the village of Bloomingdale, and the Boston Post Road which followed a route up the present East Side and headed E. to Connecticut and eventually Boston.

History. During the colonial period the Commons or Fields served as a parade ground and a public gathering place. Later it served as the site of numerous public protests, several riots, and occasional celebrations. In 1911 an oak was planted in front of City Hall to commemorate the Leisler Rebellion (1689–91), an early political clash between one faction supporting the British royal governors and another with more local loyalties. Jacob Leisler, leader of the rebellion, was hanged for treason somewhere near the present park, though he was belatedly exonerated and his followers freed from prison.

On the W. lawn of City Hall is a *monument to the Liberty Poles,* which were erected in the years preceding the Revolution by the Sons of Liberty, a group of disgruntled tradesmen, workers, and army veterans who harassed the British government, propagandized against taxation policies, and taunted the British troops.

The Liberty Boys, as they were also called, erected five successive Liberty Poles as symbols of protest and as rallying points for demonstrations. Decorated at the top with an emblem saying "Liberty" and protected at the bottom by iron hoops, the poles were deliberately provocative, erected in sight of the British barracks.

Traditionally public heroes have been driven up Broadway from Battery Park to City Hall Park and showered with miles of **ticker tape** tossed from the office buildings of the Financial District. The first so honored was Theodore Roosevelt in 1910. In recent times, however, when modern office buildings have sealed windows and computer paper has replaced old-style ticker tape, the tonnage of celebratory paper has declined. The Department of Sanitation regularly sweeps up and weighs the shredded paper and ranks the parades, the largest in the last two decades having been 971 tons on January 30, 1981, which fluttered down on the American hostages returned from Iran. Gen. Douglas MacArthur, who followed a 19-mile route through Manhattan streets including lower Broadway achieved a festive 3249 tons.

Near Broadway in the park is a bronze *statue of Nathan Hale* (1890; Frederick W. MacMonnies), a schoolteacher from Connecticut who joined the militia and volunteered to penetrate the British lines and gather information about troop movements in occupied New York.

Hale was captured and when asked for his last words before being hanged uttered the statement that ensured his place in the textbooks of American history: "I only regret that I have but one life to lose for my country." The location of the gallows is unknown, but recent scholarship favors the vicinity of 63rd St and First Ave.

The statue depicts Hale as a handsome youth (he was 21 when executed) in an impassioned attitude of defiance, his arms and ankles bound with ropes. This portrayal represents MacMonnies' romantic conception of Hale's appearance which one of his contemporaries described as "above the common stature . . . his shoulders of moderate breadth, his limbs straight and very plump," a description which would certainly have produced a less inspiring statue.

On the E. side of City Hall is a bronze *statue of Horace Greeley* (1890; John Quincy Adams Ward) showing the famous newspaperman sitting casually in a bronze upholstered chair with delightful bronze fringes, a newspaper draped over his right knee. Greeley founded the *New York Tribune* and guided it to eminence. Famous also for his advice to an unknown fortune

City Hall (built 1802–11), an elegant example of the Federal style. The uptown facade was not clad in marble since at the time hardly anyone lived north of Chambers Street to look at it. (Landmarks Preservation Commission, New York City. Photographer: John B. Bayley)

seeker, "Go West, young man," Greeley is known to have been careless about his dress and personal appearance, a quality Ward has caught in the statue.

*City Hall (1802–11; Joseph Mangin and John McComb, Jr; DL) is the dominant building in the park.

City Hall / The Governor's Room. City Hall, New York 10007. Tel: 566-5700. Open Mon–Fri, 10–3. Free.

The security guards may ask why you wish to enter, but an explanation of normal touristic desires should suffice. The public may visit the Governor's Room and the Rotunda. On days of public hearings the Board of Estimate Chamber and the Council Chamber are open. Restrooms. No restaurant, no gift shop. Accessible to wheelchairs.

Small by comparison with the buildings surrounding the park, City Hall is one of New York's architectural jewels: elegant, gracefully proportioned, and attractively situated. Oddly enough the building has not always been treasured and only within the past two decades has it been restored from shabby neglect.

History. The present City Hall is the third building to house the municipal government following the *Stadt Huys* on Pearl St and the 18C City Hall on Wall St that later became Federal Hall. John McComb, Jr. and Joseph Mangin, two established New York architects, won the design competition taking home a prize of $350, for which (plus construction costs estimated at a half million dollars) the city got one of its outstanding public buildings.

The cornerstone for City Hall was laid in 1803 and the buiding officially opened on July 4, 1811. Delays caused by a yellow fever epidemic, labor disputes, and financial difficulties held up the work. McComb, who supervised the construction, got $6 per day; John LeMaire, a French artisan, got $4 per day for his work as master stonecarver, while the laborers received something between $1 and $1.50. The marble, more than 35,000 cubic ft of it, quarried in West Stockbridge, Massachusetts, came to what nowadays seems a reasonable $35,000. The N. side of the building, originally faced in brownstone because the city fathers wished to save money and felt that the N. facade was safely out of sight, was covered with limestone in 1956.

In the 19C City Hall was used to entertain visiting celebrities, including the Prince of Wales (later Edward VII) who visited in 1860. Ulysses S. Grant, Gen. William J. Worth, and Abraham Lincoln lay in state in the Rotunda.

EXTERIOR. For the best view of the facade approach the building from the S., along the central path of the park. City Hall is an elegant example of the Federal style elaborated with French details, perhaps the contribution of Mangin, a French emigré, believed to have been the principal designer of the exterior. The French influence appears particularly in the long rows of windows ornamented with pilasters and swags instead of the usual more severe classical orders and in the general massing of the building. The tower, however, belongs to the native tradition, as does the design of the interior, probably McComb's inspiration. The dome is crowned by a copper, mass-produced statue of Justice, manufactured in Ohio at the William H. Mullins Co. workshop, which dealt in such figures.

It replaced the original Justice carved in wood (1812) by John Dixey, but destroyed by fire in 1858. A second figure seems to have been made around 1860 by someone named Stratton, possibly a member of the local family of ships' carvers who did business on South St.

INTERIOR. *Ground floor.* The walls of the lobby are still covered with the original white Massachusetts marble that once adorned the facade. To the right of the entrance is a bronze copy (1857) of a *bust of George Washington* made from a marble original by Jean-Antoine Houdon in 1787; the original, in the state capitol at Richmond, Virginia, is based on life casts Houdon made during a visit to the United States in 1785. The mayor's office is at the end of the left corridor; the office of the president of the City Council on the right. Beyond the lobby is the *Rotunda, with its beautiful circular staircase. In the center of the Rotunda supported by ten marble Corinthian columns is a dome with a clear glass oculus opening into the tower. The design for this domed space is probably McComb's and has an antecedent in the plan of Wardour House (Wiltshire, England) designed by James Paine.

Second floor. To the E. of the Rotunda on the second floor is the *City Council Chamber,* designed in about 1898 when the five boroughs were joined to make Greater New York, a union commemorated by the low-relief sculpture in the corners of the ceiling. The plaster statue of Thomas Jefferson is a copy of an original bronze (1833) by Pierre Jean David d'Angers, a student of Houdon. The ceiling painting, *New York Receiving the Tributes of the Nation* (1903), is by Taber Sears, George W. Breck, and Frederick C. Martin.

On the W. side of the building the *Board of Estimate Chamber* resembles a courtroom of the Federal period. At the W. end is a semicircular dais where the members of the board sit elevated above the public for whom white bench pews with mahogany trim are provided. The mayor gets to sit in the chair with the elaborate canopy with red hangings. The chandeliers are from the Civil War period. In niches on the walls are marble busts of two of the nation's outstanding chief justices of the U. S. Supreme Court, both by John Frazee, often called America's first native portrait sculptor: John Jay (chief justice, 1789–95) and John Marshall (chief justice, 1790–1852).

At the head of the stairs is the ***Governor's Room,** originally set aside as an office for the state governor when he visited the city.

The portraits in the room belong to the city's historical collection and include on permanent display 12 of the 13 paintings by *John Trumbull* commissioned by the city. The portrait of George Washington on the W. wall shows the general on Evacuation Day (Nov 24, 1783) standing by his horse, with a background view of Bowling Green and the Upper Bay. Over the opposite mantel is his portrait of George Clinton, Brigadier General in the American Army, with the Hudson River highlands in the background.

Other Trumbull portraits, mainly of mayors and governors, include Govs. John Jay and Daniel D. Tompkins, Mayors James Duane, Richard Varick, Edward Livingston, and Marinus Willett, and Secretary of the Treasury Alexander Hamilton. The portrait of Peter Stuyvesant is a copy by Trumbull of an earlier painting. The frames for the 1805 and 1808 commissions were made by John LeMaire, the chief carver for the building.

The furniture consists of chairs, desks, and tables made for City Hall at the time of its completion and two high-backed upholstered settees attributed to Duncan Phyfe although without documentation. The writing table used by George Washington dates from the period when Federal Hall on Wall St was the nation's capital.

The New York City Art Commission occupies the *attic floor,* once an apartment for the housekeeper. Consisting of ten unsalaried commissioners plus the mayor, the Art Commission acts as a watchdog of aesthetic quality, reviewing designs for bridges, monuments and arches, schools, courthouses, and other public buildings as well as art works placed in parks and other public places.

N. of City Hall in the park facing Chambers St is the former **New York County Courthouse** (1872; John Kellum; DL), known familiarly as the **"Tweed" Courthouse** because William M. "Boss" Tweed and his "Ring" embezzled impressive sums of money from the city during its construction.

History. In 1858 the city Board of Supervisors agreed to a preliminary expenditure of $250,000 for a much-needed new criminal courthouse, the cornerstone of which was laid in Dec 1861. By the time the building reached completion ten years later, the cost had risen to somewhere between $12 million and $13 million—the exact figures were concealed during the ensuing scandal—of which an estimated ⅔ ended up in the pockets of Tweed and his cronies. They hired contractors who padded their accounts and then kicked back to the politicians most of the difference between what the work actually cost and what the city paid for it. Thus a plasterer named Andrew J. Garvey appeared in the records as receiving $45,966.89 for a single day's work, a sum which earned him the title, "Prince of Plasterers." Although the Tweed Ring fleeced the city in other ways, it was the disclosure of cost overruns during the construction of the courthouse that precipitated Tweed's exposure, downfall, and ultimate imprisonment.

Tweed, who rose from humble beginnings to wealth, power, and fame through the machinery of Tammany Hall, the most powerful organization in Democratic Party politics, never held a high city office himself, but was a kingmaker who profited from friends in high places. His fall was swift and spectacular, and he died in prison (1876), poor and friendless.

EXTERIOR. The building is a three-story, flat-roofed structure of Massachusetts marble, formerly white but now weathered to a dark gray. In the rear is an addition (1880) by Leopold Eidlitz. In the mid-1970s the courthouse was to be razed but the high cost of demolition plus resistance by preservationists saved it, although as a symbol of municipal graft it hardly endeared itself to those in power. The beautiful rotunda has been restored and a grand stairway on the Chambers St side leading to what was originally the main entrance (removed 1955) is currently being reconstructed.

Continue through the park to *Chambers St* which runs along the N. side of the courthouse and is named after John Chambers, an 18C lawyer and official of Trinity Church.

Turn left and walk toward Broadway. The former **Emigrant Industrial Savings Bank Building** (1909–12; Raymond Almirall; DL) at 51 Chambers St between Broadway and Elk St is a familiar though unwelcome place for drivers who come here to ante up their parking fines. Founded in 1850 by the trustees of the Irish Emigrant Society to protect the financial resources of Irish immigrants and to teach those without such resources the virtues of thrift and industry, the bank succeeded from the outset, gradually widening its dealings to include people of many nationalities. The large oval stained glass skylights whose themes represent aspects of economy are perhaps as appropriate for the injudicious parker as they were for the arriving immigrant.

On the N.E. corner of Broadway and Chambers St at 280 Broadway is the former **Sun Building,** originally the A. T. Stewart Marble Palace (1846; Trench & Snook; DL), once an elegant department store proudly leading architectural fashion, from

1917 to 1950 the home of the *New York Sun,* now a city-owned office building. The bronze clock above Broadway at the corner of Chambers St bears the motto of the newspaper, "The Sun It Shines For All."

History. Alexander Turney Stewart did for merchandising at the upper end of the economic scale what F. W. Woolworth did at the lower end. He brought together many different types of merchandise under a single roof, selling clothing in fixed sizes at fixed prices and freeing shoppers from the uncertainties and psychological demands of bargaining. In addition Stewart shrewdly saw the need to make shopping itself an entertainment, and to that end built the Marble Palace.

EXTERIOR. The building is an early example of the Italianate style which replaced the Greek Revival style as the dominant architectural fashion in the city. Contemporaries admired the store for its palatial dimensions, beautiful white marble facade, and elegant details (for example the classical masks in the keystones over the second-story windows). When the building opened, there were slender Corinthian columns on the ground floor with large display windows between them. The dimensions of the windows were so large that Stewart had to order the plate glass from France. By 1862, however, fashionable society had begun shopping further uptown and Stewart moved up Broadway to a new palace, the Cast Iron Palace, between 9th and 10th Sts, retaining the Chambers St store as a warehouse. Stewart eventually built himself a mansion on Fifth Ave at 34th St, a $3 million extravagance that set the standard for younger generations of millionaires.

Look across Broadway to the N.W. corner of Broadway and Chambers St and the carefully restored BROADWAY CHAMBERS BUILDING (1901; Cass Gilbert), 277 Broadway, the first New York office building of the architect who later built the Woolworth Building a stone's throw to the south.

From the corner of Broadway and Chambers St, turn around and walk E. on Chambers St to Centre St. At 31 Chambers St (N.W. corner of Centre St) is the **Surrogate's Court,** also known as the **Hall of Records** (1899–1911; John R. Thomas, 1899–1901; Horgan & Slattery, 1901–11; DL). Like the Woolworth Building with which it is roughly contemporary, the Surrogate's Court was built as a monument, and the impulse of civic pride that inspired the design is expressed in the elegance and costliness of both the facade and the interior. Originally it was intended as a repository for municipal records and as a surrogate's court administering trusts and guardianships, but since the building has been used more and more by the court, the name was officially changed from Hall of Records to Surrogate's Court in 1963.

EXTERIOR. The facade is lavishly ornamented with sculpture appropriate to the building's first function as a guardian of historical records. Flanking the Chambers St entrance are two sculptural groups by Philip Martiny: *New York in Revolutionary Times* represented by a proud female figure wearing a helmet, and (right) *New York in Its Infancy,* a woman wearing a feathered headdress. The frieze above the portico bears eight figures representing prominent early New Yorkers including Peter Stuyvesant (third from left) and De Witt Clinton (third from right). The cornice figures facing Reade and Centre Sts represent the arts, professions, and industries.

INTERIOR (open during business hours). The walls of the Foyer are faced by yellow-toned Siena marble. Above the doorways at each end of the rooms are sculptural groups by Albert Weinert (E. door), *The Consolidation of Greater New York* and (W. door), *Recording the Purchase of Manhattan Island*. On the ceiling is a mosaic by William de Leftwich Dodge, a Paris-trained muralist; it is organized into a series of panels depicting Greek and Egyptian deities and includes corner figures of Greek gods with functions presumably appropriate to those of the building: Themis (Justice), Erinys (Retribution), Penthos (Sorrow), and Ponos (Labor). On the end walls are mosaics also by Dodge with the unimaginative but descriptive titles *Searching the Records* and *Widows and Orphans Pleading Before the Judge of the Surrogate's Court*. Above the central landing of the grand staircase in the lobby is a stucco relief of the seal of New York City upon whose shield are the sails of a windmill; between the sails are beavers and flour barrels, both important elements of the early economy of the colony. A sailor and an Indian support the shield which rests on a horizontal laurel branch bearing the date 1664, the year the British captured New Amsterdam and named it New York. Also of interest are the fifth floor *North and South Court Rooms*.

At the N.W. corner of Reade and Centre Sts stood the Manhattan Water Tank (demolished during the early years of the 20C), originally made of iron plates and eventually enclosed within a building. It was built by Aaron Burr's Manhattan Water Company, a business venture whose real aim seems to have been to secure a charter for the Manhattan Bank, now part of the Chase Manhattan Bank. The water came from the nearby Collect Pond (now drained) and was brought through wooden pipes, samples of which may be seen at the New-York Historical Society.

The **Civic Center,** focus of the municipal government, consists of a collection of buildings centered around Foley Square, N. of City Hall. The location was chosen almost by default, the boggy ground making the neighborhood unsuitable for high-rise commercial construction and the nearby slums making it unattractive for anything else. The buildings span a period from the turn of the century to recent years and reflect changing architectural fashions.

One of the main landmarks of the Civic Center is the **Municipal Building** (1907-14; McKim, Mead & White; DL) located on the E. side of Centre St at Chambers St, a building designed on the one hand to complement City Hall to its S. and on the other to set the style for other buildings in Foley Square. Applauded as a great civic skyscraper and an example of the Eclectic style at its grandest, it replaces the former Staats-Zeitung Building, home of the most important German language newspaper in the city.

EXTERIOR. Like other early skyscrapers, the Municipal Building is divided horizontally into an elaborate base (impressive to the pedestrian), a simple central tower, and a monumental top planned to take a conspicuous place in the skyline. The central arch in the ground level colonnade formerly straddled Chambers St, forming a monumental gateway to the slums of the Lower East Side, but now acts as a grand entrance to Police Plaza. Above the colonnade are shields with the insignia of Amsterdam, Great Britain, New York City, and New York State. The winged figures flanking the arch represent Guidance (left) and Executive Power (right). The panels over the smaller arches are (left) Civic Duty, which shows the City conferring the law upon its citizens and (right) Civic Pride, depicting the citizens returning the fruits of their labors to the city. Above, relief medallions depict Progress (left) and Prudence (right). Crowning the building is Adolph A. Weinman's 25-ft statue, *Civic Fame* (1913–14), holding a laurel branch and a crown with five turrets symbolizing the five boroughs. Made of copper hammered over a steel frame (like the Statue of Liberty, only gilded), the statue stands 582 ft above the street.

INTERIOR. Walk through the central arch to see the coffered ceiling and the bronze ornamental work inside the lobby. On the S. side of the building is an arcade with a vaulted ceiling, making the subway entrance there one of the most imposing in the city. Among the city offices is the *Marriage Chapel* where couples who wish to get married "at City Hall" take their vows.

Walk through the central arch to **Police Plaza,** one of the few areas within the Civic Center which is the fruit of comprehensive architectural planning. Bounded by the remnants of a former warehouse district on the E., by the entanglements of the Brooklyn Bridge approaches on the S., and by existing municipal buildings and irregular streets in other directions, the site recommended itself to planners only because the city could conveniently purchase its many small land parcels at a reasonable price. In the center of the 3-acre brick plaza stands a sculpture of five interlocking oxidized steel discs by Bernard (Tony) Rosenthal (1971-74), entitled *Five in One* and said to symbolize the five city boroughs. Each disc weighs 15,000 lb and is 20 ft in diameter, and is 10 inches thick. Its installation aroused adverse comment, perhaps because it appeared merely rusty at the time. One correspondent to the *New York Times* likened it to the "rusty propeller of a supertanker," but since then its weathering steel has taken on a dark red-brown color.

Beyond the Municipal Building on the S. side of the plaza is the *Rhinelander Sugar House Prison Window Monument*. During the 18C one of the city's prime industries was distilling rum for which raw sugar was a principal ingredient; the rum, made of sugar or molasses from the West Indies, was exported to Africa in exchange for slaves, a series of transactions known as the "Triangular Trade." The Rhinelander Sugar Warehouse built (1763) on the corner of Rose (formerly the name of the S. extension of Madison St) and Duane Sts served this purpose until the British occupation during the Revolutionary War when it became a prison for American soldiers. The sugar house was razed in 1892 but a window was incorporated in the Rhinelander Building (1895) which stood here until it was demolished (1968) for Police Plaza.

Behind Police Headquarters are five Ionic columns from the Rhinelander Building.

Look N. from the plaza. *Southbridge Towers* (1969; Gruzen & Partners), at Gold, Frankfort, Water, and Fulton Sts, is a middle-income cooperative housing project. The *Beekman Downtown Memorial Hospital* at Spruce, Gold, Beekman, and William Sts (1971; Skidmore, Owings & Merrill) is the major medical facility in the area. Look toward the bridge. N. of it is the *Murry Bergtraum High School for Business Careers* (1976; Gruzen & Partners) at 411 Pearl St on the S. corner of Madison St, whose three cylindrical towers house heavy service equipment which could not be installed in the basement because of the questionable solidity of the old landfill beneath the site. Nearby is a *New York Telephone Company building* (1976) which houses automatic switching equipment. Beneath the plaza is a municipal parking garage with space for 407 cars. *The Avenue of the Finest* runs past the S. side of the plaza, named to honor the city's police force.

Police Headquarters (1973; Gruzen & Partners), dominating the plaza and bounded by Park Row, Pearl, Henry, and New Sts, is a 15-story, $58 million building of brick and reinforced concrete, its ground level containing an auditorium, meeting rooms, and holding and interrogation rooms for prisoners.

Between Police Headquarters and St. Andrew's Church is the *U.S. Courthouse Annex* (1975; Gruzen & Partners) between Park Row, Duane, and Pearl Sts, really two buildings straddling an old power substation of the subway which could not be relocated. The S. part houses the U.S. Attorney's Building; the N. part contains the technologically advanced Federal Metropolitan Correctional Center, whose windows of unbreakable glass have a built-in alarm system.

Between the Annex and St. Andrew's Church is *Cardinal Hayes Place,* named after Patrick Joseph Cardinal Hayes (died 1938), born nearby, altar boy at the previous St. Andrew's Church, Archbishop of New York (from 1919) and cardinal (from 1924).

St. Andrew's Church (1939; Maginnis & Walsh, Robert J. Reiley) stands facing the plaza between Cardinal Hayes Place and Duane St. It bears the coats of arms of Pope Pius XI (central door)

the church was consecrated. The present building replaces an earlier one known as Carroll Hall, which became the first Church of St. Andrew, ministering to the Catholic immigrants pouring into this neighborhood in the mid-19C. In 1900, when the printing industry dominated the area, the church began offering a Printer's Mass at 2:30 A.M. for newsmen and other late-night workers, making St. Andrew's the first work-centered parish in the city.

Continue past the church and the side of the Municipal Building back to Centre St; turn right into **Foley Square,** formed by the intersection of Duane, Lafayette, Pearl, and Centre Sts, the focal point of the Civic Center.

History. Until the beginning of the 19C the square lay beneath the waters of the Collect Pond (from Dutch "kolch" designating any small body of water) or Freshwater Pond. Known for its depth (60 ft) and the purity of its water, the spring-fed pond drained W. into the Hudson and much of the land on that side was low marshland called the Lispenard Meadows. In the 18C tanners settled in the area because the water supply was essential to their business, but in 1730 Anthony Rutgers, a landowner, petitioned the city for the swamp and pond which he then began to drain, to the distress of the tanners. The city gained title to the pond in 1791. In 1796 John Fitch tested a prototypical steamboat on its waters, a vessel driven by paddlewheels and screw propellers. Though successful technologically, the boat never achieved the fame of Robert Fulton's *Clermont* which steamed up the Hudson in 1807, and Fitch eventually abandoned his craft in the pond and left the city.

Around 1800 the city began filling the pond and draining the Lispenard Meadows. By 1807 cartloads of dirt and garbage were being dumped into the pond; they eventually formed a foul-smelling island some 12–15 ft above the water. In 1809 Canal St was laid out and a sewer built beneath it to drain the springs which formerly fed the pond. By 1811 the pond had disappeared altogether.

The stench, the sinking of land still undermined by springs, and the encroachment of the dry goods trade into nearby streets drove out people who could afford to live elsewhere. By the early 19C it was a slum, inhabited by freed slaves, immigrants, and the undifferentiated poor. By 1840 it had become notorious for crime, its worst section called FIVE POINTS at the intersection of Park, Baxter, and Worth Sts. The area was so filthy that it offended even the experienced eyes and benumbed olfactory organs of native New Yorkers. Houses, mostly of wood, were rotten and overcrowded, with people packed into windowless basements or relegated to "back buildings" hastily erected in dark rear yards by eager landlords.

A central feature of Five Points was the Old Brewery, on part of the site of the present County Court House, once used for making beer but by the mid-19C the dwelling of some 1200 people. In 1852 the Ladies' Home Missionary Society bought it and eventually replaced it with the Five Points Mission and House of Industry, a nursery school with about 400 students and boarders. Before demolishing the building, however, the missionary ladies with remarkable skill at public relations opened the brewery for tours, allowing middle class visitors who were becoming increasingly curious about the seamier side of life to see just how the poor lived.

Foley Square is named after Thomas F. Foley (1852-1925), a Tammany politician considered a kingmaker though never an important officeholder himself. He was born in the Williamsburg section of Brooklyn and entered politics by way of the saloon business, moving his saloons closer to the center of the city as he moved closer to the center of power. Foley was influential in helping Al Smith become governor and in keeping William Randolph Hearst, who had attacked him in his newspapers, from becoming either governor or a U.S. senator.

Walk along the E. side of Foley Square, whose buildings have been built up so that their friezes match that of the Municipal Building. The **United States Courthouse** (1933-36; Cass Gilbert; completed by Cass Gilbert, Jr.; DL) at the S.E. corner of Pearl St is joined to its Annex in Police Plaza by a pair of aerial bridges. It is one of the last neoclassical office towers built in the city and one of the first U.S. government sponsored skyscrapers. It has a gold top like the Municipal Building and a heroic portico (50-ft Corinthian columns) facing Foley Square like the County Courthouse to its north. The building houses the U.S. District Court and the Federal Court of Appeals.

On the N.E. corner of Pearl St at Foley Square is the **New York County Courthouse** (1913–27; Guy Lowell; DL) home of the New York State Supreme Court. Guy Lowell, a Boston architect, won an architectural competition for the building with plans for a circular structure, later altered to the present hexagonal plan. The grand portico in the Roman Corinthian style is three columns deep and about 100 ft wide. The carving in the tympanum above the portico (sculptor Frederick W. Allen) shows Justice with Courage and Wisdom. Atop the pediment are statues representing Law (center) flanked by Truth and Equity. The niches of the porch shelter two female figures (by Philip Martiny) that were removed from the Surrogate's Court on Chambers St. The figure with the shield and city coat of arms (left) is Authority, while her companion (right), resting her foot upon a bundle of records, represents Justice.

INTERIOR. In the center of the building is a saucer dome supported on Corinthian columns of Tennessee marble. Ceiling frescoes by Attilio Pusterla depict famous monuments in the history of jurisprudence. The central oculus, originally open to the sky, is now shielded by glass against the elements and, presumably, the pigeons. Beneath the dome is a circular design in colored marble with bronze figures representing the signs of the zodiac.

On the W. side of Foley Square the *Jacob K. Javits Federal Building* and the *Customs Courthouse* (1967; Alfred Easton Poor, Kahn & Jacobs; Eggers & Higgins) at 26 Federal Plaza stand between Duane and Worth Sts, facing a plaza paved with old Belgian blocks salvaged from the city streets.

The smaller cubelike building houses the Customs Court; the taller with its odd-looking windows has U.S. government offices.

On the N. edge of the square stand two buildings in the Art Deco style of the 1930s. The *State of New York Building* (1930; Sullivan W. Jones & William E. Haugaard) on the N.E. corner of Worth and Centre Sts has a classic frieze and sculptured cornice. The former *Department of Health Building,* now the *Health, Hospitals, and Sanitation Departments Building* (1935; Charles B. Meyers) on the N.W. corner of the same intersection bears a molding inscribed with the names of great men of medicine.

Continue past the front of the building to Lafayette St and turn right (N.). Walk N. to Catherine Lane, named for Catherine Rutgers, née De Peyster. The next street to the N. is Leonard St, named for Leonard Lispenard, whose father owned the Lispenard Meadows through which these streets were cut. Anthony Lispenard named three streets after his sons, Leonard, Thomas, and Anthony, but the latter lost out when Anthony St was renamed Worth St after Mexican War hero William Jenkins Worth.

Between Catherine Lane and Leonard St is the former **New York Life Insurance Co. Building** (1870; Griffith Thomas; remodeled in 1895; McKim, Mead & White; DL), whose front is at 346 Broadway. The two clock towers originally had cupolas and a great iron globe with an eagle on top once graced the Broadway entrance. The first 12 floors hold offices for assorted municipal

departments while the **Clocktower** (enter from 108 Leonard St)
houses galleries of the Institute for Art and Urban Resources.

The Clocktower. 108 Leonard St, 13th floor (Broadway), New York 10013. Tel:
784-2084. Open Wed–Sat 1–6; closed major holidays; closed mid-June–Aug.
Requested donation. Catalogues. Poetry workshops, performances. No restau-
rant. No wheelchair access.
    SUBWAY: IRT Lexington Ave local (train 6) to Canal St. BMT Broadway local
(N, or R train) or Nassau St local (J train) to Canal St. BUS: M1 or M6 via
Broadway.

The Institute for Art and Urban Resources since 1971 has devoted
itself to salvaging abandoned buildings (or parts thereof) and
using them as studio and exhibition space for new and experimental artists. The Clocktower mounts about a dozen shows
yearly as well as music and poetry readings (telephone for
schedule).

One flight above the gallery the mechanism of the largest
weight-driven clock in the city ticks off the hours. In 1980 after
several decades of disrepair, the clock was returned to service by
two city employees, Eric Reiner and Marvin Schneider, who
devoted their lunch hours to the task and still rewind and reset it
every week.

Continue N. on *Lafayette St*, named for the Marquis de Lafayette,
who aided the country in the Revolutionary War and returned to
New York for a bangup welcome celebration in 1824. At 60
Lafayette St between Leonard and Franklin Sts is the **Family
Court of New York City** (1975; Haines Lundberg Waehler),
shaped like a cube partially sheered off on one surface. A statue
(1972–76) entitled *Three Forms* by Roy Gussow stands before
the entrance.

Across the street and parking lot (100 Centre St between
Leonard and White Sts) looms the bulk of the New York City
Criminal Courts Building (1939; Harvey Wiley Corbett; rede-
signed 1986, The Gruzen Partnership), formerly the Manhattan
Detention Center for Men, better known as "The Tombs."

The name originated with an earlier prison (1836–38), officially known by the
more reassuring name "The Halls of Justice," and constructed in the Egyptian
Revival style with trapezoidal windows, lotus columns, and emblems of the sun
god. The old prison acquired the name "The Tombs" partly because of the
funereal associations of the architectural style and partly because of its dismal
function and appearance, made even gloomier by the site—a hollow so deep
that the massive prison walls hardly rose above the level of Broadway some
hundred yards to the west. This "Tombs" served as the city jail until 1893
when a second prison, Romanesque Revival in style but still called "The
Tombs" replaced it. The present building is the third generation of penal
institutions on the site.

Built in the Art Moderne or Art Deco style of the 1930s with
ziggurat-shaped towers and cast aluminum detail, it is laid out in
four main blocks with the northernmost containing the prison
cells while the others have offices and courtrooms.

North of the parking area at 111 Centre St on the S.W. corner
of White St is the *Municipal and Civil Court Building* (1960;
William Lescaze & Matthew Del Gaudio), a plain white marble

cube with a vertical stripe of windows down the S. facade. On the E. side are granite reliefs (c. 1959) representing *Law* by William Zorach; on the W. facade is Joseph Kiselewski's relief (1960) depicting *Justice* flanked by an infant and a serpent.

Walk N. to White St, turn left and walk one block W. to the former **Engine Company Number 31** (1895; Napoleon Le Brun; DL) at 87 Lafayette St on the N.E. corner of White St. Built like a French Renaissance château with a steep slate roof, a corner turret, assorted dormers, and crestings of metal and stone, the building evokes a time when firefighting was a dangerous sport. In its day this firehouse was a showcase of technology, with automatic stall latches that released the horses at the sound of the alarm. Today it houses social services for residents of Chinatown.

5 Chinatown and Little Italy

SUBWAY: IRT Lexington Ave local (train 6) to Canal St. Walk four blocks E. on Canal St and two blocks S. on Mott St to Chatham Square. BMT Broadway local or express (N or R train) to Canal St. Walk E. five blocks to Mott St and S. two blocks to Chatham Square.

BUS: M1 or M6 (downtown) via Broadway to Worth St; walk E. to Chatham Square (five blocks, counting on the N. side). M15 (downtown) via 2nd Ave to Chatham Sq. M101 or M102 (downtown) via Lexington Ave / Bowery to Chatham Square.

For the visitor, Chinatown—formerly bounded by Canal, Worth, and Baxter Sts and the Bowery (an area today known as Old Chinatown) but now spilling over into the Lower East Side and Little Italy—is an exotic outpost of the Far East, its narrow, crowded streets overhung with signs bearing incomprehensible messages in Chinese characters, its busy sidewalks clogged by sacks of rice, crates of eggs, and cartons of unfamiliar foodstuffs. But for those who live in Chinatown (about 125,000 in ''old'' Chinatown, a much larger population estimated as high as 300,000 within the constantly shifting boundaries of the new, larger community) Chinatown is a ghetto, plagued by poverty, overcrowding, and physical deterioration; it is in many ways similar to other earlier immigrant areas on the Lower East Side, Hell's Kitchen, and Williamsburg, for example.

Most Chinatown housing and business space is substandard, but rents are rising, propelled by the population explosion which has taken place since 1965, when immigration laws were liberalized with the annulling of the Exclusion Acts of 1882. With this influx of primarily urban immigrants—many from Shanghai, Hong Kong, and most recently Vietnam—the tuberculosis rate has soared, reaching a level 100 times that of the rest of the country, and crime has risen sharply, though not in ways that affect the ordinary visitor.

Unlike the city's other ghettos, where physical deterioration is matched by corrosion of the spirit, Chinatown has thriving businesses that attract investors from here and abroad, while its

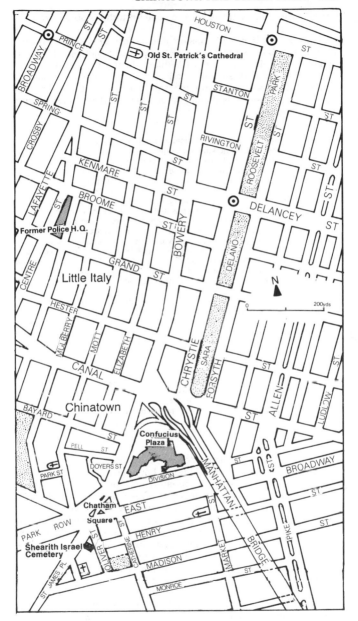

social institutions actively seek to cope with the problems of new immigrants.

Sunday is Chinatown's busiest day as former residents return to visit and Chinese from all over the greater metropolitan area come to shop. It is at its most brilliant during the Chinese New Year celebration (first full moon after Jan 21), when masked dragon dancers parade through the streets amid the din and sulphurous fumes of exploding firecrackers, and restaurants offer festive banquets.

Chinese Restaurants: In greater Chinatown it has been estimated that there are 300–400 restaurants, making food supply one of Chinatown's most important trades. At the turn of the century when laws in many states prohibited the Chinese from entering occupations in which they would compete with Caucasians, the restaurant business was one of the few available trades (the hand laundry business was another). Early Chinese restaurants catered to a Chinese clientele, generally immigrant men without wives and families, but after 1890 the Caucasian trade became profitable, led by journalists from nearby Park Row. Because most Chinese immigrants were Cantonese—one study estimates that 60% came from Toishan, a suburb of Canton—most restaurants were originally Cantonese in style; but after World War II, as refugees from all over China remained in America, it became possible to find restaurants specializing in the cooking of Shantung, Szechuan, and Hunan. Today the increased migration from Hong Kong, itself an enclave of refugees from all over China, has brought to Chinatown the sophisticated cooking of Hangzhou, Suzhou, and Shanghai.

In addition to regional restaurants, different kinds of Chinese restaurants serve different gustatory needs. First, there are numerous "regular" Chinese restaurants, serving a complete menu. For lunch, there are dim sum parlors, offering what can best be described as dumplings—noodle doughs wrapped in various shapes around meat or vegetable stuffings and either steamed or fried. Some dim sum restaurants have no menu; the waiters carry around trays with the dishes and the diner simply asks for (or points at) what looks appealing. Another lunch or snack restaurant is the noodle shop, where the staple is noodles—in soup or with meat and vegetables or steamed fish. Noodle shops, usually simple in appearance and inexpensive, draw a Chinese clientele. Rice houses—small, economical, lunch-counter restaurants—offer rice topped with meat and vegetables and also serve plain, home-style fare. Coffee shops, selling Chinese buns, almond cookies, steamed sponge cake, and some sweet types of dim sum, have become convenient places for a snack.

Begin at **Chatham Square.** Before population pressures caused Chinatown to overflow its traditional boundaries, Chatham Square marked the border between Chinatown on the W. and the Lower East Side to the east. Park Row, St. James Place, Oliver St, East Broadway, Catherine St, Division St, the Bowery, Doyers St, Mott St, and Worth St all empty into this congested intersection. On one of the traffic islands is the *Kimlau War Memorial* (1962; Poy G. Lee), an arch with a pagoda-style top dedicated to Chinese-Americans who died in the U.S. armed services. On another traffic island E. of the arch is a branch of the Manhattan Savings Bank (1977; George W. Clark Assocs.), brightly painted and topped with a traditional curved roof. Most of the buildings in Chinatown are loft buildings or Old Law Tenements, and only recently has there been an effort to make Chinatown architecturally "Chinese."

On the E. side of Chatham Square is a neighborhood once

considered part of the Lower East Side, now part of an expanded Chinatown. During the early years of the 19C, however, it was a prosperous area, home of successful merchants and ships' captains, a few of whose homes and churches still remain.

Cross the square to St. James Place and follow it a block to James St, barely more than an alley, whose name recalls the otherwise forgotten James Desbrosses, who had a distillery on the East River during the 18C. At 32 James St between St. James Place and Madison St is the **Church of St. James** (1835–37; attrib. Minard Lafever; DL), a severe brownstone Greek Revival building. The facade with its two central columns placed between flanking walls is ornamented only by rosettes on the door lintels and a carved scroll and anthemion above the central doorway. Originally the church served Irish immigrants but today the congregation is largely Spanish-speaking. The building has developed structural weaknesses, but members of the congregation and community are trying to raise money to preserve it.

A plaque on the doors of the Hall of St. James School across the street announces that Alfred E. Smith, who was baptized at St. James Church, received his entire formal education here. Smith, born at 174 South St and raised on Oliver St, rose from these lowly beginnings to become a social reformer, four-time governor of the state, and Democratic candidate for President in 1928. He is also remembered in the *Governor Alfred E. Smith Houses* (1952; Eggers & Higgins), between South and Madison Sts, Catherine Slip, and St. James and Robert F. Wagner, Sr. Places, a public housing project.

Return along St. James Place. Between James and Oliver Sts is the small, rather forlorn **First Shearith Israel Graveyard** (1683–1828; DL), the earliest surviving burial ground of the city's first Jewish congregation ("Remnant of Israel"). An earlier cemetery, then outside the city, was consecrated in 1656 on a piece of land granted to the Jews of New Amsterdam by Peter Stuyvesant, but its location is no longer known. The earliest stone (1683) of the present graveyard marks the grave of one Benjamin Bueno de Mesquita. During the Revolutionary War Gen. Charles Lee placed several guns in "the Jew Burying Ground" as part of the city's fortifications; 18 Revolutionary soldiers and patriots are buried here, among them Gershom Mendes Seixas, minister of the congregation who removed the Torah scrolls to Stratford, Connecticut, during the British occupation. As the congregation moved uptown following the general development of the city, it established two other cemeteries, one at W. 11th St and another at W. 21st St.

Continue along St. James Place to Oliver St and turn right. Follow it to 12 Oliver St at the N.W. corner of Henry St. The **Mariners' Temple** (1844; attrib. Minard Lafever; DL), originally built as the Oliver Street Baptist Church, was bought by the Mariners' Temple in 1863, serving as a social mission for seamen, immigrants, and later, Bowery derelicts. Today its congregation is largely Chinese. The Mariners' Temple, roughly contemporary with the St. James Church nearby, is constructed of stone laid in random courses, plastered over (where visible to the street), and grooved with false joints to give it the smooth appearance characteristic of the Greek Revival style.

Either walk back to East Broadway, turn right and begin walking toward the Manhattan Bridge or take the following diversion.

Diversion. Follow Henry St to Catherine St and turn right; continue two blocks to Monroe St. The huge housing project bounded by Catherine, Market, Monroe, and Cherry Sts is **Knickerbocker Village** (1934; Van Wart & Ackerman) built during the Depression to replace a slum. Unfortunately the rental fees of $12.50 per room per month priced the apartments out of reach of the former slum dwellers who then had to find other slum housing. Despite its high density—500 units per acre as opposed to the average New York City Public Housing figure of 80–100 units per acre—the project is well-maintained and successful.

Follow Monroe St to Market St and turn left. The *51 Market Street House* (1824; DL) between Monroe and Madison Sts, is one of the few remaining Federal houses in the city, unusual for its four stories. The main floor is raised above street level over a high basement, an architectural feature inherited from the Dutch, whose houses in Holland were elevated against the threat of flood. In New York this raised first floor made possible a basement entrance to the kitchen, sorely needed in a city generally lacking service alleys, and conferred added elegance upon the first floor entrance. The stairway leading to the main door, called a "stoop" (from the Dutch "stoep"), has a wrought-iron railing, a typical detail of the Federal style.

Continue up Market St to the N.W. corner of Henry St. The Catherine Market was established in 1786 between what is now Market St and Catherine St. The **First Chinese Presbyterian Church,** formerly the *Church of Sea and Land* (1817; DL) at 61 Henry St, was built to serve seamen on land donated by Henry Rutgers. Constructed of local building materials, it has brownstone quoins and trim, rubble masonry, steep gabled ends, and a square tower. The tall side windows with pointed arches are unusual in a church predating the Gothic Revival period by about two decades.

Nearby, between Market and Catherine Sts at 48 Henry St, is the *Chinatown Mission* (1830), originally built as a subsidiary chapel of Trinity Church and later the Church of Our Savior. Now part of the social ministry of the Episcopal Church, the mission is housed in three Federal houses, of which the central one is the best preserved.

Walk back to Catherine St, turn right and continue a block to East Broadway. Turn right again and walk toward the viaduct of the Manhattan Bridge.

The *Chatham Square Branch of the New York Public Library* (33 East Broadway), once the intellectual territory of Jewish immigrants, now circulates a large selection of Chinese-language books. At 53 East Broadway is the New Asia Book Store, long a source of literature from mainland China. Hoolok at 54 East Broadway is one of Chinatown's oldest noodle shops.

Continue along East Broadway to the *Sun Sing Chinese Theater* at 75 East Broadway under the approach to the Manhattan Bridge, Chinatown's opera house until 1950, when it was converted to a movie theater. Many of the films are imported from Hong Kong and often have romantic and melodramatic plots; a few sample titles suggest their flavor: *Poison Rose and the Bodyguard, The Lotus Triangle, Who Will Be My Boyfriend?* plain, unadulterated *Passion,* and the cryptically titled *Fish and Guts.*

Turn left on Market St just before the bridge and walk a block to Division St, so named because it marked the division between the farms of James De Lancey and Henry Rutgers in pre-Revolutionary New York. At one time the area now occupied by the street was used as a rope walk, where strands of hemp were twisted into rope. The area under the bridge, now a parking lot, is slated for revitalization as a shopping mall.

Turn left on Division St. On the N. side of the street is **Confucius Plaza** (1976; Horowitz & Chun), the only new housing built in Chinatown between the 1960s and the early 1980s. The project includes an elementary school and 764 apartments, 20% of which are reserved as low income housing. Today most of the residents are elderly.

Continue along Division St past the apartment complex. Oddly enough, Taiwanese sculptor Liu Shih's benign-looking *statue of Confucius* facing Chatham Square at Division St and the Bowery aroused a flurry of controversy when presented (1976) to the city by the Chinese Consolidated Benevolent Association. At the time Confucius's reputation had sunk low in the People's Republic of China for the traditional, authoritarian nature of his teachings, and Chinatown residents who followed the party line found the philosopher an unsuitable representative of China's cultural heritage.

Continue around Confucius Plaza, past the shops facing the Bowery; cross the Bowery at the traffic light opposite Bayard St. At 65 Bayard St, near Elizabeth St is the *Chinatown Ice Cream Factory,* whose spectrum of flavors runs from prosaic vanilla to exotic lichee, red bean, green tea, and ginger (open daily, 12 noon to midnight; tel: 577-9701).

Return to the Bowery; turn right and walk downtown one block. On the S.W. corner of the Bowery and Pell St (18 Bowery) is the **Edward Mooney house** (c. 1785; DL), the city's oldest row house. Mooney, a meat wholesaler and amateur racehorse breeder, built the house on land formerly owned by Tory James De Lancey, who forfeited his property and fled the country at the end of the Revolutionary War.

Dating from the beginning of the Federal period, the house is Georgian in its proportions (three full stories with a gambrel roof) and in its details: the door hood, the lintels with splayed keystones, the quarter-round and round-headed windows facing Pell St. The generous number of windows reveals Mooney's wealth, since glass, manufactured in the middle colonies only after about 1740, was an expensive commodity.

Three blocks N. at the intersection of the Bowery and Hester St is a handsome outdoor mural (side wall of the theater) entitled *Wall of Respect for the Working People of Chinatown.* It depicts Chinese workers laboring as peasants in their native land and then working in Chinatown in the garment and food service industries. The Chinese characters on the tablet read "Together we have strength." Return to Pell St.

Turn into Pell St, named after John Pell, a prosperous butcher in pre-Revolutionary days. At 10 Pell St is the Chin Family Association. Family or clan associations, or tongs, were originally formed of people with the same surname. They were especially important during the early days for male immigrants without families who found themselves isolated and unfamiliar with English and local customs. Later they became social agencies for families as well, providing for the aged and for widows, acting as employment brokerages, and organizing social functions. At 13 Pell St is the headquarters of the Hip Sing Association.

The Chinese, like other immigrant groups, drawn together by shared customs and language as well as shared problems, became a close-knit community; they formed benevolent organizations to help them adapt to an alien culture. These associations also had commercial functions as businessmen from one association banded together to enhance their commercial strength. The two most powerful associations in Chinatown are said to be the Hip Sing Association and the On Leong Merchant Association.

At 20 Pell St one floor up is the *Oriental Culture Enterprises Company,* which sells newspapers and magazines, books from China, and English-Chinese dictionaries and cookbooks. Also available are Chinatown's ten daily Chinese newspapers, whose opinions span a wide political spectrum. These journals which discourage assimilation and preach the superiority of Chinese culture are read by the many residents of Chinatown who are literate in Chinese only and have therefore a considerable conservative influence on the community. Also on sale is the *People's Daily* (in English), flown in every day from Peking.

Turn left into **Doyers Street,** named after Anthony H. Doyer, a distiller. The crooked, narrow street was originally a cart lane leading to the distillery at the S. end.

The bend in Doyers St was once known as "Bloody Angle," recalling a tong war around the turn of the century during which the Hip Sings battled the On Leongs. The tongs, first established in Imperial China to fight the Manchu dynasty, were transported to New York as early as the 1890s, and while shedding their political content maintained their clandestine character. Initially involved in vice, especially prostitution, gambling, and opium dealing and later in legitimate business, they eventually came into conflict with one another. In the 1920s tong wars, fought mainly by hired assassins wielding either guns or cleavers (hence the term "hatchetman"), were luridly exploited by the American press, and for years Chinatown bore the image of a place of sinister crimes and exotic sins. Eventually the tongs evolved into merchant associations some of which, according to students of the area, once again have connections with the underworld, using the profits from illicit enterprises to finance legal businesses and hiring youth gangs to police the area and protect tong-operated gambling dens.

On the site of the present Post Office at 6 Doyers St stood the Chatham Club where Irving Berlin, whose name at the time was Israel Baline, worked as a waiter. Across the street at 5—7 Doyers St is the site of the original Chinese Opera House, which stood here until 1910 when it was acquired for a mission run by Tom Noonan, an ex-convict who dispensed charity to the Bowery bums until his death in 1935.

Follow Doyers St to the Bowery. On the S.W. corner of the intersection is a small Federal house remaining from 1809 when Anthony Doyer built it as one of four, today recognizable only by the spacing of the windows and its diminutive size.

Turn right and walk to **Mott Street,** named after Joseph Mott, another prosperous pre-Revolutionary butcher. Mott also ran a tavern at what is now 143rd St and Eighth Ave, which served as Washington's headquarters before he moved into the Morris-Jumel Mansion.

Turn right into Mott St, Chinatown's main street. At 8 Mott St stood (c. 1875) New York's first Chinese mercantile establishment run by one Wo Kee. Upstairs nowadays is the **Chinese Museum.**

The Chinese Museum. 8 Mott St (Chatham Square), New York 10013. Tel: 964-1542. Open daily 10–6. Admission charge. No food, no telephone, no gift shop. Not accessible to wheelchairs.

This small museum, behind a video arcade and up a steep flight of stairs, offers oddly assorted exhibits including a Buddha, a rickshaw, costumes, incense, calligraphy, and an 18-ft mechanical dragon.

The identity of New York's first Chinese resident is not known, but theorists have suggested either a Buddhist monk who arrived in the late 18C or a man brought in 1808 by John Jacob Astor along with an illegal cargo of furs. In 1847 the junk *Kee Ying* arrived bearing a cargo of silk from Canton and a crew of 35 Chinese, some of whom seem to have remained. Then in the 1850s Chinese began arriving from San Francisco where they had worked in the goldfields or on the transcontinental railroad; most of them found work making cigars, carrying advertising signs, or running laundries. As racial hostilities increased on the West Coast, more Chinese immigrants came east, settling in the Chinatown area, known then as the Plow and Harrow district after a tavern of that name founded in the 17C. Wo Kee's shop and others like it that soon opened on Mott St became sources of Chinese groceries and medicines as well as social centers where on Sundays immigrants—generally men without families—could receive mail, socialize, and eat in familiar restaurants.

Continue along Mott St. Just beyond Park St is the **Church of the Transfiguration** (1801; DL) at 25 Mott St, built as the Zion Episcopal Church and now serving a Roman Catholic parish. Like the nearby First Chinese Presbyterian Church on Henry St, this modest rubblestone building belongs to the Georgian tradition with its triangular pediment, simple tower, and unusual pointed arch windows. The copper-clad spire was added in 1868.

Walk W. on Park St to Mulberry St. **Columbus Park** (opened 1897), facing Mulberry St between Bayard and Worth Sts, represents a triumph for early social reformers who spurred passage of the Small Parks Act in 1887. This park, formerly known as Mulberry Bend Park, replaced Mulberry Bend, which Jacob Riis called "the worst pigsty of all," a violent slum where as a police reporter he was called weekly to record shootings or stabbings. On the E. side of Mulberry St in a former schoolhouse (second floor), is the *Chinatown History Project.*

The Chinatown History Project. 70 Mulberry St (near Bayard St), New York 10013. Tel: 619-4785. Open Fri and Sun 12–5. No restaurant, no restrooms, no gift shop. No wheelchair access. Occasional tours of Chinatown, changing exhibits of a historical nature.

Return to Mott St and continue north. The telephone booths with pagoda tops were inspired by similar ones in San Francisco.

Some of Chinatown's larger vegetable and fish stores line Mott St, which still remains the East Coast supply center of Chinese foodstuffs. The *Lung Fong Chinese Bakery* at 41 Mott St is typical of many in this area, with an inventory of Chinese sweets, cookies, buns, and steamed pastries—many unfamiliar to western palates.

At 62 Mott St is the headquarters of the **Chinese Consolidated Benevolent Association,** the oldest and best known of Chinatown's leadership groups, an umbrella organization coordinating about 60 family, trade, recreational, tong, regional, and dialect associations. Until recent years, the organization functioned as a kind of local government that spoke for the community in the larger spheres of city politics. Today, as other agencies have been created, its influence has diminished. The *Chinese School* (opened 1915) in the same building has worked to transmit and preserve Chinese language and culture, and now enrolls about 1500 students.

Continue along Mott St to Canal Street. On the S.W. corner of the intersection is the *Chinese Merchants' Association* (1958) at 85 Mott St. The building, an architectural melange of east and west, houses an organization that evolved from the On Leong tong.

Canal St, once the N. border of "old" Chinatown, has recently seen the resurgence of the garment industry although clothing manufacture is declining throughout the city as a whole. Many loft buildings here are leased by apparel contractors who hire Oriental workers, predominantly female immigrants whose inability to speak English bars them from other jobs. It is estimated that in good times the 500 garment factories on Canal St and along Centre and Elizabeth Sts employ some 30,000 women, more than 75% of the employed Chinese women in the neighborhood.

Three blocks W. on Canal St, at the intersection of Centre St, the headquarters of the former Golden Pacific National Bank (1983; George Rycar) now the **Hongkong and Shanghai Bank,** is one of Chinatown's newer architectural attractions, vividly decorated in blue, red, gold, and green, and styled with sweeping tile roofs and galleries. The former Golden Pacific National Bank, once the pride of Chinatown, collapsed in 1985, causing economic hardship among the families who had deposited their savings in uninsured certificates.

Turn left on Canal St and walk one block W. to MULBERRY STREET, the spine of **Little Italy,** an ethnic enclave dating from the 1880s but whose population dramatically increased between 1890 and 1924 before restrictive laws stanched immigration. Nowadays after decades of decline marked by a dwindling younger population who fled the city for the suburbs leaving behind the aging and the poor, Little Italy is showing signs of gentrification. Before the city killed the proposed Lower Manhattan Expressway in 1968, Little Italy reached its nadir, with sagging real estate values and a withering economic base. However the resurgence of SoHo to the W. with its acronymic offspring LoBro and NoHo, the immigration of Chinese businesses N. of Canal St, and the efforts of community leaders have combined to give Little Italy a new if different kind of life and hope. New cafes and chic restaurants are broadening the area's culinary range while businesses offering Italian imports of high quality and attractive design now stand side by side with the old souvenir and food shops.

Festivals: Little Italy is at its most colorful during two principal festivals when old residents return to mingle with crowds of tourists. The *Feast of St. Anthony of Padua,* held evenings during the first two weeks of June, centers on Sullivan St. The *Feast of San Gennaro* held around the week of September 19, occupies several blocks of Mulberry St. Images of the saints are carried through the streets and at night arcades of lights turn the neighborhood into a carnival, with games of chance, balloons and souvenirs, and such caloric delights as Italian sausage and zeppole, a kind of deep-fried cake dusted with powdered sugar.

Walk N. on Mulberry St. On the corner of Hester St (129 Mulberry St) is UMBERTO'S CLAM HOUSE, once respected for its seafood but notorious as the restaurant where Joe (''Crazy Joey'') Gallo was shot in classic gangland style. While Gallo, alleged head of a Brooklyn Mafia family, was celebrating his 43rd birthday (April 7, 1972), he was gunned down, presumably to avenge the 1971 shooting of rival Joe Colombo at a Columbus Circle rally organized to protest the vilification of Italian-Americans as mafiosi. Although Colombo didn't die immediately his injuries forced him into involuntary retirement.

Continue N. on Mulberry St. At 142 Mulberry St is the Sun Mee Company, a spillover from Chinatown, behind whose walls bean sprouts grow in an artificially induced tropical climate. An Italian restaurant, Paolucci's (149 Mulberry St near Grand St), occupies the original *Stephen van Rensselaer House* (1816; DL) which dates from the Federal period and still retains its original dormers.

Shops near the corner of Grand and Mulberry Sts hark back to an older Little Italy. The Italian Food Center (186 Grand St) sells the olive oil, pasta, and other staples of Italian cooking as well as sandwiches and antipasti to take out. The Alleva Dairy in its old-fashioned, tiled shop at 188 Mulberry St, was founded in 1892 and today makes and sells two tons of cheeses each week. Next door (190 Grand St) Piemonte's Ravioli turns out several varieties of home-made pasta. The devotee of Italian pastries will enjoy Ferrara's (195–201 Grand St) across the street, a landmark in Little Italy (founded in 1892), or the Caffe Roma (385 Broome St, bet. Mulberry / Mott Sts).

Turn left at Grand St. At 165 Grand St on the S.E. corner of Centre St is the *former Odd Fellows Hall* (1847–48; Trench & Snook; DL), an immense brownstone pile with a mansard roof, built as the home of a fraternal and mutual aid society. The second owner of the building, R. Hoe and Co., was an important manufacturer and designer of printing presses. The two top stories were added in 1881–82.

Look W. to the intersection (S.W. corner of Centre and Grand Sts) where one of the few bishop's crook lamp posts remains (see p. 195). North of it at 240 Centre St is the **former Police**

Headquarters (1905–09; Hoppin, Koen & Huntington; DL), set apart from the surrounding tenements and loft buildings by its grand scale and Baroque ornateness. The main entrance on Centre St is embellished by a large New York coat of arms and five statues representing the five boroughs. In the shadowy side streets a few gunsmiths' shops still survive. In 1987 the building was sold to a developer for conversion to luxury condominiums.

Along its E. facade runs CENTRE MARKET PLACE named after the market that once stood here. The diagonal course of the street was dictated by the boundaries of the 18C Bayard farm.

Go N. to Broome St. Turn right and walk east. Down the block between Mott and Elizabeth Sts is *Engine Company 55* of the City Fire Department (1898; R. H. Robertson) at 363 Broome St, a fine Renaissance Revival firehouse.

Walk N. on Mott St three blocks to Prince St. On the S.W. corner is **Old St. Patrick's Convent and Girls' School** (1826; DL), an unusually large Federal building with brownstone trim, its handsome doorway framed with slender Corinthian columns and topped with a fanlight (now filled with stained glass).

Facing Mott St between Prince and Houston Sts is **Old St. Patrick's Cathedral** (1809–15; Joseph F. Mangin; DL), begun in 1809 and finished six years later, the War of 1812 having interrupted the work. Until the present St. Patrick's was completed in 1879, this was the cathedral church of the see of New York. Altered after a fire in 1866, its present appearance only hints at its former self. Above the remaining sheered-off Gothic facade was once a balustrade above which was a central pointed window framed by a broken pediment and topped off by a spire, the oddness of the whole explainable by the fact that this was America's second Gothic Revival church (the first was the Chapel of St. Mary's Seminary in Baltimore dating from 1807) and architect Mangin (designer of classically beautiful City Hall) was experimenting with an unfamiliar style.

At 256–258 Mott St is the former *Fourteenth Ward Industrial School* (1888–89; Vaux and Radford; DL), later the Astor Memorial School, a Gothic Revival reminder of Little Italy's past as an immigrant slum, now converted to cooperative apartments. Industrial schools were established by charitable organizations like the Children's Aid Society to fill the gap between the tenement and the public school, gathering in street children and teaching them the rudiments of citizenship as well as reading and writing.

Walk around to the rear of St. Patrick's on Mulberry St. In the graveyard (usually locked) lie the remains of Pierre Toussaint (1766–1853), born a slave in Haiti, revered for his ministrations to the poor and plague stricken. North of the church on Mulberry St is *St. Michael's Chapel* (1858–59; James Renwick, Jr., and William Rodrigue; DL), a small brownstone and brick church built as a chancery office and now used by Catholics of the Russian Rite.

Continue N. on Mulberry St to Houston St. At 295–309 Lafayette St (filling the block between Mulberry, Houston, Lafayette, and Jersey Sts) is the imposing brick Romanesque Revival **Puck**

Building (1885–86; addition 1892–93; Albert Wagner, Herman Wagner; DL) which long served the printing industry, first as the home of the humor magazine *Puck;* later its 30 large lithographic presses turned out steamboat and railway posters, stationery, and certificates. In 1983 it reopened as a condominium with offices, studios, galleries, and showrooms for graphic designers, filmmakers, photographers, and architects. At the corner of Houston St and above the main entrance on Lafayette St are figures of Puck, top-hatted and cherubic, by Caspar Buberl (died 1889), an immigrant from Bohemia.

The nearest uptown subways are the IRT Lexington Ave local (train 6) at Bleecker and Lafayette Sts and the IND 6th Ave (B, D, or F train) at Broadway and Lafayette St. There are uptown buses on the Bowery (M101 and M102), on Lafayette St (M1) and on West Houston St (M5, via 6th Ave). Downtown buses run on Broadway (M1, M6) and the Bowery (M101 and M102).

6 Lower East Side

SUBWAY: IND (F train) to East Broadway-Canal St.

BUS: M15 via 1st / 2nd Aves. M9 via Avenue B from Union Square to Chatham Square.

Sunday is a good day to visit the Lower East Side, since shops and markets are open and lively; many are closed on Saturday, the Jewish Sabbath. If you are interested in serious shopping, however, go during the week, when the crowds are thinner. Many churches and synagogues in the area are closed except during services because of vandalism.

The Lower East Side has historically been one of the city's poorer neighborhoods. It is short on famous landmarks, fine buildings, museums, and luxury shops (although it is a good place for bargain hunters). Its interest lies in its past, and visiting the area becomes an exercise in urban archaeology: the visitor with a historical imagination must look through layers of peeling paint and beyond shattered windows to see the once-proud synagogue, or try to visualize from the crumbling tenements what life must have been like within their walls for the immigrants who lived and labored there. There are many traces of the past: the jewelry shops near the approach to the Manhattan Bridge remain from a time when the area had an active outdoor diamond market; the stores selling bedclothes on Grand St near Allen St survive from the old bed linens market in the Romanian district. The former presence of the Second Avenue El (elevated train) can be detected from the old powerhouse at the intersection of Allen and Division Sts.

There are also human survivors, some of the early immigrants now elderly and mostly poor, a few still clinging to old-country dress and ways. However, Oriental immigrants are changing the character of the southern sections of the district, and stretches of its northern portion beyond Houston St are undergoing gentrification, either as "Alphabet City" around Avenues A–D or NoHo (North of Houston).

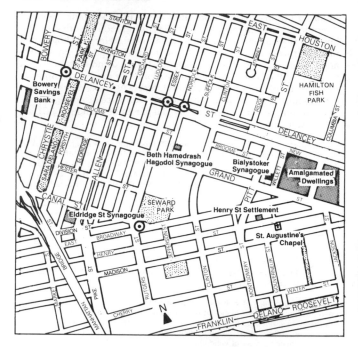

History. In the 18C, much of what is now the Lower East Side belonged to the city's great landowning families, the Rutgerses and the De Lanceys. The former settled E. of Division St; the De Lanceys until the conclusion of the American Revolution held the land W. of Division St to the East River and built the family seat between the present Delancey and Rivington Sts on what is now Chrystie St. After the war the area still remained semirural, with pleasant homes and considerable open space. By 1800, however, the city had spread as far N. as Cherry St with Federal and Greek Revival row houses springing up for the newly prosperous merchants and sea captains who enjoyed the neighborhood's proximity to the center of the shipping industry on South St.

By 1850 the pressures of immigration were beginning to be felt, and the Lower East Side was starting to deteriorate socially. The former captains' mansions on East Broadway were becoming shops; the slums of Five Points (see p. 157) were boiling over into Cherry St, and the area surrounding the present Brooklyn Bridge was becoming crowded and undesirable. The once quiet streets began to witness the violence of street gangs who harassed respectable citizens, and single family row houses were being sold off for a quarter of what they would have brought 30 years earlier.

The ethnic makeup of the district was also shifting. Between 1846 and 1860, large numbers of Irish immigrants forced out of Ireland by the potato blight, poverty, and political oppression, sought relief in the U. S. and many settled in the Lower East Side, at least until the next wave of immigration swept them out. Many joined the building and maritime trades and later became municipal workers, policemen, firemen, and eventually politicians and lawyers. At mid-century a large group of Germans, both Jews and gentiles, also arrived, a group that included skilled workers and craftsmen, who actively pursued their trades, forming trade unions and workingmen's associations. They became assimilated with relative ease and took their places in society as merchants, jewelers, clothing manufacturers, furriers, professionals, and bankers.

In 1881, however, revolutionary terrorists assassinated Czar Alexander II of Russia, and in the pogroms and repressive political actions that followed, a wave of Russian and east European Jewish immigration began that entirely changed the character of the Lower East Side and still affects the ethnic makeup of New York. Between 1881 and 1914 almost 2 million Jews came to the U. S., many of whom settled at least temporarily in the Lower East Side. After the end of World War I until the immigration quotas were imposed in 1924, another group arrived. In general the Jews who came were young; they intended to resettle permanently; they included a higher proportion of women and children than other immigrant groups. Those who arrived after 1900 tended to be better educated, more highly skilled than earlier settlers.

The life in store for them was not what the myth of America, the golden land, had led many to believe: much was demanded, little was given in return. Immigrants had to show great endurance to accept the constant crowding and lack of privacy that awaited them in the tenements, the pitiful wages that their jobs offered. They had to endure boredom and loss of identity, the inability to communicate, and the ensuing family crises, as the young quickly adapted to the New World and rejected the traditions of their parents. Coping with all these difficulties demanded the heroic expenditure of both physical and psychological energy, and naturally everyone did not survive. Many immigrants were reduced to resignation and fell prey to physical and mental illness, especially tuberculosis (the worst tenement areas were called ''lung blocks'' and claimed mortality rates twice as high as the rest of the city) and depression; suicide was not uncommon. Some turned to crime, although studies indicate that most of these criminals were native born, the children of the immigrants, and that ghetto crimes tended to involve fraud rather than violence.

Most of the Jewish immigrants found work either peddling or in the needle trades, virtually the only choices open to the uneducated poor, neither job an easy one. Since the skills demanded by the needle trades could be learned quickly and since English was unnecessary, many immigrants, both male and female, worked in the factories or sweatshops of the garment district. Starvation wages forced them to work 12- or 14-hour days under miserable conditions: the machines were powered by foot treadles; the pressing irons weighed as much as 25 lb; lighting, ventilation, and toilet facilities were pitifully inadequate. Wages were low: in 1911, fewer than 30% of the male workers who had come from eastern Europe after 1905 earned more than $12.50 per week. Women and children eked out the family income at home by sewing, making paper flowers, and shelling nuts.

The suffering of these immigrants awoke the compassion of reformers, some of them coreligionists like Lillian Wald, others nonsectarian humanitarians like Jacob Riis. American social work began on the Lower East Side, and early settlement houses included the Neighborhood Guild, founded in 1886 by a small group of middle class Christians who trucked their belongings down to the Lower East Side to live by the people they proposed to serve. Other social agencies were the Henry Street Settlement, the University Settlement, and the Educational Alliance, all of which are active today.

Following a long cultural tradition, the Jews also helped each other. Various ethnic or local groups formed *landsmanshaftn* to offer each other financial and social support. They formed labor unions in the various trades and a central organization called the United Hebrew Trades (1888). Often risking personal injury, immigrant workers both male and female went out on strike and not infrequently had to prove their physical courage in the face of threats from thugs hired to intimidate them. Women at home ''organized'' in other ways: the members of the Ladies Anti-Beef Trust, for example, instituted a meat boycott and poured kerosene over extortionately priced kosher beef.

Another bright spot in the general grayness of the slums was the intellectual life that the immigrants, despite the rigors of their working hours, carried on with undiminished passion. Lower East Side cafes became informal institutions where they could discuss socialism, industrialism, Zionism, literature, and drama. Agencies like the Educational Alliance offered lecture series, and after the turn of the century there were libraries whose reading rooms were filled to capacity nightly. Jewish workers read Tolstoy and Goethe during their lunch breaks, and companies of Jewish actors began occupying the theaters of the Bowery and Second Ave north of Houston St.

Here one could see performances by such luminaries as Jacob Adler and Boris Tomashevsky who first acted in rough comedies and gaudy melodramas and later in serious translations and adaptations of the works of Shakespeare, Ibsen, and Goethe. Among the actors and performers who rose from the ghetto theaters to the brighter lights uptown were Eddie Cantor, Fannie Bryce, Sophie Tucker, Al Jolson, and George Jessel.

Although the biblical injunction against graven images traditionally had made Jews suspect of the fine arts, a number of men and women who eventually became important American artists stepped over the invisible boundaries into what was essentially a gentile field of endeavor. While the Yiddish poet or playwright merited cultural respect no matter how poor, the painter or sculptor bore the double burden of poverty and indifference or suspicion. Among the artists who overcame these difficulties mainly through inflexible will were Jo Davidson, Jacob Epstein, William Gropper, William Zorach, Raphael Soyer, and Max Weber. Oddly enough, the Educational Alliance began to offer art classes in the 1880s (although it dropped them as a luxury in 1905 when the pressures of immigration had begun to mount), and the roll of alumni is studded with famous names: Leonard Baskin, Louise Nevelson, Ben Shahn, and Mark Rothko.

The Lower East Side was also a hotbed of political activity with clubs and organizations mostly of left-wing persuasions meeting in the cafes and meeting halls. The more successful of these put out their own propaganda and the most successful of these left-wing publications was the *Jewish Daily Forward,* but there was also the Yiddish Communist daily, *Freiheit,* and Emma Goldman's anarchist *Mother Earth,* as well as periodicals like the *Yidisher Kemfer,* which had a labor Zionist point of view. The titles of these journals reflect the aspirations of their writers: *Yidisher Kemfer* (the Jewish Fighter), the *Naye Lebn* (the New Life), the *Naye Land* (the New World), and *Tsukunft* (the Future).

The socialists of the Lower East Side had their victories at the polls, electing Meyer London (1871–1922) to Congress in 1914, 1916, and 1920 and putting three socialist assemblymen in office in 1918. Morris Hillquit (1869–1933), a leader of the American Socialist Party, ran for mayor of New York in 1917 and attracted 145,332 votes, five times the number garnered by the previous socialist candidate.

The high-water mark of immigration came in the early years of the 20C, when the Lower East Side ghetto suffered a population density of more than 700 people per acre. But while new arrivals were pressing at the barricades of Ellis Island, established residents were beginning to move on. They went out to Brooklyn across the Brooklyn, Williamsburg, and Manhattan Bridges which opened in 1883, 1903, and 1909 respectively. They took the elevated railway up to the Bronx starting in 1896 or rode the new subway through the tunnel under the Harlem River (1905) or to Brooklyn (1908). Harlem itself had a burgeoning Jewish community in 1900, and by 1910 the *Jewish Daily Forward* was bemoaning that this once green and lovely town had become airless, foul, and tenement ridden.

The immigration law of 1924 virtually stopped all new arrivals from eastern Europe and as the existing population drained away through the newly opened portals, the area became less crowded and also less vital. The first synagogues were abandoned in the 1930s. According to the 1980 census the population is approximately 35% Jewish, 35% Puerto Rican, 8% Black, 17% Chinese, and 5% other (Italian, Ukrainian, Polish, and Indian). Year by year the Jewish population dwindles. Several large public housing developments were constructed after the close of World War II, but many tenements still remain. While many synagogues have either been torn down or sold to new Christian congregations, reversing the trend of the early years of the century, others remain deserted, crumbling, and often besieged by hostile and ethnically alien neighbors. A few, notably the Eldridge Street Synagogue, have brighter futures.

Observers look back, almost nostalgically, at an era that will never return, and from this distance what was a time of struggle and dislocation for many seems attractive and almost quaint. And yet the problems today facing the new immigrants and the new ghetto dwellers—poverty, poor housing, cultural alienation, the language barrier—are essentially those the Jews encountered.

The **Educational Alliance** (197 East Broadway near Jefferson St), organized in 1889 and named in 1893, was one of the most important early agencies formed to help the massive influx of eastern European Jews adapt to the bewildering, alien culture of America. Founded by a group of German-Jewish philanthropists, many of them immigrants themselves, who had arrived a generation earlier, prospered, and moved out of the ghetto (if they had ever lived there), the Alliance started as a merger of three organizations: the Aguilar Free Library Society, the Young Men's Hebrew Association, and the Hebrew Free School Association. It proposed to bring education to the ignorant, recreation to the weary, and, most important, knowledge of American institutions and language to the foreigner, for the "uptown" Jews, as the German philanthropists came to be known, saw Americanization as the key to self-reliance and freedom from want.

The Alliance held classes for immigrant children to prepare them for the public school system and gave courses in English and civics to adults to ready them for naturalization. It showed movies about American history and held Legal Holiday parties (on July 4th, Lincoln's Birthday, and so on) which naturally had educational as well as celebratory aspects. It opened a library before the free public system was organized, and offered courses for interested adults: art, Greek and Roman history, botany, electricity and physics, lessons in piano, violin, and mandolin, stenography, American history, bookkeeping. It presented lectures which probed moral, philosophical, and literary topics. It ran social clubs for children and a children's theater, where aspiring actors and actresses could participate in plays like *Little Lord Fauntleroy* and *The Tempest.* It provided a gymnasium and facilities for taking showers, an important service in a tenement-ridden slum where bathtubs were rare. Children could escape the heat, filth, and crowding of an East Side summer by attending an Alliance camp. Wives deserted by their husbands, a common occurrence in this stressful society, could find legal assistance from Yiddish-speaking lawyers. Mothers could buy pasteurized milk from a dispensary on the roof, which in 1896 recorded an average daily attendance of 4600.

While the Alliance provided services sorely needed by the immigrant community, it still remained something of a source of distress to the people who used it, and relations between the "uptown" and "downtown" Jews were prickly for a long time. The assimilated uptowners found the new immigrants backward, "Oriental," and slovenly, people who needed lessons in hygiene as well as English. The "greenhorns," or new immigrants, found the German Jews condescending and insensitive to their natural desire to perpetuate their native, eastern European culture. Yet despite such strains, the Alliance survived to make life better for many. Today it carries on its work, although those who use its facilities are Puerto Rican, Oriental, and black as well as Jewish.

Opposite Jefferson St in the park at 192 East Broadway is the SEWARD PARK BRANCH OF THE NEW YORK PUBLIC LIBRARY (1909; Babb, Cook & Welch), founded as an early branch of the public system. It ministered to the intellectual hunger of the immigrants by offering a large collection of books in Yiddish, and frequently long lines formed at the door as people waited to get in.

The nearby Chatham Square branch also served the immigrant community and recorded in 1903 that books in English were being borrowed at the rate of 1000 per day.

Seward Park, created from land acquired in 1897 and opened officially in 1903, is named after William H. Seward (1801–72), governor of the State of New York, a U.S. senator, and eventually secretary of state under Abraham Lincoln.

Across the street from the park is the **Forward Building** (1912; George A. Boehm; DL), built to house the *Jewish Daily Forward.* Although the newspaper is now published uptown at 45 E. 33rd St, this building at 175 East Broadway was long the home of the most influential Yiddish daily newspaper. It was founded in 1897 and after a few years of floundering began to rise under the guidance of Abraham Cahan (1860–1951).

Cahan, himself an immigrant from Lithuania, dictated the editorial policy of the paper, which focused on the whole spectrum of immigrant Jewish experience. Intimate in tone, straightforward in diction, socialist in political leaning, the *Forward* told of the everyday events of the Lower East Side and described the minutiae of Jewish life. Cahan wrote about the prostitution of Allen St, about the iniquities of bosses who imposed unbearable working conditions; his paper explained baseball to the greenhorn and offered advice on the proper use of the pocket handkerchief. Although he carried lurid and sensational stories, he also presented high quality fiction and serious essays. The most famous feature of the paper, the *Bintel Brief* ("Bundle of Letters"), was a column in which readers unburdened themselves of the personal problems confronting them in their new homeland. The topics covered are an index of the miseries of immigrant life. A mother writes that her adult daughter ridicules the old-country modes of dress, speech, and even cooking (alienation between parents and children was a common source of grief during a time when parents clung to old ways and children eagerly embraced the new). A working father worries because his daughters hang around with street boys, no better than gangsters.

Cahan's detractors criticized the paper as vulgarly anti-intellectual and degradingly commercial; according to the intellectual component of the community, it had the mind of a child and the lusts of a grown scoundrel. Today it has become a weekly, claiming a readership of about 20,000, less than a tenth of its circulation of 238,000 in 1917. In part the paper is the victim of its own success. The Jewish proletariat has dwindled; the unions in the garment and millinery trades are no longer predominantly Jewish; and many of the daring socialist reforms it advocated (for example unemployment and old-age insurance and subsidized medical care) have become ordinary, bureaucratic realities.

The floors of the building not used by the newspaper offices were leased to labor organizations, and the first floor frieze (currently obscured by signs), includes portraits of Karl Marx and Friedrich Engels.

Continue along East Broadway to RUTGERS STREET which bears the name of one of early New York's illustrious families; the original landowner Hendrick Rutgers had a farm stretching from Division St to the East River. The Rutgers mansion, built in 1754, occupied the city block bordered by Cherry, Jefferson, Monroe, and Clinton Sts and remained there until 1875, when it was razed in favor of tenements and sweatshop loft buildings.

Until the mid-1980s when it became a Chinese restaurant, the GARDEN CAFETERIA (intersection of Rutgers St and East Broadway) served up blintzes, borscht, fish, dairy, and vegetable dishes. A mural on the E. wall recalled the time when an artisans' market flourished in what is now Seward Park. People wishing to hire the services of a carpenter or plasterer, for example, came here in the morning and bargained for his services.

Down the block to the E. is *St. Teresa's Roman Catholic Church* (141 Henry St), originally built as the First Presbyterian Church in 1841 but purchased by the Roman Catholic Church in 1863 to serve the growing population of Irish Catholics. As the ethnic balance of the Lower East Side continues to shift, the church now offers services in Spanish and Chinese as well as English.

NATHAN STRAUS SQUARE, at the intersection of East Broadway and Canal St, honors the Jewish philanthropist and businessman perhaps best remembered for his campaign to provide pasteurized milk to city children.

Nathan Straus (1848–1931) made his fortune in the R. H. Macy & Co. department store and went on to devote his energies and some of that fortune to the welfare of the city and its people. He was Park Commissioner from 1889–93 and president of the Board of Health in 1898. In 1923 he was chosen by popular vote as the New Yorker who had done the most for the city during its first 25 years as Greater New York.

The marble column in the square commemorates servicemen from the Lower East Side who gave their lives during the two world wars.

Walk W. on Canal St. The building at 5 Ludlow St, now a funeral parlor, formerly belonged to the *Independent Kletzker Brotherly Aid Society* and served both as a synagogue and the center for the group's mutual-aid activities. The Kletzker Society (founded 1892), an organization of immigrants from the Polish village of Kletsk, was one of an estimated 3–6000 of such *landsmanshaftn* which existed on the Lower East Side at the turn of the century. Besides providing such services as making burial and funeral arrangements and visiting the sick, these groups also served as social centers where people could enjoy the company of their compatriots and keep in touch with the old country. Formed by immigrants uprooted from the soil that had nurtured their parents and grandparents, the *landsmanshaftn* did not attract the immigrants' children who had no special love for little places like Chortkov, Kletsk, or Prszemisl, and indeed would rather forget their foreignness as soon as possible.

Continue W. on Canal St. The former **Yarmulowsky's Bank** (S.W. corner of Canal and Orchard Sts) was one of a number of small private Jewish banks that came into existence when financial conditions eased enough for local residents to save a few dollars. Unfortunately for the depositors, several of these home-grown institutions failed, taking with them the savings painfully culled from sweatshops, factories, and small businesses.

The Yarmulowsky Bank was founded at the beginning of the period of heaviest Jewish immigration and survived until August 1914, when the state banking superintendent closed it because of its "unsound" condition, with assets of $654,000 and liabilities of $1,703,000. On August 5 of that year, 2000 people demonstrated in front of the bank, and a month later an angry crowd of about 500 swarmed around the entrance of Yarmulowsky's apartment, while he and his family scurried to safety over the rooftops. Yarmulowsky was given a suspended sentence for mismanaging the bank's assets, and the depositors, who eventually did recover some of their losses, learned to be wary of such local institutions.

The lettering above the corner entrance proclaims the original function of the building, which dates from around 1895. The clock, surrounded with classical decoration, and the cupola, atop the tower, suggest the aspirations of the institution, but are far from the architectural grandeur expressed by major financial institutions, for example the Bowery Savings Bank (see p. 183).

Continue W. on Canal St to Eldridge St. Turn left (south). Although several low-income and middle-income cooperative housing projects have been constructed on the Lower East Side since the close of World War II, there are many **19C tenements** still standing and it has been estimated that half the population still lives in them. These buildings, constructed for the purpose of exploiting all available space to maximize profits, were one of the horrors of immigrant life. They can be classified as pre-Old Law (before 1879), Old Law (1879–1901), or New Law (after 1901) tenements; and in general, the earlier buildings were darker, more dangerous, and more primitive than later ones, since each successive law laid new restrictions on landlords and builders. The row of tenements at 15–21 Eldridge St was built after the enaction of the Old Law; the small building across the street at 18 Eldridge St was built before the Old Law.

The tenement became a fact of life starting in about 1850, when the migrations of German, Irish, and northern European people became significant. In that year one Silas Wood built a "model" tenement on Cherry St, between Roosevelt

St and Franklin Square, "with the design of supplying the laboring people with cheap lodging." His tenement, named Gotham Court, was made of brick and was five stories high, with about 144 apartments each containing two rooms. Six years after its completion, it housed over a thousand tenants and had become such a scandal that a Health Commission Committee inspecting the sanitary conditions of the basement had to retreat, their untried sensibilities assaulted by the odors.

In 1867 the city passed an act that promised improvement, but lacked methods of enforcement. Technically landlords were required to provide fire escapes and to connect toilets with sewers instead of cesspools, but for every requirement the law provided a loophole, and few landlords complied.

The next attempt at amelioration came in 1878 when Henry C. Meyers advertised in his plumbing magazine for a design that would best fit the standard New York 25 × 100-ft lot, simultaneously affording the greatest safety and convenience to the tenant and the greatest profit for the landlord. The prize-winning design soon became synonymous for all that was miserable in tenement design. Reformer Jacob Riis called James E. Ware's "dumbbell" plan hopeless: two tenements were constructed side by side with a narrow airshaft, often only a foot or so wide, between them, which gave the buildings their characteristic dumbbell shape, but provided virtually no air or light to the lower rooms on the airshaft. Furthermore, the shafts quickly became garbage dumps, as families pitched their garbage and sanitary waste out of the windows. The population of a five-story building based on this plan could reach 100–150 people and often did, since poor families sublet space to boarders to help with the rent. Still the Tenement House Act of 1879 did provide some improvements: cellars could not be rented out except by permission of the Board of Health; there had to be running water somewhere either in the house or yard; buildings were to contain one toilet for each two apartments. Backyard houses—buildings for multiple occupancy put up behind the original ones and having no direct access to the street (another ploy to exploit all available space)—were prohibited.

In 1901 a reformer named Lawrence Veiller helped enact a law forbidding further construction of dumbbell tenements. Instead of the narrow airshaft, the law required a light court at least 4½ ft wide. Nonfireproof tenements could not exceed five stories. Toilets were required in each apartment and windows in each room. Unfortunately the 1901 law came rather late to help most tenement dwellers, since by 1893 some 1196 dumbbell tenements already blighted the Lower East Side.

At 12–16 Eldridge St is Congregation Khal Adath Jeshurun with Anshe Lubz ("Community of the People of Israel with the People of Lubz") also known as the **Eldridge Street Synagogue** (1886–87; Herter Bros.; DL), crammed into a side street but towering above the neighboring tenements. While other Lower East Side synagogues had been built by Western European Jews, this was the first established by Eastern European Ashkenazi Jews, a congregation sufficiently wealthy to hire the prestigious firm of Herter Bros. to design their house of worship. Built in a mixture of Gothic, Romanesque, and Moorish Revival styles, it shows the mid-19C trend in synagogue architecture toward Oriental motifs.

The barrel-vaulted upstairs sanctuary was once an outstanding example of synagogue decoration, with great brass chandeliers (gaslit in early days) and Victorian glass shades, a large rose window in the W. wall, a towering ark carved in walnut, elaborately designed pews, galleries, and a vaulted ceiling.

The sanctuary was sealed in the 1930s and re-entered thereafter some 40 years later. Today there are plans underway for restoration.

Continue down Eldridge St to the intersection of Division St. Turn left and walk a block to Allen St. The warehouse at the corner of Allen and Pike Sts once held a **power station of the Second Avenue El**, which came down Allen St, turned W. into Division St, and continued on to Chatham Square and City Hall. Evidence of the original purpose of the building remains in the lettering on the wall, "Manhattan Railway Company" (several letters are currently missing) and in the circular openings that once accommodated the power lines (visible from the S. side of the building).

The extension of Allen St east of Division St is called **Pike Street** and is named, perhaps surprisingly, for the same Zebulon Montgomery Pike who left his name on Pike's Peak, a mountain in Colorado. In the flush of victory after the War of 1812, the city fathers named several streets in the vicinity for heroes of that struggle (see p. 183), among them Pike, who commanded troops in the campaign against Toronto and was killed as the retreating British blew up an ammunition dump.

Walk a block and a half S.E. (i.e., toward the river) on Pike St. CONGREGA-TION SONS OF ISRAEL KALWARIE (15 Pike St) was built in 1903 for a congregation of Jews from the town on the Polish-Lithuanian border which gave its name to the synagogue. Once tall stained glass windows illuminated the interior but vandals have smashed many, and even the upper windows with their eight-pointed rose designs and Stars of David have been within throwing range. The main entrance, once flanked by slender Corinthian columns, has been walled up against human and animal intruders. Walk up Allen St to Canal St. Turn left and return to the intersection of Canal and Eldridge Sts.

Continue three blocks W. on Canal St to the Bowery. The **Manhattan Bridge** with its ceremonial approach, arch, and colonnade (1912; Carrère & Hastings; Gustav Lindenthal, bridge engineer) was the third East River crossing.

History. Feelings ran high over the design of the Manhattan Bridge, for though the Brooklyn Bridge (opened 1883) had evoked enthusiasm both as a feat of engineering and as an object of beauty, the Williamsburg Bridge which followed it in 1903 was considered ugly. The two disputing parties were the "engineers," whose interests were primarily technological, and the "architects," whose goals were essentially aesthetic. Because of these opposing interests and the political factions expressing them, plans for the bridge went through numerous modifications as architects and bridge commissioners came and went.

An early plan was scrapped in about 1901 and the bridge redesigned by Henry Hornbostel, an architect whose belief in "artistic" engineering resulted in a proposal which included the use of eye-bars instead of the usual cables to support the roadway. City officials, however, preferred the older suspension cable system, and Carrère & Hastings (also designers of the New York Public Library and the Frick Museum) were hired to replace Hornbostel. The bridge, with its 1470-ft span, opened in 1909.

Meanwhile the World's Columbian Exposition in Chicago (1893), awakening public interest in neoclassic architecture, had given birth to the City Beautiful movement. From these enthusiasms sprang the plans for improving the approaches to the bridge, both on the Manhattan and Brooklyn sides. Carrère & Hastings, who had studied at the École des Beaux-Arts in Paris, the cradle of the neoclassical movement, were well qualified for such an undertaking.

The Manhattan approach originally featured an elliptical landscaped plaza which surrounded the actual roadway. Eight rail lines carried subways and surface railroads while the paved roadways accommodated both vehicular and foot traffic. Nowadays the subways are carried on the lower deck of the bridge, and the landscaping has been replaced by a small parking area and considerable debris.

The approach ends in a monumental arch and colonnade, the arch modeled after the 17C Porte St. Denis in Paris, the colonnade after Bernini's colonnade at St. Peter's Square in Rome. The frieze over the arch opening by Charles Cary Rumsey (1879–1922) is said to have been inspired by the Panathenaic procession on the Parthenon frieze, suitably Americanized. It depicts a group of four Indians on horseback hunting buffalo. The choice of such primitive subject matter may seem peculiar on a classical arch signaling the approach to a modern steel suspension bridge linking two boroughs of a large city, but such frontier themes were then extremely popular.

Flanking the arch opening are two large granite sculptural groups by Carl Augustus Heber: the *Spirit of Commerce* on the N. side and the *Spirit of Industries* on the south. Above the arch opening (36 × 40 ft) is a cornice and a low attic story decorated with lions' heads. The interior of the arch is barrel-vaulted and coffered. The arch is set in the middle of a colonnade of Tuscan columns (31 ft high) above which are cornices with balustrades which connect the columns to one another and to the arch.

Two monumental granite sculptural groups by Daniel Chester French originally stood on the Brooklyn side; they are now displayed outside the Brooklyn Museum.

In the 1960s a proposed expressway which was to cut through lower Manhattan threatened the existence of this fine bridge approach. Robert Moses, the Parks Commissioner and head of the Triborough Bridge and Tunnel Authority whose interest in ever larger and wider highways led to some of New York's finer arteries and some of its more blighted neighborhoods, asked the city Art Commission for permission to demolish the bridge approaches claiming that the removal of the sculpture was necessary for bridge connections to the proposed roadway. Since it appeared that the road was inevitable and that the bridge approaches were doomed, the Commission sadly gave permission, under the condition that some of the sculpture be removed to other sites where the public might still enjoy it. The Brooklyn Museum then volunteered to take the groups by French and the buffalo hunt frieze and in 1963 the sculptures from the Brooklyn side were moved there. Unlike many urban preservation stories, this one had a happy outcome, since the roadway project was defeated in 1969 and the removal of the approaches became unnecessary.

The jewelry stores on the Bowery and on Canal St in the blocks near the bridge approach remain from a time when diamond merchants carried on an active but informal sidewalk trade, often carrying their stock, perhaps a single diamond, in a vest pocket.

Walk back E. one block on Canal St to the intersection of Chrystie St; turn left and go one block N. to Hester St. SARA DELANO ROOSEVELT PARK, named after the mother of Franklin D. Roosevelt, was created in 1934 by widening Chrystie and Forsyth Sts and tearing down the seven blocks of tenements between them. When the park was named, Mrs. Roosevelt sent several telegrams to the Board of Aldermen requesting that the park be named for former Park Commissioner Charles Stover, who had devoted 40 years of his life to improving conditions on the Lower East Side, but the Board bowed to the wishes of the district alderman who favored Mrs. Roosevelt.

Cross the park and walk E. on Hester St, named for Hester Rynders, daughter of Jacob Leisler, who was hanged for treason in 1691 (see p. 148). During the late 19C **Hester Street** became synonymous with the Lower East Side. It was the home of sweatshops, tenement houses, and the area's busiest street market, crowded with housewives, peddlers, and pushcarts offering all kinds of merchandise, bread, vegetables, dry goods, and fish, sometimes the worse for the warm weather and the passage of time. Writers of the period found it the quintessential ghetto street, ringing with the shouts of vendors, the haggling and chattering of women, the cries of children who darted through the crowds playing games and making swift raids on the push-carts. A sympathetic reporter from the *Times* in 1898 found the street scene touching and attractive, the people intensely human, pious, and homeloving, worthy subjects of the student of human nature. Another reporter for the same journal with sterner standards of cleanliness, described it as the filthiest place on the western continent and called its inhabitants slatternly, lawless (they had failed to empty their garbage cans at a specified hour), and indecent.

Orchard Street, which intersects Hester St beyond Allen St, now the main shopping street of the district, is especially interesting to visit on Sundays, when the streets are jammed with bargain hunters. It gets its name from orchards on the 18C farm of James De Lancey. Like Hester St, Orchard St was once a center of the pushcart market, which stretched a few blocks N. and S. from Delancey St. The pushcarts may have been picturesque and productive of bargains, but they were obstructive and unsanitary, and consequently outlawed by the city in the late 1930s. For the immigrants they represented one of the few ways an unskilled person could eke out a living (in 1898 the daily rental of such a cart was 10¢), and so peddling from the carts became a chief occupation of the poor.

Walk N. (left) on Orchard St to Grand St; turn left and continue five blocks to the Bowery. **The Bowery,** a name long associated with loneliness and poverty, alcoholism and possibly vice, is one of Manhattan's oldest streets.

History. It began as an Indian trail and got its name during the Dutch colonial period when it led to Peter Stuyvesant's farm, or *bouwerie* (see p. 222). During the 18C, it formed part of the Boston Post Road and so figured in the Revolutionary War as an evacuation route for the retreating American troops. In the early 19C, it was still suburban, and the nearby side streets became the center of the abattoir district. There were slaughterhouses on Chrystie, Elizabeth, and Forsyth Sts as well as factories for the production of lard, soap fats, and candles.

In the mid-19C, the Bowery glittered with the lights of theaters; it saw the first blackface minstrel show in the city as well as the first stage version of *Uncle Tom's Cabin,* and toward the end of the century it boasted several Yiddish theaters. After about 1870, as the slums encroached on both sides, it began a long slide into poverty. Its popular night life gave way to cheap saloons, either beer halls or distilleries which made their own whiskey and then sold it, not infrequently adulterated. The Bowery of this period also had cheap lodgings. There were 25¢ establishments, advertising themselves as hotels, which offered private rooms to their clientele. For 15¢ a visitor could sleep in a dormitory with a bed covered by indifferently clean linen and a clothing locker. In the 10¢ lodgings the locker became unnecessary, as the patrons had nothing worth locking up, according to Jacob Riis, who knew the proprietor of three such places, a man who made enough from them to live swankly in Murray Hill. For 7¢ the lodger could rest his bones on a canvas strip stretched like a hammock between timber posts; and for 5¢ (in 1885) the lodger flopped on the floor, his space chalked out for him by the proprietor.

Gradually the Bowery developed into a skid row, with cheap food, cheap lodging, and cheap liquor readily available. During the Depression its flophouses, doorways, and all night restaurants offered the army of the city's unemployed a place to spend the night, or wait until times got better, and in the 1940s and 1950s there were still several bars per block. Until 1968 the

Salvation Army operated a mission, doling out free food, coffee, and counseling on alcoholism.

The Bowery has not yet recovered from its period as the city's skid row, but its population has changed. Many of the old residents have died or gone elsewhere, though the few who do remain live in the half-dozen or so old-style flophouses. The sidewalks are no longer crowded with alcoholics standing around sharing bottles. The new derelicts are the homeless who are dispersed throughout the city, many with drug problems, others mentally ill. They are drawn here by the few charities in the area (including the Salvation Army which now serves the Bowery's deinstitutionalized mental patients instead of its alcoholics) and by the Men's Shelter Care Center on E. 3rd St (see p. 216), the city's main processing center for homeless men.

There are positive signs also: the influx of businesses from Chinatown, the arrival of young professionals who have colonized the streets of Little Italy and the East Village near the Bowery, and the continuing success of the area's traditional lighting and restaurant supply houses.

The **Bowery Savings Bank** (1894; McKim, Mead & White; DL) at 130 Bowery on the corner of Grand St, with its imposing Roman Corinthian portico and pediment sculpted with lions and seated classic figures, embodies the spirit of the classic revival sweeping the country after the World's Columbian Exposition the previous year (see p. 180). A guidebook of 1893 points out that while the bank is an "afiduciary institution of the highest order," and its incorporators bear some of New York's finest names, it has traditionally taken care of the "savings of the poorer classes and has earned for them all that their small accumulations could safely return." The magnificent interior seems to express the affluence of the incorporators rather than the slender means of the depositors. The main banking room with its coffered ceiling, ornate metal and glass skylight, massive columns painted to resemble marble, and classically enframed windows must have dazzled those humble depositors.

The blocks N. of Grand St on the Bowery constitute the center of the city's lighting fixture trade which established itself here during the gaslight era.

Walk N. on the Bowery to Delancey St, turn right. **Delancey Street,** now a shabby thoroughfare leading to the Williamsburg Bridge, is named after the De Lancey family, early settlers of French Huguenot origin. Etienne or Stephen De Lancey, the original owner of what is now the Fraunces Tavern, had a farm in this vicinity on the W. side of Division St (so named because it marked the 18C boundary between the De Lancey and Rutgers farms). James De Lancey (1703–60), son of Etienne, who became chief justice of the New York Supreme Court and lieutenant governor of the colony, had a home at the corner of the present Chrystie and Delancey Sts.

When the street was widened to accommodate traffic to the bridge, it was renamed Schiff Parkway in honor of Jacob Schiff, financier and philanthropist, generous contributor to the Henry Street Settlement and the Educational Alliance. The name never took root, however, and so the dubious honor reverted to the De Lancey family.

The blocks E. of the Bowery, originally called First, Second, and Third Sts, and so on, were renamed following the War of 1812 for several now obscure heroes wounded or killed in the fighting. Lt.-Col. John Chrystie was killed on the Niagara frontier; Lt.-Col. Benjamin Forsyth died in upstate New York; Lt. Joseph C. Eldridge was ambushed and apparently scalped by Indians in Canada; Lt. William Henry Allen had his leg shot off during a naval battle between the *Argus* and the British brig *Pelican* and died the next day; and Lt. Augustus Ludlow was slain aboard the *Chesapeake,* but not until he had received the famous dying command of Capt. William Lawrence: "Don't give up the ship." The two are buried together in Trinity Churchyard.

The *Union Square Seventh Day Adventist Church,* originally the synagogue of *Congregation Poel Zedek Anshe Ileya* (c. 1895) on the S.E. corner of Forsyth and Delancey Sts, one block E. of Chrystie St, was once one of the largest and most active synagogues in the area, also known as the Forsyth Street Synagogue. The shops built into the Delancey St side of the building were intended to provide financial security for the synagogue.

Continue E. on Delancey St to Allen St. During the closing years of the 19C, **Allen Street,** darkened and dirtied by the Second Avenue El, became a haven for prostitution (although there were brothels also on Houston, Delancey, Rivington, Forsyth, and Chrystie Sts). A local minister complained that the women openly solicited from the stoops of tenements adjoining his church, while writer Michael Gold in his novel *Jews Without Money* recalled the time when prostitutes sat out on the sidewalks in chairs sunning themselves, their legs sprawled indolently in the way of anyone who wanted to pass by. After the street was widened in 1930 and the El torn down in 1942, the S. part near the Manhattan Bridge became a center for antiques, especially copper and brass ware. There was also a large center for bed linen run by the Romanian immigrants who settled chiefly around Allen St.

Turn N. (left) on Allen St. The vacant building at 133 Allen St with its white antiseptic-looking facade and sea horse motif above the door was once a *Municipal Bath House* built just after the turn of the century for people who didn't have bathing facilities, or perhaps even running water, at home. In 1893 there were more than 16 such facilities used by an estimated 4 million people annually.

Continue N. to Rivington St. **Rivington Street** is named after James Rivington (1724–1803), who emigrated to Philadelphia from England in 1760. Eventually he moved to New York, where he continued in the bookselling business and became publisher of *Rivington's New York Gazetteer,* a Tory newspaper which attacked the American revolutionary movement. Rivington's sentiments, as well as his abrasive personality, earned him the hostility of a group of American patriots who mobbed his shop, destroyed his presses, and stole his fonts of type, a theft made more serious by the fact that no American foundries produced type of the same high quality as Rivington's imported English fonts. Undaunted he returned to England and got new equipment, came back to New York, and started another loyalist newspaper. In 1781, he seems to have had a change of heart, for he became a spy for Gen. Washington and is credited with deciphering a British military code.

Turn right on Rivington St. *The First Roumanian-American Congregation, Shaarai Shamoyim* ("Gates of Heaven"), at 89 Rivington St, bought this building in about 1890, although the congregation itself may have been organized as early as 1860. Like many other congregations, this one did not construct its own synagogue, but remodeled a Christian church, since gentile congregations moved out as the Jewish immigrants poured into the Lower East Side. The building formerly belonged to the Allen Street Methodist Church, whose members apparently made a serious error in planning when they erected this large church, for they sold it and moved out only two years after it was finished. It is one of the few Romanesque Revival buildings in the area, with a simple brick facade and round arch windows. In the days when cantors were lionized as opera stars are today, Shaarai Shamoyim was a springboard to vocal success, and two of America's famous operatic singers appeared here before they went on to secular work, Jan Peerce (then Jacob Pincus Perelmuth) and Richard Tucker (then Reuben Ticker).

Continue E. toward Essex St. The *Economy Candy Shop* at 108 Rivington St between Ludlow and Essex Sts is a holdover from earlier days. In the immigrant world candy stores such as this one became informal gathering places for people who had no privacy at home and nowhere else to go. This one sells homemade chocolate bark, dried fruit, nuts, marzipan, halvah, and imported European and Israeli candy.

Walk E. to Essex St. East of about Essex St, the population becomes largely Hispanic.

Diversion. This section of the walk continues through poorer neighborhoods and includes several derelict synagogues.

Continue E. on Rivington St. *Schapiro's Wine Company* (126 Rivington St between Essex and Norfolk Sts), now the only remaining kosher wine firm in Manhattan, was founded by the present owner's grandfather, who performed his own charitable work, giving new immigrants a free meal, 50¢, and a bottle of honey wine. The kosher wine, billed as "The Wine You Can Almost Cut with a Knife," is made from grapes grown in upstate New York and pressed there under rabbinical supervision. The juice is then shipped to the city in tank trucks and handled only by staff members who are Jewish Sabbath observers.

Turn N. (left) on Norfolk St. Walk a block and a half, almost to Houston St. **Congregation Anshe Chesed** (1850; Alexander Saeltzer; DL) at 172–176 Norfolk St, today a derelict but moving reminder of more prosperous times, has the honor of being the oldest surviving structure in the city built as a synagogue and the original home of New York's third Jewish congregation (after Shearith Israel and B'nai Jeshurun). Designed by the architect of the Astor Library (now the New York Shakespeare Festival Public Theater), it was once resplendent with Gothic Revival trappings: pointed arch windows, quatrefoil designs, pyramidal towers, delicate tracery. Like other downtown synagogue buildings, its changing ownership reflected the successive waves of Jewish immigration in the neighborhood: built by a German congregation, Anshe Chesed ("People of Kindness"), it later housed a Hungarian immigrant group Ohab Zedek, and eventually after several more changes of ownership it became Anshe Slonim, ("People of Slonim") named for a fondly remembered native village in Poland.

Congregation Anshe Slonim, dwindling in size and resources, abandoned the building in 1974. After years of vandalization, it was sealed against intrusions and threatened with demolition in the early 1980s.

Return to Stanton St; go two blocks E. to Clinton St; turn left. **Chasam Sopher**

Synagogue (1853) at 8 Clinton St is the second oldest surviving synagogue in the city, built for a German-Jewish congregation which moved uptown in 1886. A group from Poland purchased the property and renamed it Chasam Sopher ("Seal of the Scribe") to honor Moshe Sofer (or Schreiber, in the Germanicized form), a religious leader, scholar, and rabbi, who was born in Frankfurt in 1762. Sofer devoted the later part of his life to fighting Reform Judaism and founded numerous Hebrew charitable institutions and schools. This red brick building is constructed in the round-arch Romanesque Revival style, although its appearance has been altered by the loss of the original parapets topping off the flanking towers.

Walk a block E. to Attorney St and two blocks S., through the playground. Across the street from the school, at 87 Attorney St, is another formerly fine synagogue, **Beth Haknesseth Mogen Avraham** (c. 1845) whose name means "Synagogue of the Shield of Abraham." The building started out as a Methodist Church, but was soon sold to a black congregation who renamed it the Emmanuel African Methodist Episcopal Church and eventually sold it to a group from Poland called the Erste Galitsianer Chevra ("First Galician Congregation"). The Galician Jews later changed their name to Mogen Avraham. Although the building was adapted to Jewish worship, it was never really modernized, and retained its gas-fired radiators and outdoor plumbing. The small brick building to the N. originally served as the parsonage for the Emmanuel African M. E. Church.

Return to Rivington St and go W. toward Essex St. *Streit's Matzoth Company* (150 Rivington St) is the sole remaining bakery in Manhattan producing matzoth, an unleavened bread used especially during Passover.

Continue W. to Essex St. *Bernstein-on-Essex* a few doors to the N. of the intersection of Essex and Rivington Sts (135 Essex St) has the expected kosher fare and the additional distinction of having been the city's first kosher Chinese restaurant.

Turn around and walk S. on Essex St. Occupying the blocks from Stanton to Broome Sts on the E. side of the street, the **Essex Street Market** (1940) houses a multitude of stalls whose proprietors speak Yiddish, Chinese, and Spanish and sell foodstuffs to match. The building on the N.W. corner of Broome and Essex Sts (75 Essex St) long ago housed the *Eastern Dispensary,* one of several privately endowed clinics serving the poor with free or low-cost medical care. The clinic was founded in 1832, and became the Good Samaritan Dispensary in 1891, at which time it treated about 160,000 patients annually.

Continue south. *Seward Park High School* (between Ludlow, Essex, Broome, and Grand Sts), occupies the site of the old Essex Market Court House and the Ludlow Street Jail. The jail held prisoners whose offenses came under the jurisdiction of the Sheriff of the County of New York as well as violators of federal laws. Sheriff's prisoners with enough money could buy fancier accommodations in the jail, a system which naturally led to abuse. William M. Tweed (see p. 152) availed himself of these privileges while he was serving his sentence for defrauding the city; his cell had two rooms, flowerpots on the windowsills, even a piano to ease the tedium of prison life. Tweed died in the Ludlow Street jail in 1878.

Turn left on Broome St and walk a block to Norfolk St. Turn right. **Beth Hamedrash Hagodol Synagogue** ("Great House of Study") at 60 Norfolk St between Grand and Broome Sts was built (1850; DL) as the Norfolk Street Baptist Church and sold in 1885 to the present owners, a Russian Orthodox congregation.

Unlike many other synagogues in the area, this one is still decently preserved. Few details of the original Gothic Revival exterior remain—only the stained glass in the W. window, the bands of quatrefoils on the two towers, and the moldings framing the pointed window arches—but the interior still bears traces of the time when the building was a Christian church: carved pews, a former altar rail, a vaulted ceiling, and an elaborate gallery.

Next door at 50 Norfolk St is the Hong Ning Housing for the Elderly, whose presence suggests the changing ethnic character of the Lower East Side.

Continue S. to Grand St. Mid-block between Norfolk and Essex Sts is KOSSAR'S BIALYS (367 Grand St), famous for its *bialys*, onion rolls reputedly invented by the bakers of the Polish (now Russian) town of Bialystok. The bakery opens in early morning and remains open until around midnight, selling very fresh *bialys* and bagels. The Bialystoker Synagogue is a few blocks away.

At Grand St turn left and walk E. past Clinton and Ridge Sts. At 466 Grand St between Pitt and Willett Sts is the **Arts for Living Center of the Henry Street Settlement** (1975; Prentice & Chan, Ohlhausen), a red brick building which has won awards for architectural excellence. On the W. wall is a mural (1972) *Arise from Oppression*. The center, along with the adjoining Harry De Jur Henry Street Settlement Playhouse which features the work of minority playwrights, is the focal point of the arts programs of the settlement, and has changing exhibitions of contemporary artists, usually reflecting the ethnic interests of the Lower East Side (gallery open Tues–Sat, 12–6, and before evening performances. Admission free. Tel: 598-0400).

Continue to Willett St and turn left. Just N. of the intersection of Willett and Grand Sts. is the BIALYSTOKER SYNAGOGUE (1826; DL), originally the Willett Street Methodist Church, a plain late Federal building with walls of random fieldstone masonry, trimmed with brownstone. The Bialystoker Synagogue bought it in 1905.

Willett St is named after Marinus Willett (1740–1830), an American patriot who served with distinction during the Revolutionary War and went on in politics to become sheriff of the city and eventually mayor.

Return along Willett St to Grand St and continue east. At the N.W. corner of Grand and Kazan Sts are the **Amalgamated Dwellings** (1930; Springsteen & Goldhammer), built as cooperative apartments and sponsored by the Amalgamated Clothing Workers of America. Though commended architecturally for their "complete elimination of meaningless ornament" the apartments, with an average rent of $12.33 per room per month, were said to be too expensive for most clothing workers. A larger project, called the **Hillman Houses,** (1951; Springsteen & Goldhammer), now stands on Grand St between Willett and Lewis Sts. It is named in honor of Sidney Hillman (1887–1946), a Lithuanian immigrant, union organizer, and prominent labor leader.

Kazan St is named after Abraham Kazan, instrumental in the construction of the housing project; formerly it was called Sheriff

St after Marinus Willet, who served as city sheriff before he became mayor.

The building at the intersection of East Broadway and Grand St (311–313 East Broadway), once the Young Men's Benevolent Association, is now the EAST SIDE MIKVAH, or ritualarium, the last remaining public ritual bath in the area. Although individual synagogues often have their own *mikvahs*, public ones were necessary in a neighborhood where synagogues were often converted from churches or from storefronts.

Turn right into Henry St just beyond the intersection of Grand and Kazan Sts.

At 290 Henry Street is SAINT AUGUSTINE'S CHAPEL (1827–28; DL), originally the All Saints' Free Church. According to tradition, the fieldstones for its masonry were dug from Mount Pitt, a hill located near the present intersection of Grand and Pitt Sts. During the Revolution, Mount Pitt was fortified and was one of a chain of primitive and inadequate fortifications running across Manhattan from the East to the Hudson Rivers.

Details of the facade of St. Augustine's Chapel recall several other churches in Lower Manhattan dating from the same period (the Sea and Land Church, and the Church of the Transfiguration). The windows are enframed with brick and have pointed Gothic arches. Stone lintels top the doors; the cornices are of wood. The interior details of the church mirror the simplicity of the exterior. Particularly fine are the wineglass pulpit with a three-feather Prince of Wales crest on the sounding board, and the organ by Henry Erban, both dating from 1830. The galleries, which once were used for slaves, rest on fluted cast-iron columns.

The **Henry Street Settlement Houses** (1827–34; DL) at 263–267 Henry St, between Montgomery and Grand Sts, attract attention architecturally as late-Federal residences, built in what was once a semi-rural setting at the edge of town. Although the three houses are roughly contemporary, only the center one has escaped alteration, fortunately surviving with much of its original detail intact: the wrought-iron stoop railing with open box newel posts, the areaway fence with knobby finials (sometimes said to be acorns symbolizing hospitality, an attribute also attached to the pineapple which appears as a finial on the newel post of 263 Henry St), and the louvered shutters on the first-story windows. Also original is the paneled doorway flanked by slender fluted columns with Ionic capitals. The cornice above the doorway and the lintels above the windows are later alterations.

These rather modest buildings became the home of one of the nation's pioneer social agencies. Lillian Wald (1867–1940), who founded the Henry Street Settlement, remains one of New York's great figures, a compassionate, gentle, yet shrewd and worldly woman who devoted herself tirelessly to the poor. Awakened to a sense of vocation by a visit to a poor home, she moved to a fifth-floor walkup at 27 Jefferson St and began her rounds, fighting ignorance, disease, malnutrition, rats, and bigotry. She raised money, largely through the assistance of Jacob Schiff, the philanthropist who gave two of the Henry St buildings to the settlement. Coming from a bourgeois German-Jewish family, she gradually grew to accept these strange eastern European immigrants as her own people and became an important liaison between the "uptown" and "downtown" Jews who often found themselves at odds with one another.

After Wald retired in 1933, her work was carried on by Helen Hall, whose career was as distinguished as the founder's. The organization continues its work today in the original settlement house tradition; its programs, adapted to reflect changing social conditions, include a credit union (founded in 1937 to offer the needy an alternative to street-based loan sharks), a day care center for small children, and a companions' program for the elderly.

Turn right at the intersection of Henry and Montgomery Sts and walk one block to East Broadway, so named because it was supposed to divert traffic from Broadway, which it joins via Park Row.

East Broadway still bears traces of its former importance as the center of Orthodox Judaism in New York. The two blocks between Jefferson and Montgomery Sts contain a row of storefront synagogues housing small congregations some of which share space because they cannot afford their own quarters. Most of these congregations are composed of people from the same European locale, who are unwilling to merge with other groups and lose their particular national or ethnic identity, and so struggle on at the edge of extinction. Some of the groups are Hasidic, members of an extreme and fundamentalist sect which originated in 18C Poland and holds conservative views on social matters and ultra-Orthodox views on religious questions.

However, the *Young Israel Synagogue* (225 East Broadway) belongs to a group founded in the early 20C in New York City, to counteract what its young Orthodox members considered the triple threat of Reform Judaism, rising crime among second-generation Jews, and socialism. Although the founders were deeply committed to Orthodoxy, they also considered themselves Americanized, and so shaved their beards, accepted mixed social dancing, dressed in modern style, and listened to sermons in English. Today they continue their social programs, promoting Orthodox styles of living and worship.

The building formerly belonged to the Hebrew Immigrant Aid and Sheltering Society, an organization founded in 1892 to assist immigrants as they arrived in New York, by providing such services as interpreters, lawyers, and temporary shelter (see p. 219).

7   SoHo and TriBeCa

SUBWAY: IRT Lexington Ave local (train 6) to Canal St. IND 8th Ave express or local (A or E train) to Canal St; walk 3 long blocks E. (counting on the S. side of the street) to Broadway. IND 6th Ave (D or F train) to W. 4th St; change to 8th Ave local train.

BUS: M6 southbound via 6th Ave to Canal St and Broadway. M1 southbound via 5th Ave / Park Ave South to Canal St and Broadway.

WHEN TO VISIT: Saturday is the most popular day for shopping or

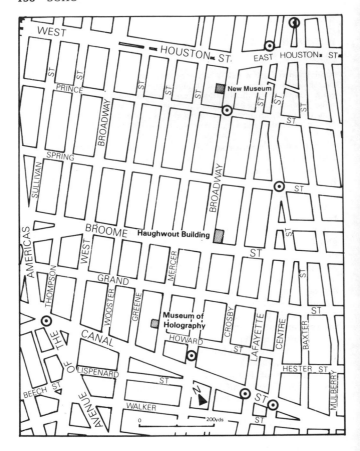

browsing in the galleries, an activity that begins around noon. For a
less crowded view, go Tues—Fri in the afternoon. Most galleries are
closed in the mornings and on Sun—Mon.

For a fleeting moment in the late 1960s, SoHo, an acronym for
SOuth of HOuston, with apologies to London's Soho, was an
artist's Eden, where rents were cheap, space was plentiful, and
society was made up mostly of other artists, all searching for
style, authenticity, identity, or whatever other goals separated
them from the rest of the populace. Today SoHo is cleaner,
slicker, more expensive, and, according to critics who should
know, the center of contemporary art in the western world,
successor to Greenwich Village in the 1920s and Paris between
the wars. The East Village had a fling as the focus of the avant-
garde in the early to mid-1980s, but the action is presently back

in SoHo, and some of the galleries previously located in the East Village have moved to SoHo.

Before its present heady revival SoHo endured its peaks and valleys. Its great farms were first subdivided and developed as a quiet residential suburb in the years after the Revolution, although the oldest remaining house dates only from around 1806. By 1825 what is now SoHo was the most densely populated part of New York. By 1840 it was highly fashionable. By the 1850s expensive hotels and retail stores of sterling reputation lined Broadway while the side streets began sporting brothels, dance halls, and casinos, some of them elegant in their own way. As the carriage trade vanished uptown, industry came in to fill the vacuum. During the decades between 1860 and 1890, most of the cast-iron architecture so admired today was constructed, the buildings serving as factories or warehouses, often with shop fronts on the ground floor. Appealing as they may seem now with their Corinthian columns, Palladian windows, or French Second Empire dormers, many functioned as sweatshops where the immigrants from southern and eastern Europe endured 12 or more hours a day of tedious labor in degrading surroundings for the sake of their offspring. SoHo and Little Italy still overlap and much of the remaining Italian population, especially visible in warm weather on the streets west of West Broadway, is descended from those overworked immigrants.

Although the sweatshops were legislated out of existence, in part by immigration quotas that stanched the flow of cheap, uneducated, and hence acquiescent labor, SoHo remained industrial until recently. Gradually the cast-iron buildings became outmoded and inconvenient, and small industry—paper-box companies, tool and die factories, wool remnant companies—began moving elsewhere. In 1959 the City Club of New York published an influential report labeling the area, then known as Hell's Hundred Acres (because of its frequent fires), or as The Valley (a lowland between the architectural highs of the financial district and midtown), an industrial slum with no architecture of note.

In the early 1960s artists attracted by those same empty commercial buildings began moving in, illegally converting the space to apartments and surreptitiously installing such amenities as plumbing, household wiring, and adequate heating. To protect themselves from profiteering landlords, artists' cooperatives began buying entire buildings and tenants' associations began lobbying for legalization of the status quo.

By 1970 SoHo had become a boom town for real estate dealers, for art dealers (some headed downtown from the pricey reaches of the Upper East Side), and for artists themselves who, if not becoming rich were at least forming a coherent artistic community with its own aesthetics and codes of living. Film, video, and "performance" art—the avant-garde media of the 1960s—became staple commodities of SoHo artistic life. Experimental dance and drama flourished. Cooperative galleries opened.

Today SoHo is still exciting, though it has become fashionable and established, and the industry of art is pushing out the

remaining firms dealing in wool remnants and electronic components. Commerce has established itself also in the form of the
many small, cleverly arrayed shops whose wares—clothing, fancy
food, artistic jewelry—constitute the accessories of a tasteful yet
casual existence. Rents have kept pace with the area's popularity
and are currently too steep again for any but highly successful
artists. Newcomers (and hard-pressed earlier arrivals) now head
for cheaper territory in Hoboken and Brooklyn while limousines
await the well-heeled at SoHo restaurants and stores.

But even though SoHo has changed, it has not entirely succumbed to the charms of the bourgeoisie; one can still observe
the energy and the ambition of this community dominated at
many levels by art.

SoHo's *cast-iron architecture, capable of arousing passionate
emotions in the hearts of admirers, has within the past two
decades emerged from a century of obscurity. In 1973 the SOHO
HISTORIC DISTRICT, bounded by W. Broadway, Houston, Crosby,
and Canal Sts, was created to protect a 26-block tract with the
largest concentration of cast-iron architecture in America, buildings which were a major architectural innovation and in their
freshly painted prime a source of personal and civic pride but
which later suffered the ravages of neglect—disfigured by ugly
ground-floor modernizations or dimmed by layers of dull paint.
Today many have been handsomely restored.

Early cast-iron architecture, adorned with the familiar quoins,
columns, and consoles of the classical tradition and painted tan,
buff, or cream, was designed to imitate marble or limestone.
Sometimes cast-iron plates were even grooved to resemble blocks
of stone mortared together. Eventually iron founders, many of
whom had previously dealt in stoves, safes, and lawn furniture,
began offering catalogues of ornaments from which the client or
architect could select, combining the elements in simple or lavish
compositions. While the earliest cast-iron buildings hark back to
Italy (Sansovino's Library in Venice and the Roman Colosseum
were much admired), later examples were based on French
Renaissance, Second Empire, or neo-Grec styles.

The term "neo-Grec" refers not to an imitation of ancient classical models but
to a style of incised ornament favored during the 1870s in Paris and imported
to New York. The designs, which may suggest classical ornamentation but may
also be geometric—circles, diamonds, dots, bandings—are cut into smooth
surfaces to a uniform depth so that they look drawn rather than carved. The
style has been said to look machine-made, thereby expressing the nation's
industrial development during the late 19C.

In one sense cast-iron architecture was standardized: the ornaments were machine-made, mass-produced, and as interchange-
able as parts of a Winchester rifle. On the other hand, their
deployment allowed the architect great scope and originality, as
the general exuberance of these SoHo buildings testifies.

James Bogardus is generally considered to be the father of cast-iron architecture, though his importance arises primarily from his patents for constructing
buildings with mass-produced cast-iron sections and as a building contractor.

He left little documentable work (see p. 204 and 208) and does not appear to have operated a large foundry of his own.

Begin at Houston St and Broadway; walk S. on Broadway. **Houston Street** is the border between SoHo and NoHo (i.e., SOuth of HOuston and NOrth of HOuston), while Broadway, S. or N. of the border, in this part of town is known as LoBro (LOwer BROadway) and is beginning to acquire an identity of its own as the revival of the avenue in the Astor Place district (see p. 219) has extended downtown. On the E. side of the street are boutiques with clothes best worn by the young and adventurous. On the W. side of Broadway, between Houston and Prince Sts, is the **New Museum of Contemporary Art,** artistically daring, and as museums go, young.

The New Museum of Contemporary Art. 583 Broadway (Houston St), New York 10012. Tel: 219-1222. Open Wed, Thurs, Sun 12–6; Fri 12–10; Sat 12–8. Suggested admission charge. Lectures, tours, performance events, poetry readings. Shop with publications, catalogues, books. Restrooms. Limited wheelchair access.
SUBWAY: IRT Lexington Ave local (train 6) to Spring St. BMT Broadway line (N or R train) to Prince St. IND 8th Ave local or express (A, C, or E train) to Spring St. IND 6th Ave express (F train) to Broadway-Lafayette. BUS: M6 southbound via 7th Ave to Broadway and Houston St. M5 southbound via Broadway to Houston St. M1 south via 5th Ave to Broadway and Houston St.

The New Museum was founded (1976) by Marcia Tucker, formerly a curator of the Whitney Museum of American Art, to collect and show truly contemporary art. Geographically the collection is international in scope but chronologically it contains only works created within the past ten years; works older than a decade are sold. The museum presents about six major shows yearly of new and experimental work. Smaller exhibitions appear in the Work Space, whose rapid turnaround time allows installation of work at the cutting edge of recent developments. The Window on Broadway features painting, video art, sculpture, and work by artists featured in the galleries inside. The Window on Mercer Street is currently given over to performance art.

The museum building (1896; Cleverdon & Putzel), originally a store and manufacturing loft, was constructed as an investment by John Jacob Astor well after elegance had departed from this part of Broadway.

Across the street at 584 Broadway (bet. Houston / Prince Sts) is the **Museum of Contemporary Hispanic Art,** also known as MOCHA.

Museum of Contemporary Hispanic Art. 584 Broadway (Houston St), New York 10012. Tel: 966-6699. Open Tues–Sun, 11–5; Thurs until 8. Admission free but donation suggested.
Occasional music and performance events. Programs for school groups. Slide archive of contemporary Hispanic artists, open by appointment. Restroom, no telephones, no restaurant. Limited wheelchair access.

Formerly known as the Cayman Gallery, the Museum of Contemporary Hispanic Art (founded 1974 by the Historical Society of the Friends of Puerto Rico) exhibits works by Latin American artists living in New York and the U.S. who show interest in Latin American culture. The museum mounts about 20 exhibitions yearly, including one invitational show which draws from Spain, South America, and Latin America as well as from the U.S. The small permanent collection includes carved Puerto Rican *santos,* Puerto Rican posters, and works by contemporary Latin American artists.

Continue S. on Broadway, long a rather drab manufacturing area, now a focal point of the SoHo art scene. As rents on 57th St squeeze out all but the most intensely successful art dealers and the East Village fades as a magnet for the avant-garde, galleries from both locales are relocating here on the E. border of SoHo. The new galleries are most densely concentrated in two recently rehabilitated buildings on the E. side of the intersection of Broadway at Prince St, 560 Broadway and 568–578 Broadway, which have essentially become vertical malls specializing in art. Other galleries are creeping around the corner toward Lafayette St, pushing the E. border of SoHo even farther east.

On the ground level of 560 Broadway is *Dean & DeLuca*, one of the city's great food stores, whose glorious displays of produce, cheeses, cakes, fish, and prepared foods are rightfully housed in a building committed to art. The store first opened in SoHo in 1977 and moved to this location in 1988.

On the S.W. corner of Prince St and Broadway, at 561–563 Broadway, is the former **"Little Singer Building"** (1904; Ernest Flagg), so called because there once existed a bigger Singer Building, demolished in 1967 (see p. 135). Despite ugly ground-floor modifications, the building (now the Paul Building) is extremely handsome, with terra-cotta panels, delicate curls of wrought iron, large expanses of plate glass, and a great arch beneath the cornice. The building wraps around the corner of Prince St, enveloping 565 Broadway (1859; John Kellum), next door, whose carved marble Corinthian columns evoke the days when Ball, Black & Co. purveyed jewelry to society.

The next block of Broadway to the S., long filled with drab small manufacturing lofts and shops, glittered with the bright lights of theaters and music halls during the late 1850s and 1860s. The Empire Hall, the Palace of Mirrors, Heller's Salon Diabolique, and Willis' Gambling House all stood in this block as well as Niblo's Garden (1827) at 568-578 Broadway, known for its extravagant productions, its 75-ft stage, and its illuminated marquee with red gas jets.

Continue S. across Spring St. The restrained cast-iron facade at *550 Broadway* was added in 1901 to modernize an older masonry building and is one of the last such facades erected, though the use of cast-iron to spruce up old-fashioned masonry or to convert a residence into a commercial building was common in earlier decades. The building itself (1854) housed Tiffany & Co. until 1870.

On the W. side of the street at 555 Broadway the handsomely maintained ROUSS BUILDING (1889; Alfred Zucker) still pro-

claims the aplomb of merchant Charles "Broadway" Rouss, who
came debt-ridden to New York from Maryland and so flourished
that he took the street's name as his own and had it emblazoned
on his storefront.

At 521–523 Broadway are the bare remains of the *St. Nicholas
Hotel* (opened 1853), an establishment of legendary luxury. All
that survives of a white marble building that once ran about 275
ft S. from the corner of Spring St is this portion.

The present shabby condition of the building makes it difficult to believe that
at one time the hotel dazzled its clientele with tapestry carpets, magnificent
chandeliers, Sheffield plate, and a bridal suite decorated in such an excess of
white satin and carved rosewood that, according to *Putnam's Magazine,* it
caused timid brides to shrink and cower. This splendor was short-lived though,
for by 1870 these blocks of Broadway had fallen to commerce and the hotel,
while remaining profitable for another decade, had lost its glamour. It closed
in 1884 to be replaced in part by a loft building.

Continue walking S. on Broadway. The *bishop's crook lamppost*
in front of 515 Broadway dates from around 1900, when it and
others of its kind replaced the older gaslights which had been
introduced in the 1860s. About 1880 arc lights, perfected by
Charles Francis Brush, were installed at the intersections along
Broadway and in Union and Madison Squares, but in 1893 there
were still 26,524 gas lamps and 1535 electric lights. In 1896 this
classic lamppost—with its tendrils, scrollwork, and acanthus
leaves—designed by Richard Rodgers Bowker began to appear
on city streets. About two dozen, documented for preservation,
still remain.

There are altogether about 200 antique fixtures among the city's 340,000
streetlights. Upholding the older fixtures are T-arm poles with scrollwork
supporting their bilateral arms, M poles with straight arms, E poles with
curved arms, and A and B poles, armless but ornamented. The older heads are
called bishop's crook and teardrop; newer ones are the shoe box and the
ubiquitous cobra head.

Continue S. along Broadway to the N.E. corner of Broome St and
the once supremely elegant **Haughwout Building** (1857; John P.
Gaynor; DL) at 488–492 Broadway. Designed in the Italianate
palazzo style common to many early cast-iron buildings and
perhaps even modeled on the Sansovino Library in Venice, the
Haughwout Building (sometimes inappropriately called the Parthenon of Cast-Iron Architecture) was nonetheless a pioneering
structure—one of the first New York buildings whose floor loads
were carried by a cast-iron skeleton instead of masonry walls and
the very first to feature a passenger elevator with a safety device,
a steam-driven, cable-and-drum contraption invented by Elisha
Otis. The economy of casting many forms from the same mold
fostered the repetition of detail on cast-iron buildings such as
this one whose basic motif—a round-arch window between slender Corinthian colonnettes flanked by larger Corinthian columns—is repeated 92 times in four tiers on two facades. It is this
repetition, the result of a practical and economic principle, that
results in the frequently invoked harmony of the building. Originally the Haughwout Building, whose ironwork was cast by

The Haughwout Building. One of the earliest (1857) of SoHo's case-iron masterpieces, the building shows how the economy of casting repeated forms from the same mold fostered the skillful repetition of architectural detail. (Landmarks Preservation Commission, New York City. Photographer: John B. Bayley)

Daniel D. Badger & Co., was painted bright cream; now it is a dingy black.

Eder V. Haughwout sold china, glassware, chandeliers, and silver (to the White House and lesser householders) from the ground-floor showroom. After he retired in 1869, the building became a loft, including among its occupants M. H. Pulaski & Co., manufacturers of embroidery, whose monogram remains etched in the glass of the entrance.

Less than a half block S. of the Haughwout Building is the ROOSEVELT BUILDING (1874; Richard Morris Hunt) at 480 Broadway, one of two cast-iron buildings by an architect remembered primarily for the grandiose homes he built for the wealthy. Its decoration (tracery arches at the fourth floor, an outleaning fifth-floor cornice, neo-Grec motifs on the ground-floor pilasters) is quite original, in no way imitating stonework as do so many cast-iron buildings. Hunt's other New York survivals are the base of the Statue of Liberty and the Fifth Ave facade of the Metropolitan Museum of Art. Roosevelt Hospital, which inherited the site from James H. Roosevelt, who lived and practiced law here (1843–61), constructed the building as an investment. It extends through the block to Crosby St, where its narrow rear facade echoes the side facing Broadway.

Return to Broome St. Turn left (W.). **Broome Street,** named in 1806 after John Broome, lieutenant governor of New York State (1804) and a prominent businessman who demonstrated his acuity by purchasing 2 million lb of tea from China at the end of the Revolutionary War, thereby initiating the romantic and lucrative China trade.

Previously called Bayard Lane, the street led across the Bayard family farm to the Bowery Rd past Bayard's Mount, once the highest point in the developed part of Manhattan. When the hill was leveled from 1807–11 and its earth dumped as landfill into the Collect Pond (see p. 157), Broome St became a major east-west access route, a function it still maintains, linking the Holland Tunnel with the Williamsburg Bridge. Its function as a crosstown artery made it the target of Robert Moses's missionary zeal; his projected Lower Manhattan Expressway, an elevated highway above Broome St, would have carried heavy traffic from tunnel to bridge across the midsection of what is now SoHo. Moses's plan, conceived as early as World War II, was rejected by the Board of Estimates in 1968.

The dilapidated former warehouse, one building in from the corner, at *448 Broome St* (1875; Frederick Clarke Withers), with its unusual floral and filigree decoration, is the only known cast-iron building by the architect responsible for the reredos in Trinity Church, the Church of the Good Shepherd on Roosevelt Island, and the Jefferson Market Court House.

Continue west. The *Global Village Video Study Center* at 454 Broome St between Mercer and Greene Sts is a nonprofit video and film center with facilities for teaching, production, and exhibition. Here independent film and video makers present and discuss their work, and in the spring the center presents an annual documentary festival in conjunction with the Public Theater. For information tel: 966-7526.

On the S. side of the street is a fine though shabby stretch of cast-iron architecture, including *453–455 Broome St* (1873; Griffith Thomas), originally built as the Welcome G. Hitchcock silk and veilings firm. Hitchcock came as a poor boy from Montrose, Pennsylvania, and according to a contemporary achieved success by "industry, economy, ability, fidelity to each and every obligation, knowledge of his business, and proper consideration of his customers." Among his partners were Aaron Arnold and James Constable, founders of the Arnold Constable department store.

Continue W. on Broome St across Greene St. At 464–466 Broome St on the N.E. corner of the intersection is a building

(1861) constructed for Aaron Arnold of the Arnold Constable Dry Goods Co., who left it to his son and daughter.

Continue W. on Broome St; turn right (N.) on Wooster St. Between Broome and Spring Sts is the **Museum of Colored Glass and Light,** a small, private, intensely personal museum.

The Museum of Colored Glass and Light. 72 Wooster St (2nd floor), New York 10013. Tel: 226-7259. Open Tues–Sun 1–6; admission charge. No wheelchair access.

    SUBWAY: IRT Lexington Ave local (train 6) to Canal St. BMT Nassau St local (J or M train) to Canal St. BMT Broadway local or express (N or R train) to Canal St. BUS: M1 or M6 to Broome St or Grand St.

In these modest upstairs rooms hung with dark curtains and illuminated by the works themselves, founder Raphael Nemeth displays and explains his art, a group of laminated, fused, and painted glass works depicting religious and traditional subjects.

Turn around and walk S. on Wooster St; cross Broome St. In the next block between Broome and Grand Sts is **The Drawing Center.**

The Drawing Center. 35 Wooster St, New York 10013. Tel: 219-2166. Open Tues–Sat 11–6, Wed 11–8. Admission by donation. Lectures, symposia, workshops on paper conservation, viewing program where artists present works for possible exhibition, slide archive. Restrooms. Limited wheelchair access.

    SUBWAY: IRT Lexington Ave local (train 6) to Canal St. BMT Nassau St local (J or M train) to Canal St. BMT Broadway local or express (N or R train) to Canal St. BUS: M1 or M6 to Broome St or Grand St.

The Drawing Center (1977) is a nonprofit exhibition space devoted to fostering appreciation of drawing as a major art form. The gallery mounts five or six exhibitions yearly—some historical, some focusing on previously unexhibited works of established artists, some devoted to the works of emerging artists—designed to show the range and diversity of the medium. Previous exhibits have included architectural and theatrical drawings, music manuscripts, artists' postcards, and sketchbooks. One recent notable show brought a selection of drawings from the Victoria and Albert Museum.

The high quality of the installations as well as the handsome exhibition space (cast-iron Corinthian columns and expanses of white wall and hardwood floor) make The Drawing Center one of SoHo's most frequently visited galleries.

Return to Broome St. At *484–490 Broome St* on the N.W. corner of Wooster St (1890; Alfred Zucker) is a fine Romanesque Revival brick and rockface brownstone building once the warehouse and salesrooms of Fleitmann & Co., dealers in dry goods and tailors' trimmings.

Walk W. on Broome St. The brick building on the S.E. corner of the intersection with West Broadway (499 Broome St) dates from around 1825, when it was owned by one Alfred Pell, who probably used it as a residence. Much of Broome St, however, early developed as a commercial street, retains its industrial flavor better than some of the surrounding territory.

Turn N. on **West Broadway**, long the main thoroughfare of SoHo, known for shopping and restaurants, and until the recent emergence of the LoBro scene, as SoHo's mecca of galleries. Like its mirror, East Broadway, the street got its name from its intended function, relieving the congested traffic on Broadway, four blocks east. It is also SoHo's widest street and is the district's western frontier (only the E. side of the street lies within the protected SoHo Historic District, so that building fronts on the W. side have been altered extensively).

Walk N. and cross Spring St. In the block of West Broadway between Spring and Prince Sts is a group of the historically most influential **SoHo art galleries.** At **420 West Broadway** are the *Sonnabend Gallery* and the *Leo Castelli Gallery,* as well as *Germans Van Eck,* the *Charles Cowles Gallery,* and the *49th Parallel,* a government-supported center for Canadian artists. Across the street at 417 West Broadway is the *Mary Boone Gallery.* Leo Castelli, still acknowledged a major force in contemporary American art, became internationally recognized as an authority on Pop Art in the 1960s representing Andy Warhol, Roy Lichtenstein, and Claes Oldenburg.

Among the shops along these blocks are those with entertaining but marginally useful paraphernalia: toilet paper holders resembling classic cars, inflatable alligators, lamps which blow bubble gum, and outsize baseballs, golf balls, and pushpins.

Continue uptown across Prince St. At 468 West Broadway is a brick Romanesque Revival building (c. 1885), its round arches relieved by cast-iron floral swags in the spandrels. Next door at *472–478 West Broadway* is a one-time brick warehouse whose first-floor pilasters have been decorated with floral designs including cast-iron sunflowers.

Continue N. to Houston St, widened when the IND subway tunnels were carved out in 1936. Many of the buildings on the S. side still present blank walls and truncated facades to the road.

Walk east. Turn right at Wooster St. At 141 Wooster St, the Dia Art Foundation has installed Walter de Maria's *New York Earth Room.* This work (1977) consists of 220,000 lb or 222 cubic yards of dirt filling the gallery space to a uniform depth of 2 inches. (Admission free; open Tues–Sat 12–6; ring bell to left of door for entry. Tel: 473-8072).

Return to Houston St and walk E. to **Greene Street,** named after Revolutionary War general Nathanael Greene. *139 Greene St* is a brick Federal house (c. 1824) still graced by its original dormers and lintels. One of the few buildings remaining from SoHo's early period of residential development, it was owned originally by one Anthony Arnoux.

Across the street is *142 Greene St.* Behind most cast-iron fronts are buildings of conventional internal structure with brick bearing walls, wooden beams, and joists supporting wooden floors, but occasional buildings, like this one (1871; Henry Fernbach), have a system of slender cast-iron columns supporting the floors, an arrangement which permits a very open interior (and hence a lot of rentable space). Such columns, usually painted white, were often fluted and embellished with elaborate Corinthian capitals. Several influential art dealers have put the open interior to good use.

Walk S. on Greene St. *Nos. 121–123 Greene St* (1883; Henry Fernbach) is a fine example of this prolific architect's work. The building is elaborated with fluted pilasters, Corinthian columns, and an ornate cornice, all painted a smooth cream color. The sidewalks are granite, some with their original self-curbing.

Continue S. to Prince St. At *109 Prince St* (N.W. corner of the intersection) is a handsome cast-iron building with a chamfered entrance (1882; Jarvis Morgan Slade) built as a warehouse. Since 1943 it has been occupied by one of SoHo's more enduring businesses, the Industrial Electronic Hardware Company, a firm that now produces electronic components. The foundry label for "Architectural Iron Works, Cheney & Hewlett" is visible on the base of the column at the corner of Greene St.

At the S.W. corner of Prince and Greene Sts is a famous trompe l'oeil **mural** (1973) by Richard Haas, sponsored by City Walls Inc., an organization dedicated to enlivening such blank outdoor surfaces. With wit and precision the mural reproduces in paint on the brick E. wall of the building (1889; Richard Berger) the cast-iron detail of the N. facade; the castiron in turn suggests masonry construction—banded corner pilasters resembling masonry blocks, colonnettes standing on pedestals and supporting impost blocks, protruding cornices ending in decorative blocks supported by consoles.

The building houses the **SoHo Center for Visual Artists** (114 Prince St, Tues–Sat noon–6; closed New Year's Day, late July– early Sept, Thanksgiving, Christmas; tel: 226-1995). Larry Aldrich, founder of the Aldrich Museum in Ridgefield, Connecticut, established the SoHo Center in 1973 as a tax-exempt foundation to provide research facilities and exhibition space for fledgling artists. The center mounts about seven group shows yearly, each lasting about six weeks, and presenting the work—predominantly paintings and works on paper—of artists who have not yet had solo shows.

The buildings on the N. side of the street, *113–115, 117–119, and 121 Prince St* (1890; Cleverdon & Putzel), were built as warehouses, but have now been converted to the kind of trendy shops that mark the SoHo revival; they offer natural foods, herbal medicines, high-style shoes, imported edibles, and exotic, newly popular vegetables. As diverse as the proliferation of goods within is the wealth of ornament lavished on the warehouse facades: geometric, floral, foliate, and heraldic motifs, egg and dart moldings, and scrollwork.

Return to the intersection of Greene and Prince Sts and continue S. on Greene St. *Nos. 114–120 Greene St* (1882; Henry Fernbach) was built as a branch of the Frederick Loeser Department Store, whose main facility was in Brooklyn. *No. 113 Greene St* (1883; Henry Fernbach), across the street, built as a shop and warehouse for Lippman Toplitz, seller of caps and imported headgear, has a handsome cast-iron ground-floor facade added to a masonry building. The unusual and restrained ornamentation includes an Art Nouveau molding with entwined leaves below the architrave and incised ornament on the vertical supports flanking the central door and at the edges of the building.

On the same (W.) side of Greene St are three cast-iron buildings (93–95, 97, and 99), all designed in the neo-Grec style by Henry Fernbach in 1881. Look at 93–97 from the S. side to see how the iron facade is bolted to a masonry structure.

Continue S. to **Spring Street,** named after a spring tapped by Aaron Burr's Manhattan Water Company, whose ostensible purpose was to supply drinking water to the city but which quickly evolved into a banking company instead. Local legend maintains that a well at Broadway and Spring St became the grave of one Juliana (or Gulielma) Elmore Sands, whose body minus shoes, hat, and shawl was found floating there on Jan 2, 1800. Her fiance was acquitted of the crime but the victim apparently remained dissatisfied, for her ghost has been seen occasionally in the area; as recently as 1974 a resident of 535 Broadway at Spring St reported that a gray-haired apparition wearing mossy garments emerged from his waterbed. But 1974 seems to have been a boom time for the spring anyhow, since that same year it burst its underground channel and flooded a basement on West Broadway.

The brick building at the S.E. corner of Spring and Greene Sts (124 Spring St) was built in 1883 as a glass factory.

Turn left (E.) on Spring St. The three cast-iron buildings on the N. side date from the late 1870s: Nos.119 (1878; Robert Mook), 115, and 113 (1878; Henry Fernbach).

Return to Greene St and continue south. The building at **72–76 Greene Street** (1872; J. F. Duckworth), a redoubtable old pile known as the "King of Greene St," is actually two structures designed as one. The monogram cast on the central pilaster between the doorways belongs to the Gardner Colby Co., which used the building as a warehouse. Most of the other buildings on the block, designed by Henry Fernbach and John B. Snook in the early 1870s, until recently were used by firms dealing in rug clippings, wool rags, and fabric remnants, but now are being converted into galleries and shops. *No. 66 Greene St* (1873; John B. Snook) was built as a store for the Lorillard tobacco company.

Further down Greene St at the S.W. corner of Broome St (469–475 Broome St) is the **Gunther Building** (1871–72; Griffith Thomas), built as a warehouse for furrier William H. Gunther. The once elegant corner turning, with its curved panes of glass, is a notable feature of this handsome cast-iron building, now needing a coat of paint. The structure houses a cooperative art gallery with studio space for its member artists.

During the 1950s a group of cooperative galleries, founded by artists reacting against what they saw as the overly commercial values of the uptown art establishment, sprang up around 10th St. Although the 10th St galleries faded in the 1960s, a second generation emerged in SoHo in the 1970s, undertaken by artists who did not find, or wish to find, acceptance in private galleries. Co-op galleries, run by their members with or without a professional manager and financed by annual dues, may be politically or artistically exclusive, limiting membership to certain political or artistic groups (women, black artists, realist painters), or they may accept a wide range of work. In general they are more informal and less polished than private galleries.

Cross Broome St. *Nos. 44 and 46–50 Greene St* are masonry structures with cast-iron ornaments. The ground-floor pilasters of 46–50 Greene St (1860) are decorated with scrollwork and ornate medallions bolted onto the long horizontal panels of the pilasters. Some of the acanthus leaves, cast separately and bolted to the capitals, have fallen off.

Other advantages of cast iron as an architectural material in a period of rapid industrial expansion were speed and convenience of construction. The elements of a facade could be separately cast, the smaller pieces bolted together at the factory, the whole facade laid out with pieces numbered and tested for fit, and then shipped to the construction site where the front was assembled and permanently bolted into place.

Continue S. to Grand St and turn left (E.).

Nos. 91 and 93 Grand St (1869; John B. Snook) are two iron-fronted buildings resolutely imitating stone. The iron plates, cast in large sections and bolted through the brick front wall of the house, are grooved to look like uniform blocks of stone mortared together. The houses, which originally cost $6000 apiece, were built in 4½ months from a design offered in the catalogue of ironworker J. L. Jackson & Bros.; attached to the W. pier of No. 91 is the company's foundry label. The columns of 89 Grand St (1885) are identical to those of 31 and 72 Grand St, no doubt cast from the same mold.

Return to Greene St and continue south. The vista along this block, little changed since the 19C, delights cast-iron buffs as it reveals the city's longest continuous row of cast-iron architecture, the buildings at 8–34 Greene St, as well as several other superlative examples of the form.

The row may be catalogued as follows: 34 Greene St (1873) by Charles Wright; 28–30 Greene St (1872) and 32 Greene St (1873) by J. F. Duckworth; 16–18 Greene St (1880) and 20–26 Greene St (1880) by Samuel A. Warner; 8 Greene St (1883) and 10–14 Greene St (1896) by John B. Snook. As the proximity of dates suggests, SoHo became industrial very rapidly in the 1870s and 1880s. Many of these buildings were erected with retail space on the ground floor and lofts for warehouses or workshops above.

The *pièce de resistance* of the block between Grand and Canal Sts, the *Queen of Greene St,* is 28–30 Greene St (1872; J. F. Duckworth), a grandly ornate Second Empire building crowned with a stupendous mansard roof and painted a pale blue. The tall broad windows flanked by half-round columns, the keystoned segmental arches, the central two-window bay rising the full height of the building to a broken pediment, and the elaborate dormers with balustrades, modillions, pediments, and finials offer a wealth of architectural ornament.

One of the attractions of cast iron as a building material was the ease of creating details in any architectural style. As long as patterns could be carved and molds made, elaborate ornaments could be cheaply reproduced, allowing businessmen who could not afford the extravagance of stonecutting the prestige of fluted Corinthian columns, floral swags, anything they wanted, all bolted onto their buildings and painted to look like stone.

The plants in the upper-story windows reveal to the casual observer as they once did to the city inspector that the loft space has been converted to living quarters.

During the 1850s when nearby Broadway sparkled with theaters, hotels, and casinos, Greene and Mercer Sts were notorious for their brothels. While the houses on the S. end of the streets near Canal St catered to sailors from the ships docked in the Hudson, the houses further N. appealed to a wealthier clientele. An 1859 *Directory to the Seraglios in New York* written by an anonymous "Free Loveyer" recommends a Miss Clara Gordon at 119 Mercer St, "beautiful, entertaining and supremely seductive," who is patronized by Southern merchants and planters, and a Mrs. Bailey of 76 Greene St, whose comfortable and quiet "resort" is within a few moments' walk of Broadway and the principal hotels.

Continue S. to **Canal Street**. Canal St owes both its name and its exceptional width to a canal proposed by the city fathers in 1805 to serve as a storm drain, a household sewer, and a conduit siphoning off the waters of the Collect Pond near present Foley Square. By the 1820s both the street and the canal had been paved over, a mixed blessing: while the covered sewer alleviated the mosquito problem, the stench it created depressed both property values and morale until adequate air traps were installed.

Turn left (E.) and walk a block along Canal St to Mercer St. On the N.E. corner of Canal and Mercer Sts at 307–311 Canal St stands the former *Marble House* (1856-65; Griffith Thomas), now in sad decline from its heyday as home of the Arnold Constable Dry Goods Store. From Mercer St, however, it becomes apparent that only the Canal St facade of Marble House actually involved marble; the sides and rear of the building made do with humble brickwork. During the 1850s and 1860s the neighborhood boasted several such fine stores, including Lord & Taylor's, ultimately the victor in its perennial rivalry with Arnold Constable's, then located a block N. at Broadway and Grand St.

Turn into Mercer St. Not far N. of Canal St is the **Museum of Holography.**

Museum of Holography. 11 Mercer St, New York 10013. Tel: 925-0526 for infotape. Open Tues–Sun noon–6; Wed 10:30–6. Admission charge, lower rates for children and seniors. No food service; no telephone. Restrooms on ground floor. Gift shop. Limited wheelchair access. Reference library and guided tours for groups by appointment.

SUBWAY: IRT Lexington Ave local (train 6), IRT Broadway-7th Ave local (train 1 or 9), IND 8th Ave local or express (A or E train), or BMT Broadway local (R train) to Canal St. BUS: M1 or M6 to Canal St.

Founded in 1976, this small museum features changing exhibitions of state-of-the-art holograms (three-dimensional images produced by laser photography). In the basement is a permanent display on the history of holography. Educational films shown continuously during gallery hours explain to the uninitiated the techniques and significance of this unique visual medium. Included in the collection and sometimes on exhibit are holographic portraits of celebrities, impressively lifelike, some apparently able to wink, riffle through books, and blow kisses as the viewer walks around them.

The building itself (1870; F. E. Graef) began as a warehouse for the India Rubber Company. It still retains its vault cover, also known as an illuminated sidewalk or light platform, with glass discs embedded in the iron stoop to permit sunlight to illuminate the storage vault below, a system invented in 1845 by one Thaddeus Hyatt.

Return S. down **Mercer Street**, still paved with its 19C Belgian blocks; it is named after Hugh Mercer, a surgeon and brigadier general in the Revolutionary War.

Continue S. to **Canal Street,** which over the years has become a bazaar for industrial wares: nuts, bolts, spare machine parts, plexiglass and lucite, sheet metal, tools, and surplus office furniture. Recently it has become also a source for more domesticated items: blue jeans and military surplus clothing, household appliances of exotic provenance, mops and brooms, and novelties like rubber monsters, flamingo ashtrays, and plastic fried eggs.

If you are particularly interested in cast-iron architecture, walk a block E. along Canal St past Broadway to Lafayette St. On the S.W. corner of the intersection is an early cast-iron building, known by its address, 254–260 CANAL ST. Its Italianate half-round window arches and the Medusa-head keystones over the fourth floor windows suggest that it may have been designed by James Bogardus (1857).

TriBeCa, an acronym for the "TRIangle BElow CAnal" St, today reminiscent of SoHo a decade ago, is a pleasing neighborhood to explore for its architecture, its galleries, its signs of new life.

SUBWAY: IRT Broadway-7th Ave local (train 1 or 9) to Canal St or Franklin St, or IRT Broadway-7th Ave express (train 2 or 3) to Chambers St. IND 8th Ave local (A, C, or E train) to Canal St, or IND 8th Ave express (A or C train) to Chambers and Church Sts.

BUS: M10 uptown via Hudson St or downtown via Varick St. M8 crosstown on Broome / Grand Sts to the E. of TriBeCa, W. on Vestry St or E. on Watts St. M1 and M6 downtown via Broadway and uptown via Church St / 6th Ave.

Consisting of about 40 square blocks bounded by Canal, West, Church, and Chambers Sts (or Park Place, depending on whom you ask), TriBeCa has since the early 1970s been absorbing the spillover from SoHo and undergoing transformation from a market and industrial area to a middle-class residential neighborhood. Historically it acheived economic importance when the Washington Market, a distribution center for meat and produce, opened in 1880, and TriBeCa is still the city's primary depot for eggs, cheese, and butter.

Begin at Canal St and Broadway. Walk S. on Broadway past Lispenard St, named for Anthony Lispenard, who immigrated from France in the 18C for religious reasons. Back then the neighborhood was known as Lispenard Meadows.

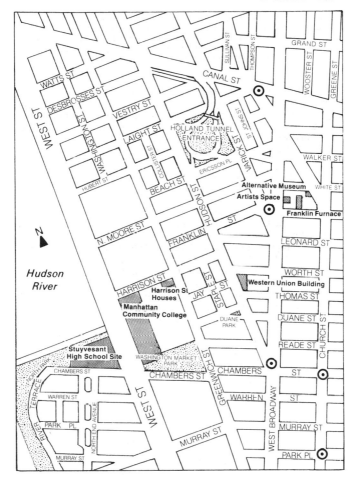

Continue past Walker St, named not for James J. Walker, high-flying mayor, but for a less flamboyant personality, Benjamin Walker, a captain of the Second New York Regiment during the Revolution and (1801–03) a representative to Congress.

Continue S. to **White Street** (namesake unknown). At 77 White St, E. of Broadway, were the premises of the now defunct *Mudd Club*, one of the earliest downtown nightclubs (1978), which lured artists, new wavers, punk rockers, and people who enjoyed proximity to the avant-garde. The club is gone but apparently lives on in the hearts of its devotees, for slogans such as ''Long Live Mudd'' and ''Punk's Not Dead'' have been spray-painted on the facade of the building.

A block S. at the S.W. corner of Broadway and Franklin St is the **James White Building** (1881–82; W. Wheeler Smith; DL), a cast-iron palazzo which arrived late in a neighborhood mostly built up before the Civil War. High up on the S. wall is a sign, faintly visible, advertising Civil War photographer Mathew Brady's studio, located above a saloon at 359 Broadway before the war. Return to White St.

Walk W. on White St. After the Civil War, many of the Greek Revival homes and shops that previously occupied this part of town were torn down in favor of larger industrial buildings, and, like SoHo to the N., TriBeCa has substantial offerings of cast-iron architecture. On the S.W. corner of Franklin Place stands 55 WHITE ST (1861; James Kellum & Son; DL), a building deemed sufficiently handsome by iron founder Daniel D. Badger to display its facade in his 1865 catalogue. At the time the building had keystones crowning the tall arches, Corinthian capitals atop the columns, and faceted quoins on the pier at the corner of Church St. Early occupants were Samuel I. and John Elliot Condict, who had a large saddlery here; in later years draper and textile firms tenanted the space.

The triangular pediment of 46–50 White St (1865) identifies WOODS MERCANTILE BUILDINGS (1865; DL). Across the street at 49 White St (bet. Broadway / Church St) is the CIVIC CENTER SYNAGOGUE (1967; William N. Breger Assocs.), an undulating expanse of marble hemmed in by its rectilinear neighbors. At 41 White St is the COLLECTIVE FOR LIVING CINEMA, an avant-garde and experimental film showcase which also screens old Hollywood movies and rarely seen foreign films. Tel: 925-2111.

White St is now the home of several art galleries and alternative art spaces which have abandoned the perceived egoism of SoHo and the isolation of the East Village for TriBeCa and its straightforward outlook (and more modest rents).

An alternative art space is, in the hierarchy of the art world, a starting point, a place where emerging artists can present their work unfettered by commercial constraints. Unlike conventional galleries which offer finished products for judgment or for sale, alternative spaces often have an unfinished, even raw, quality that encourages change and experimentation. Many began as collectives; some have strong ideological stances or focus on only one area of art (drawing, video); others work at the places where one art form impinges on another; many offer multimedia programs. Alternative art spaces are to emerging artists, more or less, what Off Off Broadway is to fledgling playwrights.

Cross Sixth Ave and continue west. At the S.W. corner of the intersection of White St, Church St, and Sixth Ave is the **Alternative Museum.**

Alternative Museum. 17 White St (intersection of Church St / 6th Ave), New York 10013. Tel: 966-4444. Open Tues–Sat 10–6. Free admission to museum, charge for concerts. Closed New Year's Day, month of Aug. Concert series of new music, workshops, publications. Restrooms. No telephones. No restaurant. No gift shop. Limited wheelchair accessibility. Museum is two steps up from street.

SUBWAY: IRT Broadway-7th Ave local (train 1 or 9) to Franklin St. IRT Lexington Ave local (train 6) to Canal St at Lafayette. IND 8th Ave local or express (A or E train) to Canal St. BMT Broadway local or express (R or N train) to Canal St. BUS: M1 downtown via 5th Ave / Broadway to White St. M6 downtown via 7th Ave / Broadway to White St. M10 downtown via 6th Ave to White St. M8 crosstown on Grand St to Canal St.

The Alternative Museum began (1975) on the Lower East Side showing the work of minority and Third World artists. Nowadays it continues this international emphasis while also providing exhibition space for artists not associated with any New York commercial gallery. Its shows are frequently political, polemical ("Disinformation: The Manufacture of Consent," "Endangered Species: Ecological Commentaries"), and almost always experimental. A New Music Program showcases jazz, folk music, and avant-garde classical styles.

Continue W. on White St. At **2 White St**, N.E. corner of West Broadway, is a small Federal house (1809; DL) which harks back to the 18C in style and character though it was built in the early years of the 19C; the gambrel roof is a rare survivor.

At West Broadway walk briefly north. At 260 West Broadway is the former **American Thread Building**, recently revivified and converted to condominiums.

Turn around and walk S. on West Broadway. **Artists Space**, as the name suggests, an alternative art space, which moved from Hudson St to this former noodle factory in 1984.

Artists Space. 223 West Broadway (bet. White / Franklin Sts), New York 10013. Tel: 226-3970. Open Tues–Sat 11–6. Closed Sun, Mon, major holidays, Aug, Dec 25–Jan 1. Free admission to gallery, admission charge for events. Exhibitions, music, films, lectures. Publications. Restrooms. No telephone, no restaurant, no gift shop. Limited wheelchair access. Entrance is five steep steps up from street. Gallery space all on one floor but video program is down a flight of stairs.
SUBWAY: IRT Broadway-7th Ave local (train 1 or 9) to Franklin St. IND 8th Ave express or local (A or E train) to Canal St. BUS: M6 uptown via 6th Ave, downtown via Broadway. M10 downtown via 7th Ave / Varick St, uptown via Hudson St / 8th Ave.

Artists Space was founded (1973) to help emerging artists cope with one of the primary obstacles confronting them—no place to show. The shows, which change frequently, are consistently interesting and innovative sometimes to the point of being raw and unfinished.

Continue S. to Franklin St. Another mainstay of the avant-garde in TriBeCa is **Franklin Furnace,** an archive and gallery of works of art in book form.

Franklin Furnace. 112 Franklin St (near West Broadway), New York 10013. Tel: 925-4671. Open Tues–Sat 12–6. Closed Sun, Mon, major holidays; check for summer hours. Free admission to exhibitions; fee charged for performances. Restroom. No restaurant, no telephones; no gift shop but posters, catalogues available. No wheelchair access (up four steps).
SUBWAY: IRT Broadway-7th Ave local (train 1 or 9) to Franklin St. IND 8th Ave express or local (A or E train) to Canal St. BUS: M6 uptown via 6th Ave, downtown via Broadway. M10 downtown via 7th Ave / Varick St, uptown via Hudson St / 8th Ave.

Founded (1976) by Martha Wilson to collect and preserve artist-designed books and other multiples produced after 1960 (magazines, pamphlets, record jackets, postcards, and the sort of printed matter often consigned to the trash can), Franklin Furnace, which calls itself "The Last WORD in Museums," now has more than 7000 of these objects, making it the largest such publicly funded archive in the world. The name, incidentally, comes from a sign, "Furnace," found on the premises by the director when she moved in.

Continue S. on West Broadway to Leonard St, named for another of Anthony Lispenard's sons. At 79 Leonard St, two blocks E. between Church St and Broadway, is *Pathfinder Books,* with a large selection of left-wing and Third World publications, records, posters, and other items.

In the same block stands a fine row of cast-iron buildings. One of them, **No. 85 Leonard St** (1860–61; James Bogardus; DL) is the only positively identified structure by James Bogardus in the city. Bogardus, the father of cast-iron architecture (see p. 192), foresaw the possibilities of bolting together sections of cast iron into facades or even whole buildings. Of course many different types of ornament could be bolted onto the sections, and this building is practically a catalogue of decorative elements: fluted columns (formerly with leafy capitals), lions' heads, rope moldings, bearded faces, dentiled moldings, faceted keystones, egg-and-dart trim, stylized leaves, and (best of all for cast-iron fanciers) Bogardus's own nameplate is embossed in the window ledge to the left of the door: *James Bogardus, Originator and Patentee of Iron Buildings. May 7, 1856.*

Return to West Broadway and continue downtown. The *Odeon* at 145 West Broadway on the S.E. corner of Thomas St, converted from a 30s vintage cafeteria, was the first of many stylish restaurants to follow the artists to TriBeCa.

Continue S. on West Broadway to Chambers St (for origin of the street name see p. 152). At 125 Chambers St stands what is possibly New York's oldest extant hotel, the Hotel Bond, currently being reconstructed. It was built around 1850 when the old Hudson River Railroad terminal, one of the routes that Cornelius Vanderbilt rode to fame, stood nearby on Warren St and West Broadway. Today a sign advertises the hotel to transients and permanent visitors.

A block S. on the wall of the building at the N.W. corner of West Broadway and Warren St a sign identifies West Broadway as College Place.

Kings College, now Columbia University, occupied the blocks bounded by West Broadway, Murray, Church, and Barclay Sts between 1760–1857, the first of its locations in the city.

Continue S. on West Broadway to Murray St, named after Joseph Murray, a pre-Revolutionary War lawyer and associate of John Chambers. In 1728 the two men were commended by the Common Council and given the "freedom of the city" (presumably an honor like getting the key to the city today) for refunding the 5-pound fees they had been paid for legal work.

Walk W. toward the river. At 75 Murray St is one of the earliest extant cast-iron fronts in the city, possibly also designed by James Bogardus. Italianate in style, it still retains Medusa-headed keystones over the arches on the third and fifth floors, appropriate enough in a medium (cast iron) which was used to imitate stone. Medusa-head keystones appeared on the defunct Laing stores (see p. 120) and on the one documentable example of Bogardus's work in the city, 85 Leonard St. The original tenants were Francis and John Hopkins, who had a glassware business.

Continue W. to Greenwich St and turn right (N.). *Public School 234* (1988; Richard Dattner), its design suggestive of an imaginative child's castle but on a far larger scale, stands on the N.W. corner of Warren and Greenwich Sts.

On the left-hand side is handsome WASHINGTON MARKET PARK (1983), a chunk of land carved out of the corner of the college campus, enclosed within a wrought-iron fence, and decorated with occasional ornaments from the former West Side Highway ramps.

As the park name suggests, **Washington Market,** which opened in 1880, stood in this vicinity, the market building itself occupying a square bounded by Fulton, Vesey, Washington, and West Sts (Washington St formerly ran one block W. of Greenwich St). A center for all kinds of produce, as well as cheese, butter, eggs, and candy, the market had spread into the surrounding streets along West St as far N. as Canal St by the third decade of the 20C. The market building was divided into stalls and offered everything from codfish tongues to bear steaks. The Hunts Point Market in the Bronx has supplanted this and most of the other old Manhattan markets.

Walk N. to Duane St, turn right and walk inland a block. **Duane Park** was created out of part of a plot of land whose history is known back to 1636, when it belonged to Annetje Jans, a Dutch farmer. The widow of a descendant, Roeloff Jans, married into the Bogardus family. Later the farm was sold to the English governor and then given to the Duke of York, who in turn gave it to Trinity Church. The city bought it in 1795 for a park, paying five dollars. The block, between the park and Greenwich St, has a collection of small late-19C Italianate and Romanesque Revival buildings. There are still a few dairy, butter, egg, and cheese distributors here, housed in small, older buildings, their trucks backed up to the old loading docks, giving a last fleeting suggestion of what this neighborhood was like years ago.

Return to **Greenwich Street** and continue north. The large apartment complexes, *Independence Plaza North and Independence Plaza South* (1975; Oppenheimer, Brady & Vogelstein), bounded by Greenwich, Duane, Washington, and N. Moore Sts, are middle-income housing, possibly the last middle-income housing that will be built in TriBeCa as the neighborhood gentrifies. The buildings stood nearly empty until federal subsidies made them rentable; now they have a long waiting list.

West of Independence Plaza, bounded by Duane, West, Greenwich, and N. Moore Sts, is **Manhattan Community College** (1983; Caudill, Rowlett, Scott, and Assocs.), part of the City University of New York. It previously occupied a group of rundown office buildings in midtown. In the plaza by the college entrance near West and Chambers Sts is Roy Shifrin's *Icarus* (1976), a bronze torso of the Greek mythological flyer who according to the sculptor "represents the uncertainties of our age."

In the shadows of Independence Plaza on Harrison St to the N. is a row of restored 18C townhouses, known as the **Harrison Street houses** (1796–1828; DL), formerly on Washington St but moved around the corner when the college was built. *Nos. 25, 37, 39, and 41 Harrison St* were built by John McComb, Jr., architect of City Hall, who lived in one. *Harrison St* takes its name from Harrison's Brewery, which stood near the river in pre-Revolutionary days and presumably belonged to one George Harrison, who also had an estate in this area.

Continue N. on Greenwich St, so named because when New York centered around Wall St and the Battery, it was the high road out of town to Greenwich Village. Many of the industrial buildings along Greenwich St were formerly occupied by food wholesalers and processors serving the nearby Washington Market, but gradually problems of space and transportation are forcing them out to New Jersey and elsewhere.

Turn right at Franklin St. Walk a block to Hudson St. The former **Powell Building** (1892; Carrère & Hastings), 105 Hudson St at the N.W. corner of Franklin and Hudson Sts, is a Renaissance Revival building in brick and terra-cotta which was enlarged four stories up and 25 feet N. in 1905.

Across the street on the N.E. corner of Hudson and Franklin Sts is *108 Hudson St* (c. 1895), which the *AIA Guide to New York City* aptly describes as having "rusticated marshmallow" columns.

Other nearby points of interest. Area at 157 Hudson St near Laight St, another hot spot of the mid-1980s (closed 1987), was known for its chameleonic decor which varied every six weeks or so from astroturf and topiary to disco glitz. One of its grandest installations was called "Art," and drew on the talents of such seasoned veterans as Larry Rivers and Andy Warhol, as well as Keith Haring, Kenny Scharf, and the other *wunderkinder* of the East Village.

On the far far west of the district is the *Market Diner*, at West and Laight Sts, an authentic Depression period, stainless steel, railroad-car diner, with authentic diner food.

Occupying the block bounded by Hudson, Varick, and Laight Sts and Ericsson Place are the ramps leading to the Holland Tunnel (just as well read about as seen). Once *St. John's Park* stood here, an elegant open space surrounded by red brick Federal row houses and anchored by St. John's Chapel, an outpost of Trinity Church that looked not unlike St. Paul's Chapel. The neighborhood was doomed in 1866 when Commodore Cornelius Vanderbilt bought the park for a million dollars, felled the trees, and constructed a freight warehouse for the Hudson River Railroad.

The **Holland Tunnel** was the first Hudson River vehicular tunnel, completed in 1927 and named after its chief engineer, Clifford M. Holland. Linking Canal St in Manhattan with 12th and 14th Sts in Jersey City, New Jersey, it may seem modest enough today, but when it opened it was heralded as a triumph of engineering. Among Holland's achievements was the design of the ventilation system, which included four ventilation towers in New Jersey and two in New York, housing immense fans which changed the air in the tunnel every 90 seconds. Operated by the Port Authority of New York and New Jersey, the tunnel carries more than 11 million cars in each direction annually. The N. and S. tubes are respectively 8558 and 8371 ft long.

Turn around and walk south. At 6 Harrison St, N.W. corner of Hudson St, is the former **New York Mercantile Exchange** (1886;

Thomas R. Jackson), a five-story gabled brick building with a handsome tower looking toward the river and rusticated granite pillars at the base. The tall second-story windows opened onto the trading floor, where on a good day at the turn of the century $15,000 worth of eggs changed hands in an hour. The exchange was organized in 1872 as the Butter and Cheese Exchange, for commercial objectives (fostering trade, reforming abuses) and also social ones (promoting good fellowship, providing for widows and orphans of members). Recently the building has been converted to condominiums.

Along with the spate of galleries which have settled here on lower Hudson St are a few remnants of the old days, for example *Puffy's Tavern*, at 81 Hudson St on the S.W. corner of Harrison St, which dates back to Prohibition and still has its old-fashioned bar, tile floor, and jukebox. It still draws old-fashioned truck drivers along with the new neighborhood professionals.

Continue south. The **Western Union Building** (1930; Voorhees, Gmelin & Walker) at 60 Hudson St between Thomas and Worth Sts and West Broadway is a noteworthy building by architect Ralph Walker whose Barclay-Vesey Building stands further downtown (see p. 138). When it opened, the Western Union Building housed telephone, telegraph, and ticker machinery, as well as a messenger service and classrooms where Western Union messenger boys could continue high school. Nineteen tones of brick shade the facade from deep red brown at the bottom to bright salmon at the top.

Walk through the lobby to West Broadway. Finished in brown brick, with recessed lighting and geometrically patterned brickwork and marble on the floor, the lobby gloriously exemplifies Art Deco materials and techniques.

Walk across *Thomas St* toward Broadway. Thomas St, incidentally, takes its name from Thomas Lispenard, a son of Anthony Lispenard (see p. 204). *No. 147 West Broadway* (1869; John O'Neil), S.E. corner of Thomas St, is a cast-iron building closer than most in its imitation of stone, down to the incised blocks on the facade and the quoins on the corners.

The building at *8 Thomas St* (1875; Jarvis Morgan Slade; DL) between Broadway and Church St has a cast-iron storefront on the bottom, topped off by four floors of Ruskinian Gothic brickwork and granite.

Across the street, on a different scale altogether, is the American Telephone & Telegraph Long Lines Building (1974; John Carl Warnecke & Assocs.), whose tall, windowless tower holds electronic equipment for the phone company.

There is a stop of the Broadway-7th Ave IRT at Canal and Varick Sts. The 8th Ave subway stops at Church and Canal Sts. The M10 bus runs uptown on Hudson St and there is a crosstown bus on Canal St.

8   Lafayette Historic Group, East Village, St. Mark's Historic District

SUBWAY: IRT Lexington Ave local (train 6) to Bleecker St. IND 6th Ave (train B, D, or F) to Broadway / Lafayette St.

BUS: M1, M5, or M6 to Houston St.

This walking tour through the Astor Place district, the East Village, and the St. Mark's Historic District explores one of New York's more motley areas. Within its boundaries, Houston St, 14th St, Fourth Ave and the Bowery, and Avenue A, live Bowery derelicts, working-class families, students, the remnants of 19C Polish, Russian, and Ukrainian immigrant communities, middle-class sometimes middle-aged "hippies," artists, merchants, a few remaining pink-haired punks, and a large black and Hispanic population E. of Tompkins Square. Culturally the area includes such established institutions as Grace Church, Cooper Union, and the New York Public Theater as well as the more experimental theaters of the East Village and the ethnic shops and restaurants around Second Ave. Architecturally it offers a beautiful 18C church, several late-Federal residences—both shabby and restored—fine examples of 19C commercial cast-iron and masonry architecture, and Louis H. Sullivan's only New York skyscraper. Because of historical circumstance—sudden and rapid development as a fine residential area in the early 19C followed by an equally rapid decline precipitated by the invasion of commerce along Broadway and the pressures of immigration around Tompkins Square—the district preserves in strange juxtaposition traces of its various stages of evolution. Long a working-class community, the East Village now is experiencing social conflicts traceable to the late 1960s, when it became the center of the "counterculture" and saw the influx of large numbers of young people whose lifestyles ran counter to the values of an aging immigrant society. The Electric Circus on St. Marks Place and the Fillmore East on Second Ave offered the flower children the latest in rock music and avant-garde entertainment, but by the mid- 1970s the counterculture had faded. The neighborhood continued to decay, beset by problems of drug abuse and crime until the 1980s, when once again its location and relatively cheap rents began attracting the young and (this time) the prosperous.

Begin at Broadway and Houston St; on the N.W. corner of the intersection is the former *Cable Building* (1894; McKim, Mead & White), built as an office building and power station for the Broadway Cable Traction Company.

Cable cars or trolleys, popular in other American cities, had to compete in New York with horse cars and horse-drawn stages in which Boss Tweed (see p. 152) held considerable interests. Most of the city's cable cars ran on Broadway and Third Ave, where electricity supplanted horse power at the end of the 19C.

Across the street at *620 Broadway* (1858; John B. Snook) is one of the city's earliest cast-iron buildings. Known as the "Little Cary Building" because its facade was cast from the same molds as the larger Cary Building (now *The Marketplace* on the W. side of Church St between Chambers and Reade Sts), the ironwork is designed to simulate masonry. The original *New York Mercantile Exchange* at 628–630 Broadway (1882; Herman J. Schwarzmann) still retains its unusual cast-iron facade adorned with roses and lilies, slender colonnettes ridged to suggest bamboo, and Oriental filigree arches below the cornice.

Continue N. on Broadway to Bleecker St and turn right (E.); walk a block to *Crosby St*, named after William Bedlow Crosby (1786–1865). Orphaned at the age of two, Crosby had the good luck to be adopted by his great-uncle Henry Rutgers, whose fortune he inherited and then devoted to good works.

The **Bayard-Condict Building** at 65–69 Bleecker St (1897–99; Louis H. Sullivan; DL), tucked away at the N. end of Crosby St, is one of Manhattan's little-known architectural treasures, the city's only example of the work of Louis H. Sullivan, a pioneer in skyscraper design. It is best seen from Crosby St near Houston St.

First called the Bayard Building in honor of one of the city's oldest families (though no Bayards were financially involved in the project), this 13-story office tower was undertaken by the United Loan and Investment Co., which hired Sullivan. Already known for his work in Chicago, Sullivan had also attracted attention for his radical theories on skyscraper design, theories which departed from the currently popular adaptation of classical and Renaissance models and stressed instead the importance of function as a determinant of form. Sullivan also recognized the importance of new building materials and their influence upon design.

His first plan for the building incorporated a freestanding steel skeleton with 14-inch structural columns and 12-inch exterior brick walls clad with terra-cotta. Unfortunately the conservative city building code ruled against the steel column system and insisted upon thickening the lower walls and columns, resulting in such a loss of floor space and rental income that the United Loan and Investment Co., now unable to afford the building, sold it to Silas and Emmeline Condict.

The EXTERIOR reflects Sullivan's famous dictum that a skyscraper should be a proud and soaring thing. Slender, vertical piers over the interior structural columns alternate with even more slender vertical columns between the windows. The sumptuous surface decoration of terra-cotta—a material that became practical as iron and steel framing techniques were developed—in leafy and geometric forms (designed by Sullivan and George Elmslie) culminates in an ornate cornice beneath which hover six angels with outspread wings. Although legend asserts that Silas Condict insisted on the angels over Sullivan's objection, the angels appear in a drawing made before Condict purchased the building.

The building, radical in its time, made little impression on other practicing architects, who continued working in more traditional styles.

Return to Broadway; turn right; walk a block north. The ornate building at 670 Broadway at Bond St is a *former Brooks Bros. clothing store* (1874; George E. Harney). The ironwork (attrib. Michael Grosz and Sons) is noteworthy for the geometrically designed bases and graceful leaf forms on the capitals of the street-level columns.

Brooks Bros. Clothiers occupied this store from 1874–84. Founded in 1818 on Cherry and Catherine Sts, the store first moved in 1863 when it was looted during the Draft Riots. Like other fashionable retailers, Brooks Brothers began a pilgrimage uptown, moving first to Broadway and Grand St, later to this site, then to the 23rd St area, and finally to its present location at 44th St and Madison Ave in 1915.

Walk a short block E. on **Bond Street** to Jones Alley. NO. 1 BOND ST, occupies the site of the home of Albert Gallatin, secretary of the treasury under Thomas Jefferson.

For a while in the 1830s and 1840s, the Bond St area was the cynosure of fashion, but the encroachment of commerce along Broadway put an end to its social eminence and its fine homes became boarding houses and offices. *Leslie's Illustrated Magazine* pointed out in 1857 that the number of teeth that are pulled out or "filled" in Bond St in one day would make a curious statistic. By 1870 it was solidly commercial.

Now converted to apartments, 1–5 BOND ST, the former **Robbins & Appleton Building** (1879; Stephen D. Hatch; DL), was built for Henry Robbins and David Appleton, proprietors of the American Waltham Watch Co.; the ground floor was also headquarters for publisher D. Appleton & Co., whose torches of learning adorn the spandrels above the main doorway. The building is a dramatic example of the French Second Empire style executed in cast iron with a mansard roof and the large expanses of plate glass, made possible by the strength of iron under compression so that a few widely spaced columns could support a sizable facade. With their gleaming plate windows and their light-colored facades (cast-iron buildings were frequently painted off-white), buildings such as this one must have dazzled onlookers.

Continue two blocks E. on Bond St to the **Bouwerie Lane Theatre** (1874; Henry Engelbert; DL), at 330 Bowery, built as the Bond Street Savings Bank, later the German Exchange Bank, and converted to its present use in 1963. The architect, working with a modest 25 × 100-ft building lot, has managed to create the impression of massive grandeur formerly associated with bank architecture, an undertaking made even more difficult since the short side of the lot faces the Bowery, the more important thoroughfare. The Corinthian columns, the cornices at every floor, the quoins and rusticated piers all masquerade as stone though they are executed in cast iron.

Cross the Bowery and continue E. to Second Avenue. Turn left (N.). Halfway up the block (W. side) between E. 2nd and E. 3rd Sts is small, gated (and locked) **New York Marble Cemetery** (1830; DL), the city's first nonsectarian graveyard, built as a commercial venture after burials were outlawed S. of Canal St. The investors in this half acre constructed 156 underground marble vaults and sold them to surgeon Valentine Mott, pastor Gardiner Spring, publisher Uriah Scribner, and tobacco magnate Peter Lorillard, among others. Of this group only the Scribners are buried here, though they were joined by Beekmans, Howes, Varicks, and Hoyts.

The following year the same corporation constructed another cemetery (walk S. to 2nd St; turn left or E. and continue a half block) on 2nd St east of Second Ave. Called the **New York** *City* **Marble Cemetery** (1831; DL) to distinguish it from its predecessor, it is laid out in rectilinear fashion with handsome monuments and gravestones, which can be seen through the fence. John Ericsson and James Monroe were once interred here but later removed; still remaining are Marinus Willett, Revolutionary army officer and mayor (1807), and members of the Roosevelt and Kip families. Here also rests Preserved Fish, member of a prominent family of lawyers and politicians, seemingly the victim of his parents' fondness for punning.

Continue on to First Ave and turn left (N.); at E. 3rd St turn right (E.) and continue a quarter block to the **First Houses** (1935-36; N.Y.C. Housing Authority; Frederick L. Ackerman; DL). The first project of the New York City Housing Authority, created during the Depression, the First Houses are rebuilt from existing tenements using work relief labor and bricks salvaged from demolished buildings. The Housing Authority purchased many of the original tenements at a fraction of their value from Vincent Astor who had inherited them from his grandfather John Jacob Astor, real estate entrepreneur and slumlord. Every third house was demolished to create light and air space for the remaining tenements which had to be rebuilt and reinforced with structural steel after the removal of adjoining structures made them unsound.

The Housing Authority opened a rental office for the 122 units in mid-January 1935 and was flooded with more than 3000 applications by March. Social workers chose the tenants, giving preference to those from the worst slums and those with small families. To the chosen, the new apartments, renting for $6.05 per room, were luxurious, each equipped with a refrigerator, a four-burner stove, and a bathroom. Though attacked as a boondoggle, the First Houses remain a source of pride to the city and a residential haven for an ethnically mixed, predominantly elderly group of tenants.

At 8 E. 3rd St near the Bowery is the NEW YORK CITY SHELTER CARE CENTER FOR MEN (c. 1915), once a branch of the Y.M.C.A, now a grim facility where the homeless may get food, counseling, and transportation to one of the 14 city-run men's shelters. Some 1500 men—drifters, ex-convicts, drug addicts, the mentally ill—daily pass through its heavy metal doors.

Across the street at 15 E. 3rd St is a onetime school, *Primary School No. 6* (c. 1875), later the *New York Turn Verein,* a sports and gymnastic club which followed the German population uptown to Yorkville.

Walk W. on E. 3rd St, which becomes *Great Jones Street* west of the Bowery. The land for the street was ceded to the city by Samuel Jones, a prominent lawyer and the city's first comptroller (1796–99), with the stipulation that it bear his name. Unfortunately New York already had a Jones St; for a while it had two, until Samuel Jones suggested calling his street "Great Jones St."

Continue west. At 44 Great Jones St is the firehouse of ENGINE COMPANY 33 (1898; Ernest Flagg and W.B. Chambers; DL), a satisfyingly flamboyant, impeccably maintained Beaux-Arts building dominated by a monumental three-story arch. Among its elegant details: a deep cornice with scroll brackets, tall French windows, and ornamental railings.

Across the street at 31–33 Great Jones St are two buildings constructed as stables; the lettering on the gables identifies them as one-time facilities for the Joseph Scott Trucking Corporation and the Beinecke Company.

Continue W. on Great Jones St to Lafayette St. On the N.W. corner is **376 Lafayette Street** (1888; Henry J. Hardenbergh; DL), originally a warehouse, designed by the architect better known for the Plaza Hotel and the Dakota Apartments.

On the N.E. corner of the intersection at 399 Lafayette St is the former **De Vinne Press Building** (1885; Babb, Cook & Willard; DL) a spare Romanesque Revival building constructed with masonry bearing walls and executed in dark brick with terra-cotta trim. Massive and simple, the De Vinne Press Building is remarkable for its appearance of weight and strength: note-worthy are the deeply recessed window arches and the restrained trim on the rounded corner turning. The building is now a rug store.

Theodore De Vinne (1828–1914) was a successful printer and distinguished scholar of the history of printing. The De Vinne Press achieved prominence through its publication of *Scribner's Monthly* and the *Century* magazine, but

De Vinne's more enduring achievements are his edition of the *Book of Common Prayer*, and the *Century Dictionary*.

Turn right (E.) and walk a half block to the ***Old Merchant's House.**

The Old Merchant's House. 29 E. 4th Street (bet. Lafayette St / Bowery), New York 10003. Tel: 777-1089. Open Sun 1–4. Closed Aug through Labor Day weekend. Small admission charge; children under 12 and members free. Groups of 20 or more by appointment weekdays. Restroom. No telephone. No restaurant. Sales table with postcards, pamphlets, catalogues. Not accessible to wheelchairs.

SUBWAY: IRT Lexington Ave local (train 6) to Astor Place. BMT Broadway local (N or R train) to 8th St and Broadway. IND 8th Ave local or express (A, C, E, or K train) to W. 4th. IND 6th Ave local (F train) or express (B train) to W. 4th St. BUS: M1 downtown via 5th Ave. M5 or M6 via Broadway. When the M1 terminates at 8th St, either walk S. to 4th St or transfer to the M6.

Known also as the Seabury Tredwell House, the Old Merchant's House (1832; attrib. Minard Lafever; DL), a three-story brick town house, is a stunning, remarkable survivor from the days when the Bond St neighborhood was the city's finest. Built on speculation by a hat merchant dabbling in real estate development, the house was purchased in 1835 for $18,000 by Seabury Tredwell. The Tredwells filled their home with fine contemporary furniture—some of it late Federal, most of it American Empire with some Victorian pieces—which still remains there today. The house stayed in the family until the last survivor, Gertrude Tredwell, died in it in 1933. Like her father, Gertrude was conservative by nature (apparently throwing out nothing) and at the end of her days lived in genteel poverty which would have prevented her from changing the house significantly even had she been temperamentally so disposed.

On view are a kitchen and family room (used by the Tredwell family for its everyday meals) on the ground floor. The next floor is the PARLOR FLOOR, with two beautiful parlors, both of which were used for more formal occasions and entertaining. They retain elaborate detailing which suggests Tredwell's affluence and also the furniture that belonged to the Tredwell family—in the FRONT PARLOR gondola chairs covered with black horsehair, a hand-carved Federal sofa with carved eagles. The REAR PARLOR, was used for family entertaining during Seabury Tredwell's lifetime but converted to a formal dining room after his death, conforming with the newly chic European custom of dining upstairs. On the next floor are BEDROOMS with Victorian and American Empire furniture. On the third floor are more bedrooms, with hall bedrooms at each end, and in the attic are four bedrooms for servants and a central servants' parlor heated by a potbellied stove (neither floor open to the public).

Further down the block at 37 E. 4th St is the SAMUEL TREDWELL SKIDMORE HOUSE (1844–45; DL) built by a distant Tredwell cousin, who made his living as a drug importer and served as a vestryman of Trinity Church. Most of its brownstone trim has succumbed to the pollutants in the city's atmosphere, but the paneled door flanked by Ionic columns is still handsome, though deteriorated. Less impressive and smaller in scale than the Old Merchant's House, it was built as part of a row of speculative dwellings.

Return to Lafayette St; turn right (N.) and walk uptown to the **Durst Building** (1891; Alfred Zucker) at 409–411 Lafayette St between E. 4th St and Astor Place, a cast-iron and brick building with terra-cotta trim, designed for Simon Goldenberg's haberdashery and workshops. On the ground floor are great iron-clad piers and freestanding iron columns ornamented with beaded rings.

Lafayette Street (originally Lafayette Place) ran only from Great Jones St to Astor Place when opened in 1826 and was, for a single generation, the city's swankiest residential address, the home of Astors, Vanderbilts, and Delanos.

In 1804 John Jacob Astor bought the land where the street now runs for $45,000; while waiting with his usual acumen for land values to rise, Astor leased it to a Frenchman who created a pleasure ground called Vauxhall Gardens with summer pavilions where visitors could buy light refreshments and a remodeled greenhouse where those so inclined could indulge in heavier drinking. In 1825 Astor reclaimed the gardens, carved out Lafayette Place, and sold building lots facing the new street for more than $45,000 apiece, the price of the entire parcel only 20 years earlier.

John Jacob Astor himself never lived on Lafayette St, but his son William B. Astor did—opposite Colonnade Row at 34 Lafayette Place, in a house described by a contemporary as a "plain but substantial looking brick mansion."

On the W. side of Lafayette St (428–434) stand the remains of **Colonnade Row** (1833; attrib. Alexander Jackson Davis; DL), once a handsome, highly desirable building, now suffering the indignities of neglect. First named La Grange Terrace after the country home of the Marquis de Lafayette, the row originally consisted of nine houses joined by a monumental two-story colonnade of Corinthian columns. The houses, built on speculation by Seth Geer, were faced with white Westchester marble cut by Sing Sing prisoners and sold for upwards of $25,000 apiece (a high price for a row house at the time) and were purchased eagerly by such notables as Franklin Delano, grandfather of Franklin D. Roosevelt, and David Gardiner, whose daughter Julia married President John Tyler in 1844. So successful were the houses that other colonnaded rows were built in Brooklyn Heights, on Broadway, and on W. 23rd St, but none has survived. Colonnade Row itself enjoyed only a brief moment of social splendor, as commerce continued moving up Broadway, depressing residential land values. By the 1860s the Astor mansion had become a restaurant, a neighborhood church had been converted to a boxing ring, and the five southernmost houses of Colonnade Row opened as the Colonnade Hotel. When Lafayette St was extended S. to the City Hall area in the 1880s, the remaining houses on the street became tenements and rooming houses or were torn down to make way for warehouses and factories. In 1901 the Wanamaker warehouse replaced the Colonnade Hotel and the district became solidly commercial.

Directly opposite Colonnade Row is the **Public Theater** (at 425

Lafayette St bet. E. 4th St / Astor Place), originally the **Astor Library,** a complicated building with a complicated pedigree (S. wing, 1849–53, Alexander Saeltzer; center wing, 1856–59, Griffith Thomas; N. wing, 1879–81, Thomas Stent; remodeled, 1966, Giorgio Cavaglieri; DL).

Although handsome and well proportioned, the building is remarkable not so much for its architectural style (it is a Victorian version of a Renaissance Italian palace), as for its rich historical associations. It opened in 1854 as the Astor Library, the only public benefaction of crusty, tight-fisted John Jacob Astor, who ostensibly dedicated it to working people but kept it open only during the day when workers couldn't use it. When the Astor Library was merged with the Lenox and Tilden collections in 1912 to form the nucleus of the New York Public Library system, the Hebrew Immigrant Aid Society took over the building and used it from 1921–65 in its work of resettling immigrants arriving from eastern Europe. In 1965, with the HIAS determined to move, impresario Joseph Papp, convinced the city to buy the building and remodel the interior under the guidance of Giorgio Cavaglieri, renovator of the Jefferson Market Courthouse (see p. 256). The building, now the headquarters of the New York Shakespeare Festival, witnessed the launching of many successful plays including such musicals as *Hair* and *Chorus Line*. In addition to plays, the Public offers jazz concerts, films, and poetry readings.

Reduced-price tickets, called Quiktix, for performances in any of its seven auditoriums are available at the box office Tues—Sun at 6 P.M. for evening performances, at 1 P.M. for matinees. The box office number is 598-7150.

Continue N. on Lafayette St to Astor Place. On the traffic island on the right (E.) side of the intersection is a 15-ft weathering steel cube (1966) by Bernard (Tony) Rosenthal. Balanced on one apex so that it will revolve when pushed, the work is entitled *Alamo,* a name derived from a remark by the sculptor's wife that the piece had the strength and feeling of a fortress. The subway entrance across the street at the Astor Place station (4th Ave and 8th St) is a cast-iron reproduction (1985) of an original kiosk and the subway station below (1904; Heins & La Farge; DL) is one of the best subway restorations in the city. Milton Glaser designed the new murals.

Across Lafayette St to the W. at 13 Astor Place is the *District 65 Building,* originally the *Mercantile Library Building* (1890; George E. Harney), home of the district offices of the United Auto Workers. The building stands on the site of the old Astor Place Opera House, now remembered chiefly for the Astor Place riot (May 10, 1849). An already bitter theatrical rivalry between English actor William Macready and his American counterpart Edwin Forrest which was fanned by working class anti-British and antiaristocratic sentiments erupted into violence during a performance of *Macbeth*. The audience inside the theater hurled garbage at Macready and a mob outside assaulted the building with bricks and paving stones. The militia summoned from the nearby Tompkins Market Armory was eventually ordered to fire into the crowd. Estimates of casualties differ, but the usual count is about 30 dead and 150 wounded.

Walk E. on Astor Place to Broadway. This segment of Broadway called **LoBro** (for Lower Broadway, an inaccurate appellation since Broadway runs S. all the way to the tip of the island) has since the early 1980s seen the renaissance of its real estate values and the rejuvenescence of its population.

Many gentrified Manhattan neighborhoods are designated by acronyms (perhaps to polish their former images), and this area can also be considered part of NoHo (North of Houston), the economic spillover from the archetypal gentrified neighborhood, SoHo.

The stores along Broadway—clothing stores with moderately priced but immoderately stylish gear, for example the *Unique Clothing Warehouse* (1984) at 718 Broadway, cookie shops, art galleries, a branch of *Conran's* (1982) with high-style, moderately priced furniture (10 Astor Place near Broadway) and one of *Tower Records* (1983), the transported California record store (692 Broadway at E. 4th St)—as well as the restaurants featuring currently favored cuisines and the clubs, all cater to the same crowd.

Along E. 8th St (N. of the District 65 Building) is the one-time annex of the famous **Wanamaker Department Store** (1904, addition 1907; Daniel H. Burnham & Co.), today used by the Parking Violations Bureau.

Turn around and walk N. on Broadway. Here begins a stretch of Broadway known during palmier days as **Ladies' Mile,** which peaked in the 1870s and 1880s, extending from 8th to 23rd Sts, and spilling over to Fifth and Sixth Aves. Ladies' Mile was *the* promenade for women of taste and means, making available to them the clothing and furnishings essential to displaying their position in society. The woman who could not be satisfied in James McCreery & Co., Arnold Constable, Lord and Taylor, B. Altman & Co., Best & Co., or Bonwit Teller was indeed difficult to please. While none of these stores has survived in this location and some have not survived at all, several of the original buildings remain, adapted to other uses. In 1989 the area was designated the Ladies' Mile Historic District.

Across E. 10th St where the Stewart House apartments presently stand was the old Wanamaker Store, a magnificent cast-iron building, constructed in 1862 as the A. T. Stewart Store by architect John Kellum. Outside were large, plate-glass Palladian windows in a gleaming white facade. Inside was a central rotunda encircled by galleries like the balconies in an opera house and illuminated by a glass dome. The Wanamaker store descended from A. T. Stewart's famous emporium which began to fail after Stewart's death in 1876 and was purchased in 1896 by John Wanamaker, the Philadelphia merchant, under whose care it first bloomed and then merely survived. In 1952 when the retail trade had moved far uptown the building was sold; while awaiting demolition, a spectacular fire ravaged it (July 15, 1956).

Continue N. along Broadway to E. 10th St, where ***Grace Church** (Protestant Episcopal) lifts its delicate spire skyward (open daily 10–5, Sat 12–4). Praised as New York's finest Gothic Revival church (1843–47; James Renwick, Jr.; DL), it was also once its most socially desirable, especially for weddings. The EXTERIOR white marble, quarried by Sing Sing convicts as an economy measure, has been dulled by pollution, but the delicate stonework and fine proportions of the church remain undiminished. The octagonal spire (1888) rising from the central tower replaces a wooden steeple—another economy measure instituted by the building committee; unfortunately the marble spire cost ⅔ the original cost of the whole church. Although early fears that the building would collapse beneath its weight were unfounded, the steeple's conspicuous list has prompted extensive repairs.

The INTERIOR is especially beautiful, with a handsome mosaic floor. The chancel window known either as the ''Te Deum'' window or the ''Church Triumphant'' window is by Clayton and

Bell (1879), an English firm with a conservative, quasi-medieval style. Henry Holiday's Pre-Raphaelite windows in the N. and S. aisles represent a bolder attempt to fuse medieval and 19C sensibilities. On the S. wall is a chantry added from Renwick's designs. In the N. transept is a bust of architect Renwick.

The family of Renwick's wife, née Margaret A. Brevoort, long held the land on which Grace Church stands. Henry Brevoort, according to legend, so loved his gardens and orchards that he refused to let the city push 11th St through his property, thereby giving Grace Church its spacious plot.

The handsome pews were sold to prominent families at the time the church opened, with some going for as high as $1400.

Leave the church and walk around to its north. The **Rectory** (DL), designed by Renwick at the same time as the church, one of the city's earliest Gothic Revival dwellings, is replete with pinnacles, gables, quatrefoil ornamentation, and traceried windows. The large urn in the Rectory Garden was brought to New York by William Reed Huntington (rector, 1883–1909).

The light gray apartment building across the street from the Rectory on the N.W. corner of Broadway (67 E. 11th St) formerly housed the James McCreery Dry Goods Store. Known as the **Cast Iron Building** (1868; John Kellum; converted, 1971; Stephen P. Jacobs), it has a handsome colonnade with ¾ round Corinthian columns on paneled pedestals along 11th St. The first floor, 20 ft high, has broad glass show windows whose light once flooded the sales counters. The fifth floor is an addition, replacing a mansard roof.

Unlike other department stores, McCreery's long adhered to its original line, dry goods, and at the end of the 19C was known for its fabrics, especially its silks and woolens, its wedding and trousseau gowns, and its ball dresses. James McCreery arrived as an Irish immigrant in 1845, began trade as a lace merchant, and rose to become a major merchandiser; he dedicated his fortune to the arts and eventually became a patron of the Metropolitan Museum of Art. McCreery's store moved uptown as fashion dictated, closing finally in 1954.

Walk around the S. side of the church on E. 10th St to Fourth Ave and turn left. **Grace Memorial House** (1882–83, James Renwick, Jr.; DL) at 94–96 Fourth Ave is now used by the Grace Church School.

By the late 1870s the parish served by Grace Church was no longer exclusively wealthy, and the church needed facilities for its poorer members. Levi P. Morton, Vice-President of the United States under Benjamin Harrison, donated money in memory of his wife for Grace Memorial House, first a day nursery, then a home for young women of modest means, and still later a rehabilitation center for girls. The building, originally two Greek Revival town houses, was altered to its present appearance by Renwick, who added the facade, the gable, and other features. NO. 96 FOURTH AVENUE was later duplicated by CLERGY HOUSE at 92 Fourth Ave (1902; Heins & La Farge) to make a symmetrical group of buildings. Later NEIGHBORHOOD HOUSE at No. 98 (1907; Renwick, Aspinwall, & Tucker) was added in the same style.

The stretch of Fourth Ave between Cooper Square and Union Square on 14th St was once **Book Row,** lined with shops for used and antiquarian books. In the 1950s some 50 dealers offered their wares, but since a used book store requires low rent and high traffic, irreconcilable conditions in New York today, such stores have all but disappeared. The primary survivor in the area is **The Strand** (828 Broadway at 12th St), which now stocks some 2 million books, including review copies, used books, paperbacks, and some antiquarian books.

Return to E. 10th St and walk E. through **St. Mark's Historic District,** which includes much of E. 10th St between Third and Second Aves, Renwick Triangle, St. Mark's-in-the-Bowery, and 232 E. 11th St. The district once lay within the boundaries of Peter Stuyvesant's original farm or *bouwerie,* purchased in 1651 from the Dutch West India Company and extending from the East River to Fourth Ave, from about present-day 5th–17th Sts.

The governor's great-grandson, Petrus Stuyvesant, decided to develop a part of the estate and in the late 1780s had his property mapped into building lots along a grid of streets oriented to the points of the compass, with the road that ran to the Bowery Rd from the old Stuyvesant mansion (whose probable foundations were uncovered in 1854 during excavations at 129 E. 10th St) incorporated into the plan as Stuyvesant St. Building began around 1800, but a few years later the city moved to impose its own scheme for development based on the Commissioners' Plan of 1811 which featured a street grid oriented to the long axis of Manhattan Island. Although the city generally closed existing streets or tore down buildings that did not conform to its plan, the Stuyvesant St neighborhood was allowed to remain, largely in deference to its wealthy families, including the Stuyvesants.

The houses at 112–128 E. 10th St and the houses directly behind them (23–35 Stuyvesant St) comprise **Renwick Triangle** (1861; attrib. James Renwick, Jr.), a group of 16 residences planned and built on land that once belonged to Hamilton Fish who sold it under the condition that no "noxious or offensive establishments"—breweries, slaughter houses, soap or glue factories, tanneries, cattle yards, or blacksmith shops—be built there. Before restrictive zoning laws, such covenants were the sole means of ensuring residential tranquility.

The houses, built in the Anglo-Italiánate style with red Philadelphia pressed brick and brownstone trim, have rusticated ground floors, bold cornices, and fully enframed upper-story windows; many have fine cast-iron railings. The dimensions of the houses conform to the triangular plot of land, with widths varying from 16–32 ft and depths from 16–48 ft.

Continue along E. 10th St to ***St. Mark's-in-the-Bowery** (Protestant Episcopal) at the N.W. corner of Second Ave (1799; DL). The church is the second oldest in the city after St. Paul's Chapel, and is built on the probable site of Gov. Stuyvesant's own chapel. The rubblestone walls and simple triangular pediment of the body of the church date from its late-Georgian, rural beginnings. The lovely Greek Revival steeple was added in 1828 (Ithiel Town), and an Italianate cast-iron portico was built in 1854 keeping the church abreast of the latest architectural fashions.

The Georgian interior (open Mon–Fri 9–4; Sun 9–1) was severely damaged in 1978 along with the steeple and roof when a worker's acetylene torch ignited the wooden gallery on the

St. Mark's-in-the-Bowery (built 1799), the second oldest church in the city. In the graveyard are the remains of Governor Peter Stuyvesant, whose "bouwerie," or farm, gave its name to the church and a nearby avenue. (Landmarks Preservation Commission, New York City)

second floor. In 1980 a new bell was installed, dedicated to the workers, many of them youthful laborers from the neighborhood, who rebuilt the church.

Flanking the main doorway are two Florentine marble lions and, outside the portico, two granite statues of American Indians by Solon Borglum, (1868–1922), brother of the more famous Gutzon Borglum, a rancher and adventurer before he took up art. At the W. end of the porch is a *bust of Daniel Tompkins* (1774–1825) by O. Grymes, erected in 1939. Lawyer, judge, legislator, and state governor, Tompkins was known for his liberal reforms in education, in the criminal code, and in human rights.

The graveyard (left side of church, sometimes locked) now paved with undulating rows of cobblestones and used as a play yard, was the scene of a ghoulish kidnapping in 1878 when department store millionaire A. T. Stewart was exhumed and carted off for $20,000 ransom. His body was recovered two years later. Resting more peaceably here are Commodore Matthew Perry, Daniel Tompkins, Philip Hone, described in Moses King's 1893 Handbook as "one of the most courtly and most distinguished New York mayors," and author of a famous diary. Also nearby, members of the Fish, Goelet, Schermerhorn, Stuyvesant, and Livingston families.

The entrance to the churchyard is on the other (N.) side of the church. Here stands the old church bell, cracked by the heat of the 1978 fire. Unlike the new electronically operated carillon, it was rung by a rope, and tolled the deaths of John F. Kennedy, Robert F. Kennedy, the Rev. Dr. Martin Luther King. Since King's assassination it has rung only for the end of the Vietnam War. Here also are the remains of Peter Stuyvesant, entombed in the church wall and a statue (to the right of the porch) of the governor sculpted in the Netherlands (1911) by Toon Dupuis. A plaque memorializes W. H. Auden, who lived in the neigborhood and was a parishioner of the church.

INTERIOR. The interior has been restored, retaining as much of the original detailing as possible. The stained glass windows on the lower level remain from the 19C, but the upper windows (1982; Harold Edelman) obviously are replacements.

St. Mark's-in-the-Bowery originally served an affluent, conservative congregation but in recent years has broadened its appeal, and now is one of the city's most active churches, both in terms of community action and in the arts. During the late 1950s and 1960s, as artists migrated to the area, theater began to flourish locally, and Theater Genesis, founded at the church in 1965, began producing experimental plays. Today the St. Mark's Poetry Project, the Danspace Project, and applied arts programs make it an important cultural center.

Second Avenue from Houston St to 14th St, once called the *Jewish Rialto,* was the home of a vital Yiddish theater beside whose musical comedies and melodramas the rest of the city theater paled. Between the turn of the century and the 1930s it nurtured such stars as Jacob Adler, Boris Thomashefsky, David Kessler, and later Molly Picon, Menashe Skulnik, Muni Weisenfreund (Paul Muni), and Luther and Stella Adler. Its modern counterpart, the Jewish Repertory Theatre (344 E. 14th St; 279-4200) offers plays in English on the Jewish experience.

Along with the theater were restaurants, Russian, Polish, Hungarian, and Romanian, serving the immigrant clientele. Most of the old-style restaurants are gone, though a few remain, for example, Hammer's Dairy Restaurant (243 E. 14th St bet. 2nd / 3rd Aves). The popular *Second Avenue Delicatessen* (2nd Ave at E. 10th St) was founded in 1954, but features (along with pastrami and corned beef) metal stars embedded in the sidewalk commemorating the greats of Yiddish theater.

Also in the neighborhood: *Entermedia,* at 189 Second Ave on the S.W. corner of E. 12th St, was originally *The Yiddish Art Theatre* (1926; Harrison G.

Wiseman), built for actor Maurice Schwartz. Across the street on the S.E. corner of the intersection was the *Cafe Royal,* the intellectual hotspot of the Yiddish-speaking intelligentsia; it closed in 1953.

Sculptor Karl Bitter, responsible for the Pulitzer Fountain near the Plaza Hotel (5th Ave at 59th St), had a studio at 249½ E. 13th St (bet. 2nd / 3rd Aves).

Return westward along Stuyvesant St, the other long leg of Renwick Triangle. At 21 Stuyvesant St near Third Ave is the **Stuyvesant-Fish Residence** (1803–04; DL) which dates from the earliest period of development of the Stuyvesant property. Built by Petrus Stuyvesant as a wedding present for his daughter Elizabeth and her husband, Nicholas Fish, the house is one of the city's grandest Federal residences, declaring the Stuyvesant wealth in its unusual height and width (28 ¾ ft). The east windows indicate that it was built as a freestanding (not a row) house. Other fine details include the handsome dormers, splayed brownstone lintels, rectangular top and sidelights, and Flemish bond brickwork.

Hamilton Fish (1808–93), born in this house to Elizabeth and Nicholas Fish, inherited from a childless relative half a million dollars and went on to become governor of New York., U.S. senator, and secretary of state.

Continue S.W. along Stuyvesant St, across Third Ave to Cooper Square (intersection of E. 7th St, the Bowery, Astor Place, and Fourth Ave) and the **Cooper Union Foundation Building** (1859; Frederick A. Peterson; DL; additions 1890s, Leopold Eidlitz; remodeling, 1975, John Hejduk), which embodies the innovative genius of its founder both in its physical plant and in the institution it houses.

Peter Cooper (1791–1883), a self-educated genius, designed the first American locomotive, promoted the Atlantic cable with Cyrus W. Field, and helped develop Morse's telegraph, but made his fortune largely through an ironworks in Trenton, New Jersey, and a glue factory in Baltimore. Unlike others of his breed, Cooper recognized that his wealth had come from the "cooperation of multitudes," and turned his millions to philanthropy. By establishing the Cooper Union as a free educational institution to give students the equivalent of a college degree while stressing also the practical arts and trades, Cooper provided for others the education he would have wished for himself. Requiring no other credentials than a good moral character, Cooper Union opened its doors to women as well as men, to adults as well as young people.

Built of brownstone in the Italianate style, the building incorporates some of the first wrought-iron beams used anywhere, beams which Cooper developed from train rails and for which he built the necessary rolling machinery in his Trenton plant. Later Cooper's beams evolved into I-beams which when translated into steel became the backbone of the modern skyscraper. The upper stories, added in the 1890s, once housed the collection of decorative arts that later became the nucleus of the Cooper-Hewitt Museum.

In 1973–74 the INTERIOR was gutted and the interior beams and columns encased in noncombustible materials; the new interior bears little relation to the old one except in its general proportions. Toward the N. end of the lobby an elaborate carved Victorian "birthday card" from the Foundation, thanks its benefactor for a donation of $150,000 on the occasion of his 80th birthday. Cooper donated over $650,000 to the school, but didn't endow it, thinking that rentals from shops in the street level arcade (E. and W. sides of the building) and offices would provide adequate operating income. On the right side of the lobby a staircase leads down to the *Great Hall,* a fine auditorium with arcades of supporting granite arches. One of Cooper's aims in founding the Union was to establish a forum where great issues of the day could be freely discussed. Here Henry Ward Beecher, William Cullen Bryant, and William Lloyd Garrison spoke against slavery before the Civil War. Here Abraham Lincoln made his famous "Might makes right" speech in 1860, winning the support of the N.Y. press and hence the presidential nomination. Later the auditorium housed the People's Institute, offering lectures to education-hungry Jews from the Lower East Side.

Just S. of the main entrance to Cooper Union is a *statue of Peter Cooper* (1894, installed 1897; Augustus Saint-Gaudens) by a sculptor who had received his early training as a night student at Cooper Union. The bronze statue sits beneath a marble canopy designed by the sculptor's friend Stanford White.

Across Third Ave to the E. (bet. E. 6th / E. 7th Sts) is the *Abram S. Hewitt Memorial Hall* of Cooper Union (1905; Clinton & Russell). Active in founding and managing Cooper Union, Hewitt established the first American open-hearth furnace with Cooper's son Edward; later he became a U.S. congressman and mayor of New York (1887–88). The building stands on the site of the former Tompkins Market Armory, home of the Seventh Regiment whose troops were called out to quell the Astor Place Riots.

Walk E. on 7th St, heart of the city's Ukrainian enclave. "Little Ukraine," a community estimated at some 20,000 people in the East Village, stretches along Second Avenue from about E. 4th St to E. 14th St. It is a flourishing community, its churches and ethnic associations full and active, its members prospering. While some of the original settlers came during the last century along with other Eastern European immigrants, the main influx of Ukrainians came fleeing Soviet domination after World War II. The community dwindled during the 1960s and 1970s, but is today expanding as younger Ukrainians remain in the area and new immigrants arrive. Many residents speak Ukrainian, take part in Ukrainian activities, and read *Svoboda,* the Ukrainian-language daily published in Jersey City.

On the S. side of E. 7th St at the intersection with Taras Sevchenko Place, renamed in 1978 for the 19C Ukrainian writer and political activist (it was formerly called Hall Place after the man who ceded the land for the street), is the new building of ST. GEORGE'S UKRAINIAN CATHOLIC CHURCH (1977; Apollinare Osadca). On the N. side of the street is the *Surma Book and Record Company* (11 E. 7th St), which specializes in Ukrainian books, records, and crafts.

McSORLEY'S OLD ALE HOUSE (formerly McSorley's Saloon) at 15 E. 7th St was founded by John McSorley in 1854 and has befriended the drinking man ever since. Peter Cooper was a customer, as was painter John Sloan who recorded its atmosphere in his painting *A Mug of Ale at McSorley's* (1913); Joseph Mitchell wrote of it in a book, *McSorley's Wonderful Saloon*. Only in 1970, when it became illegal to exclude women, did McSorley's befriend also the drinking woman.

In the block of E. 6th St between First and Second Aves stretches a row of small, inexpensive Indian restaurants. On the N. side of the street (323 E. 6th St) is the COMMUNITY SYNAGOGUE CENTER (1848), built as the United German Lutheran Church during the period when the immigrants surrounding Tompkins Square were largely German.

Return to Third Ave and E. 7th St. The grand marble edifice at the N.E. corner (59 Third Ave), the former **Metropolitan Savings Bank** (1868; Carl Pfeiffer; DL) is now a nondenominational Christian church. This French Second Empire-style building is— in marble—what the cast-iron Bouwerie Lane Theatre (also formerly a bank) pretends to be; massive and imposing, with quoins at the corners and cornices articulating every floor. It was built seven years before the Bouwerie Lane Theatre and could have been its prototype.

Turn right (N.) and walk a block along Third Ave to St. Mark's Place, actually the section of E. 8th St between Third Ave and Avenue A. Turn right into St. Mark's Place.

During the 1960s **St. Mark's Place** became the Main St of the **East Village** (the neighborhood east of the Bowery stretching from about Houston St to 14th St) and the focus of New York's "counterculture." Before that period, the East Village had been considered simply a part of the Lower East Side, and as such had witnessed from the mid-19C onward the arrival of various ethnic groups: Germans, Poles, Ukrainians, Russians, and later Puerto Ricans and blacks, now mostly concentrated in the eastern section near Avenues A–D. In the late 1950s writers and poets, some of them members of the "Beat Generation," lived in the area: Jack Kerouac, Allen Ginsberg, William Burroughs, Norman Mailer. Seen historically the influx of "hippies" in the 1960s was one more wave of immigrants, seeking cheap rents and a place to establish a new life. Like the groups that preceded them, they put their stamp on the neighborhood: the book and "head" shops (i.e., shops selling drug paraphernalia), the avant-garde theatrical establishments; and the layers of peeling pink and blue paint mark their presence just as the ethnic churches, social clubs, and restaurants recall earlier arrivals. In the early 1980s the East Village began another period of change, as young professionals, spurred by a severe shortage of rental housing, moved downtown, bringing in their wake upscale restaurants, gourmet food stores, and cafes as well as night clubs, performance spaces, and a profusion of art galleries. For a while in the early 1980s the East Village art scene was the hottest in town, with some openings drawing crowds of over a thousand people and limousines regularly parked in front of the major galleries.

When first developed in the early 19C, **St. Mark's Place** was a fashionable street, its houses set back from the sidewalks to give a street of standard width (60 ft) the impression of spacious elegance. NO. 4 ST. MARK'S PLACE (1831–32) with its rickety, lopsided dormers, retains an ornamental stone molding on its Federal-style fanlight doorway. Novelist James Fenimore Cooper rented 6 St. Mark's Place in 1834. NO. 12 ST. MARK'S PLACE (1885; William C. Frohne) was built as the social hall of a German shooting club, the *Deutsch-Amerikanische Schuetzen Gesellschaft*, its identity marked architecturally by the ornamental terra-cotta target and crossed rifles decorating the upper part of the facade.

Downstairs is the ST. MARK'S BOOKSHOP, a haven for serious browsers with a stock that reflects the intellectual tastes of the community it serves instead of the popular tastes of the larger uptown chains. The shop, which inherited some of the fixtures of Eli Wilentz's legendary Eighth Street Bookstore in Greenwich Village (closed 1979) has a good selection of books on poetry, new fiction, drama, politics, and aesthetics. There is an annex across the street.

NO. 20 ST. MARK'S PLACE (1832; DL), as yet unrestored, is the original *Daniel LeRoy House*, its Federal doorway—ornamented with splayed triple keystones—reminiscent of that gracing the Old Merchant's House four blocks south. The building at 23 St. Mark's Place once housed The Dom, a Polish-American social club, and later, as the home of the rock group, the Electric Circus, became a central institution of East Village culture.

Continue E. to Second Avenue. The *Gem Spa*, at 131 Second Ave on the corner of St. Mark's Place is a good place to buy offbeat magazines, foreign newspapers, and that nostalgic New York drink, the egg cream. Today egg creams are concocted of milk, chocolate or vanilla syrup, and seltzer, but historically they are said to have contained both cream and eggs.

Turn left on Second Ave. On the W. side of the street at 135 Second Ave between St. Mark's Place and E. 9th St is the **Ottendorfer Branch of the New York Public Library** (1884; William Schickel; DL), originally the *Freie Bibliothek und Lesehalle*, a bright red brick building with terra-cotta ornament, donated by Oswald and Anna Ottendorfer to the large local German immigrant community.

Anna Ottendorfer immigrated to the U.S. in 1844 with her first husband Jacob Uhl, who purchased the *New Yorker Staats Zeitung* and made it a thriving daily newspaper. Six years after Uhl's death in 1853, she married Oswald Ottendorfer, the paper's editor-in-chief, under whose directorship it further evolved into a respected, conservative journal. Ottendorfer personally selected the library's original collection of books.

Next door at 137 Second Ave is the **Stuyvesant Polyclinic Hospital** (1884; William Schickel; DL) founded and endowed by the Ottendorfers as the German Dispensary. Designed in an energetic neo-Italian Renaissance style, the clinic is architecturally noteworthy for its terra-cotta ornament, which includes portrait busts of physicians and scientists: Celsius, Hippocrates, Aesculapius, and Galen on the porch; Harvey, Linné (Linnaeus), Humboldt, Lavoisier, and Hufeland on the frieze beneath the cornice.

In 1866 the dispensary, which provided free outpatient care to the poor, became a branch of the German Hospital at Park Ave and 77th St (now Lenox Hill Hospital). In 1906, the German *Polyklinik*, another charitable organization which provided free care and training for medical students, bought the building. During World War I, because of intense anti-German sentiment, the clinic's name was changed to the Stuyvesant Polyclinic. Between the wars it reverted to its original name only to become the Stuyvesant Polyclinic again during World War II.

Across the street at 140–142 Second Ave is the UKRAINIAN NATIONAL HOME, a community center with an inexpensive, home-style Ukrainian restaurant whose specialties include kielbasa, varnishkes, stuffed cabbage, pierogi, and other eastern European dishes.

Walk N. to the **Ukrainian Museum** at 203 Second Ave between 12th and 13th Sts.

The Ukrainian Museum. 203 Second Avenue (bet. 12th / 13th Sts), New York 10003. Tel: 228-0110. Open Wed–Sun 1–5. Admission charge. Changing exhibitions, workshops, lectures, educational programs. Souvenirs, folk art, gifts. Accessible to wheelchairs.
SUBWAY: IRT Lexington Ave express (train 4 or 5) to Union Square. BMT Broadway local (N or R train) to Union Square. BMT 14th St-Canarsie local (L train) to First Ave. BUS: M15 downtown via 2nd Ave.

The museum contains over 2000 objects, which illustrate the range of Ukrainian crafts: embroidered and woven textiles, costumes, pysanky (Easter eggs), ceramics, woodwork, and metalwork.

Turn around and walk S. on Second Ave. Walk E. on E. 11th St to First Ave. Along the way are several old- and new-style restaurants. *Veniero's Cafe* at 342 E. 11th St, a tile-floored coffee shop and *pasticceria* founded almost a century ago by immigrants from Sorrento, makes traditional Italian pastries.

Turn S. on First Ave. Also venerable is the *De Robertis Pasticceria,* at 176 First Ave, between E. 11th and E. 10th Sts. Its tiled floors and walls and the old-fashioned showcases hark back to 1907; the pastries hark back to Italy.

Turn E. on E. 10th St. At 268 E. 10th St (bet. 1st Ave / Ave A) is the TENTH STREET BATHS, almost a centenarian (1892?) and probably the only traditional Russian-Turkish steam bath remaining in the city. Years ago many such establishments modeled after their Old World predecessors served people without bathtubs, but were consequently shunned as too old-fashioned by the children of immigrants. Many that remained acquired sexual connotations and have since closed. This one is said to have attracted gangsters who checked their weapons as the more law abiding checked their coats; the legend further asserts that the baths hired deaf-mute attendants who neither heard nor spoke evil.

Continue E. along 10th St to Avenue A. On the S.W. corner of E. 10th St and Avenue A is **St. Nicholas Carpatho Russian**

Orthodox Greek Catholic Church (1883; James Renwick, Jr. and W.H. Russell), founded by the Rutherford-Stuyvesant family as St. Mark's Chapel. The interior is distinguished by tiled walls, stained glass, and carved wooden beams.

Across Avenue A is **Tompkins Square Park,** named after Daniel Tompkins whose remains lie at St. Mark's-in-the-Bowery. Along the N. side of the park is a handsome row of houses built in 1846 when the Tompkins Square neighborhood was felt to have an auspicious future. The houses on the S. side, built just a year later, were described at the time of completion as "new and desirable tenements" but their ground floors were designed as stores to be rented for $200 a year, an indication of the coming decline of the area. By the 1850s German immigrants had begun to displace the previous residents and the one- and two-family houses were sliced up into rooming houses or razed to make way for profitable tenements. By the 1860s the area was described as dirty, seedy, and dusty; 4th St between Avenues A and B was called "Ragpickers' Row," while 11th St from First Ave to Avenue B became "Mackerelville."

Enter the 16-acre park along the N. walkway near E. 10th St. Originally part of a salt marsh known as Stuyvesant Swamp, the land was given to the city by the Stuyvesant family in 1833. It served as a recruiting camp during the Civil War and witnessed riots during the financial panic of 1873. Its present population reflects the ethnic and racial mix of the neighborhood: members of the Russian, Ukrainian, and Polish community, most of them older people, enjoy the benches and tables for chess and checkers along the S. side; younger people, many of them black or Hispanic, play basketball, skate on the walkways, and listen to music.

About halfway through the park along the walkway is a small monument whose eroded features depict a boy and girl looking at a steamboat, a memorial to the victims of the *General Slocum*, an excursion steamer that burned in the East River on June 15, 1904. Some 1200 people, most of them women and children from this predominantly German neighborhood, burned or drowned in the tragedy. Many men, kept from the outing by their jobs, lost their entire families; for the bereaved, the Tompkins Square neighborhood became too full of painful memories and an exodus to other German communities within the city followed the disaster. As the Germans moved out, Jews moved in, changing the ethnic character of the area within a few years.

Near the 9th St entrance is the *Temperance Fountain* (1888; Henry D. Cogswell), given to the city by the Moderation Society; it once had a life-size statue of Hebe (the water carrier) on its peak and a water fountain within; its aim of encouraging the healthful consumption of water instead of alcohol is still appropriate today to Tompkins Square.

Near the S.W. entrance to the park is a statue of Samuel Sullivan Cox, "the letter carrier's friend," an Ohio congressman who earned this appellation by sponsoring legislation that raised wages and gave salaried vacations to postmen. The statue (1891; Louise Lawson) was commissioned by the mailmen of America and first erected in Cooper Square where it occasioned criticism that the figure resembled a floor walker beckoning an approaching customer. When Saint-Gaudens's figure of Peter Cooper was installed there, Congressman Cox was moved here.

On the E. side of the park runs Avenue B, and E. of that, Avenues C and D.

Across the park **Christodora House** (1928; Henry C. Pelton) at the N.E. corner of E. 9th St and Avenue B, one of the few tall buildings in the area, has a history that reflects that of the area as a whole. In 1897 Sara Libby Carson and Christina MacColl founded a settlement house at 1637 Avenue B, calling it Christodora House, a name suggested by a college professor to mean "gift of the Christ."

In 1928 Christodora House moved to this 17-story brick building, financed by Arthur Curtiss James, a railroad magnate. George Gershwin, whose brother Ira headed the house Poets' Guild, is said to have given his first public concert on the third floor. Christodora House functioned successfully until after World War II when it was sold to the city, which turned it over (late 1960s) to community groups. After a group of political activists destroyed the electrical system, the building was sealed. In 1975 it sold at public auction for a mere $62,500. Rehabilitated in 1986–87, Christodora House, the onetime "skyscraper settlement house," today contains luxury condominium apartments.

Nearby are two more buildings constructed for the relief of the poor. The former NEWSBOYS' AND BOOTBLACKS' LODGING HOUSE, CHILDREN'S AID SOCIETY (1887; Vaux and Radford), at 127 Avenue B, N.E. corner of E. 8th St, has been converted to apartments. Also, the original SIXTH STREET INDUSTRIAL SCHOOL, CHILDREN'S AID SOCIETY (1890; Vaux & Radford) at 630 E. 6th St (bet. Avenue B / Avenue C) is today a shelter run by Trinity Lutheran Church. In the 1880s Calvert Vaux (of Central Park fame) and George Radford designed nine lodging houses and industrial schools in tenement districts for the Children's Aid Society.

At the far E. side of the island are the JACOB RIIS HOUSES (1966; Pomerance & Breines), one of the city's more admirable public housing projects. Jacob Riis was an early social reformer (see p. 706).

Return to Avenue A on the W. side of Tompkins Square. At the N.W. corner of the avenue and E. 7th St is the *Leshko Coffee Shop*, one of the remaining Polish restaurants in the area. A little further downtown is *Pyramid*, at 101 Avenue A, between E. 6th–E. 7th Sts, a rock and roll club that peaked in the mid-1980s.

Walk back along E. 10th St toward First Ave. Along the N. side of the park are several galleries and cafes serving the newer, gentrified population of the East Village.

The nearest subway is the BMT 14th St local (L train) at 14th St and 1st Ave. The IRT Lexington Ave local (train 6) stops at Astor Place. (E. 8th St and 4th Ave). Bus M15 runs uptown on 1st Ave and downtown on 2nd Ave.

9 Greenwich Village

History. When Washington Square was still marshland traversed by Minetta Brook, an Indian settlement called Sapokanican stood in the general area of present-day Greenwich Village. The Dutch pushed out the Indians and divided the land into large farms one of which, the Bossen Bouwerie (Wooded Farm) belonged to Wouter Van Twiller. The second governor-general of the colony, he was a maladroit administrator whose particular liabilities were greed and a fondness for wine. Under the British the area became known as Greenwich (Green Village), a name that first appeared in city records in 1713. A few large landholders dominated the rural fields—Trinity Church which held considerable property in the West Village south of Christopher St, Capt. Peter Warren, who purchased 300 acres in 1744, and such established families as the De Lanceys, Lispenards, and Van Cortlandts. By the 1790s, however, as the city spread northward, in part fleeing epidemics of yellow fever and other diseases, the large estates were being broken up.

Between 1825 and 1850 the population of the Village quadrupled. Since its inhabitants were predominantly native born, the area became known as the "American Ward," a title that lost its accuracy toward the end of the century. By 1870 the Village had become a backwater, fashionable commerce sweeping ever north along Broadway, first enveloping the area and then passing it by, leaving a vacuum filled by immigrants. First came the Irish and a black population who settled south of Washington Square; they were displaced by Italians in the 1890s and a second, poorer, wave of Irish who settled around Sheridan Square. Row houses gave way to tenements, while shops and hotels were converted to warehouses or manufacturing lofts suitable for exploiting immigrant labor.

Around the turn of the century, the Village entered its halcyon period. Because of its relative isolation, its historic charm, and the indifference or social tolerance of a foreign population who adhered to the spiritual precepts of the Roman Catholic church and the political dictates of the Democratic Party machine, the Village offered a haven for the radical, avant-garde element of American society. Here were cheap rents and freedom from the late-Victorian sexual and materialistic attitudes that dominated middle-class American culture. Soon the place swarmed with radical social and artistic activity: Max Eastman founded *The Masses* (1910), a radical paper whose publication was suppressed in 1918 because it opposed the war; the *Seven Arts* (founded 1916), whose columns integrated political and artistic ideas, met a similar fate. Clubs like the "A" Club and the Liberal Club became forums for such inflammatory topics as women's suffrage, birth control, anarchy, and free love.

Among the theater groups flourishing in the opening decades of the 20C were the Provincetown Players whose productions, staged in a converted stable on MacDougal St, displayed the talents of such playwrights and performers as Eugene O'Neill, Edna St. Vincent Millay, Susan Glaspell, and Bette Davis. The Theater Guild, which started as the Washington Square Players, moved uptown in 1919 and became an innovative force in the American theater, producing new plays and hiring unknown actors. Resident Village writers included Sherwood Anderson, Theodore Dreiser, John Dos Passos, and Van Wyck Brooks as well as poets e.e. cummings, Hart Crane, and Marianne Moore.

The isolation of the Village, however, soon came to an end. Seventh Ave South was cut through south of Greenwich Ave and W. 11th St in 1919. Sixth Ave was extended south of Carmine St in the 1920s, and in the 1930s the IND subway joined the old IRT (opened 1904), linking the Village to the rest of the city. Real estate developers began tearing down the old row houses and replacing them with high-rise, high-rent apartments, a process that accelerated distressingly after World War II.

Though its high rents exclude the struggling unrecognized artist, a trace of the old bohemianism still clings to the Village. Its jazz clubs attract both old and new performers; its theaters are still active. Because of its longstanding tolerance, the Village has a significant homosexual community and has been a base for feminist and gay activists, but it also attracts middle-class and professional people who, perhaps because of the traditional

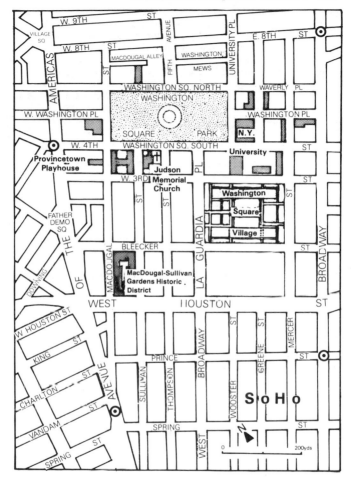

Village sense of community, have frequently and visibly exercised themselves in political and social causes.

A.   Washington Square, New York University, and the South Village

SUBWAY: IND 6th and 8th Ave lines (train A, B, C, D, E, or F) to W. 4th St station.

BUS: M1, M2, M3, M5, M6, M7.

Begin at **West 8th Street** and Sixth Ave (Ave of the Americas). Formerly the main shopping street of the Village, W. 8th St has deteriorated in recent years, its galleries and bookstores giving way to fast food outlets and, for inexplicable reasons, a glut of shoe stores.

Walk E. on W. 8th St. The *Eighth Street Playhouse* (52 W. 8th St), now an ordinary movie theater, opened in 1928 as a show-case featuring the technological advances of theatrical architect Frederick J. Kiesler. Slide shows could be projected on the side walls and the main screen could be enlarged or reduced, innovations which failed to impress several successive owners who drastically altered Kiesler's work.

Further along at 8 W. 8th St the *New York Studio School of Drawing, Painting, and Sculpture* occupies a peeling pink Art Deco building that once housed the collection of the Whitney Museum of Art, founded in 1931 by Gertrude Vanderbilt Whitney. Member of a wealthy New York family and a sculptor herself, Mrs. Whitney remodeled one of the stables in MacDougal Alley as a studio and gallery. From this beginning evolved the Studio Club and eventually the museum which remained here until 1949.

Return to the intersection of MacDougal St and W. 8th St.

Turn S. into **MacDougal Street,** named after Alexander McDougall (*sic*), a successful merchant and political activist (died 1786). As a major general in the American Revolution, he succeeded Benedict Arnold commanding the defenses at West Point; after the war he became first president of the Bank of New York.

The austere modern building on the W. side of the street (171 MacDougal St) is the *Tenth Church of Christ, Scientist* (converted 1967; Victor Christ-Janer), originally a factory and store (1891; Renwick, Aspinwall & Russell). Directly opposite the church is **MacDougal Alley,** a gated, dead-end street overhung by the bulky apartment building at 2 Fifth Ave. The houses, now remodeled in a variety of styles ranging from vaguely Federal to pseudo-Tudor, were built in the 1850s as stables for homes on W. 8th St and Washington Square and were converted to residences during the 1920s and 1930s. At No. 19 was Gertrude Vanderbilt Whitney's studio.

Continue half a block S. on MacDougal St to **Waverly Place,** renamed in 1833 (Sir Walter Scott had died the previous year), after Scott's novel. The house at 108 Waverly Place (half a block W. of MacDougal St) dates from 1826 but was altered to its present odd, crenellated form in 1906 by architect Charles C. Haight. War correspondent and novelist Richard Harding Davis (1864–1916) lived here during his early newspaper days.

Turn left and walk along the N. side of Washington Square Park. Throughout the 19C, attractive row houses faced the square on three sides, but now only **Washington Square North** suggests the former dignity and gentility of the neighborhood. The row here, on the W. portion of the street, was developed (late 1820s to 1850s) by individual owners, and the houses reflect various styles—Federal, Greek Revival, and Italianate. Nos. 21–23 are

Greek Revival mansions (1835–36) with fine freestanding columned doorways, long parlor windows, and fine ironwork, considered in its day especially suited to park settings (see p. 281). The parlor window balcony on No. 21 with anthemion and Greek key motifs combined on a wheel is especially handsome.

The earliest house on the square (No. 20) is one of the city's few remaining Federal mansions, constructed 1828–29 as a country residence for one George P. Rogers and converted into apartments in 1880 by Henry Hardenbergh, architect of the Plaza Hotel. The keystone and blocks in the arched doorway and the panels in the lintels are decorated with a bold vermiform design. The building is owned by the Catholic church and houses a center for the elderly and dormitories for nuns.

The original buildings from 18 Washington Square North to Fifth Ave have been demolished, including two matching Rhinelander family mansions and Henry James's grandmother's Greek Revival house (No. 18), which provided the setting for his novel *Washington Square.* In 1951 the entire site with adjoining property on Fifth Ave was sold for an apartment house, dismaying the local populace who then waged a battle against what they considered the wanton development of their neighborhood. The only concession the developers made was to scale down the wing facing the park, but the result is bland and unappealing.

Cross Fifth Ave to the east. One of the architectural jewels of this part of the Village is the group of houses extending from Fifth Ave east to University Place, Nos. 1–13 Washington Square North, known simply and perhaps snobbishly as **The Row.** Built in 1831–33 on land belonging to Sailors' Snug Harbor, they form one of the city's first examples of controlled urban design.

Sailors' Snug Harbor, a foundation for the benefit of aged and decrepit seamen, came into existence under the will of Robert Richard Randall (died 1801). His father, captain Thomas Randall, a privateer, amassed a fortune preying on French ships trading with Quebec and the West Indies before he left the seas for a sedate mercantile career. Among Randall's assets was a large plot of land running N. and E. from the foot of Fifth Ave, a tract which his son enlarged and endowed as a home for impoverished sailors. In 1801 the land was valued at $25,000, but by the beginning of the 20C it had appreciated to a value of $50 million. The original sailors' home, supported by income from this land, is now a Designated Landmark on Staten Island, although the sailors themselves have moved to a new facility in North Carolina.

In 1831 builders James Boorman, John Johnston, and John Morrison leased the land for the row from Sailors' Snug Harbor with certain stipulations about design and use: brick or stone construction, a 12-ft setback from the lot line, no slaughterhouses, no tallow chandleries, no forges or other offensive businesses. Thus the group of fine Greek Revival houses forms one continuous row.

The fronts are red brick; the basement stories and trim are marble, as are the freestanding porches and massive balustrades—a feature lavished on only the most expensive houses. Along the street runs an iron fence with anthemia, lyres, and Greek key motifs. Yet even this fine row has not escaped alteration. The house at No. 3 is a Victorian replacement. In 1939 Sailors' Snug Harbor gutted the interiors of Nos. 7–13 and converted them to apartments to increase the income from the property, but today the buildings are used by New York University, largely as offices.

Among the famous residents of the row have been Edith Wharton, William Dean Howells, and John Dos Passos who at No. 3 wrote *Manhattan Transfer.*

At the corner of Washington Square North and University Place, cross over to the park and walk back (S.W.) toward the center of the park along the diagonal path.

Washington Square Park was once marshland through which Minetta Brook wandered on its way to the Hudson River. Its first inhabitants, after the Indians, were some black slaves, freed by the Dutch beginning in 1644 and granted land for farming in this vicinity. Toward the end of the 18C it became a potters' field and a hanging ground. In 1826 the field was converted to a parade ground and in 1827 the park was laid out, attracting the well-to-do whose houses rose along its perimeter. In 1837 New York University constructed its first building on the E. side of the park, a handsome Gothic Revival building.

In the early 1950s Robert Moses, then Parks' Commissioner, and always a highway advocate, decided to push a highway over, under, or through the park to ease the flow of traffic downtown on Fifth Ave, a project that Villagers fought for almost a decade, this time with a successful outcome.

Today the park swarms with activity during good weather: parents and children, students, chess players, roller skaters (in defiance of posted notices), and the inevitable representatives of the city's distressed and derelict population. In recent years neighborhood residents have complained of increasing crime, particularly drug-related offenses, in the park, especially at night, and nowadays there is a heightened police presence.

Near the intersection of the diagonal walk and the central crosswalk is a rather stiff *statue of Giuseppe Garibaldi* (c. 1888; Giovanni Turini) presented to the city by its Italian-American citizens; from 1851–53, the Italian revolutionary lived in exile on Staten Island. Directly W. of the statue across the central plaza is a heroic *bust of Alexander L. Holley* (died 1882), metallurgist, inventor, and engineer, who established the Bessemer steel process in America. The bronze bust (1889) by John Quincy Adams Ward is one of the finer works by a sculptor who left more examples of his art in the city than any other person.

Walk N. to **Washington Arch** (designed 1892, dedicated 1895; Stanford White), which dominates the entrance to the park. The present grand marble arch replaces a temporary wooden one erected (1889) to commemorate the centennial of George Washington's inauguration as the nation's first President and financed by William Rhinelander Stewart, who lived at No. 17 Washington Square North and collected $2765 from friends for a triumphal arch built near the foot of Fifth Ave. Onlookers were so pleased that the structure was perpetuated in marble.

The arch is 77 ft high; the piers are 30 ft apart; the arch opening is 47 ft high. The frieze is carved with a design of 13 large stars, 42 small stars, and the initial "W" repeated at intervals between emblems of war and peace; in the spandrels of the arch are figures of Victory. Sculpted against the N. side of the E. pier is "Washington in War" (1916; Hermon A. MacNeil), the commander-in-chief flanked by Fame (right) and Valor. On the W. pier is "Washington in Peace" (1918; A. Stirling Calder), showing the statesman with Justice and Wisdom, holding a book inscribed (faintly nowadays) "exitus acta probat" ("the end justifies the deed"). The sculptor was the father of Alexander Calder.

Recently restored, the arch was formerly defaced by political, religious, feminist, and racial slogans spray-painted in several languages, a sign of the Village's political activism and linguistic competence.

Cross Washington Square North and walk N. on Fifth Ave. A half block N. on the E. side of the avenue is WASHINGTON MEWS, a private alley. The buildings on its N. side were stables, as the configuration of their doors suggests, while those on the S. were built in the 1930s on land formerly part of the back gardens of the houses facing Washington Square.

Continue N. on Fifth Ave to the corner of 8th St. The apartment tower on the S.E. corner ONE FIFTH AVE (1929; Helmle, Corbett & Harrison and Sugarman & Berger) is a handsome Art Deco building with "Gothic" details: stylized gargoyles, pointed window arches over the balconies, and simulated vertical piers achieved by using different colors of brick. During the 1920s the "A" Club met at One Fifth Ave; it claimed among its politically and socially avant-garde members Rose O'Neill, inventor of the Kewpie doll, and Frances Perkins, secretary of labor during Franklin D. Roosevelt's presidency.

Across 8th St on the N.E. corner of the intersection are the BREVOORT APARTMENTS, whose name is the only reminder in this vicinity of a family that once owned the land surrounding lower Fifth Ave. The Brevoorts' holdings, which came into the family as early as 1701, stretched N. and S. from about 8th to 13th Sts and E. and W. between Fourth and Sixth Aves.

Henry Brevoort, one of New York's few millionaires in the 1840s, built a Greek Revival mansion on the corner of Fifth Ave and 9th St, partly with the proceeds from real estate sales. The house became famous as the site of a scandalous masked ball during which two of the guests took advantage of their disguises to elope. After this incident masked balls were forbidden for a while and the sponsors of such dangerous entertainments became liable for fines of up to $1000.

The Brevoort Hotel (opened 1854), a quiet, aristocratic hotel noted for its cuisine and its appeal to English tourists, later stood on the site of the present apartments. While the upstairs dining room catered to an expensively sedate uptown clientele, the basement café became a gathering place for the Village's bohemian population and the site of various extravagant parties, climaxing on the eve of Prohibition when the hotel's liquor was sold at wholesale prices to an overflow crowd.

Walk E. on 8th St. The unusual row of houses, 6–26 E. 8th St (best seen from the N. side), are apartments remodeled by Harvey Wiley Corbett in 1916. Corbett, remembered for the Criminal Courts Building (the old "Tombs") and his work at Rockefeller Center, has here transformed a row of 19C Greek Revival houses in a picturesque, stagy manner, altering rooflines and window shapes, decorating the facades with brickwork, stucco, and wrought iron.

Continue E. to the corner of University Place; turn S. (right) and walk back toward Washington Square. The remodeled row houses at the E. entrance to Washington Mews belong to N.Y.U. (as do several of the houses within the mews).

Continue S. on University Place across Waverly Place to the Main Building of **New York University,** founded in 1831 by a group of business and professional men including Albert Gallatin, secretary of the treasury under Thomas Jefferson. The university, nonsectarian and modern in its curriculum, was to offer practical as well as classical courses to a middle-class student body, providing an alternative to Episcopalian and conservative Columbia College. Among its early faculty members were John W. Draper, professor of chemistry and physiology, who is credited with making the first photographic portrait of the human face, and Samuel F. B. Morse, painter, sculptor, and inventor of the telegraph and of Morse code.

The Main Building replaces a Gothic Revival structure torn down in 1894 that resembled King's College Chapel in Cambridge, England. Rooms in its tower were rented to students, including Winslow Homer, Walt Whitman, and inventor Samuel Colt, who worked there on the revolver ultimately named after him.

During the early 1960s, N.Y.U. provoked local hostility for its territorial expansion and its disregard for existing Village architecture. In 1964 the university hired architects Philip Johnson and Richard Foster to produce a master plan to unify the campus and end its haphazard growth, but the plan has resulted only in three bulky buildings (the Tisch building, the Meyer physics building, and Bobst Library), all faced with bright red sandstone. Soaring costs halted the plan to reface the buildings on the E. side of the square with the same stone.

Continue past the Main Building to Washington Place and turn left. The S.W. corner of the building (entrance at 33 Washington Place) has been refurbished as the **Grey Art Gallery and Study Center,** and offers interesting, unusual art exhibitions.

Grey Art Gallery and Study Center. 33 Washington Place (Washington Square East), New York 10003. Tel: 998-6780. Open Sept–June, Tues and Thurs 10–6:30, Wed 10–8:30, Fri 10–5, Sat 1–5. Summer hours (July and Aug) Mon–Fri 10–6. Closed major holidays. Suggested donation. Lectures, special events. No restaurant; telephone and restrooms in building.
SUBWAY: IRT Lexington Ave (train 6) to Astor Place. IRT Broadway-7th Ave local (train 1 or 9) to Christopher St. IND 8th Ave and 6th Ave (A, B, C, D, E, or F train) to W. 4th St. BMT Broadway local (R train) to 8th St / Broadway. BUS: M1, M2, M3, M5, downtown via 5th Ave. M6 downtown via 7th Ave / Broadway.

The building at 29 Washington Place, now called the BROWN BUILDING and belonging to N.Y.U., was built in 1900 as a manufacturing loft, the Asch Building. The building cost some $400,000 to construct but the owners declined to have a sprinkler system installed for another $5000 because they considered the stone and brick structure fireproof. It proved flammable on Saturday, Mar 25, 1911, when fire broke out at about 4:30 P.M. in the upper stories where the Triangle Shirtwaist Co. employed some 600 laborers, largely Italian and Jewish immigrant girls. Most of the doors to the stairs had been locked to prevent the employees from stealing; the stairways were narrow and winding; the fire escape could not bear the weight of the fleeing workers and tore free from the wall; fire department ladders reached up only six stories. Before the fire was brought under control, perhaps 20 minutes later, 146 workers died, most plummeting to the pavement on Washington Place ten floors below. Although the owners were acquitted of manslaughter and received some $65,000 more in insurance than they paid out in claims (making a profit of $6445 per victim), the fire brought improved safety regulations and working conditions for sweatshop employees and still remains an important landmark in the history of labor reforms.

Arthur L. Carter Hall at 10 Washington Place (1891; Richard Berger; restored 1972), half a block E., demonstrates how attractive the neighborhood's cast-iron and granite loft buildings must have looked in their prime.

Continue east. Toward the end of the 19C, as the Village waned in elegance, manufacturing lofts were built to take advantage of the cheap labor pouring into the Lower East Side. Several of these lofts remain on the blocks between Greene St and Broadway to the east.

Visible on the S.W. corner of Broadway and Washington Place is the André and Bella Meyer Physics Hall (1971; Philip Johnson and Richard Foster), one of the bright red sandstone towers of the master plan.

Both Mercer and Greene Sts are named after Revolutionary War generals: Nathanael Greene from Rhode Island and Hugh Mercer, born in Scotland.

Turn S. (right) on Mercer St and walk to the intersection of W. 4th St. *The Bottom Line*, across the street at 15 W. 4th St, is a popular cabaret theater, featuring jazz, rock, and folk music and also comedy and drama. In the late 1970s it was a showcase for the emerging talents of rock star Bruce Springsteen and new wave stars Steve Reich and Philip Glass.

Across the intersection is BROOKDALE CENTER, HEBREW UNION COLLEGE (1979; Abramowitz, Harris, and Kingsland). Within the building are the Petrie Synagogue with windows, ark, and eternal light by Yaacov Agam, and the Joseph Exhibition Center (open Mon–Fri 10–4 and some Sundays), whose changing exhibits focus on Jewish life and culture. Formerly located on W. 68th St, Hebrew Union College is an important center of Reform Judaism, whose programs reach both students and the public. The college offers courses in sacred music, communal service, and biblical archaeology as well as a graduate rabbinic program.

Founded in 1875 in Cincinnati by Rabbi Isaac Mayer Wise, Hebrew Union College was the first institution of Jewish higher education in the country, its function to train rabbis for the Reform movement. In 1922 Rabbi Stephen S. Wise founded the Jewish Institute of Religion in New York and in 1950 the two institutions, similar in orientation, merged.

Walk W. on W. 4th St toward the park. Across from The Bottom Line is *Warren Weaver Hall*, an early N.Y.U. effort at contemporary architecture (1966; Warner, Burns, Toan & Lunde). Next to it is *Tisch Hall* (1972; Philip Johnson and Richard Foster), another product of the master plan. At the W. end of the plaza in front of it is a Gothic finial removed from the original N.Y.U. Gothic Revival building on Washington Square.

Continue to the intersection of Washington Square East. The third red sandstone tower is the *Elmer Holmes Bobst Library* (1973; Philip Johnson and Richard Foster).

Beyond the library is **La Guardia Place,** named after Fiorello Henry La Guardia, mayor from 1934–45, renowned for his fighting spirit and ferocious temper, his boundless energy and ambition, and his facility in seven languages. Born on Varick Place, now Sullivan St, in 1882 to a Jewish mother and an Italian father, married first to a Catholic and then a Lutheran, La Guardia was a living example of his city's ethnic diversity. He was a liberal, a reformer, and an irate opponent of graft; he died in 1947 of cancer, with only a small house in Queens and $8000 to show for his years in office.

N.Y.U. occupies most of Washington Square South. The *Loeb Student Center* (1959; Harrison & Abramovitz) at the intersection of La Guardia Place is decorated with aluminum sculptural forms (1960) by Reuben Nakian. The building stands on the site of Marie Blanchard's famous boarding house (demolished in 1948?) whose roster of famous occupants is said to have included Adelina Patti, Theodore Dreiser, Willa Cather, O. Henry, and Eugene O'Neill. John Reed, later the author of *Ten Days that Shook the World,* described the so-called "house of genius" as sheltering "inglorious Miltons by the score and Rodins . . . one to every floor."

Cross Thompson St to the **Judson Memorial Church** (1892; McKim, Mead & White; DL), named by its founder Edward Judson after his father Adinoram Judson (1788–1850), first Baptist missionary to Burma and compiler of an English-Burmese dictionary. The younger Judson turned his missionary zeal to city dwellers and from its inception this church has involved itself in urban problems.

Designed by Stanford White, the building and adjoining square bell tower, built of amber Roman brick with terra-cotta moldings and panels of colored marble, are generally Romanesque Revival in style. The auditorium (usually open weekdays 9–5) has stained glass windows by John La Farge (best seen around midday); the marble relief on the S. wall, executed by Herbert Adams, follows designs by Augustus Saint-Gaudens.

Judson Hall, next door, was once a hotel whose revenues were intended to support the programs of the church. Both the bell tower and hall are now residences for N.Y.U.

The quadrangle of bland red Neo-Georgian buildings across Sullivan St to the W. is the *Vanderbilt Law School of N.Y.U.* (1951; Eggers & Higgins).

Continue W. a block to **MacDougal Street** and turn S. (left). Formerly magnetically attractive to the young artistic set, who sat by the hour in its coffeehouses, small bars, and restaurants, this stretch of MacDougal St has fallen somewhat in the world, though it still attracts crowds of wandering tourists at night.

Continue to the *Provincetown Playhouse* (133 MacDougal St, S. of the intersection of Washington Square South), an American theatrical landmark.

In 1915 the Provincetown Players, a group of struggling actors and writers, formed a summer theater on Cape Cod. The following year Eugene O'Neill joined them, bringing along a suitcase full of plays. One of them, *Bound East for Cardiff,* achieved such success that the group opened a New York season in 1916 using the parlor floor of a house at 139 MacDougal Street. In 1917 they remodeled a stable and bottling works at 133 MacDougal St into a theater seating 182 people. Among the plays first produced here were Edna St. Vincent Millay's *Aria da Capo,* and *The Emperor Jones* and *The Hairy Ape* by O'Neill, whose work changed the shape of American drama.

Next door, housed in rooms upstairs at 137 MacDougal St, was the Liberal Club, organized as a meeting place for those interested in New Ideas. Downstairs in the same building was Polly Holliday's restaurant, a famous eating and meeting place for artists and intellectuals. Polly's lover, anarchist Hippolyte Havel, who served as cook and waiter, gave the place its own cachet by shouting "bourgeois pigs" and other insults at the patrons, who nonetheless remained loyal; Polly later moved her restaurant around the corner to 147 W. 4th St. Another popular watering place at the corner of W. 4th St and Sixth Ave was the Golden Swan, known by its intimates as the Hell Hole, whose clientele included thugs as well as bohemians, and which later provided the setting and some characters for O'Neill's *The Iceman Cometh.*

The small Federal houses at 127–131 MacDougal St, next to the theater, their facades altered for commercial purposes, were built (1829) on speculation for Aaron Burr, who invested heavily but with little success in Greenwich Village real estate. At No. 129 the original pineapple newel posts, symbolic of hospitality, remain.

Walk on down MacDougal St and turn right at W. 3rd St. On the block of W. 3rd St between Sixth Ave and MacDougal St stood two legendary Village nightspots. *Folk City* (which moved to 130 W. 3rd St in 1960 from its original site at 11 W. 4th St) where Bob Dylan, Arlo Guthrie and others launched their careers is today a bar called the Kettle of Fish. More venerable and more enduring is the *Blue Note* (131 W. 3rd St; tel: 475-8592), which still features big name jazz stars.

Return to MacDougal St. Across the street and a half block S. is an unusual double house (1852), 130–132 MacDougal St, with an ironwork portico, where Louisa May Alcott, author of *Little Women* lived for a while.

Continue south. The next intersection on the right is *Minetta Lane*, whose name commemorates Minetta Brook which flowed from former hills near Fifth Ave and 21st St to the Hudson River near Charlton St. Once famous for its trout, the brook was called Mintje Kill ("little stream") by the Dutch and the name was later anglicized to its present form. Minetta St, which intersects Minetta Lane a half block W., follows the course of the brook. In 1987 geologists from N.Y.U. using ground-penetrating radar mapped the course of the stream bed, which was buried beneath Washington Square in the 1820s.

On the S.W. corner of MacDougal St and Minetta Lane is the *Minetta Tavern* (113 MacDougal St), whose walls are covered with pictures of illustrious clients.

Perhaps the tavern's most famous patron was Joe Gould, bohemian poet and writer. Born to an old New England family and duly sent to Harvard (class of 1911), Gould lived in the Village by his wits and on the charity of his friends for more than 30 years, gathering material for his ambitious work, *An Oral History of Our Time* (sometimes called *An Oral History of the World*). The work, consisting of innumerable conversations, some of them overheard, was reputed to have reached 11 million words when Gould died in a mental institution in 1957. Though it was rumored that he carried on his person a will leaving ⅔ of the manuscript to Harvard and ⅓ to the Smithsonian Institution, neither the will nor the work was ever found. The Lions' Club of the Village paid for Gould's funeral to which Ernest Hemingway sent gladioli.

Continue S. to **Bleecker Street,** named after Anthony Bleecker, an early-19C man of letters and owner of the land ceded to the city for the street. The *San Remo Cafe,* an Italian restaurant and bar, once occupied the N.W. corner of the intersection and was a favorite literary hangout during the 1940s and 1950s of such people as James Baldwin, James Agee, socialist writer Michael Harrington, and Gregory Corso. According to Ed Fancher, one-time publisher of the *Village Voice,* the tough bartenders occasionally beat up someone in the crowd and after one too many of these brawls the literary set vacated the San Remo for a bar called Louis' near Sheridan Square.

The *Café Borgia* (185 Bleecker St) and *Le Figaro* (186 Bleecker St) are among the Village's classic coffee houses, institutions that flourished during the ''beatnik'' period of the 1950s when Jack Kerouac and Allen Ginsberg reigned as culture heroes and such entertainments as poetry reading with or without jazz accompaniment enlivened the premises. The coffee houses that have survived the waning of this culture still offer espresso, food, and a setting for conversation. Other examples of the genre include the Peacock Caffé (29 Greenwich Ave), the Caffè Reggio (119 MacDougal St) and the Caffè Dante (81 MacDougal St).

Look right (W.) on Bleecker St. At 196 Bleecker St is the *Little Red Schoolhouse,* founded in 1932 by Elisabeth Irwin, a pioneer in progressive education.

Cross Bleecker St and walk S. a half block. Here begins the *MacDougal-Sullivan Gardens Historic District* a group of 24 houses (1844–50) sharing a common back garden. In the mid-19C this land, bounded by MacDougal, Bleecker, Houston, and Sullivan Sts, belonged to Nicholas Low, a banker, land speculator, and legislator, who subdivided the property and built the houses as an investment. Although a large immigrant population altered the social makeup of the neighborhood in the late 19C, the Low family resisted the temptation to tear down the houses and replace them with more profitable tenements. Then in 1920 William Sloane Coffin, scion of the W. & J. Sloane furniture company, hit upon the idea of modernizing old row houses to provide moderate-cost housing for professional people. He bought the block and converted the buildings to apartments, selling off the houses facing Bleecker and Houston Sts to finance the project. Although the facades of the buildings have been significantly altered, the district remains interesting as an example of early urban renewal and for the creation of a single common garden from small individual plots.

Tiro a Segno across the street at 77 Sullivan St is the century-old descendant of an Italian shooting club, whose post-hunt banquets have become more important than the hunting. It harks back to a time in the late 19C when such organizations played an important role in immigrant social life.

Return to Bleecker St and turn right (E.). Walk one block to Sullivan St named after Brig. Gen. John Sullivan, a commander in the Revolutionary War. In November 1987, a five-story building at 177 Sullivan St between Bleecker and Houston Sts collapsed when construction workers trying to reinforce the foundation undermined its integrity instead; the building had been the birthplace of Fiorello La Guardia. Nearby is the *Sullivan Street Playhouse* (181 Sullivan St), where *The Fantasticks* has been playing since May 3, 1960.

Return to Bleecker St. The **Circle in the Square** (159 Bleecker St) began (1950) in Sheridan Square, occupying the premises of a defunct nightclub, whose layout (a stage more or less in the round) suggested the name of the theater. The Circle in the Square rose to prominence with its 1952 production of Tennessee Williams's *Summer and Smoke* and its later revivals of O'Neill plays. Today it offers classic and contemporary plays and has grown to include an uptown branch on 50th St.

Across the street at 160 Bleecker St is the massive **Atrium,** originally Mills House No. 1 (1896; Ernest Flagg). Flagg designed the much lamented Singer Tower and several buildings, including homes for the Scribner family, but was also interested in high-density housing for the less affluent. Palatial in scale but cut up into tiny single rooms, it was intended for men of modest means who could not even afford boarding house rates and was named for Darius Ogden Mills, who philanthropically financed it expecting only a modest 5% profit. With some justification *Scribner's* magazine described Mills House as "A Palace at Twenty Cents a Night." Its 1500 small rooms faced either the streets or the open, grassy interior courts and the hotel had modern bathrooms, lounges, restaurants, and smoking rooms. Eventually it deteriorated into the Greenwich Hotel, whose down-and-out clientele stood around on the sidewalks with wine bottles concealed in paper bags. In 1976 the building was converted into apartments and its interior courts reconstructed.

The *Village Gate* cabaret-theater (160 Bleecker St; tel: 475-5120) at street level in the Atrium building opened in 1958 and made its fame with shows like *Jacques Brel Is Alive and Well* and *MacBird,* a political satire of the Vietnam War era; today the Village Gate has two theaters featuring musical and satirical revues, jazz, and salsa.

Continue E. on Bleecker St across *Thompson St,* named after another Revolutionary War general, William Thompson from Pennsylvania. The *Bleecker Street Playhouse,* (144 Bleecker St) now a movie theater showing foreign and classic films, owes its elegant facade to architect Raymond Hood, guiding hand behind Rockefeller Center. The building once housed Mori's, a restaurant founded by Placido Mori in 1884. Hood converted two row houses in 1913 and added the present facade in 1919.

Continue E. along Bleecker St to the massive apartment complexes across La Guardia Place. Named *Washington Square Village* and *University Village,* names which disregard architectural and social realities, the buildings, most of them owned by N.Y.U., tower above the surrounding streets. The oldest group (1956–58; S. J. Kessler, Paul Lester Weiner) are institutional in feeling; the newer buildings (S. of Bleecker St, 1966; I. M. Pei & Partners) have been admired for their design and for the technological achievement of their cast-in-place concrete. In the center of the Pei group is a monumental sculpture after a smaller work (1934)

by Pablo Picasso, entitled *Bust of Sylvette*. The original, representing the profile of a girl with a ponytail, was only 2 ft high,
painted on a piece of bent metal. The present adaptation (1968)
by Carl Nesjar and Sigurd Frager is 36 ft high and is made of
concrete with black basalt aggregate revealed by sandblasting.

Walk S. to **Houston Street** and turn right. The name "Houston"
(its first syllable is pronounced "house") is a corruption of
"Houstoun," after William Houstoun, a Georgia delegate to the
Continental Congress (1784—86), who got a New York street
named for him by marrying the daughter of Nicholas Bayard III,
owner of the land where the W. part of the street now runs.

The patch of vegetation sprouting from the concrete at the
intersection of La Guardia Place and Houston St is an environmental sculpture, *Time Landscape* (planted 1978; Alan Sonfist),
of trees, shrubs, and plants that grew on Manhattan before
Europeans arrived. Some of the trees were transplanted as
saplings from Bronx Park, where the New York Botanical Garden
now maintains the last virgin forest in the city.

Walk W. to the intersection of Sullivan St. On the S. side of
Houston St is the *Church of St. Anthony of Padua* (c. 1895).
During the first two weeks of June this church sponsors the Feast
of St. Anthony of Padua, beginning with a procession during
which the saint's image is carried through the streets. The
outdoor fair in the evenings offers rides, carnival games, and
staggering quantities of Italian street food.

Continue W. on Houston St to Sixth Ave (Avenue of the
Americas), slashed through the irregular network of Village
streets S. of Carmine St in the 1920s, creating a freeway for
traffic and a free-for-all for pedestrians, and leaving a swath of
mutilated buildings. The city has attempted to improve the
situation (1976) by providing trees and benches, by converting
some of the odd triangular spaces created by the avenue to vest-
pocket parks, and by repaving the street with asphalt and attractive concrete paving block.

Cross Sixth Ave and walk S. two blocks. In the area bounded
on the N. by King St and on the S. by Vandam St is the **Charlton-
King-Vandam Historic District,** whose Federal houses date from
the 1820s and 1830s.

History. In the 18C the district belonged to Abraham Mortier, who built (c.
1767) a fine mansion, Richmond Hill, on high ground overlooking the Hudson.
Washington used it for his headquarters; John and Abigail Adams lived there
while he was Vice-President in 1789; Aaron Burr bought it in 1793 to further
his colossal social ambitions and entertained there lavishly. Never one to
overlook his business interests, Burr had the estate mapped for development
in 1797 and laid out the present Vandam, King, and Charlton Sts. In 1817, his
political career long dead, he sold the property to John Jacob Astor who cut
down the hill and rolled the mansion down to the S.E. corner of Charlton and
Varick Sts. Astor sold off the land as 25 × 100-ft building lots to speculators
who constructed the present houses. The first homeowners were lawyers,
builders, and merchants whose livelihood was tied to the Hudson River
wharves nearby. The mansion became at various times a theater, menagerie,
and tavern, and was demolished in 1849.

The best preserved street in the district is *Charlton St* with the
longest unbroken row of Federal houses in the city (N. side).

Many are in pristine condition, retaining original details and features: brick facades laid in Flemish bond; doorway and window trim of modest brownstone, granite, or more refined marble; high stoops guarded by wrought-iron railings sometimes with hollow cage newel posts; elegant paneled front doors surrounded by leaded top- and sidelights; steep roofs pierced by dormers. The rooflines were originally joined by a continuous cornice.

Charlton, King, and Vandam Sts are all named after prominent early-19C New Yorkers. Dr. John Charlton came from Britain with the troops in the Revolution, stayed after the war, and became president of the New York Medical Society. Rufus King was the state's first U.S. senator, a minister to Britain, and a candidate for the Vice-Presidency. Anthony Van Dam was a 19C alderman.

The nearest subway stops are the IND at 6th Ave and Spring St (uptown entrance in the S. side of the library building) and the IRT at W. Houston and Varick Sts.

B. West Village from St. Luke's Place to Westbeth and Bank Street

SUBWAY: IRT Broadway-7th Ave local (train 1 or 9) to Christopher St-Sheridan Square or to W. Houston St.

BUS: M5, M6, or M10.

The route begins at St. Luke's Place and Seventh Ave South. **St. Luke's Place,** the block of Leroy St between Hudson St and Seventh Ave South, has one of the city's finest rows of Italianate houses whose aura of settled repose characterizes much of the West Village.

Built in the early 1850s for prosperous merchants, many of whose livelihoods were tied to the Hudson River, the houses still have the red brick facades typical of the earlier Greek Revival style, but incorporate such fashionable Italianate details as brownstone trim, door hoods supported by carved consoles, bold cornices, tall stoops with rather elaborate cast-iron railings, high rusticated basements, and deeply recessed doorways with double doors.

Writers Theodore Dreiser, Sherwood Anderson, and Marianne Moore, and painter Paul Cadmus have lived here but its most famous resident was James J. ("Jimmy") Walker—popular, high-living mayor of New York from 1926 until his resignation under a cloud of fiscal scandal in 1932. His home was at 6 St. Luke's Place.

The playground across the gingko-lined street is *James J. Walker Park,* originally St. John's Burying Ground of Trinity Parish (which owned the West Village up to Christopher St under a 1705 land grant from Queen Anne). In 1898, under the guidance of architects Carrère & Hastings, the deteriorating cemetery was dug up and landscaped as Hudson Park. During excavations, workers uncovered a stone marked "Leroy" which romantic

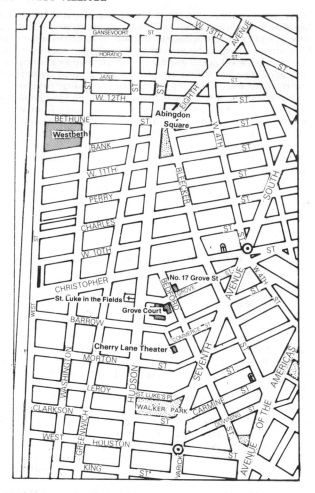

rumor identified as the grave marker of Louis Charles, son of Louis XVI and Marie Antoinette. Although the dauphin may have been smuggled out of prison after his parents' death, he surely did not die in Greenwich Village. *Leroy St* is named after Jacob Leroy, alderman and successful merchant.

Just inside the fence is an elaborate monument for Eugene Underhill and Frederick A. Ward, two firemen of Eagle Engine Company No. 13, who died in 1834 while performing their duties.

Continue W. on St. Luke's Place to Hudson St and turn right (N.). One block N. is **Morton Street,** named after Jacob Morton, a prominent early-19C lawyer. Turn right and walk E. on Morton St toward Bedford St.

Some of the houses on the W. end of Morton St, for example No. 68, remain from the early 19C, when tradespeople and craftsmen lived in the West Village, many of them sailmakers and building suppliers involved with the city's maritime trade. At No. 59 is a fine Federal doorway. Toward the E. end of the block, the smaller row houses give way to Old Law Tenements—bigger, bulkier, built right up to the sidewalk—dating from the late 19C when the Village experienced the influx of a large Italian and Irish immigrant population.

Turn left at **Bedford Street,** mapped before 1799 and named after its precursor in London. On the E. side of the block stands a row of early-19C houses (Nos. 64–70) in fine condition, though suffering various alterations. James Vandenburgh, master mason of Trinity Church, lived at No. 68 in 1821, another reminder of Trinity's influence in the West Village. The house at No. 70 belonged first (c. 1807) to a sailmaker, John P. Roome. Across the street at 75½ Bedford St is a house only 9.5 ft wide, distinguished both as the narrowest house in the Village and as a residence of Edna St. Vincent Millay. Built in 1873, it was wedged into a former carriage alley; the pink brick facing came later.

Edna St. Vincent Millay (1892–1950), poet, playwright, and actress, arrived in Greenwich Village in 1917, illuminating bohemian society with her beauty and intoxicating personality. In 1923, when she won the Pulitzer Prize, she married Eugen Boissevain and lived briefly in this house.

The *Isaacs-Hendricks House* next door (S.W. corner of Bedford and Commerce Sts) was built in 1799 by Joshua Isaacs and sold to his son-in-law Harmon Hendricks, a pioneer in the business of copper rolling and the New York agent for Paul Revere. Altered in 1836 and 1928, the house retains little of its original appearance. Both this building and the narrow house at 75½ Bedford St face the rear courtyard.

Turn left into **Commerce Street.** Formerly called Cherry Lane, the street took its present name from the sudden arrival of many downtown business firms during the smallpox epidemic of 1822. The *Cherry Lane Theatre* (38 Commerce St) was founded in 1924 by Edna St. Vincent Millay and others as an experimental theater in what was a former brewery or malt house; it has evolved into an Off Broadway house and still presents new and sometimes experimental plays. Around the sharp bend in the street (at *39 and 41 Commerce St*) are two remarkable houses (built 1831 and 1832) facing one another across a central courtyard. Although local legend says that they were built by a sea captain for his two feuding daughters, land records attribute them to Peter Huyler, a milk seller. The mansard roofs were added in the 1870s.

At the intersection of Commerce and Barrow Sts turn right and walk back to Bedford St; turn left. The inhospitable-looking building partway up the block (86 Bedford St) is *Chumley's* restaurant, a hangover from Prohibition days when, disguised as a garage, it operated as a speakeasy, catering to Edna St. Vincent

Millay and John Dos Passos, among others whose thirst was not quenched by the Volstead Act. In commemoration of those clandestine times, the restaurant does not advertise its presence with a sign, although the liquor license is visible through the barred window.

The attractive small apartment house diagonally opposite (95 Bedford St) was built in 1894 (Kurzer & Kohl) as a stable for J. Goebel & Co., dealers in wine. It was converted to a residence in 1927.

Continue to the corner of Bedford and Grove Sts. The clapboard house at 17 GROVE ST (N.E. corner of the intersection) was built in 1822 by William Hyde, a window-sash maker. Although the house has been considerably altered—a Greek Revival doorway added in the 1830s or 1840s, a third story with gingerbread cornice in 1870, and an obtrusive fire escape later—it is still the best preserved of the Village's few wood frame houses. Behind it at 100 Bedford St stands Hyde's workshop (1833), a small, picturesque building erroneously rumored to have been a slave quarters. Clifford Daily, whose greatest project stands next door, ''renovated'' it in the 1920s using moldings and other trim salvaged from demolished 19C houses.

The bizarre house known as **"Twin Peaks"** (102 Bedford St) was built in 1830 as an ordinary frame house. Designer Clifford Daily, who felt that local artists were being ''herded into barracks . . . with the result that the Village is growing into a desert of mediocrity with nothing of inspiration to Villagers who depend a great deal on their surroundings for inspiration,'' persuaded financier Otto Kahn to undertake renovation of the house, which would be turned over to artists, writers, and actors who could then live in inspirational surroundings free from financial pressures. The resulting house, said to be a replica of a house in Nuremberg, contains bricks from the old Madison Square Garden, the Brevoort Hotel, a Second Ave tenement, and an Upper West Side apartment. The opening ceremonies of this stuccoed, gabled, and half-timbered extravagance were held in 1926; Princess Amelia Troubetzky sat on one of the peaks making a burnt offering of acorns (presumably to the god Pan) while actress Mabel Normand sat atop the other peak christening the building with the customary bottle of champagne.

Return to the corner of Grove and Bedford Sts; walk W. toward the river. This block, between Bedford and Hudson Sts, is especially attractive, with a row of vine-covered Greek Revival houses (Nos. 14–16, built in 1840 by Samuel Winant and John Degraw), followed by a group of Federal houses (Nos. 4–10, built 1834 by James N. Wells), which retain many original features: hand-wrought ironwork including boot scrapers in the stoop fences at Nos. 6 and 8, small dormers, and paneled doorways. Between Nos. 10 and 12 is the entrance to one of the Village's hidden architectural enclaves, **Grove Court,** a group of shuttered brick houses built in 1853–54 as dwellings for workmen. Remarkable nowadays for its serenity, the court has a more boisterous past, earning at different times in its history the names Mixed Ale Alley and Pig's Alley.

Follow Grove St to **Hudson Street,** considered the boundary between the West Village and the Far West Village (both of which run N. as far as 14th St). Directly across the intersection is **St. Luke in the Fields** (1822; James N. Wells builder), formerly St. Luke's Chapel of Trinity Parish. It is the city's third oldest church behind St. Paul's Chapel and St. Mark's-in-the-Bowery and reflects the austerity of the Federal style adapted for a rural setting. Built of brick rather than the more customary rubble stone, St. Luke's has a low, bulky, square tower unadorned with a steeple, and its parklike setting, surviving from the builder's original plan, still gives it a pastoral atmosphere. In its early years, the church was flanked by 14 town houses planned by Wells, of which six remain (Nos. 473–477 and 487–491 Hudson St, all built in 1825) as does the handsome vicarage in the churchyard. The buildings and playground of St. Luke's School (founded 1894) now occupy much of the park. In 1981 the church was severely damaged by fire (restoration and expansion 1986; Hardy Holzman Pfeiffer Assocs.)

St. Luke in the Fields was founded independently by local residents with financial aid from wealthy Trinity Parish, but when in the late 19C the neighborhood was overwhelmed by immigrants, the fashionable congregation built a new church uptown on Convent Ave at W. 141st St, and Trinity Parish bought this one, reopening it in 1893.

For a long time St. Luke's was the source of Leake's Dole, a weekly gift of bread to poor parishioners who attended the ten o'clock Saturday service, provided by a bequest in the will of John Leake (died 1792). Leake left 1000 pounds "put out at interest to be laid out in the annual income in sixpenny wheaten loaves of bread and distributed . . . to such poor as shall appear most deserving."

Walk N. on Hudson St. No. 487 Hudson St, now the parish house of St. Luke's, was writer Bret Harte's boyhood home. Continue along Hudson St with its antique and old furniture shops.

Just E. of the intersection with Christopher St is the *Lucille Lortel Theatre* (121 Christopher St), named after its owner, who has been called "the First Lady of Off Broadway." It began as a meat-packing plant, became the *Theatre de Lys,* and fell under Lortel's jurisdiction when her late husband gave it to her as a wedding present. Her first production here was Kurt Weill's *Threepenny Opera* which opened with Lotte Lenya in 1955.

Turn W. (left) on **Christopher Street** and walk toward the river. Because of its generally permissive attitudes, the Village has long had a sizable homosexual community focused around Christopher St in the West Village and particularly visible at night. Various bars, clubs, clothing stores (and the Oscar Wilde Memorial Bookshop further E. at 15 Christopher St) cater to this clientele, though the AIDS epidemic has closed a number of the clubs on West St. In 1969 a confrontation between gays and police in the now defunct Stonewall Inn near Sheridan Square is credited with having sparked the drive for civil rights for homosexuals.

Continue W. on Christopher St. The ten-story dark brick building filling the block bounded by Washington, Greenwich, Christopher, and Barrow Sts was originally the **U.S. Appraiser's Stores** (1899; Willoughby J. Edbrooke and others; DL), a warehouse for goods passing through customs. Later it served as a federal archives building and a post office; like other large industrial buildings in the Village it has been renamed *The Archives*), renovated, and converted to condominiums. Imposing in scale and massive in appearance, it typifies the Romanesque Revival style at its best, with strong brick arches at ground level, rounded corner turnings, and successive bays of arched windows.

On the N. side of Christopher St between Greenwich and Washington Sts is *St. Veronica's Roman Catholic Church* (c. 1900), which now operates a hospice at 657 Washington St.

Continue walking W. on Christopher St straight ahead toward the river. At 180 Christopher St, intersection of West St, is a former hotel called at various times the Great Eastern and the Christopher Hotel. At its nadir it was a single-room-occupancy hotel that housed a clientele of the anonymous poor, as well as Jerome A. Johnson who shot Joe Colombo at the infamous Columbus Day rally in 1971 (see p. 169). Renamed the River Hotel, it was renovated in 1984 and briefly reopened as a commercial hotel with a glassed-in French restaurant on the top.

West St runs north and south along the river; it once serviced the HUDSON RIVER PIERS, most of which are now abandoned. Some of the piers berthed ocean liners, for example the now unused Cunard-White Star facility at the foot of W. 13th St; others accommodated more mundane freighters or served as loading piers for the Lehigh Valley Railroad. Little remains of the time when the Hudson River piers were an important factor in the city's economy—only a few truckers' coffee shops and garages, in an area potentially poised for redevelopment.

During the early 19C the **New York State Prison** was located on landfill just N. of Christopher St and, oddly, was considered an ornament to the neighborhood. In 1828–29, after serving as a terror to evildoers for a full quarter of a century (according to Moses King's 1893 handbook), the prison was closed and its inmates moved up the river to Sing Sing in Ossining, New York.

Return to Christopher St and walk inland a half block. **Weehawken Street,** one of the city's shortest, is named after the Weehawken Market, a former distribution point for produce from New Jersey (via the onetime ferry from Weehawken). The curious old house at 6 Weehawken St, today a bar, dates in part back to the 18C and was built for George F. Munson, a boat builder.

Continue along Weehawken St to W. 10th St; turn right and walk E. to Washington St. The large apartment building at 277 W. 10th St on the N.E. corner of the intersection, with its bold Romanesque Revival facade of brick and unfinished stone, was originally *Everhard's Storage Warehouse* (built c. 1894). It was renovated for condominiums as *Shepherd House* in 1978.

Walk N. along Washington St. The WEST VILLAGE HOUSES (1974; Perkins & Will), stretching along Washington St from W. 10th St to Bank St, represent the outcome of another territorial struggle between Village activists and the city bureaucracy. Led by Jane Jacobs, whose book *The Life and Death of American Cities* has become a classic, local residents succeeded in having the scale of a proposed high-rise development reduced, but the resulting walkups are institutional and bleak, with windowless walls facing blankly out on Washington St.

Continue N. along Washington St. Turn right at Charles St. The *Gendarme Arms*, a half block inland from Washington St (135 Charles St) occupies the *former Ninth Precinct Station House* (1895; John Du Fais), another example of the conversion of older commercial or public buildings to residential uses. Across the street at 140 Charles St, S.E. corner of Washington St, is a high-rise condominium, *Memphis Downtown* (1986; Rothzeid, Kaiserman, Thomson & Bee), whose 22 stories were permissible because it stands outside the Historic District boundaries of the Village. Its bulk has not endeared it to West Villagers.

Continue E. on Charles St to the next intersection at Greenwich St. The house at *121 Charles St* on the N.E. corner is oddly rural, with wide clapboards, old double-hung windows, and unexpected angles and proportions. Tucked away on a small triangular plot amidst larger commercial buildings, the house, which may date from the 18C, has been moved twice. It was brought to its present location in 1968 from York Ave and 71st St, where it was a back house with no street frontage. When the building was threatened with demolition, the owner purchased this small piece of land and had the house trucked here through five miles of city streets. Return to Washington St.

Continue N. along Washington St to **Bank Street,** once an important financial center. In 1798 the Wall Street Bank of New York established a branch bank on a nameless Greenwich Village lane to be used for emergencies (the downtown branch was threatened with quarantine for yellow fever); during the smallpox epidemic of 1822 other banks came for similar reasons.

The bulky industrial building at 155 Bank St filling the block between Bank and Bethune Sts is **Westbeth** built as the Bell Telephone Laboratories (1900; Cyrus L. W. Eidlitz), renovated in 1965 by Richard Meier, a pioneer in the reuse of old buildings. Among the technological advances engineered here were the transistor and the transatlantic telephone, but its greatest artistic contribution in the old days was the production on its sound stage of parts of *The Jazz Singer,* the first commercially successful "talkie." After the phone company moved its laboratories to New Jersey, the building was converted to studios and artists' housing with federally subsidized rents. At one time or another Robert de Niro, Merce Cunningham, and Diane Arbus lived and/or worked within its walls. Within the complex are the *Westbeth Theater Center,* an Off Off Broadway house with three theaters, an art gallery, a sculpture studio, and the Gay Synagogue. There is currently a waiting list for apartments of about eight years.

Overhead N. of Washington St are the remains of an old freight line that for more than a century ran from the old Washington Market to Spuyten Duyvil at the N. tip of Manhattan where it connected to rail lines fanning out to the north and west. The last train ran in 1980, carrying a load of frozen turkeys. Currently the right of way is owned by Conrail, the federally supported freight carrier, but railroad buffs and city planners keep hoping to salvage the tracks for some useful purpose, perhaps as a West Side commuter line.

Along the N. side of Westbeth runs **Bethune Street,** named after landowner Johanna Graham Bethune, a 19C educator and philanthropist whose charitable works included founding New York's first school for "young ladies."

Gansevoort St, four blocks N. of Bethune St, forms the S. border of the GANSEVOORT MARKET, the city's wholesale meat district (bounded roughly on its other sides by 14th St, Ninth Ave, and the Hudson River). Hectic and noisy at its early morning peak, deserted and rather forbidding the rest of the time, the market is crowded into a clutter of 19C buildings and small stone streets. The present Gansevoort Market is descended from two major 19C markets: the West Washington Market at the foot of W. 12th St, through whose buildings and piers passed cargoes of produce from southern and Caribbean ports as well as much of the city's oyster supply; and the old Gansevoort Market across from it, a large paved area where New Jersey and Long Island farmers drove their market wagons to await the beginning of the 4 A.M. workday. Herman Melville, author of *Moby Dick,* his literary career apparently in ruins, worked as a customs inspector on the former Gansevoort dock for 19 years beginning in 1866. Later, in the late 1920s when the Ninth Avenue "El" was torn down, the city decided to restructure the Gansevoort area as a meatpacking and distribution center, a function the area still maintains. Though the markets at the Hunts Point Terminal in the Bronx and the advent of meat prepacked at the slaughterhouses of the Midwest are cutting into its profits, the Gansevoort Market still supplies the meat that will grace the tables of most of Manhattan's restaurants.

Gansevoort St is named after Peter Gansevoort (1749–1812), officer in the American Revolution and later brigadier general in the U.S. Army. Return to Bethune St.

Walk inland (E.) on Bethune St. The block between Washington and Greenwich Sts is lined with handsome Greek Revival houses. Nos. 19–29 Bethune St were built in 1837 by Henry S. Forman and Alexander Douglass. Those at Nos. 24–34 date from 1845 (builder Alexander R. Holden). At No. 25 note the unusual ironwork anthemion motifs on the door.

Continue E. on Bethune St to **Abingdon Square** (intersection of Hudson and Bethune Sts and 8th Ave), named after Charlotte Warren who married the Earl of Abingdon. Although many British place names were changed in 1794, after due consideration by the City Council Abingdon Square's name was allowed to remain because the earl and his wife had been sympathetic to the American Revolution.

One of Greenwich Village's great 18C landholders was Charlotte's father, Admiral Sir Peter Warren, who owned some 300 acres and built a handsome mansion on the block now bounded by Charles, Perry, Bleecker, and Washington Sts. A true adventurer, Warren went to sea as a 12 year old, rose to his own command at age 24, made a fortune as a privateer, and less adventurously, married Susannah De Lancey. Before the Revolution he returned to England where he became a member of parliament and acquitted himself brilliantly in society. He died in 1752 at the age of 49 and is buried in Westminster Abbey. His three daughters inherited his estate, later divided by the Commissioners' Map of 1811 into small 12- and 15-acre farms. The manor house was demolished in 1865.

Abingdon Square contains the *Greenwich Village War Memorial* (1921; Philip Martiny), a bronze figure of an American soldier carrying a flag.

Leave Abingdon Square on the W.; walk W. on Bank St where there is an especially attractive group of 19C houses. The small top-story windows of No. 76 Bank St (1839-42; Andrew Lock-wood) are surrounded by cast-iron wreaths, a Greek Revival ornament seldom surviving. Return to Bleecker St.

Turn left and walk S. on **Bleecker Street,** one of the Village's most appealing shopping streets, with antique shops, clothing boutiques, small restaurants, and other attractive, generally expensive places to spend money. At the intersection of Bleecker and W. 11th Sts, look a block W. to the *White Horse Tavern* (567 Hudson St at the corner of W. 11th St), a pleasant, old-fashioned bar (founded 1880) made famous by Dylan Thomas, who frequented it in the early 1950s, until his untimely death (1953) in St. Vincent's Hospital.

Continue down Bleecker St; at the intersection of Christopher St, four blocks to the S., is one of the Village's few Art Deco buildings (95 Christopher St), a massive apartment house (1931; H. I. Feldman) executed in two tones of amber brick. A half block E. on Christopher St (81 Christopher St) stands *St. John's Evangelical Lutheran Church,* built in 1821 as the Eighth Presbyterian Church, and later St. Matthew's Protestant Episcopal Church. Like its denomination, the building has been altered several times and now retains a Federal cupola above its gray, painted-brownstone and sheet-metal body. The church housed America's first Lutheran seminary.

Continue N.E. on Christopher St to Sheridan Square where there is a stop of the IRT 7th Ave subway.

Diversion. Continue S. on Bleecker St. Just W. of the next intersection at Grove St is the former Samuel Whittemore residence (45 Grove St), once a grand late-Federal mansion (c. 1830) situated on spacious grounds with stables and a hothouse. The house retains its original arched doorway and iron torchières flanking the stoop.

At 59 Grove St (on the block E. of Bleecker St) the name of *Marie's Crisis,* a restaurant and piano bar, memorializes, though obscurely, political theorist Thomas Paine, who died in a house on this site in 1809, a victim of social ostracism and poverty. His periodical, *Crisis,* was published during the Revolutionary War to propagandize for the colonial cause.

Follow Bleecker St south across Seventh Ave. Visible from this intersection is *Greenwich House* at 27 Barrow St, a large neo-Federal building (1917; Delano & Aldrich) significant for its history rather than its appearance. Founded in 1902 by social worker Mary Kingsbury Simkhovitch, Greenwich House originally directed its major efforts toward the children of the densely concentrated immigrant and black population in the area around Jones St (a block S. of Barrow St)—a population which reached the staggering density of 975 people per acre around the turn of the century. Today Greenwich House continues to address itself to social problems, offering drug counseling, day care, adult education, and programs for the elderly.

Barrow Street is named after Thomas Barrow, a prominent early-19C artist. Originally named Reason St to honor Thomas Paine's *The Age of Reason,* the name degenerated to *Raisin St,* and was changed at the request of Trinity Church.

The section of Bleecker St between Seventh and Sixth Aves reflects the Italian population of the Village and is an attractive, lively street for household shopping; its bakeries, butchers, and grocery stores retain a strong ethnic appeal.

At the intersection of Bleecker and Carmine Sts, a block W. of Sixth Ave, is the *Church of Our Lady of Pompeii* (1926), which replaces a church where St. Frances Xavier Cabrini (born 1850), first American citizen to be canonized, once worshipped. Mayor Fiorello La Guardia named the nearby square for Father Antonio Demo (died 1936), who served this church for 35 years.

The nearest subway is the 7th Ave IRT at W. Houston and Varick Sts (walk
S.W. two blocks on Downing St).

C.   Sheridan Square to West 14th Street

SUBWAY: IRT Broadway-7th Ave local (train 1 or 9) to Christopher
St-Sheridan Square. IND 6th Ave (B, D, or F train) or 8th Ave (A, C,
or E train) to W. 4th St (walk W. on W. 4th St to 7th Ave and
Sheridan Square).

BUS: M10 downtown via 7th Ave / Broadway to Christopher St-
Sheridan Square.

The route begins at **Sheridan Square,** a triangle of asphalt
bounded by Washington Place, Barrow, Grove, and W. 4th Sts
(cross 7th Ave to the E. from the IRT subway stop and walk a
few yards along W. 4th St). *Christopher Park,* around the corner
to the N., is often mistaken for Sheridan Square, understandably
since it contains a statue (1936; Joseph Pollia) of *Gen. Philip
Sheridan* (1831-88). Sheridan, successful Union general during
the Civil War and exterminator of the American Indian thereafter,
was the unfortunate author of the (generally misquoted) remark
that "the only good Indians I saw were dead."
On the N. side of Christopher St, near the square, is the LION'S

HEAD (59 Christopher St), a legendary writers' bar, moved here from an earlier incarnation as a West Village coffeehouse.

Follow Christopher St N.E. to Waverly Place. Except for City Hall, the **Northern Dispensary** (1831; Henry Bayard, carpenter, and John C. Tucker, mason), a triangular building sited on a triangular plot, is the only public building from the Federal period still standing. Austerely constructed of red brick with its well proportioned rows of double-hung windows, the dispensary was originally two stories high, and the addition of a third story (1854) can be detected by a line in the brickwork; the cap-molded lintels and the cornice (sheet metal, not stone) are also later additions.

Chartered in 1827 to offer free medical care to the poor (its most famous patient was Edgar Allan Poe, treated for a cold in 1837), it still functions as a public clinic. The vagaries of Greenwich Village geography make it possible for the building to have two different sides facing a single street and one side facing two streets, since Waverly Place forks at its S.E. corner and Christopher St joins Grove St along its N. facade.

Follow Waverly Place along the S. side of the dispensary to **Gay Street,** still graced by several small, dormered Federal houses. During the mid-19C, Scottish weavers lived on this crooked, block-long street; off and on until about 1920 it was a residential enclave for the Village's black population. During Prohibition it harbored the Pirate's Den, a speakeasy where the waiters reputedly refused to give change. Novelist Ruth McKenney (born 1911) who lived at No. 14, made Waverly Place famous in her play *My Sister Eileen*, later adapted as the musical comedy *Wonderful Town*, which recounted her adventures in the bohemia of the 1930s.

Continue E. along Waverly Place. At No. 138 is a brick and brownstone Gothic Revival town house (1895; George H. Streeton), formerly the rectory of St. Joseph's Church, around the corner.

At Sixth Ave, turn right. Down the block (corner of Washington Place) is *St. Joseph's Church* (1833; John Doran), the city's oldest Roman Catholic Church and one of its earliest Greek Revival church buildings. The main facade belongs to the then emerging Greek Revival tradition, with its smooth surface, two large Doric columns, low pediment, and frieze. The rubblestone masonry on the side walls, corner quoins, and tall, round-headed windows hark back to the Federal period. John McCloskey (1810–85), an early rector, became America's first cardinal. The interior preserves many of the original architectural features but suffers from the addition of stained glass windows.

Turn around and walk north. At the intersection of Sixth Ave and W. 9th St is *Balducci's*, the quintessential Village grocery, risen from lowly origins as a produce stand, stocked with dewy produce, exotic cheeses, and whatever is simultaneously chic and edible. Its Italian origins show up in the apparently infinite variety of pastas.

At the intersection of Sixth Ave with W. 10th St stands the remarkable **Jefferson Market Courthouse** (1877; Vaux & With-

The former Jefferson Market Courthouse, now a branch of the New York Public Library system. Just visible behind it is the old Women's House of Detention (demolished 1973–74), famous for its Art Deco styling, infamous as a prison. (Courtesy of The New York Public Library. Photographer: Bib Serating)

ers), now a branch of the New York Public Library system. Turreted, towered, gabled, carved, and further embellished with stained glass and ironwork, the building exemplifies Victorian Gothic architecture at its most flamboyant. Voted the nation's fifth most beautiful building in 1855, it stood empty from 1945 until 1967, when Giorgio Cavaglieri remodeled it for its present use.

The courthouse stands on the site of the Jefferson Market, one of the city's primary 19C produce markets. The old market (founded 1833) had a tall wooden fire tower with a bell to alert volunteer fire fighters, the precursor of the present main tower originally used for the same purpose. Assembly rooms above the market sheds doubled as courtrooms, so that when the present courthouse was built, it became part of a complex that included a brick jail (also Victorian Gothic in style) and a reconstructed market building. In 1927 the jail was demolished and replaced by the infamous *Women's House of Detention* (1931; Sloan & Robertson), a massive, Art Deco building, long a village landmark or eyesore depending on the beholder's point of view. The women's prison, originally intended for the temporary detention of women awaiting trial, was more successful architecturally than socially, and as conditions within it deteriorated, its grim bulk bore unpleasant associations for Villagers, especially since the inmates could often be heard shouting out of the windows. In 1973–74 it was demolished, lamented only by architectural historians and admirers of the Art Deco style. Its site has been converted to a garden officially called the Jefferson Market Greening, begun and maintained by volunteers with aid from the Vincent Astor Foundation.

Cross W. 10th St on the N. side of the courthouse and turn left. In the middle of the block W. of Sixth Ave is **Patchin Place,** a secluded mews with ten brick houses built in 1848 by Aaron D. Patchin. Theodore Dreiser lived here in 1895 while still an obscure journalist, and e.e. cummings, the occupant of No. 4, presumably enjoyed its serenity for some 40 years.

Walk back around the corner of Sixth Ave and half a block N. to the entrance of **Milligan Place,** another enclave of 19C houses clustered around a tiny triangular courtyard. The street is named after Samuel Milligan, who purchased farmland here in 1799 and, according to a local legend, hired Aaron Patchin, later his son-in-law, to survey it. The houses (c. 1852) are said to have accommodated Basque waiters from the Brevoort Hotel on nearby Fifth Ave and French feather workers who dealt in ostrich and egret plumes for millinery.

Walk S. to W. 9th St and turn left (E.) toward Fifth Ave. Lining this residential side street are handsome row houses, especially Nos. 54, 56, and 58 W. 9th St (1853; Reuben R. Wood, builder), and apartments—the Portsmouth, 38–44 W. 9th St (1882; Ralph Townsend) and its neighbor the Hampshire (1883; Ralph Townsend).

At 23 Fifth Ave, on the N.E. corner of 9th St, stood a house where Mabel Dodge held her famous "evenings." In 1912 Mrs. Dodge and her wealthy husband rented the second floor of the house, which she had fitted up in white, including a white bearskin rug in front of a white marble fireplace. Inviting anarchists, poets, artists, sculptors, and journalists, she organized her evenings around a theme—psychoanalysis, birth control, or the labor movement. Featured speakers included A. A. Brill, Big Bill Haywood (leader of the Wobblies or Industrial Workers of the World), and anarchist Emma Goldman. The evenings, covered by the press, sometimes degenerated into quarrels, but were nonetheless considered symbolic of the Village's artistic and intellectual eminence.

Cross Fifth Ave and walk a block N. to 10th St. Just E. of the avenue at 7 E. 10th St stands a house that was originally the *Lockwood de Forest residence* (1887; Van Campen Taylor) with an adjoining apartment building, 9 E. 10th St (1888; Renwick, Aspinwall & Russell). The house has unusual East Indian decorative details, including an ornate teakwood bay window and a carved teakwood door frame. Artist Lockwood de Forest, worked in India and developed an interest in traditional Indian woodcarving; he also designed the teakwood trim for the family library of the Carnegie Mansion (p. 427) and with his more prominent brother gave a room from an Indian Jain temple to the Metropolitan Museum of Art.

Return to Fifth Ave. On the N.W. corner of Fifth Ave and 10th St is the **Church of the Ascension** (1840–41; Richard Upjohn), a fine brownstone Gothic Revival church by the architect who later designed Trinity Church at the head of Wall St. In 1844 it witnessed the wedding of President John Tyler and Julia Gardiner, whom a contemporary diarist described as "one of those large fleshly Miss Gardiners of Gardiners Island." She was a resident of Colonnade Row (see p. 218), and a woman who apparently knew the value of publicity, since she had already allowed herself to appear in an advertisement for a nearby department store.

The church is noted for its interior (open daily 12–2 and 5–7) with stained glass windows and an *altar mural by John La Farge and a marble altar relief by Augustus Saint-Gaudens.

Walk W. on 10th St. Next to the church at 7 W. 10th St is the **Rectory** (1839–41), a 2½-story Gothic Revival row house, romantically picturesque and daringly innovative for its day, with assymetrical massing, drip moldings, a steep roof, large chimney, pointed dormers, and a rough brownstone facade.

Across the street at *12 W. 10th St* is a town house (1846, renovated 1895; Bruce Price) once owned by Bruce Price, the father of etiquette expert Emily Post. Next to it at *14 W. 10th St* (1855–56) is a beautifully carved brownstone inhabited during the winter of 1900–01 by Mark Twain.

The row of houses at 20–38 W. 10th St is known as **Renwick Terrace** (1856–58; attrib. James Renwick, Jr.) or as the **English Terrace** since it was influenced by rows or "terraces" of town houses in London. Stylistically these Anglo-Italianate or English basement houses depart from the usual Italianate brownstone in having low stoops (three or four steps instead of ten or twelve) and round-arched single windows and doorways on the ground floor. Like other brownstones of the mid-19C, Renwick Terrace was planned as part of a unified streetscape, with cornices, rooflines, and window levels aligned to create an impressive architectural vista. Sculptor Frederick MacMonnies (d. 1937) lived here toward the end of his life.

The house at *50 W. 10th St*, built shortly after the Civil War as a stable, has been converted to a residence. The small dormered

.house at *56 W. 10th St* (1832) dates back to the Federal period and is one of the oldest houses in this part of Greenwich Village. Next to it at No. 58 is another early house, built c. 1836 and remodeled by Stanford White. Behind it stood a back house (now joined to the main building) where the Tile Club once met. This nationally important society of artists claimed such members as Augustus Saint-Gaudens, Daniel Chester French, and John Singer Sargent. Across the street stood another indication of the Village's artistic and intellectual vitality during the late 19C, Richard Morris Hunt's Studio Building (at 51 W. 10th St). Clients included Winslow Homer, John La Farge, Albert Bierstadt, Frederick MacMonnies, Saint-Gaudens, and French.

Continue W. to Sixth Ave. Walk a block N. and turn E. into W. 11th St. About a quarter of a block along the S. side of the street is the small triangular remnant of the SECOND CEMETERY OF THE SPANISH AND PORTUGUESE SYNAGOGUE, once a larger, rectangular plot. When the first graveyard of the synagogue (also called Shearith Israel) at Chatham Square (see p. 163) was full, this one was opened (1805) and used until W. 11th St was cut through in 1830, obliterating most of it. The congregation petitioned the city to retain the part of the cemetery that did not lie in the way of the street. Still buried here is Ephraim Hart, a founder of the New York Stock Exchange. Most of the bodies were removed to W. 21st St (west of Sixth Ave) where the congregation established its third graveyard, used until 1852 when the city passed a law prohibiting further burials within the city limits. Buried there is Mordecai Manuel Noah, a playwright, who conceived the notion of founding a Jewish colony on Grand Island in the Niagara River. The present Shearith Israel cemetery is in Long Island.

Continue E. along W. 11th St. The new town house (1978; Hardy Holzman Pfeiffer Assocs.) at *18 W. 11th St* replaces one that belonged to lyricist Howard Dietz, destroyed by an explosion in 1970. Members of the Weathermen, a radical sect born in the politicized 1960s, were concocting explosives in the basement; one misfired, killing three of the bomb makers and sending the others into hiding. One of them, Kathy Boudin, surfaced in 1981 when she was arrested after a bank robbery whose proceeds were intended to finance further revolutionary activities. The present house is a contemporary replacement, compatible in scale with its Greek Revival neighbors.

Continue E. to Fifth Avenue. The **First Presbyterian Church** (1846; Joseph C. Wells; S. transept, 1893; McKim, Mead & White). The chancel (added, 1919) on the W. side of the avenue between 11th and 12th Sts is one of three handsome Gothic Revival churches built in the area in the mid-19C (the others are Grace Church and the Church of the Ascension). British architect Joseph C. Wells modeled the crenellated central tower on that of Magdalen College, Oxford. The *Church House* around the corner on W. 12th St was designed by Edgar Tafel (1960) in dark brown Roman brick to blend with the brownstone of the church itself; the Gothic quatrefoil motifs in the balcony railings repeat the design of the roof cresting of the church.

Across the avenue at 47 Fifth Ave is the SALMAGUNDI CLUB (1852–53; DL), the only survivor of the great mansions that once ennobled lower Fifth Ave. Built for Irad Hawley, president of the Pennsylvania Coal Company, it belongs to the Italianate tradition, with a boldly rusticated basement, a high stoop and grand balustrade, an ornate door hood supported on foliate consoles, and lavish cast-iron work on the parlor window balconies. The Italianate brownstone came into style (late 1840s) when many New Yorkers, enjoying new wealth, sought to flaunt their money architecturally; the elaborate ornamentation of the style offered those so disposed unlimited opportunities for display.

The interior (open during exhibitions,) provides a glimpse into the pleasures of wealth in 19C New York. The ceilings are embellished with ornate plasterwork; doors are rosewood; the marble mantels are handsomely carved; Corinthian columns separate the two first-floor parlors, and elaborate chandeliers glitter overhead. For all its opulence, however, this house was nothing spectacular in its day; contemporary guidebooks wax eloquent on the nearby Lenox, Schiff, Belmont, and Haight mansions but do not deign to mention this one.

The Salmagundi Club is the nation's oldest artists' club, founded in 1870 and numbering among its alumni John La Farge, Louis Tiffany, and Stanford White. The name "Salmagundi" (whose origins cannot reliably be traced back beyond the French *salmigondis,* a salad of minced veal, anchovies, onions, lemon juice, and oil) was adopted by Washington Irving and his collaborators as the title of a periodical whose pages satirized New York life.

Continue N. to 12th St and the **Forbes Magazine Galleries** located in the former *Macmillan Company Building* (1925; Carrère & Hastings).

Forbes Magazine Galleries. 60 Fifth Ave (12th St), New York 10011. Tel: 206-5548. Open Tues–Sat 10–4. Closed Sun, Mon, legal holidays. Reserved Thurs for group tours. Free. Entry limited to 900 persons per day on a first-come first-served basis. Children under 16 must be accompanied by an adult; no more than 4 children per adult. Group tours by reservation only. Restrooms, telephone. No food service, no gift shop.

SUBWAY: IRT Broadway-7th Ave (train 1, 2, 3, or 9) to 14th St; IRT Lexington Ave (train 4, 5, or 6) to 14th St. IND 6th Ave (B, D, or F train) to 14th St. BUS: M1, M2, M3, or M5, downtown via 5th Ave. M14, crosstown on 14th St.

The Forbes Magazine Galleries (1985) serve as a showcase for the eclectic collections of magazine publisher Malcolm S. Forbes. On display are hundreds of toy boats, thousands of toy soldiers, and a gallery of trophies including some rather odd testimonials to moments of triumph along with the usual cups and urns. Also here are The Presidential Papers, documents and memorabilia revealing the personalities and problems of various American Presidents. For many visitors the highlight of the museum is the Fabergé room, a glittering collection of baubles which includes a dozen jewel-encrusted Easter eggs made for the last two Russian czars.

Walk S. to West 12th Street and turn west. The *Winfield Scott*

House (1851) at 24 W. 12th St, now a cooperative apartment, became a national historic landmark in 1974 as the onetime home of Gen. Winfield Scott (1786–1866), hero of the Mexican War and Whig candidate for President (1852). The iron railings date from the 1880s. Across the street at 31–33 W. 12th St are the *Ardea apartments* (1895 and 1901; John B. Snook & Sons), built for department store baron George A. Hearn. Next door at *35 W. 12th St* stands a narrow house (c. 1840), only 13 ft wide, with a basement and two stories plus an anachronistic mansard roof with a single dormer. In 1867 when the house, then 25 ft wide, was cut in half to widen its eastern neighbor, the mansard roof and dormer were added without altering the Federal lintels and doorway. During this period homeowners commonly topped off their Federal and Greek Revival houses with mansard roofs, partly to follow fashion and partly to gain additional space in a city where housing was already cramped.

Next to this attractive little house is a highly lauded modern apartment, BUTTERFIELD HOUSE (1962; Mayer, Whittlesey & Glass) which sits agreeably alongside the older buildings of the street. On 12th St it rises only seven stories to conform to the existing 19C scale; on 13th St it rises to 13 stories in a more commercial block. At *45 W. 12th St* is another curious small house (c. 1846) whose side wall slants to follow the course of Minetta Brook, which is now channeled underground.

At 66 W. 12th St is the main building of the **New School for Social Research** (1930; Joseph Urban). Known for his stage sets and theatrical designs, Urban made a large building as unobtrusive as possible on a street where most structures are of small scale by recessing the upper stories and using alternating courses of black and white brick and strip windows to emphasize the building's horizontal dimension.

In a classroom on the seventh floor is a group of outstanding murals by José Clemente Orozco, painted in 1930, the only murals by Orozco in the city.

The New School was founded (1919) as a small, informal adult learning center and has evolved into a university whose major commitment is still adult education. Through the years it has offered innovative courses including in the 1920s psychoanalysis and the first college level work on black culture (taught by W. E. B. DuBois). During the following decades it became a "university in exile" for intellectuals fleeing Nazi Germany.

On the first floor is a small *auditorium* designed by Urban whose theatrical credits included sets for the Metropolitan Opera and the Ziegfeld Follies.

At the corner of Sixth Ave turn right (N.) and walk a block to W. 13th St. Continue W. to the *Portico Place* apartments (converted 1982), formerly the **Village Community Church,** built as the Thirteenth Street Presbyterian Church (1846; attrib. Samuel Thompson). One of the finest Greek Revival churches in the city, at one time it simultaneously housed Presbyterian and Jewish congregations.

Its first rector was Dr. Samuel D. Burchard, for whom the row house next door at 146 W. 13th St was built in 1846. Burchard is best known for having undermined the presidential hopes of Republican James G. Blaine in 1884 by making an inflammatory speech in which he labeled the opposition, Grover Cleveland's Democratic Party, the party of "rum, Romanism, and rebellion." In the Catholic backlash that followed, Blaine lost New York City, New York State, and the nation.

Continue to Seventh Ave and turn S. (left). The complex of institutional buildings along the avenue near 12th St belongs to **St. Vincent's Hospital,** the city's oldest and the nation's largest Catholic hospital. The modern white building with scalloped overhangs on the W. side of the avenue (36 Seventh Ave) is the *Edward and Theresa O'Toole Medical Services Building* (1964; Albert C. Ledner & Assocs.), built as the headquarters of the National Maritime Union of America. Union president Joseph Curran once described the ungainly building—a squared-off, inverted, stepped pyramid—as "the box in which the Guggenheim Museum came."

The modern *George Link, Jr. Pavilion* on the N.E. corner of W. 11th St, 7th Ave, and Greenwich Ave (1983–87; Ferrenz, Taylor, Clark & Assocs.) replaces the Elizabeth Bayley Seton Building (1899; Shickel & Ditmars), a red brick and limestone hospital building which local efforts could not save.

St. Vincent's Hospital, opened by the Sisters of Charity in 1849, has served the city well, counting among its patients battlefield casualties of the Civil War, survivors of the *Titanic,* and President Grover Cleveland; among its students Georges Clemenceau; and among its grateful admirers the parents of Edna St. Vincent Millay, who gave the poet her middle name to honor the hospital whose staff had saved the life of a family member.

A little further S. is *The Village Vanguard*, 178 Seventh Ave South near W. 11th St, a jazz club whose roster of performers looks like a jazz hall of fame. It opened in 1934 and in its long career offered everything from poetry readings to comedy, to classical guitar music to free-for-all discussions with such diverse discussants as LeRoi Jones and Percy Sutton, later borough president of Manhattan, and Mario Savio, onetime bad boy of the Free Speech Movement. Most of all it is known for jazz, and has seen and heard the likes of Miles Davis, John Coltrane, Thelonious Monk, Dexter Gordon, and Lee Konitz.

Continue N. along Seventh Ave to 14th St. **Fourteenth Street** marks the N. boundary of Greenwich Village but seems miles away from its quaint and historic insularity. It is a broad, busy, rundown, gritty commercial thoroughfare, though some of the richly ornamental facades of bygone days still hover above street level.

The W. extreme of 14th St lies within the Gansevoort Market district. W. of Seventh Ave is an established Hispanic neighborhood, whose restaurants, groceries, and shops cater to local tastes. Of interest is the *Iglesia Catolica Guadalupe* (229 W. 14th St bet. 7th / 8th Aves), founded in 1902 in a brownstone row house later converted to a church by the addition of a Spanish-style facade. Here, too, is the *Casa Moneo* (210 W. 14th St), the city's best-known Spanish grocery and import store. The Little Spain Merchants Association, founded in 1975 to fight what its members considered the "blight" spreading across W. 14th St, has banned the selling of merchandise on the sidewalks between Seventh Ave and the Hudson. East of that frontier, however, bargain goods pour out from the interiors of numerous small shops.

Between Seventh and Sixth Aves the Salvation Army makes its headquarters at 120 W. 14th St in *Centennial Memorial Temple* (1930; Voorhees, Gmelin & Walker), a grandiose Art Deco monument to a spiritual soldiery. Across the street at 125 W. 14th St is the *42nd Division Armory* of the New York National Guard (1971; N.Y. State General Services Administration, Charles S. Kawecki, architect), a piece of modern military architecture that makes one long for the castles and crenellations of old.

The 7th Ave IRT stop is at 14th St and 7th Ave. IND stations are at 6th and 8th Aves.

10 Chelsea

SUBWAY: IRT Broadway-7th Ave local (train 1 or 9) to 23rd St. IND 8th Ave (C or E train) to 23rd St.

BUS: M10 via 7th Ave to 23rd St. M11 via 9th Ave to 23rd St. M2 or M3 via 5th Ave to 23rd St. M6 or M7 via Broadway to 23rd St, then walk W. to 7th Ave. M26 crosstown on 23rd St.

Chelsea owes its name and approximate boundaries to Captain Thomas Clarke, a retired British soldier, who bought (1750) a tract of land (present 14th–24th Sts, Eighth Ave to the Hudson River—though today Chelsea is considered to extend N. to about 34th St and E. to Fifth Ave), and named the estate after the Chelsea Hospital in London, a refuge for old and disabled soldiers. It owes its most attractive streets to his grandson, Clement Clarke Moore, who developed the area as a residential district, and its ethnic diversity and slums to the New York Central Railroad.

History. Moore (1779–1863), distinguished as the compiler of the first Hebrew lexicon published in the U.S. but remembered for his poem beginning '"Twas the night before Christmas," kept Chelsea for a summer home until it became clear that the pressures of the city's northward growth would engulf the rolling hills and meadows of his patrimony. He moved uptown from Greenwich Village, generously but astutely donated a block to the General Theological Seminary, and began selling building lots with design and use controls attached: no alleys, no stables, no manufactures, and a mandatory ten-ft setback for all houses.

Chelsea's residential tranquility was disrupted when the Hudson River Railroad, later absorbed by the New York Central, laid tracks down Eleventh Ave (c. 1847), attracting breweries, slaughterhouses, and glue factories, which in turn attracted job-hungry immigrants including a large group of Irish fleeing the potato famines. The Ninth Ave El (1871), an elevated railway whose overhead tracks plunged the avenue below into shadow, further depressed the area. Although the El was dismantled before World War II, the W. part of Chelsea still houses thousands of the city's poor, either in decrepit tenements or in municipal housing projects like the Robert Fulton Houses, the Chelsea Houses, and the Elliott Houses.

The E. part has fared better. During the 1870s and 1880s a theatrical district flourished on W. 23rd St, home of Edwin Booth's Theater (1869–83), Proctor's (opened 1888), and Pike's Opera (1868). Although the theater district moved uptown, Chelsea enjoyed a brief artistic revival around World War I as the center of early moviedom, before a better climate and more open space lured the industry to California. The Famous Players' Studio (221 W. 26th St) in an old armory released some of Mary Pickford's early films, and other studios like the Reliance and the Majestic (both at 520 W. 21st St) and the Kalem Company

(235 W. 23rd St) attracted such stars as Alice Joyce and Wallace Reid to Chelsea.

Chelsea has long embraced a wide range of ethnic groups, from the predominant Irish, to a French colony whose only remaining trace is the Church of St. Vincent de Paul (127 W. 23rd St), to a Greek enclave on Eighth Ave, and a Spanish community extending N. from 14th St, one of the oldest in the city. Tolerance has been extended also to union activists, to artists and their followers who overflowed Greenwich Village, and to a gay population frequenting the "leather bars" of Eleventh Ave.

Today Chelsea is in a state of flux. Its population, which reached 60,000 in the mid-1960s, was down to fewer than 44,000 in 1980, but is probably on the upswing again. To some extent the older immigrant groups have been replaced by Japanese, Chinese, and South American, mostly Ecuadoran, residents, but the number of families is still dwindling. Signs of gentrification abound. Real estate conversions—office space into expensive apartments—and brownstone renovations are transforming Chelsea's present ethnic and social mix. The theater has returned to the district. Along with several important Off Off Broadway companies, Chelsea has become home to the Joyce Theater, a major center of dance, and The Kitchen, formerly of SoHo, an experimental center for video, music, and other avant-garde pursuits which found new life in a Chelsea outpost. The Jacob K. Javits Exhibition and Convention Center, built on the old New York Central freight yards, has brought new activity to the northern edge of Chelsea, and a proposed development west of Madison Square Garden will change the far west of the district.

The **Chelsea Hotel** between Seventh and Eighth Aves on W. 23rd St (1884; Hubert, Pirsson & Co.; DL), enjoys a reputation as a literary and architectural landmark. Replete with gables, chimneys, dormers, lancet and semi-elliptical windows, terra-cotta reliefs and bands of white stonework, it is most remarkable architecturally for its cast-iron balconies, with their interlaced sunflowers stretched row upon row across the long facade. Built as an apartment house, the Chelsea Hotel has earned a minor niche in the annals of New York as the first apartment building to reach 12 stories and the first to feature a penthouse. Writers Mark Twain, William Dean Howells, and O. Henry (William Sydney Porter) lived there in its early days, but its artistic heyday came after the 1930s, when Thomas Wolfe, James T. Farrell, Mary McCarthy, Arthur Miller, Brendan Behan, Vladimir Nabokov, Gregory Corso, John Sloan, Sarah Bernhardt, and Yevgeny Yevtushenko all enjoyed its hospitality. Dylan Thomas lapsed into a fatal coma in room 205 after allegedly remarking to his female companion, "I've had my eighteenth whiskey, and I think that's the record." Andy Warhol portrayed it as a wild and impetuous place in his movie *Chelsea Girls;* in the 1960s rock musicians and their hangers-on stayed there. In 1978 Sid Vicious, lead singer of the Sex Pistols, a punk rock group, was indicted for murdering his girlfriend with a hunting knife in the hotel, but died of a heroin overdose before he could stand trial. The hotel's most eccentric resident, perhaps, was George Kleinsinger, a composer who wrote a children's musical called *Tubby the Tuba* and is said to have been fond of composing at the piano with his pet boa constrictor encircling his body.

A painted papier-mâché sculpture (1969?; Eugenia Gershoy) installed in the lobby (E. window) depicts a group of the hotel's famous residents: playwright Arthur Miller and his wife photographer Inga Morath, science-fiction writer Arthur C. Clarke, composer Virgil Thomson, and director Peter Brook. On the walls are paintings by residents.

Continue W. on W. 23rd St to the N.W. corner of Eighth Ave. Here stood Pike's Opera House (1868), bought a year later by financier Jay Gould and his partner Jim Fisk, directors of the Erie Railroad. Gould and Fisk renamed it the Grand Opera House and in addition to producing opera, revues, and plays in the theater installed the railroad offices upstairs and in the basement a printing press, a famous piece of apparatus that was used to enlarge the capitalization of the railroad. Attached to the theater by a tunnel was a brownstone mansion where Fisk kept his buxom and beautiful mistress, Josie Mansfield.

This remarkable complex of business, pleasure, and art ended abruptly in 1872, when Fisk, by now supplanted both on the board of the Erie Railroad and in the affections of Josie Mansfield, was murdered by her new lover, Edward S. Stokes. Fisk's body lay in state in the foyer of the opera house, which shortly thereafter entered a period of decline, becoming a vaudeville house and a movie theater before its demise (1960).

Turn left and walk S. on Eighth Ave to 20th St. Turn west. At 346 W. 20th St, between Eighth and Ninth Aves, is **St. Peter's Church** (Protestant Episcopal), a modest fieldstone church important as the earliest Gothic Revival church in America (1836–38; James W. Smith, builder, from designs by Clement Clarke Moore; DL). At the W. end of the group is the Rectory (1832), which first served as the church and is built in the Greek Revival style, though with engaged brick pilasters instead of the usual free-standing columns. According to legend, the foundations for the present church had already been laid when a vestryman returned from England, so enthralled with the Gothic parish churches there that he persuaded his colleagues to redesign the new church. The resulting structure, therefore, is Gothic more in its details than in its proportions and materials. The newest building, the brick *Parish Hall*, now used by the Apple Corps Theater, was started in 1854 and completed in 1871, when the churchlike facade was attached. Trinity Parish donated the wrought-iron fence (1790), formerly used in front of St. Paul's Chapel.

The **Joyce Theater** is at 175 Eighth Ave, just S. of 19th St. Formerly the Elgin Theater, a movie house reduced to pornography, it was gutted and dramatically remodeled in 1982 (Hardy Holzman Pfeiffer Assocs.) and now is one of the principal venues of modern dance in the city. Among the companies who perform here are Eliot Feld, Erick Hawkins, Dan Wagoner, and Alwin Nikolais.

Several blocks to the W. is the new home of **The Kitchen,** a center for experimental video, music, dance, performance, and film, whose purpose is to encourage media artists working in the high risk environment of the avant garde and to educate audiences to what is new in the arts.

The Kitchen. 512 W. 19th St (bet. 10th / 11th Aves), New York 10011. Tel: 255-5793. Video viewing room open Tues–Sat 1–6, free. Admission charge for performance events. Membership with benefits.

Founded in 1971 in what had once been the kitchen of the now defunct Broadway Central Hotel, The Kitchen began as a space for video art and soon expanded to include experimental music and other avant-garde performance arts. In 1974, it moved to SoHo where it remained for about a dozen years, increasingly beset by such problems as the acquisition of its major artists (people like Steve Reich and Philip Glass) by major institutions, the skyrocketing rents in SoHo, and the relocation of the avant-garde artistic community to the East Village and elsewhere. In 1986 The Kitchen moved here, occupying a former ice house and film studio.

Return to Ninth Ave and 20th St. The block bounded by Ninth and Tenth Aves between 20th and 21st Sts is known as Chelsea Square and is the home of the **General Theological Seminary** (Main Building, 1960; O'Connor and Kilham; West Building, 1836; other principal buildings, 1883-1900; Charles C. Haight). Clement Clarke Moore, who taught Hebrew and Greek here, donated the land on which the seminary (founded 1817) now stands.

Enter through the modern building on Ninth Ave. With the exception of the Gothic Revival *West Building* (1832), most of the college was built during the tenure of dean Eugene Augustus Hoffman, who hired Charles C. Haight to design the present Collegiate Gothic quadrangle. Especially attractive is the central *Chapel of the Good Shepherd* with its 161-ft tower and bronze doors by J. Massey Rhind.

Return to Ninth Ave. Just N. of the seminary on the N.W. corner of 21st St is a small Federal house, *183 Ninth Ave* (1831), with fine Flemish bond brickwork. Now used as a store, the building, with its pitched roof, dormers, and simple cornice, is still intact. The three houses adjacent—*185 Ninth Ave* (1856) and *Nos. 187 and 189 Ninth Ave* (1868)—among the few wooden houses remaining in Manhattan, were built by James N. Wells, one of Chelsea's major 19C developers and the builder of St. Luke in the Fields in Greenwich Village.

Return to West 20th St with its gracious Greek Revival and Italianate row houses, now a little run-down. The building at *402 W. 20th St* (1897; Charles P. H. Gilbert) is a late-19C house remarkable primarily for the concave facade that curves back from the corner tenement to meet the 10-ft setback of the adjoining row of older houses. The letters DONAC above the door commemorate Don Alonzo Cushman, not a Spanish grandee but a dry-goods merchant, friend of Clement Clarke Moore, parish leader, and land developer who made a fortune building in Chelsea. The house at *404 W. 20th St* (1830) is the earliest house in the area.

Stretching W. on 20th St (406–418 W. 20th St) is CUSHMAN ROW, named after developer Don Alonzo Cushman. Completed in 1840 (DL), these brick, brownstone-trimmed Greek Revival houses have retained considerable original detail: fine cast-iron wreathes around small attic windows, paneled doors, iron stoop railings and areaway fences, pilastered doorways with slender sidelights. Two of them (Nos. 416 and 418) still have their pineapple newel posts.

Further down the block (446–450 W. 20th St) are some exceptional Italianate houses built in 1853, with round-headed ground-floor windows and doorways as well as unusual trim beneath the cornices. Arched windows and doorways, exemplifying the Italianate style's attraction to circular forms, appeared only on expensive houses, since they were relatively difficult to execute.

Turn right (N.) at Tenth Ave and walk a block to 21st St. At 193 Tenth Ave (N.W. corner) is the *Guardian Angel Roman Catholic Church* (1930; John Van Pelt), an elaborate red brick and limestone Romanesque-style church with a tile roof. Before the Chelsea Piers closed (1968), the church served seamen and dockworkers residing in the neighborhood, and in the 1930s its pastor was the port chaplain.

The **Chelsea Piers** (1902–07; Warren & Wetmore), Piers 54–62, once stretched from W. 12th to W. 22nd St. Designed specifically to receive the great transatlantic liners being built around the turn of the century, the 800-ft finger piers were finished just in time to receive the *Mauretania* and the *Lusitania* (both 790 ft), then the pride of the Cunard Line. The Depression debilitated the Atlantic trade, and after World War II the Chelsea Piers never regained their importance for passenger shipping. With the decay of New York as a port in succeeding decades, this segment of Chelsea's economy atrophied (in the early 1970s the city lost 20,000 waterfront jobs), and many of the Irish-American dockworkers who once lived here moved to New Jersey, where the piers are still active.

Another group of fine Italianate houses (465–473 W. 21st St) stretches along the N. side of 21st St just E. of Tenth Ave.

Continue up Tenth Ave to *Clement Clarke Moore Park* at the S.E. corner of 22nd St, a pleasant multilevel playground (1968; Coffey, Levine & Blumberg). Across the street on the N.E. corner of the intersection is the *Empire Diner* (1943, altered 1976; Carl Laanes), a relic of the period when these "railroad car" eateries dotted the country; refurbished in black and chrome appropriate to its Art Deco origins, it serves updated diner food .

Walk W. on 22nd St. At 548 W. 22nd St (bet. 10th / 11th Aves) is a major exhibition space of the **Dia Art Foundation,** installed (1987) in a 19C brick loft building (open Thurs–Sun 12–6; tel: 989-5912).

The Dia Foundation was established in 1974 by Philippa de Menil Friedrich, daughter of a Houston art patron, and Heiner Friedrich, a German-born art dealer, to support a selected group of artists outside the usual institutional system. The foundation also maintains two installations by Walter de Maria in SoHo.

Turn around and walk E. on 22nd St. The double house (1835) at 436–438 W. 22nd St, now stripped of some of its ornamentation and converted to apartments, was once the residence of actor Edwin Forrest, remembered primarily as one of the dramatic antagonists involved in the Astor Place riots (see p. 219). The house at *414–416 W. 22nd St*, a once-elegant mansion (1835; James N. Wells), is the only surviving five-bay Greek Revival house in Manhattan. Wells himself lived here briefly; in 1864–66 the building was remodeled and in 1870 began a tour of duty as the Samaritan Home for the Aged.

Continue to Ninth Ave and walk N. to 23rd St. The original *Clarke family mansion* stood between Ninth and Tenth Aves, 22nd and 23rd Sts, until demolished in 1854. A plaque at 420 W. 23rd St records the fact.

Filling an entire block (23rd to 24th Sts, Ninth to Tenth Aves) are the **London Terrace Apartments,** an early modern apartment project (1930; Farrar & Watmaugh), built in a vaguely Romanesque (or Gothic?) style around a central garden which, along with such other amenities as a swimming pool, solarium, gymnasium, and doormen dressed as London bobbies, lured early tenants to its 1670 apartments. On the top level was a clubhouse and the Marine Roof, an area fitted out like the deck of a transatlantic liner, complete with life buoys and folding deck chairs.

The original London Terrace, torn down for the present apartments, was a row of colonnaded town houses (1845; Alexander Jackson Davis) with an extravagant 35-ft setback and handsome front gardens.

Walk N. on Ninth Ave to 28th St. On the S.E. corner of Ninth Ave and W. 28th St is the Protestant Episcopal **Church of the Holy Apostles** (1848; Minard Lafever; transepts 1858; Richard Upjohn & Sons; DL), a small brick church with a copper-covered, slate-roofed spire and bracketed eaves, set in the midst of an over-scaled modern housing project. Handsome windows by William Jay Bolton, one of America's earliest stained-glass artists, enhance the interior (open during services, Sun at 11). Composed of monochromatic central medallions surrounded by stylized roses, lilies, and foliate forms, the windows depict scenes from the life of Christ and from the Acts of the Apostles. Today the church serves the area's poor with a substantial soup kitchen.

Return S. to 26th St and walk W. to Eleventh Ave. In 1985, after a long dry spell when the city lacked an active commercial brewery, the NEW AMSTERDAM BREWERY (26th St and 11th Ave) opened; it now produces 5.3 million bottles of beer yearly.

The far W. of Chelsea, once dominated by the piers and railroads, still bears traces of that past. The **Starrett-Lehigh Building** (1931; Russell G. and Walter M. Cory with Yasuo Matsui, assoc. architect; DL), between Eleventh and Twelfth Aves, 26th and 27th Sts, is an imposing Art Deco industrial building often overlooked because of its surroundings. Admirers praise its dramatic exterior—horizontal bands of glass, concrete, and brown brick wrapped around curved corners—and its innovative concrete column-and-slab construction. Built over a spur line of the Lehigh Valley Railroad, it was intended for freight handling, warehousing, and manufacturing, and was equipped with powerful elevators that could lift loaded boxcars from the tracks to the warehouse above. The railroad tracks inside the building were never built and those at street level were torn out, but the elevators are still used, hoisting 15-ton trucks into the vast interior.

A block N. (bet. 27th–28th Sts, 11th–12th Aves) stand the **Central Stores of the Terminal Warehouse Company** (1891), 25 storage buildings (24 acres of warehousing space) walled into one massive fortress surmounted by a Tuscan tower. The great arched doorway at one time admitted locomotives on a spur line of the New York Central Railroad, while the W. facade opened onto the deepwater Hudson River piers. Cool cellars running beneath the entire structure were used to store wines, liquors, gums, and rubber.

In 1987 the dance club **Tunnel,** at 220 Twelfth Ave, opened in the lower reaches of the Terminal Warehouse, drawing artists, celebrities, and onlookers into the cavernous cellars decorated with industrial hardware, red velvet couches, chandeliers, abstract paintings, and railroad tracks running off into nothingness.

Across the street at 270 Eleventh Ave (bet. 27th / 28th Sts) is MICHAEL DEZER CLASSIC MOTORS, an entertaining showroom of 1950s vintage cars.

Before the diesel truck supplanted the locomotive as America's prime freight hauler, this neighborhood was the hub of the city's freight distribution system. The Thirtieth Street Yards of the New York Central Railroad (30th–37th Sts bet. 11th / 12th Aves with two additional blocks, 30th–32nd Sts bet. 10th / 11th Aves) received trains from a railroad that stretched far into the hinterlands. Additional yards at 60th St were connected to this facility by a freight line down Eleventh Ave, known grimly as Death Ave until the 1930s, when the tracks were dropped beneath street level. South of the yards an elevated rail viaduct (parts still visible) led to the St. John's Park Freight Terminal (1934) between Charlton and Clarkson Sts west of Washington St.

After years of controversy in governmental and financial circles, the N. section of the abandoned yards (34th–39th Sts) was designated as the site of the **Jacob K. Javits Convention Center,** a massive five-square-block complex designed by I. M. Pei & Partners (James I. Freed, partner in charge) and completed in 1986, 17 years and innumerable political squabbles after the project was conceived. The complex has vast areas of exhibition space, rooms for conventions and meetings, as well as exceptionally handsome public spaces. It is the third largest such facility in the nation, behind centers in Chicago and Las Vegas, with 640,000 square feet of exhibition space. Although the center has been criticized for being too small (some 15 of the nation's biggest trade shows cannot be accommodated), lacking adequate parking space and public transportation, a dearth of services in the surrounding neighborhood, and problems with air conditioning and labor, it currently has bookings into the next century. At night, illuminated from within, it gleams like a many-faceted jewel; on a sunny day, lit by the rays of the afternoon sun, it sparkles against the waters of the Hudson. Built as a 20C Crystal Palace of glass enframed by a metal grid, it incorporates some 16,100 glass panels, 100,000 sq ft of skylights, and a half mile of glass handrails. Surrounding the central exhibit area are three monumental public spaces—a glass-walled vestibule rising 75 ft to a glass ceiling, a central piazza whose glass ceiling soars 150 ft above the floor, and a galleria, or promenade, running the length of the building, for shops and services.

The nearest subways are the IND 8th Ave at 23rd St and the IRT 7th Ave at 28th St. The M10 bus runs uptown on 8th Ave and downtown on 7th Ave. The nearest crosstown bus is at 23rd St.

11 Union, Madison, and Stuyvesant Squares, Gramercy Park, and the Flatiron District

SUBWAY: IRT Lexington Ave local or express (trains 4, 5, or 6) to 14th St-Union Square. BMT Broadway or Broadway local (train N or R) to 14th St-Union Square. BMT 14th St-Canarsie (train L) to Union Square.

BUS: M1 downtown via 5th Ave / Park Ave South to Union Square. M2, M3, or M5 downtown via 5th Ave to 14th St; walk E. one long block to Union Square. M6 or M7 downtown via Broadway to Union Square.

Union Square, first named Union Place (1811) because it stood at the junction of the two main roads out of town is today emerging from a period of hard times, enjoying the fruits of a recent redesign and restoration (1985). In the early 1980s it was surrounded by failing businesses and deteriorating buildings, abandoned more or less by the public to drug dealers, who strolled its paths hawking their wares. Little trace remained of the repose and charm of its beginnings as a residential square, the glamour of its period as New York's theatrical district, or the fervor of its days as a political forum.

Part of the Brevoort farm in the 18C, Union Square was designated as a park in 1815 and laid out in 1831. It was enjoyed by such prominent local families as the Roosevelts and Goelets. In the decade before the Civil War the social elite displayed their privilege at the Academy of Music (14th St and Irving Place), while members of a wider swathe of society enjoyed themselves at Wallack's Theater (13th St and Broadway) and Irving Hall (later the Irving Place Theater at 15th St and Irving Place). During the later part of the century 14th St marked the midpoint of Ladies' Mile, a promenade of fashionable stores that stretched from Broadway and 8th St to 23rd St, but by 1900 both commerce and art had moved uptown to Madison Square, leaving Union Square stranded between the immigrant ghetto and industrial area to the south and the fashionable district uptown. Needle-trade workers moved in and during the early years of the 20C many old homes became tenements housing laborers and the occasional artist. In the years before World War I, the square became a center of political dissidence, for anarchists, socialists, "Wobblies," and Communists. A decade later, mass meetings sometimes developed into con-

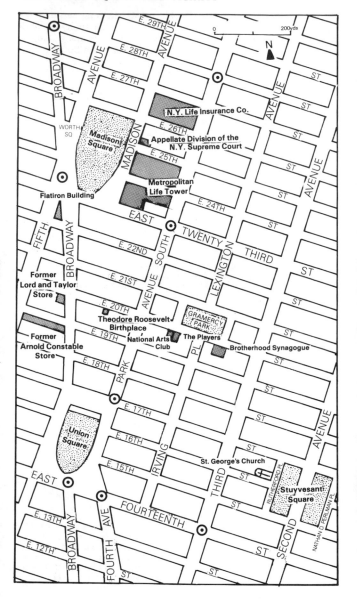

frontations with the police: most famous were a gathering protesting the execution of anarchists Nicola Sacco and Bartolomeo Vanzetti (August 22, 1927) and a Depression labor demonstration (March 6, 1930) attended by 35,000 workers and sympathizers. Public outcry after police injured 100 demonstrators at this meeting secured the square as a place of assembly, making it the heart of radical political activities in the city. During the 1930s various radical, progressive, and labor groups established headquarters in the area: the Socialist Party, the Communist Party, the American Civil Liberties Union, the Amalgamated Clothing Workers of America, and the International Ladies Garment Workers Union.

The present redesign (1984–85) alters a landscape plan developed in 1935–36, when the ground level was raised to accommodate the labyrinthine subway station beneath. Facing E. 14th St at the S. end of the park is an equestrian *statue of George Washington* (1856; Henry Kirke Brown with John Quincy Adams Ward), a 14-ft bronze work considered the sculptor's masterpiece. It commemorates Washington's entrance to the city on Evacuation Day (Nov 25, 1783), when British occupation of the city during the Revolutionary War ended. In the S.W. pedestrian triangle is Kantilal B. Patel's bronze statue of *Mohandas Gandhi* (1986), the Indian nationalist and advocate of nonviolent resistance, an appropriate resident of a park long associated with political protest.

Walk around the outside of the park to the E. (counterclockwise). Until 1984 the bulk of **S. Klein-on-the-Square,** a store for moderately priced women's apparel, dominated the E. side of the street opposite the park. In 1921, another low point in Union Square's past, Klein bought three derelict buildings and opened a discount apparel outlet, soon to be joined by Ohrbach's and Hearn's, thus making the neighborhood a center for bargain hunters as well as dissidents. Abandoned in 1975, the S. Klein store has been razed and *Zeckendorf Towers* (1987; Davis, Brody & Assocs.), a mixed use project, now stands on the site.

A little to the N. at 20 Union Square East is the *American Savings Bank,* originally the Union Square Savings Bank (1907; Henry Bacon), whose handsome Corinthian colonnade recalls Bacon's most famous accomplishment, the Lincoln Memorial in Washington, D.C.

At the edge of the park near E. 15th St (adjacent to Park Ave South) is a bronze **statue of the Marquis de Lafayette** (1876; Frédéric Auguste Bartholdi) presented in gratitude for support during the Franco-Prussian War. Bartholdi, best known for that other monument of Franco-American friendship, the Statue of Liberty, shows Lafayette offering his sword to the cause of American independence.

The *Guardian Life Insurance Co.* at 201 Park Ave South on the N.E. corner of E. 17th St (1911; D'Oench & Yost; DL) was founded as the *Germania Life Insurance Co.,* a name that became a liability during World War I.

In the center of the park stands the base (36 ft diameter; 9½ ft high) of the *Independence Flagstaff* (1926; Anthony De Francisci), whose bronze reliefs symbolize the forces of good and evil during the American struggle for independence. Formerly called the Charles F. Murphy Memorial, after the Tammany Hall boss

(1858–1924), the flagpole was financed by $80,000 of Tammany money collected on the 150th anniversary of the signing of the Declaration of Independence. The pedestal bears the text of the Declaration and a quotation from Thomas Jefferson. On the W. side of the park is a fountain (1881; Adolph Dondorf) with a figure of a woman and children. At the N. end is a **bronze statue of Abraham Lincoln** (1868; Henry Kirke Brown). Erected three years after Lincoln's assassination, the figure, dressed in a baggy suit, was criticized for its uninspiring dowdiness. North of the statue is a colonnaded pavilion dating from the 1930s.

Continue to the N. end of Union Square. A Greenmarket (open Wed, Fri, and Sat all year, 8–6) offers glorious produce from farms close to the city as well as eggs, cider, and other rural pleasures.

Just N. and E. of the park at 100 E. 17th St, the *Roundabout Theater* occupies a building (1928; Thompson, Holmes & Converse) built for Tammany Hall, the infamous Democratic political machine of Manhattan (see p. 285). The building now houses Local 91 of the International Ladies Garment Workers Union, who bought it in 1943 and quickly renamed it Roosevelt Auditorium.

Cross the parking lot N. of Union Square. At 33 E. 17th St, the ornate red brick CENTURY BUILDING (1881; William Schickel; DL) once housed the *Century Illustrated* and *St. Nicholas* magazines.

Turn left and walk toward Broadway. Visible on the W. side of Broadway are two turn-of-the-century office buildings. At *31 Union Square West* (N.W. corner of E. 16th St) is the BANK OF THE METROPOLIS (1893; Bruce Price; DL), a narrow graceful tower with an ionic portico of dark granite columns and a large cornice. Next door at 33 Union Square West is the UNION BUILDING (1893; Alfred Zucker; DL), whose primary stylistic ancestors seem to have been Moors and Venetian Goths.

Walk N. on Broadway. Hectic and dirty, even shabby today, it once was the home stretch of LADIES' MILE, with palatial department stores and fine office buildings majestically occupying the prominent intersections along Broadway and Fifth Ave. The *MacIntyre Building* (1892; R. H. Robertson) at 874 Broadway on the N.E. corner of E. 18th St is a once-elegant office tower adorned with Romanesque arches, finials, and a spectacular heraldic device.

Across the street (entrance on the S.W. corner of E. 19th St) at 881—887 Broadway stands the former **Arnold Constable Dry Goods Store** (1869, extended 1873 and 1877; Griffith Thomas), with one of the city's finest surviving mansard roofs. Thomas, architect of Marble House, the Arnold Constable store on Canal St, faced the original Broadway wing with marble—the only suitable material according to Aaron Arnold—and as the store grew, added the two-story mansard roof, expanded along 19th St, and finally duplicated the Broadway facade—in cast iron—along Fifth Ave, wrapping the mansard roof around the entire building.

On the S.E. corner of the same intersection (880–888 Broadway) is the former *W. & J. Sloane store* (1882; W. Wheeler Smith), a six-story brick building with cast-iron decoration, wide windows, and classical detailing. Originally dealers in carpets, Oriental rugs, lace curtains, and upholstery fabrics, W. & J. Sloane followed the carriage trade uptown in 1912.

On the N.W. corner at 889 Broadway is the former *Gorham Manufacturing Co.* building (1883; Edward H. Kendall; DL), a fussy brick structure with a chamfered corner turning that once rose to a tower. Built as an investment by the Goelet family, whose mansion stood across Broadway, it was an early multiuse building, with showrooms for Gorham silver and ecclesiastical metalwork downstairs and apartments on the upper floors.

Continue N. on Broadway. Another family investment, the onetime *Goelet Building, No. 900 Broadway* (S.E. corner of E. 20th St) (1887; McKim, Mead & White), is conspicuous for its fine brickwork. The former **Lord & Taylor store** (901 Broadway, S.W. corner of the E. 20th St intersection) is best seen from the E. side of the street. The building (1869; James H. Giles; DL), the fourth and grandest Lord & Taylor emporium, is a cast-iron French Second Empire extravaganza now sadly reduced in circumstance, though the handsomely restored part along Broadway suggests the grandeur of the original. The two-story arched entranceway on Broadway and the fine corner turning with its tall display windows and marble columns are gone, but the imposing corner tower and its high mansard roof remain. Known for its fine window displays and its modern equipment (including Otis elevators), Lord & Taylor's was a tourist attraction as well as one of the city's largest merchandisers of dry goods and ladies' wear.

Turn right (E.) on E. 20th St and walk a half block to the ***Theodore Roosevelt Birthplace** (original building, 1848; replicated, 1923; Theodate Pope Riddle; DL).

Theodore Roosevelt Birthplace. 28 E. 20th St, New York 10003. Tel: 260-1616. Open Wed–Sun 9–5, except Christmas, New Year's Day and Thanksgiving; last tour at 4:30. Admission charge for adults; children under 16 and senior citizens free.
    SUBWAY: IRT Lexington Ave local or express (train 4, 5, or 6) to Union Square-14th St. BMT Broadway express or local (N train) to Union Square-14th St or to 23rd St-Broadway. BUS: M2, M3, or M5 downtown via Madison Ave; M6 or M7 downtown via Broadway.

At the time of Roosevelt's birth (1858), this four-story brownstone was an upper middle class home in a comfortable residential neighborhood. Theodore's parents moved uptown in 1873, but the house remained in the family until 1896 when it was sold, altered for commercial use, and eventually demolished (1910). After Roosevelt's death (1919), his sisters bought the site and rebuilt their childhood home, a mirror image of their uncle's house still standing next door. The Roosevelt birthplace contains five rooms of period furniture, about 40% of it originally in the family, and an excellent collection of memorabilia, including a set of obelisks from a trip the family made to Egypt, Roosevelt's christening gown, and his diaries.

Return to Broadway and continue W. a short block to Fifth Ave. On the S.W. corner (150 Fifth Ave) is the former *Methodist Book Concern* (1889; Edward H. Kendall), a Romanesque Revival building whose rockface granite lower stories and handsome brickwork arches survive above an unattractively modernized ground floor. Originally the building was the headquarters of the *Christian Advocate,* a weekly Methodist journal which apprised its readers of the progress of humanity along religious and philanthropic lines. The *Advocate* carried its moral principles into its business policies, refusing advertisements of products endorsed by bishops or ministers and financial opportunities offering interest rates greater than 8% to investors.

Walk N. along Fifth Ave. At 153–157 Fifth Ave between 21st and 22nd Sts is the *United Synagogue of America Building,* originally the SCRIBNER BUILDING, small and classically elegant (1894; Ernest Flagg; DL) designed by the Scribner family's architect, who also obliged them with a printing plant, the uptown Scribner's store, and two private houses. Admired for its elegant metal and glass storefront which would have been at home on the Rue de la Paix, the Scribner Building once had a salesroom reminiscent of a library in a great private house and a metal and glass canopy over the entrance.

Continue up Fifth Ave past the Flatiron Building at E. 22nd St and the former Western Union Building (186 Fifth Ave), both better seen from Madison Square Park. Cross 23rd St and enter the park from the southwest.

Look back at the ***Flatiron Building** (1902; Daniel H. Burnham & Co.; DL), filling the elongated triangle where Broadway joins Fifth Ave at 23rd St, the world's tallest building (300 ft) when completed and one of the first to be supported by a steel skeleton. Dramatically sited and radically constructed, the Flatiron Building is nonetheless conservatively garbed in limestone and terracotta molded in ornate French Renaissance detail. The rounded corner turning (only 6 ft wide at the N. end), and the eight-story undulating bays in the midsection of the side walls soften its severity.

First called the Fuller Building after its developer, the Flatiron Building has evoked strong responses from such diverse observers as H. G. Wells (1906) who admired its "prow . . . ploughing up through the traffic of Broadway and Fifth Avenue in the afternoon light," and Edward Steichen, whose photos of it are famous. Because gusty winds often swirled around 23rd St and Broadway, the Flatiron Building was once haunted by street-corner Romeos who gathered to see a bit of ankle beneath a billowing skirt. Policemen, shooing these offenders, are said to have originated the expression "23 skidoo."

On the S.W. corner of 23rd St just W. of the Flatiron Building at 186 Fifth Ave is the *former Western Union Telegraph Company Building* (1884; Henry J. Hardenbergh). Small in scale, this red brick building with limestone trim, a gabled roof, dormers, and an odd, octagonal chimney tower at the N.W. corner, is an early work by the architect of the Dakota Apartments and the Plaza Hotel.

*Madison Square, recently restored while the neighborhood around it undergoes gentrification, once was the centerpiece of the city's most glamorous neighborhood, a garden of pleasure for the socially elite. This happy time came to an end in 1902, when the skyscraping Flatiron Building arrived, signaling in a grand way the arrival of commerce.

On the W. side of the square stood expensive hotels, including the white marble Fifth Avenue Hotel (opened 1859, bet. 23rd and 24th Sts), nicknamed Enos's Folly because Amos Enos had ventured to build so far uptown, and the Hoffman House (1865 Broadway, bet. 24th / 25th Sts), famous for the racy Bouguereau painting of nymphs and satyrs above the bar in the gentlemen's cafe. Delmonico's Restaurant hastened uptown (1876) to the S. side of 26th St between Fifth Ave and Broadway to provide a place for the cream of society to dine and dance. At the N.E. corner of the square was Stanford White's Madison Square Garden and on the E. side near 25th St his pillared and domed Madison Square Presbyterian Church. Nowadays these old buildings are all gone, but their replacements, with one exception, are graciously scaled and dignified. Dealers in insurance, giftwares, and toys have supplanted the social aristocracy, but the Madison Square district still retains the aura of its pleasant past, an aura which one hopes will survive the burgeoning condominiums now rising nearby.

Madison Square Park was, successively, a marsh, a potter's field, and a parade ground before the Commissioners' Plan of 1811 designated the whole area bounded by 23rd and 34th Sts, Third and Seventh Aves as a park. In 1844 the city fathers reduced it to its present size (from 6–7 acres) and named it after President James Madison; it opened officially in 1847. Its earliest claim to fame came in 1845 when a group of men who had been playing the new game of baseball there since 1842 codified the rules and organized the Knickerbocker Club, ancestor of all American baseball teams.

At the S. end of the park is a statue (erected 1876; Randolph Rogers) of *William Henry Seward*, U.S. senator and secretary of state under Lincoln and Andrew Johnson, best known for purchasing Alaska from Russia. The bronze figure, admired when first installed, drew scorn when it turned out that Rogers had recast the body from a figure of Lincoln made earlier for Fairmount Park in Philadelphia and simply attached Seward's head to Lincoln's neck.

Walk N.W. through the park (toward Broadway). The flagpole near the sidewalk bears a glass star, the *Eternal Light Memorial* (1924; Thomas Hastings and Paul Bartlett), commemorating American soldiers fallen in France during World War I. Visible on the traffic island between Fifth Ave and Broadway is a 51-ft granite obelisk, marking the grave of Gen. William Jenkins Worth (1857; James Goodwin Batterson), hero of the Mexican War, whose mortal remains lie virtually beneath the roaring traffic. The 19C cast-iron fence, of swords embedded in the ground, is also handsome.

A half block W. of the park at 15 W. 25th St (bet. Broadway / 6th Ave) is the SERBIAN EAST ORTHODOX CATHEDRAL OF ST. SAVA (1855; Richard Upjohn; DL), originally built as an uptown outpost of Trinity parish, purchased by the present Serbo-Croatian congregation in 1943. Like other early Gothic

Revival churches, it is a severe, simple brownstone, its somber-
ness intensified by the darkening of the brownstone. Inside (open
during services) is a reredos (1892) and altar (1897) by Frederick
Clarke Withers. The *Parish House* (1860; Jacob Wrey Mould; DL)
just E. of the church is more fanciful, with polychrome decoration,
ornamental brickwork, and carved stonework in the Victorian
Gothic manner. Between the buildings a walkway leads to *Clergy
House,* built by Upjohn at the same time as the church. Along the
walkway a statue commemorates Michael Pupin (1858–1935),
the noted Columbia University physicist who came to New York
as a Serbian immigrant. Return to Madison Square Park.

Continue clockwise through the park. At the N. end is the fine
Admiral Farragut Monument (1880; Augustus Saint-Gaudens;
base by Stanford White). The bronze figure of the admiral,
whipped by an imaginary wind, gazes off at the horizon from a
pedestal (a replica of the original) on which two low relief female
figures, Courage and Loyalty, emerge from a swirl of ocean
currents. The monument was unveiled (1881) by John H. Knowles,
the sailor who lashed Farragut to the mast of his ship during the
historic Civil War battle of Mobile Bay.

In the N.E. corner of the park is a *statue of Chester A. Arthur*
(1898; George E. Bissell), 21st President of the United States.
Visible behind the statue (N.W. corner of Madison Ave and E.
26th St) at 50 Madison Ave is the former *American Society for
the Prevention of Cruelty to Animals* (1896; Renwick, Aspinwall
& Owen), now a bank. This dignified limestone Italian Renaissance palazzo with its elaborately worked cornice at one time
housed a dispensary and hospital for animals.

Occupying the block between 26th and 27th Sts on the E. side
of Madison Ave at 51 Madison Ave is the **New York Life
Insurance Company** (1928; Cass Gilbert), designed by the architect of the Woolworth Building. Its limestone Italian Renaissance
base rises to a brightly gilded pyramidal tower, a feature Gilbert
also put on the Woolworth Building and the Federal Courthouse
at Foley Square. The grandiose lobby with its imposing scale,
coffered ceiling, bronze appointments, and great staircase suggests the wealth of the institution that commissioned the building.

The present office tower replaces Stanford White's beautiful Madison Square
Garden (1890; demolished 1925), the second of four successive buildings with
that name. The first, converted from the abandoned railroad depot of the New
York and Harlem Railroad, was leased by P. T. Barnum and known as the
Hippodrome before it became Madison Square Garden in 1879. In 1883 the
National Horse Show Association bought the site and built the second and most
famous Madison Square arena, which housed a restaurant, theater, and roof
garden as well as a sports arena. The walls were of yellow brick and white
terra-cotta; the sidewalks were arcaded and the roof ornamented with six open
cupolas, two small towers, and a large tower (249 ft to the base of the cupola)
modeled after the Giralda in Seville. On top of the tower stood Augustus Saint-
Gaudens's gilded statue of Diana, whose nudity distressed the city's more
proper citizens, though since the goddess's head was 332 ft from the sidewalk,
her anatomical charms could be glimpsed only remotely. Ironically this Madison
Square Garden was the site of White's death. In June 1906 he was murdered,
an unusual fate for an architect, shot to death in the roof garden by Pittsburgh

millionaire Harry K. Thaw, whose wife, the former showgirl Evelyn Nesbit, had in earlier days enjoyed a well-publicized affair with White.

Just S. of the New York Life Building is Madison Square's ugliest structure, the *Merchandise Mart* (1973; Emery Roth & Sons), a big, shiny, black box, especially unfortunate since the Leonard Jerome mansion was sacrificed for it. The Jerome mansion was the only Designated Landmark destroyed under a stipulation in the law allowing demolition if no financially viable use can be found.

The Jerome mansion (1859), built with the fortune Leonard Jerome reaped selling short in the Panic of 1857, featured a stables paneled in black walnut and a theater seating 600, perhaps because Jerome was notably fond of actresses. When his wife moved to Paris (1868), he rented the house to the Union League Club. Later when the Manhattan Club took over the lease, it became the alleged site of the invention of the Manhattan cocktail. Jennie Jerome, Leonard's daughter who spent part of her childhood here, became Lady Randolph Churchill, mother of Winston Churchill.

Walk S. along Madison Ave on the park side to the N.E. corner of E. 25th St (27 Madison Ave) and the **Appellate Division of the New York State Supreme Court** (1900; James Brown Lord; DL), a small building remarkable for its sculpture and decoration. Built of white marble with a Corinthian portico facing 25th St and four columns along Madison Ave, the courthouse cost $633,768 of which more than one-third went for statuary and murals.

Along Madison Ave are (on the roof balustrade, N. to S.): Confucius (Philip Martiny); Peace flanked by Wisdom and Strength (Karl Bitter), and Moses (William Couper). The four caryatids below (Thomas Shields Clarke) represent the four seasons. Along the balustrade on 25th St are (W. to E.): Zoroaster (Edward C. Potter); Alfred the Great (Jonathan Scott Hartley); Lycurgus (George Edwin Bissell); Solon (Herbert Adams); Justice flanked by Power and Study (Daniel Chester French); Louis IX (John Donoghue), Manu (Augustus Lukeman) and Justinian (Henry Kirke Bush-Brown). Formerly a statue of Mohammed stood next to Zoroaster but was removed and destroyed (1955) at the request of the city's Islamic community because religious law forbids images of the prophet. The pediment above the main doorway bears a sculptural group, the Triumph of Law (Charles H. Niehaus). Flanking the steps are Wisdom and Force (Frederick Wellington Ruckstuhl). The statuary and the stained glass dome in the courtroom were renovated in 1983 at a cost greater than the original cost of the building.

The interior of the building (open weekdays during working hours) is lavishly decorated with murals, beaded chandeliers, and paneling. In the courtroom is a fine stained glass skylight bearing the names of famous American lawyers. Occasionally historical displays are mounted in the lobby.

Directly across E. 25th St (Nos. 11–25 Madison Ave) is the North Building of the **Metropolitan Life Insurance Company** (1932; Harvey Wiley Corbett and D. Everett Waid), a massive limestone Art Deco building, best seen from the park. Its high vaulted entrances and elaborate, angled setbacks have been praised for lightening the apparent mass of the building while conforming to the zoning code. Here stood Stanford White's Madison Avenue Presbyterian Church (1906), a white marble, domed, and colonnaded temple demolished in 1919.

Adjacent to the North Building is the **Metropolitan Life Tower** (1909; Napoleon Le Brun; DL) on the S.E. corner of Madison Ave and 24th St, which took the title as the world's tallest building from the Flatiron Building, only to be topped by the Woolworth Building four years later. The tower (700 ft high, 75 ft wide on Madison Ave, 85 ft wide on 24th St) was inspired by the Campanile in St. Mark's Square in Venice and was considerably more elaborate before a remodeling in 1962.

Near the Madison Ave side of the park at its S. end is a bronze *statue of Roscoe Conkling* (1893; John Quincy Adams Ward), a U. S. senator and presidential candidate who died of exposure after trying to walk home from his downtown office in the Blizzard of 1888. The only modern work in the park is *Skagerrak* (1972; Antoni Milkowski), in the center of the park between Conkling and Seward. It consists of three rectangles (7 × 7 × 16 ft) of weathering steel and is named for a waterway separating Norway, Sweden, and Denmark.

Return to E. 26th St and walk E. across Park Ave South to Lexington Ave. At 68 Lexington Ave between 25th and 26th Sts is the former **69th Regiment Armory** (1904–06; Hunt & Hunt; DL), now used by the New York National Guard, site of the famous Armory Show (1913), where Marcel DuChamp's cubistic *Nude Descending the Stairs* stunned the New York art world. Behind the Lexington Ave facade with its copper-framed windows and mansard roof is a barrel vaulted drill hall.

Walk S. on Lexington Ave. At 147 E. 24th St (bet. Lexington / 3rd Aves) stands the last of the city's horse auction marts. It was built (1907; Horgan & Slattery) for the Fiss, Doerr & Carrol Co., which advertised itself as the largest dealer of horses in the world. The adjacent seven-story building at 155 E. 24th St was built at the same time as a stable for the horses sold "rain or shine," Mondays and Thursdays. One of the city's premier dealers in riding equipment, the *H. Kauffman & Sons Saddlery Co.,* is at 139 E. 24th St.

Continue S. on Lexington Ave. On the S.W. corner of E. 22nd St is the former RUSSELL SAGE FOUNDATION (c. 1914; tower added 1919; Grosvenor Atterbury), converted to apartments in 1975. The building, a lavishly handsome Renaissance Revival palace in the Florentine style, bears a frieze proclaiming its purpose—"For the Improvement of Social and Living Conditions." Sage, who acquired millions in the stock market after a start as a grocery clerk and, among his other achievements, gained control of the city's elevated railways (along with Jay Gould), left a fortune of some $60 million. In 1905, the year before his death, his wife, who would inherit his fortune, had written an article outlining "Opportunities and Responsibilities for Leisured Women" and, as this ponderous title suggests, she took her own responsibilities seriously, using some $15 million of her inheritance to establish the Russell Sage Foundation. Among its philanthropic acts was the construction of Forest Hills Gardens in Queens, an attempt at model housing.

Turn right and walk a block along E. 22nd St to Park Avenue South, Fourth Ave prestigiously renamed. This stretch was once filled with charitable organizations, some of which still remain. On the N.E. corner is the former *United Charities Building* at 287 Park Ave South (1891; R. H. Robertson and Rowe & Baker), once headquarters for some 45 social welfare agencies, still the home of the Children's Aid Society. On the S.E. corner is the Federation of Protestant Welfare Agencies at 281 Park Ave South (1893; Robert W. Gibson and Edward J. N. Stent; DL), located in the CHURCH MISSIONS' HOUSE BUILDING, formerly headquarters of the Episcopal Church's missionary societies. Constructed of rockface granite and Indiana limestone over a steel skeleton, the building is sometimes described as Flemish Renaissance and sometimes as Romanesque Revival. The tympanum above the entry shows St. Augustine preaching to the barbarians in England and Bishop Seabury preaching to the barbarians in America.

The *New York Bank for Savings* (1894; apartment tower and bank alterations 1987; Cyrus L. W. Eidlitz) at 280 Park Ave South, serves as a gateway to a tower of condominiums. *Calvary Church* (Protestant Episcopal) at 273 Park Ave South on the N.E. corner of E. 21st St (1846; James Renwick, Jr.) is a minor work by the architect of Grace Church and St. Patrick's Cathedral. Renwick also designed the Sunday School Building (1867), now used for offices.

Turn left and walk one block E. to **Gramercy Park,** New York's only private residential square. It was created by Samuel Bulkley Ruggles, a lawyer and small-scale urban planner, who bought a 20-acre farm in 1831, drained the marshland, and laid out a park to increase the value of his land. Around the park he designated 66 building lots and sold them with the stipulation that only lot owners could have access to the park. His wishes are still in force: except for a brief period during the Draft Riots of 1863, when troops camped inside the 8-ft iron fence, the park trustees have resisted all intrusions, including a proposed cable car line (1890) and an extension of Lexington Ave (1912) through the park. Only residents facing the square who pay a yearly maintenance fee are granted keys.

Begin walking S. along Gramercy Park West, with its fine Greek Revival town houses (numbered counterclockwise). Dr. Valentine Mott (died 1865), prominent surgeon and a founder of Bellevue Hospital, lived at No. 1 **Nos. 3–4 Gramercy Park West** (c. 1840; attrib. Alexander Jackson Davis) are distinguished by their original cast-iron verandas with profuse Greek Revival ornamentation—anthemions, meanders, and floral motifs. This lacy ironwork, more familiar in southern cities like Charleston and New Orleans, was considered a rustic touch especially appropriate to houses facing parks or enjoying deep front yards. A pair of Mayor's Lamps stand at No. 4, once the home of James Harper, mayor of the city (1844–45) and a founder of Harper & Bros., publishers.

At No. 15 on the S. side of the park is the **National Arts Club** (1845; remodeled 1874; Calvert Vaux; DL), a brownstone built during the Gothic Revival period of the 1840s as two houses and remodeled for Samuel J. Tilden during the heyday of a more flamboyant Victorian Gothic style. Tilden, scourge of the Tweed

Ring (see p. 152) and governor of New York State, who lost the Presidency by one electoral vote (1876), seems to have doubted the public's goodwill, for he had rolling steel doors installed behind the lower windows and an escape tunnel built to 19th St. Tilden, who was a successful corporate lawyer and shrewd investor, spent much of his money on his collection of rare books, which along with the Astor and Lenox endowments, formed the core of the New York Public Library collection. Architecturally the building's attractions include polychrome decoration, asymmetric bays, heavy lancet windows, and a set of medallions portraying Goethe, Dante, Franklin, and Milton. The National Arts Club bought the property in 1906; occasionally it is open to the public for exhibitions (tel. 475-3424).

Next door at No. 15 is **The Players** (1845; remodeled, 1888; Stanford White; DL) a simple Gothic Revival brownstone (note the drip moldings on the upstairs windows) until actor Edwin Booth bought it and hired Stanford White to remodel it as an actors' club. At the end of his tragic and rootless life, Booth, one of the finest actors of his time, lived on the top floor of the club overlooking the park. The fine iron railings and lanterns and the two-story porch based on an Italian Renaissance prototype are known to be White's personal work.

Cross Gramercy Park South and look into the park for a view of the *statue of Edwin Booth* in the character of Hamlet (1917, dedicated 1918; Edmond T. Quinn).

The name "Gramercy" harks back to the Dutch colonial period when the area was called Krom Moerasje ("crooked little swamp") after a marshy brook that wandered from Madison Square to the East River near 18th St. Later the neighborhood was called Crommashie Hill, and eventually Gramercy Park.

At 19 Gramercy Park South (S.E. corner of Irving Place) stands *Evyan House*, the former *Benjamin Sonnenberg mansion*, a five-story red brick house built in 1845 and updated with a mansard roof in 1860. Stuyvesant Fish, whose business interests included railroads, insurance, and banking, bought it in the 1880s and his wife here began her assault on society. After Fish moved uptown near the turn of the century the house declined until public relations counsel Benjamin Sonnenberg bought it in 1931 and restored it to its former glory, both as a house and as a center of the city's social life.

Continue east. On the S.E. corner of the block (144 E. 20th St) is the former **Friends' Meeting House** (1859; King & Kellum; DL), an austere Italianate building whose severity is broken only by the arched pediment above the doorway. Saved in 1965 from a developer, the meeting house was renovated as the Brotherhood Synagogue (1975; James Stewart Polshek). On its E. side is the Garden of Remembrance, a memorial (dedicated 1982) to the Jews who perished in the Holocaust.

In the S.E. corner of the park is Greg Wyatt's *Fantasy Fountain* (1983), whose spouting giraffes please the young at heart.

Two apartments on Gramercy Park East deserve brief note. No. 34 (1883; George da Cunha), a red brick building with an octagonal turret and a lavish mosaic lobby floor, is probably the city's first cooperative apartment. No. 36 (1908; James Riely Gordon) has elaborate terra-cotta Gothic ornament and two cast stone armored knights guarding the entrance. Return to Irving Place.

Walk S. on Irving Place, named (1831) by Samuel Ruggles for Washington Irving, writer and diplomat. The block of E. 19th St between Irving Place and Third Ave is known as *The Block Beautiful*. Remodeled in the 1920s, its little 19C houses and stables, individually undistinguished, collectively have unusual serenity and charm, though a few suffer from excessive cuteness. During the 1930s a small artists' colony flourished here, its residents including muckraker Ida Tarbell (*The History of Standard Oil*) and painter George Bellows. *Pete's Tavern*, originally the Portman Hotel and later Tom Healy's Cafe, on the N.E. corner of Irving Place and 18th St, is one of the city's oldest taverns (opened 1864), having survived Prohibition as a speakeasy. Its most illustrious client, writer O. Henry (William Sydney Porter), lived at 55 Irving Place, and described the cafe in a story, *The Lost Blend*.

Continue S. to 17th St. The house at 40 Irving Place (S.W. corner of the intersection) has been erroneously identified as Washington Irving's home. It wasn't. Built c. 1845, its most famous residents were Elsie de Wolfe (later, Lady Mendl) and Elisabeth Marbury, two ladies of taste and social ability who became famous respectively as an interior decorator and a literary agent. During their stay in this house at the turn of the century the ladies ran a Sunday salon which, according to their own recollections, attracted so many foreign celebrities that it was known as the "Immigrants' Home." Across the street a bronze *bust of Washington Irving* (1885; Frederick Beer) stands in front of the high school bearing his name.

Turn left and walk E. on 17th St. At 190 Third Ave (bet. 17th / 18th Sts) is *Fat Tuesday's*, now a jazz club. It was formerly Joe King's Rathskeller (also known as the German-American), host to several generations of beer-drinking collegians; in an earlier incarnation it was Scheffel Hall, a *biergarten* serving the large 19C neighborhood German population. The building (1894; Weber & Drosser) owes its ornate baroque facade to those early days.

Continue E. on 17th St past Second Ave to **Stuyvesant Square**, once part of Peter Stuyvesant's farm, later (1836) a Stuyvesant family gift (sold for $5) to the city. The 4-acre park, which has always been bisected by Second Ave, was landscaped in 1936 with shade trees and small pools. The bronze *statue of Peter Stuyvesant* (1936, installed 1941) is by Gertrude Vanderbilt Whitney, founder of the Whitney Museum.

To the E. are the buildings of Beth Israel Medical Center and the New York Infirmary-Beekman Downtown Hospital.

Diversion. From Stuyvesant Square, walk E. a block to First Ave. Occupying the territory bounded by First Ave and the Franklin Delano Roosevelt Drive, 14th and 20th Sts, is **Stuyvesant Town** (1947; Irwin Clavan and Gilmore Clarke), an immense middle-income housing project branded "the architecture of the Police State" by Lewis Mumford in 1948. Stuyvesant Town was built by the Metropolitan Life Insurance Company which got a sizable tax abatement for redeveloping 18 blocks of slums as affordable housing for returning World War II servicemen. In 1947 the waiting list numbered some 110,000; now a mere 8000 families wait for an opening in one of the 8736 rent-stabilized apartments. Age has softened somewhat the appearance of the project, and by modern standards the 13- and 14-story red brick buildings are not unduly institutional. North of Stuyvesant Town, between First Ave and the F. D. R. Drive, 20th and 23rd Sts, is its wealthier cousin **Peter Cooper Village** (1947; Irwin Clavan and Gilmore Clarke). Return to Stuyvesant Square.

West of Stuyvesant Square, across Rutherford Place, is the FRIENDS' MEETING HOUSE AND SEMINARY (1860; Charles T. Bunting; DL), a red brick Greek Revival building with brownstone quoins, austere like all Quaker houses of worship. A 17C schism accounts for the presence of two Quaker meeting houses built within one year and a few blocks of one another.

Rutherford Place is named after Col. John Rutherford, a member of the committee that laid out the city's streets beginning in 1807 and eventually issued the Commissioners' Plan of 1811 (see p. 222).

Across 16th St from the meeting house is **St. George's Church** (Protestant Episcopal), a formidable Romanesque Revival brownstone (1856; Otto Blesch and Leopold Eidlitz; DL), remembered as J. P. Morgan's church because as an elder he ruled it with an iron hand; he also donated the land on which the present parish house stands. The first church (1847) burned in 1865 but was rebuilt according to the original plans, although at the time of the reconstruction the rector insisted on an evangelically simple interior without the customary altar and reredos. The original church had two tall spires, but they were weakened by the fire and removed (1888). North of the church is the *Chapel* (1911; Matthew Lansing Emery and Henry George Emery), a rather elaborate Byzantine-Romanesque companion to the more somber church.

Walk W. on 16th St past the original *Rectory* at 209 E. 16th St, built in the early 1850s by Leopold Eidlitz. Because of demographic changes, St. George's is now combined with Calvary Church and the Church of the Holy Communion (W. 20th St and Sixth Ave) in a single parish.

Continue walking W. to Third Ave; turn left and walk S. to 14th Street. At 145 E. 14th St near the corner of Third Ave is the *Consolidated Edison Energy Museum* (Tues—Sat 10—4; closed major holidays; admission free; tel: 460—6244), with displays of early electrical equipment, dioramas, and recorded narrations documenting the history of electricity in the U. S. and especially in New York. One exhibit is a room-size model of the city's subterranean energy distribution system.

The *Consolidated Edison Co. Building* (N.E. corner of Irving Place and E. 14th St) is Henry J. Hardenbergh's last large work (1915—29; Henry J. Hardenbergh; tower, 1926; Warren & Wetmore), and not one of his most successful. It occupies the sites of the old Academy of Music, Tammany Hall, and Tony Pastor's Music Hall.

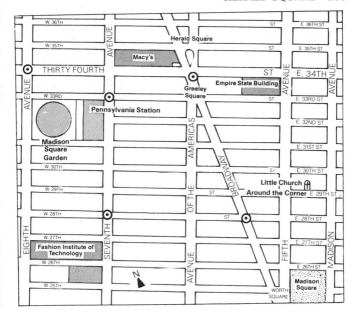

Tammany Hall, founded in 1789 as a fraternal society and political club, later grew into the Democratic Party machine, long the most potent factor in city politics. By the mid-19C, Tammany had become synonymous with corruption and crooked elections (notably with bought immigrant votes), and its leaders were known as "Bosses," e.g., "Boss Tweed."

Across the street at 126 E. 14th St, is the *Palladium,* a night spot recycled (1985; Arata Isozaki) from a namesake of the Academy of Music (1926) which had descended the cultural hierarchy to ballroom, burlesque theater, and movie house before becoming a hall for rock concerts. In 1985 amidst great fanfare the building re-opened as a nightclub set apart by its decor, created by contemporary artists.

Continue W. on 14th St to Union Square for the subway and buses.

12 Herald Square and the Garment District

SUBWAY: IRT Broadway-7th Ave local or express (train 1, 2, 3, or 9) to 34th St-Penn Station. IND 6th Ave (B, D, or F train) or IND 8th Ave (A, C, or E train) to 34th St-Penn Station. BMT (N or R train) to 34th St.

BUS: M6 or M7 via Broadway / 7th Ave. M10 via 7th Ave to 34th St. M16 crosstown via 34th St. M4 via 5th Ave to 34th St and 6th Ave.

Begin at **Herald Square,** not really a square at all but two triangles (W. 32nd to W. 35th Sts) created by the intersection of Broadway and Sixth Ave. It owes its name to the *New York Herald,* which between 1895 and 1921 occupied a fine McKim, Mead & White palazzo just N. of 35th St. Both the palazzo and the paper are gone now, the former demolished in favor of an office building, the latter, after a number of mergers, finally succumbing in 1966. Only the bell and clock that once adorned the building remain; when the Sixth Ave El was torn down (1939–40), they were installed as a memorial to *Herald* publishers James Gordon Bennett and his son James Gordon Bennett, Jr. (pedestal and redesign of square, 1940; Aymar Embury II). Two muscular bronze figures nicknamed Stuff and Guff or alternately Gog and Magog apparently hammer out the hours on the Meneeley bell (actually the bell is struck from within), while a bronze Minerva and her owl observe the proceedings (statuary, 1894; Antonin Jean Paul Carles). The S. triangle (bet. W. 32nd / W. 33rd Sts), properly called **Greeley Square,** contains a statue of *New York Tribune* founder Horace Greeley (1892; Alexander Doyle).

Beneath Herald Square stretches a labyrinthine subway station, a maze of pedestrian access tunnels and transit lines—the BMT subway, the railroad tubes connecting lines in New Jersey and Long Island with Penn Station, and the 6th Ave IND subway, which was threaded through the existing tangle (1939) about 52 ft below street level.

Herald Square also enjoys a reputation as a major retail shopping district, long dominated by Macy's and Gimbels, while W. 32nd St between Sixth and Seventh Aves offers a concentration of shops dealing in photographic equipment.

R. H. Macy & Co. (W. 34th to W. 35th St, Broadway to 7th Ave) now occupies a square block containing 2.2 million sq ft of selling space (original building facing Broadway, 1901; DeLemos & Cordes; 7th Ave building, 1931; Robert D. Kohn).

The store was founded by Rowland Hussey Macy, a Nantucket Quaker who went to sea at the age of 15 and returned four years later with $500 and a red star, now Macy's logo, tattooed on his hand. After six failures in merchandising and additional disappointments in real estate and the stock market, Macy founded (1858) his New York store on Sixth Ave near 14th St, an enterprise he developed to the point where he could bill it as "the world's largest store." Its 168 selling departments are overseen by a staff of 11,000 employees, who deal with 45 million business transactions annually.

The store's longtime conservative, middle-class image resulted in part from its founder's business principles: sell at fixed prices, undersell all competitors, buy and sell only for cash (the last a throwback to Macy's Quaker heritage). In the late 1930s, however, Macy's began to extend credit to its customers, and since 1974 the store has projected a more daring image to attract customers from the suburbs, the Upper West Side, and the newly affluent loft areas like SoHo lying S. of 34th St.

Macy's is also known for the variety of its merchandise, stocking almost half a million items, from furs and diamonds, caviar and raspberries, to all the more humble articles needful in this life. Among its more spectacular sales have been a cowboy costume for a show business chimpanzee, the plumbing fixtures for the presidential palace in Liberia, and a length of silk to outfit the members of a Saudi Arabian harem.

A decade after its founder's death the store passed (1887) to Isidor and Nathan Straus, who had leased space in the store's basement (1874) to run a china and glassware department. The Straus family maintained its association with Macy's for five generations. Isidor Straus and his wife Ida, who perished together in the sinking of the *Titanic* (1912), are honored by a plaque near the entrance.

Across 34th St to the S. is the **Herald Center**, a vertical mall replacing the former Korvettes discount store, which in turn replaced *Saks-34th St,* the original Saks department store in the city (1902; Buchman & Fox).

A block S. along Broadway between W. 32nd and W. 33rd Sts, **A & S Greeley Square Plaza**, a branch of Brooklyn's Abraham & Straus, occupies what was, before considerable alteration, the legendary *Gimbel Brothers Department Store* (1912; Daniel H. Burnham & Co.; alterations 1988–89), long famous as Macy's competitor.

Gimbels, founded by Adam Gimbel, a Bavarian immigrant who started his career in this country as a pack peddler, was hardly an upstart in the merchandising field. The store, founded in the Midwest (1842), came to New York in 1910 and rose to fame for its "feud" with Macy's, romanticized in the film *Miracle on 34th St.* Although the rivalry was generally profitable to both stores, Gimbels was bought out after 76 years of doing business in the city and closed its doors in 1986.

The branch of Abraham and Straus, the Brooklyn-based retail chain, is the first major department store built in Manhattan since Alexander's opened (1980) a satellite store in the World Trade Center.

Walk W. to Seventh Ave. The street signs for Seventh Ave as it passes through the **Garment District** are subtitled "Fashion Ave," a name imposed with some bravado on an area beset with economic problems. The American garment industry as a whole is shrinking in the face of cheap imported goods, and the New York sector is further threatened with transportation difficulties, high labor costs, and infiltration by organized crime. Nonetheless, the Garment District, bounded roughly by 25th and 41st Sts, Sixth and Ninth Aves, houses one of the city's most important industries, which moved uptown from the sweatshops of the Lower East Side around the time of World War I, following the northward progress of the major department stores and reflecting gains in working conditions achieved by the labor unions. Until recent years the entire industry—from designers to cutters, button makers, seamstresses, to marketing professionals—crowded within the borders of the district. Nowadays, with gentrification encroaching on the area and an increasingly Oriental labor force, many of the manufacturing operations have moved to cheaper quarters in Chinatown and elsewhere in the city, while the showrooms remain here.

To a certain extent the old lines of demarcation still exist. The S. part of the district is dominated by the fur industry; the area around 34th St by children's wear firms, and the section N. of 36th St by women's apparel, though these geographical divisions are only general. On the fringe of the Garment District are allied industries and trades—firms dealing in millinery, hosiery, buttons, thread, trimmings, and fabrics.

The Garment District is notorious for its congested traffic, and only the ignorant or sublimely patient driver will try to negotiate the crosstown streets during working hours, when double-parked trucks and wheeled clothing racks called hand trucks clog both the roadway and the sidewalk. The lunchtime crowd, once famous for its density, has thinned with the shrinking of the work force. The most famous of the remaining Garment District eateries is *Lou G. Siegel's* (209 W. 38th St), a kosher restaurant that still caters to buyers and bosses.

Walk S. on Seventh Ave. On the S.E. corner of W. 33rd St is the *New York Penta Hotel* (1918; McKim, Mead & White), formerly the Hotel Pennsylvania, whose telephone number was immortalized by bandleader Glenn Miller, composer of a song called *Pennsylvania 6-5000;* during the 1930s the hotel was a center for big bands as well as the gathering place for buyers who arrived in town to stock their stores from the offerings of the Garment District.

Pennsylvania Station is still across the street but it is now stripped of its former glory and relegated to a hole in the ground. Marking the entrance to 2 Penn Plaza (7th Ave and 32nd St) is a statue (c. 1910; Adolph A. Weinman) of *Samuel Rea,* president of the Pennsylvania Railroad from 1913–25, when railroads were at the peak of their power. Adolph Weinman also sculpted a row of 22 granite eagles, which once stood atop the cornice of the old station, and a great stone clock framed by two classical figures, which were carted off to a dump in Secaucus, New Jersey, when the station was demolished. Until wantonly destroyed in 1963–66, the **former Pennsylvania Station** (1906–10) was McKim, Mead & White's masterpiece, a symbol of the power of the Pennsylvania Railroad, and a happy union of history and technology. The facade with its imposing Doric colonnade and the General Waiting Room with its vaulted ceiling were modeled on the Roman Baths of Caracalla, while the steel and glass arches, domes, and vaults covering the Concourse belonged to the more recent tradition of crystal palaces and glass exhibition galleries. Not only did the station provide the visitor with a spectacular entrance to the city, but the tunnels leading to it allowed, for the first time, a convenient approach from either New Jersey via the Hudson River tubes or Long Island via a connecting crosstown tunnel and tubes beneath the East River.

The station was doomed in 1962, when the financially troubled Pennsylvania Railroad sold the air rights above the station for a new Madison Square Garden to rise above a smaller station. In unusually bitter tones, the *New York Times* declared (Oct 3, 1963) that the demolition was a monumental act of vandalism,

The Concourse of the former Pennsylvania Station in 1910. The demolition of this magnificent building and its replacement by the present nonentity mark one of the saddest episodes in the city's architectural history. (Courtesy of The New-York Historical Society, New York City)

remarking that ". . . any city gets what it admires, will pay for, and ultimately deserves."

In its place rose the present graceless **Madison Square Garden Center** (1968; Charles Luckman Assocs.). The complex includes Madison Square Garden, a 20,000-seat arena enclosed in a precast concrete-clad drum, the Felt Forum (5000 seats), an office building (29 stories), and other facilities. The New York Rangers (ice hockey) and the New York Knickerbockers (basketball) call the Garden home; other events are regularly scheduled: track meets; dog shows; ice shows; tennis tournaments; the Ringling Brothers, Barnum and Bailey circus; rock concerts; and boxing matches.

Beneath the Garden is the present **Penn Station,** still giving access to the old tracks laid down when its predecessor was completed. About 650 trains carrying some 200,000 passengers use the station daily; with additional access from the BMT, IRT, and IND subways and the PATH (Port Authority Trans-Hudson) system, the station receives a crowd of half a million people daily. Ironically, less than 20 years after the old terminal was destroyed, intercity rail traffic has increased, and the current station is too small.

Walk W. to Eighth Ave. On the W. side of the avenue (bet. W. 31st / W. 33rd Sts) is the **General Post Office** (1913; McKim,

Mead & White; DL), whose tall Corinthian colonnade once echoed that of the railroad station. Around the frieze marches a motto loosely adapted from Herodotus and only vaguely applicable to the workings of the present New York postal system: "Neither snow nor rain nor heat nor gloom of night stays these couriers from the swift completion of their appointed rounds." The interior is monumental.

Walk S. on Eighth Ave and turn left on W. 30th St. At 211 W. 30th St, between Seventh and Eighth Aves, is the small, lovely brownstone ST. JOHN THE BAPTIST CHURCH (Roman Catholic), designed (1872) by Napoleon LeBrun, architect of the Metropolitan Life Tower and a number of handsome firehouses. The interior, with its elaborate stations of the cross, marble columns with gilded capitals, and handsome vaulting is especially beautiful.

Continue walking E. to Seventh Ave and turn right (S.). The **Fur District** stretches roughly from 27th to 30th Sts between Sixth and Eighth Aves. Like the rest of the garment industry, the fur trade is shrinking. The rather dismal-looking shops whose barred windows attest to the value of the merchandise within are protected by closed-circuit TV cameras, alarm systems, and buzzer-operated locked doors. Even though robbery is a threat it is still possible on occasion to see couriers walking casually through the streets with fur coats worth tens of thousands of dollars dangling from hangers or slung over their arms.

Continue S. on Seventh Ave. The FASHION INSTITUTE OF TECHNOLOGY (1958–77; DeYoung & Moscowitz), located along the avenue from W. 26th to W. 28th Sts, is a professional school for students seeking careers in the clothing industry. In the plaza facing Seventh Ave and 27th St is Robert M. Cronbach's hammered brass *Eye of Fashion* (1976). The galleries in the Shirley Goodman Resource Center offer changing exhibitions, some of interest to observers or historians of fashion, others fascinating to the public at large.

The Galleries at F.I.T., Shirley Goodman Resource Center. Seventh Ave at 27th St, New York 10001. Tel: 760-7760. Open during exhibitions Tues 10–9; Wed–Sat 10–5. Closed Sun, Mon, legal holidays. Free.

Group tours by appointment. Occasional lectures and seminars with major exhibitions. Library, costume, accessory, textile collections available to members. Restrooms and telephones. No restaurant, no gift shop. Accessible to wheelchairs.

SUBWAY: IRT Broadway-7th Ave local (train 1 or 9) to 28th St. BMT Broadway local (N or R train) to 28th St. BUS: M4 downtown via 5th Ave, uptown via Madison Ave. M5 downtown via 5th Ave, uptown via 6th Ave. M6 or M7 downtown via 7th Ave / Broadway, uptown via 6th Ave. M10 downtown via 7th Ave, uptown via 8th Ave. M11 downtown via 9th Ave, uptown via 10th Ave. M16, M34 crosstown on 34th St.

Diversion. There is a sculptural tribute to the workers in the garment industry in front of 555 Seventh Ave (39th–40th Sts), a larger than life bronze figure of a Jewish man operating a sewing machine. Entitled *The Garment Worker* (1984), it was inspired by sculptor Judith Weller's father, who for many years was a member of the International Ladies Garment Workers Union.

Walk E. on 28th St to Sixth Ave. In the early morning hours, the **Flower Market**—not a centralized market building but a collection of wholesale and retail stores along Sixth Ave and the side streets near W. 28th St—still delights the eye with a burst of color in an otherwise drab neighborhood. Later in the day the shops revert to more sedate retail selling, and one can browse at leisure among palm fronds, rubber plants, and masses of fragrant cut flowers.

The market began about 1870, when Long Island growers brought their flowers daily to the foot of E. 34th St at the East River; gradually the district moved inland to be near what was then the center of retail selling. Nowadays the merchants are facing economic pressures that threaten to drive them from the area: rising rents, competition from wholesalers who deliver cut flowers by truck directly to the florists, and zoning changes which may permit residential development.

In the 1880s a variety theater, dance hall, and restaurant called the **Haymarket** stood at the S.E. corner of Sixth Ave and W. 30th St. It was the most notorious resort of a district known as the **Tenderloin,** which stretched from about 24th to 40th Sts (bet. 5th / 7th Aves) and was so famous for its brothels, saloons, and dance halls that Brooklyn reformer T. DeWitt Talmadge called it "Satan's Circus." Police Inspector Alexander Williams, transferred to this precinct from quieter streets, gave it its best-known name by remarking: "I've had nothing but chuck steak for a long time, and now I'm going to get a little of the tenderloin." Williams then began supplementing his modest salary with protection money extorted from the proprietors of saloons, gambling houses, and brothels, eventually coming to enjoy a city home, a Connecticut estate, and a yacht. Through the efforts of reformers and the Lexow Committee (1894), the involvement of public officials in vice and crime became a source of general indignation; Williams was retired "for the good of the force."

Continue E. to Fifth Ave; turn left and walk north. At 272 Fifth Ave on the N.W. corner of 29th St is the **Marble Collegiate Reformed Church** (1854; Samuel A. Warner; DL), a Gothic Revival contemporary of Trinity Church. The Collegiate Dutch Reformed Church, the oldest (1628) denomination in the city, is so named because its ministers, serving as equals, are called colleagues. Norman Vincent Peale, prolific author, popular speaker, and master of public relations, made the church famous during his pastorate.

The Church of the Transfiguration (Protestant Episcopal) at 1 E. 29th St in its quiet garden is better known as **The Little Church Around the Corner,** a name it earned in 1870. Actor Joseph Jefferson, trying to arrange the funeral of George Holland, another actor, was told by the minister of a fashionable nearby church who declined to perform the service that "the little church around the corner" might be willing to bury someone as socially nondescript as an actor. Jefferson replied, "God bless the little church around the corner," a remark now enshrined in a stained glass window in the S. aisle.

The main body of the church (architect unknown) dates from 1849; the Guild Hall and Rectory by Frederick C. Withers were added in 1861, while the Lich Gate, also designed by Withers, was donated (1896) by Mrs. Franklin Delano, the former Laura Astor, aunt of President Franklin D. Roosevelt. The Lich Gate, unusual in American churchyards, provided a covered resting place for the coffin before burial.

The church, Rectory, Guild Hall, Lich Gate, Lady Chapel, and Mortuary Chapel are all Designated Landmarks.

Enter the church (open 8–6 daily; during the winter months the nave is closed except during services because of heating costs). To the left of the entrance is the Chantry or Chapel of the Holy Family, first used as a parish schoolroom. The altar, called the Brides' Altar because it was donated by couples married in the church, is surmounted by a reredos containing three Scottish carved oak panels more than 400 years old depicting aspects of the Crucifixion. The Baptistry to the left of the altar contains a bronze marker commemorating actress Gertrude Lawrence (died 1952). The paintings (artist unknown) flanking the font are Flemish (17C). The LADY CHAPEL, separated from the chantry by three stained glass doors was added in 1906. Its windows reproduce (left to right) Raphael's *Madonna del Gran Duca,* the high altar of this church, and Botticelli's *Virgin and Child.*

Enter the NAVE, which contains a number of memorials to actors. Begin in the N. aisle. Montague (Henry J. Mann), a handsome matinee idol (died 1878), is depicted in the first window wearing the robes of a pilgrim. The first clerestory window honors Mary Shaw (died 1929), actress and feminist. The window depicting St. John the Beloved Disciple is dedicated to American actor John Drew (died 1927). Other windows in the N. aisle honor St. Alban, first martyr of Britain, and St. Augustine, first Archbishop of Canterbury. The *St. Faith window* nearest the pulpit in the N. aisle is said to be the oldest church window in America, made of 14C Belgian glass saved from a church destroyed during the Napoleonic wars. The window depicts St. Faith on a mound of flowers beneath a canopy of early Renaissance design. In the S. aisle the *Joseph Jefferson Memorial Window* commemorates the incident which gave the church its nickname. Jefferson, clad in the rags of his role as Rip Van Winkle is shown leading enshrouded George Holland toward the Lich Gate. The bronze tablet next to the window honoring actor Otis Skinner is the work of Paul Manship.

The Peace Shrine near the SOUTH TRANSEPT contains a wood statue of Christ designed after Thorwaldsen's *Christus Consolator.* At the end of the transept is the Madonna Shrine dating from 1930. The *Actors' Memorial Window* in the transept clerestory honors members of the theatrical profession and depicts the Flight into Egypt. On the W. wall of the transept is the **Edwin Booth Memorial Window* honoring the tragedian, who is depicted in the garb of Hamlet; it was given by the Players, a club in Gramercy Park that he founded. Next to it is the *Jeweled Window,* whose richly colored pieces of glass are said to resemble rubies and sapphires, a memorial to Joseph W. Drexel, a communicant of this church. Both the Drexel and Booth windows are the work of John La Farge. The MORTUARY CHAPEL (1908) is dedicated to St. Joseph of Arimathea. The window above its altar depicting Raphael's *Transfiguration* was originally above the high altar.

The nearest subway is the IRT Lexington Ave local (train 6) at Lexington Ave and 33rd or 28th St. Uptown buses run on Madison Ave. Downtown buses run on 5th Ave and Park Ave South.

13   East 42nd Street, Kips Bay, and Murray Hill

SUBWAY: IND 6th Ave (B, D, or F train) to 42nd St. IRT Flushing (train 7) to 5th Ave and 42nd St.

BUS: M1, M2, M3, M4, or M32 downtown via 5th Ave. M5 or M104 downtown from upper W. Side. M1, M2, M3, M4, or M32 uptown via Park Ave South / Madison Ave. M5 or M6 uptown via 6th Ave. M106 crosstown on 42nd St.

Since 1838 Fifth Ave has been the dividing line between the East Side and the West Side, a division with social as well as geographical ramifications. The East Side has a reputation for being rich and chic while the West Side is said to be a little down at the heels. This is generally true of 42nd St, too, with W. 42nd deserving its reputation for seediness and E. 42nd its acclaim as the site of such institutions as the Ford Foundation and the United Nations.

In the block of W. 42nd St just before Fifth Ave there are two noteworthy buildings. At 33 W. 42nd St (bet. 5th / 6th Aves) is the *Graduate Center of the City University of New York,* originally Aeolian Hall (1912), remodeled (1970; Carl J. Petrilli & Assocs.) with a mid-block pedestrian arcade and gallery for changing exhibitions. The *W. R. Grace Building* at 41 W. 42nd St (1974; Skidmore, Owings & Merrill) is a big white building with a self-important swooping facade.

Cross Fifth Ave and walk east. At 60 E. 42nd St (bet. Madison / Park Aves) is the *Lincoln Building* (1939; J. E. R. Carpenter), a 53-story skyscraper with a striking series of setbacks. The lobby contains a smaller bronze version of Daniel Chester French's immense seated Lincoln in the Lincoln Memorial in Washington, D.C.

Across the street ***Grand Central Terminal** (1903–13; Reed & Stem and Warren & Wetmore; DL) looms into view, standing proudly athwart Park Ave. Though railroad travel has declined in scope and grandeur since the terminal was built, Grand Central Terminal remains one of the world's great railroad stations and an enduring symbol of the city. Visually less exciting than those other emblems of New York's preeminence—the Empire State Building, the Brooklyn Bridge, and the Statue of Liberty—it is still a fine building and a marvel of engineering and urban planning, bringing the railroad into the heart of the city while enhancing property around itself.

At one time Grand Central was the terminus for two major railroads, the New York Central, which reached to the Mississippi River, and the New York, New Haven, and Hartford, which served New England; today it has become essentially a commuter station, through whose portals pass some 140,000 passengers daily, mostly from towns N. and N.E. of the city.

The station covers three city blocks—42nd–45th Sts between Vanderbilt Ave and Madison Ave—and beneath it are luggage tunnels, electric power facilities, steam, water, sewage, and

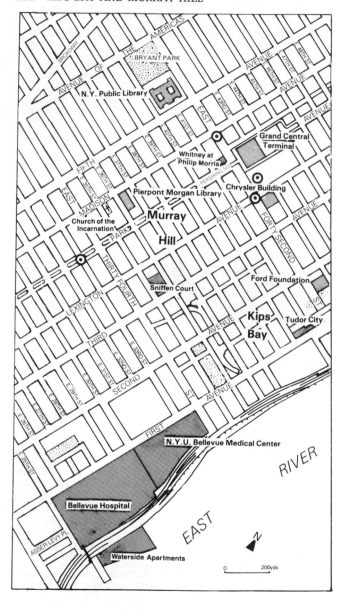

electric mains, and loops of track where trains can turn around without backing out of the station.

EXTERIOR. The best view of the terminal—albeit impaired by the presence of the Pan Am Building—is from a few blocks S. on Park Ave. Whitney Warren, primarily responsible for the south facade, saw the station as a gateway to the city and designed it with three great arched windows framed by pairs of columns to recall the triumphal arches of the cities of antiquity. Jules Felix Coutan created the sculptural group (1914) that crowns the facade. Entitled *Transportation,* it depicts Mercury (Commerce) flanked by Hercules (Physical Energy) and Minerva (Intellectual Energy). Directly beneath the clock (13 ft in diameter) stands an heroic bronze figure of *Cornelius Vanderbilt* commissioned by the Commodore himself (1869; Albert De Groot) and moved here from the former Hudson River freight station in 1929.

History. By 1869 Cornelius Vanderbilt, known as the Commodore because of his beginnings as a ferryboat entrepreneur, had seized control of all the railroads into New York by a series of bold financial maneuvers. He determined to consolidate the lines physically by erecting at Fourth Ave and 42nd St a Grand Central Depot, magniloquently named in the manner of his breed, since in 1896 42nd St was in the hinterlands. He then acquired sufficient land along Fourth Ave for storage and marshaling yards, land that constitutes practically all of the present Grand Central complex. A station designed by John B. Snook rose between 1869–71, a "head house," whose trains either backed in or backed out. Never really adequate, the original station and its sheds and yards underwent almost constant enlargement and rearrangement, including a remodeling in 1898 in which a new waiting room for immigrants was created in the basement so that passengers in the main waiting room and rotunda might not have to mix with them.. Shortly after the original depot had been completed, the Vanderbilt interests began the process of lowering the tracks below street level, first in an open cut with a roofed tunnel provided with smoke vents, ultimately in the present subterranean system that includes a tunnel from 96th St to the station and fans out at 57th St to a width of 31 tracks on the upper level and 17 tracks on the lower level.

In 1903, when the city demanded that the railroad electrify its lines or move the terminal to the outskirts, William J. Wilgus, brilliant chief engineer, submitted a proposal for submerging the tracks, introducing the two present levels of trackage and electrifying the lines as far as Mott Haven in the Bronx. He further suggested building a new terminal while using the air rights over the tracks (Madison– Lexington Aves, 42nd–50th Sts) for new, revenue-producing office and apartment buildings. A competition for the design of the station produced the innovative plan of architects Reed and Stem (Reed was Wilgus's brother-in-law) that wrapped Park Ave around the station on viaducts. Later the firm of Warren & Wetmore (Warren was a cousin of William K. Vanderbilt, then Chairman of the Board of the New York Central Railroad) was brought into the project. Though Warren & Wetmore seem to have triumphed in the power struggle between the two firms, the basic premises of the design are those of Reed & Stem: the elevated driveway around the station, the bridge across 42nd St with ramps down to street level at 40th St, and the placement of piers for future office buildings along Park Ave.

INTERIOR. Enter the terminal through the central doorway at Park Ave.

Every Wed at 12:30 P.M. a free tour of the building meets outside the Chemical Bank Commuter Express on the Concourse. For more information call the Municipal Art Society, tel: 935-3960.

Directly behind the Main Waiting Room is the MAIN CON-
COURSE (120 ft wide; 375 ft long); sheathed in marble and
simulated Caen stone, it rises to an elliptical vault (125 ft high)
colored cerulean and decorated with constellations designed by
Warren with Paul Helleu and Charles Basing. Worked into the
ornamentation throughout are clusters of oak leaves, chosen by
the Vanderbilts as the family emblem. The Concourse, with its
elegant spaces and rich materials, has suffered various commercial depredations, notably the too large, too bright Kodak billboard on the E. wall. The shopping arcade (main level), long the
site of dingy and unappealing enterprises, now offers several
attractive stores. Among the concessions on the lower level
(accessible from the Grand Staircase at the W. end of the Concourse) is the *Oyster Bar,* architecturally interesting for the
Guastavino tiles supporting its vaulted ceiling and gastronomically appealing for its many varieties (sometimes as many as 12)
of oysters, of which some 12,000 are opened and served daily.

Beneath the lower level, whose tracks once served the lowly
commuter while more glamorous long-distance arrivals and
departures took place on the upper level, a vast network of
tunnels carries mains and pipes for the steam and hot water and
cables for electricity and telephone that serve the station and
several nearby buildings. It is possible, though hardly advisable,
to walk from 43rd–49th St in these dark, sometimes rat-infested
service tunnels, which despite efforts of the management occasionally have become home for a population of derelicts to whom
their attraction is inversely proportional to the outdoor temperature.

It is not surprising that many assaults have been made on the architectural
integrity of the terminal, sitting as it does on a prime midtown site. Fortunately
most have come to naught, with the unhappy exception of the Pan Am Building,
which towers above the terminal from the north. Among the more unpleasant
of these schemes was a plan (1960) to divide the Main Waiting Room horizontally into four 15-ft stories, the upper three to contain bowling alleys. This
proposal doubtless hastened designation of the terminal as a landmark (1965),
a status the Penn Central Railroad, then operating it, soon came to resent,
recognizing the inflation in surrounding real estate generated by the station
and wanting to profit from these rising values. The railroad proposed a 54-
story tower over the Waiting Room, a design rejected by the Landmarks
Commission. After several other plans to circumvent the designation failed,
the railroad sued to have the landmark status withdrawn on the grounds of
economic hardship, but in 1978 the Supreme Court upheld the city's right to
protect architecturally or historically valuable buildings by this means.

Return to 42nd St. The intersection of Park Ave and E. 42nd St,
though not properly a square, is named *Pershing Square* in honor
of Gen. John Joseph Pershing, commander of the American forces
in Europe during World War I.

Park Avenue began as Fourth Ave on the 1811 grid, but was
not developed because a granite ridge ran its entire length. When
the New York and Harlem Railroad requested a right of way for
its tracks and permission to run its steam engines above 14th St
(1832), the city granted it Fourth Ave. The railroad then blasted
out the granite and laid the tracks in a cut from which coal smoke

and noise polluted the neighborhood. In 1857 the city set 42nd
St as the S. limit for steam engines and the trains were then
pulled by horses downtown to their terminal. Fourth Ave was
renamed in sections, with the final portion up to the Harlem River
receiving the name Park Ave in 1888.

On the S.W. corner of Park Ave and E. 42nd St (120 Park Ave)
is the PHILIP MORRIS BUILDING (1983; Ulrich Franzen & Assocs.),
clad in gray granite and remarkable architecturally for having
different facades on its different sides, the most elaborate of
which faces Park Ave. Inside, in addition to the corporate headquarters, is the **Whitney Museum of American Art at Philip
Morris.**

The Whitney Museum of American Art at Philip Morris. 120 Park Ave, New
York 10017. Tel: 878-2550. Gallery open Mon—Sat 11:00—6:00, Thurs until
7:30. Free. Sculpture Court, also free, open Mon—Sat 7:30 A.M.—9:30 P.M.,
Sun 11 A.M.—7 P.M. Gallery talks Mon, Wed, Fri at 12:30; tours by appointment; catalogues. Restrooms and espresso bar in Sculpture Garden; no telephones. Complete wheelchair access from 42nd St.

The Sculpture Court, a 42-ft gallery paved with granite, walled
with glass, and set about with ficus trees, contains changing
exhibitions of sculpture, usually large scale, by major American
artists. John Chamberlain's *City Lux*, a 12-ft wall relief (S. wall)
of crushed automobile parts was created especially for the museum.
The smaller gallery near the 42nd St entrance offers about six
shows yearly, most emphasizing 20C painting and sculpture.

Return to 42nd St and walk east. Built on the steel skeleton of
the old Commodore Hotel (1920; Warren & Wetmore) is the new
Grand Hyatt Hotel (1980; Gruzen & Partners with Der Scutt), a
chunky 30-story building sheathed in gray mirrored glass that
reflects its surroundings. Inside, the 1400-room luxury hotel
exudes the swank and glitter once associated with the Grand
Central district. The foyer is paved in Paradiso Italian marble;
the round columns are covered with bronze; the hardware is
brass. The 275-ft four-story atrium is resplendent with fountains,
plants, and a 77-ft sculpture by Peter Lobello entitled *Bronze
Tracery*.

Return to E. 42nd St and look across it to the geometric and
floral bas reliefs on the **Chanin Building** (1929; Sloan & Robertson; DL) at 122 E. 42nd St. Cross to the S. side of the street and
enter the lobby, a treasure of Art Deco design in bronze and
marble. René Chambellan, architectural sculptor known more
widely for his work at Radio City, collaborated on the design of
the interior, including the lobby, whose theme is "City of Opportunity." The bas reliefs and grille work express, respectively, the
active and the intellectual life of the individual, with the geometric patterns, in Chambellan's conception, also symbolizing emotions and abstractions of thought. The whole told the story of a
city where a man, through the exertion of his mind and hands,
could rise from a humble state to wealth and power.

The theme was especially applicable to Irwin Chanin, one of the city's first real
estate developers, whose career epitomized the astonishing growth of the

industry in the 1920s. In 1919 Chanin borrowed $20,000 to build two houses in Bensonhurst, Brooklyn. Ten years later he had created 141 buildings in the city, including hotels, the Fur Center, and several Broadway theaters.

The **Bowery Savings Bank** just to the W. at 110 E. 42nd St (1923; York & Sawyer) is one of the masterworks of the city's finest bank architects, a grand Romanesque palace with a dramatic deep arched entrance. Inside, the banking room is imposing in its proportions and in the elaboration of detail: the beamed and coffered ceiling (65 ft high, 165 ft long, 80 ft wide), the varicolored marble columns, the limestone floor inset with marble mosaics, arranged asymmetrically. The pendant lamps were modeled after those of Hagia Sophia. Among the carvings in the frieze, directly below the ceiling, are forms suggesting qualities and aspirations associated with money (the squirrel for thrift, the rooster for punctuality, the lion for power, the bull and bear representing Wall St).

Walk E. to the intersection of Lexington Ave. At 150 E. 42nd St (bet. Lexington / 3rd Aves) is the *Mobil Building*, originally the Socony Mobil Building (1955; Harrison & Abramovitz), which at the time of its completion held a number of records: the world's largest (1.6 million sq ft) metal-clad office building; the city's largest office floor (the second, 75,000 sq ft); and the city's largest central air-conditioning system. The facade, whose cost was underwritten by the steel industry, at the time threatened by the emerging potential of glass and aluminum as building materials, was designed for practicality: the repeated stamped design prevents the sheet metal from warping, and the surface scoured by the wind, stays clean. In this day of hermetically sealed environments, the windows actually open, pivoting vertically to allow the window cleaners to remain safely indoors while performing their rites.

Across the street (405 Lexington Ave, bet. 42nd / 43rd Sts) is the ***Chrysler Building** (1930; William Van Alen; DL), a beautiful skyscraper built by Walter P. Chrysler, the automobile magnate, to express both the luxury and the mechanical precision of that automobile in its Jazz Age incarnations.

History. The building was undertaken by William H. Reynolds, a real estate speculator who after a brief career in the state senate still enjoyed the title senator. Like other ambitious men of his ilk, reaching back through Frank Woolworth to the builders of the Tower of Babel, Reynolds aspired to erect the world's tallest tower, and hired maverick architect William Van Alen to design it. Walter P. Chrysler bought the lease and the plans in 1928, by which time the race for height had become a bitter rivalry between Van Alen and his former partner H. Craig Severance then at work on the company headquarters of the Bank of Manhattan (now 40 Wall St). Van Alen announced plans for a Chrysler Building of 925 ft. Severance in 1929 topped off triumphantly at 927 ft, having added a 50-ft flagpole and a lantern above the 60 stories and ten penthouses of his building. Meanwhile a team of steelworkers inside the fireshaft of the Chrysler Building constructed its 185-ft spire and, when Severance had declared himself the victor, pushed it through a hole in the roof, bringing the building's height to 1048 ft, 64 ft higher than the Eiffel Tower, previously the world's tallest structure. In 1931, however, the Empire State Building soared above them all to 1250 ft.

EXTERIOR. The slender 1048-ft tower rises to a shining stain-less-steel spire above concentric arches pierced by triangular windows. There is probably more stainless steel on the facade of the Chrysler Building than on any other building in New York, for although sleek, mirrorlike, and hence vastly appealing to Art Deco designers, stainless steel cost too much for all but the most lavish builders. Below the spire, winged gargoyles resembling hood ornaments stare off in four directions and a brickwork frieze of wheels studded with radiator caps encircles the building.

INTERIOR. Enter the *lobby, one of the city's most beautiful interiors. The walls are veneered with sensuously veined African marbles in warm tones of buff and red, and the elevator doors and walls are inlaid with African woods in intricate floral designs. Overhead a mural by Edward Trumbull, rather ponderously titled *Energy, Result, Workmanship, and Transportation* depicts two favorite Art Deco themes—transportation and human endeavor. The elevator doors have floral designs veneered of woods including Japanese ash, Oriental walnut, and English gray harewood. The interior of the elevator cabs are marquetried, no two alike.

Oddly, although modern opinion glorifies the Chrysler Building, it received mixed reviews on completion. Van Alen's career ground to a halt, as Chrysler accused the architect of taking bribes from subcontractors and would not pay his fee.

Continue E. on 42nd St. The only surviving AUTOMAT (1958; Horn & Hardart Co.) in New York stands on the S.E. corner of E. 42nd St and Third Ave (200 E. 42nd St), a latecomer to a group of some three dozen Automats dating back to 1912 but flourishing in the 1930s. Nowadays a few tourists and nostalgic New Yorkers come to drop their quarters and nickels into the slots and retrieve their food from behind little glass doors. While the Automats inspired composers and poets (David Amram wrote *Horn & Hardart Succotash Blues*, and P. D. Q. Bach, alias Peter Schickele, wrote a Concerto for Horn and Hardart), they also attracted vagrants long before the presence of the homeless became the fact of urban life it is today. Street people sat in the automats for hours with a cup of coffee (or someone else's coffee cup) or made free soup from ketchup, hot water, salt, and pepper. Today Horn and Hardart holds the local franchise from a fast food chain, and the other former Automats have been retooled to dish up burgers and fries instead of baked beans, meatloaf, and lemon meringue pie.

Continue east. At 220 E. 42nd St (bet. 3rd / 2nd Aves) is the **News Building** (1930; Howells & Hood; DL), formerly the Daily News Building, a fine Art Deco skyscraper by Raymond Hood, considered the quintessential architect of the Age of Commerce. White vertical strips of brick alternate with dark strips of windows broken up by red and black brick spandrels. The water tower and other machinery atop the roof are concealed within a vertical extension of the building—a radical notion at a time when such fripperies as temples, flèches, and choragic monuments usually served as camouflage. Handsome brickwork and a bas relief around the entrance form the only decoration of this severe, cubistic building, which appeared in 1980s Superman movies as the home of the mythical *Daily Planet*. Inside the lobby are meteorological displays including a revolving globe set into a floor recess, although the publisher thought the public would prefer "murder charts," maps of the city with the location of crimes indicated.

Midway between Second and First Aves on the N. side of E. 42nd St (main entrance, 320 E. 43rd St) is the **Ford Foundation Building** (1967; Roche, Dinkeloo & Assocs.), justly admired for its beautiful interior garden, a quiet lush landscape filled with plants, trees, and a small pond. Surrounding the garden is the cube-shaped building, with piers of pinkish-gray granite, a facade of weathering Cor-Ten steel, and such large expanses of glass that it resembles a modern Crystal Palace, all suitably elegant for a foundation that disburses millions of dollars to the arts, the humanities, and science.

Tudor City (E. 40th–E. 43rd Sts bet. 1st / 2nd Aves), an ambitious and successful private effort at urban renewal (1928; Fred F. French Co. and H. Douglas Ives), is a self-contained city with a hotel (The Tudor, 600 rooms) and apartments (3000 of them) rising on abutments over First Ave. Developer Fred French bought more than 100 crumbling brownstones and tenements and erected 12 high-rise buildings in the American Tudor style popular in the 1920s—that is, brick with an occasional stained glass window, Gothic doorway, and decorative lion or unicorn. Such former amenities as tennis courts and a miniature golf course are long gone, but the residents have triumphed in a struggle to retain the two remaining parks. Because the site of the United Nations was once occupied by a slaughterhouse, a coaling station, and breweries, the buildings of Tudor City face inward, with only occasional windows looking toward what is nowadays a splendid river view.

Walk S. on Tudor City Place to E. 41st St. The East Side from about 27th to 40th Sts, Second Ave to the East River, is known as **Kips Bay.** In 1655 one Jacobus Kip owned a farm around Second Ave and E. 35th St reaching to the East River which at the time curved inward, forming a bay. Kips Bay later became a beachhead for British troops invading the city during the Revolutionary War and the site of an American rout that caused one of George Washington's) uncontrolled outbreaks of temper. His forces, mostly ill-trained recruits exhausted from their defeat on Long Island, broke before broadsides from the British men-of-war in the bay and fled in panic. Washington, enraged, tried to turn them around, drawing his sword and threatening both foot soldiers and officers, including a brigadier general whom he beat with his cane whip. Thereafter Kips Bay remained pastoral until the mid-19C when its country estates, subdivided around the time of the Civil War, gave way to rows of brownstone houses. The arrival of the Second and Third Ave Els hastened its decline, bringing about a period of residential and industrial squalor from which it recovered only after the demolition of the Els. The bay itself has long since disappeared under tons of fill.

At E. 41st St turn right (W.) and begin walking toward Park

Ave. The entrance to the QUEENS-MIDTOWN TUNNEL cuts through the block between First and Second Aves. Operated by the Triborough Bridge and Tunnel Authority, it was completed in 1940, its two tubes (N., 6414 ft; S., 6272 ft) joining E. 37th St with Long Island City in Queens. At one time optimistic city planners hoped to bore a crosstown tunnel linking the Queens-Midtown with the Lincoln Tunnel.

West of Kips Bay is **Murray Hill**, bounded roughly by Madison and Third Aves, 34th and 42nd Sts, named after Robert Murray who had a country home there (at present E. 37th St and Park Ave) during the Revolutionary War period. Legend asserts, probably erroneously, that after the British landing at Kips Bay, Mrs. Murray detained General Howe and his chief officers at tea, thereby allowing the American troops stationed in lower Manhattan to escape up the West Side to Harlem Heights. In the mid-19C Murray Hill became fashionable and real estate values soared as the upper crust built brownstone mansions along Fifth, Madison, and Park Aves. Although most have been torn down or stripped of details, a few homes and carriage houses remain to suggest Murray Hill at its peak.

Turn S. on Park Ave and walk a block to E. 40th St. Continue W. on E. 40th St. At No. 148 (bet. 3rd / Lexington Aves) is a fine old carriage house (c. 1875) with Second Empire detailing.

Others survive at 157 and 159 E. 35th St (c. 1890) and at 149 E. 38th St (1902), all between Third and Lexington Aves. Two town houses dating from around 1900 remain at Nos.19 and 21 E. 37th St (bet. Madison / Park Aves).

Turn S. at Park Ave and walk to E. 38th St. On the S.E. corner of Park Ave and E. 38th St is the Roman Catholic *Church of Our Saviour* (1959; Paul Reilly), a new church imitating its Gothic and Romanesque forebears.

Continue S. and turn right (W.) at E. 37th St. One block W., on the N.E. corner of E. 37th St (233 Madison Ave) is the CONSULATE GENERAL OF THE POLISH PEOPLE (1905; Charles P. H. Gilbert; DL), originally the Raphael De Lamar mansion, built for an adventurer of Dutch ancestry who had interests in gold mines and considerable acuity on Wall St. The interiors are as imposing as the lavish Second Empire facade implies.

Just across the street on the S.E. corner of E. 37th St and Madison Ave is one of the city's few freestanding Italianate brownstone town houses (231 Madison Ave). Originally built (1852) for banker Anson Phelps Stokes and later the home of J. P. Morgan, Jr., it was bought in 1988 by the Pierpont Morgan Library.

Beyond it is the ***Pierpont Morgan Library** (1906; McKim, Mead & White; DL; extension to Madison Ave, 1928; Benjamin Wistar Morris), a monument to the finely honed acquisatory tastes of the great banker. Established as a museum in 1924, the library contains a priceless collection of manuscripts from the Middle Ages and the Renaissance, drawings by artists from before 1800, incunabula, autograph manuscripts and letters, musical manuscripts, early children's books, and ancient written records including Assyrian and Babylonian seals, cuneiform tablets, and Egyptian papyri.

The Pierpont Morgan Library. 29 E. 36th St (bet. Madison / Park Aves), New York 10016. Tel: 685-0008. Open Tues–Sat 10:30–5:30, Sun 1–5. Closed Mon, the month of Aug, and national holidays. Suggested donation.

Lectures, publications, concerts, seminars. Restrooms, telephones, no food service. Gift shop. No facilities for the handicapped. The entrance is seven steps up from the street and there is another narrow step up to the two rooms of the original library. Special assistance rendered by appointment.

EXTERIOR. The present entrance is in the 1928 annex. Walk down E. 36th St toward Park Ave to the middle of the block to see the original library, a simple classical building with a Palladian porch flanked by two empty niches. Sculptured panels (Adolph A. Weinman) below the frieze represent (right to left), Truth with Literature, Philosophy, History, Oratory, Astronomy, and Music Inspiring the Arts. It was McKim's idea to construct the library like the marvels of antiquity, without mortar, using marble blocks fitted closely together, a procedure only possible where costs were no great object and where labor was plentiful. The total library cost $1,154,669 of which only about $50,000 went for the extra stone-cutting. The marble lionesses guarding the doorway are by Edward Clark Potter who later placed a more famous pair in front of the New York Public Library.

INTERIOR. Enter the vestibule. To the left is the *Exhibition Hall* for changing exhibitions. Beyond, a corridor leads to the original library, two rooms connected by a vestibule. Just before the entrance to the first room is a life mask of George Washington taken by *Houdon* (1785).

The WEST ROOM, Morgan's study, is preserved as it was during his lifetime, though fabrics and wall coverings have been renewed as necessary. Displayed in the room are some of Morgan's favorite paintings and objets d'art including bronzes, faience, and metalwork. Of particular interest are (clockwise from doorway): E. wall: *Memling,* Kneeling Female Donor and Her Patron, St. Anne; *Cima da Conegliano,* Mystic Marriage of St. Catherine (c. 1510); *Memling,* Kneeling Male Donor and His Patron, St. William of Maleval. S. wall: *Perugino,* Virgin and Two Saints Adoring the Child; marble statue of St. John the Baptist (Florence, 16C). W. wall: *Lucas Cranach the Elder,* Wedding Portraits of Martin Luther and His Wife (beneath the Morgan portrait). N. wall: *attrib. Bellini,* Virgin and Child with Saints and a Kneeling Donor (c. 1505); four-paneled Altarpiece attrib. Master of St. Mark, Catalonia (1355–60). E. wall: **Memling,* Portrait of a Man with a Pink. On a table in the N.W. corner of the room: *Court painter in the circle of Clouet,* Portrait of a French Princess, probably Marguerite de Valois. The two Morgan portraits are (W. wall) J. Pierpont Morgan (d. 1913) and on the N. wall, J. P. Morgan (d. 1943).

In the EAST ROOM, the actual library, are displayed tiers of rare books and changing exhibitions of manuscripts, letters, and other items of interest. Permanently on display are a **Gutenberg Bible*

(Mainz, c. 1455), one of two and a half in the Morgan collection, an Antiphonary made for Carlo Pallavicino, Bishop of Lodi (third quarter of the 15C), and the *Stavelot Triptych* (1156), a portable altar made by Godefroid de Claire with Byzantine enamels framing relics of wood and a nail from the True Cross.

Diversion. The densest concentration of converted carriage houses on Murray Hill is the **Sniffen Court** Historic District (150–158 E. 36th St bet. Lexington / 3rd Aves, a little over two blocks E. of the Pierpont Morgan Library). Named after builder John Sniffen, this group of ten small Romanesque Revival brick carriage houses (c. 1850–60) has been attractively preserved, though some of the large arched doors for carriages have been altered. Sculptor Malvina Hoffman had her studio at the S. end of the court. Return to Madison Ave.

The apartment building at 211 Madison Ave (bet. E. 35th / E. 36th Sts) occupies the site of the Pierpont Morgan carriage house. Adjacent to it (209 Madison Ave) is the *H. Percy Silver Parish House* of the Church of the Incarnation (1868; Robert Mook; altered c. 1905, Edward P. Casey). At 205 Madison Ave on the N.E. corner of E. 35th St is the Protestant Episcopal **Church of the Incarnation** (1864; Emlen T. Littel; rebuilt and enlarged after a fire in 1882), open weekdays until 3 P.M. Founded as a mission of Grace Church, it is English Gothic in style with a brownstone front and a corner tower. The INTERIOR is noteworthy for stained glass windows by Tiffany, John La Farge, and others.

S. aisle: Henry Holiday (London), Resurrection and Ascension window; Heaton, Butler & Bayne (London), Old Testament window; Clayton & Bell (London), New Testament window depicting St. Paul preaching on Mars Hill; *John La Farge, Christian Discipleship window; Henry Holiday, Parental and Christian Nurture window; John La Farge, Grapevine window; Phillips Brooks Memorial, with marble, onyx, and glass decoration by Tiffany Glass and Decorating Co.; *William Morris, two Angels' windows dedicated to infant children; Louis Comfort Tiffany, Christian Pilgrim window.

The carved oak angels on the altar rail are by Daniel Chester French; the large mural flanking the altar and depicting the Adoration of the Magi is by John La Farge.

N. aisle (E. to W.): Edward Burne-Jones, Window of Faith and Charity; Cottin & Co. (London), Window showing Christ Feeding the Multitudes; *Tiffany Studios, Tomb of Lazarus window, the Twenty-third Psalm window.

In the gallery: Guthrie & David, Samuel window; Tiffany Studios, Dignity of Labor window. The West window, depicting the Adoration of Christ Enthroned in Heaven, is in the style of 15C English glass painters and was designed by C. E. Kempe (England).

The city's Oriental rug district has for about 50 years been centered in midtown, from about 28th–34th Sts between Fifth and Lexington Aves, although recent rent increases have driven some dealers to New Jersey and elsewhere.

At 22 E. 35th St between Madison and Park Aves is the *Collectors' Club* (1902; McKim, Mead & White; DL), originally the Thomas B. Clarke residence, a Georgian Revival house built by Clarke, an art dealer and decorator, as a showcase for his collections. The Collectors' Club, founded in 1896, is devoted to philately.

Andy Warhol, perhaps the most influential of the Pop artists, maintained **The Factory** in what was originally a substation of the New York Edison Co. (19 E. 32nd St, 22 E. 33rd St, bet. 5th / Madison Aves). The place served as studio space and production facilities for his magazine enterprises.

At the E. edge of Manhattan, between First Ave and the Franklin D. Roosevelt Drive, 25th–30th Sts is the **Bellevue Hospital Center** (1908–39, McKim, Mead & White; New Building between 27th / 28th Sts, 1974; Katz, Waisman, Weber, Strauss; Joseph Blumenkranz; Pomerance & Breines; Feld & Timoney). North of the hospital is the *New York University-Bellevue Medical Center,* 30th–34th Sts, First Ave to F.D.R. Drive (1950; Skidmore, Owings & Merrill; later additions), a white-glazed brick building housing the teaching hospital associated with N.Y.U.

History. Bellevue began as an infirmary in New York's first almshouse, erected 1736, and since then has become one of the city's principal municipal hospitals. It became an important public facility as early as 1816 when it was known as the Bellevue Establishment and had also a penitentiary, soap factory, bake shop, and church school in addition to its facilities for the ill. In 1819, during an epidemic of yellow fever, a fever hospital was built near the Bellevue Establishment and eventually took the name of Bellevue Hospital. Famous during the 19C, Bellevue was rebuilt after the turn of the century, with the first section opening in 1908. Later came a pathology building (1911), new Medical and Surgical Pavilions (1916 and 1927), and a Psychiatric Hospital (1939).

The hospital boasts a number of pioneering achievements: the first recorded U.S. instruction in anatomy dissection (1750), the first lying-in wards in the city (1799), first appendectomy in the U.S. (1867), first hospital-based ambulance service in the world (1869), first hospital cesarean section (1887), and first development of the method of heart catheterization (1956). The Bellevue Hospital emergency service, which cares for about 80,000 patients each year on a 24-hour basis, is one of the most famous in the nation.

At 203 E. 29th St near Third Ave is one of the few remaining privately owned and occupied wood frame houses in Manhattan, a small three-story white, shuttered vernacular house built around 1790, the kind of house that was unremarkable in the years up to the Civil War when Kip's Bay was semirural. Before its current owners restored it, the house had deteriorated to the point where only the basement was usable: a group of hotdog vendors stored their carts there.

East of the hospital complex, stretching from E. 25th–E. 30th Sts along the F.D.R. Drive, are the *Waterside apartments* (1974; Davis Brody & Assocs.), with shopping and restaurants, now a visual landmark along the river.

Just S. of the hospital complex, on 23rd St at Asser Levy Place (bet. 1st Ave / F.D.R. Drive), is the former **Public Baths of the City of New York,** (1906; William Martin Aiken and Arnold W. Brunner; DL), now a public swimming pool. Before reformers convinced the city to construct public bathing facilities, tenement dwellers had to make do with the shared sink in the hallway, the "floating" baths in the rivers (barges filled with river water), or the few public bathhouses built by charitable organizations. This bathhouse, with its elaborate neoclassical facade, had 155 shower stalls and a swimming pool.

Asser Levy, for whom the street is named, was among the 23 Jewish refugees who arrived in New Amsterdam in 1654. When in 1655 Gov. Peter Stuyvesant excluded Jews from military training and taxed them instead, Levy petitioned the Dutch West

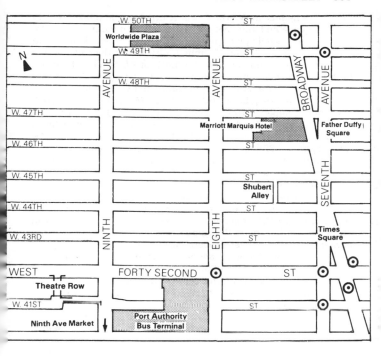

India Co. to be allowed to help defend the city, becoming thereby the first Jewish soldier in the nation.

The nearest subways are the IRT Lexington Ave local (train 6) at E. 23rd St and Park Ave and E. 33rd St and Park Ave. Uptown buses run on 1st Ave, Park Ave South, and Madison Ave. Downtown buses run on Park Ave South and 2nd Ave. The M16 crosstown bus runs on 34th St.

14   West 42nd Street and the Times Square Theater District

SUBWAY: IND 8th Ave (A, C, or E train) to 42nd St.

BUS: M11 uptown via 10th Ave or downtown via 9th Ave to 42nd St. M106, 42nd St crosstown to 9th Ave. M16, crosstown on 34th St, loops N. to 42nd St between 9th and 12th Aves.

CAR PARKING: The roof of the Port Authority Bus Terminal has a large parking lot. For patrons of Theatre Row there is a parking lot in the Manhattan Plaza apartment building. The theater district, particularly the side streets between Seventh and Eighth Aves, has numerous commercial parking lots. West of Eighth Ave the neighborhood is unpleasant and dangerous after the theater crowd has left.

This route begins on W. 42nd St at Ninth Ave and proceeds E. to Times Square and the theater district. The middle part of the tour is not especially pleasant, passing through the neighborhood of the Port Authority Bus Terminal with its resident population of the homeless and through the block of W. 42nd St between Eighth and Seventh Aves, notable for pornography. The section from Times Square north is more traditionally touristic.

The two 45-story brick towers of the MANHATTAN PLAZA apartment complex (1977; David Todd & Assocs.), occupying the block between W. 42nd and W. 43rd Sts, Ninth and Tenth Aves, could be part of any upper middle-class apartment complex. The majority of its 1688 apartments, however, are rented to performing artists who pay as rent 25 percent of their annual gross income, a boon since in the theatrical profession incomes are usually both low and insecure.

Theatre Row on the S. side of 42nd St between Ninth and Tenth Aves is one expression of the neighborhood's new vitality. A group of Off Off Broadway theaters, opened here officially in 1978, although three of the companies had started several years earlier. The goal of these theatrical pioneers, supported by the city, state, private industry, and individual donors, was to reclaim the derelict west end of 42nd St for the Theater District, and today the row boasts 13 theaters—commercial, nonprofit, and small studio theaters—and 11 nonprofit companies. Since 1978, more than a dozen restaurants have opened, real estate values have tripled, and developers, scenting the new climate, are hastening to construct new housing projects. Here the theatergoer, who a decade ago would not venture to wander W. of Times Square after dark, may sample a wide variety of theatrical fare—classic and contemporary plays, traditional and experimental musicals—while performers and playwrights will find professional support.

Ticket Central (414 W. 42nd St, tel: 279-4200), the booking office for most of the theaters, is open from 1–8 P.M. daily.

The row includes: the Samuel Beckett Theatre (410 W. 42nd St); Manhattan Punch Line (410 W. 42nd St) dedicated to satire, comedy, and the arts of the clown; the Harold Clurman Theatre (412 W. 42nd St); the Actors and Directors Lab (412 W. 42nd St), whose approach stems in part from the techniques of Stanislavsky; Playwrights Horizons (416 W. 42nd St), a showcase for new playwrights, INTAR (420 W. 42nd St), an acronym for International Arts Relations, a Hispanic cultural center; the John Houseman Theatre Center (420 W. 42nd St), home of the Acting Company, a repertory and touring company for young professionals; the Neighborhood Group Theatre Ltd (420 W. 42nd St), a small resident theater; the Lion Theatre Company, which produces at the Judith Anderson Theatre (422 W. 42nd St); the South Street Theatre Company (424 W. 42nd St); the Raft Theatre (432 W. 42nd St) which provides playwrights writing for the American theater with a professional environment; the Douglas Fairbanks Theatre (432 W. 42nd St), a commercial off-Broadway house; the Nat Horne Musical Theatre (440 W. 42nd St); and the John Houseman Theatre Center (450 W. 42nd St), a 299-seat commercial theater with rehearsal and workshop spaces.

Across the street at 407 W. 42nd St the *West Bank Cafe* adds cabaret, comedy, and jazz to the mix of traditional and experimental plays offered on Theatre Row.

Dyer Avenue, which exists primarily as part of the ramp system for the Lincoln Tunnel, seems to have been named (with a variation in spelling) after William Dyre, mayor of the city in 1680, owner of Oyster Island (now Ellis Island), and customs collector. The murals facing Dyer Ave are by Richard Haas.

The **Lincoln Tunnel,** owned and operated by the Port Authority of New York and New Jersey, links midtown with Weehawken, New Jersey, and the interstate highway system. Its three tubes were opened in 1937 (center), 1945 (north), and 1957 (south) and now carry over 32,609,000 vehicles annually. The maximum depth from mean high water to the roadway is 97 ft, and the longest tube (center) is 8216 ft from portal to portal.

Even further W. is the Midtown Mounted Division (621 W. 42nd St, bet. 11th / 12th Aves) of the New York City Police Department, a onetime telephone company building now stabling the horses which patrol the streets of midtown.

Turn around and walk E. on 42nd St toward Ninth Ave.

The name **Hell's Kitchen** once designated a slum stretching from about 30th St to 57th St west of Ninth Ave, whose housing included some of the city's worst tenements and whose industries, attracted by the tracks of the Hudson River (later the New York Central) Railroad down Eleventh Ave, included stables, slaughterhouses, gas plants, glue and soap factories. Supposedly two policemen watching a street fight on a muggy summer night gave the district its name. Said one, ''This neighborhood is hot as hell.'' ''Hell is cool,'' corrected the other. ''This here's Hell's Kitchen.''

At 495 Eleventh Ave (bet. W. 39th–40th Sts) stands what was once the *New York Butchers' Dressed Meat Company,* a slaughterhouse (1905; Horgan & Slattery), whose function was depicted by the heads of sheep and cattle on the exterior.

Local gangs preyed on the railroad yards and so terrorized the neighborhood that policemen from the nearby 20th Precinct would venture out only in groups larger than three. Bearing such colorful names as the Hudson Dusters, the Gophers, the Gorillas, and Battle Row Annie's Ladies' Social and Athletic Club, the gangs gave Hell's Kitchen a reputation as one of the most dangerous spots on the American continent. After 1910, when the New York Central Railroad hired a strong-arm squad who clubbed, shot, arrested, and otherwise incapacitated most of the old-style gangsters, life in the area mellowed for a while, only to resume its former vehemence with the arrival of bootleggers during the 1920s, whose influence is still felt in their present-day offspring, the Westies, a group currently under investigation for loan-sharking, extortion, drug trafficking, and murder.

The elimination of the Ninth Ave El and the Eleventh Ave grade-level railroad tracks, as well as the demolition of many tenements that stood in the way of the ramps for the Lincoln Tunnel, paved the way for social changes now taking place. With a proposal for the redevelopment of Times Square under serious consideration, the far West Side now is showing distinct signs of gentrification. Nowadays residents prefer the neighborhood to be called **Clinton** after a park of that name between W. 52nd and W. 54th Sts.

At Ninth Ave turn right (S.) and walk a block or so to look at the **Ninth Avenue market,** a congregation of modest, ethnic food shops whose roots go back to the turn of the century when a large pushcart market known as Paddy's Market flourished under the Ninth Ave El between about 35th and 42nd Sts. When the streets were being widened to construct the Lincoln Tunnel ramps in the late 1930s, the Port of New York Authority with the city Department of Markets went to court to evict the pushcart operators. Although business slumped temporarily as the hucksters moved to the side streets, eventually the market reestablished itself and has recently enjoyed a renaissance attracting not only local people but also knowledgeable consumers from all over the city. The ethnic orientation of the shops reflects the immigrant groups who have passed through here: Puerto Rican, Italian, Greek, West Indian, Filipino, Polish.

During the annual **Ninth Avenue Street Festival** (a weekend in mid-May), the avenue is closed to traffic and an estimated half million people stroll from 37th to 57th Sts, overeating and enjoying the jugglers, mimes, magicians, steel bands, jazz combos, and high school choruses spotted along the route.

Return to 42nd St. On the S. side of 42nd St. (330 W. 42nd St, bet. 8th / 9th Aves) is the former **McGraw-Hill Building** (1931; Raymond Hood, Godley & Fouilhoux; DL), a skyscraper in its day more revolutionary than the Daily News Building two years earlier. Because the building originally contained printing presses, it was relegated to the fringes of midtown by the Zoning Resolution of 1916, which prohibited light industry further inland, a law enacted in part to restrain the Garment District from encroaching on the theaters and restaurants of Times Square. McGraw-Hill's executives nonetheless hoped that the fortunes of the neighborhood would rise, a hope never fully realized. The building is much admired for its blue-green terra-cotta sheathing, which helps it blend with the sky and apparently reduces its bulk, as well as its horizontal bands of strip windows which were needed to illuminate the loft and factory floors. McGraw-Hill long ago departed for more genteel surroundings uptown.

On the N. side of the street (333 W. 42nd St) is **Holy Cross Church** (Roman Catholic), the oldest building on 42nd St, known primarily for its association with Father Francis Duffy (see p. 315). Considered Byzantine in style when built (1870; Henry Engelbert), the church has a simple brick and limestone facade over which rises an octagonal drum, dome, lantern, and crucifix (148 ft to the top). The interior is noteworthy for its fine stained glass windows and marble work. The chancel windows were executed by Mayer and Co., in Munich, while Louis Comfort Tiffany designed the clerestory windows and the large circular windows of St. Peter and St. Paul in the transepts, the window of St. John in the Baptistry, and the mosaics at the base of the cupola and in the sanctuary.

Walk E. along 42nd St past the side of the **Port Authority Bus Terminal,** now filling two city blocks from 40th–42nd Sts between Eighth and Ninth Aves (1950; decks added 1963; expansion to W. 42nd St 1982; Port Authority Design Staff). Vast and efficient, this terminal is a weekday way station for some 207,000 commuters delivered and received by some 7500 buses. Commuter buses make up 80% of the traffic, but most of the long-distance buses entering New York use it as well. Vehicular ramps feed directly into the Lincoln Tunnel without impeding traffic on the streets below, and subterranean pedestrian passageways connect with the 42nd St stations of the IND, IRT, and BMT subways. Near the 42nd St entrance is an audiokinetic sculpture, *42nd Street Ballroom* (1983; George Rhoads), an entertaining contraption of rolling balls and dinging bells. In the waiting room in the South Wing is a life-size bronze group *The Commuters* (1980) by George Segal, made as plaster casts of Segal's wife and friends and finished with a white patina.

Nowadays, the Port Authority Terminal, sadly, is also "home" for hundreds of homeless people who gravitate there and remain in part because the Port Authority has developed an enlightened view of their plight and in part because there are legal limits to police intervention. The crowd, which includes alcoholic derelicts, prostitutes of both sexes, runaway teenagers, drug dealers, the mentally ill, as well as the "new homeless," young adults without jobs or resources, many of them addicts, increases in winter.

The block of W. 42nd St between Eighth Ave and Broadway, though better than it was ten years ago, remains the worst in the Times Square area, a line-up of porno movies, sex shops, and similar entertainments. The crowd that prowls this dazzlingly illuminated stretch includes not only people drawn to its attractions but derelicts, aggressive panhandlers, three-card monte players, prostitutes, and drug dealers and their clients.

Since the area is the center of the theater and tourist industries and is hence integral to New York's economy, the city has repeatedly sought to clean it up or to redevelop it. In 1982 city and state agencies agreed to a massive rebuilding project which will include new office towers and the restoration or conversion of some of the once-famous theaters. Lawsuits, concern over design features, rising land costs, and softening of the market for midtown office space, as well as municipal scandals, have delayed implementation of the plan.

Continue walking east. Behind many of the marquees of the pornographic movie houses are the facades of the old theaters that once brought a more civilized kind of glitter to Times Square. On the S. side of the street is the *Empire Theatre* (1912; Thomas A. Lamb) (240 W. 42nd St), formerly called the Eltinge after Julian Eltinge, a popular female impersonator during the first decade of the 20th century. Successful as a legitimate theater until the early years of the Depression, it was later leased for burlesque, becoming a movie theater after Mayor La Guardia's crackdown. The *Liberty Theatre* next door (234 W. 42nd St), designed by architects Herts & Tallant (opened 1904), was originally part of the Klaw and Erlanger syndicate and achieved its most notable success with the musical, *Blackbirds of 1928*. After 1932 it too began showing movies.

At 220 W. 42nd St, is the **Candler Building,** named after its builder Asa Candler, then president of the Coca-Cola Company. Clad in white terra-cotta, the building (1914; Willauer, Shape & Bready) has been called Spanish Renaissance in style and is perhaps the first office building in New York with a fireproof stair tower.

Across the street at 229 W. 42nd St is the *Selwyn Theatre*

(1918; George Keister), built by Arch Selwyn, a Broadway producer who went to Hollywood; it is now a movie theater which leans toward X-rated films. The *New Apollo Theatre* at 219 W. 42nd St has its main entrance at 234 W. 43rd St. Built (1910; Eugene DeRosa) as a combination motion picture and vaudeville house, it became a legitimate theater ten years later. Its most famous production was George White's *Scandals,* which ran yearly from 1924 to 1931. After a Depression stint showing motion pictures and burlesque (it was leased by the Minskys), a period of showing pornographic films, and another interlude as a legitimate theater, it has reverted to showing films. The *Times Square Theater,* joined by a common facade to the Apollo, was built by Arch and Edgar Selwyn in 1920 as a musical house; *Gentlemen Prefer Blondes* opened here. It was converted to a movie theater in 1933.

The *Lyric Theatre* (213 W. 42nd St) was built by the Shuberts to be the home of the American School of Opera and to feature a yearly engagement of actor Richard Mansfield and his company. It opened in 1903 (architect, V. Hugo Koehler) and enjoyed an impressive history, booking such stars as Douglas Fairbanks, Otis Skinner, Fred Astaire, Flo Ziegfeld, Rudolf Friml, and the Marx Brothers before it became a movie theater in 1933. Although the original stone portico was torn off the 42nd St facade and the two-story ornamented arch is obscured by a metal sign, it is still possible to see something of the building's original grandeur by walking around to the back on W. 43rd St, where "progress" has made fewer inroads. One of Koehler's innovations was designing the auditorium parallel to the street so that the audience could take its seats from the side aisles.

The *Victory Theatre* at 207 W. 42nd St was built (1900; J. B. McElfatrick & Co.) by Oscar Hammerstein, who called it the Republic. It was 42nd St's first theater, built by the man who brought theater to Times Square. Hammerstein, however, was soon in financial distress and turned the house over to David Belasco, who quickly renamed it after himself. In 1931 the theater was taken over by burlesque, and after 1942, when it received its present name, it became a movie house.

The heart of ***Times Square** is the area where Broadway and Seventh Ave intersect, bounded roughly by 42nd and 48th Sts. Once called the Crossroads of the World, Times Square is now known for its spectacular displays of neon, its theaters, its crowds, and its seediness. The area acquired its name in 1904, when the *New York Times,* just moving to its new building, succeeded in having its name appended to the subway stop also just opening here.

Before 1904 Times Square, then Longacre Square, was dominated by horse exchanges (the used car dealers of their day), carriage factories, stables, and blacksmiths' shops. On its E. side was the 12th Regiment Armory. The Astor family owned much of the W. part of the district as part of a tract that ran from 42nd to 46th Sts along Broadway and W. to the Hudson River, a parcel John Jacob Astor had picked up for a modest $25,000 in the early 19C.

The IRT reached Times Square in 1904, nine years after the area had been electrically lighted. O. J. Gude, an advertising man, is said to have coined the term "Great White Way" in 1901, when he realized the commercial potential of electrically enhanced billboards. The first electric sign (1891) in the city at Broadway and 23rd St had extolled seaside Long Island, but it was a pallid beginning to an art form that flowered in Times Square and produced such landmark extravaganzas as a gigantic smoker emitting real smoke rings, a shower of golden peanuts cascading from an illuminated bag, and a figure of Little Lulu and a giant electric Kleenex made of some 25,000 light bulbs. One of the all-time favorites was a Wrigley's gum sign in the 1930s, with illuminated waves, glowing tropical fish each more than a story tall, and bubbles which floated up past a neon pack of gum (larger than a city bus) where a Wrigley boy fished calmly.

Times Square is always crowded, but particularly so in the evenings around theater time, and on occasions of public celebration. Every New Year's Eve the square is choked with celebrants who have come to witness the descent of an illuminated ball from the top of the Times Tower on the stroke of midnight. The crowd that packed the square at the conclusion of World War II has become legendary both for its density and for the quantity of alcohol it consumed.

On the N. side of 42nd St in the triangle created by the intersection of Seventh Ave and Broadway is **One Times Square,** formerly the Allied Chemical Tower, originally the *Times Tower* (1904; Eidlitz & MacKenzie). When the *New York Times* moved in on Dec 31, 1904, the building had a granite base, a fine marble lobby, and 25 floors sheathed in ornamented terra-cotta. The *Times* has moved to W. 43rd St, and the terra-cotta and granite have been replaced by a slick marble facing (1966; Smith, Smith, Haines, Lundberg & Waehler), a remodeling that was supposed to have a catalytic effect on the neighborhood but only despoiled it of one of its more cherished buildings.

Wrapped around the building some three stories up was the **Motogram,** a moving sign 360 ft long with letters 5 ft tall, whose 14,800 light bulbs once informed the public of important events. The sign has been replaced by a colored, electrically lighted billboard on the N. end of the building

On the S.E. corner of Broadway and W. 42nd St is the original **Knickerbocker Hotel** (1902; Marvin & Vavis, architects with Bruce Price, consultant; DL), now converted to an office building. This massive pile of brick and limestone, crowned with a mansard roof, was commissioned by John Jacob Astor and once opened its doors to such notables as Enrico Caruso and George M. Cohan. *Hotalings newsstand* and shop at 142 W. 42nd St between Broadway and Sixth Ave carries newspapers from most major American cities as well as a large selection of foreign language newspapers and periodicals.

Return to Times Square and walk N. along the W. side of Broadway; turn left into W. 43rd St. At 229 W. 43rd St is the building that houses the business and editorial offices of the *New York Times* as well as the presses on which the paper is actually printed. Founded in 1851, the *Times* rose to prominence under Adolph S. Ochs (publisher, 1896–1935) who increased its daily circulation from 19,000 to 490,000 and established it as the nation's most respected newspaper. It is still considered the newspaper of record, distinguished for its reliability, coverage of foreign news, and editorial restraint. The current daily circulation is 1,068,217.

On the S. side of W. 43rd St across from the *Times* are the stage doors of the Lyric , Times Square, and Apollo theaters. Untouched by the sleazy alterations of 42nd St, the rear facades of these buildings suggest their former elegance.

Return to Broadway and cross to the E. side. **Town Hall** (1921; McKim, Mead & White; DL) at 123 W. 43rd St between Broadway and Sixth Ave is one of the city's premier halls for music and other cultural events.

Continue up Broadway. The **Paramount Building** (1927; Rapp & Rapp) at 1501 Broadway between W. 43rd and W. 44th Sts is a Times Square skyline landmark with its 14 setbacks converging on an illuminated bulb at the top. Although the palatial Paramount Theater, one of the great movie palaces of its day, is no longer here, the lobby is still theatrical, with its heavily ornate gilded ceiling, black marble-faced walls, opulent chandeliers, and paneled bronze elevator doors. A block N. on the same side of the street at 1515 Broadway is *One Astor Plaza* (1969; Kahn & Jacobs), a large, ill-named office building: the "Astor" part comes from the Astor Hotel (1904) which once but unfortunately no longer stands here; the plaza is too small to merit naming the building after it. Architecturally the building is recognizable at some distance by the concrete fins adorning its upper stories, suggestive to one critic of an Edsel crashing into it from outer space; historically it is significant as the first building in the specially designated Times Square Theater District to take advantage of zoning bonuses that allow extra floor space to a building that includes a new legitimate theater.

Cross Broadway to the east. The *Manhattan Church of the Nazarene* at 130 W. 44th St was originally the home of the Lambs Club (1904; McKim, Mead & White; DL), the city's oldest theatrical club, founded in 1875. The club, still active, is now located at 3 W. 51st St, but the Lamb's Theater continues in this building.

During the late 19C clubs were started to meet the social needs of actors whose profession set them apart from the rest of society. An 1875 dinner held for Henry Montague, a distinguished actor, was so enjoyable that the group decided to meet monthly. Montague suggested the name, and the Lambs continued for many years, led by successive Shepherds.

On the other side of the street (123 W. 44th St) is the *1-2-3 Hotel* (1894; George Keister; DL), originally the Hotel Gerard, an ornately dormered brick and limestone residential hotel built for middle-class residents.

The *Belasco Theatre* (1907; George Keister; DL) at 111 W. 44th St was built by David Belasco as a showcase for his technical innovations; it included an elevator stage, a sophisticated lighting system, and a studio for developing special effects, as well as a grandly furnished apartment for Belasco himself. Return to Broadway.

The city's **theater district** developed around Times Square during the first three decades of this century. First came a few pioneers, creeping up Broadway from

Herald Square: Charles Frohman's Empire Theatre (1893) on Broadway at 40th St and the former Metropolitan Opera House (1883) between 39th and 40th Sts. However, Oscar Hammerstein—opera impresario, composer, cigar maker, and onetime plasterer—was the first to forge N. of 42nd St, and while his Olympia Theatre (1895) on Broadway between 44th and 45th Sts lasted only two years, Hammerstein rebounded from bankruptcy and resiliently built three more theaters in Times Square—the Victoria, the Republic, and the Lew Fields—earning himself kudos as ''the man who created Times Square.''

As advances in transportation made the district widely accessible and investors began to realize the potential profits in theaters as real estate, Times Square began to flourish. Theaters were built either by speculators aware that a hit show could gross a million dollars in a single year, roughly the price it cost to build a theater in the peak years of the 1920s, or by financial backers working with independent producers like Charles Frohman, David Belasco, and Harrison Grey Fiske. The theater became a flourishing and complex industry and Times Square began attracting agents, producers, theatrical publications, restaurants, hotels, and theatrical clubs. New York's best season came in 1927–28 when 257 productions were mounted and 71 theaters were in operation.

The Depression devasted Broadway: tickets remained unsold; actors were unemployed; even the Shuberts went into receivership. The Federal Theater Project kept some actors and writers in work during these years, but the Times Square theater district began a process of attrition that still continues, abetted by rising land values and the inroads of television and the movies.

Continue W. across Broadway. On the S. side of the street at 234 W. 44th St is *Sardi's restaurant,* onetime haunt of actors, writers, and theater people, who traditionally held opening night celebrations there while awaiting the newspaper reviews. Today its clientele includes tourists and celebrity watchers. Across the street at 225 W. 44th St is the **Shubert Theatre** (1913; Henry B. Herts; DL), named after Sam S. Shubert, who with his brothers Lee and J. J. founded a theatrical empire that still survives.

The Shubert brothers, offspring of a Syracuse peddler, came to New York around the turn of the century. Beginning with a single theater, they took on and bested the ruling monopoly of the day, the Klaw and Erlanger Syndicate, emerging as the most powerful force in the American theater. In their heyday the Shuberts controlled the production, booking, and presentation of shows, dominating the try-out circuits through their ownership of theaters outside New York and forcing producers to book exclusively through their organization. A decree issued in 1956 as the result of an antitrust action brought by the federal government required them to stop their restrictive booking practices and to sell 12 theaters in six cities. At the present time the Shubert Organization controls 16.5 Broadway theaters (Irving Berlin's estate owns a half interest in the Music Box) or 48.5% of the 34 existing houses.

The Shubert Theatre, whose upper floors house the headquarters of the Shubert Organization, has had a resoundingly prosperous career, beginning with its opening production *Hamlet,* and including *A Chorus Line,* which won the Pulitzer Prize in 1976 and ran until 1990.

To the E. of the theater is **Shubert Alley,** now a promenade for theatergoers, formerly a gathering place for singers, actors, and dancers who hoped to be cast in Shubert-produced plays. Walk through Shubert Alley to the *Booth Theatre* (1913; Henry B. Herts; DL) at 222 W. 45th St. Named after Edwin Booth and built by Lee Shubert and Winthrop Ames, the Booth is a small theater (783 seats; the Shubert has 1483), perhaps because its developers had just emerged from the spectacular failure of the New Theatre on Central Park West, a palatial marble-faced edifice that was to ennoble theatrical art far above the hustle of Broadway but which collapsed financially after two seasons.

Across Broadway on the block between Seventh and Sixth Aves (149 W. 45th St) is the LYCEUM THEATRE (1903; Herts & Tallant; DL), the oldest surviving New York legitimate theater, now a part of the Shubert Organization, whose archives occupy the one-time apartment of entrepreneur Daniel Frohman. The building stands out for its Baroque ornament: its undulating marquee; its elaborate columns decorated with fluted, foliated, and flowered columns; and its high mansard roof pierced with oval windows.

Return to Broadway; walk north. Dominating Broadway between 45th and 46th Sts is the *Marriott Marquis Hotel* (1985; John C. Portman), a 50-story tower, the largest in the Marriott chain. The luxury hotel features a dramatic atrium (on the eighth floor), a glass elevator, 1877 rooms for visitors, the 1600-seat Marquis Theatre, and a revolving lounge and restaurant on top. In October 1982, despite protests from actors, directors, producers, and preservationists, the historic Helen Hayes and Morosco Theaters were demolished in favor of the hotel, whose presence, it was hoped, would help revitalize this part of Times Square.

On the other side of Broadway at the N.E. corner of 46th St is the *I. Miller Building,* long a shoe store that catered to theater people. In niches on the facade are life-size marble statues of famous ladies of the theater: Ethel Barrymore (drama), Marilyn Miller (musical theater), Mary Pickford (film), and Rosa Ponselle (opera), sculpted by A. Stirling Calder, father of Alexander Calder.

The two blocks of W. 46th St between Seventh and Fifth Aves are New York's **Little Brazil,** popular with Brazilian tourists who shop here for electrical appliances, sporting goods, and other American products offered at prices far lower than at home. Also on these blocks are travel agencies specializing in Brazilian vacations, the Brazil Exchange (57 W. 46th St), which carries foodstuffs, records, and magazines imported from Brazil, and a group of moderately priced Brazilian restaurants.

Continue W. on W. 46th St. Until Nov 1987 the scruffy offices of *Variety* stood at 154 W. 46th St. Founded in 1905, the trade paper which tallies up box-office grosses and offers inside information on show business soon became a "must see" for performers and other entertainment professionals and is known to the general public for its snappy literary style, particularly its headlines. When the stock market crashed in 1929, the newspaper crowed: "Wall Street Lays an Egg." When the same thing happened in 1987, the headline read: "Wall Street Lays an Egg: The Sequel." The all-time classic appeared above a story reporting the reaction of midwestern audiences to cornball Hollywood country movies (July 17, 1935): "Stix Nix Hick Pix." According to the *New York Times* the public is also reputedly indebted to *Variety* for such expressions as "passion pit" (a drive-in movie), "gams" (female legs), "hoofer" (a dancer), "boffo" (a box office hit but not as big as a whammo), "sitcom" (a TV situation comedy), "chopsocky" (a martial arts film), and of course "ankle," a verb meaning to leave or quit, as in "Variety Ankles Great White Way," the headline announcing its departure. The paper is currently located in tonier surroundings at Park Ave South and 32nd St.

On the same side of the street at 120 W. 46th St stood the *High School of Performing Arts* (1894; C.B.J. Snyder; DL), a specialized public school within the city system which trains students for professional careers. The aspirations and trials of its students were recounted in the movie *Fame*. The school moved to Lincoln Center in 1984 and the building here was gutted by fire (1988).

The N. end of Times Square is properly known as FATHER DUFFY SQUARE. Near the 46th St end is a bronze *statue of George M. Cohan* (1958; Georg Lober), the song-and-dance man (1878–1942) best known for writing *Give My Regards to Broadway*, *Over There*, and *I'm a Yankee Doodle Dandy*. The statue was unveiled in a ceremony with Oscar Hammerstein II presiding, George Jessel acting as master of ceremonies, and a crowd of 15,000 attending. At the conclusion, everyone broke into *Give My Regards to Broadway*. N. of Cohan's debonair figure is another bronze statue (c. 1936, installed 1937; Charles Keck), portraying *Father Francis P. Duffy* (1871–1932), the "Fighting Chaplain" of the 69th Regiment during World War I. As pastor of Holy Cross Church, Father Duffy also served a parish that embraced the slums of Hell's Kitchen, the burlesque houses and dance halls of Times Square, and the legitimate theaters of Broadway. When the statue was unveiled, a crowd of 30,000 including prize fighters, political figures, and Broadway characters came to pay him tribute, joining the 69th Regiment and the military bands which struck up *Onward Christian Soldiers*. Father Duffy is shown in his World War I uniform grasping a copy of the New Testament, his back to a granite Celtic cross.

Just N. of Father Duffy (W. 47th St bet. 7th Ave / Broadway) is **tkts** (short for Times Square Ticket Center), a canvas and pipe kiosk with discounted theater tickets sold on the day of performance. Lines form well in advance of curtain time.

The ticket service, run by the Theater Development Fund, often sells as many as 4000 tickets in the two-hour preshow period. Tickets to Broadway and Off Broadway productions are sent over from the theaters and sold at half-price plus a small service charge, starting at 3 P.M. for evening performances and at 10 A.M. for matinees. Tel: 354-5800. A list of performances for which tickets are available is posted on the N. side of the structure. Other branches of this service are located in Two World Trade Center (mezzanine level, Mon–Sat 11–5:30, Off Broadway 11–1 only) and in Brooklyn at Court and Montague Sts (open Mon–Fri 11–5:30, Sat 11–3:30; Off Broadway 11–1 only).

The N.W. corner of Broadway and 49th St has been renamed Jack Dempsey Corner, for the prizefighter who successfully defended his heavyweight title in the first Madison Square Garden.

After the third Madison Square Garden (1925–66) was built on the N.W. corner of Eighth Ave and 49th St, Dempsey had a restaurant in the neighborhood, which while the Garden was still nearby had a high concentration of gymnasiums, fight managers' offices, and watering holes favored by the sporting crowd. Designed with an undistinguished exterior by Thomas W. Lamb, a theater architect, the third Garden was built as an institution by John Ringling, a circus entrepreneur, and Tex Rikard, sometime gambler, cattleman, and promoter of prizefights. Its staple offerings were boxing matches, ice hockey and basketball games, ice shows, the circus, rodeos, and expositions. Its social peak came with the annual horse show, for which a box cost $315 in 1939; its social nadir was probably the Six-Day Bicycle Race for which in the same year a one-week admission cost a dollar. Today **Worldwide Plaza** (1989; Frank Williams, apartment towers; Skidmore, Owings & Merrill, office tower), a mixed use project, occupies the site.

Located at Pier 86 in the Hudson River at 46th St is the **Intrepid Sea-Air-Space Museum.**

The Intrepid Sea-Air-Space Museum. 1 Intrepid Square (W. 46th St and 12th Ave), New York 10036. Tel: 245-2533. Open Wed–Sun 10–5, last admission at 4; open most major holidays that fall on Mon and Tues; call 245-0072 for recorded message. Closed other Mon, Tues, New Year's Day, Presidents' Day, Thanksgiving, Christmas. Admission charge with lower rates for groups, children, senior citizens.

Group tours by appointment; special events often scheduled around military holidays or on summer weekends. Modest cafeteria, gift shop with books, posters, ship and plane models, souvenirs. Telephones on pier and aboard ship. Restrooms on pier and aboard ship. Be prepared in winter for chilling winds on the flight deck. Complete wheelchair access to Hangar Deck; elevator, restrooms and telephones accessible to handicapped visitors. No wheelchair access to Flight Deck at present time.

No subway stop near 12th Ave. Take any subway to 42nd St (Grand Central, 42nd St-6th Ave, Times Square, or 42nd St-8th Ave) and transfer to the 42nd St crosstown bus. BUS: M106, crosstown on 42nd St to 12th Ave. M16 crosstown on 34th St makes a loop to 42nd St and 12th Ave. M27 crosstown on 49th / 50th Sts runs downtown via 12th Ave to 46th St.

The aircraft carrier *Intrepid,* whose planes destroyed 650 enemy planes and 289 enemy ships in World War II, was refurbished as a museum of technology and naval history in 1982. In the forward theater is a film with impressive clips of planes thundering onto the flight deck. Elsewhere you can see military aircraft, exhibits about the ship in World War II, wood and canvas planes from the early days of aviation, and a film on space craft. On the *flight deck* visitors can examine more real aircraft and climb up (sometimes a wait) to the captain's bridge and the admiral's bridge to see the command centers from which the ship was maneuvered.

15 Fifth Avenue, 34th–59th Street

SUBWAY: IRT Lexington Ave local (train 6) to 33rd St. IND 6th Ave local or express (D or F train, B train except during rush hours) to 34th St. BMT Broadway local (R train or N train except during rush hours) to 34th St at 6th Ave.

BUS: M2, M3, M4, M5, or M32 downtown via 5th Ave. M1 downtown via 5th Ave / Park Ave South. M10 downtown via 7th Ave. M2, M3, M5, or M32 uptown via Madison Ave. M10 uptown via 6th Ave. M16 crosstown on 34th St.

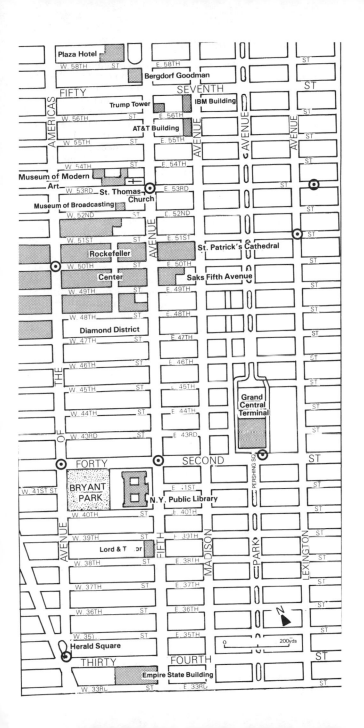

Among the streets of New York, Fifth Ave is preeminent. It is *the* avenue, the most famous, most glittering promenade in the city, known as the route of grand processions, the site of many elegant shops, and the best place to observe the chic and the famous on their daily rounds. During the closing years of the 19C and for a while at the beginning of the 20C, Fifth Ave was the city's most desirable residential address, the territory of the rich and the socially ambitious. Gradually commerce invaded, first with the old Waldorf-Astoria Hotel at 34th St, then with B. Altman & Co. a block further N., driving society uptown. Today genteel urban decay follows the same route. The shops in the 30s and low 40s, with the monumental exception of Lord & Taylor and a few others, are stocked with pseudo-Oriental rugs, electronic gadgetry, and garish bric-a-brac. Further N., however, Fifth Ave still glitters, with jewelers, international boutiques, and expensive apartment houses where tenants have been known to spend $2 million redecorating their homes. While the mansions of Vanderbilts and Goulds are gone from this area, traces remain of the heady days before the income tax: grand hotels like the Plaza, the St. Regis-Sheraton, and the Pierre Hotel further north; St. Thomas' Episcopal Church where the cream of society married one another or wed their wealth to the titles of Europe; the exclusive University Club; and the Morton Plant residence, now remodeled as Cartier's.

As a ceremonial route, Fifth Ave is used by Israelis, Puerto Ricans, Germans, Poles, and Italians to honor their countries of origin, and by people of any ethnic background to parade their finery after Easter services. Between Thanksgiving and Christmas the stores (especially Lord & Taylor, F.A.O. Schwarz, and Saks Fifth Avenue) offer extravagant window displays with elaborately costumed dolls and mechanical figures. Members of the armed forces and the Salvation Army perform on brass instruments or bang on tambourines as they solicit money for charitable causes.

Finally, Fifth Ave is famous for its skyscrapers, most notably the Empire State Building, but also the towers of Rockefeller Center and several lesser buildings.

While some stores are open on Sun, it is better to visit during the week. During the Christmas season Fifth Ave is especially beautiful but maddeningly crowded.

The ****Empire State Building** (1931; Shreve, Lamb & Harmon; DL) between 33rd and 34th Sts at 350 Fifth Ave, is no longer the world's tallest building, surpassed by the Sears Roebuck Building in Chicago and the twin towers of the World Trade Center, but for many people it remains the quintessential skyscraper. It is 1250 ft to the 102nd floor observatory or 1472 ft to the top of the TV tower (installed 1951). It weighs 365,000 tons and occupies 37 million cubic ft on a site of about two acres. The structure includes 10 million bricks, 2.5 million ft of electrical wire, and enough steel to build a double-track railroad from New York to Baltimore (187 miles).

The Empire State Building, long the world's tallest building, looking south. Also in the photo are two other former title holders: the twin-towered World Trade Center on the right and the Metropolitan Life Tower (on the left, with illuminated clock), record holder 1909–13. (Courtesy of the Empire State Building)

History. In 1827 a son of John Jacob Astor bought the site where, beginning in 1859, two younger Astors, John Jacob III and William Backhouse Astor, Jr., built adjoining mansions. William married Caroline Webster Schermerhorn, later the dowager queen of society, and after fathering four children spent a great deal of time elsewhere. The Astor mansions remained intact until Caroline's nephew, William Waldorf Astor, inheritor of the southern house, lost out in a social competition with his redoubtable aunt and determined to revenge himself by tearing down his mansion and putting up a hotel, which he named The Waldorf after the ancestral Astor home in Germany. Caroline, offended by the towering hotel, moved uptown leaving her house to her son, John Jacob IV, who tore it down and built the Astoria part of The Waldorf-Astoria, named after a city in Oregon, originally a trading post in the first John Jacob's fur empire.

The Waldorf-Astoria (opened 1893) flourished both financially and socially. Its Gentlemen's Bar was the domain of Frick, Morgan, Guggenheim, et al., its dining room was ruled by the legendary Oscar Tschirky, known better as Oscar of the Waldorf, a maître who understood the minutiae of social discrimination and deployed his expertise imperiously. In 1929 the hotel moved uptown to its present location.

The concept of the Empire State Building, the world's tallest skyscraper budgeted at $60 million, was a product of the optimistic 1920s, but the building itself was a child of the Depression, demolition beginning in 1929 just two months before the stock market crash. Because of the Depression, actual costs came only to $40,948,900, but the economic climate also prevented full occupancy until almost the beginning of World War II, a period during which the building was nicknamed "the Empty State Building." Remarkably it was finished ahead of schedule, setting construction records still unrivaled, rising an average of 4½ stories a week and 14½ stories during the ten peak working days. Steel was set in place as little as 80 hours after leaving the furnaces of Pittsburgh, and the supply and delivery of other materials were superbly coordinated with the building schedule. Lewis Hine's photographs of the "skyboys" at work on the high steel are a tribute to them and a landmark in American photography.

In 1933 Irma Eberhardt became the first successful suicide to leap from the top. In the same year Hollywood used the building for the climax of the film King Kong, showing the mythical giant ape atop the tower fighting off a squadron of army planes; a later version used the towers of the World Trade Center instead, but the 1933 version has become a classic and in its day was considered a masterpiece in composite motion picture photography. On a foggy July 28, 1945, after threading its way among the pinnacles of midtown, an Army B-25 crashed into the 79th floor, killing 14 people. In 1986 two British parachutists jumped from the 86th floor and landed safely near Fifth Ave and 31st St. The staircases annually become a racecourse as climbers compete in the Empire State Run-Up, the winners clocking times for the 86 flights of about 11½ minutes.

EXTERIOR. The facade consists of a limestone curtain wall, blonde in tone, pierced by windows set flush and trimmed with vertical strips of stainless steel running the height of the building, a design chosen after 15 discarded attempts, in part because it would facilitate rapid construction. Everything possible—windows, spandrels, steel strips, even slabs of stone—was fabricated at the site of origin and shipped to be installed without further hand-fitting or stone-cutting. The setbacks, necessitated by zoning laws, were designed by taking the allowable volume, slicing away at the width, and adding as much as possible on the top, a process that resulted in a single major setback with a 60-ft terrace at the fifth floor and a tower rising straight above that. Originally the building was to end at the 86th floor, but one of the backers determined that it needed a mast for mooring zeppelins, which added 150 ft to the projected height. Several attempts were made, but the mast never succeeded, though a Navy blimp managed to dock long enough in 1931 to dump its ballast—water—on pedestrians several blocks away.

INTERIOR. The lobby, three stories high, is lined with marble imported from France, Italy, Belgium, and Germany. In 1963 illuminated panels by Roy Sparkia and Renée Nemorov depicting the eight wonders of the world, the traditional seven plus the Empire State Building, were installed.

The ticket office for the *observatories (86th and 102nd floors) is on the Concourse Level, one floor below the main lobby (open every day 9:30 A.M.—

11:30 P.M., observatory open until midnight). Admission charge; tel: 736-3100. On a clear day visibility reaches 80 miles. The view is equally spectacular at night.

Also on the Concourse Level is the **Guinness World Record Exhibit Hall** where unusual records and record holders—tallest, fattest, smallest, fastest, most disastrous—are displayed in cleverly designed exhibits, including videos of stunts (man wrestles alligator), curiosities (spectacular displays of falling dominoes), and sports records.

The Guinness World Record Exhibit Hall. Empire State Building, 350 Fifth Ave (at 34th St), New York 10118. Tel: 947-2335. Open seven days a week 9:30–6; closed Christmas and New Year's Day; admission charge. No food service, no gift shop, no restrooms (though restrooms are located in building corridor). No wheelchair access.

Begin walking N. on Fifth Ave. Between 34th and 35th Sts on the E. side is the former **B. Altman & Company** (1906; Trowbridge & Livingston; DL), the first department store to intrude on a previously residential area, modeled like a great palazzo, perhaps to soften the blow to disgruntled neighbors. Founder Benjamin Altman, son of a Lower East Side milliner, opened his first shop on Third Ave near 9th St and worked his way uptown via a stylish store in Ladies' Mile (Sixth Ave and 19th St). When Altman died unmarried in 1913, he left his art collection to the Metropolitan Museum of Art and $20 million in Altman's stock to a foundation which channeled the interest to philanthropy. Never trendy, the store was known through the years for its high-quality conservative clothing, home furnishings, dishes, and glassware; it went out of business in 1989.

While the Altman palazzo has been reasonably maintained, two nearby stores have been less fortunate. The former Gorham Building at 390 Fifth Ave (1906; McKim, Mead & White) on the S.W. corner of 36th St, an Italian Renaissance palace built for the jeweler and silver company, and the former Tiffany's at 409 Fifth Ave (1906; McKim, Mead & White) on the S.E. corner of 37th St, modeled after the Venetian Palazzo Grimani, have suffered ugly alterations. In 1983 W. & J. Sloane, the well-known furniture store long located on the S.W. corner of Fifth Ave and 38th St, left the neighborhood.

Lord & Taylor, one of the city's best-known department stores but originally a humble Lower East Side dry goods shop, occupies the block between 38th and 39th Sts on Fifth Ave. Despite the downslide of this part of the avenue, Lord & Taylor in 1977 elected to remodel their flagship Fifth Ave store (1914; Starrett & Van Vleck) at an estimated cost of $5 million, furnishing the ground floor with mirrored columns, marble floors, and greenery. The store is known for traditional women's sportswear, American designer clothing, and conservative, high-quality home furnishings.

Continue N. on Fifth Ave. On the N.W. corner of 39th St and Fifth Ave is **Lane Bryant** (452 Fifth Ave), a store specializing in stylish clothing for larger women. Lena Himmelstein Bryant, who founded the chain of stores (1904), was an immigrant from Lithuania, a widow without financial resources who pawned her wedding gift, a pair of diamond earrings, to make the down payment on a sewing machine. She introduced attractive maternity clothing to America (though prudish newspapers refused to carry advertising for it until 1911) and with her second husband pioneered the merchandising of clothing for larger women. Insurance company statistics and on-the-spot measurements of 4500 customers confirmed that 40% of American women were larger than the standard size 36, considered ideal at the time.

Across the street on the N.E. corner of 39th St formerly stood Arnold Constable & Co., the traditional rival of Lord & Taylor's but now out of business; its space has been taken over by the **Mid-Manhattan Branch of the New York Public Library**.

On the S.W. corner of Fifth Ave and W. 40th St is the former *Knox Building* (1901-02; John H. Duncan; DL), built as a showroom for hatter Edward M. Knox. Over it looms the *Republic National Bank Tower* (1986; Attia & Perkins), which incorporates the landmark building as banking space.

The **American Standard Building,** formerly the American Radiator Building (1924; Hood & Fouilhoux; DL) at 40 W. 40th St between Fifth and Sixth Aves is a black brick and gold terra-cotta tower with a Gothic crown. The color of the facade elicited comment that the building suggested what the American Radiator Co. manufactured—the black evoking a pile of coal, the gold of its higher points the glow of flames.

Continue north. The ***Central Research Branch of the New York Public Library** on the W. side of Fifth Ave between 40th and 42nd Sts (1911; Carrère & Hastings; DL) is one of the world's leading research libraries with some 9 million volumes of printed material and 21 million other items. The building itself is an example of Beaux-Arts classical extravagance, finished in marble, and lavishly decorated inside and out.

The Central Research Building, New York Public Library. Fifth Ave at 42nd St, New York 10036. Tel: 661-7220 for recorded information. Open Mon–Wed 10–9, Thurs–Sat 10–6. Closed Sun, holidays. Hours vary for specific collections. Admission free.

Tours of building Mon–Sat 11 and 2. Exhibitions, concerts, lectures, tours of exhibitions; for recorded announcement of major exhibitions and events, call 869-8089. Shop with books, posters, catalogues of exhibitions, toys. Restrooms and telephones. Outdoor café in season, open 8 A.M.–7 P.M.

History. The research collections of the New York Public Library developed from the consolidation of two great privately endowed libraries, the Astor and Lenox Libraries, and the Tilden Trust, a bequest of $2 million and 15,000 books from Samuel J. Tilden, lawyer, governor, and unsuccessful presidential candidate. Immigrant John Jacob Astor, hardly a bookish man, was persuaded by Joseph Green Cogswell to establish a public library (see p. 219) as a fitting testimonial to his adopted country (Astor for a while favored a huge monument to George Washington), and bequeathed $400,000 and a plot of land for its foundation. The books, largely chosen by Cogswell, provided a general reference service in the fields of greatest public interest including books on the "mechanic arts and practical industry" and books on languages, since Cogswell saw the American nation coming "into near relation with countries formerly the most remote." James Lenox, on the other hand, was a scholar whose particular interests are reflected in the strengths of his collection: American literature and history, the Bible, Milton, Shakespeare, Bunyan, and Renaissance literature of travel and discovery. Lenox built his own library (1875) on the site of the present Frick Collection (5th Ave bet. 70th / 71st Sts) but at his death (1880) left his 85,000 peerless books and an endowment of $505,000 to the New York Public Library. The gift of bachelor Samuel J. Tilden, a bequest reduced from $4 million to $2 million by his relatives who contested the will, was sorely needed as by 1886 the Astor and Lenox libraries already lacked funds for new books and maintenance. In 1895 the three gifts were united as the New York Public Library, Astor, Lenox, and Tilden Foundations—the Central Research Library as it exists today. In 1901 Andrew Carnegie, made aware that the city had nothing comparable to the public circulating systems of Boston and other American cities, gave $52,000,000 for the building of branch libraries. Today the library has 80 branches including the Library and Museum of the Performing Arts at Lincoln Center and the Schomburg Center for Research in Black Culture in Harlem. The circulating collections are publicly supported while the research libraries depend upon endowment and contributions.

EXTERIOR. The building sits on a wide terrace running the length of the Fifth Ave facade. In the center a broad flight of steps leads to three deep entrance arches framed by Corinthian columns. Flanking the steps which have long attracted tourists, pigeons, footsore shoppers, and the usual urban eccentrics, are two famous couchant marble lions by Edward C. Potter (1911), originally criticized as mealy-mouthed, complacent creatures but now securely ensconced in public affection. The bronze flagstaff bases (1912) by Raffaele J. Menconi were cast in the Tiffany Studios. In niches behind the fountains against the facade are statues (1913; Frederick W. MacMonnies) of Truth, a man leaning against a sphinx, and Beauty, a woman seated on the winged horse Pegasus. Above the entrance on the frieze are six allegorical figures (left to right) representing History, Romance, Religion, Poetry, Drama, and Philosophy by Paul Wayland Bartlett. The pediment figures at the ends of the facade are Art (S) and History (N.) by George Grey Barnard. Architect Thomas Hastings, never totally happy with the facade on Fifth Ave which early critics found too ornate, undertook studies for improving it, even leaving money in his will for alterations, but today its extravagance is generally admired.

INTERIOR. The entrance hall is finished in white Vermont marble, with an elaborate vaulted ceiling, heroic marble candelabra, and wide staircases. Behind it is GOTTESMAN HALL (restored 1984) which yearly features four major exhibits of objects from the collection.

Take the elevator (end of the right corridor) to the third floor, or walk up the marble stairs that crisscross back and forth under marble barrel vaults. Visible from the stairway are the large interior courts that provide natural light for the catalogue and reading rooms.

The stairway rises to the McGRAW ROTUNDA (third floor), decorated with murals (1940) by Edward Laning depicting the Story of the Recorded Word. The *Public Catalogue* in Room 315 formerly held more than 10 million cards; these have either been photographed and bound into books (pre-1972) or recorded electronically in the library's computerized catalogue system, CAT-NYP.

New York looking south from 42nd St in 1855. The Croton Distributing Reservoir and the Crystal Palace occupy the site of

Beyond is the monumental *Main Reading Room* with a shelf collection of about 40,000 reference books. The beautifully decorated ceiling, the tall, arched windows and the furniture designed by Carrère & Hastings, make it one of the city's great interiors. Beneath the reading room are the stacks, with 88 miles of shelves.

SPECIAL COLLECTIONS. Room 318 is an exhibition room with treasures from the *Berg Collection* (Room 320) which contains some 127,000 items mostly in the fields of American and English literature: manuscripts from the 15–20C, authors' corrected proofs, family correspondence, and rare books. The *Prints Division* (Room 308) has some 180,000 prints including the Phelps Stokes Collection of American Historical Prints, one of whose treasures is an engraving by Paul Revere of the British landing in Boston in 1768. The *Spencer Collection* (Room 308) has illuminated manuscripts from the 9–16C, and finely illustrated and bound books including a 14C Tickhill psalter. The *Arents Collection* (Room 324) consists of two sections, a collection of books published in serial form, acquired unbound as originally issued, and a collection of manuscripts, printed works, and other documents (1507–present) concerned directly or tangentially with tobacco, a resource for researchers interested in the early history of America or such matters as taxation. The *Rare Book Division* (Room 303) has more than 122,000 volumes and 21,500 broadsides including such treasures as a Gutenberg Bible, the only known copy of the original folio edition (in Spanish) of Christopher Columbus's letter describing his discoveries (dated 1493), the first full folio of Shakespeare (1623), and a Bay Psalm Book (1640) from Cambridge, Massachusetts, the first book printed in America in the English language.

the Public Library and Bryant Park, while surrounding blocks remain sparsely developed. (Museum of the City of New York)

Directly behind the library is **Bryant Park,** named after William Cullen Bryant (1794–1878), editor, writer, abolitionist, and proponent of such projects as Central Park and the Metropolitan Museum of Art. A *statue of Bryant* (1911; Herbert Adams) as an elderly sage sits just behind the library (center of park) shaded by an elaborate pillared architectural setting by Thomas Hastings, one of the designers of the library. At the S. end of the park near 40th St is a heroic bronze *bust of Goethe* (1932; Karl Fischer); towards 42nd St is a bronze *statue of William Earl Dodge* (1885; John Quincy Adams Ward), wealthy industrialist and supporter of virtuous causes (founder of the American Y.M.C.A., president of the National Temperance Society). Near the N.W. corner of the park is a bronze *statue of José Bonifacio de Andrada*, scholar, poet, and patriarch of Brazilian independence, by José Lima, cast from an original (1889) and presented to the U. S. in 1954 as a gift from Brazil.

At the edge of the park near 42nd St and Sixth Ave is a **tkts** kiosk with half-price, same-day tickets for concerts, operas, and dance events (open Tues, Thurs, Fri 12–2 and 3–7; Wed and Sat 11–2 and 3–7; Sun 12–6; tel: 382-2323). Near Sixth Ave are food stands and bookstalls operated by the Strand Book Store.

The park's present formal design (1934; Lusby Simpson), essentially a grid raised 4 ft above street level and walled in by shrubbery, has been criticized for sheltering drug dealers and muggers. Plans to redesign the park, opening it up to increase security and enhancing its public appeal with a restaurant or cafe along the rear wall of the library have long been under consideration, mired in the slough of municipal politics.

History. Before these 9.6 acres became Bryant Park (1884), the land was called Reservoir Park after the Croton Reservoir (1837–1900) which stood where the library is now, a walled and buttressed mass of gray granite with a wide promenade on top from which strollers could observe local sights. In June 1842 the first Croton water poured into the reservoir, flowing from artificially created Lake Croton (which rose behind a dam in the Croton River, a tributary flowing into the Hudson north of Ossining, N.Y.), along 33 miles of aqueduct, across the Harlem River on High Bridge, through pipes in the Manhattanville Valley and into a tunnel that emptied into the reservoir. A jubilant crowd listened to speeches and a 38-gun salute as water filled the two basins within the aqueduct to a capacity of 150 million gallons, ending a period of more than 200 years when the city, dependent on shallow wells and springs, was subject to frequent outbreaks of cholera and the ravages of uncontrollable fires. The Croton system, enlarged, updated, and supplemented by the Catskill system, still forms a significant part of the city's water supply.

In 1853 a world's fair, complete with Crystal Palace, opened in the park behind the reservoir, dazzling the public with pumps, hardware, sewing machines, and less utilitarian objects. On the N. side of 42nd St stood the Latting Tower, a 350-ft iron structure with an ice cream parlor at the bottom and a view at the top, reached via an unreliable steam-propelled elevator. Both the Latting Tower (1856) and the Crystal Palace (1858) burned, possibly so their owners could recover the insurance.

On the N.E. corner of 42nd St and Fifth Ave stands *503 Fifth Ave,* almost unnoticed among its newer neighbors. With two fewer stories, it was first owned by a drug merchant and then by Levi P. Morton a banker and later, congressman, Minister to France, Vice President with Benjamin Harrison, and Governor of New York. In 1879 well-born novelist Edith Wharton, her hair piled high on her head and clutching a large bouquet of lilies of the valley, made her social debut in the house.

No. 500 Fifth Ave (1931; Shreve, Lamb & Harmon), between 42nd and 43rd Sts, is a less famous office tower by the architects of the Empire State Building.

Continue N. on Fifth Ave. The steel and glass box at the S.W. corner of W. 43rd St (510 Fifth Ave) is **Manufacturers Hanover Trust Co.** (1954; Skidmore, Owings & Merrill), perhaps ordinary today but innovative in 1954 when banks still resembled palazzos or ancient temples, symbolic of their safety and endurance. While the building was designed expressly so that it could be turned to other uses, a 30-ton Mosler safe in the window identifies it as a bank.

At 7 W. 43rd St is the *Century Association* (1891; McKim, Mead & White; DL). Founded by William Cullen Bryant, the club has long been known for its intellectual and cultural orientation and recently for its struggles both intramural and legal (1988) over admitting women as members. Members Charles Follen McKim and Stanford White here designed one of their first neo-Italian Renaissance clubhouses; the Palladian window above the doorway was once part of an open loggia.

Continue W. on 43rd St. to Sixth Ave. On the N.W. corner of

the intersection is the satellite branch of the International Center of Photography known as **ICP/Midtown.**

The International Center of Photography/Midtown. 1133 Avenue of the Americas (43rd St), New York 10036. Tel: 768—4680. Open Tues—Wed 11—6, Thurs 11—8, Fri—Sun 11—6; closed Mon, New Year's Day, July 4th, Thanksgiving, Christmas. Admission charge except Thurs 6—8. Bookstore. Restrooms, no restaurant. Complete wheelchair access.

ICP/Midtown mounts exhibitions of established and little-known, contemporary, and historically important photographers in a handsome multi-level space (opened 1989). In addition to the large galleries, with their windows opening onto a photographically appealing view of the midtown skyscrapers, are the Permanent Collection Gallery and the Screening Room on the ground floor.

Return to Fifth Ave and continue north. Next door at 15 W. 43rd St is the *Princeton Club*.

On W. 44th St between Fifth and Sixth Aves (27 W. 44th St) is the *Harvard Club* (1894; McKim, Mead & White, additions 1905 and 1915; DL), a handsome neo-Georgian clubhouse whose restrained brick and limestone facade recalls the early architecture of the college itself.

Built on land donated by J. P. Morgan (commodore 1897—99), the **New York Yacht Club** at 37 W. 44th St (1901; Warren & Wetmore; DL) is a wonderfully eccentric Beaux-Arts clubhouse, festooned with ropes and pulleys, anchors and hooks, adrip inside and out with seaweed (criticized at the time for resembling spinach); truly astonishing, however, are the three windows fashioned like the sterns of ships ploughing through ossified seas whose stony waves curl over the sidewalk. The keystone above the main entrance represents Poseidon. Until the 1983 defeat of its entry, *Liberty,* by the Australian challenger *Australia II,* the club housed the America's Cup, given in 1851 by Queen Victoria and now considered the ultimate prize in yachting.

The **Algonquin Hotel**, originally the Puritan Hotel, at 59 W. 44th St (1902; Goldwyn Starrett; DL) rose to fame as a literary hangout when H. L. Mencken stayed there in 1914; since then it has enrolled William Faulkner, Gertrude Stein, James Thurber, F. Scott Fitzgerald, Tennessee Williams, and Graham Greene on its guest register. Beginning in 1919 Robert Benchley and Dorothy Parker among others held forth at the Round Table (site of the bar in the Rose Room), amusing one another with clever conversation, whose most succulent witticisms Franklin P. Adams reported in his column in the *New York World*. Later the Round Table extended itself into the Thanatopsis Pleasure and Literary Club, which in turn evolved into the Thanatopsis Poker and Inside Straight Club. Harold Ross, founder of *The New Yorker* magazine, belonged to the coterie and created his magazine—less high-minded in its beginnings than presently—partly to enshrine the sophisticated, incisive humor of his friends. While today's clientele may glitter less brightly in the literary firmament, the hotel still attracts literary and theatrical people as well as executives. Long a family business, the Algonquin was sold in 1987 to a Brazilian subsidiary of a Tokyo corporation.

The ROYALTON HOTEL (1898: Ehrick Rossiter) across the street at 44 W. 44th St once enjoyed the presence of George Jean Nathan, who maintained an apartment there from 1908 until his death in 1959. With Mencken, Nathan was editor (1914–25) of the *Smart Set,* premier literary magazine of its day until it fizzled into triviality. Robert Benchley, writer and humorist, also maintained a suite here, furnished with the red draperies and coverings of the Victorian era and appointed with two portraits of the queen herself. More recently (1988) the Royalton was refurbished as a conspicuously high-style luxury hotel.

The *Hippodrome Garage* at 50 W. 44th St marks the site of the Hippodrome Theatre (1905; Frederick Thompson and Elmer S. Dundy), which faced Sixth Ave and was the largest legitimate theater in the world, seating a crowd of 5000 spectators. Because it was so large that the audience couldn't hear words or lyrics, it was used for spectacles—elephants pulling automobiles, horses or girls plunging into a giant tank, ballets featuring as many as 700 singers and dancers.

Walk back toward Fifth Ave along the S. side of W. 44th St. The ponderous limestone building with massive Doric columns at ground level (42 W. 44th St) is the *Association of the Bar of the City of New York* (1895; Cyrus L. W. Eidlitz; DL).

At 20 W. 44th St is a more humble institution, the *Mechanics' and Tradesmen's Institute* (1891; Lamb & Rich; DL), originally the Berkeley Preparatory School, which still offers courses to technical students. Inside is a three-story gymnasium and drill hall now converted to a library and museum. The Mechanics' and Tradesmen's Institute library on the ground floor is open by membership to the public (tel: 840-1840), and is stocked with novels, poetry, books on religion, and, oddly, a good collection on Gilbert and Sullivan. The *John M. Mossman Collection of Locks* is installed on the balcony.

The John M. Mossman Collection of Locks. 20 W. 44th St (near 5th Ave), New York 10036. Tel: 840-1840. Open Mon–Fri 10–12 and 1–4; closed weekends, July, and first Wed of every month, major holidays; admission free. Restroom, no telephone, no restaurant. Limited wheelchair access; elevator to second floor.

The collection, displayed in old cases, consists of some 400 antique and modern locks, including such surprises as a Very Complicated lock which more than justifies its name. Mossman (1850–1912) was a member of the Society of Mechanics and Tradesmen.

Return to Fifth Ave and continue north. The FRED F. FRENCH BUILDING at 551 Fifth Ave (N.E. corner of 45th St), built by a successful developer, typifies the better skyscrapers of the 1920s (1927; John Sloan and H. Douglas Ives; DL) with its ornate lobby, upper-story setbacks, and ornamental work—unusual faience polychromy delineating the setbacks and the top of the building. The panels concealing the water tower on the roof are decorated with symbolic motifs chosen by architect Ives: N. and S., the rising sun (Progress) amid winged griffins (Integrity and Watch-fulness) and golden beehives with bees (Thrift and Industry); E. and W., heads of Mercury, god of commerce. The building is probably the first New York flat-topped skyscraper.

Walk W. on 45th St. In the middle of the block is an attractive vest pocket park, known as the Plaza at 1166 (the Sixth Ave address of the building). Designed by Hideo Sasaki (1983), the plaza features an angular sculpture (1976–79), *Throwback* by Tony Smith, enhanced by plantings and flowing water. Scheduled noontime events, a cafe, and seating make this an attractive oasis.

Continue to Sixth Ave and walk uptown to 47th St. Return E. along 47th St toward Fifth Ave. Unimposing though it may be, the block of W. 47th St between Fifth Ave and Sixth Aves is the city's **Diamond District,** where daily an estimated $400 million in gems is exchanged. In the 1920s and early 1930s the diamond business centered around the Bowery and Canal St, but the refugees who fled the Amsterdam and Antwerp ghettos ahead of Hitler established themselves uptown beside the few downtown dealers already moving to 47th St. The glittering shops at street level are for the tourist trade, while the real business is trans-acted upstairs in old buildings equipped with ultrasensitive cam-eras and sophisticated alarm systems or in the trading clubs. Still, at least until 1977, when two traders were murdered for their diamonds, dealers handed over valuable stones to friends of friends on the sidewalk and consummated million-dollar agree-ments with handshakes. Virtually all the brokers and diamond cutters are Jewish, using skills passed down the generations from as far back as the 16C, when stone-cutting was one of the few trades open to Jews. The community includes a number of Hasidic Jews, highly visible with their beards, long sidelocks, black, wide-brimmed hats, and dark clothing, drawn to the trade partly by tradition and partly because the flexible hours permit them to observe the strict schedule of their religion.

Internationally famous among fanciers of cameras, video cas-sette recorders, and other electronic equipment is *Forty-seventh Street Photo,* at 67 W. 47th St, whose discounts lure shoppers to its crowded, often frenzied headquarters (open Mon–Thurs 9–6, Fri 9–2, Sun 10–4; closed Sat; tel: 398-1410).

At 41 W. 47th St between Fifth and Sixth Aves is the GOTHAM BOOK MART, a national literary landmark, established in 1920 by Frances Steloff, friend and supporter of such American writers as William Carlos Williams, Henry Miller, and T. S. Eliot. Thou-sands of new and used books (an especially wide selection of 20C poetry and prose), and literary magazines cram the shelves. The James Joyce Society was organized here in 1947 with T. S. Eliot purchasing the first membership.

The Diamond Trade Association, a center for trading uncut stones, is at 15 W. 47th St. It is not open to outsiders.

The most important institution on the street is the Diamond Dealers Club, a trading center for dealers in cut diamonds, at 580 Fifth Ave on the corner of 47th St. Members are admitted via card-controlled turnstiles and a steel door. The new facilities, where more diamonds reputedly change hands than anywhere else in the world, opened in 1985, replacing an older center at 30 W. 47th St known for its deafening noise levels.

Return to Fifth Ave. On the S.E. corner of Fifth Ave and 47th St, occupying a converted and expanded Korvette store (575 Fifth Ave), is *The Center of Fifth* (1985; Emery Roth & Sons), a 40-story tower with a glistening salmon-pink marble public atrium (restrooms on the concourse level), a leaded glass skylight (Hank Prussing) and four levels of shopping.

Continue north. In these blocks Fifth Ave still lives up to its reputation, though here and there less exclusive stores and offices have begun to intrude. After more than seven decades in this location the former *Charles Scribner's Sons* bookstore at 597 Fifth Ave (bet. 48th / 49th Sts) closed in 1989, reopening soon thereafter as *Brentano's*, another well-known bookseller. The building (1913; Ernest Flagg; DL), with a black iron and glass storefront reminiscent of *fin de siècle* Paris, is protected by its landmark designation, but the elegant two-story wood-paneled interior reminiscent of a gentleman's library is not.

For Rockefeller Center, which begins at Fifth Ave and W. 49th St, see Route 17.

Saks Fifth Avenue, (1924; Starrett & Van Vleck; DL) on the E. side of the avenue between 49th and 50th Sts, a department store known for high-fashion boutiques, excellent service, and fine merchandise, was founded by Andrew Saks, who began as a peddler in Washington, D.C. In 1923 his son Horace sold a less exclusive store, Saks Thirty-fourth, to the now extinct Gimbels for $8 million in order to follow the carriage trade uptown. The next year he opened the present store, whose windows featured a pigskin trunk ($3000), raccoon coats ($1000), and chauffeurs' livery.

**St. Patrick's Cathedral (1879; towers, 1888; James Renwick, Jr.; DL), filling the block between E. 50th and E. 51st St on Fifth Ave, is the seat of the Roman Catholic Archdiocese of New York, a famous city landmark and a symbol of the success in New York of its immigrant Irish Catholic population. Designed by James Renwick with William Rodrigue, whose contribution seems to have been minimal, it draws on the decorated Gothic style of the 13C and has been compared to French, German, and English cathedrals of that period. It is the largest Catholic cathedral in the U.S. and the eleventh largest in the world.

History. In 1828 the two major Catholic churches of New York, St. Peter's and St. Patrick's—then at the corner of Prince and Mott Sts—bought the plot where the cathedral now sits, intending it as a burial ground. Unfortunately the buyers neglected to examine the land, which turned out to be far too rocky for its intended purpose. In 1850 Archbishop John Hughes announced his intention to build a new cathedral on the site, a church "worthy of God, worthy of the Catholic religion, and an honor to this great city"—the last phrase remarkable at a time when upper class New York was largely Protestant, and considered the city's Catholic population a rabble. The established Protestants isolated the immigrant outsiders from Ireland and later Germany, Italy, and Poland, deny-ing them all but the most menial jobs and leveling against them a deep-rooted prejudice. Hughes had arrived in America from Ireland in 1817, an uneducated 20-year-old eager to become a priest. He arrived in New York 19 years later a bishop, a skillful administrator, and a flamboyant orator. Eight years after announcing his plan, Hughes solicited enough money to lay the cornerstone and begin construction (1858); in 1879 the cathedral was dedicated, having cost twice as much and taken four times as long to build (including an interruption during the Civil War) as estimated. It was consecrated, debtfree, in 1910.

Measurements. Exterior: length, 332 ft; width 174 ft; base of towers, 32 sq ft; height from street to top of spire, 330 ft; height of central gable, 156 ft. Interior: length, 306 ft; length of nave and transept, 144 ft; width of nave, 48 ft; height of nave, 108 ft.

EXTERIOR. The general plan is a Latin cross with traditional east-west orientation. The facade is of marble. The two square towers facing Fifth Ave are topped by octagonal lanterns rising to spires. Because the interior vaulting is brick and plaster, not stone, flying buttresses were not needed, but the pinnacles of the buttresses exist, perhaps because Renwick originally called for stone interior vaulting supported by flying buttresses. The bronze doors (added 1949) at the W. entrance were designed by Charles Maginnis with figures by John Angel.

Figures represent (top to bottom, left to right): St. Joseph, patron of this church; St. Isaac Jogues, first Catholic priest in New York; St. Frances X. Cabrini, founder of the Missionary Sisters of the Sacred Heart and "Mother of the Immigrant"; the Blessed Kateri Tekakwitha, an Indian maiden called the "Lily of the Mohawks"; and St. Elizabeth Ann Seton, first American-born saint.

INTERIOR. Enter the nave, articulated by two rows of clustered columns. Above the arches runs the triforium, divided into four sections by the arms of the cross. Above the triforia rise clerestory windows (14 × 26 ft in the nave, 28 × 58 ft in the transept). The ceiling is groined with (plaster) ribs with foliated bosses at the intersections.

Chapels and aisle windows in the **south aisle** (near 50th St): (1) Window of St. Vincent de Paul over the book shop. (2) Altar of St. Anthony of Padua with window showing St. Elizabeth of Hungary, St. Andrew, and St. Catherine of Alexandria. (3) Altar of St. John the Evangelist with window of the Annunciation. (4) Shrine of St. Elizabeth Ann Seton (sculptor Frederick Shrady) which dates from 1975, and window dedicated to St. Henry, 11C Holy Roman Emperor. (5) Altar of St. Rose of Lima, patroness of South America, with window depicting Pope Pius IX proclaiming the dogma of the Immaculate Conception.
  South Transept: (6) The stations of the cross were designed by Peter J. H. Cuypers in Holland and are carved in Caen stone (seven in S. transept, seven opposite them in N. transept). The windows above the stations of the cross are (S. transept) St. Luke (right of entrance) and St. John (left of entrance). Over the entrance is a window devoted to St. Patrick, depicting 18 scenes from his life, given by Old St. Patrick's Cathedral. In the W. wall of the transept is another St. Patrick's window, given by architect Renwick, who appears in the lower panels. (7) Altar of the Blessed Sacrament, with a tabernacle containing the sacrament beneath a baldachin of oak with gold leaf, which once hung over the cardinal's throne.
  South Ambulatory: (8) Altar of St. Andrew with window of St. Agnes, virgin martyr of Rome. (9) Altar of St. Theresa of the Little Flower, with window of St. Alphonsus Liguori. (10) Archbishop's sacristy with window depicting the death of St. Joseph. (11) Beyond the sacristy is a marble Pietà (1906; William

ST. PATRICK'S CATHEDRAL

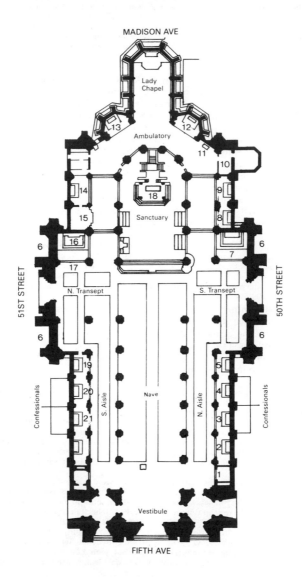

O. Partridge) based on Michelangelo's famous work. (12) Next is the altar of St. Elizabeth, mother of St. John the Baptist.

The **Lady Chapel**, begun in 1901 and completed in 1906, was designed by Charles T. Matthews and is patterned after 13C French Gothic architecture. Constructed of Vermont marble (but with plaster vaults), it is 56 × 28 ft and 56 ft high. The stained glass windows (Paul Woodroffe) over this altar and the two flanking it depict the mysteries of the rosary. The chapel pavement of polished marble contains a mosaic of the heraldic arms of Pope Leo XIII.

(13) Directly opposite the Lady Chapel is the entrance to the *Crypt* in which are buried the earthly remains of Archbishop Hughes, the other cardinals of New York, and several rectors of this church, as well as Archbishop Fulton J. Sheen. (Crypt not usually open to the public.)

North ambulatory: (14) Adjacent to the Lady Chapel on the N. side is the Altar of St. Michael and St. Louis, designed by Charles T. Matthews and executed by Tiffany & Co. (15) Beyond the usher's office and bride's room is the altar of St. Joseph. (16) Further along is the chancel organ (1928) with 2520 pipes.

North transept: (17) The altar of the Holy Family stands against the E. wall of the transept. In front of it is (18) the marble Baptistry. Carved figures of doctors of the church and theologians flank the door of the transept; the windows depict evangelists: St. Matthew (right of door) and St. Mark (left of door). Above the door is a window depicting the life of Mary. Opposite the Holy Family altar is the St. Charles Borromeo window.

(19) The focal point of the **sanctuary** is the high altar with its baldachin or canopy designed by Charles D. Maginnis, made of bronze and rising to a height of 57 ft.

Suspended from the ceiling of the sanctuary above the altar are the *galeros* or ceremonial hats of all the cardinals of New York. The clerestory windows surrounding the sanctuary depict (clockwise from N.): sacrifice of Abel, sacrifice of Noah, sacrifice of Melchisedech, apsidal windows illustrating parables of Christ and symbols of the evangelists, sacrifice of Calvary, sacrifice of the eating of the Paschal lamb, sacrifice of Abraham.

From the crossing is a good view of the **West or Rose Window,** 26 ft in diameter and filled with stained glass in geometric patterns. In the loft beneath it is the Great Organ (1930), with 9000 pipes ranging from a little over 3 in to 32 ft in length. The cathedral also has an echo organ, placed in the S. triforium near the American flag, which is used to enhance the chancel organ.

North aisle: (20) The first altar beyond the transept is the Altar of the Holy Face, formerly called the Chapel of St. Veronica and the Chapel of the Holy Relics because relics received by the archbishops of New York were kept here for veneration. Above the altar is a window depicting St. Bernard preaching the Second Crusade. To the right of the altar is a statue of St. Jude. (21) The shrine of St. John Neumann was erected in 1978 to honor this missionary in western New York State and bishop of Philadelphia, elevated to sainthood in 1977. The metal church depicted is Old St. Patrick's Cathedral where he was ordained. Above the shrine is a window depicting the martyrdom of St. Lawrence. (22) The altar of St. Jean Baptiste de la Salle stands below a window showing Pope Benedict XIII. (23) The altar of St. Brigid and St. Bernard is designed around a replica of a doorway of St. Bernard's Chapel in Mellifont, County Louth, Ireland, which dates from 1142. In front of the altar is a statue of the Infant of Prague, and above it a window depicting St. Columbanus, an Irish missionary, rebuking Burgundian King Thierry III for his scandalous life.

Continue N. on Fifth Ave. On the N.E. corner of E. 51st St is OLYMPIC TOWERS (1976; Skidmore, Owings & Merrill), an outscale luxury multiuse building (shops at ground level, offices above, and apartments on the highest floors) constructed by a consortium headed by Greek shipping colossus Aristotle Onassis.

At the turn of the century the block of Fifth Ave between 51st and 52nd Sts was Vanderbilt territory. Three brownstone mansions built by William Henry Vanderbilt for himself and two daughters occupied the W. side of the avenue. Alva Smith Vanderbilt, the socially ambitious wife of his second son, commissioned Richard Morris Hunt to do a house at 660 Fifth Ave (N.W. corner of 52nd St), a $3 million palace of limestone (not brownstone), whose turrets and Gothic traceries recalled the château of Blois in the Loire Valley of France. Alva's husband, William Kissam Vanderbilt, alarmed by the northward sweep of commerce, sold the lot on the S.E. corner of Fifth Ave and 52nd St to Morton F. Plant on the condition that the site remain residential for 25 years. Plant erected a residence, now **Cartier's** (1905; Robert W. Gibson; remodeled as a store, 1917; DL), worthy of a man of his means (a reputed $32 million in 1919) and stature (Commodore of the New York Yacht Club). However, by 1916 he found the area too commercial and started a new mansion at the N.E. corner of Fifth Ave and 86th St. William K. Vanderbilt bought the mansion, a five-story neo-Italian palazzo of marble and granite, for a million dollars and quickly rented it to Cartier's for $50,000 a year. According to legend, however, Plant traded the house to Pierre Cartier for a string of pearls, said at the time to be worth a million dollars but valued on Mrs. Plant's death (1956) at a mere $151,000. Cartier's, jewelers to the French court in the 18C and to numerous later millionaires, movie stars, and members of royalty, offers the general public the pleasure of its exquisite window displays and *Les Musts,* a boutique with more moderately priced items.

Between Fifth and Sixth Aves, 52nd St has been designated *Swing St* to commemorate its place in the history of jazz. Known simply as "The Street" among jazzmen, it attracted attention beginning in the late 1930s with its nightclubs, many of them former speakeasies, where most of the great innovators and performers of the period worked: Art Tatum, Dizzy Gillespie, Thelonius Monk, Lester Young, Kenny Clark, and of course Charlie Parker for whom the most famous jazz club of all, Birdland, would later be named. In particular the street has been identified with bop, a style which emerged in Harlem between 1940–44 and came downtown when black musicians began working in the clubs of 52nd St. The best known were the Onyx, the Spotlight, the Three Deuces, the Famous Door, and on nearby Broadway, the Royal Roost and Bop City. The period was a golden age for jazz and for 52nd St, but by 1948, when heroin abuse was widespread among jazz musicians, the street had become the territory of prostitutes, strippers, and drug pushers.

Just W. of the avenue at 21 W. 52nd St is the *"21" Club,* risen from its origins as a Prohibition speakeasy to its present status as a celebrity haunt. The cast-iron jockeys outside suggest the territorial character of the restaurant as the turf of the well-heeled and well-known.

Continue N. on Fifth Ave past *666 Fifth Avenue* (1957; Carson, Lundin & Shaw) between W. 52nd and W. 53rd Sts; its embossed aluminum facing is not unusual for the skyscrapers of the 1950s; the sculpted waterfall in the pedestrian shopping arcade is by Isamu Noguchi.

B. Dalton, Bookseller, part of a large chain, occupies the S. portion of the building. The store carries some 300,000 books, arranged by subject, as well as a growing stock of computer software and other booklike objects. Occasional signings by celebrity-authors.

On the N.W. corner of 53rd St and Fifth Ave (1 W. 53rd St) is Protestant Episcopal *St. Thomas' Church (1914; Cram, Goodhue & Ferguson; DL), a picturesque asymmetric French Gothic church placed on a small corner plot. Originally it was built without steel, following the principles of Ralph Adams Cram (also architect of St. John the Divine) who believed that if a church were Gothic in style it should be Gothic in construction, its columns supporting its weight. However, 11 years after completion the unbuttressed N. wall was bulging dangerously and steel beams were placed across the columns above the ceiling. Later, during blasting for the subway tunnel under 53rd St, a steel beam was installed under the altar.

The EXTERIOR is of Kentucky limestone. Bertram G. Goodhue (architect of St. Bartholomew's on Park Ave) planned the facade, notable for its asymmetry and single corner tower. Above the double entrance doors a gilded relief shows the four different buildings in which the congregation has worshiped, two on Houston St and Broadway, two on the present site. The central figure on the facade is St. Thomas. Left of the main portal is the *Bride's Entrance;* above the doorway some observers have discerned a stylized dollar sign, whose presence recalls medieval times when carpenters and stoneworkers left tokens of social criticism in obscure parts of their cathedrals. During the years when this stretch of Fifth Ave was the city's greenest residential turf, St. Thomas' Church hosted marriages of wealth and prestige, the most famous of which was the marriage of Consuelo Vanderbilt to the Duke of Marlborough in 1895.

The INTERIOR culminates in the 80-ft *reredos* of ivory-colored Dunville stone (Ohio) pierced by three stained glass windows. Lee Lawrie, known for his work at Rockefeller Center, and Goodhue designed it, though the central portion showing the cross and kneeling angels was copied from a smaller reredos by Augustus Saint-Gaudens in the previous church on this site (burned 1905).

Also of interest is the wood carving of the chancel, donated after World War I. The carved panels on the kneeling rail in front of the choir stalls have designs representing the human industries and important historical events, including such unexpected subjects as (from the left) Christopher Columbus's ship, Theodore Roosevelt, Lee Lawrie (between the steamship and the telephone), a radio, finance (with the initials of J. P. Morgan), and medicine.

The small carved heads above the choir stalls (difficult to see for those not in the choir) also represent contemporary personages including (S. side, second, third, and fourth figures from altar) President Woodrow Wilson, Premier Paderewski of Poland, and King Victor Emmanuel of Italy. The clerestory windows were made by Whitefriars in London and represent (N. side) the fruits of the spirit and (S. side) sacraments of the church, St. Thomas, and builders of churches.

Just off Fifth Ave on E. 53rd St is the **Museum of Broadcasting,** founded (1975) by William S. Paley to document the history of American broadcasting.

Museum of Broadcasting. 1 E. 53rd St (5th Ave), New York 10022. Tel: 752-7684. Open Tues 12–8, Wed–Sat 12–5. Mornings reserved for groups by appointment. Closed Sun, Mon, major holidays. Suggested donation. Restrooms, gift shop, no food, no telephone. Accessible to wheelchairs. **Note:** The museum will move to a new location at 23 W. 52nd St some time after autumn of 1990.

The collection, gathered from the major commercial networks, public television, and other sources, now includes more than 25,000 tapes of radio and TV shows and televised events. The radio shows date back to the 1920s, the earliest being a speech by labor leader Samuel Gompers; the TV shows begin in 1949. Visitors, if inclined, hear Lord Haw Haw or Jack Benny, or Toscanini or, in a lighter vein, the *Amos 'n' Andy Show*. They may watch Howdy Doody, Lucille Ball, Edward R. Murrow's documentary on Sen. Joseph McCarthy, the Beatles and Elvis Presley on the Ed Sullivan Show, or the funeral of John F. Kennedy.

PALEY PARK (1967; Zion & Breen, landscape architects; Albert Preston Moore, consulting architect) just E. of Fifth Ave (5 E. 53rd St) is a small, serene park with an almost Oriental ambience. Measuring only 42 × 100 ft, it is graced by ivy, a dozen honey locust trees, and a "waterwall" whose steady white noise obliterates the whine of traffic. Unusual for New York is the moveable furniture (secured at night). Before William S. Paley, chairman of the board of CBS, donated the park in memory of his father Samuel, the site was occupied by the Stork Club, a nightclub beloved of cafe society and gossip columnists.

Continue up Fifth Ave. On the N.W. corner of the next intersection at 1 W. 54th St is the **University Club** (1899; McKim, Mead & White; DL), a grand neo-Italian palazzo built during the heyday of the club, when some clubmen, Cornelius Vanderbilt for example, belonged to as many as 16 and spent in dues what the average worker earned in a year. Even then the University Club was remarkable for its grandeur. Above the main door, flanked with reeded and foliated columns, is a head of Athena modeled after a statuette owned by Stanford White. The interior (not open to the public) is remarkable for its opulent decoration: hallways paved with marble, ceiling paintings by H. Siddons Mowbray, pilasters of Italian walnut.

Turn W. (left). When St. Luke's Hospital vacated W. 54th St in 1896, new dwellings began to rise on both sides of the street. At 7 W. 54th St is the former *Philip Lehman residence* (1900; John H. Duncan), a handsome town house noteworthy for having once held the Robert Lehman collection of paintings now exhibited in the Metropolitan Museum of Art. (Duncan is better known for designing Grant's tomb.) The double house next door, Nos. 9–11 W. 54th St, was designed for James Goodwin (1898; McKim, Mead & White; DL), admired in its day as a "revival of the Georgian epoch, pure and simple." *No. 13 W. 54th St* was a Rockefeller town house, belonging most recently to Gov. Nelson Rockefeller, who died there in 1979.

Standing on the site of the senior John D. Rockefeller's town house at 17 W. 54th St are the ROCKEFELLER APARTMENTS (1936; Harrison & Fouilhoux; DL), an experiment in middle-class apartment design financed by John D. Rockefeller, Jr. The project consists of two buildings running back to back (the other faces W. 55th St) with a central garden between to admit light but not noise to the rear bedrooms. Because the cylindrical bays were designed as "dinettes," their windows face away from one another, insuring privacy. The tenants were also given rooftop sun decks, a playroom, and wood-burning fireplaces.

Return to Fifth Ave and cross it. At 4 E. 54th St is a neo-Italian town house remodeled for William H. Moore (1900; McKim, Mead & White; DL). Moore was a Chicago industrialist, involved with United States Steel, the American Can Co., and the National Biscuit Co. The building (protected by its landmark designation) now stands alone, dwarfed by its neighbors.

Return to Fifth Ave and go north. Fifth Ave between 54th and 55th Sts remains one of the city's finest shopping blocks, catering, as in the old days, to the carriage trade. Bijan, a men's clothier (by appointment only) whose blazing white facade is more suggestive of its earlier Beverly Hills incarnation than of staid Fifth Ave, Gucci, Elizabeth Arden, and Fred, Joaillier, give the block the élan of yesteryear.

On the S.E. corner of the next intersection (2 E. 55th St) is the ST. REGIS-SHERATON HOTEL (1904; Trowbridge & Livingston, with an addition to the E., 1925), a venture of John Jacob Astor IV, who realized from his experience with the Waldorf-Astoria that expensive hotels in elegant residential neighborhoods attracted a clientele eager for proximity to social splendor. The exterior has stone garlands, a mansard roof with bull's-eye windows and copper cresting, and on E. 55th St, a fine brass and glass kiosk for the top-hatted doormen. Inside, Astor provided automatic thermostats in every room, a system for heating, cooling, moistening, or drying the air (predating air conditioning), 47 Steinway pianos, a service of gold-plated flatware, and other decorative touches that cost him $1.5 million. Once famous for its restaurants including a palm room where members of both sexes could smoke publicly at all hours, the St. Regis is now known for the King Cole Room, present home of Maxfield Parrish's mural originally commissioned for another Astor enterprise, the Knickerbocker Hotel in Times Square.

Across the street on the S.W. corner of Fifth Ave (700 Fifth Ave) is the *Peninsula Hotel*, formerly the Gotham Hotel (1905; Hiss & Weekes). Built by a group of speculators, the Gotham ran into early financial difficulties: it was denied a liquor license because it stood within 200 ft of the Fifth Avenue Presbyterian Church and was saddled with unpaid bills by its socially elite but financially straitened clientele. In the mid-1980s the hotel was gutted and refurbished, opening in 1987 as the Hotel Maxim's de Paris, and in 1988 under its present name.

On the N.W. corner of Fifth Ave and 55th St is the *Fifth Avenue Presbyterian Church* (1875; Carl Pfeiffer). Next to it at 714 Fifth Ave is rising a new office tower (Kohn Pedersen Fox Assoc.)

behind the landmark facades of the former Rizzoli Building (1907–08; Albert S. Gottlieb; DL) and its neighbor the Coty Building (1907–08; Woodruff Leeming; DL). Developers have used the air rights purchased from the adjacent church for $15.75 million to construct the 44-story skyscraper.

Preservationists who wished to maintain the low profile of this part of Fifth Ave discovered that the Coty Building facade has some windows designed by René Lalique, who also designed perfume bottles for François Coty.

Continue uptown. *Harry Winston* (718 Fifth Ave, S.W. corner of 56th St) is a jeweler of international reputation.

The block of W. 56th St between Fifth Ave and the Ave of the Americas, once called "Eat Street" by columnist Earl Wilson, still has a dense concentration of restaurants—Italian, French, Korean, and Japanese, among others.

Across the avenue on the S.E. corner of Fifth Ave and 56th St (717 Fifth Ave) is the *Corning Glass Building* (1959; Harrison, Abramovitz & Abbe), a 28-story tower with greenish glass facing. On the ground floor are the showrooms of the Steuben Glass Co., whose windows, convex to prevent glare, seem invisible. Inside is a grand array of crystal figurines, sculptures, and accessories.

Continue north. Occupying most of the block between 56th and 57th Sts is **Trump Tower** (1983; Der Scutt, design architect; Swanke Hayden Connell) at 725 Fifth Ave, a flashy newcomer to a venerable block. Offspring of Donald J. Trump, the city's most visible real estate entrepreneur, the building features a lavish six-story atrium whose pink marble surfaces, cascading waterfall, and luxuriant greenery provide an opulent setting for a dozen or so luxury shops, most of them of European provenance. Above the atrium rise floors of office space and some 260 condominiums.

At the S.E. corner of 57th St at 727 Fifth Ave is *Tiffany & Co.*, another of the avenue's renowned jewelers, founded by Charles L. Tiffany, father of Louis Comfort Tiffany, remembered as a designer of glass, stained glass, jewelry, enamels, and interiors. The firm moved to this modest granite palazzo (1940; Cross & Cross) from a fancier palace on 37th St and Fifth Ave. Tiffany's sophisticated window displays are famous.

Walk back to Fifth Ave. On the S.W. corner of the intersection of 57th St, at 730 Fifth Ave, is the CROWN BUILDING (1921; Warren & Wetmore), originally the Heckscher Building. It was the first tall building to invade upper Fifth Ave and the first office building constructed under the Zoning Resolution of 1916. The Museum of Modern Art had its modest beginnings here (1929), renting space on the 12th floor for loan exhibitions.

Continue a block north. The *Solow Building* at 9 W. 57th St (1972; Skidmore, Owings & Merrill), with its glassy swooping facade is a more expensive version of the W. R. Grace Building on W. 42nd St. The red "9" on the sidewalk was designed by sculptor Ivan Chermayeff.

Continue uptown. Like so many of the city's other luxury

stores, BERGDORF GOODMAN (W. side of 5th Ave bet. 57th / 58th Sts) had humble beginnings. Herman Bergdorf, a tailor known for adapting men's suits to the female figure and also for his enjoyment of wine, founded the firm, but Edwin Goodman, who bought out Bergdorf in 1901, raised the store to its present heights, moving it in 1928 to this location. The store is known for its luxury European clothing and accessories, its fur collection, and its service. Before Bergdorf's arrived, the Cornelius Vanderbilt mansion stood here, a 137-room castle, filling the whole block with peaks, gables, dormers, and other Victorian extravagances.

Once located at the N.E. corner of Fifth Ave and 58th St, F. A. O. Schwarz, the toy store, has moved across 58th St to the General Motors Building (see p. 361).

16 United Nations, Turtle Bay, and Beekman Hill

SUBWAY: IRT Lexington Ave local or express (train 4, 5, or 6) or Flushing IRT (train 7) to Grand Central Station.

BUS: M15 uptown via 1st Ave, downtown via 2nd Ave. M101 or M102 via 3rd and Lexington Aves. M27 crosstown on 49th-50th Sts. M104 or M106 crosstown on 42nd St.

History. The neighborhood in the East 40s, today dominated by the United Nations, is known as Turtle Bay, after a cove in the East River that reached from about 45th to 48th Sts. Whether the bay, long since filled in, got its name from the abundant turtles in its waters or as a corruption of the Dutch word "deutal" (a bent blade), referring to its shape, the land around it, "Deutal Bay Farm," was granted in 1639 by Dutch Gov. William Kieft to two Englishmen, George Holmes and Thomas Hall. Later, Sir Peter Warren, a distinguished British naval officer who married a De Lancey and enjoyed a mansion in Greenwich Village (see p. 252), owned the farm, while James Beekman owned a nearby parcel from 49th to 51st Sts, in an area now known as Beekman Hill. Just before the Revolution (1775), the Sons of Liberty, a group of belligerent, radical, mostly working-class patriots, sailed a sloop from Greenwich, Connecticut, through Hell Gate to Turtle Bay. They seized a military storehouse on the Warren farm from its British guards and took its supplies back to Boston. Marinus Willett, after whom Willett St on the Lower East Side is named, led the foray. Later, Nathan Hale (see p. 148) was captured near the former Dove Tavern (3rd Ave at 66th St) and sentenced in the Beekman greenhouse as a spy and traitor to the king.

In the mid-19C several notable literary figures sought refuge in Turtle Bay, then a rural suburb. Publisher Horace Greeley brought his wife here to ease her grief at the death of several of her children. Margaret Fuller, writer and reformer, spent some years here, occasionally rowing across the river with a friend to visit the prison on Blackwell's (now Roosevelt) Island. Edgar Allan Poe and his desperately ill wife, Virginia, rented a house (1846) facing the bay near 47th St.

At Third Ave and 46th St an enrollment office for the draft into the Union Army was established during the Civil War and became the focal point of the Draft Riots of 1863, a three-day binge of rioting, looting, and burning, during which 18 blacks were lynched, the Colored Orphan Asylum on Fifth Ave was burned, and perhaps 1000 people were killed or injured.

In the later 19C, modest brownstones replaced the country homes, and although the neighborhood around the Beekman farm remained pleasant

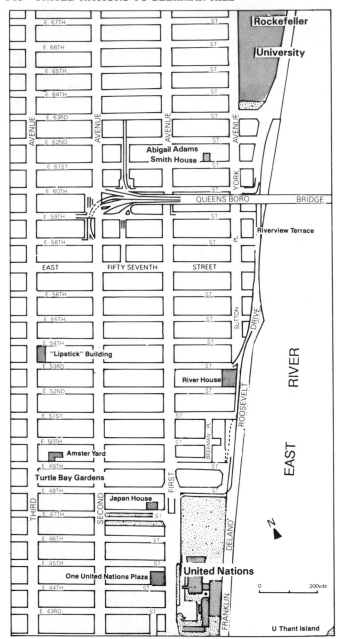

because of James W. Beekman's careful development of his property, elsewhere the area, unrestricted by residential covenants, deteriorated into slums. The shores of Turtle Bay became a garbage dump, and by 1868 the bay had been filled in. When the Third Ave elevated railway opened in 1878, followed by the Second Ave El in 1880, the far East Side saw its brownstones converted to rooming houses or razed for tenements. In addition to Italian, German, Irish, and Jewish immigrants, many of whom worked in the slaughterhouses near the present United Nations complex, the area attracted the city's night people: actors, musicians, stagehands, and waiters who worked in the restaurants near Broadway.

The resurgence of Turtle Bay began around the end of World War I with the development of Turtle Bay Gardens, the renovation of individual brownstones, and the greening of Sutton Place and Beekman Hill which began to attract such literary and theatrical people as Alfred Lunt and Lynn Fontanne, the Barrymores, Helen Hopkinson, Henry Luce, Irving Berlin, Billy Rose, and Humphrey Bogart. But only after the coming of the U.N. in 1947 were the cattle pens, slaughterhouses, breweries, and coal yards that had followed the opening of the Els dislodged from the shoreline.

Today Turtle Bay is one of the city's more genteel residential neighborhoods, its gracious brownstones and luxury high rises attracting diplomats, the affluent young, and a few celebrities.

Begin at First Ave and 43rd St. The 18 acres of ****United Nations Headquarters** at United Nations Plaza (1st Ave bet. 42nd / 48th Sts) are not part of New York City, not even part of the U. S., but belong as international territory to the member nations of the United Nations. Built (1947–53) to serve as headquarters of an organization of sovereign nations whose primary purpose is maintaining world peace, the U.N. annually attracts about a million visitors who tour its buildings and are informed of its workings.

The United Nations Headquarters. First Ave at 46th St, New York 10017. Tel: 963-7713. Buildings open weekdays 9–5; Sat, Sun, and holidays 9:15–5. Visitors must pass through electronic metal detectors. Tours in English and other languages leave from the Tour Desk in the Secretariat Building, 9:15–4:45 daily; admission charge. Children under 12 must be accompanied by an adult; children under five are not permitted on the tours. For groups larger than 15 people, call 963-4440. Tickets to General Assembly and Council sessions available free at Information desk in lobby shortly before meeting times (usually 10:30 A.M. and 3:30 P.M.).

Delegates' dining room on second floor of the General Assembly Building, open to the public from 11:30–2:30; inquire at the Information Desk for a pass; reservations suggested; call 963-7625. Coffee shop (open 9–4:30), telephones, post office, and restrooms on basement level of General Assembly Building. Large, well-stocked gift shop with many unusual handcrafted items from all over the world. Complete wheelchair access including ramps (at entrance gate on N. side of steps), elevators, restrooms, and telephones.

History. Soon after the signing of the United Nations Charter (1945), the General Assembly moved to locate the U.N. permanent headquarters in the United States. On December 11, 1946, John D. Rockefeller, Jr., offered $8.5 million to buy a large parcel of land on the East River assembled by William Zeckendorf, a real estate operator who had obtained an option to buy it for private development. With unusual rapidity Congress accepted the gift and exempted it from the usual taxes while the city agreed to contribute adjacent properties. A plan by Zeckendorf to condemn everything east of Third Ave between 46th and 49th Sts, including Turtle Bay Gardens and other areas just emerging from urban decay, was discarded in favor of a scheme sponsored by Robert Moses to widen 47th St between First and Second Aves and to route First Ave beneath United Nations Plaza in a tunnel.

The buildings were designed by an international committee of architects headed by Wallace K. Harrison, whose ties with the Rockefeller family went back to the building of Rockefeller Center.

EXTERIOR. On the W. side of the street opposite the fountain is RALPH J. BUNCHE PARK whose centerpiece is a steel sculpture, *Peace Form One* (1972–80) by Daniel Larue Johnston, near which is inscribed a quotation from Bunche's acceptance of the Nobel Peace Prize. On the wall to the N. is inscribed the verse from Isaiah 2:4 beginning "They shall beat their swords into plough shares. . ."

Across the avenue stand the U.N. buildings prefaced by a row of flags representing the member nations (arranged in alphabetical order). From left to right (N. to S.) the buildings are: the General Assembly Building with a curving roof from which protrudes the dome covering the assembly hall, the Secretariat Building, and the Dag Hammarskjöld Library. Behind the General Assembly Building, but not visible from the street, is the Conference Building. In a circular pool in front of the Secretariat is a bronze sculptural abstraction, *Single Form* (1964), 21 ft high, by Barbara Hepworth, placed there to honor Dag Hammarskjöld, secretary-general of the U.N. killed (1961) in a plane crash on a peace mission in the Congo (now Zaire). Commissioned by the U.N. (1963) of a sculptor whose art Hammarskjöld admired and collected, the work was cast in six sections whose outlines still remain.

Adjacent to the entrance to the Secretariat Building is a bronze *Reclining Figure* (1980) by Henry Moore, another memorial to Hammarskjöld who had expressed hope to the sculptor that one of his works would one day join the U.N. collection.

When built, the **Secretariat Building** seemed a daring piece of architecture, a 544-ft slab (287 ft wide and 72 ft thick) with white marble end walls and side walls of green glass set in an aluminum grid. Its long east-west exposure created air-conditioning problems that led critic Henry Russell-Hitchcock to predict, erroneously, the demise of glass-walled skyscrapers unless their western facades were shielded from the sun. Le Corbusier established the original design of the complex: a tall slab with offices for the bureaucracy, a low horizontal building for conferences, and a functionally shaped though imposing assembly building, all to be set on a landscaped site, a scheme, according to Lewis Mumford, that demonstrated architecturally that "bureaucracy ruled the world." When Le Corbusier withdrew, Wallace K. Harrison became responsible for implementing the details of the project.

Enter the VISITORS' ENTRANCE along the N. side of the General Assembly Building near 46th St. The seven nickel-bronze entrance doors were donated by Canada and their bas relief panels symbolize peace, justice, truth, and fraternity.

INTERIOR. At the left or E. end of the lobby is a mural, *Brotherhood* (1968; Rufino Tamayo, the gift of Mexico. In front of it is a bronze cast of the famous 5C (B.C.) *Poseidon* of Artemision, gift (1952) of Greece: the original is in the National Museum of

Athens. Overhead is a replica of the first *Sputnik,* launched in 1957, gift of the U.S.S.R. Hanging over the curve in the stairway is a *Foucault pendulum,* gift (1955) of the Netherlands.

In the center of the lobby is the INFORMATION DESK; apply there for tickets to any public sessions or for passes to the Delegates' Dining Room.

Near the stairway arch is a case containing a gift of the U.S., a moon rock, collected on the Apollo 14 mission (1971), man's first landing on the moon. Against the west wall is the DAG HAMMARSKJÖLD MEMORIAL CHAPEL with a stained glass memorial window on themes of Man and Peace donated by the artist, Marc Chagall. The chapel also honors other U.N. workers—soldiers, observers, and diplomats—who died in the performance of their duties. A door on the S. wall of the chapel opens into the MEDITATION ROOM (ask the guard for admission) with an abstract fresco by Swedish artist Bo Beskow and a 6-ton polished block of Swedish iron ore.

Walk through the lobby beyond the Information Desk to the TOUR DESK to purchase tickets. The tours last about an hour and are offered in several languages. For information about tours tel· 963-7713.

Leave the General Assembly and walk across the concrete plaza to the river and the ***Public Gardens.** On the paved VISITORS' PLAZA is a stainless steel sculpture by Eila Hiltunen (1983) a study for part of a monument celebrating the composer Jean Sibelius, the gift of Finland. Across the lawn to the N. is a 16-ft bronze equestrian *Monument to Peace* (1954; Antun Augustinčić) given by Yugoslavia.

Walk down the stairs past the flagpole; on the lawn near the river is Evgeny Vuchetich's bronze statue, *We Shall Beat Our Swords Into Plowshares* (1958; presented 1959), a gift of the U.S.S.R. The rose garden runs between the river promenade and the E. wall of the General Assembly Building, on which there is an abstract relief sculpture (1961) by Ezio Martinelli.

From the promenade are good ***views of the East River,** including the decaying hospitals on the S. tip of Roosevelt Island, the Queensboro Bridge to the N., and the Williamsburg Bridge to the south. The small island, with a tree, a navigational marker, a little shrubbery, and a metal peace arch south of Roosevelt Island is now called U-Thant Island, after one of the secretaries general of the U.N.; it was formerly Belmont Island, named for August Belmont, a power behind the original IRT subway line. The island is man-made, built up of material excavated from the tunnel that now carries the IRT Flushing line subway beneath the river. To the E. is the industrial architecture of Queens.

Walk N. along the promenade. The stainless steel sculpture on the N. part of the lawn, *Roots and Ties for Peace* (1983) by Yolanda d'Augsburg Ulm, was presented by Brazil. In the wooded area just N. of the lawn are (E. to W.): a memorial to Eleanor Roosevelt, a bronze statue entitled *The Rising Man* (1975; Fritz Cremer), gift of the German Democratic Republic, and a bronze

bust of Francisco de Vitoria (1976; Francisco Toledo), a 16C
Spanish Dominican theologian.

Cross U.N. Plaza to the N.W. corner of 44th St. Here stands ONE
UNITED NATIONS PLAZA (1976; Kevin Roche, John Dinkeloo &
Assocs.), a 39-story, glass-walled building providing office space
for the U.N. and a hotel for delegates and others. Because the
U.N. Development Corporation which built it has a charter forbidding the construction of any building taller than the Secretariat,
this one stops at 505 ft. The mirrored, greenish glass facade,
which conceals floor divisions and the distinction between wall
and window, has been much admired as has the decor of the
hotel lobby (enter on 44th St), executed in chrome, mirrored
glass, and marble. Those visitors anxious about their personal
safety may bypass the lobby altogether by having their limousines driven into an enclosed entranceway and alighting by the
elevator banks.

TWO UNITED NATIONS PLAZA (1983; Kevin Roche, John
Dinkeloo & Assocs.), another larger glass and metal tower, now
adjoins its predecessor to the W. along 44th St, making an
abstract formal composition that dominates the neighborhood
skyline. On the S. side of 44th St at 3 United Nations Plaza, the
UNICEF Building (l987; Kevin Roche, John Dinkeloo & Assocs.)
completes the trio. Unlike the two earlier buildings, this one, only
18 stories high slips unobtrusively into its surroundings. It is
faced with light and dark granite that reflects the facade of the
Beaux-Arts Apartments (1930; Murchison and Hood, Godley &
Fouilhoux; DL) next door.

The intersection of First Ave and E. 45th St has been renamed
Allard Lowenstein Square. The **United States Mission to the
United Nations** (1961; Kelly & Gruzen and Kahn & Jacobs) faces
U.N. Plaza on the S.W. corner of 45th St (799 U.N. Plaza), like
some other U.N. missions, surrounded by tight security. Just
visible behind the brick wall in the courtyard is a statue *Offering
of the Sacred Pipe* (1985; Allan Houser), a 7-ft bronze figure of
an Indian raising skyward a peace pipe. The sculptor was a
Chiricahua Apache.

Next door is *Uganda House* at 336 E. 45th St, built (1977)
during the regime of Field Marshall Idi Amin. Its 14-story height
was said at the time to be a deliberate attempt to overshadow
the U.S. Mission to the E. as an expression of Amin's outrage at
American denunciations of his policies. The U.S. retaliated architecturally by installing a flagpole atop the mission. When Amin
fell, the new team of Ugandan delegates discovered an elaborate
system of electronic listening devices in the walls and hidden
behind curtains. Then in 1980, when a neighboring garage was
razed in preparation for the 40-story tower at Two United Nations
Plaza, it came to light that Uganda House had no outside wall
below the fifth floor on its W. side; its insulation was attached
directly to the garage, a circumvention of the building code
possible because Uganda as a foreign government was not required
to have the city approve the building plans.

Continue N. on First Ave. The W. side of the avenue from

42nd–49th Sts was renamed (1985) *Raoul Wallenberg Walk* to honor the Swedish diplomat who saved thousands of Hungarian Jews from the Nazis during World War II. The widened section of 47th St, *Hammarskjöld Plaza,* sometimes holds a small flower market.

Down E. 47th St to the W., between First and Second Aves is **Japan House** (1971; Junzo Yoshimura and Gruzen & Partners). Designed by a Tokyo architect in a typically Japanese style, but using primarily American building materials, Japan House is the headquarters of the Japan Society, founded in 1907 to promote better understanding through cultural exchange. On the second floor is a gallery with exhibitions on Japanese life and culture.

Japan House Gallery. 333 E. 47th Street, New York 10017. Tel: 832-1155. Open during exhibitions Sat–Thurs 11–5; Fri 11–7:30. Closed major holidays. Suggested donation.

   Lectures, tours by appointment. Catalogues, posters, postcards; no restaurant. Restrooms and public telephones in basement. Accessible to wheelchairs.

Along with the exhibitions, some of the most beautifully mounted in the city, Japan House sponsors such activities as film showings, poetry readings, craft demonstrations, kabuki and No theater, and discussions on economic and social problems common to the two countries.

Continue W. to Second Ave. Walk N. to 48th St. In the block between Second and Third Aves is the former WILLIAM LESCAZE RESIDENCE at 211 E. 48th St, which began as an ordinary 19C brownstone but was aggressively transformed (1934; DL) by architect William Lescaze into an advertisement for himself and a preeminent example in the city of the International Style. Used as both a home and a studio for himself, the building made dramatic use of glass block, a trademark of Lescaze's style. The facade, pushed forward to the building line, is covered with smooth gray stucco (originally white), has industrial tubular railings instead of the familiar iron balustrades, and is especially brilliant when illuminated at night. In its day the house caused such a stir that for a while Lescaze and his wife set aside an hour on Mondays for public visitation.

At 227–247 E. 48th St and 226–246 E. 49th St (bet. 2nd / 3rd Aves) is the **Turtle Bay Gardens Historic District** (remodeled 1920; William L. Bottomley and Edward C. Dean), two rows of ten houses each, back to back with a common garden inside the block. Mrs. Walton Martin in 1919–20, inspired by houses with shared gardens in France and Italy, bought the houses and, with architect Dean, tore down the back fences, filled in the swampy areas, shaved 6 ft off each back yard to create a common garden, and redesigned the houses so that they faced inward to the garden, where she placed a replica of the fountain at the entrance of the Villa Medici in Rome. The gardens have attracted such famous residents as Judge Learned Hand, Leopold Stokowski, Katharine Hepburn, Mary Martin, Tyrone Power, and Stephen Sondheim. To essayist E. B. White, who lived there, an old willow tree in the garden symbolized the city, life surviving difficulties, growth against odds.

Walk around the block to 49th St (bet. 2nd / 3rd Aves). AMS-
TER YARD at 211–215 E. 49th St (1870; remodeled 1945; Harold
Sterner) is another enclave, also almost entirely secluded from
the street. Originally the yard (enter through an arcade on 49th
St) held a group of workshops and small houses built on the site
of what may have been the terminal stop of the Boston-New York
stagecoach route along the Boston Post Road. After the Second
Ave El was demolished in 1942, James Amster, a designer,
bought the property and developed it into an attractive group of
shops, apartments, and offices, around a central courtyard.

At 225–227 E. 49th St is the former *Efrem Zimbalist House*
(1926), home of the violinist; his wife, diva Alma Gluck; and her
daughter, novelist Marcia Davenport. The cartouche over the
door bears a violin, a staff with some unidentified musical theme,
and an open-mouthed cherub. Later Henry Luce of Time-Life Inc.
lived here, but between 1957–60 the house became the 17th
Precinct Police Station House, its paneling and artistic interiors
ripped out in favor of institutional iron stairways and bilious
green paint. Nowadays it is divided into apartments.

Return to First Ave and walk N. to *Mitchell Place* at 49th St on
the E. side of the avenue. At the N.E. corner of the intersection
stands the former Panhellenic Tower (1928; John Mead Howells),
once a residence and clubhouse for women college graduates,
now converted to the BEEKMAN TOWER APARTMENTS. William Mitchell, whose name this small street bears, was a distinguished 19C jurist, who served as a member of the state Court
of Appeals and as presiding justice on the State Supreme Court.

Walk along Mitchell Place to Beekman Place. The small park
on the S. side of Mitchell Place is called *General Douglas Mac-
Arthur Plaza*, named after the controversial general who fought
in Europe during World War I, led the allied forces in the Pacific
during World War II, and finally commanded the U.N. forces in
Korea, a post from which he was relieved by President Harry S.
Truman for disobeying (Truman's) orders.

Walk N. to 51st St along **Beekman Place.** Named after the
Beekman family, the street runs only two blocks but its location
on a high bluff overlooking the river and its history of controlled
development (no slaughterhouses here) by the Beekmans have
made it a socially desirable enclave since the 18C, except for a
brief period in the early 20C when immigrants seeking work at
the nearby slaughterhouses lived here. The neighborhood began
to turn around in the 1920s when Alfred Lunt and Lynn Fontanne
moved here. Among those who have lived here are John D.
Rockefeller III, Irving Berlin, Gloria Vanderbilt, and Rex Harrison.

The Beekman mansion Mount Pleasant (built 1765) stood near the river at
about 51st St, and for a while during the Revolution served as British headquarters. In 1783 James Beekman got his house back and here entertained
American officers and staff entering New York on Evacuation Day in the
drawing room, with punch made with lemons plucked from trees growing in
the greenhouse. A cholera epidemic apparently drove away the Beekman family
who lived there until 1854, and in 1874 the house was demolished.

At 51st St descend the steps which lead to a footbridge across the Franklin D. Roosevelt Drive and go N. along the walkway next to the drive. One of the more imposing prominences overlooking the water is **River House** (1931; Bottomley, Wagner & White) at 433–437 E. 52nd St (E. of 1st Ave). Completed the same year as the George Washington Bridge, the Empire State Building, and the Waldorf-Astoria Hotel, River House quickly became synonymous with privilege and wealth. The apartments in the tower were built on two or three floors with as many as 17 rooms (one had nine bathrooms), while those in the body of the building were only slightly more modest. Tennis courts, a swimming pool, and a dock for yachts added to the comfort and convenience of such tenants as Marshall Field and William Rhinelander Stewart. Today the pool and courts are administered by the River Club, but the building retains its reputation for exclusivity.

The serenity of the setting was disturbed somewhat by the arrival of the **Franklin D. Roosevelt Drive,** begun downtown in 1936 and completed after World War II as a major artery linking the city with outlying highways. Much of the landfill used for the roadbed is rubble from the London Blitz, brought back as ballast in returning American ships.

In 1821 someone named Youle built a shot tower near 53rd St at the river, which after falling down and being rebuilt served as a landmark for some 40 years. *Cannon Point,* as the area was known, is now only a few rocks in the river near 52nd St.

Cross back over the F.D.R. Drive to **Sutton Place,** formerly and less glamorously known as Avenue A. It was renamed after one Effingham B. Sutton, a dry goods merchant who developed the area around 1875 with a fortune he had made in the California gold rush of 1849, not by striking the mother lode but by selling picks, shovels, and provisions to prospectors who hoped to do so. His venture with Sutton Place was timed about 50 years too soon, and the street remained modest until Anne Morgan, daughter of J. P. Morgan, and Mrs. William K. Vanderbilt (Anne Harriman) arrived in 1921. The S. part of the street, now lined with attractive apartment houses, was a later extension and is called Sutton Place South (53rd to 57th Sts). *No. 1 Sutton Place South* (1927; Cross & Cross, with Rosario Candela) vies with River House as one of the city's premier apartments. SUTTON SQUARE, the block between 57th and 58th Sts, has a group of town houses sharing a common back garden, hence the name. At the foot of 57th St is a small park with a replica of the boar, *Il Porcellino,* in the Straw Market in Florence. The sculptor Pietro Tacca made three copies altogether—the one in Florence, this one, and another said to be in Country Club Plaza in Kansas City. The model for all three, itself a copy of a Hellenistic original, is in the Uffizi Gallery in Florence. On the N. side of 57th St abutting the park (1 Sutton Place) is the neo-Georgian town house built (1921; Mott B. Schmidt), for Mrs. William K. Vanderbilt. No. 3 Sutton

Place (1921; Mott B. Schmidt), originally the home of Anne Morgan, now is the residence of the secretary-general of the U.N.

At 58th St E. of Sutton Place is another small park and N. of it, parallel to the river, a small, cobbled, private street, RIVERVIEW TERRACE, with five 19C houses looking out from the top of the ridge.

From the end of 58th St is a fine view of the **Queensboro Bridge** (1909; Gustav Lindenthal, engineer; Palmer & Hornbostel, architects), which joins Long Island City in Queens with 59th St in Manhattan. As early as 1852 some of Long Island City's most powerful families—Steinways and Pratts for example—began agitating for a bridge, an enterprise furthered by Long Island Railroad tycoon Austin Corbin and later by a Dr. Thomas Rainey, who foresaw the bridge as an aid to tourism, freight handling, and the funeral business (there were 15 cemeteries on Long Island at the time). Political and financial problems delayed its construction for some 40 years and the collapse of another partially built cantilever bridge, the Quebec Bridge, called in doubt the safety of this one. An alleged engineer vouched for it saying that in his 20 years of experience he had never seen so many birds gathering on a bridge as on the Queensboro, a remark based on the superstition that large numbers of birds will only roost on a soundly engineered structure. Less whimsical was designer Lindenthal who reduced the number of elevated tracks crossing it and removed some deadload, which may have been added to pad the profits of the steel supplier. This extra steel may also have accounted for architect Hornbostel's outcry, "My God—it's a blacksmith's shop!" when he first saw the completed superstructure. Today, however, the bridge is generally admired for its intricate mesh of steelwork and its handsome ornaments, including the finials on top.

The span is 1182 ft long and 135 ft above mean high water. About 50,000 tons of steel were used in construction at a cost of $20.8 million. Bicycle riders and pedestrians can still cross the bridge but can no longer descend to Roosevelt Island, though once a building with an entrance lobby on the eighth floor and elevators down to the ground provided access from Manhattan. Beneath the Manhattan approach to the bridge are handsome vaults with high Guastavino-tiled arches now being restored as **Bridgemarket,** for meat, fish, and produce, imported specialty items (chocolates, truffles, caviar), and prepared food. Rafael Guastavino designed the space in 1909 and it was used as a food market from 1914 to the 1930s, when it was closed during the Depression.

Walk N. on First Ave and turn right on 61st St. Halfway down the block between First and York Aves, is the **Abigail Adams Smith Museum** (1799; DL).

Abigail Adams Smith Museum. 421 E. 61st Street (bet. 1st / York Aves), New York 10021. Tel: 838-6878. Open Mon–Fri 10–4; closed weekends, holidays, and month of August; admission by tax-deductible contribution.

Tours, lectures. No restaurant, no telephone. Restrooms. Small gift shop. Not accessible to wheelchairs.

The Abigail Adams Smith Museum, almost in the shadow of the Queensboro Bridge, is a fortunate survivor from the early years of the American republic. It was built as a carriage house for Col. William Stephens Smith and his wife, Abigail Adams Smith, daughter of President John Adams, and after gradually declining in fortune through the years was saved by the Colonial Dames of America, who now operate it as a museum. Set on a half acre of landscaped grounds, the house has been painstakingly restored and refurnished with period furniture (1800–30) predominantly in the Federal style.

History. In 1795 Col. Smith bought 23 acres from the Van Zandt family, on which he planned a mansion to be called Mount Vernon in honor of George Washington, his commander during the Revolutionary War. Unfortunately, Smith got into financial difficulties and had to sell this property which was known locally through most of the 19C as "Smith's Folly." In 1798 William T. Robinson bought it and completed what is now the museum building as a stable and coach house and the mansion as his residence. Later the mansion became the Mount Vernon Hotel, known for its turtle soup, and even later, a female academy, which was destroyed by fire in 1926.

The stable, meanwhile, was converted to another hotel, also known as the Mount Vernon. From 1833 to 1905 it belonged to the Towle family, who sold it to the Standard Gas Light Co. The gas company built three large tanks behind it, used the house as office space, and generally let it fall into disrepair.

In 1919 Jane Teller rented and restored it, for an antique shop displaying a collection of early American furniture. The Colonial Dames of America bought it five years later, furnished it, and opened it to the public.

Walk N. on York Ave. Between 62nd and 68th Sts on the E. side of the avenue is **Rockefeller University,** founded (1901) as Rockefeller Institute for Medical Research (name changed in 1965). The campus occupies the site of the former Schermerhorn family summer estate which still had its original farmhouse when John D. Rockefeller, Sr. bought the property. Today the university, small and prestigious, is dedicated to advanced education and research in the biomedical sciences. (The grounds are not open to the public.)

University scientists have earned 16 Nobel Prizes, seven since 1972, and more than half of the full professors have been elected to membership in the National Academy of Sciences. The 40-bed hospital (established in 1910) was the first in the country devoted exclusively to clinical research. Today more than 30 diseases are under investigation, mainly those for which there is no satisfactory prevention or cure. Among the achievements by university scientists were the first demonstration that animal cancer can be caused by a virus, the first demonstration that DNA is the substance that transmits hereditary information, and the first isolation and successful tests of antibiotics. One of its most far-reaching innovations, though not recognized as such at the time, was the development of a way to preserve whole blood, making possible the blood banks of today. In addition, Rockefeller scientists have made basic discoveries and technical advances that resulted in the development of the modern science of cell biology and have pioneered studies on the role of cholesterol in the body's metabolism.

N. of Rockefeller University between 68th and 70th Sts is the **New York Hospital-Cornell University Medical College** (1932; Coolidge, Shepley, Bulfinch & Abbott), a 6.4-acre complex for patient care, research, and teaching, occupying 11 buildings and having 45 acres of floor space and five miles of corridors. The MAIN BUILDING of glazed white brick constructed in Art Deco Gothic has been much admired for its skillful massing and spartan use of detail. At the time of completion it was also widely admired for its technical advances (air conditioning, X-ray machines, and shadowless lights in the operating rooms) and for the humane quality of its interior design—the small wards subdivided by glass partitions into four-bed sections, lounges overlooking the East River, and the noninstitutional use of color in corridors and pavilions.

History. The city's oldest, New York Hospital was founded under a charter from King George III in 1771 as a hospital for the poor and, incidentally, as a medical school. During the Revolution it was used for British and Hessian soldiers but was not reopened to the public until 1791. In 1877 a new 200-bed hospital was built on W. 15th St near Fifth Ave with such technological advances as steam heat and artificial ventilation. The present hospital (1350 beds) was built after the New York Hospital-Cornell Medical College Association was formed (1927) with donations of some $27 million by Payne Whitney, J. Pierpont Morgan, the Rockefellers, and others. In 1938 more than 100 anonymous donors gave an additional $1000 for removing from the 325-ft chimneys the swastika designs, which had acquired sinister connotations with the rise of Hitler, and replacing them with the present Greek crosses.

Today the New York Hospital-Cornell University Medical Center is also affiliated with the Hospital for Special Surgery (535 E. 70th St at York Ave), and the Memorial Sloan-Kettering Cancer Center (1275 York Ave at 68th St), as well as other institutions outside the immediate neighborhood.

17 Rockefeller Center

SUBWAY: IRT Broadway-7th Ave local (train 1 or 9) to 50th St. IRT Lexington Ave local (train 6) to 51st St. IND 6th Ave (B, D, or F train) to 47th–50th Sts-Rockefeller Center. BMT Broadway express (N train) or Broadway local (R train) to 49th St.

BUS: M1, M2, M3, M4, M5, M6, M7, M27, M32.

TOURS: NBC Studio Tours include visits to sets and control rooms; for information and schedule, tel: 664-4000. For tours of Radio City Music Hall, see p. 356.

**Rockefeller Center is a complex of 19 commercial buildings, theaters, plazas, streets, underground pedestrian passageways, and shops located on almost 22 acres of land W. of Fifth Ave in midtown Manhattan. It is the world's largest privately owned business and entertainment center, the first architecturally coordinated development in New York City, a major tourist attraction, and a financially successful venture which maintains high aesthetic standards. More than 240,000 people—including visitors and workers—use it daily (only 57 U.S. cities have a larger population); more than 240 million patrons have paid admission to Radio City Music Hall, the center's great theater. John D. Rockefeller, Jr. (1874–1960), one of America's richest men, built the center, which until 1989 remained in the hands of his heirs who controlled the stock of Rockefeller Center, Inc., the corporation that developed and still maintains the property.

History. In 1927 the Metropolitan Opera, seeking to replace its cramped and outmoded house on Broadway and 40th St became interested in some land owned by Columbia University. The land—about 12 acres between Fifth and Sixth Aves, 48th and 51st Sts—had blossomed briefly between 1801–11 as the Elgin Botanic Garden but now held speakeasies, rooming houses, and brothels. The opera company approached Rockefeller as a possible benefactor, hoping he might donate land for a plaza in front of the new opera house. Rockefeller in turn began exploring the possibilities of leasing the land himself, making the central portion available to the opera, and then subleasing the rest to commercial interests who would construct their own buildings. Since property experts led him to believe that he could realize as much as $5.5 million dollars annually on the property, he entered into negotiations with the trustees of Columbia University, signing a contract in October 1928 to lease the property for a 24-year period with renewal options to 2019, later extended to 2069. Then the stock market crashed (1929), the Metropolitan Opera Co. abruptly dropped its plans for a new house, and Rockefeller was left holding a lease under which he owed more than $3.8 million a year on property that brought in only about $300,000.

Rockefeller's only real choice, since even he could ill afford a $2 million annual deficit, was to develop the property without the opera house. He directed his planners to design a commercial center "as beautiful as possible consistent with maximum income," and work began on the city's first integrated commercial center, where skyscrapers could be planned in relation to one another with due consideration of open space, light, and traffic control. Largely responsible for the early project were real estate developers Todd, Robertson & Todd, and three principal architectural firms, Reinhard & Hofmeister; Corbett, Harrison, and MacMurray; and Hood & Fouilhoux (before 1931, Hood, Godley & Fouilhoux), who worked under the name of The Associated Architects, making it nowadays impossible to assign specific credit for individual buildings in the original development.

Between 1931 and 1940, 14 buildings were constructed, 228 were demolished to make way for them; 4000 tenants were relocated; and 75,000 workers found jobs on the site during the depths of the Depression. Although Rockefeller drove the "last" rivet in the "last" building, the United States Rubber Co. Building, in 1939, development continued after World War II, when the Warner Communications (formerly Esso) Building pushed the center beyond its original boundaries. During the 1950s and 1960s, Rockefeller Center expanded W. to Sixth Ave replacing a neighborhood of nondescript low buildings and small business tenants with a group of stiff, ponderous office towers which express more than anything the affluence of their corporate tenants.

In 1985 Columbia University sold the land it owned under the center to the Rockefeller Group for $400 million, the largest price ever paid for a single parcel of real estate in the city. On the plot, 11.7 acres, sit Radio City Music Hall, the skating rink, the RCA Building, and the other buildings of the original development.

The most dramatic approach to Rockefeller Center is from Fifth Ave between 49th and 50th Sts. Flanking a central promenade are two low buildings, the BRITISH BUILDING (completed 1933; DL) on the N. and LA MAISON FRANÇAISE (1933; DL) on the S., buildings whose modest scale reflects an earlier and more gracious Fifth Ave. By placing these low structures on the avenue, the developers gained rights to build a large tower (the RCA Building) in the center of the block, simultaneously preserving neighborhood property values by leaving the side streets unshadowed.

Over the main entrance of the British Building (formerly the British Empire Building) is a bronze panel (1933) by Carl Paul Jennewein (born 1890), whose figures represent nine major industries of the British Commonwealth; at the bottom is a bronze sun, symbolic of the empire on which the sun never set. Above the panel is a cartouche with the British coat of arms and the mottoes of British royalty and the Order of the Garter.

Cross the Promenade to La Maison Française. A bronze strip in the sidewalk near the building line at the entrance to the Promenade marks the boundary of the property formerly belonging to Columbia University. Over the main door of La Maison Française is another bronze panel (1934). Designed by Alfred Janniot (born 1889), it depicts Paris and New York joining hands above figures representing Poetry, Beauty, and Elegance. Inscribed on a ribbon behind the figure of Paris is that city's motto: "Fluctuat nec mergitur" ("It is tossed by waves but does not sink"). Above the panel soars an Art Deco version of the traditional symbol of France, a woman holding the flaming torch of liberty; beneath her is the motto of the French Republic: "Liberté, Égalité, Fraternité."

Enter the Promenade, popularly known as the ***Channel Gardens** (1933; DL), because it separates the British and French buildings; the walkway (60 ft wide and 200 ft long) is embellished with granite pools, seasonal floral displays, and fountains. The bronze fountain heads (1935), designed by René Chambellan, represent tritons and nereids riding dolphins; they symbolize (E. to W.): leadership, will, thought, imagination, energy, and alertness—qualities chosen as those contributing to human progress.

Most of the themes of the center's artwork were chosen by Prof. Hartley Burr Alexander of the University of Southern California, hired to impose thematic unity on the whole development. His original suggestion for an overall theme was "Homo fabor" ("Man the Maker"), a subject that was modified to "New Frontiers and the March of Civilization."

At the N.W. corner of the Promenade is *Nikon House* (620 Fifth Ave), a photographic showroom and gallery which mounts individual and group shows (open Mon–Fri 10–5; tel: 586-3907).

The Promenade opens into the LOWER PLAZA (DL), dominated by an 18-ft figure of Prometheus, designed by Paul Manship (1885–1966) and installed in 1934. The 8-ton gilded bronze statue rests on a pedestal shaped like a mountain peak and encircled by a ring containing the signs of the zodiac. On the red granite wall behind is a quotation from Aeschylus: "Prometheus, teacher in every art, brought the fire that hath proved to mortals a means to mighty ends." Behind the statue 50 jets of water form a summer backdrop for an electronically controlled lighting display (nightfall to 1 A.M.). During the Christmas season, a large tree is installed on the sidewalk behind the plaza and illuminated by thousands of lights, accounting in large part for the spectacular crowds who pack the area during the holidays. During the summer, the sunken plaza becomes an outdoor cafe; during the winter it is flooded and used as an ice rink.

At the top of the stairway leading to the lower level is a commemorative plaque inscribed with John D. Rockefeller, Jr.'s personal credo.

Cross ROCKEFELLER PLAZA, the street separating the Lower Plaza from the RCA Building. The idea of breaking up the long east-west block with a private street was one of the happy inspirations of the developers. Rockefeller Plaza remains one of the few private streets in the city and is closed to all traffic, vehicular and pedestrian, once a year, usually a Sunday in July, to preserve its private status.

The most famous and imposing building at Rockefeller Center is the **RCA Building** (1933; DL), directly W. of Rockefeller Plaza. The building (70 stories, 850 ft) once had the largest gross floor area of any commercial structure in the world, a dubious distinction. Roughly rectangular with its thin edge facing east-west and a broad, slablike wall on the N. and S., it owes its disproportionate length to Rockefeller's desire to include within its perimeter some potentially unprofitable lots he owned on Sixth Ave, still overhung by the elevated railway. Skillfully designed setbacks give the building the impression of soaring height. Receding wings flank the main rectangle and an 11-story wraparound structure houses the National Broadcasting Company studios, constructed free from the rest of the building to minimize vibrations.

When the Metropolitan Opera decided not to build at Rockefeller Center, architect Raymond Hood proposed that the Radio Corporation of America (RCA), still prospering during the stagnation of the Depression, be invited to replace the opera company as the center's major tenant. For years most of the radio programs of NBC, a subsidiary of RCA, were produced here, and Rockfeller Center was known popularly as Radio City.

EXTERIOR. Over the E. entrance is a stone relief by Lee Lawrie (1877–1963), whose subject is "Wisdom, which Interprets to the Human Race the Laws and Cycles of the Cosmic Forces of the Universe. Making the Cycles of Light and Sound." Wisdom, a giant with a remarkable Art Deco beard, spreads a compass above a glass screen made of 240 blocks of glass, cast in relief in 84 different molds. Only when the work was well underway did the art committee notice the embarrassing similarity between Lawrie's work and William Blake's frontispiece to *Europe: A Prophecy* (1794).

Flanking the 49th St entrance are two limestone pylons with sculptures by Leo Friedlander (1890–1966) representing "Transmission Receiving an Image of Dancers and Flashing It Through the Ether by Means of Television to Reception, Symbolized by Mother Earth and Her Child, Man." At the 50th St entrance two more pylons, also sculpted by Friedlander, represent "Transmission Receiving Music and Flashing It Through the Ether by Means of Radio to Reception." Rockefeller found these works "gross and unbeautiful," an opinion with which critics generally concur.

INTERIOR. Directly in front of the main entrance is a large mural by José Maria Sert (1876–1945), originally entitled "Triumph of Man's Accomplishments Through Physical and Mental Labor," now called "American Progress." Sert's moralistic painting (1937) is renowned primarily for what it replaces, the controversial Diego Rivera fresco destroyed by the Rockefellers.

Commissioned to paint a mural illustrating the theme "man's new possibilities from his new understanding of material things," Rivera submitted a sketch acceptable to the patrons and then produced a fresco which included a portrait of Lenin, a crowd of workers carrying red flags near Lenin's tomb, and a scene of rich people playing cards with venereal disease germs hovering over them. When asked to substitute another face for Lenin's, Rivera replied that he would prefer the destruction of the painting, at least preserving its integrity. The fresco remained shrouded in canvas during opening ceremonies, but eventually the Rockefellers had it destroyed. In the recriminations that followed, cowboy humorist and sage Will Rogers made one of his most famous *bons mots,* advising Rivera that he "should never try to fool a Rockefeller in oils."

The ceiling painting, again by Sert, is entitled "Time," while the murals against the elevator banks in the N. and S. corridors by Sert and Frank Brangwyn (1867–1956) illustrate themes of progress against such obstacles as disease, slavery, and crushing physical labor.

Continue down the N. corridor to the elevator banks, containing the first high-speed elevators in New York City. The last row of cars contains the elevators to the Rainbow Room on the 65th floor. The nightclub opened in 1934, the first dining spot atop a skyscraper, and was through the years celebrated for its view and handsome trappings. Noel Coward, Cole Porter, and Elsa Maxwell came on opening day, to be followed through the years by the great dance bands of the 30s and 40s—Duke Ellington, Glen Gray, and Ray Noble. Built as a two-story cylinder with no internal columns and called the Stratosphere Club, the place was renamed the Rainbow Room for its color organ that threw colored lights corresponding to musical pitches on the domed ceiling. It reopened in 1987, redesigned by Hardy Holzman Pfeiffer Assocs. with furniture that includes Art Deco pieces by Donald Deskey (see p. 356). Open for cocktails and dining. For reservations call 632-5000. Dress code.

Return to the main corridor. Stairways behind the elevator banks lead down to the Concourse, with more than two miles of underground passageways lined with shops, services, and restaurants. Also underground are ten large trucking ramps and loading docks which, along with facilities located beneath the new office towers on the Ave of the Americas take an estimated 700–1000 trucks off the city streets daily.

Continue through the main ground floor corridor to the Ave of the Americas entrance. Less opulently decorated than the E. facade, it features a glass mosaic by Barry Faulkner (1881–1966) made of about one million pieces of colored glass and is entitled "Intelligence Awakening Mankind." Four limestone panels by Gaston Lachaise (1882–1935) on the W. facade depict: "Genius Seizing the Light of the Sun," "Conquest of Space," "Gifts of Earth to Mankind," and "Understanding—Spirit of Progress."

Across the Ave of the Americas from the RCA Building loom the four newest additions to the center. Architectural critics have found them sadly wanting in comparison to the original development, charging that they lack sympathetic human scale, that they have driven small businesses from the area, that their plazas—cold and ill-planned—compete with one another, and that their use of modern technology has allowed them to contain maximum permissible space at the expense of light, air, and human values.

The southernmost of these towers, the CELANESE BUILDING (1973; Harrison, Abramovitz & Harris) occupies the block between 47th and 48th Sts. Like its companions, it is a slab building divided vertically into columns and vertical window strips. In the lobby is a white-on-crimson mosaic mural developed from a design by Josef Albers (1888–1976) entitled *Reclining Figure*. To the W. of the building is a covered shopping plaza which enabled developers to exceed building limits according to the Zoning Resolution of 1961. In the center of the plaza is Ibram Lassaw's (born 1913) welded bronze plate sculpture (1973), *Pantheon*.

Just N. of the Celanese Building is the McGRAW-HILL BUILDING (1972; Harrison, Abramovitz, & Harris).

In the sunken plaza is a sculpture (1973) by Athelstan Spilhaus (born 1911) entitled *Sun Triangle*, made of steel with stainless steel cladding. The three sides of the triangle point to the sun's noon position at the equinoxes and solstices. In the nearby reflecting pool whose diameter represents that of the sun are nine stainless steel globes representing the planets, their diameters also accurately proportioned. To the W. of the building is an attractive little park with a waterfall and tunnel.

Cross 49th St to the EXXON BUILDING (1971; Harrison, Abramovitz, & Harris), a 54-story rectangular slab clad in limestone, with a seven-story wraparound wing on the west. Like its neighbors, it has an austere facade of vertical columns alternating with vertical window strips. On the E. is a street-level plaza with a large fountain; on the W. is a small park. In the N. lobby are displayed a tapestry reproduction of a theater curtain designed by Pablo Picasso for a 1924 production of *Mercure,* and a three-part gilded bronze sculpture, *Moon and Stars* (1973), by Mary Callery (born 1903).

In the small park behind the building is J. Seward Johnson, Jr.'s bronze *Out to Lunch* (1980), a 340-lb bronze boy on his lunch break reading a book.

At 64 W. 50th St (bet. 6th / 5th Aves) is the *Museum of American Folk Art Book and Gift Shop* (tel: 246-5611), whose wares include handcrafted folk items and an extensive line of books about American folk art.

Return to Sixth Ave and cross 50th St to the TIME & LIFE BUILDING (1959; Harrison & Abramovitz), the earliest of the new buildings across Sixth Ave. Along its E. facade is a plaza with a central pool and basin surrounded by a low wall that serves as a bench. The undulating gray and white pattern on the pavement is similar to one that architect Wallace K. Harrison admired in Rio de Janeiro. The blue-painted steel sculpture, *Cubed Curve,* on the S.E. corner of the lot, is by William Crovello (born 1929) and was installed in 1971. Inside the lobby are (W. end of elevator banks) a glass and metal mural (1961) by Josef

Albers entitled *Portals,* and (E. end of elevator banks) an oil-on-canvas mural (1960), *Relational Painting #88* by Fritz Glarner (1899–1972).

Cross Sixth Ave to ***Radio City Music Hall** (1932; Edward Durell Stone, design architect; DL), the nation's largest indoor theater and a masterpiece of Art Deco decoration.

The hall can be seen only by attending a performance or joining a Music Hall tour; tel: 632-4000.

History. Samuel Lionel Rothafel (1882–1936), better known as Roxy, was a self-made man who began his career showing movies in the back room of a bar and rose to become a show business mogul producing radio programs and stage shows and managing a series of New York theaters including the opulent Roxy. Because he enjoyed the reputation of knowing infallibly what the public wanted, he was given broad powers by the RKO Corporation, a subsidiary of RCA, who hired him as director of the Music Hall. He contributed to the design of the theater and shaped its general policies, intending to revive vaudeville and produce spectacular variety entertainment.

Unfortunately Roxy's variety shows lost $180,000 in the first two weeks of operation, and the format was changed. Until television began competing strenuously, the Music Hall successfully presented a long list of wholesome movies coupled with stage shows, drawing an average 5 million patrons yearly to the end of 1967. By 1977 attendance had fallen to less than 2 million and the theater lost $2.3 million. In 1978 the closing of the Music Hall was announced but a wave of public support resulted in its interior being designated a landmark; in 1979 the parent company, Rockefeller Center Inc., renovated and reopened it with a new format of elaborately staged musical shows, rock concerts, and special events.

INTERIOR. The interior of the Music Hall, climaxed by the great auditorium, is one of the high points of American theater design and one of the city's grandest and most sophisticated displays of Art Deco styling.

The ticket lobby, low and relatively dark, forms a deliberate contrast to the Grand Lobby beyond. Walls are of red marble above black marble wainscoting; the low ceiling, painted black, is illuminated by dramatic circular light fixtures. The Grand Lobby inside the doors measures 140 ft long, 45 ft wide, and 60 ft high. The carpet of red, brown, gold, and black features abstract forms of musical instruments and was designed by Ruth Reeves (born 1892).

The unity of the decorative features of the hall—carpets, wall coverings, statues, murals, and furniture—was coordinated by Donald Deskey (1894–1989), who reputedly spent his last $5000 preparing his entry for the competition. Deskey had worked in Paris and attended (1925) the Exposition Internationale des Arts Decoratifs et Industriels Modernes, an exhibition generally credited with establishing the Art Deco style in the public taste.

Over the imposing staircase at the N. end is a mural by Ezra Winter (1886–1949), *The Fountain of Youth,* its subject suggested by Prof. Alexander (see p. 352) and drawn from a legend of the Oregon Indians. It depicts an old man gazing at a gleaming inaccessible mountaintop on which bubbles the fountain of youth; across the sky marches a cloudy procession representing the vanities of life. Gold mirrored panels reflect the light from two 29-ft glass chandeliers (2 tons apiece).

Staircases at the ends of the Grand Lobby lead down to the *Main Lounge* and restrooms. The lounge is richly decorated in gray and black: Donald Deskey designed the plaid carpet; the nine piers are faced with black glass and edged with chrome trim; walls are covered with black Permatex, a novel material at the time of installation. Vignettes of famous theatrical figures decorate the walls; they are drawn from Louis Bouché's (1896-1969) mural, *The Phantasmagoria of the Theater.* William Zorach's (1887–1966) cast aluminum nude, *Spirit of the Dance,* kneels in the center of the room.

Along with Gwen Lux's (born 1912) statue of *Eve* (niche at top of S. stairway leading to Grand Lobby) and Robert Laurent's (1890-1970) *Girl with Goose* (S. end of first mezzanine), this statue caused a scandal when installed, since Roxy declared the three nudes morally offensive. In view of his own racy reputation and the tameness of the statues, his outrage seems surprising. Nevertheless the nudes were removed, and only reinstated at the demand of art lovers.

Even the restrooms (E. side) are impressively decorated, though the original mural, *Men without Women,* by Stuart Davis (1894–1964) was removed from the men's smoking lounge to the Museum of Modern Art. The women's lounge has a mural by Witold Gordon, *The History of Cosmetics.* Fixtures, mirrors, and tile work were all especially designed for the Music Hall.

Equal care was lavished on the lounges and restrooms throughout the building, although fabrics and murals have faded with time. Especially attractive is the women's lounge on the first mezzanine, designed by Deskey himself.

Return to the Grand Lobby. Separating it from the auditorium are 11 double stainless steel doors with bronze bas-reliefs representing theatrical scenes, designed by René Chambellan. The most impressive space in the Music Hall is the *auditorium, which seats 6200 people. The ceiling is egg-shaped, a form Roxy demanded for its supposed acoustic superiority. The great proscenium arch (60 ft high, 100 ft wide) dominates the room. Rising outward and forward from it are the successive overlapping bands of the ceiling, painted with perpendicular rays, whose effect has been compared to the aurora borealis, a sunburst, and the rays of dawn. Roxy liked to assert that a sunrise he had witnessed at sea inspired the design for the ceiling, but the model of the auditorium, complete with ceiling, had been photographed six days before he embarked on the voyage in question.

The lighting system is installed between the bands and regulated by a large control board placed between the footlights and the audience. The stage machinery, designed by Peter Clark, includes sections that can be raised or lowered on elevators, a revolving central turntable, and a moveable orchestra pit. The stage can support 12 grand pianos, or three Roman chariots with horses, or six elephants. While animals frequently appear in the Christmas pageant, the most famous performers of the Music Hall stage are the Rockettes, a troupe of precision dancers founded in 1925 by Russell Markert, who brought them from St. Louis to New York.

Leave the Music Hall and walk E. on 50th St. Adjacent to the theater is the *Associated Press Building* (1938; DL). Above the main entrance (E. side of building, facing Rockefeller Plaza) is Isamu Noguchi's (born 1904) stainless steel panel, *News* (1940), depicting five men with the tools of the reporter's trade: pad and pencil, camera, telephone, teletype, and wirephoto.

Continue E. along 50th St to the INTERNATIONAL BUILDING (1935; DL). Over the entrance at 25 W. 50th St is a massive limestone screen by Lee Lawrie symbolizing the international purpose of the building.

The four figures in the central rectangle on the bottom row represent the four races of mankind; above them are: a trading ship; three figures representing art, science, and industry; and Mercury, messenger of trade. The upper side panels represent regions of the Earth (whale's fluke, palm trees, mosque, and Aztec temple), while the lower ones symbolize the old order (Norman tower and lion, symbol of kings) and the new industrial, republican age (smokestacks and eagle). Panels at Nos. 19 and 9 W. 50th St, also by Lawrie, represent *Swords into Ploughshares*, and *St. Francis of Assisi with Birds*.

The main entrance of the building is on Fifth Ave, where a central doorway is flanked by two projecting wings. The S. wing is known as the PALAZZO D'ITALIA (1935; DL), and like the British and French Buildings demonstrates the developers' policy to attract foreign tenants at a time when American ones were not readily available. Two bronze reliefs by Giacomo Manzu (born 1908) adorn the main entrance: a high relief of entwined grapevines and wheat stalks symbolizing fruitfulness and a smaller low relief depicting an immigrant mother and child. These works, installed in 1965, replace earlier decorations by Attilio Piccirilli (1868–1945), removed in 1940 when the U. S. was on the brink of war with Italy. In front of the central entrance of the International Building is a statue of *Atlas* (1937) supporting an armillary globe studded with signs of the zodiac. Designed by Lee Lawrie, this bronze, muscle-bound giant (height of figure, 15 ft; diameter of sphere, 21 ft; weight 14,000 lb) impresses by its sheer size. The N. wing of the building, known as the International Building North, retains its original decoration. Above the door is a glass panel by Piccirilli entitled *Youth Leading Industry* (c. 1936). Made of 3 tons of cast Pyrex, it depicts a charioteer reining in two plunging horses as a youth points out the road ahead.

INTERIOR. Enter the building through the main entrance. The lobby is tall and deep, with thin piers leading the eye to the central escalators which dominate the room like the grand staircases of 18–19C public buildings, but suggest the fondness of Art Deco designers for machinery as a stylistic motif. The ceiling is covered with copper leaf and illuminated by indirect lighting. Ride up the escalator to the blank wall at the top, decorated with a bust of the aviator Charles A. Lindbergh. The trip down the escalator offers a fine view through the rings of Atlas's sphere to the rose window and Gothic arches of St. Patrick's Cathedral across the street, an appealing juxtaposition of old and new.

18   Fifth Avenue, 59th–79th Street

SUBWAY: IRT Lexington Ave (train 4, 5, or 6) to 59th St; IND 6th or 8th Ave (E or F train) to 5th Ave-53rd St. BMT Nassau or Broadway (N or R train) to Fifth Ave.

BUS: M1, M2, M3, M4, or M5 uptown via Madison Ave, downtown via 5th Ave. M6 or M7 uptown via 6th Ave. M28 crosstown on 57th St. M32 uptown via Madison Ave as far as 60th St, downtown via 5th Ave as far as 23rd St.

History. Fifth Ave between 59th and 79th Sts, one of the city's most attractive boulevards, remained undeveloped until the city purchased land for Central Park in 1856. Before then 59th St formed the frontier between the city's most exclusive residential section and a social and geographical wasteland called "Squatters' Sovereignty" which stretched almost to 120th St and contained poor people living in wooden shacks sometimes patched together with flattened tin cans. After the park was begun the area was purged of its humble human and animal population (pigs and goats) and began to receive many of the city's wealthiest and most powerful families. From the closing decades of the 19C to the years of World War I, the area displayed an imposing collection of monumental residences.

The period during which the great mansions rose coincided roughly with the Eclectic period in American architecture. As the new millionaires, many of whom had made their fortunes during the post–Civil War boom, arrived on the social scene desirous of building suitably impressive homes, they turned for advice to the city's influential architects, who thus controlled the canons of taste. What the established architects—notably Richard Morris Hunt, Charles Follen McKim, and Stanford White—offered was Eclecticism, a self-conscious selection of styles from the classical orders of the past. The new classical architecture depended on the availability of cheap, skilled labor, supplied by the influx of immigrants, many of whom were experienced in masonry, iron-work, stone carving, painting and gilding, and ornamental plaster work. Eclecticism died after the end of World War I, when changing economic patterns and new building technology dictated the end of sumptuous masonry building and ushered in the era of the skyscraper and the high-rise apartment.

Although Eclecticism made itself felt in other parts of the city, the greatest concentration of such buildings in residential uses is here in the vicinity of Fifth Ave. So much so that novelist Edith Wharton, whose privileged background and judicious eye made her a keen commentator on social developments of the period, once described this wide-ranging selection of detail as a "complete architectural meal."

The Plaza, properly called **Grand Army Plaza**, lies between 58th and 60th Sts on the W. side of Fifth Ave. The open square, one of the few deviations from the gridiron plan of the city, provides a site for the *Pulitzer Memorial Fountain*, erected in 1916 (Carrère & Hastings) with a $50,000 donation from publisher Joseph Pulitzer. It is surmounted by Karl Bitter's *statue of Pomona,* goddess of abundance, a graceful young woman surely at home here in one of the wealthier sections of the city. Bitter, a protégé of Richard Morris Hunt, was killed by a car in 1915 as he was leaving the Metropolitan Opera and his assistants completed the statue.

Facing the plaza between 58th and 59th Sts on the W. side of Fifth Ave is the **Plaza Hotel** (1907; Henry J. Hardenbergh; DL), remarkable for the beauty of its site (vistas in two directions) and

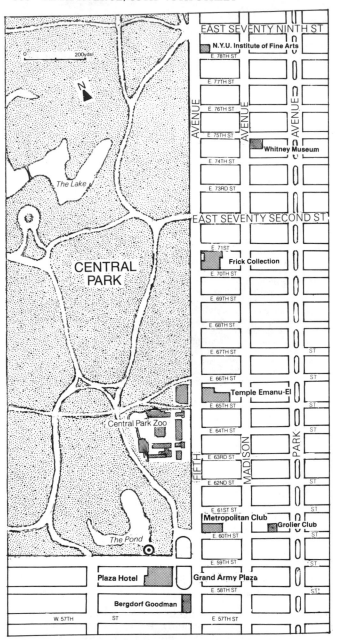

its social splendor, having attracted such visitors as Eleanor Roosevelt, Mark Twain, Groucho Marx, and Frank Lloyd Wright during its illustrious past. Architectural critics admire Harden-bergh's skill in manipulating the details of its French Renaissance design, using dormers, balustrades, high roofs, and rounded corner turnings to create a harmonious whole. In 1988, the hotel was bought by real estate magnate Donald Trump, who restored it to its former grandeur.

Across the avenue (E. side of Fifth Ave, 58th to 59th Sts) is the *General Motors Building* (1968; Edward Durell Stone and Emery Roth & Sons). This 50-story, white, marble-clad skyscraper aroused controversy when it replaced the Savoy Plaza Hotel, destroying the gracious, traditional design of the square and its hospitality to pedestrians. Artificial turf carpets the sunken plaza.

On the W. side of Fifth Ave, N. of Central Park South, is an equestrian *statue of General William Tecumseh Sherman* (1892–1903; Augustus Saint-Gaudens), the Civil War general best remembered for his destructive sweep through Georgia. Walking before the conqueror and waving an olive branch is a figure of Victory; the pine branch on the granite pedestal (Charles Follen McKim) signifies Georgia, according to the sculptor. One of the nation's finest equestrian statues, it was at the time of its unveiling covered with a layer of gold leaf. Its opulence distressed some contemporary observers who remembered the devastation and misery left in the path of Sherman's march from Atlanta to Savannah.

Near the statue stands a row of horse-drawn cabs available for a ride through the park or down the avenues. The horses are shod with rubber and the drivers, male and female, are attired in costumes ranging from the traditional black overcoat and top hat to blue jeans and fringed leather jackets.

Rates per trip, not per person, are currently $17 for the first half hour or fraction and $5 for each additional half hour or fraction. It is wise to check the cost and synchronize your watch with the driver's before you begin.

Cross Fifth Ave. On the N.E. corner of 59th St and Fifth Ave is the *Sherry-Netherland Hotel* (1927; Schultze & Weaver), once part of a trio that included the Plaza and the Savoy Plaza. Its high peaked roof adorns the skyline and at ground level, its show windows adorn the avenue with displays of Czarist jewelry, French 18C furniture, and exquisite trinkets.

Begin walking N. on Fifth Ave. On the N.E. corner of 60th St and Fifth Ave stands the **Metropolitan Club,** an imposing Italian Renaissance palazzo (1892–94; McKim, Mead & White; DL). The club was founded by J. P. Morgan and other discontented members of the Union Club after the board of governors had black-balled a candidate whom Morgan proposed for membership. One of the participants in the rejection remarked that Morgan's protegé had been voted down because, figuratively at least, he ate with his knife. The new club, whose membership boasted Vanderbilts and Goelets as well as the redoubtable Morgan, was soon nicknamed "The Millionaires' Club." An impressive wrought-iron fence and a colonnaded gateway guards the carriage entrance.

The *Hotel Pierre* (1928; Schultze & Weaver) at 2 E. 61st St, is another of the city's older, prestigious hotels, its towered top a skyline landmark. The apartment house at *800 Fifth Ave* (1978; Ulrich Franzen & Assocs.) on the N.E. corner of 61st St replaces a plain brick and limestone town house that formerly belonged to Mrs. Marcellus Hartley Dodge, a niece of John D. Rockefeller, Sr. Mrs. Dodge was a great animal lover and toward the end of her life retired to an estate in New Jersey where her dogs ran up yearly meat bills of over $10,000. Her art collection contained over 50 paintings by Rosa Bonheur, busts by the French 18C sculptor Houdon, and casts of hands that included those of Paderewski, Abraham Lincoln, and the Brownings (clasped). The construction of the apartment house marked the passing of an era.

Although the majority of buildings in the Eclectic style like the Plaza Hotel and the Metropolitan Club reflect French, Italian, or Roman originals, the *Knickerbocker Club* (1915; Delano & Aldrich; DL) at 2 E. 62nd St recalls a town house of the Federal period with its fine brickwork, marble lintels, and wrought-iron window gratings.

Diagonally across the intersection is the *Fifth Avenue Synagogue* (1959; Percival Goodman) at 5 E. 62nd St. Unlike many New York churches which are constructed as freestanding buildings and often located on the avenues, this one, standing on a cross street and attached to its neighbors on either side, has been described as particularly urban. The limestone facade has pointed oval windows filled with abstract patterns of stained glass; the shape of the windows is reiterated in the design of the sanctuary.

The intersection of Fifth Ave with 63rd St is graced with two palatial apartment houses, *Nos. 817 (1925; George P. Post & Sons) and 820 Fifth Ave* (1916; Starrett & Van Vleck). The original plans of 820 Fifth Ave show each apartment occupying a full floor and including five fireplaces, a kitchen-pantry with four sinks, six and a half bathrooms, servants' rooms, and a conservatory. The exterior details of the building—copper cornice with a frieze beneath, pedimented windows, balconies—were also features of the great town houses of the period.

Turn right into E. 63rd St. The **New York Academy of Sciences** at 2 E. 63rd St occupies what was originally the William Ziegler, Jr. house (1920; Sterner & Wolfe), residence of the Royal Baking Powder Company president. Members of the Woolworth family lived there later and gave it to the Academy.

Go N. to 64th St. At the S. corner of the intersection is 2 E. 64th St, the *former Edward Berwind mansion* (1896; N. C. Mellen), now converted to apartments. At one time reputedly the largest owner of coal mines in the nation, Berwind was also for many years the chief executive officer of the IRT (Interborough Rapid Transit). Described as Prussian in appearance, and as dour, close-mouthed, and acquisitive in business dealings, he was apparently socially charming and belonged to about 40 clubs and societies. This brick and limestone house in the style of an

Italian palazzo was his town house ; his country residence was "The Elms" at Newport, Rhode Island.

New India House (1903; Warren & Wetmore), home of the Indian Consulate and headquarters for the Indian delegation to the United Nations, stands at 3 E. 64th St, one of the few remaining buildings of modest scale designed by Warren & Wetmore, most famous for Grand Central Station. It originally belonged to Mrs. Marshall Orme Wilson, daughter of the dowager Mrs. Astor (see below) and herself a prominent figure in society. The mansion of molded limestone with a slate and copper roof, arched drawing room windows, and small oval dormers, exemplifies the Beaux-Arts style.

Return to Fifth Ave. Facing it in the park at about E. 64th St is the **Arsenal** (1848; Martin E. Thompson; DL), a building of eccentric charm surmounted by eight crenellated octagonal towers which perhaps offer a sense of security to the present tenants, the administrators of the Parks and Recreation Department. The newel posts of the central staircase represent cannon, and the balusters supporting the railing resemble rifles.

Within the building (third floor) is the *Arsenal Gallery* (Mon–Fri 9:30–4:30; closed weekends and holidays; free; tel: 360-8173) with changing exhibitions focusing on the park and city or featuring the work of local artists.

History. Although it was constructed to replace an older ammunition depot downtown on Centre St whose decrepitude made it an easy mark for thieves, the remoteness of the present building (in 1848) rendered it only dubiously effective as a place for stockpiling arms and ammunition. One critic complained in an official report to the state that the cannon in the Arsenal, four and a half miles distant from the previous depot, would be utterly useless, since a mob bent on riot could accomplish its purpose before the troops could arm themselves and drag the artillery into action.

Before becoming the home of the Parks, Recreation, and Cultural Affairs Department in 1934, the building housed the Eleventh Police Precinct, the Municipal Weather Bureau, the American Museum of Natural History, and assorted animals of what is now the Central Park Zoo.

On the site of the present Temple Emanu-El (5th Ave at 65th St) stood the dwelling of Mrs. Caroline Schermerhorn Astor (Mrs. William Astor), the acknowledged leader of New York society in the closing years of the 19C. She was forced to move uptown when her nephew William Waldorf Astor vengefully built the Waldorf Hotel next to her 34th St mansion as a reprisal against her social domination of his wife. Mrs. Astor's uptown mansion, designed by Richard Morris Hunt, was styled like a French Renaissance château and featured a two-ton bathtub cut from a single block of marble, an elaborate picture gallery, and a big ballroom. According to legend the capacity of the ballroom coincided precisely with the number of acceptable people in New York society, the "Four Hundred."

TEMPLE EMANU-EL at 1 E. 65th St, N.E. corner of Fifth Ave, is one of the largest houses of worship in the city and has a greater seating capacity than St. Patrick's Cathedral. The building (1929; Robert D. Kohn, Charles Butler, and Clarence Stein) was constructed in an adaptation of Moorish and Romanesque styles to symbolize the mingling of Eastern and Western cultures.

The auditorium is next to the corner and the taller community house behind it, with the water tanks and elevator machinery stacked on top to suggest a bell tower. Facing Fifth Avenue is a gabled facade flanked by towers with a recessed arch.

INTERIOR (open Sun—Thurs 10—5; Fri 10—4; Sat 12—5; organ recital Fri at 5 P.M. before the service). At the center of the altar on the E. wall is the Ark which contains the Torah, the scrolls of Mosaic law. In accordance with the Jewish restriction on visual images, the decoration of the sanctuary is limited to a few traditional designs: the six-pointed Star of David seen in the mosaics and stained glass windows, the Lion of Judah, and the crown, a traditional Torah ornament. The mosaics are by Hildreth Meiere.

Since 1946 the *Lotos Club,* 5 E. 66th St, has occupied the former William J. Schieffelin residence (1900; Richard Howland Hunt), originally the home of Margaret Vanderbilt Shepard. The Club was founded in 1870 as an organization devoted to literature and the arts.

Next door at No. 3 E. 66th St a modest placard marks the site of a house where Ulysses S. Grant spent his final years (1881—85) and wrote his memoirs.

At 854 Fifth Ave between 66th and 67th Sts stands the townhouse formerly belonging to R. Livingston Beekman, now the home of the *permanent Mission of Yugoslavia to the United Nations* (1905; Warren & Wetmore; DL). Designed as a reflection of 18C classic French architecture of the period of Louis XV, the house, crowned by a steep copper-covered mansard roof with two stories of dormers, maintains an air of dignity and monumentality, despite being hemmed in by two large apartment buildings.

Across the avenue at the intersection of 67th St and Central Park is the *Seventh Regiment Monument* (1926—27; Karl Illava), a memorial to the men of the 107th Infantry who died in World War I. The sculptor was a sergeant in the 107th Infantry.

Continue uptown. At the edge of the park between 70th and 71st Sts is a *memorial to Richard Morris Hunt* (1898; Daniel Chester French) opposite the site of the former Lenox Library (torn down and replaced by the Frick mansion), one of Hunt's finest achievements.

Architect Bruce Price, a student of Hunt, planned the granite monument on which rests a bust of Hunt flanked by two classically draped women: Sculpture and Painting (left) with a mallet and a palette (which once supported the remains of a figure modeled on one from the Parthenon) and Architecture (right) with a replica of Hunt's Administration Building at the World's Columbian Exposition. The figures, which weigh nearly 600 lb apiece and are about 6 ft tall, were abducted in 1962 and were nearly melted down in a belt buckle factory before they were recognized and recovered.

Across the street is the ****Frick Collection,** housed in one of the most elegant remaining Fifth Ave mansions (1914; Carrère & Hastings. Renovated as a museum, 1935; John Russell Pope; DL; addition to the E., 1977, Harry Van Dyke and John Barrington Bayley). The collection is a monument to that passion for acquiring European art harbored by so many millionaires and industrialists of Frick's generation and the furnishings of the building provide a glimpse of a culture long past. The museum contains a superb group of European paintings, mostly from the Renaissance to the end of the 19C, a fine collection of small Renaissance bronzes, antique furniture, enamels, prints and drawings, and porcelains.

The Frick Collection. 1 E. 70th St, New York 10021. Tel: 288-0700. Open Tues–Sat 10–6; Sun and minor holidays 1–6; closed Mon, major holidays, and Tues during July and Aug. Admission charge; lower rates for students and senior citizens. Children under 10 not admitted; children under 16 must be accompanied by an adult.
   Lectures, chamber music concert series in winter. No eating facilities in the museum. Limited wheelchair accessibility. Book and card shop.

History. Henry Clay Frick (1849–1919), a pioneer in the development of the coke and steel industries, began collecting art seriously around 1895, indulging his taste for Daubigny, Bouguereau, and the Barbizon school. As his taste matured, he sold earlier acquisitions and began buying the Flemish, Dutch, Italian, and Spanish paintings which presently ornament the collection. In 1905 he abandoned plans for a new house and gallery in Pittsburgh because he felt that pollution from the steel mills would be hazardous to his collection and commissioned Thomas Hastings of Carrère and Hastings to build (1913–14) this building as a dwelling and museum. Designed in an 18C French style, the mansion stands on the site of the former Lenox Library; after Frick's death both the house and the artworks were left in trust to establish a public gallery and in 1935 the house, enlarged and remodeled by John Russell Pope, was opened to the public.

ANTEROOM. This room is reserved for changing exhibitions of paintings and drawings from the part of the collection not on permanent display.
   BOUCHER ROOM. The panels by François Boucher of plump, rosy cherubs representing the Arts and Sciences are thought to have been commissioned by Mme. de Pompadour, mistress of Louis XV and patroness of the arts, for a boudoir in the château at Crécy. Among the period furniture are pieces by Jean Henri Riesener, André Louis Gilbert, and Martin Carlin.
   In the DINING ROOM are 18C English portraits: William Hogarth, *Miss Mary Edwards;* Sir Joshua Reynolds, *General John Burgoyne;* George Romney, *Henrietta, Countess of Warwick and her Children.* Thomas Gainsborough is represented by *The Mall in St. James Park,* an idealized view of upper class promenaders in an idealized park, and *Grace Dalrymple, Mrs. Elliott,* a portrait of a notoriously scandalous woman.
   In the West Vestibule are four more panels by Boucher representing *The Four Seasons.*
   The *FRAGONARD ROOM demonstrates Frick's taste toward the end of his collecting career. The four largest panels depict *The Progress of Love* and were painted for Mme. du Barry who succeeded Mme. de Pompadour in Louis XV's affections. The paintings are entitled *The Pursuit, The Meeting, Love Letters,* and *The Lover Crowned.* Mme. du Barry never accepted them, possibly because the Rococo style they represent was no longer in vogue, and Fragonard installed them in his cousin's house. Later he complemented them with *Love Triumphant, Reverie, Love the Jester, Love the Sentinel, Love the Avenger,* and *Love*

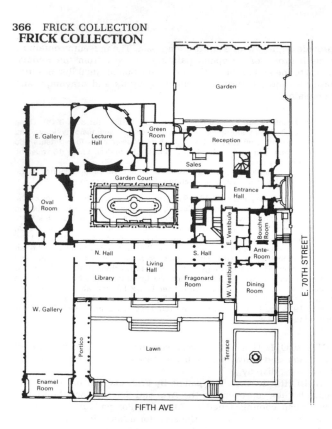

Pursuing a Dove, as well as the Hollyhock panel also displayed here.

Sculpture includes Jean Antoine Houdon's elegant bust of the *Comtesse du Cayla,* and two terra-cotta groups by Clodion, *Satyr with Two Bacchantes,* and *Zephyrus and Flora.* Among the porcelains are a Sèvres vase in the form of a ship, the single-masted shape often regarded as related to the vessel in the ancient Parisian coat of arms.

Almost every painting in the *LIVING HALL is a masterpiece any collector would treasure. There are two portraits by Titian, *Man in a Red Cap,* a young nobleman, and *Pietro Aretino,* the bawdy, scathing court poet. There are two portraits by Hans Holbein the Younger, *Sir Thomas More,* and *Thomas Cromwell,* both beheaded but only one sainted. Giovanni Bellini's *St. Francis in Ecstacy* is one of the treasures in an inestimable collection, a portrait of the saint in a luminous yet wild landscape, looking toward heaven or the source of his beatitude. El Greco painted several versions of the ascetic scholar, visionary *St. Jerome;* another is in the Lehman collection at the Metropolitan. In this room also are examples of the small Renaissance bronzes which Frick began to collect toward the end of his life, purchasing some from the estate of J. P. Morgan (died 1914), who had purchased them from European collections in great quantity.

The LIBRARY has more English paintings, as well as Chinese porcelains, and Renaissance bronzes. Here are portraits of English upper class wives and daughters by George Romney, Sir Thomas Lawrence, and Sir Joshua Reynolds, and one of Gilbert Stuart's paintings of *George Washington*. Gainsborough's *Sarah, Lady Innes* is an early portrait done around 1757. John Constable's *Salisbury Cathedral from the Bishop's Garden* is one of several he made of the cathedral from the garden of his friend the bishop. Also here, J. M. W. Turner is represented by *Fishing Boats Entering Calais Harbor* and *Mortlake Terrace*.

Frick planned the *WEST GALLERY as a setting for the major part of his collection, and the long room allows the kind of interesting juxtapositions he preferred. There are several paintings by Rembrandt, including *Portrait of a Young Artist*, *Self-Portrait* with the artist dressed up as an Eastern potentate, and the mysterious, allegorical *Polish Rider*, whose attribution has come under doubt. Fewer than 40 documented paintings of Johannes Vermeer are known, and the Frick Collection has three, including *Mistress and Maid*, an atypical painting, possibly unfinished. Also here in the WEST GALLERY are portraits by Anthony Van Dyck and Franz Hals, Velasquez and El Greco, landscapes by Corot, Turner, Constable, Hobbema, and Jacob van Ruisdael. Francisco de Goya's *The Forge*, a late painting, dark and violent, is noticeably different from Frick's other choices.

The beautifully paneled ENAMEL ROOM, the smallest room of the museum, contains painted French enamels (late 15C–17C) from the workshops at Limoges and religious paintings: Duccio di Buoninsegna, *The Temptation of Christ on the Mountain*, part of an altarpiece by this influential Sienese painter; Piero della Francesca, *St. Simon the Apostle*, and Jan van Eyck, *Virgin and Child with Saints and Donor*, with the donor (who commissioned the work) kneeling in the foreground.

The OVAL ROOM at the other end of the West Gallery was added during the remodeling of 1935. It contains a terra-cotta statue of *Diana the Huntress* by Houdon and four elegant society portraits by James A. McNeill Whistler: *Miss Rosa Corder; Valerie, Lady Meux; Mrs. Frederick R. Leyland;* and *Robert, Comte de Montesquiou-Fezensac*, who appears as the Baron de Charlus in Proust's *Remembrance of Things Past*.

The EAST GALLERY. Among the paintings here are tranquil Dutch landscapes, court portraits by Goya and Van Dyck, *The Sermon on the Mount* by Claude Lorrain, and a small, stormy painting of *The Purification of the Temple* by El Greco.

The Fricks drove their carriages into what is now the GARDEN COURT. Around the outside of the room are portrait busts of men of power; in the central part of the court near the fountain is a tranquil bronze Angel by Jean Barbet dated 1475 on its left wing.

The NORTH HALL. Here is the beautiful portrait of the *Comtesse d'Haussonville* in a shimmering blue gown, painted by

Jean-Auguste-Dominique Ingres, known for his compositional skill and his virtuosity in rendering fabric and flesh.

Cross through the Living Hall to the SOUTH HALL. Two more paintings by Vermeer are hung here, *Officer and Laughing Girl* and *Girl Interrupted at her Music,* both of them the still, luminous interior scenes for which the painter is known. There is also Boucher's appealing portrait of his wife, *Mme. Boucher,* a winsome woman but apparently not a demanding housekeeper.

Continue N. on Fifth Ave. The LYCÉE FRANÇAIS, just off Fifth Ave at 72nd St, appropriately enough occupies two Modern French-style town houses, a fashion introduced to New York in the early 1890s by Carrère & Hastings. *No. 7 E. 72nd St* (1899; Flagg & Chambers; DL) with its vermiculated stonework and bulbous mansard roof, started out as the home of Oliver Gould Jennings and was built to accommodate itself to its neighbor. *No. 9 E. 72nd St* next door (1896; Carrère & Hastings; DL) was the home of Henry T. Sloane, and was in its day praised as a compelling example of the Modern French style. The porte-cochere led to an interior court from which a grand staircase arched upward to a grand salon which spanned the whole front of the house.

A block further N. and a little off Fifth Ave at 11 E. 73rd St is the former Joseph Pulitzer residence (1903; McKim, Mead & White). Modeled on two Venetian palazzos, the house has a wide facade, arched windows, and colonnades. It stood empty much of the time the publisher owned it because his illness, near-blindness, and extreme sensitivity to sound (although muted by the double walls) made the house unattractive to him.

Continue up Fifth Ave. At 943 Fifth Ave between 74th and 75th Sts is the *French Consulate* (1926; Walker & Gillette). Beyond it at 1 E. 75th St is the home of *The Commonwealth Fund,* the former Edward S. Harkness house (1909; Hale & Rogers; DL), a remarkable example of the superb craftsmanship available at the turn of the century to those who could pay for it. Protected by a spiked iron fence and a "moat," the house, with its beautifully carved marble, resembles an Italian palazzo and is elegantly detailed from the elaborate cornice to the iron ground-floor gates. Harkness, a noted philanthropist, was the son of Stephen Harkness, one of the original partners in Standard Oil.

Further N. at 1 E. 78th St is the former **James B. Duke mansion** (1912; Horace Trumbauer; DL; interior remodeled 1958; Robert Venturi, Cope & Lippincott), now preserved as the *New York University Institute of Fine Arts.* Built of white limestone so fine that it looks like marble, it was modeled after the late 18C Labottiere mansion in Bordeaux in the classical style of Louis XV. James B. Duke rose from humble beginnings on a North Carolina farm to dominate the tobacco industry, becoming president of the American Tobacco Co. in 1890 and maintaining his position of power even after the Supreme Court ruled his company in violation of the antitrust laws. He lived in this mansion until his death in 1925; his daughter Doris Duke and his widow donated the property to N.Y.U. in 1957.

The *Cultural Services of the French Embassy,* on Fifth Ave between 78th and 79th Sts (972 Fifth Ave) are located in the former *Payne Whitney House* (1906; McKim, Mead & White; DL), one of the earliest Italian Renaissance mansions N. of 72nd St. It is especially interesting for its gracefully curved and elaborately carved facade of light gray granite, a material not generally favored because of its extreme hardness. The house belonged first to Payne Whitney, philanthropist, financier, and aficionado of horse racing who kept stables in Kentucky and on Long Island. His estate was calculated at a quarter of a billion dollars. His wife, Helen Hay Whitney, was a daughter of John Hay, secretary of state under Presidents McKinley and Theodore Roosevelt. Their daughter, Joan Whitney Payson, was the principal owner of the New York Mets baseball team until her death in 1975, and their son, John Hay (Jock) Whitney, was publisher of the *New York Herald Tribune* and ambassador to Great Britain.

The former Cook mansion next door at 973 Fifth Ave was built from 1902–05 by McKim, Mead & White and is visually continuous with the Payne Whitney House.

Looming up on the S.E. corner of Fifth Ave and 79th St is the home of the UKRAINIAN INSTITUTE OF AMERICA, the former mansion of Augustus Van Horn Stuyvesant, the last direct male descendant of the famous one-legged Dutch governor, Peter Stuyvesant. The house (1899; Charles P. H. Gilbert; DL) is a picturesque French Gothic mansion, with high slate roofs, pinnacled dormers, gargoyles, and a "moat" protected by an iron fence. Here Augustus Stuyvesant, a successful real estate dealer, spent his declining years, eventually becoming a complete recluse, limiting his social activities to meetings with the family lawyer and visits to the graves of his ancestors buried in the churchyard of St. Mark's-in-the-Bowery, where he was driven by his chauffeur in an old Rolls Royce.

The Ukrainian Institute. 2 E. 79th St, New York 10003. Tel: 288-8660. Open Tues–Fri 2–6, Sat and Sun by appointment. Voluntary donation. No restaurant, no gift shop, no telephone. Not accessible to wheelchairs.

The Institute (1948) maintains a collection of contemporary Ukrainian paintings, religious relics, and Ukrainian arts and crafts (ceramics, folk costumes, woodcuts).

19 Museum of Modern Art and Vicinity

SUBWAY: IRT Broadway-7th Ave local (train 1) to 50th St and Broadway. IND 6th Ave (B train) to 57th St. IND 6th Ave (D train) or 8th Ave (E train) to 7th Ave and 53rd St.

BUS: M1, M2, M3, M4, or M32 downtown via 5th Ave or uptown via Madison Ave. M5 downtown via Broadway / 5th Ave. M5, M6, or M7 uptown via 6th Ave. M27 crosstown on 49th and 50th Sts.

The ****Museum of Modern Art** at 11 W. 53rd St boasts an unrivaled collection of modern painting and sculpture spanning

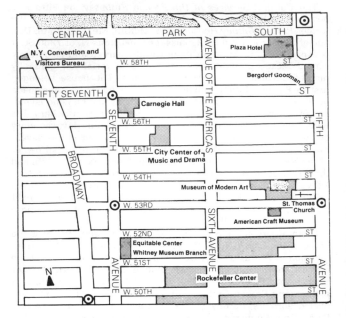

the years from about 1880 to the present. The collections also include films, photographs, prints, and drawings, and embrace the arts of architecture and industrial design.

The Museum of Modern Art. 11 W. 53rd St, New York 10019. Open Fri—Tues 11–6, Thurs 11–9, closed Wed. Admission charge. Children under 16 when accompanied by an adult, free. Thurs 5–9, admission by voluntary donation (pay what you wish but pay something). Tel: 708-9400.

Restaurant, restrooms, telephones, gift shop (Museum Store Annex at 37 W. 53rd St). Film screenings, gallery talks, and lectures. For information on exhibitions, tel: 708-9480; for information about film screenings tel: 708-9490. Accessible to wheelchairs.

In 1984 the museum opened its expanded and renovated building (1939; Edward Durell Stone & Philip L. Goodwin; East Wing, 1964, Philip Johnson; 1984 renovation and West Wing; Cesar Pelli & Assocs. with Gruen Assocs.), which includes the original building plus wings to the east and west, whose addition more than doubled the former exhibition space (currently 87,000 sq ft). Above the West Wing rises Museum Tower, a luxury apartment building which uses the air rights above the museum and generates financial support for it.

The museum has one of the most important collections of modern art in the world, containing in the permanent exhibitions representatives from most of the significant movements in painting from Impressionism through Abstract Expressionism. The paintings are displayed more or less chronologically in galleries on the second and third floors.

GROUND FLOOR. Exhibition space on the ground floor consists of the International Council Galleries used for changing exhibi-

THE MUSEUM OF MODERN ART
Lower Level

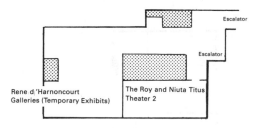

THE MUSEUM OF MODERN ART
Theater Level

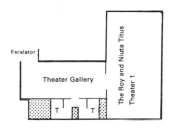

tions and the Abby Aldrich Rockefeller Sculpture Garden, a much loved feature of the old museum now incorporated in the new. In the garden are: Barnett Newman, *Broken Obelisk;* Henry Moore, *Family Group, Large Torso;* Rodin, *Monument to Balzac;* Picasso, *She-Goat;* works by Gaston Lachaise, Aristide Maillol, and others.

SECOND FLOOR. **Painting and Sculpture.** The Alfred H. Barr, Jr., Galleries are named to honor the first director of the museum, who was responsible for acquiring many of the great classics in the collection. The first four galleries are devoted to Post-Impressionism. First gallery: Cezanne: *The Bather, Pines and Rocks, Still Life with Ginger Jar, Sugar Bowl,* and *Oranges.* Toulouse-Lautrec: *La Goulue at the Moulin Rouge.* Degas: *At the Milliner's.* Second Gallery: Seurat: *The English Channel at Grandcamp.* Henri Rousseau: *The Sleeping Gypsy.* Van Gogh: *The Starry Night, Les Oliviers.* Gauguin: *Still Life with Three Puppies, The Moon and the Earth.* Works by Edvard Munch, Paul Signac,

THE MUSEUM OF MODERN ART
Ground Floor

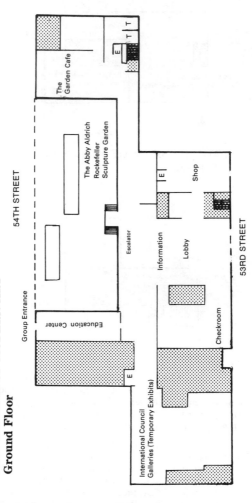

THE MUSEUM OF MODERN ART
Second Floor

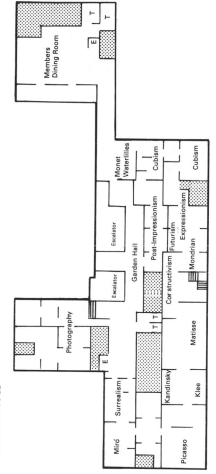

Odilon Redon. Third Gallery: James Ensor: *Masks Confronting Death*. Henri Rousseau: *The Dream*. Odilon Redon: *Vase of Flowers*. Edouard Vuillard: *Mother and Sister of the Artist*. Pierre Bonnard: *The Breakfast Room*. Fourth Gallery: Kees van Dongen: *Modjesko, Soprano Singer*. Gustav Klimt: *The Park, Hope II*. André Derain: *London Bridge, Bathers*.

The next three galleries focus on the development of Cubism. First Gallery: Picasso: *Boy Leading a Horse, Les Demoiselles d'Avignon, "Ma Jolie," Man with a Hat, Two Nudes, Guitar*. Georges Braque: *Man with a Guitar*. Juan Gris: *Breakfast*. Francis Picabia, *La Source*. Second Gallery (to the left of the first Cubist gallery): Monet, *Water Lilies*. Third Gallery: Picasso: *Guitar* (sheet metal and wire), *Card Player*. Gallery 8: Fernand Léger: *Exit the Ballets Russes, Three Women*. Picasso: *Three Musicians, Three Women at the Spring*.

The gallery between Cubism and Expressionism: Brancusi: *The Cock, Fish, Endless Column*. Marc Chagall: *Birthday, Over Vitebsk, I and the Village*.

The next two galleries focus on Expressionism and Futurism. First Gallery: Oskar Kokoschka: *Self-Portrait, Hans Tietze and Erica Tietze-Conrat*. Emil Nolde: *Christ Among the Children*. Ernst Kirchner: *Street, Dresden*. Second Gallery: Gino Severini: *Dynamic Hieroglyphic of the Bal Tabarin*. Umberto Boccioni: *Dynamism of a Soccer Player, The Laugh*. The last room in this group is devoted primarily to Mondrian: *Trafalgar Square; Pier and Ocean; Composition in White, Black, and Red;* and *Broadway Boogie Woogie*. Also Theo van Doesburg: *Composition (The Cow)*. In the hallway with the staircase are works by Kasimir Malevich, including *Suprematist Composition: White on White*, and Naum Gabo's *Head of a Woman*.

Beyond the stair hall is a large gallery devoted to Matisse: *The Red Studio, The Blue Window, Dance, Goldfish and Sculpture, View of Notre Dame, The Moroccans, Piano Lesson*. In the next gallery are works by Paul Klee: *Actor's Mask, Portrait of an Equilibrist, Around the Fish, Mask of Fear*. Also Wassily Kandinsky: *Painting 198, Painting 201, Painting 200,* and *Painting 199*, sometimes said to represent the four seasons. Lyonel Feininger: *Viaduct*. Robert Delaunay: *Simultaneous Contrasts: Sun and Moon*. František Kupka: *The First Step*.

Continue to the next gallery with works of Derain, Braque, and Soutine. Also Modigliani: *Reclining Nude* and Rouault: *Christ Mocked by Soldiers, Clown*. The corner section of this gallery is devoted primarily to works by Picasso from the 1930s: *Night Fishing at Antibes, Seated Bather, Girl Before a Mirror, Bather with a Beach Ball, Woman Dressing her Hair,* and *Charnel House*, the last painted in 1944 and possibly inspired by newpaper photos of the victims in the Nazi concentration camps. The large plaster head of Marie-Therese Walter, the artist's model and mistress, is an important recent acquisition, given by the artist's widow.

The next section, devoted to Surrealism, contains: Max Ernst, *Two Children Are Threatened by a Nightingale;* Marcel Duchamp: *To Be Looked at (from the Other Side of the Glass) with One Eye,*

Close To, for Almost an Hour; The Passage from Virgin to Bride. To the right of this room are works of Giorgio Morandi, Joseph Cornell, and Giorgio de Chirico: *Gare Montparnasse* and *The Nostalgia of the Infinite*. In the smaller gallery on the other side of the first Surrealism gallery are: Marcel Duchamp: *Bicycle Wheel;* George Grosz: *Metropolis;* Francis Picabia: *I See Again in Memory My Dear Udnie* and *M'Amenez-Y;* Man Ray: *The Rope Dancer Accompanies Herself with Her Shadows*.

The next corner gallery has several works by Jean Arp: *Bell and Navels, Human Concretion, Ptolemy*. Also Max Ernst: *The Blind Swimmer*. And several important works by Joan Miro: *Hirondelle / Amour, Dutch Interior I, The Hunter (Catalan Landscape), The Birth of the World*. Also Yves Tanguy: *Mama, Papa Is Wounded*.

In the final gallery: Pavel Tchelitchew: *Hide-and-Seek;* René Magritte: *The Empire of Light, The False Mirror, The Lovers;* Salvador Dali: *The Persistence of Memory, Untitled (Petit Theatre);* Paul Delvaux: *Phases of the Moon*.

The galleries of **Photography** include six small galleries arranged chronologically and an introductory gallery that shows a wide variety of temporary exhibitions. The historical survey in the six galleries is continually revised, with the most important photographers always represented though not always by the same photographs. The collection numbers more than 15,000 prints, spanning the whole history of photography beginning in about 1840, and includes (among others): Diane Arbus, Eugene Atget, Walker Evans, Dorothea Lange, Moholy-Nagy, May Ray, Alexander Rodchenko, Edward Steichen, and Edward Weston. The museum also has an extensive body of work of contemporary photographers: Ansel Adams, Bill Brandt, Brassai, Harry Callahan, William Eggleston, Lee Friedlander, Joel Meyerowitz, and Aaron Siskind.

The THIRD FLOOR galleries contain Painting and Sculpture, both American and European, from the years before World War II to the present, including a fine collection of Abstract Expressionism.

Prewar American Painters. Edward Hopper: *Gas* and *House by the Railroad;* Stuart Davis: *Visa*. Arshile Gorky: *Agony*. Work by Marsden Hartley, Arthur Dove, Georgia O'Keeffe, Max Weber.

Opening off these galleries are two that suggest the beginnings of Abstract Expressionist inspiration, with works by Adolph Gottlieb, Willem de Kooning, Barnett Newman, and Mark Rothko. Also Jackson Pollock: *Gothic* and *The She-Wolf*.

In the corner gallery, Postwar European and American Painters: Francis Bacon: *Dog* and *Number VII from Eight Studies for a Portrait*, examples of this painter's intense, chilling art; Jean Dubuffet: *The Cow with the Subtile Nose;* Alberto Giacommetti: *Chariot*.

The next gallery features Matisse's exuberant cutouts, *The Swimming Pool*, which were made at the end of his life when illness confined him to a wheelchair.

The following four galleries continue to document the development of American Abstract Expressionism, and the interest of

THE MUSEUM OF MODERN ART
Third Floor

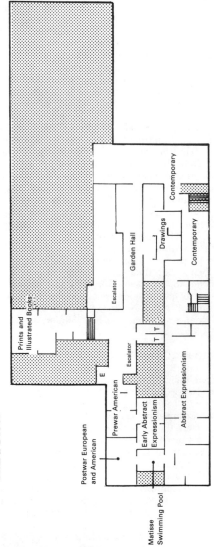

THE MUSEUM OF MODERN ART
Fourth Floor

its practitioners in expressive line and color. Among the paintings in these galleries: Mark Tobey: *Edge of August;* Jackson Pollock: *Echo Number 25*. Included here is Fernand Léger's *The Divers, II*, painted while in exile in this country. Second Gallery: Robert Motherwell: *Elegy to the Spanish Republic, 108*. Work by David Smith, Barnett Newman, Willem de Kooning, Franz Kline. Third Gallery: Ad Reinhardt, Mark Rothko. Fourth Gallery: Barnett Newman: *Vir Heroicus Sublimis,* a color field painting that influenced later Minimalists. David Smith: *Australia.* Closing out the vista along this range of galleries is Jackson Pollock's *One (Number 31, 1950),* which looks back at many of the concerns of the past decades. Monumental in scale, radical in technique, intense in its demands on the viewer, it has been called a 20C interpretation of the sublime.

The last quarter of the painting and sculpture installation across the stairwell area is devoted to artists of the past 20 years, beginning with Robert Rauschenberg and Jasper Johns, continuing through Pop Art and the color field artists, Ellsworth Kelly to Kenneth Noland, and ending with Minimalists and Conceptualists. The exhibition is flexible and changes with some frequency. Among the artists shown here are George Segal, Frank Stella, Alexander Liberman, Donald Judd, Robert Morris, Claes Oldenburg, Roy Lichtenstein, Andy Warhol, Helen Frankenthaler, and Dan Flavin.

The gallery for **Drawings** is located near the exit from the contemporary galleries. Rotating exhibitions in the galleries will be historical or thematic, concentrating on particular mediums (watercolor, collage) or subjects. The departmental collection of some 6,000 works is probably the largest single gathering of modern drawings and is outstanding in its representation of Dada, Surrealist, School of Paris, early Russian avant-garde, Italian Futurist, and American drawings. Dubuffet, Ernst, Klee, Kupka, Matisse, and others are well represented, as are Johns, Pollock, and Rauschenberg among recent major artists.

The Department of **Prints and Illustrated Books** is also located on the third floor. The first gallery contains major works from the 1880s to the 1950s including representatives from the department's great collections of Munch, Matisse, Picasso, Klee, Dubuffet, and Johns. The second gallery area, with the wood floor, has rotating exhibits of contemporary work and new acquisitions.

FOURTH FLOOR. On this floor is the **Architecture and Design** collection reached by a two-story entrance area at the top of the escalator. On its largest two walls are hung a selection of posters. Also here are examples of industrial art including the Cisitalia sports car and a Bell-47D1 helicopter designed by Arthur Young. The first gallery features drawings and architectural models of such buildings as Frank Lloyd Wright's house Fallingwater, Gerrit Rietveld's Schroder House, and Le Corbusier's Villa Savoye. The permanent Design Collection is displayed in a series of galleries organized chronologically and beginning with 19C precursors of modern design, for example Viennese bentwood furniture. The exhibitions also offer representatives of the Arts and Crafts and Art Nouveau movements, de Stijl, Bauhaus design, Scandinavian and Italian design, and computer age technology and design. Among the useful and beautiful objects are chairs, fiberglass furniture, cocktail shakers and table silver, motorcycle helmets, goalie masks, calculators, turntables, and saucepans.

The Donnell Library Center across the street at 20 W. 53rd St, a branch of the New York Public Library, is named after Ezekiel J. Donnell, a cotton merchant who in 1896 bequeathed money for a library "in which young people can spend their evenings profitably away from demoralizing influences." The center, financed by the city, lends a million books each year and has the nation's best collection of children's literature. The Rare and Old Book Collection has English and American children's books of the 18C and 19C. The library also sponsors a film series, poetry readings, and other events.

The **American Craft Museum** is adjacent to the library in the N.E. corner of the *E. F. Hutton Building* (1986; Roche, Dinkeloo & Assocs.).

American Craft Museum. 40 W. 53rd Street, New York 10019. Tel: 956-3535. Open Wed–Sun 10–5; Tues 10–8. Closed Monday and national holidays. Admission charge; lower rate for students and senior citizens; children 12 and under free; free admission for all visitors Tues 5–8.
   Gift shop, restrooms, telephones, no restaurant. Accessible to wheelchairs.

The American Craft Museum (formerly the Museum of Contemporary Crafts) inaugurated its handsome new facility in October 1986. Unlike many other museums which depend on the largesse of major corporations for midtown exhibition space, the Craft Museum owns its own space, a condominium within the E. F. Hutton Building.

In 1959 the American Craft Council, parent organization of the museum, bought a brownstone on 53rd St, whose site began looking attractive to the developers of the present office tower. Consequently the Craft Museum was able to exchange the brownstone and its air rights for a 15,000 square foot chunk of the new building and negotiate costs of finishing it.

The museum today consists of a 40-ft atrium fronting on 53rd St and giving access to three levels of galleries, which are used for installations from the permanent collection and for changing exhibitions of contemporary crafts, including work in such traditional craft media as glass, ceramics, fiber, paper, wood, and metal. The installations, often very beautiful, range from traditional and humble folk crafts to sophisticated modern works that stand between traditional craft and what is usually considered art.

In the plaza between the Hutton Building and the CBS Building is *Lapstrake* (1987) by Texas sculptor Jesús Bautista Moroles, a pile of granite slabs, alternately rough hewn and polished, suggesting perhaps an ancient architectural ruin.

Walk W. a block and a half to Seventh Ave and turn left (south).

The **Equitable Tower** (1986; Edward Larrabee Barnes Assocs.), at 787 Seventh Ave (bet. 51st / 52nd Sts), headquarters of the Equitable Life Assurance Society of the United States, one of the largest real estate investors in the country, is the first major office building to have been built W. of Sixth Ave in recent years. It is remarkable not only for pioneering the western territories of the midtown office district but for its public spaces, which demonstrate a convincing commitment to art. Here, in addition to restaurants and an auditorium, is a branch of the Whitney Museum of American Art, a series of murals by Thomas Hart Benton, and outstanding commissioned works by other notable contemporary artists. Finished in smooth beige limestone framed with orange granite, the building rises 54 stories with a few setbacks from a 723-ft arch facing Seventh Ave to a pair of 53-ft arched windows at the top that face east and west.

INTERIOR. Dominating the imposing 80-ft atrium is Roy Lichtenstein's *Mural with Blue Brushstroke,* a 68-ft painting whose images span the artist's career and include references to his early pop period and his later paraphrases of art history. In the center of the atrium is Scott Burton's *Atrium Furnishment,* a 40-ft semicircular settee and circular table (19 ft in diameter) made of marble.

The **Whitney Museum of American Art at Equitable Center** occupies two galleries near the Seventh Ave entrance to the building.

Whitney Museum of American Art at Equitable Center. 787 Seventh Ave (bet. 51st / 52nd Sts), New York 10019. Tel: 554-1000. Open Mon, Tues, Wed, Fri 11–6; Thurs 11–7:30; Sat 12–5. Free. Gallery talks Mon, Wed, Fri at 12:30. Tours by appointment; lecture series (554-1113). No food, no restrooms, no gift shop. Accessible to wheelchairs.

The North Gallery (left of the entrance) houses long-term exhibitions selected from the Permanent Collection of the Whitney Museum of American Art. The South Gallery is devoted to changing exhibitions with about five scheduled each year.

In the N. corridor Thomas Hart Benton's muscular murals *America Today* (1930–31), painted for the New School of Social Research, reflect the life of rural and urban America and the development of technology. They communicate a positive attitude which seems, with historical hindsight, at odds with Depression America, but as the artist pointed out, the Depression hit hard only when he had almost completed the work.

Purchased by The Equitable in l984 for $3.4 million, the murals have been completely restored.

In the S. corridor is Paul Manship's bronze sculpture *Day,* designed for the l939 World's Fair and installed here to provide an artistic link between the Equitable Center and Rockefeller Center, where Manship's best-known work, his bronze *Prometheus,* watches over the lower plaza.

Directly to the E. of the building is the Galleria, an open space, which will one day be provided with escalators to a concourse level. Sol LeWitt's *Wall Drawing: Bands of Lines in Four Colors and Four Directions Separated by Gray Bands* (1985) is the only work of the artist on permanent public display in the city. At the N. and S. ends respectively of the Galleria are Barry Flanagan's bronze *Young Elephant* (1985) and *Hare on Bell* (1983).

In the center of the Galleria is the entrance to the bar of the Palio restaurant, whose decor features a four-part mural by Sandro Chia (1985) showing the Sienese biennial horse race.

Cross the Galleria and enter the building to the E., the *Paine-Webber Building*, 1285 Ave of the Americas (1961; Skidmore, Owings & Merrill), the previous headquarters of The Equitable, which with the new tower to the W. now constitutes *The Equitable Center*. The *PaineWebber Art Gallery* on the ground floor of the building hosts changing exhibitions of work from its corporate collection as well as traveling shows from nonprofit institutions located away from midtown and seeking affordable midtown exhibition space: for example, the Brooklyn Museum, the Museum of American Folk Art, or the Museum of the City of New York.

PaineWebber Art Gallery. 1285 Avenue of the Americas (bet. 52nd / 53rd Sts), New York 10019. Tel: 713-2885. Open Mon—Fri 8—6. Closed holidays on which the stock market is closed. Free. No restaurant, no gift shop, restrooms on concourse level (ask the guard for the key). Accessible to wheelchairs. Guided tours arranged for groups.

Continue W. to Sixth Ave and walk north. At 1335 Ave of the Americas (bet. 53rd / 54th Sts) is the *New York Hilton Hotel* (1963; William B. Tabler), one of the first of New York's big (2200 rooms) convention hotels.

Walk a block N. and turn left into 55th St. At 135 W. 55th St between Sixth and Seventh Aves is the CITY CENTER OF MUSIC AND DRAMA (1924; H. P. Knowles, succeeded by Clinton & Russell; DL), an ornate domed structure built as the Mecca Temple of the Ancient and Accepted Order of the Mystic Shrine (Masons). The city took it over during the tenure of Fiorello La Guardia and converted it to a theater (3000 seats). The New York City Ballet and the New York City Opera called it home until their move to Lincoln Center, but local and foreign companies still perform here regularly, making it a major dance center.

Walk W. to Seventh Ave and go north. **Carnegie Hall** at 154 W. 57th St (S.E. corner of 7th Ave) was built (1891; William B. Tuthill, architect with Dankmar Adler and William Morris Hunt, consultants; restored 1986; James Stewart Polshek; DL) by Andrew Carnegie as a home for the Oratorio Society of which he was then president. He also hoped to make money on his $2 million investment. Architecturally the building is not outstanding—a bulky brownish neo-Italian Renaissance hall with a high square tower at one corner—but it is a musical landmark. The acoustics of the original auditorium (seats 2760) were legendary, delighting both audiences and performers, beginning with Tchaikovsky who appeared as guest conductor during opening week. Despite the popularity of the hall, it came close to demolition in the early 1960s when its owners began yearning for larger profits (Andrew

Carnegie didn't make money on it either), but a committee of preservationists headed by violinist Isaac Stern saved it. Although the New York Philharmonic, which first made Carnegie Hall its home and appeared here under the batons of Toscanini and Stokowski, now resides at Lincoln Center, major orchestras and soloists are still booked into the hall.

Carnegie Recital Hall, renamed Weill Recital Hall at Carnegie Hall, is a small but prestigious auditorium where less well-known artists display their talents.

The presence of Carnegie Hall has long made this part of town a center of musical activity, as music and instrument dealers gravitated to the area. Still in evidence are the *Joseph Patelson Music House* behind Carnegie Hall (at 160 W. 56th St), whose bulletin board offers announcements of interest to musicians, and *Steinway Hall,* now the Manhattan Life Insurance Building (1925; Warren & Wetmore) at 111 W. 57th St between Seventh and Sixth Aves. The showroom still occupies the ground floor, but the upstairs concert hall is gone.

Also in the immediate neighborhood is the **Museum of the American Piano,** ensconced in the back room of founder Kalman Detrich's piano workshop and showroom.

Museum of the American Piano. 211 W. 58th St (bet. 7th / 8th Aves), New York 10019. Tel: 246-4646. Open Tues—Sat 12—4; closed public holidays. Admission charge; lower rates for students, senior citizens. Ring doorbell for admission. No restaurant, no gift shop, no restrooms. Museum on ground floor; no special facilities for handicapped visitors.

This new museum (founded in 1981; opened 1984) is dedicated to preserving and documenting the craft of American piano making which flourished in the 19C but is now dying. On exhibit are representative examples of major American 19C instruments including pianos by Chickering, Osborne, Steinway, Weber, and Boardman & Gray. On one wall a display of components of typical instruments, represents the beginning of a collection which will be expanded to show the evolution of American piano technology.

Diagonally across Seventh Ave from Carnegie Hall at 205 W. 57th St are the *Osborne Apartments* (1885; James E. Ware), a fine early apartment house with a facade of reddish stone. The lobby maintains its former splendor but the rest of the ground floor has been converted into storefronts.

The ART STUDENTS LEAGUE (1892; Henry J. Hardenbergh; DL) at 215 W. 57th St between Seventh Ave and Broadway, an art school, enjoys a dignified French Renaissance building by the architect of the Plaza Hotel.

Go W. on 57th St. At 965 Eighth Ave on the S.W. corner of the intersection is the bizarre, theatrical **Hearst Magazine Building** (1928; Joseph Urban and George B. Post & Sons; DL), worthy of both its designer and original owner. Joseph Urban, famous as a set designer whose talents encompassed the high seriousness of the Metropolitan Opera and the large-scale frivolity of Florenz Ziegfeld's *Follies,* met William Randolph Hearst through Marion

Davies, a Ziegfeld showgirl who became Hearst's wife. Urban designed sets for several of Marion Davies's movies; the Hearst Magazine Building, with its oversized urns and fluted columns, its grand entranceway and massive keystone, could be yet another movie set. Original plans called for adding another seven stories to the building's present six, which would have modified its squat appearance. The statuary by Henry Kries depicts (left to right): Sport and Industry, Comedy and Tragedy, Music and Art.

20   North of Grand Central: Park Avenue and Vicinity

SUBWAY: IRT Lexington Ave express or local (train 4, 5, or 6) to Grand Central. IRT Flushing line (train 7) to Grand Central. Shuttle (S) from Times Square to Grand Central. IND 6th Ave (B, D, or F train) to 42nd St; walk E. to Vanderbilt Ave and N. to the Pan Am Building.

BUS: M1, M2, M3, M4, M5, or M32 downtown via 5th Ave. M101 or M102 downtown via Lexington Ave to 42nd St. M104 downtown via Broadway and crosstown on 42nd St. M1, M2, M3, or M4 uptown via Madison Ave to 42nd St. M5 uptown via 6th Ave to 42nd St. M101, M102, or M104 uptown via 3rd Ave to 42nd St. M106 crosstown on 42nd St.

More than 20 years after its arrival on the scene, the **Pan Am Building** (1963; Emery Roth & Sons, Pietro Belluschi, and Walter Gropius) at 200 Park Ave just N. of Grand Central Station can still evoke hostility. It is big (59 stories or more than 2 million sq ft of rentable space on a 3.5 acre site), unattractive (with a facade of precast concrete panels and windows relieved by two square-columned floors for machinery and equipment), and intrusive (spoiling the former vista down Park Ave). A heliport on top once further disrupted the neighborhood with noise and fumes, but after a fatal accident (1977), it was closed.

History. Once this neighborhood was the focal point of the New York Central Railroad's vast real estate empire. Handsome if staid hostelries rose around Grand Central Station: the former Hotel Biltmore (1914; Warren & Wetmore) on Vanderbilt Ave, named after Cornelius Vanderbilt's château in North Carolina, has been converted to office space, though the famous old clock still remains in an unobtrusive corner of the lobby (Madison Ave side); the *Commodore Hotel*, named after the railroad's founder, has been stripped to the bones and refleshed as the Hyatt Regency Hotel on 42nd St at Lexington Ave; the Yale Club (1915; James Gamble Rogers), stands at 50 Vanderbilt Ave, welcoming students and alumni of the university attended by several Vanderbilt offspring.

The **New York Central Building** (1929; Warren & Wetmore; DL), now the HELMSLEY BUILDING at 230 Park Ave (bet. 45th / 46th Sts) served as headquarters for the railroad and as a visible reminder of its power. Walk N. through the central lobby with its travertine, Jaspé Oriental marble, and bronze fittings. When it opened the architectural critic of *The New Yorker* magazine compared its dark red marble trim to "the red meat of a vigorous

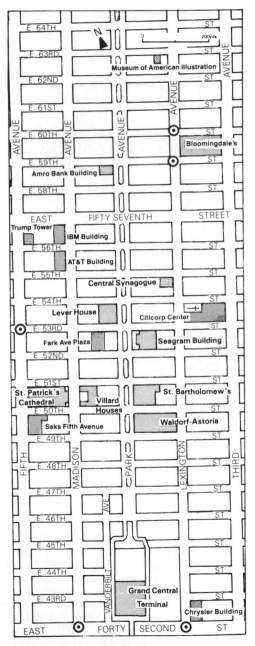

period when kings were kings and architects were princes." Burgundy and gold were also the Vanderbilt colors, and the oak leaf one of the chosen family emblems. From the N. the building, its tower gilded and dramatically floodlit at night, bestrides Park Ave, its facade pierced by two vehicular portals that carry traffic on ramps around the railroad terminal.

Park Avenue north of the Helmsley Building is now in its third stage of urban development. Before 1900, when the railroad yards ran aboveground, the street attracted modest dwellings and factories. The avenue began its upward swing when the Fourth Avenue Improvement Scheme (completed 1872–74) submerged the tracks below street level as far as 56th St, but the neighborhood remained humble until the tracks were completely decked over during the construction of Grand Central Terminal (1903–13). By the 1920s all the air rights over the tracks had been acquired by apartments and hotels, and luxury dwellings began appearing along both sides of the avenue up to 96th St where the tracks emerge from the tunnel. As Park Ave became prime residential territory land values soared, increasing over 200% between 1914 and 1930. After World War II, however, the drop in passenger revenues led the railroad to reexamine the potential of its real estate empire and to take advantage of the enormous inflation along Park Ave. Starting in the 1950s Park Ave began changing from a fine residential to a desirable commercial area, so much so that today city planners worry about its becoming the home of nothing but enormous, institutional towers. Indeed, Park Ave above Grand Central Station is the heartland of corporate America (or at least it was until corporations began finding that the taxes and other annoyances of the city outweighed its prestige) and it is the workday turf of thousands of commuters who pour daily into Grand Central from the Westchester and Connecticut suburbs.

NO. 250 PARK AVENUE (1925; Cross & Cross), originally the Postum Building, is one of only a handful of buildings remaining above 46th St from before World War II.

Across the street in front of 245 Park Ave is a tubular steel sculpture, *Performance Machine: Big O's* (1986; Lowell Jones), a kinetic work powered by a photovoltaic cell atop the building. With exquisite slowness the two intertwined rings couple and uncouple like colossal worms, their progress perceptible only at significant intervals of time.

At 270 Park Ave (bet. 47th / 48th Sts) is the former **Union Carbide Building,** (1960; Skidmore, Owings & Merrill), now the **Manufacturers Hanover Building,** 52 stories (707 ft) of matte black and stainless steel, with gray glass. Since 75% of the building stands over the railroad yards, the elevator machinery, normally installed in the basement, is aboveground and the lobby on the second floor.

In the same block but across the street is the headquarters of Chemical Bank (277 Park Ave). Inside is *Chemcourt* (entrance on 47th St), the city's largest indoor garden, a three-story greenhouse stretching a full block, luxuriant with ficus, schefflera, philodendron, and the occasional palm. Vines hang from the aluminum rafters; water cascades into marble pools. Outside is *Taxi!* (1983; J. Seward Johnson, Jr.) a lifelike sculpture of a businessman, briefcase in hand, hailing a cab at the intersection of Park Ave and 48th St.

Walk north. The **Waldorf-Astoria Hotel** (1931; Schultze & Weaver) at 301 Park Ave (bet. 49th / 50th Sts) is still architecturally and socially one of the city's finest hotels. Faced in brick and limestone over a granite base, the hotel rises to two chrome-capped 625-ft spires, the Waldorf Towers, whose private apartments, reached from a separate entrance on 50th St, once attracted such tenants as the Duke of Windsor, President Herbert Hoover, and General Douglas MacArthur. Facing Park Ave above the main door is a figure by Nina Saemundsson symbolizing the "Spirit of Achievement," though it is uncertain whether this applies to the clientele or the hotel management.

Inside, the lobby is half a flight up, since like other Park Ave buildings the hotel (1800 rooms) stands over the railroad yards and needs space aboveground for mechanical equipment. While the tracks may have been irksome for the architects, they were a convenience for former guests arriving in private railcoaches, who could be shunted onto a special siding, bypassing the terminal altogether. When the hotel opened during the Depression, President Hoover lauded it as an "exhibition of . . . confidence to the whole nation," and surely its exquisite Art Deco interiors with marble, bronze, and matched woods suggested that the management foresaw better times. Many of the public rooms, including the ballroom, have been restored to their original appearance after languishing for some 20 years in a vaguely Edwardian disguise. Of particular interest in the Park Ave foyer are the murals and "Wheel of Life" mosaic in the main lobby, both by Louis Rigal. In the LOBBY, beyond, paneled in dark wood, is a clock made for the Chicago Columbian Exposition in 1893. On it are likenesses of Washington, Lincoln, Queen Victoria, and other notables as well as bronze plaques representing various sports.

The first Waldorf-Astoria (1894) stood on the site of the Empire State Building and the names of several of the present public rooms recall those fabled days: Peacock Alley, where society's grand dames once flaunted their plumage, the Empire Room, and the Palm Garden, the old hotel's most aristocratic restaurant. Oscar's, today a modest coffee shop, commemorates that legendary maître d'hôtel, Oscar Tschirky, whose command of the subtle points of social distinction raised him to the position of social arbiter. In the olden days, the Starlight Roof, had a ceiling which could be rolled back on balmy nights, making the room worthy of its name.

Walk west on 50th St to Madison Ave and the HELMSLEY PALACE HOTEL (1980; Emery Roth & Sons). The public rooms of this luxury hotel are housed in part of the extraordinary **Villard Houses** (1886; McKim, Mead & White; DL), a U-shaped group of six sumptuous neo-Renaissance dwellings built for railroad baron Henry Villard.

History. At the peak of his power in early 1883 Villard, an Austrian immigrant, began construction on a group of houses that would convince the most casual passerby of his success. By Christmas, however, he had lost his fortune (perhaps $5 million), the presidency of the Northern Pacific Railroad, and his health. The unfinished houses were transferred to trustees to be completed and sold. Their buyers included Villard's lawyer Artemas Holmes, Harris C. Fahnestock and his son William who founded the brokerage firm Fahnestock & Co., and Mrs. Whitelaw Reid, wife of the editor of the *New York Tribune,* who bought Villard's own house for $350,000 in 1886 with wedding money from her father, millionaire Darius Ogden Mills. The houses remained residential until after World War II, when social and economic changes eroded the style of life implied by their grandeur. Random House, the publishing firm, Capital Cities Communications, and the Archdiocese of New York all used the buildings as offices, fortunately leaving them more or less intact. When the Archdiocese no longer wanted the property, exhaustive negotiations (75 official meetings and 15 public hearings) led to the present project. One of the stipulations of the conversion of the houses to a hotel was the preservation of the most important interiors.

EXTERIOR. Finished in warm Belleville (New Jersey) brownstone, the facade is modeled after the Roman Palazzo Cancelleria (1489–96), and was designed by Joseph Morrill Wells, first assistant in the office of McKim, Mead & White, an architect known for his wit as well as his talent. Once when White boasted that one of his own drawings was as good "in its way . . . as the Parthenon," Wells, eating breakfast, replied, "Yes, and so too, in its way, is a boiled egg." In the center of the complex is a courtyard, once used as a carriage turnaround. The two projecting wings with their rusticated ground floors were the Harris Fahnestock (N.) and Villard-Whitelaw Reid (S.) houses. Those in the central wing behind the graceful portico were smaller and less elaborate and have now been converted for use by the hotel.

INTERIOR. Enter the hotel from the courtyard. In the *Grand Lobby* is a red fireplace mantle with marble figures above it representing Joy, Hospitality, and Moderation, designed by Augustus Saint-Gaudens, who with Stanford White, also designed the zodiac clock near the top of the stairs.

The present *Gold Room,* used for cocktails and afternoon tea, was the Villard-Reid Music Room, its barrel-vaulted ceiling (30 ft high) gilded according to instructions by Stanford White, who completed the decor of the room after Villard's bankruptcy. In the lunettes at the ends of the vault are murals (completed 1888) by John La Farge representing Music and Drama. Beneath them are plaster casts of Luca della Robbia's marble Cantoria (1431–48) in Florence, perhaps suggested by Augustus Saint-Gaudens who had returned from study in Italy with casts of works he admired. The *Madison Room* (nearest Madison Ave) was the drawing room enlarged and redecorated by the Reids who installed marble columns with bronze doré Corinthian capitals in the new "French" taste. The small door to the right of the fireplace was concealed behind a hinged marble niche and allowed an unobtrusive escape from dull receptions. The *Hunt Room,* with its carved English oak paneling remains more or less as it was in Villard's day; the inlaid mahogany panels along the bottom of the frieze have sentimental mottoes in Latin, French, English, and German—Villard's native language (he was baptized Ferdinand Heinrich Gustav Hilgard).

The grand new hotel was at first to be called simply The Palace, a name it unfortunately shared with a Bowery flophouse, which began receiving unexpected requests for reservations from major corporations and well-heeled visitors. When the Bowery establishment refused to change its name to suit the upstart newcomer, the latter became the Helmsley Palace.

The wing N. of the courtyard, originally owned by Harris Fahnestock but later joined with the adjacent house by his son William who inherited it, now serves the **Urban Center,** a group of organizations dedicated to historic preservation, architecture, and urban planning: the Municipal Art Society, the Parks Council, the Architectural League, and the New York Chapter of the American Institute of Architects. Visitors may enjoy the Fahnestocks' reception rooms as they attend lectures, seminars, and exhibitions or browse in the superbly stocked bookstore specializing in architectural books.

The Municipal Art Society was founded (1892) during the City Beautiful movement by architect Richard Morris Hunt and others to embellish the city with sculpture, fountains, and other forms of public art. Today the organization keeps a watchful eye on the urban environment, its design, preservation, and maintenance. Among the society's causes have been battles against gaudy advertising—on Fifth Ave (1917), on river barges (1964), and on taxis (1973)— as well as campaigns for the preservation of Pennsylvania Station (1963), Grand Central Terminal (1970), and Radio City Music Hall (1978). Most recently the group has (so far successfully) sought to block construction of a brutally massive building on the site of the former New York Coliseum at Columbus Circle, whose bulk threatened to cast a long dark shadow over the southwestern corner of Central Park.

The *New York Chapter, American Institute of Architects* on the second floor, has occasional exhibitions.

Return to Park Ave. **St. Bartholomew's Church** (Protestant Episcopal) facing Park Ave between 50th and 51st Sts (1919; Bertram G. Goodhue; DL) is one of the oldest buildings along the avenue. The congregation bought the site for $1.5 million in 1914 from the F. & M. Schaefer Brewing Co., which had been making beer by the railroad tracks since 1860.

EXTERIOR. The ornate carved portico comes from the previous St. Bartholomew's Church (1902) on Madison Ave, designed by Stanford White, who styled it after a Romanesque church at St. Gilles in southern France and hired Daniel Chester French and Philip Martiny, among others, to execute the figures. Connecting the three arches of the portal is a frieze depicting events from the Old and New Testaments. The tympanum over the center doors contains a representation of the Coronation of Christ.

INTERIOR. The mosaics on the ceiling of the narthex by Hildreth Meiere tell the story of the Creation. The narthex opens into the three aisles of the nave, built facing E. in the traditional cruciform shape with a barrel-vaulted ceiling. The structural elements are stone and marble veneered over concrete and much of the wall surface has been covered with rough-textured Guastavino acoustic tiles. The *West Window* is made of stained glass given as memorials for the earlier Madison Ave church and has figures of evangelists and scenes from the New Testament. Along the N. aisle (toward 51st St) are six stained glass windows by John Gordon Guthrie illustrating the Te Deum. Dominating the interior is a mosaic of glass and gold leaf (also by Hildreth Meiere) filling the ceiling of the *apse*. It represents the Transfiguration with Christ in the center flanked by Elijah and Moses standing on the mountain and the disciples Peter (N. side), James, and John (S. side). The five tall windows in the apse below are filled with thin sheets of amber onyx and covered with grilles of the same material.

Return to Park Ave. On the S. side of the church is the *Community House* (1927; Bertram G. Goodhue Assocs. and Mayers, Murray & Philip; DL) added by Goodhue's successor firm after his death. The garden (1971) along with the Community House converts the church into an L-shaped complex whose pleasing proportions and open space provide a moment of grace along an avenue that is becoming increasingly an unrelieved wall of skyscrapers. A 1981 plan to lease the land under the garden and Community House for the development of an office tower, giving the church an estimated $7 million annual income, led to a bitter and as yet (1989) unresolved conflict between preservationists and the church vestry.

Providing a dramatic background to the church is the reddish-orange brick of the **General Electric Building** (1931; Cross & Cross; DL) at 570 Lexington Ave (S.W. corner of 51st St), whose spiked Art Deco crown suggests the fantasies of science fiction, as appropriate to the present tenant as to the original one, the R.C.A. Victor Company. The lobby, with terrazzo floors, pale purple marble panels, aluminum light sconces, and silvery barrel-vaulted ceiling openings is as coolly elegant as anything in the city.

Walk N. on Park Ave from St. Bartholomew's Church. On the S. side of 345 Park Ave along 51st St is a 12 × 20 ft bronze sculpture *Dinoceras* (1971; Robert Cook), suggestive of a struggling animal and named after a horned mammal of the Eocene period.

On the next block between 52nd and 53rd Sts stands the *Seagram Building* (1958; Ludwig Mies van der Rohe and Philip Johnson; Kahn & Jacobs), a classic, elegant metal and glass curtain-wall building. Set back 90 ft from the building line, the Seagram tower rises on square columns to a height of about 500 ft (150 ft wide by 90 ft thick). All the materials from the wall of the custom-made amber glass and bronze, to the green Italian marble seating around the fountain, to the brushed aluminum and stainless steel hardware, were chosen for their quality and meticulously deployed. The excellence of the building stems largely from the interest and sophistication of Phyllis Lambert, daughter of Seagram board chairman Samuel Bronfman, who persuaded her father to erect a monumental not just a serviceable building and who chose Mies van der Rohe as architect.

When the Four Seasons restaurant opened (1959; Philip Johnson & Assocs.) in the Seagram Building, its intentionally modern decor created a stir which has since subsided into enduring admiration. There is a sculpture of metal rods by Richard Lippold in the grill and a stage backdrop for *Le Tricorne* (1929) by Picasso in the corridor between the two main dining rooms.

Across the street from the Seagram Building at 370 Park Ave (bet. 52nd / 53rd Sts) is the **Racquet and Tennis Club** (1918; McKim, Mead & White; DL), designed after White and McKim were dead and Mead had retired. Behind the row of blind arched windows at the top are tennis and squash courts. Beneath the cornice is a terra-cotta frieze of racquets and netting. The club was built for the enjoyment of the well-to-do and well-connected athlete who could disport himself on its especially constructed, slate-based tennis courts built at a time when indoor tennis was a rarity and there were still a few kings around to play court tennis, an esoteric form of tennis played in a court similar to a squash court and known, in its heyday, as the sport of kings.

Like the Villard Houses and St. Bartholomew's Church, the Racquet and Tennis Club has become a purveyor of air rights and now squats in front of a 575-ft office tower clad in aquamarine-tinted glass. In a complicated legal maneuver the developer, Fisher Bros., got permission to build a tower called PARK AVE-NUE PLAZA (1981; Skidmore, Owings & Merrill) that contains as much space as would be permitted on the site of the office building plus the site of the racquet club, thus "shoehorning" a big building onto a small site. The building has an elegant high atrium with greenery, a sculptural waterfall, a shopping arcade, tables and chairs, and a cafe (open Mon—Fri 8—7:30).

In June 1981 the City Planning Commission proposed a new zoning law to discourage midblock "shoehorning" on the overbuilt East Side, seeking to limit the size of buildings.

Continue up Park Ave. **Lever House** at 390 Park Ave between 53rd and 54th Sts (1952; Skidmore, Owings & Merrill; DL) by the same architectural firm seems modest today, though it did not when it made its appearance on Park Ave, the first commercial structure on a residential avenue and the first steel and glass building in a file of stolid masonry apartment houses. The building takes its form from two slabs, one stretched out horizontally along the street, the other rising vertically. On the ground floor is an open interior courtyard with a garden and a pedestrian arcade. Lever House, once considered the ultimate corporate headquarters, is impressive today partly because it is so small, smaller than it legally had to be, an act of restraint on the part of the builders which has since elicited proposals from developers to tear it down and replace it with something bigger.

Walk E. on 54th St to Lexington Ave. Here, filling the block between 53rd and 54th Sts is the **Citicorp Center** (1978; Hugh Stubbins & Assocs.), a midtown office tower as representative of 1970s architectural values as Lever House and the Seagram Building were of the values of the 1950s. The Citicorp Center is a mixed-use building with offices and shops. The tower, sheathed in gleaming white aluminum, rises 915 ft from the street, resting on four 127-ft columns which support it at the midpoints of the sides, not at the corners. The top of the building slants at a 45 degree angle, the large plane surface facing south originally intended as a solar collector, now a conspicuous form on the skyline among the domes, crowns, and spires of yesteryear and the flat tops of the previous generation.

On the N.W. corner of the site, under the tower, is **St. Peter's Church** (Lutheran), founded in 1861, which has existed here since 1904 and allowed Citicorp to buy its old building with the understanding that it would erect a new one (1977; Hugh Stubbins & Assocs.). The angular form of the church faced with Caledonia granite to some observers suggests a rock, to others a granite tent; inside are the sanctuary, acoustically isolated from the street and subway, a small theater (seats 250), and the beautiful Erol Beker *Chapel of the Good Shepherd (open for meditation during the day), enhanced by Louise Nevelson's wall sculptures.

N. wall: *Cross of the Good Shepherd* and three columns, *Trinity*. E. wall: *Frieze of the Apostles*. W. wall: *Sky Vestment—Trinity*. S. wall: *Grapes & Wheat Lintel* and S.W. wall: *Cross of the Resurrection*.

St. Peter's Church is also known for its jazz vesper services (Sun at 5; check weekly listings in the newspapers or magazines for performers).

Enter the **Citicorp Building** either from Lexington Ave or from 54th St.

Public restrooms are located near the 54th St entrance.

Surrounding the atrium, lit by a skylight and furnished with plants, tables, and chairs, are attractive shops and restaurants. Occasional free concerts and other events are held here.

A block E. and a little S. across Third Ave between 53rd and 54th Sts is *885 Third Ave* known popularly as the "Lipstick Building" (1986; John Burgee with Philip Johnson), an elliptical building on a rectangular site, a round peg in a square hole, as architecture critic Paul Goldberger has remarked.

Return to Lexington Ave, and walk a block N. to the **Central Synagogue** (1872; Henry Fernbach; DL) at 652 Lexington Ave (S.W. corner of 55th St). It is the oldest synagogue in continual use in the state and was designed by the first Jew to practice architecture in New York, Henry Fernbach, known chiefly for his cast-iron work in SoHo. While Judaism has never had an architectural heritage similar to the Gothic tradition in Christianity, the Moorish style with its allusions to Judaic roots in the Middle East became the dominant style of synagogue architecture in the middle 19C, and the Central Synagogue is generally considered the finest example of Moorish Revival architecture in the city. The onion-shaped green copper domes rise to 122 ft. The interior is colorfully stenciled in red, blue, and ochre. The congregation was founded as Ahawath Chesed (Love of Mercy) in Coblenzer's Hotel on Ludlow St by 18 men, most of them immigrants from

Bohemia. Following the uptown migration of the Jewish population, the congregation moved northward gradually, acquiring the
present site in 1870.

Return to Park Avenue and walk N. one block to 56th St. On
the S.W. corner, jammed into the N. end of *430 Park Ave* is the
Mercedes-Benz showroom, remarkable mainly for being Frank
Lloyd Wright's first (1955) New York work.

On the sixth floor of the Korean Consulate, 460 Park Ave at
57th St, is the gallery of the **Korean Cultural Service,** with
changing exhibitions of Korean art.

Korean Cultural Service. 460 Park Ave (57th St), New York 10022. Tel: 759-
9550. Open Mon–Fri 10–5. Admission free. Library, lectures, catalogues. No
restaurant, no gift shop. Restrooms in corridor outside gallery.

Three blocks N. at 59th St (500 Park Ave) is the *Amro Bank
Building,* originally the **Pepsico Building** (1960; Skidmore, Owings
& Merrill). This elegant aluminum and glass box was built for
the Pepsi Cola Co., which fled to the suburbs around 1970. Its
successor, the Olivetti Corporation, left in 1978, and the building
was saved from demolition by selling its air rights to 500 Park
Tower (1984; James Stewart Polshek) now "shoehorned" above
it.

Walk a block W. to Madison Ave. Two large corporate skyscrapers have recently been completed here. The **American Telephone
and Telegraph Company Building** between 55th and 56th Sts
(1984; Philip Johnson & John Burgee), which raised a few
eyebrows when its design was announced in 1979, stands on a
131-ft masonry base of rose-gray granite with ground-floor arcades
and rises to a huge broken pediment—the cause of the elevated
brows—which elicited jokes about New York's first Chippendale
skyscraper and questions about the architect's seriousness. Since
its completion, however, the building (648 ft tall) has generally
elicited critical praise for its monumental proportions, its beautiful materials (notably the rosy Stony Creek granite sheathing),
and its public spaces, including a row of shops and a covered
colonnade. Historians have pointed to the architects' rejection of
the stark glass and steel of International style in favor of classic
principles articulated in its materials and forms (the split pediment on top, the Renaissance-inspired base). In the lobby is
Evelyn Beatrice Longman's 24-ft winged statue, *The Spirit of
Communication* (1916), known affectionately as *Golden Boy,*
which previously stood atop the former AT&T headquarters at
195 Broadway. On the N. and S. sides are colonnaded outdoor
loggias with tables and chairs.

Located within the building is the **AT&T InfoQuest Center,** a
hands-on museum of technology that should delight the techno-
phile, old or young. There are exhibits on microchips, communications technology, and computers; among the many interactive
exhibits are a number disguised as games, where those so
inclined can "direct" their own rock video, manipulate a robot,
or program a computer to respond to voice commands.

The AT&T InfoQuest Center. 550 Madison Ave (56th St), New York 10022.
Tel: 605-5555. Open Tues 10–9; Wed–Sun 10–6. Closed Mon, national holi-

days. Free. During peak hours (weekends), free admission tickets available at the kiosk on 56th St. Children under 10 must be accompanied by an adult. Groups of 10 or more must make reservations.

Restrooms, small gift shop. No restaurant. Accessible to wheelchairs: ramps, elevators, restrooms, and telephones equipped for handicapped users.

SUBWAY: IRT Lexington Ave local or express (train 4, 5, or 6) to 59th St. IND 6th Ave express (F train) or IND 8th Ave local (E train) to 5th Ave-53rd St. BMT Broadway local (R train) to 5th Ave-60th St. BUS: M1. M2, M3, M4, or M32 uptown via Madison or downtown via 5th Ave; M5 uptown via 6th Ave, downtown via 5th Ave; M28 crosstown on 57th St. M30 crosstown on 72nd St to 57th St.

More conservative than the AT&T building, the **IBM Building** (1983; Edward Larrabee Barnes, Assocs.) at 590 Madison Ave (bet. 56th / 57th Sts) is distinguished by its shape (a five-sided prism, like a right triangle with two points sliced off), its color (a dark gray-green), and its public spaces (an enormous, glass-enclosed garden atrium and an exhibition gallery). Although the IBM Building does not break radically from recent skyscraper design, it has been hailed as a dignified addition to midtown. The granite which sheathes this 403-ft skyscraper, chosen to harmonize with the greenish glass of the windows and the greenhouse park, was quarried in Quebec, Canada. The windows, set in strips around the building like those of the Citicorp Center, are sealed shut but have 4-in slots beneath them that can open to provide fresh air. On the corner of Madison Ave and 57th St is a sculptural fountain, *Levitated Mass* (1982; Michael Heizer), under which sluices a torrent of water.

Inside is one of the city's better public spaces, the 68-ft atrium covered with a saw-toothed glass roof and brightened with seasonal displays of flora. The tall stands of bamboo, struggling a bit beneath the glass, the fountain, tables and chairs, and the kiosk for snacks (closed weekends) make it a favorite midtown rest stop, both for smartly clad shoppers and the city's less fortunate inhabitants. The New York Botanical Garden maintains a shop here for gardening buffs, with supplies, plants, bulbs, and a range of horticulturally decorated gifts (open Mon–Sat 10–6).

Downstairs (enter from the atrium or 590 Madison Ave) is the **I.B.M. Gallery of Science and Art.**

I.B.M. Gallery of Science and Art. Madison Ave at 56th St, New York 10022. Tel: 407-6100 (gallery information, recorded message). Open Tues–Fri 11–6; Sat 10–5. Closed Sun, Mon, some legal holidays. Free.

Computerized information service about New York cultural events. Changing exhibitions, gallery talks, films, lectures, catalogues. Restrooms, telephones. No restaurant (but food available in atrium), no gift shop. Accessible to wheelchairs: elevator; restrooms and telephones equipped for use by handicapped visitors.

SUBWAY: IRT Lexington Ave local or express (train 4, 5, or 6) to 59th St. IND 8th Ave local (E train) to 5th Ave-53rd St. IND 6th Ave local (F train) to 5th Ave-53rd St. BMT Broadway local (N or R train) to 5th Ave. BUS: M1, M2, M3, or M4 uptown via Madison Ave, downtown via 5th Ave. M28 crosstown on 57th St. M30 crosstown on 72nd St.

The gallery, a handsomely appointed subterranean space, presents a range of superior exhibitions on everything from computer technology to folk art. In the foyer is a multimonitored computerized cultural guide with information about some 250 cultural institutions within the city—hours, prices, exhibitions, and facilities.

Begin walking E. on East 57th Street. At 45 E. 57th St (N.E. corner of Madison Ave) is the **Fuller Building** (1929; Walker & Gillette; DL), a slender Art Deco building with a clock and sculptural figures by Elie Nadelman. To some observers the patterned apex of the tower suggested a neo-Babylonian ziggurat or a Mayan temple.

The Fuller Co., at the time, was one of the nation's largest construction firms, best known perhaps for a building that for a while officially bore its name but came to be indicated by its shape, the Flatiron Building.

Today the Fuller Building houses several floors of prestigious art galleries.

At 57th St and Park Ave (N.E. corner) is the **Ritz Tower** (1925; Emery Roth and Carrère & Hastings), a vintage Park Ave masonry apartment building with all the trappings of its period—an elaborate top, swags, urns, cartouches, and balustrades marking the major setbacks. The setbacks created terraces and balconies at various levels and, in the slender tower were a number of duplex apartments with two-story living rooms that stretched along a full facade. The legendary restaurant Le Pavillon (founded during the New York World's Fair of 1939) once stood on the ground floor.

Nearby at 117 E. 57th St is THE GALLERIA (1975; David Kenneth Specter & Philip Birnbaum), the second experiment after Olympic Tower to rise under the zoning law redistricting Fifth Ave and some surrounding territory for mixed residential and commercial uses. It contains luxury apartments, a retail arcade, offices, and a health club. The elaborate penthouse on top was built for a millionaire as an office, residence, and vegetable garden, whose prospective 2000 tons of soil necessitated a frame of concrete, poured in place.

Continue E. to Lexington Ave and turn left (N.). On the E. side of the avenue between 57th and 58th Sts is ALEXANDER'S, one of the city's major department stores. Like its peers, Alexander's began (1928) as a small shop—on Third Ave—specializing in dry goods; it is known as a discount store with an eye to fashion.

To its N. is **Bloomingdale's** (bet. 59th / 60th Sts on the E. side of Lexington Ave), which in the past decades has become associated with whatever is "hot" in women's fashion. Known to its habitués as "Bloomies," it is one of the nation's most successful stores.

History. Lyman Bloomingdale, who with his brother Joseph founded the store in 1872, learned the retail business as a clerk in Bettlebeck & Co. Dry Goods in Newark, New Jersey, a firm with an all-star sales staff that also included Benjamin Altman (who later founded B. Altman & Co.), and Abraham Abraham (later of Abraham and Straus). Unlike the other 19C department stores which began downtown and trailed the middle class uptown, Bloomingdale's started at 938 Third Ave, only a few blocks from its present location. In both its arrival and its demise, the Third Ave elevated railway was a blessing to Bloomingdale's, first bringing so many shoppers from downtown when it opened (1879) that within seven years the store had to move to larger quarters on the N.W. corner of Third Ave and 59th St, a block it now completely occupies. Then, when the El was torn down (1954), the Upper East Side, formerly depressed by the inconveniences attendant upon the El, began a swift climb to respectability and affluence. Fortunately the store's management had already begun upgrading the inventory from its former good quality but sensible merchandise to the present stuff of fashion and fantasy.

The exterior of the building is a conglomeration of styles, the section at 740 Lexington Ave (1930; Starrett & Van Vleck), an Art Deco addition, its most interesting segment. The main floor, known as B'way, redesigned (1979) in black plastic, marble, and mirrored glass, is still chic and glitters as expensively as anything in New York.

Bloomingdale's has become surrounded by such mythic appeal that it appears regularly as a film location: scenes of *An Unmarried Woman, Moscow on the Hudson, Splash,* and *Manhattan,* have all unfolded in the halls and corridors of Bloomies.

Additional points of interest. There are a number of small but interesting museums in the vicinity.

The **Grolier Club**, founded 1884 (1917; Bertram G. Goodhue), takes its name from 16C French bibliophile Jean Grolier and is dedicated to the art of book production. In connection with this scholarly interest, the club presents (Oct—June) changing exhibitions highlighting books, writers, manuscripts, and old prints.

The Grolier Club. 47 E. 60th St (Madison / Park Aves), New York 10022. Tel: 838-6690. Open during exhibitions Mon—Sat 10—5. Free. Exhibition catalogs. Restroom. No food, no gift shop.
SUBWAY: IRT Lexington Ave (train 4, 5, or 6) to 59th St. BMT Broadway local (N or R train) to 59th St. BUS: M1, M2, M3, or M4 uptown via Madison Ave, downtown via 5th Ave.

The **Museum of American Illustration** serves as an exhibition space for the Society of Illustrators and offers changing exhibitions designed to encourage interest in the art of illustration.

Society of Illustrators: Museum of American Illustration. 128 E. 63rd St (Park Ave), New York 10021. Tel: 838-2560. Open Mon—Fri 10—5, Tues evenings until 8. Closed weekends, during the month of Aug, and on legal holidays. Free. Changing exhibitions. Lecture series twice yearly. Restrooms. Telephone (second floor). No restaurant. Museum shop. Ground floor exhibition space accessible to wheelchairs.
SUBWAY: IRT Lexington Ave local or express (train 4, 5, or 6) to 59th St. BUS: M1, M2, M3, or M4 uptown via Madison Ave, downtown via 5th Ave. M29 crosstown on 66th / 67th St. M30 crosstown on 72nd St and downtown via 5th Ave.

In addition to shows of individual artists and groups, historical and thematic exhibitions—Cream of Wheat Advertising, 1910—40, the Chicago School in the 1940s—the society presents the Illustrators' Annual Exhibition with the best book, editorial, advertising, and institutional illustrations of the year.

The China Institute in America, a nonpolitical, nonprofit organization (founded 1926) offers courses in Chinese culture—language, cooking, calligraphy—activities for the Chinese community, and bilingual vocational training. It also sponsors the CHINA HOUSE GALLERY, which mounts two major exhibitions yearly, for example a Chinese Lantern Festival in celebration of the Chinese New Year.

China House Gallery. 125 E. 65th St (bet. Park / Lexington Aves), New York 10021. Tel: 744-8181. Open Mon—Sat 10—5. Closed during summer. Admission by voluntary contribution. Lectures, catalogs.
   SUBWAY: IRT Lexington Ave local (train 6) to 68th St. BUS: M1, M2, M3, or M4 uptown via Madison Ave, downtown via 5th Ave. M101 or M102 uptown via 3rd Ave, downtown via Lexington Ave.

Occupying a whole block (Lexington to Park Aves, 66th to 67th Sts) is the **Seventh Regiment Armory** (1880; Charles W. Clinton), which includes a huge drill hall (187 × 290 ft), offices, and meeting rooms. The drill hall holds the annual winter antiques sale and other large-scale events. The smaller rooms were originally decorated by Louis Comfort Tiffany.

21 The Whitney Museum and Environs

SUBWAY: IRT Lexington Ave local (train 6) to 77th St.

BUS: M1, M2, M3, or M4 uptown via Madison Ave or downtown via Fifth Ave. M30 crosstown on 72nd St.

The ***Whitney Museum of American Art,** founded by Gertrude Vanderbilt Whitney houses a stellar collection of modern American art.

The Whitney Museum of American Art. 945 Madison Ave (75th St), New York 10021. Tel: 570-3676. Open Tues 11—8, Wed—Sat 11—6, Sun 12—6. Closed Mon, Christmas. Admission charge. Free Tues after 6.
   Changing exhibitions, lectures, gallery talks, symposia, performances, film, video. Pleasant restaurant, restrooms, telephones. Bookshop. Accessible to wheelchairs: ramp at entrance, elevators.

The building (1966) designed by Marcel Breuer, a member of the Bauhaus group, has made the museum an architectural presence on Madison Ave. Breuer spoke of wanting the museum to have the vitality of the streets, the latitude of a bridge, and the weight of a skyscraper. What resulted is a building of three tiers of reinforced concrete clad in gray granite and cantilevered out like the steps of an inverted pyramid. The seven windows are randomly sized and placed; the entrance is reached by a concrete bridge over a sunken sculpture garden. Currently plans are underway for an addition to the building.

History. In 1907 Gertrude Vanderbilt Whitney opened a studio in Greenwich Village (see p. 234). Linked by birth and marriage to two of the city's wealthiest and most eminent families, the Whitneys (oil and streetcars) and the Vanderbilts (shipping and railroads), she was nonetheless drawn to a kind of Bohemianism and used her considerable means to support and exhibit young American artists. The Whitney Studio Club showed Stuart Davis, Edward Hopper, Charles Sheeler, Reginald Marsh, and John Sloan, among others, and Mrs. Whitney further supported the artists by buying many of the works she exhibited. In 1929 she offered her collection to the Metropolitan Museum of

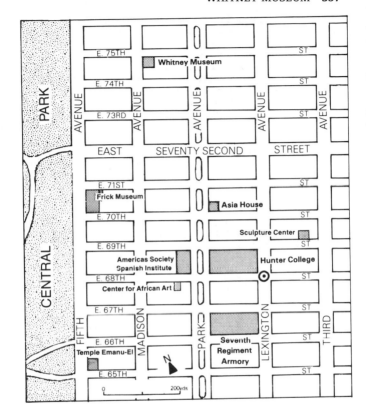

Art, which spurned it, and so understandably irritated with the establishment, she opened the first Whitney Museum on 8th St in 1931. In 1954 the museum moved uptown to 54th St next to the Museum of Modern Art, a move that almost quadrupled its attendance, and today the Whitney is the most important showcase of contemporary American art in the city. As the museum continues to expand it has elected to create branches: the Downtown Branch at Federal Reserve Plaza (see p. 134), the Whitney Museum at Philip Morris on 42nd St (see p. 297), the Whitney Museum at Equitable Center (see p. 380), and a branch in suburban Stamford, Connecticut.

In addition to a full program of changing exhibitions, many of which have attracted wide interest, a representative sample of the permanent collection is on view in the galleries on the third floor.

GROUND FLOOR: Alexander Calder's *Circus* near the main staircase, has become a familiar introduction to the museum, its whimsical performers made of wire and bits of fabric. (Video shown every two hours beginning at 11:30.)

The FIRST and SECOND FLOORS are taken up with changing exhibitions. In addition to solo shows of modern and contemporary artists (Charles Sheeler, Elizabeth Murray, Donald Judd, David Salle, Julian Schnabel, Richard Artschwager), there have been thematic shows surveying, for example, 20C American design, Shaker handcrafts, treasures of American folk art.

On the THIRD FLOOR is a permanent installation of selected major works from the collection, with some 60 paintings and sculptures. Ranging chronologically from Marsden Hartley's *Painting, Number 5* (1914–15) to Scott Burton's *Pair of Two-Part Chairs, Obtuse Angle* (1984), the exhibition offers an abbreviated view of the most comprehensive collection of 20C American art in the world. The development of American art before World War II is illustrated by examples of realism (a tradition Gertrude Vanderbilt Whitney particularly appreciated) by Edward Hopper, George Bellows, and Guy Pène du Bois. Early abstract artists include Stuart Davis, Arthur G. Dove, and Georgia O'Keeffe. Major postwar artists are represented either by multiple works or important single holdings: Alexander Calder, Willem de Kooning, Philip Guston, Al Held, Jasper Johns, Donald Judd, Ellsworth Kelly, Franz Kline, Roy Lichtenstein, Louise Nevelson, Barnett Newman, Claes Oldenburg, Jackson Pollock, Mark Rothko, David Smith, Frank Stella, and Cy Twombly.

The Madison Ave corridor from about 57th–86th Sts has one of the city's three major concentrations of **art galleries** (the others are in SoHo and on 57th St). The uptown galleries, generally older and more traditional than those in SoHo, offer works of virtually every period and movement in the history of art.

The Sunday *New York Times, New York Magazine,* and *The New Yorker* magazine offer schedules of current gallery shows. Most galleries are closed Sun and Mon and many close for vacation during part of the summer.

Walk E. to Park Ave. A relative newcomer (chartered 1982) to the East Side cultural scene is the CENTER FOR AFRICAN ART.

Center for African Art. 54 E. 68th St (Park Ave), New York 10021. Tel: 861-1200. Open Tues–Fri 10–5; Sat 11–5; Sun 12–5. Admission charge; lower rates for students, children, and the elderly. Restroom. Catalogues. Not accessible to wheelchairs.

The Center, which seeks to deepen understanding of Africa's ancient cultures, offers three exhibitions of tribal African art yearly and supplements the shows with catalogues, lectures, and films.

Occupying the block of Park Ave, 68th–69th Sts, is a group of houses built in the years after the turn of the century and now devoted to different intercultural agencies. The first is the former *Percy R. Pyne residence* (1911; McKim, Mead & White; DL), the town house of a third-generation banker who also led the life of a country squire on an estate in New Jersey.

In 1965 a developer wanted to demolish the house and its neighbors in favor of an apartment building, but the Marquesa de Cuevas, a granddaughter of John D. Rockefeller, bought them all and turned them over to their present owners.

The building currently houses the **Americas Society** and its gallery.

The Americas Society, formerly the Center for Inter-American Relations. 680 Park Ave (68th St), New York 10021. Tel: 249-8950. Open Tues–Sun 12–6. Closed Mon, holidays. Suggested donation.

Lectures, concerts, group visits, and guided tours by appointment. Restrooms, telephone. No restaurant. Catalogues, posters, books on Latin-American culture and history. Entrance up two steps from street level; gallery on ground floor.

SUBWAY: Lexington Ave IRT local (train 6) to 68th St. BUS: M1, M2, M3, or M4 uptown via Madison Ave, downtown via 5th Ave. M101, M102 uptown via 3rd Ave, downtown via Lexington Ave. M29 crosstown on 66th / 67th St.

Since 1967, the Americas Society Art Gallery has presented a continuing program of exhibitions documenting the achievements of the countries neighboring the U. S. to the north and south. The inaugural exhibition, Precursors of Modernism, was the first survey to place painting from the Americas into a single historic context. Since then the gallery has offered a wide range of shows, some devoted to emerging talents, some to prominent artists (Fernando Botero, Rufino Tamayo, Matta, even Camille Pissarro, who was born in the Virgin Islands), some to indigenous Indian cultures and their pre-Columbian heritage. A current program seeks to introduce younger artists who are virtually unknown outside their native countries, to a larger audience; it opened in 1988 with the presentation of three Venezuelan artists and in the future will spotlight other leading figures from major cultural centers.

The **Spanish Institute** at 684 Park Ave (1926; McKim, Mead & White; DL) has an exhibition program that offers some of the finest in contemporary Spanish art.

The Spanish Institute, Center for American-Spanish Affairs. 684 Park Ave (68th St), New York 10021. Tel: 628-0420. Open during exhibitions Mon–Sat 11–5. Closed Sun, holidays. Free.

Changing exhibitions, lectures and symposia on Spanish politics, economy, culture; language instruction, dance instruction, courses in art history. Telephone, restrooms. No restaurant. No gift shop, but exhibition catalogues available. Entrance up three stairs from street. Main gallery on first floor. In large exhibitions, basement galleries are used.

SUBWAY and BUS: Same as for Americas Society.

There are usually four exhibitions yearly, one in the autumn and three in the spring. Notable have been lithographs and pastels illustrating *Don Quixote* by the Surrealist Matta, drawings by the poet and playwright Federico García Lorca, and photographs by Francesc Català-Roca, works dating from 1949 and ranging in subject from portraits of artists to street scenes in places as disparate as Barcelona and Andorra. To mark its 30th anniversary, the Institute mounted an exhibition of prints by Goya, drawing on the five major print cycles made by the artist during his long career and including a group of etchings from the series ''Disasters of War,'' inspired by the atrocities that followed Napoleon's invasion of Spain.

Also in the block are the *Italian Cultural Institute* at 686 Park

Ave (1919; Delano and Aldrich; DL) and the *Consulate General of Italy* at 690 Park Ave (1917; Walker & Gillette; DL).

Continue uptown. The **Asia Society,** on the N.E. corner of Park Ave at 70th St, was founded in 1956 to further American awareness of Asian culture, arts, politics, economics, and customs. On the Park Ave facade of the new building (1981; Edward Larrabee Barnes Assocs.), incised in the red Oklahoma granite, is the society's logo, a lion adapted from an 18C bronze Nepalese guardian lion. The galleries host changing exhibitions and house a permanent collection of Asian art, given by Mr. and Mrs. John D. Rockefeller III.

The Asia Society. 725 Park Ave (70th St), New York 10021. Tel: 288-6400. Open Tues—Sat 11—6, Sun 12—5. Closed Mon, holidays. Admission charge.

Changing exhibitions, lectures, gallery tours, group tours by appointment (tel: 288-6400). Concerts, films, arts programs, performances of music, theater, and dance; special events; membership with benefits. Restrooms, telephone, no restaurant. Bookshop, excellent gift shop. Accessible to wheelchairs.

SUBWAY: IRT Lexington Ave local (train 6) to 68th St. BUS: M1, M2, M3, or M4 uptown via Madison Ave, downtown via 5th Ave. M29 crosstown on 66th / 67th St.

The collection includes some 250 objects, not all on display, given to the society in 1979 by John D. Rockefeller III, who began seriously collecting Asian art in 1951. He and his wife visited the Orient frequently over the next decades, assembling their collection in part as souvenirs of their experiences, in part to bring together a group of objects that would reflect the achievements of Asian artists. The collection therefore is small and personal in scale and yet of uniformly high quality, with pieces from Japan, Korea, China, India, and Southeast Asia.

There are early CHINESE bronze ritual wine and food vessels dating from the 11C B.C. to the early 10C B.C. and ceramics, including a storage jar with spiral decoration from the Neolithic period (c. 2200 B.C.). There are several stoneware bowls with incised decoration and celadon glazes from the Northern Sung (early 12C) and Chin (12C) periods, examples of other famous Sung glazes—"hare's fur," "oil spot," and the gray-blue crackled "Ko" type. Ming dynasty (early 15C) ceramics include Ching-te-chen blue and white ware, which Rockefeller seems to have collected in particular abundance. There are also fine Ch'ing dynasty porcelains, decorated with underglaze cobalt blue or *famille rose* overglaze enamels.

INDIAN ART is represented by some 50 pieces of sculpture from the Kushan period (A.D. late 2—3C); figures of Buddha from the Gupta period (A.D. 320—600), the golden age of Sanskrit literature; and sculpted examples of the many deities of Buddhism. In addition to the sculpture are manuscript pages from the Rajput school (16—19C in northern India), a style influenced by Mughal conventions, and from the Rajasthan (late 18C). NEPALI art is represented by several figures of the Bodhisattva Avalokiteshvara, executed in gilt bronze or silver and richly decorated, as well as illuminated leaves from 12C manuscripts.

The art of SOUTHEAST ASIA begins with several Cambodian

sculptures from the pre-Angkor period (7–8C) and includes sandstone and bronze figures from the Angkor period (11–13C), Buddhist sculptures from Thailand (7–8C), Indonesia (8–12C), and Burma (11–15C), as well as stoneware from Thailand (14–15C) and Vietnam (15C).

The JAPANESE collection draws from the full range and history of a long tradition. There is a primitive figure from the Jomon period (6–7C), as well as Buddhist figures and scrolls from the Kamakura period (12–13C) when the religion was imported into Japan. Traditional ink painting is represented by hanging scrolls from the Muromachi period (15–16C). Woodcuts, first developed as a cheaper alternative to painting, soon developed into a major art form, and the collection has prints by Kitagawa Utamaro and other artists of the Edo period (18–19C). Japanese ceramics are represented by Momoyama and Edo stonewares and Imari and elegantly decorated Kakiemon porcelains from the late 17C.

Diversion. Not far away at 119 E. 74th St (bet. Park / Lexington Aves) is the *Church of the Resurrection* (1869; Renwick & Sands), built originally as a missionary venture on the wrong side of the Park Ave railroad tracks. The slate roof is timbered and the center corbels carry shields of the parish, the Diocese of New York, and the See of Canterbury. The brasses in the church are replicas of English brass plaques dating from the 13C onward.

St. Jean Baptiste Church (1913; Nicholas Serracino; DL) at 1067–1071 Lexington Ave, S.E. corner of E. 76th St, was built to serve a Yorkville parish of French Canadian Catholics founded in 1882. The building, funded by financier Thomas Fortune Ryan, its towered and domed silhouette anchoring the intersection, harks back to Renaissance Italian precedents.

Walk S. on Lexington Ave. There is a wonderful row of carriage houses (built from c. 1884–1902; various architects; DL) on E. 73rd St between Lexington and Third Aves, Nos. 168–182 on the S. side of the street and Nos. 161–167 on the north. Because the New York street grid had no room for service alleys, certain streets were given over to carriage houses and stables. Joseph Pulitzer at one time owned No. 166. No. 177 (1906; Charles F. Hoppe; DL), a harbinger of the future, was built as a garage for automobiles. Continue S. on Lexington Ave. Turn right at 70th St.

The anachronistic but appealing *Paul Mellon House* at 125 E. 70th St (bet. Lexington / Park Aves) is one of the few town houses built after World War II (1965; Mazza & Seccia). Nearby, the *Visiting Nurse Service of New York* (107 E. 70th St) occupies the former Thomas W. Lamont residence (1921; Walker & Gillette), a Gothic-style home for a parson's son who rose to chair the board of J. P. Morgan & Company.

At 46 E. 70th St near Park Ave is The EXPLORERS' CLUB, an organization founded in 1904. Its roster includes some 3500 members from 58 countries as well as such famous explorers, past and present, as Sir Edmund Hillary and Tenzing Norgay, several of the early astronauts, and Reinhold Messner. The club (not open to the public except for occasional lectures) owns rare books, manuscripts, and paintings of historical value as well as memorabilia of famous explorers. Named Lowell Thomas House after the broadcaster and world traveler who served as honorary club president, the building (1912; Frederick J. Stener) originally was the home of Stephen C. Clark, younger son of Singer Sewing

Machine magnate Edward Clark who built the Dakota Apartments.

Not far away is the **Sculpture Center**, a non-profit organization devoted exclusively to sculpture, which maintains both a school and a gallery. Located in a carriage house built for George G. Heye, founder of the Museum of the American Indian, the gallery mounts about ten shows yearly, usually of contemporary sculpture. Exhibitions include provocative group and thematic shows as well as one-person exhibitions both of established and emerging artists.

The Sculpture Center. 167 E. 69th St (Lexington / Third Aves), New York 10021. Tel: 879-0430. Open Tues—Sat 11—5; closed during summer. Admission free. Changing exhibitions, catalogues.

22 Central Park

SUBWAY: IRT Lexington Ave local or express (train 4, 5, or 6) to 59th St. BMT Broadway local (N or R train) to 5th Ave.

BUS: M1, M2, M3, or M4 uptown via Madison Ave, downtown via 5th Ave. M30 crosstown on 72nd St. M103 crosstown on 59th / 60th Sts. M28 crosstown on 57th St.

HOURS. Central Park is open from dawn to midnight though it is closed to motor traffic from 7 P.M. Friday until 6 A.M. Monday and on major holidays from 7 P.M. the night before until 6 A.M. the following morning. It is also closed to traffic from the end of April through Nov weekdays on non-rush hours, 10 A.M.–3 P.M. and 7—10 P.M. (The short section of road which enters the Park at 59th St and 6th Ave and exits at 72nd St and 5th Ave is closed only from 7 to 10 P.M. during the seasonal closing.)

INFORMATION AND MAPS. The **Visitor Information Center** at the Dairy has maps, calendars of park events, and exhibits on the history, horticulture, and planning of the park (open Tues—Sun 11—5, except Fri when it opens at 1 P.M.; tel: 397-3156). Calendars of events are posted at most entrances and are also available at the Dairy and the Belvedere. For **recorded information** on park events tel: 360-1333.

CRIME. Despite rumors to the contrary, Central Park is quite safe and the 22nd Precinct (i.e., Central Park) has one of the lowest crime rates in the city. Nevertheless it is unwise to wander around in remote areas of the park or to visit the park at night alone, except to attend scheduled events. Company is the best security, whether strolling, jogging, or cycling; either bring your own, join organized tours to isolated areas, or stay around other people. Don't display valuables: cameras, jewelry, watches, money. Don't leave bicycles unlocked. Precinct policemen, urban rangers, and special services men patrol the park; direct-line emergency call boxes are located throughout; they require no dialing and are connected directly with the police. The call boxes are identified with a brightly colored telephone logo. The first two digits on the metal plate attached to most park lampposts (some have been ripped off) tell the approximate cross street: thus 06413 means 106th St and 70235 means 70th St.

HANDICAPPED VISITORS. Parking permits available for the physically disabled; call 408-0204.

TOILETS. Public restrooms are located at the Boathouse, Ice Cream Cafe, Mineral Springs Pavilion, Model Boat House, Puppet House, Shakespeare Theater, Skating Rinks, Swimming Pool, Tennis Courts, Zoo, and Children's

Zoo. Additional facilities at Heckscher Playground, Conservatory Garden, and Bethesda Terrace.

REFRESHMENTS can be purchased at the Loeb Boathouse, the Ice Cream Cafe, the Mineral Springs Pavilion, the Sweet Feast Cafe at Bethesda Terrace (summer only), and the Zoo Cafe. The Tavern on the Green is a large, formal restaurant within the park (see p. 48).

ORGANIZED TOURS are offered every weekend, free; call 397-3156. Also available are group tours with the Urban Park Rangers (tel: 397-3081).

SPORTS AND RECREATION. *Ball fields:* Season opens in April. Permits required for organized athletic activities; tel: 408-0209.

Bicycling: On bike paths beside roadways or on roadways when park is closed to traffic. Cyclists must ride with traffic. Bicycles may be rented at the Loeb Boathouse (N.E. corner of the Lake at 74th St), every day beginning in late March, weather permitting, 10–6; I.D. required. Telephone: 861-4137.

Carriage rides: Grand Army Plaza, 5th Ave or 6th Ave at 59th St. Rates are $17 for the first half hour or fraction, $5 for each additional quarter hour. Make sure you and the driver agree on the starting time and the cost. Tel: 246-0520.

Folk dancing (seasonal, beginning late March, early April) at King Jagiello statue, 80th St, E. of Turtle Pond. Sat 2 to sundown; tel: 535-0763; also Sun 2 to sundown; tel: 673-3930 weekdays or 995-8567 on Sun after noon.

Gondola rides: Loeb Boathouse, N.E. corner of the Lake at 74th St. Spring through fall, rides available from 5–10 weekdays, 1–10 weekends; up to six people, fee; tel: 517-2233 for reservations.

Healthwalking: 90th St and 5th Ave. Clinics and group workouts organized by New York Walkers Club; Sat at 9 A.M. Tel: (914) 439-5155.

Horseback riding: Rentals at Claremont Stables, 175 W. 89th St, tel: 724-5100. Open weekdays 6:30 A.M. to one hour before dusk; weekends 6:30 to 4 P.M. For riders experienced in English saddle.

Ice skating: Wollman Rink season ends late Feb or March depending on the weather. Admission charge. Tel: 397-3142. Lasker Rink, 106th St, mid-park. Admission charge. Tel: 397-3142. Skating permitted on other bodies of water when signs indicate ice is sufficiently thick.

Lawn Sports: Bowling and croquet greens just north of Sheep Meadow. Permits required; tel: 360-8133.

Model Yachts: Conservatory Water, 72nd St and 5th Ave. Races begin Sat at 10 A.M.

Picnicking: The *Sheep Meadow* is open for quiet recreating, walking, and picnicking when weather and maintenance needs permit; for status call 397-3111 or see a ranger.

Roller skating: On closed road N.E. of Sheep Meadow. Weather permitting beginning in March, 10–5 weekdays; 10–6:30 weekends.

Rowboats: May be rented at Loeb Memorial Boathouse, N.E. corner of the Lake at 74th St, open seven days a week beginning in April, 11–5; deposit required; tel: 517-2233.

Running: Soft track around Reservoir, 1.58 miles. Running also on park roads when closed to traffic. Group runs organized by the Road Runners Club; tel: 860-4455.

Swimming: Lasker Pool, 106th St at mid-park. Open daily in season 11–7. Tel: 397-3106 for opening date.

CULTURAL ACTIVITIES. Get seasonal schedule of events at the Dairy.

Concerts, opera, dance: The Metropolitan Opera, and the New York Philharmonic usually appear in the park during the summer; large-scale events held on Great Lawn. Summerstage events held at the Bandshell (72nd St, mid-park) include opera, dance, folk music, ethnic music, jazz. Call Park information, 397-3165.

Shakespeare in the Park: Performances Tues–Sun during summer months, except when Metropolitan Opera or New York Philharmonic is performing. Free tickets distributed from 6:15 on the night of performance; get there early as lines form well ahead of time; only one ticket per line member. For information call the Dairy, 397-3165.

Events and performances at the Belvedere Castle Sun at 2 and 3 P.M. (No registration required; free, for all ages.) For schedule call 772-0210. Past performances have featured American Indian dancers, magic shows, jugglers, woodwind quartets, ethnic music, and storytelling.

CHILDREN'S ACTIVITIES. *Puppets* at Swedish Cottage Marionette Theater (79th St, enter at Central Park West and 81st St) or at Heckscher Puppet House (in the Heckscher Playground, 62nd St, enter at 59th St and 7th Ave); call 988-9093 (Swedish Cottage) or 397-3162 (Heckscher Puppet House) for reservations and information.

Story telling at the Hans Christian Andersen statue, 74th St near the Model Boat Pond, every Sat from June–Sept 11–noon.

Workshops at the Belvedere Castle include Saturday programs, free for children ages 5–11 and their families; 1–2:30 P.M. (reservations required; tel: 772-0210.) Programs on papermaking, basket making, insects, birds, puppets.

Workshops at the Dairy are also free for children 5–11 and their families; reservations required; tel: 397-3165. Cookie making, programs on fossils, kites, al fresco drawing, park history, landscape architecture.

The *Central Park Zoo* at 64th St and 5th Ave. For information tel: 439-6515. The Children's Zoo, entrance at 64th St and 5th Ave, is open 10 to 4:30; small admission charge.

Carousel, mid-park at 64th St. Open every day of the week weather permitting; weekends only in winter; weekdays 10:30–4:45; weekends until 5:45; small fee; tel: 879-0244.

**Central Park, bounded by 59th St (Central Park South), 110th St (Central Park North), Fifth Ave and Eighth Ave (Central Park West), is the heartland of Manhattan, 843 acres set aside for the recreation of all its citizens. Although the park seems "natural," the largest surviving piece of Manhattan unencrusted with asphalt and masonry, its landscape and scenery are completely man-made, based on designs by Frederick Law Olmsted and Calvert Vaux.

History. In 1844 poet William Cullen Bryant among others began calling for a public park, observing that commerce was devouring great chunks of Manhattan and the population sweeping over the rest. Andrew Jackson Downing, an architect and the preeminent landscape designer of the period, added his voice as did several politicians, and in 1856 the city bought most of what is now the park for $5 million. The land was desolate, covered with scrubby trees, rocky outcroppings, and occasional fields where squatters grazed their pigs and goats; a garbage dump, a bone-boiling works, and a rope walk added their own atmosphere. Egbert Viele was hired to survey the land and to supervise its clearing; he was aided by the police, who forcibly ejected the squatters and their livestock.

The board of Park Commissioners (established 1857) arranged a design competition for the park in part because Andrew Jackson Downing, who probably would have been chosen, had recently drowned in a steamboat accident trying to rescue his mother-in-law. Among 33 entries the Greensward Plan (1858) by Olmsted and Vaux was chosen, a plan based on enhancing existing land contours to heighten the picturesque, dramatic qualities of the landscape.

During the initial 20 years of construction, 10 million cartloads of dirt were shifted; 4–5 million trees of 632 species and 815 varieties of vines, alpine plants, and hardy perennials were planted; and half a million cubic yards of topsoil were spread over the existing poor soil (some of it recovered from the organic refuse of the garbage dump). Sixty-two miles of ceramic pipe were laid to drain marshy areas and to supply water to lawns where hydrants were installed.

The Greensward Plan also incorporated the existing Arsenal and the Croton reservoirs, rectangular receiving pools for the aqueduct system that brought water from the Catskills. Curving drives, designed to keep would-be horseracers in check, carried traffic around these obstacles while straight transverse roads recessed below ground level took crosstown traffic unobtrusively through the park. North of the reservoir site (later filled in to become the Great Lawn as the present reservoir was created) the land was high and rocky, with good views, and the designers chose to leave this area as wild as possible. South of the reservoir were long, rocky, glacial ridges running north-south, which would be changed into open meadows, shady glens, and gently sloping hills. The formal element was to consist of a mall, an avenue of trees with a fountain at one end and statuary along its length.

In all of this Vaux and Olmsted were influenced by English landscape gardeners beginning with Lancelot "Capability" Brown, who turned against the earlier preference for symmetrical flower beds and topiary; later the English landscape tradition proceeded from Brown's pastoral ideal to a love of more rugged, craggy scenery—the kind of landscape in the N. end of the park.

Socially the park was intended as a democratic experiment, for the relief of the working classes whose daily lives were often confined to tenements and sweatshops as well as for the amusement of the wealthy who could display their clothing, carriages, and horses along the tree-lined drives. It was also a public works project employing a staff of several thousand laborers, though it unfortunately attracted politicians who saw in its labor-intensive landscape a golden opportunity for patronage (controlling immigrant votes) and for letting out lucrative contracts to cronies in the building trades.

Even before its completion the park was a target for unwanted encroachments, beginning with a Racing Track for horses, which Olmsted blocked. While an airplane field (1919), trenches (1918) to memorialize World War I, an underground garage for 30,000 cars (1921 and frequently thereafter), and a statue of Buddha (1925) have not materialized, paved playgrounds, skating rinks, swimming and wading pools, a theater, and a zoo have taken park land. Robert Moses, zealous Parks Commissioner from the La Guardia era to 1960, advocated organized sports, accepted various buildings donated by philanthropists, and tore down structures of Olmsted's vintage, replacing them with boxy brick buildings. The present park environment represents therefore a compromise between the Olmsted vision of pastoral serenity and modern interests in active sports and recreation.

Restoration of the park. Because the park is ever popular (estimates range from 13–20 million visitors yearly), it has been ravaged by overuse as well as by neglect. Recognizing its fragility, the city Department of Parks & Recreation and the Central Parks Conservancy in 1980 put in motion a long-term (estimated completion in the mid-1990s) project that will return the park to its former beauty, dredging lakes silted by erosion, resodding lawns and replanting hillsides, improving security, restoring monuments, redesigning buildings to make them harmonize better with the landscape, and encouraging public respect for the park.

A. The South End of Central Park

SUBWAY: IRT Lexington Ave local (train 6) to 68th St.

BUS: M1, M2, M3, or M4 uptown via Madison Ave or downtown via 5th Ave. M30 crosstown on 72nd St.

Begin at 72nd St and Fifth Ave. In 1862 the original 18 park gates were named, though only three of the gates are actually inscribed, and several others were named later. This is the *Inventors' Gate* (the others bearing inscriptions are the Mariners' and Engineers' Gates).

Clockwise from this point the other named gates are: *Miners' Gate* (79th St and 5th Ave), *Engineers' Gate* (90th St and 5th Ave), *Woodmen's Gate* (96th St and 5th Ave), *Girls' Gate* (102nd St and 5th Ave), *Vanderbilt Gate* (105th St and 5th Ave, named later when the gates from the former Vanderbilt mansion were installed here), *Pioneers' Gate* (Frawley Circle), *Farmers' Gate* (Central Park North and Lenox Ave), *Warriors' Gate* (Central Park North and Powell Blvd), *Strangers' Gate* (Duke Ellington Blvd or 106th St and Central Park West), *Boys' Gate* (100th St and Central Park West), *Prophets' Gate* (96th St and Central Park West), *Mariners' Gate* (85th St and Central Park West), *Hunters' Gate* (81st St and Central Park West), *Naturalists' Gate* (77th St and Central Park West), *Women's Gate* (72nd St and Central Park West), *Merchants' Gate* (Columbus Circle), *Artisans' Gate* (7th Ave and Central Park South), *Artists' Gate* (6th Ave and Central Park South), *Scholars' Gate* (60th St and 5th Ave), *Children's Gate* (64th St and 5th Ave), and *Students' Gate* (67th St and 5th Ave).

On the left side of the road is a playground (1970; Richard Dattner & Assocs.), one of 19 along the park perimeter. Nearby, inside an iron fence, stands a small-leaved Chinese elm *(Ulmus parvifolia)*, one of the oldest trees in the park. Olmsted hired Austrian nurseryman Ignaz Anton Pilat, who had studied in the Imperial Botanical Gardens in Vienna; Pilat chose the varieties to be planted, emphasizing native trees and shrubs, especially conifers to give color during the winter.

Take the first right turn in the path on the N. side of the roadway, and walk to the **Conservatory Water,** named after a conservatory planned here but eventually erected at 104th St. On the E. shore of the pond is the KERBS MODEL BOATHOUSE (1954; Aymar Embury II; refreshments and restrooms) where enthusiasts sail radio-controlled model yachts, some luxurious enough for model moguls. Regattas usually take place on Sat beginning at 10 A.M. during warm weather.

Walk around to the N. end of the pond to José de Creeft's 11-ft bronze *statue of Alice in Wonderland* (1959) sitting on a mushroom and surrounded by the Mad Hatter, the Dormouse, the Cheshire Cat, and the March Hare. Children scramble all over it, but park purists would prefer all sculpture restricted to the Mall as Vaux and Olmsted originally desired. George T. Delacorte (see p. 413) commissioned *Alice* to honor his wife, who read the classic story to all their children.

Continue around the pond to the W. shore (good view of the East Side skyline from here) to the 8-ft seated bronze *statue of Hans Christian Andersen* (1956; Georg Lober) with a 2-ft, 60-lb Ugly Duckling waddling in front. In 1973 a thief sawed the duckling off its base and stole it, but it was recovered undamaged several weeks later in a paper bag near a Queens junkyard.

Take the path that leads under the TREFOIL ARCH to the Lake. The brownstone arch with its wooden ceiling, designed by Vaux, who planned the original park architecture, is part of a scheme that revolutionized traffic planning by separating different modes of transportation within the park, an innovative notion in the 19C, as were the sunken transverse roads across the park carrying city traffic.

Beyond the arch and to the right is the LOEB MEMORIAL BOATHOUSE (1954), donated by the banking family. In front of it is a small bronze statue of a rowboat (1967; Irwin Glusker).

Boats for hire spring to fall; gondola rides by reservation; (see introduction to park facilities, p. 403). Refreshments and restrooms. Cafeteria, Boat House Cafe serving lunch and dinner at lakeside. A trolley bus runs complimentary service from 7 in the evening until the cafe closes to Fifth Ave and Central Park West. Tel: 517-2233 (517-CAFE).

N. of the boathouse up the hill along East Drive is Edward Kemeys's *Still Hunt* (1881–83), a bronze mountain lion crouched on a natural rock as if to pounce on the runners who jog obliviously along the road.

Return to the boathouse. Continue S.W. around the Lake to the formal ***Terrace.** At the center is the BETHESDA FOUNTAIN and its statue, *Angel of the Waters* (1868) by Emma Stebbins, one of the few works especially commissioned for the park, which depicts the biblical angel who stirred the waters of the Bethesda pool in Jerusalem and conferred healing powers on it. On the column beneath the angel four plump-limbed cherubs represent the particularly 19C virtues of Temperance, Purity, Health, and Peace. The fountain has recently been restored and its waterworks engineered to recirculate the water. While 19C Central Park was a place for the wealthy to strut their well-blooded horses, nowadays the Terrace seems to attract the owners of exotic dogs, who parade their well-bred, well-groomed pets past the fountain.

Long side trip for energetic walkers. Follow the shore of the lake to the beautiful cast-iron **Bow Bridge* (1859; Calvert Vaux), restored to its original tan and cream colors. It crosses the Lake to the **Ramble,** a heavily planted glen with intricately winding paths and carefully organized cascades in a meander-

Key to Statuary in Central Park

South

1	Alice in Wonderland
2	Hans Christian Andersen
3	Still Hunt
4	Angel of the Waters
5	The Tempest
6	King Jagiello
7	Obelisk
8	Daniel Webster
9	Schiller
10	Beethoven
11	Victor Herbert
12	Mother Goose
13	Eagles and Prey
14	Samuel F.B. Morse
15	Fitz-Greene Halleck
16	Sir Walter Scott
17	Shakespeare
18	Robert Burns
19	Indian Hunter
20	Columbus
21	Balto
22	Delacorte Clock
23	Dancing Bear
24	Dancing Goat
25	Tigress and Cubs
26	Sophie Loeb Fountain
27	Maine Monument

North

1	Frances Hodgson Burnett Fountain
2	Untermeyer Fountain
3	A.H. Green Memorial Bench

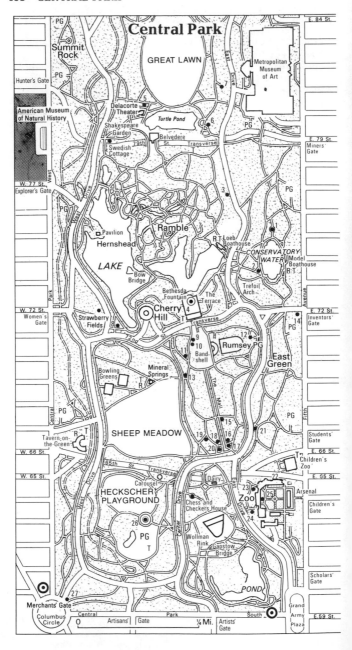

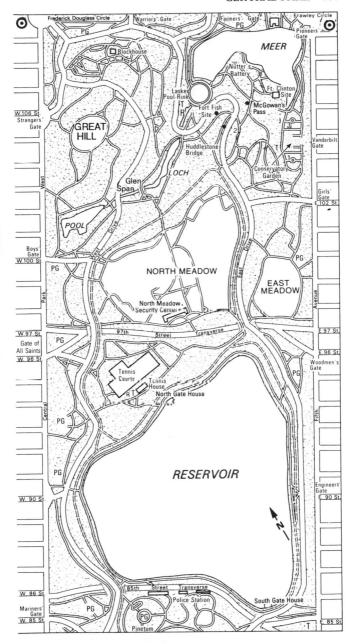

ing brook, the Gill. Vaux and Olmsted included an artificial cave near the brook, but it has been walled up.

N. of the Ramble, a favorite haunt of bird watchers, is *Vista Rock* (elevation 135 ft), site of the BELVEDERE CASTLE (1869), since 1919 used as a weather station and now home of the Central Park Learning Center. N. of the castle is the *Belvedere Lake* also known as the *Turtle Pond* and the DELACORTE SHAKESPEARE THEATER on its W. shore, with appropriate sculpture near the entrance, notably the bronze *Tempest* (1966; Milton Hebald) and *Romeo and Juliet* (1977; Milton Hebald) dedicated to Joseph Papp, theatrical producer who brought Shakespeare to the park.

The *Shakespeare Garden* (E. of West Drive, between the theater and the Swedish Cottage at the latitude of 80th St) contains plants mentioned in the dramatist's work. The *Swedish Cottage,* a replica of a Swedish schoolhouse made for the Philadelphia Centennial Exposition, houses the *Swedish Cottage Marionette Theater.*

Puppet shows Tues–Fri during the academic year for school groups, general admission weekdays in summer and Sat all year; reservations required; tel: 988-9093 for prices and schedule.

THE TURTLE POND, formerly BELVEDERE LAKE, before that, New Lake, is the last trace of the old Croton Receiving Reservoir (drained 1920) which once filled the site now occupied by the GREAT LAWN. During the Depression squatters built shanties on the dry reservoir bed. Today the squatters have given way to ball players, the Metropolitan Opera, and the New York Philharmonic.

Telephone the Dairy, 397-3165, for concert information.

To the S.E. of the lawn near the Turtle Pond is a bronze *statue of King Jagiello* (1939; Stanislaw Kazimierz Ostrowski), heroic warrior under whom Poland became a major power. Jagiello, the first Christian Grand Duke of Lithuania, married the Queen of Poland uniting their lands. He is shown holding crossed above his head the swords of his adversaries. Ostrowski originally made the statue for a Polish competition; later it was used in the Polish Pavilion at the 1939 World's Fair.

North of this statue behind the Metropolitan Museum of Art is New York's oldest piece of outdoor sculpture, the 71-ft, 224-ton *Obelisk,* erected (c. 16C B.C.) by Thutmose (Tuthmosis) III at Heliopolis. It stood there a thousand years until toppled by some irate Persians and thereafter lay on the ground until the Romans set it up near the water in Alexandria (16 B.C.) not far from a temple built by Cleopatra, thus giving it its nickname, *Cleopatra's Needle.* The khedive of Egypt gave it to New York a few years after the Suez Canal opened (1869), but it didn't arrive in the city until William H. Vanderbilt paid the $100,000 shipping bill, which included constructing a railroad track to drag it up from the Hudson. Cecil B. de Mille, the film producer, presented the plaques translating the hieroglyphs. Since its installation (1881), the pink granite has been attacked by the city's damp climate and air pollution.

Head back toward the Bethesda Fountain via the Shakespeare Theater, the Swedish Cottage, and the W. shore of the Lake. On the shore S. of 76th St is a promontory known as the *Hernshead* with the *Ladies' Pavilion* (1871; Vaux & Mould), originally a shelter for ladies awaiting streetcars at Columbus Circle, moved here when the Maine monument displaced it.

At the intersection of West Drive and the 72nd St transverse is a 24-ft pedestal bearing a 14-ft *statue of Daniel Webster* (1876; Thomas Ball). In 1863 Ball modeled for mass production a 2-ft statuette of the famous statesman and orator; the present work is a rather ungainly enlargement of that original.

The area near Central Park West and the 72nd St entrance is called **Strawberry Fields** to honor John Lennon, the songwriter, singer, and member of the Beatles, who was assassinated in the courtyard of the nearby Dakota Apartments in 1980; among his contributions to popular music was a song called "Strawberry Fields Forever." Another was titled "Imagine," the word inscribed in the star-shaped mosaic in the pavement donated by the city of Naples, Italy. The garden, landscaped and set aside as a Garden of Peace, was donated in part by his widow, Yoko Ono.

The garden opened in 1985 after its planners overcame some rather unusual obstacles beginning with the wish of conservative City Council members to name the area for Bing Crosby instead of the politically controversial John Lennon. When Yoko Ono ran an advertisement in the *New York Times* requesting rocks and plants from nations around the world, many countries sent plants suitable to other climates or soil or offered gifts inappropriate to the park—a totem pole, a tile bench, a large amethyst. Eventually the landscape architect Bruce Kelly decided on 161 varieties of plants for the 161 nations of the world. Ono chose the Italian mosaic from among the many gifts. The birds have shown an unfortunate appetite for the strawberry plants.

From here either go back to the Bethesda Fountain or continue S. to the *Tavern on the-Green*, a restaurant (expensive) at 66th St at Central Park West, with a parking lot so conspicuous that critics once called the place the "Tavern-on-the-Parking Lot." Originally a *Sheepfold* (1870; Jacob Wrey Mould) stood here and until 1934 sheltered a flock of white Southdowns who grazed in the Sheep Meadow. When the sheep were exiled to Prospect Park, commissioner Robert Moses converted the Sheepfold to a restaurant, whose personnel included doormen in top hats, riding boots, and hunting coats, cigarette girls in court costumes, and a 12-piece orchestra on the terrace dressed in forest green.

In 1956 Moses wanted to enlarge the parking lot, a process which would have involved tearing down trees and paving over a play area. A brigade of parents and conservationists fought in the courts and in the park for the playground, wheeling baby carriages in front of Moses's bulldozers, which were stealthily brought in after midnight. Eventually the publicity made Moses relent and drop plans for the lot.

Skirt the N. edge of the Sheep Meadow and cut back to the Bethesda Fountain area. On the way are the *Mineral Springs Pavilion* (skate rental in season, restrooms, and refreshments).

From the Bethesda Fountain, walk through the TERRACE BRIDGE ARCADE, with its fine Minton tile roof and ornamental stonework by Jacob Wrey Mould. On its S. side is the *Mall,* a formal avenue of trees (1212 ft long) set aside by Olmsted and Vaux for the park's statuary; the memorials deposited elsewhere result mainly from a passion for commemorative objects that gripped the city during the last half of the 19C. Near the beginning of the Mall is a *statue of Johann Christoph Friedrich von Schiller* (c. 1859; C. L. Richter), the first portrait statue erected in the park. Nearby are busts of *Beethoven* (1884; Henry Baerer) and *Victor Herbert* (1927; Edmond T. Quinn). On the E. side of the Mall is the NAUMBERG BANDSHELL (free concerts and dance events during the summer; call the Dairy at 397-3165).

Behind the bandstand is the *Pergola,* covered by Chinese wisteria, with the Mary Harriman Rumsey playground behind it, given (1936; rebuilt 1987) by the sister of former governor Averell Harriman. It replaced the Casino, an expensive play spot for adults, including former Mayor James J. Walker who entertained lavishly without always paying his bills. The *statue of Mother Goose* (1938) at the E. edge of the playground is by Frederick George Richard Roth.

Return to the Mall through the oak grove and cross over to the W. side. The roadway between the Mall and the Sheep Meadow has been set aside for roller skating and during pleasant weather skaters seemingly blessed with rubber joints dance to music from their own headsets or from the occasional blaring portable radio. Nearby is Christophe Fratin's *Eagles and Prey* (c. 1850), a bronze group of two ferocious eagles sinking their claws into a dead goat. Fratin belonged to a group of 19C French *animaliers* whose renderings of wild animals expressed a fascination with violence and terror. Facing the Mall is Byron M. Pickett's bronze statue (1870) of *Samuel Finley Breese Morse,* whose skill as a historical painter and miniaturist was eclipsed by his fame as the inventor of the telegraph and Morse code. The statue depicts Morse as an inventor, one hand on the telegraph, the other holding a dispatch.

Further down the Mall are (E. side) statues of *Fitz-Greene Halleck* (1876; James Wilson Alexander MacDonald), a minor 19C poet who also served as John Jacob Astor's private secretary; *Sir Walter Scott* (1871; John Steell); and *Shakespeare* (1870; John Quincy Adams Ward). The tricentennial of Shakespeare's birth was 1864, a time when the nation was preoccupied with proving its cultural sophistication; civic leaders felt that a statue in Shakespeare's honor would enhance the city's reputation as well as the poet's.

On the W. side are *Robert Burns* (c. 1880; John Steell) and, opposite Shakespeare, a bronze statue of *Christopher Columbus* (1892; Jeronimo Suñol). To the W. is *The Indian Hunter* (1866; John Quincy Adams Ward), a realistic bronze portrait of an Indian brave grasping his bow and arrow and leaning forward to hold his dog; Ward spent months in the Dakotas sketching Indians to prepare for this work, one of the best in the park.

Walk back N. by Shakespeare and Sir Walter Scott to the WILLOWDELL BRIDGE; beyond it is a statue of *Balto* (1925; Frederick George Richard Roth), leader of a team of huskies that carried diphtheria serum across 600 miles of stormy Alaskan wasteland to Nome in 1925. The expedition caused Balto's death, and a memorial committee commissioned Roth to make a statue of the heroic dog. The back and tail of this much-loved statue have been worn shiny by affectionate petting.

From here a path leads S. to the **Children's Zoo** and the **Central Park Zoo** (redesigned 1988; Kevin Roche, John Dinkeloo & Assocs.).

The Central Park Zoo. Central Park at Fifth Ave and 64th St. Open every day of the year at 10 A.M. Closes at 5 on weekdays, at 5:30 Sat, Sun, and holidays. Closes at 4:30 Nov–March. Open Tues until 8, May through Sept. Admission charge. Children under 12 must be accompanied by an adult. No pets, no radios.

Changing exhibitions of art, photography in Zoo Gallery. Restrooms, cafeteria, telephones, gift shop. Accessible to wheelchairs.

Although park designers Olmsted and Vaux disapproved of caging animals in urban parks, the park commissioners were deluged with gifts of animals, including white mice, cattle, and deer, and to provide shelter for them established a menagerie in the Arsenal which remained there until 1934. The Central Park Zoo, which opened in 1935, originally had both large and small animals, most confined to barred cages; the recent renovation has made the exhibits more suitable to the small scale of the zoo, retaining the popular sea lions and polar bears, but concentrating otherwise on smaller animals. The zoo is divided into three zones, temperate, tropic, and polar, with animal exhibits and environments to match: real and artificial vegetation, an elaborate sprinkler system made to exhale a humid jungle atmosphere, a man-made pseudo-Antarctic icepack. Among the animals in the new zoo are red pandas, river otters, colobus monkeys, penguins, flying geckos, poison-arrow frogs, and Indian fruit bats, all chosen for their interest to the visitor and their ability to adapt to zoo conditions. Near the penguin exhibit and the Visitors Service Building, respectively, are *Honey Bear* and *Dancing Goat* (c. 1935; Frederick George Richard Roth), fanciful fountain statues of great charm. In the Intelligence Garden is *Tigress and Cubs* (1866) by Auguste Cain, a prominent French sculptor whose commissions included works for the Jardins des Tuileries.

At the S. entrance to the **Children's Zoo** is the *Delacorte Clock* (1964–65; Andrea Spadini), commissioned by publisher George T. Delacorte, who admired the animated clocks of Europe. Every hour a parade of bronze animals about the size of the children watching them circles the clock while playing nursery tunes on musical instruments. A shorter performance takes place on the half hour.

The **Arsenal** (see also p. 363) is now the home of the city Department of Parks and Recreation and Cultural Affairs (open 9–5 weekdays for general information and permits). The Arsenal Gallery is one of the main exhibition spaces in the park.

Arsenal Gallery. Central Park at 64th Street (5th Ave), New York 10019. Tel: 360-3413. Open Mon–Fri 9–4:30. Closed Sat, Sun, national holidays. Free admission.

Art exhibits, occasional lectures and special events. No shops, no library, no food service. Restrooms. Accessible to wheelchairs by prior arrangements; call ahead for ramp installation. Elevator to third floor; restrooms equipped for visitors in wheelchairs.

The gallery mounts up to a dozen exhibitions yearly, each lasting about a month and emphasizing such themes as urban parks, recreation, and local history. But within this framework there is considerable variety: works of the city's uncelebrated older artists, photographic exhibits from the archives of the Parks Department on the building of Orchard Beach, contemporary painters of the Hudson River, the art and architecture of the Robert Moses era, and murals by New Yorkers.

Continue W. of the zoo to the **Dairy** (1870; Calvert Vaux; restored 1979), built as a refreshment stand for mothers and children and now used as the principal information center of the park.

The Dairy. Central Park Visitor Center, Central Park, New York 10019. Tel: 397-3165. Open Tues–Sun 11-5, except Fri 1–5. Maps, calendars of events, small gift shop with educational materials. Slide show on the history of the park, family workshops, tours, and activities related to the history and design of the park.

When Olmsted and Vaux designed the park, they set aside for children and their parents the southern portion, the part most accessible to the city, which was sparsely developed this far north. Here were the Dairy, the Children's Cottage with rental play equipment, the Carousel, two rustic shelters—the Kinderberg and the Cop Cot—and a ballfield or playground. At a time when fresh milk was not readily available in the city (the two prime sources were the herds of cows kept by breweries to eat the leftover mash and the surplus brought in by dairy farmers outside the city), the Dairy was more than just a romantic pastoral feature. Its herd of cows was stabled in the Children's Cottage and grazed in the field between the Dairy and what is now the Wollman Rink. The Dairy was restored in 1981, the ornate wooden loggia recreated from the original drawings and painted Victorian colors.

The *Kinderberg,* the little hill near the Dairy, once held a summerhouse, where the CHESS AND CHECKERS HOUSE (1952) now stands. Cross under Center Drive via the PLAYMATES' ARCH just N. of the Chess and Checkers House to the Friedsam Memorial **Carousel**.

The Carousel. Central Park (near 64th St, mid-park). Tel: 879-0244. Open every day, weather permitting, in spring, summer, and autumn; 10:30–4:45 weekdays, and 10:30–5:45 weekends; weekends only in winter, 10:30–4:45; small admission charge.

Originally the carousel was turned by two animals in the basement, a mule and a horse, both blind and trained to respond to one or two knocks on the floor over their heads. The present carousel (1908; Stein and Goldstein) was brought here from Coney Island after its predecessor was destroyed by fire and is outstanding for the beauty of its 58 hand-carved horses. It was restored completely (along with the machinery and the organ) in 1983.

From the carousel, walk W. toward the Heckscher Ballfield, on the site of one of the three playgrounds planned by Vaux and Olmsted. Unlike modern playgrounds equipped with swings, slides, and other mechanical aids to juvenile enjoyment, the original ones were simply meadows designated for field sports. Adults were not allowed, there were no permanent facilities (like backstops), and even the children had to have permits for all sports except sledding, a measure designed to protect the landscape. By 1927, compelled by overwhelming pressure for adult sports, the park managers installed five permanent fields with backstops, which today remain the exclusive turf of softball players.

The concrete playground to the S. dates from 1936, as does the *Queen of Hearts Fountain* (Frederick George Richard Roth) with characters from *Alice in Wonderland*. On the N.W. side of the playground is *Umpire Rock,* a large slab of gray Manhattan schist with white strips of quartz folded into it. Its surface is marked by glacial grooves, cut into the rock face by boulders and rocks called erratics that were dragged across it by the glacier some 20 thousand years ago. The park has many glacial erratics sitting around, most in their original sites, some moved by the designers, generally recognizable by their round, smooth, unfurrowed surfaces. Most came from the Palisades along the Hudson or from Westchester County.

Continue around the playground. Cross back under both Center Drive and South Drive. At the first sharp left intersection climb the hill to the Cop Cot, a rustic shelter crowning another rocky outcrop. The name means "little house on the crest of a hill" and the structure is a close replica (1984) of the original rustic summerhouse placed there when the park opened; it is built of tree limbs and trunks constructed where possible with traditional joinery techniques, mortise and tenon for example, instead of nails and bolts. The park once had a dozen such structures.

Follow the path northward back to **Wollman Rink,** restored in 1987 by Donald Trump, a real estate developer, to the embarrassment of the city government. Trump renovated the skating surface and rebuilt the rink building in five months for less than $3 million after the city had spent six years and $12.9 million without completing the job.

Walk up the hill past the chain link fence enclosing the Bird Sanctuary and cross the GAPSTOW BRIDGE spanning **the Pond** where once both swan boats and real swans plied the waters. The latter have been replaced by pigeons and seagulls; the boats disappeared in 1934. Today Henry Moore's *Two Piece Reclining Figure: Points* (1969–70, installed 1984) stands on the shore, awaiting a permanent site. The Pond, about twice its present size before the advent of the skating rink, was fed by De Voor's Mill Stream, which flowed through the park and continued S. and E. to Turtle Bay. Like other city streams it is now channeled underground but its waters have been tapped to fill the pools outside the Corning Glass Building (5th Ave at 56th St) during droughts.

From here the path leads S. to Grand Army Plaza at 59th St and Fifth Ave. Lined up along the sidewalk are horsedrawn carriages for hire, the horses shod with shock absorbent rubber shoes.

On the S. edge of the park (Central Park South at 6th Ave) stand three equestrian statues of South American liberators. Nearest Fifth Ave is a *statue of Simón Bolívar* (1919; Sally Jane

Farnham), who fought against Spanish domination in South America. Facing straight down Sixth Ave is the second equestrian statue, *José Julian Martí* (1959; Anna Hyatt Huntington), completed when the sculptor was 83 years old. Martí, a Cuban intellectual, organized Cuba's liberation from Spain while exiled in New York. He returned to Cuba in 1895 where he was mortally wounded in a skirmish that marked the opening of Cuba's war for independence. He is shown dressed in a business suit, clutching his wound, about to topple from his horse. To its W. is a statue of *José de San Martín* (c. 1950; Louis J. Daunas), who led the revolt of Argentina, Chile, and Peru against Spain. The intersection of Central Park South and Sixth Ave, officially renamed The Avenue of the Americas in 1945, is known (also officially) as Bolívar Plaza.

B.   The North End of Central Park

Note: Since this part of the park is less heavily used and has some isolated, wooded areas, visitors may feel more secure taking the route in company.

SUBWAY: IRT Lexington Ave local (train 6) to 103rd St.

BUS: M1, M2, M3, or M4 northbound via Madison Ave.

Begin at the VANDERBILT GATE, Fifth Ave and 105th St, formerly guarding the Cornelius Vanderbilt II mansion where Bergdorf Goodman now stands (58th St at 5th Ave). Made in Paris (1894) by Bergrotte and Bauviller, the handsome wrought-iron gates were donated to the city (1939) by Gertrude Vanderbilt Whitney. Inside the gate is the **Conservatory Garden** which once had greenhouses and later a fine Conservatory (1899; torn down, 1934) with impressive seasonal displays. The present garden began as a Works Progress Administration project during the Depression to provide employment, with Gilmore D. Clarke as consulting landscape architect. In the 1960s and early 1970s it fell into disrepair, its broken fountains running dry, its hedges and trees growing unpruned. In 1983 the Central Park Conservancy, a nonprofit organization dedicated to maintaining and restoring the park, began replanting the perennial gardens (redesigned by Lynden B. Miller) and, the following year, with the help of volunteers planted some 1500 wildflowers on the slope to the S.W. of the South Garden. Today the Conservatory Garden with its magnificent displays of blooms and fine collections of perennials has become a popular place to stroll, contemplate nature, and even get married. The CENTER GARDEN, with its borders of flowering quince, yew hedges, and symmetrical rows of crabapples, is one of the few formal areas in the park. On the hillside is a Chinese wisteria *(Wisteria sinensis)*, about 50 years old, on a wrought-iron arbor.

The SECRET GARDEN (S. of the Center Garden) takes its name from the *Burnett Memorial Fountain* (1936; Bessie Potter Vonnoh) of Mary and Dickon in Frances Hodgson Burnett's childhood classic, *The Secret Garden,* or perhaps from its cloistered atmosphere and long period of neglect. The statue is dedicated to Mrs. Burnett and, appropriately, the area surrounding the fountain has been specifically designed for storytelling and reading. The beds are planted with long-blooming annuals and surrounded by white and purple lilacs. Originally designed by Betty Sprout (1936), these beds were redesigned by Lynden B. Miller (1983) as English-style herbaceous borders, with some 175 varieties of perennials.

The NORTH GARDEN, formal and French in style, centers around the bronze *Untermeyer Fountain* (1947; Walter Schott) with its three playful girls dancing in a circle. The pedestal contains granite from the Yonkers home of donor Samuel Untermeyer, a successful trial lawyer. Circular beds surround the fountain, the outer ones planted with spectacular seasonal displays of tulips and chrysanthemums.

Continue past the Untermeyer Fountain and take the left fork of the path that leads up the hill toward *McGowan's Pass*. On the right is the **Meer** (completed 1866) with its severely vandalized boathouse (scheduled for restoration). At McGowan's Pass take the right fork to the remains of FORT CLINTON, built as part of a line of fortifications around the pass. The memorial cannon dates from 1905.

History. The Albany Post Road, built over an old Indian trail, once ran northward more or less along the course of East Drive from 103rd to 106th St, threading its way between two jutting hills where the remains of Fort Clinton and Fort Fish now stand. During the Revolutionary War the pass became an escape route for Col. William Smallwood's Marylanders covering the retreat of the colonial troops after the British invasion at Kip's Bay (September 15, 1776), and for the rest of the war British troops and German mercenaries were garrisoned there to protect the city from a northerly invasion. About 30 years later during the War of 1812 the pass again gained strategic importance as New Yorkers realized, following the bombardment of Stonington, Connecticut, that their city was vulnerable to a land attack from the north. A volunteer force that included gentlemanly Columbia College students as well as butchers, lawyers, Free Masons, and tallow chandlers worked by day and night to strengthen the old line of Revolutionary forts from Third Ave to the Hudson. In the McGowan's Pass area were Fort Clinton, named after Mayor De Witt Clinton; Fort Fish, named after Nicholas Fish, chairman of the defense committee; and NUTTER'S BATTERY.

Descend the hill and follow the path to The Mount where McGowan's Tavern once stood, now a composting area. The early stone tavern bought from the Dyckman family was replaced in 1790 by a frame house which members of the McGowan family ran as an inn until 1845. Two years later the Sisters of Charity of St. Vincent de Paul bought it and added other buildings for use as a convent, Mt. Saint Vincent's. When the land was incorporated in the park, park commissioners used the convent buildings for administrative offices and Olmsted lived in one with his family for a while. Later it became a Civil War hospital, a restaurant with a sculpture gallery, and after burning in 1881, a restaurant again; it was finally torn down in 1917. The nearby bench (1928) is a *memorial to Andrew Haswell Green*, park commissioner, lawyer, preservationist (he helped save Niagara Falls from exploitation), and moving force behind the consolidation of the five boroughs into one city. Five American elms planted here to symbolize the boroughs have unfortunately succumbed to Dutch elm disease. Green himself was murdered at the age of 81 by a madman who mistook him for someone else.

Take the path under the East Drive past the site of Fort Fish, and continue to the Huddlestone Bridge. Through the arch you can see the LASKER POOL-RINK, aesthetically one of the park's less attractive structures but much appreciated by local children, donated by the Loula D. Lasker Foundation.

Near the bridge is a Cascade, actually a trickle except in wet weather, one of several along a watercourse that begins at **The Pool** near Central Park West and leads to the Harlem Meer. All the bodies of water in the park are artificially created and filled with water from the city system. **The Loch,** as this stream is called, flows through a wooded area which, despite its great natural beauty, suffers neglect and vandalism. Follow The Loch to the west.

Side trip. The Springbanks Arch leads to the North Meadow and its ball fields. At the S.W. edge of the meadow across the 97th St Transverse are tennis courts and the Tennis House. (Courts open during spring, summer, and early autumn. Permits required; available at the Arsenal Mon—Fri during working hours or Sat morning. For information call 360-8133.) Beyond the tennis courts is the **Reservoir** encircled by a running track, probably the city's most heavily run 1.58 miles. Return to The Loch.

At the W. end of The Loch the rocky *Glen Span* leads through the Ravine to **The Pool,** formed by damming an old stream, Montayne's Rivulet (named after a Walloon family who farmed the area), that rose in high ground at Columbus Ave and 95th St and flowed into Harlem Creek at Fifth Ave and 107th St. Around the pond are tulip trees *(Liriodendron tulipifera)*, weeping willows *(Salix babylonica),* and a handsome bald cypress *(Taxodium distichum)* with small leaves and fuzzy orange bark.

From here either leave the park by taking the left fork on the S. side of the lake or take the right fork and walk up **The Great Hill** (134 ft), third highest elevation in the park after Summit Rock (137 ft 6 in) at 83rd St and Central Park West and Vista Rock (135 ft) at the Belvedere Castle. Workmen here in 1864 found evidence of a Revolutionary War encampment—bayonets, shot, and pot hooks. From the summit take a path on the N.W. side of the hill under the drive to the BLOCKHOUSE, built as part of the chain of fortifications for the War of 1812. At one time a cannon was mounted on the platform roof of the fort so that it could fire over the parapet in any direction. From here descend the Great Hill along its W. side to the Boys' Gate at Central Park West and 100th St.

The nearest subway is the IND 8th Ave local (C train) or the IND 6th Ave (B train) at Central Park West and 103rd St. Bus M10 runs N. and S. on Central Park West. There is a crosstown bus (M19) at 96th St.

23 Museum Mile: Fifth Avenue, 79th—104th Street

SUBWAY: IRT Lexington Ave local (train 6) to 77th St.
BUS: M1, M2, M3, or M4, uptown via Madison Ave and downtown via 5th Ave. M17 crosstown on 79th St.

The section of Fifth Ave between 79th and 106th Sts has more museums, libraries, archives, and cultural exhibitions than any comparable stretch in the city. Dominating the group is the Metropolitan Museum of Art of course, but along the E. side of the avenue are nine other institutions, most of them housed in the former homes of millionaires; the sector of Fifth Ave renamed **Museum Mile** in 1981 was once, before the debilitations of the income tax, known as Millionaire's Row. In 1979 the ten institutions formed a consortium to encourage joint ventures and shared resources.

Begin at 79th St and Fifth Ave. The palazzo-inspired house at *15 E. 79th St,* now occupied by the Rudolf Steiner School, was built (1918; McKim, Mead & White) for Thomas Newbold, a lawyer, state senator, and head of the New York State Department of Health. The uninspired brown and white brick 27-story apartment house at *980 Fifth Ave* (1968; Paul Resnick & Harry F. Green) replaces two town houses known as the Brokaw mansions, built by Isaac Vail Brokaw, a real estate dealer and clothing manufacturer, for himself and his daughter. They were demolished in 1965 despite efforts of conservationists to save them, the first blows falling surreptitiously during the weekend. The glazed brick apartment at *985 Fifth Ave* (1970; Wechsler & Schimenti) stands where Brokaw built two more houses for his sons.

Cross 80th St. A few of the old town houses remain. *No. 991 Fifth Ave* (1901; Turner & Killian), now the home of the *American Irish Historical Society,* was built as a speculative house and at one time was owned by William Ellis Corey, a president of U.S. Steel, who shocked society by marrying (1907) Mabelle Gilman, a musical comedy star. The house with its swell front, ornamental cartouches, and slate mansard roof is a fine example of the Beaux-Arts style.

The American Irish Historical Society, 991 Fifth Ave (80th St). New York 10022. Tel: 288-2263. Open Tues—Fri 10–6; free; ring bell for admission. Changing exhibits on Irish-American themes, including the careers of successful Irishmen, American or otherwise.

The 16-story apartment at 993 Fifth Ave (1930) exemplifies the work of Emery Roth père (see p. 513) who designed in the classical mode; now his firm is known for its blander, boxier towers (e.g., the General Motors Building, the tower of the Helmsley Palace Hotel).

Continue uptown. On the S.E. corner of 81st St and Fifth Ave is the *Stanhope Hotel* (1926; Rosario Candela). Its terrace is one of the more elegant places for people watching. *No. 998 Fifth Ave* (1910; McKim, Mead & White; DL) on the N.E. corner of 81st St has been called "the finest Italian Renaissance—style apartment house in New York City." Although luxury apartments like the Dakota had been built earlier, only after the turn of the century did the city's elite families succumb to the advantages of apartments. Among the first tenants here were Murry Guggenheim, Elihu Root, secretary of state and Nobel Peace Prize winner, and Levi P. Morton, banker and Vice President under Benjamin

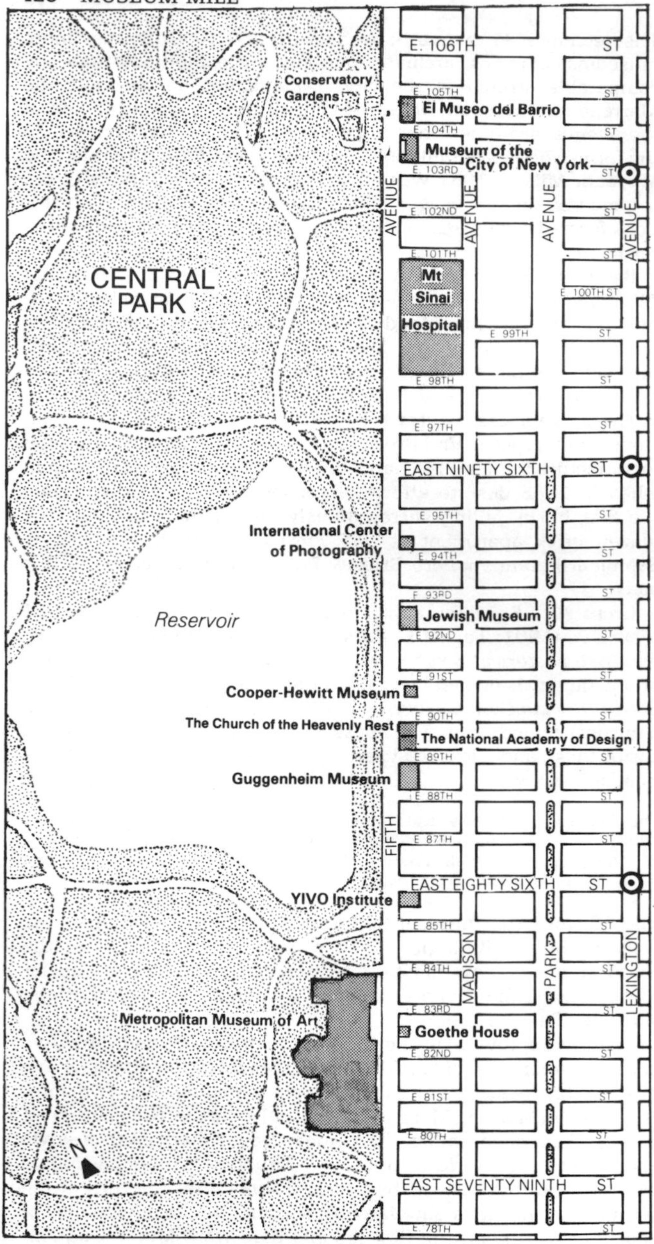

E. 106TH ST
E. 105TH ST
El Museo del Barrio
E. 104TH ST
Museum of the City of New York
E. 103RD ST
E. 102ND ST
E. 101ST
Mt Sinai Hospital
E. 100TH ST
E. 99TH ST
E. 98TH ST
E. 97TH ST
EAST NINETY SIXTH ST
E. 95TH ST
International Center of Photography
E. 94TH ST
E. 93RD ST
Jewish Museum
E. 92ND ST
E. 91ST ST
Cooper-Hewitt Museum
E. 90TH ST
The Church of the Heavenly Rest
The National Academy of Design
Guggenheim Museum
E. 89TH
E. 88TH ST
E. 87TH ST
YIVO Institute
EAST EIGHTY SIXTH ST
E. 85TH ST
E. 84TH ST
E. 83RD ST
Metropolitan Museum of Art
Goethe House
E. 82ND ST
E. 81ST ST
E. 80TH ST
EAST SEVENTY NINTH ST
E. 78TH

CENTRAL PARK

Conservatory Gardens

Reservoir

AVENUE
FIFTH
MADISON
PARK
LEXINGTON AVENUE

Harrison. The rental agent reputedly offered Root a cut-rate, hoping to lure his social peers into the building.

Another Beaux-Arts town house, handsomely ornamented with wrought iron and limestone, stands at the S.E. corner of 82nd St (No. 1009 Fifth Ave). Built speculatively (1901; Welch, Smith & Provot), it was sold to Benjamin N. Duke, brother of the tobacco king (see p. 368).

Most of the block facing Fifth Ave between 82nd and 83rd Sts remained unbuilt until the 1920s. Today with its one early-20C town house squeezed in by newer, larger apartment buildings, it illustrates changing patterns of living in the second decade of this century when expensive, impractical town houses gave way to more efficient apartments. The remaining town house at 1014 Fifth Ave (1907; Welch, Smith & Provot), a handsome Beaux-Arts building first owned by banker and broker James Francis Aloysius Clark, now belongs to the Federal Republic of Germany which operates it as **Goethe House New York.**

Goethe House New York. 1014 Fifth Ave (82nd St), New York 10028. Tel: 744-8310. Galleries open Tues and Thurs 9–7, Wed, Fri 9–5; Sat 12–5. Gallery and library closed during summer. Free.
  Changing exhibitions, lectures, concerts, films, symposia, performances. Library. Restrooms, telephone, no restaurant. No gift shop. Limited wheelchair access, gallery up several steps from street.

A branch of the Goethe Institute in Munich, Goethe House offers film programs, lectures, exhibitions, musical and theatrical performances. The library has more than 16,000 volumes on German culture and history as well as current issues of German newspapers and periodicals and an extensive record collection.

The *Marymount School* on the S.E. corner of Fifth Ave and 84th St occupies a trio of town houses (Nos. 1026, 1027, and 1028 Fifth Ave) previously occupied by wealthy but otherwise unremarkable bankers, oil refiners, real estate dealers, leather manufacturers, and dairymen. The two southern houses were built (1903; Van Vleck & Goldsmith) as a pair; the corner house (1903; Charles Pierrepont H. Gilbert) first belonged to Jonathan Thorne, an art lover who spent the last two decades of his life collecting beautiful objects with which to adorn his Beaux-Arts house.

Continue uptown. Only one early home survives in the block between 84th and 85th Sts, *No. 1033 Fifth Ave*, designed as a brownstone (1878; Stephen D. Hatch) but altered in 1912 to the then-fashionable Beaux-Arts style. The 17-story apartment at *1040 Fifth Ave* (bet. 85th / 86th Sts) is another work (1930) of Rosario Candela. Candela was born in Sicily, immigrated to the U. S. at the age of 19, and graduated from the Columbia School of Architecture (1915) three years later. In addition to building luxury apartments in the city's most elite precincts, he published two books on cryptography.

One of the finest mansions along the avenue is the *William Starr Miller mansion* (1914; Carrère & Hastings) on the S.E. corner of 86th St. Miller, who had investments in railroads and banking worth more than $3 million at the time of his death

(1935), divided his time between this house and his Newport mansion, "High Tide." His daughter married an English baron. Later Grace Wilson Vanderbilt, widow of Cornelius Vanderbilt III, bought the house (1944); after her death (1953) the YIVO INSTITUTE FOR JEWISH RESEARCH took it over.

The YIVO Institute for Jewish Research. 1048 Fifth Ave (86th St), New York 10028. Tel: 535-6700. Open Mon—Fri 9:30–5:30; free.
    SUBWAY: IRT Lexington Ave local or express (train 4, 5, or 6) to 86th St. BUS: M1, M2, M3, or M4 uptown via Madison Ave, downtown via 5th Ave. M18 crosstown on 86th St.

Built of red brick and limestone, crowned with a slate mansard roof and embellished with Ionic pilasters, brackets, scrolls, balustrades, rosettes, and bullseye windows, the mansion is reminiscent of the 16C houses in the Place des Vosges in Paris, which is not surprising since both Carrère and Hastings had studied at the École des Beaux Arts. The YIVO Institute houses a collection of modern Judaica second only to that of the Hebrew University in Jerusalem: 300,000 books, 100,000 photographs, ceremonial objects, and 22 million archival documents on the history of eastern European Jews and their descendants. There are diaries of Holocaust survivors, photographs of Jewish immigrants on the Lower East Side, sheet music from the Yiddish theater, papers of families including the owners of Grossinger's Hotel in Liberty, New York, and early sound recordings of Yiddish speakers.

The name YIVO is an acronym for Yidisher Visnshaftlekher Institut (Institute for Jewish Research), a graduate institute of Yiddish language studies and eastern European Jewish history founded in 1925 in Vilna, an intellectual center of Jewry. The Vilna institute began collecting photographs, diaries, and records, not with any premonition of the doom of the culture but simply as a scholarly exercise in preserving materials that reflected contemporary Jewish life. When the Nazis occupied Vilna, YIVO workers risked their lives, defying an order to gather materials to ship to Germany, and smuggled books out of the building into the ghetto, where they were buried in milk cans or hidden in attics. After the war some materials were recovered from these places and others, which had been sent to Germany, were recovered from the storehouse there where, ironically, they had been preserved.

Today the Institute still offers courses in Yiddish, a hybrid of medieval German and the Hebrew alphabet, as well as exhibitions which focus on eastern European and American Jewish history and culture.

Facing Fifth Ave between 88th and 89th Sts is the ***Solomon R. Guggenheim Museum,** Frank Lloyd Wright's only New York building (completed 1959), the repository of a collection of some 4000 paintings, sculptures, and works on paper from the Impressionist period to the present.

Note: The museum is currently closed for renovation. The following description reflects its appearance in 1990 and highlights the important aspects of the collection.

The Solomon R. Guggenheim Museum. 1071 Fifth Ave (89th St), New York 10128. Tel: 360-3500. Open Tues 11–7:45, Wed–Sun 11-4:45; closed Mon and holidays. Admission charge except Tues evening 5–7:45, free.

Gallery talks, lectures, changing exhibitions, films, concerts. Group visits by appointment. Restaurant. Restrooms. Telephones. Gift shop. Accessible to wheelchairs, but because of the ramp, visitors in wheelchairs are advised to inquire about special facilities at the admissions desk.

SUBWAY: IRT Lexington Ave local or express (train 4, 5, or 6) to 86th St. BUS: M1, M2, M3, or M4 uptown via Madison Ave, downtown via 5th Ave. M18 crosstown on 86th St.

One of the city's most controversial and distinctive buildings, the museum in form is a spiral with a ramp cantilevered out from its interior walls sitting above a horizontal slab. The ramp, 1416 ft long (about a quarter of a mile), rises 1.75 inches per 10 ft to a domed skylight 92 ft above the ground. The ramp diameter at ground level is 100 ft; at the top, 128 ft. Wright called the building "organic" architecture, imitating the forms and colors of nature, though his critics called it a bun, a snail, and an insult to art. Between the time of Wright's original design and the completion of the building, 16 years elapsed, many of them spent in arguments with the city Department of Buildings, whose ideas on construction differed from Wright's, and in quarrels with former museum director James Johnson Sweeney, who argued that Wright's design would create serious problems in storing and hanging the collection, reservations that have proven true. Today the interior of the building is much admired as a brilliant work of architecture though not as a display space for paintings.

In 1985 the museum announced plans to erect an 11-story addition, which will allow the public to see more of its permanent collection, a large part of which is now in storage. The addition will replace an earlier one (1968) by William Wesley Peters, Wright's son-in-law.

History. More than any other New York museum, with perhaps the exception of the Whitney, the Guggenheim has a collection that reflects the tastes of a few individuals. Solomon R. Guggenheim (1861–1949), like other American millionaires of his vintage, started out with the usual collection of Old Masters, but the focus of his collection changed entirely in the late 1920s after he met Baroness Hilla Rebay von Ehrenwiesen, an intense, highly opinionated artist who introduced him both to her friends, artists like Delaunay, Gleizes, Léger, Chagall, Kandinsky, and Rudolf Bauer, and to her taste for abstract art. In 1939 the Solomon R. Guggenheim Collection of Non-Objective Painting was shown in rented quarters at 24 E. 54th St with the baroness in charge. James Johnson Sweeney followed Rebay as museum director in 1952 and under his guidance the Guggenheim Museum became less narrowly ideological in its approach, purchasing Picassos and Cézannes, for example, which Rebay would have outlawed on grounds that they were objective. A gift of Impressionist and Post-Impressionist work from Justin K. Thannhauser, a noted dealer and collector, further enriched and broadened the collection. The bequest of Peggy Guggenheim put her entire collection of Cubist, Surrealist, and postwar painting and sculpture in the custody of the Guggenheim Foundation, though the collection remains in Venice, and is shown in New York only on occasional exchanges.

The idea of building an architecturally remarkable museum and of hiring Frank Lloyd Wright to design it apparently came from Rebay, and since Guggenheim died long before plans came to fruition, the realization of the building was left to her and to Harry Guggenheim, Solomon's successor.

The collection is shown in a series of changing exhibitions, on the spiral ramps, with the exception of two galleries reserved for paintings from the Thannhauser bequest (off second-floor ramp) and for Precursors of Modernism (off fourth-floor ramp).

JUSTIN K. THANNHAUSER GALLERY. Camille Pissarro, *The Hermitage at Pontoise*, painted before his Impressionist works, the earliest (c. 1867) picture in the collection.Vincent Van Gogh, *Mountains at Saint-Rémy*, a turbulent landscape painted from the asylum where Van Gogh was a patient in 1889. Paul Cézanne, *Man with Crossed Arms*. Paul Gauguin, *In the Vanilla Grove, Man and Horse*. Henri Rousseau, *The Football Players*, four athletes in stylized poses in a stylized setting, an unusual subject for Rousseau. Edouard Villard, *Place Vintimille*. Pablo Picasso, *Le Moulin de la Galette*, painted when Picasso was 19 years old and still under the influence of Toulouse-Lautrec. Amedeo Modigliani, *Nude*. Pierre Bonnard, *Dining Room on the Garden*. Picasso, *Woman Ironing*. The angular, distorted pose, and flat monochromatic colors typify the end of his Blue Period. Henri Matisse, *The Italian Woman*. Pierre Bonnard, *The Dining Room on the Garden*.

Other highlights of the permanent collection, generally on display on the fourth floor are works by Pioneers of Modernism. Among the artists who fell within the canons of Rebay's taste were Georges Braque, represented by *Violin and Palette* and *Piano and Mandola*, both analytical, monochromatic studies painted around 1909–10, as well as the later *Guitar, Glass, and Fruit Dish on Sideboard* (1919). Picasso is represented by *Accordionist*, painted (1911) when he and Braque were together in the Pyrenees, and by *Mandolin and Guitar*, a more colorful, lively painting whose surfaces are less fractured. Fernand Léger's *The Great Parade* (1954) is considered by many the definitive work of his career.

Also paintings by Albert Gleizes, Robert Delaunay, Ernst Ludwig Kirchner, Emil Nolde, Oskar Kokoschka, Egon Schiele, Gino Severini, and Paul Klee. Vasily Kandinsky was a particular favorite of Rebay and his work is well represented from its early Post-Impressionist and Fauve roots through his later, symbolic formal paintings of circles which had spiritual meaning to the painter.

Also represented in the collection, but usually shown in changing exhibitions, are Kazimir Malevich, Piet Mondrian, Theo Van Doesburg, and Joan Miró, the latter represented both by a visionary surrealist landscape, *The Tilled Field*, and by a ceramic mural that was designed to occupy the wall space by the ramp as it ascends from the ground floor. Among the works by the postwar painters are canvases by Willem de Kooning, Jackson Pollock, Mark Rothko, Franz Kline, and Richard Diebenkorn. Andy Warhol is represented by a silk screen with multiple images of an electric chair, *Orange Disaster* (1963), and Roy Lichtenstein by *Preparedness* which he called "a muralesque painting about our military-industrialist complex." There are also color field paintings by Morris Louis, Ellsworth Kelly, and a photorealistic view of the *Solomon R. Guggenheim Museum* by Richard Estes.

Although Hilla Rebay envisioned a collection of painting only, the museum began to purchase sculpture after her departure as its director. Alexander Archipenko's *Médrano II*, assembled of metal, wood, glass, and painted oilcloth, represents a circus dancer. Constantin Brancusi, Alberto Giacometti, Henry Moore, Jacques Lipchitz, Isamu Noguchi, Louise Nevelson, and David Smith are all represented in the collection.

A block N. between 89th and 90th Sts is the **National Academy of Design.**

National Academy of Design. 1083 Fifth Ave (89th–90th St), New York 10128. Tel: 360-6794. Open Tues 12–8; Wed–Sun 12–5. Closed Mon, major holidays. Admission charge except Tues 5–8.

Lectures, symposia, changing exhibitions, group tours by appointment. Restrooms. No restaurant. Bookshop. Accessible to wheelchairs.

SUBWAY: IRT Lexington Ave express or local (train 4, 5, or 6) to 86th St. BUS: M1, M2, M3, or M4 uptown via Madison Ave, downtown via 5th Ave. M18 crosstown on 86th St. M19 crosstown on 96th St.

The town house facing Fifth Ave (1914; Ogden Codman, Jr.) where the academy holds its exhibitions was donated (1940) by Archer M. Huntington, whose wife, sculptor Anna Hyatt Huntington, was an academy member. The academy, as the name implies, is a conservative institution, its members drawn from the ranks of the nation's established painters, sculptors, and graphic artists. Founded in 1825 as a school and exhibition center by painters Samuel F. B. Morse and Rembrandt Peale, architect Ithiel Town, sculptor John Frazee, and engraver Peter Maverick, the academy has a collection of more than 2000 paintings and 200 works of sculpture, in part the product of a ruling that members supply a representative sample of their work. The program includes loan exhibitions, works drawn from the collection, and a biennial juried show. The academy maintains an art school around the corner at 5 E. 89th St.

North of the academy on the S.E. corner of Fifth Ave at 90th St is the Protestant Episcopal CHURCH OF THE HEAVENLY REST (1929; Hardie Philip of Mayers, Murray & Philip), a Gothic church with external sculpture by Ulrich Ellerhausen and a pulpit madonna by Malvina Hoffman. The rose window is by J. Gordon Guthrie and the clerestory windows are by J. H. Hogan. Off the S. aisle is the Chapel of the Beloved Disciple.

Continue north. At 2 E. 91st St (S.E. corner of Fifth Ave) is the ***Cooper-Hewitt Museum,** presiding over the neighborhood in a mansion built for millionaire Andrew Carnegie (1901; Babb, Cook & Willard; DL).

The Cooper-Hewitt Museum: The Smithsonian Institution's National Museum of Design. 2 E. 91st Street (Fifth Ave), New York 10028. Open Tues 10–9; Wed–Sat 10–5; Sun 12–5. Closed Mon and major holidays. Admission charge. Tel: 860-6868.

Changing exhibitions, lectures, catalogues, special events, membership with benefits. Restrooms; telephones. No restaurant. Gift shop.

History. Andrew Carnegie, an immigrant from Scotland, began as a bobbin boy in a cotton factory and evolved into an industrial genius, amassing a fortune in iron, coal, steel, steamship and railroad lines. When he bought the land for his mansion, it was a rocky, semirural plot between Yorkville and Harlem, far N. of the dwellings of his financial peers, although developers had begun to erect brownstones nearby. As architects he chose Babb, Cook &

The Cooper-Hewitt Museum. Built (1901) as the mansion of steel magnate Andrew Carnegie, the building now houses the design collections of the Smithsonian Institution. The daughters of another self-made millionaire, Peter Cooper, initiated the collections. (Courtesy of the Cooper-Hewitt Museum, the Smithsonian Institution's National Museum of Design. Photographer: Dave DeSilva)

Willard, a firm respected for its industrial buildings but which later moved on to grander schemes. What Carnegie asked for was ''the most modest, plainest, and roomiest house in New York.'' What he got was this 64-room mansion, remarkably comfortable and technically advanced for its time, well-suited for his domestic needs and for the philanthropic projects he administered from his first-floor library and office. The subbasement was filled with pumps and boilers, the most advanced and sophisticated available, with two of each major piece so that a spare could be used should the primary piece malfunction. If city water or electricity were interrupted, an artesian well and generator would relieve the family and servants of any inconvenience. Up in the attic great fans pulled air through cheesecloth filters over tanks of cool water in a primitive system of air-conditioning. The house was the first private residence in the city with a structural steel frame, an Otis passenger elevator, and central heating.

Enter from 91st St. An ornate copper and glass canopy shelters the door. The marble vestibule leads to the Great Hall paneled in Scottish oak, an indication of Carnegie's affection for his homeland, to which he returned yearly. At the E. end of the hall stood the organ, its pipes in a shaft now used for the elevator. On the W. end was Carnegie's study, now used as a gallery. Carnegie, like Fiorello La Guardia, was 5 ft 2 in tall, and the doorways leading into the library and office are appropriate in scale. Along the S. side of the first floor, facing the garden, were public rooms—the Music Room on the W. with a large crystal chandelier and musical motifs, including a Scottish bagpipe, in the ceiling moldings. Next to the Music Room is the garden vestibule with leaded glass windows by Louis Comfort Tiffany. The formal dining room was E. of the vestibule and adjacent to it a breakfast room faced the garden and conservatory, which had an elevator to the potting shed below. All these rooms are currently used as exhibition space.

Upstairs were family bedrooms and a family library with elaborately carved teakwood trim designed by Lockwood de Forest who used the same material on his own town house near Greenwich Village (see p. 258). Across the garden facing 90th St is a town house, formerly belonging to Carnegie's daughter, now used for museum administration.

History. In 1897 the granddaughters of Peter Cooper (see p. 225), Sarah, Eleanor, and Amy Hewitt, impressed by the South Kensington Museum (now the Victoria and Albert Museum) in London and the Musée des Arts Décoratifs in Paris, opened the Cooper Union Museum for the Arts of Decoration. Early acquisitions included three European textile collections given by J. P. Morgan, and Italian architectural and decorative drawings belonging to the Cavaliere Giovanni Piancastelli, curator of the Borghese collection. Although the collections increased over the years in size and quality, the museum could not continue its activities because of financial pressures and closed in 1963. A committee was formed to save it, its collections entrusted to the Smithsonian Institution, and the name changed to its present form. In 1972 the Carnegie Corporation deeded the mansion to the museum.

The collections are shown in a series of changing exhibitions. Holdings include more than 30,000 examples of drawings and prints, most of them restricted to architecture, design, and ornament. There are Italian architectural drawings, French textile designs, American wood engravings, northern European woodcuts, designs for theater scenery and costumes, and a large selection of 19C American drawings. The collection of ceramics includes European and Oriental porcelain, stoneware, and earthenware including faience and majolica, and 19C figurines. There is a growing collection of glass. Also included are furniture, architectural woodwork and hardware, wallpaper, bandboxes, goldsmiths' work, jewelry, work in minor metals, locks and keys, and a vast collection of fabrics and textiles including Egyptian, Near Eastern, and Mediterranean fabrics from the 3–15C. Among the more amusing trifles in the collection are valentines, Christmas tree ornaments, feather pictures, and sand toys.

In Central Park at Fifth Ave and 91st St is the *William T. Stead Memorial* (1913; George James Frampton), a bronze tablet commemorating this British journalist who died on the *Titanic* after helping other passengers into the lifeboats; there is also a tablet commemorating him in London on the Thames embankment. The two figures beneath Stead's profile represent Fortitude (the knight) and Sympathy (the angel).

On the other side of the avenue at 1 E. 91st St (N.E. corner of Fifth Ave) is the **Convent of the Sacred Heart** (1918; Charles Pierrepont H. Gilbert & J. Armstrong Stenhouse; DL), built as the mansion of Otto Kahn—financier, philanthropist, and patron of the arts. One of the largest and most restrained neo-Italian palazzi in the city, the house has unusual arched carriage entrances. Kahn, a member of the German-Jewish elite known as "Our Crowd," was chairman of the board of the Metropolitan Opera which he saved from artistic mediocrity by bringing Giulio Gatti-Casazza as manager and Toscanini as conductor, and from financial bankruptcy by donating an estimated $2.5 million from his own pocket.

Next door are the neo-Renaissance mansions of two more eminently successful capitalists. At 7 E. 91st is the **James A. Burden House** (1902; Warren & Wetmore; DL), now part of the convent. It was built by W. D. Sloane and his wife Emily Vanderbilt Sloane for their eldest daughter, Adele, who married James A. Burden, heir to the Burden ironworks in Troy, New York. The Burden ironworks produced most of the horseshoes for the Union Army during the Civil War (at a peak rate of 3600 per hour) and eventually developed into the American Machine and Foundry Company, making James, Jr. both socially and financially a brilliant match for Adele Sloane, by reputation a beautiful and spirited woman. The architects of the house, Warren & Wetmore, who stood in the good graces of the Vanderbilts (they also built Grand Central Terminal), here built a house that has been described as a modern French interpretation of an Italian palazzo: Italian in its massing and the simplicity of details, French in the inventive ornament and the presence of a service floor between the ground floor and what in a less imposing building would be called the parlor floor.

Next door at 9 E. 91st Street is the **John Henry Hammond House** (1909; Carrère & Hastings; DL), until recently the U.S.S.R. Consulate. Built for the Sloanes' second daughter, Emily, it has an even more star-studded history than its neighbor. Emily married John Henry Hammond, whose father had served as Gen. Sherman's chief of staff in the Union Army; Emily's husband was of good enough family to have been educated at Yale and Columbia Law School but not secure enough in social class to take a house of such proportions with equanimity: "I'm going to be considered a kept man," he is said to have told his wife when shown the plans. One of the four Hammond daughters married Benny Goodman. Their only son, John, spent a lifetime discovering, nurturing, and promoting musical talent, a career which shaped the direction of American music from the early years of the Depression until his death in 1987. John Hammond's early protégés and benefactors included Benny Carter, Benny Goodman, Count Basie, Billie Holiday, and Lester Young. During the 1960s and 1970s Hammond helped launch the careers of Aretha Franklin, Bob Dylan, Paul Winter, George Benson, and Bruce Springsteen. The house became the Soviet consulate in 1942, and the driveway gate was added in 1976; it now stands empty.

Continue N. on Fifth Ave. On the S.E. corner of 92nd St is **1107 Fifth Ave** (1925; Rouse & Goldstone), a building remarkable for once having had the 54-room, three-story apartment of Marjorie Meriwether Post (the breakfast cereal heiress) and her husband, E. F. Hutton (the stock broker). The Palladian window facing the park two floors down from the cornice opened into her foyer; the port cochère on 92nd St led to the vestibule of her private elevator. The apartment has long since been subdivided.

Across the street in another recycled mansion, is the *Jewish Museum, operated under the auspices of the Jewish Theological Seminary of America.

The Jewish Museum. 1109 Fifth Ave (92nd St), New York 10028. Tel: 860-1888. Open Sun 11–6; Mon, Wed, and Thurs 12–5; Tues 12–8. Closed Fri, Sat, major Jewish holidays, and certain legal holidays. Admission charge except Tues 5–8.

Changing exhibitions, lectures, family programs, panel discussions, films, concerts. Membership with benefits. Group tours by appointment. Restrooms, telephones. No restaurant. Museum shop with books, catalogues, posters, postcards, note cards, ceremonial objects, reproductions, toys. Accessible to wheelchairs; elevator; disabled visitors are requested to telephone in advance: 860-1891.

SUBWAY: IRT Lexington Ave local (train 6) to 96th St. BUS: M1, M2, M3, or M4 uptown via Madison Ave, downtown via 5th Ave.

Note: The museum will close for expansion and renovation in Dec 1990 and hopes to re-open in the summer of 1992; highlights from the permanent collection and changing exhibitions will be on display at the New-York Historical Society (170 Central Park West at 77th St; tel: 873-3400) while the museum is closed.

The Jewish Museum offers changing exhibitions from the most extensive collection of Judaica in the world. The collection is housed in the former *Felix M. Warburg mansion* (1908; Charles Pierrepont H. Gilbert) which was donated by his widow Frieda Schiff Warburg in 1944. The proposed addition by architect Kevin Roche will copy, Gothic finial for Gothic finial, the exterior of the Warburg mansion, replacing the architecturally uninspired modern wing (1962; Samuel Glazer) presently on the site.

In the Sculpture Court leading to the main entrance are *The Sacrifice,* by Jacques Lipchitz, and *Holocaust* by Luise Kaish, as well as changing installations.

THE COLLECTIONS. Among the holdings of the museum are an outstanding group of Jewish coins and medals, archaeological artifacts, ceremonial objects, paintings, drawings, prints, sculpture, and decorative arts. The Benjamin and Rose Mintz collection purchased by the museum in 1947 includes 500 objects of Polish-Jewish culture: kiddush cups, Hannukah lamps, tefillin bags, Torah crowns and wrappers. In the Benguiat Collection is a Torah ark from the synagogue of Urbino dating from 1551. In 1904 Lesser Gieldzinski, connoisseur and advisor to Kaiser Wilhelm II, donated his collection of Judaica to the Jewish community of Danzig, where it was housed in the Great Synagogue. In 1939 the American Jewish Joint Distribution Committee along with leaders from the Danzig Jewish community, negotiated the shipment of the collection to the Jewish Theological Seminary for safekeeping. If, after 15 years, there was still a Jewish community in Danzig, the objects were to be returned; if not, they were to remain in New York "for the education and inspiration of the rest of the world." The collection, along with ceremonial objects from Danzig synagogues and individual Jews, arrived a month before the German army occupied Danzig.

On the FIRST AND SECOND FLOORS are changing exhibitions. Upstairs on the THIRD FLOOR, along with changing exhibitions, is a permanent installation of *The Holocaust* (1982) by George Segal.

On display is the plaster original (1981) of Segal's San Francisco memorial to the victims of the Holocaust; a bronze version (1984) stands in Lincoln Park near the Golden Gate Bridge.

Also on the THIRD FLOOR is a permanent archaeological exhibition, Israel in Antiquity, focusing on biblical archaeology and including photographs and maps illustrating Jewish Biblical history. Objects, primarily from the Holy Land, date from the Bronze and Iron Ages and from periods of Persian, Hellenistic, and Roman domination.

The permanent exhibition of coins and medals from the Samuel Friedenberg Collection begins with examples from the 6C B.C., and proceeds chronologically to modern coins from the British Mandate of Palestine and the State of Israel. The exhibition is accompanied by an audioguide.

Continue N. on Fifth Ave. Turn E. (right) on 93rd St. The area from about Fifth to Park Aves bounded by 90th and 94th Sts is known as **Carnegie Hill**.

At 56 E. 93rd St the **Smithers Alcoholism Center** of Roosevelt Hospital (1932; Walker and Gillette; DL) occupies a house built for William Goadby Loew—stockbroker and sportsman—and is one of the last great New York mansions, a fine example of the American Adam style with Palladian and bull's-eye windows and a white limestone facade curving around a small motor court. Later the house belonged to Billy Rose, theatrical producer, art collector, and inventor of the Aquacade.

The austere classical house next door at 60 E. 93rd St, now the PERMANENT MISSION OF ROMANIA TO THE UNITED NATIONS (1930; John Russell Pope; DL), was designed for Virginia Graham Fair Vanderbilt (Mrs. William K. Vanderbilt II). This and the Loew mansion were among the last elegant town houses built in the city because rising construction and maintenance costs as well as the vogue for palatial apartments made them obsolete.

Across the street at 75 E. 93rd St, the SYNOD OF BISHOPS OF THE RUSSIAN ORTHODOX CHURCH OUTSIDE RUSSIA has taken over the Francis F. Palmer House (1918; Delano & Aldrich; DL). While banker George F. Baker, Jr., owned the house during the late 1920s, he added the garden courtyard and the wing to the W. with a ballroom. Beneath the house ran a spur from the New York Central line under Park Ave so that Baker could take his private railroad car all the way home.

Walk S. down Park Ave to the Louise Nevelson sculpture at 92nd St in the Park Ave mall. *Night Presence IV* (1972), a work of Cor-Ten steel (22 ft high, 13 ft wide, 9 ft deep) was given to the city by the artist who said that she felt New York represented "the whole of [her] conscious life." It is one of her earliest outdoor metal works, enlarged from a small wooden sculpture (1955), with turned doorknob forms and a cutout bird silhouette.

Between Park and Madison Aves two wooden houses, **120 and 122 E. 92nd St** (1859, 1871; DL) survive from more bucolic times.

Return to 93rd St and walk back to Fifth Ave. Look uptown as you cross Madison Ave to the FACADE OF THE SQUADRON A ARMORY (1895; John Rochester Thomas; DL) along the E. side of the avenue between 94th and 95th Sts. At one time this facade with its virtuoso brickwork and fanciful towers, machicolations, crenellations, and arched doorways, was part of a building that filled the block and housed Squadron A of the First New York Hussars, later reorganized as the 105th Machine Gun Battalion. Until 1966 when threatened with demolition it hosted horse shows and polo matches. Today it is the W. wall of a playground that serves *Hunter High School* (1971; Morris Ketchum, Jr.), designed to complement the remains of the old armory.

Return to Fifth Ave and continue N. to 94th St. Occupying a gracious neo-Georgian town house is the **International Center of Photography** known familiarly as I.C.P.

The International Center of Photography. 1130 Fifth Ave (94th St), New York 10128. Tel: 860-1778. Open Tues 12–8, Wed–Fri 12–5, Sat and Sun 11–6. Closed Mon, New Year's Day, July Fourth, Thanksgiving, Christmas. Admission charge, lower rates for students and seniors. Free on Tues 5–8.

Exhibitions, lectures, workshops, seminars, courses in virtually every aspect of photography, travel workshops. Library. Membership with benefits. Restrooms, telephones, no restaurant. Museum shop. Entrance up about five steps from street, small elevator to second floor.

SUBWAY: IRT Lexington Ave local (train 6) to 96th St. BUS: M1, M2, M3, or M4 uptown via Madison Ave, downtown via Fifth Ave. M19 crosstown on 96th St.

Founded (1974) by Cornell Capa to preserve not only the work of his brother, a photojournalist killed in Vietnam, but that of other photographers whose work was in danger of being lost, I.C.P. has a growing collection of 20C photographers. Today I.C.P. is the foremost exhibitor of photography in New York, and a center for photographers, editors, artists, and others interested in the medium. Exhibitions range from the historical—shows of the work of Atget, Stieglitz, and Weegee—to the contemporary, from photojournalism to the frankly experimental.

The Federal-style house (1914; Delano & Aldrich; DL) now occupied by the museum was built for Willard Straight, diplomat, financier, and founder of the *New Republic* magazine. Straight, who spent much of his adult life in the Far East, volunteered for service in World War I and died of pneumonia contracted in the line of duty four years after the house was completed.

Continue N. on Fifth Ave. The RUSSIAN ORTHODOX CATHEDRAL OF SAINT NICHOLAS (1902; DL) just E. of the avenue (15 E. 97th St), with its five onion domes, gold crosses, red, blue, and yellow majolica tiles, and ornate terra-cotta, is an exotic form in a staid neighborhood.

Between 98th and 101st Sts along Fifth Ave is **Mount Sinai**

Hospital, whose medical school is associated with the City University of New York. Mount Sinai was founded in 1852 by a group of Jews including Sampson Simson, one of the city's wealthiest citizens, who donated land for the original buildings on 28th St. The older buildings of the present complex date from 1904; the large, dark, rusty tower (436 ft, sheathed in Cor-Ten steel) is the *Annenberg Building* (1976; Skidmore, Owings & Merrill). In the central plaza is a sculptural *Sphere* (1967) by Arnaldo Pomodoro.

Opposite 101st St at the edge of Central Park is a *memorial to Arthur Brisbane* (1939; Richard Barthé), a journalist and editorial columnist for several Hearst newspapers.

The NEW YORK ACADEMY OF MEDICINE (1926; York & Sawyer) at 2 E. 103rd St (S.E. corner of Fifth Ave) is a picturesque eclectic (Byzantine, Italian, Romanesque) building whose library contains in addition to the expected scientific tomes a surprising collection of cookbooks, the gift of Dr. Margaret Barclay Wilson, who donated (1930) 4000 volumes on food and nutrition to assist workers in dietetics. The rarest item in the collection is a manuscript on roast boar duplicated only at the Vatican. Dr. Wilson also translated and edited one of the earliest of all cookbooks, the *De re coquinaria* of Apicius Caelius.

Facing the Academy of Medicine from the other side of Fifth Ave at 103rd St is a statue of *Dr. James Marion Sims* (1892; Ferdinand von Miller II). Sims, who founded Woman's Hospital of New York, was a prominent surgeon, gynecologist, and philanthropist.

At Fifth Ave and 103rd St is the ***Museum of the City of New York** (1932; Joseph H. Freedlander; DL), founded in 1923 to familiarize New Yorkers with the history and culture of their city.

Museum of the City of New York. Fifth Ave at 103rd St, New York 10029. Tel: 534-1672. Open Tues–Sat 10–5, Sun and holidays (including N.Y. legal holidays) 1–5. Closed Mon, Thanksgiving, Christmas, and New Year's Day. (New York legal holidays include Martin Luther King Day, July Fourth, Labor Day, Columbus Day, Election Day, and Veterans Day.) Free admission, but voluntary contribution suggested.

Lectures, concerts, walking tours, gallery talks associated with exhibits, films, guided tours for groups by reservation. Programs for children. No restaurant; restrooms on ground floor; public telephone. Interesting gift shop. Accessible to wheelchairs; ramp entrance on 104th St; call ahead.

SUBWAY: IRT Lexington Ave local (train 6) to 103rd St. BUS: M1, M2, M3, or M4 uptown via Madison Ave, downtown via 5th Ave.

On the GROUND FLOOR is the FIRE GALLERY, with antique fire engines and memorabilia including sections of wooden water pipes laid down by the Manhattan Company starting in 1799. Left of the main entrance on the FIRST FLOOR is the DUTCH GALLERY with dioramas, models, and other exhibits covering the rise of the Dutch nation in the 16C, the age of exploration, Dutch and Indian life in New Amsterdam.

On the SECOND FLOOR at the N. end of the corridor are six alcoves showing New York interiors from the late 17C to the early 20C. Portraits in the corridor are by John Singleton Copley,

Gilbert Stuart, and others. In the J. CLARENCE DAVIES GAL-
LERY are historical paintings, prints, maps, and documents. The
SILVER GALLERY in the middle of the building includes beautiful work by early New York silversmiths as well as portraits of
prominent New Yorkers. The STOCK EXCHANGE GALLERY
documents the history of the New York Stock Exchange, while
the PORT OF THE NEW WORLD exhibit traces New York as a
maritime city.

On the THIRD FLOOR (N. end) is the *DOLLS' HOUSE GAL-
LERY with exhibits from the museum's outstanding collection of
dolls and toys. The permanent dolls' house exhibition has period
dolls' houses and furniture from 1769. The BENKARD MEMO-
RIAL DRAWING ROOM shows furnishings and accessories from
the early 19C.

On the FOURTH FLOOR are museum offices. On the FIFTH
FLOOR are the *JOHN D. ROCKEFELLER, SR., ROOMS, a master
bedroom and dressing room from the home of John D. Rockefeller, Sr., dating from the early 1880s.

Between 104th and 105th Sts along Fifth Ave is **El Museo del
Barrio**, the only museum in the nation devoted to the culture of
Puerto Rico and Latin America. Founded in 1969 as a neighborhood museum in a public school classroom in East Harlem, it is
housed today in a building formerly used by the Heckscher
Foundation for Children and the New York Society for the Prevention of Cruelty to Children.

El Museo del Barrio. 1230 Fifth Avenue (104th–105th Sts), New York 10029.
Tel: 831-7272. Open Wed–Sun 11–5. Closed Mon, Tues, holidays. Voluntary
contribution.
  Gallery talks by appointment; lectures and symposia on Hispanic art and
culture; concerts; film and theater festivals; school programs. Restrooms, no
telephone, no restaurant. Posters, catalogues, but no gift shop. Limited wheelchair accessibility. Museum is up a few steps from the street but is on one
floor.
  BUS AND SUBWAY: See Museum of the City of New York.

In addition to a handsomely mounted permanent exhibition of
Santos de Palo, carved wooden saints and religious figures, the
museum offers four or five exhibitions of paintings and graphic
arts yearly, some devoted to contemporary Puerto Rican and New
York artists, others to historical themes, for example the Golden
Age of Spain, an exhibition mounted to coincide with the 300th
anniversary of the death of Calderon de la Barca, the great
Spanish playwright. The f: STOP Gallery has shows of photography. The permanent collection contains some 300 paintings as
well as pre-Columbian objects, farm and household implements,
sculpture, over 5000 works on paper, historic photographs, and
handcrafts.

The nearest subway is the IRT Lexington Ave local (train 6) at Lexington Ave
and 103rd St. More pleasant are downtown buses on 5th Ave or uptown buses
on Madison Ave. There is a crosstown bus at 96th St (M19).

24 The Metropolitan Museum of Art

SUBWAY: IRT Lexington Ave express or local (trains 4, 5, or 6) to 86th St.

BUS: M1, M2, M3, or M4 uptown via Madison Ave or downtown via Fifth Ave. M17 or M18 crosstown on 79th and 86th Sts.

Founded in 1870 by a group of civic leaders, art collectors, and philanthropists, the ****Metropolitan Museum of Art** is the largest art museum in the western hemisphere and bills itself as the most comprehensive in the world. Its collections include more than 3.3 million objects spanning the course of human history, from bits of flint scraped into useful shapes by our earliest ancestors to 20C paintings and photographs.

The Metropolitan Museum of Art. 82nd St and Fifth Ave, New York 10028. Tel: 535-7710. Open Sun, Tues–Thurs 9:30–5:15; Fri and Sat 9:30–8:45. Closed Mon, New Year's Day, Thanksgiving, and Christmas. Suggested admission fee; free for members and children under 12 accompanied by an adult. The tax-deductible admission fee is mandatory, but you may pay more or less than the suggested amount. Certain galleries may be closed for a part of each day because of a shortage of guards. Inquire at the Visitors' Center or at Admissions Desks.

Restrooms, telephones. Cafeteria and bar open for continental breakfast and lunch. Museum restaurant with waiter service, open for lunch and early supper (Fri and Sat, when museum is open late). For reservations call 570-3964. Museum dining room with waiter service: Sat and Sun brunch only, 11:30–2:30; for reservations tel: 879-5500, extension 3614. Impressively stocked art, book, and gift shops located off the Great Hall.

For information about the museum's multitudinous programs and services inquire at the Visitors' Center located at the Information Desk in the Great Hall. Gallery tours in English and Spanish, other languages by special arrangement (tel: 570-3828). Lectures and concerts, films, educational programs. Recorded tours available at the Audioguide Desk in the Great Hall and at certain special exhibitions.

Special programs for the elderly and the disabled. Wheelchairs available on request at the Coat Check areas. All galleries and exhibitions accessible by wheelchair. For activities for the sight-impaired, call 879-5500, extension 3561. For access to the Telephone for the Deaf (TTY), call 570-3828 or 879-0421.

EXTERIOR: The museum building has grown, rather like Topsy, from its modest Ruskinian Gothic beginnings to encompass 1.4 million square feet and to reflect the reigning architectural styles of the past century.

The rear facade (1874–80; Calvert Vaux and Jacob Wrey Mould), originally faced Central Park and is partially visible from the Lehman wing. To it were added N. and S. wings (1894; Arthur L. T. Tuckerman, and 1888; Theodore Weston) both largely covered or demolished by later expansion. The central Fifth Ave pavilion, the present facade of the museum, was designed by Richard Morris Hunt (1902) and executed by his son Richard Howland Hunt, while the N. and S. wings facing the avenue (1911 and 1913) are the work of McKim, Mead & White. Recent expansion undertaken by Roche, Dinkeloo & Assocs. has resulted in the redesign of the Fifth Ave stairs and the addition of three glass-walled wings on the other facades: the Lehman wing (1975) to the rear, the Sackler wing (1979) to the N., and the Rockefeller wing (1982) to the south.

The large uncarved blocks above the columns of Hunt's imposing neoclassical facade were to be carved into allegorical groups representing major periods in the history of art, but funds never became available. The recent building program has aroused criticism among park conservationists, who resent the museum's intrusion into the park, a controversy begun during park designer Frederick Law Olmsted's lifetime, when he regretted allowing the museum a toehold in his territory.

The Fifth Ave entrance leads directly into the **Great Hall,** designed by Richard Morris Hunt. The weekly floral exhibits whose scale matches that of the hall were donated by Lila Acheson Wallace, a significant benefactor of the museum.

The **information desk** in the center of the room has floor plans, notices of special exhibitions and events, and information for disabled visitors. At the N. end of the hall is the Audioguide Desk for renting recorded tours.

Note: In the descriptions that follow, accession numbers, for example (17.190.499), have been used to identify small objects.

On the left side of the hallway in an architectural niche near the Great Staircase is a blue and white glazed terra-cotta *Madonna and Child* by Andrea della Robbia.

Greek and Roman Art.

First floor galleries. WEST SIDE OF CORRIDOR. The first gallery (between the entrance to the restaurants and the entrance to the Rockefeller wing), contains material representing CYCLADIC AND GREEK BRONZE AGE CULTURES (2nd–3rd millennia B.C.). One outstanding small sculpture is the *Seated Harp Player (47.100.1), which displays a surprising rendering of detail. Mycenaean pottery includes a characteristic stirrup jar (53.11.6) dating from c. 1600–1000 B.C. decorated with fish and octopus.

The second gallery contains GREEK AND ROMAN BRONZES, the earliest dating from the Geometric period (8C B.C.). Of special interest are a small bronze horse (21.88.24) and a bronze group (Centauromachy) with a centaur and a standing male figure (17.190.2072), perhaps Zeus or Herakles; this very primitive centaur is really a man with the hindquarters of a horse growing out of the middle of his back. Other works include Roman portrait busts, Greek and Hellenistic figurines, ornaments, helmets, mirrors, wine jugs, and water jars.

The third gallery, next door, contains GREEK SCULPTURE OF THE CLASSIC PERIOD, 6–4C B.C. Except for temple decorations and grave reliefs, most classic Greek sculpture was executed in bronze, very little of which has survived except in later marble copies. *Wounded Warrior Falling Backwards* (25.116) is a Roman copy of a Greek bronze by Kresilas. The wound under his right arm would have been painted red. *Wounded Amazon* (32.11.4) is probably a Roman copy of a Greek original attributed to Kresilas; like other wounded warriors portrayed in the classic period, the Amazon betrays no pain.

Next on this side of the corridor is a gallery devoted to ETRUSCAN ART, with a spectacular bronze ceremonial *chariot,

METROPOLITAN MUSEUM
First Floor

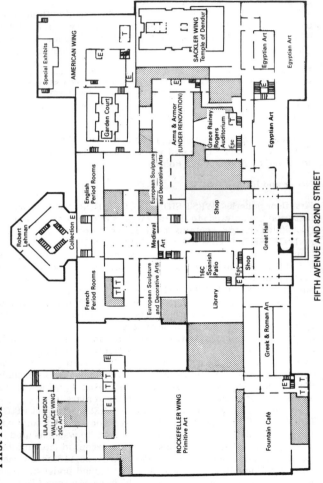

FIFTH AVENUE AND 82ND STREET

a tomb offering (late 6C B.C.), found near Spoleto; by the 6C chariots were no longer used as fighting vehicles. The Etruscan collection also contains gems, bronze mirrors, tripods, cauldrons and pails, and examples of Etruscan pottery and bronze from the 4–6C B.C.

Return down the LONG GALLERY IN THE CENTRAL CORRIDOR (leading from the restaurant toward the Great Hall) with its array of CYPRIOT SCULPTURE, notably archaically smiling votive figures, interspersed with grave reliefs and sarcophagi, most dating from 550–500 B.C. They were gathered by Luigi Palma di Cesnola, American consul in Cyprus and first paid director of the museum (1879–1904) who believed, wrongly, that Cyprus was the cradle of Greek civilization and busied himself buying Cypriot sculpture while other museums sought more important works.

On the EAST SIDE OF THE CORRIDOR (nearest Fifth Ave) the first gallery contains GREEK SCULPTURE OF THE ARCHAIC PERIOD (7–6C B.C.) including a marble *kouros (32.11.1) or nude male figure, the earliest (end of 7C B.C.) Greek marble statue in the museum. There is an especially charming Grave relief of a girl with doves (27.45) from about 450 B.C.

The next gallery contains GREEK MARBLE GRAVE SCULPTURE FROM THE 4–5C B.C. There are monuments in the shape of lekythoi or oil jars (for example 47.1 1.2) decorated with farewell scenes as well as upright gravestones.

The last gallery along this side of the hall contains GREEK SCULPTURE FROM THE HELLENISTIC PERIOD, 4–2C B.C, when major centers of Greek art flourished far from Athens. *Old Peasant Woman (09.39), perhaps an original from the 2C B.C., portrays a recognizable, unidealized person, a stooped and wrinkled old woman carrying her produce to market.

The corridor opens into a large gallery devoted to ROMAN SCULPTURE AND WALL PAINTINGS. The *Boscoreale frescoes, removed from a villa at Boscoreale near Pompeii, were buried by the eruption of Vesuvius in A.D. 79 and are the finest Roman paintings outside Italy. The room also contains the Badminton sarcophagus (55.11.5) dating from A.D. 220–230, named after Badminton House in England where it resided after its discovery in 1728. The Romans were masters of portrait statuary, and the room contains a wealth of portrait busts exhibiting varying degrees of idealization. The portrait statue of a Roman Prince (14.130.1; late 1C B.C.) in the corridor with Cypriot art possibly depicts Lucius Caesar, a grandson of the emperor Augustus. A larger than life-size portrait statue (05.30) of Trebonianus Gallus dating from A.D. 251–253 has a thickened torso signifying divinity to some critics, but suggesting to others how far the Romans had fallen from Greek ideals of proportion. On the wall near the Great Hall is a lovely marble portrait bust of a young woman (30.11.11) with virtuoso drapery (early 3C).

Just beyond this room at the edge of the Great Hall (E. side) is a

CUBICULUM or Roman bedroom, from the villa near Boscoreale. Wall paintings depict architectural scenes perhaps drawn from stage settings.

Egyptian Art.

The Egyptian galleries contain the finest collection of Egyptian art in America, numbering some 40,000 objects which date from prehistoric time to the Byzantine occupation during the reign of the emperor Justinian (A.D. 641). The galleries are organized chronologically beginning with prehistoric and predynastic material just N. of the Great Hall on the E. (Fifth Ave) side of the building; they continue in a U-shape, reaching the Temple of Dendur in the Sackler Gallery and then doubling back to the Great Hall. A recorded tour is available.

Gallery 1, **Predynastic Period,** includes a reconstruction of the tomb (c. 2440 B.C.) of Pernebi, a high official of Dynasty 5. There is a false door in the rear of the chapel which gave Pernebi's spirit access to the food offerings left for him.

Galleries 2 and 3. **Dynasties 1–11:** Near the entrance is a simple, powerful, crouching lion carved out of a block of quartzite and dating from c. 3100 B.C. Among the examples of architecture, sculpture, and objects from daily life from the 1st through the 10th dynasties (3100–2040 B.C.) are finely carved reliefs bearing the name of Cheops, builder of the Great Pyramid.

Galleries 4–5. **Dynasty 11:** On display in Gallery 4 is the finest collection of ancient Egyptian *tomb models ever found—boats, models of a granary, brewery and bakery, stable, and garden, all in a superb state of preservation.

Gallery 6. **Amenemhat I, Dynasty 12:** The first of several galleries with royal and private material excavated at Lisht, including a royal relief and altar from Amenemhat's pyramid temple.

Gallery 7. **Senwosret I, Dynasty 12:** Of special interest are the monumental Falcon panels which originally decorated the wall enclosing Senwosret's pyramid precinct at Lisht, and a wooden statue of a striding King Wearing the Red Crown of Lower Egypt.

Galleries 8–11. **Dynasty 12–Early Dynasty 18:** The display of royal jewelry includes an exquisite *pectoral with falcons and a scarab. Among the 12th dynasty royal portrait statues is a sensitively modeled black gneiss statue of Senwosret III as a Sphinx, a fragment sometimes called the first realistic portrait in the history of the world. "William," the museum's famous blue faience hippopotamus, actually an amulet for good luck, is in Gallery 9; while we often render hippos as charming, lovable (albeit ungainly) creatures, the Egyptians considered them threatening.

Gallery 12. **Queen Hatshepsut, Dynasty 18:** Among the 26 statues of this pharoah, two large seated statues at the end of the room show her as a woman; the gender of the central crystalline limestone figure is ambiguous. Elsewhere she had herself portrayed as a man, wearing a kingly beard. The statues are all broken because some years after her death her nephew,

Thutmosis III, had them removed from her temple, smashed, and buried in pits.

Galleries 13–15. **Early Dynasty 18, Hatshepsut, and Amenhotpe:** In these galleries are household belongings, funerary objects, and (Gallery 14) a *magnificent collection of jewelry, some for the living, some for the dead. In the next room is a beautiful yellow jasper fragment with delicately incised smiling lips, possibly a portrait of Amenhotpe's queen.

Gallery 16. **The Amarna Room (late Dynasty 18)** contains objects from the reigns of Akhenaton, Tutankhamun, Ay, and Haremhab. Akhenaton began his reign as Amenhotpe IV, but apparently underwent a religious conversion, banishing the established god Amun-Ra and choosing to worship instead Aton, the sun disk. Akhenaton moved his capital to the location of modern Amarna, and the wall paintings are named from that city. Akhenaton was the uncle of Tutankhamun, who ruled with the assistance of Haremhab. The E. wall is devoted to articles from the burial of Tutankhamun and the remains of his funerary banquet found (1907) in an "embalmer's cache" by an American businessman, a discovery that later helped Howard Carter to localize his excavations which resulted in the spectacular discovery of Tutankhamun's tomb in 1922.

Seated near the door in Gallery 18 is a granite statue of cross-legged *Haremhab as a Scribe of the King* (c. 1350 B.C.), writing on a scroll.

Major sculpture in Gallery 19, the **Ramesside Room, Dynasties 19–20,** includes the stele of Ptahmose, a minor 19th Dynasty official shown worshiping the god Osiris, a kneeling statue of King Sety I, and reliefs of Ramesses II vanquishing his bearded Asiatic enemies.

Gallery 21, the *Archaeological Room, Dynasties 19–26,** contains some of the best tomb groups in the world. The display shows the development of burial customs in Thebes and includes painted and decorated coffins, canopic chests, shawabtys (servant figures buried to wait on the dead), Osiride figures, and mummies.

Gallery 23, **Dynasty 30,** the last of the native Egyptian dynasties, is dominated by the dark stone sarcophagus of Wennofer.

Gallery 25, occupying the main part of the Sackler Wing, holds the **Temple of Dendur** (recorded tour available), a small temple (c. 23–10 B.C.) built by the Roman emperor Augustus, primarily as a political gesture to a people he had recently conquered. Centuries later it was given to the U.S. in gratitude for contributions to save ancient monuments upstream from the Aswan Dam. The Temple of Dendur honors two brothers who drowned in the Nile during wartime, and though the circumstances of the drowning are unclear, it is reasonably certain that the body of one washed ashore at Dendur and was buried in a chamber cut into the hillside behind the original temple site, on the W. bank of the Nile.

In the exterior rear wall a beveled block can be removed to reveal a hidden chamber ($9\frac{1}{2} \times 6 \times 2$ ft) perhaps the tomb of the drowned brothers. The emperor Augustus is represented in the reliefs on the walls as a pharaoh making offerings to the gods. Also on the exterior walls are graffiti by tourists through the centuries—the earliest left in 10 B.C., the later ones dating from the 19C.

Return to the main part of the Egyptian galleries. Just beyond Gallery 23 (with the sarcophagus of Wennofer) is Gallery 26, a lounge area, containing **Facsimiles of tomb and temple paintings,** most from the 3rd—11th Dynasties. Copied (1907—39) by museum staff members, they provide a source of information on daily life in ancient Egypt.

From here return through Gallery 23 and turn left.

Galleries 27—28, **Macedonian-Ptolemaic periods,** contain objects from the time of Alexander's conquest of Egypt (332 B.C.) to the death of Cleopatra (30 B.C.), a period in which the influence of Western art began to make itself felt in Egypt.

Gallery 31, beyond the auditorium foyer, contains **Roman art from the time of Augustus to A.D. 4C,** notably a series of *Fayum portraits.* They were found at the northern Egyptian site of Fayum where a Greek community flourished in A.D. 2C. In the center of the room is a mummy, its painted mask wrapped in place above the face, showing the features of the dead person. The portraits are startling renderings of ancient people, preserved by their technique (encaustic, a kind of colored wax) and the arid climate.

The objects in Gallery 32, **Roman and Coptic periods** (30 B.C.—A.D. 641), may seem akin to Byzantine or early medieval Western art rather than to the art of ancient Egypt. Coptic (Egyptian Christian) pieces include a carved ivory relief showing the Ascension of Christ.

Arms and Armor.

Note: The galleries of Arms and Armor are currently closed for renovation.

The collection of Arms and Armor contains about 14,000 weapons, both offensive and defensive, from small arrowheads to complex full suits of armor. Many of the arms are ceremonial in nature, chosen for their design, rather than their technical or military importance.

The centerpiece of the galleries is the EQUESTRIAN COURT, overhung with colorful banners; down the center charges a group of mounted knights in 15—16C German and Italian armor. Usually on display is a suit of fluted "Maximilian" armor (c. 1510), named after the Holy Roman emperor Maximilian I, who was often portrayed wearing it. The collection contains an important suit of English armor from the Royal Court Workshop in Greenwich, given by Henry VIII to the French ambassador.

Among the outstanding objects in the collection usually displayed in the alcove galleries is a gilded Germanic *spangenhelm (42.50.1) from the Great Migrations Period (early 6C), a style probably brought to the West during the invasion of Europe by the Huns (A.D. 375—453); this is the only one in the western

METROPOLITAN MUSEUM: AMERICAN WING
First Floor, Old & New Wings

101 – 104   Garden Court
105 – 112   Early 19C Period Rooms
116   Folk Art
118   Shaker Room
119   Vanderlyn Panorama
120   Mid-19C Furniture
121 – 125   Mid-19C Period Rooms
127   Frank Lloyd Wright Room

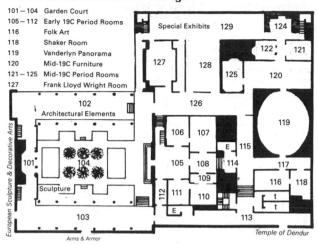

hemisphere. A *parade burgonet or helmet (17.190.1720) is signed by the Milanese master armorer Filippo Negrolo and dated 1543. Hammered from a single sheet of steel, the helmet is decorated with a mermaid over the crest, her outstretched arms holding a head of Medusa. There are also rapiers, daggers, courtswords, both useful and ornamental, and a collection of firearms from the 15–19C.

The American Wing.

The *American Wing contains a superb collection of American art, furniture, and decorative arts from the late-18th to the early-20th centuries. Floor plans are provided here to unravel the labyrinthine design of the wing which resulted when a new structure was wrapped around an older one. Period rooms are organized chronologically with the earliest exhibits on the top floor.

The *Garden Court is one of the best places in the museum to sit down. It contains 19C and early-20C sculpture and architectural elements, and examples of stained glass by Louis Comfort Tiffany, John La Farge, and Frank Lloyd Wright. At the N. end is the dignified marble facade (1824) of the United States Branch Bank once located on Wall St. At the other end is an ornamental loggia by Tiffany, salvaged from his house in Oyster Bay, Long Island. Tiffany's wisteria window (c. 1905), with its hanging clusters of blue blossoms, shows a stained glass view of the bay, but from the glass west wall of the court there are real views of Central Park. A pair of cast-iron staircases (1893–94) by Louis H. Sullivan, the outstanding American architect of his period,

METROPOLITAN MUSEUM: AMERICAN WING
Second Floor, Old & New Wings

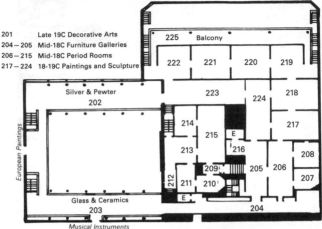

201 Late 19C Decorative Arts
204 – 205 Mid-18C Furniture Galleries
206 – 215 Mid-18C Period Rooms
217 – 224 18-19C Paintings and Sculpture

leads up to the balcony level. Sculpture (changed occasionally) includes work by William Rimmer, George Grey Barnard, Gutzon Borglum, Frederick MacMonnies, Paul Manship, Gaston Lachaise, and William Zorach. The gilded statue of Diana is a reduced replica of Augustus Saint-Gaudens's original (now in Philadelphia) that once adorned the first Madison Square Garden and shocked the walkers in the square below.

Galleries on the BALCONY (see floor plan for second floor) contain a survey of **American decorative arts** from the 17C to the 20C. Included here are examples of American pewter, silver, glass, and ceramics, ranging from humble ultilitarian wares to opulent presentation pieces, remarkable for their extravagant materials and fine workmanship.

A replica of Daniel Chester French's finest grave memorial, *Mourning Victory,* is mounted against the S. wall.

Return to the first floor and enter the **Period Rooms** through the bank facade at the N. end of the court.

Period rooms in the FIRST FLOOR galleries contain furniture from the early Federal period (1790–1820), an era marked by the influence of neoclassical tastes in England, especially by the work of Robert and James Adam. The most famous craftsman of the period was Duncan Phyfe, an immigrant from Scotland.

The doorway of the United States Branch Bank leads from the garden courtyard into the *Federal Gallery* (105) with distinguished examples of furniture from Boston, New York, Philadelphia, and Baltimore. There are elegant period rooms reconstructed from houses in Baltimore; Richmond and Petersburg, Virginia; and Haverhill, Massachusetts. Furniture in the *Neoclassical Gallery* (108) reflects the French Empire style in America, for example, a marble-topped pier table by Charles Honoré Lannuier with gilt bronze and gilded terra-cotta ornamentation. The Philadelphia Gallery (112) shows representative examples of the distinguished neoclassical tradition in that city. Galleries 113–117 contain furnishings and decorative arts from about 1780–1865 including painted furniture, Windsor and fancy chairs, and folk art. The *Shaker Retiring Room* (gallery 118) from New Lebanon, New York, is furnished in the simple, utilitarian manner associated with this austere religious sect.

Gallery 119 is given over to John Vanderlyn's *Panorama of the Palace and Gardens of Versailles (1818–19). In Gallery 120 groupings of furniture reflect the bewildering variety of 19C Revival styles (Greek, Gothic, Rococo, Renaissance, and Egyptian). Gallery 127 (accessible from the garden court if the special exhibition galleries are closed) is the *Frank Lloyd Wright Room which recreates from period photographs and architectural drawings a living room (1914) from the Francis W. Little house in Wayzata, Minnesota.

The **Period Rooms** on the SECOND FLOOR are devoted to the late Colonial period (1730–90). In the OLD WING (lower level of the second floor) are a Pennsylvania German Room (210) with painted woodwork, a gentleman's bedroom from Maryland, and an assembly room with a musicians' gallery from a tavern in Virginia. Other galleries highlight Philadelphia Chippendale furniture, New England chairs, chests, and secretaries by master craftsmen.

Three more period rooms are installed in the NEW WING OF THE SECOND FLOOR. The Van Rensselaer Hall (206) with its remarkable scenic wallpaper comes from a distinguished Georgian manor house in Albany, New York. The furnishings of the Verplanck Room (208) belonged to Samuel and Judith Crommelin Verplank, who lived at 3 Wall St. The Marmion Room (207) from a Virginia plantation is remarkable for its woodwork, some painted to simulate marble.

The *Joan Whitney Payson galleries* contain a permanent display of *American paintings and sculpture** arranged chronologically on the SECOND FLOOR AND MEZZANINE.

Gallery 217, 18C PAINTINGS AND SCULPTURE. Works of native American painters and those who immigrated from England, among them John Singleton Copley, *Mrs John Winthrop* and *Augustus Brine, Midshipman;* Copley was the preeminent painter of the period, but went to England (where he painted Augustus Brine) where his native American style took on courtly overtones.

Gallery 218, LATE-18C EARLY-19C PAINTING AND SCULPTURE. Includes Benjamin West, *The Triumph of Love;* West, a self-taught painter, perhaps America's best known before Whistler, was influential as a teacher. Among paintings by Gilbert Stuart is a fine early portrait of *George Washington,* one of the best of many, possibly done in part from life.

Gallery 219, PAINTING 1812–1840. George Caleb Bingham,

Fur Traders Descending the Missouri, a masterpiece of genre painting, remarkable for its luminous mist. Also, Hiram Powers, marble bust of *Andrew Jackson,* the old warrior, his face worn and toothless, his shoulders draped classically in marble.

Gallery 220, EARLY HUDSON RIVER SCHOOL. In the mid-19C there arose a native tradition of landscape painting detailing and dramatizing the natural beauty of the still-unspoiled continent. Thomas Cole is sometimes considered the father of the school. His *View from Mt. Holyoke, Massachusetts, After a Thunderstorm—The Oxbow* shows the power of nature as well as the painstaking rendering of its details characteristic of his style.

Gallery 221, LATE HUDSON RIVER SCHOOL. Martin Johnson Heade, *The Coming Storm;* Heade along with John Frederick Kensett, Fitz Hugh Lane, and others was deeply interested in effects of light and atmosphere. Albert Bierstadt, *The Rocky Mountains, Lander's Peak;* German-trained Bierstadt's favorite subject was the wild landscape of the American West, here rendered with visionary luminosity. Frederick Edwin Church, *The Heart of the Andes;* like his teacher Bierstadt, Church sought dramatic landscapes, only in more exotic places.

In Gallery 222 is the work of WINSLOW HOMER, now rated as one of the nation's finest painters. *Northeaster* is a powerful, austere example of his late style.

19TH CENTURY HISTORY AND GENRE PAINTINGS (Gallery 223) are shown on a rotating basis with the exception of Emanuel Leutze's *Washington Crossing the Delaware,* a romantic reconstruction of history inaccurate in its details but nonetheless deeply imprinted on the American consciousness.

Gallery 224, POST–CIVIL WAR PAINTING. Paintings by Thomas Eakins (he and Homer were the outstanding painters of the period) including *Max Schmitt in a Single Scull* with Eakins himself rowing in the middle distance, a study of perspective and light. Paintings and bronzes by Frederic Remington, definitive chronicler of cowboys, Indians, and army troopers.

From this gallery a stairway leads down to the MEZZANINE in the new wing (Gallery M1) with LATE-19C AND EARLY-20C REALISTS. Mary Cassatt, *Lady at the Tea Table;* Cassatt, a Philadelphia heiress, worked with the French Impressionists Degas, Manet, and others; women and children were among her favorite subjects. James A. MacNeill Whistler, *Arrangement in Flesh Color and Black: Portrait of Theodore Duret;* the title indicates Whistler's interest in the effects of color. John Singer Sargent, *Madame X;* a portrait scandalous in its day, both for its subject, the unconventional Mme. Gautreau, and for her demeanor in the picture—the low-cut gown, the slipped shoulder strap (repainted later).

Period Rooms and galleries on the THIRD FLOOR have exhibits from the early Colonial period (1630–1730). The central Meetinghouse Gallery (309) has chests, cupboards, and several pieces in the William and Mary style. The early Hart Room (303) comes from Ipswich, Massachusetts (before 1674), and is furnished with 17C oak and pine furniture. Elsewhere on this level are

METROPOLITAN MUSEUM: AMERICAN WING
Mezzanine, New Wing

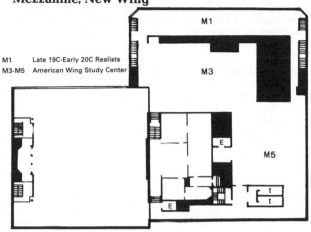

M1 Late 19C-Early 20C Realists
M3-M5 American Wing Study Center

METROPOLITAN MUSEUM: AMERICAN WING
Third Floor

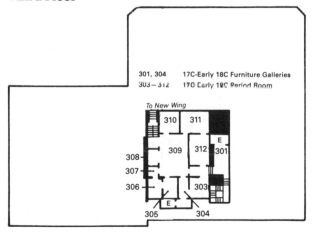

301, 304 17C-Early 18C Furniture Galleries
303 – 312 17C-Early 19C Period Room

rooms from a mid-18C Connecticut home, a New Hampshire farmhouse, and a stone house in Ulster County, New York. The Hewlett Room (310), from a house (c. 1740) on Long Island, shows Dutch influences in its architecture and furnishings.

Medieval Art.

The collection of the Department of Medieval Art contains objects from the 4–16C, from about the time of the fall of Rome to the beginning of the Renaissance, a long and complicated period of 12 centuries, whose major strands include Early Christian, Byzantine, Migration, Romanesque, and Gothic art. A bequest (1917) by J. P. Morgan of more than 4000 objects forms the heart of the collection, part of which is on display in The Cloisters near the N.W. tip of Manhattan.

GALLERY 1, **Early Christian Art** (S. side of Grand Staircase, just W. of Great Hall). Near the entrance are tomb reliefs and sarcophagus fragments. Along the staircase wall are examples of early Christian plain and gold glass and gold jewelry. *Marble Bust of a Lady of Rank* (late 5–early 6C) is a sensitive portrait of a woman in a heavily draped mantle; Byzantine and Avaric jewelry from the 6–9C; a sarcophagus lid from the late-3–early-4C which illustrates the parable of the sheep and goats; Byzantine art from the 9–13C including ivory plaques, enamels, icons, lockets, jewelry. On the other side of the hall are articles from the second Cyprus treasure including six silver plates with scenes from the Life of David; Byzantine bronze steelyard weights; silver from the 3–6C B.C.; Byzantine ivory plaques and caskets; and bronze lamps; and the Antioch Chalice, a liturgical vessel of silver inside an elaborately decorated cup of silver gilt.

GALLERY 2, the **Romanesque Chapel** (on the E. wall of Gallery 3, the Tapestry Hall). On the front wall of the chapel is a wooden statue from the Auvergne of the Virgin with the Child enthroned in her lap, an image in which Mary represents the Throne of Wisdom and Christ, the new Solomon. On a side wall is a 12C stone head of King David from the cathedral of Notre Dame, Paris.

GALLERY 3, the **Medieval Tapestry Hall** with stained glass and tapestries. Among the tapestries is a rare Annunciation Tapestry probably from Arras, the most important center of weaving during the first half of the 15C. The so-called Rose Tapestries depict finely dressed courtiers against a background of stripes and stylized rosebushes. In the center of the room is a monumental seated Virgin and Child from Burgundy (c. 1440–50), remarkable for its naturalism.

At the far end of GALLERY 4, the **Medieval Sculpture Hall,** is an impressive 17C *choir screen from Valladolid, Spain. Also Gothic sculpture in marble, alabaster, limestone, and wood, as well as furniture, ceramics, paintings, and tapestries. In a free-standing case nearby is a Reliquary Crib of the Infant Jesus (15C South Netherlandish), a popular devotional object during the early 16C. On the other side of the entrance door is Alabaster Mourner from the Tomb of the Duc de Berry.

GALLERY 5, the **Medieval Treasury,** contains precious objects of gold, silver, ivory, and enamel. Cases on one side of the room have enamel plaques from the Mosan Valley. On the other side of the door are ivory plaques and caskets, including a rare *situla,* or holy water bucket. Among the objects from Romanesque Spain is an ivory plaque with the Journey to Emmaus, when the risen Christ appeared to two disciples. The large reliquary head of St. Yrieix from 13C Limoges probably held a piece of the saint's skull or head, as reliquaries were often crafted to suggest the original relic. Also carved ivories, including a small *Corpus of Christ (1978.521.3) from the later 13C, a sensitively carved piece intended for an altar cross and remarkable for its anatomical detail.

Beyond the Treasury is the gallery of **Late Medieval Secular Art,** displaying everyday objects from the 14th to the 16th centuries, including examples of late-medieval ironwork, kitchen tools, games, and hunting equipment. Also a good selection of Spanish lusterware.

European Sculpture and Decorative Arts.

The galleries of European Sculpture and Decorative Arts, some of which will be reinstalled in the near future, contain one of the largest collections in the museum and include period rooms, furniture, a wide variety of decorative arts—silver, ceramics, metalwork—and some sculpture from the Renaissance to 1900. The galleries are organized more or less geographically with those devoted to the arts of the Renaissance in northern Europe beginning adjacent to the medieval section, followed by the Italian and English galleries. English and French period rooms are located along the W. side of the museum, with further examples of French and German furniture and porcelain near the period rooms. Completing the exhibition are the 16C Spanish patio and an adjacent gallery (Renaissance bronzes) and the ground floor galleries of porcelain, silver, and minor decorative arts (scheduled for reinstallation on the second floor).

Begin just next to the Tapestry Hall in the medieval section. GALLERY 1 contains **Sculpture and Decorative Arts from Northern Europe, 16–17C** including domestic implements, silver relief plaques, earthenware and stoneware vessels, silver gilt cups and tankards, and a collection of Renaissance bronzes by Flemish, German, and Netherlandish artists. In a freestanding case is an *Automaton: Diana on a Stag* (17.190.746) made by Joachim Fries in Augsburg (c. 1620), a piece of equipment which could be filled with wine and rolled around the table as part of a drinking game.

GALLERY 2 contains a display of **16–17C English Decorative Arts** including stoneware, silver, porcelain, and furniture, notably an oak table (64.101.1065) and an imposing tester bed (53.1) from the late 16C. On the E. side of this gallery are three period rooms: the *Chapel of the Château de la Bastie d'Urfé* near Lyons (GALLERY 3), the *Elizabethan Room* (GALLERY 4), with carved oak paneling from a house in Yarmouth, and the *Swiss Room* (GALLERY 5) from the mid-17C with a corner stove of faience tiles.

Galleries 8–10 are devoted to **Italian Decorative Arts.** Gallery 8, with its two gondola prows, serves as an antechamber to the *bedroom from the 18C Venetian Palazzo Sagredo* (GALLERY 9), on the Grand Canal near the Rialto. Such niceties as the ceiling painting and the 32 fluttering stucco cupids were created for other eyes than those of the home owner, as it was customary at the time to receive formal visits in bed.

GALLERY 10 contains *18C Italian furniture* and a set of allegorical frescoes from the workshop of Giovanni Battista Tiepolo. (Gallery 11 contains the collection of secular medieval decorative arts.)

Galleries 13–20 are devoted to **17–18C English Decorative Arts.** (To see the collection chronologically begin at Gallery 20 near the sculpture gallery.) GALLERY 13: Neoclassical English furniture, late 18C. GALLERY 15 is furnished with groupings of mahogany furniture from the mid-18C, much of it with Oriental or French rococo influence.

In this gallery is one entrance to the first of the **English Period Rooms,** the *DINING ROOM FROM LANSDOWNE HOUSE (1768), Berkeley Square, London (GALLERY 16), decorated by Robert Adam in neoclassical style. The silver on the table is by Paul Lamerie and others. More 18C English silver including work by the great Huguenot silversmiths active in London at the beginning of the century (Simon Pantin, Paul Lamerie, Lewis Mettayer, Pierre Harache) as well as Chelsea and Bow porcelains are shown in cases near the other doorway to the Lansdowne room (selections of porcelain and silver rotated occasionally).

GALLERY 17, the TAPESTRY ROOM FROM CROOME COURT (1760), shows the contemporary English fashion for rooms "in the French taste," and is remarkable for the *Gobelins tapestries that cover the walls and the seating.

GALLERY 18 contains ENGLISH DECORATIVE ARTS FROM THE EARLIER 18C with examples of needlework and furniture. The focal point of GALLERY 19 is a *STAIRCASE FROM CASSIOBURY PARK, a former country house in Hertfordshire. Carved (c. 1674) by *Grinling Gibbons* or Edward Pearce, the staircase has oak leaf and acorn decoration referring to the Royal Oak where Charles II hid during the Civil War. GALLERY 20 is a DINING ROOM FROM KIRTLINGTON PARK, north of Oxford (c. 1748), notable for its carved wood doors and rococo plaster decoration from designs by Thomas Roberts, a local master.

GALLERY 22 is the Josephine Bay Paul Gallery of **18C French sculpture.** The finest piece in the gallery is Jean Louis Lemoyne's *The Fear of Cupid's Darts,* made for Louis XV around 1740.

The Wrightsman Galleries of ***French 18C Period Rooms** are superb. Turn left on entering the galleries and walk to GALLERY 33, Introductory Gallery and PARIS SHOPFRONT, the only Parisian shopfront (c. 1775) remaining from the reign of Louis XVI. In the windows are examples of Parisian silver, rare survivals from a period when a great deal of it was melted down on royal orders to finance royal wars. Two small paneled rooms open from the left side of the corridor. The ROOM FROM THE HÔTEL DE

CRILLON (GALLERY 34) is a mirrored boudoir from the residence of the Duc d'Aumont in the present Place de la Concorde among whose furnishings are a daybed and armchair that belonged to Marie Antoinette. The BORDEAUX ROOM (GALLERY 35) is a circular salon with carved neoclassical paneling; a Beauvais tapestry carpet covers the floor and the table is set with pieces of black Sèvres porcelain.

Beyond the Bordeaux Room is (23) the LOUIS XV ROOM, with corner panels carved with trophies of the four seasons. Hyacinthe Rigaud painted the portrait of *Louis XV as a Boy*. In the SÈVRES ALCOVE are porcelains including a rose vase (58.75.89a,b) in the form of a ship, considered a tour-de-force of Sèvres work. The *SÈVRES ROOM (23a) with polychromed paneling from the Hôtel de Lauzun on the Île Saint-Louis, Paris, houses a collection of furniture set with Sèvres plaques.

Antoine Lavoisier and His Wife as portrayed by Jacques Louis David look down over the LOUIS XVI GALLERY (24). Furniture includes two secretaries and a commode by *Adam Weisweiler* with panels of Japanese lacquer. The first doorway on the right opens into (25a) a ROOM FROM THE HÔTEL DE VARENGE-VILLE, the Paris town house of the Duchesse de Villars, wife of one of Louis XIV's great generals. Louis XV's own writing table from the study at Versailles stands in the center on a Savonnerie carpet, one of 92 woven for the Grande Galerie at the Louvre. Adjacent is the PAAR ROOM (25b) from the Palais Paar in Vienna, built (c. 1630) for the Baron Johann Christoph von Paar, postmaster of the Holy Roman Empire, and remodeled 1765–71.

The carved and gilded paneling in the CABRIS ROOM was executed in Paris (c. 1775–78) for a home in Grasse, some 12 miles from Cannes. The final gallery (26) is the DE TESSÉ ROOM, the grand salon of a Paris town house still standing on the Quai Voltaire.

GALLERY 29 is the LOUIS XIV STATE BEDCHAMBER, its centerpiece a bed with needlework hangings surrounded by four extraordinary needlework wall panels.

Adjacent to these rooms are the **Jack and Belle Linksy Galleries,** containing European paintings, sculpture, and decorative arts, a private collection of high quality donated to the museum in 1982. To see the rooms in chronological order, enter from the Medieval Sculpture Hall.

To the left of the anteroom in the RED ROOM are Renaissance paintings and small bronzes from the Middle Ages and Renaissance. Outstanding among the Italian paintings are Carlo Crivelli, *Madonna and Child,* and a half-length *Madonna and Child* by Vittorio Crivelli; Giovanni di Paolo, *Adoration of the Magi,* and Andrea del Sarto, *Portrait of a Man,* as well as an early portrait by Fra Bartolomeo. Two miniature panels by Cranach illustrate events from the New Testament, *Christ Blessing the Children,* and *Christ and the Adulteress.* The most dramatic medieval object is a Romanesque bronze showing a Monk-Scribe Astride a Dragon (Rhenish, 12C).

Return through the anteroom to the blue-gray CENTRAL ROOM which contains examples of jewels and goldsmiths' work. In the

GOLD ROOM are 17C Dutch paintings, notably Jan Steen, *The Dissolute Household*, and a triple portrait by Gerard ter Borch, *The Van Moerkerken Family*. The single most extravagant decorative object in the collection must be the smoky rock-crystal *ewer, probably made for the imperial court at Prague (c. 1680) and mounted in London in the early 19C.

The next room contains PORCELAINS from Menency and Saint-Cloud, a group of Russian figures showing different ethnic types, Neopolitan figures from the Capodimonte factory, and a group of Danish figures.

Return through the Gold Room to the IVORY ROOM with its exhibit of French 18C decorative arts and paintings, which includes three canvases by François Boucher, *Angelica and Medoro, Jupiter in the Guise of Diana,* and *Calisto.* The still life by Luis Egidio Meléndez, *La Merienda*, is one of the largest and most elaborate of some eighty-five.

Off this room is the second of two displaying the Linsky PORCELAINS. This one is devoted to German works from Fulda, Nymphenburg, Höchst, Ludwigsburg, and a collection of some 30 Meissen figures, including a series of J. J. Kändler's appealing characters from the commedia dell'arte. Notable also is a small but dramatic stoneware portrait bust of Augustus the Strong.

Installed in GALLERY 57 adjacent to the 16C Spanish Patio are sculptures from the museum's outstanding collection of **16—17C bronzes.** Among the classic pieces by masters of the genre are Bartolomeo Bellano, *David with the Head of Goliath* (64.304.1); Antico, *Paris* (55.93), Andrea Riccio, *Striding Satyr* (1982.45), and a *Rearing Horse* (25.74) thought to be after a model by Leonardo.

The **16C Spanish Patio** (GALLERY 56) from the castle of Los Vélez in S.E. Spain was donated by George Blumenthal, president of the museum 1933—41, who had previously installed it in his home on Park Ave. The patio (1506—15) was decorated in part by Italian craftsmen who executed the marble work around the doorways and on the arcades. It now serves as a sculpture garden containing a group of Renaissance works, notably Tullio Lombardo's *Adam* (36.163).

The Robert Lehman Pavilion.

The ***Robert Lehman Pavilion** contains the superb Italian, Flemish, and 19C French paintings, ceramics, Renaissance bronzes, and drawings collected by Robert Lehman who promised them to the museum in 1969 with the stipulation that they remain permanently together and that seven period rooms from the Lehman town house be recreated within the museum.

The LEHMAN WING (1975; Roche, Dinkeloo & Assocs.) is set against the original Victorian Gothic W. wall of the museum (1880; Calvert Vaux and Jacob Wrey Mould; DL). The lower galleries are used for changing exhibitions from the more than 1600 drawings in the collection; the upper galleries contain the period rooms where the paintings are hung.

The GRAND GALLERY, nearest the central courtyard, contains **19—20C French painting** arranged chronologically. Jean Baptiste

Camille Corot, *Diana and Actaeon*. Claude Monet, *Landscape near Zaandam*. Pierre Auguste Renoir, *Young Girl Bathing*. Vincent van Gogh, *Madame Roulin and Her Baby*. Balthus, *Figure in Front of a Mantle*.

In the two rooms (N.W. side of courtyard), arranged as in the Lehman town house, are **Sienese and Italian Renaissance painting** with works by Giovanni di Paolo, Lorenzo Veneziano, Carlo Crivelli, and Lorenzo Monaco.

Continue past the DINING ROOM to the SPECIAL GALLERY with Jean Auguste Dominique Ingres's *Portrait of the Princesse de Broglie,* one of his most beautiful aristocratic portraits. There are also paintings by Paul Cézanne, André Derain, Matisse, Degas, Van Dongen, Vuillard, Signac, Bonnard, and Seurat.

The *RED VELVET ROOM contains **15C Italian paintings.** Sassetta, *The Temptation of St. Anthony Abbot,* shows the saint in a strange desert landscape; a figure of the devil in the lower left of the painting has been erased. Giovanni di Paolo's *Expulsion from Paradise* is remarkable for its iconography, with God showing the sinful Adam and Eve the barren world which they will inhabit, a world surrounded by the concentric circles of the universe, the outer ring inscribed with the signs of the zodiac. Giovanni Bellini, *Madonna and Child;* the garlands of leaves and fruit above the Virgin's head may have symbolic meaning. Sandro Botticelli, *Annunciation;* the complex organization of the space and the transparent colors indicate that it is a late painting. Jacometto Veneziano, *Portrait of Alvise Contarini* and a companion portrait, *Nun of San Secondo.* Lorenzo Costa, *Portraits of Alessandro di Bernardo Gozzadini and Donna Canonici.*

Beyond the STAIRCASE LANDING is the SITTING ROOM with **16–18C Spanish and 17C Dutch painting.** Velázquez, Hooch, Ter Borch, and Goya are represented. Also El Greco, *Saint Jerome as a Cardinal;* Rembrandt, *Portrait of Gérard de Lairesse.*

The final room, the *FLEMISH ROOM, contains **15C northern European painting** and decorative arts. There is an *Annunciation* by Hans Memling, and a pair of panels (painted on both sides) by Gerard David, one with *Christ Bearing the Cross and the Crucifixion* and the other with *The Resurrection with Pilgrims of Emmaus* (the outer sides depict the Archangel Gabriel and the Virgin of the Annunciation). Also a painting by Petrus Christus, *St. Eligius,* patron saint of goldsmiths, in his shop. Lucas Cranach, *Nymph of the Spring,* and *Venus and Cupid the Honey Thief.* Hans Holbein, a small *Portrait of Erasmus of Rotterdam.*

Primitive Art.

The Michael C. Rockefeller Wing devoted to the art of Africa, the Americas, and the Pacific Islands, contains some 2000 objects spanning 3000 years and three continents. Within an architecturally dramatic setting (1982; Roche, Dinkeloo & Assocs.), millions of dollars of sophisticated technology have been lavished on the preservation of these "primitive" objects.

History. The wing houses the collection of the museum along with art from the Museum of Primitive Art, founded by Nelson A. Rockefeller in 1954. It is named as a memorial to Rockefeller's son, who drowned in 1961 on an expedition to Papua, New Guinea.

The first of two galleries devoted to **African Art** (adjacent to the entrance from Greek and Roman Art) focuses on the art of WESTERN SUDAN AND THE GUINEA COAST. There is wooden sculpture by the Dogon, Bamana, and Senufo peoples of Mali and bronze sculpture from Benin (modern Nigeria). Notable among the many wooden sculptures are a *7-ft male Dogon figure with upraised arms. Dogon sculpture is among the largest in Africa and, preserved by the dry climate, also among the oldest. At the far end of the room, Bamana figures from Mali include a mother and child. On the left wall, Senufo helmet masks (Ivory Coast), in the forms of monumental bird figures which were carried on the heads of dancers.

The second African gallery opens to the left and is devoted to the arts of CENTRAL AFRICA, THE GUINEA COAST, AND EQUATORIAL AFRICA. In the Central African section are stools and chairs, including a rare stool (1979.290) with a caryatid figure by the Buli master of the Luba people (Zaire). The mysterious Songe mask (1979. 206.83) with stylized features and a design of incised lines was probably worn at ceremonies for the death of a king. In a case on the side wall a Kongo fetish of a man or spirit rides on a dog (1978.412.531); nearby is a Kongo figure of wood, nails, cloth, beads, and shell (1979.206.127) believed to embody a spirit with good and evil powers. In a freestanding case is a Fang reliquary head (1979.206.229) from Gabon that was once owned by sculptor Jacob Epstein. In the middle section of the gallery is a highly stylized Nigerian headdress of the Yoruba people (1976.329), made up of geometric forms. In a freestanding case are Akan terra-cotta heads (1978.412.352, 353), made to commemorate deceased members of the royal family. In the section devoted to the Guinea Coast is an extraordinary early-16C *pendant mask of ivory (1978.412.323) from the court of Benin in Nigeria; it was worn on the belt of the ruler as part of his regalia and apparently represents a queen. There is also a fine collection of bronze and brass objects from the court of Benin, for example (side wall) a bronze Horn Player (1978.412.310) and a group of dark brass heads (1979.206.86, 87, 36). On the end wall is a Bangwa dancing figure (1978.412.576) from Cameroon.

The galleries devoted to **Art of the Americas** lie behind the African galleries. Enter the MESOAMERICAN GALLERY from the first African gallery. The collection of Aztec stone sculpture includes animals, female figures (perhaps agricultural or fertility goddesses), and a collection of grim coiled rattlesnakes. The equally grim Toltec panel of an Eagle Devouring a Human Heart (93.27.2) dates from the 9—12C. Among the ceramics are examples from Huastec, Tlatilco, Colima, Nayarit, and Jalisco cultures. Olmec artifacts include a jade mask (1977.187.33) as well as pendants, ornaments, and "baby" figures (for example 1979.206.1134). The wooden Seated Figure (1979.206.1063), probably a priest or dignitary, ceremonially posed and elegantly dressed, is one of the few Maya wooden objects that have survived time, moisture, and infestation; it dates from the 6C. From Veracruz (Remojadas) comes a rare "smiling" figure (1979.206.1211).

The second gallery of the Americas opens from the first. Against the rear wall in a section devoted to CENTRAL AMERICA, are stone sculptures and ceramics from Ecuador and northern Peru, including vessels from the Chavin period, one of the most artistically fertile periods in ancient South America. In the TREASURY are ornaments and small objects of gold: Mohican ear spools (66.196.40,41) of gold with stone and shell inlay, a fine pendant (69.7.10) of a ferocious figure with an elaborate headdress from the Tairona of Colombia, pectorals, an eagle pendant (1979.206.735), and other animal pendants. Near the exit is a gold funerary mask (1974.271.35) of the Peruvian Chimu people. Also, southern Peruvian ceramics, feather hangings, and ornaments.

From the second Americas gallery enter the third display area with a small section devoted to ESKIMO AND NORTHWEST COAST INDIAN cultures of NORTH AMERICA. The Haida sea-bear mask of copper with inlaid shell eyes and teeth (1979.206.830) is exceptional.

The rest of the wing focuses on the cultures and **Art of the Pacific Islands.** Adjacent to the North American exhibit is a recreation of a ceremonial house with ceiling paintings on bark by the Kwoma people of New Guinea. Among the objects in the Polynesian section are a rare 18C ivory figure (1979.206.1470) from Tonga, and an anthropomorphic pendant (1979.206.1587) of a type known formerly only from the writings of the 18C explorer Captain Cook.

The main gallery in this area with its glass wall facing south contains large funerary festival carvings from northern NEW IRELAND; these are the most complex of Oceanic works of art and were used in feasts honoring the dead. Also standing slit gongs and figures from the NEW HEBRIDES, and an impressive collection of artifacts from NEW GUINEA. The Michael C. Rockefeller collection of Asmat art includes *nine memorial poles from 12–21 ft tall facing the glass wall as well as reclining two-headed ancestor poles, costumes of straw and reed with woven masks, spears and shields, sago pounders, and canoe ornaments. On a low platform parallel to the window is a 25-ft crocodile effigy (1978.412.843a,b) from the Karawari River region of New Guinea.

20th Century Art.

The Lila Acheson Wallace Wing (1987; Roche, Dinkeloo & Assocs.), named after one of the museum's greatest benefactors, has been called the best space for displaying 20th century art in the city, although the collection is overshadowed by the holdings of other major New York museums.

To see the galleries in chronological order, begin on the First

Floor. Because some of the paintings within the galleries are rotated occasionally, the description below may not precisely describe the current arrangement. Not all of the paintings mentioned may be on display at any one time.

The general plan of the galleries is as follows. FIRST FLOOR: Galleries 1–9, Chronological Survey of Painting, 1905–45. Gallery 10, Design and Architecture. Gallery 11, Changing Exhibitions. MEZZANINE: Sculpture Gallery and two smaller flanking galleries for Klee Collection and changing exhibitions from the Department of Prints, Drawings, and Photographs. SECOND FLOOR: Galleries 15–22, Continuation of Chronological Survey of Painting, 1945–present. Gallery 22, the Lila Acheson Wallace Gallery overlooking the park.

ROOM 1: The first of four rooms which survey currents in 20C painting. The survey begins with the French Impressionists and their Belgian, British, Austrian, and American contemporaries. Included are Pierre Bonnard, *The Terrace at Vernon,* a scene of the terrace and garden of his home in the Seine valley, painted with techniques developed by the Impressionists; James Ensor, *Banquet of the Starved.*

ROOM 2: PAINTING IN EUROPE. André Derain, *The Table,* showing the influence of the Cubists. Pablo Picasso: *The Blind Man's Meal* from the Blue Period; *Gertrude Stein,* his most famous portrait, executed in Paris when Picasso was 24 and Stein was 32, given by Stein to the museum, and *A Woman in White,* a calm portrait of Olga Koklova, whom he married in 1918. Amedeo Modigliani, *Juan Gris,* a portrait of the Spanish artist, and *Jeanne Hébuterne.* Also paintings by De Chirico, Vlaminck, Van Dongen.

ROOM 3: PAINTING IN EUROPE, EARLY 20C ART AND CUBISM. One of the high points of the collection is Henri Matisse's *Nasturtiums and "Dance."* The painting *Dance,* with its circle of naked dancers, belongs to the Museum of Modern Art; it leans against the wall in Matisse's studio where there is also a chair and a vase of nasturtiums. ROOM 4 is used for changing exhibitions from the collection.

ROOM 5: This long gallery offers a survey of mainstream American painting between 1905 and about 1945 (exact dates change occasionally). There are paintings by Maurice Prendergast, Childe Hassam, John Sloan, William Glackens, and Reginald Marsh, which focus on New York City and its daily life. Also George Bellows, *Tennis at Newport;* several paintings by Edward Hopper: *From Williamsburg Bridge, Tables for Ladies,* and *The Lighthouse at Two Lights;* American regional painters including John Steuart Curry and Grant Wood; American avant-garde paintings by Raphael Soyer, Paul Cadmus, Isabel Bishop, Stuart Davis, and Florine Stettheimer. Toward the end of this survey are Lyonel Feininger, Thomas Hart Benton, and Charles Sheeler. Usually in this gallery are early figural paintings by Willem de Kooning.

ROOM 6 is used for changing exhibitions. The next galleries, ROOMS 7–9, often feature the work of artists nurtured by Alfred Stieglitz: Arthur G. Dove, *Portrait of Ralph Dusenberry,* an abstract assemblage suggesting the subject's interests and personality; Marsden Hartley, *Portrait of a German Officer*. Other artists usually exhibited here include John Marin, Diego Rivera, Charles Demuth, and Georgia O'Keeffe, Stieglitz's widow and the original overseer of the collection.

ROOM 10 has changing exhibitions of decorative and industrial arts from about 1900 to the present. Exhibitions change about twice yearly. ROOM 11 is also reserved for changing exhibitions.

On the **Mezzanine level** is a large central SCULPTURE GALLERY, reserved for generally large-scale paintings and pieces of sculpture (changed occasionally). Usually on display are *Reclining Nude* by Henry Moore and a gigantic silkscreen and acrylic, *Mao* (1973), by Andy Warhol. Flanking the sculpture gallery are two small rooms, ROOM 12, reserved for selections from the Berggruen Klee Collection, and ROOM 14, the Gioconda and Joseph King Gallery, which features two or three yearly exhibitions from the Department of Prints and Photographs.

The chronological survey of modern, primarily American, painting continues on the **Second Floor** with paintings from 1945 to the present. ROOM 15: Jackson Pollock, *Pasiphaë,* an early work that anticipates his Abstract Expressionist style; Willem de Kooning, *Seated Woman*. ROOMS 16 and 17 focus on the work of first-generation Abstract Expressionists. Jackson Pollock's *Autumn Rhythm* (1950) and Willem de Kooning's *Easter Monday* are major paintings by the dominant figures of the movement. There are also works by Clyfford Still, Mark Rothko, and Robert Motherwell.

ROOM 18: Abstract and Color Field paintings by Franz Kline, Ellsworth Kelly, Frank Stella, Morris Louis. ROOM 19: R. B. Kitaj, *John Ford on His Deathbed*. ROOM 20: Romare Bearden, *The Block,* a collage of a Harlem street; James Rosenquist, *House of Fire;* Roy Lichtenstein, *Stepping Out*. ROOM 21 is reserved for changing exhibitions of living artists. ROOM 22: The last gallery of the survey, with paintings by Red Grooms, Jim Dine, Jasper Johns, and others, is installed in a lovely room with a view of Central Park and the skyline to the south.

SECOND FLOOR.

The museum holds one of the world's great collections of ****European Paintings,** which began with trustee William T. Blodgett's purchase of 174 paintings (c. 1870) at a time when Old Masters were just becoming popular with the city's burgeoning millionaire population. The museum has since received major bequests from railroad financier H. B. Marquand, Benjamin Altman, J. P. Morgan, H. O. Havemeyer, and Michael Friedsam, as well as from Jacob S. Rogers, a locomotive manufacturer known as the meanest man in Paterson (New Jersey), who gave $5 million to the museum instead of to his relatives. With the exception of the Altman and the Lehman collections, gifts conditional upon specific arrangement within the museum, paintings are arranged chronologically and by school.

METROPOLITAN MUSEUM
Second Floor, European Paintings

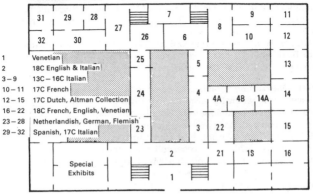

Audio tours of some parts of the collection are available at the Audioguide desk in the Great Hall. The Harry Payne Bingham Galleries to the right of Gallery 1 are used for the study collection or for special exhibitions. The collection of European paintings spans roughly the late-14—18C; 19C paintings and sculpture are displayed in the André Meyer Galleries.

GALLERY 1: 18C VENETIAN PAINTING including Giovanni Battista Tiepolo. GALLERY 2: 18C ENGLISH AND ITALIAN PAINTING. Here are aristocratic portraits by Sir Joshua Reynolds and Thomas Gainsborough, and Giovanni Paolo Panini's panoramic depiction of the monuments of ancient and "modern" (i.e., 18C) Rome.

Galleries 3–9 contain **Italian Painting**. GALLERY 3: 13–14C ITALIAN PAINTING. Berlinghiero, *Madonna and Child,* one of three known paintings by this important early Tuscan painter; Giotto, *The Epiphany,* a nativity scene by the painter considered even near his own time as a precursor of something new; Sassetta, *Journey of the Magi;* Giovanni di Paolo, *Paradise.* GALLERY 4: ITALIAN SECULAR PAINTING OF THE 15C. GALLERY 4A: Ceiling panels from the Palazzo del Magnifico in Siena by Bernardo Pintoricchio; frescoes from the Villa Mattei in Rome by Baldassare Peruzzi. GALLERY 4B: ITALIAN RENAISSANCE PAINTINGS FROM THE ALTMAN COLLECTION.

Benjamin Altman, founder of the department store and a bachelor who devoted himself totally to his work and his art collection, left a $15 million collection of paintings and porcelains to the museum on the condition that it be maintained intact in two suitable adjoining rooms, one for the paintings, statuary, Limoges enamels, and rock crystals, another for the Chinese porcelains. Although the porcelains and decorative arts have been moved elsewhere, the paintings are displayed in their own galleries.

Andrea Mantegna, *Adoration of the Shepherds.* Sandro Botticelli, *The Last Communion of St. Jerome;* usually this saint is depicted as a scholar. Fra Angelico, *The Crucifixion*. GALLERY 5: *15C VENETIAN PAINTING. Carlo Crivelli, *Madonna and Child,* delicately colored and stylistically archaic. Giovanni Bellini, an early and a late *Madonna and Child*. Vittore Carpaccio, *Meditation on the Passion* with Job and St. Jerome in front of symbolic landscapes. Antonello da Messina; Cosimo Tura.

GALLERY 6: 15C ITALIAN PAINTING. Filippino Lippi, *Madonna and Child*. Domenico Ghirlandaio, *St. Christopher with the Infant Christ,* a large fresco. Luca Signorelli, *Madonna and Child,* with an unusual gold background. Piero di Cosimo, *Young St. John the Baptist*. John the Baptist is a patron saint of Florence and often appears in Florentine painting as a young man. Also Lorenzo di Credi, Cosimo Rosselli, and Perugino.

GALLERY 7: *16C ITALIAN PAINTING. Agnolo Bronzino, a very aristocratic *Portrait of a Young Man*. Raphael, *Madonna and Child Enthroned with the Young Baptist and Saints* and a smaller painting that was part of the same altarpiece, *The Agony in the Garden*. Andrea del Sarto, *Holy Family with Infant St. John*.

GALLERY 8: *16C VENETIAN PAINTING. Titian, *Venus and the Lute Player; Venus and Adonis,* a subject drawn from Ovid; Venus embraces her lover before he goes off to the fatal boar hunt. Paolo Veronese, *Mars and Venus United by Love* and *Alessandro Vittoria,* a portrait of a famous Venetian sculptor. Tintoretto, *The Miracle of the Loaves and Fishes*.

GALLERY 9: 16C ITALIAN PAINTING. Correggio, Moretto da Brescia, and Giovanni Battista Moroni.

French Painting is in Galleries 10–11. GALLERY 10: 17C FRENCH PAINTING. Nicolas Poussin, *The Blind Orion Searching for the Rising Sun* and *The Rape of the Sabine Women*. Claude Lorrain, *View of La Crescenza* and *The Trojan Women Setting Fire to Their Fleet*. GALLERY 11: Georges de la Tour, *The Penitent Magdalen*.

Dutch Painting occupies galleries 12–15. *GALLERY 12: Jan Steen, *Merry Company on a Terrace*. Johannes Vermeer, *Young Woman with a Water Jug* and *Portrait of a Young Woman*. Only about 40 universally accepted Vermeers are known to exist; the Metropolitan has five.

GALLERY 13: 17C DUTCH LANDSCAPE PAINTING. Paintings by Salomon van Ruysdael, Meindert Hobbema, Aelbert Cuyp, Jacob van Ruisdael.

GALLERY 14: 17C DUTCH PAINTING FROM THE BENJAMIN ALTMAN COLLECTION. Frans Hals, *Young Man and Woman in an Inn* and *Merrymakers at Shrovetide*. The Altman collection is remarkable for its Rembrandts, among other paintings. Rembrandt, *Self-Portrait, Man with a Magnifying Glass, Lady with a Pink, The Toilet of Bathsheba, Portrait of a Young Man (The Auctioneer)*. Vermeer, *A Girl Asleep*. Jacob van Ruisdael, *Wheatfields*. Also works of Nicholas Maes, Aelbert Cuyp.

In GALLERY 14A are other NETHERLANDISH AND NORTHERN EUROPEAN PAINTINGS FROM THE ALTMAN COLLECTION. Judith Leyster, *Boy with a Lute,* formerly attributed to

Hals. Albrecht Durer, *Virgin and Child with St. Anne*. Hans Memling, *Tommaso Portinari* and his wife, *Maria Baroncelli*. Also paintings by Dieric Bouts, Gerard Dou.

*GALLERY 15: DUTCH 17C PORTRAITS. Frans Hals, *Portrait of a Man*. Rembrandt, *Man in Oriental Costume—the Noble Slav; Flora; Aristotle with a Bust of Homer*, purchased by the museum in 1961 for the then remarkable price of $2.3 million. Aristotle, wearing a glittering gold chain with a medallion of his pupil the conqueror Alexander, contemplates a bust of Homer.

GALLERY 16: 18C ENGLISH PORTRAITS. GALLERY 18: 18C FRENCH PAINTING. Jean Baptiste Siméon Chardin, *Boy Blowing Bubbles*. Paintings by Hubert Robert, Jean Baptiste Greuze.

GALLERY 21: Jean Honoré Fragonard, *The Love Letter*. François Boucher, *The Toilet of Venus*. Antoine Watteau, *Mezzetin,* a figure from the commedia dell'arte.

GALLERY 22: 18C VENETIAN PAINTING. Francesco Guardi, *Fantastic Landscape*; Gian Domenico Tiepolo, the son and assistant of Giovanni Battista Tiepolo, *A Dance in the Country*.

In the other wing of galleries, opening to the left of Gallery 2, are **Renaissance paintings from northern Europe, Spanish paintings, and 18C Italian paintings.**

GALLERY 23: *15C FLEMISH PAINTING. (Recorded tour available.) Jan van Eyck, *The Crucifixion* and *The Last Judgment*. Petrus Christus, *Lamentation over the Dead Christ* and *Portrait of a Carthusian*. Attrib. Van Eyck or Petrus Christus, *Annunciation*. Rogier van der Weyden, *Christ Appearing to His Mother* and *Francesco d'Este*. Hugo van der Goes, *Portrait of a Man*. Gerard David, *Rest on the Flight into Egypt* and triptych with the *Adoration of the Shepherds, St. John the Baptist, St. Francis Receiving the Stigmata*.

GALLERY 24: Gerard David, *Annunciation*. Hieronymus Bosch, *The Adoration of the Magi*. Quentin Massys, *The Adoration of the Magi*.

GALLERY 25: 16C GERMAN AND FLEMISH PAINTING. Lucas Cranach, *John, Duke of Saxony*. Hans Holbein the Younger, *Edward VI when Duke of Cornwall* and *A Member of the Wedigh Family*. Jean Clouet, *Guillaume Budé*.

*GALLERY 26: Pieter Breughel the Elder, *The Harvesters*. Joachim Patinir, *The Penitence of St. Jerome*. Lucas Cranach, *The Judgment of Paris*.

GALLERY 27: 17C FLEMISH PAINTING. Anthony van Dyck, *James Stuart, Duke of Richmond and Lennox*. Peter Paul Rubens, *Venus and Adonis* and *Rubens, His Wife Helena Fourment, and their Son, Peter Paul*.

GALLERY 28: Van Dyck, Jordaens.

GALLERY 29: Note: At the present time the **Spanish paintings** have been moved during construction of the new galleries for European Decorative Arts. The following description reflects their previous and presumably subsequent location. El Greco, *Portrait of a Man, Cardinal Don Fernando Niño de Guevara, View of Toledo, The Miracle of Christ Healing the Blind*. Francisco de Zurbarán, *The Young Virgin*.

GALLERY 30: 17C ITALIAN PAINTING. Caravaggio, *The*

Musicians. Annibale Carraci, *The Coronation of the Virgin.* Mattia Preti, *Pilate Washing His Hands.* Salvator Rosa, *Self-Portrait.* Guido Reni, *Charity.*

GALLERY 31: 17C SPANISH PAINTING. Diego Velázques, *Juan de Pareja.* GALLERY 32: Bartolomé Esteban Murillo, *Virgin and Child.*

Prints, Drawings, and Photographs are shown in changing exhibitions in the galleries between the Recent Acquisitions gallery and the André Meyer galleries.

19C European Paintings and Sculpture.

In 1980 the André Meyer Galleries of **19C European Paintings and Sculpture** opened allowing the public to see for the first time about 75% of the museum's outstanding collection from this period. The focus of the installation is the central gallery where the Impressionist and Post-Impressionist paintings are hung, while peripheral galleries contain minor painters, precursors of the period, and sculpture, with separate rooms devoted to Rodin, Degas, Courbet, and Corot. Recorded tour available.

The first two galleries contain **Precursors of Impressionism.** GALLERY 1 (enter from the galleries of Greek vases) contains works of NEOCLASSICAL PAINTERS. Jacques Louis David, *The Death of Socrates.* Jean Auguste Dominique Ingres, *Portrait of Joseph Antoine Moltedo* (1807–14), a successful industrialist.

GALLERY 2, the long gallery adjacent, is devoted to works of influential ROMANTIC PAINTERS. Francisco Goya, *The Bullfight;* portrait of *José Costa y Bonells,* called Pepito; *Don Manuel Osorio Manrique de Zuniga, Majas on a Balcony. Majos* and *majas,* working class men and women, were recognizable by their general flamboyance of appearance and behavior. Eugène Delacroix, *Basket of Flowers* and *The Abduction of Rebecca,* a romantic subject taken from Scott's *Ivanhoe.* J. M. W. Turner, *The Whale Ship* and *The Grand Canal, Venice,* a view from the Grand Canal toward the doge's palace. John Constable, *Salisbury Cathedral from the Bishop's Garden;* Constable, a friend of the bishop of Salisbury who appears in the lower left, painted this scene several times; there is a version in the Frick Collection.

GALLERY 3 is devoted to **Gustave Courbet** and the paintings on display (about 20) constitute one of the world's largest holdings of his work. Gustave Courbet, *Woman with a Parrot, Young Ladies from the Village, Portrait of Jo, Lady in a Riding Habit (L'Amazone),* and *The Source of the Loue.*

Turn left into GALLERY 7, the first of three devoted to the **Barbizon School.** Here are hung landscapes by Charles François Daubigny and Théodore Rousseau. Rousseau, *The Forest in Winter at Sunset,* generally considered his masterpiece; the painter refused to sell it during his lifetime.

To the right GALLERY 8 features the work of **Camille Corot** and includes figure paintings as well as the more familiar landscapes. Corot, *Hagar in the Wilderness, Woman Reading.* GALLERY 9 (straight ahead), also devoted to the BARBIZON SCHOOL, contains the work of Jean François Millet and Honoré Daumier along with lesser painters. Notable are Millet, *Autumn Land-*

METROPOLITAN MUSEUM
Second Floor

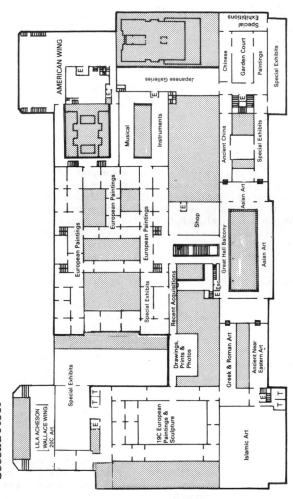

scape with a Flock of Turkeys and *Haystacks: Autumn.* Daumier, *The Third Class Carriage.* Arnold Böcklin, *Island of the Dead.* The Swiss symbolist painter made five versions of this subject, this one, the first, at the request of a newly widowed Florentine patroness who wanted to commemorate her bereavement.

Turn left into GALLERY 6, devoted to **Salon Painting,** a name given to conservative 19C painting, much of it commercially successful in its day, much of it judged sentimental today. Rosa Bonheur, *The Horse Fair.* Jules Bastien-Lepage, *Joan of Arc.* Pierre August Cot, *The Storm.* Henri Alexandre Georges Regnault, *Salome.*

GALLERY 5, **Second Empire Painters.** Franz Winterhalter, *Countess Maria Ivanovna Lamsdorf.* In the center of the room is a marble group by Jean Baptiste Carpeaux, *Ugolino and His Sons,* a highly romantic rendering of a subject drawn from the lower depths of Hell in Dante's *Divine Comedy.* Edward Burne-Jones, *Le Chant d'Amour,* a picture whose subject reflects the Pre-Raphaelite romantic fascination with the Middle Ages.

GALLERY 10, between the Second Empire Room and the gallery of Rodin sculpture contains paintings by **Symbolist Painters.** Gustave Moreau, *Oedipus and the Sphinx.* Frederick Leighton, *Lacrymae.* Several allegorical paintings by Pierre Puvis de Chavannes, a painter known for his flat, stylized, symbolic figures; Puvis's work influenced younger artists, including Gauguin who studied with him.

GALLERY 11 has some 40 works by **Rodin** in bronze, marble, terra-cotta, and plaster. Included are a terra-cotta study for a Head of Balzac, on whose monument Rodin worked long and intensively; the statue was not cast during Rodin's lifetime. Bronzes from his unfinished project *The Gates of Hell* include Adam and Eve (both modeled 1880–81 and cast 1910), commissioned for a building in Paris that was never built.

GALLERY 12: ****Impressionist and Post-Impressionist Paintings.** Édouard Manet, *Woman with a Parrot, Mlle. Victorine in the Costume of an Espada, The Spanish Singer, Boating.* Pierre Auguste Renoir, *Mme. Charpentier and Her Children,* a portrait of the wife of the publisher of Maupassant and Zola; *A Waitress at Duval's Restaurant; Tilla Durieux,* painted at the end of Renoir's life, when arthritis forced him to work with his brush strapped to his hand.

Paul Cézanne, *The Gulf of Marseilles Seen from L'Estaque,* a landscape of which Cézanne made multiple paintings, studying the changing forms of the houses and mountains from slightly different viewpoints. Also, *Dominique Aubert, The Cardplayers, Mont Sainte-Victoire, Mme. Cézanne in a Red Dress, Still Life with a Ginger Jar and Eggplants.*

Georges Seurat, *Invitation to the Sideshow* and *Study for a Sunday Afternoon on the Island of La Grande Jatte,* the final sketch for the famous painting in the Art Institute of Chicago. Paul Gauguin, *Ia Orana Maria.* Henri Rousseau, *The Repast of the Lion.*

Claude Monet, *Rouen Cathedral, Bridge over a Pool of Water Lilies, Morning on the Seine near Giverny, Haystacks in the*

Snow. The Terrace at Sainte-Adresse, an early painting in which Monet's mature style can begin to be seen in the detached strokes of color in which the sea, flowers, and pennants are rendered. *La Grenouillère, The Park Monceau, Poplars.* Camille Pissarro, *The Boulevard Montmartre on a Winter Morning.*

Vincent van Gogh, *Cypresses,* painted in the asylum at Saint-Rémy. *Sunflowers, The Potato Peeler* and, on the other side, *Self-Portrait with a Straw Hat, Mme. Ginoux (L'Arlésienne), Irises,* painted at the end of his life at Saint-Rémy during a period of calm.

GALLERY 13 (along with the two following galleries, 13a and 13b) contains the museum's outstanding collection of the work of **Edgar Degas,** much of it the bequest of Mrs H. O. Havemeyer, wife of the sugar tycoon, who, encouraged by Mary Cassatt, changed the focus of her husband's collection from Oriental art to paintings, particularly Impressionist and Post-Impressionist work. Edgar Degas, *Woman with Chrysanthemums* and *Jacques Joseph Tissot,* a portrait of a fellow painter who fled to England for political reasons. In a case near the entrance is a bronze *Little Fourteen Year Old Dancer.* In the last two rooms are more small bronzes, paintings, and pastels by Degas which are rotated for reasons of conservation.

Islamic Art.

The museum's collection of Islamic art, the most comprehensive in the world, is displayed in galleries in the S. wing of the second floor and arranged chronologically and geographically to suggest the entire range of Islamic art which developed over a span of some 1300 years in countries as far apart as Spain and western China. Outstanding areas of the collection include glass and metalwork from Egypt, Syria, and Mesopotamia; 16–17C carpets; and royal miniatures from the courts of Persia and Mughal India.

GALLERY 1, **Introductory Gallery** presents exquisite objects suggesting the full sweep of the collection (display changed periodically; some objects mentioned later may be here from time to time).

GALLERY 2, to the right of the introductory gallery, contains objects found in the museum's **Nishapur Excavations** (1935–39 and 1947). Today Nishapur is a small town in Iran, but in the 10C it was a great center of Islamic art; Mongol invaders destroyed it in the early 13C. The central cases display a sampling of the great variety of ceramic types produced at Nishapur between 9–12C. Outstanding is a white slip-painted bowl with an elegant Arabic inscription (65.106.2) dating from the 10C. The inscription in Kufic reads: "Planning before work protects you from regret; prosperity and peace." A doorway on the far wall leads to a reconstruction of a small *ivan* or hall from the 10C with carved stucco panels once polychromed.

GALLERY 3, **Early Centuries of Islam (7–11C).**

Here are represented the cultures of the Umayyad dynasty (A.D. 661–750), whose capital was at Damascus, its offshoot the Spanish Umayyad dynasty (756–1031), the Egyptian Fatimid dynasty (969–1171), its cultural children

Islamic Sicily and southern Italy, as well as the Abbasid dynasty (750–1258) having as its capital city Baghdad and (836–889) Samarra on the Tigris River.

Cases along the W. wall contain glassware, textiles, and ceramics, including a silver gilt plate (63.186) and a fine bronze ewer (47.100.90). Cases along the E. wall contain a collection of glassware, delicately carved ivory plaques and boxes, and a group of gaming pieces. Near the middle of the room a pair of doors exemplifies the beveled style of carving of 9C Iraq (31.119.1,2).

GALLERY 4A, directly beyond GALLERY 3, is devoted to the **Seljuk (11–13C) and Mongol (13–14C) Periods** and concentrates on ceramics of the Seljuk period. Of special interest are the ceramic tabouret (69.225) and the large bronze incense burner in the form of a lion (51.56) in the S.W. case. Also in this room, in the N.E. case, the earliest known complete (except one pawn) chess set (1971.193, a–ff), which dates from the 12C.

GALLERY 4B, to the W., also devoted to the Seljuk and Mongol Periods contains metalwork, painting, and sculpture as well as ceramics. On the left end wall near the entrance is a particularly fine stucco head with Turkic features (42.25.17) and on the far left wall are ceramic pieces of the *mina'i* (i.e., overglaze enameled) type. The technique, which involved firing the piece twice at higher and then at lower temperatures, allowed artists to increase their range of colors. On the right wall are stone and tile niches and on the far right wall, a ceramic ewer with carved and pierced outer shell (32.52.1). Cases in the center of the room contain leaves; also, from 14C manuscripts of the *Shah Nameh* of Ferdowsi, the Iranian national epic, and other 13–14C manuscript leaves.

GALLERY 4C contains objects which originally formed part of **Mosque Settings** including a historical progression of calligraphic styles as represented in Koran leaves; also, Koran stands, enameled glass mosque lamps, and wood panels. The centerpiece of the room is a Mihrab (39.20) or prayer niche that indicates the direction of Mecca, executed in small pieces of ceramic arranged to form floral and geometric patterns and Arabic inscriptions.

GALLERY 5, which opens off Gallery 4B, contains mainly works from the **Ayyubid (1171–1250) and Mamluk (1250–1517) Periods in Egypt and Syria** and the **Nasrid Period (1230–1492) in Spain.** In the center is a superb Mamluk geometric carpet (1970.105) from the last quarter of the 15C. Also displayed are examples of ceramics, textiles, brass, and architectural ornament including the monumental carved, painted, and gilded ceiling from early 16C Spain.

GALLERY 6, **Timurid Period (1395–1501) and Savafid Period (1501–1736) in Iran,** contains a number of beautiful miniatures (changing exhibitions) from such manuscripts as the *Mantiq at-Tayr* ("Language of the Birds") dated 1483, the *Haft Paikar* ("Seven Portraits"), from circa 1426, and the Houghton *Shah Nameh,* executed over a period of years and consequently affording a picture of the development of Savafid painting over the second quarter of the 16C.

GALLERY 7, **Other Arts of the Savafid Period,** contains ceramics, carpets, metalwork, and book bindings. Of particular interest are (left wall, fifth case clockwise) a ceramic plate (65.109.2) following Chinese blue and white porcelain ware in its color scheme and design of intertwined dragons; Timurid jug (91.1.607) in N.W. case; a helmet with mail (91.1.749); a Tabriz carpet (10.61.3) with a geometric star pattern filled with dragons and phoenixes. There is also a changing exhibition of carpets on sliding rug racks.

GALLERY 8, **Art of the Ottoman Empire** (1281–1924). Ceramics including many beautiful pieces of painted and glazed ware from Iznik (16–17C), carpets, and textile fragments, and an impressive suit of Mamluk armor for man and horse.

GALLERY 9, **Mughal Period in India** (1526–1858), has examples of carpets, miniature painting, jewelry, and jade carving. Opposite the entrance on a marble platform is a dramatic wool carpet (17.190.857 alternating with 17.190.858) from the period of Shah Jahan. On the right wall is a display of jade with colors ranging from green so dark as to appear almost black, through smokey green, to white. Among the textiles is a beautifully decorated man's robe (29.135).

GALLERY 10, adjacent to the introductory gallery, is the luxurious paneled **Nur ad-Din Room** (1707) from Damascus, a traditional reception room of a well-to-do gentleman of the Ottoman period.

Ancient Near Eastern Art.

In the galleries of Near Eastern art are pre-Islamic works from Mesopotamia and ancient Iran, along with selected objects from Anatolia, Syria, and southern Arabia—modern Iraq, Iran, Turkey, Syria, and Yemen. Chronologically it encompasses more than 5000 years, from the 5th millennium B.C. through the Arab conquest of Sasanian Iran in A.D. 651. Yet, in spite of being so remote both in time and place, the collection contains many objects that appeal to modern sensibilities. Begin with the Raymond and Beverly Sackler Gallery for Assyrian Art and then proceed chronologically through the new installation.

Lining the walls and guarding the doorways of the Raymond and Beverly Sackler Gallery for **Assyrian Art** are 20 large reliefs and two imposing carvings from the palace of King Assurnasirpal II (883–859 B.C.) in Nimrud (northern Iraq). The door guards are immense human-headed mythical winged creatures, a bull and a lion, endowed by the artist with five legs so that the animals look correct whether viewed from the front or the side.

The first gallery of Ancient Near Eastern Art (beyond the room with small archaeological objects and ivories from Nimrud) contains works from the earliest urban societies through the Sumerian, Akkadian, and Babylonian periods in Mesopotamia (5th–1st millennium B.C.). Along the N. wall are exhibited cylinder seals, which first appeared in the mid-4th millennium B.C. Pressed on clay tablets, or used to seal vessels and doors, they marked legal or commercial agreements. The white gypsum

Standing Male Figure (40.156) was probably a substitute wor-
shipper, set in a temple to pray when it was inconvenient for
humans to do so. He has wide eyes made of shell set in bitumen,
the remaining pupil of black limestone, and is dressed in a
sheepskin skirt with tufts at the border. A headdress ornament
with gold pendants shaped like poplar leaves (33.35.3) found in
the royal tombs at Ur (c. 2600–2500 B.C.) shows the skill of
Sumerian metalworkers, as does a cult stand (1974.190) shaped
like an ibex. Near it in a freestanding case is a bronze foundation
peg shaped like a roaring lion (48.100) to frighten off evildoers.
On the other side of the room, a neo-Sumerian statue of Gudea,
governor of Lagash (59.2), and nearby a statue of Ur-Ningirsu
(47.100.86), a Mesopotamian ruler.

Ancient Anatolia, which coincides roughly with modern Turkey, embraced civilizations going back to the sixth millennium
B.C., from which the collection has stone and ceramic female
figurines. From early Bronze Age civilizations comes a yoked pair
of long-horned bulls (55.137.5) dating from around 2300–2000
B.C., as well as rattles and weapons.

In the Central Gallery are pre-Islamic Iranian antiquities. On
the E. wall panels of glazed and molded brick depict lions who
symbolized Ishtar, the Mesopotamian goddess of love and war
(31.13.2); the panels once faced a wall along a processional road
in Babylon built during the reign (c. 604–562 B.C.) of Nebuchad-
nezzar II. In the center of the room are the powerful bronze head
of a ruler (47.100.80), a modeled stone ram (1978.58), a gilded
silver axe head (1982.5), as well as a fine ceramic jar (59.52)
with silhouettes of mountain goats. In the case opposite the lions
is a silver kneeling bull demon (66.173). On the same side of the
room: a ceramic female figure (64.130), a bronze helmet with
four raised figures (63.74), a gold cup with gazelles (62.84), and
a display of pottery.

In the last gallery are beautiful objects in gold and silver from
the Achaemenid dynasty (550–331 B.C.) founded by Cyrus the
Great, for example a gold vessel with the head and forepaws of a
roaring lion (54.3.3). From the later Sasanian dynasty (A.D.224–
651) comes the *head of a Sasanian king* (65.126), hammered
from a single piece of silver.

Greek and Roman Art.

Five rooms are devoted to the museum's fine collection of Greek
vases, arranged chronologically beginning in the elevator lobby
adjacent to the department of Islamic art.

In the lobby are three large sepulchral vases from the Geometric period (8C B.C.) which served as tomb monuments.

Enter ROOM 1 (room number above entrance door) with wares
from the PROTOGEOMETRIC PERIOD (11–10C B.C.) to the
ATTIC BLACK-FIGURED WARE OF THE 6C B.C. Wall cases at
the left of the entrance contain (cases 1–2) Attic Protogeometric
and Geometric pottery, Corinthian, Laconian, Boeotian, Euboean,
Chalcidian, and Rhodian pottery (cases 3–6). Among the black-
figured vases are a column krater, or bowl, for mixing water and

wine (case 8, 24.97.95), depicting the struggle between Zeus and the titans, and another column krater (case 9, 31.11.11) showing Hephaestus brought back to Olympus. The monumental neck amphora (case 11, 11.210.1) showing the hero Herakles battling a centaur, probably Nessos, is from the earlier orientalizing period (7C B.C.). Also noteworthy (case 13, 01.8.6) is a cup with a gorgon's head (interior) and Achilles pursuing Troilus and Polyxena (exterior).

ROOM 2 also contains ATTIC BLACK-FIGURED VASES, including a group (cases 1–6) of prize amphorae of the type awarded at the Pan-Athenaic festival. Especially famous is one depicting a *foot race (case 2, 14.130.12). In case 9 there is a lekythos or oil jug (56.11.1) depicting a bridal procession.

ROOM 3, primarily devoted to ATTIC BLACK-FIGURED WARE, contains central cases with selections of black-figured pottery and a study collection. To the left of the exit door are several psykters or wine-coolers designed to float upright in a larger vessel filled with ice water or snow. On the other side of the doorway is a red-figured amphora (63.11.6) depicting the struggle between Herakles and Apollo over the Delphic tripod, one of the earliest red-figured vases in existence.

The next gallery (ROOM 4) devoted to RED-FIGURED WARE contains (case 19) the *Euphronios vase (1972.11.10), the most famous piece in the collection.

In 1972 the museum purchased it legally in Switzerland for a million dollars; though said to be from a collection in Beirut, many people, including officials of the Italian government, believed that it had been dug up by tomb robbers in Italy (the Etruscans prized the work of Euphronios) and smuggled out of the country. Dating from c. 515 B.C. this calyx krater shows an episode from the Trojan War, the death of Sarpedon, whose body is lifted by Sleep and Death as Hermes looks on. Admired for the overall design, for the virtuosity of the brushwork, and the skillful rendering of anatomical detail, the vase is considered to be Euphronios's masterpiece.

Nearby is an amphora (case 3, 56.171.38) by the Berlin painter (so-named because the Berlin State Museum has another of his amphorae) showing a *Youth Singing and Playing the Kithara,* a wonderful image of ancient music, the singer moving to his song as musicians do today.

ROOM 5 contains ATTIC AND SOUTHERN ITALIAN RED-FIGURED WARE from the late 5–4C B.C., by which time vase painting had declined as a major art. A column krater (case 18, 50.11.4) shows a painter coloring a marble statue of Herakles while Herakles and Zeus look on, a reminder that Greek statues were indeed painted, their present whiteness the result of time. Also displayed in this room is a small collection of ANCIENT GLASS, ranging from early-Mycenaean to late-Roman times.

Asian Art.

The collection of Asian Art covers a time span from the 2nd millennium B.C. to the 19C A.D. with objects from China, Japan, Korea, India, and Southeast Asia, including paintings, sculpture, decorative arts, ceramics, bronzes, jades, and textiles. The collection of monumental Chinese Buddhist sculpture is outstanding as is the collection of Chinese paintings.

The collection of CHINESE CERAMICS AND BRONZES is arranged along the E. side of the Great Hall balcony, with the exception of the Altman Collection of porcelains grouped around the Great Stairway and the objects now displayed in the galleries for ancient Chinese arts (opened 1988). Also on the balcony are examples of small-scale INDIAN AND SOUTHEAST ASIAN SCULPTURE.

Adjacent to the balcony is the GALLERY OF CHINESE STONE SCULPTURE, with large-scale works mostly from the 5–6C. The galleries beyond are the Weber Galleries of **The Arts of Ancient China,** which contain works from the Neolithic period (4000–1500 B.C.) through the T'ang Dynasty (A.D. 618–906).

In the NEOLITHIC GALLERY are painted grain jars and pottery vessels from the Yellow River region of N.W. China. GALLERY II has Bronze Age (1500–2000 B.C.) artifacts, including a Tuan-fang altar set, a food vessel (1988.20.2) ornamented with images of birds, a pair of monumental wine vessels (1988.20.5a,b), and an immense three-legged cauldron from the 5C B.C. Also, decorated garment hooks and weapons, jade ornaments, and small sculptures that show the influence from northern nomads from the steppes. In the HAN DYNASTY GALLERY (206 B.C.–A.D. 220) is a group of architectural models, houses and farm buildings (complete with livestock), that show something of the domestic side of Han life. There are also vividly painted animal-shaped containers and vases, rare outside China. Also appealing to modern sensibilities for their presentation of human character are ceramic tomb figurines, including a dancing woman with a long robe and hanging sleeves, and a pair of men playing some kind of game, one clearly happier than the other with the outcome.

The GALLERY OF THE SIX DYNASTIES PERIOD (A.D. 220–618) emphasizes a collection of early Buddhist sculpture from northern China, created during a period after the collapse of the Han Dynasty when Buddhism became a significant intellectual and religious force. A 3C "soul jar" with its upper portion decorated as a celestial city was believed to contain the soul of the deceased. Here also are objects like a pole stand in the form of a tiger exemplifying the taste of nomadic tribes for images of fierce animals. In the fifth gallery, devoted to the T'ang Dynasty (A.D. 618–906) are objects from an era when China enjoyed political and cultural influence and its capital (modern Sian), the end of the Silk Road trade route, was the most advanced city on earth. Here are gold and silver vessels and ornaments and jade belt plaques, illustrative of the wealth and cosmopolitan spirit of the age. A gilt bronze statuette of the Shakyamuni Buddha shows the achievement of early T'ang sculpture, which conveys a sense of monumentality at a small scale. Also included are T'ang tomb figures including horses and a camel in three-color glaze.

The large LATER CHINESE BUDDHIST SCULPTURE GALLERY (A.D. 500–1500), opening off the center of the chronological galleries, features a large standing Maitreya or Buddha of the

Future (5C), and a dry lacquer seated Buddha from the 7C. The figure was made by molding layers of lacquer-soaked cloth over a wooden base to the desired form. Near the doorway are two 9C life-size ceramic *lohans.*

In galleries of **Chinese Paintings** some 80 works of Chinese painting from the Sung, Yüan, Ming, and Ch'ing dynasties are shown on a rotating basis along with sculpture and objects from comparable periods, important loans, and special exhibitions. In the right or east gallery is a permanent display of jades.

The Astor Court between the two galleries is a small ***Chinese garden court** modeled on the Garden of the Master of the Fishing Nets in Suzhou, W. of Shanghai, first built in the 12C by a public official who retreated there from the rigors of his administrative job. Like other Chinese gardens, this one is carefully designed so that contrasting principles—light and dark, hard and soft, high and low, crooked and straight, dynamic and static—balance and complement one another; in this the garden becomes a microcosm for the universe as construed by Chinese philosphers, ruled by the complementary principles of Yin and Yang. The garden is the center of an implied architectural whole; in China many rooms would have been built around the courtyard and, in prosperous families, many courtyards and sets of rooms would extend and enlarge the house as needed. Here, in the museum, the architecture consists of three typical garden structures: the viewing pavilion or *ting,* the winding walkway, and the small main hall (called the Ming Room), with formally arranged furniture. Against the S. wall stands a fantastically shaped Taihu rock, one of several in the courtyard harvested from the bottom of Lake Tai, whose waters and sands give these rocks their characteristic forms. To the connoisseur the proportions of the rock are significant: it should appear lean and bony, be broader at the top than at the base, have holes so that it rings when struck, and have "walkable" passages through its surface where the mind may wander and climb.

Musical Instruments.

The *Collection of Musical Instruments displayed in the André Mertens Galleries is outstanding for its scope and for the beauty of the individual instruments.

The galleries are arranged in a rectangle with instruments from Europe and the U. S. on the W. (left) side, from the Americas and the Pacific on the N., and from the Near East, Africa, and Asia on the east.

In the 1870s Mrs. Mary Crosby Brown, wife of a New York banker, began collecting instruments from all over the world, enlisting the help of missionaries, foreign officers in her husband's bank, scholars, and diplomats. By 1914 she had gathered some 3000 instruments which form the nucleus of the present collection. The instruments have been chosen for their technical and social importance, as well as their physical and tonal beauty. Especially noteworthy are the rare violins, the oldest extant piano, and the courtly instruments from the Middle Ages and the Renaissance.

The INTRODUCTORY GALLERY (cases 1–3) provides an overview of the collection and includes Western and Oriental brass instruments, a Javanese *saron* in the form of a dragon (89.4.1462), drums from Europe, Thailand, and Melanasia, and a group of unusual keyboard instruments.

EUROPEAN GALLERIES. The instruments are arranged by family or by material. There are ivory and ceramic instruments, post horns, hunting horns, a shofar, and a falconer's horn. Among the keyboard instruments is a *piano (89.4.1219) by Bartolommeo Cristofori, who invented the instrument (c. 1700); it is the oldest (1720) piano in existence. Other early keyboard instruments include a Venetian spinettino (53.6) made (1540) for the duchess of Urbino and an elaborately decorated *double virginal (29.90) by Hans Ruckers the Elder, a famous Flemish harpsichord builder. Along with lutes, mandolins, citterns, guitars, and American folk instruments are baroque violins by Stradivari and Amati. While most Stradivari violins have been modified to produce a louder, more brilliant sound, the finest one in the collection (55.86) is unique in having been restored to its original appearance and tone.

GALLERIES OF THE AMERICAS, ASIA, AND AFRICA. Instruments from the Americas (cases 19–21), include pottery whistles, whistling jars, and rattles in human and animal forms. The next cases contain instruments of the South Pacific (22–23), North Africa (24), the Near East (25), and Iran and Turkey (26). Among the African instruments (cases 27–31) are whistles, Benin bells, rattles, thumb pianos, and a marimba with gourd resonators (89.4.492). From the Orient come Japanese instruments (cases 32–34), Chinese and Korean instruments (cases 35–37) including a beautiful sonorous stone (89.4.64), gong chimes, bronze bells, drums, a jade flute (65.149), and a mouth organ (89.4.96) of bamboo pipes in a lacquered bowl. Cases 39–41 contain Tibetan instruments including trumpets made from the thigh bones of priests, and instruments of Southeast Asia. Indian instruments (cases 42–46) include the now relatively familiar sitars, as well as drums and trumpets, other bowed and plucked stringed instruments, and a large bronze temple gong (89.4.278).

GROUND FLOOR.

Located on the ground floor adjacent to the Grace Rainey Rogers Auditorium, the **Costume Institute** contains a collection of more than 35,000 articles of clothing including regional costumes and sophisticated articles of urban dress. The costumes, representing cultures of Asia, Africa, Europe, and the Americas, include such diverse examples as bullfighters' capes, a bridal robe from Korea, and tribal headgear from Central Africa. Among the urban clothing are American and European dresses from the late 17C to the present time, lingerie, accessories, clothing for sports (skating dresses, fencing costumes), and notable examples of elegant couturier clothing.

The collection is shown in special exhibitions changed approximately once a year and often mounted with great style. (Recorded tour available.) Past exhibitions have included The World of Balenciaga, American Women of Style, and The Glory of Russian Costume, which was viewed by some 830,000 visitors.

European Decorative Arts.

The galleries on the ground floor (go down the staircase from the Medieval Tapestry Hall) are devoted to European decorative arts, primarily ceramics, silver, and glass.

Note: These objects are scheduled for reinstallation when the new decorative arts galleries are completed.

There are examples of French ceramics from early 16–17C tin- and lead-glazed earthenware from provincial centers to elegant porcelains from the factories at Vincennes and Sèvres. German and Austrian ceramics include salt-glazed cups, tankards, and jugs, faience from Fulda and Hoechst, 18C Swiss and German porcelain figurines and Meissen wares including part of a Swan table service (1737–1741) and a family of large porcelain goats cast from models by J. J. Kändler.

Among the other European ceramics are 17C delftware, Dutch and German tiles, 15–16C Italian majolica, and a few examples of Medici porcelain. The display of English ceramics contains examples of salt-glazed wares, tin-enameled earthenware, porcelains from Chelsea and Bow, Wedgwood jasperware, and Bristol ware. There are examples of 16–19C European glass, French and English silver, watches and clocks, French and English enameling and goldsmithing, and numerous little baubles from the Morgan bequest of 1917 including snuff boxes, Renaissance jewels, and enameled jeweled cups.

25   Yorkville and East River Islands

SUBWAY: IRT Lexington Ave local or express (train 4, 5, or 6) to 86th St. Walk five blocks E. to East End Ave; enter Carl Schurz Park and walk N. along the promenade.

BUS: M15 uptown via 1st Ave or M18 uptown via York Ave (from 57th St) to 88th St; walk E. to Carl Schurz Park. M31 crosstown on 86th St; enter Carl Schurz Park at 86th St and East End Ave, walk N. along the promenade.

Yorkville, today not easily distinguishable from other middle-class neighborhoods, was once home to three major ethnic groups: Germans, Czechoslovakians, and Hungarians. Although most of the eastern European population has moved out to the suburbs and Yorkville itself with the spate of new luxury high rises has become suddenly chic and too expensive for many of the aging survivors, traces of the old way of life remain.

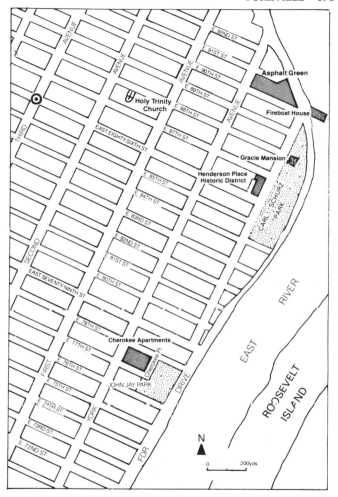

History. In the late 18C Yorkville was a small hamlet between New York and Harlem, its country estates attracting wealthy families of Germanic origin— Schermerhorns, Rhinelanders, and Astors. When the New York and Harlem Railroad arrived in 1834, Yorkville quickly became a suburb drawing middle-class Germans, among them people like the Rupperts, who operated a brewery, but the main concentration of Germans remained on the Lower East Side, notably around Tompkins Square in a neighborhood called "Kleindeutschland." By 1900, as waves of eastern European and Italian immigrants poured in, the downtown Germans began moving out, a migration hastened by the *General Slocum* disaster (1904), when an excursion steamer jammed with holiday tourists, mostly women and children from Kleindeutschland, burned and sank in the East River, killing more than a thousand people. Many of the surviving husbands, prevented from attending the excursion by work, found their homes unbearable and moved to Yorkville to be with their countrymen.

Though Yorkville was never rich it remained a solid neighborhood through the years of the Depression, a place where people worked close to home—either in small businesses or for the brewery—and enjoyed themselves at local restaurants, beer gardens of the Bavarian variety, or cafes modeled after those in Vienna. At some restaurants, presumably those for tourists, the doormen wore lederhosen and plumed Tyrolean hats.

In the years before World War II, Yorkville was a center of both Nazi and anti-Nazi activity, the home of the Nazi-supported German-American Bund with its official paper, the *Deutscher Weckruf und Beobachter* (at 178 E. 85th St) and the German-American Business League, which published a list of Nazi-approved American business firms. The German Central Book Store (218 E. 84th St) carried books banned by Hitler, while the German Workers Club (1501 Third Ave) served as an anti-Nazi labor organization.

After World War II, the area saw a last wave of German immigration and later an influx of Hungarians following the uprising of 1956. After that ethnic newcomers were largely Hispanics filtering down from Spanish Harlem on the N. edge of Yorkville, but nowadays the area is increasingly attracting affluent young working couples and single people to the high-rise buildings which are rapidly changing the face of the neighborhood. The older, poorer German population is believed to live mostly in the unrenovated, rent-controlled apartments above the shops, and the Germanically oriented shops and services are increasingly being replaced by newer businesses, strudel and sauerbraten giving way to croissants and carpaccio.

Begin at the N. end of Carl Schurz Park along the East River opposite 90th St. Visible to the N.W. (York Ave to Franklin Delano Roosevelt Drive, 90th–91st Sts) is a strange parabolic structure of exposed concrete over an arched steel frame, formerly the **Municipal Asphalt Plant** (1944; Kahn & Jacobs; DL), used until 1968, when larger facilities were needed. In 1972 a citizens' group wanted to use it for a public park and recreational facility. With the city's permission they tore up the former parking lot to create an athletic field, known as the Asphalt Green, and installed facilities for the arts and athletics in the concrete parabola.

At the N. end of the park along the river is the **Fireboat House Environmental Center,** (rebuilt 1981; Steven Robinson), a community center for studies on energy and the river environment. The boathouse was built (c. 1930) as one of 22 fireboat stations around the city. When faster and more powerful diesel boats started replacing the earlier steam models in the 1950s, stations were gradually phased out and by 1976 when this one was abandoned only four remained.

Walk S. along the promenade by the river. **Carl Schurz Park** bears the name of the most notable German-American of the 19C: hero of the German revolutionary movement of 1848, immigrant (1852), supporter of Abraham Lincoln, brigadier general in the Civil War, U.S. senator, secretary of the interior, editor of the *New York Evening Post* and *The Nation* and, at the end of his life, resident of Yorkville. The park reaches from 90th St to Gracie Square at 84th St, offers fine river views, and is pleasantly landscaped (remodeled during construction of the F. D. R. Drive, 1938). The promenade, *John Finley Walk,* honors John Huston Finley (1863–1940), president of the City College of New York, editor of the *New York Times,* state commissioner of education, and an unflagging pedestrian who on several occasions walked the 32 miles around Manhattan Island.

From the walkway look north. The small island N. of the Fireboat House at the confluence of the East and Harlem Rivers is **Mill Rock,** part of a group of islands and reefs in the Hell Gate section of the Harlem River. The East River, spanned by the Triborough Bridge with the curve of Hell Gate Arch behind it, runs along the E. side of Mill Rock and out into Long Island Sound.

The little island, thought once to have been a pirate's refuge, got its name from a mill (c. 1701–07) powered by tidal currents. During the War of 1812 a blockhouse along with fortifications on both shores protected the N. entrance to New York harbor, but was destroyed by fire in 1821. In 1860 a private citizen bought it and moved there with his family and several cows. The U.S. government reclaimed it in 1911 for $25,000 and used it as a base of operations for surveying the harbor and removing hazards until the city took it over in 1953, placing it under the jurisdiction of the Parks Department because Commissioner Robert Moses was afraid that some commercial operator would adorn it with a giant billboard. In 1979 the Parks Department entrusted its care to the Neighborhood Committee for the Asphalt Green who plan to use it for environmental and nautical studies.

To the W. of Mill Rock runs the Harlem River along the shore of Manhattan. The large island just N. of Mill Rock is **Wards Island,** now joined by landfill to Randalls Island at its northern end.

These islands are of interest only to the extremely thorough visitor, and the following description is given to satisfy the curiosity of the average tourist who might wonder what is on them but not wish to visit. They are accessible either from the pedestrian footbridge at 103rd St or via the M35 bus, which runs from 125th St and Lexington Ave across the Triborough Bridge to Wards and Randalls Islands and then across a second arm of the Triborough Bridge to Astoria in Queens.

Look N. along the Harlem River. The *Wards Island Pedestrian Bridge* (1951), painted aqua, joins 103rd St in Manhattan with Wards Island, now used for parks, mental hospitals, and a firemen's training center.

History. Wards Island, used by the British as a military base during the Revolution and called Buchanan's Island or Great Barn Island, a corruption of Great Barent Island, belonged to farmers Jasper and Bartholomew Ward after the war. Around 1810 a cotton mill stood there, but when the mill closed after the War of 1812, the island remained deserted until the city took it over for a potter's field, digging up 100,000 bodies on the present site of Bryant Park and moving them there. The state immigration service (1847) operated a refuge for sick and destitute aliens until 1860, when the island became a backup station for the immigration facilities in Battery Park. When Ellis Island opened in 1892 the abandoned immigration buildings were taken over by the New York City Asylum for the Insane, and a few years later the state took control of the mental hospital, changing its name to *Manhattan State Hospital*. Once scheduled for demolition, the hospital is still there with expanded facilities, the *Rehabilitation Building of the Manhattan Psychiatric Center* (1970; Caudill Rowlett Scott), a "half-way house," and the *Manhattan Children's Treatment Center* (1972; Richard G. Stein & Assocs.), for teaching and treating retarded and disturbed children. On the N.E. part of Wards Island is a *Firefighters' Training Center* (1975; Hardy Holzman Pfeiffer Assocs.) which replaces an earlier one on Roosevelt Island. The center, not open to the public, includes a model city of vitrified tile block which can be set on fire and extinguished for practice. The island also houses a Municipal Sewage Disposal Plant, 77.5 acres on the N.E. corner.

Randalls Island, the northernmost part of the island, once a separate body of land separated from Wards Island by Little Hell Gate but now joined to it with landfill, is the home of the headquarters of the Triborough Bridge and Tunnel Authority and holds also the junction of the three arms of the Triborough Bridge, the tracks of the old New York Connecting Railway, a park with athletic facilities, and Downing Stadium, named for John J. Downing, a Parks Department employee for 41 years. The stadium is used for summer concerts, athletic events, and festivals.

History. In 1668 British governor Richard Nicolls granted the island to Thomas Delavall, a tax collector; later (1772) Captain James Montresor bought it and lived there, giving it his name until Jonathan Randel took possession in 1784. The city paid Randel (or Randal) $60,000 for it in 1835, misspelling his name on the deed, a mistake which has endured to the present. From then until the Triborough Bridge project (begun 1929), the island shared the dreary history of other East River islands: it held a potter's field (1843) with bodies exhumed from a graveyard at 50th St and Fourth (now Park) Ave, an almshouse (1845), a House of Refuge for the Society of the Reformation of Juvenile Delinquents (1851), and a state asylum for the feebleminded. The Bartholdi Crèche founded in 1886 maintained a seaside cottage there at the turn of the century for mothers with sick children who could not afford to leave the city.

The channel N.E. of Mill Rock is called **Hell Gate,** and leads to the sea via the protected waters of Long Island Sound. Ever since Adraien Block sailed the *Tyger* through it in 1612, Hell Gate has had a reputation for treachery, but the name comes from the Dutch *Hellegat* which means "beautiful pass" and originally applied to the entire East River. Hell Gate is only 22.5 miles from the open sea via New York Bay and Sandy Hook (the southern route) but more than 100 miles via Long Island Sound (the northern route), a discrepancy which accounts for three hours' difference in the tides at the two ends of the East River. These conflicting tides along with reefs and rocky islets once made Hell Gate so tortuous that hundreds of wrecks are believed to lie beneath its waters including a Revolutionary frigate, *Hussar,* that went down in 1780 with a payroll estimated as high as $500 million in gold and silver coins for British troops in America. In 1985, Barry L. Clifford, a salvage expert, claimed that he discovered the wreck using the type of sonar that helped locate the *Titanic.* So far, neither the wreck nor the gold has surfaced.

Today, Hell Gate, still difficult to navigate, is tamer than it was in the days of the *Hussar,* its treacherous rocks blasted away (1851–mid-1920s); gone are the Hen and Chickens, Hog's Back, Frying Pan, Pot Rock, Bald-Headed Billy, and Way's Reef, and gone are some of the river's better place names.

Two bridges span Hell Gate. The southernmost is the **Triborough Bridge** (1936; Othmar Ammann, chief engineer), whose Y-shaped structure touches three boroughs—Manhattan, Queens, and the Bronx. The Bronx arm begins on a viaduct between E. 132nd and E. 134th Sts (Bronx) and with seven truss spans (1683 ft) over land and water crosses the Bronx Kills (span, 383 ft) to Randalls Island. The bridge has been designed so that it may be converted into a lift bridge if the Kills, now a ditch, is ever made navigable. The Manhattan arm crosses the Harlem River at E. 125th St to Randalls Island, with three truss spans (total length 772 ft) and a 310-ft vertical lift bridge over the river. Within each of the twin 215-ft towers is a thousand-ton cement counterweight and a 200-horsepower motor which can lift the six-lane roadway and the span to a height of 135 ft above the river (closed, the span is 55 ft above mean high water). The Queens arm, above Hell Gate, is a 1380-ft suspension bridge joining Randalls Island and Astoria, Queens. The towers rise 315 ft and the roadway is 143 ft above mean high water. The three arms converge above Randalls Island in an intricate whorl of 22 lanes and ramps punctuated by two toll plazas, the most complex traffic sorter of its day. All the roadways have footwalks, so pedestrians as well as motorists may descend to Randalls Island from the bridge.

History. Construction began on Black Friday, October 25, 1929, when the stock market began its plunge, but when funds ran out in 1932 only a $3 million lump of cement on Wards Island, a future anchorage, remained to show three years' work. In 1933 the Triborough Bridge Authority was created to finance and build the stalled bridge and under Roosevelt's Public Works Administration got a $37 million construction loan. Robert Moses, soon the propulsive force of the TBA, pushed the bridge to completion despite political interference from a hostile Roosevelt administration and in addition built the stadium on Randalls Island, an extension of the East River Drive (later renamed after Roosevelt) past 96th St, a marina in Flushing Bay, and made improvements in Astoria Park including a large pool used for the Olympic trials of 1936.

Hell Gate Arch (1917; Gustav Lindenthal, engineer, and Henry Hornbostel, architect), visible beyond the Triborough Bridge, is a 1017-ft span carrying four railroad tracks across the East River from Wards Island to Queens. It stands as a monument to Lindenthal, structurally beautiful and imaginatively engineered, the high point of a career later mired in the frustrations of city politics, and to Alexander Cassatt, president of the Pennsylvania Railroad (1899–1907), who planned the New York Connecting Railroad, a direct rail link between New England and the rest of the northeast corridor (Philadelphia, Baltimore, and Washington) of which the bridge is the most prominent part.

The design of the arch is unusual in that the upper arc curves upward at the ends, a pleasing effect which also allows overhead clearance for locomotives and aids the bridge's rigidity by allowing deeper stiffening trusses. The handsome granite-faced towers with their arched openings reminded early observers of the portico to a mammoth temple. Among Lindenthal's engineering achievements were the bridging of an underwater fissure in the bedrock beneath the Wards Island foundation and the discovery of a way to build the arch without using scaffolding to support the unfinished span, which would have closed Hell Gate to navigation. When the final steel section was hoisted in place at the center, an adjustment of only $5/16$ of an inch was needed to close the arch.

Note: Directly across the East River is the northern end of Roosevelt Island; for a description see Route 32.

Begin walking S. along the promenade. Facing the river near the N. end of the park is **Gracie Mansion** (1799; additions, 1966;

Mott B. Schmidt; restored 1984, Charles A. Platt; DL), official residence of the mayor of New York. Built as the country home of merchant Archibald Gracie whose offices were on Whitehall St and whose town house stood on State St across from Battery Park, the house, with its 16 rooms and fine detailing (leaded glass sidelights and semicircular fanlight above the main doorway, elegant railings around the roof and above the main floor), exemplifies Federal domestic architecture at the elegant end of the scale. Gracie extended his hospitality to Louis Philippe, later King of France, the Marquis de Lafayette, Alexander Hamilton, John Quincy Adams, and Washington Irving until his shipping business foundered during the War of 1812. Bankrupt, Gracie sold the mansion in 1819; the city bought it in 1887, using it eventually to house the Museum of the City of New York (1924–30). In 1942 it became the mayor's residence after Fiorello La Guardia rejected another major contender, the Charles M. Schwab 75-room French château (Riverside Drive at 73rd St, now demolished). "What," said the 5-ft 2-in fiery proletarian mayor, "me in that?" In 1966 reception and conference rooms were added and in 1984 an extensive, gracious renovation was completed.

The Gracie Mansion Conservancy offers house tours from April–Oct, Wed; admission charge; reservations necessary. Tel: 570-4751.

Walk S. along the Finley Walk in Schurz Park. Across the East River lies the N. tip of Roosevelt Island with its lighthouse and hospital buildings. Opposite the lighthouse turn inland and walk down the curved double staircase to the walkway leading to 86th St, the main street of German Yorkville.

On the N. side of 86th St between York and East End Aves is the **Henderson Place Historic District,** once part of John Jacob Astor's country estate. It was purchased in 1881 by John C. Henderson who, having made his fortune in furs and fur hats, decided to speculate on some row houses for people of moderate means. Some 20 of the original 32 houses (1882; Lamb & Rich) remain, small (typical lot size 18 × 46 ft), charming, Queen Anne–style town houses with turrets, paired entranceways, double stoops, and carefully considered details. The houses facing East End Ave have been altered and those on the W. side of Henderson Place (a half block W.) exist in the shadow of a gargantuan apartment building. There is also a good view of the houses from 87th St.

Walk N. to 88th St. At 312–316 E. 88th St between First and Second Aves is the (Protestant Episcopal) CHURCH OF THE HOLY TRINITY (1897; Barney & Chapman; DL), a neo-Francis I church with a fine belfry. The brown brick church ornamented with terra-cotta has a copper crested roof and red slate shingles and is part of a homogeneous group that includes a parsonage, the bell tower, and a parish house. In 1897 Serena Rhinelander gave the diocese part of the Rhinelander farm (purchased by the family, 1798) in memory of her father and grandfather. The church and the *Rhinelander Children's Center of the Children's Aid Society* (1891; Vaux & Radford) at 350 E. 88th St are the fruits of her gift. The facade of this Vaux and Radford building was stuccoed over and cannot be restored.

Two blocks N. and not really worth the walk, *Yorkville Towers and Ruppert Towers* (1976; Davis, Brody & Assocs.), two immense apartment houses, stand on part of the site where Jacob Ruppert's Brewery (90th–93rd Sts, Second–Third Aves) once dominated the neighborhood, offering jobs to the German population and filling the streets with the aroma of roasting hops. The Dutch opened the first commercial brewery in North America (1632) in lower Manhattan and at its peak the city had more than 100 breweries.

Return to 86th St along Second Ave. At 244 W. 86th St, S.W. corner of Second Ave, stands **The Manhattan** apartments (1880), probably the city's oldest large apartment building, built by the Rhinelander family as an investment.

Most of the few surviving German small businesses are clustered along **86th Street** between Second and Third Aves. The *Elk Candy Co.* (240 E. 86th St) has a good supply of old-fashioned marzipan pigs, vegetables, and hot dogs. Here and there are a few restaurants heavy on hearty food. *Bremen House* (220 E. 86th St) still sells slices of strudel, German books and phonograph records, *rehrucken* pans, and chocolates emblazoned with a likeness of Mozart. The linked tenements in which these shops are installed, collectively called *The Montgomery* (c. 1883), belong to the sturdy housing stock of old Yorkville.

To the W., the *Cafe Geiger* (206 E. 86th St) dispenses confections which hark back to a time when slenderness was not a national ideal. In between are Indian boutiques and Japanese, French, Italian, and Chinese restaurants. In the midst of this ethnic multiplicity is *Corso,* the city's most famous Puerto Rican nightclub (205 E. 86th St), synonymous with salsa, a polyglot music of Latin and African rhythms and American jazz imported from Cuba

Two blocks S. at 339 E. 84th St (bet. First / Second Aves) is the *Zion St. Mark's Church* (1888), which began as the *Deutsche Evangelische Kirche von Yorkville* during the first period of German immigration.

The HUNGARIAN SECTION of Yorkville, around Second Ave in the upper 70s and low 80s, like the German and Czech sections, is a pallid remnant of its former self. The abortive Hungarian Revolution (1848) touched off the first wave of Hungarian immigration, which peaked just before World War I, increasing again after the 1956 invasion of Hungary by the Soviet Union. According to the 1980 census, 100,000 Hungarian-Americans, including second and third generation families, live in greater New York, but the 1990 figures when tallied will surely show a smaller number. The original center of the Hungarian population was, as with other groups, the Lower East Side, particularly Avenues A and B near Houston St. But immigrants began to move uptown around 1905.

Most of the social clubs have disappeared, but St. Stephen of Hungary Roman Catholic Church (1928; Emil Szendy), 414 E. 82nd St (bet. 1st / York Aves), is still the largest house of worship for local Hungarians. Not far away is *St. Elizabeth of Hungary Roman Catholic Church* (1918) at 211 E. 83rd St (bet. Second / Third Aves), with beautiful mosaics inside. Also nearby are churches for Hungarian Baptists, Jews, and those who follow the Byzantine rites.

Along Second Ave remains an occasional butcher shop specializing in sausages, pork products, liverwurst, and paprika-coated bacon, for example, the *Hungarian Meat Market* (1560 Second Ave at 81st St) as well as the occasional pastry shop offering tortes and strudel. *Paprikas Weiss* (1546 Second Ave, bet. 80th / 81st Sts), whose founder began importing Hungarian paprika because his wife needed it for cooking, still offers Hungarian specialties—spices, cooking utensils, strudel, embroidered blouses—but supplements these eastern European staples with Italian olive oil and pasta. At 323 E. 79th St between First and Second Aves is the *First Hungarian Literary Society,* a remnant of the old-time social clubs, where pinochle has been played on occasion along with the literary discussions.

At 79th St walk E. to **York Avenue,** a block E. of First Ave and formerly called Avenue A. In 1928 the avenue was renamed to honor World War I hero Alvin C. York, who singlehandedly (Oct 8, 1918) killed 25 Germans and took 132 prisoners in a battle of the Meuse-Argonne campaign.

The *City and Suburban Homes* (1901–13; Harde & Short, Philip Ohm) and the former *Junior League Hotel,* later the East End Hotel for Women (1910–12; Philip Ohm) filling the block between 79th and 78th Sts, York Ave and the Franklin Delano Roosevelt Drive represent an early attempt at working-class housing.

The block is divided into several six-story walkup apartment groups which were built as part of a philanthropic program by the City and Suburban Homes Co. to show that well-designed tenements could also produce acceptable profits. Facing the river is the former hotel, a residence for single women built by the Junior League, an organization created to encourage affluent young women to work for charitable causes. The hotel originally housed stenographers, dressmakers, librarians, and milliners, among others, who paid $4–7 per week, including board. Before the advent of the F.D.R. Drive, the hotel had balconies and rooftop pergolas facing the river. Today the entire block is threatened with demolition.

Walk E. on 78th St to *Cherokee Place,* named after a branch of Tammany Hall (see p. 285), the Cherokee Club, which once stood on 79th St between First and Second Aves. *John Jay Park,* along the E. side of Cherokee Place between 78th and 77th Sts, is a popular neighborhood gathering spot with trees, a playground, and a swimming pool; it is named after the first Chief Justice of the U.S., drafter of the Constitution, and governor of New York State (1795–1801). In the park are two black steel sculptures *Kryet-Aekyad #2* and *Eaphae-Aekyad #2* (1979; Douglas Abdell). The strange names of these pieces are taken from the sculptor's private language in which the "Aekyads" are "letter sculptures," and can function as the basis of more complex structures, just as letters function as the basis of words and sentences. (*Eaphae-Aekyad #2* is on loan from the artist.)

Across from the park (507–523 E. 77th St bet. York Ave /
Cherokee Place) are the CHEROKEE APARTMENTS (1912; Henry
Atterbury Smith; DL), a six-story complex originally called the
Shively Sanitary Tenements because they incorporate the environmental notions of Dr. Henry Shively. Built for tubercular
patients, the buildings have high architectural standards with
small balconies accessible from triple-hung windows, well-conceived ironwork, and Guastavino-tiled tunnels leading to the central courtyards. In the courtyards corner stairways rise to the
upper floors, roofed against the rain with iron and glass. But the
original purpose of all these features—courtyards, balconies,
open passageways, and triple-sash windows—was to enhance air
circulation.

Walk back to First Ave. South of Little Hungary is the remnant
of the CZECH QUARTER, centered around First Ave from the
mid-60s to mid-70s, a section of the avenue once called Czech
Broadway. Like other immigrant groups, the Czechs and Slovaks
first settled on the Lower East Side, with the Slovak enclave E. of
Avenue A between 4th and 7th Sts. New immigrants continued
to arrive from the 1920s to the late 1940s, with a later influx
after the Russian invasion of Czechoslovakia in 1968. Today,
however, the area has more tall apartment buildings than tenements and is rapidly becoming more chic than Czech. Among the
remaining ethnic institutions is the *Jan Hus Presbyterian Church*
(347 E. 74th St bet. 1st / 2nd Aves), whose namesake was burned
as a heretic for his efforts at religious reformation. A comedy and
improvisation company occupies the Church House (351 E. 74th
St), but the senior citizens' center still draws a Czech-speaking
clientele. Among the few Czech restaurants still in the area is
Vasata at 339 E. 75th St (bet. 1st / 2nd Aves).

At 321 E. 73rd St (bet. 1st / 2nd Aves) stands what was once
Bohemian National Hall (1896; William C. Frohne), built at the
turn of the century to house an array of Czech social, athletic,
and intellectual clubs. In the basement was a bowling alley and
shooting gallery; upstairs were a restaurant, club rooms, and on
top a ballroom and theater.

To the S. and E. at 1334 York Ave, near 72nd St, is **Sotheby's,**
legally Sotheby Parke Bernet Inc., the American branch of the
world's oldest firm of fine arts auctioneers (founded 1744). The
American firm, the Parke-Bernet Galleries, originated in 1883 as
the American Art Association (AAA), an exhibition gallery, but
was catapulted into the top ranks of auction houses when one
George Seney, a bank president, got caught with his hand in the
till and had the AAA auction off his possessions to pacify his
creditors, a sale that brought $405,821. Otto Bernet began in
1896 at the age of 14 working at the gallery by day and studying
art appreciation at night. Hiram Haney Parke, gentlemanly in
bearing though humble in background and one of the country's
greatest auctioneers, came to the firm from Philadelphia. In 1937
Parke and Bernet founded their own immediately successful firm,
which later (1964) merged with Sotheby's of London. In recent
years the galleries have had spectacular sales, including (1987)

a painting of *Irises* by Vincent van Gogh for $53.9 million, the highest price ever paid for a work of art at auction, and the blockbuster sale of Andy Warhol's collections in 1988.

Exhibition hours Tues–Sat 9:30–5; Sun 1–5; tel: 606-7000.

A bit further downtown is the Roman Catholic *Church of St. John Nepomucene* (411 E. 66th St, N.E. corner of 1st Ave). Above the arches of the nave are folk designs; a mosaic above the altar depicts scenes from the lives of St. Cyril and his brother St. Methodius who in the 9C brought Christianity to Moravia. Cyril is said to have invented the Cyrillic alphabet and to have translated the gospel and liturgy into Old Slavonic.

The nearest subway is the Lexington Ave at 66th St, three blocks west. There are uptown buses on 1st Ave and downtown buses on 2nd Ave as well as crosstown buses on 72nd and 67th–68th Sts.

26 Harlem and Hamilton Heights

Geographically Harlem is defined by the East and Harlem Rivers, the cliffs of Morningside Heights and St. Nicholas Terrace, and by 110th and 168th Sts. The E. and S.E. section, once heavily Italian with a few Germans spilling over from the Yorkville area, today is predominantly Puerto Rican and is known as El Barrio or Spanish Harlem. A dwindling Italian community still remains around Pleasant Ave and E. 116th St. Central Harlem, from 110th–145th St, is mostly poor and black with Puerto Rican enclaves and small neighborhoods of relative affluence—Sugar Hill, Striver's Row, and the "Gold Coast," a group of middle-income developments along the Harlem River N. of 125th St.

As this may suggest, Harlem is not merely a homogeneous slum or a jobless ghetto shaken by drug addiction and crime, its streets marked by burned-out buildings and rubble-strewn lots. While all these things do exist, there are also parks and wide boulevards, adequate public transportation, rows of fine brownstones, handsome churches, and evidence of flourishing artistic and educational institutions.

History. When upper Manhattan still enjoyed its pristine topography, an Indian village stood on the banks of the Harlem River between about the location of 110th and 125th Sts. In 1658, attracted by the fertile soil and the strategic advantages of the terrain, Dutch farmers incorporated the village of Nieuw Haarlem and hired a contingent of soldiers to build and defend their settlement. In 1672 black slaves, originally brought to this country by the Dutch, built a wagon road from Nieuw Haarlem to New Amsterdam about 10 miles south at the tip of Manhattan. Increasingly this beautiful outlying land attracted gentlemen farmers or wealthy merchants who developed estates and built country mansions of which the only survivor is the Morris-Jumel Mansion.

In 1827 the state prohibited slavery, but its black population remained in a kind of civil limbo until the Emancipation Proclamation (1863) gave citizenship to all former slaves. At the close of the Civil War, New York's black population, estimated at 15,000, was concentrated in various ghettos in lower Manhattan, notably around Thompson St in Greenwich Village. By the end of the century the black population was centered around the Tenderloin (W. of Broadway between 32nd and 42nd Sts) and Hell's Kitchen districts (the 40s and 50s W. of Seventh Ave). As demolition for the construction of the old Penn Station displaced them, blacks moved up into the San Juan Hill neighborhood, N. and W. of Columbus Circle.

Meanwhile, Harlem had begun its metamorphosis to a suburb as the New York and Harlem Railroad reached out along Park Ave from City Hall to the Harlem River (1837), opening the area for development, but simultaneously raising a barrier between the east and west sides of Harlem and creating a strip of blight where factories, squatters' shacks, and tenements quickly sprang up.

East Harlem, further blighted by the arrival of the Third and Second Ave elevated railroads in 1879 and 1880, was soon established as a working class neighborhood. Speculators erected rows of tenements along the avenues which became home to immigrants from Russia, Germany, Italy, Ireland, Hungary, Scandinavia, England, and Spain.

In western Harlem, however, encouraged by the opening of the IRT subway along Lenox Ave in 1901, speculators, anticipating the full-blown arrival of the middle class from downtown, put up substantial apartment buildings and handsome row houses. Oscar Hammerstein had opened the Harlem Opera House at 205 W. 125th St in 1889 expecting the same thing. When it didn't happen the real estate market collapsed, leaving landlords with unrentable buildings. Black realtor, Philip A. Payton, stepped into the gap, taking over building management and guaranteeing high rents to landlords who would accept black tenants, making decent housing available to blacks for the first time in New York.

Although rents were inflated because they could not get comparable housing elsewhere, black people poured into Harlem from other parts of the city, and also from the rural south and from the West Indies. During the 1920s the black population of Harlem increased from 83,248 to 203,894 with a density of 236 people per acre, twice that of the rest of the city. White business and property owners fought bitterly to keep Harlem white, but failed simply because it was too profitable to rent to blacks, although the arriving blacks were effectively barred from holding jobs in white-owned businesses. Since many of the new arrivals were either single or had small families, landlords began subdividing apartments, increasing their own profits but beginning a policy of overcrowding and poor building maintenance that continues today.

The 1920s were years of optimism and great artistic activity as writers, artists, and intellectuals made the pilgrimage to Harlem, by then the capital of black America. According to poet Langston Hughes, it was a time when local and visiting royalty were not uncommon in Harlem, when every year a Broadway hit play had an all-black cast, when black authors were being published with greater frequency than ever before. Marcus Garvey awoke black self-respect and militancy with his back-to-Africa movement, but black and white intellectuals still enjoyed cordial relations. Harlem was famous for its music, and whites flocked uptown to enjoy the jazz at its famous night-clubs—the Cotton Club, Connie's, and Smalls' Paradise—many of which were white-owned and which had white-only audiences. Casinos, ballrooms, and cabarets, some catering to whites and some refusing entrance to them, provided a glittering nightlife.

With the Depression, the gaiety ended and the poverty behind the glittering surface became apparent. People marginally employed were the hardest hit, and blacks, excluded from virtually all but menial jobs, were among the first to suffer. The 1930s were the years of "rent parties," where guests paid an entrance fee to hear the music, drink the bathtub gin, and help pay off the month's rent. Literary output dried up, housing deteriorated, racial tensions heightened, and Harlem became the ground for several unpleasant incidents and riots.

The physical and social scars of the Depression are still visible. During the period of civil rights activism of the 1960s, Harlem became the focus of both political and social activity. The Black Muslims founded the Temple of Islam at 116th St and Lenox Ave, and black civil rights leader Malcolm X worked there until he broke with the Muslims and founded his own Organization of Afro-

American Unity in 1964. In February 1965, he was assassinated at the Audubon Ballroom on W. 166th St between Broadway and St. Nicholas Ave at a political rally. After the riots of 1968 federal, state, and local money was channeled into Harlem to improve housing and education, and to solve social problems. While some gains were made, the programs did not produce the results hoped for. Unemployment, crime, and drug addiction rates are still high; housing, education, and other public services are still below standard. Efforts are being made to bring Harlem back to the center of black cultural life, a position it lost in the late 1950s and early 1960s when black artists, actors, musicians, and dancers were drawn to the commercially more successful cultural scene in midtown or Greenwich Village.

Although both Harlem's population and fortunes declined steadily from the end of World War II to the 1970s, there are signs that better times may be on the way. For many years Harlem families in troubled neighborhoods moved out when they could afford to do so but in recent years, a significant number of middle class black families have bought town houses for redevelopment in the neighborhoods of Striver's Row, Sugar Hill, Hamilton Terrace, and Mount Morris Park. The new residents have been attracted by adequate public transportation, proximity to midtown, and the architectural variety and reasonable price of its town houses.

Visiting Harlem. Because of its high crime rate and the attention it receives in the press, Harlem has a lurid reputation, but it is certainly possible to walk around in much of the area and feel secure, although hostility to whites does exist. The area of Frederick Douglass Blvd (Eighth Ave) between the top of the park and about 122nd St is better avoided, but Hamilton Heights, the area around the Schomburg Library, the 125th Street corridor, and elsewhere are safe. A car is useful, offering both flexibility and security.

Several commercial tours also touch on the major sights of Harlem; see p. 55.

The following route, therefore, lists points of interest in reasonable geographical order but is not intended as a walking tour; the distances covered are quite great. To drive to Harlem, follow Eighth Ave and Central Park West uptown to W. 110th St.

At the N.W. corner of Central Park is FREDERICK DOUGLASS CIRCLE, named after the escaped slave, journalist, orator, and crusader for abolition. Along the park are handsome brownstones and elevator buildings built at the turn of the century for middle- and upper-class families, for example, the *Semiramis Apartments* (c. 1905) at 137 Central Park North. Like hundreds of other Harlem buildings, it was seized for taxes by the city (1974) but has been rehabilitated as condominiums (1987). Playwright Arthur Miller was born at No. 45. At Frederick Douglass Circle and Cathedral Pkwy is *Towers on the Park* (1987; Bond Ryder & James), a condominium project marking the N.W. corner of Central Park.

Go W. to Manhattan Ave and **Morningside Park,** designed by Frederick Law Olmsted and Calvert Vaux (preliminary plan, 1873; revised plan, 1887), whose sheer cliffs separate the poor in the Harlem Valley from the university community on Morningside Heights.

The park is not safe; its natural wooded beauty, sadly, has become a liability.

The park became a cause célèbre in 1968, when Columbia University, cramped on Morningside Heights, sought two acres of its land for a gymnasium; student riots preserved the park. The heroic bronze *statue of Washington and Lafayette* (1890; unveiled 1900) at Manhattan Ave and W. 114th St is by Frédéric Auguste Bartholdi.

Harlem street names. The major avenues have been renamed as they pass through Central Harlem. Eighth Ave is Frederick Douglass Blvd. Seventh Ave was named Adam Clayton Powell, Jr. Blvd shortly after the black leader's death in 1972. The extension of Sixth Ave north of Central Park is Lenox Ave, named after the family who established the Lenox Library, now part of the New York Public Library. Similarly, 116th St east of Lexington has become Luis Muñoz Marin Blvd after the first governor of Puerto Rico, and 125th St is officially Martin Luther King, Jr. Blvd. For the sake of brevity and clarity, with no wish to offend, all these boulevards shall be referred to by their numerical names.

Nearby reminders of bourgeois turn-of-the-century Harlem are the rusticated limestone *115th St Branch of the New York Public Library* (1908; McKim, Mead & White; DL) at 203 W. 115th St (bet. 7th / 8th Aves) and the *First Corinthian Baptist Church*, 1910 Seventh Ave (S.W. corner of W. 116th St), built as the *Regent Theater* (1913; Thomas W. Lamb). Here Samuel Lionel Rothafel, later famous as "Roxy," began the New York phase of his career as a movie theater mogul, saving this neo-Venetian picture palace from financial failure.

At 1923 Seventh Ave on the N.E. corner of the same intersection are the *Graham Court Apartments* (1901; Clinton & Russell; DL), the most elegant of the early Harlem apartment houses, the first in a series of three palatial court-centered apartments financed by the Astor family (the other two are the Apthorp and the Astor Court on Broadway and 90th St). The arch on Seventh Ave originally opened to a courtyard.

Roman Catholic ST. THOMAS THE APOSTLE CHURCH at 260 W. 118th St, on the S.W. corner of St. Nicholas Ave (1907; T. H. Poole) is an eclecticly Gothic building with an arcaded porch and grand entrance stairway.

Follow St. Nicholas Ave N. to Morningside Ave at W. 125th St. ST. NICHOLAS AVE was named in 1901 after the patron saint of New Amsterdam, whose image as figurehead graced the ship that brought the first settlers from the Netherlands.

Just across 125th St, Morningside Ave becomes Convent Ave and rises steeply to Hamilton Heights. CONVENT AVENUE is named after the Convent of the Sacred Heart (established 1841) which stood between St. Nicholas Ave and Amsterdam Ave (then called Tenth Ave) until it burned in 1888.

Along Convent Ave between W. 130th and W. 135th Sts is the South Campus of the ***City University of New York,** originally the City College of New York.

CCNY was founded in 1849 after the state legislature authorized the Board of Education to establish a free academy for qualified city students. Because of its policy of free admissions for city residents, City College was long a stepping stone out of the ghetto. In 1903 more than 75% of the students were Jewish, and in 1910 almost 90%, of whom most came from eastern European families.

Nowadays though tuition is no longer free, and the student body is more black and Hispanic than Jewish, CCNY still provides an educational outlet to the city's aspiring young.

The grounds are divided into a North and South Campus, the South Campus originally having belonged to the Academy and Convent of the Sacred Heart, which moved to Westchester County as the Manhattanville College of the Sacred Heart in 1952. The Nursery (1912) on the N.E. corner of Convent Ave and W. 133rd St originally served as the gatehouse of the college. *Aaron Davis Hall* (1978; Abraham W. Geller & Assocs. and Ezra D. Ehrenkrantz & Assocs.) for the performing arts, at the S.E. corner of Convent Ave and W. 135th St, has three theaters and an outdoor amphitheater.

At the S.W. corner of W. 135th St and Convent Ave between the two campuses is a GATEHOUSE (1890; DL) for the Croton Aqueduct, a brownstone and granite structure that marks the end of the masonry aqueduct leading into Manhattan from High Bridge. From here the water is piped underground to the next gatehouse at 119th St and Amsterdam Ave.

The *North Academic Center* on the W. side of Convent Ave between W. 135th and W. 138th Sts. (1984; John Carl Warnecke & Assocs.) stands on the site of Lewisohn Stadium given to the college in 1915 by Jewish philanthropist Adolph Lewisohn as an athletic field but fondly remembered as the place the New York Philharmonic held summer outdoor concerts.

The **North Campus,** between W. 138th and W. 140th Sts, was designed in 1905 by George B. Post in a neo-Gothic style and constructed of Manhattan schist dug out during the tunneling for the Broadway-Seventh Ave IRT subway. Shepard Hall, just inside the archway, is the main building.

North of the campus along Convent Ave between W. 141st and W. 145th Sts is the *Hamilton Heights Historic District,* an enclave of fine row houses built between 1886 and 1906.

The centerpiece is **Hamilton Grange,** the country home of Alexander Hamilton (1801; John McComb, Jr.; DL), squeezed into its current site in 1889 from a location about 100 yards north. The Grange, one of the finest Federal houses of its day, was Hamilton's home at the end of his life, which ended (1804) when he was fatally wounded in a duel by Aaron Burr, his political enemy. The National Park Service now administers the site.

Hamilton Grange. 287 Convent Ave (bet. W. 141st / W. 142nd Sts), New York 10031. Tel: 283-5154. Open Wed–Sun 9–5. Free. Restrooms, telephones, no restaurant. Not accessible to wheelchairs.

The heroic bronze *statue of Hamilton* (1889) in front is by William O. Partridge. The house has been restored, but with the exception of a few pieces of furniture and a clavichord it is not furnished.

On the N.E. corner of W. 141st St is ST. LUKE'S (PROTESTANT EPISCOPAL) CHURCH (1892; R. H. Robertson), the brownstone Romanesque Revival home of the congregation founded on Hudson St in Greenwich Village. The tower was never finished.

Across the street at 280—298 Convent Ave (1902; Henri Foucheaux) is a row of limestone-faced Beaux-Arts houses.

Further up the street are Nos. 311—339 (1890; Adolph Hoak), a picturesque Romanesque row, and Nos. 320—328 (1890; Horace B. Hartwell) and Nos. 330—336 (1892; Robert Dry), all constructed at about the same time.

Just W. of Convent Ave at 467 W. 142nd St is OUR LADY OF LOURDES CHURCH (1904; O'Reilly Brothers), an astonishing exercise in architectural recycling, made up of the parts of three different, unrelated buildings. The National Academy of Design (1865; Peter B. Wright) which once stood at Park Ave South and E. 23rd St contributed its gray and white marble Ruskinian-Gothic facade. The apse and parts of the E. wall came from the Cathedral of St. John the Divine, when the E. wall there was altered to make way for the Lady Chapel. The pedestals flanking the main entrance were salvaged from department store millionaire A. T. Stewart's mansion (1867; John Kellum) on the N.W. corner of 34th St and Fifth Ave.

The heights between St. Nicholas and Edgecombe Aves, from about 143rd to 155th Sts is known as **Sugar Hill**, a place where the poor of central Harlem could see the more affluent black bourgeoisie living the sweet life. Among the prominent figures, athletes, and show business people who have lived there are Duke Ellington, Count Basie, Sugar Ray Robinson, and Supreme Court Justice Thurgood Marshall.

Go N. to W. 150th St and E. to St. Nicholas Place bordering Colonial Park. At 10 St. Nicholas Place on the N.E. corner of W. 150th St is the former *James A. Bailey house* (1888; Samuel B. Reed; DL), a rockface limestone gabled and towered mansion, built by circus entrepreneur James Anthony Bailey, partner of P. T. Barnum and cofounder of the Barnum & Bailey Circus, "the greatest show on earth."

Go N. on St. Nicholas Ave (the left fork) to W. 162nd St; turn right (E.) and right again (S.) onto Jumel Terrace. (Street parking usually available.)

Situated in small Roger Morris Park with a commanding view is the ***Morris-Jumel Mansion** (N.W. corner of W. 160th St and Edgecombe Ave). One of the city's few remaining pre-Revolutionary buildings (1765; remodeled with portico added, 1810; DL), it is now a museum.

The Morris-Jumel Mansion. W. 160th St and Edgecombe Ave, New York 10032. Tel: 923-8008. Open Tues—Sun 10—4. Admission charge. Knock on the door if the building appears to be closed.

No food, no telephone. No restrooms. No gift shop. Visitors may picnic in the surrounding park. Special events, workshops, and crafts demonstrations.

Built as the summer home of Lt.-Col. Roger Morris and his wife Mary Philipse, the house retains its original Georgian hipped roof, wooden corner quoins, and wide-board facade (though the rear of the house is shingled for economy). Morris served under

Gen. Edward Braddock during the French and Indian War and was a friend of George Washington who is thought to have been romantically linked to Mary Philipse before her marriage. When the war broke out, the family returned to England as did many wealthy loyalists. Washington used the house as his headquarters between September 14 and October 18, 1776, during his vain defense of Manhattan. The house gradually deteriorated, becoming a tavern, until Stephen Jumel, a wealthy French wine merchant, and his wife bought it and had it restored, adding the portico and enlarging the doorway in the Federal style.

Mme. Jumel, *née* Betsy Bowen of Providence, Rhode Island, who had a reputation for an imperious tongue, a scandalous love life, and boundless social ambition, became one of the richest women in America upon Jumel's death in 1832. About a year afterward 77-year-old Aaron Burr married her (she was then about 60), apparently for her money; the marriage was stormy and unsuccessful. Mme. Jumel lived on in the mansion after she and Burr separated and she died there in 1865 at the age of 93.

The furnishings include many original Jumel pieces as well as others chosen to illustrate the 100-year period in which the mansion served as a private residence.

Across Jumel Terrace between W. 160th and W. 162nd Sts is **Sylvan Terrace,** once the carriage drive of the Morris-Jumel mansion. Two rows of modest wooden houses, built (c. 1882) for workers, face one another across the street.

On the E. of the mansion lies Edgecombe Ave, whose name (from Saxon "combe," hill) implies its situation on the side of a ridge or bluff. HIGHBRIDGE PARK (1888; Calvert Vaux & Samuel Parsons, Jr.) which runs from W. 155th St to Dyckman St along the E. side of the escarpment, gets its name from High Bridge near W. 174th St, the oldest remaining bridge joining Manhattan to the mainland, in this case the Bronx. **High Bridge** was originally called Aqueduct Bridge (1839–48; John B. Jervis; DL) and was part of the Croton system bringing water into the city from tributaries of the Hudson River in Westchester County. Built of closely spaced granite piers supporting 15 arches and resembling the aqueducts of the Roman *campagna*, the bridge once attracted tourists who enjoyed views from the promenade across the top (closed many years ago because of vandalism and crime). In 1923, during construction of the Harlem Ship Canal, the Navy replaced several of the center spans with a steel arch to provide a wider ship channel. The campanile, HIGHBRIDGE TOWER (1872; attrib. John B. Jervis; DL), at W. 173rd St in the park, was once a water tower with a 47,000 gallon tank providing pressure to keep the water flowing in its regular 13 ft-per-mile downhill course to the reservoirs in Central Park.

Return down Edgecombe Ave along the E. side of the park to W. 155th St. Here the rocky spine of Harlem is, or was, known as *Coogan's Bluff,* a name kept in front of the public when the New York Giants played in the Polo Grounds.

West 155th St sweeps down the E. flank of the bluff into the Harlem Valley. Across the Harlem River the top of Yankee Stadium rises into view. On its N. side between the W. branch of the Harlem River Drive and Eighth Ave are the POLO GROUNDS TOWERS (1968) occupying the site of the former ballpark. The stadium (1912) in turn took its name from an actual polo grounds here, used in the 1880s when the area was still rural.

Turn right (S.) on MACOMBS PLACE, which takes its name

from Alexander Macomb, a hero of the War of 1812, who had his home nearby. The *Macombs Dam Bridge* across the Harlem River at W. 155th St (opened 1895) is the modern descendant of a toll bridge and dam built (c. 1813) by his son John, who thereby harnessed the river's power to run a mill but simultaneously obstructed shipping and turned much of the river upstream into a large millpond. In 1838 irate citizens bashed a hole in Macomb's dam with picks and shovels, restoring the river's navigability, an action later upheld by the courts.

Between W. 151st and W. 153rd Sts, Macombs Place and the Harlem River Drive, is one of Harlem's oldest redevelopment projects and still one of the best, the **Harlem River Houses** (1937; Archibald M. Brown, Horace Ginsbern, Charles F. Fuller, Richard W. Buckley, John L. Wilson, Frank J. Forster, and Will R. Amon; DL). These four-story red brick walkups, grouped either around central open spaces or facing the river, represent a period of high hopes for public housing and redevelopment which were not later fulfilled. At a time when black families living in filthy Old and New Law tenements often paid half their incomes for rent and "rent parties" were a major social institution, the fortunate 574 black families in these houses paid from $19.28 to $31.42 for rent and enjoyed such amenities as playgrounds, steam heat, cross ventilation, and tiled bathrooms. Only blacks living in substandard housing with incomes less than five times the rent who could reasonably prove their ability to continue paying the rent were eligible, and so relatively few families qualified.

The **Dunbar Apartments** (1928; Andrew J. Thomas; DL), six well-designed low-rise buildings bounded by W. 149th and W. 150th Sts, Seventh and Eighth Aves, represent a private attempt to solve ghetto housing problems. John D. Rockefeller, Jr., constructed them as a housing cooperative for which tenants had to pay $150 down plus $50 a room and a monthly fee. All the apartments sold quickly and the project succeeded until the Depression, when most of the tenants lost their jobs and defaulted on their mortgages. Rockefeller foreclosed in 1936, returning the tenants' equity and thereafter offering the apartments on a rental basis. Named for black poet Paul Laurence Dunbar, the buildings, grouped around a central courtyard, attracted an illustrious clientele: poet Countee Cullen, labor and civil rights activist A. Philip Randolph, dancer Bill "Bojangles" Robinson, and arctic explorer Matt Henson.

Continue downtown on Eighth Ave to W. 139th St and the ST. NICHOLAS HISTORIC DISTRICT (The King Model Houses), an enclave of handsome row housing in depressed surroundings. In 1891 David H. King, Jr., prominent as the builder of Stanford White's original Madison Square Garden, decided to put up four rows of housing designed by different architects but on the same scale. McKim, Mead & White designed the neo-Italian Renaissance group on the N. side of 139th St between Eighth and Seventh Aves; facing it and on the N. side of W. 138th St is a neo-Georgian row by Bruce Price and Clarence S. Luce in lighter brick with profuse terra-cotta and limestone trim. The row by James Brown Lord on the S. side of W. 138th St is also neo-

*Striver's Row on W. 139th St. Built in 1891 during a real
estate boom, these townhouses were intended for well-to-do
whites, but the "strivers" who inhabited them after about
1919 have been successful blacks, who began migrating to
Harlem after the turn of the century. (Museum of the City of
New York)*

Georgian, but of red brick with brownstone trim. Built during the
Harlem real estate boom, the houses were intended for upper
middle class white families; beginning in 1919 they attracted
upper middle class and presumably ambitious black families,
hence their nickname, **Striver's Row.** Among the strivers have
been W. C. Handy, Noble Sissle, Eubie Blake, and a number of
professional and civic leaders.

A little S. and E. at 132 W. 138th St between Seventh and
Lenox Aves is the *Abyssinian Baptist Church* (1923; Charles W.
Bolton), a neo-Gothic church built of New York bluestone (a fine-
textured bluish grey sandstone). The church is famous for its
former preacher, Adam Clayton Powell, Jr. It was founded downtown on Worth St in 1808 and gradually moved uptown with the
black centers of population, stopping along the way on Thompson
St, Spring St, and in the Hell's Kitchen area of W. 40th St
between Seventh and Eighth Aves.

The present building was erected during the pastorate of Adam Clayton Powell,
Sr. His son, Adam Clayton Powell, Jr., a charismatic preacher, began working
for black civil rights during the Depression and became a U.S. Congressman in
1945. He sponsored legislation focusing on civil rights and education, the
minimum wage, and segregation in the armed forces, and became a powerful
figure both in Congress and in Harlem. Always a controversial man, Powell
was censured by the House for financial irregularities in 1967 and stripped of
his office, although the Supreme Court reinstated him in 1969. (The church
maintains a memorial room with memorabilia and photos of his career.)

Go E. to Lenox Ave and turn south. Over the main doorway of HARLEM HOSPITAL on Lenox Ave between W. 137th and W. 135th Sts is a sculptural group of a black family by John W. Rhoden. Founded as a municipal hospital in 1887, Harlem Hospital is now the main facility serving the local populace.

Diagonally across the street at 515 Lenox Ave between W. 135th and W. 136th Sts is **The Schomburg Center for Research in Black Culture** (1978; Bond Ryder Assocs.), a branch of the New York Public Library.

The Schomburg Center for Research in Black Culture. 515 Lenox Avenue (135th St), New York 10037. Tel: 862-4000. Open Mon–Wed 12–8; Thurs–Sat 10–6; call for summer hours; free.

Changing exhibitions, lectures. Restrooms, telephone. No restaurant. No gift shop. Accessible to wheelchairs.

The Arthur A. Schomburg Collection, whose nucleus was gathered by Schomburg, a black Puerto Rican informed by a schoolteacher that blacks had no history, is the world's largest collection documenting the history and literature of all peoples of African descent. The library contains some 75,000 volumes, 300,000 photographs, 3000 prints and posters, personal papers, extensive holdings in West Indian history and literature, recordings of African folk music, jazz, Afro-American blues and spirituals, and an important collection of African and Afro-American artifacts.

Next door at 103 W. 135th St is the 135TH STREET BRANCH OF THE NEW YORK PUBLIC LIBRARY (1905; McKim, Mead & White; DL), where the Schomburg collection was first housed after the library acquired it (1926) with a grant from the Carnegie Corporation. An extension to the N. of this building, the COUNTEE CULLEN BRANCH OF THE NEW YORK PUBLIC LIBRARY (1942; Louis Allen Abramson) at 104 W. 136th St (S.W. corner of Lenox Ave) is named after the poet, editor, and social critic, an important figure of the Harlem Renaissance. The extension stands on the site of a mansion built in 1913 by Mme. C. J. Walker, a St. Louis laundress who discovered a hair-straightening process and reaped a fortune. Her daughter, A'Lelia Walker Robinson, was Harlem's outstanding hostess during the 1920s and for a time established one floor of the mansion as a cafe and gathering place for black poets and intellectuals.

Another nearby literary landmark is the *Harlem Branch of the Y.M.C.A.* (1932; James C. Mackenzie) at 180 W. 135th St between Lenox and Seventh Aves. In 1945 the Harlem Writers' Workshop was founded at the Y, which also served as the temporary home of many aspiring blacks drawn to Harlem, including Langston Hughes and Ralph Ellison.

Continue W. to Seventh Ave and turn left (south).

During the Roaring '20s, entrepreneurs taking advantage of white curiosity billed W. 133rd St between Lenox and Seventh Ave as "Jungle Alley," a place where whites could see "the primitive essence" of Harlem; of course it was a tourist trap whose nightclubs—Dickie Wells', the Nest, Mexico's, Pod's—arranged to show the unsuspecting just what they wanted to see.

Harlem's most famous nightclub during the 1920s was the Cotton Club, located at Lenox Ave and 143rd St. Whites owned it and enjoyed its entertainments. Blacks, preferably light-skinned ones, worked there on the stage, backstage, and out front as waiters and bouncers. The chorus line of light-skinned black women (which Lena Horne joined for a while) was so famous that white women tried to "pass" to get in. Cab Calloway performed here, and Duke Ellington, whose band played here from 1927–31, achieved his first brilliant success both musically and commercially through his association with the club. The Depression killed the Cotton Club, and most of the other Harlem night spots.

The WILLIAMS CHRISTIAN METHODIST CHURCH (2225 Seventh Ave, bet. W. 131st / W. 132nd Sts) began as the Lafayette Theater (c. 1910), which hit its stride offering black revues in the 1920s. While the shows, especially the midnight shows, were a local social event and the Lafayette was the major showcase of black talent, it was owned and operated by whites. Bessie Smith, Duke Ellington, "Bojangles" Robinson, Fletcher Henderson, and Earl Hines all appeared here, as well as a lot of raw untested talent. During the Depression the Lafayette housed the W.P.A. Federal Negro Theater among whose productions was a 1937 *Macbeth* directed by Orson Welles with an all-black cast.

Outside the theater at Seventh Ave and W. 131st St once flourished the *Tree of Hope,* purported to bring good luck to black actors and actresses out of work. When a job came through, the lucky performer kissed the tree in gratitude. Age and pollution killed both the original and its replacement, donated by dancer Bill "Bojangles" Robinson (1878–1949).

Continue S. towards 125th St. At 151 W. 128th St, N.E. corner of Seventh Ave, is the *Metropolitan Baptist Church* (1884; John R. Thomas; DL), a low, massive Romanesque church with a heavy half-conical roof. It was built as the New York Presbyterian Church when Harlem was still well-to-do and bourgeois.

Any visitor to Harlem notices its empty, derelict buildings and rubble-strewn vacant lots, the legacy of generations of landlord-tenant hostilities. The combination of long-standing building code violations, landlord neglect, tenant abuse, and tax delinquency resulted in the abandonment of many buildings by landlords who found it cheaper to walk away from their property than to pay the taxes on it. The empty buildings then become havens for drug addicts and targets for criminals who rip out the plumbing, wiring, and other things of value. Landlords have been known on more than a few occasions to hire arsonists to burn their buildings down, thereby collecting on the insurance. By this depressing route of tax default and abandonment, the city has become the *in rem* owner of hundreds of buildings and Harlem's largest landlord.

Continue down Seventh Ave to 125th St, officially Martin Luther King, Jr., Blvd, Harlem's main commercial strip. On the N.E. corner of the intersection (163 W. 125th St) in a monumental plaza is the former Harlem State Office Building (1973; Ifill Johnson Hanchard), renamed (1983) the Adam Clayton Powell, Jr. State Office Building.

Diagonally across the intersection at the S.W. corner (2090 Seventh Ave) is the THERESA TOWERS (c. 1910), now an office building (altered 1971) but originally the Theresa Hotel. The

Theresa became famous as the place Fidel Castro chose to stay when he visited the United Nations in 1960.

Go W. on 125th St. In the next block (253 W. 125th St) between Seventh and Eighth Aves is the APOLLO THEATER (1913; DL), which opened as a burlesque house for whites only; in 1934 Leo Brecher and Frank Schiffman, previously operators of the Lafayette Theater, opened it to blacks and began presenting revues, singers, and bands. Bessie Smith and Billie Holiday, Duke Ellington, Count Basie, Charlie Parker and Dizzy Gillespie, as well as latter-day soul and rock stars Gladys Knight and Aretha Franklin all appeared here before poor box office receipts closed it (1976) for a decade. In recent years the theater has been refurbished and the old Amateur Night has been revived. On Wednesday nights would-be stars sing, dance, or strut through comedy routines before an audience that showers them with hoots and catcalls or enthusiastic applause.

Turn around and go E. on 125th St to the **Studio Museum in Harlem.**

The Studio Museum in Harlem. 144 W. 125th Street (bet. 7th / Lenox Aves), New York 10035. Tel: 864-4500. Open Wed–Fri 10–5; Sat–Sun 1–6; admission charge.
   Restrooms, telephone. Gift shop. No restaurant. Changing exhibitions, children's programs, workshops, seminars. Accessible to wheelchairs.

Founded in 1968 to collect and exhibit the work of black artists, the museum fills its handsome exhibition space with changing exhibitions; some feature emerging artists, African art, or other cultural themes of interest to blacks. The permanent collection includes works of Romare Bearden as well as historic photographs of Harlem and black life by James Van DerZee.

There are several handsome churches in the vicinity. The EPHESUS SEVENTH DAY ADVENTIST CHURCH (1887; J. R. Thomas), originally the Reformed Low Dutch Church of Harlem, at 267 Lenox Ave on the N.W. corner of W. 123rd St, was the second church of that denomination to serve the burghers of Harlem; the first was established in 1660. On the S.E. corner of the same intersection at 36 W. 123rd St is the picturesque Romanesque Revival BETHEL GOSPEL PENTACOSTAL ASSEMBLY (1889; Lamb & Rich), built as the Harlem Club for businessmen and civic leaders. *St. Martin's Episcopal Church* (1888; William A. Potter; DL) on the S.E. corner of Lenox Ave and W. 122nd St, a handsome Romanesque church with a fine carillon of 40 bells, began as the Holy Trinity Episcopal Church. The parish was established 20 years earlier; five years after the church was built it had a communicant list of 1000 and enjoyed increasing prosperity. The MOUNT OLIVET BAPTIST CHURCH at 201 Lenox Ave on the N.W. corner of W. 120th St was built as Temple Israel (1907; Arnold W. Brunner) for a prestigious congregation of German Jews.
   A little out of the way is the Roman Catholic ALL SAINTS' CHURCH on the N.E. corner of Madison Ave and E. 129th St, a splendid Gothic group of ecclesiastical buildings in the Renwick tradition (Church: 1894; Renwick, Aspinwall & Russell. Rectory at 47 E. 129th St: 1889; Renwick, Aspinwall & Russell. School at 52 E. 130th St: 1904; W. W. Renwick). Especially handsome is the 129th St facade and the row of rose windows in the clerestory along Madison Ave. Return to Fifth Ave and 125th St.

Straddling Fifth Ave between 120th and 124th Sts is **Marcus Garvey Park,** originally called Mount Morris Park but renamed (1973) to honor the black leader. Garvey, flamboyant, fond of titles and prerogatives, a charismatic leader, arrived in Harlem from the West Indies in 1914 dedicated to the improvement of his race. He encouraged blacks to be proud of their color and to work toward their own social and political institutions, but his major interest was in leading his people back to Africa, of which he dubbed himself Emperor and Provisional President. To this end he formed two steamship companies whose vessels, along with many others of the period, attempted to subvert Prohibition by carrying some $3 million worth of liquor from New York to Cuba, a voyage which ended in the confiscation of the liquor by the government. Later Garvey, convicted of mail fraud and imprisoned, was deported to Jamaica; he died an exile in London in 1940.

In 1839 the city established the park, mainly because its steep, rocky terrain was unsuitable for building. When the surrounding blocks were leveled and built upon, the central hill in the park (called Snake Hill by the Dutch) achieved a prominence that made the park visually dramatic. Its dominant man-made feature is a cast-iron **watchtower** (c. 1855; attrib. James Bogardus; DL), the sole survivor of many that once served as fire lookout and warning stations (even the bell remains). Near the park, are fine rows of houses, some rehabilitated.

Go S. on Fifth Ave to 116th St. A block W. (102 W. 116th St, S.W. corner of Lenox Ave) is the *Malcolm Shabazz Mosque No. 7*, originally the Lenox Casino, converted to a temple (1965) by the addition of an aluminum onion-shaped dome. Elijah Muhammad established it as his Temple of Islam and Malcolm X preached there before his break with Muhammad and the Black Muslims.

Continue down Fifth Ave. At the N.E. corner of Central Park (110th St) is FRAWLEY CIRCLE, named (1926) after James J. Frawley, a Tammany politician, state senator, and public administrator. SCHOMBURG PLAZA (1975; Gruzen & Partners and Castro-Blanco, Piscioneri & Feder), its two 35-story octagonal towers rising high above anything else in the neighborhood, serves to demarcate the corner of the park. It was a project of the state Urban Development Corporation.

Spanish Harlem, E. of Park Ave and N. of 96th St, no longer has the largest number of Hispanic residents in the city (the Bronx has), but it is still the cradle of Latin American culture here, known also as "El Barrio," the neighborhood, the district. Unlike central Harlem it was never elegant but from the time of its development housed poor immigrants—Italians, Scandinavians, Irish, Jews—in its long rows of tenements. Puerto Ricans, who form the largest group among the city's Hispanic population, began immigrating to mainland U. S. after 1917 when they became American citizens, but the largest influx came after World War II, peaking in the mid-1950s and fluctuating with economic conditions since that time. The neighborhood around Pleasant Place and 114th St still has a dwindling number of Italians, most of whom originated in Sicily and southern Italy, and elsewhere in Spanish Harlem are enclaves of Cubans, Dominicans, and Asians.

Spanish Harlem has a fairly high incidence of crime. It is wiser to tour by car or in company.

The *Aguilar Branch of the New York Public Library* (174 E. 110th St bet. 3rd / Lexington Aves) was established in 1886 as a private library to satisfy the intellectual hunger of the predominantly Jewish immigrants who lived nearby. Named after Grace Aguilar, an English novelist of Spanish Jewish parentage, the building (1899, expanded 1905; Herts & Tallant) now serves as part of the public system.

Among the large housing projects in East Harlem several stand out. One is the *1199 Plaza* apartment complex (bet. 107th / 110th Sts, 1st Ave and the Franklin Delano Roosevelt Drive), a mix of brick towers (32 stories) and lower residential buildings (1975; The Hodne / Stageberg Partners, architects; Herb Baldwin, landscape architect) on a landscaped site that divides public and private spaces in the best traditions of city planning. The name refers to District 1199 of the National Union of Hospital and Health Care Employees, sponsors of the project.

LA MARQUETA, one of the more colorful, boisterous spots in the neighborhood, even the city, is an enclosed market under the Park Ave railroad viaduct between 110th and 116th Sts (open 8–6 every day except Sun and major holidays). Merchants cater to local tastes, offering plantains, mangoes, and banana leaves, or eels, octopus, and salt cod along with more familiar staples; butchers offer whole pigs or virtually any of the parts thereof. Other merchants fill their stalls with religious items, plaster figurines of saintly or secular figures, herbal preparations, clothing, and jewelry. The market is currently (1989) under renovation.

The *Harlem Courthouse* at 170 E. 121st St on the corner of Sylvan Place was built (1893; Thom & Wilson; DL) in the eclectic (Victorian Gothic and Romanesque) style then popular. Once known as the Fifth District Prison (it had holding cells), it remained a magistrate's courthouse until 1961; since then it has served the city Parole Board, Sanitation Department and Department of Air Pollution.

The second of East Harlem's most impressive slum clearance projects is *Taino Towers* (bet. 122nd / 123rd Sts, 2nd / 3rd Aves), which dates from 1977 (Silverman & Cika) and was sponsored by a group of local residents and community leaders. The name "Taino" refers to the pre-Columbian natives of Puerto Rico who, incidentally, called their island Borinquen, a name also perpetuated in various Puerto Rican endeavors in the city.

27 Columbus Circle to Lincoln Center

SUBWAY: IRT Broadway-7th Ave local (train 1 or 9), IND 8th Ave express or local (train A or C), or IND 6th Ave express (D train), all to 59th St-Columbus Circle.

BUS: M5 or M7 uptown via 6th Ave; M104 or M10 uptown via 8th Ave; M103 crosstown on 59th St or M28 crosstown on 57th St.

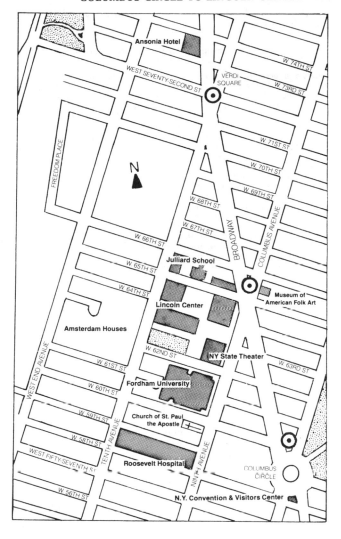

Begin at Columbus Circle, the intersection of Central Park South (59th St), Central Park West (Eighth Ave), and Broadway. In the triangle N. of the circle is GULF & WESTERN PLAZA (1970; Thomas E. Stanley), a white rectangular slab of an office building set down on a triangular site. On the Broadway side is the *Paramount Theater*, mostly underground, with a cylindrical "hat box" sticking up through the pavement. The redevelopment of the *site of the former New York Coliseum* (1965; Leon & Lionel

Levy), replaced by the Javits Center, is currently (1990) a politically charged issue.

For the Columbus Monument, the Maine Memorial, and the New York City Department of Cultural Affairs see Rte 29.

Points of Interest W. of Columbus Circle. West of Columbus Circle on a slight rise near Ninth Ave and the upper W. 50s was a black neighborhood known around the turn of the century as SAN JUAN HILL because of the black veterans of the Spanish-American War who lived there and also, apparently, because of racial battles in the area. It was one of the neighborhoods whose population eventually moved uptown to Harlem.

ROOSEVELT HOSPITAL, along Ninth Ave between W. 57th and W. 59th Sts, was founded in 1871 and is now part of the St. Luke's-Roosevelt Hospital Center. The oldest building remaining is the *William J. Syms Operating Theater* (1892; W. Wheeler Smith; DL) on the S.W. corner of W. 59th St; named for its donor, a retired gun merchant, it is remarkable architecturally for the high semiconical skylight which formerly illuminated the operating theater, a large operating room with a gallery of steeply raked tiers of seats where observers, mostly medical students, could learn surgery.

Between Eleventh and Twelfth Aves, W. 58th to W. 59th Sts, is a CONSOLIDATED EDISON POWERHOUSE (1904; McKim, Mead & White), originally the main powerhouse for the first New York subway, the *Interborough Rapid Transit*, which opened in 1904 and ran between City Hall and W. 145th St. The electricity was generated from furnaces (once there were six tall smokestacks on the building) fueled by coal brought upriver on barges and transported to the powerhouse on electric conveyor belts. Today the city buys power for the subways from Consolidated Edison Co.

On the W. side of Columbus Ave at 60th St is the (Roman Catholic) CHURCH OF ST. PAUL THE APOSTLE (1885; Jeremiah O'Rourke), the home of the Paulist Fathers or Missionary Society of St. Paul, founded (1858) by Father Isaac Thomas Hecker to spread Catholicism and an awareness of its thought and traditions in the essentially Protestant societies of the U.S. and Canada. The Gothic exterior is unremarkable except for the bas-relief on the E. facade (Lumen Martin Winter) depicting the conversion of St. Paul; it contains 50 tons of travertine fixed against a mosaic background of Venetian glass tesserae in 15 shades of blue.

Inside, however, are a number of monuments by prominent American artists (described clockwise from entrance). The bronze panel on the S. wall depicting the Raising of the Daughter of Jairus is by Charles Keck. The baptismal font in the second bay, designed by John La Farge, is constructed of Tennessee, Numidian, and Colonna marble; the mural above it is a copy from Bellini. The Altar of the Blessed Virgin at the far end of the S. aisle was designed by Stanford White, as were the High Altar and the Altar of St. Joseph in the N. aisle. Frederick MacMonnies executed the bronze kneeling angels on top of the baldachin; the sanctuary lamp was designed by Stanford White, and executed by Philip Martiny. The murals (dark and difficult to see) high on the walls of the Sanctuary representing the Angel of the Moon (S. wall) and the Angel of the Sun (N. wall) are by John La Farge and William Laurel Harris, respectively. The altar of St. Patrick in the N. aisle (second bay from the main entrance), executed in Connemara marble, is also by John La Farge. Bertram Goodhue designed the floor whose mosaics touch on the apostleship of St.

Paul. The East Window was designed by John La Farge as were the two blue windows at the W. end of the church.

About a block E. and N. of the church at 1865 Broadway (N.W. corner of W. 61st St) is *Bible House* (1966; Skidmore, Owings & Merrill), headquarters of the American Bible Society, a white precast concrete building with huge exposed beams on the Broadway side.

Bible House. 1865 Broadway (61st St), New York 10023. Tel: 581-7400. Open Mon–Fri 9–4:30. Closed weekends, national holidays. Free. No restaurant, no restrooms, public telephone outside building.

Bible House offers a permanent exhibition of rare or unusual Bibles—an 1849 Nu Testament in Fonetic Shorthand, Helen Keller's imposing stack of Braille volumes, original fragments of the Dead Sea scrolls—as well as a full-scale reproduction of the Gutenberg printing press. Changing exhibitions (about two each year) are usually based on Bibles drawn from the collection and organized thematically.

Return to Columbus Ave, originally Ninth Ave, renamed above 59th St in 1890 (as were West End Ave, Amsterdam Ave, Central Park West, and Central Park South at various times) to enhance its prestige and the value of its real estate. Oddly, those who petitioned the city for the name change regarded it as second in importance only to the advantages of increased rapid transit in its beneficial effect on property values.

At 47 Columbus Ave (bet. W. 61st / W. 62nd Sts) is the former SOFIA BROTHERS WAREHOUSE (1930; Jardine, Hill & Murdock; DL), a much admired Art Deco building, constructed as one of the city's first high-rise, "automatic" (i.e., elevator-equipped) parking garages and recycled (1985) as a luxury apartment building.

Pressed up against the warehouse at 44 W. 62nd St is *Lincoln Plaza Tower* (1973; Horace Ginsbern & Assocs.), a 30-story apartment building with curved balconies and cylindrical columns—one of many residential buildings to arise after the construction of Lincoln Center set the neighborhood on its present upward course.

The LINCOLN CENTER CAMPUS OF FORDHAM UNIVERSITY, a Jesuit institution founded in 1841 with its main campus in the west Bronx, occupies the blocks bounded by Columbus and Amsterdam Aves, W. 60th and W. 62nd Sts. Built as part of the Lincoln Center urban renewal project, the campus has two main buildings: the *Fordham Law School* (1962; Voorhees, Walker, Smith, Smith & Haines) on the S., and the *Leon Lowenstein Center* (1969; Slingerland & Booss) on the north.

Facing Columbus Ave at 61st St in front of the Law School is Lila Katzen's *City Spirit* (1968), whose curved forms signify, to the sculptor, the interlocking elements of the city. Closer to 62nd St is *Circle World #2,* (1969; Masami Kodama), a cube of black granite inserted in a broken circle of pink granite. In the plaza of the Lowenstein Center is a 28-ft bronze statue of *Peter, Fisher of Men* (Frederick Shrady), casting a 14-ft bronze net across the plaza's reflecting pool.

Walk N. on Columbus Ave. ****Lincoln Center for the Performing Arts,** bounded by Columbus and Amsterdam Aves, W. 62nd and W. 66th Sts, is a 14-acre complex of six buildings devoted to drama, music, and dance.

Lincoln Center for the Performing Arts. 140 W. 65th Street (Broadway), New York 10023. Tel: 877-1800.

Box office information. Box office openings differ from house to house; they close weekdays between 6 and 9 P.M., depending on performance schedules.

Alice Tully Hall. For information tel: 362-1911. Box office opens Mon–Sat at 11; is open Sun 12–6. Credit card sales: Center Charge, tel: 874-6770, Mon–Fri 10–6, weekends 12–6.

Avery Fisher Hall. For information tel: 874-2424. Box office open Mon–Sat 10–6; Sun 12–6. Credit card sales: Center Charge, tel: 874-6770, Mon–Fri 10–6, weekends 12–6.

Juilliard School. For information tel: 799-5000. For ticket information call 874-7515.

Metropolitan Opera. For information and credit card sales tel: 362-6000. Box office hours: Mon–Sat 10–8; Sun 12–6. Group sales, tel: 870-7447.

New York Public Library at Lincoln Center. For information tel: 870-1630. Galleries open Mon, Tues, Thurs 10–8, Wed and Fri 12–6, Sat 10–6; closed Sun and holidays. Tickets for free concerts in Bruno Walter Auditorium: apply in person after 3 o'clock on the day of the program or Sat after noon at the Amsterdam Ave entrance.

New York State Theater. For information tel: 870-5570. Box office open Mon 10–8, Tues–Sat 10–9, Sun 11:30–7:30. Group sales for New York City Ballet, tel: 870-5660. For New York City Opera information, tel: 870-5630. Tickets for the New York City Opera may be purchased by credit card at the box office or by calling Ticketmaster, tel: 307-7171.

Vivian Beaumont Theater. For information and credit card sales tel: 239-6200.

Restaurants are located in Avery Fisher Hall and the Metropolitan Opera House and on the plaza, weather permitting. The Fountain Cafe on the plaza is open mid-May to Oct, 11 A.M. to midnight. The Panevino Ristorante (moderate) in Avery Fisher Hall is open daily from 11:30 to 4 P.M. for lunch, from 4 to curtain time for dinner, and for supper from curtain time to one hour post-performance. The Adagio Buffet (moderate) is open before performances from 5 until curtain time; reservations and information, tel: 874-7000. The Grand Tier Restaurant (moderately expensive) in the Metropolitan Opera is open two hours before performances for Metropolitan Opera ticket holders only (reservations; tel: 799-3400).

Restrooms located on the Concourse level near the garage entrance. Performing Arts Shop, concourse level under the Plaza, Mon–Sat 10 A.M. through first intermission of performance; Sun 12–5; tel: 580-4356. Metropolitan Opera Shop in Metropolitan Opera House lobby, Mon–Sat 10 A.M. through first intermission of performance; tel: 580-4090. Gallery at Lincoln Center on the concourse level under the Plaza, Mon 4–8, Tues–Sat 11–8; tel: 580-4673.

Tours and Visitors' Services. Two kinds of tours are offered, general tours of the buildings, which sometimes include glimpses of rehearsals, and backstage tours of the Metropolitan Opera House. The general tours leave from the Concourse Level (accessible from the foyer of the Metropolitan Opera House, down one flight) from 10 to 5. Admission charge. For information tel: 877-1800, ext. 516. Backstage tours (1½ hours long) of the Met, organized by the Metropolitan Opera Guild leave from the entrance foyer of the Met, Mon–Fri at 3:45, Sat at 10:30. Advance reservations necessary; admission charge. For reservations and information, tel: 582-3512.

Information for the physically handicapped is available at the Administrative Offices (140 W. 65th St); tel: 877-1800, ext. 553.

SUBWAY: IRT Broadway-7th Ave local (train 1) to 66th St. Underground concourse to all buildings.

BUS: M7 via Broadway and Columbus Ave. M5 uptown via 6th Ave /
Broadway; downtown via Riverside Drive / Broadway / 5th Ave. M30
crosstown on 72nd St. M29 crosstown on 65th St. M104 via Broadway.

Lincoln Center is the premier performing arts center in the
nation, possibly the world. It is the home of the Metropolitan
Opera, the New York Philharmonic, the New York City Ballet, the
New York City Opera, and the Chamber Music and Film Societies
of Lincoln Center, the Lincoln Center Theater, the School of
American Ballet, the City Center of Music and Drama, and the
Juilliard School, as well as the site of the New York Public Library
at Lincoln Center, a branch specializing in the performing arts.
The center is currently erecting a major new building adjacent to
the Juilliard School which will house rehearsal studios, dormitories for Juilliard and the School of American Ballet, a film theater,
broadcasting facilities, a branch of the New York Public Library,
and archival space for the Philharmonic and other Lincoln Center
organizations.

Its ten performing arts companies stage about 3000 performances annually, offering during peak season some 150 events a
week, which range from classical ballet, theater, and music to
rock and jazz concerts, musical theater, and smaller, less conventional offerings. Most of the houses are filled to near capacity.

Architecturally Lincoln Center evokes for most people the
image of its three largest halls—the Metropolitan Opera House,
Avery Fisher Hall, and the New York State Theater—which
surround a plaza with a fountain (architect, Philip Johnson) and
a pavement design of concentric circles and spokes. The three
halls, classical in inspiration, all have large expanses of glass
looking out on the plaza; they all have colonnades of one sort or
another; they all are finished with travertine, a creamy white
marble from ancient quarries near Rome.

History. Three events in 1955 paved the way for Lincoln Center: the designation of Lincoln Square (the neighborhood surrounding the intersection of
Broadway and Amsterdam Ave at W. 65th St) as a target for urban renewal,
the recognition by the Metropolitan Opera that Lincoln Square might be a site
for a new and desperately needed opera house, and the impending homeless-
ness of the New York Philharmonic, since Carnegie Hall was scheduled for
demolition. Heading the building committee was John D. Rockefeller III, while
Wallace K. Harrison, who had worked with the Metropolitan Opera for a
quarter of a century and had participated in the development of Rockefeller
Center and the United Nations Headquarters, was chosen to head the board of
architects. In 1959 President Dwight D. Eisenhower dug up the first shovelful
of earth beginning a period of construction that ended with the opening of the
Juilliard School in 1969. By 1987 most of the companies had outgrown their
facilities and the trustees got out the shovel again to break ground for the new
building currently under construction (scheduled completion 1990).

Despite its obvious successes, or perhaps because of them, Lincoln Center
has not escaped controversy. Urban planners have objected to the burden
placed on public transportation by the concentration of halls and theaters.
Social critics have decried the destruction of a lower income neighborhood
rebuilt for the affluent: 1647 families had to find new homes when their
buildings were demolished to make way for the center. Though time and
familiarity seem to have mellowed its big, glossy marble buildings, architectural critics have never liked Lincoln Center, at worst citing it for mediocre and
slick classicism, at best faintly praising the scale and relationship of its plazas

and open spaces. Artists have sometimes found it too institutional, too rich, too powerful.

The fact remains, however, that Lincoln Center, despite its plague of initial cost overruns and continuing operating deficits, is a vital cultural institution. An audience of about 5 million people attends yearly. Its payroll of over $100 million supports over 6000 employees—musicians, actors, and dancers; stagehands, ushers, and ticket takers; costume makers, set builders, office personnel, and other staff. Its physical presence has inspired continuing renewal of the West Side. Its artistic and educational programs are vital to the cultural life of the city.

The **Metropolitan Opera House,** the centerpiece of Lincoln Center (1966; Wallace K. Harrison), 10 stories high, faces Broadway from the W. side of the plaza. The main facade has five marble arches separated by columns, while the long side walls with their closely spaced mullions reach back the equivalent of 45 stories. Through the main facade gleam two murals by Marc Chagall, except when curtains are drawn to protect them from the sun.

History. The Metropolitan Opera was founded by a group of "new" capitalists—i.e., Goulds, Whitneys, J. P. Morgan, and the occasional Vanderbilt—who were denied boxes at the Academy of Music on 14th St because the "old" nobility held title to them all. The first house (1883; J. C. Cady and Louis de Coppet Bergh) on Broadway at 39th St featured an auditorium whose deep Diamond Horseshoe gave box holders an unrivaled opportunity to look at one another but otherwise had disastrous sightlines, with some 700 seats having partial or obstructed view of the stage. Backstage the house was cramped and outdated by the 1920s when the opera began searching for a new home. Nevertheless, the house enjoyed the affection of the public until it closed in 1966.

The new house opened September 16, 1966, with the premier performance of Samuel Barber's *Antony and Cleopatra,* commissioned for the occasion, with the title roles sung by Leontyne Price and Justino Diaz.

The INTERIOR, finished in red plush, gold leaf, and marble, recalls the color scheme of the old Met and attempts to reconcile the grandeur of traditional opera houses with a more contemporary approach, an attempt that critics generally feel has failed on the side of overdecoration and timidity. The crystal sunburst chandeliers were donated by the Austrian government. The concrete forms for the sweeping curves of the Grand Staircase were executed by boatbuilders.

The predominantly red Chagall mural on the S. side, *Le Triomphe de la Musique,* depicts singers, ballerinas, and musicians, and contains references to opera, folk music, and jazz, as well as images of the New York skyline. Former Metropolitan general manager (1935–72) Sir Rudolph Bing appears in gypsy costume (central figure in the group of three on the left). The yellow mural, *Les Sources de la Musique,* shows a combined King David-Orpheus figure holding a lyre, a Tree of Life afloat in the Hudson River, and references to Wagner, Verdi, Bach, and the operas *Fidelio* and *The Magic Flute.*

Among the works of art in the foyers and corridors is a bronze (1911) by Wilhelm Lehmbruck, *Die Kniende* ("Kneeling Woman") at the top of the Grand Staircase. Two figures by Aristide Maillol, *Summer* (1910) and *Venus without Arms* (1920) are displayed on the S. and N. ends of the Grand Tier level. In the foyer of the

Lincoln Center for the Performing Arts, the exterior of the Metropolitan Opera House. Through the windows are visible the murals by Marc Chagall and the Austrian crystal sunburst chandeliers. The central fountain has become a popular meeting place and a symbol for the city at large. (Winnie Klotz, Metropolitan Opera Association, Inc.)

Dress Circle is Maillol's *Kneeling Woman: Monument to Debussy* (1931). A gallery on the concourse level (one floor below the main foyer) contains paintings of Metropolitan stars and operatic composers. The heroic bronze *bust of Caruso* by Onorio Ruotolo and the marble *bust of Giulio Gatti-Casazzi,* general manager 1908–35, were familiar fixtures in the lobby of the old Met. The *portrait of Gluck* displayed in the N. passage (beyond the bust of Gatti-Casazza) is by Joseph Sifrede Duplessis (1725–1802) and is believed to be the original, the one in Vienna being a copy.

Backstage the building is superbly equipped, with a 110-ft fly loft above the main stage, three auxiliary stages as large as the main playing area, 20 rehearsal rooms three of which are large enough to duplicate the main stage, and an orchestra pit that can hold 110 musicians. The stage equipment, including six 60-ft hydraulic lifts and a revolving stage, was a gift from the government of West Germany.

The *auditorium,* also decorated in red, has 3788 seats arranged in the traditional manner though with a widened horseshoe to improve sightlines. Immense by European standards (cf. Covent Garden's 2158 seats), it offers a single row of boxes with otherwise "democratic" seating, in contrast to the old Met which provided segregated elevators and less comfortable seats for patrons of the cheaper levels of the house. The free form sculpture for the proscenium arch (1966) is by Mary Callery.

The Metropolitan Opera is known for the general grandeur of its productions, usually chosen from the traditional repertoire, and for its star-studded casts. James Levine is the musical director.

On the S.W. corner of the Lincoln Center site is DAMROSCH PARK (1969; Eggers & Higgins) with the Guggenheim Bandshell, used for outdoor concerts, the Big Apple Circus at Christmas time, and other events. The park is named for Walter Damrosch, director of the New York Symphony Orchestra (1903–27), composer, and pioneer of orchestral radio concerts.

On the S. side of the plaza stands the **New York State Theater** (1964; Philip Johnson & Richard Foster), home of the New York City Opera and the New York City Ballet. Over the glass front wall rises a colonnade of paired square columns, interrupted by an outdoor balcony used as a promenade during intermissions.

INTERIOR. On the front wall of the ground-level foyer are an *Untitled Relief* (1964; Lee Bontecou) and a painting entitled *Numbers* (1964) by Jasper Johns. On the stairway landings are two abstract sculptures of gold leaf on fiberglass by Kobashi entitled *Song* and *Dance*. Reuben Nakian's bronze *Voyage to Crete* (1963) stands inside the doors (left) leading to the orchestra level. Also displayed on the same level are Jacques Lipchitz's *Birth of the Muses* (1949) and an untitled *Sculpture* (1963) by Edward Higgins. One floor up is the Grand Promenade, with a marble floor, gold leaf–covered ceiling, beaded metallic curtains, and tiers of balconies for strolling. Since the state owns the building, the mayor and governor may use the foyer for receptions, as can private individuals—though for a fee. Two large, curvaceous statues at either end, one pair representing *Two Nudes*, the other, *Two Circus Women* (originals 1930 and 1931 by Elie Nadelman) were duplicated in Carrara marble at twice the original size by Italian artisans. Perhaps the most controversial objects in the theater, they have been called "absolutely pneumatic" by detractors who also likened their polished whiteness to yogurt, while admirers have found them to combine "high style, sly levity, and swelling monumentality."

The *auditorium* (seats 2792), designed without a center aisle for better sightlines, is decorated in a garnet color, with big jewellike lights studding the tiers of balconies and a central chandelier that resembles a colossal, many-faceted diamond. The stage, engineered specifically to meet the demands of dancers, features a "sprung" floor with air spaces between its layers and is covered with dark gray linoleum.

The resident New York City Ballet founded in 1948 by general manager Lincoln Kirstein and artistic director George Balanchine, is especially famous for its performances of Balanchine's abstract, neoclassical ballets. The New York City Opera is a company of predominantly young, predominantly American singers who perform an imaginative, adventurous repertoire as well as standard operatic favorites.

Facing the New York State Theater is **Avery Fisher Hall,** originally Philharmonic Hall (1962; Max Abramovitz), a glass box around which is wrapped a peristyle of 44 tapered travertine columns. Renamed (1973) after Avery Fisher, manufacturer of high-fidelity components and donor of $10 million to Lincoln Center, the hall is the professional home of the New York Philharmonic.

From its opening (September 23, 1962) until its present redesign, the hall's acoustics proved a nightmare to musicians, audiences, and its designers. Musicians complained of being unable to hear one another, while trained listeners in the auditorium were troubled by a lack of low frequency sounds, a strident quality in the upper registers, and an echo. When adjustment of the original 106 sound-reflecting "clouds" hung over both the stage and the auditorium area failed to improve the acoustics, engineers resorted to increasingly radical measures, changing wall contours, replacing heavily upholstered seats with thinly padded, wooden-backed chairs, and filling in the space between the "clouds" with plywood. Even so, in 1974 the Boston and Philadelphia Orchestras, still dissatisfied, went back to Carnegie Hall for their New York appearances. Finally in 1976, using half of Avery Fisher's gift, architects Philip Johnson and John Burgee with acoustical guidance from Cyril Harris, consultant for the Metropolitan Opera House, had the hall completely gutted and rebuilt, to the general satisfaction of all concerned.

INTERIOR. In the entrance foyer at ground level are (E. end) Seymour Lipton's *Archangel* (1964), an abstract sculptural work of bronze and Monel metal, and (W. end) Dimitri Hadzi's dark bronze *K458—The Hunt* (1964), whose title recalls a Mozart string quartet. In the main foyer (up the escalator) is a two-part hanging work by Richard Lippold entitled *Orpheus and Apollo,* constructed of 190 strips of polished Muntz metal, a copper alloy, suspended from the ceiling by steel wires. At the S. end (Broadway side) of the Grand Promenade (one level higher) is a bronze *Tragic Mask of Beethoven,* by Antoine Bourdelle, and (on the W. side) a *bronze head of Gustav Mahler,* made by Auguste Rodin in 1901.

The *auditorium* (seats 2742) is used by the Philharmonic, now under the directorship of Zubin Mehta, about four times weekly during the season, and by soloists, other orchestras, and jazz and pop groups the rest of the time.

Between Avery Fisher Hall and the Vivian Beaumont Theater is a reflecting pool containing a two-piece bronze work by Henry Moore, *Lincoln Center Reclining Figure* (1965). Moore himself described the piece as "a leg part and a head and arms part." Near the entrance to the library is Alexander Calder's *Le Guichet* (1965), a stabile of blackened steel (22 ft long, 14 ft high). The name means "the ticket window."

The **Vivian Beaumont Theater** (1965; Eero Saarinen), named after a generous donor, has been praised as the center's visually most successful building but has suffered financial and artistic difficulties that have, until recently, resisted changes in leadership and in artistic direction. Finally in 1986, under the direction of Gregory Mosher and Bernard Gersten the theater, by then closed and on occasion described as "the black hole of New York's dramatic firmament" reopened and since then has attracted favorable attention from both audiences and critics.

Situated W. of the reflecting pool, the main facade appears as a horizontal slab of travertine projecting over a glass wall. Inside the entrance is a sculptural work, *Zig IV* (1961) by David Smith.

The theater itself, designed in consultation with Jo Mielziner, at a time when thrust stages were in vogue, was conceived as a compromise between a traditional proscenium arch and a thrust stage, with complex machinery for converting it from one form to the other. The stage area is much larger than that of any other legitimate theater in the city and the auditorium is arranged as an amphitheater (seats 1089). Soon after the Beaumont opened it was discovered that the sightlines and acoustics were wanting and that some of the audience could not see action taking place at the rear of the deep stage. The lighting system, originally computerized, was changed to a conventional control system when the automatic system caused erratic, unforeseen lighting changes.

Also in the building is the *Mitzi E. Newhouse Theater,* a small house (seats 280) for experimental drama.

To the left of the theater and wrapped around it is the **New York Public Library at Lincoln Center** (1965; Skidmore, Owings & Merrill), a library and museum of the performing arts, with a circulating collection of some 50,000 volumes and 12,000 records, and a research library devoted to the performing arts.

Exhibitions pertaining to the performing arts are mounted in the *Main Gallery* and the *Vincent Astor Gallery*. The Heckscher Oval in the Children's Library often has special exhibitions of puppets, story theaters, and memorabilia appealing to children. Free recitals take place in the Bruno Walter Auditorium.

The research collection is superb. Included in the dance collection, for example, along with some 40,000 volumes are 200,000 clippings, 2000 original stage and costume designs, and 92,000 theater programs. There are cylinders of Metropolitan Opera performances dating back to the turn of the century, recorded broadcasts of the American musical theater from the Railroad Hour radio show, Kirsten Flagstad's private tape collection, and the Rodgers and Hammerstein Archives of Recorded Sound, with over 450,000 tapes, disks, cylinders, phonograph records, and videotapes.

The Juilliard School, founded in 1905 as the Institute of Musical Arts by Frank Damrosch and James Loeb and endowed in 1920 through a bequest from merchant and philanthropist Augustus D. Juilliard, lies on the N. side of W. 65th St. Of all the buildings in the center the Juilliard School (1969; Pietro Belluschi) is the most complex, housing ALICE TULLY HALL, home of the Chamber Music Society of Lincoln Center, and the school itself, which offers professional training for performance in music, dance, and drama. Facilities of the school include the JUILLIARD THEATER (seats 1026), with a moveable ceiling which can be raised or lowered to vary the reverberation time to suit spoken drama, instrumental, or vocal music, as well as a small recital hall (seats 278), a drama workshop theater (seats 206), 82 soundproof practice rooms, three organ studios, 200 pianos, 35 teaching studios, and 16 two-story studios for dance, drama, or orchestral rehearsals.

Outside the building on the terrace facing Broadway stands a work of three tall zig-zag columns of polished stainless steel entitled *Three by Three Interplay* (1971; Yaacov Agam). In the foyer of Alice Tully Hall is Antoine Bourdelle's bronze *Beethoven à la Colonne* (1901). Louise Nevelson's wood construction, *Night-sphere-Light* (1969) covers the W. wall of the Juilliard Theater lobby; an untitled abstraction of black Swedish granite by Masayuki Nagare stands on the landing of the main staircase in the 65th St lobby.

Just W. of Lincoln Center, between 64th and 65th Sts on Amsterdam Ave, is the Fiorello H. La Guardia High School for Music and the Arts (1984), a public high school open to talented city students by examination and audition. Among its graduates are Susan Strasberg, Al Pacino, and Murray Perahia.

A block uptown at 122 Amsterdam Ave (bet. W. 65th / W. 66th Sts) is MARTIN LUTHER KING, JR., HIGH SCHOOL (1975; Frost Assocs.). The memorial sculpture, by William Tarr, constructed of self-weathering steel, resembles a huge printer's block, with letters and numbers suggesting milestones in the career of the slain civil rights leader. Before the tenements of the Lincoln Square Urban Renewal Area were razed in the 1950s, Hollywood temporarily used the shabby streets for the set of its movie *West Side Story*. Return to Broadway.

The S. triangle created by the intersection of Broadway and Columbus Ave (at 63rd St) has been designated Dante Park and contains a *bronze statue of Dante Alighieri* (1921; Ettore Ximenes), erected to commemorate the 600th anniversary of the poet's death. The family of tenor Richard Tucker placed a bronze bust of him in the N. triangle near 66th St not long after his untimely death in 1975. Tucker, who appeared in 499 performances in 21 seasons with the Met was, as a native New Yorker, one of the company's most popular singers.

On the E. side of Broadway between W. 65th and W. 66th Sts at Two Lincoln Square, is the *Church of Christ of Latter-Day Saints and the Mormon Visitors' Center* (1975; Schuman, Lichtenstein & Claman). Within is a permanent exhibition introducing Mormonism (10–8 daily, free).

The **Museum of American Folk Art** occupies the courtyard, the result of a negotiated settlement between the city and the building owners, who originally constructed a barren, unusable mall. The museum will remain here while building a new permanent home on W. 53rd Street and thereafter use the Lincoln Square space as a satellite.

Museum of American Folk Art. Two Lincoln Square (Columbus Ave and 66th St), New York 10023. Tel: 977-7298. Open seven days a week from 9 A.M. to 9 P.M. Free.

Restrooms. Gift shop with books, catalogues, toys, handmade objects and crafts, reproductions, postcards. No telephone. No restaurant. Accessible to wheelchairs. Special exhibits in braille, large print gallery guides and labeling. Changing exhibitions, lectures, educational programs, craft demonstrations, performances by folk musicians, storytellers.

SUBWAY: IRT Broadway-7th Ave local (train 1 or 9) to 66th or 72nd St; IRT Broadway-7th Ave express (train 2 or 3) to 72nd St. IND 8th Ave local (C train) to 72nd St; IND 6th Ave express (B train) to 72nd St. BUS: M5 or M7 uptown via 6th Ave / Broadway. M10 uptown via 8th Ave / Central Park West, downtown via Central Park West / Broadway / 7th Ave. M104 uptown via Broadway. M66 crosstown on 66th / 67th Sts. M30 crosstown on 72nd St.

Founded in 1961, the Museum of American Folk Art is one of the nation's leading centers of folk art scholarship. Its collections, which span the mid-18C to the present, contain works that reflect the museum's broad conception of folk art. Along with portraiture and needlework are carved animals, decoys, trade signs, cigar store Indians, and statues of both utilitarian and purely decorative intent. Among the textiles are beautiful quilts, samplers, braided rugs, and Navajo blankets. Among the most famous objects are a 19C gate of painted wood, whose wavy horizontal slats form the red stripes of the American flag; a 9-ft copper weathervane in the form of an Indian, known as St. Tammany; and Ammi Phillips's *Girl in Red Dress with Cat and Dog,* all three considered outstanding examples of their type.

In its handsome new exhibition space, the museum will present four major exhibitions yearly, with objects from the permanent collection on display at all times.

The American Broadcasting Company occupies most of W. 66th St between Central Park West and Columbus Ave. The earliest building of the complex (56 W. 66th St) was originally the First Battery Armory of the N.Y. National Guard (1901; Horgan & Slattery). The newest, *Capital Cities / ABC Incorporated* headquarters (1988; Kohn Pedersen Fox Assocs.), at 55 W. 66th St, looms ponderously over the block.

Other points of interest. Around the turn of the century the West Side saw the simultaneous arrival of the subway and a number of large, ornate apartment buildings, which reflected a general change in the nature of domestic living.

The Dorilton (1902; Janes & Leo; DL) at the N.E. corner of Broadway and 71st St was the first. Its high stone arch, swelling mansard roof, and copious decoration—called importune by some, incendiary or voluptuous by others—all announced the building as a major social presence.

The triangle created by the intersection of Broadway and Amsterdam Ave at 72nd St is *Sherman Square,* named after Gen. William Tecumseh Sherman (see p. 361). While no remembrance of Sherman marks the traffic island, there is a *subway kiosk* (1904; Heins & La Farge; DL) dating back to the original opening of the IRT, a little neo-Dutch colonial structure with limestone quoins and a Dutch gable, no doubt intended to recall the founding of the city by the Dutch. Once three such "control houses," so-called because riders entering them passed into territory "controlled" by the IRT, stood along Broadway, but the other two at 103rd and 116th Sts have not survived.

The **Ansonia Hotel** (1904; Graves & Duboy; DL) at 2107 Broadway (bet. 73rd / 74th Sts) is another grand old dowager among West Side apartment houses, not a hotel of the usual sort. Although apartments had been built in the city toward the close of the 19C, people of means regarded multiple dwellings as the natural preserve of the working class and shunned close proximity to their neighbors and to their live-in servants who could no longer be relegated to the attic or basement. Apartment hotels, like the Ansonia, however, offered suites and single rooms either furnished or not, and their services included restaurants and full domestic staffs so that live-in servants were less necessary. Onetime New York home of Caruso, Toscanini, Ziegfeld, Stravinsky, Pinza, and Pons, the Ansonia still draws a musical clientele. Imperiously facing down Broadway from its commanding site at a bend in the avenue, the Ansonia delights the eye with its copious Beaux-Arts decoration, rounded corner towers, and high mansard roof. The developer, William Earl Dodge Stokes, named the hotel for his grandfather, Anson G. Phelps, founder of the Ansonia Brass & Copper Co., in Ansonia, Connecticut. Stokes kept ducks, chickens, and a pet bear on the roof.

The triangle N. of 72nd St is known as **Verdi Square** (DL), appropriately named in a neighborhood that attracted musicians long before Lincoln Center was established nearby. The *Verdi Monument* (1906; Pasquale Civiletti) depicts the composer in Carrara marble on a granite pedestal against which stand life-size figures of Aida, Otello, Falstaff, and Leonora (heroine of *La Forza del Destino*).

At 2100 Broadway (N.E. corner of W. 73rd St) is the *Central Savings Bank* (1926–28; York & Sawyer; DL), founded as the German Savings Bank in 1859 but renamed in a period of anti-German feeling during World War I. York & Sawyer along with Samuel Yellin, responsible for the decorative ironwork, also designed the Federal Reserve Bank in the Financial District.

Several other major apartment buildings from the turn of the century, similar in scale and style to the Ansonia adorn the neighborhood. The HOTEL BELLECLAIRE (1903; Stein, Cohen & Roth; DL) at Broadway and 77th St, is an early work of Emery Roth (see p. 513), better known for his work on Central Park West. It provided cafes, dining rooms in Moorish and Louis XV styles, a library, and a telegraph office. Russian author Maxim Gorky was put up here during his visit in 1906 by American socialist millionaire Gaylord Wilshire.

The **Apthorp** (1906–08; Clinton & Russell; DL) at Broadway and 79th St, proclaimed the largest in the world upon completion, was developed by the Astor family, whose real estate holdings formed the basis of their fortune. The *Belnord* (1908–09; H. Hobart Weekes; DL) at Broadway and 86th St also advertised itself as the world's largest. Both are built around central courtyards.

SUBWAY: IRT Broadway-7th Ave local (train 1 or 9) at 79th St or 86th St. IND 8th Ave local or 6th Ave local (C or B train) at Central Park West and 72nd St, 81st St, or 86th St.

BUS: Uptown and downtown buses, the same as those serving Lincoln Center. M30 crosstown on 72nd St.

28   Columbus Circle to the American Museum of Natural History

SUBWAY: IRT Broadway-7th Ave express or local (train 1, 2, 3, or 9) to 59th St-Columbus Circle. IND 8th Ave express or local (A or C train) to 59th St-Columbus Circle; IND 6th Ave express (D train) to 59th St-Columbus Circle.

BUS: M5 or M7 uptown via 6th Ave; M104 or M10 uptown via 8th Ave; M103 crosstown on 59th St or M28 crosstown on 57th St.

At 59th St, Eighth Ave becomes Central Park West, renamed after the opening of the park in 1876 to boost land values. The ploy, or more likely the presence of Central Park, succeeded, for the street is now an elegant boulevard whose venerable institutions and stately apartment buildings serve the cultural and spiritual needs of many New Yorkers as well as the domestic needs of a select few. The older buildings date back to the last decade of the 19C, after the arrival of the Ninth Ave elevated railroad in 1879 made the Upper West Side accessible to the middle class. The newer ones, with a few exceptions, date from before 1931, rather remarkable considering the city's penchant for tearing down and building up. Among the newer buildings facing the park are several splendid examples of Art Deco apartment architecture; among the older ones are some fine masonry buildings, and along the side streets are long blocks of brownstone row houses dating to the late 19C, many with imposing stone stoops and exuberant ornamentation. The survival of this architectural stand of virgin forest has prompted local concern for historic preservation of the district.

Begin at **Columbus Circle,** where W. 59th St, Broadway, and Eighth Ave merge in a snarl of traffic. Atop a 77-ft granite column decorated with ships' prows stands a *statue of Christopher Columbus* (1892; Gaetano Russo), given by the Italian-American community to commemorate the quadricentennial of Columbus's discovery. At the base of the column a winged boy peruses a globe, while two bronze tablets depict the explorer's departure from Spain and his arrival in the New World.

Visible just inside the park is the *Maine Memorial,* which commemorates the sinking of the U.S. battleship *Maine* (February 15, 1898), an incident that helped trigger the Spanish-American War. The memorial (1913; statuary by Attilio Piccirilli) consists of a granite stele (43.5 ft) with bronze and marble sculptures. On the top 15-ft Columbia Triumphant stands in a shell pulled by three hippocampi. At the base facing Broadway a boatload of marble figures includes Victory (a youth kneeling in the prow), accompanied by Courage (a male nude), and Fortitude (a mother comforting a weeping child). Behind them stands a robed figure representing Peace. Another group, facing the park, includes Justice, History, and a Warrior whose upraised hand once clenched a bronze sword. The reclining youth looking down-

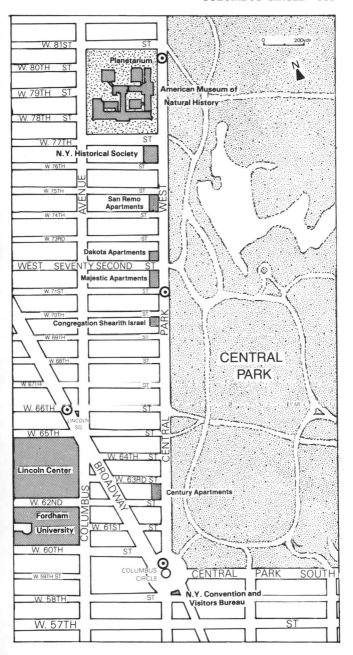

town represents the Atlantic, while the Pacific, facing uptown, appears as an aged man.

The Coliseum on the W. side of the intersection and the Gulf & Western Building on the triangle N. of the circle are discussed in Rte 28.

Look downtown to the headquarters of the NEW YORK CITY DEPARTMENT OF CULTURAL AFFAIRS (1965; Edward Durell Stone) at 2 Columbus Circle, housed in a white marble box on stilts pierced with rows of round holes and tall open arches. The building, whose vaguely Islamic appearance formerly elicited jokes about Persian brothels, was built by A & P supermarkets heir Huntington Hartford to house his collection; when that didn't work out, the building became the New York Cultural Center with exhibitions, concerts, and lectures. When that in turn failed, the owners, the Gulf & Western Co., gave it to the city for its present use.

On the ground floor is the **Visitors Information Center** of the New York Convention & Visitors Bureau, open Mon–Fri 9–6; Sat–Sun 10–6; tel: 397-8222. The Bureau lists hotels, restaurants, major attractions, and stores, and offers information about transportation and sightseeing.
    On the second floor the *City Gallery* (open Mon–Fri 10–5:30; free; tel: 974-1150) offers exhibitions focusing on the city and its artists.

Begin walking N. up Central Park West, preferably on the park side for the best view of the buildings. The **Century Apartments** (1931; Jacques Delamarre and the Irwin S. Chanin Construction Co.; DL) at 25 Central Park West (bet. 62nd / 63rd Sts) is a handsome Art Deco building, with machinelike trim at the top, six rows of bay windows across the front, and cantilevered terraces at the base of the twin towers. The building is named after the Century Theater, a grandiose neoclassical fiasco (1909; Carrère & Hastings), planned as a national theater which would be untainted by commerce. Unfortunately it was too large and too far uptown to make a profit, even when Florenz Ziegfeld staged spectaculars there.

The *West Side Y.M.C.A.* at 5 W. 63rd St is housed in a massive building (1930; Dwight James Baum), within whose somber brick walls are swimming pools, handball and squash courts, and an indoor track. At 10 W. 64th St is the Frederick Henry Cossett Dormitory, offering rooms by the day and week. A plan evolved in 1966 to create a landscaped mall between Central Park and Lincoln Center to the W., which would have destroyed this and all its neighbors.

Filling the block front between W. 63rd and W. 64th Sts are two buildings of the ETHICAL CULTURE SOCIETY, founded in 1876 by Felix Adler to further morality independently of organized religion. The Ethical Culture school system began with the city's first free kindergarten (1878) and continued to educate working men and women as well as conventional students, early establishing itself as a force in experimental education and a pioneer in the use of education as a social tool. Today the society operates the Fieldston Schools in the Bronx as well as the Ethical Culture School here, all known for their progressive outlook. The more northerly of the two buildings at 2 W. 64th St (1910; Robert D. Kohn with Estelle Rumbold Kohn, sculptor; DL) is a formal limestone Art Nouveau structure, much admired at the time of completion.

Standing boldly atop the *Liberty Warehouse* (1891?) at 43 W. 64th St, between Central Park West and Broadway, her arm proudly upraised, is a 55-ft replica of the larger, more famous, more dramatically sited Statue of Liberty in the harbor. Based on one of the intermediate scale models sculptor Frédéric Auguste Bartholdi made for visualizing his completed statue, the figure was commissioned by warehouse owner William H. Flattau and cast in a foundry in Akron, Ohio. It was shipped to New York by rail on a flatbed car, sliced in half lengthwise because it was too large to fit through the railroad tunnels, and then welded together again. Inside is a circular staircase, sealed by Flattau in 1912 because visitors were distracting his workers; outside is green paint, not verdigris.

The *Prasada Apartments* at 50 Central Park West on the S.W. corner of W. 65th St (1907; Charles W. Romeyn & Henry R. Wynne) feature a monumental entrance.

Holy Trinity Lutheran Church on the N.W. corner of W. 65th St dates from 1903. The apartment house at 55 CENTRAL PARK WEST (1940; Schwartz & Gross), another Art Deco–inspired building, has a splendid ironwork canopy over the entrance and brickwork which shades from red at the bottom to tan at the top, to give the impression, critics have said, of a ray of sunshine perpetually shining on the facade.

Walk down W. 66th St as far as No. 56, once the *First Battery Armory of the New York National Guard* (1901; Horgan & Slattery), now altered (1978) into television studios for the American Broadcasting Company. Across the street at 71 W. 66th St is another fanciful facade, originally the street side of the St. Nicholas Skating Rink (1896; Ernest Flagg and Walter B. Chambers), and later altered into an arena. Nowadays ABC uses it for broadcast engineering operations. The most recent addition, *Capital Cities / ABC Incorporated* headquarters (1988; Kohn Pedersen Fox Assocs.), 55 W. 66th St, looms ponderously over the block.

Return to Central Park West and continue north. West 67th St is a charming anomaly, its housing consisting not of the usual brownstones but of studio buildings constructed expressly for the needs of working artists. The earliest such building here is *27 W. 67th St* (1905), erected by ten artists who occupied half and rented out the rest, thereby realizing a 23% profit on their investment. Most famous of the studio buildings is the HOTEL DES ARTISTES (1915; George Mort Pollard) at 1 W. 67th St, just off the park, with large two-story windows opening into the studios, and fanciful neo-Gothic statuary above the second story. Among its famous and / or artistic tenants have been Noel Coward, Isadora Duncan, Norman Rockwell, former mayor John V. Lindsay, and Howard Chandler Christy, whose murals still adorn the ground floor Café des Artistes.

Return to Central Park West and keep walking uptown. At 68th

St turn left and continue to 40 W. 68th St, originally the Free Synagogue (1923; S. B. Eisendrath and B. Horowitz) and now the HEBREW UNION COLLEGE-JEWISH INSTITUTE OF RELIGION, a rabbinical training school. Under the leadership of its founder, Stephen Wise, civic reformer and ardent Zionist, the Free Synagogue became a forum for both public and religious issues. In addition to founding the synagogue (1907), Rabbi Wise organized the first section of the Federation of American Zionists and headed the delegation of the American Jewish Congress at the Paris Peace Conference following World War I. The present *Stephen S. Wise Synagogue* at 30 W. 68th St just E. of the original building was added in 1941 (Bloch & Hesse).

At the S.W. corner of W. 70th St (99 Central Park West) is the newest home (1897; Brunner & Tryon; DL) of **Congregation Shearith Israel**, the nation's oldest Jewish congregation, which dates back to 1654 when the first Jewish refugees arrived in New Amsterdam fleeing the Inquisition (see p. 112). Under Dutch rule the Jews had to worship in secret, but later, in 1682, under a more tolerant British governor, they founded Congregation Shearith Israel (Remnant of Israel) and held organized services, first in a rented room on Beaver St, then in the upper story of a flour mill on Mill Lane and South William St. The first synagogue building (1730) at what is presently 26 S. William St is gone but some of its artifacts and two large millstones from the Dutch mill are preserved in the Little Synagogue here (open during services, Fri evening and Sat morning; tel: 873-0300 for times), which reconstructs the original sanctuary. Congregation Shearith Israel maintains the three graveyards that mark its progress uptown (see index).

Turn W. into W. 71st St, whose BROWNSTONE ROW HOUSES, some of them a little seedy, hark back to a gentler era.

"Brownstone" is a Triassic sandstone whose characteristic chocolate color comes from the presence of iron ore. A "brownstone," in the local dialect, is a one-family row house faced with this material, usually dating from the late 19C, usually four or five stories high and two or three windows wide, featuring a tall stoop and a cornice at the top. Most brownstones were built by masons or builders, but the one at 20 W. 71st St, the best-preserved house on the block, enjoyed the talents of an architect (1889; Gilbert A. Schellenger), who designed a row of four houses here for the builders. Most brownstones were built in such small groups, and their widths became fractions of the standard city building lot (25 × 100 ft). The most spacious are 25 ft wide, while smaller varieties are 20 ft (a fifth of four lots), 18¾ ft (a quarter of three lots) or 16⅔ ft (a third of two lots). Because these houses were built for prosperous middle class families, the interiors were executed in fine materials and the facades often elaborately decorated; note for example the cupids at the cornice of No. 24, the cartouches on Nos. 26, 28, and 30, and the lions' heads on Nos. 33–39.

Continue N. on Central Park West past the MAJESTIC APARTMENTS (115 Central Park West, bet. 71st / 72nd Sts), the second of four double-towered buildings that give the skyline along the park its distinction. Stylistically related to the Century Apartments nine blocks downtown, the Majestic was also built (1930; Jacques Delamarre; DL) by the Irwin S. Chanin Co. René Chambellan, better known for the fountains at Radio City, designed the brickwork patterns. Corner windows were frequently used in Art Deco buildings, whose steel cage construction allowed corners to be opened up (unlike masonry construction where corners were load-bearing).

Across the street at 1 W. 72nd St are the **Dakota Apartments** (1884; Henry J. Hardenbergh; DL), architecturally one of the city's finest apartment buildings and socially the preeminent West Side address.

History. In 1884 apartments were just beginning to find favor with the well-to-do. Rutherfurd Stuyvesant had (1869) remodeled some houses on E. 18th St near Irving Place as "French flats," and quickly rented them all. Alert to potential profits, other builders followed, so when Singer Sewing Machine heir Edward S. Clark undertook a magnificent apartment house on W. 72nd St, he was not acting without precedent. His choice of location, however, was daring—uptown, surrounded by shanties and vacant land, so far N. and W. of civilization that detractors called it "Clark's Folly," one of them remarking that the building might as well be in the Dakota territory. Clark liked the notion and instructed his architect to garnish the building with ears of corn, arrowheads, and a bas relief of an Indian's head above the main gateway.

From the beginning the Dakota has been a luxury building, its apartments originally fitted out with carved marble mantles, oak and mahogany paneling, inlaid marble floors, and hardware of solid brass. On the eighth and ninth floors, undesirable in the days before elevators, were rooms for servants, while the basement held boilers and generators to light the building, since the Edison Co. lines reached only as far as Spruce St. Not surprisingly the building has attracted a striking clientele, notably people involved in the arts. Among them have been Boris Karloff, Zachary Scott, Leonard Bernstein, Lauren Bacall, Roberta Flack, and scientist Michael Idvorsky Pupin. John Lennon, songwriter and member of the Beatles, was shot and killed in the courtyard by a deranged admirer on December 8, 1980. The Dakota also served as a suitably Gothic setting for the horror movie *Rosemary's Baby*.

Built around an open central courtyard, the Dakota is finished in buff-colored brick with terra-cotta and stone trim and embellished with balconies, oriel windows, ledges, turrets, towers, gables, chimneys, finials, and flagpoles. It is generally acknowledged to be the masterpiece of an architect outstanding for his sense of composition.

Henry Hardenbergh also built row houses and apartments on W. 73rd St behind the Dakota and further W. (15A-19 W. 73rd St, 41-65 W. 73rd St, and 101 and 103 W. 73rd St just beyond Columbus Ave), in what has been designated as a historic district.

Continue N. on Central Park West. At 145–146 Central Park West (bet. W. 74th / W. 75th Sts) is the third of the boulevard's twin towers, the SAN REMO APARTMENTS (1930; Emery Roth; DL), finished in neoclassical garb with cartouches over the entrances and finialed temples on top.

The firm of Emery Roth & Sons has built more than 100 glass and steel skyscrapers since World War II, but Emery Roth himself, who worked in New York between 1903 and the late 1930s, gave the city a series of masonry apartment buildings and hotels ornamented with neoclassical detail. He came to the U.S. in 1886 at the age of 13, and four years later began working as a draftsman on the Chicago World's Columbian Exposition. Like other conservative architects, he was deeply impressed by the dignity of the Beaux-Arts buildings that dominated the exhibition, a style later reflected in his own work.

The San Remo (built 1930). One of Central Park West's dramatically silhouetted twin-towered apartment houses, it was constructed after the arrival (1925) of the IND subway stimulated a building boom along the Park. (Landmarks Preservation Commission, New York City. Photographer: John B. Bayley)

The San Remo is named after a hotel of that name which stood here before the turn of the century.

Continue to W. 76TH STREET and turn left. The block between Central Park West and Columbus Ave has been designated a historic district because of its impressive row housing, built between 1889 and 1900. The earliest, Nos. 31–37 (George M. Walgrove), have neo-Grec trim and a then newly fashionable rockface finish; Nos. 8–10 were built by John H. Duncan (better known for Grant's Tomb) in a neo-Baroque style. Elsewhere on the block are neo-Italian Renaissance, Romanesque Revival, and neo-Gothic facades.

Parallel to Central Park West and a block W. is **Columbus Avenue**, which in recent years has taken on some of the style of the Upper East Side. The blocks between about 67th St and 86th St have designer children's clothing, art galleries, upscale ice cream, bed linens, and tableware. There is also a run of attractive cafes, restaurants, and bars that cater to a mostly young, affluent clientele.

Return to Central Park West. Facing the park on the S.W. corner of W. 76th St is the *Universalist Church of New York* (1898; William A. Potter), formerly the Church of the Divine Paternity, and originally the Fourth Universalist Society. Andrew Carnegie worshipped here.

A block further uptown is the ***New-York Historical Society**

(1908; York & Sawyer; N. and S. wings, 1938; Walker & Gillette; DL), a paragon of neoclassical severity, faced in hard gray granite and barely ornamented.

The New-York Historical Society. 170 Central Park West (bet. 76th / 77th Sts), New York 10024. Tel: 873-3400. Open Tues–Sun 10–5; closed Mon, national holidays. Admission charge.
   Exhibitions, lectures, concerts. Group visits by appointment. No restaurant. Restrooms, telephones, gift shop. Accessible to wheelchairs but inquire about facilities at Admissions Desk or by calling.
   SUBWAY: IND 8th Ave local (C train) to 81st St. IRT Broadway-7th Ave local (train 1 or 9) to 79th St. BUS: M7 uptown via 6th Ave / Amsterdam Ave; downtown via Columbus Ave / 7th Ave. M10 via 8th Ave / Central Park West. M11 uptown via 9th Ave / Columbus Ave, downtown via Amsterdam Ave / 10th Ave. M18 crosstown on 86th St. M104 via Broadway.

Founded in 1804, the New-York Historical Society, which retains the old hyphenated spelling of the city's name, preserves and documents the history of the city, state, and nation. It maintains within the building a major research library and a museum whose interesting permanent collections are augmented by an ambitious schedule of changing exhibits.

On the FIRST FLOOR is an outstanding collection of *American silver with pieces from the Colonial through the Victorian periods. Among the ornate pieces of Tiffany silver from the mid- to late-19C is the throttle handle from the first New York subway. In the Rotunda is a collection of sculpture, including Antoine Houdon's portrait busts of George Washington, Benjamin Franklin, and Thomas Jefferson.

The Neustadt Collection of *Tiffany lamps and stained glass on the SECOND FLOOR is the most comprehensive group of Tiffany lamps and windows ever assembled. In the Hall is a rotating exhibit of *watercolors by John James Audubon, painted for his monumental series, *Birds of America.*

On the THIRD FLOOR in the East Hall is the *Toy Treasury*, a collection of some 150 toys dating from the early 19C to the early 20C. Along with the dolls, teddy bears, and miniature furniture are cast-iron banks and enviable model fire engines.

The FOURTH FLOOR galleries contain American portraits and landscapes. The *East Gallery* offers likenesses of founding fathers and prominent men and women of the Federal period, as well as elegant examples of American period furniture. Featured here is Thomas Cole's five-part allegory, *The Course of Empire,* which chronicles the rise and fall of a mythical civilization. The *Hudson River School Gallery* includes landscapes by Cole, as well as work by John Frederick Kensett, Asher B. Durand, Jasper Cropsey, and Albert Bierstadt. Nearby is the *Genre Gallery*, whose assorted paintings and sculptures include scenes of American life by William Sidney Mount, Albert Bierstadt, and Francis William Edmonds, as well as sculpture by John Rogers and Augustus Saint-Gaudens. The *Portrait Gallery* in the East Hall spans the mid-18C to the late 19C and reflects changing styles of American portraiture. Highlights of this display include John Durand's *Beekman Children,* and a Colonial portrait of *Edward Hyde,* a governor of New York who dressed in women's attire.

In the next block is another of New York's best-loved museums, The ***American Museum of Natural History**, with the **Hayden Planetarium**.

The American Museum of Natural History/The Hayden Planetarium. Central Park West at 79th Street, New York 10024. Tel: 769-5600. For recorded information, call 769-5100. Open Sun, Mon, Tues, Thurs 10–5:45; Wed, Fri, Sat 10 A.M.–9 P.M. Closed Thanksgiving and Christmas Day. Admission to museum by contribution (pay what you wish, but you must pay something). Free 5–9 on Fri and Sat. Fixed admission charge at the planetarium serves as entrance to museum also. For planetarium hours and information, see p. 518. Special exhibitions, guided tours, lectures, films, concerts, educational programs, symposia. Cafeteria (no bag lunches) and restaurant. Restrooms. Telephones. Gift shop, children's shop.

SUBWAY: IRT Broadway-7th Ave local (train 1 or 9) to 79th St. IND 6th Ave express (B train, rush hours only), 8th Ave local (C train) to 81st St. BUS: M7 and M11 uptown via Amsterdam Ave, downtown via Columbus Ave. M10 via Central Park West. M104 via Broadway. M17 crosstown on 79th St.

The American Museum of Natural History, along with the Hayden Planetarium, should delight anyone interested in the natural sciences from anthropology to zoology. The collection contains some 36 million specimens (not all, fortunately, on display) ranging from the world-famous dioramas of animal habitat groups and the dinosaur exhibits to the world's largest cut gem.

The Building. The museum occupies the equivalent of four city blocks (W. 77th–W. 81st Sts bet. Central Park West / Columbus Ave), an area formerly called Manhattan Square and intended by the designers of Central Park as a park annex. The first museum building (1877) is now almost walled in by the wings and additions that have made the present museum an architectural hodge-podge of some 22 buildings.

First wing and general plan, 1872-77; Calvert Vaux and Jacob Wrey Mould. W. 77th St wings, 1892-98; J. Cleveland Cady & Co. and 1899; Cady, Berg & See. Columbus Ave wing and powerhouse, 1908; Charles Volz. Additions, 1924, 1926, 1933; Trowbridge & Livingston. Theodore Roosevelt Memorial facing Central Park West, 1936; John Russell Pope; DL.

The oldest visible part of the facade (1892; J. Cleveland Cady & Co.; DL) facing W. 77th St is also the most attractive. This wing (60 × 110 ft), Romanesque in style, faced with pink granite from New Brunswick, has two round towers, a seven-arched arcade, and a central granite stairway that once swept up over the carriage entrance. The facade facing Central Park West (1922; Trowbridge & Livingston) is faced with smooth blocks of the same granite. The central portion is the Theodore Roosevelt Memorial, its heroic arch framing a 16-ft group showing *Theodore Roosevelt* (1940; James Earle Fraser), the 26th President, as an explorer; the flanking guides symbolize Africa and America.

Enter from Central Park West. The barrel-vaulted lobby (second floor) of the Roosevelt Memorial, known as the Rotunda, is finished in English Renfrew marble (short end walls) containing fossils of colonial animals related to sponges. The long side walls

MUSEUM OF NATURAL HISTORY
Lower Level

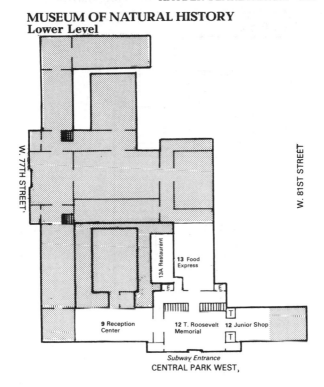

are Portenelle marble, a Portuguese limestone, with fossils of oyster-like bivalves. The murals depict scenes from Roosevelt's life.

First Floor (down a flight): Hall 12, the Theodore Roosevelt Memorial, reflects the interests and background of this ardent naturalist, explorer, and conservationist. One diorama shows how the southern tip of Manhattan may have looked in about 1660 (Roosevelt's ancestors were early Dutch settlers).

Hall 19, BIOLOGY OF BIRDS, an older exhibit, with dioramas, skeletons of giant flightless birds, living and fossil, and hundreds of mounted specimens which illustrate the major families of birds.

The **Hayden Planetarium** (Hall 18), named after investment banker Charles Hayden who donated the original equipment, is actually located in a separate building (1935; Trowbridge & Livingston) on the N.E. of the museum complex, but may be reached from the first-floor corridor as well as from the street. Its focal point is the *Sky Theater* (capacity 660), where a Zeiss Model VI planetarium projector aided by a computer-automated control system creates dazzling celestial effects.

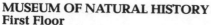

MUSEUM OF NATURAL HISTORY
First Floor

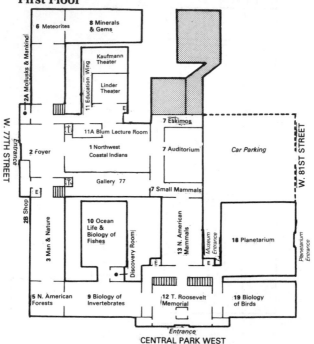

Sky Shows, changed about four times yearly, are scheduled twice each after-noon (1:30 and 3:30) on weekdays and hourly from 1 to 5 on weekends; Sat morning shows at 11 from Oct–June. The planetarium is closed Thanksgiving and Christmas and several other days during the year for installation of new shows. Admission charge. On Fri and Sat evenings the Laserium, a light show with rock music, beams up at 6:30, 9, and 10:30; box office opens at 6:00; tickets in advance through Ticketron; for Laserium information call 769-5921. Planetarium shop with T-shirts, posters, cards, toys, books, souvenirs, tele-scopes. For planetarium information call 769-5920.

On the first floor are the GUGGENHEIM SPACE THEATER, with 22 screens for panoramic slide shows and the Copernican orrery (a moving model of the solar system). On the second floor are the HALL OF THE SUN and "Astronomia," an eclectic display of astronomical fact and fiction.

Return to the Museum of Natural History. In Hall 13, *NORTH AMERICAN MAMMALS, beautiful dioramas show major species in their native habitats.
  Hall 9, BIOLOGY OF INVERTEBRATES, which includes a model of a giant squid (39 ft) and hand-blown glass models of microscopic organisms, anemones, and jellyfish leads to Hall 10, OCEAN LIFE AND THE BIOLOGY OF FISHES.

The *Discovery Room* near the entrance (open Sat–Sun 12–4:30 except holidays) accommodates 25 children (with accompanying adults) who may experiment with scientific entertainments (admission by ticket, free at the first-floor information desk).

The centerpiece of dimly lit HALL 10 is a 94-ft *model of a blue whale. Displays on the upper-level gallery focus on the biology and classification of fish (fossil fish, jawless and jawed fish, cartilaginous and bony fish). The lower level has dioramas of fish and marine mammals.

In the entrance corridor to Hall 5, NORTH AMERICAN FORESTS, is a display, 24 times larger than life, of creatures of the forest floor, with gigantic earthworms and other specimens. Dioramas reproduce the primary North American forest environments.

Between this hall and Hall 3, MAN AND NATURE, is a cross-section of a Giant Sequoia (harvested 1891), 16 ft 5 inches in diameter, cut from a tree that weighed 6000 tons. Displays in Hall 3 focus on soil use, the water cycle, glaciation, and the relation of plants to soil, and the geological history of New York State.

In the 77th St foyer, a Chilkat Indian chief and his followers paddle a 64½-ft seagoing war canoe on a ceremonial visit. Across from the gift shop is the entrance to the **Nature Max Theater,** whose four-story screen is the largest in the city (call 769-5650 for schedule; admission charge).

To its left is the HALL OF NORTHWEST COAST INDIANS (Hall 1), with artifacts of Indian tribes living from S.E. Alaska to northern California but forming a single cultural group.

Return to the Foyer. Hall 2A, MOLLUSKS AND MANKIND, is devoted to the biology (life cycles, anatomy, formation of pearls) and human uses of mollusks (shells for collectors, as objects of spiritual power, status, or wealth).

GALLERY 1 is used for changing exhibits.

The centerpiece of Hall 6, *METEORITES, is Ahnighito (the Eskimo name means "the Tent"), the largest piece of the Cape York meteorite discovered in 1897 and brought back from northern Greenland by Robert Peery. In front of the photo montage of the back side of the moon stands a case containing three *moon rocks, representing the three major lunar types.

In Hall 8, the *HARRY FRANK GUGGENHEIM HALL OF MINERALS and the MORGAN MEMORIAL HALL OF GEMS (opened in 1976), directly beyond the Hall of Meteorites, some 6000 of the museum's 120,000 specimens of minerals are handsomely displayed. Some are spectacularly large: a ½ ton copper block with malachite and azurite crystals, a giant topaz crystal (597 lbs or 1,330,040 carats). Others are merely beautiful. Near the entrance to the *J. P. MORGAN HALL OF GEMS stands a 4700-lb slab of nephrite (from Poland). In the hall itself are diamonds, star sapphires including the Star of India (563 carats, mined 300 years ago in Sri Lanka), and the Brazilian Princess Topaz (21,005 carats), the world's largest cut gem.

Older visitors may remember the jewel robbery (1964), in which three Florida beachboys, one picturesquely named Murph the Surf, stole the Star of India

MUSEUM OF NATURAL HISTORY
Second Floor

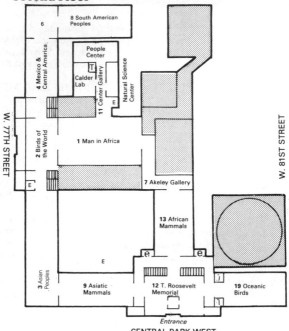

sapphire, the DeLong Star ruby, and other gems. Eventually, however, the thieves were apprehended and 85–90% of the jewels, in terms of cash value, were recovered. Naturally the security of the room has been strengthened and it is now considered impregnable.

Second Floor. Dioramas in Hall 19, the WHITNEY HALL OF OCEANIC BIRDS, display birds of the Pacific in a latitudinal sequence from Antarctica northward.

Hall 13, the *AKELEY MEMORIAL HALL OF AFRICAN MAMMALS, is known for its beautiful and dramatic dioramas including habitat groups of gorillas, lions, giraffes, and zebras. As with all dioramas in the museum, settings are accurately recreated from photographs and sketches made on the site and vegetation is carefully simulated: a blackberry bush in the gorilla diorama has 75,000 artificial leaves and flowers, which took eight months to make and cost $2000 (in the 1930s). Special efforts have been made to present the animals in characteristic actions: hyenas and vultures devouring a dead zebra, giraffes browsing, wild dogs hunting in a pack. (The second floor of the gallery is reached from the third-floor corridor.)

Hall 9, ASIATIC MAMMALS, considered the best collection of such mammals in the world, includes Indian elephants (center of room) and dioramas with habitat groups of tigers, wild boars, Sumatran and Indian rhinoceroses, and a particularly dramatic recreation of a sambar attacked by a pack of wild dogs.

The *GARDNER D. STOUT HALL OF ASIAN PEOPLES (Hall 3), documents traditional Asia using costumes, artifacts, paintings, and photographs. The display focuses on anthropological themes (the relationship of the individual to family and society, the unifying beliefs of a culture, and the adaptation of a society to its environment).

The first part of the hall is organized historically and includes prehistoric development, archaeology, and the rise of civilization. The rest of the hall is organized geographically. Exhibits focus on Korea, Japan, China, and Southeast Asia. The galleries devoted to India elucidate village life and include a fine diorama of an Indian village wedding, examples of crafts, theater masks and costumes, a display on Hinduism, polychromed wooden horses and musicians from a 19C temple, and wooden dancing figures (southern India, 17C).

Other sections are devoted to Islamic cultures, Armenia, the Arabian peninsula, Caucasian Georgia, and Samarkand. Included in a more extensive section on Siberia are carvings in wood, bone, and ivory, a diorama on Siberian shamanism, and artifacts of tribes who hunt, fish, and herd reindeer.

The religious aspect of the culture of Tibet appears in the collection of religious paintings and in ritual implements. Harnesses, animal bells, and similar objects demonstrate the importance of nomadic herding and trading, while a group of masks and hats and a pair of long curved trumpets (overhead) represent Tibetan monastery life.

Hall 2, BIRDS OF THE WORLD, contains a small fraction of the museum's 1 million bird specimens representing 98% of the known bird species.

Hall 1, MAN IN AFRICA, begins with two introductory rooms devoted to the origins of man and society in Africa and to river valley civilizations (the Nile, Niger, Zambesi, and Congo). The main part of the exhibition is organized environmentally, treating Grasslands, Forest-Woodland, and Desert cultures.

Hall 4, MEXICO AND CENTRAL AMERICA, uses archaeological finds (primarily pottery and stone carvings), replicas of large monuments still in Central America, and architectural scale models to document the pre-Columbian cultures of Meso-America. The rear of the room is devoted to Maya and Aztec cultures. Dominating the Aztec section is a full-size replica of an Aztec stone of the sun, sometimes mistakenly thought to be a calendar. Other objects include Toltec pottery, clay and stone sculpture from the Vera Cruz area, a tall terra-cotta figure (Toltec) of a man wearing the skin of a sacrificial victim, objects from the culture of Teotihuacan, and a large Olmec head (reproduction) found in the Gulf Coast region.

The newest exhibit hall, *SOUTH AMERICAN PEOPLES (1989) is divided into three sections. The introductory area offers archaeological materials from the period when people first arrived

MUSEUM OF NATURAL HISTORY
Third Floor

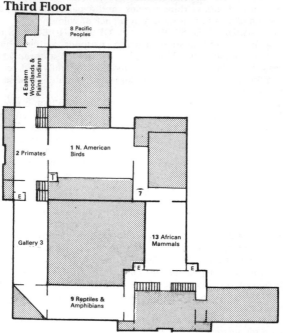

on the South American continent (c. 12,000 B.C.) up to about 2000 B.C. Here also are exhibitions on South American flora and fauna and the artifacts made from them. In the second section, Andean archaeology, are textiles and intricately worked gold ornaments found in a 2200 year old Peruvian mummy bundle, and the remarkably preserved body of the "Copper Man," a Chilean miner killed in a tunnel collapse about 1500 years ago. The final section, Amazonian ethnology, illustrates the culture of Indians of the Amazon rain forest. and artifacts. Films and photographs document blowgun hunting and tribal puberty rites.

Third Floor. Exhibits in Hall 9, REPTILES AND AMPHIBIANS (opened 1977), include mounted skins, wax-impregnated specimens, and models and plastic casts of specimens from the collection of the Department of Herpetology. Directly in front of the entrance is a giant Galapagos tortoise, which died some decades ago in the Bronx Zoo.

Gallery 3 is used for special exhibitions.

Hall 2, the HALL OF PRIMATES, uses taxidermic specimens and skeletons to explore the characteristics and relationships of different groups of primates. Beginning with the lowly tree shrew

MUSEUM OF NATURAL HISTORY
Fourth Floor

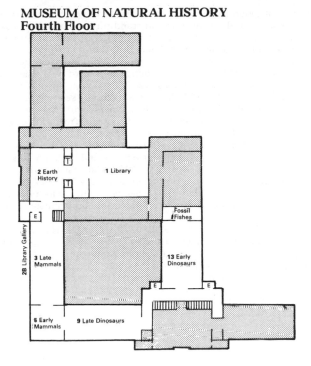

(near the restrooms) the exhibit leads up to the final case on man.

Hall 4 documents the EASTERN WOODLANDS AND PLAINS INDIANS of the U. S. and Canada, from prehistoric times to the early 20C. Among the exhibits on Eastern Woodlands Indians are displays of beautiful *costumes and imaginative, grotesque masks used in religious ceremonies. Behind this hall is the room devoted to the Plains Indians, nomadic or seminomadic tribes living W. of the Mississippi, including a diorama depicting the interior of a Blackfoot tepee.

The FRANK M. CHAPMAN MEMORIAL HALL OF NORTH AMERICAN BIRDS (Hall 1), completed in the late 1960s, is the first bird exhibit completely devoted to habitat groups: game birds, Canada geese, storks and limpkins, western marsh birds, golden and bald eagles, whooping cranes, the California condor, wild turkeys, and peregrine falcons.

A small corridor with birds and mammals of New York State leads to the upper level of the Akeley Memorial Hall of African Mammals (for a description, see Second Floor, Hall 13).

Fourth Floor. Hall 13, the *HALL OF EARLY DINOSAURS is a longstandng favorite with visitors. The museum has the world's finest collection of fossil bones, about 5% of which are currently on display. On the central island stand three magnificent fossilized skeletons from the Jurassic period (180–120 million years ago): a Brontosaurus (66 ft long, probable live weight 35–40 tons), a Stegosaurus, and an Allosaurus. At the rear of the room is the gallery of Fossil Fish, its entrance framed by a 9½-ft jaw of a prehistoric shark with fossil teeth.

Hall 9, *LATE DINOSAURS, contains fossil skeletons from the Cretaceous period (120–65 million years ago), the zenith of reptilian evolution. The central island contains Trachodonts (webfooted, duck-billed dinosaurs), a Triceratops, and a spectacular *Tyrannosaurus rex found (1902) in Montana. On the W. (right) wall are several nests of dinosaur eggs, found during a museum expedition to the Gobi Desert in 1923, the first ever found in association with the dinosaur laying them. The HALL OF EARLY FOSSIL MAMMALS (Hall 5) is organized to illustrate principles of vertebrate paleontology and early phases of mammalian differentiation.

In the HALL OF LATER FOSSIL MAMMALS (Hall 3) is the largest single block of fossil bones (5½ × 8 ft) on exhibition anywhere; they come from the famous Agate Springs (Nebraska) fossil quarries. Beyond it is the *Asphalt Group, with bones of extinct animals buried in the Rancho La Brea tar pits in Los Angeles. The display includes a sabre-toothed tiger mired in the pit and a wolf observing its trapped prey.

The HALL OF EARTH HISTORY (Hall 2) includes exhibits on the materials of the earth's crust and on the forces shaping it. Dioramas with specimens and models arranged in habitat groups illustrate marine environments from the Cambrian period to the end of the Cenozoic era. One end wall is devoted to the geology of oil fields, while other exhibits catalogue fossil invertebrates (coelenterates, arthropods, echinoderms, molluscs, sponges, etc.).

SUBWAY: IRT Broadway-7th Ave local (train 1 or 9) at 79th St and Broadway. IND 6th Ave (B train) at 81st St or IND 8th Ave local (C train) at 81st St.

BUS: M7 or M11 downtown via Columbus Ave or uptown via Amsterdam Ave. M10 downtown via Central Park West and 7th Ave. M17 crosstown on 79th St.

Other points of architectural interest on Central Park West. At 211 Central Park West (N.W. corner of 81st St) is the *Beresford* (1929; Emery Roth; DL), a massive pile from which rise three towers topped with vaguely Baroque crowns, another skyline landmark along the park. The *Eldorado* (1931; Margon & Holder; DL) between 91st and 92nd Sts at 300 Central Park West is the northernmost of the twin-towered apartment houses along the park. The *Ardsley* (1931; Emery Roth) at 320 Central Park West on the S.W. corner of 92nd St is admired by enthusiasts of Art Deco architecture for its elaborate brickwork and the terrazzo reliefs at street level. The *First Church of Christ, Scientist* (1903; Carrére & Hastings; DL) at 1 W. 96th St is a fine, Baroque-style church often said to recall the London churches of Nicholas Hawksmoor.

SUBWAY: The nearest subways are the IRT Broadway-7th Ave local (train 1 or 9) at 79th St, 86th St, or 96th St and Broadway; or IND 6th Ave (B train) and the IND 8th Ave local (C train) both of which stop at 81st St, 86th St, and 96th St on Central Park West.

BUS: M7 downtown via Columbus Ave or uptown via Amsterdam Ave. M10 downtown via Central Park West and 7th Ave. M11 uptown via Amsterdam or downtown via Columbus Ave.

29 Morningside Heights

SUBWAY: IRT Broadway-7th Ave local (train 1 or 9) to 110th St (Cathedral Parkway).

BUS: M4, M5, M11, M104 to 110th St (Cathedral Parkway).

Bounded by Cathedral Parkway (110th St) on the S. and the deep valley of 125th St on the N., **Morningside Heights** sits on the rocky ridge that runs the length of Manhattan. Harlem lies on low ground to the E., and on the W. the terrain slopes down to the Hudson. The area remained isolated, lacking adequate public transportation, until the 9th Ave El opened in 1880; in its pastoral serenity dwelt the owners of small farms and houses and the squires of country estates as well as the orphans of the Leake & Watts Asylum and the inmates of the Bloomingdale Insane Asylum. Riverside Drive opened in 1880, touted as a new Fifth Ave, a prophecy that never quite materialized, and Morningside Park, elegantly landscaped in the 19C but now dangerous and rundown, was planned in 1887. By the end of the century it seemed that the Heights would become a cultural, intellectual, and spiritual center of the city, as Columbia University, the Cathedral of St. John the Divine, and St. Luke's Hospital all moved there.

That promise has been partially fulfilled. Major institutions—not only Columbia but also Barnard College, Teachers College, St. John the Divine, St. Luke's, the Riverside Church, Union Theological Seminary, and the Jewish Theological Seminary—dominate the social and economic tone of the area. They boast beautiful and impressive buildings and own an estimated 70% of the property. But shabby neighborhoods and impoverished slums impinge on the Heights from three sides. The disparity between the wealth and power of the institutions and the poverty of the surrounding communities has in the past engendered antagonism, especially apparent during the 1960s, when the institutions, seeking to secure their frontiers and to expand, tried to encroach on nearby park areas and residential space. Although the tensions have eased, they are still evident in the locked churches and the visible security measures taken in many public buildings.

The ****Cathedral Church of St. John the Divine** (1892–1911; Heins & La Farge; continued 1911–42; Cram & Ferguson), cathedral of the Episcopal Diocese of New York, rises in uncompleted splendor on Amsterdam Ave at 112th St. The enormous stone arches erected to support the unbuilt dome and tower of

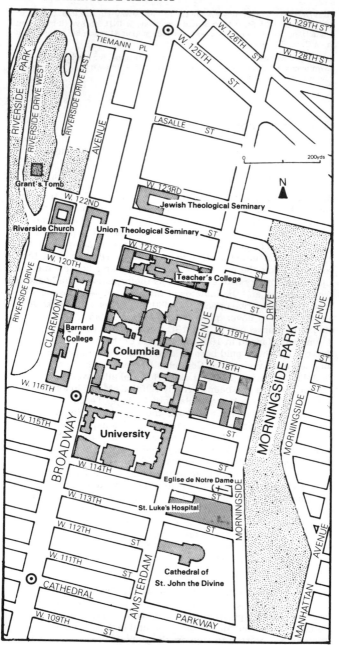

the crossing stand exposed to the eyes of the passerby who in all probability will never see another masonry cathedral in construction. Begun in 1892, the church is about ⅔ finished, and construction of the towers has started. It will cost an estimated $400 million to complete the entire cathedral, and even if all the money were miraculously to become instantly available, it would still take about 50 years to finish the work. Even in its unfinished state, however, St. John the Divine is the largest Gothic church in the world.

HOURS. The cathedral is open daily from 7–5, and visitors may wander at will except during services. Tours Mon–Sat at 11 A.M. and Sun at 12:45; however, it is wise to call the information desk in advance (tel: 316-7540). Visitors may see the stoneyard Mon–Fri 9–5. There is an information desk inside the main doors. The gift shop in the N. Transept has a large selection of books, cards, posters, reproductions, toys, herbs and spices, and other attractive items. There is an excellent guidebook on the history and iconography of the cathedral. Restrooms on ground level behind the gift shop.

History. Although the idea of an American Episcopal cathedral in New York had been suggested as early as 1828, only after Bishop Horatio Potter proposed it to the diocesan convention in 1872 did it become a viable notion. Although the convention voted unanimously for the project, the financial panic of 1873 made fund raising impossible. Eventually (1887) a wooded plot of some 13 acres belonging to the Leake & Watts Orphan Asylum was purchased for the then momentous sum of $885,000 and the next year 60 entrants submitted designs in an architectural contest, from which the firm of Heins & La Farge emerged victorious. Like many of the other entries, the Heins & La Farge design, a Romanesque plan incorporating Byzantine elements, placed the long axis of the building along the spine of Morningside Heights, which would have given the church a spectacular flight of entrance stairs down to 110th St, but the tradition of building cathedrals with the nave running E.-W. was so strong that it eventually prevailed. In 1892 under Potter's nephew, Bishop Henry Codman Potter, the cornerstone was laid.

Excavations for such a heavy building proved difficult, and J. P. Morgan poured half a million dollars into an ever deeper hole before workers struck bedrock some 70 ft below the surface. In 1911, almost 20 years after the digging had begun, only the choir and the four stone arches to support the dome were in place. Five years later, in the wake of personal disputes and changing canons of taste, the Heins & La Farge Romanesque plan was discarded, and Ralph Adams Cram (of the firm of Cram & Ferguson) redesigned the church on Gothic principles, solving the problems of the original plan, notably the width of the nave and the size of the crossing.

Cram added about 80 ft to the length of the nave, divided it into five aisles instead of the usual three, and proposed the use of alternate thick and slender piers to help in vaulting over its great width (146 ft; Westminster Abbey, 70 ft). He also made several proposals for covering the crossing, whose size presented aesthetic problems as well as difficulties in engineering. His ultimate solution involved reducing the 100-ft square to a 60-ft square by using intersecting arches and covering this smaller opening with a stepped-back 400-ft tower.

Ground was broken for the nave foundations in 1916; the nave itself was begun in 1925 and completed about 10 years later, but excavations for the N. transept went slowly and the money raised for its construction ran out when the walls had reached a height of about 40 ft. In 1939 the Romanesque choir was bricked up and remodeled to conform to Cram's Gothic interiors. Seven new clerestory windows were installed but since the original Heins & La Farge roof still overhangs them, they are artificially lighted.

During World War II major construction was halted. In the 1960s a plan for completing the crossing in a contemporary style with an unattached 800-ft campanile (i.e., 250 ft higher than the Washington Monument, or 184 ft shorter than the Eiffel Tower) was submitted but not approved. Then in 1967 during

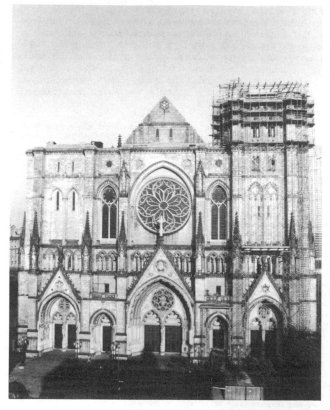

The Cathedral of St. John the Divine in 1988. The building, including the South West Tower now enveloped by scaffolding, was erected using traditional methods of masonry construction, basically the same techniques available to the builders of Europe's medieval cathedrals. The new addition to the tower was begun in 1982. (Robert F. Rodriguez)

an era of intense national social awareness, the bishop announced that the cathedral might never be completed but would devote its energies to the poverty in the community surrounding it. After more than a decade of social involvement, the trustees in 1978 announced a fund-raising campaign for completion of the crossing and the W. facade, including the two towers. Today some 30 apprentice stonecutters, many from nearby neighborhoods, are at work under the tutelage of master masons in a shed adjacent to the cathedral cutting the 21,000 pieces of Indiana limestone needed for the S.W. tower, whose first stone was mortared into place in Sept 1982. So far the apprentice program has trained about 100 people, many of whom are still working on the project. High-wire artist Philippe Petit, who first attracted attention walking the gap between the towers of the World Trade Center, opened the ceremonies walking across Amsterdam Ave, 15 stories above the road, with a ceremonial trowel for the bishop of New York, who awaited him on the cathedral roof.

MEASUREMENTS. Area of cathedral: 121,000 square ft. Length of nave, 248 ft, of choir, 145 ft, total length, 601 ft. Width of W. front, 207 ft, of nave and aisles, 146 ft, of crossing, 100 ft. Height of nave roof, 177 ft, of nave vault, 124 ft. The W. towers, when completed, will be 291 ft tall.

EXTERIOR. The general appearance of the West Front suggests medieval French cathedral architecture, though no single direct antecedent exists. The doors of four of the five portals are Burmese teak, while those of the central portal are bronze. The bronze lights on the front steps, salvaged when Penn Station was demolished (1963–66), were installed in 1967. The *North Tower Portal* is the only one whose statuary (sculptor John Angel) is complete.

Figures in the buttress niches (beginning with the rear buttress facing E.) are the apostles St. Peter, St. Andrew, St. James, St. John, and St. Philip. The figures flanking the doorway (left to right) are the martyrs St. Thomas Becket, St. Catherine of Alexandria, St. Stephen, St. Alban, St. Lawrence, St. Vincent of Saragossa, St. Joan of Arc, and St. Denis. On the central post is St. Peter. The pierced window in the arch above the door contains a Crucifixion; on the gable is a statue of the archangel Michael.

CENTRAL PORTAL. The great bronze doors (sculptor Henry Wilson) were cast in Paris by Barbedienne, the firm that cast the Statue of Liberty. Their 60 panels depict scenes from the Old Testament (N. doors) and the New Testament (S. doors). The frieze above the doors shows the peoples of all nations standing before the Lamb. The figure on the central post, his eyes raised heavenward, is St. John the Divine. Directly above him in the tympanum is a Majestas, showing Christ in Glory surrounded by the seven lamps and the seven stars of St. John's revelation. The spandrels contain symbols of the four Evangelists. The central coat of arms in the gable belongs to the See of New York.

SOUTH PORTAL. Only the figure of St. Paul on the central post and the portrayal of the Holy Family in the pierced window have been completed. Both are by John Angel.

INTERIOR. The W. doors open into the *Narthex.*

Just inside the Narthex are displayed some of the icons formerly mounted on the walls of St. Saviour's Chapel, one of the apsidal chapels. They are of Greek, Russian, and Byzantine origin, and date from the 15–18C. Nearby is the Peace Altar (1986; George Nakashima), cut of walnut boards from a tree 300 years old.

The piers of the nave are alternately massive (16 ft) and slender (6 ft), an arrangement reflected both in the cathedral's exterior buttressing and in the design of the nave vaulting. The thick piers have an inner core of granite and are faced with limestone. The slender piers, made of solid granite, are constructed of 53 courses of single blocks each weighing about four tons, a method of construction necessitated by the city building engineer who would grant a permit only if each course was monolithic. The outer aisle on each side of the nave is divided by an arcade into seven bays, illuminated by stained glass windows—chapel windows 25.5 ft high and clerestory windows 44 ft high. The general

CATHEDRAL OF ST. JOHN THE DIVINE

theme of the windows is that of the religious spirit in human activity, and the iconography of the windows and other furnishings within each bay contributes to its individual theme. A general theme of the cathedral's iconography is that of internationalism, of the cathedral as a house of prayer for all nations. This theme is reflected especially in the windows, in the decoration of the apsidal chapels, and in the Pilgrim's Pavement.

In the pavement of the **Nave** (area 32,400 square ft) are medallions commemorating important people and locations in Christian history. The medallions of the central aisle represent places identified with Christ's earthly life while those in the side aisles recall places and people venerated by pilgrims through the ages.

The bays in the NORTH AISLE (from W. to E.) are the Sports' Bay, Arts' Bay with the Poets' Corner (1984) whose tablets commemorate major American writers, Crusaders' Bay, Education Bay, Lawyers' Bay (with a fine carved walnut reredos representing the themes of lawgiving and justice), Ecclesiastical Origins' Bay (tracing the growth of the Church of England and its translation to the New World), Historical and Patriotic Societies' Bay (which contains the tomb of Bishop William Thomas Manning, 1866–1949, with a recumbent marble figure of the bishop executed by Constantin Antonovici), and Fatherhood Window (this bay has only a clerestory window). Also displayed in the bays in the N. and S. aisles, are contemporary works of religious art and the Mortlake Tapestries, woven in England from a series of cartoons by Raphael and entitled *The Acts of the Apostles*.

Commissioned by Pope Leo X in about 1513, the cartoons, from which numerous sets of tapestries were woven, were dispersed throughout Europe and eventually lost. Sir Francis Crane, manager of the Mortlake tapestry works, rediscovered them in Genoa in 1623 and had them sent to England to be woven for Prince Charles (later Charles I). Since some of the original borders depicted scenes from the life of Leo X, the Mortlake weavers added new borders with floral patterns, cherubs, and the arms of the Earldom of Winchelsea and Nottingham.

In the partially finished NORTH TRANSEPT is a giftshop with a wide selection of books and gifts.

In the **Crossing** the visitor can see the "bones" of the cathedral, the great granite piers, the uncompleted arches, and the remarkable temporary dome of red-brown Guastavino tile hastily installed in the summer of 1909 as a cheap alternative to covering the crossing with a conventional flat wooden roof supported by steel beams. The pulpit (1916), carved of Tennessee marble, was designed by Henry Vaughan, a Boston architect influential in reawakening the Gothic taste of the period. Displayed in the Crossing are the cathedral's other important set of tapestries, the ***Barberini Tapestries,** woven in the first half of the 17C on the papal looms founded by Cardinal Barberini. They depict scenes from the life of Christ and a map of the Holy Land; the cartoons by Jean-François Romanelli are now in the Vatican.

The **Choir** shows both the work of Heins & La Farge and Ralph Adams Cram. The lower part up to the balustrade below the clerestory windows remains from the original Romanesque plan (completed 1911); the work above (altered 1939–41) is Cram's Gothic remodeling. Dominating the choir are eight *granite columns from Vinalhaven, Maine, originally quarried as monoliths but cut in two after the first two columns cracked while being turned and polished on a special lathe (lower sections, 38 ft high, 90 tons; upper sections, 17 ft high, 40 tons). Because the land slopes sharply downhill at this end of the church, the foundations for the columns go down 135 ft. Although the choir is relatively short (145 ft), a kind of false perspective makes it seem longer: the arcades at the E. end are closer together and the floor slopes upward in that direction. The choir stalls were designed by Heins & La Farge after those in the Cathedral of San Domenico in Taormina, Sicily.

Among the interesting objects in the choir are the two menorahs (seven-branched candlesticks) near the altar. Designed after those in the Temple of Jerusalem as pictured on the Arch of Titus, they are the gift (1930) of former *New York Times* publisher Adolph Ochs. The Magna Charta pedestal (S. side of main altar) was once part of the Altar of the Abbey of Bury St. Edmunds on which (November 20, 1214), according to the inscription, "the barons swore fealty to each other in wresting the Great Charter from King John."

The original *organ* (Ernest M. Skinner, 1910) was remodeled and rebuilt in 1954 to achieve a better balance between the bass and treble. At that time a new stop, the State Trumpet, was added, whose 61 silver pipes are placed directly under the Rose Window in the West Front. The **Rose Window* itself, best seen from the E. end of the nave, was designed by Charles Connick, is 40 ft in diameter, and contains more than 10,000 pieces of glass. From the central figure of Christ radiate symbols representing the gifts of the Holy Spirit, the Beatitudes, and the heavenly choir. The lesser Rose Window below it, also by Connick, develops the symbolism of the number seven: from a central monogram of Christ radiate seven fountains, seven growing vine forms, seven pairs of doves, and seven stars.

Enter the N. AMBULATORY from the archway in the Crossing. The first structure in the ambulatory is the *Baptistry* (1928; Frank Cleveland of Cram & Ferguson) donated by members of the Stuyvesant family whose Dutch origins are symbolized in the decoration of the room.

Over the entrance arch are the arms of the Netherlands with statues of St. Nicholas (right) and St. Catherine (left). On the E. wall of the entrance is a statue of Judith Bayard, wife of Peter Stuyvesant last Dutch governor of New York; on the W. wall opposite is a figure of Louise de Coligny, wife of William of Orange. Inside the octagonal room a frieze (John Angel) depicts the history of illustrious men associated with the Netherlands under whose flag New York was first settled. The coat of arms of the Stuyvesant family is in the spandrel of the ground level arcade in the N.E. wall. The baptismal font, also octagonal in form and about 15 ft high, is built of Champville marble and modeled on the font in the baptistry of the cathedral of Siena, Italy. The sculptured panels at its base depicting scenes from the life of John the Baptist are the work of Albert H. Atkins.

A doorway in the W. side of the Baptistry leads into the *Columbarium,* a repository for the ashes of the dead.

Standing above a marble credenza in the N. Ambulatory is a diptych of the *Annunciation,* attributed to *Simone Martini* (1283?–1344). An opening on the right of the ambulatory leads into the *Presbytery.* The parapet at the ascent to the presbytery (in two sections at the S. and N. sides) is carved with figures representing notable men of the first 20 centuries of the Christian era. The block on the floor at the extreme left remains uncarved, awaiting the selection of a figure from the 20C.

The **Chapels** opening from the ambulatory are called the *Chapels of Tongues,* since each represents a different national or ethnic group, in keeping with the international ideal of the cathedral.

At the present time, for security reasons, the chapels are frequently locked but are still visible through the gates.

The first chapel in the N. Ambulatory is (1) *St. Ansgar's Chapel* (1918), named after the 9C Frankish missionary to Denmark, Sweden, and Germany. Designed by Henry Vaughan, it is stylistically reminiscent of 14C English Gothic. The windows are by C. E. Kempe of London. The (2) *Chapel of St. Boniface* (1916), next along the ambulatory, is named after the Apostle of Germany (c. 680–755), martyred by a heathen mob while preaching in West Friesland. Vaughan was again the architect, and Kempe designed the windows commemorating great missionaries. The 11-ft bronze statue of Michael the Archangel was made and donated in 1963 by Eleanor M. Mellon. The chapel hosts rotating art exhibits. *St. Columba's Chapel* (1911) next door (3) is named after the Irish saint (521–97) who founded the monastery of Iona and worked to convert the Celts. The statues by Gutzon Borglum flanking the entrance represent influential figures in English church history. The altarpiece is a 15C polyptych by Giovanni di Paolo. Architects Heins & La Farge designed this chapel in the Romanesque style they chose for the cathedral as a whole.

St. Saviour's Chapel, the central chapel (4) and the first one built (1904; Heins & La Farge), is dedicated to the eastern church, though its style is Gothic. The window depicting the Transfiguration is by Hardman, of Birmingham, England. The 20 figures flanking the entrance represent the heavenly choir and were designed by Gutzon Borglum, as were the figures of scholars, bishops, and saints of the eastern church on either side of the window. The heavenly choir occasioned controversy when installed, since the figures are all female. The icons, displayed behind the altar, on the side walls, and sometimes at the entrance to the nave of the cathedral, are Greek, Russian, and Byzantine, dating from the 15–18C. The shrine on the S. wall is dedicated to certain African saints while that on the N. wall opposite is dedicated to Athenagoras, the late Ecumenical Patriarch of the Orthodox Church.

In the ambulatory directly opposite the entrance to the chapel is the *tomb of Bishop Horatio Potter* (1802–87), designed after the tomb of Edward the Confessor in Westminster Abbey and occupying the spot behind the high altar traditionally reserved for a cathedral's founder.

The next chapel (open only for prayer and meditation) is the *Chapel of St. Martin of Tours* (5), the 4C Gallic bishop. Designed by Ralph Cram (1918) in a style reminiscent of 13C French Gothic, it is noteworthy for its beautiful windows (Charles Connick) depicting scenes from the lives of three French saints (left to right): St. Louis, St. Martin, and St. Joan of Arc. The statue of Joan of Arc (donated 1922) on the right wall is by Anna Hyatt Huntington, and stands above a stone taken from the saint's cell in Rouen. A small chip of Reims cathedral blasted away during World War I is embedded in the trefoil above the altar cross.

St. Ambrose' Chapel (6) is named after the 4C bishop of Milan and is designed (1914; Carrère & Hastings) in a style Cram called "purely Renaissance." Italian paintings include: *The Annunciation* by Andrea Sabbatini (1480?–1545); *The Baptism of Christ,* studio of the brother and sons of Paolo Veronese (16C); *Virgin and Child,* attributed to Perugino (1446–1523). The statue of St. Anthony is by Luca della Robbia (1400?–82).

Although the *Chapel of St. James* (1916), the last in the S.

Ambulatory, is dedicated to the people of Spain, it is decorated in a style recalling 14C English Gothic (architect Henry Vaughan). The Sacristy window (Henry W. Young) depicts figures in the history of Spain, particularly those associated with the discovery of the New World, including Christopher Columbus. In the central bay of the S. aisle is the tomb of Bishop Henry Codman Potter (1834–1908); behind the sarcophagus are three paintings depicting scenes from the life of St. Peter by Luca Giordano (1632–1705). The *Ecce Homo* is by Luis de Morales (1510?–86).

Continue along the S. Ambulatory and return to the crossing. The *Bays in the S. Aisle,* like those on the N. side of the nave, are devoted to religious aspects of various human activities. They are (E. to W.): Motherhood Window (only clerestory window); Armed Forces' Bay with a 13C recumbent effigy of a knight in chain mail; Religious Life Bay, with the Earth Shrine (1986), and a memorial to St. Francis of Assisi, whose respect for the earth and its creatures is symbolized by a figure of the *Wolf of Gubbio* (1986; Kappy Wells); Medical Bay, with an ornate carved oak reredos complementing that in the Lawyers' Bay opposite (the Medical Bay contains the AIDS memorial, 1985, a book commemorating those who have died of AIDS); Press or Communications Bay (with a marble statue of the *Return of the Prodigal* by William O. Partridge (1861–1930); Labor Bay, with a memorial to N.Y. Firemen by Ralph Feldman, dedicated 1976; Missionary Bay, with the Holocaust Memorial (1978; Elliott Offner), the figure of a victim of Auschwitz; and finally the All Souls' Bay.

Leave the cathedral by the W. doors and walk S. on Amsterdam Ave to 110th St to see the Auxiliary Buildings within the cathedral close. *Synod House,* at the corner of Amsterdam Ave and Cathedral Parkway, a Gothic structure (1913; Cram & Ferguson), houses the offices of the bishops of the diocese. Of particular interest is the W. entrance built like a medieval porch, its sculptural figures illustrating the progress of Christianity. Near the sidewalk is a *Peace Fountain* (1985; Greg Wyatt), a bronze sculpture depicting the battle between good and evil, as represented in the figures of Satan and the Archangel Michael. The pedestal, in the form of a double-helix, represents DNA, carrier of the genetic code. The giant crab symbolizes the origin of life in the oceans. Around the rail are 66 small bronze animal sculptures, cast from originals made by children and chosen in a juried contest. The sculpture contest will continue for 10 years and expand to the entire nation, eventually resulting in the installation of 120 children's sculptures. In the center of the lawn is the *Outdoor Pulpit* (dedicated 1916), an open-work Gothic spire 40 ft high, designed by architects Howells & Stokes. Before the advent of modern traffic, outdoor services were held on the lawn with a small choir and brass band.

Continue along the close road to *Diocesan House* (1909–12; Heins & La Farge), once a training school for deaconesses. The building now contains the cathedral library and archives. *Cathedral House,* across the road and E. of Diocesan House, was originally the *Bishop's House* (1914; Cram & Ferguson), built in the manner of a Gothic chateau with money donated by J. P. Morgan. Morgan defended its elegance by opining that bishops should live "like everyone else," though he must have had a rarefied view of how "everyone else" lived. Today the bishop occupies only the third floor.

Directly E. is the *Deanery* (1914; Cram & Ferguson), and beyond it to the left is the *Cathedral School* (1913; Walter Cook and Winthrop A. Welch), formerly a day school for choir boys, now a coeducational elementary and middle school from whose enrollment the choir still draws its treble voices. The left fork of the road continues past the school to the *Biblical Garden,* whose plantings include only flora mentioned in the Bible (most of which spend the winter in nurseries). The close road now leads back to Amsterdam Ave.

Walk N. on Amsterdam Ave to the corner of 113th St. The small square building on the S.W. corner of the intersection is a *Gatehouse* (c. 1890) marking the end of a section of masonry aqueduct beneath Amsterdam Ave. Most of the water supplied from the city's reservoirs is carried by pipes, but during the later years of the 19C when labor was relatively cheap and pipe was expensive, the city built a number of masonry aqueducts. A second gatehouse stands at 119th St, where the pipes end and the masonry begins.

Turn right at 113th St and walk E. Although much of *St. Luke's Hospital-Roosevelt Hospital Center* on the N. side of 113th St is new, part of the original *central pavilion may still be seen, overshadowed by the modern wings.

The original hospital on this site, Saint Luke's, consisted of a central pavilion for administration and nine semidetached outbuildings, designed in the Beaux-Arts style by Ernest Flagg and built between 1893 and 1896. The hospital was founded in 1846 by the Episcopal Church; in 1986, the 780-bed facility merged with Roosevelt Hospital in an effort to streamline the city's patchwork system of private, voluntary, and municipal hospitals.

Walk E. on 113th St to Morningside Drive. Just across the drive is **Morningside Park,** a rocky cliff of Manhattan schist, which plunges steeply down to the Harlem Plain.

History. In the mid-19C its precipitous slopes proved too steep for even the most ardent real estate developer, and so the area was handed over to landscape architects Frederick Law Olmsted and Calvert Vaux to be converted to a park (final plan 1887). Realizing that the most attractive feature of the area was the view to the E., the designers planned a walkway on top of the cliff studded with balconies facing the Harlem Plain below. Jacob Wrey Mould, who designed the railings surrounding the Terrace in Central Park, planned the massive, buttressed masonry wall that supports the overlooks. Down the hillside they laid out curving walks conforming to the topography of the slope and placed small open meadows along the southern and eastern edges of the park. They proposed planting the cliff face with vines and creepers which could survive in its shallow soil and planned an alpine rock garden for the N. panhandle of the park at 123rd St.

Today Morningside Park has fallen on hard times. Its paths, choked with weeds, attract urban predators; it is unsafe to walk there. Public School 36 has usurped the site of the alpine garden in the N. and concrete playgrounds have been built in the S. portion. In 1968 Columbia University began construction of a gymnasium within the park, but after loud protests from the public and the student body the work was abandoned; though covered partially by undergrowth, the foundations remain unreconstructed.

Down in the park, at its eastern edge (Morningside Ave and Manhattan Ave at 114th St), is a statue of *Washington and Lafayette* (1890; Frédéric Auguste Bartholdi) shaking hands in greeting, a less successful evocation of Franco-American friendship than the Statue of Liberty. Charles Broadway Rouss (see p. 195) gave the statue to the city in 1900.

Also in the park (foot of the stairs at 116th St and Morningside Ave) is the *Bear and Faun Fountain*, also known as the Seligman Fountain (c. 1910; Edgar Walter), a bronze Faun sequestered in the hollow of a bronze boulder on top of which stretches a bronze bear, its paw dangling over the edge; the rocks of the park form the pedestal on which the group rests. The work was given by the National Highways Protective Society to honor its vice-president, Alfred L. Seligman, who died in an auto accident.

Continue N. on Morningside Drive. At the N.W. corner of 114th St is the Roman Catholic ÉGLISE DE NOTRE DAME (apse 1909–10; Dans & Otto; remainder, 1914-28; Cross & Cross; DL). Originally built for a French-speaking congregation, the building recalls churches of Napoleonic France (the Church of the Madeleine in Paris has been mentioned). A handsome portico with four Corinthian columns faces Morningside Park. The interior (open for services, Sun 8:30, 10, 11:15, 12:30, and 5:30; weekdays 8, 12:05, and 5:30) is remarkable for its replica of the grotto at Lourdes, donated by Mrs. Geraldine Redmond, a parishioner whose son had been healed by its miraculous waters. Since plans for a large drum and dome over the crossing which would have brought natural light into the building never materialized, the interior is artificially lighted.

Two blocks N. at the intersection of 116th St and Morningside Drive is the *Carl Schurz Memorial* (sculptor, Karl Bitter, architect Henry Bacon; 1913). Forced to flee Germany because of his revolutionary political sentiments, Schurz (1829–1906) emigrated to the U. S. where he became a leader of the Republican Party, a friend of Abraham Lincoln, a major-general in the Union Army during the Civil War, a senator, and an editor. Bitter's bronze statue depicts Schurz as a strong, idealistic man; the low relief panels on the monument, influenced by the sculptor's admiration for archaic Greek sculpture, portray the liberation of oppressed peoples: American Indians, Asians, and blacks.

Directly across Morningside Drive are the outposts of ***Columbia University,** whose main campus lies between Amsterdam Ave and Broadway, W. 114th–120th Sts.

Free tours of the university are given, weather permitting, during the academic year Mon–Fri at 3, and at 10 A.M. and 2 P.M. from late May through Aug (hiatus in late Dec and early May during the exam period); it is always advisable to telephone ahead; tel: 280-2845; tours leave from the Office of

Information and Visitors' Services, 201 Dodge Hall, and are available in several languages by prior arrangement.

Columbia University, one of the oldest, wealthiest (the endowment is currently $1.4 billion), and most famous American universities, was founded as a gentlemen's college to "instruct youth in the learned languages and in the liberal arts and sciences." It is known for its professional schools—medicine, law, business, education, journalism, and architecture—and for the School of General Studies, where adults of any age can work toward degrees. Coeducational Columbia College, Barnard, for women, and the School of Engineering and Applied Science are the undergraduate colleges. The university has a student body of some 18,000 (10,000 men; 8,000 women) and a faculty of 5,000 members in teaching and research.

History. By the mid-18C it became apparent to contemporary observers that while New York outstripped its American rivals commercially, it lagged behind culturally, its populace (according to observers from Boston or Philadelphia) afflicted by ignorance, their lives dominated by a sordid thirst for money. Consequently a group of citizens set out to establish a center of learning that would lighten the intellectual gloom, in the process outshining Harvard, Yale, and the College of New Jersey (later Princeton). Among them were several vestrymen of Trinity Church who arranged a transfer of five acres of church property to the proposed college, a plot not far from the present World Trade Center bounded by Church, Murray, and Barclay Sts and the Hudson River, then located at about West St. It was Columbia's first piece of valuable real estate. The college was chartered by King George II in 1754 and named King's College, the fifth such institution in the colonies. The first president was Dr. Samuel Johnson, an Anglican pastor from Stratford, Connecticut, and the first class of eight men, who bore such resounding old New York names as Verplanck, Van Cortlandt, and Bayard, met in the schoolhouse of Trinity Church.

Among the early students were Alexander Hamilton (1755–1804), who enrolled in 1775 and stayed about a year, later becoming the first secretary of the U.S. Treasury; John Jay (1745–1829), first chief justice of the U.S. Supreme Court; Gouverneur Morris (1752–1816), statesman and diplomat, minister to France; and Robert R. Livingston (1746–1813), first U.S. secretary of foreign affairs.

After the Revolution, the college, renamed Columbia, entered a period of intellectual dormancy which lasted well into the 19C. In 1814 the trustees appealed to the state for financial aid and received, instead of the share in the proceeds of a state lottery for which they had hoped, a plot of land between 47th and 51st Sts, W. of Fifth Ave, formerly the Elgin Botanic Garden. Appraised by the state at $75,000, it seemed worth much less to the trustees, since it was rocky, remote from the city, and overgrown with weeds. In the long run it turned out to be worth much more: today Rockefeller Center stands on that 11.5-acre parcel which in 1985 the university sold to the Rockefeller Group for $400 million.

In 1857 the college moved uptown, not to the Rockefeller Center site but to buildings formerly owned by an asylum for the deaf and dumb between Madison and Fourth (now Park) Aves, bounded by 49th and 50th Sts. The school remained there until its relocation on the Morningside Heights campus in 1897. In 1902 Nicholas Murray Butler became president, and under his energetic guidance Columbia achieved its present high reputation. Its faculty has been illustrious, including such luminaries as John Dewey, Michael Pupin, Harold C. Urey, Isidor I. Rabi, Edward McDowell, and Franz Boas. Dwight D. Eisenhower resigned his presidency of the university (1948–53) to become President of the United States.

On the N.W. corner of Morningside Drive and 116th St is the house (1912; McKim, Mead & White) of the university president.

Adjacent to it on 116th St is a dormitory, *Johnson Hall,* named after the university's first president, Samuel Johnson.

Next to Johnson Hall on the N.E. corner of 116th St and Amsterdam Ave is the **Law School** (1961; Harrison & Abramovitz), a massive, white, high-rise building linked to the School of International Affairs (1971; Harrison & Abramovitz) on the N. by a wide bridge passing over Amsterdam Ave. In front of the Law School stands Jacques Lipchitz's *Bellerophon Taming Pegasus* (cast 1973, installed 1977), best seen from the W. side of Amsterdam Ave or the upper-level plaza (take the stairway on 116th St). According to the sculptor, the monumental statue (30 ft high, 28 ft wide, 23 tons) symbolizes the control by law over the forces of disorder in human society.

An overpass crosses Amsterdam Ave at 117th St. On it is *Three-Way Piece: Points* (1967; Henry Moore), a swelling, volumetric bronze abstraction resting on three points. Not far away in Revson Plaza on the N. side of the Law School, accessible from the overpass, is *Tightrope Walker* (1979; Kees Verkade), an elongated aerialist with a second figure balanced on his shoulders. The statue, whose figures suggest poise and daring, was donated as a monument to William "Wild Bill" Donovan, Columbia alumnus, World War I leader. Nearby is *Flight* (1981) by Gertrude Schweitzer.

Cross Amsterdam Ave to the main campus. The MORNINGSIDE HEIGHTS CAMPUS of Columbia was designed (1893) by McKim, Mead & White, but is principally the work of Charles Follen McKim, who envisioned a densely developed area with small side courtyards and a narrow central quadrangle. McKim's original intentions can be seen in the brick and limestone classroom buildings with green copper roofs on the periphery of the main quadrangles, and in the placement of St. Paul's Chapel, Low Library, Earl Hall, and University Hall. The only side courtyard actually built is the one bounded by Schermerhorn, Avery, and Fayerweather Halls and St. Paul's Chapel (and it has been altered by the Avery Library extension), since after McKim's death (1909) the university elected to retain the central open space and expand instead into surrounding city streets, a policy that has not been without social repercussions in an area where the general populace is poor in comparison to the university.

The university purchased the land from the Bloomingdale Insane Asylum in two parcels (1892 and 1903) for a total of $3.9 million. The original campus, built on the first parcel N. of 116th St, contains the college's finest buildings, Low Library and St. Paul's Chapel.

Continue along College Walk, the pedestrian extension of 116th St, to the center of the campus. The principal building in the lower or South Quadrangle is **Butler Hall** (formerly South Hall), the main university library (1934; James Gamble Rogers). Named after president Nicholas Murray Butler, the library can accommodate 4 million volumes. The present Columbia collection, housed in several smaller libraries as well as Butler Hall, num-

Low Library (built 1895–97) at Columbia University is the focal point of McKim, Mead & White's Morningside Heights campus. On the steps sits Daniel Chester French's statue of Alma Mater, originally covered with glittering gold leaf. (Office of Public Information / Columbia University)

bers about 5,552,000 volumes and is one of the largest in the nation.

Dominating the Upper Quadrangle (N. of College Walk) is **Low Library** on whose broad steps sits Columbia's most famous piece of sculpture, *Alma Mater* (1903; Daniel Chester French). The statue, originally covered with gold leaf, was regilded in 1962 to the dismay of students and faculty members who demanded the removal of the gaudy gold in favor of the familiar gray-green patina. In 1970, the figure was slightly damaged by a bomb set off during student uprisings. *Alma Mater* sits on a throne flanked by torches implying enlightenment; her right hand holds a sceptre topped with a crown, an emblem referring to Columbia's beginnings as King's College. An owl, symbolic of wisdom, peers from the folds of her robe near her left knee; a laurel garland wreathes her head; a book, signifying knowledge, lies open on her lap.

Low Memorial Library (1895–97; McKim, Mead & White; DL) dominates the quadrangle by virtue of its scale (dome, 136 ft above the terrace), its site atop three flights of stairs, and its imposing classicism. Seth Low, president of Columbia from 1890–1901, donated the building to honor his father, Abiel Abbot Low (1811–93), the wealthy tea merchant and China trade pioneer whose warehouses still grace the South Street Seaport area. The younger Low resigned his office to become mayor of New York (1901–03), a position he won not because of special political acuity but because his opponents were flagrantly corrupt. Low Library remained the main university library until 1934 when Butler Hall superseded it; now it houses administrative offices and the Columbiana Collection.

EXTERIOR. Low Library has its stylistic origins in the Roman Pantheon; its general plan is that of a Greek cross with an octagonal transition to a saucer dome. The outer dome of solid masonry covers an inner dome (diameter, 70 ft) of plaster on a steel frame, which forms the ceiling of the main reading room.

INTERIOR (open weekdays 9–5 during the academic year). The former Reading Room, with its 16 polished granite columns capped by gilt bronze Ionic capitals, its galleries and heroic marble statuary, and its domed ceiling rising above semicircular clerestory windows, exemplifies the most elegant work of McKim, Mead & White.

Room 210 on the first floor houses the COLUMBIANA COLLECTION (open Mon–Fri 1–5), which contains books, portraits, and memorabilia relating to the history of the university. In the basement are restrooms. At one time the subbasement contained a large canvas tank and a stationary rowing rack for the Columbia crew.

The picturesque (though rather shabby) three-story gabled brick building just E. of Low Library is *Buell Hall,* the only building remaining from the days of the Bloomingdale Asylum.

In front of Philosophy Hall is a cast of Rodin's most famous work, *The Thinker* (modeled 1880, cast 1930), originally a small figure intended to represent the poet Dante contemplating the tragic human condition.

Just to the left (N.) of Buell Hall is ***St. Paul's Chapel** (1904–07; Howells & Stokes; DL), one of the campus's most beautiful buildings, originally affiliated with the Episcopal Church but now used for diverse religious services.

EXTERIOR. Constructed of brick and limestone, the building is shaped like a short Latin cross (140 ft long, 80 ft wide, 112 ft high) with a vaulted portico on the W. and a semicircular apse on the east. A dome (interior diameter, 48 ft; height, 91 ft) covers the crossing. The capitals of the columns flanking the entrance are decorated with heads of cherubim by Gutzon Borglum.

The chapel is generally open weekdays until 10:30 P.M., Sat 11–1, and Sun 10–7. Tel: 280-5113.

INTERIOR. The walls of the chapel are of tan brick and the fine Guastavino tile vaulting is in warm tones of salmon and buff. In accordance with the educational aspirations of Columbia, the three apse windows (John La Farge) show St. Paul preaching to the Athenians on the Areopagus; the windows in the transepts show teachers of the Old Testament (N. transept) and the New Testament (S. transept).

Continue N. along the sidewalk from the chapel to *Avery Hall* (1912; McKim, Mead & White), one of the early classroom buildings in the style designated by McKim. It houses the School of Architecture and the nation's largest architectural library (not open to the public).

Visible to the N. from the front of Avery Hall is the *Sherman Fairchild Center for the Life Sciences* (1977; Mitchell / Giurgola Assocs.), the only building among recent additions to the campus to meet with approbation from the city's architectural critics.

Turn left in front of Avery Hall and walk west. In front of Uris Hall stands a 3-ton, hollow, black-painted steel sculpture (24 ft long, 11 ft wide, 12 ft high) by Clement Meadmore, installed in 1968 and entitled *Curl*. Meadmore, an Australian sculptor now living in New York, has left a similar work at the corner of Riverside Drive and 156th St.

Turn left again and walk S. along the side of Low Library toward College Walk. Between the library and Lewisohn Hall to the S.W. reclines a statue of *The Great God Pan,* by George Grey Barnard. Cast of bronze and weighing more than 3 tons, it was completed around 1898, intended for a fountain in the courtyard of the Dakota apartments.

Turn right at College Walk and continue toward Broadway. On the left is the *School of Journalism* (1912–13; McKim, Mead & White), founded by publisher Joseph Pulitzer in 1912, which comes into the public eye each spring when it announces the Pulitzer Prizes. On the S. side of the building is a statue (1914) of Thomas Jefferson by William Ordway Partridge (1861–1930), an alumnus of Columbia. Partridge's statue (1908) of Alexander Hamilton stands in front of Hamilton Hall on the E. side of the quadrangle.

On the N. side of College Walk, opposite the School of Journalism, is Dodge Hall, with the Office of Information and Visitors' Services. The walkway leads out to Broadway through a gate guarded by two classically draped figures representing *Science* (1925) and *Letters* (1916?), both by Charles Keck.

Turn right (N.) on Broadway. The campus of **Barnard College** lies on the W. side of the street between 116th and 120th Sts. Visitors are welcome to explore.

HISTORY. Frederick A. P. Barnard (1809–89) became president of Columbia in 1864 after a string of men distinguished more for their piety than their administrative abilities. Among his liberal innovations was the institution of a women's course, which the trustees grudgingly accepted in 1883. Since women were not allowed to enter the classrooms and faculty members were not allowed to counsel or advise women outside class, the course was not notably successful. Nevertheless it was due to Barnard's efforts that the women's college was founded in 1889.

The older buildings reflect the predominant style at Columbia, but two newer buildings toward the N. end of the campus (at about 119th St) are attractive, imaginative additions: the Millicent McIntosh Center for student activities and the 14-story science building, Helen Goodhart Altschul Hall (both 1969; Vincent G. Kling & Assocs.).

On the wall of the Mathematics Building on the E. side of Broadway at about 117th St is a large plaque commemorating the Battle of Harlem Heights, fought close to this site on September 16, 1776. It was Washington's only significant victory in the campaign for Manhattan, where his efforts resulted in a series of lost battles followed by spectacularly successful retreats.

On September 15, the British Army had landed at Kip's Bay (near the present site of 34th St on the East River) and had routed the defenders, nearly trapping the main body of American forces in lower Manhattan. The following day a force of American troops, encamped on Harlem Heights (roughly at 130th St, E. of Broadway) moved S. to encounter a British force in a buckwheat field where the Barnard campus is presently located. The Americans hoped to lure some of the British down into the valley where 125th St lies, to outflank them, and eventually to cut them off, but the plan failed because the flanking party fired prematurely, making their whereabouts known. Nevertheless the Americans did hold off the British for several hours in the buckwheat field and forced them to retreat. While the battle had no great significance in the course of the war, it bolstered sagging American morale and demonstrated to Washington that his soldiers, despite several disastrous recent performances, were capable of standing up to the British.

Continue N. along Broadway, which now begins to slope downhill. Near the corner of 120th St is the side of the *Marcellus Hartley Dodge Physical Fitness Center* (1974; Eggers Partnership), a gymnasium built after student and community hostility doomed the one proposed for Morningside Park.

Just N. of the gymnasium are the *Pupin Physics Laboratories* (120th St and Broadway), built in 1925 but named 10 years later after Michael Idvorsky Pupin (1858–1935), a Serbian immigrant who became one of America's foremost inventors in the field of electricity and a revered professor of electrical engineering. In this building in the late 1930s and early 1940s, Harold C. Urey, Enrico Fermi, and I. I. Rabi did the work in nuclear fission that won them the Nobel Prize. They are among 42 Nobel laureates who have taught or studied at Columbia.

The row of red brick buildings on the E. side of Broadway between 120th and 121st Sts houses **Teachers College,** an affiliate of Columbia University. Founded in 1889 by Nicholas Murray Butler, the college grew from humble beginnings as the Kitchen Garden Club of the Church of St. Mark's-in-the-Bowery, an organization for introducing manual training into the public school system and teaching working class girls the elements of housekeeping and gardening. Since the days when John Dewey belonged to the faculty, Teachers College has earned a reputation for spearheading progressive causes in education.

Most of the red brick buildings date from around the turn of the century. On the N.E. corner of the intersection is *Horace Mann Hall* (1901; Howells & Stokes and Edgar H. Josselyn), formerly the Horace Mann School, founded in 1887 and taken over by the college as an experimental school. Halfway down the block to the E. on 120th St is *Main Hall* (1892; William A. Potter), the campus's earliest building, an elaborate composition of dormers, gables, pointed-arch windows, porches, and turrets.

Cross Broadway to the W. side. **Union Theological Seminary** (1910; Allen & Collens, altered 1952 by Collens, Willis & Beckonert; DL) occupies the blocks between 120th and 122nd Sts. Founded in 1836 as a graduate school for Protestant ministers, the seminary has long enjoyed a reputation for liberal religious thought and involvement in social action. Its library (open to enrolled students and qualified scholars) is outstanding, containing the van Ess Collection, rich in manuscripts and incunabula, and the McAlpin Collection of British History and Theology. Among its faculty and graduates have been such luminaries as Reinhold Niebuhr, Norman Thomas, and Henry Sloane Coffin.

The classroom and residential buildings are organized in a quadrangle around a central courtyard dominated by the Brown Memorial Tower on Broadway and the James Memorial Tower on Claremont Avenue. Constructed of rockface granite with limestone trim, the buildings belong to an era when American universities imitated the Gothicism of Oxford and Cambridge, presumably in hopes of acquiring their academic tradition along with their appearance. The interior quadrangle and the James Chapel are especially attractive (for admission inquire weekdays 9–5 at the Security Desk in the Rotunda near the Broadway-120th St entrance).

On the N.E. corner of 122nd St and Broadway is the **Jewish Theological Seminary** (1930; Gehron, Ross, Alley), a large prosaic example of neo-Georgian architecture. Founded in 1886 to provide the Jewish population with American-trained rabbis and scholars, it has become a major center of Jewish education. Its library has the most comprehensive collection of Judaica and Hebraica in the western hemisphere and contains more than 250,000 volumes, including a fine collection of manuscripts from the repository of the Old Cairo Synagogue.

Walk W. on 122nd St. The building housing the **Manhattan School of Music** (N. side of 122nd St, between Broadway and Claremont Ave) was built in 1910 (Donn Barber) for the Institute of Musical Art; later with substantial additions (1931; Shreve, Lamb & Harmon) it was the home of the Juilliard School of Music. The latest addition, the Mitzi Newhouse Pavilion (1970; MacFadyen & Knowles), was added by the present occupant.

Riverside Drive (opened 1880) and **Riverside Park** were planned by Frederick Law Olmsted at a time when it seemed that the Upper West Side might become one of the city's most desirable areas. Olmsted laid out a wide drive following the natural contours of the land (instead of the profitable perpendiculars of the 1811 grid); he divided the roadway into carriage and foot promenades; and he insisted that park and drive be unified, that the imaginary boundary between them be erased. Although expensive homes did line the drive by the 1890s, the area lacked a tradition of fine old families and never did rival Fifth Ave in glitter and snob appeal.

Continue W. on 122nd to Claremont Ave. Up a flight of stairs in the park is a *statue of Daniel Butterfield,* designed by Gutzon Borglum and erected in 1918. Butterfield (1831–1901) was a Union general in the Civil War but achieved his greatest fame off the battlefield as the composer of Taps, the bugle call played as the flag is lowered at nightfall and at funerals. Visible across *Sakura Park* is *International House* (1924, Lindsay & Warren), a residence for graduate students from almost 100 countries, built with funds provided by John D. Rockefeller, Jr., who was chairman of the building committee. The building was constructed during the years between World Wars I and II to foster international understanding across the chasms of cultural difference. Mrs. Rockefeller, later a founder of the Museum of Modern Art, had the assembly hall modeled on the Beneficent Street Church in Providence, Rhode Island, which she had attended as a child, and insisted that the rooms be furnished in an American colonial style—her way of introducing foreigners to the American experience.

Walk S. on Riverside Drive to the main entrance of *Riverside Church.

Open Mon–Sat 9–4:30. Sun services in the nave begin at 10:45. A guided tour is given on Sun at 12:30 after the worship service. The Visitors' Center in South Hall, on the main level, has a small bookshop (books, sermons, notecards) and public telephones. Visitors are welcome to have lunch in the cafeteria during the week and after the Sun service. Restrooms located downstairs on the Cloister level.

The Riverside Church (1930; Allen & Collens and Henry C. Pelton; south wing, 1960; Collens, Willis & Beckonert) occupies a commanding site overlooking the Hudson River. Originally affiliated with the Baptist Church, its membership is now interdenominational, interracial, and international; Riverside Church has long been known for its liberal appeal and community service.

The church began as a small Baptist congregation meeting on Stanton St on the Lower East Side. About 1850 the group moved to Norfolk St and occupied the landmark building now owned by Beth Hamedrash Hagodol (see p. 186). As the immigrant population overwhelmed the Lower East Side, the Baptists moved uptown, first to 46th St just W. of Fifth Ave, later to Park Ave, and finally to the present location.

Despite its Gothic inspiration and particular indebtedness to the cathedral of Chartres, the Riverside Church is a modern, steel-framed building, its Gothicism relegated to surface details. Although criticized when completed for its disproportionately tall tower (392 ft), for its cultural servitude to Europe, and for its eclecticism, the church is nonetheless distinguished for its fine stained glass, stone carving, and woodwork, which represent the finest materials and craftsmanship available.

MEASUREMENTS. Length (excluding S. wing), 265 ft; width, 100 ft; height of tower, 392 ft; length of nave, 215 ft; width of nave, 89 ft; height of nave, 100 ft; seating capacity of nave, 2500 people.

EXTERIOR. The building, faced with Indiana limestone, has its long axis parallel to Riverside Drive. The 22-story tower at the S. end contains classrooms and offices as well as the carillon. The principal entrance on the W. is elaborately carved and is clearly intended to recall the portals at Chartres. The tympanum depicts a seated Christ surrounded by emblems of the four Evangelists. Above the tympanum are five archivolts (moldings around the arch), the first and fifth depicting angels, the middle ones portraying scientists, philosophers, and religious leaders drawn from the whole sweep of human history—classical, Christian, and modern. The chapel door, just S. of the West Portal, is thematically devoted to the Nativity.

Visitors may also enter the church through the Cloister entrance on Claremont Ave (E. side), near which is a bronze *Madonna and Child* (1927) by Jacob Epstein, modeled on an Indian mother and child, a work intended to emphasize the humanity and humility of Christ.

Inside the revolving door is the NARTHEX. In the E. wall are two windows of 16C Flemish glass, the only windows not made specifically for the church. A small chapel in the N.E. corner of the narthex contains Heinrich Hofmann's (1824–1902) painting, *Christ in Gethsemane*. A door in the S. wall of the narthex leads into CHRIST CHAPEL, inspired by the 11C Romanesque nave of the Church of St. Nazaire at Carcassone, France.

The carved stone reredos portrays (bottom to top): the Last Supper, the Transfiguration, and Christ as Shepherd. The stained glass windows in the S. wall depict scenes from the life of Christ. The emblems of the apostles form the basis of the design in the rose window and the wrought-iron rear doors.

NAVE. On the N. of the narthex is the nave, finished in Indiana limestone and divided into three aisles by an arcade, above which is a triforium gallery and a clerestory. The clerestory windows are copies of the famous 12–13C windows at Chartres, while those on the aisle level present modern motifs as well as historical ones. The 51 colored stained glass windows in the church were made by firms in Boston, Chartres, and Reims.

Aisle windows, W. wall (S. to N.): Agriculture, Reformers, Development of the Bible, State and Government, and Builders. Aisle windows, E. wall (S. to N.): International Character of Religion, Christ and Humanity, Scholars, Music, and Children. The capitals of the columns in the nave tell the prophecies of Jeremiah and the story of their fulfillment.

Continue along the nave to the CHANCEL. The pulpit (weight, 9 tons) at the W. side of the chancel is carved from three blocks of limestone; its niches (both upper and lower levels) contain figures of prophets; 10 of the figures on the upper level stand beneath canopies representing the major cathedrals of France. In the center of the chancel floor a marble maze has been adapted from the labyrinth at Chartres, whose route medieval penitents traced out on their knees. The *chancel screen portrays seven aspects of the life of Christ, shown in each panel, surrounded by people who have fulfilled the divine ideal, including Pasteur, Savonarola, Florence Nightingale, and J. S. Bach. The panels represent (left to right): Physicians, Teachers, Prophets, Humanitarians, Missionaries, Reformers, and Lovers of Beauty.

On the S. wall of the nave at the gallery level, best seen from the chancel, is a work by Jacob Epstein, *Christ in Majesty*; finished in gold leaf, it measures 19.5 × 6 ft.

Return to the narthex to ascend the *carillon tower (open daily 11–3, Sun 12:30–4; admission charge; purchase tickets in the Visitors' Center). An elevator ascends 20 stories; stairs (147 steps) lead to the bell chamber and an open observation platform with spectacular views of upper Manhattan and the rivers. The Laura Spelman Rockefeller Memorial Carillon, gift of John D. Rockefeller, Jr., in memory of his mother, contains 74 bells, ranging from the 20-ton Bourdon (the largest tuned bell ever cast) to a 10-lb treble bell. Cast in three stages (1925, 1930, and 1956; Gillet & Johnston Foundry, England, and Van Bergen Foundry, Holland), it is the first carillon to exceed a range of five octaves.

Leave the church by the W. Portal and walk south. At 475 Riverside Drive (120th St) just S. of the church is the *Interchurch Center* (1958; Voorhees, Walker, Smith, Smith & Haines), housing the offices of Protestant, Jewish, and Eastern Orthodox religious organizations. On the ground floor are a chapel and two small exhibition rooms (Mon—Fri 9—4:30; closed holidays; free; public telephones in the main lobby; restrooms on the lower level; occasional lectures and demonstrations; tel: 870-2932). In the larger room are changing exhibits of art, generally religious or spiritual in nature; the smaller Bible Room has the final manuscript copy of the Revised Standard Version of the Bible, displayed in changing exhibitions.

Walk N. on Riverside Drive past Riverside Church toward Grant's Tomb. On the N.W. corner of the church is the *Women's Porch,* with sculptured figures of four biblical women typifying ideal womanhood. Facing N. are Mary and Martha, the sisters of Lazarus; facing W. are Eunice and Lois, mother and grandmother of Timothy. On the ridgepole of the roof is an Angel of the Resurrection.

On the W. side of Riverside Drive at about 122nd St is ***Grant's Tomb.**

General Grant National Memorial. Riverside Drive and 122nd St, New York 10027. Tel: 666-1640. Open Wed—Sun 9—5, free. Not accessible to wheelchairs. No food, no phone, no restrooms. Small gift shop with postcards, books, slides, information on Grant and the Civil War. Tours of monument if booked in advance. Annual celebration on April 27, Grant's birthday.

Officially named the General Grant National Memorial (1891—97; John H. Duncan; DL), one of the city's most imposing formal monuments, the massive granite sepulchre contains the remains of Ulysses S. Grant (1822—85) and his wife, Julia Dent Grant. Intended to be unmistakably tomblike, despite objections that it would give a funereal tone to the neighborhood, it was once a popular site of pilgrimage but now rather sparsely visited.

History. After an illustrious career as commander-in-chief of the Union Armies in the Civil War and a scandal-ridden period as President (1868—76), Ulysses S. Grant died in 1885. He had requested burial in New York, at the U.S. Military Academy in West Point, or in Galena, Illinois. Because Galena seemed too remote and Mrs. Grant could not be buried at West Point, New York was chosen. In 1885, Grant's body was temporarily interred in a brick structure at 123rd St, and five years later John H. Duncan won the architectural competition for a tomb to cost about half a million dollars (eventually 90,000 subscribers contributed about $600,000). Duncan's design was based largely on reconstructions of the Mausoleum at Halicarnassus (now in Turkey). Ground was broken in 1891 and the general's remains were quietly brought to the finished tomb in 1897. Despite the scandals that marred his administration, Grant himself remained a revered figure, and even while the tomb was under construction two attempts were made to claim his remains for other locales.

EXTERIOR. The monument consists of a cubelike base topped by a drum supporting a stepped conical dome. A broad flight of steps flanked by two large eagles leads to the Doric portico and entrance. The raised stone blocks above the portico were originally intended to support equestrian statues of Union generals. Above the cornice a tablet contains Grant's words, "Let us have peace," spoken upon accepting the presidential nomination of 1868; figures of two lamenting women recline against the tablet. The stepped cone, derived from reconstructions of the tomb of Mausolus (died c. 532), was to have been crowned by a statue of Grant in a triumphal chariot.

INTERIOR. The austere interior, inspired by Napoleon's tomb at the Hôtel des Invalides in Paris, is cruciform in plan and dominated by the sunken crypt set directly below the dome. Above the windows, mosaics (1966; Allyn Cox) depict Grant's victories at Vicksburg (E.) and Chattanooga (W.), and the surrender of Robert E. Lee at Appomattox (N.). The coffered dome rests on pendentives with sculptured women (by J. Massey Rhind) symbolizing phases of Grant's life: birth and infancy (S.E.), military career (N.E.), civil career (N.W.), and death (S.W.). The two exhibition rooms on the N. wall are devoted to Grant's civil and military career. A double staircase in the N. arm (currently closed) leads down into the crypt containing the imposing polished red granite sarcophaghi of Gen. and Mrs Grant. Niches in the wall at the crypt level contain bronze busts (1938; William Mues) of Grant's generals Sherman and Sheridan and generals Thomas, Ord, and McPherson (done by Jens Juszko). Originally the windowpanes were clear glass over which were drawn dark purple curtains symbolizing mourning, but the curtains deteriorated and the windows were redesigned by the Tiffany studios and glazed with purple glass, which in its turn was found to be too somber and dark. The present yellow color seems to be some sort of compromise.

The park surrounding the monument, now known as *Grant Centennial Plaza*, was established to commemorate Grant's establishment (1872) of Yellowstone, the first national park. The free-form, free-spirited mosaic benches (1972–74) were created as part of a community participation project.

Directly behind the tomb a fence encloses the *Commemoration Tree*, a ginkgo given (1897) as a gift by China to honor Grant.

Across Riverside Drive to the W. (about opposite the public restrooms in the park) a fence near the footpath encloses a small stone urn "Erected to the Memory of an Amiable Child," St. Claire Pollock, age 5, killed in a fall from the rocks on July 15, 1797, his body found washed up on the rocks. His uncle, George Pollock, a wealthy linen merchant, had bought the land from Nicholas de Peyster and built his home at what is now Riverside Park and 123rd St, on a high piece of land commanding a view of the river. The house (c. 1783), called Strawberry Hill, stood at the N. end of the landscaped oval behind Grant's Tomb. After the child's death, Pollock sold the house to Joseph Alston, husband of Aaron Burr's daughter Theodosia, and returned to Ireland, requesting, however, that the child's grave remain untouched. In the mid-19C the house became the Claremont Inn, popular with travelers, and numbering among its illustrious guests Joseph Bonaparte. It remained until 1951 when it burned and was demolished by the city.

SUBWAY: The nearest stop is the IRT Broadway-7th Ave local (train 1 or 9) at 116th St and Broadway.

BUS: M4 and M5 from Riverside Drive; M104 from Broadway.

30 Washington Heights Museum Group (Audubon Terrace)

SUBWAY: IRT Broadway-7th Ave local (train 1) marked 242nd St to 157th St. IND 6th Ave express (B train marked Washington Heights) to 155th St; walk two blocks west.

BUS: M4 uptown via Madison Ave and Broadway or M5 uptown via 6th Ave / Riverside Drive / Broadway to 155th St.

The **Washington Heights Museum Group,** which embraces the Museum of the American Indian, the Hispanic Society of America, the American Numismatic Society, and the American Academy of Arts and Letters, occupies a plot of land between W. 156th St and W. 155th St along the W. side of Broadway, once part of the estate of John James Audubon. Sometimes collectively referred to as *Audubon Terrace,* the buildings stand on a piece of land that once formed part of the estate and game preserve of John James Audubon the ornithologist and painter. The buildings were financed largely by Archer Milton Huntington, son of Collis P. Huntington, transcontinental railroad builder and steamship magnate. The younger Huntington's interests, however, ran to poetry, archaeology, and scholarship, not railroads, and he is remembered more for the money he gave away—to libraries and museums—than for the money he made. In 1904 he started buying up parcels of Audubon Park for a kind of American acropolis, a concentration of cultural and intellectual institutions which would serve scholars and be available to the public also.

Originally the buildings faced N. to 156th St, where Audubon Park was still undeveloped. Later, about 1911, the architects changed their plan, presumably deciding that the apartment buildings growing up around Audubon Terrace were insufficiently scenic, and changed the Terrace to look inward upon itself. Nowadays the museum buildings, grand and classical in manner, facing each other across a paved brick courtyard, seem incongruous in a modest neighborhood remote from the intellectual life of the city.

On the S. side are the Museum of the American Indian, Heye Foundation (1916), the Hispanic Society of America (1908)—

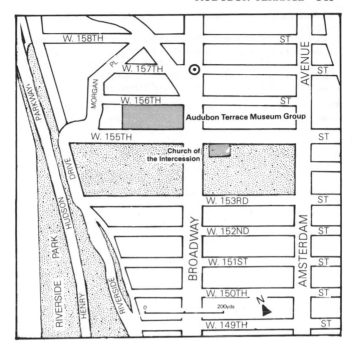

founded by Archer M. Huntington—and the American Numismatic Society (1908), all designed by Charles Pratt Huntington, nephew of the donor, and the Administration Building (1923; William M. Kendall) of the American Academy of Arts and Letters. On the N. side of the courtyard are (E. to W.) the former headquarters of the American Geographical Society (1916; Charles Pratt Huntington), now occupied by Boricua College, the courtyard of the Hispanic Society, and the auditorium and gallery of the American Academy of Arts and Letters (1930; Cass Gilbert).

Dominating the plaza is a group of statues by Anna Hyatt Huntington, already well-known as a sculptor at the time of her marriage to Archer M. Huntington. The largest is a bronze equestrian *statue of El Cid Campeador* (1927) surrounded by four seated warriors, a piece which celebrates the legendary medieval hero who defended Spain against the Moors and replicates Mrs. Huntington's original, erected the same year in Seville. Mrs. Huntington, previously known for her sculpture of animals, contributed also the two limestone lions flanking the entrance of the Hispanic Society (1930), and the four limestone animal groups (bears, jaguars, boars, and vultures) on the terraces of the N. building (1936), as well as the limestone equestrian reliefs of Don Quixote, Cervantes's legendary knight of La Mancha, and Boabdil, the last Moslem king of Granada (1942 and 1944); the inscriptions beneath them are taken from the poetry of her husband.

Now part of the Smithsonian Institution, the *National Museum of the American Indian, founded in 1916 by George G. Heye, is the largest Indian museum anywhere. Its collections include objects belonging to aboriginal peoples, ranging from the Eskimos of the Arctic to the inhabitants of Tierra del Fuego.

Note: In 1992 the Museum will close at this location. Part of the collection will be shown in changing exhibitions at the former Custom House opposite Battery Park. Eventually (late 1990s?) the permanent collection will move to a new building on the Mall in Washington, D.C., though the satellite space at the Custom House will remain permanently open.

The **National Museum of the American Indian**. Broadway at 155th St, New York 10032. Tel: 283-2420. Open Tues–Sat, 10–5; Sun 1–5. Closed Mon and major holidays. Admission charge. Restrooms, gift shop. No restaurant.
   SUBWAY: IRT Broadway local (train 1, marked 242nd St) to 157th St. BUS: M4 or M5.

On the FIRST FLOOR ethnological displays focus on Indians of the eastern and midwestern U. S., including New England tribes. Highlights include Iroquois False Face masks, wampum Treaty Belts given to William Penn in 1683, and a costume of *mishinghali'kun*, a Lenni Lenape ceremonial figure. Displays on the Great Lakes tribes (Ojibwa, Kickapoo, Sauk, and Winnebago Indians, among others) have examples of clothing, farm implements, tools for gathering wild rice, toys, and games. More familiar perhaps are artifacts of the Plains Indians (Sioux, Dakota, Crow, Blackfoot)—buffalo hide robes, a feathered war bonnet, tomahawks, war clubs, and scalps. Indians of the Basin-Plateau region of Idaho and Wyoming (Shawnee, Ute, Nez Percé, and Paiute tribes) are represented by clothing, artifacts and a display on peyote in Indian religion.

The exhibitions on the SECOND FLOOR include archaeological displays (left of stairway) and ethnographic materials from North American Indians of the Southwest and Far West. Among the archaeological displays are a diorama of 16C Indian life in the Inwood section of Upper Manhattan; objects from mounds in Alabama and Oklahoma. The ethnographic displays (other side of stairway) include Navaho weaving, Hopi kachina dolls, an array of Northwest Coast Indian masks, and Eskimo artifacts including fur parkas, masks, and carvings.

On the THIRD FLOOR are displays relating to the Indians of Central and South America. Among the highlights are pottery and sculpture from Colombia and Ecuador (A.D. 500–1500), Peruvian fabrics and clothing (case 204), Chilean silver and weaving, and, most bizarre, several trophy heads, both shrunken and of normal dimensions.

The **Hispanic Society of America** (founded 1904) houses a collection gathered mainly by Archer M. Huntington whose fascination with Spanish and Portuguese culture dated from his first visit to

Spain, when as a young man of 22 he began collecting archaeological fragments from Italica, the earliest Roman colony in Spain.
Today the collection ranges from prehistoric times through the
periods of Roman and Moorish domination, to the present. The
library contains over 100,000 volumes and manuscripts, mainly
on Spanish and Portuguese history, literature, and art.

The Hispanic Society of America. Broadway at 155th St, New York 10032. Tel:
926-2234. Open Tues—Sat 10—4:30, Sun 1—4:30. Closed Mon and major
holidays. Requested donation.
  Restrooms, telephone, no restaurant facilities. Sales desk with postcards,
publications. Not accessible to wheelchairs.
  SUBWAY: IRT Broadway-7th Ave local (train 1) marked 242nd St to 157th
St. IND 6th Ave express (B train marked Washington Heights) to 155th St;
walk two blocks west. BUS: M4 via 5th Ave or M5 via 6th Ave / Riverside Dr /
Broadway to 155th St and Broadway.

The Main Court, two stories high and illuminated in part by
skylights, with its archways of deep red terra-cotta ornately
worked in Spanish Renaissance style, is one of the city's more
remarkable interiors. Featured here are two Goya portraits, a
13C Mater Dolorosa of polychromed wood, pieces of antique
furniture, and changing displays of prints, drawings, and manuscripts. Outside the arches are reliquaries of silver and silver gilt,
architectural fragments, fabrics including Hispano-Moresque and
Mudejar silk, and marble tomb statuary (16—17C). Off the Main
Court a small corridor contains tiles and glazed 18—19C earthenware from Valencia and Toledo. The corridor opens into the
Sorolla Room, decorated by a series of murals (commissioned
1911) by Joaquín Sorolla y Bastida, which depict street scenes
and festivals of regional Spain.
  Upstairs are a display of Hispano-Moresque tiles, mosaics,
lusterware, and other ceramics; a small collection of historic
glass; and paintings by Spanish artists, including El Greco,
Velázquez, and Zurbarán.

The **American Numismatic Society** (founded 1858) contains an
extraordinary numismatic collection and the world's finest numismatic library, whose 70,000 items include books, periodicals,
and auction catalogues. Although basically the Society is scholarly in nature, the permanent exhibition on coinage, from prehis-
tory to the present, should both profit (intellectually) and delight
anyone interested in either history or money.

American Numismatic Society, 155th St and Broadway, New York 10032. Tel:
234-3130. Open Tues—Sat 9—4:30; Sun 1—4. Closed Mon and holidays. Free;
ring bell for entrance. Curatorial assistance and access to special sections of
the collection upon request. Restrooms, telephone, no eating facilities, no gift
shop.
  SUBWAY: IRT Broadway-7th Ave local (train 1) marked 242nd St to 157th
St and Broadway. IND 6th Ave express (B train) to 155th St; walk two blocks
west. BUS: M4 via 5th Ave or M5 via 6th Ave / Riverside Dr / Broadway to
155th St and Broadway.

The museum has two galleries. In the East Gallery are changing
displays of coins and medals. In the West Gallery is the permanent exhibition entitled "The World of Coins," which surveys the

history of coinage from about 1000 B.C., when coins were invented more or less contemporaneously in China, India, and Asia Minor, to the present day when computers and the marvels of modern technology have created money without physical form, theoretically making coins obsolete. Examples of ancient, medieval, and modern coins are displayed in a setting that makes their historical and artistic significance intelligible to the numismatically innocent, while visitors eager for more detailed information can tap into the data base of a computer installed for that purpose.

The American Academy of Arts and Letters was founded in 1904 by the National Institute of Arts and Letters to recognize outstanding achievement in the arts.

The American Academy / Institute of Arts and Letters. Broadway and 155th St, New York 10032. Tel: 368-5900.Call for admission, days and hours of special exhibitions. Not accessible to wheelchairs. Research library by appointment.
   SUBWAY: IRT Broadway-7th Ave local (train 1 marked 242nd St) to 157th St. IND 6th Ave express (B train marked Washington Heights) to 155th St; walk two blocks west. BUS: M4 via 5th Ave or M5 via 6th Ave / Riverside Dr / Broadway to 155th St and Broadway.

Founded in 1898 to honor artists, writers, and composers, the Academy has 250 members of whom 50 are elected for further distinction by election to the American Academy of Arts and Letters. (The "Academy" and the "Institute," formerly separate organizations, were unified in 1977). The Academy-Institute also includes 75 foreign honorary members and 10 American honorary members (choreographers, filmmakers, and photographers). Among those so honored have been Pearl S. Buck, Aaron Copland, Lillian Hellman, Edward Hopper, Walter Lippmann, John Steinbeck, Samuel L. Clemens (Mark Twain), and Andrew Wyeth.
   The Academy-Institute holds annual exhibitions which reflect its activities and focus on the work of its members. On display are American sculpture, painting, and manuscripts. The library contains first editions, manuscripts, musical scores, notebooks, and other memorabilia pertaining to members and their work, a collection available to scholars by appointment.
   The Administration Building (1923; McKim, Mead & White) stands on the S. side of the courtyard. The other building, on the N. side, contains the North Gallery and auditorium (1930; Cass Gilbert). Among the significant features of the buildings, Italian Renaissance in style, are the bronze doors, decorated with symbolic reliefs. The doors at the entrance of the Administration Building were designed by Adolph A. Weinman and those leading to the galleries by Herbert Adams.

The building on the N.E. corner of the complex, now occupied by *Boricua College,* was constructed as the home of the American Geographical Society, which moved to the University of Wisconsin at Milwaukee for financial reasons, taking with it the largest map collection (some 325,000 maps) in the western hemisphere. Boricua College, a four-year liberal arts school, offers courses designed to meet the educational needs of Spanish-speaking students.

Other nearby points of interest. Directly across Broadway on the S.E. corner of W. 155th St is the CHURCH OF THE INTERCESSION (1914; Cram, Goodhue & Ferguson; DL), formerly a chapel of Trinity Parish, built by the preeminent ecclesiastical architect, Bertram Grosvenor Goodhue. The church complex, which includes a bell tower, cloister, parish house, and vicarage, has been praised for the site design which recalls the times when the neighborhood was still rural and evokes the Gothic Revival ideal of the country church. Noteworthy in the interior are the wooden ceiling supported by stone piers, the wood carving, the high altar inlaid with some 1500 stones collected from the Holy Land and other shrines of early Christianity, and the wall tomb of architect Goodhue, decorated with reliefs of some of his buildings. Behind the church is part of the original graveyard including the burial plot of John James Audubon.

TRINITY CEMETERY occupies a plot of land from Riverside Drive to Amsterdam Ave, 153rd to 155th Sts (open 9–4:30 daily, entrance on 155th St near Riverside Drive).

Joggers run in the western part of the cemetery but it is still probably not a place to wander around alone. The plot E. of Broadway near the church is less frequently used.

In 1842 Trinity Parish, realizing the scarcity of land in lower Manhattan, bought a 23-acre parcel from Richard F. Carman (the area was then known as Carmanville) and set aside part for the cemetery. Its hummocky topography sloping toward the Hudson suggests the 19C landscape before developers exercised their leveling powers. Trinity Cemetery (not to be confused with Trinity Churchyard downtown on Broadway and Wall St) is the only graveyard in Manhattan still accepting burials, although the only usable space belongs to Gallatins, Astors, Harsens, and others who purchased family plots many years ago. When Broadway was extended northward, the parcel was cut in two and Trinity corporation built a suspension bridge (1871; Vaux & Withers) joining the two halves, so that visitors could wander between them without having to descend to the street. Although the bridge was demolished in 1911, the high granite wall supporting its ornamental iron fence with gateways (1876) and the gatehouse and keeper's lodge (1883; Vaux & Radford) still remain.

In the eastern sector of the cemetery, near the Church of the Intercession, is the grave of John James Audubon (1785–1851) who after long struggles achieved fame and financial security with his *Birds of North America*. The gravestone, a tall brown Celtic cross decorated with reliefs of animals and birds, rests on a pedestal with sculpted rifles and powder horn, palette and paintbrushes: the naturalist, also something of an adventurer, tended to exaggerate his exploits. Also in the easterly parcel is the grave of Fernando Wood (1812–81), whose tall marker is surmounted with a shrouded urn. Wood was mayor of New York during the "Boss" Tweed years, having made his fortune selling questionable liquor to sailors and investing the returns in ships and real estate.

Enter the western parcel, between Broadway and Riverside Drive, from Riverside Drive near the cemetery offices. In this parcel of the graveyard is a mausoleum, built by the parish in part to help defray maintenance costs. Clement Clarke Moore, writer of the verses beginning "'Twas the night before Christmas…," is buried in the N.W. part of the cemetery (lower slope near the Riverside Drive retaining wall and 155th St). Local children still visit his grave Christmas Eve to hear the minister recite his famous words. Further up the hill is the Astor plot containing the remains of John Jacob Astor (1822–90), philanthropist and grandson of the patriarch, and his wife, Charlotte Gibbes Astor. Astor, who administered the family estate for the later years of his life, funded such charities as the Children's Aid Society, the New York Cancer Hospital, and the Astor Library. Higher up the slope lies Eliza Brown Jumel (1775–1865), who married first a successful wine merchant (rumor had it that she allowed him to bleed to death) and then Aaron Burr whose interest in her money became too evident for the marriage to last out a year. Alfred Tennyson Dickens, son of the novelist, godson of the poet, lies on the hillside near Broadway and the 155th St gate. He died of a heart attack at the Hotel Astor while on a lecture tour and was buried here with great ceremony; Andrew Carnegie was one of the honorary pallbearers.

North of Audubon Terrace at 264 W. 156th St is the CHURCH OF OUR LADY OF ESPERANZA, built in 1912 by Charles Pratt Huntington who designed the museum group. Inside the entrance a stairway leads up to the small sanctuary, decorated in gold and green, whose stained glass windows, skylight, and hanging lamp were donated by the King of Spain.

31 Washington Heights, The Cloisters, and Inwood

SUBWAY: IRT Broadway-7th Ave local (train 1 or 9) to 168th St; IND 8th Ave express (A train) to 168th St.

BUS: M4 via Madison Ave or M5 via Broadway and Riverside Drive to the George Washington Bridge Bus Station.

Note: Since the distances on this route are long and the traffic not too heavy, the route lends itself to car travel. The first portion passes through borderline neighborhoods of minor touristic interest. Visitors whose prime interest is in museums and architectural landmarks should start at Fort Tryon Park, for which separate directions are given.

Upper Manhattan, largely unknown to visitors except for the Cloisters, has some of the city's best scenery, several museums, an 18C farmhouse, and a population of about a quarter of a million people. The area from 155th St to Dyckman St is known as *Washington Heights;* N. of that it is called *Inwood.*

At the N. tip of Manhattan, where the island narrows to a slender peninsula, the leveling effects of the city's developers are less evident than elsewhere in the city. Elevations rise to more than 200 ft, hardly alpine but high enough to affect the street plan, whose pleasant deviations from the downtown grid follow early roads built over Indian trails, which in turn followed the contours of the land. Two ridges of MANHATTAN SCHIST, the bedrock upon which the city's first skyscrapers depended, run N. and S.—the Fort Washington ridge on the W. and the Fort George ridge on the E., which ends at Dyckman St. Between them is a basin known as the Inwood lowlands, beneath whose soil and architectural accretions lies a base of INWOOD MARBLE, a stone more easily eroded than the schist. To the S. of Inwood, the Broadway valley between the ridges forms the natural roadbed for that avenue, formerly called the Boulevard in this part of town until, in 1899, its full 15½-mile length from Bowling Green to Spuyten Duyvil was given one name. At about Dyckman St the road formerly swung E., following low ground along the Harlem River, which it crossed at King's Bridge.

As the names of the ridges suggest, the high ground had strategic importance during the Revolutionary War and was fortified with three outposts: Fort Washington overlooking the Hudson River, whose outlines are still recognizable in Bennett Park just W. of Fort Washington Ave at 183rd St; Fort Tryon a little to the N. in the park now bearing the same name; and Fort George on the E. ridge near the intersection of Fort George Ave and Fort George Hill (formerly an extension of St. Nicholas Ave, renamed in 1962). The area remained rural well into the 19C, attracting gentlemen farmers and others who located their country homes here, among them publisher James Gordon Bennett and naturalist John James Audubon.

C. K. G. Billings, heir to a Chicago gas fortune, owned the land where Fort Tryon Park now stands, and to celebrate the opening of a $200,000 stable completed in 1903, Billings, also known as the "American Horse King," threw a dinner for 36 of his friends at Sherry's restaurant, an affair known in the annals of New York society as "The Horseback Dinner." The Horse King's companions enjoyed various courses served on little tables attached to the saddles of the horses (brought upstairs in the freight elevators) upon which they sat during the entire meal. Lest the guests snigger at the incongruity of it all, the walls of the restaurant were masked in painted woodland scenery and the floor covered with grasses and other suitable materials, perhaps creating the impression that the whole affair was taking place al fresco.

The completion of the IRT subway in 1906, however, hastened the end of aristocratic exclusivity at the N. end of the island, and the process of urbanization was essentially completed by the arrival of the IND line in 1932. John D. Rockefeller, Jr., had bought the Billings estate in 1917, and the city had begun purchasing large tracts of land, now parks, along the rivers around the turn of the century. Upper Manhattan was developed as a working-class residential community and has remained one, though the population, once largely Irish but with Armenian and

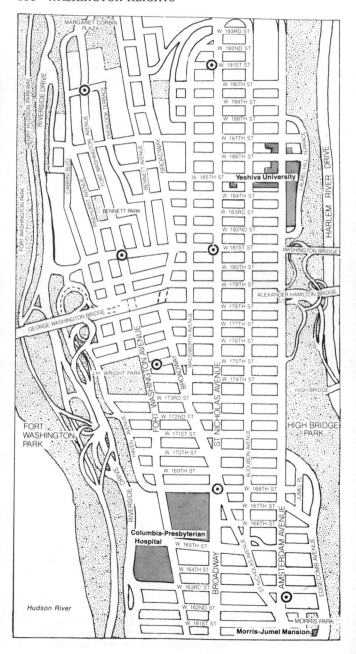

Greek communities, is no longer predominantly white. During the 1930s an influx of Jews fleeing Nazi Germany temporarily conferred the name The Fourth Reich on the Heights. Nowadays Washington Heights is a warren of ethnic enclaves, many of whose residents are black and Hispanic, including Puerto Ricans, Dominicans, and Cubans. The area also claims Koreans, Soviet Jews, and the remnants of earlier Irish and German Jewish populations, as well as "yuppies" drawn uptown by more moderate rents.

At 165th St and Broadway stands the former *Audubon Ballroom* (1913; Thomas W. Lamb) and San Juan Theater. Malcolm X, black activist and civil rights leader, was assassinated there in 1965. The ballroom and adjoining theater, originally called the Audubon Theater, an impressive movie palace in its youth, were acquired by the city in the mid-1970s. Columbia University currently plans a research complex on the site, which will stretch from 165th to 168th St and include biomedical research laboratories and commercial labs.

The COLUMBIA-PRESBYTERIAN MEDICAL CENTER, which fills the blocks from 165th to 168th Sts, between Broadway and Riverside Drive, is one of the largest and most prestigious medical centers in the nation (1928–47; James Gamble Rogers, Inc.; additions: 1947–64; Rogers & Butler; 1964–74; Rogers, Butler & Burgun), on a commanding site along the hillside overlooking the Hudson River. Since 1911 it has embraced both the teaching and research facilities of Columbia University's College of Physicians and Surgeons and the clinics and facilities for patient care of the Presbyterian Hospital.

The Presbyterian Hospital was founded in 1868 by James Lenox and located downtown between Park and Madison Aves from 70th to 71st Sts. Now, with the corporate title of The Presbyterian Hospital in the City of New York, it has about 1400 beds and a staff of 1137 attending physicians and 384 interns and residents who care for about 150,000 patients annually. The hospital also includes Babies Hospital, whose old-fashioned name harks back to its foundation in 1887; the Dana W. Atchley Pavilion for ambulatory patient care; Harkness Pavilion for private patients; the Edward S. Harkness Eye Institute; the Neurological Institute, founded in 1909 as one of the first nongovernmental hospitals in the nation treating diseases of the nervous system, and the New York Orthopaedic Hospital, founded in 1866 by, among others, Theodore Roosevelt, father of the President of that same name, who was deeply interested in the problems of the crippled. The Vanderbilt family endowed the main outpatient facility (1888) which bears their name. The Sloane Hospital for Women, the Squier Urological Clinic, and the Radiotherapy Center also come under the corporate aegis of the Presbyterian Hospital. The Columbia University College of Physicians and Surgeons, along with its Schools of Public Health, Dental and Oral Surgery, and Nursing, and the Institutes of Cancer Research and Human Nutrition are nationally recognized for the quality of their teaching and research.

WADSWORTH AVE, which forks off Broadway to the right just above 173rd St, was named to honor the heroism of James Samuel Wadsworth, father of six and Republican candidate for governor in 1862, who rose to the rank of brigadier general in the Union Army during the Civil War despite a total lack of military training. Wadsworth died in the battle of Chancellorsville when, after two horses had been shot from under him, his third mount galloped in uncontrollable panic straight at the Confederate lines.

Return to Broadway on the N.E. corner of Broadway and 175th St stands the former movie palace, *Loew's 175th St Theater* (1930; Thomas W. Lamb), whose facade mixed Oriental, Indian, Mayan, Islamic, and classical motifs. The architect, known for other theaters in the city, said he chose this exotic mélange to create an atmosphere in which the mind was free to frolic. In the theater's heyday, the lobby was a modern, gilded version of a Moorish seraglio and the auditorium was redolent with Byzantine and Romanesque elements. These luxurious trappings were turned to religious uses in the 1970s, when the auditorium was used as a church by a charismatic preacher, Frederick Eikerenkoetter, known familiarly as the Reverend Ike.

The approaches to the ***George Washington Bridge** (1931; Othmar H. Ammann, engineer, and Cass Gilbert), cut across town between 179th and 180th Sts. Like the Brooklyn Bridge, the George Washington Bridge, which crosses the Hudson River to Fort Lee, New Jersey, represented a step forward in technology while becoming also an object of beauty and imaginative inspiration. Its 3500-ft span doubled the record for suspension bridges while its soaring steel towers and curving cables inspired Charles Edouard Jenneret (Le Corbusier) to call it "the only seat of grace in the disordered city."

History. A trans-Hudson Bridge had been contemplated as early as 1868, when the state of New Jersey authorized one at the S. boundary of Union Township, a move which the State of New York ignored. Conflicting interests and difficulties in financing and engineering kept the involved agencies squabbling until the Port of New York Authority was formed in 1921 and brought the project to fruition. The man eventually chosen as chief engineer, Othmar H. Ammann, had emigrated from Switzerland in 1904 expressly to participate in American bridge projects, the most daring and advanced of that time, and had studied the political, financial, and structural problems surrounding previous attempts at a Hudson River crossing; it was he who proposed an automobile crossing, not a railroad bridge, thus cutting costs and anticipating America's romance with the internal combustion engine. The Port Authority funded the bridge ($59 million) by selling bonds, a difficult task in the years before 1929 when stock prices were booming. Groundbreaking ceremonies took place in 1927 and four years later 5000 people came to listen to speeches marking the completion of the project. When the bridge was then opened to the public, the first to cross were two boys from the Bronx on roller skates. Between 1958 and 1962 a lower deck was constructed without disturbing traffic on the existing bridge, a feat accomplished by raising 76 steel sections from below, either from the shores or from barges. The lower deck, snidely nicknamed the Martha Washington Bridge, brought the total cost to $215.8 million and took longer to build than the original structure but increased its capacity 75% to its present level of about 50 million cars yearly (in the eastbound, toll, direction).

On the New York side the huge U-shaped anchorage in Fort Washington Park also serves as a roadway arch. To avoid placing such a bulky object on the New Jersey Palisades, Ammann had workers tunnel into the rock of the cliffs, place eye-bar chains in the tunnels (which were large enough to accommodate four trolley tracks), attach the cables to the chains, and fill the tunnels with cement. The New Jersey tower stands 76 ft out in the river, but the New York tower is on land because a deep fissure runs beneath the river. The original plans called for clothing the towers in masonry for which Cass Gilbert produced appropriate designs, but by 1931 the Port Authority having just bought the Holland Tunnel was unwilling to spend money for cosmetic purposes.

Statistics. The bridge is 4760 ft between anchorages, with decks 115 ft and 212 ft above mean high water. The four steel cables (two on each side of the road) are composed of 26,474 wires apiece making the total length of steel wire in the cables 105,000 miles, almost half the distance to the moon. The towers rise to a height of 604 ft above the water. The bridge contains 113,000 tons of steel, 28,000 tons of cable wire, and 200,000 cubic yards of masonry.

At the E. end of the George Washington Bridge, between Fort Washington and Wadsworth Aves, is the **George Washington Bridge Bus Station** (1963; Pier Luigi Nervi and the Port of New York Authority), the concrete wings of its butterfly-shaped roof rising to allow the fumes from the buses to escape from beneath. The station, which connects with the Eighth Ave IND subway, serves some 11 million commuters yearly. The **Bridge Apartments** (1964; Brown & Guenther) between 178th and179th Sts, Wadsworth and Audubon Aves, represent an early attempt to use the air rights over a highway for residential purposes. Unfortunately the roadway is not completely decked over and the noise, smell, and dirt from this major artery rise to assault the senses of those living above.

At 181st St and Pinehurst Ave a set of steps descends via a footbridge at Riverside Drive and an underpass at the Henry Hudson Parkway to Fort Washington Park along the river. Just under the tower of the bridge stands the **Little Red Lighthouse** (1921), which once warned river traffic of shoals off Jeffrey's Hook. When the navigational lights on the bridge took over that function, the lighthouse went up for auction (1951) but was saved by the pleas of admirers, many of whom had read Hildegarde Hoyt Swift's children's tale *The Little Red Lighthouse and the Great Gray Bridge*. Today the lighthouse (interior not open to the public) is maintained by the Parks Department. (This section of the park tends to be quiet and isolated.) Return to Pinehurst Ave.

Bennett Park, between 183rd and 185th Sts, Fort Washington and Pinehurst Aves, stands on the site of Fort Washington, a Revolutionary War fortification.

After defeats on Long Island and in Manhattan, Washington led his troops N. leaving behind a garrison at Fort Washington, a crudely fortified earthwork with five bastions under the command of Col. Robert Magaw. On November 16, 1776, the Americans were attacked by Hessians led by Gen. von Knyphausen, who scaled the outworks on Long Hill (the ridge in what is now Fort Tryon Park) from the north and east. General Cornwallis invaded Manhattan across the Harlem River at what is now about 201st St; the 42nd Highlanders crossed the Harlem more or less where High Bridge now stands, and British troops led by Lord Percy marched up from downtown, while warships bombarded the fort from the Hudson. The defenders of the outworks were killed or pushed back into the fort, which quickly surrendered after it became clear that the American troops were outnumbered. The loss of 54 lives and the capture of 2634 of Washington's best-equipped troops was a severe blow to the ragged, inexperienced American army.

Later the land where the fort stood came into the possession of James Gordon Bennett, founder of the *New York Herald*. His son, an expatriot, gave the park to the city in 1903 in honor of his father. In the small park are paving stones marking the outlines of the fort and a rocky outcropping which is the highest natural elevation in Manhattan, 267.75 ft (some sources say 265.05 ft).

PINEHURST AVE running along the W. side of the park is named after the estate of one C. P. Bucking. Facing the park are the *Hudson View Gardens* (116 Pinehurst Ave) built in 1925 (George F. Pelham) in the then-popular Collegiate Gothic style.

At 701 Fort Washington Ave, N. of 190th St and just S. of Fort Tryon Park, is MOTHER CABRINI HIGH SCHOOL, named after St. Frances Xavier Cabrini (canonized 1946), the first American saint, founder of the Missionary Sisters of the Sacred Heart, known for her many charitable works including her assistance to immigrants. Her remains are buried in the chapel beneath the altar.

Other points of interest: Yeshiva University between 183rd and 187th Sts along Amsterdam Ave (seven blocks E. of Fort Washington Ave) evolved from the first Jewish parochial school (1886) in the nation and a theological seminary founded ten years later. The *Main Building* (1928; Charles B. Meyers Assocs.) on the S.W. corner of 186th St and Amsterdam Ave is an exotic Near Eastern conglomeration of minarets, towers, arches, domes, and buttresses executed in orange stone, ceramic tile, copper, and brass. The school provides undergraduate and graduate education in the arts, sciences, and Jewish studies, while the associated Rabbi Isaac Elchanan Theological Seminary trains rabbis and cantors.

The YESHIVA UNIVERSITY MUSEUM (1973) offers changing exhibitions on Jewish history, culture, and religion.

Yeshiva University Museum. 2520 Amsterdam Ave (185th St), New York 10033. Tel: 960-5390. Open Tues, Wed, Thurs 10:30–5; Sun 12–6. Closed Jewish holidays. Admission charge. Lectures, guided tours, family events, membership with benefits. Cafeteria and restroom facilities in university building across the street. Gift shop. Limited wheelchair accessibility.

SUBWAY: IRT Broadway-7th Ave local (train 1, marked 242nd St / B'way) to 181st St. IND 8th Ave express (A train) to 181st St. Walk east to Amsterdam Ave. BUS: M101 via Third Ave to 185th St.

In the permanent collection are ten accurate models of historic synagogues from ancient times to the 19C, including the Touro Synagogue (1763) of Newport, Rhode Island, the oldest extant Jewish house of worship in the country. All the models are not always on display. Changing exhibitions have included ethnological shows (for example, the Ashkenazy Jews), historical ones (daily life in ancient Israel), and eclectic ones (an interactive show of Jewish law and doctrine illustrated with electronic art developed at the Massachusetts Institute of Technology). The shows link Jewish customs or history with biblical law and seek to further knowledge and appreciation of Jewish culture. Smaller exhibitions show the work of major Jewish artists.

Two bridges cross the Harlem River nearby: the Washington Bridge (1888) at 181st St, and the Alexander Hamilton Bridge (1964) between 178th and 179th Sts, which carries the Cross Bronx Expressway into Manhattan. The **Washington Bridge** (best

The Cloisters, which houses part of the Metropolitan Museum's medieval collection, incorporates architectural elements from churches, monasteries, and other medieval European buildings. Pictured here is the Bonnefont Cloister from late 12th and early 13th century France. (Marilynn K. Yee / NYT PICTURES)

seen from the boat tour around the island, the Major Deegan Expressway across the Harlem River, or Laurel Hill Terrace, located a block E. of Amsterdam Ave between 183rd and 188th Sts) is one of the city's most handsome. A double steel arch (each arch 510 ft across) spans the river and the railroad tracks on its E. bank. The present design is a simplified version of a prize-winning plan submitted to the city by C. C. Schneider. Granite viaducts with masonry arches lead from high bluffs on both the Manhattan and Bronx sides, 151.6 ft above mean high water, making the bridge 16 ft higher than the Brooklyn Bridge and 6 inches higher than the Statue of Liberty. Return to Fort Washington Ave and 181st St.

The 66 acres of *Fort Tryon Park** contain the Cloisters and offer landscaped terraces, lawns, gardens, and wonderful views of the Hudson River. It is one of the city's better-maintained parks and on weekends one of its most popular.

> SUBWAY: IND 8th Ave express (A train) to 190th St. Exit by elevator and either walk through the park or take the M4 bus directly to the Cloisters.
>
> BUS: M4 via Madison Ave and Broadway.
>
> CAR: N. on Henry Hudson Parkway, first exit past George Washington Bridge. Sign indicates park entrance. Cars come into the park beneath a dramatic masonry arch bridging a deep cut in the ridge. Free parking, but usually crowded on pleasant weekends.

John D. Rockefeller, Jr., bought the park land (some of it from

Fort Tryon Park

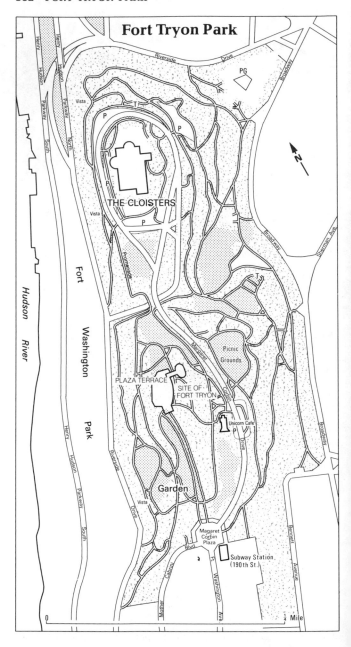

the C. K. G. Billings estate (see p. 555) in 1909 for $1.7 million and spent an additional $3.6 million to improve it before donating it to the city in 1930. The landscape architect was Frederick Law Olmsted, Jr., son of the designer of Central Park. Visible from Riverside Drive near the car entrance are the gateposts and part of the arcaded drive of the Billings estate.

From the plaza at Fort Washington Ave and Mother Cabrini Blvd a roadway and a footpath enter the park.

The roadway is named after Margaret Cochran Corbin, a 26-year-old Revolutionary War heroine who fought beside her husband John in the Battle of Fort Washington until he was killed; she took over his gun and continued firing until she herself was severely wounded. After the war, still known familiarly as "Captain Molly," she became a domestic servant remarked upon for her unbridled tongue and indifference to the niceties of dress. She died in 1800 and was buried in modest circumstances until the Daughters of the American Revolution had her body exhumed and reinterred in the Post Cemetery at West Point.

The footpath leads past flower gardens and the cafeteria (open all year 10–5 with slight variations according to the weather) to the **site of the old fort.** Built in the summer of 1776 as an outwork to Fort Washington to the S., it fell (Nov 16, 1776) to Hessian mercenaries. After the American defeat, the British renamed it Fort Tryon in honor of William Tryon, last British governor of New York (1771–78). From the site of the fort a path leads N. along the side of the hill to the Cloisters, offering beautiful views of the river and the New Jersey Palisades.

****The Cloisters,** the only branch museum of the Metropolitan Museum of Art, is located at the N. end of Fort Tryon Park. Named after the medieval cloisters incorporated within the building, it has outstanding medieval collections, lovely gardens, and beautiful natural surroundings.

The Cloisters. Fort Tryon Park, New York 10040. Tel: 923-3700. Open March through Oct, Tues–Sun 9:30–5:15; Nov through Feb, Tues–Sun 9:30–4:45. Closed Mon, Thanksgiving, Christmas, New Year's Day. Admission by voluntary contribution; you must pay something, but the amount is discretionary.

Limited free car parking around museum. Restrooms, telephone. No restaurant facilities, but picnicking permitted in park; cafeteria in park S. of museum. Gallery tours (3 P.M. Tues, Wed, and Thurs in spring, summer, fall; in winter, Wed only); programs of recorded music, concerts, special events, and exhibitions. Handicapped visitors should notify museum in advance to arrange access; restrooms and telephone accessible to visitors in wheelchairs.

SUBWAY: IND 8th Ave express (A train) to 190th St-Overlook Terrace. Exit by elevator, take M4 bus or walk through park to museum. BUS: M4, marked "Ft Tryon Park / The Cloisters," goes to door of museum. CAR: Henry Hudson Parkway north to first exit after the George Washington Bridge.

The museum building, large parts of the collection, and Fort Tryon Park were donated by John D. Rockefeller, Jr., who also bought land directly W. of the Hudson and donated it as a park to the state of New Jersey, thereby ensuring an unspoiled view across the river from the museum. Despite its medieval appearance, the building (1934–38; Charles Collens of Allen, Collens & Willis) was not copied from a single model, but was developed

THE CLOISTERS
Main Floor

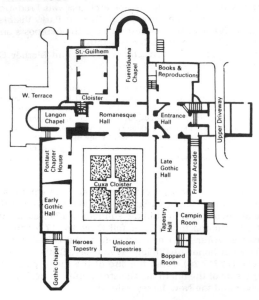

around medieval architectural elements—parts of cloisters from five ruined medieval monasteries, a Romanesque chapel, a 12C Spanish apse—with an effort to make modern additions as unobtrusive as possible. The courtyard gardens and the exterior landscaping have all been planned with medieval originals in mind and with allowances for New York's harsh winters.

Note: The following description proceeds chronologically, beginning with the Romanesque Hall and ending with the Late Gothic Hall and Froville arcade. This is not precisely the order in which the rooms are arranged and it may be necessary to consult the museum map.

The ROMANESQUE HALL incorporates three portals suggesting the evolution of the sculptured church doorway in the 12–13C: a 12C French Romanesque doorway, the late 12C Reugny doorway, transitional between the Romanesque and Gothic styles, and a magnificent 13C Burgundian Gothic doorway with jamb figures of two kings. Also displayed are 13C Spanish frescoes of a lion and winged dragon.

The FUENTIDUEÑA CHAPEL comes from a 12C Spanish church about 100 miles N. of Madrid. The apse, on exchange loan from Spain, is decorated with limestone sculpture including large pier figures of St. Martin (left) and an Annunciation group (right). The frescoes date from the 12C and depict the Virgin and Child with the three magi and the archangels Michael and Gabriel, the

Temptation of Christ, and the Healing of the Blind Man and Raising of Lazarus.

The SAINT-GUILHEM CLOISTER is built around a series of capitals, shafts, and columns (completed before 1206) from a Benedictine abbey near Montpellier. The capitals are carved with various motifs including historical themes, stylized acanthus leaves, naturalistic vine leaves, and animals; several of the column shafts are handsomely carved.

Incorporated in the walls of the LANGON CHAPEL is stonework from the 12C church near Bordeaux. The two large crowned heads on the capital of the column nearest the altar on the right may represent Henry II of England and his wife Eleanor of Aquitaine who visited Langon in 1155. The ciborium (canopy) over the altar is from a church near Rome. The wooden Romanesque *Enthroned Virgin and Child* is one of the few surviving wood sculptures from an artistically important area of Burgundy.

With the exception of the plaster vaults and the floor, the CHAPTER HOUSE FROM PONTAUT is an architectural reconstruction, stone by stone and brick by brick, of the chapter house from a 12C abbey in Gascony. It served as a meeting room where the monks gathered to discuss monastery business and in its original setting had a dormitory above it.

The pink and white marble elements of the CUXA CLOISTER come from an important 12C Benedictine monastery in the eastern Pyrenees. The present reconstruction is about half the size of the original and is made according to evidence of fragments, excavations on the site, and notes and drawings from the 18–19C. The simplest and perhaps the earliest capitals are undecorated; more elaborate ones include a capital with rearing lions at the corners and a group with leaf forms and primitively designed heads. In the center is a garden with fragrant plants.

The NINE HEROES TAPESTRY ROOM features the major part of a 14C set of French tapestries, one of only two known existing sets from that period. The Nine Heroes—Hector, Alexander, and Julius Caesar (pagan), David, Joshua, and Judas Maccabeus (Hebrew), and Arthur, Charlemagne, and Godfrey of Bouillon (Christian)—were a popular theme of medieval legend and frequently appear in 14C painting and sculpture. The set, cut up and dispersed over the centuries, has been reassembled from 95 fragments over a period of 20 years and now constitutes about ⅔ of the original work.

In the EARLY GOTHIC HALL is sculpture from the 13–14C as well as painting and architectural elements (ceiling beams and stained glass windows). From this room a short stairway leads down to the GOTHIC CHAPEL with tomb sculpture and stained glass. The *Tomb effigy of Jean d'Alluye* shows the young man fully armed, with his hands joined in prayer and his feet resting against a crouching lion. Other important pieces in this room are the tombs of the Spanish counts of Urgel, among the finest surviving examples of their kind. The five lancet windows have 14C Austrian stained glass.

Next in chronological order is the *BONNEFONT CLOISTER, outside the Glass Gallery. The gray-white marble columns and

THE CLOISTERS
Ground Floor

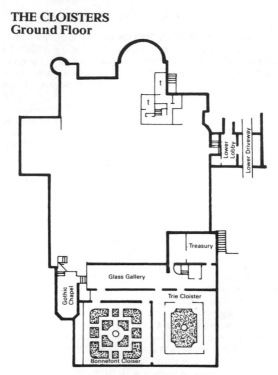

capitals of this cloister come from a Cistercian abbey near Toulouse. The capitals (first half of the 14C) are carved to represent
natural and imaginary plants. The garden (good views of the
river and George Washington Bridge) suggested by medieval
gardens depicted in paintings, is planted with herbaceous plants
which were cultivated during the Middle Ages.

Next to the Bonnefont Cloister is the TRIE CLOISTER from a
former Carmelite convent S.W. of Toulouse, destroyed except for
the church in 1571 by the Huguenots. The capitals, probably
carved between 1484 and 1490, show scenes from the Bible,
saints' legends, and coats of arms of local families and are
arranged where possible in chronological order of the scenes
depicted, beginning at the N.W. corner near the entrance from
the Bonnefont Cloister. The plants of the garden were selected
from those shown in the Unicorn tapestries.

In the GLASS GALLERY windows are 75 panels and roundels
of stained glass (15–early-16C), usually found in secular buildings but with sacred subjects, as well as examples of 15–
early-16C sculpture. Beyond the doorway to the Trie Cloister is
elaborately carved woodwork from a house at Abbeville which
once opened onto a spiral staircase.

In the *TREASURY (three rooms) are smaller objects of exceptional quality and value used for religious and state ceremonies; there are examples of Limoges enamels, illuminated manuscripts including the *Belles Heures* of the Duke of Berry, carved ivories, bronzes, reliquaries, a flabellum used for keeping flies off the eucharistic vessels, chalices, and other precious objects of small scale. The walrus tusk *ivory cross*, a 12C English Romanesque cross with more than a hundred carved figures, attributed to the abbey of Bury Saint Edmunds, is one of the outstanding objects in the collection.

Return to the main floor and the BOPPARD ROOM, containing six late-Gothic stained glass panels (15C). Originally made for the church of a Carmelite convent at Boppard on the Rhine, the windows depict bishops and saints. The 15C alabaster altarpiece from Spain has scenes from the lives of St. Martin and St. Thecla. An imposing brass eagle lectern and a 6-ft painted Spanish Easter candlestick stand before the altar. The 15C tapestries of the adjoining TAPESTRY HALL include one celebrating the Glorification of Charles VII and another from Tournai with the coat of arms of John Lord Dynham.

The **HALL OF THE UNICORN TAPESTRIES contains a famous series of six late-medieval tapestries along with fragments of another which depict *The Hunt of the Unicorn, a legendary creature rich in both religious and secular symbolism during the Middle Ages. The appeal of the tapestries almost five centuries later comes from subject matter, the naturalistically rendered animals and flowers, and the profusion of detail: over 100 different species of plants appear of which 85 are recognizable. John D. Rockefeller, Jr., donated the tapestries to the Cloisters.

The SPANISH ROOM, also known as the CAMPIN ROOM, with its 15C painted Spanish ceiling, has been decorated like a room in a house whose furnishings serve as a backdrop to the *Annunciation altarpiece by Robert Campin (c. 1425), an early Flemish masterpiece. The altarpiece has three panels: two kneeling donors on the left, the central Annunciation, and St. Joseph in his workshop on the right.

The LATE GOTHIC HALL, sometimes used for changing exhibitions, contains late-15C works, including sculpture and painting, from the Cloisters and Metropolitan Museum collections. Notable are a carved oak relief depicting *The Death of the Virgin* from Cologne; a Hispano-Flemish altarpiece depicting *The Lamentation;* and a polychromed and gilded wood group of *The Three Magi,* often thought to have descended from the Sons of Noah and thus been representative to medieval viewers of the three races of mankind.

The FROVILLE ARCADE, just outside the Late Gothic Hall, is built around nine pointed arches from the 15C Benedictine priory of Froville in eastern France. The arches, grouped in threes and separated by buttresses as they were in their original setting, are typical of 14–15C cloisters which depended for effect on their proportions rather than on great skill in decoration or stonecutting as did earlier Gothic and Romanesque arcades.

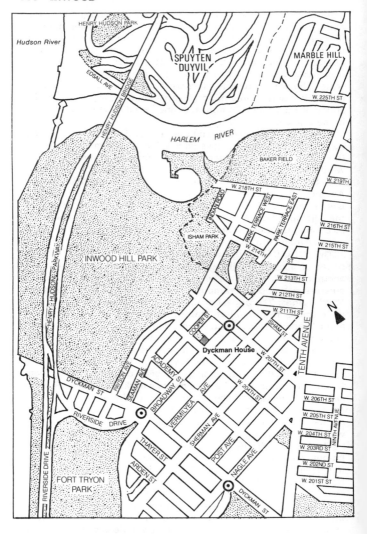

From the Cloisters paths lead N. and E. to Broadway and Dyckman St in the **Inwood** section of Manhattan. Occupying the very
N. tip of Manhattan, Inwood is ⅖ greenbelt, with Inwood Hill
Park, the city's only primeval park, and Isham Park taking up its
entire N.W. corner. The neighborhood was developed largely in
the 1930s and still has many buildings from the period. Many of
the older residents are Irish and German-Jewish; many of the
younger ones Central American including Dominicans and Cubans,
who began immigrating in the 1960s. In the N.E. corner is a

transport hub with subway yards and a brick bus barn. Nearby are a Con Ed generating station and a number of garages, car washes, and other service industries.

From the intersection of Broadway and Dyckman St, walk N. along Broadway (three blocks) to **Dyckman House** (1783; DL) at the N.W. corner of 204th St, the only Dutch Colonial farmhouse remaining on Manhattan.

Dyckman House. 4881 Broadway (204th St), New York 10034. Tel: 304-9422. Open Tues–Sun 11–4. Closed Mon, holidays. Admission free.
   Restroom. No public telephone, no restaurant. Not accessible to wheelchairs.
   SUBWAY: IND 8th Ave express (A train) to 207th St-Broadway. IRT Broadway-7th Ave local (train 1) to Dyckman St and walk N. three blocks. BUS: M104 to 125th St, transfer to the M5 to 168th St, transfer to M100 to Dyckman House; takes up to an hour from midtown depending on traffic and bus connections.

Situated in a residential neighborhood of apartments and small stores, the house is a surprising survivor from the 18C, remaining only through the determination of two Dyckman descendants who bought it in 1915, restored it, furnished it with family furniture, and donated it to the city, thereby rescuing it from the ambitions of an apartment developer. Though needing restoration, the house remains attractive; its modest garden and park benches draw local folk, who rest and gossip there in pleasant weather.
   Once the center of the 300-acre Dyckman farm, whose meadows reached to the Harlem River, the present house was built to replace an earlier Dyckman homestead destroyed by the British during the Revolutionary War and is believed to incorporate materials from the original house, which was probably not on this site. Constructed of brick and wood on a fieldstone foundation, it has the overhanging eaves and gambrel roof of the Dutch Colonial style.

The Dyckman family was one of early Manhattan's most prominent, its first representative one Jan Dyckman, who arrived (1661) from Westphalia in Germany via Holland. A bookkeeper and woodcutter, Dyckman went into partnership with Jan Nagel (after whom nearby Nagle Ave is named) and began buying land for a farm. The two first acquired 74 acres, which they leased in 1677 to tenant farmers for two hens a year for seven years provided that the tenants plant 50 fruit trees a year, a policy which eventually resulted in extensive peach, apple, and cherry orchards. Eventually the Dyckman farm became the largest in Manhattan and remained active for 200 years, until 1868. The builder of the present house was William Dyckman, a grandson of Jan Dyckman.

On the ground floor is a winter kitchen, its staircase built around a slab of Inwood marble too large to dig out. An assortment of 18–19C kitchen equipment suggests the domestic activity that took place here. On the first floor, the central hallway extends from front to rear porches, both accessible by Dutch doors. The front parlors both have fireplaces. A rear room, probably originally a bedroom, is now furnished as the farm office. A small room behind the dining room contains relics, many of them from the Revolutionary War, excavated in the neighborhood during the first decades of the 20C. Upstairs are bedrooms with clothing, toys, and furniture.

Behind the house are a reconstructed smokehouse and a well. In another corner of the garden is the reconstruction of a small military shed, similar to those used by the British during the Revolutionary War, when both British and Hessian soldiers camped on the Dyckman farm.

Like Dyckman St and Nagle Ave, other street names in this part of Inwood commemorate early landowners. VERMILYEA AVENUE is a corruption of the name of Isaac Vermeille, who settled nearby in 1663. POST AVENUE is named after a family whose early settlers called themselves Postmael. John Seaman, a captain who arrived in 1630 and 20 years later owned 12,000 acres on Long Island, gave his name to SEAMAN AVENUE near which his descendants lived. SHERMAN AVENUE is named not after the famous Civil War general but after a humble family who lived along a little waterway called Shermans Creek, which flowed into the Harlem River; the Shermans seem to have settled along the creek in about 1807 and in 1815 occupied a fisherman's shack at the bottom of Fort George Hill. SICKLES STREET brings to mind the family of that name whose American progenitor, Zacharias Sickels, followed Peter Stuyvesant here from Curaçao in 1655. ARDEN STREET recalls Jacob Arden, a butcher, whose land lay between 170th and 177th Sts. Arden probably died fighting in the Revolutionary War. The Francis Thayer who gave his name to THAYER STREET was an attorney active in local and civic affairs around 1911, when the street was mapped. Ellwood St was named in 1911 also, but no one knows the honoree. When the street was being cut and graded, however, workers found the remains of crude military huts, presumably from Hessian soldiers during the Revolutionary War, a belief based on the fact that the British and their allies occupied this part of New York for most of the war, but no British uniform buttons were found among the artifacts uncovered. Public School 52, which once stood on ACADEMY ST, was razed in 1957. Two small streets, Beak and Cumming Sts, were named in 1925, probably for early landowners.

As the dates of these street names suggest, the Inwood section of Manhattan was developed relatively late. Many of its apartment buildings show the brickwork patterns, typical setbacks, construction materials, and window forms of the Art Deco architecture of the 1930s.

Two blocks N. of Dyckman House, Isham St crosses Broadway. The street is named after a prominent family who owned the surrounding land and in 1912 gave 20 acres to the city for **Isham Park.** The main part of the park adjoins Inwood Hill Park and is indistinguishable from it, while the smaller sections to the E. lie S. of 214th St.

At the top of the terraced hill E. of Park Terrace West once stood a great marble house built in 1855 by the Seaman family and apparently used as a summer country retreat. The house and grounds remained intact until around the turn of the century, although by 1897 the Suburban Riding and Driving Club had taken over the main building. The gatehouse, a deep marble arch on the W. side of Broadway and 215th St, now has been recycled as an auto body shop. (To get to the mansion site, walk a block W. of Broadway along Isham St; turn right or N. onto Park Terrace West and walk up the hill into the small park on the right side of the road.)

Park Terrace West reaches a dead-end at 218th St. To the N. lie the Columbia University athletic grounds. **Baker Field,** including Lawrence A. Wein Stadium (1905–30; rebuilt 1986), named for a generous alumnus, is the stadium within whose precincts the Columbia University football team has pursued its recently melancholy fortunes. Also on the grounds at 5145 Broadway (opposite W. 220th St) is the *Allen Pavilion, Presbyterian Hospital,* (1988; Skidmore, Owings & Merrill), a community hospital and acute care facility.

INDIAN ROAD, formerly Isham Ave, is a small street intersecting 218th St at its W. end along the border of the large park. It was renamed in 1911, when evidence of an Indian settlement was uncovered in the park lowlands. The Indians belonged to the Weequaesgeek tribe that also inhabited much of what is now Westchester County, and the settlement was called "Shorakapkock" (generally translated "between the hills"), a name reflected in modern Kappock St in the nearby Bronx. At the W. end of the ballfields near the beginning of the woods is a boulder in the pathway bearing a plaque marking the site as the place where Peter Minuit bought Manhattan Island from the Indians for $24, although historians generally believe that the famous transaction took place downtown in the vicinity of the Dutch settlements around the Battery.

The major part of the park is **Inwood Hill Park,** 196 acres stretching W. to the Hudson River, N. to the Harlem River, and S. to Dyckman St, Manhattan's only true wilderness, with a wide variety of trees and wildflowers, steep rocky slopes (which saved the park from development), and caves where Indians once sought shelter. Its topography, like the rest of Washington Heights-Inwood, consists of two ridges with a valley between, and on the lagoon at its N. edge remains the sole surviving patch of salt marsh in Manhattan. Geologically the park is a textbook of the city at large: there are outcroppings of Manhattan schist, exposures of Inwood marble, and boulders of Fordham gneiss, as well as glacial striations and potholes, scoured out of the bedrock by the gravel-bearing water of the melting glacier.

The park became the last refuge for Manhattan's Indians as the white settlers pushed them back. There are still caves where the Indians either stored food or retreated for emergency shelter, and pottery shards, arrowheads, and other artifacts have been found there. In 1677, after the Indians were finally driven out, the arable lowlands were given to the settlers of the area, then called Nieuw Haarlem, with Jan Dyckman and Jan Nagel getting the largest tracts. A number of Indians remained in the area into the 19C, some of them intermingling with the black slave laborers who worked the Dyckman and Nagel farms.

During the Revolution a five-sided earthen fort occupied the high ground sometimes known as Cock Hill (perhaps a corruption of the Indian "Shorakapkock"), part of a chain of fortifications commanding the river. British and Hessian troops occupied the area, and pewter buttons bearing Hessian regimental insignias, as well as blue-patterned earthenware and musket shot, have been found in the park. Until the 1930s the park remained in its pristine state. When the Henry Hudson Parkway was developed and pushed through the virgin park, some of the park was landscaped, and during the WPA era the paths were laid out; nowadays the park is overgrown and wild again, but the ten miles of walking paths remain. The park is quite empty and isolated during the week, but on weekends nearby residents are out in force.

Beyond the grassy fields of the park flows the **Harlem River,** where the Columbia University boat crews train and race. It was not navigable to the Hudson River until 1895, when a channel was cut through a bulbous promontory that formerly extended N. of where Baker Field and Ninth Ave are presently located. Before then a narrow stream, **Spuyten Duyvil Creek,** flowed in a looping curve marked by the present boundary of Manhattan.

Some historians believe that Henry Hudson first anchored in Spuyten Duyvil Creek and was there received by a party of friendly Indians. Although no one really knows the origin of the creek's strange name, one explanation was offered by Washington Irving in his *Knickerbocker's History of New York:* Anthony Van Corlaer, sent by Peter Stuyvesant to warn the settlers north of the creek of an imminent British attack, reached the waterway in the midst of such a storm that he could find no one to ferry him across. Emboldened by a few swigs from his flask, Van Corlaer swore he would swim across "en spijt den Duyvil" (in spite of the devil), threw himself into the wild waters, and drowned. Others suggest that "spuyten" could refer to a cold spring that once spouted in the area presently covered by the ballfields and "duyvil" could be a corruption of *duyvel*, a Dutch word for meadow.

When the ship channel (400 ft wide and 15 ft deep) was finished, Spuyten Duyvil Creek was filled, making the area now known as Marble Hill physically a part of the Bronx; the residents petitioned successfully to remain politically a part of Manhattan.

To the W. can be seen the curve of the **Henry Hudson Bridge,** (1936; Emil F. Praeger) spanning the Harlem River with a fixed steel arch 2000 ft long and at its highest point 142.5 ft above the river. The bridge (span 800 ft) is part of the West Side Improvement project, conceived and brought to fruition by Robert Moses during the 1930s, and joins two sections of the Henry Hudson Parkway which links the West Side Highway with the Saw Mill Parkway to the north. It opened on Dec 12, 1936. The bridge was built originally as a single-deck, four-lane structure, because the bankers underwriting the project would only authorize $3.1 million in bonds, unable to believe that commuters would choose a toll bridge over the nearby free bridge on Broadway. When the bridge quickly proved itself financially viable, the second deck was added.

To visit **Marble Hill,** a quiet neighborhood whose apartment houses are relieved by occasional old frame buildings, take the M100 bus via Broadway across the Harlem River to 225th St. This 52-acre piece of Manhattan now geographically indistinguishable from the Bronx was given its name at the end of the 19C because of its terrain and its former quarries, although, as its street names indicate, it was settled early by the Dutch.

JACOBUS STREET got its name from Jacobus Dyckman who ran a tavern until 1769; TEUNISSEN PLACE recalls Tobias Teunissen who immigrated in 1636 and was killed in an Indian raid (1655) during which more than a hundred settlers were taken captive. More fortunate was Adriaen Van der Donck, the city's first lawyer, who in 1646 received a land grant that reached from Spuyten Duyvil to Yonkers. He left behind several indications of his presence: ADRIAN STREET in Marble Hill is named after him and LEYDEN STREET honors his alma mater. Even the name Yonkers is a corruption of his title *jonkheer* ("young gentleman").

Today Marble Hill still is occasionally called Kingsbridge as is the surrounding part of the Bronx because a bridge named after William of Orange (King William III) crossed the Harlem River at its shallowest point near present 230th St and Broadway.

The Philipse family, landed Westchester aristocrats, received the franchise from the king (1693) and established one of the first toll bridges in America; 20 years later they replaced it with a wider span which endured until 1917 when traffic to the port during World War I made it obsolete. In 1758 irate citizens built a competing Free Bridge (also known as Dyckman's Bridge or Farmer's Bridge) at 225th St and Broadway which remained until 1911. Before its construction the Philipses squeezed outlying farmers for tolls of from 6 to 15 pounds sterling yearly to bring their produce into city markets, annoying under normal circumstances but outrageous during the French and Indian War when the British requisitioned the crops, and the farmers, generally apolitical, found themselves paying tolls to supply the British army. One John Palmer began agitating for a free bridge, showing a lack of humility which aroused the influential Frederick Philipse to engineer Palmer's draft into the British army. Palmer paid a mercenary to fight for him; Philipse had him drafted again. Palmer hired another mercenary and got the bridge finished. One can imagine Palmer's jubilation when the fledgling American government confiscated the Philipse lands after the Revolution and made the bridge tollfree.

Over the years the residents of Marble Hill (currently about 7000) have been embroiled in a debate over the political affiliation of their 52 acres. The battle reached a climax in 1939 when Bronx Borough President James J. Lyons climbed to high ground in Marble Hill, planted the Bronx flag, and claimed the territory for his borough. In 1984 the State Supreme Court ruled that Marble Hill belonged politically to the borough of Manhattan, but is part of Bronx County, constituting the single exception to the coincidence of the five counties and the five city boroughs.

32   Roosevelt Island

ROOSEVELT ISLAND TRAM: Station, at 2nd Ave and 60th St, open from 6 A.M. until 2 A.M.; weekends until 3:30 A.M. Tram leaves every 15 minutes on the quarter hour. Fare is one subway token. Tokens not for sale at tram station.

SUBWAY: IND 6th Ave express, 63rd St line (B or Q train marked 21st St / Queensbridge) to Roosevelt Island. Or IND 6th or 8th Ave (train F and E) or BMT Broadway (N train) to Queens Plaza, then transfer to Q102 bus to Roosevelt Island.

CAR: Take the upper level of the Queensboro Bridge (59th St) to Queens; take a right turn on 21st St and a left turn on 36th Ave to the tollfree blue bridge. Parking at Motorgate Garage on the island. Car traffic restricted on Roosevelt Island but minibus service available from Motorgate.

Roosevelt Island, a 2½-mile strip of land in the East River, long used as a place of exile for madmen, criminals, and incurables, emerged in the 1970s as "Instant City," a planned community of some 5100 people of mixed economic background. Only 300 yards off the shore of the East Side, the island is quiet and remote in feeling, untouched by the frantic energy of Manhattan to which it belongs politically. In its midsection rise the towers of the new town whose housing, schools, transport, even rubbish removal were all planned by urban strategists, according to a master plan by Philip Johnson and John Burgee, a plan imperfectly implemented because of the city's fiscal problems in the 1970s. Down the island's midline runs a modern Main Street and girding the shoreline is a promenade, planned for its views and ornamented with occasional pieces of sculpture. At the ends of the island, however, remain monuments of older, less orderly times—a decaying smallpox hospital on one end, a lighthouse built by a lunatic on the other.

History. In 1637 Dutch governor Wouter van Twiller bought the island from the Indians; because the Dutch used it to pasture swine, they called it Varcken (Hog) Island, a name the English corrupted to Perkins Island. The Blackwell family owned and farmed it from the late 1600s until 1828 when the city bought it for penal uses, an objective for which according to one 19C clergyman, J. F. Richmond, it was more than suitable: "separated on either side from the great world by a deep crystal current, [it] appears to have been divinely arranged as a home for the unfortunate and suffering, a place of quiet reformatory meditation for the vicious." By the end of the 19C, its institutions included a workhouse, an almshouse, a madhouse, and the penitentiary where "Boss" Tweed served time and Mae West (1927) lingered eight days for her presumably indiscreet performance in a play entitled *Sex*. By 1921 when its name was changed from Blackwell's Island to Welfare Island, the place was notorious, the workhouse overcrowded and obsolete, the prison ruled by hard core inmates who dealt in narcotics and lived well on the profits. In 1934 a new commissioner of corrections, Austin H. McCormick, raided it and cleaned it up. The following year, when the Riker's Island Penitentiary opened, Welfare Island became a sanctuary for the aged and the ill, with a hospital for chronic diseases, the New York City Home for Dependents, a cancer hospital, and a charity hospital.

In the boom years of the late 1960s, city planners unwilling to leave so much valuable real estate lying fallow began plans for redevelopment, renaming the island Roosevelt Island to polish its image (1973) and opening apartments for rental in 1975. Originally the master plan called for two "towns" separated by a park and having a combined population of 18,000, a number deemed adequate for supporting restaurants, stores, and cultural activities. With construction delays, rampant inflation, and the fiscal collapse of the Urban Development Corporation, the quasi-public agency undertaking development of the island, only one town has been built (2138 apartments).

The **Roosevelt Island Tramway** (1976; station by Prentice & Chan, Ohlhausen) crosses the river at 16 miles per hour, controlled automatically from the Roosevelt Island terminal, though the cabin attendant can override the automatic system. The tram has a rescue car with its own drive system and an emergency generator so that passengers won't dangle midriver during a power failure. Despite these precautions, however, the Swiss-made tram has suffered maintenance delays and breakdowns including a hiatus in service when a film company leased the tram to make a thriller. Under optimal circumstances the ride takes three and a half minutes.

From the cablecar station, walk S. along the promenade. The low modern building near the terminal is a *Sports Park* (1977; Prentice & Chan, Ohlhausen), with a gymnasium and other facilities used by the island's schools. South of it is the *Goldwater Memorial Hospital* (1939; Isadore Rosenfield, senior architect of the New York Department of Hospitals; Butler & Kohn; York & Sawyer; addition, 1971), originally called the Welfare Hospital for Chronic Diseases. It has a central north-south corridor with short projecting wings to give patients, most of them chronically ill, maximal sunshine and river views.

Further S. still are the eerie ruins of the old **City Hospital** (1859; James Renwick, Jr.). Built as Island Hospital when the island was called Blackwell's Island and renamed Charity Hospital when the island was called Welfare Island, it was in the 19C the city's largest and possibly the nation's largest. Convicts from the island's penitentiary quarried the granite for its walls and were among its first patients. After the Civil War, the hospital treated thousands of Union soldiers and, through the years, thousands of the city's poor. By the time Blackwell's Island became Welfare Island (1921), many of the old institutional buildings had become obsolete including City Hospital, which eventually closed in 1957 when the patients were moved to Elmhurst Hospital in Queens.

South and east of it are the remains of the *Strecker Memorial Laboratory* (1892; Withers & Dickson; DL). Romanesque Revival in style, the laboratory was the gift of a daughter of an otherwise unknown Mr. Strecker; it housed on the first floor an autopsy room and a mortuary as well as a laboratory for the examination of specimens and on the second floor had facilities for pathological and bacteriological research.

The last ruin at the S. end of the island facing the E. channel of the river is *Smallpox Hospital* (1856; James Renwick, Jr.; S. Wing added 1904; York & Sawyer; N. Wing added 1905; Renwick, Aspinwall & Owen; DL). This hospital replaced a group of wooden shacks on the riverbanks where smallpox sufferers were formerly quarantined. Although vaccination was common by the mid-19C, immigrants still brought the disease to New York and as late as 1871 it reached epidemic proportions. In 1886 a new hospital for quarantining smallpox victims was built on North Brother Island, lessening the danger of spreading the disease to the Blackwell's Island population which numbered some 7000 by the end of the century, and the hospital was converted to a nurses' home.

Proposed for the S. end of the island is *Landmark Park*, which would incorporate these old buildings and include a memorial to Franklin Delano Roosevelt. The Strecker Laboratory and the Smallpox Hospital are both city designated landmarks and as such are protected, but City Hospital is currently slated for demolition. At the S. tip of the island is the *Delacorte Fountain* (1969; Pomerance & Breines), given by George T. Delacorte, founder of Dell Publishing and donor of the Shakespeare Theater in Central Park and other philanthropic gifts. The geyser, with a 250-ft plume of chlorinated water, has been smashed by a hit-and-run tugboat and clogged by the polluted waters of the East River, sucking into its intake system all kinds of flotsam, including, according to its donor, drowned bodies.

Return along the promenade to the tram station and either continue walking N. or take one of the free electric minibuses along Main St. North of the station, just before the main residential area, is the *Blackwell Farmhouse* (1796–1804; DL), a simple, clapboard country house used as headquarters of the Roosevelt Island Historical Society.

The Blackwell family came to the island through marriage. Captain John Manning, the British officer who botched the defense of the fort at the Battery and then formally surrendered New York to the Dutch in 1673, an interlude that lasted from Aug 1673 to Nov 1674, retired in humiliation to the privacy of this island which he had bought five years earlier. His stepdaughter married Robert Blackwell and the house, built later for James Blackwell, remained in the family until the city bought the island for the penitentiary and the house became the home of the warden.

On the right side of Main St are the *Eastwood Apartments* (1976; Sert, Jackson & Assocs.), built for low and middle income tenants. The U-shaped buildings face industrial Long Island City in Queens and the smokestacks of a Consolidated Edison generator, Big Allis, named for the Allis Chalmers company which built it. The richer tenants in the *Rivercross Apartments* (1975; Johansen & Bhavnani) across Main St to the W. look out on Manhattan's gilded East Side. To the N. of this cooperative apartment are two more middle- to upper-income complexes, *Island House* (1975; Johansen & Bhavnani) with a glassed-in swimming pool facing the river, and *Westview* (1976; Sert, Jackson & Assocs.).

Between these last two is the **Chapel of the Good Shepherd** (1889; Frederick Clarke Withers; restored 1976, Giorgio Cavaglieri; DL), now used as a community center. The church bell (1888) stands on the plaza.

Walk toward the East River through the apartment complex to the West Promenade, whose 3.6 mile loop around the island attracts joggers and strollers. Continue past Westview, dark brick with bright-red panels, and return to the main street. The parking garage, *Motorgate* (1974; Kallmann & McKinnell), holds 1000 cars and can be expanded to accommodate another 1500.

Keep walking N. past the *AVAC Building* (1975; Kallmann & McKinnell), an acronym for Automated Vacuum Collection, where garbage from the apartment chutes arrives through underground tubes at rates up to 60 miles per hour to be separated, shredded or compacted, packed into containers, and shipped off the island by the Department of Sanitation.

The second phase of residential development, Northtown II (Gruzen Samton Steinglass), is currently under construction N. of the Roosevelt Island Bridge, opposite about 72nd St in Manhattan. This area will have apartments with market rate rents and some subsidized rentals for lower income, elderly, and disabled people, and when fully occupied will increase the population by about 45%.

Two more landmarks and a hospital stand at the N. end of the island. The **Octagon Tower,** originally part of the New York City

Lunatic Asylum (1839; Alexander Jackson Davis; DL), once stood as a central rotunda (dome added c. 1880; Joseph M. Dunn) at the intersection of two low granite wings demolished in 1970.

The asylum was founded to fill a desperate need for accommodating the insane who, up until then, were housed in overcrowded wards at Bellevue Hospital. Their early treatment in the asylum could hardly have been enlightened since they were supervised by inmates from the penitentiary, but physical activity and labor were considered therapeutic and so patients were put to work in vegetable gardens or building seawalls to reclaim land. At the end of the 19C the asylum had 10 wooden pavilions, a laundry and bathhouse (patients were bathed once a week), an Amusement Hall with a stage and piano, and a Catholic church. Later the asylum became Metropolitan Hospital for charity patients.

Today only the shell of the tower is left, and it was badly burned in 1982.

Continue N. past the *Bird S. Coler Hospital* (1952), a city hospital for the chronically ill. At the very N. tip of the island in Lighthouse Park (1979) is a rock **lighthouse** (1872; James Renwick, Jr.; supervising architect; DL) with a curious inscription:

> This is the work
> Was done by
> John McCarthy
> Who built the light
> House from the bottom to the
> Top all yo who do pass by may
> Pray for his soul when he dies.

Local legend states that the asylum warden allowed McCarthy, a patient, to build a small fort on the point where the lighthouse stands because he feared a British invasion. When the lighthouse was planned, McCarthy was persuaded to demolish the fort and build the lighthouse in its place. The structure is 50 ft high and is built of the gray Fordham gneiss quarried on the island, predominantly by convicts, and used for most of the older institutional buildings of the period.

II BOROUGH OF THE BRONX / BRONX COUNTY

Home of the Bronx cheer (or raspberry), the Bronx Zoo (or New York Zoological Gardens), the Bronx Bombers (or New York Yankees), the Bronx has suffered a certain amount of ignominy at the hands of rhymester Ogden Nash who wrote (1931) "The Bronx? No thonx." Later he changed his mind, "The Bronx? God bless them."

The Bronx is the only borough of New York City attached to the mainland of North America, and even so it is surrounded on three sides by water: the Hudson River on the W., the Harlem and East Rivers on the S., and Long Island Sound on the east. Its area of 43.1 square miles and population of 1,169,115 (a decrease of 20% in the last decade) make it the second smallest borough in both categories.

The eastern sector is largely flatland, some of it originally salt marsh, sliced into long peninsulas by inlets and tidal rivers. Tons of garbage, euphemistically known as landfill, have been dumped onto the marshes since World War II and the areas along Eastchester Bay including Throgs Neck, parts of Baychester, and Co-Op City are now densely populated residential areas. West of the flatlands are three north-south ridges which give the middle and western sections of the borough their hilly terrain. The westernmost runs through the Riverdale area near the Hudson and west of Broadway, with Broadway following the lowland valley. The second ridge crosses Van Cortlandt Park and runs S. to the Macombs Dam Bridge area with the Grand Concourse laid out along its spine. The third and lowest proceeds through the Bronx River Park and Crotona Park, falling away to the flatlands along the East River.

Most of the Bronx is residential, developed with apartment houses which range from onetime luxury Art Deco buildings along the Grand Concourse and the finely kept high-rises overlooking the Hudson River to the big, institutional towers of Co-Op City and the crumbling five-story walkups of Crotona Park. A small part of the borough is industrial, mainly the strip along the East River which includes Mott Haven, Port Morris, and Hunts Point.

The Bronx is fortunate in having beautiful parks, 5861 acres of them or about 23% of its total area, most acquired by the city fathers in the years between 1880 and 1900. A plan to link them by wide, tree-lined boulevards has resulted in two attractive parkways, the Mosholu Parkway and the Bronx-Pelham Parkway. Unfortunately the city's straitened finances and changing government priorities have brought hardship to the parks, along with many other facilities in the outer boroughs.

Long considered the stronghold of working-class families— Jews, Italians, Irish, and others who had improved their lot sufficiently to escape the Lower East Side—the Bronx today encompasses a population that is increasingly poor and mostly nonwhite and now has slums of its own. Areas of the south, central, and western sectors whose scarred, burned, and abandoned buildings rise from rubble-filled lots have evoked comparisons with Dresden at the end of World War II, although the devastation which accelerated alarmingly in the 1970s has abated and the borough appears to be recuperating.

Touring in the Bronx. There are sights in the Bronx that are easily accessible and highly enjoyable. The Bronx Zoo and New York Botanical Garden next to it are among the finer attractions in the city and are clean, well-kept, and secure; they can be reached by express bus, commuter train, or subway from midtown. For other sights a car is desirable mainly because distances are great; a few neighborhoods are not safe for pedestrians. Riverdale offers fine views of the Hudson River, an assortment of educational institutions and examples of upper class domestic architecture including Wave Hill. Historic houses stand in Van Cortlandt Park and Pelham Park, near which is City Island, only recently affected by development.

History. In 1639 the Dutch West India Co. purchased from the Indians the land that now constitutes the Bronx, and in 1641 Jonas Bronck, a Dane who arrived in the New World by way of Amsterdam, purchased 500 acres along the river which soon was known as the Broncks' River. The borough today takes its name from the river. A few years later other early settlers arrived in the area, including religious dissenter Anne Hutchinson who was expelled as unfit for society by the thoocrats of the Massachusetts Bay Colony who would tolerate neither her liberal religious views nor her quick tongue. With her children and a band of followers, she settled on the shores of what is now Pelham Bay in 1644. John Throgmorton, an Anabaptist, arrived in the same year with 35 families who shared his religious views, unfortunately during a period of Indian uprisings. Indians attacked both colonies and though some of Throgmorton's followers were able to escape, Anne Hutchinson's colony was annihilated except for one of her daughters, Susannah, taken hostage by the Indians. After a two-year stay with her captors, Susannah was returned, unwillingly, when the Dutch and the Indians made a treaty to settle their differences. The place names "Throgs Neck" and "Hutchinson River" remain as evidence of these early sojourners.

Other British settlers including Thomas Pell and the Morris brothers arrived but both the Dutch and the Indians were (understandably) so entrenched that it was not until 1664 when the British took over that settlement of the Bronx began in earnest. From the end of the Revolution until the mid-19C, a remarkable span of three centuries, the Bronx remained quietly rural, its land divided between modest farmers and large landowners whose style of life imitated that of the English landed gentry. Villages evolved along the post roads to Albany and Boston—Mott Haven, Kingsbridge, Morrisania, East Chester, Pelham—later to become the commercial centers of borough neighborhoods. The railroads following the general course of the roads also fostered development in both the E. and W. sectors of the borough, and Riverdale became a fashionable country retreat for the wealthy, accessible not only by rail but also by steamboat. In the half century from 1790–1840, the population of the Bronx increased by less than four thousand.

Thereafter, however, advances in transportation and technology resulted in the influx of a population that ended with the Depression in the early 1930s and created the Bronx so fondly remembered by those who grew up there in the first half of this century. The first newcomers to the territory were the Irish, who started to arrive in the 1840s to labor on the railroads and on the Croton Aqueduct. After 1848 Germans followed, most remaining farmers as they had been in their native land. The two decades from 1840–60 saw the population quadruple (from 5346 to 23,593). In 1888 the Third Ave Elevated Railway reached the hinterland of 169th St and a flood of newcomers began settling

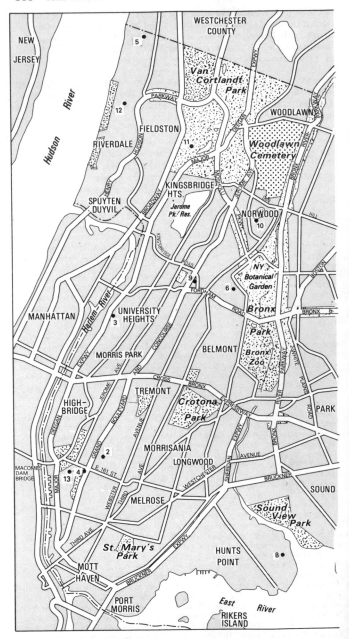

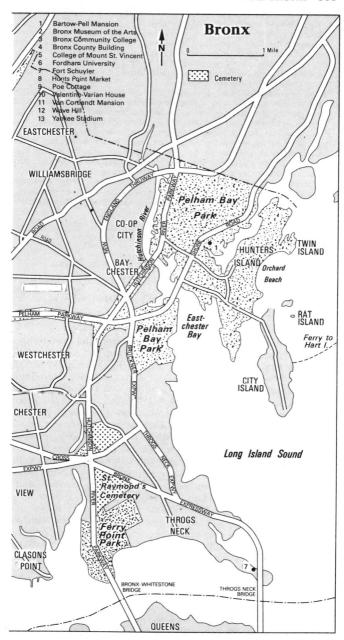

near it—more Irish and Germans, Jews, Italians, Poles, and Greeks—attracted to the Bronx because it seemed almost rural.

Politically the Bronx joined New York in two sections: first the western towns of Kingsbridge, West Farms, and Morrisania (1874), then (1894) the eastern towns of Eastchester, Westchester, and part of Pelham voted to become part of the city. According to the provisions of the Greater New York charter in 1898, these two separately annexed areas officially became the borough of the Bronx, with a population of 200,507 at that time.

The golden age of the Bronx lasted from about 1920 to the early 1950s. For these decades it was an area divided into tightly knit neighborhoods, usually dominated by one ethnic group, which became the center of social life. City services—education, transportation, parks—made life comfortable and attractive. The arrival of the automobile, however, and the construction of superhighways, enabled the population, or at least the upwardly mobile part of it, a greater choice of where to live and the lure of Westchester County and Long Island attracted many borough residents. Public transportation began to deteriorate; the last trolley ceased running in 1948. Jobs became less plentiful. As middle class whites left, areas of the S. and W. were taken over by a population increasingly dependent on public services that the city has been increasingly unwilling or unable to provide, setting in motion the cycle of urban blight that became so devastating in the 1970s.

33 The South Bronx: Mott Haven, Port Morris, Hunts Point, Melrose, Morrisania, Highbridge, University Heights, and Belmont

The **South Bronx** reaches geographically from the Harlem River on the W. to the Bronx River on the E., from the East River to a N. boundary presently put at Fordham Rd. It includes the old neighborhoods of Mott Haven, Port Morris, Melrose, Morrisania, and Hunts Point, as well as Highbridge and University Heights near the Harlem River. In the early 1970s the name, South Bronx, evoked images of looted, burned, abandoned housing standing in bleak open lots whose soil was invisible beneath tons of rubble, of street crime, of a populace whose weaker or more restrained members huddled in half-vacant, half-destroyed tenements while vandals from their own neighborhoods stripped vulnerable buildings of plumbing, wiring, and any fixture that would bring money on a flourishing market. It has been called "Fort Apache," and it connoted the end of the line. Despite the general accuracy of this picture, however, the South Bronx was not, even at its most distressed, an area of uniform devastation; here and there remained enclaves of hope—stable neighborhoods, good new housing, rehabilitated older buildings whose renovation was undertaken by committed developers or local organizers, cultural organizations and religious groups active in promoting community pride. The picture today is not nearly so bleak as it was ten years ago, but the ravages of the past will take decades to repair.

Touring. Significant distances and the high crime rate of devastated neighborhoods make a car desirable. Get a borough map as streets are laid out irregularly.

Mott Haven in the S.W. corner of the Bronx has been industrial since Jordan Mott, inventor of a cast-iron, coal-burning stove, built a factory (1828) on the Harlem River at 134th St. Mott purchased the land from Gouverneur Morris, scion of the aristocratic and powerful family (see p. 586). When asked if he would mind if the land, formerly part of Morrisania, were renamed Mott Haven, Morris allegedly snapped, "I don't care what he calls it; while he is about it, he might as well change the name of the Harlem and call it the Jordan." The Mott Iron Works flourished until 1906, attracting successive waves of immigrants, first Irish and German, to live in the tenements rapidly being built for them.

The former **Mott Iron Works** still stands on Third Ave between the Harlem River and E. 134th St, the various buildings in the complex reaching from opposite the Bruckner Blvd to the site of the former Mott Haven Canal. The company name is bricked into the south wall.

In 1969 the area along *Alexander Ave* between E. 137th and 141st Sts was declared a historic district, cited for its handsome row housing (1870s and 1880s) and for two churches: *St. Jerome's Roman Catholic Church* (1898; Dehli & Howard) on Alexander Ave between E. 137th and 138th Sts and the *Tercera Iglesia Bautista* (Third Baptist Church), originally the Alexander Ave Baptist Church (1902; Ward & Davis). Other important buildings on Alexander Ave include the *40th Precinct Police Station* (1924; Thomas E. O'Brien) between 138th and 139th Sts and the *Mott Haven Branch of the New York Public Library* (1905; Babb, Cook & Willard) between 140th and 141st Sts, which resembles a humbler version of Andrew Carnegie's mansion and was designed by the same architects.

In the late 19C the piano industry also flourished in Mott Haven drawing on the skills of German immigrant laborers. Along 132nd St between Lincoln and Alexander Aves three former factories (1885–90) still stand: the Krakauer Brothers Piano Company, the Estey Piano Company, and the former Kroeger Piano Company (Alexander Ave at 132nd St). The Steinway and Sohmer factories produced their instruments across the river in Queens.

The yellow brick *Bertine Block* rowhouses (408–440 E. 136th St) between Willis Ave and Brown Place, built (1878–95) for developer Edward D. Bertine, exemplify the substantial housing constructed for the middle class population of the Bronx.

Indicative of new philosophies in renewal housing are the *Plaza Borinquen town houses* on several sites (e.g., E. 137th St bet. Willis Ave and Brown Place), three-story red block houses (1974; Ciardullo-Ehmann) designed to keep residents close to the streets (as opposed to shutting them up in high towers surrounded with open space).

The two- and three-story townhouses (1888–97) on E. 140th St between Willis and Brook Aves are typical of pre-renewal, pre-project housing in the Bronx. Some have picturesque Dutch and Flemish details.

Nearby is ST. ANN'S CHURCH (Protestant Episcopal) and

graveyard, 295 St. Ann's Ave (139th to 141st Sts); a modest fieldstone church (1841; DL), the oldest in the Bronx. The hummocky churchyard of hard-packed dirt, now denuded of grass, holds the graves of Morris family members including Gouverneur Morris II, who sold Mott Haven to Jordan Mott. A railroad pioneer, a genius in the eyes of his acquaintances, and something of a rake, Morris built the little church to honor his mother, Anne Carey Randolph Morris, said to be a descendant of the Indian princess Pocahontas. Several prominent Morrises lie in the graveyard, among them the first Gouverneur Morris (1752–1816) who helped draft the U.S. Constitution and Lewis Morris (1726–98), a signer of the Declaration of Independence.

Early in this century tenements rose on the previously rolling farmland and, as a church brochure (1918) says, "the original American families" left; the first immigrants, apparently Germans, German Jews, Italians, and Irish, were in turn replaced by later arrivals, blacks and then Puerto Ricans. The area bottomed out in the 1970s, decimated by drugs and arson, but is on the upswing today, with the church serving as a center of community activism.

North of Mott Haven is **Melrose**. The Hub, the intersection of E. 149th St and Westchester, Third, Willis, and Melrose Aves was long the commercial center of the community, its importance dictated by the convergence of trolley and subway lines. Alexander's first department store was founded here at 2952 Third Ave.

Hilly ST. MARY'S PARK, bounded by St. Ann's and Jackson Aves, St. Mary's and E. 149th Sts, takes its name from a modest Gothic-style wooden Episcopal church that stood on Alexander Ave near 142nd St until 1959. The park, now in a neighborhood populated largely by Puerto Ricans, has long served the children of working class families. Once the hill was called Janes' Hill after Adrian Janes whose iron works stood nearby. The amalgamated Janes, Kirtland & Co. Iron Works, formerly on Westchester Ave between Brook and St. Ann's Aves, produced architectural ironwork, most notably (1863) the 8.9 million-lb dome of the U.S. Capitol Building in Washington, D.C.

ST. ANSELM'S CHURCH (Roman Catholic) at 673 Tinton Ave between E. 152nd St and Westchester Ave (1918; Gustave Steinback), an imposing neo-Byzantine brick church, was established by the Benedictine Order who founded the parish in 1892 and began the building in 1915. Long one of the leading parishes in the Bronx, St. Anselm's served German, Italian, and Irish working class families. After World War II blacks, Puerto Ricans, and other Hispanic groups replaced the older immigrants, and the Benedictines eventually gave up the church (1976). In 1979 under Cuban-born pastor Father Raul de Valle, the church, long in decline, was restored to its former beauty. Its rich interior appointments—marble columns, mosaics, bronze lamps, stained glass clerestory windows over which semicircular arches sweep up to a great dome—come as a surprise in this deprived neighborhood.

East of Mott Haven is **Port Morris**, developed by the Morris family in the 19C as a deep water port. Its main industry was long Richard Hoe & Co., Printing Machinery and Saws, a firm whose founder invented the rotary printing press. The Hoe factory was demolished in 1977.

East of Port Morris and S. of the Bruckner Expressway, is the neighborhood of **Hunts Point,** now an industrial area with economically depressed residential enclaves, once (before the Civil War) a fashionable place for waterside summer estates.

One Thomas Hunt had a house here in the late 17C, its site now incorporated in Hunts Point Park. Later the estate belonged to poet Joseph Rodman Drake (died 1820) who is buried in *Drake Park*, Hunts Point and Oak Point Aves, along with members of the Hunt family and other elite early Bronxites. Drake wrote of his borough in the early 19C, "Yet I will look upon thy face again / My own romantic Bronx, and it will be / A face more pleasant than the face of men." The street names around the park recall other 19C American poets: Whittier, Bryant, Longfellow, and Fitz-Greene Halleck.

Richard Hoe lived in this neighborhood in a house called "Brightside." His brother Peter Hoe's Gothic Revival mansion, *Sunnyslope* (c. 1860; DL), still stands at 812 Faile St on the N.E. corner of Lafayette St in the Hunts Point section. Formerly a synagogue (Temple Beth Elohim), it has been converted to the Bright Temple African Methodist Episcopal Church.

Hunts Point today is known as the site of the *New York City Terminal Market* (Halleck St bet. Lafayette / East Bay Aves), the city's primary fruit and vegetable wholesale market (1965; Skidmore, Owings & Merrill), and the *Hunts Point Cooperative Meat Market* (Hunts Point Ave, S. of East Bay Ave), which dates from 1976 (Brand & Moore). Other significant establishments in Hunts Point are a Consolidated Edison plant, a sewage treatment center, and the Spofford Juvenile Detention Center, on Spofford Ave at Tiffany St.

West of Hunts Point Ave stands the former **American Bank Note Company** (1911) at Lafayette Ave and Tiffany St. Within its impregnable walls were printed not only bank notes (of South and Central American provenance) but stock certificates and lottery tickets. Nearby, at the corner of Lafayette Ave and Baretto St is the *Corpus Christi Monastery* (1890; William Schickel), a convent of Dominican nuns.

Across the Bruckner Expressway, N.W. of Hunts Point, is **Longwood.** Near the intersection of E. 163rd St and Westchester Ave are two projects of renovated housing, modest in scale when compared to the behemoths constructed by the federal government and other agencies, but enthusiastically greeted by urban planners, who see them, and other projects like them, as the best sign of health in the blighted South Bronx. On the block of Kelly St between Intervale Ave and E. 163rd St is the *Banana Kelly Project,* named after the bend or "banana" in the street. Its several buildings were rehabilitated beginning in 1979 with private and public funds generated by local organizers, who completed the renovations at an astonishingly low $26,000 per apartment (the usual estimates for gut rehabilitation—that is, rehabilitation including plumbing, wiring, heating, and other basic services—ran at about $80–85,000 per apartment).

A block E. at 878 Tiffany St is *St. Athanasius Church,* the home of Father Louis Gigante, a charismatic community and parish leader who has had a significant impact on the South Bronx.

In front of the church is Tiffany Plaza (1981), S.E. corner of Fox St, its pink and white stucco ornament recalling Hispanic church architecture and reflecting the ethnic background of most of the parishioners. If one site might be taken to symbolize the potential resurrection of the South Bronx, it is this plaza, created through community and city effort, with its fountains and trees untouched by vandalism.

The seven-block Longwood Historic District a few blocks S. and W. (bounded roughly by Longwood and Leggett Aves, Hewitt Place and Fox St) contains some of the best domestic architecture built (1897–1901) when the Bronx was becoming an urban extension of Manhattan. Longwood is one of the few South Bronx neighborhoods that has survived the general devastation, emerging scarred but intact. Its houses are mostly bay-fronted double houses joined at the rooflines, capped by cone-shaped or other distinguished peaks. The residents are mostly elderly people, some of whom moved to Longwood during the 1940s, when Harlem was falling on hard times, who have kept alive the traditional neighborliness that once characterized the Bronx as a whole.

Morrisania,, N. of Melrose, centered around E. 170th St between Teller and Crotona Aves, was originally the town of Morrisania, incorporated in 1785.

History. The original American members of the Morris family, Richard and Lewis Morris, were born in Wales (presumably the place names Tinton Ave and Wales Ave reflect this fact) and made their way to the Bronx after successful careers as merchants and privateers in Barbados. Their original holdings, purchased from Jonas Bronck's lands in about 1670, were increased by a royal grant from William III, and the Morrises became one of the first families of New York, their descendants achieving national prominence. The first Gouverneur Morris, great-grandson of the first Richard Morris (Richards, Lewises, and Gouverneurs abound in the family), a framer of the U.S. Constitution, delivered the eulogy at George Washington's funeral.

The Lewis Morris who first owned Morrisania died in 1691. His grandson, the fourth Lewis Morris, also signed the Declaration of Independence and after the Revolution attempted to sell his estate as a site for the nation's capital. Eventually the neighborhood became German, and then Jewish, Irish, and Italian. Today it is among the more depressed areas of the South Bronx.

The former *Ebling Brewery* (c. 1875), St. Ann's to Eagle Aves, N. of 156th St, remains from the South Bronx's days as a German neighborhood. On the Eagle Ave side caves for aging the barrels of beer were dug into the hillside.

The former *Bronx Borough Courthouse* (1906; Michael J. Garvin; DL) stands abandoned at 161st St and Third Ave, a battered Beaux Arts survivor from more prosperous times.

Engine Company 82, Ladder Company 31 of the New York City Fire Department at 1213 Intervale Ave, N.W. corner of E. 169th St, became famous in Dennis Smith's novel *Report from Engine Co. 82,* which described the horrors of firefighting in the South Bronx in the early 1970s.

Crotona Park, which gives its name to the neighborhood N. of Morrisania, is bounded by Fulton, Third, Tremont, and Arthur Aves, and the perimeter roads Crotona Park, North, East, and South. Laid out (1883) on land formerly belonging to the Bathgate family, the park was named for a Greek city famed for its athletes. A Works Progress Administration (WPA) swimming pool, the Crotona Play Center (1936), and other sports facilities followed. None has survived unscathed.

Charlotte Street, a short street running S.E. from the E. border of Crotona Park, became a national symbol of urban despair after President Jimmy Carter's 1978 visit exposed the derelict buildings and the trashy, rubble-strewn lots to glaring publicity. Although Carter's proposed 732-unit housing project was turned down by the city, 94 single-family, prefabricated ranch houses, the kind typical of the suburbs, have risen from the rubble. Looking incongruous in the midst of a devastated urban area *Charlotte Gardens,* with its picket fences and green lawns, was financed with federal, city, and state assistance, and its houses are in great demand. To those who own and live in them, even to those who merely observe their presence, the houses suggest more than a transported suburbia; they represent the wholesale upgrading of an entire block, the kind of transformation impossible to local residents investing in "sweat equity," who can improve their properties only slowly, brick by brick, apartment by apartment. They also deal conclusively with the problem of density, reducing the population and the cost of city services, increasing the amount of open space.

Along the Harlem River, N. of Mott Haven, lies the neighborhood of **Highbridge**, taking its name from the aqueduct crossing the Harlem River (see p. 487) in the N. part of the district. Its most famous landmark, however, is YANKEE STADIUM, "the house that Ruth built," at E. 161st St on the S.W. corner of River Ave.

It dates back to 1923, when former Yankee owner Jacob Ruppert (of brewery fame) had it tailored with a short right field fence to increase the percentages of his great left-handed home-run hitter, Babe Ruth. Since then other stars— Joe DiMaggio, Mickey Mantle, and Roger Maris to name the most illustrious— have swung for its fences. In 1976 (Praeger-Kavanagh-Waterbury), the city renovated the stadium (capacity 54,028), believing that its presence would bolster a failing neighborhood. The rebuilding cost city taxpayers a staggering $100 million, and three years later another million went toward patching up cracks that appeared in the structure.

Not far from the stadium, across from Macombs Dam Park (see p. 487, for the name), at 1005 Jerome Ave (bet. Anderson Ave / E. 165th St) are the PARK PLAZA APARTMENTS (1928; Horace Ginsbern), one of the best and earliest Art Deco apartment buildings in the Bronx, whose neo-Mayan decorative touches Ginsbern used elsewhere in the vicinity.

Three blocks E. of the stadium is the **Grand Concourse**, its full name The Grand Boulevard and Concourse, laid out (1892) by Louis Risse, who called it the "Speedway Concourse" and provided separate lanes for carriages, cyclists, and pedestrians who used the thoroughfare as a route to Van Cortlandt Park. With the opening of public transportation, the avenue attracted large apartment buildings, many with grand facades, that make the street even now a showcase of Art Deco architecture. In the late 1920s and 1930s the avenue was the borough's finest residential boulevard, the Park Ave of the Bronx, its residents mostly well-to-do Jewish families drawn from the managerial and professional classes. Public buildings enhanced its monumentality: the *Bronx General Post Office*, 558 Grand Concourse, N.E. corner of 149th St (1935; Thomas Harlan Ellett; DL), which has handsome Works Progress Administration murals by Ben Shahn; *Cardinal Hayes High School* (1941; Eggers & Higgins), 650 Grand Concourse and E. 153rd St, with its rear windows overlooking the railroad tracks running S. to Grand Central; and the *Bronx County Building*, 851 Grand Concourse, S.W. corner of E. 161st St (1934; Joseph H. Freedlander & Max Hausle; DL), a big block of a building with a severe Art Deco facade relieved by sculpture at the entrances (Adolph A. Weinman) and a frieze (Charles Keck).

Across the street on the S.E. corner of the same intersection (E. 161st St and the Grand Concourse) is another of the Concourse's classic Art Deco apartment buildings known by its address, *888 Grand Concourse* (1927; Emery Roth), done by an architectural firm that put grander apartments on Central Park West. Inside the revolving door is a once-grand Art Deco lobby.

On the N.E. corner of the same intersection (900 Grand Concourse) is the former *Concourse Plaza Hotel* (1922), in its heyday a center of borough social activities and the temporary home of well-to-do travelers as well as ballplayers who needed to stay close to Yankee Stadium. By 1975 it had deteriorated to the point of abandonment and was sealed by the city; it has since been rehabilitated with city and federal funds and now houses the elderly.

The *New Family and Criminal Courts Building* (1977; Harrison & Abramovitz), on E. 161st St two blocks east of the Concourse (bet. Sherman / Sheridan Aves), is the only recent major institutional addition to the Concourse area.

North of the Bronx County Building at Grand Concourse and E. 164th St is JOYCE KILMER PARK, named after the poet of *Trees*, at one time known to most American schoolchildren. Toward its N. end stands the *Lorelei Fountain* (1899; Ernst Herter), a monument to Heinrich Heine, a better poet than Kilmer. Herter intended the fountain for Düsseldorf, Heine's birthplace, but it was rejected there and some New Yorkers of Germanic origin bought the work, hoping to install it where the Sherman statue now stands (Fifth Ave near the S.E. corner of Central Park), a site denied either because the statue lacked artistic value or because Heine was a German Jew. The main figure is that Teutonic siren, famous in one of Heine's lyrics, who with her beauty and song led incautious sailors to a watery death. The statues have been sadly vandalized, and though the Lorelei has been restored, the Rhine maidens are still headless.

Now reinstalled in a former synagogue, the **Bronx Museum of the Arts** at 1040 Grand Concourse at 165th St is one of the important cultural institutions of the borough.

The Bronx Museum of the Arts. 1040 Grand Concourse (165th St), Bronx, N.Y. 10456. Tel: 681-6000. Open Sat, Mon–Thurs 10–4:30; Sun 11–4:30. Closed Fri, holidays. Suggested donation.
Restrooms, small gift shop, telephone. Restaurant / cafe planned for new

wing. Accessible to wheelchairs (via new wing). Changing exhibitions, children's programs, educational programs.

SUBWAY: IND 6th Ave (D train) to 167th St-Grand Concourse. IRT Lexington Ave (train 4) to 161st St-Grand Concourse. BUS: Bx1 or Bx2 to 165th St-Grand Concourse. Bx6 to 161st-Grand Concourse. #4 Liberty Express to 165th and Grand Concourse. CAR: From Manhattan: Franklin Delano Roosevelt Drive to Major Deegan Expressway. Exit at Grand Concourse. Continue to 165th St. Or West Side Highway onto Cross Bronx Expressway; exit at Jerome Ave; right on Jerome to 165th St; left to Grand Concourse.

Founded in 1971 as part of a community effort to revitalize the borough, the Bronx Museum of the Arts is the only visual arts museum serving its people, a challenge it meets with energy and dedication. From modest beginnings the museum has grown rapidly and in 1988 opened a new wing with expanded facilities. Its schedule of exhibitions focuses on modern and contemporary art and on historical or cultural themes that relate to the Bronx and its people. There have been such topical exhibitions as A Portrait of the Jewish Bronx; Hidden Heritage: Afro-American Art, 1800–1950; and Devastation / Resurrection: The South Bronx. Along with these shows of local interest have been more general explorations: a show of Latin American Artists 1920–70, a study of abstract painters who returned to figural painting, and an exhibition of Italian photography.

In addition, the museum is acquiring a permanent collection emphasizing 20C works on paper by artists from Africa, Latin America, and southern Asia, as well as Americans who trace their heritage back to these areas.

Although the neighborhoods E. and W. of the Grand Concourse began deteriorating rapidly during the mid-1960s as the middle-class and working-class population moved out (many to Co-Op City), the Grand Concourse itself was better able to withstand the stresses of these years. Yet even its most famous and impressive structures, Roosevelt Gardens at the Concourse and 170th St, for example, barely survived. After years of abuse by its owners coupled with rising rents for its tenants, the building was abandoned and eventually closed by the city and sealed, blue sheet metal nailed over the windows. In 1982 after large-scale rehabilitation it reopened as cooperative apartments, one of the first signs of the revival of the avenue.

Other noteworthy apartment buildings on the Concourse are **1500 Grand Concourse** (1935; Jacob M. Felson) at N.E. corner of E. 172nd St, **1675 Grand Concourse** (1936; Jacob M. Felson), S. W. corner of E. 174th St; the **Mt. Hope Court** apartments (1914; Otto Schwarzler), **1882 Grand Concourse** at E. Tremont Ave, also known as the Bronx Flatiron Building, and **2121 Grand Concourse** (1936; Horace Ginsbern).

North of Highbridge lies the neighborhood of **University Heights,** named after the University Heights campus of New York University, on University Ave between W. 180th St and Sedgwick Ave, since 1973 taken over by *Bronx Community College,* part of the City University of New York. The older buildings designed by the firm of McKim, Mead & White are believed to have been the work of Stanford White: *Gould Memorial Library, Cornelius Baker*

Hall of Philosophy, and the *Hall of Languages* (all 1900; DL). At W. 181st St and University Ave is the *Hall of Fame for Great Americans* (1901, 1914; McKim, Mead & White; DL), a majestic classical arcade with bronze busts of famous Americans (open daily 9—5; free; tel: 220-6312). The great Americans honored include scientists, inventors, writers, and statesmen, their likenesses sculpted by such major artists as Daniel Chester French, James Earle Fraser, and Frederick W. MacMonnies. The colonnade sits on the brow of a hill and offers a sweeping view across the
distance with the towers of the Cloisters rising above the trees.

The remains of the *Old Croton Aqueduct* are visible in University Heights, especially along University Ave north of W. Tremont Ave. A battered gatehouse (1890) from the second phase of aqueduct construction, the *New Croton Aqueduct* (1885—93), a system of tunnels, stands on W. Burnside Ave at the S.W. corner of Phelan Place.

The former **American Female Guardian Society and Home for the Friendless** (1901; William B. Tuthill) built as a mansion and converted to Muhammad's Mosque of Islam, overlooks Macombs Dam Park. The **Park Plaza Apartments** (1928; Horace Ginsbern; DL) at 1005 Jerome Ave near E. 165th St, are one of the finest Art Deco apartments in the borough, garnished by Mayan motifs and terra cotta ornament.

While surrounding neighborhoods labor under the burdens of crime, drugs, and poverty, **Belmont,** bounded by E. Fordham Rd, the Bronx Zoo, E. 187th St, and Arthur Ave, is famous in large part for not experiencing these sorrows. Many of the people who live there, predominantly Italians but also Yugoslavians, Albanians, and some black and Hispanic families, have lived there for decades; their community commitment and refusal to leave though hemmed in by decaying neighborhoods has preserved the integrity of the society. Arthur Ave is an active commercial center and draws people from all over the city, especially on Saturdays, to buy Italian food from the open-air fruit, vegetable, and seafood stalls or in the covered market (Arthur Ave near E. 186th St). Among the food stores are importing companies displaying dried herbs, stacked tins of olive oil, and barrels of olives, and fish markets offering scungilli, calamari, baccalà, and other temptations for the Mediterranean palate.

34   Central Bronx

The main geographical and cultural feature of the **Central Bronx** is Bronx Park, which includes the Bronx Zoo and the New York Botanical Garden. Nearby are the campus of Fordham University and the neighborhood of Belmont, geographically part of the South Bronx since it lies S. of Fordham Rd, but psychologically part of the less battered Central Bronx. Formerly the Cross-Bronx Expressway was considered the S. boundary of the district, but its own deleterious effects on surrounding neighborhoods and the wave of looting, burning, and abandonment of the 1970s pushed the frontier N. to Fordham Rd.

A. The Bronx Zoo

SUBWAY: IRT Broadway-7th Ave express (train 2) to Pelham Parkway; IRT Lexington Ave express (train 5) to E. 180th St, transfer to IRT Broadway-7th Ave express (train 2) to Pelham Parkway. Walk W. to the Bronxdale entrance to the zoo.

EXPRESS BUS: Liberty Lines operates express service between midtown Manhattan and the zoo (BxM11 bus) on a regular schedule at approximately 20 minute intervals from 8 A.M. The last bus from Manhattan to the zoo is at 2:30 P.M.; the last bus returning from the zoo is at 5:20 during the week, 6:45 on Sat, and 6:15 on Sun. Exact fare required, currently $3.50. The outbound stops are on Madison Ave; the inbound ones on 5th Ave. For information about fares, schedule, and stops in Manhattan, tel: 652-8400.

CAR: The zoo is at Fordham Rd and Southern Boulevard adjacent to the Bronx River Parkway. From the EAST SIDE take the Bruckner Expressway east to Bronx River Parkway north. Take exit marked "Bronx Zoo" and turn left to Bronxdale parking lot. From the WEST SIDE, take West Side Highway to the Cross-Bronx Expressway. Go E. to Bronx River Parkway north. Take exit marked "Bronx Zoo" and turn left to Bronxdale parking lot.

PARKING. Large lots along Bronx River Parkway (Bronxdale) near exit 6 and on Southern Boulevard at 182nd St (Crotona). Smaller lot at main gate (Fountain Circle) often full. Parking fee.

The New York Zoological Park, known popularly as the ****Bronx Zoo,** is the largest urban zoo in the U.S., covering 265 acres and having 3600 animals of 561 species. It is clean, well-managed, attractively designed, and one of the city's major tourist attractions.

Open every day of the year (rides and some exhibits closed in winter) Mon–Sat 10–5; Sun and holidays 10–5:30; every day in winter 10–4:30. General admission: Tues–Thurs free; Fri–Mon admission charge. Senior citizens and children under two always free. Reduced admission rates during winter months. Additional fees for Bengali Express monorail, Safari train, Skyfari aerial tramway, World of Darkness, and Children's Zoo for which tickets must be purchased one hour before closing time. Inquire at entrance gate about Zoo Pass (Fri–Mon, April–Oct) with reduced prices for entrance and rides.

Cafeteria near Wildfowl Pond; Flamingo Pub with simple fare in more relaxed surroundings near Flamingo Pond; Zoobar outdoors near Children's Zoo with children's food favorites. Some facilities closed in winter. Picnic tables at Wildfowl Terrace and Zoobar. Souvenir shops. Guide book. Zoo map included with entrance fee. Baby strollers for rent at Zoobar; wheelchairs may be reserved in advance (tel: 220-5188). For recorded announcement of hours, fees, special events tel: 367-1010; for other information tel: 220-5100.

History. In the years since its opening (1899), the zoo, established and operated by the New York Zoological Society, has changed both physically and in its philosophy. During earlier decades administrators emphasized rarity and quantity and in 1910 the zoo had 5163 specimens of 1160 species. Today there are fewer animals and fewer kinds but larger numbers of many species, with herds and flocks replacing single animals where possible, a policy which has increased breeding potential (700–1000 live births each year). The zoo has also replaced most of the older cages with more natural habitats, an approach extended indoors in such exhibits as the Aquatic Birds Building, World of Darkness, and World of Birds.

The main entrance to the zoo at *Fountain Circle* is marked by the 36-ft bronze *Rainey Memorial Gate* (1934; Paul Manship, sculptor), whose stylized tree of life motif has 22 full-size animals. In the center of the Fountain Circle parking lot stands a white limestone *fountain* (17—early 18C) from Como, Italy, with sporting dolphins, sea horses, mermaids, and mermen, a gift (1902) from William Rockefeller. The stone jaguars near the stairs are the work of Anna Hyatt Huntington (1937) and were modeled after Señor Lopez, the first big cat in the Carnivore House (opened 1903).

*World of Birds (1972; building by Morris Ketchum, Jr. & Assocs.) is a handsome indoor display (c. 100 species) exploring the complexities of bird life. An artificial waterfall plummets 40 ft from a 50-ft fiberglass cliff and at 2 P.M. a daily shower drenches the rain forest exhibit (but not the visitors).

In **World of Darkness** (1969; building by Morris Ketchum, Jr. and Assocs.), another indoor exhibit (40 species), low levels of white, blue, green, and red light turn day into night so that visitors may see nocturnal animals at their liveliest. Included is the world's largest captive breeding collection of bats. Vampire bats in a simulated cave are fed a daily ration of blood from a local slaughterhouse (bat demonstrations at 11 A.M. and 3 P.M.).

Some exhibits are arranged as continents. **Africa,** for example, includes among other things LION ISLAND, the AFRICAN PLAINS, and a GIRAFFE HOUSE. Other continental exhibits include **South America** and **Wild Asia** (open May–Oct). The Bengali Express, a monorail (25-minute guided tour) circles the 40 acres of Wild Asia and is the only way to see it. Monorail tours leave from the Asian Plaza beginning at 10:30 every morning in good weather. *Jungle World* is an indoor exhibit recreating tropical Asian habitats and featuring mammals, birds, and reptiles. The animals of Wild Asia include elephants, gaur (largest of the world's cattle), antelope, Siberian tigers, rhinoceroses, and many species of deer of which the Formosan sika deer is the rarest, having been declared extinct in nature in 1973.

The ELEPHANT HOUSE (1908; Heins & La Farge) with its green-tinted dome and sculpted pachyderms is undergoing renovation as a visitors' reception center. *Baird Court,* once the main exhibit area of the zoo, consists of the Lion House (1903), the Primate House (1901, later renamed the Monkey House), the Administration Building (1910), the Main Bird House (1905), and the Heads and Horns Building (1922), in addition to the Elephant House. This formally designed area, named after Spencer Fullerton Baird, a 19C naturalist, is now used largely for administrative offices.

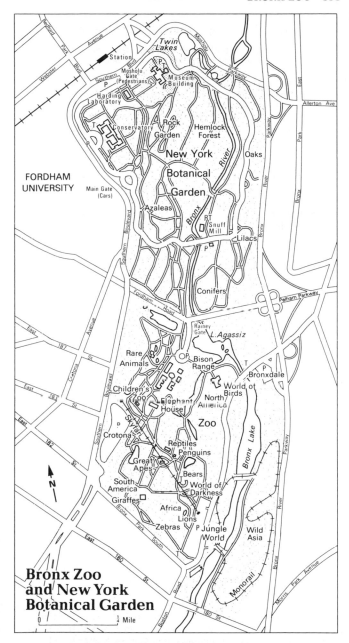

Twin Lakes

Station

Mosholu Gate (Pedestrians)

Museum Building

Harding Laboratory

Conservatory

Rock Garden

Hemlock Forest

New York

Botanical

Garden

Oaks

FORDHAM UNIVERSITY

Main Gate (Cars)

Azaleas

Snuff Mill

Lilacs

Conifers

Pelham Parkway

Rainey Gate

L. Agassiz

Rare Animals

Bison Range

Bronxdale

Children's Zoo

World of Birds

Elephant House

North America

Zoo

Crotona

Reptiles

Penguins

Great Apes

Bears

Bronx Lake

South America

World of Darkness

Giraffes

Africa

Lions

Zebras

Jungle World

Wild Asia

Monorail

N

Bronx Zoo and New York Botanical Garden

0   ¼ Mile

B.   New York Botanical Garden

TRAIN: Conrail Harlem Line local from Grand Central Station to
Botanical Garden station. This is more convenient and involves a
shorter walk than the subway.

SUBWAY: IRT Lexington Ave express (train 4) to Bedford Park
Boulevard. IND 6th Ave express (D train) to Bedford Park Boule-
vard. From the subway station walk east eight blocks. If you cross
Paul Ave you are going the wrong way.

BY CAR: Take Pelham, Bronx River, or Mosholu parkways to Southern Boulevard exit. Follow signs to vehicular entrance. Ample car
parking on grounds (parking fee includes one adult entrance to
conservatory).

The *New York Botanical Garden, with its 250 acres of garden
and lawn, conservatory, arboretum, and wilderness, is an appealing tourist attraction but also a major educational institution
sponsoring biological and environmental research, expeditions,
and scientific publications.

The New York Botanical Garden. 200th St at Southern Blvd, Bronx, N. Y.
10458. Tel: 220-8700. *Grounds* open daily; April–Oct 8–7; Nov through March
8–6. Voluntary contribution for admission to grounds; free Visitor Map and
Guide. *Conservatory* open Tues–Sun 10–5 with last admission at 4; closed
Mon, Thanksgiving, Christmas, and New Year's Day. Admission charge for
conservatory, except Sat 10 A.M.–noon, free.
   Restaurant in Snuff Mill open 9–5 daily. Picnic area near Twin Lakes.
Restrooms in Conservatory, Snuff Mill, and the Museum and Watson Buildings.
Lectures, guided tours of grounds and Conservatory, plant information, children's programs: for information about educational programs call 220-8747 or
inquire at the Watson Building reception desk. Garden shop with plants, books,
prints, and gardening items.

History. In 1884 the city bought 661 acres from the Lorillard family, tobacco
dynasts, of which 250 became the site of the Botanical Garden. Urged by
Nathaniel Lord Britton, a Columbia University botanist, the state legislature
founded the garden (1891) and was happy to see such eminences as Andrew
Carnegie, J. P. Morgan, and Cornelius Vanderbilt sit on the board of directors.
The 34-room Lorillard mansion burned in 1923, but in 1938 the city transferred
other buildings from the estate to the Garden, including the Snuff Mill, the
carriage house (now a maintenance center), and a stone cottage (used for
private functions).

Begin at the **Enid A. Haupt Conservatory** (1902; William R.
Cobb for Lord & Burnham, greenhouse manufacturers; altered in
1938 and 1953; restored, 1978; Edward Larrabee Barnes &
Assocs.; DL).

Inquire about tours. Descriptive brochure available.

   The *Conservatory is perhaps the most spectacular area of the
garden. The 11 glass pavilions hark back to the heyday of
Victorian architecture, recalling London's former Crystal Palace
and the greenhouses of the Royal Botanical Gardens in Kew
outside London. Housed within are an important collection of
palms (more than 100 varieties), tropical and desert flora (a 200-
year old saguaro cactus skeleton), and gloriously displayed seasonal exhibits (chrysanthemums, poinsettias, Easter lilies).

Outside the Conservatory are extensive displays of seasonal bedding plants and a series of demonstration gardens, each of which shows a specific type of gardening style. Behind the Conservatory are the PERENNIAL GARDEN and an HERB GAR-DEN in a traditional knot design, with plants grown for flavor, fragrance, and medicinal properties, as well as the CHEMURGIC GARDEN, whose plants are used industrially.

Not far from the Conservatory an avenue of tulip trees leads to the MUSEUM BUILDING (1890s), which once was a museum but now houses the garden shop, the library (a million items, including books, pamphlets, nursery and seed catalogues—the largest horticultural collection in the Western Hemisphere), and the herbarium, a systematic collection of some 5 million dried plant specimens from around the world. In front of the building stands a bronze *Fountain of Life* (1905; Carl Tefft), vitality in this case symbolized by plunging horses, nude figures, a mermaid, and merman.

South of the Museum Building is Rhododendron Valley with laurels and rhododendrons (late May–early June flowering), and the ROCK AND NATIVE PLANT GARDENS. Between these gardens and the Bronx River is the New York Botanical Garden FOREST, 40 acres of uncut woodland, the only virgin forest remaining in New York City (it is not advisable to wander there alone). Along with a dense grove of hemlock are examples of American beech, red oak, cherry birch, and white ash.

The **Snuff Mill,** about a half mile walk away, was built by the Lorillard brothers Peter and George (1840; restored 1954; DL), who harnessed the waterpower of the Bronx River to grind their tobacco with millstones instead of rubbing it over a grater as other firms did. This innovation, devised by their father, Pierre Lorillard, in part accounted for the success of the family business, as was evident to diarist Philip Hone, who remarked on Pierre Lorillard's death (1843): "He led people by the nose for the best part of a century and made his enormous fortune giving them to chew that which they could not swallow."

From the *High Bridge* there is a good view of the *Bronx River gorge.* The river originates near the Kensico Dam in Westchester County and empties into the East River near Hunts Point. Throughout the gorge the effects of the Wisconsin glacier are visible in the striation of the rocks, scattered boulders, and rocky outcrops. (The road over the bridge leads back to the edge of the Rock Garden and the conservatory area.)

Across from the Stone Cottage is the LILAC COLLECTION surrounding the site of Peter Lorillard's "Acre of Roses," whose petals he needed to perfume snuff manufactured in the nearby mill. Nearby is the ROSE GARDEN, reconstructed after the designs of Beatrix Farrand who began the garden in 1916.

Trees in the outlying areas of the Garden are grouped by families.

The third major neighborhood institution is **Fordham University,** E. of Webster Ave between E. Fordham Rd and Southern Boulevard.

Founded in 1841 by the Right Reverend John Hughes, later the city's first
Roman Catholic archbishop, it was headed in its early years by John McCloskey,
later the nation's first cardinal. In 1846 it became a Jesuit institution as it is
today.

The best of the campus buildings architecturally are the early
ROSE HILL MANOR HOUSE (1838; DL) now used as an admin-
istration building, originally a wealthy merchant's home, and
KEATING HALL (1936; Robert J. Reiley), an example of the
Collegiate Gothic style. The University Church, officially named
Our Lady, Mediatrix of All Graces (1845; William Rodrigue; DL)
was one of the original buildings; the transept, chancel, crossing,
and latern were added in 1929.

Just E. of the zoo and gardens lies the neighborhood of **Morris
Park,** bounded by Sacket Ave on the S., Eastchester Road on the
E., White Plains Rd on the W., and on the N. (at least according
to those who live there) Lydig Ave. The neighborhood is probably
the most stable in the Bronx, a cohesive, middle-class Italian
community, untouched either by the extremes of urban decay or
gentrification. The community dates back to 1889, when John
Albert Morris built a track for thoroughbred racing on 307 acres
he had purchased. The track prospered, attracting hotels and
restaurants for Manhattan society folk who made the journey
either on the train or by carriage. The Laconia Hotel and Restaurant, which dates back to this time, is still standing at 1571
Bronxdale Ave, between Pierce and Sacket Aves, but has been
converted to a home. After Morris's death, the city took over
Morris Park from a bankrupt real-estate syndicate and began
constructing streets and in 1913 auctioned plots of land to buyers
who included Astors and other notable families. The Aeronautic
Society of New York held meets on the former racetrack, with
Alexander Graham Bell one of the entrants foiled by his malfunc-
tioning plane. Morris Park remained sparsely settled until after
World War II, when Italian families from Manhattan moved in.
Morris Park Ave is the main shopping street, and shoppers arrive
from far away to buy from its Italian butchers, bakers, and cheese
makers.

At the N. edge of Morris Park, S. of Pelham Parkway and
running E. from White Plains Rd is **Lydig Ave,** another neighborhood shopping street. The area was settled by Italian and Jewish
immigrants in the 1920s, when the subways reached the area.
Lydig Ave abounds with kosher poultry shops, meat markets,
delicatessens, appetizing stores, bakeries, even Jewish takeout
shops, mostly of the mom-and-pop variety, many of them in
business for three decades. In the shops and on the streets older
residents of the Pelham Parkway area speak Russian or Yiddish,
but recently the area has seen an influx of Asians, Albanians,
and Russians.

35 Eastern Bronx: Throgs Neck, Parkchester, Westchester, Co-Op City, Pelham Bay Park, and City Island

Throgs Neck, formerly sometimes spelled Throggs Neck, is a peninsula stretching out at the S.E. extremity of the Bronx into Long Island Sound. It is bounded by Westchester Creek on the W., Eastchester Bay and Long Island Sound on the E., the East River on the S., and Bruckner Boulevard and Layton Ave on the N. Its population of 30,000 residents is mostly of Italian, Irish, and German descent.

Its name recalls John Throgmorton (or Throckmorton), who arrived here with a band of followers in 1643 only to be chased out by the Indians. In the 19C the wealthy, including Collis P. Huntington (railroads) and H. O. Havemeyer (sugar), had summer homes here. Nowadays it is a modest residential neighborhood through the center of which cut the approaches to the Throgs Neck Bridge (1961; Othmar H. Ammann).

At the end of Pennyfield Ave beneath the bridge is FORT SCHUYLER, now the Maritime College of the State University of New York. The fort (1834–38; I. L. Smith; DL) dates from a period between the War of 1812 and the Civil War when the city, not in any immediate danger, was completing the system of coastal fortifications begun around 1812. Fort Schuyler, paired with Fort Totten on Willets Point in Queens, was designed to rake the lower part of Long Island Sound with cross fire. Before this period the waters of Hell Gate were considered sufficient protection, but with the development of steam propulsion, the military establishment closed this back door into the city. Although garrisoned during the Civil War, Fort Schuyler never saw action and was abandoned in 1870 to lie empty until restored (1934) by public funds and converted to the Maritime College. In 1967, architect William A. Hall converted the gun galleries into a library.

Visitors may walk along the ramparts and enjoy a fine view of the N. shore of Long Island.

Parkchester, bounded by E. Tremont Ave, Purdy Ave, McGraw Ave, and White Plains Rd, was the first of the East Bronx's large-scale housing projects (1938–42; Board of Design, Richmond H. Shreve, chairman) and remains one of the best, earning the approbation of city planners and residents with its curving roads and expanses of lawn. Today the population of about 45,000 lives in 12,270 apartments in 171 buildings, with 533 parking spaces and five parking garages with room for 3500 cars. The land for the project, purchased by the Metropolitan Life Insurance Co. which administered it for some 30 years, formerly belonged to the New York Catholic Protectory, an institution for impoverished children, among whose wards was Hank Greenberg, now enshrined in baseball's Hall of Fame.

Before the arrival of Parkchester, the eastern Bronx was sparsely developed, with small residential neighborhoods, occasional business centers, and large expanses of marshland.

Westchester Square, at the intersection of Westchester Ave and E. Tremont Ave, was the village green of the colonial town of Westchester, earlier called Oostorp by the Dutch who founded it in 1653. Today it is an undistinguished commercial center. The area to the N., Westchester Heights, has in recent decades become home to several large state mental institutions and to the *Albert Einstein College of Medicine* of Yeshiva University (Morris Park Ave, S.W. corner of Eastchester Boulevard). The *Bronx State Hospital Rehabilitation Center* (1971; Gruzen & Partners), the *Bronx Children's Psychiatric Hospital* (1969; office of Max O. Urbahn), and the *Bronx Developmental Center* (1976; Richard Meier & Assocs.) all occupy a tract of land bounded by the Hutchinson River Parkway and Eastchester Rd. All have been praised for their design which minimizes their institutional quality.

Looming up from the marshland near the Hutchinson River Parkway are the towers of **Co-Op City** (1968–70; Herman J. Jessor), the nation's largest housing development—35 bulky apartment towers, 236 clustered town houses, eight parking garages, a firehouse, a heating plant, three shopping centers, and an educational park with five schools. The more than 15,000 apartments house more than 57,000 mostly working class and middle class people—bus drivers, construction and office workers, teachers, nurses—and a large population of elderly people, many of them Jewish, who fled here from decaying neighborhoods elsewhere in the Bronx, ironically pushing the old neighborhoods downward even faster. If Co-Op City were a city, it would be the twelfth largest in the state. The sheer size of the project startles people unfamiliar with the urban scale of things, and Co-Op City has had in the past problems unrelated to size, garnering a reputation for corruption from well before the first spadeful of marsh muck was turned and achieving further notoriety (or fame) as the site of a successful tenants' rent strike in 1975–76. Despite its drawbacks, tenants find it preferable to the neighborhoods they left. While 15 years ago, the community became a refuge of the white middle class fleeing other Bronx neighborhoods, today Co-Op City seeks to retain its racial balance and diversity, a source of pride to its residents.

Pelham Bay Park, the largest of six tracts purchased by the city in 1883, consists of 2118 acres of salt marsh, lagoon, forest and upland, meadow, and seashore. In addition to Orchard Beach, its most famous recreational facility, there are two golf courses, bridle paths, and facilities for hiking, bicycling, tennis, boating, and running. There is also a Police Shooting Range (not open to the public).

SUBWAY: IRT Lexington Ave (train 6) to Pelham Bay Park and then bus Bx12 into the park itself. During the summer buses run hourly on the hour from the subway stop to the golf courses.

CAR: From Manhattan, Triborough Bridge to Bruckner Expressway and New England Thruway; take Orchard Beach exit.

History. Anne Hutchinson and her followers are believed to have settled somewhere near the park site (see p. 579). In 1654 an Englishman Thomas Pell bought more than 9000 acres from the Siwanoy Indians including the present parkland but had to swear allegiance to the Dutch to keep his land.

Presumably he was relieved when the British took over the colony and he was granted (1666) a royal patent for the land.

The park is divided into two sections by the mouth of the Hutchinson River opening into Eastchester Bay. In the N. section are the golf courses, Orchard Beach, and the **Bartow-Pell Mansion,** which lies just E. of Shore Rd near the golf courses.

Open Wed, Sat, and Sun 1–5. Admission charge; children under 12 accompanied by an adult, free. Tel: 885-1461.

> SUBWAY: As for Pelham Bay Park. At the subway stop, either take a taxi (about 2½ miles) to the mansion, or in summer take one of the hourly buses to the golf course. The regular Bx12 bus runs into the park but continues on to City Island without passing the mansion during the off-season.

> CAR: Follow directions above for Pelham Bay Park; follow Shore Rd in the park N. across the bridge to the golf course. The mansion is on the right just past the golf course clubhouse; parking available.

The present mansion, third on the site, was built by Robert Bartow, a descendant of the Pell family, and is an unusually fine Greek Revival stone manor house dating from 1836–42 (DL). The city bought the house and grounds as part of a program for developing parks in 1888 when the land still belonged to Westchester County, but let it stand vacant until in 1914 the International Garden Club took it over, restored it, and planted its now lovely gardens. Behind the house, past the flower beds, herb garden, and immaculate lawn, a walkway leads to the family graveyard where the descendants of Thomas Pell are buried. Mayor La Guardia spent two summers in the house, no doubt enjoying the superb view of Long Island Sound and the clean, salt air.

The interior of the house has been furnished with period pieces from private collections and from city museums including examples of American Empire furniture (c. 1810–40): canopied sleigh beds, Aubusson carpets, Sheraton mirrors. The elliptical stairway and elegant carved woodwork exemplify Greek Revival domestic architecture at its best.

On *Hunter's Island* E. of the lagoon, now joined to the rest of the park by landfill, one John Hunter built a Georgian mansion (c. 1812) famous for lavish hospitality during his lifetime; later the house became an inn and after being abandoned and vandalized was finally demolished in the late 1930s. Traces of gardens and plantings (spruce groves particularly) and the foundations of the house are still visible.

Twin Islands, the point of land at the N.E. end of Orchard Beach now also joined to the park by landfill, has several glacial boulders including the Lion or Sphinx boulder (N.E. end of the point) revered by the Siwanoy Indians. The sweeping crescent of ORCHARD BEACH is a Robert Moses artifact made by filling the space between Hunter's Island and Twin Islands on the N. and Rodman's Neck on the S. with white sands dredged up at the Rockaways and carted here. Its colonnaded bathhouses (1936;

Aymar Embury II) are reminiscent of another Moses project, Jones Beach. Called the "Riviera of the Bronx" by its devotees, Orchard Beach was restored recently (1981–84) and regularly draws 45,000 bathers, who segregate themselves into groups indicative of the demographic makeup of the Bronx.

The dominant topographical feature of the S.W. sector of the park (take Shore Rd back across the Pelham Bay bridge) sometimes called Garbage Mountain, began as an imposing mound of trash which was closed to dumping in 1979 and seeded with grass. The *Pelham Bay War Memorial*, a tall column (c. 1925; Belle Kinney, sculptor) crowned by a winged figure, stands S. of the road which leads to *Isaac L. Rice Stadium* (1916; Herts & Robinson), built with a $1 million gift by Rice's widow. Editor, lawyer, inventor, and industrialist (electric storage batteries for cars and submarines), musician, and chess master (he devised Rice's gambit, an opening), Rice was a man of many interests and talents, some of which are reflected in the names of the streets S. of the park: Watt Ave, Ohm Ave, Ampere Ave, and presumably also Stadium Ave, Research Ave, and Library Ave.

City Island Ave in the midsection of the park leads across a bridge to ***City Island,** a small but growing community with a long maritime history.

In 1761 the local inhabitants conceived a plan to develop a port rivaling that of New York, a scheme that clearly failed; but the island has been economically healthy for several centuries. The first industry, a solar salt works (c. 1830), gave way to a profitable oystering industry in mid-century, and to a more profitable shipbuilding industry thereafter. Vincent Astor's *Nourmahal,* Jules Bache's *Colmena,* J. P. Morgan's *Corsair,* and other pleasure boats slid down the ways at City Island. In 1902 Ratsey & Lapthorn Inc., the American branch of the famous English sailmaker, opened a sail loft on Scholfield St and still turns out suits of sails though business has dwindled from its former peak. Many of the famous America's Cup defenders were built by boatyards on City Island. Today City Island is in the midst of a real estate boom, which began around 1982 when some 70 condominiums began rising on land formerly owned by the United Shipyard.

Along the main street, City Island Ave, which runs from the bridge to Belden Point at the S. tip, stand numerous seafood restaurants, ranging from the fairly elegant to the small and humble.

From the foot of Fordham St a ferry departs for *Hart Island,* where the city potter's field (not open to the public) has been since 1869 when Louisa Van Slyke, an orphan who died in the city Charity Hospital, was the first of about a million unclaimed or unknown men and women and stillborn babies buried there. At one time inmates from the Reformatory Prison on the island buried the dead, but today, with the reformatory long since closed, prisoners from the Rikers Island Penitentiary perform the job assisted by bulldozers, burying about 2700 bodies a year.

N. of the ferry slip is the *Pelham Cemetery* with some Pell family gravestones dating back to the mid-18C. *Rat Island*, a 2-acre rocky islet visible offshore, has at various times sheltered yellow fever victims from Pelham, convicts escaping from the Hart's Island Reformatory, and has been an artists' colony. At *175*

Belden St (c. 1880; DL) is a clapboarded Victorian cottage, one of few remaining in the city.

36   Northwest Bronx: Riverdale and Fieldston

Riverdale has been called the Gold Coast of the Bronx. It stretches along the E. bank of the Hudson River from Spuyten Duyvil to the Westchester County line and is bounded on the E. by Van Cortlandt Park. The Henry Hudson Parkway slices through it lengthwise and along that roadway have arisen numerous high-rise apartment buildings (mostly in the years since World War II) which have lessened Riverdale's exclusivity. From the parkway, Riverdale looks like any comfortable upper middle-class neighborhood, but its handsome old estates and turn-of-the-century mansions, further W. by the river, testify to its wealthy past.

Although Riverdale would certainly be safe walking territory (except for dangers imposed by residents' dogs), distances are so great and the terrain so hilly that a car is necessary. Wave Hill may be reached using public transportation with a reasonable hike. The roads are scarred by potholes and frost heaves, whose existence in such an expensive neighborhood suggests that the residents prefer to discourage casual sightseers. The streets are confusing and a map is useful, though commercially published borough maps do not seem to be strictly accurate.

> CAR: Take the Henry Hudson Parkway across the bridge to the Kappock St exit. Follow Kappock St past Knolls Crescent to Johnson St which then becomes Palisade Ave.

Palisade Ave skirts the river and offers a good view of the undeveloped New Jersey palisades whose remarkable beauty T. H Huxley found equal to that of some of the finest Himalayan landscapes.

Go N. on Palisade Ave. *Henry Hudson Park,* bounded by Kappock St, Independence Ave, and Palisade Ave, has as its outstanding feature a 100-ft column on which rests a statue of *Henry Hudson* (1938; Karl Bitter and Karl Gruppe) looking out to the river he discovered. Gruppe, Bitter's student, made the statue from a plaster model the sculptor had made some years earlier. (Bitter was hit by a car and killed in 1915 as he was leaving the opera.)

Continue N. on Palisade Ave. Expensive houses built during the decades following World War I line the road along the river, and further inland stand a number of tall apartment houses, most dating from a later period.

Turn inland at W. 247th St. At the S.W. corner of Independence Ave (690 W. 247th St) sits the *Greyston Conference Center of Teachers College* (1864; James Renwick, Jr.; DL) originally the residence of William E. Dodge and one of the earliest houses in Riverdale.

Dodge, whose money came from copper and other metals, asked James Renwick to design him a Gothic Revival summer cottage on the site; he later added enough gables, dormers, and wings to make the cottage a mansion. His daughter, Grace Dodge, became one of the moving forces behind the formation of Columbia Teachers College and bequeathed both her interest in education and the mansion to her nephew who eventually willed the latter to Teachers College for a conference center.

Return to Palisade Ave and continue N.; turn W. again into W. 248th St. On the left is part of the campus of the Riverdale Country School, formerly the property of George W. Perkins, benefactor of Wave Hill (see below). On the left, at 4715 Independence Ave, just S. of W. 248th St, is *Alderbrook* (c. 1880), a brooding Gothic Revival mansion, formerly home of sculptor Elie Nadelman (died 1946) and, earlier, of Percy Pyne, whose town house on Park Ave (see p. 398) is now a landmark.

Continue to Independence Ave and turn left. The *former Count Anthony Campagna Residence*, 640 W. 249th St, S.E. corner of Independence Ave (1922; Dwight James Baum), with a grand cobblestone drive and red-tile roof, commissioned by a successful builder, is one of the more theatrical houses in Riverdale.

On the other side of Independence Ave stands the **Wave Hill Center for Environmental Studies** (675 W. 252nd St, entrance on Independence Ave at W. 249th St), whose mansions and lawns enjoy a beautiful view of the Hudson River and a rich history.

Wave Hill. 675 W. 252nd St (Independence Ave), Bronx, N. Y. 10471. Tel: 549-2055. Open daily 10–4:30; after Memorial Day, grounds are open until 5:30, Wed until dusk, Sun to 7; greenhouses open daily 10–12 and 2–4. Free during the week; admission charge weekends and holidays, children under 14 always free.

SUBWAY AND BUS: IRT Broadway-7th Ave (train 1 or 9) to 231st St station. Change to bus M10 (doesn't run weekends or holidays) or M100 city line bus at the N.W. corner of 231st St and Broadway. Leave bus at 252nd St and walk across parkway bridge; continue two long blocks on 252nd St to Independence Ave. Turn left to Wave Hill gate at 249th St. Or, IND 8th Ave (A train) to last stop, 207th St. Change to the M10 (except weekends and holidays) or M100 bus and proceed as above.

EXPRESS BUS: Liberty Lines runs Mid-Manhattan Riverdale Express via East Side and West Side routes. Tel: 652-8400 for information and schedule.

CAR: From Manhattan take Henry Hudson Parkway to 246th St exit. Continue on service road to 252nd St. At 252nd St turn left over the parkway and turn left again. Turn right at 249th St and continue straight to Wave Hill gate. From points N., take Henry Hudson Parkway to 245th St exit and turn left immediately at stop sign. Turn left again at traffic light. Proceed S., turning right at 249th St, straight to Wave Hill gate.

Near the entrance is a 12-ft sculpture by Claes Oldenburg, *Standing Mitt with Ball*, on long-term loan. The oldest building on the 28-acre estate is *Wave Hill manor* (central wing, 1844 with later additions; DL), a handsome fieldstone mansion built by William Lewis Morris. In 1903 it passed into the hands of George F. Perkins whose interests in conservation led him to purchase also two nearby estates, now part of the campus of Riverdale Country Day School. Perkins, a J. P. Morgan partner, added greenhouses, gardens, stables, an underground recreation building with a bowling alley, and a neo-Georgian mansion called Glyndor. He worked personally with Albert Millard, previously a royal landscape gardener in Vienna, to lay out gardens emphasiz-

ing the beauties of the site. Orchards and vegetable gardens
planted on the lower slopes of the estate (now wooded) and
greenhouses used for cultivation of both flowers and vegetables
made the estate relatively self-sufficient. Such guests and tenants
as Theodore Roosevelt, William Makepeace Thackeray, and T. H.
Huxley enjoyed its hospitality at one time or another, and for a
while Toscanini lived there as did the British ambassadors to the
U.S. In 1928 Bashford Dean, curator of arms and armor at
the Metropolitan Museum (and also of reptiles and fishes at the
Museum of Natural History), rented the house and had eminent
Riverdale architect Dwight James Baum design him an Armor
Hall, now used for lectures and chamber music. In 1960 Perkins's
daughter gave the estate to the city for an environmental center.

Activities include art exhibitions, outdoor sculpture shows, concerts, horticultural exhibitions, and programs for school children. The greenhouses include a
palm house, tropical house, exhibitions of cacti and succulents, and a new
solar-heated area. The herb garden behind the greenhouses contains 150
varieties. Near it a historical exhibition illustrates the history of Wave Hill and
Riverdale. The wild garden offers plants in a natural setting, and the aquatic
garden features a lily pond.

Return to Independence Ave and continue N. to W. 252nd St;
turn left into Sycamore Ave which then curves around to the
right (N.). STONEHURST, 5225 Sycamore Ave (1861; DL),
screened in summer by foliage, another Bronx fieldstone manor,
first belonged to Robert Colgate, 19C paint and lead manufacturer; later Nicholas de B. Katzenbach, U.S. attorney general
under President Johnson, lived there.

Continue up Sycamore Ave. The *Salanter Akiba Riverdale
Academy,* cut into the hillside at 655 W. 254th St between
Independence and Palisade Aves (1974; Caudill Rowlett Scott
Assocs.) is an Orthodox Jewish school, the merger of three
Hebrew day schools in the East Bronx from which Jews began
migrating in the 1950s. Turn left to Palisade Ave and follow it
around the campus. The neo-Tudor Administration Building (1905),
originally the mansion of Henry W. Boettger, was Toscanini's last
Riverdale home.

Follow Palisade Ave past Ladd Rd with its modern houses, past
the Monastery and Retreat of the Passionist Fathers and Brothers
to W. 261st St. Near the intersection is the *Hebrew Home for the
Aged* (5901 Palisade Ave) with handsome new additions (1968;
Kelly and Gruzen; additions, 1975).

At 261st St turn right. There is a side entrance (unmarked) to
the COLLEGE OF MOUNT ST. VINCENT along 261st St (turn
right) but the main gate is on Riverdale Ave at 263rd St. The
college, founded as the Convent and Academy of Mount St.
Vincent by the Sisters of Charity, moved here from its former
quarters in Central Park when the park was developed. They took
over **Fonthill**, actor Edwin Forrest's picturesque Gothic Revival
home (1846; DL) modeled after its English predecessor, Fonthill
Abbey. The house, now used as a library, is dominated by six
octagonal, machicolated towers upon which the eccentric Forrest
bestowed individual names. The *Original College Building* (1857–

59 with later additions; Henry Engelbert), a handsome brick building with Victorian charm, has a 180-ft tower overlooking the river. The best view of these buildings is from the most westerly campus road, closest to the river. (Although the college is officially open only to those connected with it and parking is controlled, benign-looking visitors are usually allowed to view the campus; check with the gatekeepers.)

To return to the parkway, take 261st St inland (E.) to Riverdale Ave and turn right; follow Riverdale Ave to exit 16 of the parkway.

Between the Henry Hudson Parkway and Broadway is the neighborhood of **Fieldston,** known for its educational institutions and fine houses. Among the former are *Horace Mann High School* (231 W. 246th St, corner of Tibbett Ave), *the Fieldston Schools* (Manhattan College Parkway at Fieldston Rd), run by the Ethical Culture Society, and *Manhattan College* (Manhattan College Parkway, Tibbett Ave, and W. 242nd St), a Catholic college founded as an academy in 1849.

The main street, Fieldston Rd, shaded by an umbrella of venerable trees, is lined with handsome, rather formal suburban houses from the 1920s and 1930s in a variety of then-popular styles—Spanish colonial, Georgian, etc.

There is an entrance to the parkway at W. 246th St; turn right from Fieldston Ave.

37 Northern Bronx: Van Cortlandt Park, Woodlawn Cemetery, Kingsbridge Heights, and Norwood

SUBWAY: IRT Broadway-7th Ave (train 1 or 9) to 242nd St-Van Cortlandt Park.

BUS: M100 via Broadway to Isham St in the Inwood section of Manhattan; change to the Bronx bus, Bx20, to Van Cortlandt Park.

CAR: From the West Side, take the Henry Hudson Parkway north to the 246th St exit; go right to Broadway. From the East Side, take the Franklin Delano Roosevelt Drive north to the Willis Ave Bridge and then follow the Major Deegan Expressway north to Van Cortlandt Park South; follow it W. to Broadway and go N. to the park entrance at 246th St. Street parking along Broadway.

Van Cortlandt Park, bounded by Broadway, the city line, Van Cortlandt Park South, Jerome Ave, and Van Cortlandt Park East, occupies about two square miles in the north-central Bronx and has facilities for tennis, swimming, golf, running, and other sports. On weekends and holidays the *Parade Ground* near Broadway attracts baseball and soccer players as well as devotees of cricket and rugby, mostly West Indians. The *old Croton Aqueduct* (1837–42) runs north-south through the E. part of the park, punctuated with red brick service towers, and the aqueduct trail has become a favorite path for park runners. Also slicing through the park are the tracks of the Metro North Putnam division commuter line; the Henry Hudson Parkway, part of Robert Moses's West Side improvement scheme of the 1930s; and the Major Deegan Expressway, another Moses-sponsored highway.

The **Van Cortlandt Mansion** (c. 1748; DL) stands in the S. part of the park, not far from Broadway.

Open Wed–Sat 10–4:30, Sun noon–4:30. Admission charge. Tel: 543-3344. Walk around the house to the main entrance which faces S. and ring the handbell to alert the guard. No restaurant (restaurants in neighborhood), no telephone (phones in park). Gift shop planned; restrooms. Call ahead for wheelchair access to first floor; stairs to second, third floor.

History. In 1646 the Dutch West India Co. granted Adriaen Van der Donck, the first lawyer in the colony, a large tract of land which included the present park site. After his death some of the land passed to Frederick Philipse whose adopted daughter Eve, or Eva, married Jacobus Van Cortlandt. He bought 50 acres of what is now the park from his father-in-law and later added other parcels in the area which remained in the possession of the Van Cortlandt family until 1889. The first American Van Cortlandt, Oloff Stevensen Van Cortlandt, came as a soldier for the Dutch West Indies Co. (1638) and stayed, amassing one of the four biggest fortunes in the colony by the time of his death (1684). His descendants—merchants, shipbuilders, and frequent holders of city office—married into the Jay, Philipse, Van Rensselaer, Schuyler, and Livingston families, increasing their wealth and influence. Frederick Van Cortlandt, who built the mansion, was the grandson of Oloff Stevensen Van Cortlandt.

The house is built of rubble stone masonry with brick around the windows, above which are keystones with grotesque carved faces, unique in colonial architecture but not uncommon in Holland. It is furnished with English, Dutch, and Colonial furniture, including pieces which belonged to the Van Cortlandt family. Visitors can see an 18C kitchen with the appropriate tools and utensils, two parlors, a dining room where George Washington and Rochambeau dined, and bedrooms, including one where Washington slept during his peripatetic conduct of the Revolution.

In front of the manor once grew a formal garden in the area below the terrace. Today some of that land has been taken over by a swimming pool. In the rear is the *Sugar House Window*, taken from the old warehouse on Duane St built by the Rhinelanders to store sugar from the West Indies. In 1776 the British used the warehouse as a prison for American soldiers and when it was torn down a section of its wall and window, with iron bars, was rebuilt here. Also in the rear of the house is a statue of lawyer and soldier *Josiah Porter* (1902; William Clark Noble).

About a half mile N. of the mansion is VAULT HILL, site of the family burial ground; here Augustus Van Cortlandt, city clerk during the Revolution, secreted the municipal records in a strongbox on display within the mansion. (Several of the vault markers have been brought inside also, loosened from their original fastenings by vandals and the vault itself has been sealed.)

Woodlawn Cemetery, first called Wood-Lawn, bounded by Jerome Ave, E. 233rd St, Webster Ave, Bainbridge Ave, and E.

211th St, lies on the Fordham ridge, near the N. border of the borough.

Open daily 9–4:30. Tel: 920-0500. A free map with grave locations is available at the gate.

SUBWAY: IRT Lexington Ave (train 4) to Woodlawn-Jerome Ave stop near the main gate of the cemetery on Jerome Ave. TRAIN: Take the Harlem Division train from Grand Central Station to the Woodlawn stop. The Webster Ave entrance to the cemetery is just W. of the tracks at E. 233rd St and Webster Ave. CAR: Bronx River Parkway to E. 233rd St exit. Major Deegan Expressway to E. 233rd St or Jerome Ave to intersection of Bainbridge Ave. Car parking inside gates.

In 1863 the Rev. Absalom Peters and the cemetery trustees bought 313 acres of farmland for a rural cemetery which mourners from New York could reach by special Harlem River Railroad train in 35 minutes. Pleasantly landscaped in the manner of Green-Wood in Brooklyn, the park saw its first burial in 1865 and since then has become the final resting place of more than 250,000 people.

The cemetery is less noteworthy for the landscaping (though it is sufficiently unspoiled to have become a favorite haunt of bird-watchers) or for the Victorian excesses of its mausoleums, than for the prominence of those buried therein. Oliver Hazard Perry Belmont, financier and horse lover, lies in a mausoleum (1905; R. H. Hunt) modeled after the chapel at the Château d'Amboise in France along with his wife, Alva Vanderbilt Belmont (formerly married to William Kissam Vanderbilt), suffragist and tyrannical mother of Consuelo Vanderbilt, whom she aggressively married off to the Duke of Marlborough. Others interred here are: Jules S. Bache, head of the brokerage, whose mausoleum recalls the temple of Isis at Phylae; F. W. Woolworth, and Samuel Kress, dime store millionaires; Herman Armour, meatpacker, whose pinkish mausoleum (by James Renwick, architect of St. Patrick's Cathedral) has reminded some observers of ham, others of liverwurst; financier Jay Gould, whose railroads included the Erie and the Union Pacific; John "Bet a Million" Gates, whose interests included Texaco Oil, American Steel and Wire, and who made his mark introducing barbed wire to Texas; and Roland H. Macy, department store founder.

The list also includes Ralph Bunche; Fiorello La Guardia; William "Bat" Masterson, sheriff and U.S. marshall, gambler, Indian scout, and sports writer; suffragist Elizabeth Cady Stanton; Joseph Pulitzer; Elizabeth Cochran (Nellie Bly), journalist who went around the world in 80 days; Herman Melville; Victor Herbert; Fritz Kreisler, Admiral David Glasgow Farragut; Diana Barrymore; Vernon and Irene Castle, ballroom dancers who introduced the Castle Walk and the Castle Waltz; William C. Handy, composer of The St. Louis Blues; and Duke Ellington. Perhaps the strangest epitaph in the cemetery is that of one George Spenser (1894–1909): "Lost life by stab in falling on ink eraser, evading six young women trying to give him birthday kisses in office of Metropolitan Life Building."

Also near Van Cortlandt Park: In the middle-class neighborhood of **Kingsbridge Heights** perched on the hills and ridges S. of Van Cortlandt Park is the *Jerome Park Reservoir*, occupying part of the site of a racetrack built by Leonard W. Jerome. Known best as the father of Jennie Jerome (see p. 279), he was equally fond of horses and women, a founder of the American Jockey Club, and the moving force behind the racetrack, where he and his well-to-do colleagues raced their thoroughbreds from 1876—90. In 1905 the reservoir was built as part of the Croton system, covering 94 acres and holding 773 million gallons of water. A second basin to the E. (which extended to Jerome Ave) has now been filled and its land given over to De Witt Clinton High School, the BRONX HIGH SCHOOL OF SCIENCE (1959)—probably the city's most prestigious public school and alma mater of several Nobel Prize winners—and Herbert H. Lehman College (Bedford Park Boulevard West at Goulden Ave), until 1968 the uptown campus of Hunter College, now part of the city university system. The college has an ambitious program of performing arts with plays, concerts, and popular music; some events free (tel: 960-8833).

Filling the rest of the site are subway yards and the imposing *Kingsbridge Armory* (1912; Pilcher & Tachau; DL), at 29 W. Kingsbridge Rd between Jerome and Reservoir Aves, reputedly the largest in the world.

Poe Park, a small green space on the E. side of the Grand Concourse at Kingsbridge Rd, contains the POE COTTAGE (c. 1812; DL), a humble white frame farmhouse now rather forlornly preserved amid the apartments and commercial buildings of this borderline neighborhood.

Edgar Allan Poe Cottage. Poe Park, East Kingsbridge Rd and the Grand Concourse, Bronx, N. Y. 10458. Open Wed—Fri, Sun 1—5; Sat 10—4. Admission charge; children under 12 free. Tel: 881-8900.

SUBWAY: IRT Lexington Ave (train 4) to Kingsbridge Rd-Jerome Ave; walk three blocks E. to the Grand Concourse. IND 6th Ave (D train) to Kingsbridge Rd-Grand Concourse. CAR: Major Deegan Expressway to Fordham Rd. Go E. to the Grand Concourse and turn left (N.) to Kingsbridge Rd.

For details about the Bronx Heritage Trail and public transportation between the Poe Cottage and other historic Bronx sites, see p. 608.

Edgar Allan Poe came to this little house in 1846 hoping that the country air would cure his dying wife's tuberculosis. Already famous but still stalked by poverty and his own bleak disposition, the poet watched his wife die during the first winter, but stayed on to write *Ulalume* and *The Bells* and, perhaps, part of *Annabel Lee*, a eulogy to his bride whom he had married when she was just 13 years old. Poe left in 1849 and headed south, dying in Baltimore in October of that year. The house has been converted to a simple museum, with a few period furnishings, memorabilia, and an audiovisual exhibit that evokes Poe's tragic life and literary achievement.

The neighborhood of **Norwood** is bounded by Bronx Park, Mosholu Parkway, Woodlawn Cemetery, and Van Cortlandt Park, and is known to many of its inhabitants as St. Brendan's Parish. The population of Norwood is about 16,000 and many of its residents are of Irish descent.

Just S. of Gunhill Rd is the third of the Bronx's historic houses, the VALENTINE-VARIAN HOUSE, now converted to the **Museum of Bronx History.**

Musem of Bronx History. 3266 Bainbridge Ave (bet. Van Cortlandt Ave / E. 208th St), Bronx, N. Y. 10467. Tel: 881-8900. Open Sat 10–4, Sun 1–5. Admission charge; children under 12 free. It is wise to telephone ahead to be sure that the museum is open scheduled hours.

SUBWAY: IND 6th Ave (D train) to 205th St-Bainbridge Ave; IRT Lexington Ave (train 4) to Mosholu Parkway, then walk E. on 208th St. CAR: Major Deegan Expressway to Van Cortlandt Park exit. Follow Van Cortlandt Park South and Gun Hill Rd to Bainbridge Ave; turn right and follow Bainbridge Ave to the museum. Street parking.

Isaac Valentine, a well-to-do farmer, built this sturdy fieldstone farmhouse (1775; DL) on land purchased from the Dutch Reformed Church. During the Revolution the family fled, endangered by skirmishes nearby, and for a while the house was occupied by British and Hessian soldiers. In 1791 Isaac Varian bought the house along with some 260 acres of land and it remained in the family until 1964 when the owner set out to sell it to a developer eager to construct apartments. Fortunately a clause in the will under which the owner had taken title to the property stipulated that while the land could be divided, the house had to be preserved. In 1965 it was moved across the street to its present site and has since served as a museum with prints, paintings, photographs, and other artifacts of Bronx history. The research collection is the foremost source of documents relating to the Bronx.

The **Bronx Heritage Trail** is a self-guided tour of the Valentine-Varian House, the Poe Cottage, and the Van Cortlandt mansion, all accessible by public transportation. Begin by taking the 6th Ave IND (D train) to Bainbridge Ave-205th St and the Valentine-Varian House. Across the street from the house is the stop for bus Bx20 which goes to the Poe Cottage. From there continue by bus Bx20 to Broadway and 246th St, near the Van Cortlandt Mansion. The IRT Broadway-7th Ave (station at 242nd St) goes downtown on the West Side.

Behind the Valentine-Varian House an earthen embankment curves around a large playground on the site of the former (1888–1923) Williamsbridge Reservoir, part of the city water system. During its period of service the reservoir held water from the Bronx River that flowed into it from behind the Kensico Dam through the Bronx River pipeline. When the reservoir was abandoned, tunnels were cut through the dam and playground equipment installed. The former *Keeper's House* (c. 1890) still remains on Reservoir Oval East at the intersection of Putnam Place.

The startling upswept roof of *St. Brendan's Church* (Roman Catholic), Perry Ave between E. 206th and E. 207th Sts, looks like the prow of a ship, understandable since St. Brendan is the patron saint of navigators and, according to legend, voyaged to America. The church (1966; Belfatto & Pavarini) also has fine stained glass windows (open during services).

MONTEFIORE HOSPITAL AND MEDICAL CENTER, E. Gun Hill Rd between Kossuth and Tryon Aves, was founded in 1884 on the centenary of the birth of Sir Moses Montefiore, Anglo-Jewish leader and philanthropist. It was the first hospital in the country to use insulin therapy for diabetes and radioisotopes in cancer therapy. The first heart pacemaker was developed here as were pioneering techniques in microsurgery and organ transplant. Begun as a home on the East Side (Avenue A and 84th St) for Jewish invalids and chronically ill patients, the hospital moved first to 138th St and Broadway (1889) and then to the Bronx (1912), searching for open space and fresh country air for its many tubercular patients. It is affiliated with Yeshiva University's Albert Einstein College of Medicine and has earned a reputation as one of the city's more socially active hospitals, assuming responsibilities for the care of neighborhood patients long before federal policy began pushing large, academic institutions to do so. It is the largest employer in the Bronx with some 8000 employees.

In 1984 the hospital marked its centenary by embarking on a major building project. The North Building (1912; Arnold W. Brunner) has been torn down to be replaced by a new eight-story building, and many of its existing facilities along Bainbridge Ave and Gun Hill Rd are being renovated.

III BOROUGH OF BROOKLYN / KINGS COUNTY

Once a separate city, Brooklyn today still preserves a separate identity and an almost mystical hold on the hearts and imaginations of its admirers. Some of its mystique derives from a brighter past, illuminated by the radiance of memory and nostalgia for which the departed Brooklyn Dodgers are the most powerful symbol. It evokes fierce pride, even chauvinism, in some of its residents (past, present, and spiritual) who defend its populace as the most stalwart, its nurturing qualities as the most conducive to worldly success, its neighborhoods as the most halcyon. People write books, songs, poems, about Brooklyn as they do not, for example, about Queens or the Bronx.

To outsiders, however, Brooklyn is an alien country, whose natives speak a unique, comic dialect. The very name conjures up images of endless blocks of row houses and apartments, some handsome and gracious, others gutted, barricaded, or in the final throes of urban decay. Its stereotypical inhabitant is an aggressive, humorous, streetwise, and ambitious character, not precisely like any of the many famous people who were born or lived there but something like all of them: Mickey Rooney, Mae West, Beverly Sills, Sol Hurok, Isaac B. Singer, S. J. Perelman, Richard Wright, Floyd Patterson, John Steinbeck, Clara Bow, Aaron Copland, Jackie Gleason, George Gershwin, Irving Thalberg, Barbra Streisand, Woody Allen.

Geographically Brooklyn occupies the western tip of Long Island and is bounded by the East River, the Narrows, and upper New York Bay on the W. and N. and by the Atlantic Ocean on the S. and the borough of Queens on the east. Rocky ridges created by the Wisconsin glacier run E. and W. through its central and western portions, while the southern and eastern part of the borough is largely coastal plain, created by the glacial outwash. Many neighborhood names describe local geography: Brooklyn Heights, Park Slope, Stuyvesant Heights (now part of the conglomerate Bedford-Stuyvesant), Crown Heights, Bay Ridge, Flatbush, Flatlands, and Midwood. Even the name "Brooklyn," first applied to the 17C village near the present intersection of Fulton and Smith Sts, refers to a topographically similar Dutch town, Breuckelen ("Broken Land"). As one would expect, the waterfront has attracted industry and shipping; the downtown area is focused around Fulton St; and the rest of Brooklyn is largely residential, the pattern of its settlement influenced by transit lines—first horsecars, then elevated railways, and eventually subways—fanning outward through the borough. Its area of 78.5 square miles makes it the second largest borough geographically, while its 2,230,936 inhabitants (a loss of 14.3% since 1970) make it the largest in population.

History. The Dutch first settled Brooklyn in the 17C, buying land from the Canarsie Indians and chartering five of its six original villages: Breuckelen (1657); 't Vlacke Bos, now Flatbush (1652); Nieuw Utrecht (1662); Nieuw Amersfoort, now Flatlands (1666); and Boswijck, now Bushwick (1660). The sixth charter for 's Gravensande, now Gravesend, went to Lady Deborah Moody in 1645, an Englishwoman. Dutch culture, agrarian and conservative, endured in Brooklyn long after the Revolution, especially inland, although New Yorkers, many of them of British origin, were attracted to the waterfront and northern districts. Brooklyn rejected overtures to join New York politically in 1833, accepting Gen. Jeremiah Johnson's opinion that the two cities had "nothing in common, either in object, interest, or feeling—nothing that even apparently tends to their connection unless it be the waters that flow between them," and in the following year (1834) became an independent city, covering 12 square miles and boasting a population of some 30,000 inhabitants. As the century progressed Brooklyn gradually absorbed outlying towns: New Lots, Flatbush, Gravesend, New Utrecht, and Flatlands, and in 1898, its destiny dictated by geography, Brooklyn voted by a slim majority to join Greater New York.

The late years of the 19C and the early ones of the 20C were a golden period for Brooklyn, its cultural institutions (The Brooklyn Museum, the Brooklyn Academy of Music, the Brooklyn Botanic Garden, the Long Island Historical Society) finding fertile soil in which to flourish, its major industries (oil and sugar refining, brewing and distilling, publishing, glass and ceramics, cast iron) providing jobs for its large resident population. Major public works projects (Prospect Park, the Brooklyn Bridge, the development of the Atlantic Basin) as well as the construction of sound housing along the rapid transit lines testified to its economic health.

After the turn of the century Brooklyn's demography began changing as immigrants poured in from Europe and after the 1930s from the American South. By 1930 half Brooklyn's adults were foreign born, most gravitating to ethnic neighborhoods like Bushwick, Brownsville, Bensonhurst, and Greenpoint. The Depression hit the new immigrants hard and by the mid-1930s some of these areas had become slums. Established middle class families moved further out to suburban neighborhoods in Flatbush, Flatlands, or Canarsie. Despite the setbacks of the Depression, however, Brooklyn remained economically sound through World War II when the exodus to the suburbs of much of the remaining middle class, governmental policies favoring other regions of the country, and changes in the structure of capitalism eroded Brooklyn's economic base. In the past two decades the port has lost more than 10,000 jobs, the breweries of Bushwick have shut down, the Navy Yard was abandoned by the Defense Department, and large neighborhoods have become derelict, bombed-out slums, most poignantly Brownsville, long a working class Jewish area noted for its social and intellectual vitality. On the positive side, individual efforts— by cultural groups, by families undertaking the renovation of brownstones, by businesses like the Brooklyn Union Gas Co. which disseminates information on restoration, and by civic organizations like the Bedford-Stuyvesant Restoration Corporation—have made some progress confronting Brooklyn's massive urban problems.

Touring in Brooklyn. Where distances are short and neighborhoods are secure, walking tours have been suggested and subway stops indicated. For outlying areas a car is necessary. Guided Brooklyn tours are also available; see p. 55).

38   Fulton Ferry

SUBWAY: IND 8th Ave (A train) to High St-Brooklyn Bridge. Follow Cadman Plaza West toward the bridge.

TO WALK ACROSS THE BROOKLYN BRIDGE: IRT Lexington Ave (train 4, or 5) to Worth St-Brooklyn Bridge, or BMT Nassau St (J or M train) to Chambers-Centre Sts in Manhattan. To walk across from Manhattan, climb the stairs to the bridge promenade that are under the bridge opposite the William St extension. The stairs are also accessible from the plaza behind the Municipal Building; walk

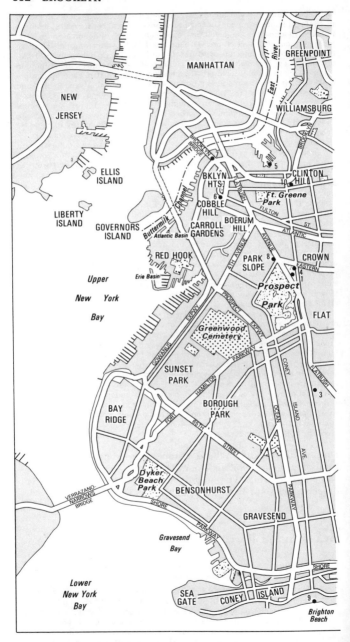

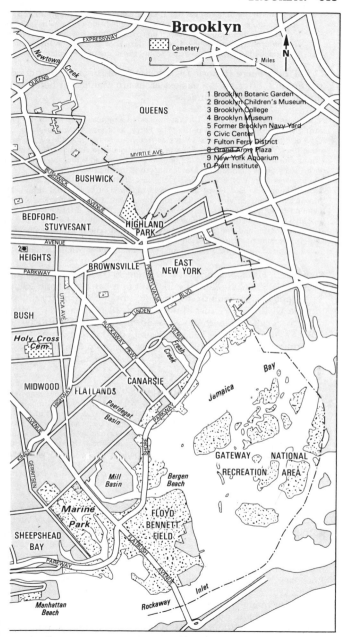

Brooklyn

Cemetery

0   1   2 Miles

N

1 Brooklyn Botanic Garden
2 Brooklyn Children's Museum
3 Brooklyn College
4 Brooklyn Museum
5 Former Brooklyn Navy Yard
6 Civic Center
7 Fulton Ferry District
8 Grand Army Plaza
9 New York Aquarium
10 Pratt Institute

QUEENS

EXPRESSWAY

Newtown Creek

QUEENS

MYRTLE AVE.

BUSHWICK

BUSHWICK AVENUE

BEDFORD-
STUYVESANT

HIGHLAND
PARK

AVENUE

HEIGHTS

AVENUE

BROWNSVILLE

EAST
NEW YORK

PARKWAY

PENNSYLVANIA

UTICA AVE.

BUSH

LINDEN

ROCKAWAY PKWY.

AVENUE

Fresh Creek

Holy Cross
Cem.

MIDWOOD

FLATLANDS

CANARSIE

Jamaica Bay

HIGHWAY

Paerdegat
Basin

PARKWAY

GATEWAY NATIONAL

KINGS

GERRITSEN

AVENUE

Mill
Basin

Bergen
Beach

RECREATION AREA

Marine
Park

FLOYD
BENNETT
FIELD

SHEEPSHEAD
BAY

FLATBUSH

PARKWAY

Inlet

Manhattan
Beach

Rockaway

through the building via the S. arch (past the subway station) and take the pedestrian underpass beneath the bridge approaches; there are signs pointing to the stairs up to the bridge. To walk across from the Brooklyn end, follow Cadman Plaza East beneath the Brooklyn-Queens Expressway to Front St and the stairs to the promenade.

The ***Fulton Ferry Historic District** lies N. of Brooklyn Heights on low ground, offering the easiest access to Manhattan before the advent of bridges and tunnels.

As early as 1642 one Cornelis Dircksen operated a regular rowboat service and during the pre-Revolutionary period The Ferry, as it was known, became the focus of industry and business, with slaughterhouses, taverns, a brewery, and a distillery. After the disastrous Battle of Long Island in August 1776, Washington's forces, barely escaping annihilation, were ferried across the river from here in rowboats manned by Massachusetts fishermen serving in the army. When a new ferry was established at the foot of Main St in 1796, the district became known as Old Ferry until it was renamed after Robert Fulton who introduced steam service in 1814 to supplement his other ferries, which included boats powered by horses on treadmills. The area thrived until the Brooklyn Bridge destroyed its economy. By the time the last ferry crossed in 1924 the district had degenerated to a skid row with the requisite flophouses and greasy spoons. Today Fulton Ferry is enjoying a renaissance with the development of a park, refurbished office buildings, and thriving restaurants.

Begin at *1 Front St* (corner of Cadman Plaza West), a cast-iron palazzo (1869; William Mundell), built as a bank, the Long Island Safe Deposit Company during the high tide of prosperity following the Civil War. Across the street at 28 Cadman Plaza West (S.E. corner of Elizabeth St) is the former EAGLE WAREHOUSE AND STORAGE CO. (1893; additions, 1910; Frank Freeman), a monumental brick building with a machicolated top, standing on the site of the original offices of the *Brooklyn Eagle*, converted to condominiums in 1980.

History. The *Eagle* was founded (1841) as an organ of the Brooklyn Democratic Party, and its first editor was Henry C. Murphy, elected mayor of Brooklyn in 1842. Walt Whitman edited it between 1846–48 but was relieved of his job either because of his strong antislavery views or because he was "slow, indolent, heavy, discourteous, and without steady principles," as his publisher stated. The paper, directed at a stable, business-oriented, Protestant readership, thrived as long as this population dominated Brooklyn, reaching its peak between 1890–1930. In 1950 the *Eagle* won a Pulitzer Prize for a series of articles uncovering crime, gambling, and police corruption; five years later (March 16, 1955), during a labor strike, the paper died.

The low buildings leading down the N.E. side of the block toward the river date from the 1830s; the one at 1 Cadman Plaza West, corner of Water St, was a hotel and now houses a restaurant. Across the street (8 Cadman Plaza West, S.E. corner of Furman St) is the former *Brooklyn City Railroad Company* (1861; remodeled 1975; David Morton; DL), originally headquarters for a horsecar firm, whose tracks (hence the name "railroad") fanned out into the city of Brooklyn. After the demise of the horsecars, a toilet seat manufacturer used the building; a recent remodeling has converted it to apartments.

Behind this building (block bounded by Doughty, Vine, and Furman Sts and Columbia Heights) is the former Squibb Building, once home of a pharmaceutical plant, now used by the Watchtower Bible and Tract Society of Jehovah's Witnesses.

On the waterfront itself at the foot of Cadman Plaza West stands a fireboat house built in 1926 for Marine Company 7 of the city fire department, two years after the ferry stopped running and the former Victorian ferry house was demolished.

Fulton Ferry Park (1976) offers spectacular, highly photographic views of the Brooklyn Bridge. The guardrails in the park were salvaged (1970) from the grassy center islands on Park Ave; a plaque commemorates the evacuation of the American forces after the Revolutionary War Battle of Long Island. Moored to the pier is *Bargemusic,* with concerts of soloists and small ensembles; tel: (718) 624-4061.

The ****Brooklyn Bridge,** still thought by many to be the world's most beautiful (1883; John A. Roebling and Washington Roebling; reconstruction, 1955; David B. Steinman, consulting engineer; DL), was the world's first steel suspension bridge, an engineering triumph (in 1883 only Trinity Church was higher) and a product largely of immigrant labor. The view from the pedestrian promenade is wonderful, both down to the river and up to the cables and granite arches. (Follow Cadman Plaza East beneath the bridge roadway to a flight of steps on the left which lead up to the promenade. The promenade descends in Manhattan near City Hall Park. Watch out for bicyclists.)

History. John A. Roebling, an immigrant from Prussia in 1831, started his American career as a farmer but soon began working on canal systems where he developed the wire rope that later would make the bridge possible. His plans (1869) for an East River bridge included the towers with their pointed openings, the iron trusses that stiffen the roadway, and the system of inclined stays that run diagonally from the towers giving the bridge its particular beauty and, he contended, making it so stable that if all the cables snapped the bridge would sag but not fall. Only a week after the plans gained final approval, a boat docking at Fulton Ferry crushed his right foot and he died of tetanus three weeks later. His son Washington Roebling took over actual supervision of the work which went slowly, hampered by blowouts of the compressed air in the caissons, fire, the dangers of "caisson disease" (the bends) whose cause was not yet understood, fraud, a taxpayers' suit against the bridge, and lack of funds. During the last decade of construction (it took 14 years), Emily Roebling became the liaison between her husband, invalided by the bends, and the bridge workers, while Roebling himself watched the project from his window with a telescope.

The bridge opened May 24, 1883, amidst triumphal celebrations. Since then it has inspired artists (John Marin, Joseph Stella) and writers (Walt Whitman, Hart Crane, Thomas Wolfe, and Vladimir Mayakovsky). Folklore surrounds it, beginning with the tragedies in the Roebling family and the death of 20 workers during its construction. The week after it opened 12 pedestrians died, crushed by a panic-stricken mob who believed it was collapsing. In 1884 P. T. Barnum took 21 elephants over it, declaring himself satisfied thereafter as to its stability. In 1885 one Robert Odlum, a swimming instructor, jumped to his death wearing a bright red swimming shirt and trunks. Steve Brodie, a personable unemployed Irishman, claimed to have survived a jump in 1886; to prove it he opened a tavern featuring an oil painting of the event and an affidavit from the barge captain who allegedly fished him out of the river.

Both bridge anchorages have imposing vaulted spaces within them. For many years the vaults on the Manhattan side, cool, dark, and partly underground, were used as storage by a commercial wine merchant, though they were sealed during prohibition; an alternative use for them is presently being sought. The Brooklyn Anchorage, however, after years of use storing vehicle tires and other mundanities, was historically restored by the Borough of Brooklyn and the City of New York (1983; Smotrich and Platt, Architects) for the Brooklyn Bridge Centennial Celebration. Today, equipped with a brick floor and theatrical lighting, the Brooklyn Bridge Anchorage hosts performance events, art exhibitions, even wedding receptions. It can be reached from the foot of Cadman Plaza West which becomes Old Fulton Street close to the river.

The centenary of the bridge (1983) was celebrated with a grand display of fireworks, a harbor parade, a sound and light show, and the commission of a musical composition, as well as the usual speeches.

STATISTICS. Length of river span, 1595.5 ft. Total length of bridge, 5989 ft. Width of bridge floor, 85 ft. The bridge is supported by four cables, each 15.75 inches in diameter and 3578.5 ft long; each contains 5434 wires or a total wire length of 3515 miles per cable. The Brooklyn foundations reach a depth of 44 ft 6 in below high water and the Manhattan foundations, 78 ft 6 in. The towers are 276 ft 6 in above high water while the roadway is 119 ft above the water at the towers. The total weight of the bridge exclusive of masonry is 14,680 tons.

Follow Front St under the bridge approach; turn left at Dock St and right at Water St. The brick *Empire Stores* at 53–58 Water St (bet. Dock / Main Sts) date from the years after the Civil War (W. group, 1870; E. group, 1885) when they were used to warehouse goods brought to the waterfront on railroad cars which were then loaded aboard barges. Later the Arbuckle Brothers kept them filled with coffee.

The nine acres between the Empire Stores and the water are *Empire Fulton Ferry State Park,* as yet undeveloped, a place for solitude, an occasional summer ball game, and good views of the river and the squat, brooding facade of the Empire Stores. The former Tobacco Inspection Warehouse (c. 1860) at 25–39 Water St between Dock and New Dock Sts, has been proposed as a maritime museum.

The nearest subway stop is the IND 8th Ave express and local (A or C train) at High St / Brooklyn Bridge station, located at Cadman Plaza West opposite the park.

39 Brooklyn Heights

SUBWAY: The nearest stops are the IRT Broadway-7th Ave (train 2 or 3) at Clark St (rather deserted during off hours; access to street via an elevator), and the IND 8th Ave (A train) at High St-Brooklyn Bridge. The IRT stop at Borough Hall serves both the Broadway-7th Ave (train 2 or 3) and the Lexington Ave (train 4 or 5) and is more heavily used.

Brooklyn Heights, bounded by the East River, Fulton St, Atlantic Ave, and Court St, is an old residential neighborhood distinguished by its tree-shaded streets and its many well-preserved 19C houses of brick, brownstone, and even wood. New York's first suburb, it also became (1965) its first designated Historic District, a classification that preserves the facades of its buildings from wanton change. Part of the village of Brooklyn, Brooklyn Heights began to thrive after 1814 when Robert Fulton's steam ferry began scheduled crossings to New York. Not long thereafter prominent landowners (whose names are commemorated in local streets) divided their property into standard 25 × 100-ft lots for development, a process largely completed by 1890. Victorian Brooklyn Heights was known for its fine families, its churches, and its clergymen.

When the subway arrived (1908) the Heights lost its patrician edge and in the early 20C many of the private homes had been converted to rooming houses; a few had even become seamen's clubs or missions. The Heights remained in social limbo until the 1950s when the borough's first brownstone revival began, led primarily by young married couples willing to put labor and money into preserving the old houses. Today, however, taxation and strictures on landmark buildings have made single-family houses increasingly expensive and the trend is once more toward the subdivision of houses into apartments.

Begin in front of the Clark St entrance to the *St. George Hotel* (bet. Hicks / Henry Sts), named after a nearby 18C tavern. This blockbuster of a hotel, built in various stages (1885; Augustus Hatfield; additions 1890–1923; tower, 1930; Emery Roth) has been converted to cooperative apartments and Jehovah's Witnesses residences. For a while it was the city's largest hotel (2632 rooms), famous during the 1920s for its mirrored swimming pool and Art Deco ballroom; today the hotel occupies only the section over the subway entrance.

Walk E. along Clark St to Henry St and turn right (S.). In the long block of Henry St running S. of Clark St are two modest Gothic churches among the many that gave 19C Brooklyn the name "Borough of Churches." The *First Presbyterian Church*, 124 Henry St (1846; W. B. Olmsted; memorial doorway, 1921; James Gamble Rogers) has beautiful stained glass windows from the Tiffany Studios (installed around 1901), including an unusual skylight. Across the street is the *German Lutheran Church* (1887) at 125 Henry St.

Turn around and walk N. on Henry St. On the right (E.) is a long block with urban renewal housing. The S. part of the project, *Cadman Towers* (bounded by Clark and Henry Sts and Cadman Plaza West with additional row housing along Clark St, Monroe Place, and Cadman Plaza) is one of Brooklyn's more successful public housing efforts (1973; Glass & Glass and Conklin & Rossant), combining high- and low-rise buildings, shopping and parking.

From Henry St turn left into Orange St. The **Plymouth Church of the Pilgrims,** on Orange St between Henry and Hicks Sts, a red brick Italianate barn of a church (1849; Joseph C. Wells), is best known as the church of Henry Ward Beecher, who used its pulpit for 40 years (1847–87) to address the great issues of the day: slavery, war, temperance, and morality.

At the height of his popularity "Beecher boats" ferried throngs of New Yorkers across the river to hear him, while policemen patrolled the crowds who gathered hours before the service. Always theatrical, Beecher once brought a slave girl to the church with the avowed intention of selling her to the highest bidder; roused to indignation by Beecher's imitation of a slave auctioneer, the congregation purchased her freedom. Beecher's sister was Harriet Beecher Stowe, author of the famous antislavery novel, *Uncle Tom's Cabin*. A sensational trial for adultery, of which he was acquitted, temporarily damaged his later career.

The church has opalescent stained glass windows (c. 1915) in the sanctuary designed by the Lamb Studios, the oldest known American stained glass studio (founded 1857), depicting the history and influence of Puritanism. In the garden to the left of

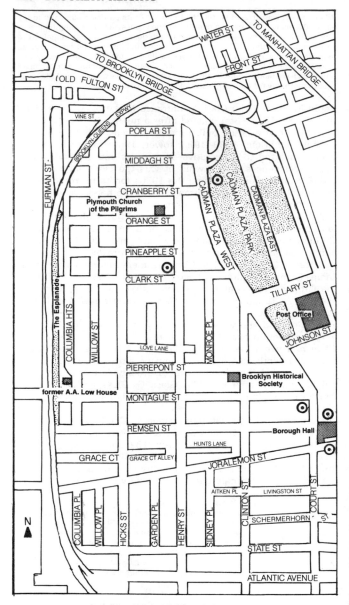

the sanctuary is a statue of Beecher by Gutzon Borglum, who also executed the bas-relief of Lincoln, one of many notables who trekked to Brooklyn to hear Beecher. Hillis Hall, given by coffee merchant John Arbuckle, has stained glass windows from the Tiffany Studios, originally in the Church of the Pilgrims (see p. 622), which merged with Plymouth in 1934.

Return to Henry St and keep going north. As you pass Cranberry St look E. (toward the housing project). Until 1964 the Rome Brothers' Printshop stood a block E. at 170 Fulton St on the S.W. corner of Cranberry St (now part of the renewal project). Here in 1855 Walt Whitman set type for his *Leaves of Grass*. The *Henry Street Studios,* 20 Henry St at the N.W. corner of Middagh St, occupy the former Mason Au & Magenheimer Candy Company (1885; Theobald Engelhardt; reconstructed, 1975); an old advertisement for Peaks and Mason mints still remains at the top of the S. wall.

Walk N. a block to Poplar St and turn left. Incorporated in the condominiums, Bridge Harbor Heights, between Hicks and Henry Sts is a former Victorian orphanage built in 1883 for indigent newsboys by the Brooklyn Children's Aid Society.

Turn left on Hicks St and walk one block south. John and Jacob Middagh Hicks, early developers of Brooklyn Heights, named Hicks St after themselves. After years of decrepitude, Nos. 38 and 40 Hicks St (c. 1830 and c. 1831), between Poplar and Middagh Sts, were restored in the early 1980s, a late but laudatory act of the Brooklyn Heights revival movement. Once confined to row houses the movement has spread to larger buildings, now being revitalized as cooperative apartments.

At Middagh St, turn right and walk a block W. to Willow St. The house on the S.E. corner of Willow and Middagh Sts, 24 MIDDAGH STREET, is a well-preserved clapboarded house (1824) with fine carved Federal detailing around the door, dormer windows, and quarter-round attic windows visible from Willow St. The cottage behind it, now joined to it by a wall, was originally the carriage house. In 1848 Henry Ward Beecher lived at 22 Willow St across the intersection.

While many Brooklyn Heights streets are named after prominent 19C families, five—Pineapple, Orange, Cranberry, Poplar, and Willow—have botanical names. Legend attributes them to the ire of one Miss Middagh, who allegedly tore down street markers bearing the names of neighbors she disliked and substituted the present ones. In fact, however, the street names seem to have been bestowed by the developers of the area.

Continue walking S. on Willow St to Cranberry St. *No. 19 Cranberry St,* on the N.W. corner, has a fine Federal fan-style doorway; the mansard roof was added later. NO. 57 WILLOW STREET (c. 1824) on the N.E. corner of Orange St, originally the Robert White home, exemplifies the Federal style with dormers, pitched roofs, Flemish bond brickwork, tooled stone lintels, and a parapet between the chimneys concealing the roof gable.

Continue on to Orange St and turn right; walk a block to Columbia Heights. The Hotel Margaret (1889; Frank Freeman) occupied the N.E. corner of the intersection until it burned in 1980; today The Margaret apartments (1988; Ehrenkrantz Group), owned by the Jehovah's Witnesses, a fundamentalist sect, occupies the site.

Walk S. on Columbia Heights past several residential facilities of the Witnesses. To the N. can be seen the former Squibb factory now used as a home for its publication, the *Watchtower*. The Jehovah's Witnesses Residence Hall at 124 Columbia Heights stands on the site of the house (110 Columbia Heights) from which Washington Roebling watched the construction of the Brooklyn Bridge. On the E. side of the street at 107 Columbia Heights is a high-rise dormitory, also a residence hall for Jehovah's Witnesses. A little to the S. (119 Columbia Heights) is a newer *Jehovah's Witnesses Library and Dormitory* (1970; Ulrich Franzen & Assocs.), hailed as a triumph of the Landmarks Law, since the facility respects the scale and proportions of the existing 19C buildings.

Turn left at Clark St and walk a block inland. The former *Leverich Towers Hotel* (1928; Starrett & Van Vleck), at 25 Clark St on the N.E. corner of Willow St, once glittered as one of Brooklyn's brighter social spots, its four corner towers spotlighted at night. Today it also belongs to the Jehovah's Witnesses and serves as yet another residence hall. The territorial expansion of the sect and its members' efforts at proselytizing have made it sometimes an unwelcome presence in the neighborhood.

Walk a block E. to Hicks St and turn right. Among Brooklyn's best Gothic Revival row houses are two (c. 1848) at 131 and 135 Hicks St (bet. Clark / Pierrepont Sts). Note the dark brownstone facades, the Tudor arches above the doors, the small-paneled casement windows with horizontal hoods and molds.

Return to Willow St and walk south. Three houses (c. 1880) on Willow St (108–112 Willow St) (bet. Clark / Pierrepont Sts) best exemplify in Brooklyn the offbeat architectural style known as Queen Anne that flourished (1880–1900) after its introduction to this country from England at the Philadelphia Centennial Exposition (1876).

The style combines medieval and Renaissance elements in a freehanded, nonacademic manner. These houses, which form one visual unit, display a surprising variety of forms (gables, bay windows, chimneys, dormers; round, square, and elliptical openings) and materials (brick, stone, terra-cotta, ironwork, shingles).

Continue S. on Willow St past a trio of pristine small Federal row houses (c. 1829) at 155–159 Willow St (bet. Clark / Pierrepont Sts). The paneled front doors with flanking colonnettes, sidelights, and leaded transoms are especially handsome. The glass set into the sidewalk near 157 Willow St illuminates a passageway that once led to the stables, though legend asserts that it led to No. 151, a way station in the underground railroad for slaves fleeing northward.

At Pierrepont St turn right and walk toward the water. *6 Pierrepont St* (c. 1890) between Willow St and Pierrepont Place is an unusual Romanesque Revival town house with a rockface entrance stairway and posts carved with flourishing stone plant forms.

Continue W. to Columbia Heights. Outstanding among the many fine Italianate town houses in the area are *210–220 Columbia Heights* (1852–60) on the N.W. corner of Pierrepont St, amply proportioned with wide doorways; the elaborate door hoods are carved with acanthus leaves.

Turn around and walk back E. on Pierrepont St; cross Willow and Hicks Sts. The former *Herman Behr mansion* (1890; Frank Freeman) stands at 82 Pierrepont St on the S.W. corner of Henry St. With an addition in 1919 this handsome Romanesque Revival mansion became the Palm Hotel whose disagreeable reputation in its twilight days was later redeemed by the Franciscans of nearby St. Francis College who took it over as a residence for novitiates. It has now been converted to apartments.

Continue walking east. In the block between Henry and Clinton Sts are several fine townhouses. *No. 104 Pierrepont St* (c. 1857), a four-story brownstone with elaborately carved console brackets on the first and second stories, was first owned by one Thomas Clark, listed in an 1858 city directory as proprietor of a "fancy store." *No. 108–114 Pierrepont St* (1840) was once a Greek Revival double house with a central cupola; drastic remodeling has made it a strange hybrid, half Greek Revival, half Romanesque Revival. The doorway pediment and corner quoins on one half remain from the original facade. The other half was given its present Romanesque Revival form for publisher Alfred Barnes by adding brownstone facing, terra-cotta ornament, a turret, and a rounded bay.

MONROE PLACE, short, wide, and quiet, is named after James Monroe, fifth President of the nation, who finished his life in straitened circumstances in New York. On the N.W. corner of Monroe Place and Pierrepont St is the *Appellate Division of the New York State Supreme Court* (1938; Slee & Bryson). Minard Lafever's (1844) *Church of the Saviour*, also called the First Unitarian Church, stands on the N.E. corner. Some windows (the Low, Woodward, Farley, Frothingham memorials and possibly the other opalescent windows) are by the Tiffany Studios. *No. 46 Monroe Place* has Brooklyn Heights's only remaining ironwork basket urn, topped with the traditional pineapple for hospitality.

Return to Pierrepont St. A block E. is the **Brooklyn Historical Society** (1878; George B. Post; DL), formerly the Long Island Historical Society, at 128 Pierrepont St, S.W. corner of Clinton St, a grand building housing a grand collection of materials on local history.

The Brooklyn Historical Society. 128 Pierrepont St (at Clinton St), Brooklyn, N. Y. 11201. Tel: (718) 624-0890. Gallery open Tues–Sat 12–5; library open Tues–Sat 10–4:45. Closed Sun, Mon, holidays; when national holidays fall on Mon, the Society is usually closed the preceding Sat. Library closed in August. Free admission to building, but there is a charge for nonmembers using the research library.

Restrooms; no food service. Gift shop with books, posters, souvenirs. Membership with benefits. Lectures, changing exhibits, bus and walking tours. Library. Entrance and gallery several steps up from street; elevator to library.

The facade of this eclectic, asymmetrical building with its slate-roofed tower is ornamented with terra-cotta reliefs including busts of worthies peering out from between the window arches (sculptor Olin Levi Warner), and a Viking and an Indian overlooking the main door. On the ground floor is the Brooklyn History Gallery, whose exhibits chronicle 350 years of the borough's changing population and major events. The library on the second floor, fitted out with black ash paneling, brass hardware, and elaborate Corinthian columns, makes research a pleasant labor. Its collections of local history and its genealogical materials are outstanding.

From the turn of the century until 1944 when the club closed, members of the Crescent Athletic Club (1906; Frank Freeman) swam, played squash, and exercised in the gymnasium of what is now *St. Ann's Episcopal School* across the street on the N.W. corner of Clinton St at 129 Pierrepont St.

At **One Pierrepont Place** (1988; Haines Lundberg Waehler) is Brooklyn Heights' largest office building, also known as the Morgan Stanley Building.

Turn right and walk a block to MONTAGUE STREET, long the main commercial street of Brooklyn Heights, its older stores and arriviste boutiques reflecting the current population of Brooklyn Heights, an established middle-class with traditional family values and a more recent influx of high spending "yuppies."

On the N.W. corner of Clinton and Montague Sts is Protestant Episcopal *Holy Trinity Church* (1847; Minard Lafever), a brownstone Gothic Revival church. Cast terra-cotta ornament, windows by William Jay Bolton, a reredos by Frank Freeman, and a bust of pastor John Howard Melish (N. side of the entrance vestibule) by William Zorach adorn the interior.

Walk W. on Montague St. At Henry St turn left and walk S. to the N.E. corner of Remsen St. *Our Lady of Lebanon Church* (1846; Richard Upjohn), originally the Congregational Church of the Pilgrims, has since 1944 served a community of Middle Eastern Catholics practicing the Maronite rite. Simple and bold in form, faced with ashlar stonework instead of the usual brownstone, the church represents a brief departure from Upjohn's more familiar Gothic Revival style. The doors in the W. and S. portals come from the luxury liner *Normandie* which burned (1942) and sank at its Hudson River berth; a projecting chunk of stone, inside near the corner tower, comes from Plymouth Rock in Massachusetts, where the first pilgrim settlers are said to have disembarked in 1620. The steeple has been removed.

Return to Montague St and keep walking west. The *Hotel Bossert,* 98 Montague St on the S.E. corner of Hicks St (1909; addition on the S., 1912; Helmle and Huberty) got its name from founder Louis Bossert, a Bushwick millwork manufacturer. In the 1920s and 1930s the Marine Roof, decorated by theatrical designer Joseph Urban, afforded visitors a vista of the Manhattan skyline while they dined and danced; it has been converted to residential space by the Jehovah's Witnesses.

Along the waterfront at the foot of Montague St runs the *Esplanade, known locally as the Promenade (1951; Andrews and Clark, engineers; Clarke & Rapuano, landscape architects), a five-block walkway between Remsen and Orange Sts cantilevered over the Brooklyn-Queens Expressway. The superb views of the Manhattan skyline compensate for the fumes rising from the road below. A plaque at the entrance recalls the original Pierpont mansion Four Chimneys which stood nearby.

*NOS. 2–3 PIERREPONT PLACE at the entrance to the Promenade, two superb Renaissance Revival brownstones (1857; Frederick A. Peterson) by the architect of Cooper Union, belonged originally to Abiel Abbot Low (teas) and Alexander M. White (furs), as an 1858 city directory lists them. Low, a Yankee from Salem, Massachusetts, got into the China trade early, made a fortune, and settled here with his family including son Seth, later mayor of Brooklyn and of New York City. From his opulent home, four stories elaborated with quoins, a heavy cornice, Corinthian pilasters at the entrance, and a conservatory added on the S. end, Low could watch his ships setting out to sea. Alfred Tredway White, housing reformer, lived at No. 2 from 1868–80. A playground now stands on the site of No. 1, Henry E. Pierrepont's mansion.

PIERREPONT PLACE, like Pierrepont St, takes its name from Hezekiah Beers Pierpont, landowner and gin distiller, who early saw the advantages of opening Brooklyn Heights for suburban development. He backed the Fulton Ferry (1814) and by 1823 was offering 25 × 100-ft lots to "gentlemen whose duties require their daily attendance in the city." His estate faced the harbor and ran N. and S. from Remsen St to Love Lane, and westward to a point beyond Clinton St. Hezekiah spelled his last name with one "r" but his children reverted to an earlier, fancier spelling.

Walk S. on Montague Terrace, like Montague St named after Lady Mary Wortley Montagu, née Pierrepont, the English writer. The final "e" is a misspelling. Thomas Wolfe lived here (1933–35) while writing *Of Time and the River*.

Turn left into Remsen St, named after Henry Remsen, a landowner. *Nos. 18 and 16 Remsen St* have handsome scroll pediments above the doorways.

Turn right on Hicks St and walk a short block to GRACE COURT ALLEY, running E. of Hicks St, originally a mews for the horses and carriages of the Remsen and Joralemon St gentry; the stables converted to apartments now house the gentry itself.

Across the street on the S.W. corner of Grace Court, Richard Upjohn designed GRACE CHURCH (1847), a year after his experiment with the Church of the Pilgrims (see p. 622), returning to his usual Gothic Revival manner. A glorious old elm tree shades the courtyard S. of the church; three Tiffany windows adorn the sanctuary.

Continue S. to Joralemon St, named after Teunis Joralemon, a 19C landowner.

Turn right on Joralemon St and walk toward the harbor. On the sloping W. end of the street, between Hicks and Furman Sts, stands a row of 24 modest Greek Revival houses, *29–75 Joralemon St*, many with their original iron railings and doorway trim. *No. 58* across the street, shuttered with steel, its windows rimmed with soot, has become a ventilator for the IRT subway, whose Battery-Joralemon St tunnel runs deep below.

Continue down Joralemon St toward the river. The RIVERSIDE BUILDINGS (4—30 Columbia Place, S.W. corner of Joralemon St), accurately named until the Brooklyn-Queens Expressway usurped the shoreline, are another stand of model tenements built by Alfred Tredway White (1890; William Field & Son), whose good works also enhance Cobble Hill (see p. 629).

Return to Willow Place, turn right and walk south. Gothic Revival town houses were never as common in New York as other styles, so *2—8 Willow Place* are unusual survivals (c. 1847), their Gothicism expressed mainly in the clustered colonnettes and pointed arches of the porches and the recessed decorative panels above. *Nos. 43—49 Willow Place* make up Brooklyn's sole remaining colonnade row, four Greek Revival houses (1847) joined by a wooden colonnade. Unlike the city's other such rows, which were intended for the wealthy, this one housed more humble folk, accountants and merchants.

Turn left on State St; walk E. past Hicks St, Garden Place, and Henry St to Sidney Place; turn left. *Sidney Place,* originally called Monroe Place after the fifth President, was given its present name after 1831 by attorney George Wood, who wished for obscure reasons to honor Sir Philip Sidney, 16C English statesman and man of letters.

Turn left into Sidney Place and walk N. past a handsome row (31—49 Sidney Place) of Greek Revival houses, built together in 1845 with unusually generous front gardens. Roman Catholic *St. Charles Borromeo Church* (1869; P. C. Keely), a Gothic Revival brick church, stands on the N.E. corner of Aitken Place, renamed for its pastor Ambrose S. Aitken.

Look N. to *135 Joralemon St,* a clapboarded frame house in the Federal style similar to 24 Middagh St (see p. 619). The cast-iron porch was added in the mid-19C, when the first-floor windows were elongated.

Follow Aitken Place to Clinton St, named after De Witt Clinton, governor of New York State, mayor of New York City, and builder of the Erie Canal. Rows of 19C houses line the block down to State St. Across Clinton St at the N.E. corner of Livingston St is the former **St. Ann's Church** (Protestant Episcopal), now the Auditorium of Packer Collegiate Institute. An exuberant Ruskinian Gothic building (1869; James Renwick, Jr., its brownstone facade banded with white limestone and topped with spires and traceried openings, the church is smaller but more flamboyant than Renwick's famous Manhattan churches, for example Grace Church on Broadway and St. Patrick's Cathedral.

Go N. to Joralemon St and turn right. The PACKER COLLEGIATE INSTITUTE at 170 Joralemon St between Clinton and Court Sts, with its Gothic Revival campus (1854; Minard Lafever), started out as a girls' school but is now a private secondary school.

The nearest subways are the Court St-Montague St station next to Holy Trinity Church (BMT Nassau St, M train; or Broadway local, R train) and the IRT

Borough Hall-Court St station (7th Ave, train 2 or 3; Lexington Ave, train 4 or 5). If the entrances on Joralemon St are closed, take the stairway in front of the Brooklyn Municipal Building.

40   The Civic Center and Downtown Brooklyn

SUBWAY: IRT Broadway-7th Ave (train 2 or 3) or IRT Lexington Ave (train 4 or 5) to Borough Hall. IND 8th Ave (A train) or 6th Ave (F train) to Jay St-Borough Hall.

The **Civic Center,** today devoted to borough affairs, was formerly the seat of government of the independent City of Brooklyn established in 1834, the descendant of the town of Brooklyn or Breuckelen, chartered by the Dutch in 1658. Long the focal point of Brooklyn's far-flung system of elevated railways, the Civic Center got a facelift in the 1950s when the trestles were torn down and the streets widened during the construction of Cadman Plaza. The main shopping street, once the main shopping street of all Brooklyn, is Fulton St.

Points of interest. Borough Hall, originally the City Hall of the independent city of Brooklyn (1846–51; Gamaliel King; cupola, 1898; Stoughton & Stoughton; DL), at 209 Joralemon St, intersection of Fulton and Court Sts, like certain other things in Brooklyn, began as a copy of its counterpart in New York across the river. Indecision and bureaucratic bungling resulted in three subsequent sets of plans, and today its stark Greek Revival mass with an imposing stairway and entrance colonnade supports a Victorian cupola, an afterthought.

Across the street (210 Joralemon St) is the **Brooklyn Municipal Building** (1926; McKenzie, Voorhees & Gmelin), home of many borough offices.

Cadman Plaza, officially S. Parkes Cadman Plaza, named after a noted Brooklyn Congregationalist minister and radio preacher (see p. 145), is bounded by Cadman Plaza West, Joralemon, Adams, Court Sts, and the viaducts to the Brooklyn Bridge. The *New York State Supreme Court* (1957; Shreve, Lamb & Harmon) is at 360 Adams St in the S. part of the plaza. The verdigris lamp standards at the S. end of the building were saved from the former (1905) Kings County Hall of Records, which went down with the redevelopment of the area in the 1950s. Near the entrance to the Supreme Court Building a plaque honors Washington A. Roebling, engineer and supervisor of the Brooklyn Bridge. To the W. in the park is a bust of assassinated Senator *Robert F. Kennedy* (1972; Anneta Duveen).

Continue N. past the courthouse. The best piece of sculpture in the plaza is John Quincy Adams Ward's 8-ft bronze *statue of Henry Ward Beecher* (1891). It stands on a granite pedestal by Richard Morris Hunt, with figures of children bringing floral tributes.

The **Brooklyn General Post Office,** 271 Cadman Plaza East, N.E. corner of Johnson St (1885–91; Mifflin E. Bell, first designer; William A. Freret, successor; addition to the N., 1933; James

626 NEW YORK CITY TRANSIT EXHIBIT

Wetmore, supervising architect; DL), is a grand example of Romanesque Revival architecture, with a steep slate-covered roof, dormers, turrets, and a massive arcaded windows at ground level. At the N. end of the plaza is the *Brooklyn War Memorial* (1951; Eggers & Higgins, architects; Charles Keck, sculptor), commemorating heroes of the Second World War.

A few blocks away is *St. James Cathedral,* formerly St. James' Pro Cathedral (1903; George H. Streeton), on Jay St between Cathedral Place and Chapel St, the first Roman Catholic church built in Long Island. The Georgian-style brick church with a verdigris copper steeple became Brooklyn's cathedral more or less by default in 1972 when plans for an imposing cathedral in the Fort Greene area were scrapped.

The *former City of Brooklyn Fire Headquarters,* 365–367 Jay St, between Willoughby St and Myrtle Ave (1892; Frank Freeman; DL), a Romanesque Revival masterpiece, is rated the best work of Brooklyn's best architect. Built of rock-face granite, dark brown brick, and red sandstone with terra-cotta ornament and a red tile roof, the firehouse has a large archway for the fire engines (horses in the old days) and a tall tower for spotting fires. Today it is being converted into housing and a community center.

Within walking distance is the **New York City Transit Exhibit**, down a flight of stairs in the former IND Court Street subway station.

The New York City Transit Exhibit. N.W. corner of Boerum Place and Schermerhorn St, Brooklyn, N.Y. 11201. Tel: (718) 330-3060. Open Mon–Fri 10–4, Sat 11–4; closed Sun, holidays. Admission charge.

Guided tours for groups, lectures, workshops, children's events. Restrooms, gift shop, telephones; no restaurant.

SUBWAY: IRT Broadway-7th Ave local or express (train 2, 3, or 4) to Borough Hall. IND 8th Ave (A train) or 6th Ave (F train) to Jay St-Borough Hall. BMT Nassau line (M train) or Broadway line (R train) to Lawrence St.

This low-key subterranean exhibit (1976) offers subway devotees the chance to explore the history of the world's second-largest mass transit system. Exhibits include classic subway cars, a model of the subway system as it exists today (263 miles of track in four boroughs, excluding Staten Island), historical photographs, examples of turnstiles and collection boxes, and displays of the mosaics from IRT and BMT Stations intended partly as decoration, partly as visual aids for immigrants who could not read English.

The **Brooklyn Friends Meeting House** (1857; attrib. Charles T. Bunting, builder; DL) at 110 Schermerhorn St on the S.E. corner of Boerum Place reflects the simple, even stark character of Quaker architecture.

Return N. along Boerum Place to Fulton St. In 1984 the section of Fulton St between Boerum Place and the Flatbush Avenue Extension was converted into a pedestrian shopping street, the **Fulton Mall,** in an effort to stem the headlong deterioration of the downtown shopping district. In the 30s and through the late 40s, this stretch of Fulton St was the center of downtown Brooklyn, with large department stores like Frederick Loeser &

Company, Abraham & Straus, and Namm's attracting shoppers from all over Brooklyn. Although the removal of the el threw light upon the scene, the suburbanization of the borough in the 1950s weakened Fulton St as a retail hub; Namm's and Loeser's closed, and the area began deteriorating until in 1973 a group of merchants banded together to work for renewal. Today shoppers can stroll down clean brick sidewalks and choose from a variety of stores, most of them offering goods in the moderate price range. *Gage & Tollner's* restaurant, 374 Fulton St between Smith St and Boerum Place (1889; DL), is a Brooklyn gustatory landmark, known also for its dark paneled dining room and crystal light fixtures once illuminated by gas.

The *Abraham & Straus* department store (known as A & S), occupying eight assorted buildings along Fulton St between Gallatin Place and Hoyt St, is the area's largest and grandest institution.

Founded as a small dry goods business in 1865 by Abraham Abraham, who clerked in Newark with Benjamin Altman and Lyman Bloomingdale, his later rivals in business, Abraham & Straus moved to Fulton St in 1883, the year the Brooklyn Bridge opened. Though others thought the location too far from the center of things, Abraham's vision of the significance of the bridge proved correct, as did his belief that the subway from New York would help trade. Joseph Wechsler, Abraham's original partner, sold his interest in 1893 to three Macy's partners including Isidor and Nathan Straus, though A & S did not become part of Macy's.

The oldest part of the building, encrusted with terra-cotta ornament, is at the N.E. corner of Livingston St and Gallatin Place and dates from 1895; the Art Deco Main Building (Starrett & Van Vleck) dates from 1929 and 1935.

At the corner of DeKalb, Fulton, and Fleet Sts is the *Dime Savings Bank* (1907; Mowbray and Uffinger), a monumental building in the classic mode with an Ionic colonnade outside. Inside is a low leaded glass dome and a decor of impressive gilded dimes, perhaps implying fiscal growth. While commercial banks in the high rent financial district were usually ensconced on the ground floor of taller buildings, savings banks, especially those located in outlying areas, could afford to build exclusively for their own use. They also felt it necessary to communicate architecturally their fiscal stability, especially during times of economic upheaval.

The *Albee Square Mall* (1978; Gruen Assoc.), on DeKalb Ave at Albee Square West, stands on the site of the former RKO Albee movie theater, demolished in 1977, the last of a group that included the Brooklyn Strand, the Brooklyn Paramount, the Loew's Metropolitan, the Fox, the Orpheum, and a number of burlesque houses. Only the Albee Square Mall, an indoor shopping mall named for Edward F. Albee, grandfather of the playwright, and the name of Fox Square (intersection of Flatbush Ave, Fulton St, and Nevins St) remain to commemorate the heyday of the silver screen in Brooklyn, though the Brooklyn Paramount Theater and its offices (1928) have been converted to Founder's Hall and Tristram W. Metcalf Hall of Long Island University, Brooklyn

Center, along the E. side of the Flatbush Ave Extension. Lovers of theater pipe organs may be pleased to know that the mighty Wurlitzer organ, known affectionately as "The Beast," built (1928) to accompany movies in the theater, still remains installed (on an elevator under the floor) in the university gymnasium.

The nearest subway stops are the IRT Broadway-7th Ave and Lexington Ave (train 2, 3, 4, or 5) at Nevins St-Flatbush Ave. Also the IND 6th Ave (B or D train) and the BMT Broadway and Nassau St lines (M, N, or R train) all at DeKalb Ave-Flatbush Ave.

41   Cobble Hill, Boerum Hill, and Carroll Gardens

SUBWAY: Broadway-7th Ave IRT (train 2 or 3) to Borough Hall. IND 6th Ave (F train) to Bergen St.

North of Red Hook and S. of Brooklyn Heights are several historic neighborhoods, formerly considered part of South Brooklyn but renamed presumably to expunge unpleasant associations as they undergo gentrification. **Cobble Hill,** running from Atlantic Ave southward to Degraw St is the most northerly. Through the years it has been the home successively of English, Irish, Swedish, Italian, and most recently Middle Eastern immigrants.

The name Cobble Hill dates back to the Revolutionary War when "Cobleshill" rose where Court St now intersects Atlantic Ave and Pacific St. The Cobble Hill Historic District extends from Atlantic Ave to Degraw St, Hicks to Court St, except for the N.W. corner occupied by Long Island College Hospital. It contains numerous late-19C brick and brownstone town houses built mostly by property speculators.

Atlantic Ave between Court and Hicks St is the center of Brooklyn's Arab population, whose members include Syrians, Palestinians, Yemenis, Iraqis, Jordanians, and Egyptians, most of them Christian, except for the Yemenis who are Moslem. The Brooklyn colony began after Little Syria (N. of Battery Park around Washington St in Manhattan) was destroyed by the excavations for the Brooklyn-Battery Tunnel, and many of the present residents had parents or grandparents in Manhattan. Food merchants on Atlantic Ave sell an exotic variety of fruits, nuts, coffee, dates, and olives, while other importers display brass water pipes, belly dancing costumes, backgammon sets, and records of Middle Eastern music. There are Arab bakeries, falafel stands, and pastry shops, as well as more formal restaurants, many of them Lebanese. On the third Sun in Sept the Arab community holds the Atlantic Antic, a street fair whose attractions have included belly dancing and camel rides.

Begin at Henry St and Atlantic Avenue and walk south. Visible at the S.E. corner of Hicks St and Atlantic Ave is the large red brick Atlantic Ave building of *Long Island College Hospital* (1974; Ferrenz & Taylor), newest addition to an institution founded in the 19C by German immigrants. The next block S. used to be devoted to the ministry of St. Peter's Church (a block W.) which operated *St. Peter's Hospital* (1888; William Schickel & Co.) at 274 Henry St.

Turn the corner to the right on Warren St. Halfway down the block on the S. side is **Warren Place,** lined with handsome cottages constructed for working people (1879) by Alfred Tredway White as part of a large project that also includes the **Tower Buildings** (1879) filling the W. half of the block between Warren and Baltic Sts and the **Home Buildings** (1877) along Hicks and Baltic Sts (439–445 Hicks St and 134–140 Baltic St). The complex, designed by William Field & Son, included 226 tenement apartments and 34 cottages on which White, who disclaimed philanthropy, sought a modest 5% return. The apartments had stairwells entered from outdoor balconies as a fire safety provision, good light and ventilation, and bathing facilities in the basement. The cottages had indoor toilets, unusual in low income housing of the period, and rented for $18 a month.

Just N. of the Tower Buildings is Roman Catholic *St. Peter's Church* (1860; P. C. Keely), at Hicks St on the N.E. corner of Warren St, now called St. Paul's, St. Peter's, Our Lady of Pilar Church. Nearby is St. Peter's Academy (1866).

Return to Henry St and continue south. The houses at 412–420 Henry St (1888; George B. Chappell) once belonged to F.A.O. Schwarz, the toy seller.

Continue S. to Degraw St and turn left. On the N.W. corner of Degraw St and Strong Place is the *St. Frances Cabrini Chapel,* originally the Strong Place Baptist Church (1852; Minard Lafever), a stone church with a buttressed square tower designed by one of the city's eminent architects. The earlier *Strong Place Baptist Church Chapel,* 56 Strong Place (1849; Minard Lafever), is now a day care center.

Walk N. on Clinton St. CHRIST CHURCH (Protestant Episcopal) at 320 Clinton St, N.W. corner of Kane St, was designed (1842) by Richard Upjohn, architect of Trinity Church on Wall St, and has furnishings designed by Louis Comfort Tiffany, including an altar and altar railings, the reredos, pulpit, lectern, and chairs. The Upjohns lived a block away at 296 Clinton St, N.W. corner of Baltic St, in a house (1843) designed by the father and enlarged by the son.

Continue north. *Verandah Place,* which runs S. of Congress St between Henry St and Clinton St has stables and small town houses. Thomas Wolfe lived at No. 40 for a while, in the basement. In *You Can't Go Home Again* he described it as more like a dungeon than a room, its windows barred "to keep the South Brooklyn thugs from breaking in." Today the street is charming.

Handsome Italianate town houses line Congress St between Clinton and Henry Sts. Abraham J. S. DeGraw originally lived at 219 Clinton St (S.E. corner of Amity St), a house built for him in 1845; but Ralph L. Cutter, a dry-goods merchant, altered the mansion (1891; D'Oench & Simon), adding the tower for viewing the harbor and installing Brooklyn's first residential elevator.

Turn right on Amity St. *No. 197 Amity St* (bet. Clinton / Court Sts), now faced with motley permastone, is distinguished by being the birthplace in 1854 of Jennie Jerome, mother of Winston Churchill. A few years thereafter her father Leonard Jerome moved the family to a new mansion on Madison Square.

St. Paul's, St. Peter's, Our Lady of Pilar Church (Roman Catholic) at the S.W. corner of Court St and Congress Ave, half a block E. and a block S., is the second Catholic church built in Brooklyn (1838; Gamaliel King), once a brick Greek Revival building, now much altered and expanded, veneered with brownstone and topped off with a steeple (c. 1860). The long name reflects merging congregations.

Boerum Hill is not far away. Walk S. a block to Wyckoff St; turn left and walk E. two blocks to Hoyt St. Walk N. on Hoyt St. Bounded by Court St, Fourth Ave, State St, and on the S., Wyckoff and Warren Sts, Boerum Hill, once lumped together with the rest of South Brooklyn, is often regarded as a new Brooklyn Heights or Cobble Hill, a comparison some of its residents reject. Boerum Hill does have its upper middle-class professionals and its historic brownstones, but it also has two large public housing projects and various social service organizations. This social and ethnic mix sets it apart from the Heights and is a source of pride to those who live there. Architecturally the E. side of the block of Hoyt St between Bergen and Wyckoff Sts (Nos. 157–165 Hoyt St) is one of the more interesting blocks in the district, with row houses built between 1854 and 1871.

The district is named after a Dutch family who farmed the land during the Colonial period, but the district did not grow until 1840–70, when middle-class business people built the three- and four-story Italianate and Greek Revival row houses that characterize the area. Today the population is a polyglot mix of white Anglo-Saxon Protestants, Chinese, Arabs, Italians, and second and third generation Irish.

To reach the **Carroll Gardens Historic District,** return two blocks along Wyckoff St and follow Court St eight blocks S. (counting on the E. or left side) to Carroll St. Turn right for a detour to **440 Clinton Street** on the S.W. corner of Carroll St, now a funeral home, originally the John Rankin Residence (1840; DL), a freestanding masonry Greek Revival town house touted as the finest in the city. Its brickwork and gray granite trim are handsomely preserved.

Turn around and walk E. on Carroll St to the historic district centered around President and Carroll Sts between Smith and Hoyt Sts. Here are rows of brownstone row houses with deep front gardens developed between 1859 and 1884 by a group of enlightened real estate entrepreneurs who planned both the self-contained quality of the district and the careful relationship of each house to its neighbor.

The nearest subway stop is the IND station at Carroll-Smith Sts (6th Ave F train and Brooklyn crosstown local G train).

42 Red Hook

Red Hook is not easily reached by public transportation. Nor is it a pleasant neighborhood in which to walk. A car is recommended.

BUS: From Borough Hall, the B61 bus runs as far S. as Beard St via Columbia / Conover Sts. The B77 bus, accessible from the last stop of the Brooklyn crosstown local G train or the IND 6th Ave F train at Smith and 9th Sts, runs S. to the Erie Basin (double-check bus route with driver as all buses do not run at all times).

Red Hook, named "Roode Hoek" by the Dutch—"hoek" meaning a point of land and "roode" describing either the soil color or the onetime cranberry bogs—originally referred to all the land below Atlantic Ave from the Gowanus Canal to the Buttermilk Channel. Today, however, as Cobble Hill and Carroll Gardens have been renamed to divorce them from disagreeable associations with Red Hook, the name now refers only to the section S. of the Gowanus Expressway. It has long been a commercial area dependent on its piers and waterfront industry, having received its initial impetus from the opening of the Erie Canal in 1825.

The pier and terminal facilities in the *Atlantic Basin area* were developed in the early 1840s by the Atlantic Dock Co. and the *Erie Basin* with its rocky breakwater in 1864 by William Beard, a railroad contractor. During the Civil War the warehouses served as a supply base for the Union Army and also as military prisons and hospitals. After the turn of the century the Brooklyn docks became one of the world's great grain ports, and the concrete silos of *former Port of New York Grain Elevator Terminal,* part of the New York State Barge Canal System, though endangered, still stand between the Henry St Basin and lower Columbia St.

Several old warehouses still remain: the *Brooklyn Clay Retort & Firebrick Works* (c 1860) at 76–86 Van Brunt St, 99–113 Van Dyke St, and 106–116 Beard St. The granite factory and warehouses produced and stored brick fired from New Jersey clay, ferried from Perth Amboy to the Erie Basin. Also near the basin are the *Beard & Robinson Stores* (1869) at 260 Beard St, and the *Van Brunt's Stores* (c. 1869) at 480 Van Brunt St.

In the 1920s the Tebo Yacht Basin, now gone, oversaw the dry-docking of the yachts of the wealthy, including J. P. Morgan's *Corsair.* During World War II, the Todd Shipyards, facing the Erie Basin, turned out landing craft for the Allied invasion; just after the war the rusted hull of the *Normandie,* which had burned (1942) at Pier 88 in the Hudson, was towed here to be readied for scrapping. Since World War II with the rise of containerized cargoes, the Brooklyn piers, lacking sufficient upland space for the handling of containers, have diminished in importance. Although there is a container port in Red Hook operated by the Port Authority, most port activity takes place across the Hudson River in New Jersey.

For years the residential communities of Red Hook rivaled Hell's Kitchen in density and bleakness. In the opening years of the century Red Hook was mostly Italian and Irish, and a few survivors from these days still remain, especially near the waterfront, in "the back" as it is called. Al Capone's family moved here to 38 Garfield Place from the area around the old Navy Yard and it was on Red Hook's mean streets that Capone is said to have received the gash that earned him the nickname "Scarface." Longshoremen, rope makers, ship chandlers, and others tied to the port lived there, sometimes without ever leaving the neighborhood, for it was and still is isolated, beyond the reach of the subway, accessible only by long bus rides.

Red Hook has never been affluent, but the area was further debilitated by the arrival of the Brooklyn-Queens Expressway (1958), a Robert Moses inspiration, and the Gowanus Expressway (1941) which cut off the shopping neighborhood around Columbia St, overshadowed blocks of housing on Hicks St, and polluted the air. More recently the loss of jobs on the docks has further depressed the area. Early slum clearance projects like the *Red Hook Houses* (1939), stretching from Clinton St to Dwight St, may have been heralded when completed, but today these blockbusters (2881 apartments) reflect rather than relieve the surrounding squalor. Newer housing attempts (1972; John Ciardullo Assocs.) on Visitation Place between Van Brunt and Richards Sts, and on Verona St, and Dwight St are more humane in scale.

In 1936 the Red Hook Play Center, at Bay and Henry Sts, with its Olympic-size swimming pool, replaced a Hooverville which had sprung up as the Depression deepened and still offers one of the few recreational facilities in an isolated neighborhood.

Optimists hope that the brownstone revival to the N. as well as several industrial ventures—the Port Authority shipping terminal (1981) in the Atlantic Basin area, Fishport, a fish market and processing center at the Erie Basin Terminal near Columbia St, and the Red Hook Container Terminal off Hamilton Ave—will help bring prosperity to the area.

43 Fort Greene, Clinton Hill, and the Navy Yard

SUBWAY: The stop nearest the first point of interest listed below is the Atlantic Ave-Long Island Railroad Station stop, reached via the IND 6th Ave (D train), the BMT Nassau St (M train), the IRT Broadway-7th Ave (train 2 or 3), or the IRT Lexington Ave (train 4 or 5).

CAR: Follow the Flatbush Ave Extension and Flatbush Ave to Hanson Place and turn left.

Fort Greene, the neighborhood bounded roughly by the Navy Yard on the N., Atlantic Ave on the S., the Flatbush Ave Extension and Clinton Ave on the W. and E., was built for the upper middle class in the late 19C, left to deteriorate, and then rediscovered by the middle class of another generation, though its renaissance seems more tentative than those of Park Slope, Cobble Hill, and Brooklyn Heights.

Distances are quite short between points of interest, and the area is pleasant S. and E. of the park, making it attractive for a walking tour. The park itself is fairly safe, but probably better enjoyed with a companion.

The neighborhood has two distinct parts. North of the park are massive public housing projects, notably the Walt Whitman Houses and the Raymond V. Ingersoll Houses, originally called the Fort Greene Houses (1944), bounded by Myrtle and Park Aves, Carlton Ave, and Prince St, part of a crash housing program for World War II industrial workers employed in the Navy Yard.

South of the park and E. of it are handsome brownstones, many being renovated. Near Atlantic Ave is the Atlantic Avenue Terminal area, dominated by the old passenger terminal of the Brooklyn spur of the Long Island Railroad, an area targeted for rehabiitation.

Points of interest (listed from S. to N. and from W. to E.). The *Hanson Place Seventh Day Adventist Church,* originally the Hanson Place Baptist Church, 88 Hanson Place, S.E. corner of S. Portland Ave (1860), is a handsome Greek Revival Church.

SOUTH PORTLAND AVE and SOUTH OXFORD ST, especially the former, between Lafayette and DeKalb Aves exemplify the spirit of neighborhood renewal, their tree-shaded brownstones dating from the 1860s. The N.-S. streets in Fort Greene bear the names of fashionable London streets: Adelphi, Carlton, Portland, Oxford, Cumberland, Waverly. The E.-W. avenues bear the names of American Revolutionary War heroes: Gates, DeKalb, Greene, Willoughby, Lafayette.

Fort Greene Park, bounded by DeKalb and Myrtle Aves, St. Edwards St, and Washington Park, was designed by Frederick Law Olmsted and Calvert Vaux (1860). Stanford White (1908) designed the granite column (148 ft 8 in) whose crowning bronze brazier (by Adolph A. Weinman) was intended to support an eternal flame. A crypt below (not open to the public) contains the remains of some of the 12,000 American soldiers who died on British prison ships in Wallabout Bay between 1780 and 1783. The dead, who had succumbed to starvation, disease, flogging, and exposure, were first buried in shallow graves along the water by their companions; later the bones were moved to a private estate in Brooklyn and in 1873 to the present crypt. During the Revolution, Fort Putnam occupied the park site; it was renamed Fort Greene after Nathanael Greene during the War of 1812.

From the summit of the hill (100 ft) there is a fine view across to Manhattan and W. to *Brooklyn Hospital.* The old building dates from 1920 (J. M. Hewlett).

The street E. of the park, known as WASHINGTON PARK, actually a section of Cumberland St, was once Fort Greene's grandest address, its Italianate brownstones housing such notable figures as publisher Alfred C. Barnes (No. 182); William C. Kingsley (No. 176), political force behind the Brooklyn Bridge; and Abner Keeney (No. 175), his partner in a contracting business. Together Kingsley and Keeney paved Brooklyn's streets, laid its sewers, built a reservoir at Hempstead, and did considerable work in Prospect Park.

Clinton Hill, E. of Fort Greene, formerly the home of Brooklyn's oil king Charles Pratt and other families of wealth, who referred to the neighborhood simply as "The Hill," is now the home of Pratt Institute, St. Joseph's College, the Roman Catholic Bishop of Brooklyn, and a generally middle-class population.

> SUBWAY: From Manhattan, IND 6th Ave local (F train) or 8th Ave local (E train) to Queens Plaza. Change to IND Brooklyn-Queens crosstown local (G train) to Clinton-Washington Ave. Or take the IND 8th Ave express (A train) to the Hoyt-Schermerhorn station in Brooklyn, and change there to the G train.

Points of interest. At the N.W. corner of Lafayette and Vanderbilt Aves is *Our Lady Queen of All Saints Church* (1913; Gustave Steinback), built by George Mundelein, pastor of this parish and later Bishop of Chicago. Twenty-four saints adorn the church. Diagonally across the intersection is *200 Lafayette Ave* (1812; DL), originally the Joseph Steele home, a Greek Revival yellow clapboard house with Italianate details probably added later.

The *site of the Roman Catholic Cathedral* for the Diocese of Brooklyn, never built, is in the block of Clermont St between Greene and Lafayette Aves. The diocese bought the land in 1860 and hired Patrick Charles Keely to design a church to be called the Church of the Immaculate Conception; construction began, and by 1887 the walls had reached 10 or 12 ft, and the bishop's residence (now the Chancery) still standing at 367 Clermont Ave had been completed. Funds ran out and in 1931 the walls, long a playground for children, were torn down and Bishop Loughlin Memorial High School (1933) built instead, its name commemorating the founder of the ill-fated cathedral.

The **Church of St. Luke & St. Matthew** (1889; John Welch; DL) at 520 Clinton Ave, near Fulton St, was built for an Episcopal congregation by a Brooklyn architect known for his Greek and Gothic Revival churches. Considered Welch's masterpiece, this eclectic Romanesque Revival church now serves a largely West Indian congregation. The interior has windows by the Tiffany Studios.

Along Clinton Ave are the former homes of the wealthy and the merely well-to-do; note especially the former *John Arbuckle home* (1888; Monstrose W. Morris) at 315 Clinton Ave, between Lafayette and DeKalb Aves. Arbuckle made his fortune in coffee and sugar importing; his warehouses stood in the Fulton Ferry district.

The former **Pratt family houses** stand on the block of Clinton Ave between DeKalb and Willoughby Aves. On the W. side (232 Clinton Ave) stands the *Charles Pratt mansion* (c. 1875), home of the founder of the Pratt Astral Oil Works in Greenpoint which he merged secretly and advantageously with John D. Rockefeller's Standard Oil Company in 1874. Ranged along the other side of the street are the homes Pratt built for three of his five sons; the youngest following fashion put his on Park Ave at 68th St (the fifth house has been demolished). The *George DuPont Pratt house,* 245 Clinton Ave (1901; Babb, Cook & Willard, later extensions to the S.), built by the architects of the Andrew Carnegie mansion, now belongs to St. Joseph's College as does the Charles Pratt mansion. Next door is the *Charles Millard Pratt Home,* now the residence of the Roman Catholic Bishop of Brooklyn (241 Clinton Ave), built in 1893 by architect William B. Tubby, a Romanesque Revival brick house with a tile roof and an arched port-cochère on one side balanced by a semicircular conservatory on the other. The *Caroline Ladd Pratt house* (1898; Babb, Cook, & Willard) at 229 Clinton Ave, now a residence of the Pratt Institute, first belonged to Frederick B. Pratt. The columned arbor on its N. serves as an entranceway to the gray and white Georgian Revival house.

Three blocks E. lies the campus of **Pratt Institute**, filling the blocks between Willoughby and DeKalb Aves, Hall St, and Classon Ave.

Charles Pratt, a self-made man, founded the Pratt Institute as a trade school for young people situated as he had been in his youth. It opened with a drawing class in 1887 and soon expanded to include courses in engineering and science, a school for librarians, and courses in home economics.

Ryerson Walk, once Ryerson St, bisects the campus. On its E. side are MEMORIAL HALL (1927; John Mead Howells; DL) and the two original college buildings, the MAIN BUILDING (1887; Lamb & Rich; DL), a sturdy Romanesque Revival, and the EAST BUILDING (1887; William Windrim). In the Main Building is the *Pratt Institute Gallery* which mounts eight or nine shows yearly, presenting sculpture, graphics, painting, book art, photography, and works in other media.

Open during the academic year Mon–Fri 9–5. Call for summer hours. Admission free. Occasional lectures, tours, performances. Tel: (718) 636–3517.

The East Building, originally called the Mechanical Arts Building, contains the engine room and boiler for the original plant designed in such a way that Pratt could convert his educational experiment to a shoe factory if it failed. Across the lawn on the W. side of Ryerson Walk is the LIBRARY (1896; William B. Tubby; expanded 1983; DL), another of Pratt's philanthropies, founded as Brooklyn's first free public library and annexed to the college only in 1940. THRIFT HALL, now containing offices, on the E. side of Ryerson Walk at DeKalb Ave (1916; Shampan & Shampan), opened as a savings and loan company (in a building where Memorial Hall now stands) organized by the philanthropic Pratt to make low-cost mortgages available to workers.

Nearby (half a block S. and two blocks W. of Thrift Hall) is the former *Graham Home for Old Ladies* (1851) at 320 Washington Ave between DeKalb and Lafayette Aves, once a shelter for elderly females indigent but too genteel for the public poorhouse. John B. Graham was a paint manufacturer.

Underwood Park on Lafayette Ave between Waverly and Washington Aves stands on the site of the John T. Underwood mansion, home of the typewriter manufacturer. The *Apostolic Faith Mission,* 265 Lafayette Ave on the N.E. corner of Washington

Ave (1868), now brightly painted, was surely more somber when it served as the Orthodox Friends Meeting House. At the next corner, 279 Lafayette Ave, N.W. corner of St. James Place (1887; Francis H. Kimball; DL) is the *Emmanuel Baptist Church,* looking like a French 13C Gothic church with Romanesque influence, a mix chosen to suggest that the church was constructed over a long period of time like its European predecessors.

The nearest subway stop is the IND Brooklyn-Queens Crosstown local (G train) Clinton-Washington stop on Lafayette Ave. To get to Manhattan from here, take the G train two stops W. to the Hoyt-Schermerhorn stop and change to the IND 8th Ave (A train).

The former **Brooklyn Navy Yard,** today an industrial park (closed to the public), stretches from the East River inland to Flushing Ave, from Kent Ave to Navy and Hudson Sts.

History. In 1781 John Jackson and William Sheffield started on the shores of Wallabout Bay a small shipyard whose facilities included a sawmill and a pond for seasoning ship timbers. During the War of 1812, the yard, purchased (1801) from Jackson by the U.S. Navy for $40,000, became an important base for servicing ships, though the first warship built there, the 74-gun ship-of-the-line *Ohio,* was launched only in 1820. Among the long line of distinguished ships produced in the yard are the battleship *Maine,* blown up in Havana harbor (1898), the *Arizona,* sunk at Pearl Harbor, and the battleship *Missouri,* on whose decks Japan signed the surrender ending World War II. Activity peaked in the Navy Yard during World War II, when 70,000 workers on continuous shifts turned out battleships and destroyers and overhauled some 5000 vessels. It closed in 1966 with the loss of thousands of jobs. Nowadays its space is leased as an industrial park.

Visible from Flushing Ave between Ryerson St and Williamsburgh Place is the *former U.S. Naval Hospital,* originally the U.S. Marine Hospital (1838; Martin E. Thompson; DL), austerely constructed of Sing Sing marble, now closed and boarded up. Nearby stands the brick Second Empire—style home of the hospital's chief of surgery (1863; True W. Rollins and Charles Hastings, builders; DL) officially known as the *Surgeon's House, Quarters R-l, Third Naval District.*

The oldest structure in the yard is the former COMMANDANT'S HOUSE also known as Quarters A (1806; attrib. Charles Bulfinch associated with John McComb, Jr.; DL), S. of Evans and Little Sts in the W. part of the yard, barely visible through the gates. The three-story white clapboarded house with handsome porches and elegant details—hewn oak floor beams 32 ft long, interior wood trim of carved mahogany—is one of the city's finest Federal structures. Also designated as a landmark is DRY DOCK #1 of the shipyard, on Dock St at the foot of 3rd St (1851; William J. McAlpine, engineer, and Thornton MacNess Niven, architect and master of masonry; DL), the oldest granite-walled dry dock in the nation, still usable.

44 Southwestern Brooklyn: Sunset Park and Bay Ridge

The neighborhood of **Sunset Park,** named after its park, lies along Gowanus Bay between the Gowanus Expressway to the N., Bay Ridge to the S., and about 5th St to the east. Like other Brooklyn neighborhoods, it suffered from the construction of the expressway in 1941. Long a Scandinavian and Finnish quarter whose residents were attracted by the waterfront economy, it is now largely Hispanic.

Points of interest. *Green-Wood Cemetery, Fifth to McDonald Ave, 20th–37th Sts, has more than 20 miles of paths winding through its 478 acres and includes the highest elevation in Brooklyn (216.5 ft).

Only the Main Gate (Fifth Ave at 25th St) is open for visiting hours; daily 8–4. The guard at the gatehouse will direct you to the office for permission to view the cemetery. For information, tel: (718) 768-7300. On weekdays a map is available at the office inside the Main Gate. Privately sponsored tours Sun afternoons in spring and autumn; by reservation only; tel: (718) 439-8828.

The nearest subway to Green-Wood Cemetery is the BMT Broadway local (N or R train) to 25th St and Broadway (Brooklyn). Bus B63 runs E. across Atlantic Ave and then S. along 5th Ave past the Main Gate.

The cemetery (opened 1840), whose landscaped hills and winding roads offer fine views of the harbor, broke with earlier burial traditions—family plots, churchyards —and soon became a popular outing spot for Victorian strollers who liked taking fresh air in a funereal atmosphere.

The *MAIN GATE, Fifth Ave at 25th St, designed (1861; Richard Upjohn & Son; DL) by the architect of Trinity Church, represents the full flowering of the Gothic Revival style. Built of brownstone with multicolored slate roofs on the flanking gatekeeper's lodge and office, the gate bristles with spires, turrets, finials, and crockets, its portals covered by tall traceried gables. *Other gatehouses:* Gate and Gatehouse at 20th St opposite Prospect Park West (1920; Warren & Wetmore), Gate and Gatehouse at 37th St and Fort Hamilton Parkway (1875; Richard M. Upjohn).

Buried there, among a half million others, are Lola Montez, James Gordon Bennett, Samuel F. B. Morse, ''Boss Tweed,'' Henry Ward Beecher, and Peter Cooper. The cemetery is interesting not only for its inhabitants but for its Victorian statuary, which has attracted art historians and scholars. To memorialize the particular lives and deaths of those buried the monuments take the shape of sinking steamboats, mangled railroad cars, fire hydrants, empty children's beds, empty chairs, and flights of angels kneeling, standing, or stooped with grief.

High, sloping SUNSET PARK, Fifth to Seventh Aves, 41st–44th Sts, also has fine views of the harbor and the Bush Terminal docks but is not one of the city's best-maintained parks.

The closest subway stop is at 45th St and 4th Ave on the BMT N or R trains. Bus B63 (see directions to Green-Wood Cemetery) continues S. past the park.

In the early decades of the 20C *Finntown,* one of two major Finnish settlements in New York (the other was in Harlem), lay on the N. and E. sides of Sunset Park. In the neighborhood were half a dozen public saunas, many small restaurants, and mama-papa stores facing clean, neat sidewalks swept by housewives who also scrubbed their stoops. A few traces remain today. The *Alku Toinen Finnish Cooperative Apartments* (816–826 43rd St bet. 8th / 9th Aves) date from 1916 and are said to be the city's first cooperative apartments. "Alku" means "beginning" in Finnish; other Finnish apartment houses were given names translatable as "Poorhouse," "Old Maids' Home," and "Drop of Sweat." Other survivals are a Finnish cooperative grocery store at 41st St and Seventh Ave, several Finnish churches, *Imatra Hall* (740 40th St bet. 7th / 8th Aves), home of an organization descended from the Finnish Aid Society Imatra (founded 1890), named after a Finnish waterfall, and a Finnish newspaper, the *Finnish New York News,* published in Swedish.

Today Sunset Park, and Bay Ridge to the S., are increasingly becoming home to a significant Chinese population, which in Brooklyn is estimated (1987) at 60,000. Attracted here by low rents, the Chinese garment industry has also begun to set up factories in old warehouses and factories.

The *Bush Terminal* district along the waterfront from about 28th–50th Sts is one of the major port facilities in Brooklyn, founded in 1890 by Irving T. Bush on land his father used for an oil business. At its peak the terminal employed some 30,000 workers, but container shipping has rendered much of it obsolete. South of the Bush Terminal is the former *Brooklyn Army Terminal* or New York Port of Embarkation and Army Supply Base (Second Ave bet. 58th / 65th Sts), built at the end of World War I to relieve the strain on the city's port facilities. The city bought the terminal in 1981 and has redeveloped it as the Harborside Industrial Center. Aficionados of industrial architecture find much to admire in the warehouses (1918; Cass Gilbert) with their eight-story skylit central atriums.

Today **Bay Ridge,** bounded by the Gowanus Expressway, the Narrows, and Gravesend Bay, is a quiet residential community with fine waterfront property. The Dutch settled the area as the town of Nieuw Utrecht (1662) which also included Borough Park, Bath Beach, and part of Bensonhurst. Bay Ridge remained rural until late into the 19C, attracting only an occasional rich industrialist to the high ground overlooking the Narrows, and a population of Scandinavians, mostly Norwegian sailors and shipbuilders, to its more modest areas inland. The Scandinavian community remained essentially stable until after World War II, when it was augmented by Irish and Italians, while today Asians and Hispanics continue to arrive. In 1964 the Verrazano Bridge arrived. Minor fame came to Bay Ridge as the setting for the 1978 movie *Saturday Night Fever,* whose dance scenes were filmed in a discotheque at Eighth Ave and 64th St.

THE BMT N and R trains stop at Bay Ridge Ave and 4th Ave. Express bus B27 from 57th St-Madison Ave in Manhattan runs along Shore Rd in Bay Ridge to

Fourth Ave. Also Brooklyn local bus B37 runs from the Borough Hall area to Bay Ridge. However, a car enables you to see more of the neighborhood.

Points of interest. *Owl's Head Park* at Colonial Rd and Wakeman Place used to be part of the estate of Democratic politician Henry C. Murphy, first editor of the Brooklyn *Eagle* and supporter of the Brooklyn Bridge. South of the park at the foot of Bay Ridge Ave are traces of an old pier where ferries departed for Staten Island before the advent of the Verrazano Bridge. Along Shore Road overlooking the Narrows and Staten Island are well-kept, well-to-do houses and apartments that have replaced the mansions. Bay Ridge's oddest house is a block inland from Shore Rd at 8220 Narrows Ave and 83rd St, an immense cottage with an extravagant fieldstone chimney. Another house, remarkable for its survival, is the *James F. Farrell residence* (119 95th St, N. side of block bet. Marine Ave and Shore Rd), a wooden Greek Revival dwelling (c. 1845), with wooden clapboards, shutters, trim, and cornice still intact.

At the S. end of Shore Rd is FORT HAMILTON PARK, a small triangular park between Fourth Ave and the bridge approach, containing a granite obelisk (1931) commemorating the service of the U.S. Navy in World War I.

West of the bridge approach at 9818 Fort Hamilton Parkway is *St. John's (Protestant Episcopal) Church* (1834), a modest country church that became known as the "church of the generals" because of its proximity to neighboring Fort Hamilton. Robert E. Lee served as vestryman and Stonewall Jackson was baptized here at the age of thirty.

Overhead soars the **Verrazano-Narrows Bridge** (1964; Othmar H. Ammann, engineer), a 4260-ft span linking Staten Island and Brooklyn, the world's longest suspension bridge, 60 ft longer than the former title holder, the Golden Gate Bridge in San Francisco.

Proposed as early as 1926, the bridge became mired in politics, and bridge commissioner Robert Moses spent almost 20 years subverting and crushing opposition to the project. Ground was broken in 1959 and as a consolation to the Italian community of Bay Ridge, some of whose homes were destroyed for the approaches, the bridge was named after Giovanni da Verrazano, the Florentine explorer who discovered New York Bay in 1524.

STATISTICS: Length of span, 4260 ft; length of bridge including approaches, 13,700 ft. Height of roadway above mean high water, 228 ft. Height of towers, 693 ft. Weight of each tower, 27,000 tons.

Fort Hamilton, named after Alexander Hamilton, was built facing Fort Wadsworth on Staten Island in 1825–31 to protect the entrance to New York harbor. The 155-acre government reservation includes the *Fort Hamilton Veterans' Hospital* (1950; Skidmore, Owings & Merrill), and the *Fort Hamilton Officers' Club,* originally Casemate Fort (1825–31; DL), one of the city's earliest granite fortifications (not open to the public).

The **Harbor Defense Museum** (enter through the 101st St gate) offers changing exhibitions on military history and the coastal defense of New York.

The Harbor Defense Museum of New York City. Fort Hamilton (101st St and Fort Hamilton Parkway), Brooklyn, N. Y. 11252. Tel: (718) 630-4349. Open Mon, Thurs, Fri 1–4, Sat 10–5, Sun 1–5. Closed holidays except Memorial Day, July 4th, and Veterans Day; closed for 10 days over the Christmas holiday. Free.

Tours by appointment. Brochure for self-guided tour of post. Restroom, telephone, and cafeteria on post nearby. Cafeteria closed Sun. Merchandise includes prints, maps, toy cannons, books, pins, T-shirts. Full wheelchair access. Restrooms equipped for handicapped visitors available.

SUBWAY: BMT Broadway local (R train) to 95th St-Fort Hamilton (4th Ave) in Brooklyn. BUS: Brooklyn buses B8, B16, B37, B63, B70. CAR: Brooklyn Bridge to Brooklyn-Queens Expressway; east to Belt Parkway, exit at Fort Hamilton-4th Ave. Take 4th Ave; right onto Marine Ave; right again onto Fort Hamilton Parkway; follow to end. Once within the fort, follow signs past Officers' Club to the museum.

The only military museum in the city, it is housed within the walls of the original fort in a renovated battery known as the Caponier (literally "chicken coop"), a term which describes its low structure. Its function as a flank battery was to protect the fort against attack from land. The exhibits consist of arms and armor, guns, uniforms, banners, and other military equipment. There is a steel helmet and body armor from the 16C, a polished brass Gatling gun, a torpedo mine, early machine guns, and an 1841 flank howitzer, part of the original armament. Also photos and memorabilia.

On Fifth Ave between Bay Ridge Parkway and about 82nd St and on Eighth Ave between about 59th and 55th Sts are the remnants of the **Scandinavian communities** of Bay Ridge. Delicatessens carry authentic Scandinavian sausages as well as fish (salt herring, dried cod, canned sardines), bread, cheese, and even canned reindeer meat. The delectable products of several Scandinavian bakeries suggest why that breakfast pastry known as a sweet roll elsewhere in the nation is called a Danish in New York. At 8104 Fifth Ave the *Nordisk Tidende* or "Norwegian News," (founded 1891) is still published.

45 Park Slope

SUBWAY: IRT Broadway-7th Ave (train 2 or 3) to Grand Army Plaza. IND 6th Ave (D train) to 7th Ave-Flatbush Ave. BMT Nassau St (M train) to 7th Ave-Flatbush Ave.

Park Slope, a district rising from the lowlands around the Gowanus Canal to the hilltops of Prospect Park, can be divided into three separate neighborhoods. The North Slope, between the park and Sixth Ave, has one of the nation's highest concentrations of Victorian architecture, fine brownstones developed after the Civil War for wealthy families seeking an alternative to Manhattan's Fifth Ave. West of about Fifth Ave is a "no man's land," a dilapidated semiindustrial area with abandoned housing and a flourishing drug trade. The South Slope, beginning around Third St, has been a working-class district since it was developed in the 19C for workers on the Brooklyn docks. Until the 1940s it was also home of a small enclave of Newfoundlanders known locally as "blue noses" who earned their livelihood on the fishing boats out of Sheepshead Bay. The following walking tour focuses on the Victorian residential architecture of the North Slope.

Begin at Grand Army Plaza (see p. 643 for description of the plaza). THE MONTAUK CLUB, 25 Eighth Ave, N.E. corner of Lincoln Place (1891; Francis H. Kimball), served Brooklyn's social, business, and political elite during its heyday before World War I and now opens its doors to a more ordinary membership. The building, an eclectic composition of Venetian Gothic and American Indian motifs, pays tribute to the Ca d'Oro in Venice and also to the Montauk Indians of eastern Long Island whose history appears in the terra-cotta frieze.

Walk S. along the W. side of the plaza. *No. 276 Berkeley Place* (1891; Lamb & Rich), a sturdy Romanesque Revival house, belonged originally to George P. Tangeman, whose fortune was derived from the Royal and Cleveland Baking Powder companies. Unlike the millionaires of New York's Fifth Ave, who dealt in railroads, real estate, and oil, Park Slope's industrialists generally owed their wealth to more homely commodities—chewing gum, hot dogs, cleansing powder.

Walk W. (away from the park) to Eighth Ave; turn left and go S. a block to Union St. Among the attractive late-19C houses along Union St between Eighth and Seventh Aves are Nos. 889–903 (1889; Albert E. White) and Nos. 905–913 (1895; Thomas McMahon).

Continue S. along Eighth Ave to President St and turn right. The *former Stuart L. Woodford residence*, 869 President St between Eighth and Seventh Aves (1865; Henry Ogden Avery), remarkable for its oriel windows and the radial ornament over the ground-floor windows and door, formerly belonged to the U.S. ambassador to Spain.

Return to Eighth Ave and continue S. a block to Carroll St. On the N.E. corner of the intersection stands the *former Thomas Adams, Jr., residence,* 115 Eighth Ave (1888; C. P. H. Gilbert), a brownstone Romanesque Revival mansion with an elaborately carved entrance arch on Carroll St, home of the inventor of Chiclets chewing gum, now apartments. On the S.W. corner of the same intersection stood the mansion (demolished 1950) of Charles Feltman, alleged inventor of the hot dog, whose Coney Island restaurant earned him fame and fortune.

Enthusiasts of row house architecture will find an interesting group on *Fiske Place* a half block W. of Eighth Ave between Carroll St and Garfield Place. Nos. 12–16 (1896) were designed by an unknown architect apparently experimenting with triangular, semicircular, and rectangular window forms, an experiment whose results so pleased him that he repeated it a block W. at Nos. 11, 15, and 17 Polhemus Place.

Another architecturally interesting block is *Montgomery Place* between Eighth Ave and Prospect Park West. Developer Harvey Murdock, who apparently had an eye for the picturesque, chose C. P. H. Gilbert to design most of the houses on the street (Nos. 11, 17, 19, 14–18, 21, 25, 36–46, 48–50, and 54–60). Murdock himself lived at No. 11.

Return to Carroll St and Eighth Ave. The block of **Carroll Street** between Eighth Ave and Prospect Park West, developed by eminent 19C architects, is architecturally one of Park Slope's most interesting. Noteworthy are Nos. 838–846 (1887; C. P. H. Gilbert), three houses each an imposing 40 ft wide; Nos. 864–872 (1887; William B. Tubby), picturesque brick and shingled Queen Anne houses; Nos. 855–861 (1892; Stanley M. Holden), Romanesque Revival houses with carved leaf forms and faces ornamenting the windows; and No. 863 (1890; Napoleon Le Brun & Sons), by a firm known for its firehouses.

On the S.W. corner of Prospect Park West and Carroll St are two limestone Renaissance Revival apartments, formerly private houses, Nos. 18 and 19 Prospect Park West (1898; Montrose W. Morris), the former retaining its glass canopy.

Continue down Prospect Park West. The *Woodward Park School,* 49 Prospect Park West between 1st and 2nd Sts (1892; Montrose W. Morris), belonged first to Henry J. Hulbert, whose financial interests included paper, Pullman cars, and life insurance. Long the biggest building around, the mansion was provided with towers which allowed Hulbert a fine view of the harbor. His next door neighbor at 53 Prospect Park West was William H. Childs, inventor of Bon Ami, precursor of the modern battery of cleansing powders. Today the red brick and limestone mansion (1901; William B. Tubby) serves as the *Brooklyn Ethical Culture Society Meeting House.* (For the nearby Litchfield Villa in Prospect Park, about opposite 4th St, see p. 647.)

The nearest subway stops are those at Grand Army Plaza.

46 Prospect Park

SUBWAY: IRT Lexington Ave express (train 4) or IRT Broadway-7th Ave express (train 2 or 3) to Grand Army Plaza. IND Sixth Ave (F train) to 7th Ave in Park Slope.

CAR: From Manhattan take the Manhattan Bridge to Flatbush Ave and follow it S. to Grand Army Plaza. From points E. take the Brooklyn-Queens Expressway and get off at the Tillary St exit; turn left onto Flatbush Ave Extension and follow it to Grand Army Plaza. Parking on Prospect Park West, or in Brooklyn Museum parking lot (charge).

**Prospect Park, 526 acres of meadows, woods, and lakes designed by Frederick Law Olmsted and Calvert Vaux, is one of the chief ornaments of Brooklyn. Laid out by its designers (1866–67) after they had cut their teeth on Central Park, the park is thought by many to be their masterpiece. Today, in addition to the beautifully enhanced landscape, there are recreational facilities such as picnic grounds, baseball diamonds, a zoo, and a skating rink, but fortunately the park has by and large escaped the attention of self-memorializing philanthropists.

CRIME: Prospect Park has in the past had an unpleasant reputation but is not the urban jungle many people believe it to be. In recent years the crime rate has dropped significantly and police statistics indicate that the park is safer than even the "better" neighborhoods surrounding it. Use common sense. Do not wander in its more isolated areas alone, and don't go there at night. As elsewhere, company is the best security.

TOURS: The Urban Park Rangers offer guided tours to different attractions in the park and to other Brooklyn parks; call (718) 287-3400.

RECREATIONAL FACILITIES: Ice skating at Wollman Rink, opens around mid-Nov and continues through Feb, sometimes longer; skate rental available. For information call (718) 788-0055. Horses to ride on the bridle path can be rented at the Equestrian Club of Brooklyn, 51 Caton Place at E. 8th St; lessons available. Call (718) 438-8849.

WEEKLY INFORMATION ABOUT PARK EVENTS: Call (718) 788-0055. PPEC (Prospect Park Environmental Center) sponsors tours, workshops, bus trips, and other events; call (718) 788-8500 or 788-8549 for recorded information.

History. In 1859, sparked by the success of Central Park across the river, Brooklyn civic leaders headed by James S. T. Stranahan, moved to purchase a $4-million parcel of land for a "pleasure ground." Egbert Viele, formerly the chief engineer of Central Park, developed a plan which included much of the present park as well as the area now occupied by the Brooklyn Museum and the Botanic Garden. Fortunately the Civil War halted construction, giving the commissioners time to reconsider Viele's plan. Unhappy with it, they hired Calvert Vaux who convinced them to change the site to its present form, eliminating Flatbush Ave which would have cut a swath down the middle, and adding land for a large lake. Vaux brought in Frederick Law Olmsted and the two worked on Prospect Park from 1866 to 1873, authorizing some $5 million in improvements, enhancing the natural contours of the land, providing rustic park shelters, building archways and roads, planting and replanting trees and shrubs. Work continued into the 1890s, though the exact date of completion is unknown.

At the end of the century the firm of McKim, Mead & White designed the Peristyle and a number of park entrances, and oversaw the formal placement of statuary in the Concert Grove. Later intrusions have been fenced ballfields on the Long Meadow, the zoo, and the skating rink, enjoyed by their users but unloved by those who cherish the original design.

After a period of neglect and serious vandalism, Prospect Park today is enjoying a resurgence. The Prospect Park Administrator's Office (created 1980) oversees a master plan to restore and preserve landscaping and park structures. Increased security including antigraffiti stakeouts are making the park's buildings more difficult targets for vandals, who in the past have spray-painted monuments and stolen plaques for the value of the metals in them.

Begin at ***Grand Army Plaza** (1870; Frederick Law Olmsted and Calvert Vaux), Flatbush Ave, at the intersection of Prospect Park West, Eastern Parkway, and Vanderbilt Ave, a monumental oval plaza with a triumphal arch honoring the Union forces in the Civil War, Brooklyn's answer to the Place de l'Étoile. John H. Duncan designed the 80-ft arch (1892) on top of which rides a bronze *Columbia* (1898; Frederick W. MacMonnies) in a four-horse chariot (quadriga) accompanied by trumpeters. The figure is commonly believed to represent Victory, but according to park archives she represents Columbia, the Union. On the pedestals two monumental groups also by MacMonnies (both 1901) represent the *Army* (W.) and the *Navy* (E.), while above the inner doorway to the arch are bas-reliefs of Lincoln and Ulysses S. Grant (1894; Thomas Eakins and William R. O'Donovan).

The **Grand Army Plaza Arch** is open for art exhibitions between Sept and Nov, April and June (when the weather permits; the interior is neither heated nor

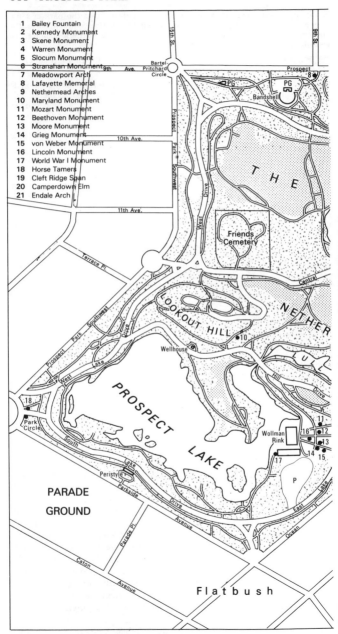

1 Bailey Fountain
2 Kennedy Monument
3 Skene Monument
4 Warren Monument
5 Slocum Monument
6 Stranahan Monument
7 Meadowport Arch
8 Lafayette Memorial
9 Nethermead Arches
10 Maryland Monument
11 Mozart Monument
12 Beethoven Monument
13 Moore Monument
14 Grieg Monument
15 von Weber Monument
16 Lincoln Monument
17 World War I Monument
18 Horse Tamers
19 Cleft Ridge Span
20 Camperdown Elm
21 Endale Arch

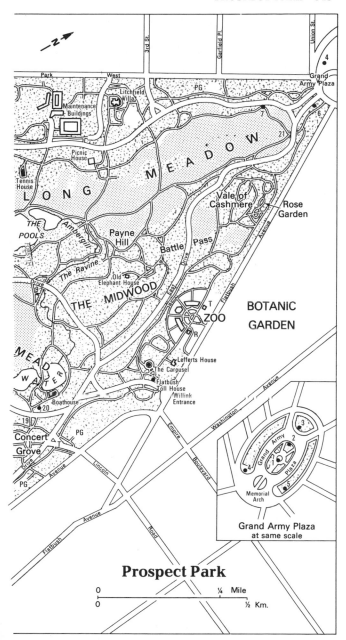

Prospect Park

0   ¼ Mile

0   ½ Km.

Grand Army Plaza
at same scale

air-conditioned). Weekends only, 11—4:30; free. For information tel: (718) 788-0055.

North of the arch is an ellipse surrounded by formally planted London plane and Callery pear trees around the central *Mary Louise Bailey Fountain* (1932; Eugene F. Savage, sculptor; Edgerton Swartwout, architect), with a grotesque openmouthed Neptune and sportive Tritons. North of it stands the city's sole official *monument to John F. Kennedy*, a modest marble tablet with a small bronze bust (1965; Neil Estern); still further N. across the road is a *bust of Alexander Skene* (1905; J. Massey Rhind), onetime dean and president of Long Island College Hospital.

Walk back toward the park. On the W., across the road, is Henry Baerer's (1896) bronze *statue of Gouverneur Kemble Warren*, Civil War engineer and soldier, defender of Little Round Top in the Battle of Gettysburg, some of whose boulders have been incorporated in the statue's base. In the same position on the other side of the arch is a bronze *statue of Henry Warner Slocum* (1905; Frederick W. MacMonnies), a Civil War general who hailed from Brooklyn and served under Sherman on his infamous march to the sea. In New York, Slocum is best remembered perhaps for the ill-fated steamboat named after him (see p. 230).

Enter the park through its most formal approach whose eagle-topped Doric columns and 12-sided classic temples (1894; Stanford White) express the reigning classicism of the period. Just inside the park entrance stands a *statue of James S. T. Stranahan* (1891; Frederick W. MacMonnies), park commissioner, public servant, and originator of Brooklyn's boulevard systems.

Take the right pathway (nearest Prospect Park West). A berm or earth mound girds the entire park, designed by Olmsted and Vaux as a visual and acoustic barrier distancing the park from its urban surroundings. Take the left fork of the path and cross under the roadway (here, as in Central Park, Vaux and Olmsted have separated vehicular and pedestrian traffic); walk through the *Meadowport Arch* (1872; Calvert Vaux) and into the Long Meadow.

Over a mile in length, the **Long Meadow** provides 90 acres of gently rolling grassland whose pastoral serenity Olmsted felt to be essential to an urban park, so essential that he had workers remove a narrow glacial ridge to enlarge the sweep of the land, creating what is the longest unbroken park vista in North America. He planted trees either singly (and some have grown to wonderful proportions) or in selected groups, using in many cases a tree-moving machine he and Vaux invented in 1867. Workmen with picks and shovels scooped out and packed into place the dips and rises that today seem to have been put there by nature itself.

Follow the path past the *Picnic House* (1927; J. Sarsfield Kennedy, restoration completed 1984), used for various park programs (restrooms in basement). Visible to the right is the TENNIS HOUSE (1910; Helmle & Huberty), of brick and limestone with open Palladian arches. It was built in the days when lawn tennis was a portable sport played on lawns and nowadays houses the Prospect Park Environmental Center, also known as PPEC. The center offers walking tours, courses, exhibitions, and programs for children and adults; tel: (718) 788-8500.

Side trip. Take the path along the road and cross under it to the paved Ninth St playground, a place for roller hockey after school or for jazz and classical concerts (summer) in the nearby bandshell. At the Ninth St entrance is Daniel Chester French's (1917) *Lafayette Memorial,* a 10-ft bronze tablet with a high relief of Lafayette in the uniform of an American Revolutionary soldier. The park maintenance buildings between Eighth and Seventh Sts (inside the park) used to be the stables of the Litchfield estate. The LITCHFIELD VILLA itself, since 1890 the headquarters of the Park Department for Brooklyn (in the park opposite about Fourth St), was built (1857; Alexander Jackson Davis; DL) as a home for Edwin C. Litchfield, a lawyer who made a fortune developing midwestern railroads. In 1853 he hired Davis to design this Italianate mansion, romantic, asymmetrical, towered, turreted, and balconied. Davis called it Ridgewood; the Litchfields called it Grace Hill (Mrs. Litchfield's maiden name was Grace Hill Hubbard). After the Civil War Litchfield donated 24 acres of his land to Prospect Park but, according to the Brooklyn *Eagle,* the park commissioners lusted after Litchfield's castle with a craving like that of David for Naboth's vineyard, and appropriated his estate and home, allowing the family to rent it back for $2500 a year. The columns on the porches have bunches of corn and wheat on the capitals instead of the classic acanthus leaves, perhaps a reminder of the Midwest where Litchfield achieved financial success. Return to the Long Meadow.

Cross the Long Meadow to the POOLS, modified glacial kettles, natural bodies of water unlike, for example, the Lake.

Take the path along the shore to the *Ambergill,* a small stream flowing into the woods past *Payne Hill* (on the left as you enter the woods) named for John Howard Payne, *Home Sweet Home's* composer, whose statue once stood here.

Follow the Ambergill into the RAVINE, keeping the brook on your right; the steep hills and plantings here were designed to satisfy the 19C taste for wild, romantic scenery and to complement the gentler landscape of the Long Meadow.

Continue along the stream past the stone staircase to the *Nethermead Arches* (1870; Calvert Vaux), whose three spans accommodate walkers, horseback riders, and the brook. Inside the arches are vaults with fine brickwork. Beyond is the **Nethermead** or lower meadow, surrounded by woods and seemingly isolated from the city.

Continue along the path to the right, following it along Central Drive to an unused paved road leading up Lookout Hill. On the W. side of the drive is the fenced FRIENDS' CEMETERY (generally locked; apply to the keeper if he is available; Urban Park Rangers sometimes lead tours to the cemetery), a 15-acre Quaker burial ground established (1846) before the park was built and still in immaculate condition. Actor Montgomery Clift is buried here about halfway up the hill near the right (N.) fence.

Take the unused carriage drive up LOOKOUT HILL, the highest elevation (170 ft) in the park, planned as a gathering place with separate concourses for carriages and pedestrians. Before the vegetation became so dense, the hilltop, rather abandoned nowadays, offered views of the city and harbor.

Walk down the E. stairway. Near the bottom of the hill, not far from the bridge, is the *Maryland Monument* (1895; Stanford White), a memorial to the heroism of a Maryland regiment whose holding action allowed the main body of Washington's troops to escape encirclement by the British during the Revolutionary War. Continue downhill to the lake. Off to the right (as you face the water), hugging the hillside is the *Well House* (1869) whose pumps once raised water to a reservoir on top of Lookout Hill. From here it flowed down into the Pools and thence through the Ravine into the Lullwater and Prospect Lake. City water came into the park at the turn of the century and the well was covered over.

From the foot of the hill cross the Terrace Bridge (designed by Calvert Vaux) and continue straight on to the **Concert Grove,** laid out as a formal garden with avenues of trees and statues of musicians. At the edge of the lake stands the *Wollman Rink and Skating Shelter* (1960; Hopf & Adler), replacing a small cove and an offshore island that once served as a natural bandstand. In the grove today are *busts of composers: Mozart* (1897; Augustus Mueller), *Beethoven* (1894; Henry Baerer), *Thomas Moore* (1879; John G. Draddy), *Grieg* (1914; Sigvald Absjornsen), and *von Weber* (1909; Chester Beach). Directly behind the rink is Henry Kirke Brown's (1869) *Abraham Lincoln,* formerly in Grand Army Plaza.

Walk around the rink past the parking lot to the *World War I Memorial* (1921; Augustus Lukeman, sculptor; Daniel Chester French, architect), a shrouded bronze angel sheltering a soldier.

Nearby along the shore stands a rustic log shelter, similar to those designed by Vaux and Olmsted as part of the original park furniture. From here either follow the lakeshore S. to the Park Circle exit or return to Grand Army Plaza past the zoo, the Lefferts Homestead, and the Vale of Cashmere.

To Park Circle: Continue along the shoreline and cross left under the drive, following the path to the PERISTYLE, sometimes called the Grecian Shelter (1906; McKim, Mead & White; DL), its limestone columns finished off with terra-cotta Corinthian capitals. Further along is the Park Circle entrance (1897; McKim, Mead & White) adorned with Frederick W. MacMonnies' wonderful, athletic *Horse Tamers* (1897), two bronze groups flanking the roadway.

To Grand Army Plaza: Walk back to the Concert Grove. Along its main axis furthest from the rink are the remnants of the *Oriental Pavilion* (1874; Calvert Vaux; restored 1988), a fine example of Victorian exotic tastes in architecture, its hipped roof and posts modeled on a medieval Hindu temple.

At the pavilion turn left and walk under the CLEFT RIDGE SPAN (1872; Calvert Vaux), the first poured concrete structure in the U.S. and probably in the world. Its vaulted interior is finished with polychrome blocks of molded concrete. Beyond on the left is a Himalayan pine and (on the right) the park's most famous tree, a gnarled and twisted ***Camperdown elm,** planted in 1872.

Poet Marianne Moore wrote about it; its devotees raised money to fill its
hollows and truss its branches, and the Friends of Prospect Park have held
benefit road races to maintain it and its fellows. Created by grafting a prostrate
Scotch elm onto an upright elm trunk, the tree is descended from a crawling
elm that grew (c. 1850) near Camperdown House in Dundee, Scotland.

Continue straight ahead to the **Boathouse** (1905; Helmle, Huberty, and Hudswell; DL) faced with white terra-cotta, formerly
the site of a boating office and a soda fountain. It is now the
Visitor Center.

The Boathouse Visitor Center. Prospect Park, Brooklyn, N.Y. 11215. Tel: (718)
287-3474. Open Wed–Sun 12–6:30 in summer. After Labor Day, weekends
only, 12–6:30. Park maps and information; rotating exhibitions, usually dealing
with park design or history. Restrooms, gift shop. No restaurant. Limited
wheelchair access, a few small steps to entrance.

The *Lullwater Bridge* (1869; restored 1986), a single steel arch,
crosses the pond.

   Past the boathouse take the right fork of the path under the
East Wood Arch toward the zoo. On the left is the *Carousel*
(closed for restoration), whose horses were salvaged from the
McCullough Brothers' merry-go-round at Coney Island. Nearby
is the octagonal *Flatbush Toll House* (c. 1855) which formerly
stood on the boundary between the independent towns of Brooklyn and Flatbush. On the right is the LEFFERTS HOMESTEAD
(1783; DL), a clapboard Dutch farmhouse burned by the American troops under George Washington during the Revolution and
rebuilt afterwards.

The Lefferts Homestead. Prospect Park, Brooklyn, N. Y. 11215. Open April–
Dec, Wed–Sun 10–4; late Dec–March, weekends only, 10–4. Admission free;
tel: (718) 965-6505. Sun afternoon programs, usually craft-oriented, focus on
colonial holidays.

The overhanging Dutch roof and six small columns supporting it
are typical Dutch details while the front door with its leaded
transom and sidelights was added later. Inside are examples of
18–early-19C American furniture and homely objects (a quilting
frame, spinning wheels, bedwarmers, dolls, and toys) to suggest
the life of the Lefferts family, one of the most prominent in
Flatbush.

The **Prospect Park Zoo** is closed for renovation. Like the recently reopened zoo
in Central Park, the Prospect Park Zoo will be redesigned and turned over to
the New York Zoological Society for operation.

Continue N. toward Grand Army Plaza. East Drive follows the
course of a colonial road that passed through a narrow rocky
defile in the hills left by the glacial moraine. Known today as
BATTLE PASS after a Revolutionary War skirmish, an outnumbered American force led by Gen. John Sullivan tried here to
hold off Hessian mercenaries attacking from the south. The
colonials got off only one volley before they were overrun and
captured or killed.

   Beyond Battle Pass on the right of the road is a meadow with a
path leading to the *Vale of Cashmere* (c. 1894), a secluded hollow

planted with azaleas and rhododendrons, once ornamented with rustic arbors and pedestals bearing Grecian urns. At its N. end a flight of stairs leads up to the Rose Garden (1894), now a stretch of lawn with empty lily pools. From the garden continue N. past the *Endale Arch* (1867) to the park exit.

47 The Brooklyn Public Library, the Brooklyn Museum, and the Brooklyn Botanic Garden

SUBWAY: IRT Broadway-7th Ave (train 2 or 3) to Eastern Parkway-Brooklyn Museum.

CAR: Flatbush Ave to Grand Army Plaza; follow Eastern Parkway signs around the traffic circle. For museum and botanic garden, follow Eastern Parkway to Washington Ave and turn right. Metered street parking. Large enclosed pay parking lot behind the museum adjacent to the gardens.

The triangle of land bounded by Flatbush Ave, Eastern Parkway, and Washington Ave was originally named **Institute Park,** and contains three of Brooklyn's major cultural institutions: the Brooklyn Museum, the Brooklyn Botanic Garden, and the Central Library of the Brooklyn Public Library.

The **Main Branch (Ingersoll Memorial) of the Brooklyn Public Library,** Grand Army Plaza at Flatbush Ave and Eastern Parkways (1941; Githens & Keally), is a handsome, streamlined, Art Deco building, the largest of 53 Brooklyn branches. C. Paul Jennewein sculpted the bas-reliefs, and Thomas H. James, the screen above the entrance.

Open Mon–Thurs 9–8; Fri–Sat 10–6; Sun 1–5. Closed holidays, and on Sun in summer. Tel: (718) 780-7722.

Highlights of its holdings include the morgue of the Brooklyn *Eagle,* which ceased publication in 1955, and the Brooklyn Photography Collection with more than 25,000 photos of Brooklyn and its people dating back to 1870.

Between the library and the Brooklyn Museum along Eastern Parkway is a playground on the site of a 19C reservoir. Frederick Law Olmsted and Calvert Vaux designed EASTERN PARKWAY in 1868, coining the word "parkway," and laying out the roadway with its side service roads and islands of trees and greenery. It was intended, along with Ocean Parkway, as part of a system of residential arteries which never came into being.

Located on Eastern Parkway at Washington Ave, the ***Brooklyn Museum** is one of the borough's major cultural resources, noteworthy for its Egyptian collection, its American paintings and decorative arts, its changing exhibitions of contemporary art, and its educational programs. Today the museum is embarked upon a major campaign for expansion.

The Brooklyn Museum. 200 Eastern Parkway (Washington Ave), Brooklyn,
N. Y. 11238. Tel: (718) 638-5000. Open 10—5 every day except Tues, Thanksgiving, Christmas, and New Year's Day. Suggested contribution. Free for
members and children under 12 accompanied by an adult.

Changing exhibitions. Gallery talks, lectures, films, children's programs.
Museum cafe, open until 4 P.M. Restrooms, public telephones. Excellent gift
shop. Accessible to wheelchairs. Handicapped parking.

ACCESS: SUBWAY: IRT 7th Ave express (train 2 or 3) to Eastern Parkway-
Brooklyn Museum. Or IRT Lexington Ave express (train 4 or 5) to Nevins St,
cross platform and transfer to 7th Ave express. CAR: From Manhattan via
Brooklyn Bridge, left onto Tillary St, right onto Flatbush Ave to Grand Army
Plaza to 200 Eastern Parkway. Museum on right at Washington Ave. PARKING
LOT entrance behind the Museum off Washington Ave.

Exterior. The Brooklyn Museum (1897; McKim, Mead & White,
additions and alterations to 1978; DL), a neoclassical pile complete with Ionic portico and an imposing pediment, represents
only a quarter of the architects' original grand plan. The *statues
of Manhattan and Brooklyn* (1916; Daniel Chester French) flanking the main entrance on Eastern Parkway formerly stood near
the Manhattan Bridge, but were placed here (1963) when the
bridge ramps were widened. On the frieze are heroic sculptures
of great thinkers and artists including four Chinese figures
(sculptor, Karl Bitter) representing Law, Art, Religion, and Philosophy (beginning at the far left of the facade), Mohammed
(Charles Keck) left of the pediment, and (right of the pediment)
Homer, Pindar, and Minerva by Daniel Chester French, followed
by Plato, Phidias, Praxiteles, and Demosthenes by Herbert Adams.
On the pediment itself eight heroic figures by Adolph A. Weinman and Daniel Chester French represent (left to right) Sculpture, Painting, Architecture, Art and Science, Geography,
Astronomy, and Biology. Until 1936 a broad flight of stairs led to
the third-floor level. Today the main entrance is on the first floor,
but the grand staircase will be restored as part of the current
program of expansion.

Interior. The main exhibition area on the FIRST FLOOR is devoted
to the **Cultures of the Americas** surrounded by other ethnographic displays. In the central gallery are artifacts from Indian
cultures of North and South America, beginning with Eskimo
artifacts and proceeding southward. **Indians of the North American continent** include tribes of the Northwest coast (wood carvings, masks, and several imposing totem poles). The art of the
Indians of the Southwest includes a large collection of Kachina
dolls which represent spirits and were used to teach children the
names and qualities of these supernatural beings. The display on
Plains Indians has pipes, decorated leather clothing, and weapons. Indians of meso-America and eastern **South America** are
represented by pottery and feather arts. In a large case nearby
are beautiful woven and painted fabrics and silver from the
cultures of the Central Andes including the *Paracas textile.
Along the outside walls of two sides of the gallery is an imposing
display of wood sculpture representing the **Cultures of Oceania:**
New Zealand, Polynesia, New Guinea, Indonesia, and Melanesia.

A doorway near the totem poles leads into the **African Hall**

BROOKLYN MUSEUM
First Floor

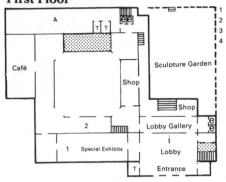

1 Robert E. Blum Gallery
2 African Art
3 Oceanic and New World Art
4 Education Wing

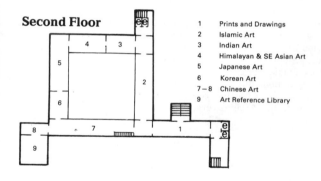

1 Prints and Drawings
2 Islamic Art
3 Indian Art
4 Himalayan & SE Asian Art
5 Japanese Art
6 Korean Art
7 – 8 Chinese Art
9 Art Reference Library

with spears, ceremonial masks, body ornaments, shields, dolls and figurines, fabrics, and musical instruments crafted from traditional and modern materials.

The other principal exhibition area on this level is the outdoor **Frieda Schiff Warburg Sculpture Garden** (1966; Ian White, designer) with fragments of demolished New York buildings, including McKim, Mead & White's Pennsylvania Station and Steeplechase Park at Coney Island.

The SECOND FLOOR houses the museum's collection of prints and drawings and Islamic and Oriental art. In the **Prints and Drawings Galleries** are changing exhibitions, some of which are taken from the museum's more than 20,000 prints and drawings (14C to the present). In the recently refurbished galleries of **Islamic art** are displays of ceramics, textiles, rugs, illustrated manuscripts, and calligraphy. The galleries of **Oriental Art** include

Chinese, Japanese, and Korean sculpture, ceramics, prints, paintings, Indian stone and bronze sculpture, and terra-cottas.

THIRD FLOOR galleries are devoted to ancient civilizations and include the ***Egyptian collection.** To view it chronologically begin with the *gallery of Predynastic Egypt,* which is to the left of the entrance gallery. Here are tools, including a hunter's knife from about 3100 B.C. with an ivory handle carved with rows of animals. Among the pottery objects is a female figure with upraised arms, possibly a deity.

Return to the first gallery, the *Old Kingdom gallery,* with its large stone sarcophagus (48.110), limestone reliefs, alabaster storage jars, and a figure of the royal official Methethy in his maturity (51.1). The adjacent *gallery of Old and Middle Kingdoms* (marked gallery 4) has block statues and the sunken relief slab of Sebek-Hotep III, later recycled as the base of a mill.

The small alcove gallery contains a diorite figure of King Sesostris II (c. 1878–1843 B.C.), a great soldier apparently because the nine bows beneath his feet represent nine enemy tribes of Egypt. Here also is a Royal Mother and Child (c. 2040–1785 B.C.), a rare figure made of metal, and faience hippos and a faience hedgehog whose spine was believed to contain an oil that cured baldness.

Return through the gallery with the millstone to the *Funerary Gallery* which contains reliefs from the walls of Tell el Amarna (mid-13C B.C.) where Akhenaton established his capital. There are also mummy cartonages, canopic jars used to contain the innards of mummies, and a statue of Sa-iset, (c. 1240–1212 B.C.) with an elaborate wig and pleated robe.

A long gallery at the end beyond the Neolithic Gallery contains *Egyptian Art from Dynasty 25 to the Roman Conquest* and includes a set of uncompleted reliefs from the Theban tomb of Nespeqashuty (664–610 B.C.) A faience lion flask (53.223) from 525–504 B.C. was probably an ointment vessel. The Brooklyn *symplegma,* an erotically intertwined anatomically astonishing group of small figures, dates from 305–30 B.C. The Head of Sarapis (58.79) from the 1C A.D., a god of combined Greek and Egyptian qualities, was designed to appeal to both ethnic groups during the reign of the Ptolemies, successors to Alexander the Great. Sarapis combined properties of Osiris, Zeus, and Asklepios, the healer. The naturalistic wood sculpture of a cat (37.1945E) is one of the five largest such figures that have survived from ancient Egypt. The "Brooklyn Black Head" (58.30), a black diorite fragment from Memphis, may represent a foreign conqueror, possibly Julius Caesar. The hair is sculpted of individual curls in the Egyptian manner (rather than the Greek flowing style). A small head of Alexander the Great dating from some two centuries after his death was part of a complete statuette with clothing of some different material.

In the **Hagop Kevorkian Gallery of the Ancient Middle East** are 12 Assyrian reliefs of gypseous alabaster from the palace of Ashurnasirpal II (9C B.C.) in Kalhu (Nimrud).

The galleries around the auditorium-court have **Greek, Roman, and Coptic art.**

The FOURTH FLOOR is devoted to **decorative arts** including period rooms, two of them from early Brooklyn. The two-room *Jan Martense Schenck House (c. 1675) which originally stood in the Flatlands section of Brooklyn has been reconstructed and filled with period furniture. The *Nicholas Schenck House* (c. 1775) from the Canarsie section of Brooklyn, is a small farmhouse with a gambrel roof. Remodeled in the 19C, it looks now as it did in 1830; much of its furniture belonged to old Brooklyn families. At its nadir it served as the concession stand for Canarsie Park. The other American period rooms are organized chronologically and geographically, covering an area that extends from New England to South Carolina. Of particular interest is the *Moorish Room from the John D. Rockefeller town house on W. 54th St in Manhattan with the dark Moorish tiles, brocaded walls, and wood paneling that pleased the exotic tastes of the period. Also on this floor are the galleries of metalware, glass, and ceramics, as well as the Costumes and Textiles exhibitions.

The FIFTH FLOOR is devoted to painting and sculpture. The Brooklyn Museum has a fine collection of ***American Painting** known for its 18–19C portraits and landscapes. In the first two galleries are 18C AND EARLY-19C PAINTINGS with portraits by Benjamin West, John Singleton Copley, Charles Willson Peale, Thomas Sully, and Gilbert Stuart, as well as early landscapes including one of Edward Hicks's many treatments of *The Peaceable Kingdom*. In Gallery III are genre paintings and scenes of everyday life including Francis Guy's *Winter Scene in Brooklyn,* which depicts a simpler life on Front St (which runs from the Brooklyn Bridge to the Navy Yard), then the center of the town of Brooklyn.

The Long Gallery has 19C Landscapes and Historical Paintings by members of the HUDSON RIVER SCHOOL and other romantic landscape painters: Asher B. Durand, Thomas Cole, George Inness, and Jasper Francis Cropsey. Daniel Huntington's *The Republican Court* painted in 1861 shows the cream of American society during the presidency of George Washington.

The next corner gallery has several large Hudson River School Landscapes, the most dramatic of which is Albert Bierstadt, *A Storm in the Rocky Mountains—Mount Rosalie* (1866). Also: Frederick Edwin Church, *South American Landscape*; Thomas Cole, *The Pic-Nic*; John Frederick Kensett, *Lake George;* and Winslow Homer, *In the Mountains.*.

The next gallery has paintings by William Merritt Chase, Eastman Johnson, and Thomas Eakins, *William Rush Carving His Allegorical Figure of the Schuylkill River.* The museum also owns Eakins' portrait of *Letitia Bacon* and his luminous painting *Oarsmen on the Schuylkill,* not currently on display.

The next gallery has a group of early 20C painters usually associated with the urban scene. Childe Hassam, *Late Afternoon, New York: Winter.* John Sloan, *Haymarket.* William Glackens,

BROOKLYN MUSEUM
Third Floor

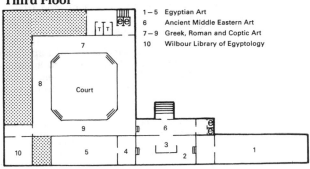

1 – 5	Egyptian Art
6	Ancient Middle Eastern Art
7 – 9	Greek, Roman and Coptic Art
10	Wilbour Library of Egyptology

Fourth Floor

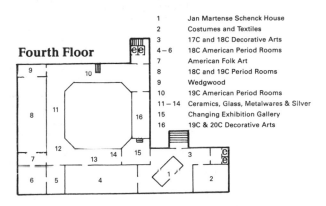

1	Jan Martense Schenck House
2	Costumes and Textiles
3	17C and 18C Decorative Arts
4 – 6	18C American Period Rooms
7	American Folk Art
8	18C and 19C Period Rooms
9	Wedgwood
10	19C American Period Rooms
11 – 14	Ceramics, Glass, Metalwares & Silver
15	Changing Exhibition Gallery
16	19C & 20C Decorative Arts

Fifth Floor

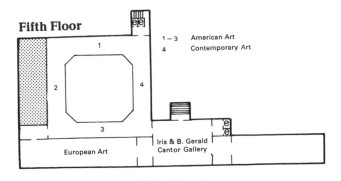

1 – 3	American Art
4	Contemporary Art

Nude with Apple. Also, John Singer Sargent, *Paul Helleu Sketching with His Wife*.

The European Art gallery contains works ranging from the early Italian Renaissance to the Impressionist and Post-Impressionist periods, including a group of Spanish colonial paintings.

The ***Brooklyn Botanic Garden,** 50 carefully tended and intensively planted acres hedged around by asphalt and apartment houses, is an unexpected Eden, clearly enjoyed by neighborhood visitors as well as horticulturists and plant lovers from further away.

The Brooklyn Botanic Garden. 1000 Washington Ave (Eastern Parkway), Brooklyn, N. Y. 11225. Tel: (718) 622-4433. Open Tues—Fri 8—6; weekends and holidays 10—6; closed Mon but open on Mon holidays. Admission to grounds free but nominal entrance fee on weekends and holidays for Japanese Garden and at all times for Conservatory.

Restrooms in Administration Building and Conservatory; telephones. Terrace cafe (sandwiches, hamburgers, snacks) open March—mid-Nov. Public tours Sun at 1; meet in front of the Garden Shop in the Administration Building. Films, lectures, exhibits of painting and photography, festivals with entertainment, food, etc. Extensive educational programs; research facilities.

SUBWAY: IRT Broadway-7th Ave express (train 2 or 3) to Eastern Parkway-Brooklyn Museum. IND 6th Ave (D train) to Prospect Park. BMT Nassau St line (Q train) to Prospect Park. CAR: From Manhattan take the Triborough Bridge to the Brooklyn-Queens Expressway (Route 278). Exit 27 to Atlantic Ave, turn right onto Washington Ave. CAR PARKING: Enclosed pay parking lot on Washington Ave between the Garden and the Brooklyn Museum.

History. The Botanic Garden was founded (1910) as a department of the Brooklyn Institute of Arts and Sciences for the education and enjoyment of the public, a remarkable goal at a time when botanic gardens were still primarily attached to universities. Initially funded with a donation from Brooklyn philanthropist Alfred Tredway White and a matching sum from the City of New York, the Garden, waste land at first, was enriched in its early years with the by-products of nearby breweries and stables. Its collections have since been expanded to include more than 13,000 species of plants in 13 specialized gardens and groupings of generically related types.

Begin at the *Administration and Classroom Building* (completed 1918; McKim, Mead & White). Outside the main entrance is *Magnolia Plaza* where 80 magnolia trees of 11 species bloom beginning in early April along with daffodils planted on Boulder Hill (to the right). The figures on the armillary sphere representing signs of the zodiac are by Rhys Caparn, daughter of Harold Caparn, landscape architect for much of the Garden.

Continue past the brook to *Cherry Walk* and the **Cherry Esplanade* (on the right), famous for its deep pink Kwanzan cherry trees, spectacular in early May against a backdrop of red foliage provided by Schwedler maples planted on Armistice Day, 1918.

Diagonally across from the Rose Arc (on the left) is the *Cranford Rose Garden* (1927) with over 1000 varieties of roses (more than 6000 plants) including many of the All-America rose selections.

The Rose Garden is open June—Oct, Tues—Fri 9—4, weekends and holidays 10:30—4. Children must be accompanied by a responsible adult.

Continue toward the hillside. On the left is the lilac collection arranged, like much of the Botanic Garden, as an arboretum with permanent plantings showing botanic relationships between species. Behind the fence on the left is the *Local Flora Section* featuring wildflowers, shrubs, and trees normally found within a 100-mile radius of the Botanic Garden. In the *Osborne Memorial Section* (1939) are rhododendrons, flowering crabapples, cherries, viburnums, and hollies. At the top of the stairs the *Overlook,* bordered by fastigiate gingkos, leads E. past the Rose Garden to the *Herb Garden* (1938), whose formally planted Elizabethan Knots were intended to be seen from above, presumably from one's castle window. The garden contains over 300 different herbaceous plants with culinary and medicinal uses.

Follow the path along to the **Japanese Garden,* designed and constructed in the traditional Hall-and-Pond style (1914—15) by Takeo Shiota and considered by its maker to be his masterpiece.

Open April—Oct 10:30—4:30, weather permitting. Nominal entrance fee weekends and holidays.

The Viewing Pavilion with its circular window represents the home of the host and the shelter across the lake a Waiting House where in an actual Japanese tea garden guests would wait to be received by the host. In the lake, its flowing shape derived from the Japanese character for "heart" or "mind," stands a vermilion *torii* or gateway indicating the presence of a shrine, here a Shinto shrine to a harvest god on the hillside beyond. On the hillside five small cascades with echo caverns beneath them splash downward in a landscape of dwarfed trees and shrubs. During World War II the Japanese Garden was neglected, even vandalized, but since 1953 it has been restored and is now maintained by gardeners trained in Oriental techniques of horticulture.

Outside it is a 3-ton Komatsu stone lantern (1652) given to the city by Japan (1980). A path near the lantern leads to the *Shakespeare Garden,* with some 80 varieties of plants mentioned in the bard's works. In the nearby *Fragrance Garden for the Blind* (1955) grow plants chosen for touch, taste, and smell, labeled in Braille and planted in raised beds.

Beyond the Administration Building is the **Steinhardt Conservatory** (1988).

Open Tues—Sun and Mon holidays, April—Sept 10—5:30, Oct—March 10—4:30. Admission charge. Restrooms, telephones. Accessible to wheelchairs, elevator at entrance to Bonsai Museum.

On the UPPER LEVEL to the left of the entrance is the *Bonsai Museum with the Garden's world-renowned collection, both indoor and outdoor bonsai, temperate and tropical species. The central exhibit is a Trail of Evolution which traces the development of plant life from the Precambrian era, some 3½ billion years ago, to the present, from simple single-celled organisms, to "modern" flowering plants. Also on this level is the Aquatic House with two pools, one shallow, one deep, and displays on bogs, insectivorous plants, and orchids.

On the LOWER LEVEL are three environmental pavilions, Tropical, Desert, and Temperate, with appropriate plantings. Special features are displays of plants producing medicines or pharmaceuticals, a fern grotto, and a limestone cave with a display of mushrooms.

Return to the pathway and continue past the *Children's Garden,* a cherished local institution where hundreds of local children annually learn to grow vegetables and flowers, absorbing in the process the human virtues associated with gardening. The pathway next leads past dogwoods, azaleas, forsythia, and the iris garden (late May—early June) to the *Rock Garden* with plants normally found on mountain slopes, whose low growth protects them from wind. The *Monocot bed,* on the other side of the path, is a display border of plants with parallel-veined leaves and includes irises, daylilies, and narcissi as well as more exotic grasses, cannas, and yuccas. The *Hedge Wheel* has 18 rows of evergreen and deciduous shrubs planted like spokes to show their use in hedges.

48   East Central Brooklyn: Crown Heights, Bedford-Stuyvesant, Brownsville, and East New York

SUBWAY: The IRT 7th Ave express (train 2) stops at Grand Army Plaza on the W. edge of Crown Heights and at Eastern Parkway-Brooklyn Museum.

CAR: Manhattan Bridge to Flatbush Ave. Follow Flatbush Ave south to Eastern Parkway at Grand Army Plaza. Eastern Parkway cuts through the center of Crown Heights.

Crown Heights, formerly considered part of Bedford, is bounded roughly by Atlantic Ave on the N., East New York Ave and Empire Boulevard on the S. and S.E., Ralph Ave on the E., and Flatbush Ave on the west. The name seems to be a corruption of the 19C place name "Crow Hill," which either described a range of hills S. of Eastern Parkway or was a racial slur directed at the black communities of Weeksville and Carrsville settled in the 1830s and 1840s. For most of the 20C Crown Heights existed as a lower middle-class Jewish neighborhood, but today it is predominantly black, its population including West Indians and a significant group of French-speaking Haitians as well as Jamaicans, Trinidadians, Barbadians, and Grenadians, all of whom spill over into surrounding areas.

On the main commercial strips near Nostrand and Utica Aves are West Indian restaurants, bakeries, grocery stores, and record shops. Climaxing the year is Carnival weekend over the Labor Day holiday (early Sept) when revelers celebrate the long weekend with steel bands, masquerades, street dancing, and a final chaotic parade down Eastern Parkway. (For carnival information, call the Brooklyn Arts & Cultural Assoc., tel: 718\783-9469.)

In addition to the blacks a growing Asian population includes a significant number of Vietnamese. Among the remaining Jews is the largest enclave of Lubavitch Hasidim in the city, and during the Jewish holidays the headquarters of the Lubavitch Movement at 770 Eastern Parkway near Kingston Ave draws thousands of the faithful.

History. The Lefferts homestead (1783), now in Prospect Park, survives from the days when the Lefferts farm was one of the largest on western Long Island. After the Brooklyn Bridge opened in 1883, well-to-do-families built imposing homes along Eastern Parkway which had been laid out (c. 1868) according to designs by Frederick Law Olmsted and is now a historic landmark. When the IRT subway was dug beneath the parkway in 1920, some of these mansions were replaced by apartment buildings which drew a population of solid middle class people, many of them professionals. Until 1956 Crown Heights was the home of the Brooklyn Dodgers, whose departure may have hastened the decline of the area, even then gaining a reputation as a ghetto. In the 1970s, however, its stock began to rise again as the attractive brownstone architecture and a revived interest in Brooklyn brought middle class families seeking housing more affordable than that in nearby Park Slope. Among the new arrivals is a small community of artists fleeing the high rents and cramped spaces of lower Manhattan.

Points of interest. It is advisable to tour by car.

The area around Grant Square (Dean St and Bedford Ave) when considered part of Bedford in the 19C was highly respectable. The *Union League Club* (Bedford Ave, S.E. corner of Dean St), now a senior citizens' center, was its premier institution. Founded in 1888 as a social and political organization for Republicans of high social standing, the club built this headquarters four years later (1892; Lauritzen & Voss), a brownstone Victorian pile adorned with medallions of Ulysses S. Grant and Abraham Lincoln and garnished with stone lions and American eagles. The club commissioned William Ordway Partridge (1896) to design the *equestrian statue of Ulysses S. Grant* that now stands in the square. A block N. stand the *Imperial Apartments* (1198 Pacific St, S.E. corner of Bedford Ave) which date from the same period (1892; Montrose W. Morris; DL) and same social milieu as the Union League Club. In addition to fine apartments Bedford also had a number of mansions (F. W. Woolworth lived here before he moved to Fifth Ave, as did Abraham Abraham, a partner in the Wechsler and Abraham department store, precursor of Abraham and Straus).

The *Twenty-Third Regiment Armory of the New York National Guard* (1322 Bedford Ave, bet. Atlantic Ave / Pacific St) with its imposing crenellated tower, slit windows, and arched entry (1892; Fowler & Hough; DL) dates from the same period of prosperity. The Armory is now a part of the city shelter system and houses some 500 homeless men nightly.

In the block bounded by Montgomery St, McKeever Place, Sullivan Place, and Bedford Ave was the *site of Ebbets Field,* home of the former Brooklyn Dodgers, now, sadly, the Los Angeles Dodgers.

Built by Charles Ebbets and the McKeever Brothers in 1913, Ebbets Field held 32,111 fans while its parking lot accommodated 700 cars, a pittance by modern standards, and the inadequacy of the stadium and facilities eventually resulted in the departure of the team from Brooklyn. Although owner Walter O'Malley negotiated with the city from 1954–57 for a new stadium (some doubt his intention ever to stay), opposition of key city officials, offers from the city of Los Angeles, and the general appeal of the West, which seemed free from the problems of crime, housing, and race that afflict Brooklyn, convinced O'Malley to leave. The loss of the team, which had distinguished itself by the ardor of its fans and by signing the first major league black player, the legendary Jackie Robinson, did not harm Brooklyn so much economically as sentimentally, but it was a loss that cut across social, racial, and economic boundaries.

The **Brooklyn Children's Museum,** in Brower Park at the intersection of Brooklyn and St. Marks Aves, was the first museum (1899) anywhere devoted solely to the education and delight of children, or as its Victorian founders phrased it, to "stimulate their powers of observation and reflection." Formerly housed in two Victorian mansions belonging to L. C. Smith, typewriter manufacturer, and historian James Truslow Adams, it now occupies subterranean quarters (1976; Hardy, Holzman, Pfeiffer) beneath the park. It is a resource for parents and children of Brooklyn and the whole tri-state area, of whom some 24,000 visit yearly in school groups.

The Brooklyn Children's Museum. 145 Brooklyn Ave (at St. Marks Ave), Brooklyn, N. Y. 11213. Tel: (718) 735-4400. Open during the school year Mon, Wed, Thurs, Fri 2–5; weekends and school holidays 10–5. During the summer vacation, open 10–5 every day except Tues. Fri evening family program 7–9. Suggested contribution. Children's resource library, workshops, films, special events. Restrooms, telephone, gift shop. No restaurant. Tel: (718) 735-4400.

SUBWAY: IRT Broadway-7th Ave (train 2) to Kingston Ave; walk W. to Brooklyn Ave, right six blocks to St. Marks Ave. IND 8th Ave (A train) to Kingston-Throop; walk W. to Brooklyn Ave, left six blocks to St. Marks Ave. BUS: B47 to St. Marks Ave. CAR: Atlantic Ave to Brooklyn Ave; turn S. on Brooklyn Ave and continue four blocks to St. Marks Ave. Street parking.

Visitors enter through a 1907 trolley kiosk and a sewer culvert with a stream whose waterpower children can harness with sluices, gates, and waterwheels. The inside of the museum is brightly painted and divided into different levels with exhibits which change from time to time stashed away in different sections of the museum. Many of the exhibits are hands-on, and at various times in the museum's recent history children could climb in a molecular maze of clear plastic modules, watch a liquid light show, a steam engine, a working windmill, or a greenhouse. They could play musical instruments, "sing" with an artificial set of lungs and larynx, and test their measuring skills in the Dr. Dimension and the Rulers of the Universe exhibit. There are also cultural artifacts, for example, a collection of masks, including some from Africa and the Orient, which are displayed in ways relevant to children. The artifacts for these exhibits are drawn from a collection of some 20,000 objects, most from the realms of ethnography (the masks) or natural history (a mammoth's tooth, a pickled human brain).

The *Hunterfly Road houses,* best seen from Bergen St between Rochester and Buffalo Aves, four modest houses (c. 1830) currently being restored, once stood along Hunterfly Road, a colonial highway joining Bedford and Canarsie, and were part of Brooklyn's first black community, Weeksville, named after James Weeks, an early landowner. Built in an informal vernacular style by laborers and farmers, the houses now belong to the Society for the Preservation of Weeksville and Bedford-Stuyvesant History and will eventually become a museum, showing how their inhabitants lived and worked.

Of the town little is known: it seems to have been settled by outsiders rather than slaves freed by state law in the 1820s; perhaps 30–40 families lived within its boundaries; it had a school and churches; it took up arms for self-defense during the Draft Riots (1863) as white mobs attacked and murdered blacks in Manhattan; it was swallowed up by burgeoning white communities toward the end of the 19C as new streets opened. Of Carrsville to the S., another early-19C black community, no physical trace remains.

Bedford-Stuyvesant, today the city's largest black ghetto, used to be two neighborhoods, Bedford on the W. settled by the Dutch in the 17C, and the Stuyvesant Heights district to the E. settled later. Its boundaries are generally agreed to be Flushing Ave on the N., Broadway and Saratoga Ave on the E., Atlantic Ave on the S., and Classon Ave on the west.

Like other outlying Brooklyn areas, Bedford-Stuyvesant went through several stages of development, first as farmland, later as a suburb with freestanding frame houses, then as an urban neighborhood with prosperous middle class brick and brownstone row houses, and finally as a black ghetto. Unlike other neighborhoods, however, Bedford (the origin of the name is obscure) had a significant black population long ago, slave laborers on Dutch farms making up 25% of the population in 1790. Between the two World Wars Jews, Italians, Irish, and West Indians began settling in the aging yet still attractive neighborhood, and after World War II the dramatic increase of black arrivals made Bedford-Stuyvesant the nation's second largest black community after Chicago's South Side.

Points of interest. It is advisable to tour by car.

The *former Boys' High School,* 823 Marcy Ave between Putnam Ave and Madison St (1891; James W. Naughton; DL), built by the longtime Superintendent for Buildings of the Brooklyn Public School system, is a grand Romanesque Revival building with a history of distinguished graduates, including Isaac Asimov, William J. Levitt (of Levittown fame), and Norman Mailer. It was joined with Girls' High in the 1970s.

On the N. side of *Tompkins Park,* between Marcy and Tompkins Aves, is one of two trees in New York that has been designated a landmark (c. 1880), a *Magnolia grandiflora* that qualifies as Brooklyn's second most famous botanical specimen after the Camperdown elm in Prospect Park. Vaux and Olmsted designed Tompkins Park, but probably wouldn't recognize it today. The tree was saved by Hattie Carthan, the "tree lady" of Brooklyn, who in 1965 at the age of 64 began working to preserve and plant trees in Bedford-Stuyvesant. When the giant magnolia was marked for destruction in 1968 (an apartment complex would have risen in its stead), Mrs. Carthan persuaded the Landmarks Preservation Commission to designate it a living landmark. Eventually she engineered the purchase of three city-owned brownstones on Lafayette Ave and oversaw their conversion to the Magnolia Tree Earth Center. When she died in 1984, her efforts had also brought some 1500 thriving trees to the streets of Bedford-Stuyvesant.

In the east-central part of the district N. of Fulton St is the STUYVESANT HEIGHTS HISTORIC DISTRICT, an L-shaped area bounded partially by Chauncey and Macon Sts, Stuyvesant and Tompkins Aves, built up during the last decades of the 19C with handsome row housing. Local street names, bestowed during a period of patriotic fervor, recall historic naval figures: Thomas MacDonough, Stephen Decatur, William Bainbridge, Isaac Chauncey; the avenues commemorate New York governors: Morgan Lewis, Enos T. Throop, Daniel D. Tompkins, and Peter Stuyvesant. Sumner Ave used to be called Yates Ave after Gov. Joseph C. Yates, but the name was changed to avoid confusion with Gates Ave. Noteworthy blocks in the historic district are the block of Bainbridge St between Lewis and Stuyvesant Aves dating from the 1890s, and the W. side of Stuyvesant Ave between Bainbridge and Decatur Sts.

The BEDFORD-STUYVESANT RESTORATION CENTER, 1360 Fulton St, S.E. corner of New York Ave (1976; Arthur Cotton Moore), is a $6-million complex of stores, offices, and a theater named after Billie Holiday, the great jazz singer. The project, utilizing derelict industrial and commercial buildings, is a major achievement of the Bedford-Stuyvesant Restoration Corporation, founded (1967) after a widely publicized visit of Senator Robert F. Kennedy focused attention on the area.

In eastern Brooklyn are three principal neighborhoods: Highland Park, Brownsville, and East New York, carved out of the old Dutch settlement of New Lots. New Lots itself, settled around 1670 by a group of Dutch farmers from the Old Lots section of present-day Flatbush, remained part of Flatbush until 1852 and joined the city of Brooklyn in 1886. None of these neighborhoods is of particular interest to visitors though Brownsville is of historical importance.

The northern section, N. of Atlantic Ave, is called either **Highland Park,** after the park of that name, a steep hill rising from Jamaica Ave, or **Cypress Hills,** after the cemetery of that name, most of which lies in Queens (as does part of Highland Park).

Brownsville, today synonymous with urban squalor, is named after Charles S. Brown who subdivided the existing farmland for housing in 1865; it was long one of the city's centers of Jewish population. In 1887 a group of realtors put up cheap housing and encouraged Jews to move out from the Lower East Side, an exodus hastened by the construction of the Fulton St elevated line in 1889; some of the early Jewish fortunes including that of the Chanin brothers come from this boom period. By 1900 Brownsville, home to 15,000 sweatshop workers, was a slum without sidewalks or sewers, with unpaved streets and only one public bathhouse. Between the 1920s and World War II, however, things improved remarkably as the population prospered mainly by dint of individual effort. The principal shopping street was Pitkin Ave, named after John R. Pitkin, founder of East New York. A pushcart market sprang up on Belmont Ave between Christopher St and Rockaway Ave, selling leftovers from the nearby produce market at Junius St by the railroad siding; it survives today, as a sidewalk market without pushcarts, catering to a Hispanic clientele. Loew's Pitkin Theatre (1501 Pitkin Ave at Saratoga Ave), for a while the

Hudson Temple Cathedral, now a furniture store, was built in 1925 (Thomas W. Lamb), one among many movie palaces of the era.

From the Brownsville ghetto came a generation of eminent actors, artists, businessmen, and politicians, including Danny Kaye; painter Max Weber; Aaron Copland; Joseph Hirshhorn, whose art collection was financed by uranium; and Sol Hurok, who launched his career as an impresario by persuading violinist Efrem Zimbalist to play for a local cultural society. After World War II, the Jews, drawn by the suburbs or by pleasanter parts of the city, began leaving, replaced by a poorer mostly nonwhite population. During the 1970s efforts at slum clearance eradicated some of the worst housing without really making a dent in the profound depression of the area. Among the better projects are Rutland Plaza (East New York Ave and Rutland Rd, E. 92nd to E. 94th Sts) which dates from 1976 (Donald Stull and Assocs.) and Marcus Garvey Village (1976; Institute for Architecture and Urban Studies, David Todd & Assocs.), a community of low-rise apartments.

East New York, between Jamaica Ave and Jamaica Bay, E. of about Junius St, was founded as a commercial venture by one John R. Pitkin, a Connecticut businessman whose schemes for a town rivaling New York were dashed by the panic of 1837. It was developed later as a working-class neighborhood and attracted Jews, Russians, Germans, and Italians, many arriving from Brownsville. During the 1960s and early 1970s most of the former Jewish residents, some pressured by blockbusting real estate dealers, sold their property and moved away and today the area is mostly black.

Points of interest. The determined local historian might wish to visit two relics from the period when Dutch influence was still strong. The *Christian Duryea House* (c. 1787), 562 Jerome St between Dumont and Livonia Aves, is a Dutch-style farmhouse, which has survived architecturally more or less (without the overhanging eaves) as it was in the 1700s, though today it sits in the midst of vacant apartment buildings and run-down brownstones. Preservationists would like to save it as a relic of the city's agricultural past.

The *New Lots Reformed Dutch Church* (1823; DL), 630 New Lots Ave, S.E. corner of Schenck Ave, was built of local oak by local farmers tired of trekking to the Flatbush Reformed Church. The simple church with pointed arch windows sits in an old graveyard.

49   Northern Brooklyn: Greenpoint, Williamsburg, and Bushwick

Greenpoint, the neck of land N. of the Brooklyn-Queens Expressway between Newtown Creek and McCarren Park, was undoubtedly verdant in 1630 when the Dutch bought it from the Indians. After 1832, however, when Eliphalet Nott and Neziah Bliss surveyed the land and laid out streets and lots for development, Greenpoint gradually became industrial, attracting shipbuilding to its shoreline and such industries as publishing, porcelain, glass, iron, and oil refining to inland areas.

SUBWAY: IND 8th Ave local (E train) or IND 6th Ave local (F train) to Queens Plaza. Change to BMT Brooklyn-Queens crosstown (G train) in direction of Smith-9th Sts, Brooklyn. Get off at Greenpoint Ave.

The birthplace of Mae West, Greenpoint in popular legend is also the cradle of Brooklynese, a dialect of American English that substitutes "d" for "th" as in "dem Bums" and interchanges "oi" and "er," as in "Hoiman hersted to Hoist," meaning that onetime Dodger star Babe Herman lifted a short fly ball to fielder Don Hurst. Linguists have shown in scholarly studies, however, that no dialect peculiar to Brooklyn exists, though they do identify "metropolitan New York City speech" which is spoken in Long Island and nearby New Jersey as well.

The following short walking tour of Greenpoint includes remnants of the old industrial era, several blocks of remarkably attractive and well-kept 19C homes, and the commercial institutions of a middle-class Polish-American community along Manhattan Ave.

Begin at the subway station, Manhattan Ave at Greenpoint Ave. One of Greenpoint's finest blocks architecturally is the section of Kent St between Manhattan Ave and Franklin St. To reach it walk a block N. of the subway station and turn left. *St. Elias Greek Rite Church* (1870) at 149 Kent St, a brick, Ruskinian Gothic building, began as the Greenpoint Reformed Church. Along the other side of the street are handsome 19C houses, built for working class and middle class families. The architectural mix includes neo-Grec houses (*148–152 Kent St*, dating from 1889) and Italianate houses (*144 and 146 Kent St*, dating from 1874). *Nos. 134–136 Kent St* (1885), also neo-Grec in style, have fine ironwork, while *94–100 Kent St* (1864), basically Italianate, have mansard roofs. On the other side of the street is the Church of the Ascension (1865; Henry Dudley), at 129 Kent Ave, built when the area was less urban than today, finished in rough granite.

Continue W. to Franklin St. Turn right and go a block north. Not far from the river at 184 Franklin St between Java and India Sts are the now dilapidated ASTRAL APARTMENTS (1886; Lamb & Rich; DL), built by Charles Pratt for the workers in his oil refinery. Designed after the Peabody Apartments in London, they were a milestone in the tenement reform movement, giving every room daylight and fresh air. Pratt's Astral Oil works were located nearby on the East River at Bushwick Creek from Kent Ave to N. 12th St; in 1870 the refinery could process 1500 barrels of petroleum daily, yielding 1100 barrels of Astral Oil, Pratt's high quality kerosene which replaced whale oil and other fuels as an illuminating oil. The street names here—Java, India—recall the 19C spice trade that flourished along the waterfront.

Return along Franklin St; continue past Kent St and Greenpoint Ave to Milton St. Turn left. Another architecturally attractive block is MILTON STREET between Franklin and Manhattan Aves (turn left), with more well-tended late 19C row houses and several churches. Noteworthy among the houses are *118–120 Milton St* (c. 1880), small and mansarded, and *122–124 Milton*

St, a brick and brownstone Queen Anne pair with attractive ironwork (c. 1880). The *Greenpoint Reformed Church* (c. 1880), 138 Milton St, moved to this Italianate Greek Revival building from its former site on Kent St. *St. John's Lutheran Church* (1892), 155 Milton St, served a German immigrant congregation, who called their house of worship the Evangelish-Luterische St. Johannes Kirche. Closing off the end of Milton St is the red brick *St. Anthony of Padua Church* (1874; P. C. Keely), 862 Manhattan Ave, a neighborhood landmark.

Along Manhattan Ave, the commercial center for the nearby Polish population, are Polish restaurants, butcher shops and grocery stores, the Chopin Theater, and several stores selling Polish and eastern European clothing and souvenirs. The Polish community contains not only second generation immigrants who are largely assimilated, but a new influx of young people who left Poland more recently. This group maintains active ties with Poland, keeping alive the mother tongue and customs of the old country.

Turn right and continue down Manhattan Ave to Calyer St. On the corner is the *Greenpoint Savings Bank* (1908; Helmle & Huberty).

Turn right into Calyer St and right again into Lorimer St, with another attractive row of small town houses. Continue along Lorimer St until it dead-ends into Noble St. Either follow Noble St (right turn) back to Manhattan Ave and turn left to return to the subway station or take the following diversion.

During the Civil War period the Continental Ironworks stood on West St between Oak and Calyer Sts and several 19C industrial buildings now used for warehousing still remain from that period. In 1861 the works began production of the hull of the *Monitor*, and on January 30, 1862, the ironclad ship (see p. 108) slid down the ways into the East River. To see the buildings, follow Noble St past Franklin St to West St; turn left and walk a block to Oak St. The next street is Calyer St, which will take you back to Manhattan Ave.

Other points of interest. Near the S. edge of Greenpoint stands the ***Russian Orthodox Cathedral of the Transfiguration** (1921; Louis Allmendinger; DL), 228 N. 12th St at Driggs Ave, its five verdigris onion domes hovering above the neighboring low industrial and residential buildings. Outside, the building, finished in yellow brick, is modest; inside (entrance on Driggs Ave, services Sun at 11) it is richly decorated in bright colors with wall paintings of saints, stained glass windows, and columns painted to simulate marble supporting a high, sky-blue dome. During services the lighted crystal chandeliers, ornately vested priests, the incense and music, seem doubly exotic in this humble neighborhood.

Another important neighborhood church is the imposing, ornate *St. Stanislaus Kostka* (c. 1878), 607 Humboldt St, on the corner of Driggs Ave, a Roman Catholic church which serves the largest Polish congregation in Brooklyn and perhaps in the city.

In MONSIGNOR MCGOLRICK PARK (bet. Driggs / Nassau Aves, Russell / Monitor Sts) is *the Monitor monument* (1938; Antonio de Filippo), a bronze sailor straining at a bronze hawser. The park also contains a landmark *shelter* (1910; Helmle & Huberty; DL) inspired by the Trianon at Versailles, but now in shabby condition.

The neighborhood of **Williamsburg** begins at the bridge of that name and stretches E. to Bushwick Ave and S. to Flushing Ave.

SUBWAY: BMT Nassau St local (J or M train) to Marcy Ave.

CAR: Williamsburg Bridge to Hooper St. Go left to Lee Ave, the center of Hasidic commercial activity. A car is recommended for those points of interest beyond this area.

History. Once part of the town of Bushwick, Williamsburg became independent about 1810 and took its name from Col. Jonathan Williams who surveyed it. A ferry from Corlear's Hook on Manhattan gave inland farmers a market for produce, but Williamsburgh (spelled with an "h" until it became part of the City of Brooklyn in 1855) remained isolated until the opening of the bridge (1903). A distillery (c. 1819) later superseded by a brewery, was its first industrial plant, but in the mid-19C it still attracted sportsmen—Commodore Vanderbilt, William C. Whitney, Jim Fisk—to its resort hotels, while affluent businessmen built mansions along its avenues. The opening of the bridge, dubbed "the Jews' Highway" by the press, brought a flood of the poor from the Lower East Side and sealed its fate as a slum.

Williamsburg was the first American home of the Satmarer Hasidic Community, an ultra-orthodox Jewish sect (Hasidim means "pious ones") founded in 18C Poland and now including groups from Hungary and elsewhere as well. Sect members are highly visible because of their clothing: men wear black garments with wide-brimmed or sable hats, full beards and sidelocks, while the women, modestly garbed in dark, long-sleeved dresses, if married have shaven heads covered with wigs and scarves. The boys wear sidelocks and *yarmulkes*.

Points of interest. Along Lee Ave, advertising their wares with signs in Hebrew and Yiddish, are kosher butchers, clothing stores selling Hasidic garments and wigs, and other stores geared to the Hasidic clientele. Along Bedford Ave Jewish institutions and schools have taken over several former mansions and clubs from pre-bridge days: *Young Israel of Brooklyn* (561 Bedford Ave at the S.E. corner of Rodney St) occupies the original Hawley mansion (c. 1875), later the Hanover Club; the *Yeshiva Yesoda Hatora of K'hal Adas Yereim* (505 Bedford Ave, N.E. corner of Taylor St) once belonged to Frederick Mollenhauer (1896), a sugar refiner. Rebbe Joel Teitelbaum, who established the Hasidic community here around 1940, lived in the building (500 Bedford Ave at the N.W. corner of Clymer St) now used by the *National Committee to Aid New Immigrants*.

Near the foot of the Williamsburg Bridge stand two venerable landmarks in a desolate neighborhood. The *Williamsburgh Savings Bank* (1875; George B. Post; additions 1906, 1925; Helmle, Huberty & Hudswell; DL), 175 Broadway, N.W. corner of Driggs Ave, has a grand dome and monumental entrance more appropriate to the bygone era when Hawleys and Havemeyers lived here than to today. Up the street is the *American Savings Bank*, 135 Broadway, N.E. corner of Bedford Ave (1868; King & Wilcox; DL), a Second Empire masterpiece, once the Kings County Savings Bank, its ornate Victorian interior still intact.

The *Peter Luger Steak House*, 178 Broadway, founded in 1887, still attracts a loyal clientele; inside ornate pressed tin ceilings and dark wood-paneled walls suggest its beginnings as a cafe and billiard parlor.

Washington Plaza, S. 4th St to Broadway between New and Havemeyer Sts is the formal Brooklyn entrance to the bridge, once the hub of the borough's trolley network, now a dilapidated turnaround for buses. Henry M. Shrady's (1906) equestrian *statue of George Washington at Valley Forge,* slathered with graffiti, needs care.

The name of Havemeyer St recalls the firm of Havemeyers and Elder, which constructed (1860), on the East River in Williamsburg a large, technologically advanced sugar plant with its own docks and warehouses.

The *Williamsburg Houses,* between Maujer and Scholes Sts, Leonard St and Bushwick Ave (1937; Board of Design with Richmond H. Shreve, chief architect) has been lauded as the city's best public housing project, ever. Its cost, $12.8 million in 1939, adjusted for inflation, also makes it the most expensive. The small buildings with private entries, outdoor courtyards for recreation, floor plans admitting generous amounts of air and light, caused a critic of the period to remark that in many ways the houses were better than the average Park Ave luxury building.

Bushwick, famous for breweries, was one of Brooklyn's original six towns, chartered in 1660 as *Boswijck,* meaning "town of the woods." The neighborhood stretches N.E. of Broadway to the Queens border and the Brooklyn-Queens Expressway; it is industrial in its northern reaches and residential further south.

> CAR: A car is recommended. Take the Williamsburg Bridge to Broadway; follow Broadway south to Myrtle Ave. Turn left on Myrtle Ave and right on Bushwick Ave.

Bushwick long had a German population, beginning after the Revolution when some of the Hessian mercenaries billeted there chose to remain, mostly as farmers. But beer came to Bushwick in the 19C with the arrival of a new wave of immigrants fleeing Germany after the abortive 1848–49 uprisings. Brewers like Otto Huber, Caspar Illig, Joseph Fallert, Ernest Ochs, and Samuel Liebermann, founder of the Rheingold Breweries, established factories on Brewers' Row (Scholes and Meserole Sts, Bushwick Place and Lorimer St), and many of these men lived in Bushwick, giving it its staid Germanic atmosphere. Peter Cooper (see p. 225) in the 1840s had a glue factory on the site of the housing project named after him, while other industries thrived along Maspeth Creek. A few buildings from former breweries remain E. of Bushwick Ave, between Forrest and Jefferson Sts. Most have been demolished as the area awaits redevelopment.

Points of interest. On Bushwick Ave S. of Myrtle Ave remain occasional staid mansions, most falling into decay, left behind by departing brewers, manufacturers, and other prosperous families. Some have been taken over by Black Muslim and Rastafarian groups. The former *William Ulmer residence,* 670 Bushwick Ave on the S.W. corner of Willoughby Ave, built by a brewer, was later owned by Arctic explorer Frederick A. Cook. The former *Catherine Lipsius residence,* 680 Bushwick Ave on the S.E.

corner of the same intersection (c. 1886; Theobald Engelhardt), built by a brewer's widow, was once an elegant Italianate home.

Across the street along Bushwick Ave between Suydam and Hart Sts is the Ansaru Abdulla Black Muslim community, with a bookstore, restaurant, and mosque.

The SOUTH BUSHWICK REFORMED CHURCH (1853; DL) stands on the N.W. corner of Bushwick Ave and Himrod St, a white frame Greek Revival survivor of the days when Dutch influence was still strong in Brooklyn. The scale of the building, its grand Ionic columns and high tower, suggest the affluence of the mid-19C congregation. Himrod St is named after its first minister.

Further S. are former homes of other affluent men: the *Gustav Doerschuck residence* (c. 1890) at 999 Bushwick Ave (N.W. corner of Grove St) and the *Louis Bossert residence,* 1002 Bushwick Ave, S.E. corner of Grove St, which dates from 1890 and has been converted to a church. Bossert, a millwork manufacturer, built the once-elegant Bossert Hotel in Brooklyn Heights.

ST. BARBARA'S CHURCH (Roman Catholic) on Central Ave, N.E. corner of Bleecker St (1910; Helmle & Huberty), a Spanish baroque church of buff brick with wedding cake terra-cotta ornamentation, rises like an apparition from the rubble of surrounding lots. Its present congregation is largely Hispanic; earlier parishioners were Italian and before that German.

50   South Central Brooklyn: Flatbush, Borough Park, and Bensonhurst

Flatbush is a quiet, residential area, stretching S. of Prospect Park to Kings Highway, bounded on the E. and W. by Nostrand and McDonald Aves. Its southern portion is often called *Midwood.*

> SUBWAY:IND 6th Ave express (D train) to Church Ave.
>
> CAR: Manhattan Bridge to Flatbush Ave. Follow Flatbush Ave south past Prospect Park to Church Ave.

The Dutch settled Flatbush in 1634, chartering the town in 1652 and calling it *'t Vlacke Bos* or "wooded plain." The good farmers of Flatbush were determined to remain apart from the burgeoning city of Brooklyn nearby, and until 1893 even imposed a toll on visitors entering their community. Annexed to the city of Brooklyn in 1894, Flatbush continued to remain rural and isolated until steam railways—the Brooklyn, Flatbush, and Coney Island Railroad later electrified as the Brighton Line of the BMT and IND—made rapid transportation possible. Thereafter it evolved into a well-to-do suburb which still maintains elements of gentility.

Points of interest. The *Flatbush Reformed Dutch Church* (1793–

98; Thomas Fardon; DL), 890 Flatbush Ave, S.W. corner of Church Ave, was established by Peter Stuyvesant in 1654, and the present fieldstone building, its third home, has stained glass windows depicting the homes of old Flatbush families. Some of the windows, including the one depicting Samson, were made by the Tiffany Studios. The tower contains a Dutch bell, donated in 1796, which tolled the death of George Washington (1799) and every President since then. The nearby *Parsonage,* on Kenmore Terrace at the N.E. corner of E. 21st St, is a Greek Revival house (1853) with a colonnaded verandah.

Erasmus Hall Academy, the original building (now a museum and offices) of the school that has evolved into Erasmus Hall High School at Flatbush Ave, S.E. corner of Church Ave, dates back to 1786. Funded by Alexander Hamilton, Aaron Burr, and John Jay among others, the academy opened in 1787 with a student body of 26 boys, and is now part of the city public school system. Among its illustrious alumni is chess champion Bobby Fischer who dropped out to work on his game. The original white clapboard Federal building (1787; DL) is now surrounded by a Gothic quadrangle dating from 1905–25; a statue of Dutch philosopher Desiderius Erasmus (copied from a 1622 Dutch original) stands in the courtyard.

Midwood (roughly bounded by Kings Highway, Coney Island Ave, Avenue H and Glenwood Rd, and Nostrand Ave) comes from the Dutch *Midwout,* a name that meant "Middle Wood" and described vegetation considerably denser than currently, though its residential streets are shady and suburban in appearance. Midwood became a township in 1652 but began to flourish until after about 1910 when the Brighton line BMT reached deep into Brooklyn. Although Midwood was in decline in the 1970s, its stores closing and homeowners selling out, today the neighborhood has turned around and is enjoying a period of prosperity. The population is primarily Jewish, including an influx of Orthodox Jews from Borough Park, but includes Italian and Irish residents and a small but growing population of Pakistanis and Indians along Coney Island Ave, as well as a significant Soviet immigrant community on Ocean Avenue.

Among Midwood's famous sons is filmmaker Woody Allen, who graduated from Midwood High School and used the Kent Movie Theater on Coney Island Ave for some interior shots in *The Purple Rose of Cairo.* Midwood's link to film fame, however, dates back to the turn of the century when Vitagraph opened a studio (1906) on E. 14th St, near Avenue M, and such silent stars as Rudolph Valentino and Erich von Stroheim are said to have passed through its gates. Today the studio is used in part for taping a TV soap opera.

Walk S. on Flatbush Ave. The *Flatbush Town Hall,* 35 Snyder Ave near Flatbush Ave (1876; John Y. Cuyler; DL), was built by the citizens of Flatbush two years after they voted down a proposal to join the city of Brooklyn. The red brick and stone Victorian Gothic building now serves the Flatbush Historical Society and other community groups.

Prospect Park South, a designated historic district, is Flatbush's most elegant neighborhood, bounded by Church Ave, Beverley Rd, Coney Island Ave, and the BMT / IND Brighton Line.

To reach it from the Flatbush Town Hall, you must walk back to Church Ave, turn left and continue W. to Buckingham Rd. Turn left on Buckingham Rd and right on Albemarle Rd. The presence of the BMT / Brighton Line occasions this zigzag route.

The community consists of large houses dating from around the turn of the century set on streets planted with stately maples. The developer Dean Alvord, who planted the trees, put in the utilities, paved the roads, and established building restrictions that defined the community, presumably was an anglophile since the streets are named Stratford, Argyle, Westminster, Rugby, Marlborough, and Buckingham and since most of the houses he offered his buyers were vaguely English in style: Georgian, Tudor, Elizabethan. There are, however, occasional homes in Swiss chalet-style and even one with Japanese influence. One particularly interesting stretch is the piece of Buckingham Rd between Church Ave and Albermarle Rd, for example, *100 Buckingham Rd* (1908; A. A. Harmon), designed by the architect whose firm also designed the Empire State Building. *No. 131 Buckingham Rd* (1902; John Petit) was built by John Petit with the aid of three Japanese consultants for F. S. Kolle, a German émigré radiologist.

Other attractive houses line Stratford, Westminster, and Argyle Rds between Albemarle and Beverley Rds.

Another development that dates from about the same period is *Beverley Square West,* undertaken in 1898 by architect Theodore Benton Ackerson. A community of large houses all with stained glass windows and spacious gardens, Beverley Square West stands on land that was formerly the farm of Catherine Lott. Architect Ackerson's own home was at 346 Argyle Rd.

BROOKLYN COLLEGE, between Flatbush and Ocean Aves around Avenue H, was founded (1930) in downtown Brooklyn as a coeducational liberal arts college and today enrolls about 16,000 undergraduates and 2000 graduate students.

SUBWAY: IRT 7th Ave or Lexington Ave express (train 3 or 4; make sure you get a train marked Flatbush Ave; train 3 during the day; train 4 at night and Sun morning) to Flatbush Ave / Brooklyn College stop, the end of the line.

The 26-acre campus opened in 1937 on a former golf course sometimes also used for tent shows of the Barnum & Bailey Circus. The *Brooklyn Center for the Performing Arts at Brooklyn College* (BCBC) offers concerts, dance programs, and theatrical events in the George Gershwin Theater and Walt Whitman Hall (tel: 718\434-2222).

Borough Park, like Bensonhurst to its S., was developed during the 1920s following the extension of the subway system from

Manhattan and attracted a predominantly Jewish population. Its boundaries are generally considered to be 39th St and 65th St on the N. and S., Seventh Ave on the W., and MacDonald Ave on the east.

During the 1960s as more prosperous Jews moved to the suburbs, poorer families began moving to Borough Park from elsewhere in Brooklyn, notably from Williamsburg and Brownsville, and in contrast to earlier immigrants who had adopted American culture, the new residents resolutely maintain their old world customs including their style of dress. Many are orthodox Jews and Hasidim (see p. 666). The process of population displacement continues and today the Borough Park Jews who formerly shared the territory with Italians are increasingly surrounded by blacks and Hispanics. The neighborhood is primarily residential and lower middle class, divided by the street grid into monotonously regular blocks of small one- and two-family houses and apartments.

Thirteenth Avenue is the neighborhood's main commercial street, with discounted clothing shoes, dry goods, and electronics stores. As in other predominantly Jewish areas, the shops close Fri afternoon around three and reopen on Sun.

Bensonhurst, S. of Borough Park, is bounded by 14th Ave to the N.W., 61st St and McDonald Ave on the N.E., Avenue U and 26th Ave on the S.E., and Gravesend Bay on the southwest. It dates back to 1652 when Cornelis van Werckhoven, a member of the Dutch West India Co., bartered the land from the Canarsee Indians for an assortment of knives, shoes, shirts, and combs, and established a homestead. The town which grew up around the present intersection of New York Ave and 18th Ave was chartered in 1657 and named Nieuw Utrecht after Van Werckhoven's home town. It remained rural for a long time, and in 1887 one square mile of the community consisted of nine farms, four owned by members of the Benson family. When the Benson holdings were broken up in 1889, Bensonhurst was opened to development. In the early years of the 20C, it became a resort area . For several generations thereafter Bensonhurst was predominantly a community of Italians and Jews, but recent arrivals have been immigrants from China, Russia, and Sicily. In a four-block area off Bath Ave there is a small community of blacks, whose ancestors arrived during the "underground railroad" days of the Civil War period, when a North Carolinian horse trainer settled in the area.

At the end of August the community celebrates the week-long Feast of Santa Rosalia, which brings many visitors to the heart of the Italian community. Along Eighteenth Ave between about 67th and 75th Sts are cafes selling espresso and elaborate pastries, shops selling Italian shoes and clothing, and grocery stores with Italian cheeses and cold cuts.

SUBWAY: IND 6th Ave (B train) to Bay Parkway.

Points of interest. *The New Utrecht Reformed Church* (1828; DL) on Eighteenth Ave between 83rd and 84th Sts, with its rubble-stone walls, pointed windows, and square central tower, recalls St. Augustine's Chapel on the Lower East Side, built at about the same time. On the grounds stands a Liberty Pole whose ancestors date back to the celebrations of November 1783, when the British Army departed after the Revolution. The original Liberty Poles, intended for flying dissident banners, were erected by patriotic colonists in part as rallying points, in part to antagonize the British garrisons. The *Parsonage* (c. 1885) on 83rd St and the *Parish House* (1892) on 84th St, both between Eighteenth and Nineteenth Aves, date from the end of the century when Benson-hurst was said to be one of the most beautiful residential communities in the city.

Bath Beach, along the shore E. of the Verrazano-Narrows Bridge, has been effectively obliterated by the Belt Parkway, though at the turn of the century it was a fashionable seaside resort.

51 Southern Brooklyn: Gravesend, Coney Island, Brighton Beach, Manhattan Beach, and Sheepshead Bay

Gravesend (center at the intersection of McDonald Ave and Gravesend Neck Rd), called *'s Gravensande* by the Dutch, the only one of Brooklyn's original six towns not settled by them, was established by an English woman, Lady Deborah Moody, who in 1643 with her Anabaptist followers fled the religious intolerance of the Massachusetts Bay Colony.

History. In 1645 the town was granted a charter and enjoyed both religious freedom and a degree of self-government. Unlike the other early settlements which grew up haphazardly, Gravesend was formally planned in the manner of English colonial towns in Massachusetts or Connecticut with a central green. Along with the original cemetery where Lady Deborah Moody is buried (though the precise location of her grave is not known), the square remains the only trace of the original town plan. The area has fallen on hard times; travel in company.

Points of interest. The GRAVESEND CEMETERY (1650; DL) is at the S.W. corner of the square (between McDonald Ave and Van Sicklen St) but is kept locked. Nearby (27 Gravesend Neck Rd) is the *Hicks-Platt House* which dates from the mid-17C (considerable alteration) and in the 1890s was passed off by real estate entrepreneur William Platt as Lady Moody's house. A little further out Gravesend Neck Road (N.W. corner of E. 1st St) is the present Trinity Tabernacle of Gravesend, formerly the *Gravesend Reform Church* (1894), successor of the congregation's earlier buildings at Neck Road and McDonald Ave.

*Coney Island, joined to the mainland by the filling of part of Coney Island Creek, is no longer the "world's largest playground" as it once billed itself, but still survives as an archetype of American honky-tonk. The 2½ mile Boardwalk remains, now frequented by joggers, gangs of teenagers, and elderly strollers, as does the Cyclone, once the ultimate terror of roller coasters. The rusting steelwork of the parachute jump still lifts itself skyward, though the parachutes are long gone. During the season (late May through early Sept), people still crowd the wide, sandy beach, but nowadays the waters are not remarkable for their purity nor the crowds for their gentility.

> SUBWAY: IND 6th Ave express or local (B, D, or F train). The D train goes to Coney Island weekends and at night. The B and F train run at all times. BMT Broadway express (N train). BMT Nassau St local (M train) goes to Coney Island during the day on weekdays.

> CAR: Take the Belt System around the shoreline (good views of the Verrazano Bridge, Narrows, and lower harbor) to the Coney Island / Ocean Parkway exit (#7) and go south. Or take the Brooklyn-Queens Expressway to the Prospect Expressway and follow Ocean Parkway through Brooklyn to Coney Island. Large pay parking lot (includes one adult Aquarium admission) at the Aquarium (Surf Ave at W. 8th St).

At the eastern tip of the peninsula the *Kingsborough Community College* (master plan 1968; Katz, Waisman, Weber, Strauss and others) occupies the site of a World War II naval training station in an area once called Orient Beach. To its W. are Manhattan Beach and Brighton Beach, both residential communities with public bathing beaches. Coney Island proper is a relatively poor community with the highest concentration of old people in the city, most housed in high-rise urban renewal apartments. On the western edge of the peninsula is Sea Gate, a private community whose guards keep out the rest of the world.

History. The Dutch called the island *Konijn Eiland* (Rabbit Island), presumably because of the local fauna. Its history as a resort began with the Coney Island Hotel (1829) at Sea Gate, soon followed by other establishments whose restaurants and bathing pavilions attracted a genteel clientele. By 1870, however, Coney Island had declined and under the corrupt administration of Gravesend political boss John Y. McKane gambling and prostitution flourished. Around the turn of the century while Coney Island was still a recognized hangout for mobsters, the construction of three spectacular amusement areas ushered in its golden age. George C. Tilyou's Steeplechase Park (1897), Luna Park (1903), the most ambitious, and Dreamland (1904). Technological advances permitted new and ever more thrilling rides, notably the ferris wheel and the roller coaster. In 1910 a reform administration swept away the worst of the vice and with the arrival of the subway (1920) Coney Island became the playground of the common man, the "empire of the nickel." During the 1920s and 1930s huge crowds thronged the boardwalk (opened 1921) or lay thigh to thigh on the sand, although by this time the amusement areas were beginning to deteriorate. Dreamland burned in 1911 and Luna Park succumbed to a series of fires in the 1940s after losing money for decades. The rise of the automobile after World War II, the flight to the suburbs, and a preference for the more wholesome atmosphere of Disneyland and its imitators hastened the decline of Coney Island. In 1966 Steeplechase Park closed; the city now owns the land and for more than 15 years has had plans for making it a public park, but no visible action has been taken.

Begin at the ***New York Aquarium,** clean, attractive, and under-used because of its remoteness from the city.

The New York Aquarium. Boardwalk and W. 8th St, Coney Island, Brooklyn, N. Y. 11224. Open Sept–May 10–5 weekdays, 10–6 summer weekdays; 10–7 summer weekends and holidays. Admission charge. Tel: (718) 265-3400.
    Changing exhibitions, educational programs. Cafeteria and snack bar. Restrooms, telephones. Picnic tables. Gift shop. Accessible to wheelchairs.

SUBWAY: IND 6th Ave local (F train) to W. 8th St station; or IND 6th Ave express (D train) to Brighton Beach and transfer to BMT Nassau St local (M train) to W. 8th St station. A pedestrian bridge leads from the subway station across Surf Ave to the Aquarium entrance. CAR: Same directions as for Coney Island.

The New York Aquarium (1902) is the oldest public aquarium in the U.S.; the facility was moved to its new building (1955; Harrison & Abramovitz) from its former home in Battery Park. On display are beluga whales, electric eels, sea lions, seals, dolphins, and penguins. An outdoor exhibition for children allows them to handle horseshoe crabs and starfish. In the summer (May–Sept) dolphin and sea lion shows are held daily, weather permitting.

From the aquarium walk W. along the ***Boardwalk**. The amusement area stretches from about W. 8th to W. 16th St, dominated by Astroland and the Wonderwheel (1920; DL), a large ferris wheel with enclosed cabins, and an array of other rides. The Cyclone roller coaster, an old-fashioned wood-frame roller coaster which dates back to 1927 (DL), is considered by some classicists to be the best roller coaster in the country.

The American Coaster Enthusiasts, an organization devoted to the admiration of, riding on, and ranking of roller coasters, consistently name the Cyclone to its list of the nation's ten best. In 1988 it was declared a city landmark. The ride is 3000 ft long and takes one minute and 50 seconds. During the first drop, the cars plummet 85 ft at a 60-degree incline, reaching speeds of 60 miles per hour. The Cyclone is one of some 85 wooden track coasters remaining from an estimated 1500 that once thrilled riders across the nation.

Astroland is open daily from noon–midnight (depending on weather early in the season) mid-June to mid-Sept; weekends only from Palm Sunday to mid-June. Tel: (718) 265-2100.

Inland, between W. 8th and W. 12th St, N. of Surf Ave and the subway tracks (elevated here), the *Luna Park Houses* (not worth the detour) occupy the site of one of the major amusement parks. The drab renewal project is a sad contrast to the former fantasy architecture created by Frederick Thompson and Skip Dundy, entrepreneurs of Luna Park, who embellished their wonderland with a Venetian lagoon, a Chinese theater, an Electric Tower, and a multitude of turrets, towers, onion-shaped domes, and minarets all illuminated with strings of light bulbs.

Continue along the Boardwalk to Stillwell Ave and walk inland. *The Bowery,* a block off the beach between W. 12th and W. 16th Sts, once Coney Island's sin strip, lined with peepshows and entertainments that shocked turn-of-the-century moralists, today features carnival amusements. A block further inland at Surf Ave and Stillwell Ave is *Nathan's Famous,* a stand-up eatery founded in 1916 as Nathan's and soon famous for its five cent hot dogs— still available but not for a nickel.

Nathan was Nathan Handwerker, a sometime employee of Charles Feltman, who is credited with inventing the hot dog (presumably by putting a frankfurter in a roll). Handwerker put himself on the map by undercharging Feltman by a nickel.

SURF AVENUE separates the boardwalk area from the rest of the community, a seedy street with garishly illuminated discos and bars, a few small businesses, and a flea market under the tracks of the elevated railway.

Return to the Boardwalk and continue W. Jutting out into the ocean at 17th St is STEEPLECHASE PIER. Fishermen angle for bluefish, flounder, and striped bass in the surf. Opposite the pier is the *site of Steeplechase Park*, named after an outdoor horse race with wooden horses on a scaled-down roller coaster track. At the W. edge of the site is the abandoned *Parachute Jump* which first appeared at the 1939 World's Fair, its 11 colored parachutes with double seats giving riders "all the thrills of bailing out without any of the usual hazards or discomforts." In the same area is a small house tucked under the framework of the Thunderbolt Roller Coaster, which was closed in 1982 though the house is still occupied.

Along the Boardwalk opposite 19th St is the *Abe Stark Center* (1969; Daniel Chait), an ice-skating rink operated (Nov–April) by the city Department of Parks and Recreation.

Toward the W. end of the peninsula are a number of *urban renewal projects* undertaken by the state Urban Development Corporation in the 1970s, the best of which are *Sea Rise I* (1976; Hoberman & Wasserman) and a group of *Townhouses* (1975; Davis, Brody & Assocs) on Bayview Ave at W. 33rd St.

Brighton Beach lies E. of Coney Island and can be reached by walking E. along the Boardwalk past the Aquarium.

In the past decades the neighborhood has seen the influx of Russian immigrants, mostly Jews, and today it is estimated that of the 25,000 recent Soviet émigrés living in the city, about half live around the Brooklyn shore and about 8000 in Brighton Beach which has thus earned the nickname "Little Odessa by the Sea." Along Brighton Beach Ave are food stores with black bread, herrings, kasha, and even such delicacies as sturgeon and caviar. Souvenir shops display amber necklaces, needlework, and nested dolls, while its cafes attract a Russian-speaking clientele who can be seen taking tea or vodka to refresh themselves after a stroll.

The BRIGHTON BEACH BATH AND RACQUET CLUB (bounded by Brighton Beach Ave, Coney Island Ave, the Boardwalk, and Sea Coast Terrace), long a private club with swimming, tennis, dancing, entertainment, mah jong, and beauty contests, is scheduled for demolition and redevelopment as high-rise apartments.

Manhattan Beach to the E. between Ocean Ave and MacKenzie St is the most pleasant of the city's subway beaches.

Sheepshead Bay, a modest residential community of about 2 square miles, E. of Coney Island on the S. edge of Brooklyn, has long been home to a population of New Yorkers of Italian and Irish extraction, though today there is an enclave of West Indians and Haitians. Moored along the waterfront (Emmons Ave between Ocean Ave and 27th St) is a small fleet of fishing boats, many for hire, which depart early in the morning and return in the late afternoon with their catch, sometimes offered for sale along the pier.

The bay which juts inward from the E. got its name either because its shape resembled a sheep's head or because sheepsheads (described as black-banded fish with sheeplike teeth), once abounded in its waters. A quiet fishing village existed here until the land boom of 1877 followed by the opening of a race track in 1890 began attracting the city's celebrities like Diamond Jim Brady and Lillian Russell.

Points of interest. The enthusiast of Brooklyn history or colonial architecture might wish to seek out the *Wyckoff-Bennett House* (c. 1766; DL) at 1669 E. 22nd St, S.E. corner of Kings Highway, considered the finest Dutch colonial farmhouse still standing in Brooklyn. The house, built for Henry and Abraham Wyckoff and sold to the Bennett family four generations ago, has the overhanging eaves and columned porch typical of the style. During the Revolutionary War Hessian soldiers who were quartered here scratched their names on two panes of glass: "Toepfer Capt of Reg de Ditfurth" and "MBach Lieutenant v Hessen Hanau Artilerie."

The *Elias Hubbard Ryder House,* 1926 E. 28th St (bet. Avenue S and Avenue T), was built c. 1834; (DL) and is a late survival of the Dutch Colonial style, evidence that rural vernacular architecture changes slowly.

Gerritsen Ave, the major N.-S. road E. of the Ryder House, runs S. to **Gerritsen,** a small, tidy community of bungalows and narrow streets crowded onto a neck of land between Shell Bank Creek and Marine Park.

52 Southeastern Brooklyn: Flatlands and Canarsie

Flatlands, one of the original Dutch towns in Brooklyn, also called Nieuw Amersfoort, was chartered in 1666, and took its name from its terrain, low coastal plains adjoining the salt marshes to the south. It is bounded by the Long Island Railroad on the N., Ralph Ave and the Paerdegat Basin on the E., Nostrand and Gerritsen Aves on the W., and Jamaica Bay on the south. During the 17C a small Dutch town centered on what is now the junction of Flatbush Ave and Kings Highway. Today the area is primarily residential with some industrial development.

Marine Park, lying W. of Flatbush Ave and S. of Avenue U along the shore, consists of some 2000 acres donated mostly by the Whitney family during the 1920s. The park has a two-mile oval for running and cycling as well as baseball diamonds and basketball courts.

Along the other (E.) side of Flatbush Ave, S. of the Shore Parkway, is **Floyd Bennett Field,** now part of the Gateway National Recreation Area, but originally developed as New York's first municipal airport (1931), and named to honor the pilot who flew Admiral Byrd over the North Pole in 1926.

It failed as a commercial airport because it was too far from central New York, although during the days before World War II when aviators competed for long-distance flight records, the field served as the takeoff point for Wiley Post (1933) who flew solo around the world (7 days, 18 hours, 49 minutes, 30 seconds) and for Howard Hughes and companions who halved that record five years later.

Today there are Coast Guard and Naval Reserve stations on the peninsula, and part of the Gateway National Recreation Area, run by the National Park Service (seasonal walks and nature programs, ethnic festivals, dog shows, etc.; tel: (718) 338-3799).

Flatbush Ave leads S. across the *Gil Hodges Bridge,* formerly the Marine Parkway Bridge (toll) built across Rockaway Inlet (1937) to Jacob Riis Park in Queens (see p. 706). The bridge has three spans totaling 4022 ft and a 540-ft central lift span. Gil Hodges was the first baseman for the Dodgers during the team's final years in Brooklyn and later managed the New York Mets.

Other points of interest. Some landmark houses and a church remain of interest primarily to the local historian. The *Flatlands Dutch Reformed Church,* 3931 Kings Highway (bet. Flatbush Ave / E. 40th St), is one of three in Brooklyn established (1654) by Peter Stuyvesant and is the third church building on this site (1848; DL), a simple white clapboard Greek Revival building with a cemetery whose markers bear prominent old Brooklyn names: Lott, Kouwenhoven, Wyckoff. The earliest church on the site had stocks and a whipping post. Pieter Claesen Wyckoff arrived as an indentured servant (c. 1637) and rose to such prominence that he is buried beneath the pulpit.

His home, the *Pieter Claesen Wyckoff House* (c. 1641; DL), possibly the oldest building in the state, is a low, wood-shingled farmhouse, recently restored and opened as a museum.

Pieter Claesen Wyckoff House. 5902 Clarendon Rd (Ralph and Ditmas Aves), Brooklyn, N. Y. 11203. Tel: (718) 629-5400 for hours.

Two other landmark houses in the vicinity are the *Hendrick I. Lott House,* 1940 E. 36th St, between Fillmore Ave and Avenue S. (small wing 1070, larger wing 1800 DL), a Dutch colonial with overhanging eaves supported with round pillars in the front and square ones in back; and the *Stoothof-Baxter-Kouwenhoven House* (c. 1747; new wing 1811; DL), 1640 E. 48th St, between Avenue M and Avenue N, whose three names belong to three prominent and related Brooklyn families who owned it for a century and a half.

Mill Island is a peninsula divided from Marine Park by Mill Basin, along whose shores many residents keep boats tied up at their own docks. BERGEN BEACH, the next peninsula to the E., was a summer resort in the early 20C.

Canarsie, which reaches from Foster Ave to Jamaica Bay between Paerdegat and Fresh Creek Basins, is named after its first inhabitants, the Canarsee Indians, a tribe of the Leni Lenape or Delawares of the Algonkian linguistic group. Both the Indians and the Dutch who bought the land from them cultivated maize, squash, and beans on the fertile plains and fished the bay for shellfish; the Dutch cut the salt hay from the marshes for fodder. Canarsie remained rural well into the 20C when it became a suburb reached primarily by automobile, built up with two-family row houses. Most recently it has become home to a Jewish community fleeing Brownsville and East Flatbush. The *Canarsie Pier*, part of the Gateway National Recreation Area (foot of Rockaway Parkway), attracts fishermen and strollers.

IV BOROUGH OF QUEENS / QUEENS COUNTY

The borough of Queens, the largest in the city, covers 118.6 square miles (37.2% of the city's total area) in the W. portion of Long Island. It is bounded by Brooklyn on the W., with Newtown Creek forming part of the border, by the East River on the N., by the Atlantic Ocean on the S., and by Nassau County on the east. Topographically it resembles the rest of Long Island with a chain of hills created by glacial deposits running across the N. and a low outwash plain in the south. The N. shore is indented by Flushing and Little Neck Bays while the Rockaway peninsula juts westward across the mouth of Jamaica Bay in the S. to form a 10-mile ocean-front, Atlantic Beach.

Home to 1,891,325 people, Queens is the second most populous borough, surpassed only by Brooklyn. It is largely residential with more than 300,000 one- and two-family houses as well as apartment towers of various heights, but lacks the concentration of 19C brownstones and tenements that characterize Brooklyn and the Bronx. Some of its neighborhoods—Douglaston, Forest Hills, Kew Gardens—are almost suburban in character with detached houses, attractive gardens, and garages for that definitive suburban vehicle, the family car. At the other end of the economic scale are slums in South Jamaica, in the Rockaways, and in surrounding older industrial areas.

While Queens has earned its reputation as a bedroom community in the past half century, those areas developed earlier became industrial, with concentrations of factories in the vicinity of Long Island City and Maspeth, and along the right-of-way of the Long Island Railroad (LIRR). As elsewhere in the city, aging physical plants, problems of transportation, taxation, and labor have made Queens less attractive to industry than other areas of the country. Commercial centers are scattered throughout the borough, usually located at the crossroads of earlier towns, established independently before the creation of Greater New York in 1898: the most important ones are Astoria, Corona, Flushing, Jackson Heights, and Jamaica.

Queens has the highest median income of any borough. Among its suburban amenities are 6474 acres of parkland, almost as much as in the other four boroughs combined, two racetracks, two major tennis centers, several golf courses, and a wildlife refuge.

Because of its spaciousness, Queens has also become the resting place of uncounted souls whose remains lie buried in the belt of cemeteries that begins on the Brooklyn-Queens border and stretches eastward along the Interborough Parkway, an area known by the waggish as the "terminal moraine" and which includes such cemeteries as Union Field, Bethel, Mt. Carmel, Mt. Neboh, Cypress Hills, Mt. Lebanon, and Mt. Judah. Other large graveyards in the borough, which also owe their impetus to an 1851 law which prohibited further burials in Manhattan, are St. John's, Mt. Olivet, Lutheran, Mt. Zion, Calvary, and New Calvary.

More than any other borough, Queens bears the stamp of Robert Moses, who as parks commissioner preserved acres and acres of land—forests, meadow, beaches, marshes—while as master roadbuilder (and head of various public authorities) he blighted equally large areas by lacing the borough with highways: Grand Central Parkway, Interborough Parkway, the Clearview Expressway, the Cross Island Parkway, Laurelton Parkway, the Long Island Expressway, the Brooklyn-Queens Expressway, and the Whitestone Expressway.

History. The first inhabitants of Queens were the Rockaway Indians, whose name lives on in the peninsula stretching across Jamaica Bay, and the first settlers were the Dutch who arrived in c. 1635. Governor Kieft purchased title to the land from the Indians in 1639 and shortly thereafter the first towns were chartered: Mespat (now Maspeth) in 1642, and Vlissingen (Flushing) in 1643. Middleburg, which became Newtowne in 1655, was founded in 1652 between the two earlier settlements, its first residents immigrants from France and England as well as Holland. Indeed, as settlement continued, the Dutch staked out their claims in the W. part of Long Island while the English colonized the E. portion including the towns of Hempstead and Jamaica (1650).

In 1683, 19 years after the British took title to the former Dutch colony of New Amsterdam, these towns were organized as Queens County, one of 12 making up the British province of New York. The name honors Catherine of Braganza, queen of Charles II. During the Revolution most residents of Queens were British sympathizers and after the war many loyalists emigrated to Newfoundland.

Although a few industries established plants in Queens during the 19C, notably the Steinway piano factory and the Edward Smith & Co. paint factory, the borough remained rural and agricultural until almost the turn of the century. As the railroads began pushing E. across Long Island the beaches of both the N. and S. shores began attracting summer residents: at the turn of the century the land LaGuardia Airport now occupies held an amusement park and the Rockaways, whose remoteness is enshrined in the place name of its easternmost settlement, Far Rockaway, attracted the well-to-do who enjoyed the grand hotels or the privacy of their own mansions. The major roads were used by farmers taking their produce to New York markets or by residents in outlying communities seeking the amenities of the commercial districts closer to the city.

In 1898 Queens voted to become part of Greater New York, although several of the eastern towns chose to remain independent—Hempstead, N. Hempstead, and Oyster Bay—and were then absorbed into Nassau County. At the time (1900) the population of the borough was only 152,999, a figure which tripled in the next 20 years and doubled again between 1920–30, as bridges, tunnels, and rapid transit opened Queens to development. In 1910 the Queensboro Bridge and the East River tunnel of the Pennsylvania Railroad allowed direct access to Manhattan, while the subways came during the next decades with the BMT and IRT both reaching the outer areas of the borough and the IND going all the way to Jamaica in 1937. The Triborough Bridge (1936), the Bronx-Whitestone Bridge (1939), the Queens-Midtown Tunnel (1939), and most recently the Throgs Neck Bridge (1961) made Queens readily accessible by car.

In 1939–40 the first of two world's fairs was held in Flushing Meadows and several of these public works projects along with the development of La Guardia Airport were undertaken to coincide with its opening. After World War II, when the populations of the other boroughs (except Staten Island) were either remaining stable or shrinking, Queens experienced its second great boom, one that took the form of suburban development as builders grabbed whatever open space remained and erected acre after acre of tract housing, small homes on small lots, monotonously repeated row upon row, block upon block. Despite the blandness of much of Queens's suburban development, its very newness has saved the borough from some of the problems of urban blight that afflict Manhattan, Brooklyn, and the Bronx.

Touring in Queens. Although security is not such a problem in Queens as in parts of Manhattan, Brooklyn, and the Bronx, distances are such that a car is certainly convenient and probably necessary. The orientation of most museums and other attractions in Queens is toward the community in which they are located, and most of the sights of the borough are of interest primarily to the truly zealous tourist, or the visitor intent on seeing the city as a whole. While a casual glance at a road map may make it appear that Queens is laid out in a recognizable rectilinear pattern, it is deceptively difficult to find one's way around. Numbered avenues generally run E. and W., but they are sometimes interspersed with Roads, Drives, and even an occasional Court bearing the same number; streets run generally N. and S. and seem to be more regular than avenues in their numbering. The pattern is further complicated by the vestiges of old roads, dating from the colonial period and themselves often following Indian paths, wandering across the modern grid according to topographical variations long erased by landfill or leveling. New highways running through old neighborhoods have disrupted the continuity of street layouts as well as the social fabric of the neighborhoods themselves. Finally developers have created special patterns, arcs or crescents, for example, in communities like Forest Hills Gardens, Rego Park, or Kew Gardens that were developed all at once as planned communities or for real estate speculation.

53 Northwestern Queens: Hunter's Point, Long Island City, Sunnyside, Woodside, Ravenswood, Astoria, and Steinway

Long Island City, manufacturing center of the borough, raises its bleak, industrial skyline just across the East River from midtown

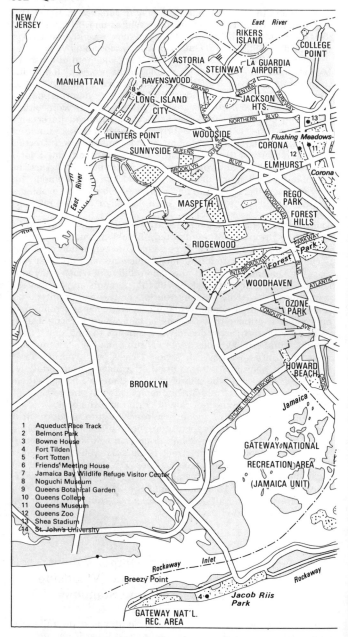

NEW JERSEY

MANHATTAN

East River

RIKERS ISLAND

COLLEGE POINT

ASTORIA
STEINWAY

LA GUARDIA AIRPORT

RAVENSWOOD

GRAND

JACKSON HTS.

LONG ISLAND CITY

CENTRAL PARKWAY

NORTHERN BLVD.

13

HUNTERS POINT

WOODSIDE

Flushing Meadows

SUNNYSIDE

QUEENS

CORONA

12   11

BROOKLYN

QUEENS BLVD.

ELMHURST

Corona

East River

MASPETH

WOODHAVEN

REGO PARK

FOREST HILLS

RIDGEWOOD

PARKWAY

Forest Park

BLVD.

INTERBOROUGH

WOODHAVEN

ATLANTIC

OZONE PARK

CONDUIT   AVE.

BROOKLYN

HOWARD BEACH

CROSS

SHORE (BELT) PARKWAY

Jamaica

GATEWAY NATIONAL

RECREATION AREA

(JAMAICA UNIT)

1   Aqueduct Race Track
2   Belmont Park
3   Bowne House
4   Fort Tilden
5   Fort Totten
6   Friends' Meeting House
7   Jamaica Bay Wildlife Refuge Visitor Center
8   Noguchi Museum
9   Queens Botanical Garden
10 Queens College
11 Queens Museum
12 Queens Zoo
13 Shea Stadium
14 St. John's University

Rockaway   Inlet

Breezy Point

Rockaway

4   Jacob Riis Park

GATEWAY NAT'L. REC. AREA

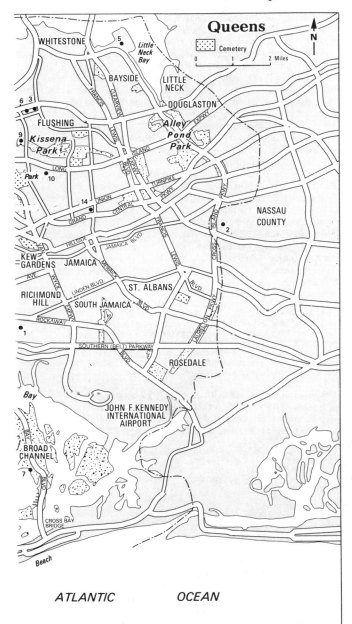

Queens

▦ Cemetery

0 ———— 1 ———— 2 Miles

N

WHITESTONE

5

Little Neck Bay

BAYSIDE

LITTLE NECK

DOUGLASTON

6 3

FLUSHING

Alley Pond Park

9

Kissena Park

NASSAU COUNTY

Park

10

2

14

UNION

CENTRAL

GRAND

HILLSIDE

JAMAICA BLVD.

KEW GARDENS

JAMAICA

MERRICK

ST. ALBANS

LINDEN BLVD.

RICHMOND HILL

SOUTH JAMAICA

BLVD.

ROCKAWAY

1

SOUTHERN (BELT) PARKWAY

ROSEDALE

Bay

JOHN F. KENNEDY INTERNATIONAL AIRPORT

BROAD CHANNEL

7

CROSS BAY BRIDGE

Beach

ATLANTIC   OCEAN

Manhattan and Roosevelt Island, the stacks of the Con Ed generator, known as Big Allis, familiar on both sides of the river. Long Island City owes its name to a period of political independence (1870–98) after it broke away from the town of Newtown and before it joined Queens in 1898 as part of the consolidation of Greater New York. Although Long Island City like the rest of the metropolis has suffered a loss in manufacturing jobs, it is beginning to emerge as an artistic and merchandizing community. It is also a hub of transportation: the IRT and BMT elevateds, the Long Island Railroad (now part of the Metropolitan Transit Authority), and the tracks of Metro North (formerly Conrail and the Penn Central Railroad) converge here before making the river crossing to Manhattan.

Nowadays it is subdivided into three areas, from S. to N.: Hunter's Point, Long Island City, and Ravenswood.

Hunter's Point, in the S.W. corner of Long Island City and just across Newtown Creek from the Greenpoint section of Brooklyn, is a mixed industrial-residential district. One block, 45th Ave between 21st and 23rd Sts, has been declared the *Hunter's Point Historic District* on the strength of a group of Italianate row houses (early 1870s) which owe their good condition to their building material, Westchester stone, harder and less friable than the usual brownstone.

Hunter's Point takes its name from British sea captain George Hunter who owned land in the vicinity during the colonial period, but its development dates from about 1860 when the first steam ferry made regular crossings to Manhattan. Around the landing at 34th St a prosperous community arose, with inns and hotels for travelers and comfortable homes for commuters. This pleasant state of affairs lasted until 1909 when the opening of the Queensboro Bridge led to the rapid industrialization of Hunter's Point and the development of more attractive residential areas further east.

Between 46th Rd and 46th Ave, **P.S. 1** occupies the former Ward 1 School (1892), now refurbished (1976; Shael Shapiro) as an experimental art center with studio and exhibition space for painting, sculpture, and performing arts.

Institute for Art and Urban Resources: P.S. 1, 46-01 21st St, Long Island City, Queens, N.Y. 11101. Tel: (718) 784-2084. Open Wed–Sun 12–6. Closed late June–Oct; free.

SUBWAY: IRT Flushing line (train 7) to 45thRd / Courthouse Square. BUS: Q19A, Q39, Q67.

Rising high above the old skyline and perhaps auguring the future is the 48-story **Citicorp** tower (1989; Skidmore, Owings & Merrill), 44th Drive to 45th Ave near Jackson Ave, the tallest building in the outer boroughs.

Nearby is the ornate **N.Y. State Supreme Court, Long Island City Branch** (1876; George Hathorne; rebuilt 1908; Peter M. Coco; DL), rebuilt in its present English Renaissance style after a fire. Willie ("The Actor") Sutton is said to have uttered his celebrated defense of his profession here; he robbed banks, he said, because "That's where the money is."

The IRT Flushing line of the subway crosses the East River at

Hunter's Point in the Steinway Tunnels, named after piano maker William Steinway who backed a trolley car connection to Manhattan in 1892. Franchise disputes, an explosion, and the Panic of 1893 halted the project; the tunnels (completed 1907), sat empty until 1913 when they were converted for subway use and opened (1915) for service.

North of Hunters Point, around the bridge approaches is **Long Island City** proper, an area of railroad yards and factories (old and recycled), and a hub of transportation.

The **Queensboro Bridge** (1909; Gustav Lindenthal, engineer; DL) sweeps overhead at 41st Rd, linking Queens to 59th–60th Sts in Manhattan (see p. 348). Just N. of it, (Vernon Blvd to 21st St, 40th Ave to Bridge Plaza) are the *Queensbridge Houses* (1939; William F. R. Ballard, chief architect), once the largest public housing project in the nation (3161 apartments in 26 buildings on 62.5 acres).

Not far from the foot of the bridge is a group of rehabilitated industrial buildings, which now constitute the *International Design Center* (1985–; I.M. Pei & Partners, master plan; Gwathmey Siegel & Assocs., design architects; Stephen Lepp Assocs., construction architects), a complex of showrooms for the design and furniture industries. The best view is from the south. The former Adams Gum Building (1919; Ballinger and Perot) at 30-30 Thomson Ave (bet. 30th Place / 31st St) home of Chiclets and Dentyne is now Center One; Center Two (1914) housed the American Eveready Battery factory, and Center Three was the Loose-Wiles Sunshine Bakery (1914; William Higginson), illuminated by a legendary thousand windows. Open interior courts have been glassed over to create soaring interior spaces with natural light and open corridors.

Sunnyside, a modest residential community centering around the intersection of Roosevelt Ave and Queens Blvd, is hemmed in by cemeteries, industrial zones, and the former *Sunnyside Yards of the Pennsylvania Railroad* (bet. Skillman and Jackson Aves). The yards opened in 1910 along with the tunnel beneath the East River to Pennsylvania Station, which allowed direct train travel from New England to New York for the first time. Today lines leading into the yards accommodate the trains of Conrail, a commuter and freight line to points N. and E., the Long Island Railroad, and Amtrak, the long-distance national railroad.

SUNNYSIDE GARDENS, bounded by Skillman and 39th Aves, 43rd–50th Sts (1924; Henry Wright, Clarence Stein, and Frederick Ackerman), is a community of detached homes and small apartment buildings, an early and successful experiment in urban planning undertaken by a limited-profit agency which developed these 70 acres of unpromising land during the boom years of the 1920s. More notable for its site planning than its architecture, the development has houses facing both the street and the back gardens and also includes park and recreational areas. During the Depression many homeowners, unable to pay their mortgages, took collective action against the sheriffs serving eviction notices, sandbagging their doors, installing barbed wire, and physically harassing law enforcement officers; but more than 60% of the original owners lost their homes through foreclosure. In the 1960s as younger families began to move out to more affluent suburbs, they left a large number of older residents as well as vacancies which were filled by lower income residents. Sunnyside Gardens is now gradually overcoming this period of decline, helped in part by the Sunnyside Foundation.

Woodside, N.E. of Sunnyside and geographically indistinguishable from it, is a lower middle class residential community developed after 1917 when the Flushing line of the IRT put it within minutes of Manhattan.

Ravenswood is the neighborhood lying along the river N. of the Queensboro Bridge. **Big Allis,** the Con Ed generator familiar from Manhattan's East Side, public housing including the Ravenswood Houses and some new waterside enterprises mark the area.

The **Isamu Noguchi Garden Museum** (1985; Shogi Sazao) gathers some 300 works of the artist, including models, sculptures, and photographs that span 60 years of his career.

Isamu Noguchi Garden Museum. 32-37 Vernon Blvd (10th St), Long Island City, Queens, N.Y. 11101. Tel: (718) 204-7088. Entrance on 33rd Rd near 11th St. Open Wed and Sat 12—5. Closed holidays. Suggested contribution.
  BUS: Take the Steinway Transit Q101 (not the bus labeled Rikers Island) from 59th St / 2nd Ave on the S. side of the Queensboro Bridge; ask for a transfer. At Broadway / Steinway St in Queens transfer to the Q104. Get off at 32nd Ave / Vernon Blvd. For more information, call Steinway Transit: (718) 445-3100.

Installed in a former photoengraving factory, this museum with 12 galleries and an outdoor sculpture garden shows the totality of Noguchi's work, with examples of his basalt and granite stone sculpture, geometric steel works, and polished marble forms. There are also models of public sculpture, set designs, and a gallery of early work. A sense of Oriental tranquility pervades the garden, with its stone sculpture, trickling fountain, and carefully placed trees.

Another sign of the growing importance of Long Island City in the cultural life of the city is **Socrates Sculpture Park,** a windswept field facing the East River.

Socrates Sculpture Park. 31-29 Vernon Blvd (Broadway), Long Island City, Queens. Tel: (718) 956-1819. Open summer, daily, 10—dusk. Winter, weekends only, 10—dusk. The sculpture is installed in a open field; there are no other facilities.
  BUS: Take the Steinway Transit Q101 (not the bus labeled Rikers Island) from 59th St / 2nd Ave on the S. side of the Queensboro Bridge; ask for a transfer. At Broadway / Steinway St in Queens transfer to the Q104. Get off at Broadway / Vernon Blvd. For more information, call Steinway Transit: (718) 445-3100.

Socrates Sculpture Park, dedicated to the philosopher who dedicated himself to a search for truth, is one of the few places in New York to see large-scale sculpture by emerging artists throughout the year. The site itself is striking—remote, a little wild, exposed. Formerly a marine terminal, then an abandoned lot filled with garbage and rubble, the park was leased in 1986 for five years from the city and developed largely by sculptors Mark di Suvero and Isamu Noguchi, whose studios are nearby. The rocks by the waterside, near what is left of the pilings surrounding the old slip, have been brightly painted by Anthe Zacharias.

A vestige of one of Queens' former industries, the **Sohmer Piano Company** (1886; addition 1910) remains close by (31-01 Vernon Blvd at 31st Ave), though it no longer produces pianos.

North of Long Island City and just across the East River from Wards and Randalls Islands is **Astoria**. Originally called Hallett's Cove after William Hallett to whom Gov. Peter Stuyvesant granted a patent for 1500 acres in 1654, Astoria got its present name in 1839 when it was incorporated as a town, a name accepted despite the bitter opposition of John Jacob Astor's local detractors. The town grew as a suburb after a steam ferry began crossings to Manhattan and during the 1840s became the center of a thriving shipping business, some of whose entrepreneurs traded in exotic woods. Successful shippers built their mansions along the waterfront, though none has survived. Today Astoria has a huge Con Edison plant occupying 383 acres along the East River, a peninsula whose outer edge is still called Berrian's Island though it is no longer separated from Long Island.

Astoria Park, bounded by Shore Blvd, 19th St, Astoria Park South, and Ditmars Blvd, was developed in the 1930s during the construction of the Triborough Bridge. The facilities include playing fields, tennis courts, and an Olympic-size swimming pool.

The *Remsen House,* 9-26 27th Ave, S.W. corner of 12th St (c. 1835), survives from the period when the bulbous peninsula of Hallett's Point protruding into the East River just S. of Astoria Park had a fashionable summer colony and grand houses. Most of the homes have been demolished but this formerly handsome Greek Revival house with its pilastered doorway, tall parlor-floor windows, and iron fence survives from those genteel times. Across the street is the former *Doctor Wayt house,* 9-29 27th Ave, N.W. corner of 12th St, an Italianate mansion once grander. In healthier condition is the two-story colonnaded former *Robert Benner house* at 25-37 14th St between Astoria Park South and 26th Ave, partially hidden behind a spreading beech and looking as if it belonged in Georgia instead of Astoria. Benner was a Manhattan lawyer.

Astoria is known today as the city's largest Greek enclave, a clean, attractive neighborhood where an estimated 75% of the Greek-Americans own their own homes and run their own businesses. Before the relaxation of immigration laws in 1965, the population of Astoria consisted mainly of Italians who had previously lived elsewhere in New York, though a small group of Greeks did settle here before World War II. Its present population is about 100,000 of whom 45,000 are Greek-born or of Greek descent. St. Demetrios, one of 11 Greek Orthodox churches in the area, a domed Byzantine-style church (31st St and 30th

Drive) is said to have the largest community of Greek congregants outside of Greece.

SUBWAY: BMT Broadway local (R train) to Astoria Blvd-Hoyt Ave.

CAR: Queensboro Bridge to Northern Blvd; turn left (N.) at 31st St in Queens and follow it N. to Ditmars Blvd. Or take the Triborough Bridge to 31st St and turn left (N.) to Ditmars Blvd.

PARKING: Difficult, especially on weekends, though there is a municipal lot on 33rd St, S. of Ditmars Blvd.

For a short walking tour, begin at Astoria Blvd and Hoyt Ave South on 31st St and follow 31st St north (street numbers will decrease) to Ditmars Blvd; turn right (E.) and continue to Steinway St. Along 31st St, the main commercial thoroughfare, are Greek-orientated shops with icons, decorated candles, records, and books, as well as several restaurants and pastry shops. Butchers, whose staple is lamb, sometimes arrange rather startling displays of sheeps' heads in the show windows, while fish markets offer prickly sea urchins and squid, along with more familiar fare. The Ditmars Theater, 31st St between 23rd Ave and Ditmars Blvd, shows Greek films. The Lefkos Pirgos coffee shop (22-84 31st St) sells baklava and other pastries to accompany strong Greek coffee. The Kalamata Market (38-01 Ditmars Blvd) is well stocked with feta cheese, Athenian honey, and other Greek specialties. Restaurants and coffee shops stay open late and nightclubs get lively around 11 P.M. with Greek music and dancing by the patrons or by professional belly dancers (though belly dancing is a Middle Eastern rather than a Greek speciality). Some of the clubs emigrated from the former belly dance center on Eighth Ave around 28th St in Manhattan, following the exodus of the Greek population.

In the days before Hollywood became the nexus of the American film industry the **Kaufman Astoria Studios** (1919) between 34th and 38th Sts along 35th Ave employed the talents of such stars as Gloria Swanson, Maurice Chevalier, Paul Robeson, the Marx Brothers, and Rudolf Valentino. Originally owned by the Famous Players-Lasky Corporation, which became a part of Paramount Pictures, the 13-building complex was first used to produce feature films; later as the Eastern Service Studios its facilities were devoted to educational and comic shorts, and during World War II the U.S. Army took over the property, turning out training films and propaganda. After the government abandoned the property in 1971, the Astoria Motion Picture and Television Foundation was formed to restore the studios, giving the developmental rights to George Kaufman, who renovated eight sound stages and renamed them the Kaufman Astoria Studios, now the most successful film making property on the East Coast.

The Foundation now has a theater with a full schedule of screenings and operates the **American Museum of the Moving Image**.

The American Museum of the Moving Image. 35th Ave at 36th St, Astoria, Queens, N.Y. 11106. Tel: (718) 784-4520. Open Wed and Thurs 1-5; Fri 1-8; Sat 10-8; Sun 10-5. Admission charge.

Lectures, screenings, changing exhibitions. Cafe, restrooms, gift shop, public telephone. Accessible to wheelchairs.

SUBWAY: BMT N train to Broadway, walk four blocks to 35th Ave; turn right and walk two blocks S. to 36th St. BMT R train to Steinway St stop. Walk two blocks W. to 36th St; turn left and walk two blocks S. to 35th Ave. BUS: Steinway Transit Q101 (not the bus labeled Rikers Island) departs from 59th St at 2nd Ave in Manhattan. Get off at 35th Ave in Astoria and walk W. on 35th Ave. Jitney from the International Design Center New York, 919 Third Ave at 56th St, leaves at half hour intervals on the hour and half hour.

Devoted to the history and art of movies, the museum has props and reassembled movie sets, instruction on using sound effects machines and making films, and exhibits of film memorabilia. For movie schedule call (718) 784–4742.

East of Astoria lies **Steinway,** developed by piano manufacturer William Steinway who moved his factory from Manhattan to a 400-acre site along Bowery Bay in 1872, surrounding it with a company town that had a park, library, ball fields, a kindergarten, and some row housing that still stands. Steinway was attracted by the availability of land and lumber in Queens, but he also chose this then isolated spot to remove his workers from the influence of union organizers.

The *Steinway Mansion* (1850s; DL) still stands at 18-33 41st St (bet. Berrian Blvd / 19th Ave), on a hill overlooking the East River. Benjamin Pike, an optician, built the Italianate villa for himself, with rough stonework, romantically asymmetric bays, arcades, and towers. Once graced by lawns, tennis courts, orchards, and stables, it now stands obscured by trees in a rather sinister neighborhood whose tone is established by a sewage treatment plant, some junkyards, and ferocious guard dogs.

The Steinway factory is at the N.W. corner of 19th Ave and 39th St and the *Steinway Company Housing* (c. 1880) is on the S. side of 20th Ave between Steinway St and 41st Ave.

The **Lent Homestead** (c. 1729; DL), 78–03 19th Rd at 78th St, is the second oldest dwelling in Queens, a Dutch-style farmhouse of fieldstone with hewn timbers and shingles built by Abraham Lent, grandson of Abraham Riker whose family once owned Rikers Island. It has been handsomely modernized though the shingles and original timbers at one end and the shape of the large, dormered, overhanging Dutch roof remain to testify to its antiquity.

Nearby at the intersection of 19th Ave and Hazen St is the bridge to **Rikers Island,** politically part of the Bronx but joined to Queens by a bridge (not accessible to the public). On the island are several city penal institutions, the most noteworthy being the Men's House of Detention, with about 5000 prisoners. Built in 1935 to replace the old Welfare (now Roosevelt) Island prison, it was heralded as a model penitentiary, but today is obsolete and the object of controversy. Other facilities on the island are the Correctional Institution for Men, the Correctional Institution for Women, the Adolescent Detention Center, the Rikers Island Hospital, and the Anna Kross Center. The island at low tide lies only about 100 ft from the runways of La Guardia Airport and has long relied for security on the currents and tides of the river, today, according to prison employees, less treacherous than in the past.

Rikers Island is named after Abraham Rycken (later spelled Riker) and his descendants who owned it for generations after 1664.

Near Rikers Island is *North Brother Island,* site of the former Riverside Hospital for communicable diseases, whose most famous resident was "Typhoid Mary" Mallon, a cook who unknowingly communicated the disease, probably starting several epidemics. The burning excursion steamer, the *General Slocum,* beached here in 1904, but not before more than a thousand passengers had lost their lives, most of them women and children on an outing from the Tompkins Square neighborhood of the Lower East Side. *South Brother Island,* also part of the Bronx, is about seven acres of wasteland.

54   Central Queens: Jackson Heights, Maspeth, Ridgewood, Corona, Elmhurst, Forest Hills, Kew Gardens, and Rego Park

The first settlement in central Queens was the Dutch town (1642) of Middleburg between Maspeth and Flushing, renamed New-towne (1655) by the English. Its boundaries encompass the contemporary communities of Jackson Heights, Corona, Elmhurst, Forest Hills, Maspeth, Ridgewood, and Rego Park, which range economically from the exclusivity of Forest Hills Gardens to the industrial blight and economic depression of parts of Ridgewood and Maspeth.

Less than two miles E. of Astoria and Long Island City is **Jackson Heights,** bounded roughly by Northern Blvd, Roosevelt Ave, 73rd and 82nd Sts, was developed (1913–1930s) by the Queensboro Corporation, who named it after John C. Jackson, planner of Northern Blvd. It is the "home" of the garden apartment, a concept developed by architect Andrew J. Thomas, who brought the advantages of luxury city apartments to people of modest means. Himself a child of the tenements, Thomas saw the true unit of planning as the city block, not the individual building, a concept he was able to explore because the developer owned a lot of land and was willing to develop it over a period of years as an investment. Thomas created blocks of buildings with wide open central courtyards and smaller garden courts along the street; he emphasized corners by towers; he grouped clusters of buildings together by historical style to give each group its own identity.

Among his projects are *Linden Court* (1919), the earliest, mid-block between 37th and Roosevelt Aves, 84th–85th Sts; the *Spanish Gardens Apartments* (1923), mid-block between 37th and Roosevelt Aves, 83rd–84th Sts; the *Towers Apartments* (1925), where Douglas Fairbanks and Charlie Chaplin once lived; and the *Chateau Apartments* (1923), facing each other across 34th Ave bet. 80th / 81st Sts.

Jackson Heights was advertised by its developers as a "restricted garden residential section"—a phrase implying that Jews, blacks, and Catholics were unwelcome. Today, however, the area is one of the city's melting pots; the older Italian, Jewish, and Irish population along Roosevelt and 37th Aves has been joined by newer arrivals: Indians, Chinese, and Spanish-speaking immigrants from Mexico, Ecuador, Colombia, Argentina, and Peru;

the most recent arrivals are "yuppies" seeking lower rents beyond Manhattan's rivers.

LaGuardia Airport on Grand Central Parkway bordering Flushing Bay and Bowery Bay in the **Jackson Heights** section was developed before World War II along with the neighborhood surrounding it and is chronologically the city's second municipal airfield after the economically unsuccessful Floyd Bennett Field.

In the 1880s William Steinway (pianos), George Ehret (beer), and Henry Cassebeer (patent medicines) developed the area between Bowery Bay (site of the bridge to Rikers Island) and Flushing Bay as a resort which they called Bowery Bay Beach, a name changed (1891) to North Beach when the Bowery in Manhattan picked up tawdry connotations. The amusement park (picnic tables, rides, dance halls) occupied the site until Prohibition took its toll and was converted (1929) to a private flying field named the Glenn H. Curtiss Airport, later North Beach Airport. Taken over by the city, it was enlarged by purchase and landfill and opened to commercial traffic in 1939. In 1947 the airport was leased to the Port Authority and named LaGuardia Airport, and in the 1960s was modernized and expanded. Today the facility occupies 650 acres, employs 8400 workers, has nine large hangars and a fuel storage facility fed by pipeline from Linden, New Jersey, with a capacity of 5.1 million gallons.

Passenger terminals are the *Central Terminal Building* (1965; Harrison & Abramovitz), which handles most scheduled airlines, the *Marine Air Terminal* (1939; Delano & Aldrich; DL), the original terminal, close to the water where the "flying boats" landed and now used by commuter airlines, air taxis, private aircraft, and the U.S. Weather Service; the *Delta Airlines Terminal* (1983); and the *Eastern Airlines / Shuttle Terminal* (1981), with frequent service to and from Boston and Washington. In the Art Deco Marine Air Terminal is a mural by James Brook entitled *Flight* (1942, restored 1980).

Maspeth, bounded by Newtown Creek, an oily tidal arm of the East River, is now heavily industrial though it has had a surprisingly stable population of ethnically mixed European residents— Poles, Italians, Lithuanians, and Germans. The town was settled early (1642) and named after an Indian village, called Maspaetches (spelled various ways) which meant "bad water place" and referred to the swamps around Maspeth Creek.

Ridgewood, founded by Dutch farmers in the 17C, is bounded by Metropolitan and Flushing Aves on the N., the Long Island Railroad tracks on the N.E. and S., and the Brooklyn border on the W., following Cypress, St. Nicholas, and Wyckoff Aves. Ridgewood became industrialized in the early years of the 20C, its breweries and knitting mills manned by an influx of German immigrants. Though the breweries have gone the way of others in the city, a small cottage knitting industry still survives. In the 1930s the Germans were joined by Rumanians, Italians, and Yugoslavians while newer immigrants are Korean and Hispanic. In the 1960s and 1970s the deterioration of adjoining Bushwick in Brooklyn (crime, drugs, arson) threatened to spread to Ridgewood. In 1979 Ridgewood voters changed the area's ZIP code from a Brooklyn to a Queens number, hoping to dissociate themselves, at least in the eyes of the post office, from Bushwick. In 1983 many rows of Ridgewood's yellow and brown brick town houses were placed on the National Register of Historic Places, an act that pushed up property values. One of the more interesting rows is on Stockholm St between Onderdonk and Woodward

Aves, built between 1862 and 1893 by architect Louis Berger. The yellow fire brick comes from what was once Kreischerville on Staten Island.

At 1820 Flushing Ave, at Onderdonk Ave, is the Vander-Enke Onderdonk House (1709), a stone farmhouse, restored by the Greater Ridgewood Historical Society, now a museum and cultural center. One of the rooms has been furnished in Victorian style; the rest of the house is an architectural museum, with exposed rafters, walls, and a foundation under the E. wing dating from 1660. In the future the museum will contain exhibits of memorabilia pertaining to the house and local history. For hours, tel: (718) 456-1776.

Settled in the 17C by Dutch and English farmers, **Corona,** is now a densely populated community bounded roughly by Northern Blvd, Junction Blvd, the Long Island Expressway, and Grand Central Parkway. During the 19C it was called West Flushing and in 1856 became the site of the Fashion Race Track, named after a race horse. It was subdivided for development in 1870 and took the name Corona, apparently expressing aspirations for eminence; around the turn of the century it was populated by Italians and Jews and today is seeing an influx of Asians, South Americans, and Indians in its northern portions. For a long time, however, it was known chiefly as the site of the Corona Dump, but in the aftermath of two Worlds' Fairs in Flushing Meadows it has become the site of major sports facilities, a museum, and a large park. Louis Armstrong lived at 34-56 107th St (bet. 34th / 37th Aves) from 1943 until his death in 1971. In 1893 the Tiffany Studios opened a factory at 96-18 43rd Ave, that produced much of the Art Nouveau glass and bronze sold in tonier surroundings on Madison Ave. The firm went bankrupt in 1932 and today the Roman Bronze Works foundry owns the building.

Flushing Meadows-Corona Park occupies 1316 acres running north-south along what was once the Flushing River, a navigable waterway to the old town of Flushing, and is girded by the Grand Central Parkway and the Van Wyck Expressway.

SUBWAY: IRT Flushing Line (train 7) to Willets Point-Shea Stadium.

Originally the land of Flushing Meadows was salt marsh, inundated by tides and therefore useless for housing. Saved thus from development, the marsh became the Corona Dump and the river an open sewer. By the 1920s trainloads of trash and garbage which arrived daily from Brooklyn smoldered nightly as they were burned, giving the place a Dantesque aura and inspiring novelist F. Scott Fitzgerald to name it the Valley of Ashes. The marsh disappeared beneath tons of filth, one mound rising high enough to earn the name Mt. Corona. Thirty years of effort created the present part, a project which involved channeling park of the Flushing River into a conduit as large as a tube of the Holland Tunnel, building sewage plants to decontaminate Flushing Bay, and removing hundreds of thousands of tons of garbage.

North of Flushing Meadows Park and across the tracks of the Port Washington branch of the Long Island Railroad is *Shea Stadium* (1964; Praeger-Kavanagh-Waterbury), home turf of the New York Mets, one of the city's two professional baseball teams. The stadium holds 55,300 spectators.

The *National Tennis Center* lies just S. of the railroad tracks and has been the site of the U.S. Open Championships since the tournament moved here in 1978 from Forest Hills. The stadium holds 20,000 and the adjoining grandstand, 6500. For ticket information call (718) 271-5100.

The widest section of the park between the Long Island Expressway and the railroad tracks was the site of the 1964–65 World's Fair. The grounds, on which stand several monumental relics of the fair, have been reused for recreational and educational facilities.

The fair mall began near the E. edge not far from the Van Wyck Expressway. Its first artifact is Donald De Lue's 45-ft statue, *The Rocket Thrower,* a modestly draped, heavily muscular bronze athlete hurling a missle through a circle of stars. On the lawn to the right is a *statue of George Washington* (1959) by the same sculptor. Straight down the mall is the fair's most imposing artifact, the *Unisphere* (1964; Peter Muller-Munk, Inc, designer) constructed by the U.S. Steel Corporation (12 stories high, 120 ft in diameter, and weighing 700,000 lbs), whose meridians and continents challenge the climbing skills of local youngsters.

Off to the left, forlorn and derelict, is the *New York State Pavilion* (1964; Philip Johnson & Richard Foster), hailed for structural innovations two decades ago. The concrete tubular columns originally supported two roofs, one above the other, sheathed in colored transparent plastic.

To the right of the mall near the New York City Building stands José de Rivera's *Free Form,* a curved scythe of polished metal.

The **Queens Museum** stands at the head of the mall in the building that once held New York City's exhibition at the 1939–40 World's Fair.

The Queens Museum, New York City Building, Flushing Meadows Park, Queens, N. Y. 11368. Open Tues–Fri 10 5; Sat–Sun 12–5:30; suggested contribution; tel: (718) 592-2405. Lectures, films, programs for children. Gift shop, restrooms, telephones. No restaurant. Complete wheelchair access.

This small museum has changing exhibitions on art and local history including major traveling shows. Its *pièce de résistance* is a 15,000 square ft *panorama of New York City executed for the fair and regularly updated; from a glass-enclosed balcony visitors may admire its bridges, rivers, parks, streets, and 835,000 buildings.

Two overpasses lead to the W. section of the park beyond Grand Central Parkway. Near the road is the *Queens Zoo,* currently closed for renovations.

Beyond the Terrace on the Park, a catering service, is the **New York Hall of Science,** which reopened in 1986 to the delight of technophiles (and the scientifically innocent as well) all over the city. The building (1964; Harrison & Abramovitz) was constructed as the Hall of Science for the City of New York during the 1964 World's Fair, which accounts for its dramatic appearance, an undulating curtain of cast concrete studded with pieces of cobalt blue glass. The rockets displayed out front are left over from that celebration and will be renovated as part of a major construction project in progress at the museum.

New York Hall of Science. 47-01 111th St, Flushing Meadows-Corona Park, Queens, N. Y. 11368. Tel: (718) 699-0675. Open Wed—Sun 10—5. Groups Mon—Fri 10-2 by appointment; call: (718) 699-0301. Closed Mon, Tues, major holidays. Suggested donation.

Restrooms, telephones, snack bar with vending machines. Gift shop. Lectures, workshops (on rockets, kite making, etc.), films, special events, science library.

SUBWAY: IRT Flushing line (train 7) to 111th St. The museum is a five-block walk south from the station. CAR: Westbound, take 108th St exit of the Long Island Expressway or eastbound take Grand Central Parkway Midtown Tunnel exit. Parking lot near museum entrance.

This museum offers two floors of beautifully designed, entertaining exhibits which illustrate principles of physics and biology. One section of the main display area is devoted to the Realm of the Atom. Other exhibits on this floor demonstrate the principle of Feedback, the process by which living creatures and certain electronic systems adjust themselves to changes in the environment. A biology demonstration shows microscopic organisms in a drop of water going on about their daily lives, enlarged and displayed on video screens for all to see. The exhibits on Structures allow visitors to swing on ropes or bounce up and down on a seesaw to see how forces of the environment affect manmade structures, whether small like chairs or large like skyscrapers.

On the Balcony level is a spectacular long-term exhibition "Seeing the Light." Visitors can climb inside a prism of mirrors to see themselves reflected an infinite number of times or dance in front of a video camera that records movement but "remembers" what it saw a moment before. Optics, resonance and reflections, lasers, and visual perception are treated with equal originality and sophistication.

Elmhurst lies W. of the park around Queens Blvd and Grand Ave, near the center of the old town of Newtowne. Although its dense development today masks its rural antecedents, Elmhurst while still part of Newtowne boasted fine apple orchards, from which Newtown Pippins were exported to England for cider. Of interest to the local historian are the *Reformed Dutch Church of Newtown* and its Fellowship Hall, 85—15 Broadway at Corona Ave (church, 1831; hall, 1858; DL), both white clapboarded structures with Victorian stained glass, and the *St. James Fellowship Hall,* originally the St. James Episcopal Church, Broadway at the S.W. corner of 51st Ave (1734), the original church of a parish established in 1704. The original steeple is gone and the building was updated with carpenter-gothic ornament. The church which replaced this one as the house of worship for the parish was built in 1849 at the N.E. corner of Broadway and Corona Ave, but it later burned.

More expressive of contemporary life in Elmhurst are Lefrak City, between Junction Blvd and 99th St, 57th Ave and the Long Island Expressway, a huge brick housing development built (1962—67;

Jack Brown) by real estate entrepreneur Sam Lefrak, and Queens
Center, on Queens Blvd at the N.E. corner of 59th Ave, a
shopping mall (1973; Guren Assocs.) with a branch of Abraham
& Straus.

Forest Hills, bounded by Yellowstone Blvd, Metropolitan Ave,
and Queens Blvd, is famous for tennis and for city planning. The
West Side Tennis Club, bounded by 69th Ave, Burns St, Dart-
mouth St, and Tennis Place, with its lawns, clay courts, and neo-
Tudor clubhouse, was the scene of the U.S. Open Championships
until 1978 when heightened interest in tennis made the stadium
(c. 13,500 spectators) less profitable than a larger one.

Forest Hills Gardens, 71st Ave to Union Turnpike, Long Island
Railroad tracks to Greenway South, is today a pleasant upper
class community with winding, tree-lined streets, many of whose
houses imitate English rural prototypes. Originally the project
(begun 1913; Grosvenor Atterbury, architect; Frederick Law
Olmsted, Jr., landscape architect) was to be an experiment in
middle income housing for commuters and was sponsored by the
Russell Sage Foundation. When it was about half finished, a
residents' organization took over, imposed restrictive covenants,
and turned Forest Hills Gardens into what it is today.

In front of the *Queens Borough Hall* (1941; William Gehron &
Andrew J. Thomas) on Queens Blvd between Union Turnpike
and 82nd Ave stands Frederick MacMonnies's marble statue
Civic Virtue (1922), a late and unsuccessful work by a fine
sculptor, originally placed in front of City Hall in Manhattan.

When installed, the statue disturbed onlookers in part for the near-nudity of its
central figure, a muscular male whose modesty is protected by wisps of
seaweed and bubbles of foam, and in part because of the symbolism of the two
writhing female forms (Civic Vice?) on whom the hero appears to be trampling.
MacMonnies defended his work by pointing out that Virtue's foot does not
actually tread upon the women, but since feminist groups, the Women's
Christian Temperance Union, and the president of Harvard all objected, the
statue was moved to a less conspicuous site in Queens.

In the S. part of Forest Hills is *Forest Park,* a 538-acre reserve
with woods, walking trails, and a golf course, whose rocky terrain
was created by the terminal moraine which forms the spine of
Long Island.

Kew Gardens, E. of Forest Park, is similar to nearby Forest Hills,
though less wealthy. It is bounded by Union Turnpike and Park
Lane South on the N. and W., by Queens Blvd on the N. and N.E.,
by Maple Grove Cemetery and 127th St on the E., and 85th St
and Babbage St on the south. Albon Platt Man, a Manhattan
lawyer, developed the neighborhood before World War I for the
express purpose of creating a garden spot away from the conges-
tion of Manhattan. Before World War II Kew Gardens attracted
refugees from Nazi Germany who arrived early enough to be
financially secure. Today there are Iranian émigrés among other
groups.

Rego Park, with its curved streets, was laid out and developed by the Real Good Construction Co., whose acronym accounts for the community's name.

55 Northeastern Queens: College Point, Whitestone, Bayside, Little Neck, Douglaston, and Flushing

College Point lies along the shore of Long Island Sound N. of Flushing and owes its name to St. Paul's College, an Episcopalian divinity school founded (1836) by Rev. William A. Muhlenberg, which never actually opened its doors. The Reverend's sister built a house (1848), known later as the Chilsholm mansion, on the site; Mayor La Guardia used it in the summer of 1937 to escape the city heat. Today the site is Hermon A. MacNeil Park.

In the 17C William Lawrence had an estate here; his descendants sold off part of the land to one Eliphalet Stratton who developed it and named the community Strattonsport. During and after the Civil War era it was a busy industrial community whose rubber factories, ribbon mills, and breweries employed a population of Swiss and German immigrants. Its picnic grounds and beer gardens attracted Manhattanites of Germanic descent who came on the excursion steamers that plied Long Island Sound. Today College Point is still residential with a surprisingly small-town atmosphere, perhaps the result of its physical isolation before it was connected to Flushing by a causeway (now College Point Blvd) over the marshes. The former *Flushing Airport* for private planes occupies 300 acres near the Whitestone Parkway and is slated for development as an industrial park.

The *Poppenhusen Institute*, 114–04 14th Rd, S.E. corner of 114th St (1868; Mundell & Teckritz; DL), now abandoned, was built primarily as an adult evening school by German-born Conrad Poppenhusen who pioneered the hard-rubber industry in this country. Along with a trade school, a language school, and a free kindergarten for the children of working mothers, the institute once had a library, savings bank, and jail whose cells, according to local tradition, not infrequently held those visiting New Yorkers who had drunk too deeply in the nearby beer gardens. Later the family bought large tracts of land, and Conrad Poppenhusen became the majority stockholder in the Long Island Railroad. The Poppenhusen Memorial (1884) at College Point Blvd at College Place and 11th Ave marks the approximate site of his home, and several buildings from his *India Rubber Co.* (1889, 1921) still stand at 127th St and 20th Ave.

The India Rubber Co. later became the Hard Rubber Comb Co. and then the I. B. Kleinert Rubber Co., the maker of dress shields.

The *First Reformed Church of College Point and Parish House,* 14th Ave at the N.W. corner of 119th St (1872), are fine examples of the carpenter-gothic tradition, worth seeking out for anyone interested in vernacular architecture.

East of College Point along the N. shore of Long Island lies the community of **Whitestone,** its boundaries marked by the footings of the Bronx-Whitestone and Throgs Neck Bridges, the East River, and on the S., 25th Ave. Settled in 1645 by Dutch farmers who paid the Indians an axe for every 50 acres of land, the community took its name from a large, white boulder that once stood at the landing place and served as a navigational aid for passing ships. In 1735 the discovery of a large clay deposit made the area a manufacturing site for pottery and clay pipes. During the governorship of De Witt Clinton, Whitestone called itself Clintonville, reverting to its old name in 1845. In the mid-19C the area became known as Iron Springs, after a spring discovered on a farm at 14th St and Old Whitestone Ave was touted as healthful for anemic patients. Today Whitestone has pleasant residential neighborhoods, the private upper class community of Malba on the W. almost beneath the Bronx-Whitestone bridge, Beechhurst in the N. along Powell's Cove Blvd between the bridges, and the Le Havre Houses, formerly known as the Levitt Houses, along 166th St and Utopia Parkway, an apartment complex built by Alfred Levitt (1958; George G. Miller), brother of the founder of Levittown.

Near the footings of the Whitestone Bridge is *Francis Lewis Park,* directly on the waterfront. At the E. end of Whitestone, in the Beechhurst section, is the *Hammerstein House* (1924; Dwight James Baum; DL) at 168-11 Powells Cove Blvd, built by Arthur Hammerstein, uncle of composer Oscar Hammerstein II. Hammerstein named the 15-room house "Wildflower" for a hit Broadway musical he produced (1923) and whose profits enabled him to build the neo-Tudor mansion which once sported gardens and a breakwater for docking yachts and seaplanes. Hammerstein had to sell "Wildflower" in 1930 to support his theatrical enterprises; it later became a yacht club and a restaurant and is now slated to be restored as the clubhouse of an apartment development to be built on the site.

Bayside, Douglaston, and **Little Neck** are residential areas whose small apartment buildings and detached houses give them a distinctly suburban character. In the N.E. corner of Bayside, the *Fort Totten Battery* (1864; William Petit Trowbridge, engineer; DL), named after military engineer Joseph Totten, faces Fort Schuyler in the Throgs Neck section of the Bronx and at one time protected the N.E. entrance to New York harbor (see p. 597). In 1983 the federal government gave to the city 11.4 acres including the battery. The former *Officers' Club* on Fort Totten Rd, is a picturesque wooden crenellated building (c. 1870, enlarged 1887; DL), used today by the Bayside Historical Society. The post is used by the U.S. Army and the Coast Guard and is not open to the public except on special occasions; however, you may ask the guard to view the fortifications ringing the post.

Flushing, first settled in 1642 and chartered in 1645, lies E. of the Flushing River. The name is a corruption of the Dutch Vlissingen, a town in Holland from which some of its early settlers emigrated. It has been associated with the development of religious freedom in the U. S. ever since the 17C struggles between Peter Stuyvesant and the Quakers whom he wished to suppress. During the 19C Flushing was a summer colony and remained a quiet residential town until the highways constructed for the first New York World's Fair led to its rapid development. Today it is still residential though not particularly quiet, intersected by major avenues and girded by expressways. The present boundaries of the town are the Flushing River and the Van Wyck Expressway on the W., 25th Avenue on the N., Francis Lewis Blvd on the E., and Union Turnpike on the south. In recent years Flushing has seen an influx of Asian immigrants, including Koreans, Chinese, Indians, and Japanese.

Flushing has a busy if not elegant commercial strip, Main St, whose stores reflect the ethnic diversity of the population; the Oriental food markets and restaurants have made the area gastronomically interesting. There are also a number of historic sites sufficiently close together to be visited on foot.

SUBWAY: IRT Flushing line (train 7) to Main St, the last stop.

CAR: Take either the Long Island Expressway to exit 23 and go N. on Main St; or follow Northern Blvd to Main St.

TRAIN: Long Island Railroad Port Washington Line to Flushing Main St.

Begin at Main St and Roosevelt Ave and walk N. (street numbers will decrease). *St. George's Episcopal Church* (1854; Wills & Dudley; DL), on Main St between 38th and 39th Aves, built of brownstone and Manhattan schist with a wooden steeple added later, replaces an earlier church of 1761, where Francis Lewis, signer of the Declaration of Independence, served as vestryman.

Continue N. to Northern Blvd. A famous 18C nursery flourished on the site of the RKO Keith Theater (Northern Blvd at Prince St); here William Prince planted the first specimen around 1737 and by 1750 the eight-acre tract, then called the *Linnaean Botanic Garden,* was a major commercial supplier. Though the gardens are gone, the offspring of Mr. Prince's industry account for many of the 140 genera and 2000 species of trees and shrubs that enhance Flushing.

Turn right. At 137-16 Northern Blvd, between Main St and Union St, is the FRIENDS' MEETING HOUSE (1694; enlarged 1716–19; DL), a simple wooden building with a steep hipped roof and very small windows.

Friends Meeting House. 137-16 Northern Blvd (Main St), Flushing, Queens, N.Y. 11354. Open first Sun of every month except Jan, Feb, Aug 2–4. Also open by appointment. Free. Tel: (718) 358-9636. Tours on request.

The back of the house faces Northern Blvd while the front opens onto a small graveyard whose stones were unmarked until 1848 in accordance with the Quaker belief that death equalizes everyone. Except for a period during the British occupation (1776–83) when it served as a prison, hay barn, and hospital, the Meeting House has been used continuously for religious services since its construction, though it must have been uncomfortable during its first 50 winters as iron stoves were not installed until 1760; central heating followed two centuries later (1965).

Across Northern Blvd is the most imposing 19C structure in town, the former FLUSHING TOWN HALL, 137-35 Northern Blvd, N.E. corner of Linden Place (1862; Cornelius Howard, builder; DL), a tan brick building with chocolate brown trim, described as Romanesque Revival but overlaid with Victorian detail—heavy cornice, gables, turrets, and a porch. Once it held a courtroom, bank offices, a library, a meeting hall, and a jail and during its prime hosted Flushing's most important events—town meetings, opera performances, balls—and its most illustrious visitors—Theodore Roosevelt, U. S. Grant, Tom Thumb, P. T. Barnum, and Jenny Lind.

Continue down Northern Blvd past the Flushing Armory (1905), 137-58 Northern Blvd, and the high school to Bowne St; turn right and walk a block to 37th Ave. The boulder about 100 yards down the street on the right, *Fox Oaks Rock,* gets its name from George Fox, English founder of the Religious Society of Friends (i.e., Quakers) who came to North America in 1672 and preached here under a stand of oaks.

On the S.E. corner of Bowne St and 37th Ave is the oldest dwelling in Queens, the **Bowne House** (1661, with later additions; DL), built by John Bowne and inhabited by nine generations of his family until 1945 when it was opened as a museum. It is important not only for its antiquity but for its association with religious freedom in this country.

Bowne House. 37-01 Bowne St (37th Ave), Flushing, Queens, N.Y. 11354. Open Tues, Sat, Sun 2:30–4:30; admission charge. Tel: (718) 359-0528. Booklets, postcards. No restaurant, no telephone. Not accessible to wheelchairs.

In the kitchen John Bowne, a convert to Quakerism, allowed illegal meetings of the group whose heretical beliefs, fanaticism, and ecstatic form of worship (hence the name "Quakers") drew the wrath of conforming Christians, notably Peter Stuyvesant, who particularly abhorred the sect. He fined Bowne and banished him to Holland where Bowne pleaded his cause with the Dutch West India Company. The company administrators, in business for a profit, considered increased immigration to an underpopulated colony more important than religious conformity and advised Stuyvesant to moderate his antagonism.

In the garden is a plaque inscribed with the *Flushing Remonstrance,* a reply by the people of the town to Peter Stuyvesant's edict (1657) that the Dutch Reformed Church was the only permitted religion in the colony.

Walk out through the garden to 37th Ave and past the playground to the *Kingsland Homestead,* once the William K. Murray House (1774; DL).

The Kingsland Homestead. 143-35 37th Ave (actually on 37th St W. of Parsons Blvd), Flushing, Queens, N.Y. 11354. Open Tues, Sat, Sun 2:30–4:30. Admission charge. Tel: (718) 939-0647. Lectures, exhibitions of local history and decorative arts, publications. No restaurant, no telephone. Not accessible to wheelchairs.

The house was built by Charles Doughty, a Quaker farmer. Doughty's son-in-law, Joseph King, inherited the house and settled down there after an adventurous career as a sea captain. King's daughter Mary married Lindley Murray, of the family for whom Manhattan's Murray Hill was named.

The Queens Historical Society opened it as a museum in 1968 with a small collection of memorabilia from Joseph King, historical photographs, maps of Queens and neighboring Nassau County, a Victorian period room, and special exhibitions on local history and decorative arts.

Next to the house is Queens's most famous tree, a **weeping beech** (1847; DL) which now flourishes in mournful splendor in its own small park. Legend asserts that a Belgian, Baron de Man, noticing a droopy seedling along his newly planted avenue of beeches, commanded his gardener to destroy it, but instead the gardener put it in a secluded spot where it flourished, apparently assuming its unusual form through spontaneous mutation. The cutting from which this tree grew came from Belgium, brought back in a flowerpot by nurseryman Samuel B. Parsons who supplied trees and shrubs for Central and Prospect Parks. Today the tree is more than 60 ft tall with a spread of about 85 ft and a trunk circumference of 14 ft.

Return to Bowne St. Several blocks S., at 45-57 Bowne St near Holly and 45th Aves, is the ornate, white-towered *Hindu Temple Society of North America,* built (1977; Baryn Basu Assocs.) in the Dravidian style of some 2000 years ago. Inside are sculptures of Vishnu, Lakshmi, Shiva, and other Indian deities.

Other Oriental temples serving Flushing's immigrant population are the Japanese *Nichiren Shoshu Temple* (1984; Ashihara Assocs.) at 42-32 Parsons Blvd and Ash Ave and the Korean *Won Buddhist Temple, Song Eun Building* (1986; Bo Yoon & Assocs.) at 43-02 Burling St.

QUEENS COLLEGE, its campus bounded by Reeves and Melbourne Aves, Main St, and Kissena Blvd, opened in 1937 and is part of the City University of New York. The college offers degrees in science and liberal arts, attracting some 15,000 students. In the Paul Klapper Library is the *Frances Godwin and Joseph Ternbach Museum at Queens College,* with a small permanent collection of European art, ancient and antique glass, prints by American artists commissioned by the WPA, and a few examples of Oriental, primitive, and Egyptian art. The museum also offers changing exhibitions of painting, sculpture, and drawing.

The Frances Godwin and Joseph Ternbach Museum at Queens College. Mattis Room, Paul Klapper Library, Queens College, Flushing, Queens, N. Y. 11367. Open Mon and Wed, 9–8; Tues and Thurs 9–6, and Fri 9–5. Tel: (718) 520-7049.

The QUEENS BOTANICAL GARDEN, a 39-acre plot, includes along with its 22-acre arboretum of maples, magnolias, dogwoods, and other specimens, a large rose garden, several demonstration backyard gardens, seasonal plantings, and specialized gardens for birds and bees.

The Queens Botanical Garden. 43-50 Main St (Dahlia Ave), Flushing, Queens, N.Y. 11355. Tel: (718) 886-3800. Open 9 A.M.–dusk daily. Free. Group tours, educational programs, lectures. Gift shop, plant shop. No restaurant. Restrooms, telephone. Limited wheelchair access.

Kissena Park (bounded by Kissena Blvd, Booth Memorial Ave, Rose and Oak Aves, and Fresh Meadow Lane) is a 219-acre park with a small spring-fed lake on the site of Samuel Parsons' Nurseries, founded 1838, whose proprietor brought Flushing its famous weeping beech (see p. 700). A group of horticulture students discovered within the park a grove of rare Oriental trees, planted a century ago, presumably during Parsons' tenure.

56 Southern Queens: Jamaica, Richmond Hill, Woodhaven, Ozone Park, St. Albans, and Howard Beach

Most of what is now southern Queens was contained within the original boundaries of the town of Jamaica (called Rustdorp by the Dutch), settled by the English in 1656 and chartered in 1660. The community today called Jamaica is a busy commercial center, with deteriorating economic conditions and slums in South Jamaica. The outlying districts—Ozone Park, Richmond Hill, Woodhaven, St. Albans, Queens Village, and Howard Beach—are primarily residential. Richmond Hill is known for its shingle-style Victorian houses, and its development dates back to the years after the Civil War (1868) when a banker, Albon P. Man, bought part of the Lefferts family farm and undertook to subdivide it. Woodhaven, also quiet and residential, was founded by the same John R. Pitkin who tried to build a rival to Manhattan in East New York, today a battered Brooklyn slum. Pitkin called his town Woodville and it began to prosper after two companies established factories for metal stamping on Atlantic Ave. Ozone Park and Howard Beach to the S. were farming and fishing communities until the 20C and Howard Beach enjoyed a period of popularity as a resort community before Jamaica Bay became polluted. Ozone Park, with its rows and rows of small houses, is noted primarily for its proximity to John F. Kennedy Airport.

Jamaica, centered around Jamaica Ave and Parsons Blvd, was settled by the Dutch in 1656 and chartered in 1660. The origin of the name is uncertain, though the accepted source is an Algonkian word for "beaver," which gives the name a different etymology from that of the island in the West Indies, whose origin is a Carib word meaning "land of wood and water." Early in the 18C, Jamaica, then as now located at the intersection of major roads, became a trading center for Long Island farmers taking their produce to Brooklyn and Manhattan. Large-scale development did not take place until the Long Island Railroad was electrified in 1910 and the subways arrived in the 1920s. During the 1930s and 1940s Jamaica was one of the major urban centers of Queens and in the late 1950s was the fourth largest retail center in the city. From then on, with shopping malls rising elsewhere in Queens and the middle class moving further out on Long Island, Jamaica began to deteriorate. A branch of Macy's located at 165th St and 89th Ave closed in 1978 when neighborhood shoppers could no longer support it, and the Gertz department store at Brewer Blvd and Jamaica Ave closed its doors in 1980 after 69 years in business. In 1979 the track of the elevated train from Sutphin Blvd to 168th St along Jamaica Ave was torn down, in the hope that Jamaica Ave would be transformed, just as Third Ave in Manhattan bloomed commercially once the "el" there was removed (1955).

The main commercial district lies along Jamaica Ave between Sutphin Blvd and 171st St. The KING MANSION, 150-03 Jamaica Ave in King Park at 153rd St (N. section 1730; W. section, 1755; E. section 1806; DL), is a large white-shingled house once owned by Rufus King, Federalist statesman, member of the Continental Congress, and father of a New York governor.

Nearby on Jamaica Ave are two landmarked churches. On the corner of 153rd St is the *First Reformed Church of Jamaica* (1859; DL), and between 153rd St and Parsons Blvd is *Grace Episcopal Church* (1862; Dudley Field; additions 1901–02; Cady, Berg & See; DL), a Gothic Revival brownstone church with an 18C graveyard (c. 1734) among whose residents is Rufus King.

The *Jamaica Arts Center* occupies the Register Building (1898; DL), at 161-04 Jamaica Ave between 161st and 162nd Sts, once the city office for registering titles and deeds; the center has an active program of changing exhibitions (fine arts, local history) with a Community Gallery for the work of local artists or students enrolled in the center's classes and workshops.

The Jamaica Arts Center. 161-04 Jamaica Ave (161st St), Queens, N. Y. 11432. Tel: (718) 658-7400. Open Tues–Sat 10–5; free.

The *Prospect Cemetery*, established before 1669 at 159th St and the S.W. corner of Beaver Rd, is the oldest public burial ground in Queens; it contains members of the Van Wyck and Sutphin families, who gave their names to an expressway and a local boulevard.

North of Jamaica, bounded roughly by Union Turnpike, Home Lawn St, 188th St, and Hillside Ave is the enclave of **Jamaica Estates,** whose steep hills were created by the Wisconsin glacier, whose terminal moraine rested at Hillside Ave. The Estates were at one time 503 acres of hardwood forest purchased (1903) from the city by Timothy Woodruff, lieutenant governor of the State of New York under Theodore Roosevelt. Woodruff and his partners developed the land as a wealthy community, giving the streets names that suggest Woodruff may have been an Anglophile: Kent, Wareham, Cambridge, Hovenden, Edgerton. Many of the houses are neo-Tudor in style; most have large lawns with large trees.

In the N.W. corner of the neighborhood is the campus of **St. John's University,** a Roman Catholic college founded in 1870 by the Vincentian Fathers, and now enrolling some 19,000 students, most of them from families in the city.

> SUBWAY AND BUS: IND 8th or 6th Ave local (E or F train) to Kew Gardens; change to Q44A bus to 173rd St-Union Turnpike.
>
> CAR: Grand Central Parkway east to Utopia Parkway exit.

The school has a tradition of public service, and nearly 25% of its law school graduates are state officials, including the present governor, Mario M. Cuomo, and his predecessor, Hugh L. Carey.

Sun Yat Sen Hall, the pagoda-style building which houses the university's Department of Asian Studies, contains the *Chung-Cheng Art Gallery,* with a collection of Chinese and Japanese art.

Chung-Cheng Art Gallery at St. John's University. Sun Yat Sen Hall, St. John's University, Jamaica, Queens, N.Y. 11439. Tel: (718) 990-6161, extension 6582. Open Mon—Fri 10—8. Free. Lectures, gallery talks. Small gift shop. Limited wheelchair access.

Included in the collection, begun with a donation of artifacts from the 1964 World's Fair, are samurai swords, porcelain and cloisonné ware, ivory carvings, and lacquerware. Changing exhibitions show the work of contemporary Asian artists.

Southeast of Jamaica is **St. Albans,** a residential community of middle-class black families, home at one time or another to Count Basie, Billie Holiday, Ella Fitzgerald, and other black celebrities.

To its W. is **Ozone Park,** one of the city's most stable neighborhoods, harboring some 70,000 residents. It is bounded by Atlantic Ave on the N., 106th St on the E., the Belt Parkway on the S., and the Brooklyn border on the west. Ethnically the neighborhood has traditionally attracted Italian and Polish families, but in the last decade Asians and Hispanics have moved there. Its most desirable enclave is *Tudor Village,* a development dating from the 1920s with brick Tudor-style homes (Pitkin to North Conduit Aves between 81st and 86th Sts).

Ozone Park's commercial origins date back to the 1870s when two Swiss and French businessmen founded a large factory for producing stamped tin and agate ware in what was at the time a sparsely populated part of Queens County. The firm, Grosjean-Lalance, built more than 100 cottages for workers, and gradually a factory town arose, first commercial buildings, later schools and churches. The first factory building was in Woodhaven, N. of present Ozone Park; it burned in 1876, though its replacement at Atlantic Ave and 92nd St still stands, including its machicolated clocktower. The firm closed its doors in 1955.

AQUEDUCT RACETRACK, bounded by Rockaway Blvd, Southern Parkway, the IND Rockaway line right-of-way, and 114th St, dates back to 1894 (reconstructed, 1959; Arthur Froehlich & Assocs). The track is named after an aqueduct that runs along Conduit Ave, the service road S. of the Southern Parkway, bringing water from sources further E. on Long Island to the Ridgewood Reservoir near the Brooklyn-Queens border. Known as "The Big A" to its fans, Aqueduct is the only raceway remaining within the city limits, real estate values having made racetracks less profitable than developments.

Rochedale Village, for example, occupies the turf once belonging to the Jamaica Racetrack near Baisley Pond Park.

The season at Aqueduct runs from Jan to May, and again from Oct to Dec. For information call (718) 641-4700.

John F. Kennedy International Airport at the S. end of the Van Wyck Expressway, bounded by Southern Blvd, Rockaway Blvd, and Jamaica Bay, is New York's largest airport, covering 4930 acres, an area equivalent to all of Manhattan from the Battery to 42nd St.

Construction began in 1942 when the first landfill was dumped onto the salt marshes bordering Jamaica Bay in preparation for a planned 100-acre New York International Airport on the site of the Idlewild golf course. Commercial flights began in 1948, and since then the facility has become the city's most important airport, serving primarily long-distance domestic and international flights. In 1989 it witnessed 305,100 take-offs and landings that involved 30,323,100 passengers.

The airport has two pairs of parallel runways aligned at right angles and a fifth general aviation runway for private, business, and commuter planes, a total of nine miles of runways served by 22 miles of taxiways. In addition to eight passenger terminals there are 13 hangars for servicing aircraft, an air cargo center, a police building, a telephone office building, a medical building, a hotel, a bus garage, a federal office building, a post office, and seven food production centers.

Traffic approaches the airport from the Van Wyck Expressway in a counterclockwise direction. The *International Hotel* on the Van Wyck Expressway at Southern Parkway (1961; William B. Tabler) and the *Federal Office Building* (1949; Reinhard, Hofmeister & Walquist) just beyond it on the W. side of the traffic circle form an architecturally undistinguished introduction to the airport. The access road leads past the *Citibank Building,* (1959; Skidmore, Owings & Merrill), a glass box raised on stilts, to the CENTRAL TERMINAL AREA, an 840-acre complex of parking lots, terminals, and service buildings. The first architecturally notable terminal is the *Pan American Airways Building* (1961; Tippetts-Abbett-McCarthy-Stratton, and Ives, Turano & Gardner, associated architects), originally a low pavilion with a disclike roof resembling some alien spacecraft settling to rest; the facility has now been expanded.

The access road continues past the *International Arrivals Building* (1957; Skidmore, Owings & Merrill), host to a number of foreign-based carriers. The scene within the terminal is usually hectic to the point of chaos.

Beyond is the sweeping concrete form of the *Trans World Airlines International Building* (1962; Eero Saarinen & Assocs.), architecturally the most controversial of the terminals. Trans World Airlines now uses the former *National Airlines Sundrome* (1972; I. M. Pei & Partners) for its domestic flights.

Further along the access road are the *British Airways Terminal* (1970; Gollins Melvin Ward & Partners), and the *American Airlines Terminal* (1960; Kahn & Jacobs) with the world's largest stained glass wall (designer, Robert Sowers). Unfortunately only employees of the airline can admire its colored light from the inside since it opens on offices and private rooms. The curved *United Airlines Building* (1961; Skidmore, Owings & Merrill) has also received the approbation of architectural critics for its skillful handling of detail.

Between parking lots 2 and 4 are three CHAPELS (all 1966) for the major faiths of the country: Roman Catholic *Our Lady of the Skies* (George J. Sole), the *Protestant chapel* (Edgar Tafel & Assocs.), and the *Jewish chapel* (Bloch & Hesse).

Note: During construction of a major new terminal, the chapels have been moved to the International Arrivals Building.

57 Jamaica Bay and the Rockaways

Jamaica Bay, a shallow bay of about 20 square miles spotted with marshy islands, lies S.W. of Kennedy Airport. Today it is part of the Gateway National Recreation Area which maintains a wildlife refuge there on its largest land mass, an island known in its various parts as Black Bank Marsh, Rulers Bar Hassock, Big Egg Marsh, and Broad Channel.

Broad Channel, the only settlement in Jamaica Bay, dates back to the 1880s when it began as a fishing village. After 1915 the area was modernized, streets laid out, houses electrified, and water plants constructed. During Prohibition it became known as "Little Cuba" and its visitors enjoyed the consumption of bootleg liquor in its yacht clubs and speakeasies. Railroads arrived in the 1860s and 1870s, passing through the bay to the Rockaways, and in 1925 the Cross Bay Boulevard made Broad Channel accessible to motorists. Today the island has perhaps a thousand families, many of them of Irish descent, living in small houses or shacks on pilings which give the community a pleasingly archaic appearance.

About a mile N.W. of the subway station of the IND Rockaway line (A or C train), which took over the trestles and right-of-way of the Long Island Railroad, is the *Visitor Center of the Jamaica Bay Wildlife Refuge,* whose ponds and marshlands form a full-time or seasonal habitat for more than 300 species of birds. Located on the Atlantic flyway, the refuge is most interesting during the autumn and spring migrations when thousands of ducks and geese stop over in its wetlands. The refuge, whose 2868 acres of upland and 9152 acres of marsh and water make it only slightly smaller than Manhattan, is under the jurisdiction of the National Park Service, and park rangers offer hikes and nature walks; tel: (718) 474-0613 for schedule of events.

The southernmost portion of Queens is the **Rockaway peninsula,** a narrow spit of land reaching westward from the mainland of Long Island across the mouth of Jamaica Bay. The earliest settlement in the area was that of Hempstead (Heemstede in Dutch), settled and chartered in 1664 by the British. The remoteness and inaccessibility of the area made it an exclusive summer resort until, beginning in 1868, railroads put it within reach of the common man, thereby driving the more aristocratic visitors E. to the Hamptons and other areas further out on Long Island, beyond the reach of the less affluent. For a while the Rockaways enjoyed a period as a middle-class resort, and today much of the W. part of the peninsula has become public park, absorbed into the Gateway National Recreation Area. East of the Cross Bay Bridge are the communities of Hammels and Arverne, economically depressed areas with a few large-scale housing projects that seem foreign to this low, windswept land.

West of the Cross Bay Bridge are **Belle Harbor** and **Neponsit,** which retain traces of former gentility, and **Jacob Riis Park,** named after the 19C journalist who crusaded for better housing and parks for the poor. Now admirably maintained by the National Parks Service as part of the Gateway National Recreation Area, Riis Park offers a mile-long sandy beach, one of the finest ocean beaches in the metropolitan area. It is understandably mobbed in summer and in cooler weather attracts people who stroll on the boardwalk, fly model airplanes in the parking lot, and fish in the surf.

SUBWAY AND BUS: IND 8th Ave Rockaway line (A train) to Rockaway Park-Beach 116th St and Q22 bus to the park. Or IRT 7th Ave express (train 3) to Flatbush Ave-Brooklyn College; transfer to Q35 bus to the park.

BUS: During the summer the Transit Authority of the City of New York operates express bus service from Brooklyn to Riis Park. Express B9 from 60th St and B46 from Utica Ave operate weekends only during July and Aug, throughout the day. For information on stops and transfer points tel: (718) 330-1234.

CAR: Gil Hodges (formerly Marine Parkway) Bridge (toll) to the (pay) parking field.

At the W. end of Jacob Riis Park is the *site of Fort Tilden,* built in 1917 as part of the city's outer coastal defenses and paired with Fort Hancock at Sandy Hook, New Jersey. It is named after Samuel J. Tilden, New York State governor and unsuccessful presidential candidate (1876), who left much of his money to the New York Public Library. Park Rangers lead seasonal walking and bicycling tours of Fort Tilden; for information and reservations tel: (718) 474-4600.

The W. tip of the peninsula is known as *Breezy Point,* though the term also sometimes refers to the Breezy Point Cooperative which embraces the private communities of Roxbury, Breezy Point, and Rockaway Point, whose beginnings reach back to a turn-of-the-century tent colony for Irish-Americans. Gradually cottages replaced the tents of the "Irish Riviera" and in 1961 the Breezy Point summer colony became a cooperative and bought the land (about 500 acres) under the houses. Today the co-op still owns the land and the members own their homes, some 2800 one-family houses. The streets are locked to outsiders and guarded by a checkpoint at the entrance.

V   BOROUGH OF STATEN ISLAND / RICHMOND COUNTY

To the world at large Staten Island is simply the end point of one of the greatest, cheapest rides in the domain of tourism, the Staten Island ferry, enjoyed by 3.5 tourists annually. The island is 13.9 miles long and 7.3 miles wide in its largest dimensions, and separated from Manhattan by Upper New York Bay, from Brooklyn by Lower New York Bay and the Narrows, and from New Jersey by the Kill Van Kull and the Arthur Kill (the word "kill" is a Dutch term for "channel"). It is the third largest borough in area (60.9 square miles) but the smallest in population (estimated at 400,000), though it is the only one still growing.

Down the center of the island as far as LaTourette Park runs a spine of rocky hills whose highest point, Todt Hill (409.2 ft) is also the highest point in the city and the highest point on the Atlantic seaboard south of Maine. Along the crest of these hills during the years before and after the turn of the century, the wealthy built mansions and today many still survive along Howard Ave in Grymes Hill and in the neighborhoods of Emerson Hills and Dongan Hills, though some have been adapted to use as schools or charitable institutions and others have surrendered part of their land to newer, often less imposing, homes. East of the central ridge lie low coastal plains which have been densely developed with back-to-back rows of tract housing and continuous commercial strips. The S. of Staten Island, once dominated by the sea, still retains some of its former charm, though the fishing villages and oystering communities no longer exist. The W., fronting the Arthur Kill, is lowland, much of it salt meadow: some has been filled and used for more tracts of housing, some has been put to commercial and industrial uses, some is befouled with the city's largest garbage dump. The far N., site of several of the oldest settlements on the island, has industrial areas and housing, much of it old and battered, looking across the Kill Van Kull at the oil tanks in New Jersey.

Joining the island to its neighbors are four major bridges whose construction spans 36 years, all engineered by Othmar H. Ammann The Outerbridge Crossing (1928), a 750-ft span, joins the Charleston section of Staten Island with Perth Amboy in New Jersey and is named after Eugenius H. Outerbridge, the first chairman of the New York Port Authority. The Outerbridge Crossing (11.3 million vehicles eastbound yearly) and the Goethals Bridge, similar in design, were the first facilities built by the Port Authority of New York and New Jersey. The Goethals Bridge (1928) a cantilever structure (span 672 ft) reaches from Howlands Hook to the Bayway section of Elizabeth, New Jersey, and carries an estimated 12 million vehicles (eastbound) yearly. The Bayonne Bridge (1931) is a graceful steel arch (span 1675 ft) linking Port Richmond with Bayonne, New Jersey (2.4 million eastbound vehicles yearly). The most recent arrival, the beautiful Verrazano-Narrows Bridge (1964), crosses the Lower Bay (span 4260 ft) from Fort Wadsworth to Bay Ridge in Brooklyn. Its arrival triggered the present land boom.

Most of the industry of Staten Island remains confined to its outer margins. In the N.W. is Howland Hook with a major truck terminal along with Port Ivory, whose exotic name is derived from its use by Procter & Gamble, producer of Ivory Soap, detergents, and similar household products. Along the N. shore are commercial and industrial areas, most of which have seen better days, while the W. coast is occupied by tank ports, Consolidated Edison plants, and a 3000-acre dump, the Fresh Kills Landfill, where 10,000 tons of garbage daily find their final resting place. Inland are separate towns or neighborhoods, mostly built up with small, single-family houses, but as development continues apace the former separate communities are beginning to merge into one giant tract of suburban sprawl.

History. Both Giovanni da Verrazano (1524) and Henry Hudson (1609) made note of Staten Island during their explorations of the New World. The former stopped off at a spring to refill his water casks (the location is thought to be in present-day Tompkinsville) and the latter gave the borough its name, Staaten Eylandt, after the States General, governing body of the Netherlands. In the years that followed, the Dutch attempted at least three times to colonize the island but hostile Indians, roused to anger by the provocative actions of the colonists, attacked the settlements. It wasn't until 1661 that a group of French and Dutch farmers were able to establish the first permanent settlement, Oude Dorp (Old Town), near present Fort Wadsworth. When the British took over New Amsterdam, Staten Island took the name of Richmond after the Duke of Richmond, illegitimate son of Charles II.

During the British colonial period, Staten Island continued to develop as an agricultural community with its less-fertile areas devoted to raising stock, while its long coastline and protected waters made fishing, oystering, and shipbuilding also important factors in the economy. Along the kills several tidal mills were built for grinding grist and sawing lumber.

In the early summer of 1776 the arrival of some 30,000 British soldiers and Hessian mercenaries disrupted the agrarian quiet of the island, which soon became a vast military camp from which the British would stage operations on Long Island. Although the population was largely loyalist and welcomed the arrival of the British forces, the billeting of so many soldiers strained the resources of the 3000 islanders and tensions inevitably developed. At the end of August the British attacked and took the W. end of Long Island, using barges built on Staten Island, and in September the Billopp House in present-day Tottenville became the site of abortive negotiations to end the war. Throughout the rest of the fighting the British maintained fortifications at Fort Hill in St. George, and Staten Island is said to have been the site of the last shot fired in the war, a derisive blast from an unknown soldier departing down the bay aimed at the crowds lining the shore and jeering a farewell.

After the war Staten Islanders continued farming, oystering, and fishing, largely unaffected by the heady changes across the bay, although the federal government did see the strategic importance of the island and fortified it during the War of 1812. In 1829 teen-aged Cornelius Vanderbilt born near Stapleton, started a regular ferry service to Manhattan, the first step in a business empire that would eventually make him the borough's wealthiest and most famous son. Soon Staten Island burgeoned as a seaside resort, especially New Brighton where such hotels as the Pavilion attracted prominent New Yorkers and a large clientele from the South. A literary circle formed around eye surgeon Samuel MacKenzie Elliott whose practice was located in Manhattan. Dr. Elliott treated historian Francis Parkman (who later claimed that he had been nearly blinded by the doctor), James Russell Lowell, Henry Wadsworth Longfellow, and Richard Henry Dana. (The Samuel MacKenzie Elliott Residence dating from c. 1850 still stands at 69 Delafield Place, between Bard and Davis Aves, a designated landmark.) Judge William Emerson had a summer house called "The Snuggery" on what is now Emerson Hill where he entertained his brother Ralph Waldo Emerson and hired Henry David Thoreau for a short time in 1843 to tutor his son. Enthusiasts of sport as well as literature were attracted to the island and it is the home of the first American canoe club and the site of the first lawn tennis court (1880).

Less leisured visitors were Giuseppe Garibaldi who remained here for three years during his exile from Italy, Herman Melville who frequently visited his brother Tom, governor of Sailors' Snug Harbor from 1867–84, and Frederick Law Olmsted who tried his hand at farming before finding his life's work as a landscape architect.

During the Civil War the island again became a training ground and assembly point for troops who set up camps in the open fields and apple orchards and whose presence provoked hostility in a population with strong Confederate sympathies. Many southerners sent their families to the safety of hotels they had formerly visited for pleasure. During the Draft Riots (July 1863) abolitionist Horace Greeley came here and was hidden from angry mobs by his friend George W. Curtis, whose house still stands in the West Brighton section (234 Bard Ave, N.W. corner of Henderson Ave). In Stapleton, Factory-ville (now West New Brighton), and New Brighton, mobs burned and pillaged buildings and attacked those blacks who had not escaped into the woods or across the kill to New Jersey.

Toward the end of the 19C, Staten Island became less rural, but again changed more slowly than the other boroughs. Industries began to dot the N. and W. parts of the shoreline—brick and linoleum factories, breweries, dye works, chemical plants—but the Atlantic seacoast still attracted summer visitors. South Beach on the Lower Bay and Midland Beach, just S. of it, became popular resort areas, the latter offering an amusement park with rides and pavilions. The first railroad (1860) was extended along both sides of the island linking formerly isolated communities, and charitable institutions aware of the growing shortages of land in Manhattan began buying sites for hospitals, orphanages, and schools. Nevertheless, in 1898 when Staten Island became part of Greater New York it had only about 67,000 inhabitants, a population slightly larger than that of Manhattan in 1800.

Today Staten Island is struggling to maintain its heritage and preserve what natural beauty remains, while growing in some orderly fashion. The National Park Service controls some of the oceanfront through the Gateway National Recreation Area, including Great Kills Park and Miller Field, and recent laws have been enacted to preserve wetlands from indiscriminate use. Since the opening of the Verrazano Bridge which brought the growth spurt long desired by some, the borough has seen a tenfold increase in crime and a fivefold increase in the number of people on welfare. Parts of Stapleton are covered with big housing projects and New Brighton has been described as Staten Island's only ghetto. Port Richmond, once a thriving commercial area for the north shore, is pocked by empty stores and abandoned buildings. Pollution is also a problem, some of it coming from the industrial plants of New Jersey, ironically nicknamed the Garden State. When the wind is from the west the residents of Tottenville can inhale the fumes of Perth Amboy. Rural and small-town Staten Island are virtually gone and the island has become another outpost of suburbia.

Touring in Staten Island. Unless you have considerable determination, a car is necessary though the Richmondtown Restoration, probably the most appealing of the island's attractions, is accessible by public transportation. Also essential is a map, since the development of the island has been haphazard and the street plan has no particular pattern. Most of the sights are pleasant but small scale, of interest either to the visitor with particular historical interests or a desire to see the city as a whole, far from the beaten path.

58   Northern Staten Island: St. George, New Brighton, West Brighton, Tompkinsville, Stapleton, Grymes Hill, and Rosebank

The ***Staten Island Ferry,** plying the waters between the Battery in Manhattan and St. George on Staten Island, makes a 5-mile, ½-hour, 25¢ trip with a view guaranteed to quicken the pulse of the most blasé passenger: Governors Island off one side, and Ellis Island, the Statue of Liberty, and the Verrazano-Narrows bridge off the other: the skyline of lower Manhattan at one end and the steep hills of Staten Island with the spires and towers of St. George at the other. Ferries run 24 hours; for information call the St. George Terminal, (718) 390-5253.

The Tourist Information Center located in the passenger terminal provides information on Staten Island events and points of interest (open weekdays 11–7, weekends and holidays 11–6; tel: 718 \ 720-1800).

The ferry owes its current location to one Erastus Wiman, a Toronto-born entrepreneur, who developed the island's system of transportation in the late 19C. In 1883 Wiman foresaw Staten Island's future link with New York City and moved the ferry station from Tompkinsville to St. George, shaving a few minutes off the trip to the Battery. He also apparently gave the village of St. George its name, succeeding in buying land he needed for a railroad tunnel from George Law, a prominent resident of Grymes Hill, only after he agreed to name the town after Law, canonizing him in the process.

Once a seaside boomtown, **St. George** is the seat of borough government and the gateway to Staten Island, a nexus of bus and train lines. Just S. of the ferry terminal at 1 Bay St is a *U.S. Coast Guard station* with the roof of the original Chief Physician's House (1815) visible above the wall enclosing it. *Bay Street Landing* and *Harbor Point* are residential condominiums occupying former coffee warehouses.

On the S. side of Richmond Terrace facing the terminal is the *Staten Island Borough Hall* (1906; Carrère & Hastings; DL), and adjacent to it, the *County Court House* (1919; Carrère & Hastings). The Family Court House, 100 Richmond Terrace (bet. Wall St / Hamilton Ave), dates from 1930 (Sibley & Fetherston). Nearby are the Department of Health and the College of Staten Island.

Plans are being developed for the St. George Seaport, on the 55 acres W. of the terminal, which will include a shopping mall and housing. On this site Erastus Wiman built the Staten Island Amusement Co.; in its three-story casino with an electrically illuminated fountain, all comers were entertained with lacrosse, baseball, a 60-piece band, and stage spectacles. The 1888 show "The Fall of Rome" had scenic effects, show girls, and elephants which were stabled in New Brighton and driven daily past political cartoonist William A. Rogers's house on St. Marks Place.

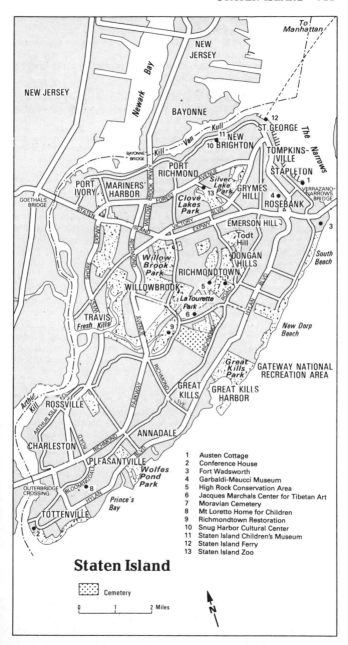

Staten Island

1   Austen Cottage
2   Conference House
3   Fort Wadsworth
4   Garbaldi-Meucci Museum
5   High Rock Conservation Area
6   Jacques Marchals Center for Tibetan Art
7   Moravian Cemetery
8   Mt Loretto Home for Children
9   Richmondtown Restoration
10 Snug Harbor Cultural Center
11 Staten Island Children's Museum
12 Staten Island Ferry
13 Staten Island Zoo

Cemetery

0   1   2 Miles

Soon the pachyderms began appearing in Rogers's cartoons, eventually becoming the symbol of the Republican Party.

Up the hill to the N. is the *Staten Island Museum,* sponsored by the Staten Island Institute of Arts and Sciences, which offers changing exhibitions of fine arts, photography, natural history, decorative arts, and Staten Island history.

The Staten Island Museum. 75 Stuyvesant Place (Wall St), Staten Island, N. Y. 10301. Tel: (718) 727-1135. Open Tues–Sat 10–5; Sun 1–5; closed Mon, holidays. Voluntary donation.

Restrooms, gift shop. No restaurant (restaurants in neighborhood), no telephone. Not accessible to wheelchairs; three steps at entrance, staircase to second-floor exhibits. Workshops, lectures, gallery talks scheduled with changing exhibitions, children's activities.

In the 19C, ten Greek Revival mansions stood along Richmond Terrace which borders the shoreline to the N., overlooking the Kill Van Kull whose formerly pleasant vistas have been replaced by a view of oil tanks. Nine of the mansions have departed along with the bucolic scenery. The lone survivor is now a catering firm, the Pavilion on the Terrace (1835), at 404 Richmond Terrace (bet. St. Peter's Place / Westervelt Ave); in happier times it was the residence of one William J. Taylor.

Six blocks beyond at 806 Richmond Terrace (bet. Clinton Ave / Tysen St) is the former *John Neville residence* (c. 1770; DL) with a veranda facing the kill. Later the house became the Old Stone Jug Tavern, whose hospitality embraced the sailors who had retired to nearby Sailors' Snug Harbor.

Today the beautiful 19C buildings of ***Sailors' Snug Harbor** (Richmond Terrace between Tysen St and Snug Harbor Rd), and its 80 acres of grounds have become the **Snug Harbor Cultural Center,** an immense restoration project continuing to grow.

Snug Harbor Cultural Center. 1000 Richmond Terrace, Staten Island, N. Y. 10301. Tel: (718) 448-2500. Grounds open daily, 8 A.M. to midnight. Exhibitions, Wed–Sun 1–5; closed New Year's Day, Thanksgiving, Christmas. Admission to grounds, free; fee for special events; voluntary donation requested for visual arts exhibitions.

Changing exhibitions, outdoor sculpture festival, concerts, performances. Free guided tours Sat, Sun at 2; tours depart from Visitors Center near parking lot by West Lawn. No restaurant. Restrooms, telephones, gift shop (open Wed–Sun 12–5). Wheelchair access limited to grounds and Veterans Memorial Hall, formerly the Chapel, today used as a small concert hall.

BUS: From St. George Terminal, S1 to Snug Harbor Gate. CAR: Five miles from Verrazano Bridge (Bay St exit), along Bay St to Richmond Terrace. On-site parking available, enter West Gate on Kissel Ave off Delafield Place.

Sailors' Snug Harbor was established by the will of Robert Richard Randall whose father, Thomas, had made a fortune at sea in activities most optimistically described as "profitable commerce" or "privateering," but which with equal accuracy could be called simple piracy. The son died in 1801 leaving the income from that fortune whose capital was invested mostly in Manhattan real estate (see p. 235) to found a home for "aged and decrepit sailors." After litigation during which disappointed relatives sought the income for themselves, trustees of the will bought a Staten Island farm (1831) and erected the row of Greek

Revival temples facing the water. The iron fence surrounding the property (1842; Frederick Diaper) was put up not so much to bar intruders as to keep the old salts from making effortless forays to neighboring watering holes.

The earliest building, the central one, dates from 1831–33 and is attributed to Minard Lafever and Samuel Thompson & Son, with the flanking buildings added in the 1840s and 1880s. After almost a century of serenity, these lovely buildings were threatened with demolition as the trustees of the Harbor needed more modern, more easily maintained facilities for the geriatric patients. After protracted negotiations the city brought the land and buildings and the few remaining sailors were moved to a new home in North Carolina. Today several independent arts organizations have filled the vacuum left by the departed sailors and Snug Harbor Cultural Center is operated on a nonprofit basis on behalf of the city Department of Parks.

The buildings are now undergoing extensive restoration. Of particular architectural interest are Main Hall, the central building facing Richmond Terrace (1831; Minard Lafever; DL), the Gatehouse on Richmond Terrace (c. 1874; DL), and the Chapel (1856; James Salmon, builder; DL), now known as Veterans Hall. The beautiful grounds with their mature trees and plantings slope graciously down toward the water.

Part of the grounds has become the **Staten Island Botanical Garden.**

The Staten Island Botanical Garden, 1000 Richmond Terrace, Staten Island, N. Y. 10301. Tel: (718) 273-8200. Open daily dawn to dusk; free.

The garden has some 28 acres of natural marsh habitat, with greenhouses, a perennial garden, and a bonsai collection.

The newest resident (1986) of the Snug Harbor Cultural Center is the **Staten Island Children's Museum,** located toward the rear of the complex behind the Chapel in what was formerly a maintenance building.

The Staten Island Children's Museum, 1000 Richmond Terrace, Staten Island, N. Y. 10301. Tel: (718) 273-2060. Open during the school year Wed–Fri 1–4; summer vacation Tues–Fri 1–4; all year Sat, Sun, and school holidays 11–5. Closed New Year's Day, Easter, July 4th, Thanksgiving, Christmas. Admission charge.

Changing exhibitions, children's programs and events. No restaurant, no telephone. Restrooms. Gift shop. Accessible to wheelchairs.

Recently voted one of the nation's best, the Staten Island Children's Museum offers a feast of changing hands-on exhibits on the humanities, science, and the arts. Some exhibits have explored the world of the disabled by simulating the environments of the blind, the deaf, and the physically handicapped; others have dealt with architecture, time, sound, and rhythm.

The **Staten Island Zoo,** in 8-acre Barrett Park, is a small urban zoo famous for its snakes.

The Staten Island Zoological Park. 614 Broadway (Colonial Court; rear entrance on Clove Rd at Martling Ave), Staten Island, N. Y. 10310. Tel: (718) 442-3100. Open daily 10–4:45. Admission charge; free Wed. Closed Thanksgiving, Christmas, New Year's Day.

Lectures, children's programs. Food concession, gift shop with souvenirs. Restrooms, telephones. Accessible to wheelchairs.

BUS: S53 Port Richmond bus from Brooklyn. CAR: Staten Island Expressway to Slosson Ave exit, N. to Martling Ave. Right onto Martling.

The reptile house contains such fearsome delights as boa constrictors, a blood python, puff adders, a black mamba, cobras, and some 30 varieties of rattlesnakes, the largest collection in the world. Also on view are small mammals, birds, a colony of vampire bats, and for the children, farm animals in a petting zoo.

WAGNER COLLEGE, bounded by Howard Ave, Campus Rd, Pleasant Valley Ave, and a network of small streets on the E., sits atop **Grymes Hill** enjoying a fine view of the harbor. It was founded in 1883 in Rochester, N.Y., as Wagner Memorial Lutheran College and moved to Staten Island in 1918, its campus the former Cunard Estate. No longer a sectarian school, the college enrolls about 2500 students. The *Sir Edward Cunard Residence*, "Bellevue" (c. 1851) in the East Campus on Howard Ave (c. 1851) has become Cunard Hall, the administration building of the college.

Howard Ave, originally called Serpentine Rd either after serpentinite, a local greenish, striated building stone, or after the winding course of the road itself, has one of the island's fine residential neighborhoods, the old mansions today interspersed with schools and newer homes.

Tompkinsville and **Stapleton,** next to one another along the N.E. shore of Staten Island, are residential-industrial communities, somewhat rundown. At one time the deep water piers extending into the bay were municipal piers built (1921–23) by Mayor John Hylan to bring trade to the waterfront. Dubbed "Hylan's Folly" (along with another ill-fated project, the Bronx Terminal Market), they were designated (1937) a free port where foreign cargoes could be unloaded and stored for trans-shipment without paying duty. When this, too, failed, some of the piers were converted (mid-1970s) to a facility for container shipping.

Tompkinsville is named for Daniel D. Tompkins, governor when it was organized as a village; two of the streets are named for his children, Hannah and Minthorne. The *Bay Street Landing* apartments were formerly the American Dock Company Piers, whose warehouses handled cocoa and coffee.

Stapleton was developed by Minthorne Tompkins (the same whose name graces Minthorne St) and William J. Staples who bought the land from Cornelius Vanderbilt. The Stapleton piers are being rebuilt as a home base for the battleship *Iowa* and several support vessels, making the city once more a Navy port.

The *Edgewater Village Hall* (1889; DL) in Tappen Park (Bay St to Wright St, Water St to Canal St) is the only vestige of a 19C village which preceded modern Stapleton, birthplace of the "Commodore," Cornelius Vanderbilt.

Uphill from the park along Van Duzer St are several old houses including *390 Van Duzer St* (1835; DL), between Wright and Beach Sts, built by Richard G. Smith and his wife Susannah, daughter of Governor Tompkins. More curious is *364 Van Duzer St* (c. 1855; DL) in the block between Beach and Prospect Sts. The land was sold by Minthorne Tompkins and William J. Staples to a Capt. Robert M. Hazard, who built the house, apparently a Greek Revival house (the double portico, the Doric columns, the tall parlor windows) which retains the overhanging eaves of the Dutch colonial style.

Further S. on Bay St (N.W. corner of Vanderbilt Ave) is the *Bayley Seton Hospital* (1834–53; Abraham Maybie; DL), formerly a U.S. Public Health Service Hospital, whose earliest buildings (hidden by trees but visible from the Bay St driveway) date from 1834–37 when the hospital opened as the Seamen's Fund and Retreat. During the 1930s as the U.S. Marine Hospital, the facility was expanded (1933–36; James A. Wetmore, Louis A. Simon, supervising architects), assuming its present appearance. The National Institutes of Health, now located in Bethesda, Maryland, began as a small research facility in the laboratories here. Originally the Marine hospital was on Bedloes Island but was moved here in 1883 to make room for the Statue of Liberty.

Behind it (119 Tompkins Ave, between Vanderbilt Ave and Tompkins St) is the former *Mariners' Family Asylum of the Port of New York*, built by a charitable organization in 1855 as a refuge for the aged female relatives of seamen of the port.

Rosebank, bounded roughly by The Staten Island Expressway, Hylan Blvd, Vanderbilt Ave, and Bay St, has long been a blue-collar neighborhood populated predominantly by Italians. Farmed by the Dutch, Rosebank became a summer community for wealthy Manhattanites beginning about 1830; in the late 1840s the Irish arrived, driven from their homeland by the potato famine, their presence reflected in street names like Shaughnessy Lane and Donley Avenue.

The *Garibaldi-Meucci Museum* is a tribute to Staten Island's most famous, if temporary, Italian immigrant.

The Garibaldi-Meucci Museum. 420 Tompkins Ave (Chestnut Ave) Staten Island, N. Y. 10301. Tel: (718) 442-1608. Open Tues–Fri 10–5, Sat and Sun 1–5. Closed Mon and major holidays. Free.
No restaurant, no public telephone. Restroom. No gift shop. Accessible to wheelchairs.

The building is a simple farmhouse (1845; DL). Between 1851 and 1853 Giuseppe Garibaldi, impoverished and anxious to return to the homeland from which he had been exiled after the collapse of the Republic in 1845, lived here with his friend Antonio Meucci. Garibaldi and Meucci, inventor of a prototype telephone, supported themselves making candles in a factory nearby. In 1891 the house and its contents were sold at auction and 17 candles made by Garibaldi brought $6.75. The museum has letters, photos, and memorabilia documenting the life of the great Italian patriot. There is a small exhibit on Meucci who was declared the first inventor of the telephone by the Supreme Court in 1886, though by that time it was too late for him to benefit from his invention. Upstairs there is a restored bedroom.

The **Alice Austen Cottage** "Clear Comfort" (1691–1710; alterations through the 18C to 1844; DL) is another old Staten Island home now restored as a museum.

The Alice Austen Cottage. 2 Hylan Blvd (Bay St), Staten Island, N.Y. 10301. Tel: (718) 816-4506. Open May 1–Nov 15, Thurs–Sun 10–5. Free.
  Gallery talks, lecture series, family programs, events, workshops. No restaurant. No public telephone. Restrooms. Gift shop. Accessible to wheelchairs by prior arrangement (museum accessible, gravel pathways difficult to navigate, but arrangements can be made for different entrance route).

The cottage was begun in the late 17C, and is worthy of note for its antiquity, but it is famous today as the home of photographer Alice Austen (1866–1952) who went to live there when she was two and stayed until she was forced to leave by illness and poverty at age 70. When she was near death her contributions to the art of photography were recognized, and using the proceeds of an article about her remarkable career published in *Life* magazine (1951), she was able to leave the public poorhouse for the last months of her life. The Staten Island Historical Society has some 3500–4000 glass negatives in which she depicted in great detail the world around her from 1880–1930; prints from these negatives form the basis of changing exhibitions of Austen's work. The garden offers lovely views of the Verrazano-Narrows Bridge and the harbor.

  Inland from the Austen cottage is the former *New York Yacht Club* (c. 1845, additions; DL) at 30 Hylan Blvd. Originally the Henry McFarlane residence, it served the yacht club between 1868–71.

Granite, Victorian Gothic *St. John's Episcopal Church* at 1331 Bay St, S.E. corner of New Lane (1871; Arthur D. Gilman; DL), replaces the earlier frame church in which Cornelius Vanderbilt (born 1794) was the first baby baptized.

  South of the church (Bay St at the N.E. corner of Nautilus St) is the former *Rosebank U.S. Government Quarantine Station* where passengers from abroad suspected of carrying communicable diseases were kept under observation; the station has been converted to housing for the U.S. Coast Guard. About a quarter mile offshore are *Hoffman and Swinburne Islands,* constructed artificially in 1872 for a quarantine station but abandoned in the 1920s when laws restricted immigration. Now deserted and undeveloped, they are part of the Gateway National Recreation Area.

By the mid-19C the original Quarantine Station (1799) in Tompkinsville angered nearby residents because workers went in and out freely, spreading disease to the local population. Frustrated by politicians who would not move the Station, a mob took matters into their own hands in 1858 and burned it down, first removing the few patients to the grounds, where they lay on beds reportedly enjoying the fire.

The top of the hill in **Von Briesen Park** (Bay St at School Rd), once the estate of Arthur Von Briesen, offers superb views of the harbor, the Verrazano-Narrows Bridge, and the fortifications to its south. Jutting out into the bay beneath the Verrazano-Narrows Bridge are the stern granite walls of BATTERY WEED (1847–61; DL) of the **Fort Wadsworth** Military Reservation, built just before the Civil War and later named after Stephen H. Weed, killed in the Battle of Gettysburg.

The Dutch fortified the site against Indian attacks as early as 1663 with a blockhouse and the British later elaborated the facilities. In 1812 the U.S. government erected Fort Richmond facing Fort Hamilton in Brooklyn across the Lower Bay and armed it with 30 cannons. Inside are a central courtyard and three tiers of arched galleries looking out over the harbor in three directions. The oldest continuously staffed military reservation in the nation, Fort Wadsworth is scheduled to become part of the Gateway National Recreational Area but is not now open to the public.

59 Central Staten Island: Dongan Hills and Richmondtown

Dongan Hills, bounded by Richmond Rd and Todt Hill Rd, is one of the most affluent residential areas on the island, its large houses supplanting former grand estates. During the 17C a mining town sprang up in this area to exploit nearby lodes of hematite and was named for Thomas Dongan, 17C governor of the province of New York.

The *Billiou-Stillwell-Perine House* at 1476 Richmond Rd, between Delaware and Cromwell Aves, began (1662–1830; DL) as a one-room stone farmhouse whose big Dutch fireplace was large enough to roast an ox. Pierre Billiou, leader of the Oude Dorp settlement (1661), built the oldest part (with its medievally steep roof) and the Stillwells and Perines added on to it later.

During the 17C when the Dutch worked the iron deposits in the vicinity, **Todt Hill** was known as Yserberg ("Iron Hill"); the origin of its present somber name (i.e. "Death Hill") is unknown.

The *Moravian Cemetery* at Todt Hill Rd and Richmond Rd contains the *Vanderbilt Family Mausoleum* (1886; Richard Morris Hunt), an ornate granite tomb containing the remains of the first Cornelius Vanderbilt and some of his descendants. The *Old New Dorp Moravian Church* (1763) in the cemetery, with its overhanging Dutch eaves, has been replaced by the New Dorp Moravian Church at 1265 Todt Hill Rd, N. of Richmond Rd, a Classical Revival church (1844) given by the Commodore's son William H. Vanderbilt. The Vanderbilt family association with the Moravian sect dates back to the conversion of Jacob Van Der Bilt in the 18C.

"Stone Court," the residence of Ernest Flagg with its Gate and Gatehouse (1898; Ernest Flagg; DL) at 209 Flagg Place, off Todt Hill Rd, for many years the home of the architect, is now in part the St. Charles Seminary and in part a development called

"Copper Flagg Estates." The 32-room mansion with its colon-naded veranda, twin chimneys, clapboarded upper stories, and walls of painted serpertinite—a striated local stone—suggests the homes of Dutch colonists in the Caribbean. A swimming pool, orchards, gardens, and a stone water tower once graced the grounds.

Flagg, who was interested in housing for social classes other than the wealthy, built the experimental **Todt Hill** cottages (1918–24; DL) adjacent to his home. The **McCall's Demonstration House** (1925; Ernest Flagg; DL) at 1929 Richmond Rd was designed at the request of the magazine as an example of economy, convenience for the housewife, and the use of modern building technology.

At the N. end of Altamont St (but more easily seen from Beacon Ave and Boyle St) stands a little wooden lighthouse, called either the *New Dorp Lighthouse* or the Moravian Light (c. 1854; DL), actually a white clapboard house topped by a short square tower which once held a beacon.

The *High Rock Park Conservation Center* is located in the greenbelt adjacent to the Moravian Cemetery. Marked trails meander through this 94-acre forest and bird refuge, which has ponds, a loosestrife swamp, and a garden for the blind.

The High Rock Conservation Center. 200 Nevada Ave (top of the hill), New Dorp, Staten Island, N.Y. 10301. Tel: (718) 987-6233. Open daily 9–5. Free.
   Visitor center. Self-guided tours. Guided hikes Sat and Sun at 2. Young Naturalist Program.
   CAR: Follow Richmond Rd to Rockland Ave; turn right to Nevada Ave; turn right on Nevada Ave to park entrance. Parking lot on Summit Ave.

The *Staten Island Light House* (1912; DL) on Edinboro Rd is visible from Lighthouse Ave, a right turn from Richmond Ave near LaTourette Park. Surrounded by houses and parks, the beacon in its octagonal yellow brick tower shines out from its 231-ft elevation across the harbor, working in conjunction with the Ambrose Light Tower in the bay.

Further up Lighthouse Ave (338 Lighthouse Ave near Windsor Ave) is one of the more unexpected sights of the island, the **Jacques Marchais Center of Tibetan Art.**

The Tibetan Museum, Jacques Marchais Center. 338 Lighthouse Avenue, Staten Island, N. Y. 10306. Tel: (718) 987-3478. Open Sept–May, Sat and Sun 1–5; June–Aug, Fri–Sun 1–5. Closed weekdays, holidays. Admission charge.

This museum, housed in two stone buildings designed to resemble a Tibetan monastery and set in a terraced garden with pieces of Oriental sculpture, contains the largest private collection of Tibetan art outside Tibet, gathered by Jacques Marchais, the professional name of Mrs. Harry Klauber, a dealer in Oriental art. Her interest in Oriental art began with 12 bronze figures collected by her grandfather, a merchant sea captain who had traveled to Darjeeling where he became acquainted with Tibetan lamas.

The *****Richmondtown Restoration,** a 100-acre area in LaTourette

Park at Richmond Hill Rd is an ambitious project of the Staten Island Historical Society, with 25 historic buildings, many of which are open to the public to illustrate the evolution of village life from the 17th through the 19th centuries.

Richmondtown Restoration / Staten Island Historical Society. 441 Clarke Ave, Staten Island, N.Y. 10306. Tel: (718) 351-1611. Open Sept–June, Sat and Sun 1–5; July and Aug, Wed–Fri 10–5; Sat and Sun 1–5; Mon holidays 1–5. Closed Thanksgiving, Christmas, New Year's Day. Admission charge. Food concession open all year. Special programs during the Christmas season; craft demonstrations. Maps and schedules available at the Visitors' Center.

BUS: S113 from the St. George terminal of the Staten Island ferry to the restoration.

History. The village dates back to around 1690 when it was called "Coccles-town," probably because of the oysters and clams found nearby, a name that degenerated to "Cuckoldstown" but was prudently changed to Richmondtown by the end of the Revolution. During the war Staten Island was occupied by the British and some of the structures in Richmondtown were destroyed, including the original Dutch Church and the courthouse. In 1729 Richmondtown became the seat of the county government. During the 1830s, when New York City across the bay was undergoing rapid growth, Staten Island became a suburban retreat and the site of new industries; at this time a new civic center was built in Richmondtown, including the restored Greek Revival County Courthouse (1837), and later the County Clerk's and Surrogate's Office (1848) and the jail (1860). When Staten Island became a borough in 1898 St. George superseded it as the seat of government, curtailing its development, but making it an attractive prospect for restoration a few decades down the line.

Just beyond the parking lot is the Visitors' Center in the *Third County Court House* (1837; DL), a Greek Revival structure with a central section of local traprock. To its left near Tysen Court is the *Reseau-Van Pelt Cemetery,* a small graveyard originally set aside on a remote part of a farm and used for family burials. Across Center St from the Third Court House is the *Second County Clerk's and Surrogate's Office* (1848; DL) now the STATEN ISLAND HISTORICAL MUSEUM. A permanent exhibit follows the evolution of the borough; changing exhibitions are drawn from the Historical Society's collections.

Across Court Place is the *Stephens-Black House* (c. 1838–40; DL) and *Store* (c. 1840–60; DL), a modified Greek Revival home (period rooms) on its original site and a general store outfitted with its original coffee grinder, iron stove, and cracker barrel. Next to it is the small *Colon Store* (c. 1840–50), now used as a tinsmith shop but built as a general store in the Pleasant Plains area of the island (N. of Tottenville) and moved here. Just beyond it is the *Transportation Museum* (1967–68), whose collection includes carriages, firefighting equipment, and antique commercial vehicles, shown in changing exhibitions; it also contains the Museum Store.

Walk up Court Place past the Stephens-Black House and Store to the *Eltingville Store* (c. 1860; DL), originally a one-room frame country store on Amboy Rd, now fitted out as a print shop with an early 19C press. Equally small is the adjacent *Carpenter Shop* (c. 1835; DL), once part of a farmhouse in New Springville, now featuring exhibits of traditional carpentry techniques. On the same side of the street at the corner of Richmond Rd is the

Bennett House (1839, with c. 1854 addition; DL), on its original site. The large brick oven in the basement suggests that the house had an early bakeshop. Upstairs are exhibits of dolls, toys, and other remnants of 19C childhood. A snack bar is in the basement.

Facing the Bennett House on the other side of Richmond Rd is the *Guyon-Lake-Tysen* House (c. 1740, with kitchen addition c. 1820 and dormers c. 1840; DL), one of the outstanding examples of Dutch Colonial architecture in the city with a characteristic gambrel roof and springing eaves. The house has a large kitchen with fireplace and beehive oven, Georgian paneling and furnishings in the West Rooms, and Adams period paneling and furnishings in the East Rooms.

Next door is the *Britton Cottage* (c. 1670, with additions in c. 1755, c. 1765, and c. 1800; DL), whose oldest section is believed to have been the Town House where public meetings were held. Facing the Britton Cottage across Richmond Rd are the *Edwards-Barton House* (c. 1870; DL), a Gothic Revival house on its original site decorated with Victorian furnishings, and the *Guyon Store* (c. 1815–20, with addition c. 1835–50; DL), also on its original site, used as a barter market until 1835 when it was converted into a house. It is now used for special events and is open during the summer season.

Across Richmond Rd from the Guyon Store, between the Britton Cottage and the pond is the *Basketmaker's House* (c.1810–20; DL), a Dutch-influenced house moved here from New Springville. It is furnished to suggest a Methodist household of c. 1815–25, for whom basketmaking was a source of supplemental income. Next door is the *Kruser-Finley House* (c. 1790, with addition c. 1820) and Shop (c. 1850–60). Oral tradition says the house, which was moved here from Egbertville (an area near the intersection of Richmond Rd and Rockland Ave), belonged to a cooper; the shop, furnished to represent the workplace of a saddle, trunk, and harness maker, has craft demonstrations.

Walk toward Richmond Hill Rd past Dunn's Mill, a partial reconstruction of an early 19C sawmill. The *Treasure House* (c. 1700, with additions c. 1740, c. 1790, and c. 1860; DL) originally housed Samuel Grasset, a tanner and leatherworker, and later was used by a series of saddlers and shoemakers. According to tradition, around 1850 a cache of British coins was discovered within the walls, hidden during the Revolution.

Set back from the road is the *Christopher House* (c. 1720 with c. 1730 addition; DL), a fieldstone farmhouse, moved here from Willowbrook. The *Boehm House* (c. 1750, with addition c. 1840; DL), belonged to Henry M. Boehm, a teacher, and was moved here from Greenridge (a locality W. of Richmondtown on the Arthur Kill Rd). It stands on the foundation of the home of Dr. Thomas Frost, a physician whose original house burned down in 1883. The oldest part is faced with wide boards in contrast to the narrow, sawn clapboards of the later section. Inside is an exhibition on traditional building methods and modern restoration techniques.

Facing Arthur Kill Rd is one of the most important structures in Richmondtown, the little frame *Voorlezer's House* (c. 1695; DL), built by the Dutch Reformed congregation for its *voorlezer* or lay reader, who lived and also taught school there, making it the oldest elementary school building still standing in the nation.

The *Parsonage* (1855; DL) on Arthur Kill Rd at Clarke Ave, a gabled, two-story Gothic Revival house on its original site, was built for the minister of the Dutch Reformed Church but became a private residence in 1875 when the church could no longer support a resident pastor.

Near the restoration stand two churches of interest primarily to enthusiasts of local church architecture. *St. Andrew's (Protestant Episcopal) Church,* 4 Arthur Kill Rd, S.E. corner of Old Mill Rd (1872; William H. Mersereau; DL), at the marshy edge of LaTourette Park, is a picturesque church that looks as if it had been transplanted from rural England with its random-fieldstone walls, bulls' eye windows, asymmetrical massing, and steep gables, all intact. It was founded in 1708 and built, originally, in 1712. Fire damaged the colonial church in 1867 and 1872 and the present structure stands on its foundations. In the churchyard are buried prominent Staten Islanders including Dr. Richard Bayley, father of St. Elizabeth Ann Seton and officer of the Quarantine Station.

At the other end of the restoration is *St. Patrick's Church* (1860–62; DL), at 53 St. Patrick's Place between Center St and Clarke Ave, a white brick Romanesque Revival church with unusually narrow round-headed windows. It was built just before the Civil War, when the Roman Catholic population of Staten Island was increasing rapidly.

David LaTourette once farmed the land now devoted to LATOURETTE PARK, and his masonry Greek Revival mansion (1836; DL) in the park E. of Richmond Hill Rd has become the clubhouse for the public golf course which occupies the N.E. part of the park.

The *Sylvanus Decker Farmhouse,* 435 Richmond Hill Rd between Forest Hill Rd and Bridgetown St (c. 1880; DL), a white clapboarded farmhouse, was left to the Staten Island Historical Society in 1955 by Richard Decker and is now a private dwelling.

60   Southern Staten Island: Pleasantville and Tottenville

At the S. tip of the island are **Pleasantville** and **Tottenville,** founded as fishing villages. The streets of Tottenville were once paved with oyster shells, and even now Main St is a throwback to an earlier, quieter time—tree-shaded, lined with 19C houses whose gingerbread ornament recalls the skill of local craftsmen.

North of Tottenville in Pleasantville is the *Mount Loretto Home for Children* (1897; Schickel & Ditmars) on Hylan Blvd between Sharrott and Richmond Aves, occupying a 650-acre estate run by the Mission of the Immaculate Virgin for children from broken homes. Father John C. Drumgoole founded the mission (1870) in Manhattan as a refuge for homeless newsboys and moved here ten years later. The *Residence for the Mission of the Immaculate Virgin* was originally (c. 1845) the Prince's Bay Lighthouse and

Keeper's House (off Hylan Blvd W. of Sharrott Ave), its beacon now replaced by a statue of the Virgin Mary.

The indentation in the coast at the foot of Sharrott Ave is *Prince's Bay* in whose now-polluted waters once flourished oysters so fine that the menus of fancy New York restaurants designated them by name.

At the foot of Hylan Blvd is Conference House Park whose westernmost tip is Wards Point, jutting into the confluence of the Arthur Kill and Raritan Bay. Overlooking the water is the stone **Conference House** (c. 1680; DL), also known as the Billopp House, scene of an unsuccessful peace conference during the Revolutionary War.

The Conference House. 7445 Hylan Blvd, Staten Island, N. Y., 10307. Tel: (718) 984-2086. Open Wed–Sun 1–5. Closed major holidays. Admission charge.

BUS: S103 from the St. George ferry terminal to the last stop on Craig Ave near the park. TRAIN: Staten Island Rapid Transit from St. George to Totten-ville Station; follow Bentley St to Craig Ave; turn right and continue to Hylan Ave; follow Hylan Ave a block to the park (the walk is about 1 mile altogether).

Set in an idyllic spot, its lawns sloping gently to the water's edge, the house has been restored and appointed with 18C furniture. The 17C basement kitchen, floored with Holland bricks made for the restoration, is especially interesting.

History. At some time around 1680 British sea captain Christopher Billopp built the manor which he called Bentley on land granted by Gov. Thomas Dongan. According to legend Billopp is responsible for Staten Island's belonging to New York instead of New Jersey. In 1664 when the British took over New Amsterdam the proprietors of New Jersey, the Lords of Berkeley and Carteret, claimed the island as theirs. To settle the dispute the Duke of York said he would award it to that province whose citizen could circumnavigate the island in less than 24 hours, a contest won for New York by Christopher Billopp. The manor house remained in the hands of his descendants and during the Revolution (September 11, 1776) was the sight of a conference between Admiral Lord Richard Howe, Benjamin Franklin, Edward Rutledge, and John Adams. Howe, who commanded the fleet anchored offshore, offered amnesty to those Americans who would lay down their arms and promise allegiance to the king, while the American representatives declined any offer of pardon that would not acknowledge the independence of the colonies.

Gradually the house fell into disrepair and in the early years of the 20C was used as a factory for making rat poison, an activity that ended in 1918 when the explosion of a powder plant across the river blew out all its windows. Although plans for saving the manor house had been bandied about since 1846, work was not begun until 1926 when the Conference House Association was formed to rehabilitate and maintain it.

61 Western Staten Island: Charleston, Rossville, and Travis

Western Staten Island, mostly lowland, encompasses the communities of Charleston and Rossville and, N. of Fresh Kills, Travis, once called Linoleumville. Because no one until recently found the salt marshes worth protecting, much of the S.W. part of the island has been used either for dumping or storing things.

There are gas and oil storage areas, a graveyard for ships near St. Lukes Ave where rusting barges wallow on the tidal flats of the Arthur Kill, a huge garbage dump N. of Rossville, a city sewage disposal plant, railroad yards, and an industrial park.

In the 19C **Charleston,** then called Kreischerville, was a brick-making town, its industry founded by Balthazar Kreischer who in 1854 discovered extensive clay deposits and started a factory. The *Kreischer House* (c. 1885; DL), built for his son Charles, a rural Victorian Gothic mansion with "stickwork" trim, applied like wooden lace to the irregular forms of its facade, stands at 4500 Arthur Kill Rd near Englewood Ave. The Kreischers also built (c. 1855) workers' housing (Kreischer St near Androvette St) and a church, originally St. Peter's German Evangelical Lutheran Church (1883), which survives today in greatly altered form as the Free Hungarian Reformed Church in America, 25 Winant Pl near Arthur Kill Rd.

Further N. are the *Clay Pits,* E. of Arthur Kill Rd on both sides of Clay Pit Rd, a remote and strangely beautiful area known to conservationists for its pine barrens, forested with stunted trees and low bushes. The Clay Pit Ponds State Park has 250 acres of wilderness, with trails for horseback riding and walking. Seventy acres of the park have been designated by the state as a unique natural area, an area formerly used for farming and clay mining, activities which depleted the soil and left pockets in the clay. The holes in the clay filled with water, developing the ponds for which the park is named. (During summer months park rangers schedule nature walks; tel: 718\967-1976.)

North of Bloomingdale Rd along Arthur Kill Rd opposite Zebra Place is tiny *St. Luke's Cemetery* (c. 1847) over which loom the liquid-gas tanks of the Public Service Electric and Gas Company of New Jersey.

Further N. at Rossville Ave is the Sleight Family graveyard (DL), also known as the Blazing Star Burial Ground. Before Rossville was named (c. 1837) for Col. William E. Ross, it was known as Old Blazing Star, after a tavern of that name. Linoleum-ville was early called New Blazing Star; the Blazing Star ferry once made regular crossings to New Jersey. Buried in the Blazing Star burial ground are early Staten Islanders: Winants, Seguines, Poillons, and Sleights—families also enshrined in local place names. The earliest grave dates from 1750.

To the W. the derelict hulks of the *Witte Marine Salvage Corporation,* 2543 Arthur Kill Rd, can be seen at their last port of call.

INDEX

NOTES

NOTES

NOTES

NOTES

NOTES

NOTES